Handbook of Coping

Handbook of Coping

Theory, Research, Applications

Edited by
Moshe Zeidner and Norman S. Endler

JOHN WILEY & SONS, INC.

New York • Chichester • Brisbane • Toronto • Singapore

Library of Congress Cataloging-in-Publication Data:

Handbook of coping : theory, research, applications / edited by Moshe
    Zeidner and Norman S. Endler.
        p.   cm.
    Includes index.
    ISBN 0-471-59946-8 (alk. paper)
    1. Adjustment (Psychology)   2. Stress (Psychology)
3. Adaptability (Psychology) I. Zeidner, Moshe. II. Endler,
Norman S., 1931–   . III. Series.
BF335.H26   1996
155.2′4—dc20   95-10655

Printed in the United States of America

10 9 8 7 6 5 4 3 2 1

To Eti and Beatty,
our partners in life and key resources,
for their incredible ability to adaptively cope with us.

Contributors

Glenn Affleck, PhD
Professor, Department of
  Psychiatry
University of Connecticut Health
  Center, School of Medicine
Farmington, Connecticut

Terry A. Beehr, PhD
Professor, Department of Psychology
Central Michigan University
Mt. Pleasant, Michigan

Jeri Benson, PhD
Professor, Department of Educational
  Psychology
University of Georgia
Athens, Georgia

Yitzchak M. Binik, PhD
Professor, Department of Psychology
McGill University
Montreal, Quebec

Monique Boekaerts, PhD
Professor, Department of Education,
  Center for the Study of Education
  and Instruction
University of Leiden
Leiden, The Netherlands

Jamila Bookwala, MA
Doctoral Student, Department of
  Psychology
University of Pittsburgh
Pittsburgh, Pennsylvania

Sue Cartwright, PhD
Research Fellow, University of
  Manchester
Institute of Science and Technology
Manchester, Great Britain

Cary L. Cooper, PhD
Professor, Institute of Science and
  Technology
University of Manchester
Manchester, Great Britain

Paul T. Costa, Jr., PhD
Chief, Laboratory of Personality and
  Cognition
Gerontology Research Center,
  National Institute of Aging,
  National Institute of Health
Baltimore, Maryland

Denise T. D. de Ridder, PhD
Research Associate, Department of
  Clinical and Health Psychology
Utrecht University
Utrecht, The Netherlands

Gerald M. Devins, PhD
Professor and Research Scientist,
  Clarke Institute of Psychiatry
Toronto Hospital (General Division)
Toronto, Ontario

Norman S. Endler, PhD
Distinguished Research Professor,
  Department of Psychology
York University
North York, Ontario

Gary W. Evans, PhD
Professor, Design and Environmental
    Analysis
College of Human Ecology
Cornell University
Ithaca, New York

Herman Feifel, PhD
Emeritus Clinical Professor of
    Psychiatry and the Behavioral
    Sciences
University of Southern California
    School of Medicine
Los Angeles, California

Gordon L. Flett, PhD
Associate Professor, Psychology
    Department
York University
North York, Ontario

Victor Florian, PhD
Professor, Department of Psychology
University of Bar-Ilan
Ramat Gan, Israel

John R. Freedy, PhD
Professor, Medical University of
    South Carolina
Department of Psychiatry and
    Behavioral Sciences
Charleston, South Carolina

Irene Hanson Frieze, PhD
Professor, Department of Psychology
University of Pittsburgh
Pittsburgh, Pennsylvania

Bonnie L. Green, PhD
Professor, Department of Psychiatry
Georgetown University
Georgetown, Washington, DC

Knut A. Hagtvet, PhD
Professor, Department of General
    Psychology
University of Bergen
Bergen, Norway

Paul L. Hewitt, PhD
Associate Professor, Department of
    Psychology
University of British Columbia
Vancouver, British Columbia

A. Elizabeth Hirky, MA
Graduate Student
Department of Epidemiology and
    Social Medicine
Albert Einstein College of Medicine
    of Yeshiva University
Bronx, New York

Stevan E. Hobfoll, PhD
Professor and Director, Applied
    Psychology Center
Kent State University
Kent, Ohio

Charles J. Holahan, PhD
Professor, Department of Psychology
University of Texas at Austin
Austin, Texas

Mardi J. Horowitz, MD
Professor and Director, Center for the
    Study of Neuroses
Langley Porter Psychiatric Institute
University of California at San
    Francisco
San Francisco, California

M. Jane Irvine, DPhil, CPsych
Assistant Professor, Departments of
    Psychiatry and Behavioural Science
University of Toronto and
Research Scholar, Heart and Stroke
    Foundation of Canada
The Toronto Hospital
Toronto, Ontario

Marla Jackson, BA
Research Assistant, Department of
    Psychology
The Toronto Hospital
Toronto, Ontario

Joel Katz, PhD, CPsych
Assistant Professor, Departments of
  Behavioural Science and
  Anaesthesia
University of Toronto and
Medical Research Council of Canada
  Scholar, Department of Psychology
The Toronto Hospital
Toronto, Ontario

Paul M. Kohn, PhD
Professor, Department of Psychology
York University
North York, Ontario

Heinz Walter Krohne, PhD
Professor, Institute for Psychology
Johannes Gutenburg University
Mainz, Federal Republic of Germany

Stephen J. Lepore, PhD
Assistant Professor, Department of
  Psychology
Carnegie-Mellon University
Pittsburgh, Pennsylvania

Howard Leventhal, PhD
Professor, Department of Psychology
Rutgers University
New Brunswick, New York

Stan Maes, PhD
Professor, Faculty of Social and
  Behavioral Sciences—Clinical and
  Health Psychology Sections
University of Leiden
Leiden, The Netherlands

Gerald Matthews, PhD
Senior Lecturer, Department of
  Psychology
University of Dundee
Dundee, Scotland

Robert R. McCrae, PhD
Research Psychologist, Personality
  Stress and Coping Section,
Gerontology Research Center,
  National Institute of Aging,
  National Institute of Health
Baltimore, Maryland

Joseph E. McGrath, PhD
Professor, Department of Psychology
University of Illinois at Champaign
Champaign, Illinois

Mario Mikulincer, PhD
Professor, Department of Psychology
University of Bar-Ilan
Ramat Gan, Israel

Rudolf H. Moos, PhD
Professor, Department of Psychiatry
Stanford University School of
  Medicine and Department of
  Veterans Affairs
Stanford, California

James D. A. Parker, PhD
Assistant Professor, Department of
  Psychology
Trent University
Peterborough, Ontario

Gregory R. Pierce, PhD
Assistant Professor, Department of
  Psychology
Hamilton College
Clinton, New York

Laura S. Porter, MA
Graduate Student, Department of
  Psychiatry and Behavioral Science
State University of New York at Stony
  Brook
Stony Brook, New York

Paul Ritvo, PhD, CPsych
Assistant Professor, Department of
  Behavioural Science
University of Toronto and
Adjunct Professor, Department of
  Psychology
Dalhousie University
Toronto, Ontario

Donald Saklofske, PhD
Professor, Department of Educational
  Psychology
University of Saskatchewan
Saskatchewan, Saskatoon

Barbara R. Sarason, PhD
Professor, Department of Psychology
University of Washington
Seattle, Washington

Irwin G. Sarason, PhD
Professor and Chair, Department of
    Psychology
University of Washington
Seattle, Washington

Jeanne A. Schaefer, PhD
Research Health Scientist
Department of Veterans Affairs and
    Stanford University Medical
    Center
Palo Alto, California

Christine Schwarzer, PhD
Professor, School of Education
University of Dusseldorf
Dusseldorf, Federal Republic of
    Germany

Ralf Schwarzer, PhD
Professor, Department of Psychology
Free University of Berlin
Berlin, Federal Republic of Germany

Susan D. Solomon, PhD
Chief, Violence and Traumatic Stress
    Research Branch
National Institute of Health
Rockville, Maryland

Mark R. Somerfield, PhD
Guest Researcher, Gerontology
    Research Center
National Institute of Aging,
    National Institute of Health
Baltimore, Maryland

Charles H. Stinson, MD
Associate Adjunct Professor, Center
    on Stress and Personality
Langley Porter Psychiatric Institute
University of California at San
    Francisco
San Francisco, California

Arthur A. Stone, PhD
Associate Professor, Department of
    Psychiatry and Behavioral Science
State University of New York at Stony
    Brook
Stony Brook, New York

Stephen Strack, PhD
Director of Internship Training, U.S.
    Department of Veterans Affairs
Veterans Administration Outpatient
    Clinic
Los Angeles, California

Laura J. Summerfeldt, MA
Doctoral Student and Research Assistant
Department of Psychology, York
    University
North York, Ontario

Howard Tennen, PhD
Professor, School of Medicine,
    Department of Psychiatry
University of Connecticut Health Center
Farmington, Connecticut

Adrian Wells, PhD
Senior Clinical Research Psychologist,
    Department of Psychiatry
Warneford Hospital
University of Oxford
Oxford, England

Thomas Ashby Wills, PhD
Associate Professor, Department of
    Epidemiology and Social Medicine
Albert Einstein College of Medicine
    of Yeshiva University
Bronx, New York

Moshe Zeidner, PhD
Professor, School of Education
University of Haifa
Mt. Carmel, Israel

Hans J. Znoj, PhD
Visiting Scientist
Langley Porter Psychiatric Institute
University of California at San
    Francisco
San Francisco, California

Foreword

To those who came of age professionally during the mid-1970s and afterward, the concept of coping is a natural part of the landscape of psychology. It wasn't always so. The vast majority of the work done in this area has occurred within the past two decades. Once ignored, coping is now the subject of intense scrutiny and debate.

The publication of this book allows us to stand back and look at the literature of coping—to consider its origins, its present state, and its future. Observers certainly would vary in what they see as the critical milestones in the development of this literature, but most would agree that one such milestone was the book *Psychological Stress and the Coping Process* (New York: McGraw-Hill) by Richard Lazarus, which was published in 1966. Lazarus proposed a view of coping that synthesized the psychodynamic with the cognitive. The model he set forward proved to be eminently compatible with the cognitive revolution that was to change the face of personality and social psychology in the mid-to-late 1970s. In part because of this confluence of similar ideas from many sources, the evolving literature of coping has taken a cognitive cast.

In this view, stress is not a direct reflection of objective events; it stems in part from the frame of mind of the person experiencing the events. The sense of threat that triggers the stress experience is partly attributable to personal vulnerabilities, which vary from one person to another. In the same way, what coping responses emerge is determined partly by people's knowledge of coping options and partly by their beliefs about the usefulness of those options. Both stress and coping, then, spring in part from the mental sets brought by the person to the event. This view is very much in line with the current *Zeitgeist* in personality-social-health psychology.

Today, after a virtual explosion of work in the 1970s and onward, the topography of research and theory pertaining to coping has changed in a number of ways. It has become more apparent that coping can potentially serve several goals. It has also become painfully clear that many responses labeled "coping" by researcher and subject alike are more harmful than helpful. Many additional questions as yet remain unanswered, ranging from the conceptual to the methodological to the metaphysical. Everyone who works in this area has nagging questions like the ones that follow:

- What is the ordinary balance of helpful coping to harmful coping? Do the ways people cope more typically facilitate positive outcomes or do they more typically interfere? (Or is coping really irrelevant—just whatever happens to go on while time passes and adaptation eventually takes place?)
- Are some coping responses helpful in some circumstances but harmful in others? Is it critical that the coping responses selected by the person match the class of situation being confronted?
- What outcome measure (or measures) should serve to validate coping as being successful or unsuccessful? Distress? Health? Task performance while under stress? Extent of rigidity of personality over time?
- How long a time lag should there be between assessment of coping and assessment of the consequences of coping? Are there critical periods within which coping is most important, and after which it matters less?
- Should coping be thought of as a volitional strategy or tactic, or should it be thought of as a *reaction?*
- Does coping differ in fundamental ways from "behavior in general," or is coping simply behavior that occurs under conditions of adversity?
- Do the people's reports about the ways they coped tell us how they really coped, or only how they *think* they coped?
- Does it make any sense to use the word *cope* when people are responding to challenges (opportunities), as opposed to threats (situations with potential for harm)?

These questions hang like smoke rings in the air in front of me when I think about coping. Sometimes I think about how to deal with them. Other times, I'm afraid I pretend they aren't there, because I don't know what the answers are and I don't even know quite where to look for them. I don't believe that the analysis of coping has reached a point where clear answers are available to these questions (or to several others that could easily be added to the list). On the other hand, I'm aware that some of the pathways to the answers are being staked out for further exploration. Many of the people who are blazing the trails to those answers have contributed their insights to this book.

This book has been created as a response to the vast proliferation of literature bearing on coping. This literature has been published in a wide range of books and journals, representing many different facets of psychology and related fields. The literature has become so diverse (as well as so extensive) that it is frankly unmanageable. A volume that integrates and coalesces the current state of knowledge as embodied in this far-flung literature is long overdue. This book is intended to serve this purpose. Rather than attempt a full integration of the sprawling literature themselves, the editors, Moshe Zeidner and Norman Endler, have chosen instead to recruit a range of talented individuals who have specialized knowledge and interests in particular facets of the literature. The result is a summarization of the important themes and issues in this area of research and theory, separated into distinct facets. The chapters raise critical questions and provide what are some of today's best guesses about the answers. I'm sure I speak for the authors in saying that this volume should be regarded as a way station rather than a final destination (some of today's best guesses will surely prove to have been wrong, or at least incomplete, 10 years hence). Yet it is a very timely way station, a much needed compendium on a very important set of topics.

It is also of at least passing interest that many of the contributors to this volume represent a second or even third generation of coping researchers (scientific generations being somewhat shorter in length than familial generations). One of the happy consequences of this fact is that the persons responsible for these chapters can be expected to continue to contribute insights about the structure and functions of coping and the application of coping models to clinical management of problems in living for many years to come. As I have looked forward to this volume, I will also look forward to seeing its second edition, with further developments in the story of coping.

CHARLES S. CARVER

University of Miami
Miami, Florida
October 1995

Preface

Since the 1970s, there has been an upsurge of interest among psychological and health science professionals in various facets of coping with psychological stress and in adaptational outcomes. Coping has also become a major topic of research interest in various subareas within psychology (e.g., personality and social psychology, health psychology, behavioral medicine) and in allied fields (e.g., psychiatry, social work, sociology, pastoral counseling, education). During the 1980s and 1990s, research on stress and coping has proliferated, and the number of publications in this area has been prodigious. The practical implications of this area of research are now readily apparent for many fields, such as health, education, industry, and interpersonal relationships. Concomitantly, researchers have developed and investigated a variety of coping models (theories) and possible applications.

Over the years, there has been a heightened awareness of the important potential role coping can play in determining how stress affects us and how it can shape adaptational outcomes. It is now widely recognized that coping processes may moderate the effects of stress on both psychological and physical well-being. Accordingly, specific coping strategies can either facilitate or hinder adaptation to physical or psychological stress. It is commonly recognized that it is not stress per se that determines adaptive outcomes, but rather how we cope with ongoing challenges and stressors that is critical in affecting our psychological and physical health. This may explain, in part, the flurry of research activity on coping dispositions, strategies, and skill training over the past years.

In view of the burgeoning interest and massive research on various aspects of coping, the time seems ripe for this *Handbook of Coping: Theory, Research, Applications,* aimed at reflecting the current state of the field on coping with stress. The Handbook's goal is to provide researchers, students, professionals, and clinicians in the field with substantial state-of-the-art overviews, reviews, and critical assessments and reflections on the conceptual and methodological issues and complexities particular to coping research. The handbook is intended to provide the foundations of knowledge, research, assessment methods, and clinical guidelines for the development of a more comprehensive understanding.

The book is divided into five broad but overlapping parts. These reflect recent advances in the conceptual, methodological, research, individual differences, and clinical areas. Part One provides a historical and contemporary conceptual overview of the coping domain, as a useful introduction and integrative organizing framework for the chapters to come. The authors of Chapters 1 to 3 discuss major conceptualizations, models, and key constructs (e.g., coping strategies, resources, resilience), and also indicate where we are, where we have been, and where we are headed in the coping field.

The contributions in Part Two delineate basic design issues, assessment tools, and data analytic procedures that are critical for the systematic scientific study and assessment of coping behaviors. The various chapters focus on the importance of the dynamic interplay and integration between theory, design, assessment, and data analysis in sound coping research methodology.

Part Three focuses on key facets of coping with stress on both a personal and communal level. Domain-specific coping with a wide spectrum of stressors is explored (e.g., pain, substance abuse, chronic health problems, multiple stressors, normative events such as hassles, and nonnormative and traumatic stressors such as criminal victimization). The contributions explore domain-specific conceptual and methodological issues, relating them to fundamental issues in stress and coping. The chapters review and integrate relevant empirical findings and point out the direction for future research in the specific facet of coping considered.

Part Four focuses on individual differences within the context of personality and social factors. Issues discussed include coping styles and dispositions, the relationship between coping and both personality traits and social support, and coping behaviors in children and adults across the life span. The issue of individual differences in coping has been relatively neglected in coping research. The chapters in this part both rectify this and reflect the recent resurgence of interest in personality.

Part Five focuses on clinical parameters, including coping adaptiveness, specific interventions, and training techniques for enhancing coping skills.

The handbook presents the reader with a cross section of recent developments in key substantive, methodological, and clinical issues in the coping area. It provides a comprehensive reference source and overview of coping theory, research, assessment, and practical applications. Respected authorities in the field of stress and coping were invited to contribute a chapter reviewing theory, research, and applications relevant to their particular area, and were asked to set out a framework for future research directions. The sheer volume of research on coping with stress makes it virtually impossible to survey and do justice to all the significant areas of coping. Thus the coverage of various aspects was limited by the space constraints of a one-volume handbook. There is some overlap among chapters. However, this allows each chapter to stand on its own, and increases the accessibility of each one.

The *Handbook of Coping* should be of interest to professionals and graduate students in the various behavioral, social, and health sciences, especially those with a serious interest in the study of personality and adaptive behavior. It should be suitable for seminars and graduate courses focusing on stress and adaptation, clinical psychology, counseling and developments, consulting psychology, personality theory, and research. The Handbook should also be useful as a reference work for general readers who wish to gain familiarity with the current status of coping research and applications. Practicing clinicians (e.g., psychiatrists, psychologists, social workers) may find useful information on preventive approaches and intervention strategies in ameliorating stress and enhancing coping and adaptive outcomes.

We are grateful to many colleagues and friends for supporting us throughout this project. Primarily, we are indebted to all the distinguished authors who prepared chapters that appear in this volume. We appreciate their critical contributions and their willingness to cope with a challenging and difficult task. Special thanks are due to Professor Charles Carver, a recognized authority on coping, who graciously agreed to write the Foreword. Herb Reich, Senior Editor at John Wiley & Sons, has been most supportive, patient, and helpful in all phases required to bring this project to publication. We extend special thanks also to Laura Summerfeldt for her critical help at various stages of the project. We also wish to thank our families for coping with us. The University of Haifa and York University provided the congenial academic environments necessary to undertake and complete this work. This has been a challenging, thought-provoking and rewarding experience for both of us; we trust readers will find it to be the same. We hope this volume will help integrate and guide current coping theory, research, and applications. We will be well rewarded if the book advances our understanding of coping and assists us in enhancing and facilitating adaptive coping with stress.

MOSHE ZEIDNER
NORMAN S. ENDLER

Mt. Carmel, Israel
North York, Ontario
October 1995

Contents

Handbook of Coping

PART ONE

Conceptual Issues

CHAPTER 1

Coping and Defense: A Historical Overview

JAMES D. A. PARKER and NORMAN S. ENDLER

The study of people's responses to stressful and upsetting situations has generated a vast literature on a variety of overlapping concepts. Much of this work has a relatively long history, which makes the process of disentangling notable developments all the more difficult. Research on the concept of "defense," for example, extends back to the 19th century and reflects events surrounding the origins of psychoanalysis. Some of the work that has examined the way people cope with stressful situations, on the other hand, has a history spanning only a few decades. The category for "coping" was not included in *Psychological Abstracts* until 1967 (see Popplestone & McPherson, 1988). Since the late 1960s, several related categories have been added (e.g., coping styles, coping resources), in response, no doubt, to the avalanche of research that has appeared on coping-related topics. This chapter presents a general historical overview of research related to the study of people's reactions and responses to stressful and upsetting situations (for more details on this history, see Cramer, 1990; Endler & Parker, 1995; Haan, 1977; Lazarus, 1993; Lazarus, Averill, & Opton, 1974; Parker & Endler, 1992; Popplestone & McPherson, 1988; Vaillant, 1986).

PSYCHOLOGICAL DEFENSE

One of Freud's earliest contributions to the study of psychopathology centered on the observation that unpleasant or disturbing thoughts are sometimes made unavailable to consciousness (Breuer & Freud, 1893/1955). A great deal of Freud's early psychoanalytic writings focused on outlining the various psychological maneuvers used by individuals to fend off, distort, or disguise unacceptable ideas or feelings. As Freud's theories evolved, the concepts of defense and repression came to play an increasingly important role (for more discussion on this point, see, Brenner, 1957; Madison, 1956; Sandler & Freud, 1985; Van der

The writing of this chapter was partially supported by a research fellowship from the Ontario Mental Health Foundation to James D. A. Parker, and a research grant from the Social Sciences and Humanities Research Council of Canada to Norman S. Endler (# 410-94-1473).

3

Leeuw, 1971). In his history of the psychoanalytic movement, for example, Freud (1914/1955) declared that the "theory of repression is the foundation stone on which the structure of psycho-analysis rests" (p. 16).

Although Freud used the concepts of repression and defense interchangeably in early psychoanalytic writings (see, e.g., Freud, 1896/1955), he introduced an important modification in 1926 (Freud, 1926/1959), when he designated the word "defence" as the general term for the ego's struggle against unpleasant ideas and feelings. In the same work, Freud also redefined the concept of "repression," noting that it should be treated as one of several special types of defense (other types of defense discussed by Freud at that time included "isolation" and "undoing").

The publication of Anna Freud's *The Ego and the Mechanisms of Defense* (A. Freud, 1936/1946) was an important event in the evolution and popularization of psychoanalytic ideas about the concept of defense. Most of the important theoretical developments that have attracted the attention of subsequent defense mechanism researchers can be traced to this work. Along with summarizing 10 defense mechanisms described by her father in his various writings (regression, repression, reaction formation, isolation, undoing, projection, introjection, turning against the self, reversal, and sublimation), Anna Freud also introduced several new mechanisms (identification with the aggressor, ego restriction, denial in fantasy, intellectualization, and altruistic surrender). Although other psychoanalytic theorists have identified additional defenses (e.g., Fenichel, 1945; Horney, 1937), subsequent research on the concept of defense has tended to focus on the list of core mechanisms assembled by Anna Freud (see, e.g., the detailed review of recent defense mechanism research presented by Cramer, 1990).

Anna Freud's (1936/1946) work also was important because she promoted several ideas about the concept of defense that would have widespread impact in the medical and social sciences. One contribution was the observation that although a variety of potential defense mechanisms exist, individuals tend to use a select few. Faced with stressful or traumatic situations, each person has preferred techniques for dealing with these problems: "We may say that Anna Freud discovered the fact that every man uses only a *restricted repertory* of defense mechanisms" (Waelder, 1960, p. 181). The idea that individuals have habitual strategies for dealing with stressful situations has interested not only researchers working with the defense mechanism construct, but many coping researchers as well (see, e.g., Carver, Scheier, & Weintraub, 1989; Endler & Parker, 1990a, 1990b, 1993, 1994; Miller, 1980, 1987; Miller & Mangan, 1983).

A related idea discussed by Anna Freud (1936/1946), also having a prolonged influence in the literature, was the suggestion that particular defense "styles" may be linked with specific psychological problems:

> A powerful psychoanalytic concept, which greatly influenced personality and clinical psychology, was that each form of psychopathology was associated with a particular *defensive style*. For example, hysterical neuroses were linked to repression, obsessive-compulsive neuroses to intellectualization and undoing, paranoia to projection. (Lazarus, 1993, p. 234)

Although the idea that particular types of psychopathology are associated with specific defense mechanisms did not stand up to rigorous empirical verification, a widespread interest remains among many researchers and clinicians in the relationship between specific psychiatric diagnoses and characteristic defense mechanisms (for a recent discussion on this point, see Vaillant, 1984). The *Diagnostic and Statistical Manual of Mental Disorders* (DSM-IV; American Psychiatric Association, 1994) contains an appendix with a proposal for a new axes on defensive functioning. In recent years, a number of proposals have been made to include a separate axis for defense mechanisms in revisions to the DSM (see, e.g., Giovacchini, 1981; Skodol & Perry, 1993; Vaillant, 1984).

Another influential idea publicized in Anna Freud's (1936/1946) work was that some defense mechanisms should be conceptualized as *potentially* more "pathological" than others. She noted, for example, that "repression is not only the most efficacious, it is also the most dangerous mechanism" (A. Freud, 1936/1946, p. 54). This idea was quickly embraced by a number of post-Freudian theorists who began to stress the adaptive (nonpathological) features of some defensive responses (cf. Groot, 1957; Hartmann, 1939, 1939/1958). A rather extensive literature on the classification of defense mechanisms according to the potential for pathology has evolved. A number of theorists have proposed models that distinguish between "adaptive" and nonadaptive" defenses (cf. Haan, 1963, 1965, 1977; Kroeber, 1963; White, 1948), whereas others have proposed models that organize defenses along a hierarchy of psychopathology (cf. Bond, Gardiner, Christian, & Sigel, 1983; Menninger, 1954; Perry & Cooper, 1989; Semrad, Grinspoon, & Fienberg, 1973).

Of the many theorists who have taken a hierarchical approach to the concept of defense, the model developed by Vaillant (1971, 1977) has probably had the most extensive impact on the defense literature. Vaillant has proposed a hierarchical model that extends from "immature" to "mature" defenses. Mature defenses are defined as activities like sublimation, humor, and suppression, whereas immature defenses are defined as activities like projection, hypochondriasis, and passive aggression. An intermediate class of defense has also been proposed ("neurotic" defenses) that includes activities like intellectualization, repression, and reaction formation. Implicit in this model, as with most hierarchical defense models, is the view that individuals who utilize mature defenses have better mental health and more gratifying relationships than individuals who utilize immature defenses. A sizable literature has developed over the past few decades to test this defense/pathology model empirically (for reviews of this literature, see Vaillant, 1986; Vaillant, Bond, & Vaillant, 1986; Vaillant & Drake, 1985).

ASSESSING THE DEFENSES

Almost from the moment Freud published his theoretical modifications on the concepts of defense and repression (Freud, 1926/1959), a literature emerged that sought to improve therapists' ability to identify various defenses in their patients' behavior (see, e.g., Sharpe, 1930). The theoretical literature on defense mechanisms is relatively small when compared with the size of the literature that has emerged on the *assessment* of defense mechanisms (for reviews, see Cramer, 1990; Endler & Parker, 1995; Haan, 1982; Kline, 1991; Vaillant, 1986). There are three basic traditions in the assessment literature on defense mechanisms: observer-rated approaches, self-report approaches, and projective approaches. Although there is a long history of using various projective techniques to assess numerous defense mechanisms (e.g., the Rorschach and Thematic Apperception Test), the history surrounding this literature will not be examined here. The interested reader can consult a wealth of sources to learn more about the various projective measures that have been developed to assess various defense mechanisms (see, e.g., Aronow & Reznikoff, 1976; Cramer, 1988, 1990; Holt, 1956; Lerner, 1990, 1991; Schafer, 1954).

Observer-Rated Approaches

One of the first observer-rated systems for identifying a cross section of defense mechanisms was developed by Haan (1963; see Morrissey, 1977, for a detailed review of this research). Following the traditional psychoanalytic literature on the topic of defense, Haan (1963) developed definitions for 20 "ego mechanisms": 10 *defense mechanisms* (e.g., denial, projection, repression) and 10 *coping mechanisms* (e.g., sublimation, substitution, suppression). Haan's work appears to have been the inspiration for the development of several other rating systems over the past two decades (see, e.g., Beardslee, Jacobson, Hauser, Noam, & Powers, 1985; Jacobson et al., 1986; Perry & Cooper, 1989; Semrad et al., 1973).

Throughout the 1970s and 1980s, Vaillant (1971, 1977) has worked on developing a rating system for the assessment of defense mechanisms that conforms to his hierarchical model of defense (e.g., mature defenses, neurotic defenses, and immature defenses). Vaillant's rating system was originally validated using autobiographical data collected from a sample of 95 men about how they had reacted to various stressful situations during their lives (Vaillant, 1971, 1977). A novel feature of Vaillant's rating system is that it was designed to be used with various types of clinical information (e.g., open-ended interviews, interview transcripts). Vaillant's (1971, 1977) overall research findings suggested that mature defenses were related to good adult adjustment and immature defenses to poor adjustment—a result that is consistent with his hierarchical defense model.

Self-Report Approaches

Since the 1960s, a sizable body of research on defense mechanisms has focused on developing self-report measures. One of the first self-report measures of defense mechanisms was a group of scales developed by Haan (1965) using items from the *Minnesota Multiphasic Personality Inventory* (MMPI) and the *California Personality Inventory* (CPI; Gough, 1957). These defense scales were developed following a model of defense (Haan, 1963; Kroeber, 1963) that distinguished between coping mechanisms (adaptive activities) and defense mechanisms (non-adaptive activities). The criterion group for these self-report defense scales comprised subjects rated high (top 25%) or low (bottom 25%) on various defense mechanisms by raters using Haan's (1963) observer-rated defense scales. Using MMPI and CPI items that successfully distinguished between high and low defense groups, Haan (1965) developed nine coping mechanism scales (e.g., objectivity, intellectuality, suppression) and seven defense mechanism scales (e.g., denial, projection, regression). Haan's work was later extended by Joffe and Naditch (1977), who used a larger group of subjects and more rigorous empirical procedures to develop 20 self-report defense scales (10 coping mechanism and 10 defense mechanism scales).

One of the most widely used self-report measures of defense has been the *Defense Mechanism Inventory* (DMI; Gleser & Ihilevich, 1969). A bibliography of DMI research by these authors (Ihilevich & Gleser, 1993) includes over 200 items. The scale was developed to assess five defense mechanism clusters: "turning against the self," "turning against the object," "projection," "reversal," and "principalization." Although the DMI was developed to assess five distinct defense mechanisms, high intercorrelations have been reported among some of the scales (for reviews of this scale, see Cramer, 1990; Endler & Parker, 1995). This finding has led some researchers to suggest that the DMI may assess a general unidimensional aggression/inhibition defense dimension, rather than five separate defense clusters (Juni & Masling, 1980).

Bond, Gardiner, Christian, and Sigel (1983) developed the *Defense Style Questionnaire* (DSQ) to assess a cross section of defense mechanisms. The original scale consisted of 81 items that were selected from a larger pool of items based on ratings of appropriateness by a group of clinicians. A second-order factor analysis of 24 DSQ subscales produced a four-factor defense model: immature defenses, image-distorting defenses, self-sacrificing defenses, and adaptive defenses. Scoring for the DSQ has been modified to reflect a more parsimonious three-factor hierarchical model of defense (Andrews, Pollock, & Stewart, 1989; Bond, 1986). The new scoring system was developed to be consistent with the glossary of defense mechanisms developed for the DSM-III-R (for a copy of this glossary, see Vaillant, 1986). The new scoring system for the DSQ allows for the assessment of a mature defense dimension (e.g., sublimation or humor), a neurotic defense dimension (e.g., reaction formation or undoing), and an immature defense dimension (e.g., projection or somatization).

In addition to developing measures that assess a cross section of defense mechanisms, many researchers have focused on developing methods for assessing specific defenses. The concept of repression, in particular, has received special research attention (Singer, 1990). Although highly critical of the outcome of this work, Holmes (1974, 1990) has pointed out that the experimental study of the repression construct represents a large and important body of psychological research. Along with developing self-report measures of repression, researchers have used three distinct laboratory approaches to the study of this variable: differential recall of unpleasant and pleasant experiences, differential recall of uncompleted and completed tasks, and changes in recall associated with the introduction and elimination of stress (Holmes, 1990).

The most common method for assessing repression, however, has probably been the Repression-Sensitization scale (R-S; Byrne, 1961; Byrne, Barry, & Nelson, 1963). The R-S scale, which comprises items from the MMPI that ask about the presence of symptoms, identifies individuals believed to use a variety of strategies to avoid awareness of impulses and affects. This scale was developed following the proposal that persons who do not acknowledge having many symptoms can be described as "repressors," whereas persons who acknowledge symptoms can be described as "sensitizers." Although a sizable literature on personality and health has developed using the R-S scale (see Weinberger, 1990), several basic problems with the measure have been widely discussed in the literature. Many researchers, for example, have found that the measure correlates quite highly with measures of anxiety and social desirability (see Bell & Byrne, 1978 for a review of this research). As a consequence, it has been proposed that the R-S scale is primarily a measure of anxiety (Cramer, 1990; Slough, Kleinknecht, & Thorndike, 1984). Holmes (1990) has suggested that there is also a serious conceptual problem with the R-S scale: "There is no way to distinguish between individuals who actually have symptoms and do not report them ('repressors,' or more likely deniers) and individuals who do not have symptoms and therefore cannot report them (nonrepressors)" (Holmes, 1990, p. 94).

In response to some of the problems that have been reported with the R-S scale, Weinberger, Schwartz, and Davidson (1979) redefined the definition of repressors as individuals who score low on a measure of anxiety *and* high on a measure of social desirability such as the Marlowe-Crowne Social Desirability Scale (Crowne & Marlowe, 1960). Low-anxious (or low symptom) individuals were identified as those respondents low on both the anxiety scale and the social desirability measure. Davis (1990) and Weinberger (1990) review almost a decade of research that tends, overall, to support the construct validity of using self-report measures of anxiety and social desirability (defensiveness) to assess repressive style.

COPING RESEARCH

In the 1960s, a new line of research, initially related to work being conducted on defense mechanisms, began to coalesce under the "coping" label. Before this period, the word coping had been used informally in the medical and social science literature (for more discussion on the history of the coping construct, see Lazarus, 1993; Lazarus et al., 1974; Lazarus & Launier, 1978; Roth & Cohen, 1986; White, 1974). In the 1960s, however, the concept of coping began to acquire a technical meaning for some researchers. A number of writers began to label certain "adaptive" defense mechanisms (e.g., sublimation or humor) "coping" activities (see, e.g., Alker, 1968; Haan, 1963; Hunter & Goodstein, 1967; Kroeber,

1963; Speisman, Lazarus, Mordkoff, & Davison, 1964; Visotsky, Hamburg, Goss, & Lebovits, 1961; Weinstock, 1967). According to Haan (1965): "Coping behaviour is distinguished from defensive behaviour, since the latter by definition is rigid, compelled, reality distorting, and undifferentiated, whereas, the former is flexible, purposive, reality oriented, and differentiated" (Haan, 1965, p. 374). It is important to emphasize that this early coping work was still within the tradition of defense mechanism research.*

For a number of researchers in the 1960s and early 1970s, the initial work on adaptive defenses led to an independent interest in the study of the *conscious* strategies used by individuals encountering stressful or upsetting situations (see, e.g., Sidle, Moos, Adams, & Cady, 1969). Conscious strategies for reacting to stressful or upsetting situations were conceptualized in this new literature as coping responses. Very quickly, this type of coping research became a large and self-contained research area distinct from the older literature on defense mechanisms (see an early review of the coping area by Lazarus et al., 1974).

The first generation of coping researchers shared a number of concerns that had a lasting impact on the coping area. Although virtually an unlimited number of coping strategies are available to an individual in a particular stressful situation, the first generation of coping researchers began to identify and study a limited number of basic coping responses (see Averill & Rosenn, 1972; Cohen & Lazarus, 1973; Kahn, Wolfe, Quinn, Snoek, & Rosenthal, 1964; Lazarus et al., 1974; Pearlin & Schooler, 1978; Sidle et al., 1969). Two coping dimensions, in particular, were identified by researchers early on and have continued to attract much of the research attention: *emotion-focused* coping and *problem-focused* coping.

To summarize a sizable, and not always consistent literature (for reviews, see Lazarus & Folkman, 1984; Parker & Endler, 1992), the problem-focused coping dimension involves strategies that attempt to solve, reconceptualize, or minimize the effects of a stressful situation. The emotion-focused coping dimension, on the other hand, includes strategies that involve self-preoccupation, fantasy, or other conscious activities related to affect regulation. Almost all coping measures developed in the past few decades include scales that assess these two coping dimensions (see, e.g., Billings & Moos, 1981; Carver, Scheier, & Weintraub, 1989; Endler & Parker, 1990a, 1990b; Epstein & Meier, 1989; Folkman & Lazarus, 1980, 1985, 1988; Nowack, 1989; Patterson & McCubbin, 1987)—one sign of the importance of these dimensions to researchers in the coping area.

Avoidance-oriented coping, another basic dimension identified by the first generation of coping researchers, has continued to generate considerable research attention (for reviews, see Roth & Cohen, 1986; Suls & Fletcher, 1985). Depending on the theorist, the avoidance coping dimension has been conceptualized as involving person-oriented and/or task-oriented responses (for discussion on this point, see Parker & Endler, 1992). An individual can react to a stressful

---

* A source of confusion in the coping and defense literature, a number of researchers involved in the study of defense mechanisms continue to use the word coping to signify adaptive defenses (see Haan, 1982, 1992).

situation by seeking out other people (social diversion) or can engage in a substitute task (distraction). Along with assessing problem-focused and emotion-focused dimensions, most of the coping measures that have been developed include scales that assess avoidance coping responses (see, e.g., Amirkhan, 1990; Billings & Moos, 1981; Endler & Parker, 1990a, 1990b; Feifel & Strack, 1989; Nowack, 1989).

The type of stressful situations attracting the attention of the early coping researchers also played an important role in shaping future research activities. Within the defense mechanism literature, there had long been a tradition of studying reactions to severe or life-threatening situations (see, e.g., Grinker & Spiegel, 1945; Hamburg, Hamburg, & DeGoza, 1953; Lindemann, 1944). For the first generation of coping researchers, however, attention focused almost exclusively on the study of coping reactions to life-threatening or traumatic life events (see, e.g., the early coping research by Bazeley & Viney, 1974; Dimsdale, 1974; Greenberg, Weltz, Spitz, & Bizzozero, 1975; Henderson & Bostock, 1975; Klein, 1974; McCubbin, Hunter, & Dahl, 1975; Viney & Clarke, 1974). The study of coping responses to life-threatening or traumatic events became so common, in the early 1970s, that some theorists began to define the coping area as the study of responses and reactions to *extreme* situations (see, e.g., Hamburg, 1974; White, 1974).

Although coping researchers would eventually turn their attention to studying a broad range of stressful situations, their initial preoccupation with extreme situations had the unforeseen effect of promoting the study of situational variables in coping research at the expense of person (predispositional) variables. In the older defense mechanism literature, derived from classic psychoanalytic theory, person variables were of prime importance. By focusing attention on coping activities in highly stressful situations, however, the early coping researchers inadvertently increased the likelihood that person variables would be found to be poor predictors of specific coping activities. Although individuals may have habitual coping preferences, life-threatening or extreme situations typically permit only a narrow range of possible coping responses.

Not surprisingly, during the 1970s and early 1980s, more and more coping researchers came to believe that "coping patterns were not greatly determined by person factors" (Folkman & Lazarus, 1980, p. 229). Researchers began to stress the importance of studying the situational context in which coping took place (Billings & Moos, 1981; Felton & Revenson, 1984; Folkman & Lazarus, 1985; Pearlin & Schooler, 1978; Stone & Neale, 1984). Reviewing the early history of the coping area, Lazarus has said:

In the late 1970s a major new development in coping theory and research occurred in which the hierarchical view of coping, with its traits or style emphasis, was abandoned in favour of a contrasting approach, which treated *coping as a process.* From a process perspective, coping changes over time and in accordance with the situational contexts in which it occurs. (Lazarus, 1993, p. 235)

Consistent with the view that situational factors determine specific coping responses, many researchers began to focus attention on studying variables, such as the cognitive appraisals of stressful situations (e.g., Lazarus & Folkman, 1984) and coping resources (e.g., Antonovsky, 1979). Over the years, both psychological and environmental factors have attracted research attention in the study of coping resources. Psychological factors might include variables like self-esteem or self-efficacy, whereas environmental factors might include social support networks, financial resources, or education (for a review, see Eckenrode, 1991; Wethington & Kessler, 1991).

During the late 1960s and early 1970s, important events were going on in psychology as a whole, that functioned to discourage interest in person variables among the early coping researchers. The history of the coping area mirrors events going on in personality psychology. In the 1960s, situationism became a serious challenge to the hegemony of the trait approach for the study of personality (for more details on this history, see Endler & Parker, 1992). Although comprising a heterogeneous collection of theorists and researchers, situationism emphasized that external environmental factors were the major determinants of personality (Endler, 1983). The rise of situationism meant that, for the first time in the history of modern psychology, the volume of research on the effects of environmental factors on personality rivaled that generated by psychologists studying traits (Endler, 1983; Endler & Parker, 1992; Parker, 1991). By the early 1970s, some personality researchers were writing about the imminent demise of the trait approach (Mischel, 1973). It would be naive to believe that the theoretical debates going on among personality researchers did not have an impact on the coping area.

Predictions about the imminent demise of individual differences research has proven to be incorrect. During the 1980s and early 1990s, trait research has flourished again in the personality area (Angleitner, 1991; Digman, 1990; Endler & Parker, 1992; Wiggins & Pincus, 1992). Not surprisingly, there has been a renewed interest in person variables by some coping researchers, although it needs to be emphasized that many researchers in the coping area continue to downplay the importance of person variables (see Folkman, 1992; Lazarus, 1993). Carpenter (1992), for example, has noted that "historically, efforts to understand coping as personality attributes, or even as styles, have not been very successful" (p. 4).

The distinction between those coping researchers who emphasize the importance of predisposition variables (traits) and those researchers who emphasize situational factors (coping as a process) has sometimes been referred to in the coping literature as the distinction between an *interindividual* and an *intraindividual* approach to coping (Endler & Parker, 1990b; Endler, Parker, & Summerfeldt, 1993; Folkman, Lazarus, Dunkel-Schetter, Delongis, & Gruen, 1986; Lazarus, 1993; Parker & Endler, 1992). The *interindividual* approach to coping attempts to identify basic coping styles: habitual coping strategies used by particular individuals across different types of stressful situations. The *intraindividual* approach to coping, on the other hand, attempts to identify basic coping behaviors or strategies used by individuals in particular types of stressful or upsetting situations. This approach "assumes that individuals have a repertoire of coping options available to them from which they can build what they believe to be the most effective strategy, depending on the nature of the situation" (Cox & Ferguson, 1991, p. 20). Although almost an unlimited number of potential coping strategies and reactions are available to a person in a particular situation, there is an assumption that these activities can be classified into a small number of basic coping dimensions.

COPING ASSESSMENT

As with the history surrounding the study of defense mechanisms, work on the assessment of various coping constructs has dwarfed the theoretical literature on the topic. Over the past few decades, a vast literature has developed on coping assessment. The size and complexity of this assessment literature warrant a few historical comments. Unlike the assessment of defense mechanisms, where researchers have utilized a variety of methods, most researchers in the coping area (whether they advocate an interindividual or intraindividual approach) have used self-report measures to assess coping reactions and responses.

Intraindividual Coping Measures

Situation-Specific Measures
The first type is intraindividual measures that assess basic coping strategies or responses for responding to a *specific* stressful situation (e.g., pain symptoms, job loss, cancer). The items used with these measures assess coping activities congruent with the particular situation. Over the past two decades, a plethora of situation-specific measures have appeared that assess coping responses to various types of illness or health problems (see, e.g., Butler, Damarin, Beaulieu, Schwebel, & Thorn, 1989; Feifel, Strack, & Nagy, 1987; McCubbin et al., 1983). Job loss and unemployment are other stressors that have generated a large number of situation-specific coping measures (for a detailed review of this literature, see Latack & Havlovic, 1992).

The study of the relationship between coping and health, in particular, has evolved into one of the most popular topics in the coping area (Auerbach, 1989; Endler, Parker, & Summerfeldt, 1993; Parker & Endler, 1992; Taylor, 1990). A variety of models have appeared that conceptualize coping as an integral part of the interaction of psychological, environmental, and biological factors influencing health and well-being (see Lazarus & Folkman, 1984; Thomae, 1987). In reviewing this voluminous literature, Aldwin (1994) has noted that three general coping and health models have tended to be utilized. The first model, used most often in the coping and health literature, assumes that coping strategies or behaviors have a direct effect on specific health variables (e.g., blood pressure, rate of recovery). The second model, used less frequently in the coping literature, takes the view that coping behaviors have an indirect effect on health by creating a change in some health-related behavior (e.g., maintaining regular contact with health professionals). The third model, also used less often in the literature, takes the view that coping strategies moderate or buffer the stress generated by a specific health problem.

Multiple Situation Measures

The second type of intraindividual measure assesses a number of basic coping strategies or responses that could be used in a *variety* of stressful situations. The items used with these measures assess a broad range of potential coping activities so that the scales can be used with individuals experiencing an array of different stressful situations. Respondents are usually asked to identify a recent stressful event and to respond to the coping items with reference to this specific event. Both types of measures (multiple and specific situation scales) can be used on multiple occasions with the same respondents to study coping responses over the course of a specific stressful episode or similar stressful situations. Thus, researchers can obtain an indirect measure of coping processes.

The intraindividual coping measure that has had the greatest impact on the coping area is the *Ways of Coping Checklist* (WCC; Folkman & Lazarus, 1980), later revised and renamed as the *Ways of Coping Questionnaire* (WCQ; Folkman & Lazarus, 1988; for reviews of these scales, see Ben-Porath, Waller, & Butcher, 1991; Parker, Endler, & Bagby, 1993; Stone, Greenberg, Kennedy-Moore, & Newman, 1991; Stone & Kennedy-Moore, 1992; Stone, Kennedy-Moore, Newman, Greenberg, & Neale, 1992; Tennen & Herzberger, 1985). Because the WCC and WCQ have been used to study coping in hundreds of published studies, and have also been used as models for the development of other coping measures (see, e.g., Amirkhan, 1990; Billings & Moos, 1981), a few historical comments about the development of these scales needs to be made.

The WCC (Folkman & Lazarus, 1980) was a 68-item self-report measure (yes/no format) developed to assess two basic coping strategies: problem-focused coping and emotion-focused coping. Respondents were asked to respond to the coping items with respect to how they have reacted to a particular stressful situation. Scoring for the WCC was developed from a factor analysis of the coping items in a sample of 100 middle-aged adults (Aldwin, Folkman, Shaefer, Coyne, & Lazarus, 1980). Although the sample size was probably too small to derive a stable factor structure, Aldwin et al. (1980) found seven interpretable factors: one problem-focused factor and six emotion-focused coping factors.

Attempts to cross-validate the WCC's factor structure have met with mixed results (for a review, see Tennen & Herzberger, 1985). For example, in a study with 425 medical students, Vitaliano, Russo, Carr, Maiuro, and Becker (1985) factor analyzed the WCC and found six factors. From these six factors, five interpretable coping scales were created. Problem-Focused, Seeking Social Support, Blamed-Self, Avoidance, and the Wishful Thinking scales were created using a pattern of items different from scales with these names identified by Folkman and Lazarus (1980), and Aldwin et al. (1980). Vitaliano et al. (1985) also found moderate to high correlations between the coping scales whether they used the scoring for the original coping scales (Folkman & Lazarus, 1980; intercorrelations, .24 to .95) or the revised coping scales (intercorrelations, .31 to .87).

Folkman and Lazarus (1985) subsequently modified the WCC by dropping some items and adding new ones. The response format was changed from a yes/no format to a 4-point Likert frequency scale and the revised 66-item scale (now known as the Ways of Coping Questionnaire; WCQ) was administered to 198 undergraduates on three separate occasions. A factor analysis of the 324 completed questionnaires was used to develop 8 coping scales: Problem-Focused, Wishful Thinking, Distancing, Emphasizing the Positive, Self-Blame, Tension-Reduction, Self-Isolation, and Seeking Social Support. Moderate internal consistency reliabilities for the subscales were reported by Folkman and Lazarus (1985), ranging from a low of .56 to a high of .85.

Folkman et al. (1986) administered the WCQ to 85 married couples on five different occasions over 6 months and selected 50 items to be factor analyzed from the pool of coping responses. This analysis produced an 8-factor solution that was used to construct eight scales: Confrontive Coping, Distancing, Self-Controlling, Seeking Social Support, Accepting Responsibility, Escape-Avoidance, Planful Problem Solving, and Positive Reappraisal. This scoring system for the measure was eventually adopted by Folkman and Lazarus (1988) in the test manual for the WCQ. The eight coping scales had moderate alpha coefficients in the derivation sample, ranging from .61 to .79; however, test-retest reliability data for the WCQ has not been reported in the literature (see the test manual for the WCQ, Folkman & Lazarus, 1988). In addition, some researchers have had problems replicating the WCQ factor structure (see Parker et al., 1993).

Folkman and Lazarus (1985) have suggested that the issue of test-retest reliability is difficult to apply to the WCQ because it assesses *situation-specific* coping activity. Thus, research on the reliability of the WCQ has been restricted to questions about internal reliability. The problem of whether test-retest data can be collected for situation-specific scales is similar to one encountered by researchers developing self-report measures for state anxiety (cf. Endler, Edwards, & Vitelli, 1991). State anxiety is influenced by the particular situation in which it is assessed. However, some researchers developing state anxiety measures have been able to demonstrate adequate test-retest reliability by collecting state anxiety data in two or more similar situations. A similar procedure could be followed by those developing situation-specific coping measures.

Interindividual Coping Measures

Person variables and coping research continue to be controversial topics in the coping literature. Folkman (1992), for example, has recently said that "measures of coping traits and dispositions are generally not predictive of how a person copes in an actual, naturally-occurring, stressful event" (p. 33; see also the recent comments by Carpenter, 1992; Lazarus, 1993). During the 1980s and early

1990s, the topic of coping styles (or predispositions) has again attracted the attention of some coping researchers (for some interesting comments on this recent literature, see McCrae, 1992; Miller, 1992). Much of the recent research on coping styles has focused on developing reliable and valid interindividual coping measures.

The *Coping Inventory for Stressful Situations* (CISS), for example, was developed by Endler and Parker (1990a, 1990b, 1993, 1994) in a series of factor analytic studies to reliably assess three basic coping styles: task-oriented coping, emotion-oriented coping, and avoidance-oriented coping. The factor structure of the CISS has been cross-validated in samples of undergraduates, normal adults, and psychiatric inpatients (Endler & Parker, 1990a, 1994). Factor structures for men and women were also compared in the various samples and found to be virtually identical (Endler & Parker, 1990a).

FUTURE DIRECTIONS

The lack of interest by most coping researchers in integrating the interindividual and intraindividual approaches is a distinctive feature of the contemporary coping area. In recent years, researchers working within the two coping traditions appear to have grown more distant from each other (cf. Folkman, 1992; Lazarus, 1993). Reminiscent of events going on at the height of the "person-situation debate" in the personality area (for a review of this debate, see Endler & Parker, 1992; Kenrick & Funder, 1988), coping researchers rarely assess both situational and stylistic coping variables in their research. When both types of variables are used in a particular study, it is usually because the researcher wants to demonstrate the importance of one variable over the other (cf. Ptacek, Smith, Espe, & Raffety, 1994).

Coping researchers might benefit by examining some of the lessons that personality researchers learned from the person-situation debate earlier in this century. Rather than focusing attention on either trait or situational variables, many personality researchers began to emphasize the importance of the simultaneous study of both variables; the interactional model of personality (Endler, 1983; Endler & Magnusson, 1976) was seen to be an important advance in the study of personality. The interactional model proposed that behavior was

> . . . a function of a continuous multidirectional process of person-by-situation interactions; cognitive, motivational and emotional factors have important determining roles on behavior, regarding the person side; and the perception or psychological meaning that the situation has for the person is an essential determining factor of behavior. (Endler, 1983, p. 160)

As the vast amount of research reviewed in this book makes clear, both situational and stylistic variables have been found to play roles in specific coping responses. We believe the coping area will have made a substantial advance when researchers assess routinely both types of coping variables.

REFERENCES

Aldwin, C. (1994). *Stress, coping, and development: An integrative perspective.* New York: Guilford.

Aldwin, C., Folkman, S., Shaefer, C., Coyne, J., & Lazarus, R. (1980, September). *Ways of Coping Checklist: A process measure.* Paper presented at the American Psychological Association Annual Convention, Montreal, Canada.

Alker, H. A. (1968). Coping, defense and socially desirable responses. *Psychological Reports, 22,* 985–988.

American Psychiatric Association. (1994). *Diagnostic and statistical manual of mental disorders* (4th ed.). Washington, DC: Author.

Amirkhan, J. H. (1990). A factor analytically derived measure of coping: The Coping Strategy Indicator. *Journal of Personality and Social Psychology, 59,* 1066–1074.

Andrews, G., Pollock, C., & Stewart, G. (1989). The determination of defense style by questionnaire. *Archives of general psychiatry, 46,* 455–460.

Angleitner, A. (1991). Personality psychology: Trends and developments. *European Journal of Personality, 5,* 185–197.

Antonovsky, A. (1979). *Health, stress, and coping.* San Francisco: Jossey-Bass.

Aronow, E., & Reznikoff, M. (1976). *Rorschach content interpretation.* New York: Grune and Stratton.

Auerback, S. M. (1989). Stress management and coping research in the health care setting: An overview and methodological commentary. *Journal of Consulting and Clinical Psychology, 57,* 388–395.

Averill, J. R., & Rosenn, M. (1972). Vigilant and nonvigilant coping strategies and psychophysical stress reactions during anticipation of electric shock. *Journal of Personality and Social Psychology, 23,* 128–141.

Bazeley, P., & Viney, L. L. (1974). Women coping with crisis: A preliminary community study. *Journal of Community Psychology, 2,* 321–329.

Beardslee, W., Jacobson, A., Hauser, S., Noam, G., & Powers, S. (1985). An approach to evaluating adolescent adaptive processes: Scale development and reliability. *Journal of American Child Psychiatry, 24,* 637–642.

Bell, P. A., & Byrne, D. (1978). Repression-sensitization. In H. London & J. E. Exner (Eds.), *Dimensions of personality* (pp. 449–485). New York: Wiley.

Ben-Porath, Y. S., Waller, N. G., & Butcher, J. W. (1991). Assessment of coping: An empirical illustration of the problem of inapplicable items. *Journal of Personality Assessment, 57,* 162–176.

Billings, A. G., & Moos, R. H. (1981). The role of coping responses and social resources in attenuating the impact of stressful life events. *Journal of Behavioral Medicine, 4,* 139–157.

Bond, M. (1986). An empirical study of defense styles. In G. E. Vaillant (Ed.), *Empirical studies of ego mechanisms of defense* (pp. 1–29). Washington, DC: American Psychiatric Press.

Bond, M., Gardiner, S. T., Christian, J., & Sigel, J. J. (1983). An empirical examination of defense mechanisms. *Archives of General Psychiatry, 40,* 333–338.

Brenner, C. (1957). The nature and development of the concept of repression in Freud's writings. *Psychoanalytic Study of the Child, 12,* 19–46.

Breuer, J., & Freud, S. (1955). On the psychical mechanisms of hysterical phenomena: Preliminary communication. In J. Strachey (Ed. and Trans.), *The standard edition of the complete psychological works of Sigmund Freud* (Vol. 2). London: Hogarth Press. (Original work published 1893)

Butler, R. W., Damarin, F. L., Beaulieu, C., Schwebel, A. I., & Thorn, B. E. (1989). Assessing cognitive coping strategies for acute postsurgical pain. *Psychological Assessment, 1,* 41–45.

Byrne, D. (1961). The Repression-Sensitization Scale: Rationale, reliability, and validity. *Journal of Personality, 29,* 334–349.

Byrne, D., Barry, J., & Nelson, D. (1963). The revised Repression-Sensitization Scale and its relationship to measures of self-description. *Psychological Reports, 13,* 323–334.

Carpenter, B. N. (1992). Issues and advances in coping research. In B. N. Carpenter (Ed.), *Personal coping: Theory, research, and application* (pp. 1–13). Westport, CT: Praeger.

Carver, C. S., Scheier, M. F., & Weintraub, J. K. (1989). Assessing coping strategies: A theoretically based approach. *Journal of Personality and Social Psychology, 56,* 267–283.

Cohen, F., & Lazarus, R. S. (1973). Active coping processes, coping dispositions, and recovery from surgery. *Psychosomatic Medicine, 35,* 375–389.

Cox, T., & Ferguson, E. (1991). Individual differences, stress and coping. In C. L. Cooper & R. Payne (Eds.), *Personality and stress: Individual differences in the stress process* (pp. 7–30). Chichester, UK: Wiley.

Cramer, P. (1988). The Defense Mechanism Inventory: A review of research and discussion of the scales. *Journal of Personality Assessment, 52,* 142–164.

Cramer, P. (1990). *The development of defense mechanisms: Theory, research, and assessment.* New York: Springer-Verlag.

Crowne, D. P., & Marlowe, D. A. (1960). A new scale of social desirability independent of psychopathology. *Journal of Consulting Psychology, 24,* 349–354.

Davis, P. J. (1990). Repression and the inaccessibility of emotional memories. In J. L. Singer (Ed.), *Repression and dissociation: Implications for personality theory, psychopathology, and health* (pp. 387–403). Chicago: University of Chicago Press.

Digman, J. M. (1990). Personality structure: Emergence of the five-factor model. *Annual Review of Psychology, 41,* 417–440.

Dimsdale, J. E. (1974). The coping behavior of Nazi concentration camp survivors. *American Journal of Psychiatry, 131,* 792–797.

Eckenrode, J. (1991). *The social context of coping.* New York: Plenum.

Endler, N. S. (1983). Interactionism: A personality model, but not yet a theory. In M. M. Page (Ed.), *Nebraska Symposium on Motivation, 1982: Personality—Current theory and research* (pp. 155–220). Lincoln: University of Nebraska Press.

Endler, N. S., Edwards, J. M., & Vitelli, R. (1991). *Endler Multidimensional Anxiety Scales (EMAS): Manual.* Los Angeles: Western Psychological Services.

Endler, N. S., & Magnusson, D. (1976). Toward an interactional psychology of personality. *Psychological Bulletin, 83,* 956–974.

Endler, N. S., & Parker, J. D. A. (1990a). *Coping Inventory for Stressful Situations (CISS): Manual.* Toronto: Multi-Health Systems.

Endler, N. S., & Parker, J. D. A. (1990b). Multidimensional assessment of coping: A critical evaluation. *Journal of Personality and Social Psychology, 58,* 844–854.

Endler, N. S., & Parker, J. D. A. (1992). Interactionism revisited: The continuing crisis in the personality area. *European Journal of Personality, 6,* 177–198.

Endler, N. S., & Parker, J. D. A. (1993). The multidimensional assessment of coping: Concepts, issues and measurement. In G. L. VanHeck, P. Bonaiuto, I. Deary, & W. Nowack (Eds.), *Personality psychology in Europe* (pp. 309–319). Tilburg, The Netherlands: Tilburg University Press.

Endler, N. S., & Parker, J. D. A. (1994). Assessment of multidimensional coping: Task, emotion, and avoidance strategies. *Psychological Assessment, 6,* 50–60.

Endler, N. S., & Parker, J. D. A. (1995). Assessing a patient's ability to cope. In J. N. Butcher (Ed.), *Practical considerations in clinical personality assessment* (pp. 329–352). New York: Oxford University Press.

Endler, N. S., Parker, J. D. A., & Summerfeldt, L. J. (1993). Coping with health problems: Conceptual and methodological issues. *Canadian Journal of Behavioural Science, 25,* 384–399.

Epstein, S., & Meier, P. (1989). Constructive thinking: A broad coping variable with specific components. *Journal of Personality and Social Psychology, 57,* 332–350.

Feifel, H., & Strack, S. (1989). Coping with conflict situations: Middle-aged and elderly men. *Psychology and Aging, 4,* 26–33.

Feifel, H., Strack, S., & Nagy, V. T. (1987). Degree of life-threat and differential use of coping modes. *Journal of Psychosomatic Research, 31,* 91–99.

Felton, B. J., & Revenson, T. A. (1984). Coping with chronic illness: A study of illness controllability and the influence of coping strategies on psychological adjustment. *Journal of Consulting and Clinical Psychology, 52,* 343–353.

Fenichel, O. (1945). *The psychoanalytic theory of neurosis.* New York: Norton.

Folkman, S. (1992). Making the case for coping. In B. N. Carpenter (Ed.), *Personal coping: Theory, research, and application* (pp. 31–46). Westport, CT: Praeger.

Folkman, S., & Lazarus, R. S. (1980). An analysis of coping in a middle-aged community sample. *Journal of Health and Social Behavior, 21,* 219–239.

Folkman, S., & Lazarus, R. S. (1985). If it changes it must be a process: A study of emotion and coping during three stages of a college examination. *Journal of Personality and Social Psychology, 48,* 150–170.

Folkman, S., & Lazarus, R. S. (1988). *Manual for the Ways of Coping Questionnaire.* Palo Alto, CA: Consulting Psychologist Press.

Folkman, S., Lazarus, R. S., Dunkel-Schetter, C., DeLongis, A., & Gruen, R. (1986). The dynamics of a stressful encounter. *Journal of Personality and Social Psychology, 50,* 992–1003.

Freud, A. (1946). *The ego and the mechanisms of defense.* New York: International Universities Press. (Original work published 1936)

Freud, S. (1955). Further remarks on the neuro-psychoses of defence. In J. Strachey (Ed. and Trans.), *The standard edition of the complete psychological works of Sigmund Freud* (Vol. 3). London: Hogarth Press. (Original work published 1896)

Freud, S. (1955). History of the psychoanalytic movement. In J. Strachey (Ed. and Trans.), *The standard edition of the complete psychological works of Sigmund Freud* (Vol. 14). London: Hogarth Press. (Original work published 1914)

Freud, S. (1959). Inhibitions, symptoms, and anxiety. In J. Strachey (Ed. and Trans.), *The standard edition of the complete psychological works of Sigmund Freud* (Vol. 20). London: Hogarth Press. (Original work published 1926)

Giovacchini, P. L. (1981). The axes of DSM-III. *American Journal of Psychiatry, 138,* 119–120.

Gleser, G. C., & Ihilevich, D. (1969). An objective instrument for measuring defense mechanisms. *Journal of Consulting and Clinical Psychology, 33,* 51–60.

Gough, H. G. (1957). *Manual for the California Personality Inventory.* Palo Alto, CA: Consulting Psychologist Press.

Greenberg, I. M., Weltz, S., Spitz, C., & Bizzozero, O. J. (1975). Factors of adjustment in chronic hemodialysis patients. *Psychosomatics, 16,* 178–184.

Grinker, R. R., & Spiegel, J. P. (1945). *Men under stress.* New York: McGraw-Hill.

Groot, J. L. (1957). On defense and development: Normal and pathological. *Psychoanalytic Study of the Child, 12,* 114–126.

Haan, N. (1963). Proposed model of ego functioning: Coping and defense mechanisms in relationship to IQ change. *Psychological Monograph, 77*(8), 1–27.

Haan, N. (1965). Coping and defense mechanisms related to personality inventories. *Journal of Consulting Psychology, 29,* 373–378.

Haan, N. (1977). *Coping and defending: Processes of self-environment organization.* New York: Academic Press.

Haan, N. (1982). Assessment of coping, defense, and stress. In L. Goldberger & S. Breznitz (Eds.), *Handbook of stress: Theoretical and clinical aspects* (pp. 254–269). New York: Free Press.

Haan, N. (1992). The assessment of coping, defense, and stress. In L. Goldberger & S. Breznitz (Eds.), *Handbook of stress: Theoretical and clinical aspects* (2nd ed., pp. 258–273). New York: Free Press.

Hamburg, D. A. (1974). Coping behavior in life-threatening circumstances. *Psychotherapy and Psychosomatics, 23,* 13–25.

Hamburg, D. A., Hamburg, B., & DeGoza, S. (1953). Adaptive problems and mechanisms in severely burned patients. *Psychiatry, 16,* 1–12.

Hartmann, H. (1939). Psycho-analysis and the concept of health. *International Journal of Psychoanalysis, 20,* 308–321.

Hartmann, H. (1958). *Ego psychology and the problem of adaptation.* New York: International Universities Press. (Original work published in 1939)

Henderson, A. S., & Bostock, F. T. (1975). Coping behaviour: Correlates of survival on a raft. *Australian and New Zealand Journal of Psychiatry, 9,* 221–223.

Holmes, D. S. (1974). Investigation of repression: Differential recall of material experimentally or naturally associated with ego threat. *Psychological Bulletin, 81,* 632–653.

Holmes, D. S. (1990). The evidence for repression: An examination of sixty years of research. In J. L. Singer (Ed.), *Repression and dissociation: Implications for personality theory, psychopathology, and health* (pp. 85–102). Chicago: University of Chicago Press.

Holt, R. R. (1956). Gauging primary and secondary processes in Rorschach responses. *Journal of Projective Techniques, 5,* 14–25.

Horney, K. (1937). *The neurotic personality of our time.* New York: Norton.

Hunter, C. G., & Goodstein, L. D. (1967). Ego strength and types of defensive and coping behavior. *Journal of Consulting Psychology, 31,* 432.

Ihilevich, D., & Gleser, G. C. (1993). *Defense Mechanisms Inventory bibliography.* Odessa, FL: Psychological Assessment Resources.

Jacobson, A. M., Beardslee, W., Hauser, S. T., Noam, G. G., Powers, S. I., Houlihan, J., & Rider, E. (1986). Evaluating ego defense mechanisms using clinical interviews: An empirical study of adolescent diabetic and psychiatric patients. *Journal of Adolescence, 9,* 303–319.

Joffe, P. E., & Naditch, M. (1977). Paper and pencil measures of coping and defense processes. In N. Haan (Ed.), *Coping and defending: Processes of self-environment organization* (pp. 280–297). New York: Academic Press.

Juni, S., & Masling, J. (1980). Reaction to aggression and the Defense Mechanism Inventory. *Journal of Personality Assessment, 44,* 484–486.

Kahn, R. L., Wolfe, D. M., Quinn, R. P., Snoek, D., & Rosenthal, R. A. (1964). *Organizational stress: Studies in role conflict and ambiguity.* New York: Wiley.

Kenrick, D. T., & Funder, D. C. (1988). Profiting from controversy: Lessons from the person-situation debate. *American Psychologist, 43,* 23–34.

Klein, H. (1974). Delayed affects and after-effects of severe traumatisation. *Israel Annals of Psychiatry and Related Disciplines, 12,* 293–303.

Kline, P. (1991). The relationship between objective measures of defences. In M. Olff, G. Godaert, & H. Ursin (Eds.), *Quantification of human defence mechanisms* (pp. 22–40). New York: Springer-Verlag.

Kroeber, T. C. (1963). The coping functions of the ego mechanisms. In R. W. White (Ed.), *The study of lives: Essays on personality in honor of Henry A. Murray* (pp. 178–189). New York: Atherton Press.

Latack, J. C., & Havlovic, S. J. (1992). Coping with job stress: A conceptual evaluation framework for coping measures. *Journal of Organizational Behavior, 13,* 479–508.

Lazarus, R. S. (1993). Coping theory and research: Past, present, and future. *Psychosomatic Medicine, 55,* 234–247.

Lazarus, R. S., Averill, J. R., & Opton, E. M. (1974). The psychology of coping: Issues of research and assessment. In G. V. Coelho, D. A. Hamburg, & J. E. Adams (Eds.), *Coping and adaptation* (pp. 47–68). New York: Basic Books.

Lazarus, R. S., & Folkman, S. (1984). *Stress, appraisal, and coping.* New York: Springer.

Lazarus, R. S., & Launier, R. (1978). Stress-related transactions between person and environment. In L. A. Pervin & M. Lewis (Eds.), *Perspectives in interactional psychology* (pp. 287–327). New York: Plenum.

Lerner, P. M. (1990). Rorschach assessment of primitive defenses: A review. *Journal of Personality Assessment, 54,* 30–46.

Lerner, P. M. (1991). *Psychoanalytic theory and the Rorschach.* Hillsdale, NJ: Analytic Press.

Lindemann, E. (1944). Symptomatology and management of acute grief. *American Journal of Psychiatry, 101,* 141–147.

Madison, P. (1956). Freud's repression concept: A survey and attempted clarification. *International Journal of Psychoanalysis, 37,* 75–81.

Menninger, K. A. (1954). Regulatory devices of the ego under major stress. *International Journal of Psychoanalysis, 35,* 412–420.

McCrae, R. R. (1992). Situational determinants of coping. In B. N. Carpenter (Ed.), *Personal coping: Theory, research, and application* (pp. 65–76). Westport, CT: Praeger.

McCubbin, H. I., Hunter, E. J., & Dahl, B. B. (1975). Residuals of war: Families of prisoners of war and servicemen missing in action. *Journal of Social Issues, 31,* 95–109.

McCubbin, H. I., McCubbin, M. A., Patterson, J. M., Lauble, A. E., Wilson, L. R., & Warwick, W. (1983). CHIP—Coping Health Inventory for Parents: An assessment of parental coping patterns in the care of the chronically ill child. *Journal of Marriage and the Family, 45,* 359–370.

Miller, S. M. (1980). When is a little information a dangerous thing? Coping with stressful life-events by monitoring vs. blunting. In S. Levine & H. Ursin (Eds.), *Coping and health* (pp. 145–169). New York: Plenum.

Miller, S. M. (1987). Monitoring and blunting: Validation of a questionnaire to assess styles of information seeking under threat. *Journal of Personality and Social Psychology, 52,* 345–353.

Miller, S. M. (1992). Individual differences in the coping process: What to know and when to know it. In B. N. Carpenter (Ed.), *Personal coping: Theory, research, and application* (pp. 65–76). Westport, CT: Praeger.

Miller, S. M., & Mangan, C. E. (1983). Interacting effects of information and coping style in adapting to gynaecologic stress: Should the doctor tell all? *Journal of Personality and Social Psychology, 45,* 223–236.

Mischel, W. (1973). Toward a cognitive, social learning reconceptualization of personality. *Psychological Review, 80,* 252–283.

Morrissey, R. F. (1977). The Haan model of ego functioning: An assessment of empirical research. In N. Haan (Ed.), *Coping and defending: Processes of self-environment organization* (pp. 250–279). New York: Academic Press.

Nowack, K. M. (1989). Coping style, cognitive hardiness, and health status. *Journal of Behavioral Medicine, 12,* 145–158.

Parker, J. D. A. (1991). *The search for the person: The historical development of American personality psychology.* Unpublished doctoral dissertation, York University, Toronto.

Parker, J. D. A., & Endler, N. S. (1992). Coping with coping assessment: A critical review. *European Journal of Psychology, 6,* 321–344.

Parker, J. D. A., Endler, N. S., & Bagby, R. M. (1993). If it changes, it might be unstable: Examining the factor structure of the Ways of Coping Questionnaire. *Psychological Assessment, 5,* 361–368.

Patterson, J. M., & McCubbin, H. I. (1987). Adolescent coping style and behaviors: Conceptualization and measurement. *Journal of Adolescence, 10,* 163–186.

Perry, J. C., & Cooper, S. H. (1989). What do cross-sectional measures of defense mechanisms predict. In G. E. Vaillant (Ed.), *Empirical studies of ego mechanisms of defense* (pp. 47–59). Washington, DC: American Psychiatric Press.

Pearlin, L. I., & Schooler, C. (1978). The structure of coping. *Journal of Health and Social Behavior, 19,* 2–21.

Popplestone, J. A., & McPherson, M. W. (1988). *Dictionary of concepts in general psychology.* New York: Greenwood Press.

Ptacek, J. T., Smith, R. E., Espe, K., & Raffety, B. (1994). Limited correspondence between daily coping reports and retrospective coping recall. *Psychological Assessment, 6,* 41–49.

Roth, S., & Cohen, L. J. (1986). Approach, avoidance, and coping with stress. *American Psychologist, 41,* 813–819.

Sandler, J., & Freud, A. (1985). *The analysis of defense: The ego and the mechanisms of defense revisited.* New York: International Universities Press.

Schafer, R. (1954). *Psychoanalytic interpretation in Rorschach testing.* New York: Grune and Stratton.

Semrad, E., Grinspoon, L., & Fienberg, S. E. (1973). Development of an Ego Profile Scale. *Archives of General Psychiatry, 28,* 70–77.

Sharpe, E. F. (1930). Survey of defence-mechanisms in general character-traits and in conduct: Evaluation of pre-conscious material. *International Journal of Psychoanalysis, 11,* 361–374.

Sidle, A., Moos, R. H., Adams, J., & Cady, P. (1969). Development of a coping scale. *Archives of General Psychiatry, 20,* 225–232.

Singer, J. L. (1990). Preface: A fresh look at repression, dissociation, and the defenses as mechanisms and as personality styles. In J. L. Singer (Ed.), *Repression and dissociation: Implications for personality theory, psychopathology, and health* (pp. xi–xxi). Chicago: University of Chicago Press.

Skodol, A. E., & Perry, J. C. (1993). Should an axis for the defense mechanisms be included in DSM-IV? *Comprehensive Psychiatry, 34,* 108–119.

Slough, N., Kleinknecht, R. A., & Thorndike, R. M. (1984). Relationship of the Repression-Sensitization Scales to anxiety. *Journal of Personality Assessment, 48,* 378–379.

Speisman, J., Lazarus, R., Mordkoff, A., & Davison, L. (1964). Experimental reduction of stress based on ego-defense theory. *Journal of Abnormal and Social Psychology, 68,* 367–380.

Stone, A. A., Greenberg, M. A., Kennedy-Moore, E., & Newman, M. G. (1991). Self-report, situation-specific coping questionnaires: What are they measuring? *Journal of Personality and Social Psychology, 61,* 648–658.

Stone, A. A., & Kennedy-Moore, E. (1992). Assessing situational coping: Conceptual and methodological considerations. In H. S. Friedman (Ed.), *Hostility, coping and health* (pp. 203–214). Washington: American Psychological Association.

Stone, A. A., Kennedy-Moore, E., Newman, M. G., Greenberg, M., & Neale, J. M. (1992). Conceptual and methodological issues in current coping assessments. In B. N. Carpenter (Ed.), *Personal coping: Theory, research, and application* (pp. 15–29). Westport, CT: Praeger.

Stone, A. A., & Neale, J. M. (1984). New measure of daily coping: Development and preliminary results. *Journal of Personality and Social Psychology, 46,* 892–906.

Suls, J., & Fletcher, B. (1985). The relative efficacy of avoidant and nonavoidant coping strategies: A meta-analysis. *Health Psychology, 4,* 249–288.

Taylor, S. E. (1990). Health psychology: The science and the field. *American Psychology, 45,* 40–50.

Tennen, H., & Herzberger, S. (1985). Ways of Coping Scale. In D. J. Keyser & R. C. Sweetland (Eds.), *Test critiques* (Vol. 3., pp. 686–697). Kansas City, MO: Test Corporation of America.

Thomae, H. (1987). Conceptualizations of responses to stress. *European Journal of Personality, 1,* 171–192.

Vaillant, G. E. (1971). Theoretical hierarchy of adaptive ego mechanisms. *Archives of General Psychiatry, 24,* 107–118.

Vaillant, G. E. (1977). *Adaptation to life.* Boston: Little, Brown.

Vaillant, G. E. (1984). The disadvantages of DSM-III outweigh its advantages. *American Journal of Psychiatry, 141,* 542–545.

Vaillant, G. E. (1986). *Empirical studies of ego mechanisms of defense.* Washington, DC: American Psychiatric Press.

Vaillant, G. E., Bond, M., & Vaillant, C. O. (1986). An empirically validated hierarchy of defense mechanisms. *Archives of General Psychiatry, 43,* 786–794.

Vaillant, G. E., & Drake, R. E. (1985). Maturity of ego defenses in relation to DSM-III Axis II personality disorder. *Archives of General Psychiatry, 42,* 597–601.

Van der Leeuw, P. J. (1971). On the development of the concept of defense. *International Journal of Psychoanalysis, 52,* 51–58.

Viney, L. L., & Clarke, A. M. (1974). Children coping with crisis: An analogue study. *British Journal of Social and Clinical Psychology, 13,* 305–313.

Visotsky, H. M., Hamburg, D. A., Goss, M. E., & Lebovits, B. Z. (1961). Coping behavior under extreme stress: Observations of patients with severe poliomyelitis. *Archives of General Psychiatry, 5,* 423–448.

Vitaliano, P. P., Russo, J., Carr, J. E., Maiuro, R. D., & Becker, J. (1985). The Ways of Coping Checklist: Revision and psychometric properties. *Multivariate Behavioral Research, 20,* 3–26.

Waelder, R. (1960). *Basic theory of psychoanalysis.* New York: International Universities Press.

Weinberger, D. A. (1990). The construct validity of the repressive coping style. In J. L. Singer (Ed.), *Repression and dissociation: Implications for personality theory, psychopathology, and health* (pp. 337–386). Chicago: University of Chicago Press.

Weinberger, D. A., Schwartz, G. E., & Davidson, R. J. (1979). Low-anxious, high-anxious, and repressive coping styles: Psychometric patterns and behavioral and physiological responses to stress. *Journal of Abnormal Psychology, 88,* 369–380.

Weinstock, A. R. (1967). Family environment and the development of defense and coping mechanisms. *Journal of Personality and Social Psychology, 5,* 67–75.

Wethington, E., & Kessler, R. C. (1991). Situations and processes of coping. In J. Eckenrode (Eds.), *The social context of coping* (pp. 13–29). New York: Plenum Press.

White, R. W. (1948). *The abnormal personality: A textbook.* New York: Ronald Press.

White, R. W. (1974). Strategies of adaptation: An attempt at systematic description. In G. V. Coelho, D. A. Hamburg, & J. E. Adams (Eds.), *Coping and adaptation* (pp. 47–68). New York: Basic Books.

Wiggins, J. S., & Pincus, A. L. (1992). Personality: Structure and assessment. *Annual Review of Psychology, 43,* 473–504.

CHAPTER 2

Coping, Stress Resistance, and Growth: Conceptualizing Adaptive Functioning

CHARLES J. HOLAHAN, RUDOLF H. MOOS, and JEANNE A. SCHAEFER

Psychology traditionally has focused much of its attention on pathological processes. Thus, psychologists understand vulnerabilities and illness better than adaptive strengths and health; they are better prepared to treat disorder than to promote well-being and personal growth (see Antonovsky, 1987; Seeman, 1989). For psychology to broaden its vision to encompass positive, growth-oriented functioning that is more than the simple absence of disorder, it needs a conceptualization of adaptive process.

We believe that contemporary research on stress and coping provides a model of the mechanisms and processes central to conceptualizing adaptive process in psychology. After a comprehensive review of stress and coping research, Kessler and his associates (Kessler, Price, & Wortman, 1985) concluded, "Diverse strands of research are beginning to converge on a common conception of the stress process. . . . At its center is the notion that stress exposure sets off a *process of adaptation*" (p. 565). Research on stress and coping, in its progression from illness, to resilience, and finally to growth, mirrors a process of expansion and discovery necessary throughout the field of psychology.

Psychological research on stress has grown exponentially during the past quarter century; during this period, conceptualizations of the stress process changed dramatically (see Goldberger & Breznitz, 1993). Early stress research presumed a straightforward link between life change and dysfunction that overlooked individual variability in response (Rahe & Arthur, 1987). Thus, despite the conceptualized consistency of stressor effects in early research, anomalies persisted. The amount of variance predicted in distress was typically less than 10%, and individuals showed highly variable reactions to stressors (Cohen & Edwards, 1989). Many people remained healthy despite exposure to stressful

Parts of this manuscript were adapted from Holahan and Moos (1994), Moos and Schaefer (1993), and Schaefer and Moos (1992). Preparation of the manuscript was supported in part by Department of Veterans Affairs Health Services Research and Development Service funds and NIAAA Grants AA02863 and AA06699. We thank Penny Brennan, Ralph Swindle, and Christine Timko for helpful comments on sections of the manuscript.

circumstances, and some people matured more rapidly after effectively managing stressful events.

At first, researchers assumed that these anomalies reflected measurement error, but eventually understood them as important findings in their own right. The relatively poor empirical predictions of early stressor-illness studies led researchers to focus increasingly on the moderating role of adaptive resources and coping strategies. Stress research has evolved from putting an early emphasis on people's deficits and vulnerabilities to placing increasing emphasis on individuals' adaptive strengths and capacity for resilience and constructive action in the face of challenge (Holahan & Moos, 1994).

In this chapter, we analyze the coping process, emphasizing the relevance of coping research to understanding adaptive functioning more generally. We begin by considering general conceptualizations of coping, and present an integrative conceptual approach. Next, we describe the relation between different coping strategies and adaptive functioning. We then present two models of adaptive functioning—reflecting both *stress resistance* and *crisis growth*—that depend on coping as a central mechanism. Finally, we highlight key issues that refine our general understanding of coping and adaptation.

CONCEPTUALIZING THE COPING PROCESS

Coping is a stabilizing factor that can help individuals maintain psychosocial adaptation during stressful periods; it encompasses cognitive and behavioral efforts to reduce or eliminate stressful conditions and associated emotional distress (Lazarus & Folkman, 1984; Moos & Schaefer, 1993). At a general level, conceptualizations of coping may be categorized according to their assumptions about the primary determinants of coping responses. *Dispositional* approaches assume that relatively stable person-based factors underlie the selection of coping behaviors. *Contextual* approaches assume that more transitory situation-based factors shape people's choices of coping responses.

Dispositional Approaches

The ego-psychoanalytic model is paradigmatic of the dispositional approach to conceptualizing coping. Ego processes are unconscious cognitive mechanisms (though their expression may involve behavioral components) whose main functions are defensive (to distort reality) and emotion focused (to reduce tension). Psychoanalytically oriented investigators assume that people have relatively stable preferences for particular defense and coping styles for dealing with conflict and that these styles vary in their maturity (see Bond, Gardner, Christian, & Sigel, 1983; Vaillant, 1977).

Several contemporary investigators outside the psychoanalytic tradition also have conceptualized coping in dispositional terms. Common to these conceptualizations is the assessment of coping by interviews and personality tests in the tradition of trait assessment (Stone, Greenberg, Kennedy-Moore, & Newman, 1991). For example, Carver, Scheier, and Weintraub (1989) developed a dispositional measure of coping by asking individuals what they usually do in stressful circumstances. Endler and Parker (1990) developed a multidimensional measure of stylistic coping by asking individuals how they generally cope when they encounter a difficult or stressful situation. Other dispositionally oriented conceptualizations index characteristic styles of cognitively seeking out or avoiding threat-relevant information (Miller, 1987) and automatic thoughts in everyday life that reflect common constructive and destructive ways of thinking (Epstein & Meier, 1989).

Contextual Approaches

Emblematic of the contextual approach is the appraisal-based model of Lazarus and his associates (Folkman, 1992; Lazarus, 1981; Lazarus & Folkman, 1984). Lazarus views coping as a response to specific stressful situations rather than as a stable feature of personality. Active and conscious cognitive appraisals of potential threat function as a mediating link between life stressors and the individual's coping responses. Coping is regarded as a dynamic process that changes over time in response to changing demands and changing appraisals of the situation.

Several other investigators also have proposed contextually oriented conceptualizations of coping. Common to these conceptualizations is the measurement of coping by indexing the thoughts and actions individuals report they actually used to cope in specific stressful situations (Stone et al., 1991). For example, Feifel and Strack (1989) assessed coping responses across five conflict situations: decision-making, defeat in a competitive circumstance, frustration, authority conflict, and peer disagreement. Other contextually oriented techniques ask individuals to describe how they actually dealt with a specific stressful event (Carver et al., 1989) or with an important recent problem (Amirkhan, 1990).

An Integrative Conceptual Framework

Contemporary theorists generally recognize that the dispositional and contextual approaches have complementary strengths in describing the coping process. Dispositional approaches tap generalizable, preferred coping styles that transcend particular situational influences (Epstein & Meier, 1989). Contextual approaches reflect how a person copes with a particular type of stressful event and are responsive to changes in coping efforts during a stressful episode (Carver et al., 1989; Folkman, 1992). Thus, we conceptualize the coping process using the general conceptual framework shown in Figure 2.1, which emphasizes that both enduring personal and more changeable situational factors shape coping efforts.

The environmental system (Panel 1) is composed of ongoing life stressors, like chronic physical illness, as well as social coping resources, such as support from family members. The personal system (Panel 2) includes an individual's

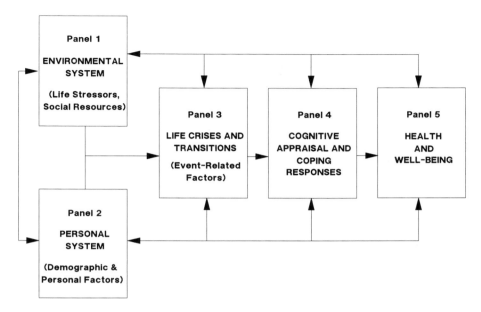

Figure 2.1 A general conceptual framework of the coping process (from Moos & Schaefer, 1993).

sociodemographic characteristics and personal coping resources, such as self-confidence. These relatively stable environmental and personal factors influence the life crises and transitions individuals face (Panel 3), which reflect significant changes in life circumstances. In turn, these combined influences, shape health and well-being (Panel 5) both directly and indirectly through cognitive appraisal and coping responses (Panel 4). The framework emphasizes the central mediating role of cognitive appraisal and coping responses in the stress process. Moreover, the bidirectional paths in the framework indicate that reciprocal feedback can occur at each stage.

COPING AND ADAPTATION

Classifying Coping

Before considering the relation between different coping strategies and adaptive functioning, it is necessary to describe how coping strategies typically are categorized. Most investigators have used one of two main approaches to classify coping. The first approach emphasizes the *focus* of coping: a person's orientation and activity in response to a stressor. An individual can approach the problem and make active efforts to resolve it or try to avoid the problem and focus mainly on managing the emotions associated with it. An alternative approach emphasizes the *method* of coping people employ; that is, whether a response entails primarily cognitive or behavioral efforts (see Moos & Schaefer, 1993).

We have combined these two approaches to develop a more integrated conceptualization of coping. We consider an individual's orientation toward a stressor, and we separate coping into approach and avoidance domains. In addition, each of these two domains is divided into categories that reflect cognitive and behavioral coping. Accordingly, we propose four basic categories of coping processes: cognitive-approach, behavioral-approach, cognitive-avoidance, and behavioral-avoidance. Table 2.1 lists eight coping subtypes from the Coping Responses Inventory (Moos, 1993) that assess these four basic categories of coping strategies.

Coping and General Adaptation

Approach Coping

In general, people who rely more on approach coping tend to adapt better to life stressors and experience fewer psychological symptoms. Approach coping strategies, such as problem solving and seeking information, can moderate the potential adverse influence of both negative life change and enduring role stressors on psychological functioning (Billings & Moos, 1981; Pearlin & Schooler, 1978). A higher proportion of problem-focused coping relative to total coping efforts also has been associated with reduced depression (Mitchell, Cronkite, & Moos,

TABLE 2.1   Four Basic Categories of Coping Strategies with Eight Associated Coping Subtypes

Basic Coping Categories	Coping Subtypes
Cognitive Approach	Logical Analysis ("Did you think of different ways to deal with the problem?") Positive Reappraisal ("Did you think about how you were much better off than other people with similar problems?")
Behavioral Approach	Seeking Guidance and Support ("Did you talk with a friend about the problem?") Taking Problem-Solving Action ("Did you make a plan of action and follow it?")
Cognitive Avoidance	Cognitive Avoidance ("Did you try to forget the whole thing?") Resigned Acceptance ("Did you lose hope that things would ever be the same?")
Behavioral Avoidance	Seeking Alternative Rewards ("Did you get involved in new activities?") Emotional Discharge ("Did you yell or shout to let off steam?")

Note: Sample coping items are shown in parentheses. From *Coping Responses Inventory: Adult Form Manual* by R. H. Moos, 1993, Odessa, FL: Psychological Assessment Resources.

1983). Similarly, active coping strategies involving negotiation and optimistic comparisons have been linked to reductions in concurrent distress and to fewer future role problems (Menaghan, 1982).

Avoidance Coping

In contrast, avoidance coping, such as denial and withdrawal, generally is associated with psychological distress—particularly when adjustment is assessed beyond the initial crisis period (Holmes & Stevenson, 1990; Suls & Fletcher, 1985). Because emotionally focused coping often entails avoidant-oriented fantasy and self-blame, it also often correlates with more depression (Endler & Parker, 1990). Menaghan (1982) explained that efforts to manage unpleasant feelings by resignation and withdrawal may increase distress and thus amplify future problems.

For example, lawyers who used more avoidance coping strategies in response to life stressors showed more symptoms of psychological and physical strain (Kobasa, 1982). In addition, older adults who relied on ineffective escapism— avoidant, helpless, and reckless coping behaviors—experienced more current and future emotional distress (Rohde, Lewinsohn, Tilson, & Seeley, 1990). Similarly, the use of avoidance coping, such as wishful thinking and self-blame, in dealing with negative life events predicted subsequent psychological disturbance among elderly persons (Smith, Patterson, & Grant, 1990).

Coping and Specific Adaptive Tasks

Clinical Depression

Among individuals treated for depression, greater use of problem solving and less reliance on emotional discharge were related to better outcome at a 1-year follow-up (Billings & Moos, 1985). Moreover, depressed patients who relied less on emotional discharge at a 1-year treatment follow-up reported less depression and fewer physical symptoms 4 years posttreatment (Swindle, Cronkite, & Moos, 1989). Similarly, depressed patients who relied more on self-consolation and distraction at baseline showed poorer treatment outcome several months later (Parker, Brown, & Bignault, 1986). In this respect, Gaston, Marmar, Thompson, and Gallaher (1988) pointed out that depressed patients who rely more heavily on avoidance processes have more difficulty forming a positive psychotherapeutic relationship.

Physical Illness

In the initial interval after a health crisis, avoidant forms of coping, such as denial, sometimes can be beneficial; however, they are generally detrimental in the longer term (Suls & Fletcher, 1985). Among patients recovering from cardiac surgery, approach-oriented coping is positively related (Scheier et al., 1989) and avoidance coping is negatively related (Mayou & Bryant, 1987) to subsequent quality of life. For cancer patients, positive reinterpretations are associated with less emotional distress (Dunkel-Schetter, Feinstein, Taylor, & Falke, 1992) and escape-avoidance with more distress (Carver et al., 1993; Stanton & Snider, 1993). Similarly, among patients with rheumatoid arthritis, information seeking predicts increased positive affect, whereas wish-fulfilling fantasy and self-blame predict decreased positive affect (Revenson & Felton, 1989).

Alcohol Abuse

Perri (1985) identified coping strategies used by people who succeeded in self-management of a drinking problem. Abstainers and nonproblem drinkers used a variety of active coping efforts; in particular, behavioral processes such as removing alcoholic beverages from their home and seeking advice and support. We obtained comparable findings on the relationship between coping processes and the outcome of treatment for alcohol abuse. Reliance on cognitive approach coping was associated with better treatment outcome at a 2-year follow-up; the use of avoidance coping was associated with worse outcome at both 2-year and 10-year follow-ups. In longitudinal analyses, we found that cognitive approach coping at 2 years predicted less alcohol consumption and depression at 10 years; more avoidance coping at 2 years predicted more depression at 10 years (Moos, Finney, & Cronkite, 1990).

Smoking

Cognitive and behavioral coping skills also have been associated with maintenance of smoking cessation. Compared with nonquitters, persons who succeeded in quitting smoking used more problem solving and cognitive restructuring, and relied less on wishful thinking, self-criticism, and social withdrawal (Carey, Kalra, Carey, Halperin, & Richards, 1993). Shiffman (1985) also found that both cognitive and behavioral approach responses were effective in averting smoking relapse; the combination of both types was better than either one alone. Shiffman noted that cognitive approach coping is especially important in that it can be used flexibly in many circumstances; it is less under situational control and thus not as likely to be disrupted by increased life stressors or reduced social support.

COPING-BASED MODELS OF ADAPTIVE FUNCTIONING

Coping and Stress Resistance

Coping processes are central to stress resistance (Holahan & Moos, 1994). Resilience in the face of adversity involves a dynamic interplay between personal and social resources and coping efforts (Coyne & Downey, 1991; Kessler et al., 1985). Moreover, personal and social resources are linked to staying healthy under adaptive challenge in significant part because they encourage more adaptive coping strategies. Lazarus and Folkman (1984), defining resources as what an individual "draws on in order to cope," argue that resources "precede and influence coping" (p. 158). Likewise, Thoits (1986) views social support as a source of coping assistance, and Bolger (1990) proposes that "coping is personality in action under stress" (p. 525).

Personal Coping Resources

Personal resources include relatively stable personality and cognitive characteristics that shape the appraisal and coping process. A variety of dispositional factors that relate broadly to personal control appear especially important as coping resources, including *self-efficacy* (Bandura, 1982), *optimism* (Scheier, Weintraub, & Carver, 1986), *hardiness* (Kobasa, 1982; Kobasa, Maddi, & Kahn, 1982), a *sense of coherence* (Antonovsky, 1987), and an *internal locus of control* (Lefcourt, 1992).

Perceived self-efficacy promotes more vigorous and persistent efforts to master new tasks. Persons with higher levels of self-efficacy tend to approach challenging situations in an active and persistent style, whereas those with lower levels of self-efficacy are less active or tend to avoid such situations (Bandura, 1982, 1989). Optimists tend to use problem-focused coping strategies, whereas pessimists prefer emotion-based strategies, such as denial and fatalism (Carver et al., 1989; Taylor et al., 1992). Thus, compared with pessimists, optimists rely more on coping processes that are likely to foster favorable outcome expectancies, more persistent coping, and better outcomes (Scheier, Weintraub, & Carver, 1986).

Social Coping Resources

Social resources can strengthen coping efforts by providing emotional support that bolsters feelings of self-esteem and self-confidence, as well as by providing informational guidance that aids in assessing threat and in planning coping strategies (Carpenter & Scott, 1992; Cohen & McKay, 1984). In longitudinal studies, high family support predicts an increase in approach coping and a decline in avoidance coping over time (Fondacaro & Moos, 1987).

Among women with rheumatoid arthritis, spouse support was linked to more reliance on cognitive restructuring and information seeking and to less wishful thinking (Mann & Zautra, 1989). Similarly, late-life problem drinkers who have better relationships with their spouse and friends are more likely to rely on positive reappraisal and support seeking and less likely to use cognitive avoidance and emotional discharge (Moos, Brennan, Fondacaro, & Moos, 1990). Moreover, in an occupational context, student nurses used more approach coping responses in dealing with serious work problems when support from supervisors was high (Parkes, 1986).

A Coping-Based Model of Stress Resistance

In a series of longitudinal studies of two community samples, we examined personal and social stress-resistance resources. Self-confidence and an easygoing disposition, family support, and less reliance on avoidance coping strategies predicted lower levels of depression over a 1-year period, even when prior depression was controlled (Holahan & Moos, 1986, 1987b). Examining the interrelationships among the predictive factors, we found that individuals with more personal and social resources were more likely to rely on approach coping and less likely to use avoidance coping (Holahan & Moos, 1987a).

Based on these and related findings (for example, Cronkite & Moos, 1984) and consistent with the general conceptual framework shown in Figure 2.1, we proposed an empirical model of stress resistance (Holahan & Moos, 1990). In the model, personal and social resources relate to subsequent depression both directly and indirectly through adaptive coping responses. The relative strength of the predictive association is presumed to vary with the level of intervening stressors. Because coping is a stabilizing factor that helps maintain psychological adjustment during stressful periods, the adaptive advantage of coping should be greatest under high stressors.

We tested these hypotheses with almost 400 community respondents in a 4-year longitudinal model (Holahan & Moos, 1991). Structural equation modeling (see Jöreskog & Sörbom, 1986) was used to estimate the parameters and overall goodness of fit of the model in a two-group analysis, in which respondents were divided into high and low stressor groups. The high stressor group experienced two or more negative life events, and the low stressor group experienced no negative life events during the year prior to the follow-up assessment. These conservative models remove the influence of prior depression from both coping and depression at follow-up.

Self-confidence, an easygoing disposition, and family support operated prospectively over 4 years, either directly or indirectly through coping responses, to protect individuals from becoming depressed. Under high stressors, resources predicted future psychological health indirectly, through their link to more adaptive coping strategies. Under low stressors, resources related directly to psychological health. The findings demonstrate the central role of coping in stress resistance. Under high stressors, adaptive personality characteristics and family support function prospectively as coping resources; coping, in turn, mediates between initial resources and later health status.

Consistent findings have emerged pointing to the mediating role of coping in the context of dispositional optimism. Among women coping with breast cancer and with breast biopsy, more active coping efforts serve as mediating routes through which optimism relates to better psychological adjustment (Carver et al., 1993; Stanton & Snider, 1993). Similarly, among freshmen adjusting to college, active coping strategies mediate the relation between optimism and subsequent adjustment (Aspinwall & Taylor, 1992).

Coping and Crisis Growth

Although conceptualizations of stress resistance provide a foundation for understanding adaptive functioning, stress resistance research remains tied, in part, to an illness perspective because of its focus on *not becoming sick* (Antonovsky, 1987). In studies of adaptation to life stressors, investigators typically equate good outcome with the absence of psychopathology and physical symptoms. The painful aspects of life crises cannot be denied; yet, individuals often emerge from a crisis with new coping skills, closer relationships with family and friends, broader priorities, and a richer appreciation of life (see Lindemann, 1979; Stewart, Sokol, Healy, & Chester, 1986). As Haan (1982) succinctly stated, "Stress benefits people, making them more tender, humble, and hardy" (p. 255).

When asked about the outcome of life crises they have experienced, a substantial number of people, often 50% or more, report some positive outcomes. A dynamic interplay between coping responses and coping resources is central to such growth. Resilience develops from confronting stressful experiences and coping with them effectively; novel crisis situations promote new coping skills, which can lead to new personal and social resources (Schaefer & Moos, 1992).

New Coping Skills

People who respond to crises by seeking information and taking direct action often learn new problem-solving coping strategies. Affleck and his colleagues (Affleck, Tennen, Croog, & Levine, 1987) found that a majority of heart attack victims reported benefits from the life crisis, such as the development of new health-related coping skills. Crises also may lead a person to search cognitively for the positive aspects of a situation and to find some deeper meaning in it. Taylor (1983) reported that some cancer patients are able to view the threat posed by their illness as a "catalytic agent for restructuring their lives" (p. 1163). She noted that cancer patients' search for meaning helped them to understand the crisis and its implications and, in turn, to regain mastery over the crisis and over their lives.

Enhanced Personal and Social Resources

Self-reliance often increases when people acquire new skills, become more independent, and successfully manage new roles or seemingly overwhelming tasks and changes. Wallerstein (1986) found that many women who experienced a marital breakup became more assertive, developed more realistic views of themselves, and experienced increased self-esteem with successful new careers. Taylor (1983) reported that for many cancer patients, their illness brought a new attitude toward life and reordered goals and priorities. Weiss (1979) found that adolescents in single-parent families assumed more responsibilities than their peers in intact families and became more independent, self-reliant, and competent.

Life crises also often necessitate help-seeking that can foster deeper social bonds and enduring confidant relationships. Dhooper (1983) noted that nearly half of the spouses of first-time heart attack victims reported that their family was strengthened by the crisis experience. Elder and his associates (Elder, Caspi, & Downey, 1984; Elder, Caspi, & van Nguyen, 1986) found that some children from economically deprived families became more competent and resilient than did their counterparts from nondeprived families. The investigators attributed beneficial outcomes to the shared responsibilities and family cooperation required to cope with financial problems.

A Coping-Based Model of Crisis Growth

Applying these views, we framed two contrasting empirical models of improvements in psychological functioning. First, we proposed a model for *prototypic growth* under low stressors. We reasoned that factors that maintain stable functioning during stressful periods would help to improve health during less stressful times. Second, based on crisis theory (see Schaefer & Moos, 1992) and consistent with the role of bidirectional influences in the general conceptual framework shown in Figure 2.1, we proposed a model for *crisis growth* under high stressors. We predicted that improvement in functioning under high stressors involves a strengthening of personal and social resources in the context of feedback from required coping efforts. We tested these hypotheses in our community sample of 400 respondents in a 1-year longitudinal framework (Holahan & Moos, 1990).

As predicted, the way personal and social resources related to improved functioning differed under low and high stressors. Reflecting prototypic growth, 70% of individuals whose functioning improved had experienced few stressors—no or only one negative event during the year. In addition to a low risk from negative life change, these individuals also had high personal and social resources. These results supported Antonovsky's (1987) contention that the "negative resource" of avoiding stressors may not foster improved functioning without being accompanied by positive personal or social resources.

More important, findings also supported the prediction that stressors can provide an opportunity for crisis growth. One-third of respondents whose functioning improved over the year experienced two or more stressors, and more than half of this multiple-stressor group experienced three or more stressors. Growth occurred even though many stressors involved profound adaptive demands, such as serious financial setbacks and the deaths of friends or family members.

Consistent with crisis theory, the individuals under high stressors whose functioning improved were the only group of respondents whose resources increased significantly during the year. The changes in resources for these individuals reflected increases in self-confidence, easygoingness, and family support. This increase in resources, in turn, was tied to improved functioning. Especially important, adaptive coping was significantly related to the increase in resources under high stressors. Positive feedback from successful mastery experiences is central to strengthening resources under adaptive challenge (see Bandura, 1990; Turner & Avison, 1992).

REFINING THE GENERAL FRAMEWORK

Although we can draw overall conclusions about the relative efficacy of approach and avoidance coping strategies, such generalizations necessarily oversimplify the coping process. A full appreciation of coping adaptiveness requires an analysis of specific coping responses in the context of particular stressor characteristics (see McCrae, 1984). Individuals adapt best when their coping efforts match situational demands—coping needs to fit the situation (Miller, 1992; Moos & Schaefer, 1993). Key situational factors that can influence the effectiveness of particular coping strategies are the time-frame and the controllability of the stressor.

There is some evidence that avoidance coping may be adaptive with some acute stressors. Denial is predictive of better medical outcome during acute hospitalization for coronary heart disease (Levenson, Mishra, Hamer, & Hastillo,

1989; Levine et al., 1987). Cognitive avoidance or inattention also may be adaptive with short-term stressors, such as pain, blood donation, and uncomfortable medical diagnostic procedures (Suls & Fletcher, 1985). In the long run, however, repressive coping may be associated with reduced adherence to medical requirements, prolonged pain and distress, and less resistance to disease (Jamner, Schwartz, & Leigh, 1988; Suls & Fletcher, 1985).

Moreover, the adaptive significance of approach versus avoidant coping strategies may depend on the controllability of the stressor that is confronted (Folkman, 1992; Roth & Cohen, 1986). Vitaliano, DeWolfe, Maiuro, Russo, and Katon (1990) found that problem-focused coping was associated with less depression and emotion-focused coping with more depression only when a stressor was appraised as changeable. Similarly, Compas, Malcarne, and Fondacaro (1988) found that youth who generated more problem-focused strategies had fewer behavior problems when they believed they had control over a stressor. In contrast, when they believed they lacked control, those who generated fewer problem-focused strategies had fewer behavior problems.

In the aftermath of irreversible stressors, the behavioral avoidance coping strategy of seeking alternative rewards, in contrast to directly confronting the stressor, may be a beneficial coping strategy (see Moos, 1993). Involvement in alternative rewards may provide both diversion and new sources of satisfaction. However, although seeking alternative rewards does not involve direct attempts to change a stressor, it requires active engagement with the environment and with other people.

Conversely, the behavioral approach coping strategies of seeking information and support may lead to increases in distress when they are used in unresponsive social contexts. Individuals who are stressed may request help from those who cannot or will not assist them, or from persons who criticize how they are handling the situation. Seemingly supportive family members and friends may minimize or trivialize distressed persons' problems and thereby discourage additional efforts to alleviate them (Dakof & Taylor, 1990).

In terms of our mediational model of coping (Holahan & Moos, 1990, 1991), appraisals of event controllability affect both the degree to which social support influences coping and the effectiveness of coping responses. Findings with a large sample of college students in a prospective framework (Valentiner, Holahan, & Moos, 1993) showed that parental support predicted adaptive coping only when students confronted a controllable event. Moreover, choice of coping strategy predicted changes in psychological adjustment over a 2-year period only in the context of controllable stressors. When events were uncontrollable, parental support no longer was associated with adaptive coping, but instead was related directly to changes in psychological adjustment.

These findings suggest that individuals who are flexible in their choice of coping should show better adaptation than persons who have a more restricted or rigid coping repertoire (see Miller, in press). These issues can be examined by tracking an individual's coping preferences across different situations (see Feifel & Strack, 1989) and by developing indexes of versatile or flexible coping (see Mattlin, Wethington, & Kessler, 1990).

CONCLUSION

We are optimistic about the prospects for continued progress toward a broadly applicable framework of coping, resilience, and growth. Promising new developments suggest that psychology's historical neglect of people's adaptive strengths is being replaced by a more balanced view of the person. Our psychological lexicon is expanding to include new constructs pertaining to resilience and growth, such as self-efficacy (Bandura, 1982), competence (Sternberg & Kolligian, 1990), learned resourcefulness (Rosenbaum & Ben-Ari, 1985), optimism (Scheier & Carver, 1985), and wisdom (Baltes, Smith, Staudinger, & Sowarka, 1990).

Broader developments both within and outside of psychology are likely to encourage continued progress toward the study of adaptive functioning. Within psychology, increasing interest in life-span development (Datan, Rodeheaver, & Hughes, 1987), health psychology (Rodin & Salovey, 1989), and preventive interventions (Heller, 1990) promises a sustained need for empirical knowledge about adaptive processes in everyday contexts. In the larger society, national policy objectives in the areas of education, aging, drug abuse, and health care call for new behavioral science knowledge that emphasizes competent and resilient functioning and goes beyond traditional illness models (see Brickman et al., 1982).

The conceptual framework we have described can help guide new research on the stress and coping process. A key issue involves a fuller understanding of interdependencies among the variables in our framework. More research is needed on how different types of life stressors and social resources influence each other. For example, ongoing stressors and a lack of social resources can predict new stressful events; in turn, such events can contribute to a rise in chronic stressors and an erosion of social resources (Moos, Fenn, & Billings, 1988). Moreover, stressors and a lack of support may be more closely connected in domains where there is a single source of both stressors and support, such as the family domain (Brennan & Moos, 1990).

A key facet of the stress process in families involves interdependencies among the functioning and coping responses of family members. Being married to a person who is distressed is associated with a spouse's own depressed mood. This adverse effect is strengthened when one partner relies on avoidance coping, and further exacerbated when both partners rely on avoidance coping (Cronkite & Moos, 1984). Similarly, emotional disturbance among children in both normal and alcoholic families is associated with their parents' use of avoidance coping (Holahan & Moos, 1987b; Moos, Finney, & Cronkite, 1990).

We also need to learn more about how the type and degree of adaptive challenge are linked to enhanced resilience. Life stressors may ultimately foster enhanced resilience when they provide an opportunity to learn new coping skills (Caspi, Bolger, & Eckenrode, 1987). Thus, more manageable stressors may promote growth more readily than less manageable ones do (Ruch, Chandler, & Harter, 1980). Moreover, longitudinal research across a sufficient time period is needed to describe the patterned course of psychological growth. Positive outcomes to life crises may emerge only after a process of emotional assimilation that follows an initial stage of emotional distress and disorganization (Stewart, Sokol, Healy, & Chester, 1986).

At an applied level, the conceptualization of coping described here has implications for clinical interventions at both the individual and contextual levels. Each path in the general conceptual framework shown in Figure 2.1 identifies a process that is potentially alterable. An appreciation of the coping process can broaden our understanding of the determinants of psychiatric disorders (Taylor & Brown, 1988) and of the process of recovery from psychopathology (Needles & Abramson, 1990; Swindle, Cronkite, & Moos, 1989) and addiction (Moos, Finney, & Cronkite, 1990).

Recognizing that stressful or relapse-inducing life situations inevitably occur, clinicians can identify coping skills and associated coping resources that can help clients deal with these situations more effectively (see Moos, 1988, 1993). In clinical case descriptions, such information can help clinicians understand how their clients manage specific stressful circumstances, identify coping factors associated with symptom remission and relapse, and plan intervention programs that target clients' precise coping deficits. Especially important, a focus on coping processes encourages a competence-enhancing view of the client's adaptive strengths and of his or her potential for resilience and personal growth.

REFERENCES

Affleck, G., Tennen, H., Croog, S., & Levine, S. (1987). Causal attribution, perceived benefits, and morbidity after a heart attack: An 8-year study. *Journal of Consulting and Clinical Psychology, 55,* 29–35.

Amirkhan, J. H. (1990). A factor analytically derived measure of coping: The Coping Strategy Indicator. *Journal of Personality and Social Psychology, 59,* 1066–1074.

Antonovsky, A. (1987). *Unraveling the mystery of health: How people manage stress and stay well.* San Francisco: Jossey-Bass.

Aspinwall, L. G., & Taylor, S. E. (1992). Modeling cognitive adaptation: A longitudinal investigation of the impact of individual differences and coping on college adjustment and performance. *Journal of Personality and Social Psychology, 63,* 989–1003.

Baltes, P. B., Smith, J., Staudinger, U. M., & Sowarka, D. (1990). Wisdom: One facet of successful aging? In M. Perlmutter (Ed.), *Late life potential.* Washington, DC: Gerontological Society of America.

Bandura, A. (1982). Self-efficacy mechanism in human agency. *American Psychologist, 37,* 122–147.

Bandura, A. (1989). Self-regulation of motivation and action through internal standards and goal systems. In L. A. Pervin (Ed.), *Goal concepts in personality and social psychology* (pp. 19–85). Hillsdale, NJ: Erlbaum.

Bandura, A. (1990). Conclusion: Reflections on nonability determinants of competence. In R. J. Sternberg & J. Kolligian (Eds.), *Competence considered* (pp. 315–362). New Haven: Yale University Press.

Billings, A., & Moos, R. H. (1981). The role of coping responses and social resources in attenuating the stress of life events. *Journal of Behavioral Medicine, 4,* 157–189.

Billings, A., & Moos, R. (1985). Life stressors and social resources affect posttreatment outcomes among depressed patients. *Journal of Abnormal Psychology, 94,* 140–153.

Bolger, N. (1990). Coping as a personality process: A prospective study. *Journal of Personality and Social Psychology, 59,* 525–537.

Bond, M., Gardner, S. T., Christian, J., & Sigel, J. (1983). Empirical study of self-rated defense styles. *Archives of General Psychiatry, 40,* 333–338.

Brennan, P. L., & Moos, R. H. (1990). Life stressors, social resources, and late-life problem drinking. *Psychology and Aging, 5,* 491–501.

Brickman, P., Rabinowitz, V. C., Karuza, J., Coates, D., Cohn, E., & Kidder, L. (1982). Models of helping and coping. *American Psychologist, 37,* 368–384.

Carey, M. P., Kalra, D. L., Carey, K. B., Halperin, S., & Richards, C. S. (1993). Stress and unaided smoking cessation: A prospective investigation. *Journal of Consulting and Clinical Psychology, 61,* 831–838.

Carpenter, B. N., & Scott, S. M. (1992). Interpersonal aspects of coping. In B. N. Carpenter (Ed.), *Personal coping: Theory, research, and application* (pp. 93–109). New York: Praeger.

Carver, C. S., Pozo, C., Haris, S. D., Noriega, V., Scheier, M. F., Robinson, D. S., Ketcham, A. S., Moffat, F. L., Jr., & Clark, K. C. (1993). How coping mediates the effect of optimism on distress: A study of women with early stage breast cancer. *Journal of Personality and Social Psychology, 65,* 375–390.

Carver, C. S., Scheier, M. F., & Weintraub, J. K. (1989). Assessing coping strategies: A theoretically-based approach. *Journal of Personality and Social Psychology, 56,* 267–283.

Caspi, A., Bolger, N., & Eckenrode, J. (1987). Linking person and context in the daily stress process. *Journal of Personality and Social Psychology, 52,* 184–195.

Cohen, S., & Edwards, J. R. (1989). Personality characteristics as moderators of the relationship between stress and disorder. In R. W. J. Neufeld (Ed.), *Advances in the investigation of psychological stress* (pp. 235–283). New York: Wiley.

Cohen, S., & McKay, G. (1984). Social support, stress, and the buffering hypothesis: A theoretical analysis. In A. Baum, J. E. Singer, & S. E. Taylor (Eds.), *Handbook of psychology and health* (Vol. 4, pp. 253–267). Hillsdale, NJ: Erlbaum.

Compas, B. E., Malcarne, V., & Fondacaro, K. (1988). Coping with stressful events in older children and young adolescents. *Journal of Consulting and Clinical Psychology, 56,* 405–411.

Coyne, J. C., & Downey, G. (1991). Social factors and psychopathology: Stress, social support, and coping processes. *Annual Review of Psychology, 42,* 401–425.

Cronkite, R. C., & Moos, R. Y. (1984). The role of predisposing and moderating factors in the stress–illness relationship. *Journal of Health and Social Behavior, 25,* 372–393.

Dakof, G. A., & Taylor, S. E. (1990). Victims' perceptions of social support: What is helpful from whom? *Journal of Personality and Social Psychology, 58,* 80–89.

Datan, N., Rodeheaver, D., & Hughes, F. (1987). Adult development and aging. *Annual Review of Psychology, 38,* 153–180.

Dhooper, S. S. (1983). Family coping with the crisis of heart attack. *Social Work in Health Care, 9,* 15–31.

Dunkel-Schetter, C., Feinstein, L. G., Taylor, S. E., & Falke, R. L. (1992). Patterns of coping with cancer. *Health Psychology, 11,* 79–87.

Elder, G. H., Jr., Caspi, A., & Downey, G. (1984). Problem behavior and family relationships: Life course and intergenerational themes. In A. Sorensen, F. Weinert, & L. Sherrod (Eds.), *Human development and the life-course: Multidisciplinary perspectives* (pp. 293–340). Hillsdale, NJ: Erlbaum.

Elder, G. H., Jr., Caspi, A., & van Nguyen, T. (1986). Resourceful and vulnerable children: Family influences in hard times. In R. K. Silbereisen, K. Eyferth, & G. Rudinger (Eds.), *Development as action in context* (pp. 167–186). Berlin, New York: Springer.

Endler, N. S., & Parker, J. D. A. (1990). Multidimensional assessment of coping: A critical evaluation. *Journal of Personality and Social Psychology, 58,* 844–854.

Epstein, S., & Meier, P. (1989). Constructive thinking: A broad coping variable with specific components. *Journal of Personality and Social Psychology, 57,* 332–350.

Feifel, H., & Strack, S. (1989). Coping with conflict situations: Middle-aged and elderly men. *Psychology and Aging, 4,* 26–33.

Folkman, S. (1992). Making the case for coping. In B. N. Carpenter (Ed.), *Personal coping: Theory, research, and application* (pp. 31–46). New York: Praeger.

Fondacaro, M., & Moos, R. (1987). Social support and coping: A longitudinal analysis. *American Journal of Community Psychology, 15,* 653–673.

Gaston, L., Marmar, C. R., Thompson, L. W., & Gallaher, D. (1988). Relation of patient pretreatment characteristics to the therapeutic alliance in diverse psychotherapies. *Journal of Consulting and Clinical Psychology, 56,* 483–489.

Goldberger, L., & Breznitz, S. (Eds.). (1993). *Handbook of stress: Theoretical and clinical aspects* (2nd ed.). New York: Free Press.

Haan, N. (1982). The assessment of coping, defense, and stress. In L. Goldberger & S. Breznitz (Eds.), *Handbook of stress: Theoretical and clinical aspects* (pp. 254–269). New York: Free Press.

Heller, K. (1990). Social and community intervention. *Annual Review of Psychology, 41,* 141–168.

Holahan, C. J., & Moos, R. H. (1986). Personality, coping, and family resources in stress resistance: A longitudinal analysis. *Journal of Personality and Social Psychology, 51,* 389–395.

Holahan, C. J., & Moos, R. H. (1987a). Personal and contextual determinants of coping strategies. *Journal of Personality and Social Psychology, 52,* 946–955.

Holahan, C. J., & Moos, R. H. (1987b). Risk, resistance, and psychological distress: A longitudinal analysis with adults and children. *Journal of Abnormal Psychology, 96,* 3–13.

Holahan, C. J., & Moos, R. H. (1990). Life stressors, resistance factors, and psychological health: An extension of the stress-resistance paradigm. *Journal of Personality and Social Psychology, 58,* 909–917.

Holahan, C. J., & Moos, R. H. (1991). Life stressors, personal and social resources, and depression: A four-year structural model. *Journal of Abnormal Psychology, 100,* 31–38.

Holahan, C. J., & Moos, R. H. (1994). Life stressors and mental health: Advances in conceptualizing stress resistance. In W. R. Avison & I. H. Gotlib (Eds.), *Stress and mental health: Contemporary issues and prospects for the future* (pp. 213–238). New York: Plenum.

Holmes, J. A., & Stevenson, C. A. (1990). Differential effects of avoidant and attentional coping strategies on adaptation to chronic and recent-onset pain. *Health Psychology, 9*, 577–584.

Jamner, L. D., Schwartz, G. E., & Leigh, H. (1988). The relationship between repressive and defensive coping styles and monocyte, eosinophile, and serum glucose levels: Support for the opioid peptide hypothesis of repression. *Psychosomatic Medicine, 50*, 567–575.

Jöreskog, K. G., & Sörbom, D. (1986). *Analysis of linear structural relationships by maximum likelihood, instrumental variables, and least squares methods* (4th ed.). Mooresville, IN: Scientific Software.

Kessler, R. C., Price, R. H., & Wortman, C. B. (1985). Social factors in psychopathology: Stress, social support, and coping processes. *Annual Review of Psychology, 36*, 531–572.

Kobasa, S. C. (1982). Commitment and coping in stress resistance among lawyers. *Journal of Personality and Social Psychology, 42*, 168–177.

Kobasa, S. C., Maddi, S. R., & Kahn, S. (1982). Hardiness and health: A prospective study. *Journal of Personality and Social Psychology, 42*, 168–172.

Lazarus, R. S. (1981). The stress and coping paradigm. In C. Eisdorfer, D. Cohen, A. Kleinman, & P. Maxim (Eds.), *Models for clinical psychopathology* (pp. 177–214). New York: Spectrum.

Lazarus, R. S., & Folkman, S. (1984). *Stress, appraisal, and coping*. New York: Springer.

Lefcourt, H. M. (1992). Perceived control, personal effectiveness, and emotional states. In B. N. Carpenter (Ed.), *Personal coping: Theory, research, and application* (pp. 111–131). New York: Praeger.

Levenson, J. L., Mishra, A., Hamer, R. M., & Hastillo, A. (1989). Denial and medical outcome in unstable angina. *Psychosomatic Medicine, 51*, 27–35.

Levine, J., Warrenburg, S., Kerns, R., Schwartz, G., Delaney, R., Fontana, A., Gradman, A., Smith, S., Allen, S., & Cascione, R. (1987). The role of denial in recovery from coronary heart disease. *Psychosomatic Medicine, 49*, 109–117.

Lindemann, E. (1979). *Beyond grief: Studies in crisis intervention*. New York: Jason Aronson.

Mann, S. L., & Zautra, A. J. (1989). Spouse criticism and support: Their association with coping and psychological adjustment among women with rheumatoid arthritis. *Journal of Personality and Social Psychology, 56*, 608–617.

Mattlin, J. A., Wethington, E., & Kessler, R. C. (1990). Situational determinants of coping and coping effectiveness. *Journal of Health and Social Behavior, 31*, 103–122.

Mayou, R., & Bryant, B. (1987). Quality of life after coronary artery surgery. *Quarterly Journal of Medicine, 239*, 239–248.

McCrae, R. R. (1984). Situational determinants of coping responses: Loss, threat, and challenge. *Journal of Personality and Social Psychology, 46*, 919–928.

Menaghan, E. (1982). Measuring coping effectiveness: A panel analysis of marital problems and coping efforts. *Journal of Health and Social Behavior, 23*, 220–234.

Miller, S. M. (1987). Monitoring and blunting: Validation of a questionnaire to assess styles of information seeking under threat. *Journal of Personality and Social Psychology, 52,* 345–353.

Miller, S. M. (1992). Individual differences in the coping process: What we know and when we know it. In B. N. Carpenter (Ed.), *Personal coping: Theory, research, and application* (pp. 77–91). New York: Praeger.

Miller, S. M. (in press). To see or not to see: Cognitive informational styles in the coping process. In M. Rosenbaum (Ed.), *Learned resourcefulness: On coping skills, self-regulation, and adaptive behavior.* New York: Spring Press.

Mitchell, R. E., Cronkite, R. C., & Moos, R. H. (1983). Stress, coping, and depression among married couples. *Journal of Abnormal Psychology, 92,* 433–448.

Moos, R. H. (1988). Life stressors and coping resources influence health and well being. *Psychological assessment, 4,* 133–158.

Moos, R. H. (1993). *Coping Responses Inventory: Adult Form Manual.* Odessa, FL: Psychological Assessment Resources.

Moos, R. H., Brennan, P. L., Fondacaro, M., & Moos, B. S. (1990). Approach and avoidance coping responses among older problem and nonproblem drinkers. *Psychology and Aging, 5,* 31–40.

Moos, R. H., Fenn, C., & Billings, A. (1988). Life stressors and social resources: An integrated assessment approach. *Social Science and Medicine, 27,* 999–1002.

Moos, R. H., Finney, J. W., & Cronkite, R. C. (1990). *Alcoholism treatment: Context, process and outcome.* New York: Oxford University Press.

Moos, R. H., & Schaefer, J. A. (1993). Coping resources and processes: Current concepts and measures. In L. Goldberger & S. Breznitz (Eds.), *Handbook of stress: Theoretical and clinical aspects* (2nd ed., pp. 234–257). New York: Free Press.

Needles, D. J., & Abramson, L. Y. (1990). Positive life events, attributional style, and hopefulness: Testing a model of recovery from depression. *Journal of Abnormal Psychology, 99,* 156–165.

Parker, G., Brown, L., & Bignault, I. (1986). Coping behaviors as predictors of the course of clinical depression. *Archives of General Psychiatry, 43,* 561–565.

Parkes, K. R. (1986). Coping in stressful episodes: The role of individual differences, environmental factors, and situational characteristics. *Journal of Personality and Social Psychology, 51,* 1277–1292.

Pearlin, L. I., & Schooler, C. (1978). The structure of coping. *Journal of Health and Social Behavior, 19,* 2–21.

Perri, M. G. (1985). Self-change strategies for the control of smoking, obesity, and problem drinking. In S. Shiffman & T. A. Wills (Eds.), *Coping and substance use* (pp. 295–317). New York: Academic Press.

Rahe, R. H., & Arthur, J. (1987). Life change and illness studies: Past history and future directions. In F. Lolas & H. Mayer (Eds.), *Perspectives on stress and stress-related topics* (pp. 108–125). New York: Springer-Verlag.

Revenson, T. A., & Felton, B. J. (1989). Disability and coping as predictors of psychological adjustment to rheumatoid arthritis. *Journal of Consulting and Clinical Psychology, 57,* 344–348.

Rodin, J., & Salovey, P. (1989). Health psychology. *Annual Review of Psychology,* 533–579.

Rohde, P., Lewinsohn, P. M., Tilson, M., & Seeley, J. R. (1990). Dimensionality of coping and its relation to depression. *Journal of Personality and Social Psychology, 58,* 499–511.

Rosenbaum, M., & Ben-Ari, K. (1985). Learned helplessness and learned resourcefulness: Effects of noncontingent success and failure on individuals differing in self-control skills. *Journal of Personality and Social Psychology, 48,* 198–215.

Roth, S., & Cohen, L. J. (1986). Approach, avoidance, and coping with stress. *American Psychologist, 41,* 813–819.

Ruch, L., Chandler, S., & Harter, R. (1980). Life change and rape impact. *Journal of Health and Social Behavior, 21,* 248–260.

Schaefer, J. A., & Moos, R. H. (1992). Life crises and personal growth. In B. N. Carpenter (Ed.), *Personal coping: Theory, research, and application* (pp. 149–170). New York: Praeger.

Scheier, M. F., & Carver, C. S. (1985). Optimism, coping, and health: Assessment and implications of generalized outcome expectancies. *Health Psychology, 4,* 219–247.

Scheier, M. F., Matthews, K. A., Owens, J. F., Magovern, G. J., Lefebvre, R. C., Abbott, R. A., & Carver, C. S. (1989). Dispositional optimism and recovery from coronary artery bypass surgery: The beneficial effects of physical and psychological well-being. *Journal of Personality and Social Psychology, 57,* 1024–1040.

Scheier, M. F., Weintraub, J. K., & Carver, C. S. (1986). Coping with stress: Divergent strategies of optimists and pessimists. *Journal of Personality and Social Psychology, 51,* 1257–1264.

Seeman, J. (1989). Toward a model of positive health. *American Psychologist, 44,* 1099–1109.

Shiffman, S. (1985). Coping with temptations to smoke. In S. Shiffman & T. A. Wills (Eds.), *Coping and substance use* (pp. 223–242). New York: Academic Press.

Smith, L. W., Patterson, T. L., & Grant, I. (1990). Avoidant coping predicts psychological disturbance in the elderly. *Journal of Nervous and Mental Disease, 178,* 525–530.

Stanton, A. L., & Snider, P. R. (1993). Coping with breast cancer diagnosis: A prospective study. *Health Psychology, 12,* 16–23.

Sternberg, R. J., & Kolligian, J. (Eds.). (1990). *Competence considered.* New Haven, CT: Yale University Press.

Stewart, A. J., Sokol, M., Healy, J. M., & Chester, N. L. (1986). Longitudinal studies of psychological consequences of life changes in children and adults. *Journal of Personality and Social Psychology, 50,* 143–157.

Stone, A. A., Greenberg, M. A., Kennedy-Moore, E., & Newman, M. G. (1991). Self-report, situation-specific coping questionnaires: What are they measuring? *Journal of Personality and Social Psychology, 61,* 648–658.

Suls, J., & Fletcher, B. (1985). The relative efficacy of avoidant and nonavoidant coping strategies: A meta-analysis. *Health Psychology, 4,* 249–288.

Swindle, R. W., Cronkite, R. C., & Moos, R. H. (1989). Life stressors, social resources, coping, and the 4-year course of unipolar depression. *Journal of Abnormal Psychology, 98,* 468–477.

Taylor, S. E. (1983). Adjustment to threatening events: A theory of cognitive adaptation. *American Psychologist, 38,* 1161–1173.

Taylor, S. E., & Brown, J. D. (1988). Illusion and well-being. A social psychological perspective on mental health. *Psychological Bulletin, 103,* 193–210.

Taylor, S. E., Kemeny, M. E., Aspinwall, L. G., Schneider, S. G., Rodriguez, R., & Herbert, M. (1992). Optimism, coping, psychological distress, and high-risk sexual behavior among men at risk for acquired immunodeficiency syndrome (AIDS). *Journal of Personality and Social Psychology, 63,* 460–473.

Thoits, P. A. (1986). Social support as coping assistance. *Journal of Consulting and Clinical Psychology, 54,* 416–423.

Turner, R. J., & Avison, W. R. (1992). Innovations in the measurement of life stress: Crisis theory and the significance of event resolution. *Journal of Health and Social Behavior, 33,* 36–50.

Vaillant, G. E. (1977). *Adaptation to life.* Boston, MA: Little, Brown.

Valentiner, D. P., Holahan, C. J., & Moos, R. H. (1993). *Social support, event controllability, and coping: An integrative model.* Manuscript submitted for publication.

Vitaliano, P. P., DeWolfe, D. J., Maiuro, R. D., Russo, J., & Katon, W. (1990). Appraised changeability of a stressor as a modifier of the relationship between coping and depression: A test of the hypothesis of fit. *Journal of Personality and Social Psychology, 59,* 582–592.

Wallerstein, J. S. (1986). Women after divorce: Preliminary report from a ten-year follow-up. *American Journal of Orthopsychiatry, 56,* 65–77.

Weiss, R. S. (1979). Growing up a little faster: The experience of growing up in a single-parent household. *Journal of Social Issues, 35,* 97–111.

CHAPTER 3

Personality and Coping:
A Reconceptualization

PAUL T. COSTA, JR., MARK R. SOMERFIELD, and ROBERT R. McCRAE

Stress has been a major topic in psychological research since the work of Selye in the 1950s. Research on coping, however, became popular only in the 1980s, after groundbreaking publications by Moos (1976), Pearlin and Schooler (1978), and Folkman and Lazarus (1980). A PsycLIT search on *coping* identified 113 articles in 1974 and 183 in 1980; by 1984 this figure had risen to 639, and that level of research interest has been sustained to the present.

The stress and coping paradigm that was so eagerly adopted in the early 1980s had several attractive characteristics. It emphasized transactional appraisal and thus fit well within the cognitive revolution in psychology. It offered personality psychologists a dynamic alternative to then-unpopular trait psychology. Best of all, it appealed to clinicians and health psychologists who wanted a scientific basis for interventions to help manage stress and promote health.

Unfortunately, the enormous quantity of research on coping has yielded rather modest returns (Aldwin & Revenson, 1987; Costa & McCrae, 1989). We have, to be sure, learned something about the situational determinants and personality correlates of coping responses, and occasional studies have shown that certain ways of coping are modestly associated with health or well-being outcomes (Aspinwall & Taylor, 1992). But we are far from the goal of being able to identify the optimal way of coping for a given individual with a given problem, and we have few new interventions that make a major difference in people's lives.

The premise of this chapter is that progress has been hampered and unrealistic expectations have been fostered by the assumption that stress and coping are special processes, governed by their own laws, and lying outside the normal range of human adaptation. By contrast, we have come to see stress and coping as an intrinsic part of the fabric of action and experience. We argue that psychologists cannot expect to understand stress and coping fully until they have a complete psychology of human behavior, and that they should not expect to understand all

Official contribution of the National Institutes of Health; not subject to copyright in the United States.

ways of coping by using a single methodology. Our reconceptualization also has more positive implications: It means that researchers can make progress by building on what is already known about the determinants of behavior and experience. Our focus in this chapter will be on personality traits as influences on adaptation.

ALTERNATIVE CONCEPTUALIZATIONS OF STRESS AND COPING

The Accepted View of Coping

In defining a distinct field of study, stress and coping researchers have laid claim to a particular aspect of human adaptation, distinguished on the one hand from routine processes like learning and social interaction, and on the other hand from maladaptive and psychopathological phenomena. They have also defined their field in functional terms, studying all those reactions and processes that are thought to help solve problems and reduce distress. The predominant methodology for studying stress and coping is based on these assumptions.

One of the conceptual distinctions that has shaped the field of stress and coping concerns the difference between coping and adaptation: "There is an emerging consensus that 'coping' and 'adaptation' should be distinguished. . . . Adaptation is a broader concept that includes routine, even automatic, modes of getting along, whereas coping always involves some sort of stress" (Lazarus & Folkman, 1984, pp. 283–284).

Adaptation is so broad a term that it covers virtually the whole of psychology (if not biology): Perception, learning, motivation, and emotion are all involved in the individual's continuous interaction with the environment. Important as an understanding of adaptation is, it is too vast a topic to inform a research agenda. Stress and coping researchers therefore limited themselves to those instances of adaptation that were particularly problematic, requiring new responses or special efforts, often in the face of disturbing emotional reactions.

At the same time, these researchers wished to differentiate their work from that of psychiatrists and clinical psychologists, who are also concerned with problems in living. In the accepted view, coping is regarded as a psychologically "normal" process found in psychiatrically healthy individuals. This distinction is sometimes made explicit by contrasting coping with defense (Haan, 1977). It is also implicit in the assumption that coping is a discrete response to an environmental stimulus, a more or less rational response to an objective problem. Coping, then, has been regarded as a special category of adaptation elicited in normal individuals by unusually taxing circumstances.

The individual can respond to a stressor in a wide variety of ways. Social comparison, creative problem solving, denial of affect, and religious faith may all be used to handle stress, and they are therefore all regarded as coping mechanisms. Further, because all ways of coping are functionally similar, it is possible to use a single method to study them, and the method that has been used in the vast majority of studies is a coping questionnaire (e.g., Carver, Scheier, & Weintraub, 1989; Folkman & Lazarus, 1988; McCrae, 1982). Subjects are typically asked to recall a single stressful event and then indicate if, or to what extent, they used each of a series of coping strategies in dealing with it. The goal of coping research has been to understand which coping mechanisms people choose when facing different stressors, and which are most effective in promoting health or well-being.

An Alternative View

Probably most stress and coping researchers would agree that the line between routine problem solving and coping is blurred, as is the boundary between ineffective coping and psychological maladjustment. We would go further, suggesting that these distinctions are arbitrary, artificial and, in the long run, counterproductive.

There are of course some events so stressful that they elicit responses qualitatively different from those of daily life. Traumatic and unexpected events, such as the accidental death of a close friend or relative, often produce intrusive thoughts (Palmer, Tucker, Warren, & Adams, 1993) that have no clear analogue in normal experience. But in most cases, there is no clear demarcation between stressful and normal experience.

Some evidence for this contention comes from a consideration of the stressors that are examined in research on coping. The Holmes and Rahe (1967) Social Readjustment Rating Questionnaire includes such mundane items as "vacation" and "Christmas." Many researchers have shifted attention from major life events to daily hassles (Kanner, Coyne, Schaefer, & Lazarus, 1981), and many deal with chronic medical conditions (Felton & Revenson, 1984) that, by definition, pose recurring rather than novel problems. When subjects are allowed to nominate their own stressor, they often choose ordinary events, such as being a mother of teenage boys or being snubbed by friends (McCrae, 1984).

The continuity of coping with normal adaptation can also be seen by examining individual coping mechanisms. Information seeking is a commonly noted way of coping, yet it is also a basic part of everyday life. Should a call to directory assistance be regarded as coping with the stress of not knowing a telephone number? Positive thinking is a technique for controlling stress by cognitive reappraisal, but how does it differ from dispositional optimism? When is complaining to friends about the job idle gossip, and when is it seeking social support?

It might be argued that the hallmark of stress is emotional arousal. Getting a telephone number for an ambulance when a family member has collapsed may be different from getting the number for a pizza shop. Positive thinking in the face of a fatal diagnosis may be different from positive thinking about next week's weather. But this argument implies that emotional responses are absent in ordinary circumstances, or that moderate levels of emotional arousal have no impact on adaptive behavior. Neither of these is likely to be true. Affect is a ubiquitous part of life, and to varying degrees it influences behavior: We feel discouraged and pass up an opportunity; get angry and yell at our boss; feel lonely and visit a friend.

Cognition, behavior, and affect are inextricably interwoven in daily life, and psychologists have been studying their interactions since the days of Yerkes and Dodson (1908).

If coping fades imperceptibly into ordinary adaptation, then stress shades into psychopathology: Both are likely to be manifested in anxiety, depression, and impaired functioning. The putative difference is that stress is a response to an external provocation, whereas psychopathology reflects inadequacies in the individual. It is more realistic, however, to view anxiety and other stress reactions as the result of an interaction of person and environment, and to note that individuals show a continuous distribution of stress proneness. For some hardy individuals, all life's problems are taken in stride; for very vulnerable individuals, even minor disturbances of daily routine can be traumatic.

The degree to which individuals are prone to experience events as stressful is closely related to the broad personality dimension of neuroticism (McCrae, 1990), the same dimension that most strongly distinguishes psychotherapy patients from volunteers (e.g., Miller, 1991). There are real and important differences between normal and psychiatrically impaired individuals, but the differences are more quantitative than qualitative: There is no categorical difference between ineffective coping and psychological maladjustment.

Implications of the Alternative View

Our reconceptualization of stress and coping as an integral part of the spectrum of adaptation is not as heretical as it might at first seem. Lazarus (1990) has recently suggested that the study of stress can and should be subsumed under the "broader and richer rubric, emotion. . . . I propose that we would be wiser to move away from stress toward the measurement of emotion" (p. 12). Similarly, we can reconceptualize coping as attempts at emotional regulation and problem solving—processes that range from getting dressed to constructing elaborate delusional systems.

An immediate consequence of this reformulation is a new perspective on the task that stress and coping researchers have set themselves. The management of distressing emotions is the single most important focus of the disciplines of clinical psychology and psychiatry, which have been grappling with this problem for decades with only modest success. To expect that stress and coping researchers could solve the problem in a few years was quite unrealistic, tenable only under the mistaken assumption of a categorical distinction between normal and abnormal psychological processes.

A second implication is that the functional grouping of certain behaviors as ways of coping is superficial. Ways of coping are adaptational processes, and these processes should be studied with a variety of specialized methodologies. No one would imagine that the same research paradigm would be equally applicable to the processes of deconditioning phobias, forming romantic attachments, and learning French verbs. Why, then, do we imagine that researchers will learn much by applying the same questionnaire methods to the study of relaxation, seeking social supports, and acquiring information? Every form of coping may require its own methodology if we are to progress beyond the grossest generalizations.[1]

If our new perspective on coping and coping research leads to conceptual and methodological critiques, it also points to new solutions. If stress and coping are normal emotional and behavioral processes, then we already know a good deal about them. Cognitive and educational psychologists should be able to help us understand problem-solving abilities. Psychotherapists can share insights on the management of distressing emotions. And personality psychologists can contribute information on the relations between basic personality dispositions and the forms of adaptation to which they give rise. In the remainder of this chapter, we will examine stress and coping from the perspective of five basic dimensions of personality.

PERSONALITY, STRESS, AND COPING

By *personality,* we mean "a system defined by personality traits and the dynamic processes by which they affect the individual's psychological functioning" (McCrae & Costa, in press, p. 33). This abstract definition is made more concrete by research on the structure of personality conducted over the past decade that specifies the most important groups of personality traits. According to the five-factor model (McCrae, 1992a), most traits can be understood as aspects of five broad trait dimensions: Neuroticism (N), Extraversion (E), Openness to Experience (O), Agreeableness (A), and Conscientiousness (C). Some alternative labels and adjective and questionnaire scale definers of these factors are given in Table 3.1. Some or all of these factors recur in different form in most major personality questionnaires; they can be assessed by self-report or observer ratings; they are quite stable in adults (McCrae & Costa, 1990).

Personality traits, according to our definition, are supposed to affect psychological functioning, and there is ample evidence that they do. For example, O facilitates divergent thinking (McCrae, 1987); E influences the development of vocational interests (Costa, McCrae, & Holland, 1984); N is associated with an exaggerated recollection of health problems (Larsen, 1992). It seems reasonable to hypothesize that personality traits will also affect coping behavior.[2]

---

[1] Mechanisms—like social withdrawal—that individuals may not identify as coping responses (Repetti, 1992), probably cannot be studied properly with questionnaire methods and call for naturalistic methodologies (e.g., diaries). Other mechanisms, such as positive reappraisal, that may occur without awareness (see Houston, 1987) may be best studied with thought-sampling procedures.

[2] Much of the research on personality and coping has not focused on broad traits, but on presumably mid-level personality constructs such as optimism (Scheier, Weintraub, & Carver, 1986), locus of control (Roberto, 1992), and self-efficacy (Chwalisz, Altmaier, & Russell, 1992). Studies have linked these constructs either to situational coping (e.g., Scheier et al., 1986) or to broad traits like N (Smith, Pope, Rhodewalt, & Poulton, 1989). A few studies have examined the more comprehensive model that considers higher-level traits, mid-level expressions of these traits such as optimism,

TABLE 3.1 Examples of Adjectives and Questionnaire Scales Defining the Five Factors

	Definers	
Factor	Adjectives	Scales
Neuroticism (or Negative Affectivity vs. Emotional Stability)	Anxious Self-pitying Tense Touchy Unstable Worrying	Anxiety Angry Hostility Depression Self-Consciousness Impulsiveness Vulnerability
Extraversion (or Surgency, Dominance vs. Introversion)	Active Assertive Energetic Enthusiastic Outgoing Talkative	Warmth Gregariousness Assertiveness Activity Excitement Seeking Positive Emotions
Openness to Experience (or Intellect, Culture vs. Conventionality)	Artistic Curious Imaginative Insightful Original Wide interests	Fantasy Aesthetics Feelings Actions Ideas Values
Agreeableness (or Love, Friendly Compliance vs. Antagonism)	Appreciative Forgiving Generous Kind Sympathetic Trusting	Trust Straightforwardness Altruism Compliance Modesty Tender-mindedness
Conscientiousness (or Dependability, Will to Achieve vs. Undirectedness)	Efficient Organized Planful Reliable Responsible Thorough	Competence Order Dutifulness Achievement Striving Self-Discipline Deliberation

Note: Scales are facet scales from the Revised NEO Personality Inventory. Adapted from McCrae and John (1992).

A few years ago such a hypothesis was radical. After Mischel's (1968) influential critique, the very existence of traits was widely doubted in the 1970s, and stress and coping researchers distanced themselves from the earlier conception of traitlike coping styles. Folkman and Lazarus (1980) in particular claimed that there was little cross-sectional consistency in coping that could be attributed to person variables, and urged researchers instead to focus on the ongoing

---

and the lower-level processes of appraisal and coping (e.g., Amirkhan, Risinger, & Swickert, 1995). More of this type of research is needed to explore the mechanisms through which traits influence adaptation.

transactions between the environment and the individual's appraisal of it. Personality traits, "individual differences in the tendencies to show consistent patterns of thoughts, feelings, and actions" (McCrae & Costa, 1990, p. 23) seemed to operate, if at all, only under routine conditions. Habitual actions might be traitlike, but responses to stress were thought to be governed by special transactional processes.

This view has been challenged. In responses to Lazarus' (1990) target article on stress measurement, the importance of personality traits was emphasized by several commentators, including Ben-Porath and Tellegen (1990), Krohne (1990), and Watson (1990). All these authors pointed out that personal dispositions interact with the situation in shaping perceptions of stress.[3] Caspi and Moffit (1993), in an ingenious attempt to explain the stability of personality traits, have inverted the assumption that stressful circumstances overpower personality traits. Instead, they argue, ambiguous and threatening life transitions accentuate preexisting traits: Our real dispositions are best revealed under stress.

Evidence of Associations between Personality and Coping

These conceptual shifts are justified in part by a growing body of research demonstrating that there is some consistency in coping responses, and that coping styles are related to the five basic factors of personality (cf. Hewitt & Flett, Chapter 18, this volume). If, as we have argued, coping is not a distinct species of behavior, then expectations about personality and coping should be informed by the general literature on personality and behavior. What we know from a long controversy on this topic is that individual instances of behavior are multiply and chaotically determined, but that they show some consistency when aggregated over many occasions (Epstein, 1979). Further, personality traits are among their important determinants (Kenrick & Funder, 1988).

By design, most coping inventories do not aggregate over instances; instead, they seek to pinpoint the exact responses made to specific stressors. Critics have questioned how accurately subjects recall specific coping responses (e.g., Stone, Greenberg, Kennedy-Moore, & Newman, 1991), and how well defined the putatively specific stressor actually is (Somerfield, 1994), but to the extent that recall is accurate and assessments are specific, this approach minimizes the likelihood of finding associations with stable personality traits. We should therefore expect to find small correlations when specific coping responses are considered. When coping styles or dispositions are measured (Carver et al., 1989; Endler & Parker, 1990) larger associations may be seen.

A large number of studies have shown links between N and aspects of the stress and coping process. Hooker, Monahan, Shifren, and Hutchinson (1992) showed strong relations between perceived stress and N in spouse caregivers.

---

[3] In response, Lazarus (1990) acknowledged that personality traits and their concrete expressions (e.g., goals and beliefs), together with environmental conditions, do indeed influence appraisal and coping processes.

Smith, Pope, Rhodewalt, and Poulton (1989) found that trait anxiety, a measure of neuroticism, was associated with relatively less use of problem-focused coping and seeking social support, and more use of wishful thinking and avoidance. Endler and Parker (1990) reported strong correlations between Eysenck Personality Questionnaire N and the Emotion scale of the Multidimensional Coping Inventory, a dispositional measure of coping. These findings are hardly surprising, because one hallmark of stress is psychological distress, and neuroticism is sometimes defined as the propensity to experience negative affects (Watson & Clark, 1984). Any attempt to understand the situational determinants of stress and coping must take N into account (McCrae, 1990).

The role of E is somewhat less clear; Amirkhan, Risinger, and Swickert (1995) have suggested that it is a "hidden" personality factor in coping. They reported that E was related to social support seeking in both correlational and experimental studies. Gallagher (1990) showed that individuals who score high on E tend to appraise academic stressors as challenges rather than threats. Rim (1987) reported that E was related to problem-focused coping and positive thinking, and Martin (1989) found that E was a predictor of active coping among survivors of a myocardial infarction. In general, E appears to be associated with active, social, and optimistic ways of dealing with stress.

N and E have been familiar dimensions of personality for decades, largely because of the influential work of Hans Eysenck. The three remaining dimensions are much less familiar, and have rarely been examined in research on personality and coping. Lonky, Kaus, and Roodin (1984) examined existential coping with the experience of loss. They found that affirmative coping, defined in terms of relatedness, transcendence, rootedness, identity, and meaning as judged from interview responses, was predicted by a questionnaire measure of Openness to Experience. Interpersonal trust, a facet of Agreeableness, was positively related to seeking social support in a study by Grace and Schill (1986). Because Conscientiousness involves such traits as persistence, self-discipline, and planning, one might hypothesize that it would be related to effective coping, and in one of the few studies to include a measure of C, Vickers, Kolar, and Hervig (1989) reported a correlation of .44 ($p < .001$) between C and problem solving in coping with military basic training. In a more recent study, Spirrison, McGrath, and Caruso (1994) reported a correlation of .62, $N = 118$, $p < .001$, between NEO-PI-R Conscientiousness and the Behavioral Coping scale of Epstein and Meier's (1989) Constructive Thinking Inventory.

Personality and Coping in the Baltimore Longitudinal Study of Aging

Most of our own research on personality and coping has been conducted on participants in the Baltimore Longitudinal Study of Aging (BLSA; Shock et al., 1984). These volunteers range in age from 20 to 90; they are generally healthy and well-educated, and have agreed to return to the Gerontology Research Center every 2 years for biomedical and psychosocial testing. The BLSA began in 1958, and new participants are continually recruited. In addition to in-person testing, a subset of participants have agreed to complete questionnaires at home periodically; their spouses and peers have also participated in some of these questionnaire studies, forming what we have called the Augmented BLSA.

In 1980, 255 men and women (Subsample A) completed a coping questionnaire in response to a single major life event, classified as either a loss, threat, or challenge. The questionnaire consisted of all the items from the Ways of Coping (Folkman & Lazarus, 1980) plus 50 additional items written to tap coping mechanisms suggested by a review of the literature. A second group of 151 men and women (Subsample B) completed the 50 items with respect to three different, self-selected stressors: a loss, a threat, and a challenge. In both samples, items were combined to form 27 provisional scales measuring a diverse set of coping mechanisms, ranging from rational action to escapist fantasy to sedation.

Analyses of these data showed that older individuals coped as well as did younger individuals (McCrae, 1982) and that there were consistent situational effects on the choice of coping mechanisms. For example, faith and fatalism were used when facing a loss; perseverance and humor were used under conditions of challenge (McCrae, 1984).

Coping responses, however, were not exclusively determined by situation. There was appreciable consistency within the individual across different kinds of stressors. One piece of evidence for this assertion came from analyses of the responses to the three stressors reported by Subsample B. The 81 correlations between responses to threats, losses, and challenges on 27 coping mechanisms ranged from $-.01$ to $.59$, with a median of $.29$; 83% of these correlations were significant (McCrae, 1992b). Thus, there appears to be some consistency in the way an individual responded to three categorically different stressors in one time period.

Cross-time consistency was evaluated with new data collected in 1987. In that study, 113 subjects from Subsample A and 78 from Subsample B completed a new questionnaire dealing with a single event. The coping questionnaire consisted of the Ways of Coping, the additional 50 items, and 28 new supplementary items. Retest correlations for the 27 coping mechanisms after an interval of 7 years ranged from $-.10$ to $.60$, with a median of $.26$; across the two samples, 65% of the correlations were significant (McCrae, 1989). Some enduring characteristics of the individual may account for these consistencies across stressor and time.

Our hypothesis was that personality traits, known to be stable over long periods of adulthood, might account for some of the stability of coping behaviors. McCrae and Costa (1986) examined the personality correlates of coping mechanisms using an early version of the Revised NEO Personality Inventory (NEO-PI-R; Costa & McCrae, 1992), which measured only three of the five factors: N, E, and O. In both subsamples, E was associated with rational action, restraint, substitution, and positive thinking. O was positively related to the use of humor, and negatively related to the use of faith. N was correlated with a variety of generally ineffective coping mechanisms, including hostile reaction, self-blame, escapist fantasy, withdrawal, and indecisiveness.

The analysis of many discrete ways of coping instead of a few broad classes of coping mechanisms (such as problem-focused and emotion-focused; Folkman & Lazarus, 1980) allows some relationships to emerge that might otherwise be obscured. Positive thinking and self-blame are both emotion-focused ways of coping, but the kinds of people who think positively are generally not the same people who blame themselves. An emotion-focused coping scale that summed these two items would probably not be related to any dimension of personality.

A logical extension of this specificity strategy is to examine coping items individually. NEO-PI-R data were available for 275 BLSA participants who completed the coping questionnaire in 1987. Each of the 146 coping items was correlated with the five orthogonal NEO-PI-R factor scores; correlations significant at $p < .01$ are summarized in Table 3.2. Most of these correlations are small, as would be expected from the analysis of single items referring to a single instance of coping. The pattern of results, however, is perfectly understandable, providing clear support for Bolger's (1990) contention that "coping is personality in action under stress" (p. 525). Coping responses, like other patterns of thoughts, feelings, and actions, reflect the pervasive influence of personality traits.

Individuals high in N react badly to stress, blaming themselves and taking it out on others. They indulge in wishful thinking and become passive and withdrawn. Extraverts respond like extraverts, talking, joking, and relating to others. People open to experience rethink the problem from different perspectives, seeking new information and trying novel solutions. Individuals high in A adopt a stoic and compliant attitude that calls to mind reaction formation or reversal (cf. Costa, McCrae, & Dembroski, 1989); those who are low in A express their anger directly. Finally, C is positively associated with perseverance and personal growth, and is negatively associated with a variety of passive and ineffective responses. A number of items positively associated with N are negatively associated with C (e.g., "lost temper," "criticized, lectured self"), but the pattern is subtly different. Men and women who score high in N seem *unable* to deal effectively with stress; those who are low in C seem *unwilling* to do so, preferring to make jokes, excuses, or feckless efforts instead of tackling the problem head on.

A methodological limitation to this study is the use of self-reports for the assessment of both personality traits and coping responses. Is it possible that these correlations are due to some self-presentational bias? One way to examine this question is by using observer ratings of personality instead of self-reports. Sixty of the 275 individuals were rated by their spouses on the observer rating version of the NEO-PI-R. Examining individual items in so small a sample would not be meaningful, but the items shown in Table 3.2 can be aggregated to form scales of N-related coping, E-related coping, and so on. When these five self-report coping scales are correlated with spouse-rated personality factors, the corresponding correlations are .36, .01, .27, .32, and .32 for N, E, O, A, and C, respectively; except for E, all are significant at $p < .05$. Personality as seen by the spouse predicts self-reported coping responses.

TABLE 3.2   Coping Responses Associated with Revised NEO Personality Inventory Factors

NEO-PI-R Factor	Coping Response	r
Neuroticism		
	60. Wished you were a stronger person	.30
	52. Took it out on others	.24
	94. Reacted childishly	.24
	104. Blamed yourself, felt guilty	.24
	78. Became irritable	.22
	82. Acted strangely out-of-character	.21
	119. Lost temper	.21
	127. Had fantasies of all problems solved	.21
	2. Went over problem again and again	.20
	66. Fantasies of how things would turn out	.19
	36. Got away from it for awhile	.19
	5. Bargained or compromised	.18
	65. Daydreamed	.18
	11. Criticized, lectured self	.17
	110. Daydreamed to forget troubles	.17
	108. Wished the problem would be gone	.16
	116. Withdrew from others	.16
	140. Stood by, let things happen	.16
	—vs.—	
	123. Didn't allow self to get emotional	−.18
Extraversion		
	41. Joked about it	.20
	42. Maintained pride	.18
	50. Talked about feelings	.17
	32. Let feelings out	.17
	72. Sought reassurance, support	.16
	138. Were able to laugh	.16
Openness		
	23. Inspired to do something creative	.20
	88. Saw the humor	.19
	76. Saw problem in artistic, philosophical perspective	.19
	131. Did something to relieve tension	.18
	22. Told self things to feel better	.18
	92. Thought about positive aspects	.18
	28. Did something totally new	.17
	117. Took strength from others' examples	.17
	91. Sought help solving problem	.16
	21. Accepted sympathy	.16
	—vs.—	
	57. Promised self things would be different next time	−.21
	90. Had no emotional reaction	−.19
Agreeableness		
	118. Put faith in God, others	.23
	123. Didn't allow self to get emotional	.22
	39. Found new faith	.21
	73. Found situation pleasant	.20

TABLE 3.2   *(Continued)*

NEO-PI-R Factor	Coping Response	r
Agreeableness (Continued)		
	19. Slept more	.17
	99. Kept doing the same things, tried harder	.16
	—vs.—	
	62. Wished you could change what happened	−.21
	20. Got mad at people who caused problem	−.19
	119. Lost temper	−.16
	32. Let feelings out	−.16
Conscientiousness		
	133. Became better, stronger as result	.25
	1. Concentrated on next step	.20
	—vs.—	
	19. Slept more	−.25
	41. Joked about it	−.22
	94. Reacted childishly	−.18
	84. Expressed feelings directly	−.18
	6. Did something that wouldn't work	−.18
	116. Withdrew from others	−.17
	119. Lost temper	−.17
	127. Had fantasies of all problems solved	−.17
	16. Felt bad that couldn't avoid problem	−.17
	33. Realized brought problem on self	−.16
	60. Wished you were stronger person	−.16
	56. Refused to believe it happened	−.16
	11. Criticized, lectured self	−.15

Note: $N = 275$ men and women. All correlations significant at $p < .01$. Items 1–68 are taken from the Ways of Coping Questionnaire (Folkman & Lazarus, 1988); items 69–118 are from McCrae (1982).

SOME IMPLICATIONS FOR COPING RESEARCH

In the recent past, researchers have spotlighted a portion of the adaptive spectrum called stress and coping. In the glare of that spotlight, links to routine adaptive processes and to psychopathological reactions were lost. If we turn off the light and view the entire spectrum, its seamless continuity is apparent.

Thus, as Lazarus (1990) has argued, stress can be viewed as part of the full complex of human emotions, which are intimately tied both to personality dispositions and to psychopathology. Approaches that emphasize the continuity of normal and abnormal psychology (e.g., Costa & Widiger, 1994) suggest a grand integration, in which normal affects, emotional responses to extraordinary events, and clinical anxiety and depression can all be understood in a single framework.

Broadening the scope of stress and coping enables us to draw on what is already known about personality, affect, and problem solving, but it also poses methodological challenges. How can we most effectively study so all-inclusive a topic? Perhaps instead of studying many ways of dealing with a narrow band of adaptive problems, we should study a few processes in depth to uncover the complex relations among personal and environmental factors in adaptation.

Research on social comparison, for example, has made progress toward a cumulative, integrated, and dynamic science of these processes (see Taylor, Buunk, & Aspinwall, 1990). Over a period of 10 years, Taylor and her colleagues completed a series of investigations, applying both open-ended approaches (Wood, Taylor, & Lichtman, 1985) and the more conventional close-ended approaches (e.g., Buunk, Collins, Taylor, VanYperen, & Dakof, 1990). In an integrative analysis of this work and related research, Taylor and Lobel (1989) highlighted the conceptual and operational complexities inherent in studying the "single" coping mechanism of social comparison, which, as they illustrated, takes on different forms that serve different needs. Similarly intensive programs of research on other coping mechanisms may be advisable.

Personality and Problem Solving

Coping questionnaires usually phrase items in general terms (e.g., "Found satisfaction somewhere else in life," "tried to analyze the problem logically to find the best solution") applicable to any kind of stressor. This strategy works relatively well for emotion-focused coping, but much less well for problem-focused coping. Whereas the ways of dealing with distress are as universal as human emotions, effective ways of solving problems are specific to the situation.

Detailing the information and skills needed for handling specific problems could be designated applied stress and coping research (Costa & McCrae, 1993), and applied research is probably conducted most productively one problem at a time. Consider the complexities of cancer diagnosis, an early substressor of having cancer. Within a relatively brief period, cancer diagnosis can require, among other tasks, regulation of one's own emotional response, a reasoned choice from among different treatment options (e.g., lumpectomy vs. mastectomy), and detailed practical arrangements to get one's affairs in order in preparation for a lengthy hospitalization (Somerfield, 1994). Any one of these sub-substressors could be the focus of a problem-focused study of coping with cancer.

The widespread reliance on "general-duty" (Pearlin, Mullan, Semple, & Skaff, 1990) coping questionnaires to the exclusion of other approaches has arguably delayed progress in applied coping research. These questionnaires, as Leventhal and Nerenz (1985) have noted, may indicate that respondents frequently used some general category of coping behavior, but they do not provide any information on what precisely they did. Yet it is this specific information that is of practical value: Patients facing chemotherapy for cancer do not need to be told that they should seek information, persevere, and take one step at a time. They need concrete information on how to manage distressing treatment-related side effects such as nausea, vomiting, and dysphoria (Carey & Burish, 1988).

The semistructured interview is probably the best way to explore problem-specific coping mechanisms in applied research (Somerfield & Curbow, 1992).

Open-ended queries can be used to survey the often idiosyncratic ways that people manage particular problems; coping checklist items can serve as a systematic source of cues for recalling specific coping efforts (Coyne, Sonnega, & Carter, 1993). To ensure a more informative assessment, probes of endorsed items should be used to ascertain the specific character of coping efforts (Stone & Neale, 1984).

What contribution can personality psychology make to applied coping research? A first step is to identify general principles that relate problem-solving efforts to aspects of personality. People high in C are more likely to make and stick with plans of action. People high in O are willing to try new approaches. People high in A may be able to elicit and accept social support. It might be hypothesized that open, agreeable, and conscientious people in fact solve problems better than closed, disagreeable, and undirected people.

Although personality traits are not easily altered and do not offer a ready avenue of intervention, information on personality may be very useful in tailoring interventions to the individual. Christensen and Smith (1995) have shown that C is a predictor of adherence to medical regimens; if one's patients are low in C, special efforts will be needed to ensure compliance, such as enlisting the aid of a family member. Support groups are often an effective way to exchange information with and gain emotional support from people who share a similar problem (Thoits, 1986), but not all individuals respond well to group interactions; very introverted individuals might prefer written materials they could study at home. Applied stress and coping researchers need to recognize individual differences in approaches to problem solving.

REFERENCES

Aldwin, C. M., & Revenson, T. A. (1987). Does coping help? A reexamination of the relation between coping and mental health. *Journal of Personality and Social Psychology, 53,* 337–348.

Amirkhan, J. H., Risinger, R. T., & Swickert, R. J. (1995). Extraversion: A "hidden" personality factor in coping? *Journal of Personality, 63,* 189–212.

Aspinwall, L. G., & Taylor, S. E. (1992). Modeling cognitive adaptation: A longitudinal investigation of the impact of individual differences and coping on college adjustment and performance. *Journal of Personality and Social Psychology, 63,* 989–1003.

Ben-Porath, Y. S., & Tellegen, A. (1990). A place for traits in stress research. *Psychological Inquiry, 1,* 14–40.

Bolger, N. (1990). Coping as a personality process: A prospective study. *Journal of Personality and Social Psychology, 59,* 525–537.

Buunk, B. P., Collins, R. L., Taylor, S. E., VanYperen, N. W., & Dakof, G. A. (1990). The affective consequences of social comparison: Either direction has its ups and downs. *Journal of Personality and Social Psychology, 59,* 1238–1249.

Carey, M. P., & Burish, T. G. (1988). Etiology and treatment of the psychological side effects associated with cancer chemotherapy: A critical review and discussion. *Psychological Bulletin, 104,* 307–325.

Carver, C. S., Scheier, M. F., & Weintraub, J. K. (1989). Assessing coping strategies: A theoretically based approach. *Journal of Personality and Social Psychology, 56,* 267–283.

Caspi, A., & Moffitt, T. E. (1993). When do individual differences matter? A paradoxical theory of personality coherence. *Psychological Inquiry, 4,* 247–271.

Christensen, A. J., & Smith, T. W. (1995). Personality and patient adherence: Correlates of the five-factor model in renal dialysis. *Journal of Behavioral Medicine, 18,* 305–313.

Chwalisz, K., Altmaier, E. M., & Russell, D. W. (1992). Causal attributions, self-efficacy cognitions, and coping with stress. *Journal of Social and Clinical Psychology, 11,* 377–400.

Costa, P. T., Jr., & McCrae, R. R. (1989). Personality, stress, and coping: Some lessons from a decade of research. In K. S. Markides & C. L. Cooper (Eds.), *Aging, stress, social support and health* (pp. 267–283). New York: Wiley.

Costa, P. T., Jr., & McCrae, R. R. (1992). *Revised NEO Personality Inventory (NEO-PI-R) and NEO Five-Factor Inventory (NEO-FFI) professional manual.* Odessa, FL: Psychological Assessment Resources.

Costa, P. T., Jr., & McCrae, R. R. (1993). Psychological stress and coping in old age. In L. Goldberger & S. Breznitz (Eds.), *Handbook of stress: Theoretical and clinical aspects* (2nd ed., pp. 403–412). New York: Free Press.

Costa, P. T., Jr., McCrae, R. R., & Dembroski, T. M. (1989). Agreeableness vs. antagonism: Explication of a potential risk factor for CHD. In A. Siegman & T. M. Dembroski (Eds.), *In search of coronary-prone behavior: Beyond Type A* (pp. 41–63). Hillsdale, NJ: Erlbaum.

Costa, P. T., Jr., McCrae, R. R., & Holland, J. L. (1984). Personality and vocational interests in an adult sample. *Journal of Applied Psychology, 69,* 390–400.

Costa, P. T., Jr., & Widiger, T. A. (Eds.). (1994). *Personality disorders and the five-factor model of personality.* Washington, DC: American Psychological Association.

Coyne, J. C., Sonnega, J., & Carter, K. (1993, August). *Couples coping with congestive heart failure: A contextual approach.* Paper presented at the meeting of the American Psychological Association, Toronto, Canada.

Endler, N. S., & Parker, J. D. A. (1990). Multidimensional assessment of coping: A critical evaluation. *Journal of Personality and Social Psychology, 58,* 844–854.

Epstein, S. (1979). The stability of behavior: I. On predicting most of the people much of the time. *Journal of Personality and Social Psychology, 37,* 1097–1126.

Epstein, S., & Meier, P. (1989). Constructive thinking: A broad coping variable with specific components. *Journal of Personality and Social Psychology, 57,* 332–350.

Felton, B. J., & Revenson, T. A. (1984). Coping with chronic illness: A study of illness controllability and the influence of coping strategies on psychological assessment. *Journal of Consulting and Clinical Psychology, 52,* 343–353.

Folkman, S., & Lazarus, R. S. (1980). An analysis of coping in a middle-aged community sample. *Journal of Health and Social Behavior, 21,* 219–239.

Folkman, S., & Lazarus, R. S. (1988). *Manual for the Ways of Coping Questionnaire.* Palo Alto, CA: Consulting Psychologist Press.

Gallagher, D. J. (1990). Extraversion, neuroticism, and appraisal of stressful academic events. *Personality and Individual Differences, 11,* 1053–1057.

Grace, G. D., & Schill, T. (1986). Social support and coping style differences in subjects high and low in interpersonal trust. *Psychological Reports, 59,* 584–586.

Haan, N. (1977). *Coping and defending.* New York: Academic Press.

Holmes, T. H., & Rahe, R. H. (1967). The social readjustment rating scale. *Journal of Psychosomatic Research, 11,* 213–218.

Hooker, K., Monahan, D., Shifrin, K., & Hutchinson, C. (1992). Mental and physical health of spouse caregivers: The role of personality. *Psychology and Aging, 7,* 367–375.

Houston, B. K. (1987). Stress and coping. In C. R. Snyder & C. E. Ford (Eds.), *Coping with negative life events: Clinical and social psychological perspectives* (pp. 373–399). New York: Plenum.

Kanner, A. D., Coyne, J. C., Schaefer, C., & Lazarus, R. S. (1981). Comparison of two modes of stress measurement: Daily hassles and uplifts versus major life events. *Journal of Behavioral Medicine, 4,* 1–39.

Kenrick, D. T., & Funder, D. C. (1988). Profiting from controversy: Lessons from the person-situation debate. *American Psychologist, 43,* 23–34.

Krohne, H. W. (1990). Personality as a mediator between objective events and their subjective representation. *Psychological Inquiry, 1,* 26–29.

Larsen, R. J. (1992). Neuroticism and selective encoding and recall of symptoms: Evidence from a combined concurrent-retrospective study. *Journal of Personality and Social Psychology, 62,* 480–488.

Lazarus, R. S. (1990). Theory-based stress measurement; Author's response. *Psychological Inquiry, 1,* 3–13, 41–51.

Lazarus, R. S., & Folkman, S. (1984). Coping and adaptation. In W. D. Gentry (Ed.), *Handbook of behavioral medicine* (pp. 282–325). New York: Guilford.

Leventhal, H., & Nerenz, D. R. (1985). The assessment of illness cognition. In P. Karoly (Ed.), *Measurement strategies in health psychology* (pp. 517–554). New York: Wiley.

Lonky, E., Kaus, C. R., & Roodin, P. A. (1984). Life experience and mode of coping: Relation to moral judgment in adulthood. *Developmental Psychology, 20,* 1159–1167.

Martin, P. (1989). Personality and coping in survivors of a myocardial infarction. *Journal of Social Behavior and Personality, 4,* 587–601.

McCrae, R. R. (1982). Age differences in the use of coping mechanisms. *Journal of Gerontology, 37,* 454–460.

McCrae, R. R. (1984). Situational determinants of coping responses. Loss, threat, and challenge. *Journal of Personality and Social Psychology, 46,* 919–928.

McCrae, R. R. (1987). Creativity, divergent thinking, and openness to experience. *Journal of Personality and Social Psychology, 52,* 1258–1265.

McCrae, R. R. (1989). Age differences and changes in the use of coping mechanisms. *Journal of Gerontology: Psychological Sciences, 44,* P161–P169.

McCrae, R. R. (1990). Controlling neuroticism in the measurement of stress. *Stress Medicine, 6,* 237–241.

McCrae, R. R. (Ed.). (1992a). The Five-Factor Model: Issues and applications [Special issue]. *Journal of Personality, 60*(2).

McCrae, R. R. (1992b). Situational determinants of coping. In B. N. Carpenter (Ed.), *Personal coping: Theory, research, and applications* (pp. 65–76). New York: Praeger.

McCrae, R. R., & Costa, P. T., Jr. (1986). Personality, coping, and coping effectiveness in an adult sample. *Journal of Personality, 54,* 385–405.

McCrae, R. R., & Costa, P. T., Jr. (1990). *Personality in adulthood.* New York: Guilford.

McCrae, R. R., & Costa, P. T., Jr. (in press). Toward a new generation of personality theories: Theoretical contexts for the five-factor model. In J. S. Wiggins (Ed.), *The five-factor model of personality: Theoretical perspectives.* New York: Guilford.

McCrae, R. R., & John, O. P. (1992). An introduction to the five-factor model and its applications. *Journal of Personality, 60,* 175–215.

Miller, T. (1991). The psychotherapeutic utility of the five-factor model of personality: A clinician's experience. *Journal of Personality Assessment, 57,* 415–433.

Mischel, W. (1968). *Personality and assessment.* New York: Wiley.

Moos, R. H. (Ed.). (1976). *Human adaptation: Coping with life crises.* Lexington, MA: Heath.

Palmer, A. G., Tucker, S., Warren, R., & Adams, M. (1993). Understanding women's responses to treatment for cervical intra-epithelial neoplasia. *British Journal of Clinical Psychology, 32,* 101–112.

Pearlin, L. I., Mullan, J. T., Semple, S. J., & Skaff, M. M. (1990). Caregiving and the stress process: An overview of concepts and their measures. *The Gerontologist, 30,* 583–594.

Pearlin, L. I., & Schooler, C. (1978). The structure of coping. *The Journal of Health and Social Behavior, 19,* 2–21.

Repetti, R. L. (1992). Social withdrawal as a short-term coping response to daily stressors. In H. S. Friedman (Ed.), *Hostility, coping, and health* (pp. 155–165). Washington, DC: American Psychological Association.

Rim, Y. (1987). A comparative study of two taxonomies of coping, personality and sex. *Personality and Individual Differences, 8,* 521–526.

Roberto, K. A. (1992). Coping strategies of older women with hip fractures: Resources and outcomes. *Journal of Gerontology: Psychological Sciences, 47,* P21–P26.

Scheier, M. F., Weintraub, J. K., & Carver, C. S. (1986). Coping with stress: Divergent strategies of optimists and pessimists. *Journal of Personality and Social Psychology, 51,* 1257–1264.

Shock, N. W., Greulich, R. C., Andres, R., Arenberg, D., Costa, P. T., Jr., Lakatta, E. G., & Tobin, J. D. (1984). *Normal human aging: The Baltimore Longitudinal Study of Aging* (NIH Publication No. 84-2450). Bethesda, MD: National Institutes of Health.

Smith, T. W., Pope, M. K., Rhodewalt, F., & Poulton, J. L. (1989). Optimism, Neuroticism, coping, and symptom reports: An alternative interpretation of the Life Orientation Test. *Journal of Personality and Social Psychology, 56,* 640–648.

Somerfield, M. (1994). *On the use of checklist measures of coping in studies of cancer adaptation.* Manuscript in preparation.

Somerfield, M., & Curbow, B. (1992). Methodological issues and research strategies in the study of coping with cancer. *Social Science and Medicine, 34,* 1203–1216.

Spirrison, C. L., McGrath, P. B., & Caruso, J. C. (1994, April). *Coping ability and neuroticism: Comparison of the CTI and NEO-PI-R.* Paper presented at the meeting of the Society for Personality Assessment, Chicago, IL.

Stone, A. A., Greenberg, M. A., Kennedy-Moore, E., & Newman, M. G. (1991). Self-report, situation-specific coping questionnaires: What are they measuring? *Journal of Personality and Social Psychology, 61,* 648–658.

Stone, A. A., & Neale, J. M. (1984). New measure of daily coping: Development and preliminary results. *Journal of Personality and Social Psychology, 46,* 892–906.

Taylor, S. E., Buunk, B. P., & Aspinwall, L. G. (1990). Social comparison, stress, and coping. *Personality and Social Psychology Bulletin, 16,* 74–89.

Taylor, S. E., & Lobel, M. (1989). Social comparison activity under threat: Downward evaluation and upward contacts. *Psychological Review, 96,* 569–575.

Thoits, P. A. (1986). Social support as coping assistance. *Journal of Consulting and Clinical Psychology, 54,* 416–423.

Vickers, R. R., Jr., Kolar, D. W., & Hervig, L. K. (1989). *Personality correlates of coping with military basic training* (Report No. 89-3). San Diego, CA: Naval Health Research Center.

Watson, D. (1990). On the dispositional nature of stress measures: Stable and nonspecific influences on self-reported hassles. *Psychological Inquiry, 1,* 34–37.

Watson, D., & Clark, L. A. (1984). Negative affectivity: The disposition to experience aversive emotional states. *Psychological Bulletin, 96,* 465–490.

Wood, J. V., Taylor, S. E., & Lichtman, R. R. (1985). Social comparison in adjustment to breast cancer. *Journal of Personality and Social Psychology, 49,* 1169–1183.

Yerkes, R. M., & Dodson, J. D. (1908). The relation of strength of stimulus to rapidity of habit formation. *Journal of Comparative and Neurological Psychology, 18,* 459–482.

PART TWO

Assessment and Research Methods

CHAPTER 4

The Methodology of Research on Coping: Conceptual, Strategic, and Operational-Level Issues

TERRY A. BEEHR and JOSEPH E. McGRATH

Discussion of many traditional research issues regarding strategy, design, and operations, which are generic over substantive topical areas, can be found in most methodology textbooks. Here, we will concentrate on conceptual, definitional, and methodological matters that are specific to stress and coping. They raise some troublesome epistemological questions.

CONCEPTUAL AND DEFINITIONAL ISSUES IN STRESS COPING RESEARCH

We offer the following parable to focus some definitional issues:

The Parable of Six Brothers and a Condominium

Six brothers—Adam, Ben, Cedric, Daniel, Edward, and Frank—inherited a condominium on a Florida key. One summer, two hurricanes hit their key. Anxious Adam, always frightened by hurricanes, evacuated to the mainland before the hurricanes hit but still experienced intense emotional distress. Macho Ben toughed it out; he laid in food, water, and other provisions, but his car was demolished in one storm. Sensible Cedric, somewhat worried about hurricanes but mainly disliking the Florida climate and culture, sold out to his brothers and had moved to Maine two years earlier. Dogged Daniel was seriously injured in one hurricane, but worked very hard to rehabilitate a shattered hip, became a leader in a hurricane safety movement and, incidentally, fell in love with and married his orthopedic therapist. Edward the unready lost his car in the first hurricane, so he evacuated, with car, when warned of the second. Frank the flake was on a safari in Africa and didn't learn about the hurricanes until 2 months later.

We might ask, which brothers coped with the potential stressor of the hurricane, which coped successfully, and which did not "cope" at all? We return to this parable later.

Stress and Coping as Value Terms

It is tempting to treat coping as if the term designated certain kinds of behavior, distinguishable from other behaviors occurring in stress situations. To designate something as a coping behavior, however, requires inferences about what the focal person was *trying to do*. Researchers can observe only two classes of events: (a) *sets of conditions* that *may* prove demanding, challenging, or stressful; and (b) *behaviors by the focal person* that the researcher interprets as being in response to or because of those conditions.

Characteristically, stress researchers have regarded the first class of events as potential stressors (Stress Producing Events and Conditions, or SPECs; see McGrath & Beehr, 1990), and have divided the latter class of events, the behaviors of a focal person, into three kinds of variables:

1. Reactions interpreting SPECs and estimating their implications, usually regarded as cognitive appraisal of the potential threat and/or opportunity represented by the SPEC (Folkman & Lazarus, 1980; Lazarus, 1966).
2. Reactions (affective, visceral, other behaviors) indicating the impact of stress on the person (distress or strains).
3. Reactions attempting (perhaps even unwittingly) to deal with the SPEC in the environment. These are usually regarded as evidence of coping, that is, of the focal person's attempts to deal with or counteract the negative effects (or take advantage of the positive possibilities) of the SPEC (McGrath, 1970).

It would be convenient if the three reactions were clearly distinguishable in terms of behavioral domains for example by reflecting cognitive, affective, and conative responses, respectively. But all three responses may partake of all three facets of that trinity, at least sometimes. Instead, the distinction among those three sets of responses is "in the eye of the beholder"—*interpretations* on the part of the researcher about the focal person's responses.

We argued earlier (McGrath, 1981) that research on stress and coping is heavily value laden. Furthermore, even the distinction between coping and noncoping behaviors in the face of a SPEC is a researcher's value-laden interpretation, not given in the nature of the behavior itself. To assert that something is a coping reaction (rather than a stress reaction, or a behavior that has no reference at all to a given set of SPEC conditions) is to presume to know what the focal person is experiencing (or, perhaps, should be experiencing).

This requirement—for the researcher to make strong epistemological assumptions about the systems being studied—appears to be an inevitable accompaniment of the logical-positivistic approach to inquiry. We accept that; but it is essential that coping researchers recognize explicitly that key "empirical" distinctions rest on interpretations and assumptions, not just direct "objective" observations.

The Stress Cycle and Its Context

Given this preamble, we will treat the methodological issues of coping within the framework of a stress cycle (see Beehr & Bhagat, 1985; McGrath, 1970; McGrath & Beehr, 1990):

1. Conditions arise that are assumed to constitute a SPEC.
2. The conditions are (or are not) interpreted as a SPEC by some focal person(s).
3. The focal person does (or does not) react to that SPEC—at physiological, psychological, behavioral, and/or interpersonal levels—in ways that may be regarded as evidence of stress.
4. The focal person may (or may not) attempt to cope with the stress (again, at physiological, psychological, behavioral, and/or interpersonal levels).

Such stress-and-coping cycles occur in a complex context including physical, sociocultural, and temporal aspects.

Temporal Context

Time plays a vital and pervasive role in the stress-and-coping cycle (cf. McGrath & Beehr, 1990). A major temporal feature here involves the temporal relations between the SPEC events and the coping activities. Coping can encompass activities with prospective, concurrent, or retrospective temporal relations with the SPEC:

1. Long before it occurs, or might occur (preventive coping); see brother Cedric's actions; also see following paragraph.
2. When it is anticipated soon (anticipatory coping), descriptive of brother Adam's reaction.
3. While it is ongoing (dynamic coping), as in brother Ben's hurricane activity.
4. After it has happened (reactive coping), as shown in brother Edward's behavior.
5. Long afterward, by contending with long-run effects (residual coping), which is part of brother Daniel's story.

All these behaviors constitute coping by preventing or counteracting negative effects of a SPEC or potential SPEC. But if all these things are coping, what is not coping?

Is brother Frank's African sojourn preventive coping? If it is not because Frank did not do it "on purpose" to avoid the effects of the hurricane, then how shall we regard Cedric's sale, which he did for other reasons although he appreciated its hurricane-preventive effects? Do we need a category of "unintended coping"? Or, do we want to limit coping to only post-SPEC actions, in which case, Adam's evacuation and Ben's provisioning must not be regarded as coping behavior? And shall we regard Daniel's serendipitous romance as a coping gain, or as an "accidental" co-occurrence unrelated to coping?

We have no solid empirical basis for deciding these vexing questions. They must be decided by fiat; the researcher, explicitly or implicitly, must presume to know (a) about the nature of the environment (SPECs); (b) about the thoughts, intentions, and purposes of the focal person; and (c) about desirable and undesirable subsequent states for that person. This is a heavy epistemological burden indeed.

Social Support

A major avenue by which people prevent or overcome negative effects of SPECs is through social support, which can play a direct positive role in coping behavior by reducing the negative effects of the stressor; less directly, it can provide resources that let the focal person execute effective coping behaviors; and/or indirectly, it can moderate various stress-coping relations (see Beehr & McGrath, 1992, for a summary).

Social support resources are "outside" the focal person and may even be outside the entire stress cycle. They are not responses by the focal person but by others, and the focal person has only limited control of them; yet social support has been advocated as a potential coping technique (e.g., Latack, 1986). Thus, their availability as coping responses is problematic.

Furthermore, if such external sources can have positive effects on the stress-and-coping cycle, then in principle they can have equally profound negative effects—also only partly under the focal person's control. People can potentially make any situation more stressful for focal person, both by failure to provide the resources that could have helped and by providing conditions that create or add to stress. It is not always clear whether obtaining social support is part of coping or whether failure to obtain it is an additional SPEC.

METHODOLOGICAL ISSUES AT STRATEGIC AND DESIGN LEVELS

To conduct research on coping is to examine one or more of three basic sets of questions, regarding the origins, the nature, and the consequences of coping behavior, as shown in the following examples:

1. What causes coping activities; do the same things cause coping across people and settings (A and B of Figure 4.1)?
2. What kinds of coping activities are there, how are they related to one another, and what are their relative effectiveness and costs (C of Figure 4.1)?
3. When do coping activities have positive or negative consequences for the person, for others in the situation, and for the situational context itself (D of Figure 4.1)?

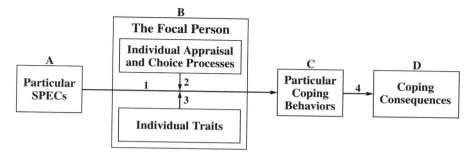

Coping as Dependent Variable: Arrows 1, 2, 3
1. Can, should SPEC be experimentally manipulated?
2. Can appraisal and choice be experimentally manipulated?
3. Can traits be experimentally manipulated?

Coping as Independent Variable: Arrow 4
4. Can C (coping) be manipulated?

Figure 4.1 Methodological issues about control of behavior.

Assumptions about the Nature of Coping Behaviors

The methodological choices in research on coping depend on assumptions about the nature and control of behavior in general, and of coping in particular. This involves three characteristics of any behavior pattern: (a) locus of control, (b) spontaneity or naturalness, and (c) mutability.

Locus of Control of Behavior

A coping behavior can be:

1. Mainly under the control of the person's own deliberate choices.
2. Mainly under the control of the person, but determined more or less automatically by his or her personality traits.
3. Mainly under control of the situation, which might elicit certain patterns of coping behavior from anybody.
4. Jointly under the control of two or all three of those sources.
5. Under none of the preceding sources of control.

Some versions of psychology might deny the very possibility of some of these alternatives. For example, radical behaviorism might contend that there is no internal or self-control, eliminating Alternative 1 and probably favoring Alternative 3. But most theory and research on stress and coping would probably expect coping, like other behaviors, to result from interactions between person and environment. Thus, for any given case, we expect some form of three-way interaction of features of the situation, attributes of the focal person, and features of the coping activity itself.

Spontaneity and Mutability of Behavior

Two other assumptions about the nature of coping behavior affect research methods. First, researchers make assumptions about the extent to which coping patterns are relatively spontaneous, or natural, versus deliberate. Second, researchers make assumptions about the extent to which coping patterns are relatively immutable versus easily modifiable (by experience or deliberate tutelage).

Researchers who regard coping as mainly controlled by personality may assume that coping consists of relatively spontaneous and immutable behavior patterns. In contrast, researchers who regard coping as mainly controlled by the focal person's deliberate choices may assume that coping consists of deliberate, and presumably relatively malleable, behavior patterns. If coping is mainly elicited by situational features, then coping is a spontaneous and nondeliberate pattern for any given set of situational conditions, and thus is amenable to change only by changing the situation (not, e.g., by training the focal person).

For the fourth or mixed case, in which control of behavior is presumed to reside jointly in situation, personality, and person's deliberate choices, various assumptions can be made about the spontaneity and mutability of patterns of coping behavior (e.g., Holahan & Moos, 1986). In the fifth case, where coping is regarded as not under the control of the person, the situation, or combinations (hence, not controllable), the question of the nature and mutability of patterns of coping behavior is moot.

The important point is that *the set of assumptions the researcher makes about the locus, spontaneity, and mutability of coping patterns shapes his or her methodological choices.* A researcher who regards the coping responses of a focal person as relatively spontaneous and stable responses to a specific situation is likely to frame the study as the exploration of individual differences in coping patterns for given populations in given circumstances—and study *coping as a dependent variable.* If, instead, the researcher regards coping behavior as relatively mutable patterns deliberately constructed by the person, that researcher is likely to frame the study as explorations of the relative effectiveness of different kinds of coping patterns in different kinds of circumstances; that is, the study of *variations in coping patterns as independent variables.* Still another set of assumptions, that coping behaviors are spontaneous but mutable patterns differing in their effectiveness for a given situation, might lead the researcher to attempt to construct and implement methods for training focal persons in the most effective coping patterns for given sets of circumstances, and thereby to use *coping training as experimental treatment.*

A relatively extreme position on these assumptions regards coping behavior as arising from stable characteristics of the person, or even *as* these characteristics themselves; that is, *coping behaviors as traits.* One of the better known examples is the concept of hardiness (e.g., Kobasa, 1979; Kobasa, Maddi, & Puccetti,

1982). Some people are seen as more hardy or more able to resist the harmful effects of SPECs than others, with their hardiness at any given time being regarded as their nature at that time (whatever the long-term etiology of the hardiness may have been). If such traits are regarded as very difficult to change, then coping must be seen as naturally occurring, relatively immutable, and not easily induced. Similarly, there has been research on physical hardiness or physical fitness, as a characteristic that makes people able to resist the potentially harmful effects of certain SPECs (Roth & Holmes, 1985).

A sharp dichotomy between mutable and immutable coping patterns oversimplifies the process. In theory, personality characteristics can be changed, although not easily; after all, an entire industry—psychotherapy—depends partially on this assumption. And even though physical fitness seems to have traitlike properties, it is theoretically possible to change one's degree of physical fitness, again with an accompanying industry banking on that theory.

Some of these issues are reflected in Figure 4.1; some implications are examined in the following discussion.

Coping as Dependent Variable

Coping as a criterion or dependent variable can only sensibly be addressed under certain combinations of assumptions about the nature of coping. If the individual is in unilateral control of his or her own behavior, then he or she can choose how to cope with a given SPEC. But if behavior is environmentally determined (perhaps by features of the SPEC), situations or circumstances "elicit" particular coping responses. It is also possible, in principle, that neither the person's deliberate choices nor the demands of the environment exert much control over the coping behavior. An individual's coping behaviors may reflect a habitual pattern that may occur without any conscious choice or response selection on the part of the person and without any apparent control by the particular environmental situation. This type of "habitual" behavior may be considered a coping *trait,* a stable characteristic of the person (for studies that examine relationships between stable individual differences and coping, see Havlovic & Keenan, 1991; McCrae & Costa, 1986; Siegler & George, 1983).

If neither features of the current situation nor choices of the person seem to control coping behaviors, that may be because the behavior is simply random. But randomness has seldom been psychologists' favorite explanation for the occurrence of one behavior rather than another.

Another issue regarding coping as a dependent variable concerns learning. If practitioners desire to teach people coping behaviors, they assume people can learn a different way of coping. Still another possibility for what causes coping is the SPEC itself; stressful environmental features might be examined as potentially leading to coping (e.g., McCrae, 1984). Furthermore, SPECs with certain characteristics (e.g., interpersonal versus impersonal, long-term versus short-term, work-related versus family-related versus leisure-related, severe versus mild, common versus unusual) may result in characteristic coping reactions for most people.

Researchers testing such ideas can encounter serious practical and ethical problems, as well as methodological ones. To test the proposition that characteristics of environmental stressors cause particular kinds of coping behavior, standard methodological practice would suggest that the method of choice is to manipulate the SPECs experimentally, so as to determine their effects on coping. Because SPECs are, by definition, expected to be harmful or stressful to the individual, deliberately exposing people to them is hard to justify ethically. An alternative would be to expose people to experiences that are only mildly and/or briefly stressful (e.g., Sales, 1970); but to do so leaves us uncertain about whether results actually pertain to effects of high levels of stress—our primary interest. This is made even more problematic because a prominent theoretical paradigm posits a nonmonotonic relation between magnitude of stress and certain outcomes (e.g., quality of task performance). With such a "mild stress only" strategy to achieve appropriate ethical standards for experimental manipulations, we could never assess the crucial right-hand, high-stress side of that nonmonotonic function. The easy way out is to employ nonexperimental field studies, but the resulting weak causal inference is not completely satisfying.

A better solution to this problem might be to use "naturally occurring" SPECs that are under control of third parties. For example, in a workplace or school system, managers or school officials might decide to introduce some changes that researchers considered stressful to employees or to students. This might afford the alert researcher an experimental or quasi-experimental opportunity to study coping while, to some degree, relieving the experimenter of the ethical responsibility for manipulating the environment in potentially stressful ways. Better yet, managers might be contemplating changes in the environment that could make it less stressful. In such a case, it might be possible to enlist manager collaboration to randomly construct the sequence in which the impending change will be implemented in different subsections of the organization (e.g., Jackson, 1983, 1984). Serendipitously, a field experiment is born!

Coping as Independent Variable: Evaluating the Effectiveness of Particular Coping Practices

A major issue in coping research is the effectiveness of various coping activities. As previously noted, this involves the issues of spontaneity and mutability of coping behavior. On the one hand, if coping behavior reflects spontaneous and immutable behavior patterns, then those patterns cannot be manipulated by a researcher in an experimental or quasi-experimental research strategy. In this case, only nonexperimental (correlational) designs can be used to study coping, and the range of choices of research strategies has been narrowed considerably for the researcher. Much research addressing the potential effectiveness of coping has employed such nonexperimental field studies (e.g., Parasuraman & Hansen, 1987; Shinn, Rosario, Mørch, & Chestnut, 1984).

Alternatively, if people can alter their coping behaviors, then in principle it is also possible for an experimenter to induce such changes in coping behaviors by using experimental or quasi-experimental designs to test the effects of different patterns of coping (e.g., Ganster, Mayes, Sime, & Tharp, 1982; Long & Haney, 1988). If subjects can be randomly assigned to conditions (to various types or levels of coping and various control or placebo conditions), then true experiments are possible, with resulting higher confidence in the attributions about direction of causality. Although for reasons already discussed, it is usually difficult to do true experiments on stress and coping, it is more often possible to conduct quasi-experimental research in this domain (e.g., Beehr, 1984; Beehr & O'Hara, 1987). The potential advantages of quasi-experimental designs over nonexperimental designs in allowing stronger causal inference, and the advantages of research in natural settings over laboratory research in affording more contextual realism, are well known and we have discussed them at length elsewhere (cf. Brinberg & McGrath, 1985; Runkel & McGrath, 1972). Conducting quasi-experimental studies of coping in natural settings may offer the best overall strategy, but the merits of any particular strategy and design must be assessed in relation to the specific case.

Threats to Validity

All empirical studies are subject to a number of potential threats to both the internal and external validity of their findings (Cook & Campbell, 1979). For an extensive discussion of those threats, the problems to which they give rise, and ways to circumvent them, readers may consult Cook and Campbell (1979), Runkel and McGrath (1972), or other general methods sources. Several threats to validity that pose special difficulties for research on stress and coping are discussed here.

Internal validity refers to the degree of confidence researchers can have about whether a particular set of empirical findings reflect a directional causal relation between independent and dependent variables. Cook and Campbell (1979) note 11 threats to internal validity. Three seem especially likely to be problems in research on stress and coping.

History refers to naturally occurring events (external to the variables examined in the study) between the onset of stress and the coping response, or between the onset of coping and the measurement of its consequences. These events, rather than the factors in the study hypotheses, might be responsible for the measured levels of coping behavior and/or its outcomes. An important example would be a change in the magnitude, periodicity, and/or predictability of the stressor while the study is taking place. The SPEC or stressor may be eliminated or lessened through some event other than the person's coping. This might encourage the researcher to conclude (incorrectly) that successful coping was occurring. The reverse case could occur if the SPEC increased in intensity due to some "external" events, in spite of what would have been effective coping efforts. This could lead to an opposite (incorrect) conclusion that effective coping did not occur.

This is a particularly instructive example because much research on stress and coping tends to ignore the "objective" stressors and focus on subjective stress effects. It is common for stress treatments to teach people how to reduce their personal anxiety, depression, blood pressure, tension, and so forth, without examining closely the environmental stressors that might have given rise to those conditions (Beehr, Jex, & Ghosh, 1995). Studies of emotion-focused coping are more likely to fall prey to this threat than are studies of problem-focused coping; the latter usually explicitly examine the problem or SPEC. To minimize the effects of stressor-altering historical events on the causal inferences about the effectiveness of coping, researchers need to measure the SPECs periodically (to ascertain that the environmental SPEC is still operating at the same magnitude).

Maturation can threaten internal validity, because as the participants develop and mature, they may become accustomed to the SPEC enough to be able to withstand it without suffering adverse consequences. The effects of time and experience alone might be mistaken for effects of coping strategies. Alternatively, time and experience might be essential for people to develop and implement effective coping strategies. This raises another question: Should maturation, in the form of the passage of time and the accrual of experience with the stressor condition, be regarded as a threat to validity of inference about coping behavior, or should it be thought of as a vital part of the development of the coping response itself?

Selection effects are a likely threat to validity in research on coping effectiveness, because there is a temptation (and often even a research requirement) to teach coping only to volunteers. Volunteers might be more enthusiastic or committed to successful coping than others, and by definition, it is difficult to get full data for a comparison group of nonvolunteers. Moreover, to deliver the treatment that is thought to be effective to a random half of the volunteers and a placebo treatment to the other half without their knowledge raises ethical questions.

Although other general threats to internal validity must be considered in coping research as well as in all other research, they do not seem to pose special threats on that topic. The overall problem of internal validity, however, is especially problematic for stress and coping research because, for pragmatic and ethical reasons, it is often not possible to employ the best forms of study design (namely, true experiments). As noted earlier, quasi-experimental designs are more likely to be available (both feasible and ethical) in studies of stress and coping. They offer some but not all the protections against threats to internal validity that true experiments can provide.

Without random allocation of cases to conditions in a true experiment, there is no strong basis for concluding that cases in the different treatment conditions were more or less comparable at the outset of the study. Hence, there is no basis for attributing posttreatment effects to the experimental treatments. Without random assignment, causal attributions can only be achieved in part, by much more complex designs (cf., Cook & Campbell, 1979; Cook, Campbell, & Peracchio, 1990).

There are situations in which it is practical and also ethical to have a "no treatment" control group when studying stress coping, but they often go unrecognized. If a large number of people want to learn coping techniques, but there are only resources available to do a good job with a small proportion of them at any one time, it might be fair to use a random procedure to choose the subset to be treated first. This gives everybody an equal chance of getting the beneficial training initially. Furthermore, those assigned to the control group can be promised (and given) the treatment (taught the coping skills) at a later time—as soon as resources are available—and they can thereby become a second experimental sample, for a within-groups comparison. It can be done; a recent review of empirical research on a narrower but related topic (behavioral based treatments of occupational stress) uncovered nine published studies using random assignment in the past 10 years (Beehr et al., 1995).

Short of random assignment in "true" field experiments, however, some of the threats to internal validity of coping evaluations can be lessened with various quasi-experimental designs. Three types of quasi-experimental designs seem especially feasible, widely applicable, and valuable in research on coping with stress (Beehr, 1984): (a) nonequivalent control group designs, (b) regression-discontinuity designs, and (c) interrupted time series designs (see Cook & Campbell, 1979; Cook, Campbell, & Perrachio, 1990).

External Validity

External validity is concerned with generalizability of internally valid findings to other populations, times, and conditions. Even when the findings from an internally valid study support a relatively strong inference about the effect of some pattern of coping on changes on stress variables, those findings say nothing about whether the same relation would hold with other participants, at other times, and in other settings. The basic issue is whether the relation between coping and stress interacts, in the statistical sense, with the nature of the people doing the coping (the study's participants), the nature of the setting, and/or features of the time period during which the experiment took place (e.g., Cook & Campbell, 1979; Cook, Campbell, & Perrachio, 1990; Beehr & O'Hara, 1987). The researcher cannot test for such a statistical interaction except by conducting multiple experiments using different types of subjects, in multiple places, and at multiple times. Instead, to estimate the study's generalizability, the researcher must examine the selection process by which he or she gained access to the subjects involved and chose the times and places in which to conduct the study.

Limitations on external validity may arise in a number of ways. Consider, for example, the much used dichotomy of problem-focused versus emotion-focused coping (e.g., Lazarus, 1966; Folkman & Lazarus, 1980). Problem-focused coping is more likely to work in some *situations* and with some *people* than others (see Zeidner & Saklofske, Chapter 22, this volume). Problem solving might be effective with SPECs such as interpersonal conflict whose roots lie in misunderstanding the other person's position, when the focal person is flexible and has credibility. Attempts at mutual problem solving might reveal the misunderstanding and eliminate the SPEC.

In other situations or for other people, however, problem solving might not be an effective form of coping. In the stressful life situation involving the death of a spouse, for example, the stress of grief for the loved one cannot easily be resolved, even though many auxiliary problems involving new forms of day-to-day living might be amenable to problem solving. Results of studies of problem solving in one situation and with one type of person might not generalize well to other situations and people.

External validity can be threatened by a third type of interaction—between *history* or time period and the experimental treatment (Cook & Campbell, 1979). An example might be drawn from workplace stress. Employees might cope with occupational stress by quitting their jobs entirely (e.g., as in Gupta & Beehr, 1979). But quitting a job is a more effective coping technique when used in times of economic boom than in times of economic decline, if the person wishes to obtain another, preferably less stressful job. Rather than reducing the individual's stress overall, quitting one's job during times of high unemployment might make things worse by inducing the SPEC of unemployment, which has been shown to evoke substantial stress responses (e.g., Cobb & Kasl, 1977; Vinokur, Caplan, & Williams, 1987). Thus, the timing of use of withdrawal as a form of coping may affect the outcome.

Fundamentally, the researcher's confidence in the external validity of a coping study's results can be increased only through convergence of findings from replications of the study conducted with many different groups of individuals, in many settings, and in many locations.

Concluding Comments Regarding Strategy and Design

Methodological choices may be affected by whether the researcher views coping behavior as the result of unalterable traits, as arising naturally from the situational conditions, as amenable to experimental intervention, and so forth. Different assumptions make different strategies and designs more and less sensible, more and less feasible.

METHODOLOGICAL ISSUES AT THE OPERATIONAL LEVEL

Even if the potential pitfalls of research design and strategy for coping research are resolved, another set of questions must be addressed: What should be measured and how should it be measured?

A relatively large number of possible measures of coping behavior have been or could be used to assess whether, and how successfully, some human system (individual, group, organization) has coped with some SPEC. Table 4.1 (adapted from McGrath, 1970) classifies such measures in a matrix of four operational forms of measurement and four system levels at which coping can take place.

TABLE 4.1   Potential Indexes of Coping Responses

	Operational Forms of Measurement			
System Level of Measure	Subjective Reports (e.g., questionnaires, interviews)	Observations (direct observations of focal persons actions)	Trace Measures (trace evidence of focal persons behavior)	Archival Records (documents, records of focal persons actions)
Physiological (e.g. use of drugs, alcohol medications)	Questionnaires, interviews about use	Direct observation of use	Biochem. analyses of medications, etc. in body	Medical records, check stubs for costs
Psychological (e.g. planning, problem solving, evaluation of situation)	Questionnaires, interviews re. planning, etc.	Direct observation of planning, problem-solving actions	Evidence of planning, problem solving (e.g. planning documents)	Records of meetings & phone calls re. planning
Task Performance (e.g. task/goal accomplishment self help treatment, visits to physicians)	Questionnaires, interviews re. task/goal attainment visits to physicians	Direct observation of task performance, problem-solving activity	Evidences of task action (e.g. empty pill bottles)	Records of treatments, job performance
Interpersonal Behavior (e.g. seeking social support role clarification, conflict resolution)	Questionnaires, interviews re. seeking social support, conflict resolution	Direct observations re. interpersonal actions	Evidences of interpersonal activity (e.g. records of group meetings)	Records of meetings with supportive others, role changes

Note: Adapted from McGrath (1970), Table 5.

The four operational forms of measures (based on Webb, Campbell, Schwartz, & Sechrest, 1966), are subjective reports, observations, trace measures, and measures derived from archival records. The four system levels are physiological, psychological, task performance, and interpersonal.

Each operational form of measure offers methodological advantages but suffers from some limitations (discussed in detail elsewhere; Runkel & McGrath, 1972; Webb et al., 1966). The use of multiple methods of measuring important dependent variables, e.g., coping, takes advantage of the strengths and offsets the weaknesses of any one class of measures.

The system levels are to some degree arbitrary and in the eye of the beholder. There is not always a clear line between levels (e.g., between physiological and psychological processes, between psychological processes and task performance processes, or between any of those and interpersonal processes). Nevertheless, researchers often act as if these were clear-cut distinctions, and make strong assumptions about the "location" of the variables they are studying; that is, at which system level the coping is taking place. Furthermore, those assumptions sometimes carry with them prescriptions for where and how to intervene in the attempt to modify coping.

At first glance, there appears to be some degree of contingency between operational forms and system levels of measures of coping. For example, observations apparently are the method of choice for assessing coping at the level of task performance. In contrast, self-reports are often chosen for assessing various psychological processes. But those characteristic form-level combinations are due more to the methodological habits of the field than to any necessary contingency between level of process and form of measurement. Furthermore, it is desirable to develop alternative measures, using different operational forms, for any given coping reaction, for a number of conceptual and methodological reasons (discussed in detail by Runkel & McGrath, 1972; Webb et al., 1966).

We consider, briefly, each of the four operational forms of measures of coping behavior shown in Table 4.1, and encourage readers to consider the meaning and implications of each of the 16 cells in that table.

Subjective Reports

Subjective reports are by far the most popular form of measurement of coping activities. They include any direct report by people regarding their own coping responses, usually elicited via questionnaires or interviews. They offer both major advantages and limitations (see Runkel & McGrath, 1972; Webb et al., 1966). Their chief limitation is their reactivity. Among their chief strengths are their content versatility and low cost.

Observational Measures

Researchers often speak as if direct observation is both the most desirable and the most frequent form in which they obtain scientific data. Perhaps the idealized notion is that of data obtained by observation via a mechanical or electronic "instrument," with a little assist (in calibration and interpretation) from a human observer. Such observations are highly touted as "objective," presumably not subject to the kind of human biases necessarily involved in self-reports. But in the social and behavioral sciences, those presumptions are inaccurate.

Not all coping processes are overt and directly observable. Nor can even an ingenious researcher always construct observation procedures with good assessments of all processes of interest. Moreover, even when such indexes can be conceived, they cannot always be implemented for both practical and ethical reasons. Observation is costly and obtrusive. Furthermore, such observations, though less subject to the focal person's biases, are subject to the observer's biases.

Trace Measures

Trace measures are evidences (accretions or erosions) left behind unwittingly by the behavior of interest; they surely are an underused resource (Webb et al., 1966). But trace measures pose especially difficult problems with regard to construct validity. In behavioral science research in general and coping research specifically, trace measures usually can be construed as indicators of a range of different constructs, some of which are and some of which are not germane to the researcher's purposes.

Measures Derived from Archival Records

Archival records are infrequently used in psychology although they are more popular in other areas of social and behavioral science. Their main strength lies in their "independence" of the research process. They are records made for purposes other than the research at hand. They therefore are presumed to be independent of the biases of both the focal person and the researcher, but of course, they are influenced by the purposes and values of whoever generated the records. Frequently, they exist at a level of aggregation too gross for the research purpose (e.g., production records recorded only per month, or only for the whole plant, rather than daily and for each work group).

Concluding Comments about Operational Level Issues

This brief sketch of possible forms and levels of measures of coping is not intended to provide a list of available ("off the shelf") measures of coping, but rather to spur coping researchers to recognize possibilities and explore a wider variety of potential operationalizations of coping measures than has been used in the past. The 16 types of coping measures in Table 4.1 have not been used with equal frequency in coping research; nor are they equally easy to conceive or use. Indeed, some researchers might protest our urging the use of some of the entries in the table, on methodological or conceptual grounds. Here again, the meaning of concepts and measures in the coping area is to a very large extent in the eye of the beholder.

CONCLUSION

Let us conclude by returning to our initial parable of the six brothers. What can we say of it now, having covered many issues about stress and coping?

We can maintain that all six brothers coped, effectively, with their hurricane situation—or, that none of them did. We can regard the parable as evidence (in various operational forms, at various system levels) about both the differential conditions that gave rise to and shaped coping behavior of the six brothers (coping as dependent variable), and the differential consequences that ensued from each of their patterns of coping (coping as independent variable).

There are potential lessons in that parable for research on stress coping. First, we cannot distinguish on *logical grounds* (though we can on *value* grounds) between Frank's being on safari and Ben's toughing it out, as instances of coping behavior. Nor can we regard Cedric's anticipatory sale and his therefore being in Maine during hurricane season as positive consequences of hurricane coping, unless we are willing to accept Daniel's romance and marriage (along with his broken hip) as positive consequences of hurricane coping. Finally, we cannot contend *on any but value-driven bases* that Adam's anxiety (even in the face of successful problem-focused coping) is a better or worse outcome than Ben's triumph over the storm (plus a demolished car), Cedric's escape, Daniel's pains and gains, Frank's obliviousness, or Edward's one-trial learning.

These hypothetical events make salient a key lesson: What is stressful, what is evidence of stress, and what is evidence of coping all depend heavily on the purposes and perspectives of both the focal person experiencing stress and the researcher studying it. The researcher's interpretation of the nature of stress and coping influences his or her choices of research strategy, study design, and operations; and these, in turn, determine what can be learned from that research.

Research methods often cannot be divorced from the substance of what is to be studied, nor from the conceptual foundations underlying the research. The study of coping presents a strong case in point.

REFERENCES

Beehr, T. A. (1984). Stress coping research: Methodological issues. In A. S. Sethi & R. S. Schuler (Eds.), *Handbook of stress coping* (pp. 277–300). Cambridge, MA: Harper & Row.

Beehr, T. A., & Bhagat, R. S. (Eds.). (1985). *Human stress and cognition in organizations.* New York: Wiley.

Beehr, T. A., Jex, S. M., & Ghosh, P. (1995). The management of occupational stress. In C. M. Johnson, W. Redmon, & T. Mawhinney (Eds.), *Performance management: Behavior analysis in organizations.* New York: Springer.

Beehr, T. A., & McGrath, J. E. (1992). Social support, occupational stress, and anxiety. *Anxiety, Stress, and Coping, 5,* 7–19.

Beehr, T. A., & O'Hara, K. (1987). Methodological designs for the evaluation of occupational stress interventions. In S. V. Kasl & C. L. Cooper (Eds.), *Stress and health: Issues in research methodology* (pp. 79–112). Chichester, England: Wiley.

Brinberg, D., & McGrath, J. E. (1985). *Validity and the research process.* Newbury Park, CA: Sage.

Cobb, S., & Kasl, S. V. (1977). *Termination: The consequences of job loss* (DHEW [NIOSH] Publication No. 77-224). Washington, DC: U.S. Government Printing Office.

Cook, T. D., & Campbell, D. T. (1979). *Quasi-experimentation: Design and analysis issues for field settings.* Chicago: Rand McNally.

Cook, T. D., Campbell, D. T., & Peracchio, L. (1990). Quasi experimentation. In M. D. Dunnette & L. M. Hough (Eds.), *Handbook of industrial and organizational psychology* (2nd ed., Vol. 1, pp. 491–576). Palo Alto, CA: Consulting Psychologist Press.

Folkman, S., & Lazarus, R. S. (1980). An analysis of coping in a middle-aged community sample. *Journal of Health and Social Behavior, 21,* 219–239.

Ganster, D. C., Mayes, B. T., Sime, W. E., & Tharp, G. D. (1982). Managing organizational stress: A field experiment. *Journal of Applied Psychology, 67,* 533–542.

Gupta, N., & Beehr, T. A. (1979). Job stress and employee behaviors. *Organizational Behavior and Human Performance, 23,* 373–387.

Havlovic, S. J., & Keenan, J. P. (1991). Coping with work stress: The influence of individual differences. *Journal of Social Behavior and Personality, 6,* 199–212.

Holahan, C. J., & Moos, R. H. (1986). Personality, coping, and family resources in stress resistance: A longitudinal analysis. *Journal of Personality and Social Psychology, 51,* 389–395.

Jackson, S. E. (1983). Participation in decision making as a strategy for reducing job-related strain. *Journal of Applied Psychology, 68,* 3–19.

Jackson, S. E. (1984). Correction to "participation in decision making as a strategy for reducing job-related strain." *Journal of Applied Psychology, 69,* 546–547.

Kobasa, S. C. (1979). Stressful life events, personality and health: An inquiry into hardiness. *Journal of Personality and Social Psychology, 37,* 1–11.

Kobasa, S. C., Maddi, S. R., & Puccetti, M. C. (1982). Personality and exercise as buffers in the stress-illness relationship. *Journal of Behavioral Medicine, 5,* 391–404.

Latack, J. C. (1986). Coping with job stress: Measures and future directions for scale development. *Journal of Applied Psychology, 71,* 377–385.

Lazarus, R. S. (1966). *Psychological stress and the coping process.* New York: McGraw-Hill.

Long, B. C., & Haney, C. J. (1988). Coping strategies for working women: Aerobic exercise and relaxation interventions. *Behavior Therapy, 19,* 75–83.

McCrae, R. R. (1984). Situational determinants of coping responses—loss, threat, and challenge. *Journal of Personality and Social Psychology, 92,* 433–448.

McCrae, R. R., & Costa, P. T. (1986). Personality, coping and coping effectiveness. *Journal of Personality, 54,* 385–405.

McGrath, J. E. (1970). *Social and psychological factors in stress.* New York: Holt, Rinehart & Winston.

McGrath, J. E. (1981). Methodological problems in research on stress. In H. W. Krohne & L. Laux (Eds.), *Achievement, stress, and anxiety* (pp. 19–48). Washington, DC: Hemisphere.

McGrath, J. E., & Beehr, T. A. (1990). Time and the stress process: Some temporal issues in the conceptualization and measurement of stress. *Stress Medicine, 6,* 93–104.

Parasuraman, S., & Hansen, D. (1987). Coping with work stressors in nursing: Effects of adaptive versus maladaptive strategies. *Work and Occupations, 14,* 88–105.

Roth, D. L., & Holmes, D. S. (1985). Influence of physical fitness in determining the impact of stressful life events on physical and psychological health. *Psychosomatic Medicine, 47,* 164–173.

Runkel, P. J., & McGrath, J. E. (1972). *Research on human behavior.* New York: Holt, Rinehart & Winston.

Sales, S. M. (1970). Some effects of role overload and role underload. *Organizational Behavior and Human Performance, 5,* 592–608.

Shinn, M., Rosario, M., Mørch, H., & Chestnut, D. E. (1984). Coping with job stress and burnout in the human services. *Journal of Personality and Social Psychology, 46,* 864–876.

Siegler, I. C., & George, L. K. (1983). The normal psychology of the aging male: Sex differences in coping and perception of life events. *Journal of Geriatric Psychiatry, 16,* 297–299.

Veninga, R. L., & Spradley, J. P. (1981). *The work-stress connection: How to cope with job burnout.* New York: Ballantine Books.

Vinokur, A., Caplan, R. D., & Williams, C. C. (1987). Effects of recent and past stress on mental health: Coping with unemployment among Vietnam veterans and nonveterans. *Journal of Applied Social Psychology, 17,* 708–728.

Webb, E. J., Campbell, D. T., Schwartz, R. D., & Sechrest, L. (1966). Unobtrusive measures: A survey of non-reactive research in social science. Skokie, IL: Rand McNally.

CHAPTER 5

The Interplay among Design, Data Analysis, and Theory in the Measurement of Coping

JERI BENSON and KNUT A. HAGTVET

In designing a study, many researchers tend to focus their attention primarily on substantive aspects, paying secondary attention to the methodology used. Research in the field of coping (as well as other disciplines) could benefit by elevating the role of methodology to coequal status with the substantive area. Toward this end, our chapter focuses on the importance of the interplay among research design, data analysis, and theory by illustrating how the construct of coping can be validated using traditional and more recent methodological designs. We believe that the recent methodological designs will prove quite useful in furthering our understanding of coping as these procedures require thorough knowledge of substantive theory to implement them. Because this volume is on coping, our chapter is limited to the psychometric designs and statistical procedures available to study the construct validation of coping measures.[1]

VALIDITY

In general there are two important aspects of validation to keep in mind. First, validity is the most important psychometric concept as it is the process by which test scores take on meaning. Researchers do not validate a scale, but an interpretation about the scores derived from the scale (Cronbach, 1971; Nunnally, 1967). Second, validation is a matter of degree, not an all-or-nothing property. Thus, one study does not validate nor fail to validate the scores from a scale. Numerous studies are needed, utilizing different approaches, different samples,

The authors would like to acknowledge Øyvind Martinsen for his assistance in preparing the figures for this chapter.
[1] Although our comments are provided with reference to scales measuring coping, they are relevant to the development, validation, and evaluation of any scale designed to measure a construct.

and different populations to build a body of evidence that supports or fails to support the validity of the scores derived from the scale. As such, validation is a continual process (Nunnally, 1967). Even when a large body of evidence exists that supports the validity of the scores from a particular scale (e.g., Wechsler Intelligence Scales), validity studies are continually needed as our interpretation of the trait can change due to changes in social or cultural conditions. Thus, for a scale to remain valid over time, its validity must be reestablished periodically.

THE THEORY OF CONSTRUCT VALIDATION

In the measurement of constructs, it should be remembered that a construct represents an abstract variable derived from theory or observation. As such, a construct represents a hypothesis about the observables thought to represent the construct. Therefore, it is important not only to be able to define and develop measurements of constructs, but also to find and demonstrate functional relations between measures of different constructs. How then are constructs defined and validated? Nunnally (1967) has suggested a three-step approach:

1. Specify the domain of observables for the construct.
2. Determine to what extent the observables are correlated with each other.
3. Determine whether or not the measures of a given construct correlate in expected ways with measures of other constructs.[2]

The third step is the essence of what Cronbach and Meehl (1955) have termed a "nomological network." To specify a nomological network for a given construct, one needs not only strong theory, but a thorough understanding of the theory. It is essential to have explicit statements regarding the way the construct of interest is influenced by and influences other constructs or variables. Therefore, the stronger the substantive theory regarding a construct, the easier it is to design a validation study with the potential for providing strong empirical evidence. The weaker or more tenuous the substantive theory, the greater the likelihood that equally weak empirical evidence will be gathered and very little advancement will be made in understanding the construct.

Researchers in the field of coping seem to have invested much time and effort in relating supposed measures of constructs to each other (Step 3 from Nunnally), whereas too little attention has been given to defining and clarifying the domain of observables that encompasses the construct of coping and studying the relations among the coping-relevant observables (Steps 1 and 2 from Nunnally). Thus, although we will present each of Nunnally's three steps, we will emphasize Steps 1 and 2.

---

[2] We suggest that the reader not think of Nunnally's word "correlate" in the narrow statistical sense, but allow it to take on a broader meaning such as "to behave."

Domain of Observables

Step 1 focuses on the development of a theoretical as well as an empirical definition of the domain to be measured. The question to ask at this stage is, How should the theoretical and empirical domain of the construct be conceptualized? Answers to this question come from previous theory and research as well as one's own observations. However, we have noted that researchers frequently develop scales without giving careful consideration to the theoretical and empirical domains to be measured. Therefore, we would like to emphasize the importance of this step by describing each domain and providing a conceptual frame of reference (as shown in Figure 5.1) for understanding the relationship among the theoretical and empirical domains as well as the measurement domain.

First, at the theoretical level are the constructs (C). Constructs are abstractions used by researchers to describe their theories. Each construct is assumed to have a boundary that defines the limits of the theoretical domain. Although the domain of some constructs can be narrowly defined (e.g., reaction time), others such as coping are potentially quite large. Regardless of the size of the theoretical domain, however, Nunnally (1967) suggests that a reasonably well-specified domain is necessary to know exactly which studies need to be designed to test the adequacy of the theoretical domain (Step 2).

At the empirical level, each construct is assumed to have its own separate empirical domain (E), which contains all the potential observables (items or indicators) that are thought to represent the construct. The empirical domain comprises

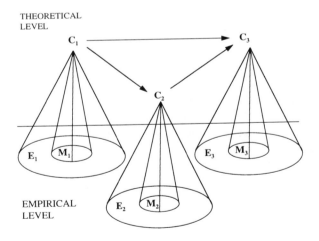

C = theoretical constructs
E = empirical domain
M = measurement of empirical domain (specific set of items)

Figure 5.1 Conceptualization of measurement domains.

all the possible ways to measure the construct as suggested by the definition of the theoretical domain. This would include different items and item formats (e.g., self-ratings, observations), which are assumed to be equivalent, both conceptually and empirically. Finally, there is the specific measurement domain (M), which consists of a representative sample of observables from E. As a specific instrument, M represents an operational definition of the theoretical domain by specifying exactly which observables comprise the construct.

It is a logical requirement that the boundaries of the theoretical and empirical domains for one construct do not overlap with the boundaries of other constructs (the concept of divergence). Furthermore, scales that claim to be different measures of the same construct should overlap if they are a part of the same theoretical domain (the concept of convergence). These two requirements are not easily satisfied in the measurement of personality (Nicholls, Licht, & Pearl, 1982) and coping (Lazarus & Folkman, 1984). For a discussion of these requirements from a measurement point of view, the reader is referred to Wicklund (1990).

Thus, in Step 1, coping researchers must explicitly conceptualize the theoretical domain of coping and the corresponding empirical domain of observables they assume to represent the construct of coping. Currently, there are many definitions of the theoretical domain of coping (Billings & Moos, 1984; Carver, Scheier, & Weintraub, 1989; Endler & Parker, 1990a; Lazarus & Folkman, 1984). Therefore, it may be time to evaluate these different theoretical domain definitions to identify the potential overlap and unique features of each. The studies described in Step 2 permit the testing of the boundary of the empirical domain of coping. The results from these studies then provide for inferences to be made regarding the appropriateness of the definition and hence boundary of the theoretical domain.

Relations among Observables

Step 2 focuses on what we have labeled "internal domain" studies. These studies are referred to as internal because they involve only the observables (items) for a given scale or scales (the M's in Figure 5.1). The relevant question at this stage is, Do the measures of observables behave in the way expected by the theoretical domain definition for a given construct? Here we will assume that "observables" are defined as self-report items for ease of communication, but observables could be represented in many different ways.

In a construct validation study, if all or some of the hypothesized relations among the items are not empirically supported, then all or some part of the theory may be incorrect. Alternatively, all or some of the items may not be good indicators of the empirical domain. Thus, to study the internal domain of a construct, statistical designs are used to evaluate the hypothesized relations among the items as well as assess the quality of the items themselves. In the following sections, we will discuss two traditional correlational designs (basic correlations and multitrait-multimethod matrices) and two more recent designs (confirmatory factor analysis and multifaceted measurement). The recent designs not only provide empirical evidence for evaluating the internal domain of coping but also provide evidence as to the nature of the theoretical domain of coping.

Correlational Designs

To evaluate the quality of the items developed to measure coping, procedures like item analysis or exploratory factor analysis[3] are frequently used. Benson and Clark (1982) have provided a framework for scale development including the use of item analysis to select items that lead to homogeneous scales (or subscales if several dimensions define the construct). When the items correlate highly with the total score and correlate at a similar magnitude with each other, the items can be spoken of as measuring the same construct, but we cannot yet say what that construct is. Thus, high internal consistency only implies that some construct or correlated constructs are being measured. Although high internal consistency is a *necessary* condition for construct validation, it does not provide *sufficient* evidence that a construct has been validated. To establish the sufficient condition for construct validity requires more in depth theoretical and empirical analyses, which are aspects of Nunnally's Step 3.

Among the more typical forms of validity evidence seen in the measurement literature in coping are correlations among various measures of coping. However, correlations among similar measures of coping provide very limited evidence for the existence of coping as a construct. First, a few distinctions need to be made between different forms of validity and the correlational designs each uses. If we consider three measures of coping: the Ways of Coping Questionnaire (WCQ) (Folkman & Lazarus, 1985), the COPE Scale developed by Carver et al. (1989), and the Coping Inventory for Stressful Situations (CISS; Endler & Parker, 1990a), correlations of a given coping scale (COPE or CISS) with another measure of coping (WCQ) actually provide evidence of concurrent validation. Concurrent validation is a form of criterion-related validity (Crocker & Algina, 1986, pp. 224–230).

In concurrent validity, the logic involves defining a predictor (usually the new measure) and a criterion (usually existing measure). However, there are explicit criteria for the criterion. The criterion must be highly reliable and, most important, it must be considered "the standard"—meaning its validity is without question. Therefore, when one correlates the COPE or the CISS (the new measure) with the WCQ (the existing measure), it is theoretically important to define which measure is the predictor and which is the criterion. When the correlation results are provided, what do they tell us about the construct validity of the scale of interest? Basically, very little. Showing that two variables are related does not validate one or the other scale. If the criterion were the WCQ and the WCQ was the accepted standard for measuring the construct of coping, then

---

[3] Exploratory factor analytic procedures will not be addressed in this chapter due to space limitations. However, Comrey (1978) has detailed appropriate use and reporting of exploratory factor analysis results.

high correlations between the COPE or CISS and the WCQ would provide some evidence that the newer scales were measuring the same thing, as defined by the WCQ. Because of the questionable psychometric properties of the WCQ, however, (Endler & Parker, 1990b; Parker, Endler, & Bagby, 1993), specifying the WCQ as the criterion may not be wise.

Multitrait-Multimethod Designs

The multitrait-multimethod matrix (MTMM) approach developed by Campbell and Fiske (1959), was one of the earliest designs proposed for validating constructs. Campbell and Fiske identified several issues to address in validating constructs. First was the need to separate the "method" of measurement from the construct being measured. When the method of measurement interacts with the construct being measured, "method variance" is created and biases the validation results. Second was the need to show evidence of convergence and divergence of the constructs under study. Although the MTMM approach incorporates both of these concerns through the use of correlational data, the MTMM procedure is considered superior to the basic correlational design just discussed because the MTMM approach involves an "expected set" of relationships that needs to be empirically supported.

To use an MTMM design to assess the notion of convergence and divergence for the construct of coping and to evaluate the extent to which method variance may be influencing the measurement, one would need to have at least two different methods for measuring coping and at least two different traits. We will illustrate the use of a MTMM design by adopting an approach suggested by Marx and Winne (1978) in the study of self-concept. Instead of having two maximally different methods of measuring coping (as suggested by Campbell and Fiske), we will use two different versions of how coping can be measured (e.g., COPE and CISS). The traits will be defined as the common dimensions thought to be measured by these two instruments.[4] This approach is illustrated in Table 5.1.

The value of an MTMM approach in assessing construct validity is that it brings together the concepts of reliability and validity within one study. The reliability coefficients are shown along the main diagonal of Table 5.1 as XX for each trait within each assessment method. There are three convergent validity coefficients, which are underlined and denoted in the table as CV. The CV coefficients represent the correlation between the same traits (task-oriented, emotion-oriented, and avoidance-oriented coping) as measured by the two methods (COPE and CISS). There are three sets of divergent coefficients (DV1, DV2, DV3). The first DV1 coefficient under Method A represents the correlation between emotion- and task-oriented coping as measured by the CISS; whereas the first DV1 coefficient under Method B represents the correlation

---

[4] Carver et al. (1989) reported the results of a second-order factor model that resulted in four factors, three of which were common to the three factors of the CISS. Thus, although the re-labeling of the COPE factors was done for illustration purposes, there is some empirical justification for this as well.

TABLE 5.1   Construct Validity of Coping using MTMM

	Method A (CISS)			Method B (COPE)		
Traits measured by (CISS)	T	E	A	T	E	A
Task-oriented (T)	XX					
Emotion-oriented (E)	DV1	XX				
Avoidance-oriented (A)	DV1	DV1	XX			
Traits measured by (COPE)						
Active + Planning (T)	*CV*	DV2	DV2	XX		
Social + Emotions (E)	DV3	*CV*	DV2	DV1	XX	
Behavioral + Mental Disengagement (A)	DV3	DV3	*CV*	DV1	DV1	XX

Note: For illustration purposes, it is assumed that the active and planning subscales of the COPE are conceptually similar to the task-oriented subscale of the CISS; the social support and emotion venting subscales of the COPE are conceptually similar to the emotion-oriented subscale of the CISS; and the behavioral and mental disengagement subscales of the COPE are conceptually similar to the avoidance-oriented subscale of the CISS.

between emotion- and task-oriented coping as measured by the COPE. The DV2 and DV3 coefficients represent the correlations between the different traits as measured by the different methods. The first DV2 coefficient (in the triangle above the CV coefficients) represents the correlation between emotion-oriented coping measured by the CISS and task-oriented coping measured by the COPE. The first DV3 coefficient (in the triangle below the CV coefficients) represents the correlation between emotion-oriented coping measured by the COPE and task-oriented coping measured by the CISS.

To evaluate whether the same traits (or constructs) converge and the different traits diverge, Campbell and Fiske (1959) provide an expected hierarchy of relationships among the correlations in the matrix: (a) the reliability coefficients should be high and similar in magnitude for each trait across the methods; (b) the convergent coefficients should be significantly greater than zero; (c) the convergent coefficients should be higher than the DV1 coefficients; and (d) the convergent coefficients and the DV1 coefficients should be higher than the DV2 and DV3 coefficients.

To evaluate whether "method variance" effects have influenced the correlations one would need two *different* methods to measure each trait. Method variance provides information on whether the "mechanism" for obtaining the measurement (e.g., self-report, clinical observation) has affected the measurement of the construct. Method variance cannot easily be studied in the illustration we provided in Table 5.1 because the same method was used to gather data on the constructs (e.g., self-report). However, if for example, the pattern of correlations in the DV1 triangle for Method A were all very high and the pattern of correlations in the DV1 triangle for Method B were low, this would be evidence of method variance. In this example, the different traits measured by Method A are not differentiated and the source of the high correlation among the traits may be due to the method of measurement. Additional information on using and evaluating MTMM matrices can be found in Crocker and Algina (1986, pp. 232–234) and Marsh and Hocevar (1983).

A major drawback to the correlational designs just presented is that they are not able to capture the complex pattern of relations among items and between items and subscales. Statistical designs are needed that directly address the complex relations within and between constructs. As stated in our introduction, the methodological design chosen to address a research question is just as important as the substantive research question. Thus, there is a need to be acquainted with advances made in research methodology that incorporate the correlations among variables with respect to the multivariate or multifaceted nature of our measurements. In the next two sections, two multivariate procedures, applied to different measurement designs, will be presented to show their usefulness to researchers studying the internal domain of a construct. The first procedure is based on a factor analytic design, whereas the second procedure uses an analysis of variance design.

Confirmatory Factor Analysis

Confirmatory factor analysis (CFA) initially conceived by Jöreskog (1969) is a psychometric procedure that explicitly tests a prespecified factor model on which a scale is based. Compared with a traditional exploratory factor analytic design, CFA can be much more useful in defining which items (the M's in Figure 5.1) best represent the empirical and theoretical domains (the E's and C's in Figure 5.1).

The use of CFA requires strong substantive theory to prespecify the model or models to be tested. Thus, CFA eliminates some of the subjectivity problems associated with traditional factor analysis procedures such as the number of factors to extract and the method of rotation to use. To implement CFA procedures, a model based on theory is postulated that explicitly states the number of factors thought to be represented by the items, which factor(s) each item is thought to represent, the relationship among the factors, and the relationship among the item residuals (errors), if any. Although a CFA design could be applied to many aspects of the measurement of coping, we limit ourselves to one illustration.

We will consider the CISS of Endler and Parker (1990a). Here the authors developed the 48-item CISS, guided by theory as well as logical and empirical results from an earlier version of their scale. The construct of coping as measured by the CISS is thought to be represented by three factors of 16 items each. To test whether the 48 items are all equally good indicators of the empirical domain and whether the theoretical domain is represented by three factors, we would start by specifying an initial model as diagrammed in Figure 5.2 as Model 5.2(a).

Model 5.2(a) assumes that simple structure holds; that is, the items written for each factor (shown by the squares) reflect only one factor (shown by the circles). Furthermore, we assume the factors themselves are correlated (shown by the curved arrows connecting the circles) and that the item residuals (shown by the arrows to the left of the boxes) are uncorrelated. The item loadings are illustrated by the arrows coming from the circles and pointing to the boxes. This specific model is then tested and a likelihood ratio chi-square statistic provides evidence

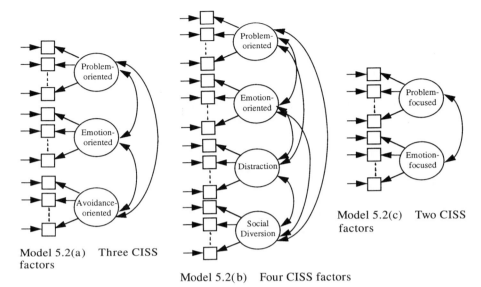

Figure 5.2   Alternative confirmatory factor analysis (CFA) models of the Coping Inventory for Stressful Situations (CISS).

as to whether the model reproduces the data sufficiently well to be considered an acceptable model.

The determination of an "acceptable model" is based on substantive and statistical criteria. Substantively, does the model as a whole make sense to other researchers in the field? Are the resulting item loadings and factor correlations predicted by theory? Statistically, an acceptable model is one where (a) the model converged (e.g., no improper solutions were noted); (b) likelihood ratio chi-square statistic is nonsignificant; and (c) the parameters of the model (loadings, factor correlations, item residuals) are statistically significant or not significant as predicted by theory.[5]

As stated in the beginning of this section with reference to Step 2, internal domain studies provide evidence whether the observables (e.g., the items) behave according to theory. In the present illustration, Model 5.2(a) provides information as to whether the 48 specific CISS items are equally good indicators of each respective latent factor. For example, low loadings on a factor or evidence of a complex loading (where the item is associated with more than one factor) would indicate (a) the items are in need of revision or deletion, or (b) the theory that generated the items is in need of revision, or (c) both the theory and items need revision. Thus, CFA designs permit an evaluation of the hypothesized relations among the items and an assessment of the items themselves. In addition, if the

---

[5] Many other issues are related to substantive and statistical fit of a model (Bollen & Long, 1993), but these few points reveal the information available from using a CFA design.

overall statistical fit of Model 5.2(a) is acceptable, then that is also evidence for the tenability of dimensionality of the theoretical domain.

The problem of equivalent models, which frequently occurs in data analysis, is easily demonstrated in the methodology of CFA (or covariance modeling in general). For any given factor model, there will often be other equally plausible models that are indistinguishable from the original model in terms of goodness-of-fit of the model to the data (MacCallum, Wegener, Uchino, & Fabrigar, 1993). Therefore, it is suggested as good practice to design research in which several competing theoretically based models are specified a priori. Then the model that has the lowest chi-square statistic and meets the other previously listed statistical and substantive criteria is selected as the best representation of the data. Thus, the basic research problem becomes more of falsifying alternative models than testing the fit of a single model.

An alternative theory-based model to compare with Model 5.2(a) would be Model 5.2(b) (shown in Figure 5.2). Model 5.2(b) is based on an alternative formulation of the CISS suggested by Endler and Parker (1990a), where the avoidance-oriented coping factor is broken down into two subdimensions, distraction and social diversion. The fit of Model 5.2(b), which is actually a four-factor model, could be compared with Model 5.2(a), which is a slightly more restricted and parsimonious representation of coping. Model 5.2(c) illustrates an even more parsimonious model. Model 5.2(c) depicts Lazarus and Folkman's (1984) early theoretical position that postulated the theoretical domain of coping consisted of two latent dimensions, problem-focused and emotion-focused coping. To convert Model 5.2(a) into Model 5.2(c), we would need to force the avoidance items from Model 5.2(a) onto either the problem-focused or emotion-focused factor. Here the question is, would the two-factor model provide just as good a fit to the data as the three-factor model or the four-factor model? If the two-factor model fits as well as the other two models, that would indicate the theoretical domain of coping is less complex than initially conceived and should lead to a revision of the definition of the theoretical and empirical domain (Step 1 of Nunnally).

Introduction to the specifics of how to set up and run CFAs is beyond the scope of this chapter; however, it is hoped that these illustrations will draw attention to this methodological procedure. The following references are suggested for interested readers: An excellent text on the topic is Bollen (1989); a thorough book chapter on issues that arise in CFA analyses and some solutions to those issues is given by Bentler and Chou (1988); the most up-to-date reference on using CFA, as well as more general structural equation models, is the edited book by Bollen and Long (1993).

Multifaceted Measurement Designs

Instead of using a procedure based on factor analysis to study the internal domain of a construct, a multifaceted measurement design could be used employing an analysis of variance (ANOVA) framework. From a psychometric perspective, an ANOVA design offers the possibility to empirically evaluate the conceptual distinctions made in coping research between such components as problem-focused versus emotion-focused coping, or more broadly, dispositional versus situational coping strategies.

To illustrate how an ANOVA design can be used psychometrically, a three-facet measurement design will be portrayed with facets derived from the study by Carver et al. (1989). A facet of measurement in this context is equivalent to a within-subject factor in the ANOVA terminology. Facets can be nested or crossed with each other and their levels can be considered random or fixed (Ferguson & Takane, 1989, pp. 279–281). In our illustration, the three facets of our ANOVA design are: Version of coping (V) which has two levels—Dispositional and Situational; type of Coping Strategy (C) with two levels—Active coping (AC) and Planning (PL)—which were crossed with versions of coping; and the items or indicators (I). In this measurement design, the items are nested within type of coping strategy (I:C), but crossed with versions. By treating versions as crossed with type of coping strategy, we assumed (as did Carver et al.) that the rewriting of dispositional items into situational items remained the same, only the frame of reference changed.

For simplicity, our illustration will use only two of the 13 COPE dimensions for each version (Dispositional AC and PL and Situational AC and PL) and two instead of four items within each of the four subscales. This resulted in a 8 by 8 correlation matrix (2 items by 2 coping strategies by 2 versions), which was used as a basis for generating a random sample of 200 subjects using values from Carver et al. (1989) and a data generator (GENRAW; Jöreskog & Sörbom, 1986). By using this generated sample, we will be able to illustrate two important features of the multifaceted measurement design: estimation of the relative importance of different design-based linear composites and generalizability of the different design-based linear composites. These two features take advantage of different sources of information produced by the ANOVA design and are presented in detail in the following two sections.

Relative Importance of Design-Based Linear Composites

Burt (1947) and Bock (1960), among others, have described how the relative importance of different multifaceted design-based composites can be estimated. The present three-facet measurement structure has four implicit design-based linear composites as depicted by the four rows of contrasts in Table 5.2. The three facets of the design are shown by the column headings in Table 5.2.

The four design-based linear composites were formed to evaluate the following four research questions:

1. Is there support for individual differences in terms of the "general" component of coping going through the entire design? This is reflected in the overall sum score composite for persons, P, by the weights 1 1 1 1 (Row 1 of Table 5.2), which is obtained by adding the four equally weighted subscale scores in our design.

TABLE 5.2   Three-Facet Design for Measuring Coping with Design-Based Composites of Interest

Version (V) Coping strategy (C)	Dispositional AC	PL	Situational AC	PL
No. of Items (I:C)	1	3	1	3
1	2	4	2	4
P	1	1	1	1
PV	1	1	−1	−1
PC	1	−1	1	−1
PVC	1	−1	−1	1

Note: P = person; V = version of coping scale: dispositional vs. situational; C = coping strategy: active coping (AC) vs. planning (PL); I:C = items within coping strategy. The linear composites are defined in terms of the facets P, V, and C, which are of substantive interest. Linear composites associated with the facet I:C (not presented) are by design reflecting measurement errors only.

2. Is there support for individual differences in terms of the distinction between dispositional and situational versions of coping? This is reflected in the corresponding linear difference score composite, PV, by the weights 1 1 −1 −1 (Row 2 of Table 5.2), which is obtained by subtracting the score for the situational part from the dispositional part of the design.

3. Is there support for individual differences in terms of the distinction between Active coping and Planning independent of the type of version? This is reflected in the linear difference score composite, PC, by the weights 1 −1 1 −1 (Row 3 of Table 5.2), which is obtained by subtracting the sum of the two Planning coping scores from the sum of the two Active coping scores.

4. Is there support for individual differences in terms of the distinction between Active coping and Planning dependent on type of version? Due to this dependency, we subtract the Active coping versus Planning distinction under the situational version from the corresponding distinction under the dispositional version; thus, (1 −1) − (1 −1). By deleting the parentheses, we obtain the linear difference score composite, PVC, by the weights 1 −1 −1 1 (Row 4 of Table 5.2). For this illustration, our interest is restricted to the variance accounted for by each of the preceding four design-based linear composites obtained from ANOVA.

The results from the analysis of the generated data for our three-facet measurement design are shown in Table 5.3. For each linear composite, a corresponding source of variation, degrees of freedom (*df*), number of linear composites (*LC*), and mean square (*MS*) from an ANOVA framework is provided. For our purpose of describing individual differences, only sources of variation reflecting the linear composites involving persons, presented in the preceding four research questions, are of relevance (e.g., only the first four sources of variation in Table 5.3). The two remaining sources reflect different types of measurement errors.

TABLE 5.3   Analysis of Three-Facet Measurement Design

Source	df	LC	MS	Trace Comp.	%	P	PV	PC	PVC
P	199	1	9.02	9.02	41.47	7.11			
PV	199	1	5.13	5.13	23.57		3.87		
PC	199	1	1.91	1.91	8.77	.70		.70	
PVC	199	1	1.26	1.26	5.78		.24		.24
PI:C	398	2	1.21	2.41	11.08	1.21		1.21	
PVI:C,e	398	2	1.01	2.03	9.23	—	1.01	—	1.01
Total	1599	8		21.76	100.00				
Generalizability coefficients (p^2)						.79	.75	.37	.19

Note: LC = Number of linear composites; MS = mean squares; P = persons; V = version of coping scale: dispositional vs. situational; C = coping strategy: active coping vs. planning; I:C = items within coping strategy. The universe of generalization is defined by the following assumptions: V = fixed, C = random and I = random.

[a] The variance components are in the metric of an average score, or in the ordinary ANOVA metric.

The relative importance of the different linear composites is given under the Trace heading in Table 5.3. The trace components here are identical to the variance accounted for by the linear composites associated with each source of variation of individual differences.[6] Our results indicate that in terms of the percentage of variance explained, the individual differences reflected by the general component (P) and the distinction between dispositional and situational coping (PV) are by far the two most important composites accounting for 41% and 24% of the variance respectively. Much less variance is explained by the linear composites of active coping and planning independent of version (PC) or dependent on version (PVC), 9% and 6% respectively. To provide a comprehensive interpretation of the four linear composites requires information as to their reliability or generalizability.

Generalizability of Linear Composites

Generalizability theory (*G*-theory) (Cronbach, Gleser, Nanda, & Rajaratnam, 1972) can be applied to interpret results from the present multifaceted design. Brennan (1992) characterized *G*-theory in terms of its parents: classical test theory and ANOVA. It should be noted that ANOVA, in this context, deviates clearly from its application in experimental research where the focus is testing group differences by means of an *F*-test. As will be shown, different sorts of variance components, focusing on individual differences, constitute the building blocks in the present type of analysis.

---

[6] Trace components are derived by multiplying the number of linear composites (*LC*) associated with a source of variation of individual differences and its mean square. The variance accounted for by the three difference score composites corresponds to the three interaction terms in ANOVA terminology involving persons: PV, PC, and PVC, respectively (Bock, 1960; Burt, 1947).

To begin, G-theory involves conceptualization of two types of universes. The first is the "universe of admissible observations." A typical generalizability study would start with a broad universe of admissible observations including several sources of variation or facets (e.g., items, raters, points in time, situational contexts, types of coping, versions of coping).[7] For illustrative purposes, we will restrict the universe of admissible observations in our example to the three facets of Version (Dispositional and Situational), Coping strategy (Active and Planning), and Items within each coping subscale. Second, to estimate the generalizability of the design-based linear composites previously presented requires defining a "universe of generalization." This definition involves deciding whether the facets in our measurement design are defined as random or fixed. In the present scenario, the version of coping (V) is considered fixed because it exhausts the entire universe of versions to which we would like to generalize. We considered coping strategy to be a random facet because the strategies we selected may be exchangeable with other strategies (Shavelson & Webb, 1991). Items within coping strategies will, by their very nature as equivalent measures of the same construct, be considered random. Given this set of assumptions, the observed mean squares in Table 5.3 can be decomposed into expected mean squares in terms of latent weighted variance components as presented in Appendix 5.A. Once the relevant expected mean squares have been established, generalizability coefficients (G-coefficients) for sum score composites and various difference score composites (Eikeland, 1973) as shown in Table 5.2 can be estimated. In Table 5.3, the observed mean squares for the first four sources of variation are decomposed in accordance with the expected mean squares structure in Appendix 5.A.

Given the universe of generalization and decisions made about the number of levels/conditions to be included in each facet, a G-coefficient can be estimated. Because the number of conditions in each facet is already given for the present design, decisions about the adequacy of the measurement of the four composites can be made. As shown at the bottom of Table 5.3, the G-coefficients suggest that the generalizability for both the general component (p^2_p = .79) and the distinction between dispositional and situational coping, (p^2_{pv} = .75) are promising. The distinction between Active coping and Planning, either independent (p^2_{pc} = .37) or dependent (p^2_{pvc} = .19) upon the version, were not supported. These coefficients are obtained for each linear composite by the ratio of its "true score" or "universe score variance" to its expected observed score variance. For the results obtained in Table 5.3, these would be $7.11/9.02 = .79$; $3.87/5.13 = .75$; $.70/1.91 = .37$; $.24/1.26 = .19$ for the P, the PV, the PC, and the PVC linear composites, respectively. Technically, the generalizability coefficient is an intraclass correlation coefficient (Cronbach et al., 1972, p. 11).

If it is theoretically important to be able to show that Active coping and Planning are separate dimensions, as discussed by Carver et al. (1989), the measure-

---

[7] The study of Carver et al. (1989) has the potential of being a G-study because they sampled a wide variety of coping strategies within both the dispositional and situational domains. For obvious reasons, all these facets could not be included in the present illustration.

TABLE 5.4   Estimated Variance Components and G-Coefficients for the PC Composite as the Number of Items Increases within Coping Subscales

No. of Items	i = 2	i = 4	i = 8	i = 12	i = 16
PC	.70	1.40	2.81	4.21	5.62
PI:C	1.21	1.21	1.21	1.21	1.21
Expected Observed Score Variance	1.91	2.60	4.01	5.41	6.82
G-Coefficient (p^2)	.37	.54	.70	.78	.82

Note: The PC composite is equivalent with the persons by coping strategy interaction.

ment of their separability can be improved by increasing the number of items within each subscale. By using the decomposed variance structure for the PC composite as a guideline (given in Appendix 5.A), decisions about optimal test length necessary to distinguish these two dimensions can be derived. In Table 5.4, estimates of G-coefficients for different numbers of items within coping subscales are given. These estimates are obtained by inserting the different values for the number of items in the decomposed structure for the mean square of the PC-source of variation in Appendix 5.A (2, 4, 8, 12, and 16) and holding the v-parameter value of 2 (number of versions) fixed in all estimations. These estimations subsequently increased the "universe score variance" and the expected observed score variance for the different number of items. Consequently also, the estimates of the G-coefficient for this composite (the ratio of universe score variance to the corresponding expected observed score variance for each number of items) increased, as is shown in Table 5.4.

The results shown in Table 5.4 suggest that if the Active coping and Planning subscales are increased up to 12 or 16 items each, the distinction between these subscales may be obtained with generalizability coefficients of .78 and .82 respectively (assuming the additional items are equivalent to the two items in the original design).

These results reveal an important distinction between G-theory and factor analysis. In G-theory language, factor analysis is analyzing a fixed universe of items. Thus, the factor analytic procedure does not provide information about the necessary length of a scale (number of items) to measure a factor adequately. However, G-theory takes advantage of the implicit definition of the universe of generalization related to measuring a factor. That is, if items of a factor or a facet do not measure the facet well, this may be caused by underrepresentation of the factor or facet in the corresponding empirical subdomain. In this situation, G-theory can be used to estimate how well the facet would be measured if more information in terms of equivalent items is added.[8] Thus, G-theory is superior to factor analysis, in that G-theory can estimate the necessary length of a subscale to measure different factors reliably as well as reliably discriminate between

---

[8] The Spearman-Brown formula to estimate reliability as a simple function of "test length" is not applicable to a multifaceted test design (Cronbach et al., 1972).

factors. We suggest that the lack of empirical support for the distinction between Active coping and Planning in our preceding illustration, where only two items per subscale were used, was due to underrepresentation of the factor in the corresponding empirical subdomain. Carver et al. (1989) reported a similar lack of distinction between these two subscales with four items per subscale. Therefore, if these two subdomains are thought to be distinct, then more than four items are needed to accurately measure this distinction.

A more formal presentation of *G*-theory and the details of the procedures necessary to implement this and other measurement designs can be found in the following introductory and advanced readings of *G*-theory: Brennan (1992), Crocker and Algina (1985), Cronbach et al. (1972), Feldt and Brennan (1989), Shavelson and Webb (1991). For illustrative studies using multifaceted measurement designs, see Crocker, Llabre, and Miller (1988) and Hagtvet (1989).

In sum, a prespecified structured measurement design can show how the internal domain of a construct can be assessed when there is strong theory to generate the design and analyses. Evidence showing that relations among observables behaves according to theory is necessary, but it is not sufficient alone to claim a construct has been validated. Ultimately, to claim a construct has been validated one must show empirical evidence of the distinction among different constructs. The following section presents Step 3 of Nunnally's three-part construct validation process.

Relations among Constructs

The types of designs relevant for the third step in the validation process may be labeled external-reference studies. The question at this stage is, How well does coping as a construct "fit" in a network of expected relations with other constructs? This is the heart of Cronbach and Meehl's (1955) nomological network. An illustration of a simple nomological network may make clear the logic embedded in Step 3. "To determine construct validity a measure must fit the theory about the construct, but to use the theory as evidence, it is necessary to assume the theory is true" (Nunnally, 1967, p. 93). This inherent circularity is presented in the following four hypotheses (adapted from Nunnally, 1967, p. 93):

1. The constructs of anxiety and coping correlate.
2. The STAI is a valid measure of anxiety.
3. The WCQ is a valid measure of coping.
4. The STAI and WCQ correlate.

Empirically, all that is really tested is Hypothesis 4, but an inference is usually made that if Hypothesis 4 is supported, Hypothesis 1 is true. But let's consider a few of the possibilities that exist among the four hypotheses. Hypothesis 1 "may" be correct, and so if Hypothesis 4 is maintained, that offers no proof as to the truth of Hypotheses 2 and 3. Alternatively, the STAI and WCQ could correlate, but their correlation could be due to other constructs and not the ones given in Hypothesis 1. If Hypothesis 2 is correct and 3 is incorrect, then there would be no necessity for the STAI to correlate with the WCQ (Hypothesis 4). However, they may correlate because of other constructs, which would mean the WCQ is operating as proxy for some unknown variable.

In the following sections, we present two traditional designs and one newer approach that can be used to provide the external evidence in support of construct validity.

Group Differentiation

Group differentiation studies permit an analysis of how the theory operates for groups of individuals known or thought to differ on the trait. That is, does the scale differentiate between groups of individuals in ways predicted by the theory? For example, Lazarus and Folkman's (1984) theory of coping suggests that individuals who have more social support and social resources in turn utilize more effective coping strategies. Billings and Moos (1984) have noted that depressed persons typically have very little social support available and have studied the coping behaviors of this clinical population compared with nonclinical populations. As predicted by theory, they found that depressed patients use more emotional and avoidance coping (which are considered less effective coping strategies) and have less personal and contextual resources than the nonclinical subjects (Billings & Moos, 1985; Holahan & Moos, 1987). Thus, their line of research provides some empirical support to the theory of coping. Another grouping variable that could be studied under this type of procedure might be those individuals experiencing severe stressful events (loss of a family member or job) compared with the coping strategies of those experiencing the stress of daily living (marital strains, relations on the job). If the theory suggests different coping strategies are utilized by these two groups, then the instrument used to measure coping should empirically reveal these group differences.

Correlational Designs

A frequently used procedure to provide evidence of construct validity is to correlate a given measure of coping with other variables or personality constructs. As stated earlier in the chapter, correlations between coping measures and other different constructs represent a very limited method of supporting construct validity because zero-order correlations can not capture the multivariate relationships that exist in a nomological network as complex as coping. Furthermore, if the theoretical relations among the constructs are not well thought out, zero-order correlations can be quite misleading. For example, Zeidner and Hammer (1992) reported partial regression coefficients (and semipartial correlations) to account for the influence of other variables on their correlations of interest. However, even when partial correlations are considered, so many relationships usually are reported that it is hard to digest their meaning (e.g., in any one study there may be from 5 to 20 variables, resulting in 10 to 190 possible correlations). What may be more helpful substantively is to use multivariate methods that test all the relationships simultaneously and take into account the influence of measurement error and the influence of other variables on the construct of interest.

Structural Equation Modeling (SEM)

SEM, developed primarily by Jöreskog (1973), is a multivariate statistical technique that combines the fields of factor analysis, path analysis, and econometric modeling. SEM extends what was presented under CFA. In CFA, the interest is on the internal structure of the measurement of a construct where the structure is prespecified based on underlying theory. In SEM, the interest is extended to the relations among a set of different constructs, taking into account their prespecified measurement structure. SEM is a general data analytic technique that subsumes many statistical and psychometric procedures (e.g., analysis of variance and covariance, correlation, regression, factor analysis, and reliability estimation) and has been applied in many disciplines in the behavioral and medical sciences (see Bentler, 1989, for an overview). In the remainder of this section, we will illustrate how SEM can provide a useful design and data analytic strategy to study the conceptual idea of the nomological network of Cronbach and Meehl (1955).

Cronbach and Meehl suggested that to validate a construct one must be able to specify how that construct relates to other constructs (shown by the C's in Figure 5.1). Since we know that zero-order correlations can be influenced by measurement error as well as be influenced by other variables, we need a statistical procedure that can account for these methodological problems. Whereas disattenuating partial correlations may correct for unreliability and the influence of other variables, we are still left with simple bivariate relationships of a multivariate phenomenon. Therefore, multivariate methods are called for when studying a phenomenon conceptualized in a nomological network of constructs such as coping behaviors.

To illustrate how one might design and analyze a SEM of coping behavior, we will draw on the work of Zeidner and Hammer (1992). Their study is particularly interesting because it took place during a severe life-threatening event, SCUD missile attacks in the Haifa area of Israel during the Persian Gulf War (January–February 1991). This dramatic event provided data from which to study how individuals use various coping strategies in a real disaster situation. In their study, they provided a path model to summarize the relationships they found among the personal variables of coping resources, optimism, and perceived control; the mediating variables of type of coping strategies (as measured by the COPE); and the outcome variables of state anxiety, physical symptoms, and perceived cognitive functioning. A path model depicting the hypothesized relationships suggested by Zeidner and Hammer's review of the literature is presented in Figure 5.3 as Model 5.3(a).

In the figure, the constructs for Model 5.3(a) are shown in circles (which are analogous to the C's in Figure 5.1) and each construct is measured by some number of observed variables (the M's in Figure 5.1). Zeidner and Hammer used a regression-based path analytic approach to analyze the relationships depicted in Model 5.3(a). This procedure assumes that each of the constructs is perfectly

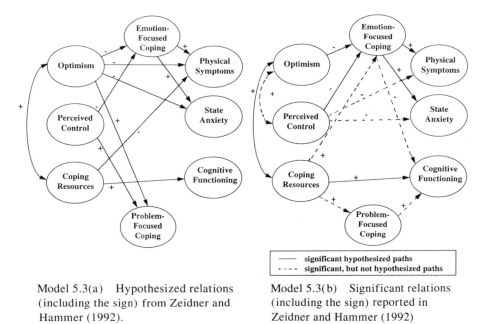

Model 5.3(a)   Hypothesized relations
(including the sign) from Zeidner and
Hammer (1992).

Model 5.3(b)   Significant relations
(including the sign) reported in
Zeidner and Hammer (1992)

Figure 5.3   Structural model of coping behaviors based on Zeidner and Hammer (1992).

measured. Because Zeidner and Hammer reported the internal consistency coefficients for each construct, which ranged from .60 for optimism to .85 for state anxiety, we know that there is some measurement error influencing their results. Prior research in SEM has shown that measurement error can bias the relationships (path coefficients) among the constructs and that this bias is propagated throughout the model (Kaplan, 1988). Therefore, we will illustrate how data from a study like that of Zeidner and Hammer can be transformed into a SEM that will take into account measurement error and provide an analysis of the simultaneous influence of multiple predictors on multiple outcomes. Here we are using a SEM to determine whether the construct of interest can be differentiated from other constructs and whether the construct, when studied within a network of other constructs, will behave as predicted by theory.

To handle the measurement error problem, each construct should be measured by at least three items or indicators. In this way, there is sufficient statistical information to estimate the strength of the association between each indicator and the construct (similar to factor loadings). Adapting the variables used by Zeidner and Hammer (1992), we have listed 31 indicators in Appendix 5.B that could be used in testing our proposed SEM.

In any structural model analysis, a two-step approach should be used where the first step is to evaluate the fit of each construct with the indicators proposed in Appendix 5.B. Thus, a CFA would be performed for each of the eight constructs in Model 5.3(a). For example, it may be that a subset of the items for emotion-focused or problem-focused coping can be used. When acceptable measurement models have been established (in terms of minimal measurement error and maximal indicator/construct association), then the second step is to estimate the relations among the constructs that form the nomological network (Jöreskog, 1993).

To study the relationships in the nomological network, all relevant paths among the constructs are to be specified prior to analysis. Thus, if SEM is used as it was designed, it is a theory-driven analysis, where the prespecified relations are based on prior research, theory, or their combination. In addition, because there are often several competing theoretical positions regarding the construct of interest—in this case coping—it is also important to specify more than one theoretically based model for comparison. For example, the paths shown in Model 5.3(a) are the hypothesized relations Zeidner and Hammer (1992) provide from their review of the literature. The fit of Model 5.3(a) could be compared with the fit of Model 5.3(b) (Figure 5.3), which depicts the significant univariate relationships found by Zeidner and Hammer. If Model 5.3(a) statistically fits better than Model 5.3(b), then it provides some support for how a given set of personal variables (optimism, perceived control, and coping resources) impacts coping strategies. However, little support is provided for how the coping strategies impact a given set of outcome variables (physical symptoms, state anxiety, and cognitive functioning) because there are few paths from the coping strategies to the outcome variables in Model 5.3(a). Alternatively, Model 5.3(b) posits not only relations among the personal variables, but more relations among coping and the outcome variables. Thus, if the overall statistical fit of Model 5.3(b) is superior to Model 5.3(a), then strong evidence exists that the "network" of relations involving the construct of coping operates as hypothesized by theory and previous research.

The determination of an acceptable model is not based just on the overall statistical fit of one model over another, but also on separate components of fit. For example, the path coefficients linking the constructs must possess the magnitude and direction predicted by theory. Also, as stated in the section on CFA models (Step 2, internal domain studies), several indexes of model-data fit need to be evaluated prior to determining whether a model fits or fails to fit the data. Finally, to strengthen the conclusions derived from any SEM, longitudinal designs are preferred to cross-sectional designs because stronger inferences about the process of behaviors underlying the model are possible (MacCallum et al., 1993).

A final caveat needs to be made. As was illustrated in the four hypotheses presented at the beginning of this section, establishing the validity of a construct (e.g., coping) requires us to assume the other constructs used in the "network" are also valid. For example, if we fail to obtain a high positive path coefficient between problem-focused coping and cognitive functioning, it may be due to the lack of validity for either or both constructs, or inaccuracy in the theory that links these constructs. In such a situation, we might consider that the measurement of coping might best be operationalized by the CISS of Endler and Parker (1990a) where there are three theoretical dimensions of coping behavior (emotion, task, and avoidance). A similar set of SEMs could be tested as the ones previously outlined using the CISS to assess coping behavior. In sum, establishing externally referenced construct validation evidence not only is a complex process but involves complex relationships that require multivariate procedures such as SEM.

CONCLUSION

Our chapter focused primarily on the methods of assessing construct validation as conceived by Cronbach and Meehl (1955) and further conceptualized by Nunnally (1967). Drawing on these two sources, it becomes evident that the construct validation procedure explicitly calls for an interplay among design, data analysis, and theory as coequal components in the research process. While paying attention to Nunnally's three-step approach to assessing construct validation, we have purposely emphasized Step 1 (domain definition) and Step 2 (internal domain studies) to better clarify the measurement of coping. The combined use of CFA, MTMM, and generalizability studies has the potential to refine and improve the measurement of complex constructs such as coping before initiating external domain studies (Step 3). Finally, the more recent methodological approaches referred to in our chapter do not provide an easy way to sound knowledge. For successful implementation, these procedures demand a thorough understanding of the phenomenon being researched prior to any empirical analyses. Thus, as we begin instrument development and validation studies, we are reminded of the wise words of Tukey (1977): "It is important to understand what you can do before you learn to measure how well you seem to have done it" (p. v).

APPENDIX 5.A

Expected Mean Squares for the Three-Facet Measurement Design in Table 5.3

MS_p	: $v\sigma^2_{pi:c,e} + iv\sigma^2_{pc} + civ\sigma^2_p$
MS_{pv}	: $\sigma^2 + i\sigma^2_{pvc} + ci\sigma^2_{pv}$
MS_{pc}	: $v\sigma^2_{pi:c,e} + iv\sigma^2_{pc}$
MS_{pvc}	: $\sigma^2 + i\sigma^2_{pvc}$
$MS_{pi:c}$	: $v\sigma^2_{pi:c,e}$
$MS_{pvi:c,e}$	: σ^2

Note: For each component, a letter (p, v, c, or i) is assigned respectively, which is used to designate a source of variation when used as a subscript, and also to designate the number of levels of the source when used as a weight or a coefficient. The rules for writing observed and expected mean squares can be found in Millman and Glass (1967).

APPENDIX 5.B

Indicators of Constructs in Figure 5.3

Personal Variables

Optimism	3 indicators based on creating item parcels from the 8 LOT items (item parcels can be created by summing subsets of the 8 items to reduce the number of observed variables and produce indicators that are more like continuous variables).
Perceived Control	Only 1 indicator. To estimate the loading between the item and its construct, the residual must be fixed by taking the product of the variance of the item times $(1-r_{xx})$, where the reliability of the item might be assumed to be some conservative value (e.g., .75).
Coping Resources	5 indicators represented by the sum of the scores on the five subscales of cognitive, social, emotional, spiritual, and physical

Mediators

Coping Behavior/Strategy: based on items from the COPE, split into two main theoretical components of coping:

Emotion-focused	8 indicators based on the summed score from the 8 subscales
Problem-focused	5 indicators based on the summed score from the 5 subscales

Outcomes

Physical Symptoms	4 indicators based on creating item parcels from the 12 Personal Stress Symptom Scale (item parcels can be created by summing subsets of 3 items each)
State Anxiety	2 indicators based on creating item parcels from 5 items in the State Anxiety Subscale of the State-Trait Personality Inventory
Cognitive Functioning	3 indicators based on creating item parcels from the 6 items

Note: All variables and constructs are taken from Zeidner and Hammer (1992).

REFERENCES

Benson, J., & Clark, F. (1982). A guide for instrument development and validation. *American Journal of Occupational Therapy, 36,* 789–800.

Bentler, P. (1985). *Theory and implementation of EQS: A structural equations program.* Los Angeles, CA: BMDP Statistical Software.

Bentler, P., & Chou, C.-P. (1988). Practical issues in structural modeling. In S. Long (Ed.), *Common problems/proper solutions: Avoiding error in quantitative research* (pp. 161–192). Newbury Park, CA: Sage.

Billings, A., & Moos, R. (1984). Coping, stress and social resources among adults with unipolar depression. *Journal of Personality and Social Psychology, 46,* 877–891.

Billings, A., & Moos, R. (1985). Psychosocial process of remission in unipolar depression: Comparing depressed patients with matched community controls. *Journal of Consulting and Clinical Psychology, 53,* 314–325.

Bock, R. D. (1960). Components of variance analysis as a structural and discriminal analysis for psychological tests. *British Journal of Statistical Psychology, 13,* 151–163.

Bollen, K. (1989). *Structural equations with latent variables.* New York: Wiley.

Bollen, K., & Long, S. (1993). *Testing structural equation models.* Newbury Park, CA: Sage.

Brennan, R. L. (1992). *Elements of generalizability theory.* Iowa City, IA: ACT Publications.

Burt, C. (1947). Factor analysis and analysis of variance. *British Journal of Psychology, 1* (Stat. Sect.), 3–26.

Campbell, D., & Fiske, D. (1959). Convergent and discriminant validation by the multitrait-multimethod matrix. *Psychological Bulletin, 56,* 81–105.

Carver, C., Scheier, M., & Weintraub, J. (1989). Assessing coping strategies: A theoretically based approach. *Journal of Personality and Social Psychology, 56,* 267–283.

Comrey, A. (1978). Common methodological problems in factor analytic studies. *Journal of Clinical and Consulting Psychology, 46,* 648–659.

Crocker, L., & Algina, J. (1986). *Introduction to Classical and Modern Test Theory.* Fort Worth, TX: Holt, Rinehart & Winston.

Crocker, L., Llabre, M., & Miller, D. (1988). The generalizability of content validity ratings. *Journal of Educational Measurement, 25,* 287–299.

Cronbach, L. J. (1971). Test validation. In R. L. Thorndike (Ed.), *Educational measurement* (2nd ed., pp. 443–507). Washington, DC: American Council on Education.

Cronbach, L. J., Gleser, G. C., Nanda, H., & Rajaratnam, N. (1972). *The dependability of behavioral measurements: Theory of generalizability for scores and profiles.* New York: Wiley.

Cronbach, L. J., & Meehl, P. E. (1955). Construct validity of psychological tests. *Psychological Bulletin, 52,* 281–302.

Eikeland, H.-M. (1973). Generalizability estimates for difference scores: An aspect of the construct validity of tests. In S. Fhanér & L. Sjøberg (Eds.), *Measurement in differential Psychology: A symposium* (pp. 19–22). *Gothenburg Psychological Reports, 3*(6).

Endler, N., & Parker, J. (1990a). *Coping Inventory for Stressful Situations (CISS) Manual.* Toronto, Canada: Multi-Health Systems.

Endler, N., & Parker, J. (1990b). Multidimensional assessment of coping: A critical evaluation. *Journal of Personality and Social Psychology, 58,* 844–854.

Feldt, L. S., & Brennan, R. L. (1989). Reliability. In R. L. Linn (Ed.), *Educational measurement* (3rd ed., pp. 105–146). New York: American Council on Education.

Ferguson, G. A., & Takane, Y. (1989). *Statistical analysis in psychology and education* (6th ed.). New York: McGraw-Hill.

Folkman, S., & Lazarus, R. (1985). If it changes it must be a process: A study of emotion and coping during three stages of a college examination. *Journal of Personality and Social Psychology, 48,* 150–170.

Hagtvet, K. A. (1989). *The construct of test anxiety.* Bergen, Norway: Sigma Forlag.

Holahan, C., & Moos, R. (1987). Personal and contextual determinants of coping strategies. *Journal of Personality and Social Psychology, 52*, 946–955.

Jöreskog, K. G. (1969). A general approach to maximum likelihood factor analysis. *Psychometrika, 34*, 183–202.

Jöreskog, K. G. (1973). A general method for estimating a linear structural equation system. In A. Goldberger & D. Duncan (Eds.), *Structural equation models in the social sciences* (pp. 85–112). New York: Academic Press.

Jöreskog, K. G. (1993). Testing structural equation models. In K. Bollen & J. Long (Eds.), *Testing structural equation models*. Newbury Park, CA: Sage.

Jöreskog, K. G., & Sörbom, D. (1986). *PRELIS: A preprocessor for LISREL*. Mooresville, IN: Scientific Software.

Kaplan, D. (1988). The impact of specification error on the estimation, testing and improvement of structural equation models. *Multivariate Behavioral Research, 23*, 69–86.

Lazarus, R., & Folkman, S. (1984). *Stress, appraisal and coping*. New York: Springer.

MacCallum, R., Wegener, D., Uchino, B., & Fabrigar, L. (1993). The problem of equivalent models in applications of covariance structure analysis. *Psychological Bulletin, 114*, 185–199.

Marsh, H. W., & Hocevar, D. (1983). Confirmatory factor analysis of multitrait-multimethod matrices. *Journal of Educational Measurement, 20*, 231–248.

Marx, R. W., & Winne, P. H. (1978). Construct interpretations of three self-concept inventories. *American Educational Research Journal, 15*, 99–109.

Millman, J., & Glass, G. (1967). Rules of thumb for writing the ANOVA table. *Journal of Educational Measurement, 4*, 41–51.

Nicholls, J. G., Licht, B. G., & Pearl, R. A. (1982). Some dangers of using personality questionnaires to study personality. *Psychological Bulletin, 92*, 572–580.

Nunnally, J. (1967). *Psychometric Theory*. New York: McGraw-Hill.

Parker, J., Endler, N., & Bagby, R. (1993). If it changes, it might be unstable: Examining the factor structure of the Ways of Coping Questionnaire. *Psychological Assessment, 5*, 361–368.

Shavelson, R., & Webb, N. (1991). *Generalizability theory: A primer*. Newbury Park, CA: Sage.

Tukey, J. W. (1977). *Exploratory data analysis*. Reading, MA: Addison-Wesley.

Wicklund, R. A. (1990). *Zero-variable theories and the psychology of the explainer*. New York: Springer-Verlag.

Zeidner, M., & Hammer, A. (1992). Coping with missile attack: Resources, strategies and outcomes. *Journal of Personality, 60*, 709–746.

CHAPTER 6

A Critical Survey of Coping Instruments

RALF SCHWARZER and CHRISTINE SCHWARZER

As we go through life, we can resist temptation, exercise to deal with depression, reinterpret loss, talk ourselves through challenges, avoid confronting an opponent, seek help, and so forth. Coping with an adversity includes numerous ways of dealing with diverse person-environment transactions. Thus, coping does not represent a homogeneous concept. Instead, it is a diffuse umbrella term. Coping can be described in terms of strategies, tactics, responses, cognitions, or behavior. Actual coping is a phenomenon that can be noticed either by introspection or by observation, and it includes internal events as well as overt actions. It has been broadly defined as ". . . cognitive and behavioral efforts to manage specific external or internal demands (and conflicts between them) that are appraised as taxing or exceeding the resources of a person (Lazarus, 1991, p. 112).

THEORETICAL ISSUES IN COPING ASSESSMENT

At least three important ingredients that should be considered in the conceptualization of coping: (a) Coping need not be a completed "successful" act, but an effort has to be made; (b) this effort need not be expressed in actual behavior, but can be directed to cognitions as well; and (c) a cognitive appraisal of the taxing situation is a prerequisite of initiating coping attempts.

A serious problem, however, is that cognitive coping and cognitive appraisal can be confounded. For example, appraising a situation as a threat may trigger coping (further thoughts or defenses that imply a reappraisal of the same situation as being more or less threatening). In such cases, a distinction between appraisal and coping cannot be practically made, but it remains at least of heuristic value. Lazarus (1991) tries to disentangle this overlap somewhat, stating: ". . . *Coping* refers to what a person thinks or does to try to manage an emotional encounter; and *appraisal* is an evaluation of what might be thought or done in that encounter" (p. 113).

Other conceptual problems arise when coping is to be separated from coping resources (e.g., hardiness, dispositional optimism, self-efficacy, sense of coherence, social support). Resources can be personal or social or other antecedents of appraisals and coping (cf. Schwarzer, 1994). An optimistic attitude toward life may result in a more favorable appraisal of a taxing situation, in adopting an efficient problem-solving strategy, or in creating optimistic coping self-talk. The existence of a social network may result in successful support-seeking behaviors when need arises. Although in reality, coping resources and actual coping may be difficult to disentangle, it is important to make this distinction in theory and research. Resources are relatively static antecedents, whereas coping is a process that depends on these resources. If, for example, a coper makes an optimistic statement, it may mainly reflect a personality trait, or it may have just been generated as a product of effortful stress management.

The measurement of coping is complicated by the preceding conceptual issues. Furthermore, there are problems that will be discussed under the headings of stability, generality, and dimensionality of coping.

Stability

The assessment of coping can be a description of the cognitions and behaviors of a person dealing with a stressful encounter. This approach does justice to coping being a process, and it allows the identification of contingencies between changing situations and changing actions—be it by time sampling or event sampling. For example, one can assess whether a person always applies and reapplies the same set of strategies, or whether he or she applies a broad range of tactics that are well adapted to changing encounters. This idiographic approach to stability and change can be adopted for single cases in clinical settings, but it is not common in research. Rather, the focus in empirical studies is on individual differences. Stability then refers to the pattern similarity of interindividual differences at multiple points in time. If, for example, some persons cope in a vigilant manner whereas others do so in a more avoiding manner, and if this behavior recurs at later observations, the researcher is inclined to attribute stable coping preferences to these individuals. When we measure coping with standardized instruments, we therefore imply that people can be characterized by some preferred ways of coping with adversity, and that they continue to apply the same strategies over time. This dispositional implication helps to reduce the complexity of coping assessment, but at a high price: It assumes that uniqueness of situation-specific coping responses only represents a negligible aspect.

A further difficulty that makes stability a crucial issue is that people usually go through stages when managing a taxing demand. For example, someone confronted with surgery has to proceed from the preparation stage to the confrontation stage, and then to the recovery stage. A coping strategy that was adaptive in the first stage may not be so in the second, and a completely different approach might be practical in the third. Therefore, if stages can be identified, it is important to assess coping within each of them and to group individuals in terms of them. This remains an issue for further research.

Generality

Closely related to stability is another problem, the consistency of coping responses across different situations. Do people apply the same strategy when they face an exam, the bereavement of a loved one, or an argument with their spouse? They may not show exactly the same responses, but maybe they can be characterized by a general tendency to select appropriate behaviors either from the class of avoidance or from the class of confrontation strategies. If all responses could be explained by the challenging events, this would reflect a pure situation determinism. In contrast, the common person-situation interaction perspective would consider joint influences from both sources. A moderate amount of generality implies that people construct a series of person-dependent strategies for a number of situations. The measurement of coping can be fruitful only under the assumption that individuals generalize across situations to a certain degree and come up with a limited set of strategies that they reapply at different occasions.

Dimensionality

These sets of strategies can be grouped according to their purpose, meaning, or functional value. Because the number of specific responses is endless, it appears to be useful to classify them in one way or the other. Empirically, this can be accomplished by factor analysis, but factor solutions typically differ from sample to sample and from stressor to stressor. There are many attempts to reduce the total of possible responses to a more parsimonious set of dimensions. Some researchers have come up with two basic dimensions—such as instrumental, attentive, vigilant, or confrontative coping on the one hand, in contrast to avoidant, palliative, and emotional coping on the other (for an overview, see Krohne, 1993; Laux & Weber, 1993; Suls & Fletcher, 1985).

The number of dimensions that have been established theoretically or found empirically also depends on the level within a hierarchy of coping concepts. Krohne (1993) distinguished a behavioral from a conceptual level, each consisting of two subclasses. Reactions and acts constitute the behavioral level at the bottom of this hierarchy. A coping reaction is considered as a single behavioral element (e.g., tuning to a music channel instead of an information channel in a laboratory stress experiment). Several similar reactions can be grouped into an act, such as executing a specific problem-solving behavior. At the conceptual level, researchers can identify a set of acts reflecting a particular strategy, such as making use of social resources or turning to religion. Strategies, in turn, can be grouped into superstrategies, two of which are vigilance and cognitive avoidance. According to Krohne's coping theory, these two superstrategies constitute orthogonal dimensions of attention orientation and can be understood as personality dimensions: "*Vigilance* refers to those strategies which are characterized by intensified intake and processing of threatening information. *Cognitive avoidance* is marked by a turning away from the threat-related cues" (Krohne, 1993, p. 21).

Another conceptual distinction has been suggested between *assimilative* and *accommodative* coping, the former aiming at an alteration of the environment to oneself, and the latter aiming at an alteration of oneself to the environment (Brandtstädter, 1992). This pair has also been coined *"mastery* versus *meaning"* (Taylor, 1983, 1989) or *"primary control* versus *secondary control"* (Rothbaum, Weisz, & Snyder, 1982). These coping preferences may occur in a certain time order when, for example, individuals first try to alter the demands that are at stake, and, after failing, turn inward to reinterpret their plight and find subjective meaning in it.

A well-known approach has been put forward by Lazarus and Folkman (1984), who discriminate between *problem-focused* and *emotion-focused* coping. The first is seen as being action centered in the sense that the troubled person-environment relationship is changed by instrumental actions. These actions need not necessarily be successful and may even have detrimental side effects; however, it is the attempt that counts. In contrast, the second kind of coping includes mainly cognitive coping strategies that do not directly change the actual situation, but rather help to assign a new meaning to it. They are not passive, but may require an internal restructuring and may cost considerable effort.

A different view has been suggested by Klauer, Filipp, and Ferring (1989) in the context of coping with chronic disease. The authors start out with a multidimensional structure to describe actual coping. Three dimensions have been established and empirically confirmed:

1. *Focus of attention* that differentiates whether attention is directed at the disease or elsewhere.
2. *Sociability* that describes whether the patient turns toward others or withdraws.
3. *Response level* that describes whether coping is reflected by overt behaviors or by cognitive (intrapsychic) responses.

This structure results in eight possible coping strategies.

There are many other attempts to conceptualize coping dimensions, and those mentioned previously may serve as examples. They are a prerequisite of coping measurement because a pure inductive collection of many single responses that have been factor analyzed would result in an unstable solution and could hardly be replicated in further studies. The high degree of situational or intraindividual variability in coping obviously implies a multilevel conceptualization with a few stable dimensions at higher levels that are theoretically linked to a variety of specific strategies and acts at lower levels. The following sections survey the coping inventories used frequently and scrutinize their contributions to the stability, generality, and dimensionality issues.

MEASUREMENT OF COPING: A SURVEY OF INVENTORIES

The Miller Behavioral Style Scale: Monitoring and Blunting

Attentional style is a basic dimension of coping. The question is whether individuals under stress tend to tune into the threat, search for information, and visualize scenarios to control the situation, or whether they tune out from the threat, distract themselves, avoid further information, and postpone instrumental action. Adopting a vigilant attentional style was coined *"monitoring,"* and adopting an avoiding attentional style was called *"blunting"* by Miller (1987), who conceived these as typical individual differences in a stress situation. To assess these styles, she developed the Miller Behavioral Style Scale (MBSS), an instrument consisting of four hypothetical situations, two of them referring to physical threat and two to ego-threat. One of the physical threat scenarios is phrased, "Imagine that you are afraid of flying and have to go somewhere by plane." Following these situations are eight coping options, half of them reflecting a monitoring and half a blunting attentional style. Monitoring is expressed in items such as "I would carefully read the information provided about safety features in the plane." Blunting is signified in items such as "I would watch the in-flight film even if I had seen it before." Each of the four stress situations is followed by eight coping responses, which provides an inventory consisting of 32 items. Scores are supplied by adding up the corresponding items yielding a monitoring and a blunting sum score.

The MBSS was originally validated by two experiments (Miller, 1987). In the first, a *physical threat situation* was created by announcing an electrical shock. Individuals characterized by high monitoring and low blunting were searching for information about the imminent shock (that was never given). On the other hand, high blunters who were also low monitors tended to distract themselves. In the second experiment, which was an *ego-threat situation,* students underwent an academic achievement test where they could obtain on-line information about their current achievement status. The monitors made frequent use of this opportunity, whereas the blunters did so less often. Additional studies have confirmed the diagnostic value of the MBSS (see Miller, Combs, & Kruus, 1993).

Attentional style has proven a useful dimension of individual coping differences, and its measurement with the MBSS has stimulated research on this topic. The main limitation of this inventory lies in its range of content because it restricts itself to those stress situations that elicit anxiety. Other stress situations that are appraised as challenge, harm, or loss, for example, are not suitable for it.

The Mainz Coping Inventory: Vigilance and Cognitive Avoidance

According to the two-dimensional coping theory of Krohne (1993) mentioned briefly earlier in this chapter, an instrument has recently been developed to assess *vigilance* and *cognitive avoidance* in threat situations (Krohne, Schumacher, & Egloff, 1992). Eight hypothetical situations are selected that supposedly elicit anxiety, half of them emulating physically threatening situations and the other half ego-threatening situations. One of the four *physical threat situations* is phrased, "Imagine that you are riding in a car as a front-seat passenger next to an obviously inexperienced driver. Road conditions are poor due to snow and ice." One of the four *ego-threat situations* is phrased, "Imagine that you have to take an important exam three weeks from now." Researchers who consider adopting this instrument may select only one of its two parts depending on whether their study is restricted to physical threat or to ego-threat.

Each situation is followed by 18 coping acts that are subdivided into those reflecting vigilance and those reflecting cognitive avoidance. For the physical threat situation (car scenario), the 9 vigilant coping acts include items such as "I watch the driver carefully and try to tell in advance when he is going to make a mistake." The 9 avoidant coping acts include items such as "I tell myself 'Thank goodness, he is not driving fast.'" A true-false response format is provided for each coping act. The 9 vigilant coping acts refer to recall of previous negative events, self-pity, information search, social comparison, planning, flight tendencies, informational control, anticipation of negative events, and situation control. The 9 avoidant coping acts refer to general bagatellization, self-enhancement, bagatellization by reinterpretation, distraction, playing down by incompatible reactions, denial, focus on own strength, focus on positive aspects, confidence. Whether these are coping acts or coping strategies instead seems to be a matter of definition, and the author uses both expressions (Krohne, 1993). Most of these expressions can be found in other coping inventories, some linked to different dimensions. For example, situation control can also be labeled mastery, and reinterpretation can also be labeled meaning.

Sum scores can be created separately for the type of situation and type of coping: There are subscales for (a) vigilance in ego-threat situations, (b) cognitive avoidance in ego-threat situations, (c) vigilance in physical threat situations, and (d) cognitive avoidance in physical threat situations. The focus of the assessment lies on these four sum scores, which represent the two dispositional superstrategies—vigilance and cognitive avoidance—for two distinct classes of situations. The 18 coping acts do not represent dimensions on their own, but merely serve as test items to generate scores for the superstrategies.

Krohne reports favorable psychometric properties of the instrument. In particular, the subdivision into the two hypothesized superstrategies vigilance and cognitive avoidance was confirmed by factor analysis in a sample of women responding to ego-threat as well as to physical threat. For men, however, the structure could be confirmed only in the physical threat situation. This is a very recent instrument, and further validation studies need to be conducted.

The limitation of this approach lies in its mere focus on threat, in the same manner as for the monitoring and blunting concept. Krohne's coping mode theory stems from his research on anxiety and personality and, thus, represents a dispositional approach to threat management. Another limitation of the instrument lies in its validation within German samples only. The research has been published in English, but the scale itself awaits cross-cultural validation.

The Billings and Moos Coping Measures:
An Early Approach

In the context of research on chronic stress and coping in families, Billings and Moos (1981) have designed a measure to assess coping with life stress. After indicating a recent life crisis, 194 families (men and women) responded to 19 coping statements with "yes" or "no." Inspired by the stress and coping theory of Lazarus (1966), the researchers grouped the items intuitively according to the method of coping and the function of coping. The methods were (a) active cognitive, (b) active behavioral, and (c) avoidance. The functions were (a) problem-focused and (b) emotion-focused coping. (The authors use the term "focus" instead of "function," the latter being the term preferred by Lazarus.) Each of the 19 items fitted into one of the methods and one of the functions. The internal consistencies are partly satisfactory. This instrument is based on a rational construction and is in line with other theories, but empirically its structure has not been confirmed.

The authors have followed up their work in subsequent research where they applied an extended version of their instrument in a study with 424 depressives (Billings & Moos, 1984), in which they used 32 items and preferred a 4-point Likert scale response format. After an item analysis, 28 items remained and formed five scales that were grouped into three major forms of coping. *Appraisal-focused coping* consisted of a 4-item scale that referred to a logical analysis of the stress at hand, with items such as "considered several alternatives for handling the problem." *Problem-focused coping* included two subscales, (a) information seeking with 7 items, such as "tried to find out more about the situation," and (b) problem solving with 5 items, such as "made a plan and followed it." Finally, *emotion-focused coping* also consisted of two subscales, (a) affective regulation with 6 items, such as "tried to see the positive side of the situation," and (b) emotional discharge with 6 items, such as "let my feelings out somehow."

In terms of theory, this instrument conforms well with the majority of current measures. Empirically, the scales show unsatisfactory internal consistencies. In addition, there is insufficient evidence about time stability, and, in particular, the intuitive dimensional structure requires a rigid test in various samples before it can be generalized. The value of this inventory lies in its theoretical perspective and in the stimulation it provided at a time when almost no satisfactory coping scales were available.

The Ways of Coping Questionnaire (WCQ):
The Standard in the Field

Already in the 1970s, the stress and coping research group of Lazarus developed the Ways of Coping Checklist (WCC) in line with the transactional phenomenological stress theory that suggested two main functions of coping: problem solving and emotion regulation (cf. Lazarus, 1991). From a pool of 68 items with a yes-no response format, 40 items formed the problem-solving subscale, and 24 the emotion-focused subscale (Folkman & Lazarus, 1980). Because this classification did not reflect the complexity and richness of coping processes, a series of factor analyses with different data sets were carried out, generating over time the current version of the instrument now called the Ways of Coping Questionnaire (WCQ). The WCQ consists of 50 items (plus 16 fill items) within eight empirically derived scales (Folkman & Lazarus, 1988). A difficulty with the instrument has always been that the number of extracted factors changed from sample to sample or from stressor to stressor (Parker & Endler, 1992). But this seems to be a general problem with most coping measures, reflecting the unresolved disposition versus situation issue.

The response format of the scales has been changed to the 4-point Likert rating scale. Responses are made with reference to a real-life stress situation experienced by the respondent (e.g., during the preceding week), that the respondent has written down. Following are the eight scales with sample items:

1. *Confrontive Coping* (6 items). "Stood my ground and fought for what I wanted."

2. *Distancing* (6 items). "Went on as if nothing had happened."

3. *Self-Controlling* (7 items). "I tried to keep my feelings to myself."

4. *Seeking Social Support* (6 items). "Talked to someone to find out more about the situation."

5. *Accepting Responsibility* (4 items). "Criticized or Lectured Myself."

6. *Escape-Avoidance* (8 items). "Hoped a miracle would happen."

7. *Planful Problem Solving* (6 items). "I made a plan of action and followed it."

8. *Positive Reappraisal* (7 items). "Changed or grew as a person in a good way."

The intercorrelations among these scales are rather low, confirming their desired distinctiveness. Internal consistencies are not always satisfactory, and test-retest reliabilities are not reported. According to the theory, a high stability is not desired because individuals are expected to adjust their actual coping responses to the requirements of each specific situation. A problem with this measure, as well as with all measures that are based on many factors, is that theoretical cross-linked relationships between scales are not considered. For example, mobilizing social support is seen here as a distinct strategy, but actually it can serve a number of purposes, such as solving a problem, obtaining information, calming down, or distracting oneself. Carver, Scheier, and Weintraub (1989) have accounted for this problem by establishing separate social support factors for problem-focus and emotion-focus. Parker and Endler (1992) argue that social support should not be conceived as a distinct coping dimension but as social resources that may be available for a number of different coping strategies. A different view is to divide all coping strategies into social and nonsocial acts, thus doubling the amount of coping options (Klauer, Filipp, & Ferring, 1989).

Another difficulty with a high number of extracted factors is that they do not appear to be all of the same weight or of the same theoretical level. Some may be closer to a higher-order factor or to a general factor, accounting for a larger amount of variance, whereas others may be rather peripheral. It remains undetermined in what way the eight factors are embedded into the initial dimension of problem-focused and emotion-focused functions. There seems to be no empirical evidence for testing such a hierarchy with confirmatory factor analysis.

The authors of the questionnaire encourage researchers to adjust the WCQ to the specific study context to achieve a close match between the stress experience and the coping statements. This has been done, for example, by Dunkel-Schetter, Feinstein, Taylor, and Falke (1992), who have developed a version for cancer patients. It consists of 49 WCQ items, some of them slightly reworded, that were given to 603 cancer patients. A factor analysis yielded five factors: seek and use social support (11 items), cognitive escape-avoidance (9 items), distancing (12 items), focus on the positive (8 items), and behavioral escape-avoidance (9 items). This version has also been used by Stanton and Snider (1993).

Broad Range Coping Responses for Different Cognitive Appraisals of Stress

In contrast to the majority of coping inventories that aim at rather dispositional coping styles, McCrae (1984) has favored a situation-specific approach. He argued that the nature of the stressor would fundamentally determine how people cope with it. He asked 255 persons to name a recent life event, and this was later classified as being either a *challenge* (75 events), a *threat* (114 events), or a *loss* (66 events), according to the stress appraisals suggested by Lazarus (1966). Afterward, participants responded to a broad range of 118 coping items, 68 taken from the WCQ and 50 added by the author. By factor analysis, scales were constructed in a "rational" way, by using the 34-factor solution only to guide the assignment of items to 28 scales. Of these scales, many consisted of only one or two items, and some of the internal consistencies were unsatisfactory. In a second study, 151 persons were asked to recall either a challenge, threat, or loss that they had experienced within the past 6 months; that is, they had to elicit the cognitive appraisal themselves. The author concludes that there was no difference between assessing the nature of the stressor and the explicit cognitive appraisal. In both cases, subsets of the instrument received situation-specific responses.

This approach adds an important aspect to the measurement of coping. The nature of the stressful encounter can be considered a key element in actual coping responses. According to Lazarus's (1991) stress theory, its cognitive appraisal should be the critical antecedent of coping but this relationship is not well researched. McCrae (1984) is one of the few who followed up this line of thinking and deserves much credit for it. The resulting instrument, however, hardly seems to be acceptable due to its methodological limitations (see also McCrae & Costa, 1986).

The Coping Strategy Indicator (CSI):
A Factor-Analytical Approach

Commonly, scale development starts out in a rational way and continues in an empirical way. An example of this approach is the Coping Strategy Indicator (CSI) presented by Amirkhan (1990). The author collected 161 coping behaviors from existing scales and from previous own research, and then reduced this accumulation step by step in a series of factor analyses with independent large samples. The participants were solicited at public sites, such as supermarkets and health clinics. The 357 respondents in the first sample were asked to recall a critical event that they had experienced within the past 6 months ("a problem you think was important and caused you to worry"). Then they responded to the 161 coping items on a 3-point scale. By factor analysis, 3 out of 17 dimensions were associated with eigenvalues above unity, and manifested the basis for all further inquiry. The three subscales of the CSI were implanted at this early stage, although they only accounted for 21% of the variance: *problem solving, seeking support,* and *avoidance.* At the next stage, the 63 best factor indicators were given to 520 respondents. Another factor analysis yielded the same factors as before, backed up by confirmatory factor analysis. This procedure was repeated at Stage 3 with 954 respondents, who received the 36 best factor indicators. The final version consisted of 33 items, 11 for each subscale. Problem solving is denoted by items such as "tried to solve the problem"; seeking support is marked by items such as "confided your fears and worries to a friend or relative"; and avoidance is indicated by items such as "daydreamed about better times." In another sample of 92 persons, good psychometric properties of the instrument were determined.

It is desirable that different diagnostic instruments arrive at similar major dimensions of coping behavior. In the present case, this may be partly because pre-existing measures were taken to provide the raw material for the new one. It is also desirable to employ large independent samples for identifying those dimensions, and there is no better statistical procedure than confirmatory factor analysis. In spite of this, the present results are not convincing because all factor solutions were characterized by poor goodness-of-fit indexes, and, in addition, only 21%, 33%, or 37% of variance were accounted for at three stages of the instrument development. It would have been necessary to conduct more fine-grained analyses with hierarchical structures that would have resulted in lower-level subscales. In the validation section, it was surprising to find the "seeking social support" scale of Folkman and Lazarus (1988) to be more closely associated with Amirkhan's problem-solving scale ($r = .55$) than with his seeking support scale ($r = .46$). The enormous effort to construct this instrument is admirable, but the product is hardly convincing, neither in theoretical nor in empirical terms.

The Life Events and Coping Inventory (LECI):
Targeting Children

Children may experience stress in a different manner from adults. Research with age-specific stress and coping inventories, therefore, is appropriate. Dise-Lewis

(1988) has presented an instrument that has been generated and validated within samples of junior high school students aged 11 to 14 years. Initially, 104 students were interviewed with open-ended questions to explore their experience of stress ("events that produce stress") and their ways to handle it (what they "can do to cope with or reduce stress"). The item pool was refined and enriched with the help of 90 students, resulting in a checklist of 125 life events and 42 (later 49) coping strategies. Normative data were then gathered in a sample of 502 students who checked those events they had experienced within the recent year, and who rated their stressfulness and the appropriate coping strategies. Retest reliabilities were determined for a subsample of 85 students, and concurrent validity data for a subsample of 198 students.

A factor analysis with oblique rotation of the 49 coping strategies resulted in a five-factor solution that accounted for half of the variance. The first factor was labeled *"aggression"* and included 7 items, such as "hit someone or hurt someone physically." The second factor, *"stress recognition"* (13 items), contained behaviors such as "to cry." The third one was coined *"distraction,"* with 11 items, such as "do a hobby or something I enjoy." The fourth factor, called "self-destruction," included 8 items, for example, cigarette smoking. Finally, 9 items ("just hold in") referred to the fifth factor, called *"endurance."* Distraction and endurance were the most frequently selected coping strategies by children.

Because of the stepwise instrument development with large and independent samples, this inventory includes an abundant and well-established source of coping strategies for a specific age group. However, the construction was mainly empirical, and it is not well balanced with rational procedures. The final five factors do not conform well with theory and research by others. The factor analysis is not cross-validated and will probably fail to show up again in different samples, which is a common experience in this field of study. The coping strategies are applied to many different stressful encounters. Also, we do not know whether there are stressor-specific coping preferences in children.

The Adolescent Coping Orientation for Problem Experiences Inventory (A-COPE): An Age-Specific Inductive Approach

Coping with life stress may be different at different stages of life. In adolescence, girls and boys face challenging developmental tasks, such as fitting into a peer group, differentiating from the family, and advancing identity formation. To identify the major coping strategies and behaviors in dealing with developmental stress in adolescence, Patterson and McCubbin (1987) have designed an inventory that covers a variety of such behaviors. The instrument was generated in an inductive way. First, a sample of 30 high school students in grades 10 to 12 were interviewed. They described what they did to manage the hardships and to relieve the discomforts of (a) personally experienced stress, (b) stress experienced by other family members, and (c) critical life changes in general. The responses resulted in a 95-item inventory that was administered to a different sample of 467 students, who responded to these coping behaviors on a 5-point frequency scale. Those 27 items that yielded almost no variance were excluded.

The remaining 68 items were factor analyzed repeatedly, resulting in a final set of 54 coping behavior items that loaded on 12 factors (labeled "coping patterns" by the authors). Most of the reliabilities (internal consistencies) of these 12 subscales are in the .70s. The factors are:

1. *Ventilating Feelings.* Six coping behaviors that focus on the expression of tensions and frustrations (swearing, letting off steam, yelling at people, etc.).

2. *Seeking Diversions.* Eight coping behaviors that reflect how to keep oneself busy or escape from sources of tension (sleeping, watching a movie, playing video games or using drugs).

3. *Developing Self-Reliance and Optimism.* Six coping behaviors that include efforts to be more organized and in charge of the situation (trying to make one's own decision, figuring out how to deal with the problem, trying to think of the good things in life, or working harder at a job).

4. *Developing Social Support.* Six coping behaviors focused on staying connected with other people through expression of affect or mutual problem solving (apologizing or talking to a friend about one's feelings).

5. *Solving Family Problems.* Six coping behaviors directed at working out difficult issues with family members (talking to one's father, trying to reason with parents, going along with parents' requests).

6. *Avoiding Problems.* Five coping behaviors that reflect how adolescents use substances as a way to escape or to avoid persons difficult to deal with.

7. *Seeking Spiritual Support.* Three coping behaviors: going to church, praying, and talking to a minister.

8. *Investing in Close Friends.* Only two coping behaviors: being close with someone you care about, and being with a boyfriend or girlfriend.

9. *Seeking Professional Support.* Only two coping behaviors: getting professional counseling and talking to a teacher.

10. *Engaging in Demanding Activity.* Four coping behaviors that involve challenges to excel at something or achieve a goal (working hard on school projects, getting body in shape, etc.).

11. *Being Humorous.* Only two coping behaviors: keeping a sense of humour and trying to be funny.

12. *Relaxing.* Four coping behaviors directed at ways to alleviate tensions (eating, daydreaming, riding around in a car, etc.).

In a further sample of 709 adolescents, this inventory was validated within a longitudinal study on health-risk behaviors. The frequency rank order of these coping patterns showed that relaxing, developing social support, investing in close friends, and developing self-reliance were used most often, whereas avoiding problems and seeking professional support were reported least often. Girls in particular preferred to turn to their social bonds. Substance use was more pronounced in those who were inclined to ventilate their feelings and who invested in close friends, whereas less substance use was reported by those who tried to solve family problems.

This inventory is a good example for the measurement of coping with general life stress at a specific developmental stage. It seems to be appropriate for research on adolescent stress and health risk behaviors. Its main weakness lies in its inductive development. It has not been influenced by major theories of stress and coping, but relies basically on the responses of the 30 adolescents who assembled the first item pool. It is likely that other researchers using the initial set of 95 coping behaviors with other samples would come up with different factors, in particular when using theory-guided confirmatory factor analysis. Therefore, this inventory is not well compatible with the leading coping instruments. Instead, it represents a unique and stimulating approach but may be restricted to the original study context.

The Life Situations Inventory (LSI): Coping within Five Conflict Areas in Later Life

Based on principal coping inventories, Feifel and Strack (1989) developed their Life Situations Inventory (LSI) to assess three forms of coping: *problem-solving, avoidance,* and *resignation.* Similar factors as those identified by various studies conform with leading theories. The approach aimed at coping with real-life circumstances in middle-aged and elderly men.

The authors began with a collection of more than 70 coping behaviors found in other instruments. By a rational selection procedure, they eliminated those items that appeared to be redundant or did not fit the three theoretical coping forms well enough. They ended up with 28 items that they administered to 182 men. The stress situations were not presented in the questionnaire, but were individually generated by the participants. However, five conflict areas were given as a guideline for the recall of personal problems: (a) decision making, (b) defeat in competition, (c) a frustration-producing situation, (d) difficulty with an authority figure, and (e) general disagreement with a peer. Subjects were asked to write down a significant conflict they had experienced recently within each area. Then they responded to how they had coped with it by answering the 28 LSI items. Thus, these 28 items were repeated five times, once for each stress situation. The instruction for the decision-making problem, for example, was "Take a few minutes and think about a situation in which you had trouble making a decision. That is, you had to make a choice, and you were not sure what to do. It might have been a decision involving just yourself, or involving your job, family, or friends. Be sure that the decision . . . is one that was important to you" (Feifel & Strack, 1989, p. 28). Participants came up with decision problems, such as finding a new place to live or investing in the stock market. Each of the 28 LSI questions was presented with a 4-point response format indicating the degree of endorsement. Examples are "How much did you try to settle things as soon as possible?" (problem solving), "How much did you try not to think about the situation?" (avoidance), and "How much did you feel that the final decision was beyond your control?" (resignation).

The 5-situations-by-28-items data set was examined by using item analysis, resulting in three scales after eliminating seven items. The problem-solving scale consisted of 8 items, the avoidance scale also of 8 items, and the resignation scale of 5 items. The pooled within-situations correlations between the scales was $r = .01$ for problem-solving with avoidance, $r = .22$ for problem-solving with resignation, and $r = .51$ for avoidance with resignation.

The development of this inventory represents a well-balanced approach where rational and empirical steps were taken and where scales emerged that are in line with current thinking. On the other hand, these scales are not very innovative. A unique feature lies in the self-generation of the five stress situations. This distinguishes the instrument from others which offer hypothetical scenarios that may be alien to the respondents. The disadvantage of real-life situations is, however, that comparisons between persons are not accurate because individual differences in the stress experiences may result in subsequent coping differences. Personal coping style is responsible then not for choosing one strategy or the other, but for determining the match between the situation and the behavior. Another problem is that different cognitive appraisals can be made within each conflict area. Loss appraisals across different areas might correspond with each other more closely than, for example, threat and loss appraisals within one area. Instead of content, the cognitive appraisal might be a better categorization of stress situations. Further, the specific stage in which a conflict is examined appears to be important: Whether one recalls the anticipation stage, the confrontation stage, or the recovery stage makes a difference for appraisal and coping.

The Coping Inventory for Stressful Situations (CISS): Three Coping Dispositions

The weakness of most of the measures lies in their unsatisfactory psychometric properties, unstable factor structures, and lack of cross-validation. These shortcomings have been prevented with the Coping Inventory for Stressful Situations (CISS), which was developed in an accurate and rigorous way (Endler & Parker, 1990a, 1990b), and in a balanced approach, including rational and empirical steps. Coping behaviors were compiled that fitted the two generally accepted coping functions—problem solving and emotion regulation. A 70-item pool based on existing instruments and on additional collections was presented to 559 undergraduates who responded on 5-point frequency scales. A general instruction was used, aiming at a "typical" coping response (". . . how much you engage in these types of activities when you encounter a difficult, stressful, or upsetting situation"). Factor analyses, performed for men and women separately, yielded three factors: *task-oriented, emotion-oriented,* and *avoidance-oriented coping*. A revised 66-item version was given to 394 college students and to 284 adults. For each subsample, divided by sex, factor analyses were conducted that replicated the three factors, producing the final 48-item inventory with 16 items per scale. The avoidance dimension could be further subdivided into a *Distraction* scale and a *Social Diversion* scale. Very good psychometric properties were identified in several validation samples. Construct validity was documented by appropriate correlations with the Ways of Coping Questionnaire (Folkman & Lazarus, 1988) and various personality traits.

Recent studies have used the CISS to predict state anxiety before an academic exam (Endler, Kantor, & Parker, 1994; Zeidner, 1994). As a trait measure, its predictive value for a situation-specific emotion obviously has to be very limited. Rather, coping dispositions play a role as distal antecedents in more complex path models that also include situation-specific coping responses.

Technically, the CISS is a state-of-the-art inventory based on stable factors that were replicated across various samples and that met the congruency test criteria. It represents a fine model of classical test construction. However, it is not better than others for resolving today's critical issues in coping assessment. It is limited to three factors, although other researchers have shown that this small range does not reflect the complexity and heterogeneity of actual coping. Further elaboration is necessary to identify subgroups of coping strategies that remain stable across individuals and situations. The instrument is disposition-oriented and, therefore, covers only one facet of coping. A more situation-oriented CISS version is required; this is what is currently being developed (Endler et al., 1994).

The COPE Scale: Theoretically Derived Dimensions

The distinction between problem-focused coping and emotion-focused coping is widely acknowledged, but many authors, including Carver et al. (1989), felt that this was too simple. They believe that both coping functions have to be subdivided because there are a variety of distinct ways to solve problems or to regulate emotions. The COPE inventory has gone through several generations in its development, and a number of theoretically important factors were identified. By using rational construction procedures, diverse scales were composed, which were then tested in a sample of 978 undergraduates. The students were asked what they usually do when they are under considerable stress. A factor analysis produced almost the same structure as was hypothesized. (It is not reported how many items were initially used, and where the 13 scales came from after only 11 meaningful factors had been extracted.) The final version of the COPE inventory (Carver et al., 1989) contains 13 scales with 4 items each (the authors now distribute a version with two additional experimental scales).

Following is a list of the scale labels together with one example each. The first five categories were established as subdimensions of problem-focused coping, and the next five as subdimensions of emotion-focused coping:

1. *Active Coping.* "I do what has to be done, one step at a time."
2. *Planning.* "I make a plan of action."
3. *Suppression of Competing Activities.* "I put aside other activities in order to concentrate on this."

4. *Restraint Coping.* "I force myself to wait for the right time to do something."

5. *Seeking Social Support for Instrumental Reasons.* "I talk to someone to find out more about the situation."

6. *Seeking Social Support for Emotional Reasons.* "I talk to someone about how I feel."

7. *Positive Reinterpretation and Growth.* "I learn something from the experience."

8. *Acceptance.* "I learn to live with it."

9. *Turning to Religion.* "I put my trust in God."

10. *Focus on and Venting of Emotions.* "I let my feelings out."

11. *Denial.* "I refuse to believe that it has happened."

12. *Behavioral Disengagement.* "I just give up trying to reach my goal."

13. *Mental Disengagement.* "I daydream about things other than this."

In addition to these 52 items, one coping behavior was kept as a single item that pertained to alcohol or drug use. After the analysis, this was extended to another 4-item scale, along with one 4-item scale concerning joking about the stressor (Carver et al., 1989, p. 280). Most of the preceding scales were found to have satisfactory psychometric properties, and evidence for validity is provided (cf. Carver & Scheier, 1993; Carver, Scheier, & Pozo, 1992).

The authors argue that this is a theoretically based approach, and certainly, it is more rational than many others. But the use of exploratory factor analysis discounts this strategy because it is hardly suitable to test a theory, in particular when used in a default manner with the eigenvalue criterion. Instead, a hierarchical confirmatory factor analysis would have been appropriate. Theoretically, five of the factors were established as subdimensions of problem solving, and five more as subdimensions of emotional coping. This makes good sense, but requires a test of the two levels. A second-order factor analysis did not replicate this hypothesized structure (Carver et al., 1989, p. 274; see also Zeidner & Hammer, 1992).

The COPE scale is conceived as a more fine-grained dispositional measure of individual differences in coping than previous instruments, and it reflects a balanced view about the disposition versus situation issue. In a separate study, a situational version of the instrument was administered to 128 students together with the dispositional version (Carver et al., 1989). The situational version was rephrased to denote a recent real-life experience instead of a generalized response to all kinds of stress. Subjects were asked to think about their most stressful event of the past two months. Low to moderate correlations between the two versions were found, which was expected and which underscores the role of situation variability. However, to decide whether a "trait version" or a "state version" of the inventory is most suitable, it is necessary to examine the predictive power of both versions in a series of studies with different stressful encounters. The same remains to be answered for the possible influence of personality dispositions on adaptation. For example, monitoring and blunting were almost unrelated to dispositional coping, but optimism was closely linked to it. It may be that the direct or indirect influence of such traits accounts for more outcome variance than situation-specific actual coping. The COPE instrument is a good tool to continue research on these issues.

The Measure of Daily Coping: Open-Ended Response Formats

Inspired by the transactional stress theory (Lazarus, 1966, 1991), Stone and Neale (1984) attempted to develop an instrument to assess daily coping for use in longitudinal studies. In a pilot study, subjects were asked how to handle a recent problem and were asked to respond to 87 coping items. This was reduced to a 55-item checklist in the subsequent study. Eight categories were established that were labeled (a) distraction, (b) situation redefinition, (c) direct action, (d) catharsis, (e) acceptance, (f) social support, (g) relaxation, and (h) religion. Because the psychometric properties repeatedly turned out to be unsatisfactory, the authors gave up their intention to construct psychometric rating scales with multiple items, and decided to apply the eight categories directly with an open-ended response format. It was filled out by 120 married individuals for 21 consecutive days. Participants checked the appropriate categories and wrote down descriptions of their coping behaviors where applicable. The authors claim content validity for this measure and argue that this approach has advantages over traditional ones. In particular, they question the usefulness of internal consistency in coping measurement, of retrospective assessment, and of representing coping processes that change over time by one static value for a specific coping strategy.

The fact that Stone and Neale (1984) failed to develop reliable and valid psychometric coping scales and had to resort to a written structured interview can be considered as a blessing today because their article has become influential and has sparked an ongoing debate about the merits of situation-oriented coping assessment (Folkman, 1992; Stone & Kennedy-Moore, 1992). It is argued, for example, that inter-item covariation does not make sense when one strategy has been used at the expense of others within the same subcategory (e.g., after "did what I had to do" has been selected successfully, it is no longer necessary to "think about different solutions to the problem"). Within a traditional psychometric scale designed to tap problem solving it would be expected that these items are highly correlated. In an actual coping situation, however, they may be unrelated because the first one is sufficient and the second may then be neglected. Another issue pertains to the duration of the stressful encounter and the opportunity for coping acts. If subjects recall an event experienced within the past year, those who report an ongoing long-term event could come up with more coping strategies than those who report a very brief event or one that had just started. In addition, recall and labeling of coping efforts could be influenced by its outcome. If "thinking about the problem" is followed by failure, it may be labeled "rumination"; if followed by success it could be interpreted as "planning" or "instrumental problem solving" (Stone & Kennedy-Moore, 1992). It has also been found that the inapplicability of part of the items within a specific stress context biases the scores (Ben-Porath, Waller, & Butcher, 1991; Stone, Greenberg, Kennedy-Moore, & Newman, 1991). For example, the item "learned to know myself better" may be applicable when harm or loss is experienced or when patients suffer from a fatal disease, as opposed to the item "made a person change her mind" that appears to be more applicable in demanding interpersonal relationships. When the entire item pool of a coping scale is presented, some of the items turn out to be inapplicable to the situation and not only are useless, but may even bias the results. These are merely a few critical points put forward by those favoring a situation-oriented approach. Due to space limitations, this highly important issue cannot be discussed here in more detail.

The Stress and Coping Process Questionnaire (SCPQ): A Three-Stage Assessment

Inspired by the transactional stress theory of Lazarus (1991), Swiss researchers have designed a unique rationale for the assessment of stress and coping (Reicherts & Perez, 1991; for an English version, see Perez & Reicherts, 1992). Its aim is to measure coping within the time course of various hypothetical stressful encounters as it relates to cognitive appraisals, emotions, and attributions. The instrument consists of 18 such episodes, tapping two classes of stress: (a) *aversive or ambiguous situations,* and (b) *loss or failure situations.* Each episode is subdivided into three stages as the encounter unfolds. An example for failure is the following episode:

- At *Stage 1,* the instruction is phrased "Try to clearly imagine the following situation: Previous relations with your boss have been quite complicated. Now your boss gives you a task which you are supposed to work on for the next two days. This job is very inconvenient for you because you have a lot of routine work to do at the moment." Next comes a two-page questionnaire that requires answers about emotions, judgments, intentions, and actions.

- At *Stage 2,* the instruction is phrased "Imagine the situation carries on in the following way: Your boss tells you that your routine work also has to be done. As you begin to work on the new task, it becomes evident how difficult and time consuming it really is. It seems that you will only finish it if you ignore your other work, and even then you may have to do overtime on it." Again, a two-page questionnaire has to be completed.

- At *Stage 3,* the instruction says "Imagine the situation finally turns out as follows: You didn't carry out the job in the assigned time. Also, a lot of routine work remained unfinished." Now, the third two-page questionnaire asks for feelings, attributions, and intentions.

An important aspect of this instrument lies in its distinction between *coping intentions* and *coping strategies.* It is assumed that individuals act according to their intentions or goals. This is more specific than merely stating that there are different coping functions, as Lazarus and Folkman (1984) do. This point is also made by Leventhal, Suls, and Leventhal (1993) and by Laux and Weber (1993). Four intentions are provided, each of them with 4-point rating scales: (a) to actively confront the other and to clear up what is at stake, (b) to maintain a friendly atmosphere and to prevent an argument with the other, (c) to remain calm and composed, and (d) to keep my self-esteem. The authors believe that four basic intentions are associated with coping. One focuses on the person-environment adaptation, subdivided into mastery-orientation (assimilative) and meaning-orientation (accommodative). The third is to keep one's emotional balance, and the fourth is to maintain self-esteem.

In terms of coping behaviors, a distinction is made between self-directed and environment-directed strategies, the latter again subdivided with respect to either aversive/ambiguous or to loss/failure situations. *Self-directed strategies* are search for information, suppression of information, reevaluation, palliation, self-blame, and other-blame. *Environment-directed behaviors* are instrumental actions, avoidance, hesitation, prevention, reorientation, and so forth.

Some validation studies with small samples have been conducted yielding satisfactory psychometric properties, in particular, high retest reliabilities. The newness of the inventory and its presentation in the German language may have impeded a large-scale evaluation up to now. In addition, this inventory is designed in a very complicated manner requiring not only an effort for the interviewee, but also for the researcher in analyzing and interpreting the data. No other measure is as closely composed in line with transactional stress theories, but this is at the expense of not being as parsimonious as other measures. A great advantage is the consideration of coping intentions and of different stages. The latter, however, is of limited value because this remains a scenario approach with hypothetical situations that change in a hypothetical way. If the aim is to tap transactional processes, it might be better to conduct research in real-life situations. Nevertheless, this is a unique approach that challenges other assessment tools.

DISCUSSION: UNRESOLVED ISSUES

The present survey of instruments is not exhaustive. It is arbitrarily limited to some examples that have been published within the past 10 years and that expose certain features of interest. Our portrayal has to be brief and cannot pay attention to all aspects. As a result of this overview, we will delineate a number of critical issues that have not been resolved sufficiently by the available operationalization.

Rational versus Empirical Scale Development

The procedure to generate a coping inventory can be more deductive (based on theoretical assumptions), or more inductive (starting with observations). Both directions are needed but a firm balance between them is rarely found (Burisch, 1984; Gough & Bradly, 1992). In addition, the conceptual and technical quality of these steps is not always satisfactory, a point well made by Parker and Endler (1992). Some authors collect items from preexisting questionnaires fitting to some theoretical distinctions, add a few items of their own, compute a factor analysis, and construct scales that match their judgment rather than the empirical factor solution. Others do not collect their items in light of theory, but they compile unsystematically a database that may have a range too narrow or too broad or that is otherwise biased; they then run sophisticated statistical analyses and value the resulting coefficients more than may be justified. In particular, some authors tend to pay lip service to a stress and coping theory that focuses on context specificity, reciprocal processes, and dynamics of the unfolding encounter, but what they actually come up with is a kind of coping style inventory that assesses a stable personality trait instead. Researchers often need a much clearer distinction between personal coping resources, coping behaviors, and coping outcomes.

Dispositional versus Situational Coping Assessment

Assessing either dispositional or episodic coping has indeed been the main issue in recent years (see, e.g., Cohen, 1987; Folkman, 1992; Stone & Kennedy-Moore, 1992). Do individuals make rigid or flexible use of habitual coping strategies across situations and across time points? Or is each coping episode highly idiosyncratic and chiefly determined by the actual situation? The question can be reframed by asking whether we prefer to study interindividual or intraindividual differences. Another perspective would be to focus either on trait coping or on state coping. These alternatives have implications for the development of measures and for the psychometric properties that we can ask for. Dispositional measures should be constructed according to high psychometric standards, but this is a trade-off because such inventories cannot account for the array of coping responses on a microanalytic level when dealing with the complexity of a stressful encounter (Folkman, 1992). "Psychometric rigor may prove to be a strait-jacket which can confine research and ignore the study of process" (Leventhal et al., 1993, p. 95). High internal consistency, for example, can be expected when all coping responses within the same category (such as avoidance) are likely to be used, not when only one of them is preferred which may render the others redundant (Stone & Kennedy-Moore, 1992). High test-retest reliability is a contradiction to the variability inherent in continuous coping within a stress episode, but it would be somewhat more applicable when comparing individuals who cope with the same kind of stress at two distinct points in time. Thus, coefficients should not be evaluated regardless of the measurement context. If we could trade in reliability for validity, we would gain something valuable, but this can only be accepted if there is empirical proof of it.

However, it could be that we are not interested in an accurate description of the coping process. Science has to aim more toward prediction and explanation than toward mere description. If adaptation outcomes are better predicted by dispositional coping strategies than by situation-oriented measures, then dispositional strategies deserve more scientific attention.

Real-Life Events versus Hypothetical Scenarios

The nature of a stressful encounter and its cognitive appraisal influence the way people cope with it. Imagining a possible future situation may provoke similar reactions to recalling a past situation experienced as being stressful. Asking all respondents to imagine the same fictitious stress situation has the obvious research advantage of improved internal validity. In contrast, people who recall a prior real-life situation experience something that has a unique personal significance for them but maybe not for others, which complicates comparability between situations. This can be somewhat alleviated by classifying the recalled events into distinct *cognitive appraisals* (such as challenge, threat, or loss) or to elicit certain types of events in the first place (McCrae, 1984). But this has been rarely done. Real-life events are often taken as "generic" stress, and then it becomes impossible to relate coping to its context. If the research goal is to identify dispositional coping strategies, one may resort to hypothetical scenarios as prototypical stress situations, but if the aim is to describe actual coping, the situation parameters have to be carefully studied. Sometimes life stress is defined by the selection of the sample, for example, when cancer patients, refugees, or rape victims are studied. The issue here is whether population-specific/domain-specific inventories should be developed or whether general coping inventories should be preferred to allow for group comparisons. Again, the need of a yardstick is a matter of the research question.

When context-specific research is being conducted, further distinctions have to be made in terms of episode, domain, and stage. An *episode* is a stressful encounter that has a beginning and an ending (such as an academic exam or a dentist appointment). A *domain* refers to the area of human functioning where the problem arises (career, health, interpersonal relationships, etc.). *Stages* subdivide an episode and are in particular important because individuals do not cope in the same manner all the time. It may be that a patient undergoing surgery is vigilant during the preparation stage, avoiding during the confrontation stage, and seeking support during the recovery stage. If the researcher aims at an accurate description of the actual coping process, it is indispensable to identify the domain, the episode, and the stage, and to assess coping at multiple points in time. Retrospective reports of coping may pertain to any stage, but most likely they will be biased toward the most recent one.

Multidimensionality and Hierarchy

Some reports come up with 2 or 3, others with 8, 13, or even 28 coping scales, no matter whether they were developed in a more rational or in a more empirical way. Dispositional instruments tend to include less dimensions; situation-oriented measures tend to have more. There is agreement about some major factors, such as either problem focus and emotion focus, or vigilance and avoidance, or a combination of both sets. Obviously, these are conceptually at a high level of abstraction, whereas others are more proximal to the coping responses.

Several authors, among them Krohne (1993) and Leventhal et al. (1993), have suggested establishing hierarchies to account for this evidence. With this purpose in mind, some researchers have conducted second-order factor analyses, but the solutions have not been found stable across samples. Carver et al. (1989), for example, extracted for their COPE scales four second-order factors; Zeidner and Hammer (1992) found only two such factors based on a modified version of the COPE inventory. Another example is the Ways of Coping Questionnaire, which consists of eight strategies originally expected to be related to problem-focused and emotion-focused coping. However, this has not been demonstrated empirically. A likely reason for the common failure to link two levels of coping strategies to each other lies in the technique of exploratory factor analysis that is unsuitable for such a design. Instead, item sets should be constrained to fit into a multidimension-multistrategy model to be tested by confirmatory factor analysis.

Most inventories include a scale to measure the seeking or mobilization of *social support,* but it has been found that this is not a stable, replicable factor. This has to do with the phenomenon that social support is a multidimensional construct in itself (Schwarzer, Dunkel-Schetter & Kemeny, 1994; Schwarzer & Leppin, 1991). Instrumental support assists in problem solving, emotional support may comfort the person, and so on. It is therefore not surprising that Carver et al. (1989) have found two support factors. The more general question is whether this construct has been conceptualized at the appropriate level within a system of coping concepts. Parker and Endler (1992) argue that social resources can be used as part of many strategies, and they suggest dropping it from the strategy list and adding it to the resource list (see also Hobfoll, 1988; Stephens, Crowther, Hobfoll, & Tennenbaum, 1990). Klauer et al. (1989) have divided all coping attempts into social and nonsocial ones (see also Filipp, Klauer, & Ferring, 1993). Directing one's coping efforts toward a social network represents a medium of action that is distinct from other media of action.

A related issue lies in the meaning of coping dimensions. Problem solving and emotion regulation, for example, are understood as *coping functions* (Folkman, 1992; Lazarus, 1991); vigilance and cognitive avoidance are interpreted as *attentional styles* (Krohne, 1993, and Chapter 17, this volume; Miller et al., 1993). It has hardly been recognized, however, that a specific coping act can serve different functions (e.g., by seeking information, a person not only can calm down and reduce threat, but also can prepare for subsequent action). Furthermore, individuals pursue a variety of goals that may differ from time to time and from situation to situation. Identifying personal *coping intentions,* therefore, is a prerequisite for a judgment about certain coping efforts (Laux & Weber, 1993; Perrez & Reicherts, 1992). In establishing a hierarchy of coping acts, the researcher should top it with "generalized coping intentions" (Leventhal et al., 1993), followed by strategies, acts, and even more specific behaviors. The assessment of coping should then take place as a multilevel process while the stressful encounter unfolds. Perrez and Reicherts (1992) come closest to this suggestion; they have developed a computer-assisted data collection procedure (called COMES) that allows the inputting of self-reported coping information during stressful interactions. The trade-off is that such databases are not only complicated to obtain, but also difficult to score, analyze, and interpret. In light of this disadvantage, traditional psychometric scales will continue to serve a purpose and will remain attractive in future research.

CONCLUSION: TOWARD A CLOSER MATCH BETWEEN CONCEPT AND MEASUREMENT

If we acknowledge the need to combine multidimensionality with hierarchy, we remain open to consider all kinds of coping measures within a single conceptual framework. The guideline for future research would be to establish a multilevel assessment rationale according to the researcher's specific coping theory. Rather than lumping together heterogeneous measures in an eclectic way, it is superior to relate, for example, dispositional coping to situational coping assessment, to describe actual coping with one part of the inventory, and to identify stable coping preferences with the other. Hypothetical scenarios may be used to identify one's personal inclination for coping, but nothing can replace real-life events for ecological validity of the assessment procedure. We need more attention to the passage of time and to the accumulation of coping experience as prerequisites for actual coping responses. A hierarchy of coping instruments, therefore, must include some parts that are administered at multiple points in time, which in turn poses demands on the parsimony of the tools. It is of less importance to what degree rational or empirical construction techniques are being used, compared with the necessity that both perspectives have to operate reciprocally in a spiral-shaped process. Coping research has to escape from narrow-minded empiricism. It can only make a significant leap forward when multilevel instruments that match the complexity of coping are embedded in a multiwave design, analyzed by causal modeling approaches.

REFERENCES

Amirkhan, J. H. (1990). A factor analytically derived measure of coping: The Coping Strategy Indicator. *Journal of Personality and Social Psychology, 59,* 1066–1074.

Ben-Porath, Y. S., Waller, N. G., & Butcher, J. N. (1991). Assessment of coping: An empirical illustration of the problem of inapplicable items. *Journal of Personality Assessment, 57,* 162–176.

Billings, A. G., & Moos, R. H. (1981). The role of coping responses and social resources in attenuating the stress of life events. *Journal of Behavioral Medicine, 4,* 139–157.

Billings, A. G., & Moos, R. H. (1984). Coping, stress, and resources among adults with unipolar depression. *Journal of Personality and Social Psychology, 46,* 877–891.

Brandtstädter, J. (1992). Personal control over development: Implications of self-efficacy. In R. Schwarzer (Ed.), *Self-efficacy: Thought control of action* (pp. 127–145). Washington, DC: Hemisphere.

Burisch, M. (1984). Approaches to personality inventory construction. A comparison of merits. *American Psychologist, 39*(4), 214–227.

Carver, C. S., & Scheier, M. F. (1993). Vigilant and avoidant coping in two patient samples. In H. W. Krohne (Ed.), *Attention and avoidance: Strategies in coping with aversiveness* (pp. 295–320). Seattle, WA: Hogrefe & Huber.

Carver, C. S., Scheier, M. F., & Pozo, C. (1992). Conceptualizing the process of coping with health problems. In H. S. Friedman (Ed.), *Hostility, coping, and health* (pp. 167–187). Washington, DC: American Psychological Association.

Carver, C. S., Scheier, M. F., & Weintraub, J. K. (1989). Assessing coping strategies: A theoretically based approach. *Journal of Personality and Social Psychology, 56*(2), 267–283.

Cohen, F. (1987). Measurement of coping. In S. V. Kasl & C. L. Cooper (Eds.), *Stress and health: Issues in research methodology* (pp. 283–305). New York: Wiley.

Dise-Lewis, J. E. (1988). The Life Events and Coping Inventory: An assessment of stress in children. *Psychosomatic Medicine, 50,* 484–499.

Dunkel-Schetter, C., Feinstein, L. G., Taylor, S. E., & Falke, R. L. (1992). Patterns of coping with cancer. *Health Psychology, 11,* 79–87.

Endler, N. S., Kantor, L., & Parker, J. D. A. (1994). State-trait coping, state-trait anxiety and academic performance. *Personality and Individual Differences, 16,* 663–699.

Endler, N. S., & Parker, J. D. A. (1990a). *Coping Inventory for Stressful Situations (CISS): Manual.* Toronto, Canada: Multi Health Systems.

Endler, N. S., & Parker, J. D. A. (1990b). Multidimensional assessment of coping: A critical evaluation. *Journal of Personality and Social Psychology, 58,* 844–854.

Feifel, H., & Strack, S. (1989). Coping with conflict situations: Middle-aged and elderly men. *Psychology and Aging, 4*(1), 26–33.

Filipp, S. H., Klauer, T., & Ferring, D. (1993). Self-focused attention in the face of adversity and threat. In H. W. Krohne (Ed.), *Attention and avoidance: Strategies in coping with aversiveness* (pp. 267–295). Seattle, WA: Hogrefe & Huber.

Folkman, S. (1992). Improving coping assessment: Reply to Stone and Kennedy-Moore. In H. S. Friedman (Ed.), *Hostility, coping, and health* (pp. 215–223). Washington, DC: American Psychological Association.

Folkman, S., & Lazarus, R. S. (1980). An analysis of coping in a middle-aged community sample. *Journal of Health and Social Behavior, 21,* 219–234.

Folkman, S., & Lazarus, R. S. (1988). *Manual for the Ways of Coping Questionnaire.* Palo Alto, CA: Consulting Psychologist Press.

Gough, H. G., & Bradly, P. (1992). Comparing two strategies for developing personality scales. In M. Zeidner & B. Most (Eds.), *Psychological testing: An insider view* (pp. 215–246). Palo Alto, CA: Consulting Psychologist Press.

Hobfoll, S. E. (1988). *The ecology of stress.* Washington, DC: Hemisphere.

Klauer, T., Filipp, S. H., & Ferring, D. (1989). Der "Fragebogen zur Erfassung von Formen der Krankheitsbewältigung" (FEKB): Skalenkonstruktion und erste Befunde zu Reliabilität, Validität und Stabilität [The "inventory to assess forms of coping": Scale development and first results pertaining to reliability, validity, and stability]. *Diagnostica, 35,* 316–335.

Krohne, H. W. (1993). Vigilance and cognitive avoidance as concepts in coping research. In H. W. Krohne (Ed.), *Attention and avoidance: Strategies in coping with aversiveness* (pp. 19–50). Seattle, WA: Hogrefe & Huber.

Krohne, H. W., Schumacher, A., & Egloff, B. (1992). *Das Angstbewältigungs-Inventar (ABI)* [The Mainz Coping Inventory (MCI)] (Mainzer Berichte zur Persönlichkeitsforschung). Mainz: Johannes-Gutenberg-Universität, Psychologisches Institut.

Laux, L., & Weber, H. (1993). *Emotionsbewältigung und Selbstdarstellung* [Coping with emotions, and self-presentation]. Stuttgart: Kohlhammer.

Lazarus, R. S. (1966). *Psychological stress and the coping process.* New York: McGraw-Hill.

Lazarus, R. S. (1991). *Emotion and adaptation.* London: Oxford University Press.

Lazarus, R. S., & Folkman, S. (1984). *Stress, appraisal, and coping.* New York: Springer.

Leventhal, E. A., Suls, J., & Leventhal, H. (1993). Hierarchical analysis of coping: Evidence from life-span studies. In H. W. Krohne (Ed.), *Attention and avoidance: Strategies in coping with aversiveness* (pp. 71–100). Seattle, WA: Hogrefe & Huber.

McCrae, R. R. (1984). Situational determinants of coping responses: Loss, threat, and challenge. *Journal of Personality and Social Psychology, 46,* 919–928.

McCrae, R. R., & Costa, R. T. (1986). Personality, coping, and coping effectiveness in an adult sample. *Journal of Personality, 54,* 385–405.

Miller, S. M. (1987). Monitoring and blunting: Validation of a questionnaire to assess styles of information seeking under threat. *Journal of Personality and Social Psychology, 52*(2), 345–353.

Miller, S. M., Combs, C., & Kruss, L. (1993). Tuning in and tuning out: Confronting the effects of confrontation. In H. W. Krohne (Ed.), *Attention and avoidance: Strategies in coping with aversiveness* (pp. 51–70). Seattle, WA: Hogrefe & Huber.

Parker, J. D. A., & Endler, N. S. (1992). Coping with coping assessment: A critical review. *European Journal of Personality, 6*(5), 321–344.

Patterson, J. M., & McCubbin, H. I. (1987). Adolescent coping style and behaviors: Conceptualization and measurement. *Journal of Adolescence, 10,* 163–186.

Perrez, M., & Reicherts, M. (1992). *Stress, coping, and health.* Seattle, WA: Hogrefe & Huber.

Reicherts, M., & Perrez, M. (1991). *Fragebogen zum Umgang mit Belastungen im Verlauf (UBV)* [Coping Process Questionnaire]. Bern: Huber.

Rothbaum, F., Weisz, J. R., & Snyder, S. (1982). Changing the world and changing the self: A two-process model of perceived control. *Journal of Personality and Social Psychology, 42,* 5–37.

Schwarzer, R. (1994). Optimism, vulnerability, and self-beliefs as health-related cognitions: A systematic overview. *Psychology and Health, 9,* 161–180.

Schwarzer, R., Dunkel-Schetter, C., & Kemeny, M. (1994). The multidimensional nature of received social support in gay men at risk of HIV infection. *American Journal of Community Psychology, 22,* 319–339.

Schwarzer, R., & Leppin, A. (1991). Social support and health: A theoretical and empirical overview. *Journal of Social and Personal Relationships, 8,* 99–127.

Stanton, A. L., & Snider, P. R. (1993). Coping with a breast cancer diagnosis: A prospective study. *Health Psychology, 12,* 16–23.

Stephens, M. A. P., Crowther, J. H., Hobfoll, S. E., & Tennenbaum, D. L. (1990). *Stress and coping in later-life families.* New York: Hemisphere.

Stone, A. A., Greenberg, M. A., Kennedy-Moore, E., & Newman, M. G. (1991). Self-report, situation-specific coping questionnaires: What are they measuring? *Journal of Personality and Social Psychology, 61,* 648–658.

Stone, A. A., & Kennedy-Moore, E. (1992). Assessing situational coping: Conceptual and methodological considerations. In H. S. Friedman (Ed.), *Hostility, coping, and health* (pp. 203–214). Washington, DC: American Psychological Association.

Stone, A. A., & Neale, J. M. (1984). New measure of daily coping: Development and preliminary results. *Journal of Personality and Social Psychology, 46,* 892–906.

Suls, J., & Fletcher, B. (1985). The relative efficacy of avoidant and nonavoidant coping strategies: A meta-analysis. *Health Psychology, 4,* 249–288.

Taylor, S. E. (1983). Adjustment to threatening events. A theory of cognitive adaptation. *American Psychologist, 38,* 1163–1171.

Taylor, S. E. (1989). *Positive illusions: Creative self-deception and the healthy mind.* New York: Basic Books.

Zeidner, M. (1994). Personal and contextual determinants of coping and anxiety in an evaluative situation: A prospective study. *Personality and Individual Differences, 16,* 898–918.

Zeidner, M., & Hammer, A. L. (1992). Coping with missile attack: Resources, strategies, and outcomes. *Journal of Personality, 60,* 709–746.

CHAPTER 7

An Approach to Assessing Daily Coping

LAURA S. PORTER and ARTHUR A. STONE

Since the 1980s, there has been a great deal of research on the role of coping as a potential moderator of the stress-health link. With the burgeoning interest in coping, attention has naturally focused on its measurement, resulting in the development of numerous new assessment devices. The assessment of coping is dependent, to a large degree, on the way in which it is conceptualized. There are two broad approaches to coping: as a trait or style, and as a process (Folkman, Lazarus, Dunkel-Schetter, DeLongis, & Gruen, 1986; Lazarus, 1993). Although the two approaches are usually treated as representing opposing theories, they are not mutually exclusive, and they most likely interact to explain individual differences in coping and stress outcomes (e.g., Bolger, 1990; Carver, Scheier, & Weintraub, 1989; Lazarus, 1993). The trait-oriented approach views coping styles as personality dispositions that transcend the influence of situational context or time, thus emphasizing stability in coping rather than change. In contrast, the process approach conceptualizes coping not as an enduring personality style but as specific thoughts and behaviors that are performed in response to stressful situations and that change over time and situations.

The trend in coping assessment has been from a trait-oriented to a process-oriented approach. Early coping theory, based on psychoanalytic ego psychology, favored a trait-oriented conceptualization and spawned trait assessment measures. Individuals were classified according to their tendency toward certain coping processes, often on the basis of clinical interviews or projective tests from which coping processes were inferred but not studied directly. These measures assessed coping along a single dimension, such as repression-sensitization (Shipley, Horwitz, & Farby, 1978), and included unconscious defenses as well as conscious thoughts and behaviors. Also, coping styles were often judged a priori as to their healthiness in a hierarchical system, with some processes labeled as more adaptive or functional than others (Lazarus, 1984).

More recent developments in coping assessment have been greatly influenced by the transactional theory of stress and coping (Lazarus & Folkman, 1984), which views coping as a process. Transactional theory posits that coping changes over time in response to changing objective demands and subjective appraisals of the person-situation interaction. The efficacy or healthiness of a coping strategy

133

is not determined a priori, but depends on the person, the type of situation, and the time frame and outcome modality studied (Lazarus, 1993).

Empirical questions resulting from the transactional theory require assessments of coping capable of detecting situation-specific effects. Trait-oriented measures assess broad coping styles without providing a description of the specific coping strategies employed in particular situational contexts and are unsuitable for this task (for example, repression-sensitization, Shipley et al., 1978, coping avoiding, Goldstein, 1959, 1973, and monitoring-blunting, Miller, 1987). Moreover, trait measures cannot assess changes in coping during different stages of a stressful event. In response to the new measurement demands raised by transactional theory, several new situation-specific, self-report coping questionnaires have emerged during the past 15 years. Unlike typical trait assessments, these questionnaires rely on self-report and are thus limited to behaviors and cognitions within the subject's awareness. These easily administered nonpsychodynamic self-report questionnaires have quantified coping and opened the way for an enormous increase in coping research.

One of the most frequently used self-report, situation-specific questionnaires is Folkman and Lazarus's (1980) Ways of Coping (WOC) scale, but others have been developed with similar formats (e.g., Billings & Moos, 1981; Carver et al., 1989; Endler & Parker, 1990; Pearlin & Schooler, 1978). Prior to responding to coping items, subjects provide an open-ended description of a problematic situation they encountered recently and also often answer several closed-ended questions about the quality of the event. They then indicate, often with yes/no response options, whether or not they had used particular coping strategies in handling a specific stressful event. Examples of items in the WOC are "Stood my ground and fought for what I wanted," "Made light of the situation; refused to get too serious about it," "Talked to someone about how I was feeling," and "I made a plan of action and followed it."

Unlike the WOC, which was designed for the exclusive purpose of measuring situation-specific coping, two other self-report measures, the COPE (Carver et al., 1989) and the Multidimensional Coping Inventory (MCI; Endler & Parker, 1990), are based on the assumption that there are individual differences in the propensity to use particular coping strategies. Therefore, although similar in format to the WOC, the MCI was designed to measure dispositional coping rather than situation-specific coping, where the COPE can be used to examine both coping dispositions and situation-specific coping tendencies. (A new version of the MCI is also available, the CISS, that measures situation-specific coping; see Schwarzer & Schwarzer, Chapter 6, this volume.) Thus, although the trend in coping research has been away from the trait-oriented approach, this perspective has not been abandoned.

Coping items were developed for these questionnaires primarily from literature reviews and from speculations and clinical observations of coping processes, and are based on theory (e.g., emotion-focused and problem-focused coping). One scale (Pearlin & Schooler, 1978) is based on a broad sampling of items that were generated from interviews of a large, representative sample of subjects about coping responses to problems in various areas. However, there is a trend toward creating new coping scales based on the deductive selection of items from a variety of existing scales. Rationally developed item pools such as these are particularly suspect to questions concerning the adequacy with which they sample the domain of possible coping responses (Stone & Kennedy-Moore, 1991).

Scaled scores are created from item responses that are intended to indicate the degree to which different kinds of coping were used. Individual coping items are classified into coping scales on the basis of theory and/or a factory analysis of the items. The most widely recognized categories of coping efforts, emotion focused and problem focused, correspond to two major functions of coping, the regulation of emotions or distress and managing the problem that is causing the distress, respectively (Folkman, 1984; Folkman et al., 1986; Lazarus, 1993). More detailed taxonomies are also common. For example, Folkman et al. (1986) differentiated between eight categories of coping in a study that employed the WOC: confrontative coping, distancing, self-control, seeking social support, accepting responsibility, escape-avoidance, planful problem-solving, and positive reappraisal.

Along with diversity in the nomenclature and number of identified coping constructs, other variations in the use of and formats of situation-specific coping questionnaires may have implications for the interpretation of their results. Researchers use different time frames in association with these questionnaires. Subjects are often asked to recall a problem that occurred within the past month. There is a large degree of variation between studies, however, with some subjects reporting on an event that occurred anytime in the past year and a half (e.g., McCrae, 1984) and others reporting on an event from the previous week (e.g., Folkman et al., 1986). Subjects have also been asked about the most stressful time ever (e.g., Felton, Revenson, & Hinrichsen, 1984), and how they typically cope with stressful events (e.g., Vingerhoets & Flohr, 1984). When subjects are asked how they typically cope rather than how they actually coped with a specific event, the coping measure becomes traitlike rather than situation-specific. Furthermore, even when subjects are asked to report on a specific event, the time frame is important: The more time that has elapsed, the more people tend toward dispositional accounts of their own behavior (Moore, Sherrod, Liv, & Underwood, 1979; Peterson, 1980), and the more traitlike the assessment becomes.

The diverse studies in which these questionnaires have been used are no doubt at least partly responsible for the variability in their format and use. Despite their widespread appeal, however, the length of these questionnaires limits their application to daily studies; the revised version of the WOC, for instance, consists of 66 items. Although a simple reduction of items could make existing questionnaires suitable for daily use, this procedure runs the risk of eliminating important coping content (Stone, Kennedy-Moore, Newman, Greenberg, & Neale, 1993). For this and other reasons, Stone and Neale (1984) developed a new assessment measure that would adequately sample the domain of coping while remaining succinct enough for subjects to complete on a daily basis without undue exigency. In the remainder of this chapter, we will detail the rationale for devising the daily coping assessment instrument, describe the steps involved in its development, and present the results of a preliminary study that provide support for its validity and its feasibility for daily use. We will then discuss subsequent analyses of the Daily Coping Assessment (DCA) to address coping questions, and we will end with a discussion of the benefits and limitations of a daily approach to coping assessment, along with some potentially fruitful future directions for coping research.

RATIONALE FOR THE STUDY OF DAILY COPING

There are three major rationales for devising an assessment of coping that can be used on a daily basis (Stone & Shiffman, 1993). First, the dynamic processes underlying coping efforts are presumed to shift so rapidly that they can only be captured through frequent assessments. The transactional theory of coping (Lazarus & Folkman, 1984) emphasizes the interactions between environmental events, their appraisal, and efforts to cope with the strains caused by the events. These interactions result in continuous change throughout the coping process. Assessments of coping that condense several days or weeks of coping and changing appraisals into a single measure do not lend themselves well to examining the processes involved in these interactions. A more fine-grained analysis of coping is required to capture the changes that occur and to investigate the impact of daily experience on mood and health. Furthermore, a repeated measures format allows analysis of within-subject variability as well as the opportunity to examine how individuals cope with various kinds of problems rather than a single stressful event. This is particularly important because some of the response biases that could influence between-subject reports are eliminated when individuals serve as their own controls. In essence, the within-subject analyses address this question: Compared with times when an individual uses one coping strategy, what is the effect of that subject using other (or no) coping strategies? This is in contrast to the between-subjects question: What are the differences between subjects who cope one way versus another?

The second rationale for the daily assessment of coping is to minimize the biases and distortions introduced by retrospective recall over longer time periods. Research on autobiographical memory shows that recall, especially over long intervals, leads to the introduction of systematic, predictable bias as well as simple forgetting. Recall relies on heuristic strategies that can systematically bias recall in ways that are particularly problematic for research on stress and coping. For example, emotionally charged or salient events are more likely to be recalled, and are judged to be more frequent, than less salient ones (Strongman & Russell, 1986), and mood-congruent memories are more accessible than mood-incongruent material (Bower, 1981; Donner & Young, 1991; Eisenhower, Mathiowetz, & Morganstein, in press). Because these biases result from the way memory naturally operates rather than from any conscious distortion or deception on the subject's part, they are difficult to remove by subject selection. One way to reduce the bias, and thus enhance the validity of the data, is to reduce the recall interval from a month or a week to a day, as bias tends to increase in proportion to recall interval.

The third rationale for studying coping on a daily basis parallels the recent shift in the field of behavioral medicine to a focus on micro processes that can better detect causal relationships in naturalistic designs. Daily measurements of coping allow for more fine-grained analyses of the relationships between coping and indexes of health, which often change on a day-to-day bass, than would be possible with less frequent assessment intervals. For instance, the number of desirable and undesirable daily events has been associated with the onset of upper respiratory infection (Stone, Reed, & Neale, 1987), and coping strategies have been differentially associated with same-day mood (Stone, Kennedy-Moore, & Neale, 1992) in studies employing a daily design. The frequency of assessment should be determined by the timing of the phenomenon under study, with some outcomes requiring more intensive assessment measures than others (Stone & Shiffman, 1993).

DEVELOPMENT OF THE DAILY COPING ASSESSMENT

The Daily Coping Assessment (DCA) was originally conceptualized as a short checklist with a series of specific coping questions, each representing a different coping style. Its development began with a review of the coping literature and a compilation of a preliminary list of items to represent the domain of coping. These items were taken from existing coping inventories and from the empirical literature on strategies of coping with surgery, illness, natural disasters, pain, threat, and stress. Selection of items was based on a working definition similar to that used by Lazarus and Folkman of coping as "those thoughts and behaviors which are consciously used by an individual to handle or control the effects of anticipating or experiencing a stressful situation." For practical reasons, this definition excluded psychodynamic processes of which a person is not aware (e.g., denial) as well as simple reactions to situations that are not meant to handle the stressful situation or its effects.

The first list contained 87 items that were classified as belonging to one of 10 rationally derived coping modes: distraction, direct action, situation redefinition, acceptance, catharsis, brooding, religion, relaxation, seeking social support, and a miscellaneous "other" category. A preliminary pilot study was conducted to test whether the items selected were understood and checked with reasonable frequency and to assess the internal consistency of the scales. A questionnaire was developed on which subjects described a recent problem and then indicated which items they used "to handle" the problem. Subjects responded well to the questionnaire: The narratives of their problems were generally extensive, they checked an average of 23 of the 87 coping items, and the directions and the task itself did not present any problems. However, internal consistency coefficients were low. Alphas ranged from .47 to .79 with an average of .61. These coefficients, especially some of the lower ones, indicated that the coping items were not uniquely indexing the 10 categories.

Based on these preliminary results and several informal sorting tasks, the 87-item checklist was reduced to 55 items through a process of combining items with similar content. In addition, one category, brooding, was eliminated because its content overlapped completely with the other categories. A second, more methodologically rigorous, study was then conducted with the revised checklist to show that the items properly represented the nine coping modes. Again, alpha coefficients were unacceptable, ranging from .36 to .78 with an average across scales of .57.

At this point, a sorting methodology was employed to further examine how items fit into coping classes. Subjects were instructed in the nine coping categories and their definitions, and they were then asked to sort each of the 55 items into one of the nine categories. The percentage of "correct" sorts, those agreeing with the original categorization, ranged from 56% to 88%. Thus, although there was a good deal of agreement, there was also a substantial amount of disagreement. For example, items that were originally classified as situation redefinition were also viewed by the subjects as direct action and acceptance, and items that had been thought to represent direct action were also classified as seeking social support. Furthermore, in looking at individual items, the researchers noted considerable variability in whether they were sorted into one category or many. These data helped to explain the lack of high internal consistency in the previous study: Subjects were using different coping behaviors or thoughts in different ways or with different intentions.

At this point, the concept of internal consistency was reevaluated as it applies to coping scales. Internal consistency is a statistic defined by the pattern of item endorsement, and it is severely attenuated when only a few items on a scale are checked. Unlike typical trait assessment, the use of a particular coping strategy may be reflected by endorsement of only one or two items on a scale, thereby reducing internal consistency. Furthermore, subjects perceived the intent of the items in different ways, and several items could validly index more than one scale, which also reduced the magnitude of internal-consistency coefficients. For these reasons, traditional scale-construction techniques, that rely on multiple items to index a single concept and on each item being associated with only one scale, were rejected. Instead, an open-ended approach was adopted, using a simple yes-no question about whether a certain mode of coping was used and requesting additional information for positive responses.

The open-ended assessment instrument that was developed was intended to allow subjects to indicate which class of coping they used as well as their specific thoughts and actions. This was accomplished by presenting one-sentence descriptions of the coping strategies and asking subjects to check whether or not they did or thought anything that fit into the categories. Responses were scored dichotomously (0 = no, 1 = yes). A positive response was followed by an open-ended question requesting a description of the particular thought(s) or action(s). The descriptions were used to confirm subjects' correct use of the coping categories; other analyses were based on the dichotomous scores. This open-ended approach allowed subjects themselves to indicate the coping function of their thoughts and actions as opposed to having it specified by the investigators in their analyses. The coping categories and the descriptions of them provided on the form are presented in Table 7.1.

TABLE 7.1   Coping Strategies

Label	Description
Distraction	Diverted attention away from the problem by thinking about other things or engaging in some activity
Situation Redefinition	Tried to see the problem in a different light that made it seem more bearable
Direct Action	Thought about solutions to the problem, gathered information about it, or actually did something to try to solve it
Catharsis	Expressed emotions in response to the problem to reduce tension, anxiety, or frustration
Acceptance	Accepted that the problem had occurred, but that nothing could be done about it
Seeking Social Support	Sought or found emotional support from loved ones, friends, or professionals
Relaxation	Did something with the explicit intent of relaxing
Religion	Sought or found spiritual comfort or support

A study was undertaken to determine if the new coping assessment instrument was feasible for daily use and to provide preliminary validity data on the instrument. Subjects were 60 married couples, the first of a sample of community residents who participated in a longitudinal study of the relationship between life stress and health. Results reported in the following section are based on the complete version of this same dataset. The data collected on a daily basis included a daily life events checklist, a mood scale, a health reporting form, and the coping assessment instrument. Data were analyzed from the first 21 days of reporting. Because no problems were reported on some of those days, the total number of days analyzed was 2,520. The questions pertaining to coping formed several sections. First, the subject was asked to describe "the most bothersome event or issue of the day"; it could be something that had happened in the past, happened that day, or was anticipated as happening in the future. On the next page were eight questions pertaining to the subject's psychological appraisal of the problem and possible responses, which were scored numerically. These are described in Table 7.2.

The next two pages contained questions about how the situation was "handled" (the word coping was intentionally avoided because of the successful connotation it has for many people). Each of the eight coping styles was described, and the subjects indicated whether or not they used that style to handle the problem. If they responded positively, the particular action or thought was to be written in spaces provided under each question. There was no limit on the number of coping styles a subject could check. A ninth category allowed subjects to report coping responses that did not fit into any of the eight categories.

TABLE 7.2   Appraisal Questions and Responses

1. How much control did you have over its occurrence? (Quite a lot/Complete; Some; No control)

2. How desirable or undesirable was it? (Extremely desirable; Moderately desirable; Slightly desirable; Slightly undesirable; Moderately undesirable; Extremely undesirable)

3. How much did it change or stabilize your lifestyle, home situation, work, etc.? (Extremely changing; Moderately changing; Slightly changing; Slightly stabilizing; Moderately stabilizing; Extremely stabilizing)

4. Was it an anticipated problem or situation? (Completely unexpected; Somewhat unexpected; Somewhat anticipated; Completely anticipated)

5. How meaningful was it? (Extremely meaningful; Somewhat meaningful; Slightly meaningful)

6. Was the problem or situation a single event or a more long-lasting chronic situation? (Single event; Long-lasting)

7. Has this problem or situation happened before? (No; Yes; How many times)

8. On a scale from 1 to 100 (where 100 is the death of a friend or family member and 1 is a minor annoyance) how stressful would you rate this problem or situation?

Overall the coping categories were used with reasonable frequency: Distraction was used with 27% of the problems, situation redefinition with 25%, direct action with 46%, catharsis with 25%, acceptance with 30%, seeking social support with 15%, relaxation with 17%, religion with 6%, and other methods of coping with 7%. The average number of coping strategies used for each problem was 1.89. No coping responses were reported for 7% of the problems; 40% of the problems had one reported coping style, 27% had two, 15% had three, and 11% had from four to seven styles.

One way to demonstrate content validity was to evaluate whether subjects' written descriptions of their coping efforts were appropriate to the categories in which they had been placed. The researchers selected a sample of 374 problems, and all the descriptions of specific coping thoughts or actions were transcribed onto index cards and independently sorted into the coping categories by two members of the research team. There was fairly high agreement between how subjects classified their responses and how the researchers classified them, with an overall agreement rate of .69. The agreement rate varied across the eight categories: the highest rates were found for direct action, relaxation, and religion; the lowest ones were found for acceptance and social support. Many of the errors matched those found in the sorting study. In other words, these data provide an important confirmation of item validity and suggest that the subjects were using the questionnaire appropriately.

According to the transactional view of stress and coping (Lazarus & Folkman, 1984), psychological appraisals of the problem should be strongly related to coping efforts, and the demonstration of such relationships provides further support for the use of this instrument. There was a consistent pattern of more use of catharsis, seeking social support, relaxation, and religion with problems with "severe" appraisals (more desirable or undesirable, more changing or stabilizing, or more meaningful). These four coping strategies were reported more frequently with problems with these appraisals in comparison with problems with responses of "slightly" or "somewhat" on the appraisal questions. An opposite pattern of results was found for situation redefinition, which was reported more with slightly desirable or undesirable problems in comparison with the more severe ratings of desirability. Direct action, the most frequently reported coping item, was not reliably associated with any of the appraisal questions. Appraisals of the problems were, then, highly related to many of the coping strategies.

The interrelationships among coping categories provide another measure of the validity of this instrument. Correlations and conditional probabilities were used to explore these associations, and they made conceptual sense. For instance, direct action was negatively correlated with distraction, situation redefinition, and acceptance: When direct action was used, other more emotion-focused strategies were used less often. Conditional probabilities presented these associations in a clearer manner. The probability of a subject using direct action given that he or she had also used distraction was .35, which compared with the overall probability of using direct action, .46, was low. The probabilities indicated that coping with specific problems may be accomplished by using particular combinations of coping styles.

Despite the emphasis on situation-specific rather than traitlike types of coping, the demonstration of some within-subject consistency in coping with a given problem seemed plausible. Because the form was used longitudinally, there was the possibility that a problem could be designated as "the day's most bothersome problem" on several occasions. When this happened, it was possible to assess how consistent individuals were in dealing with the same problem. Twenty-five subjects had at least two problems that were identical. For these subjects, the average number of days reported with similar problems was 6.1, with a minimum of 2 days and a maximum of 11. For each subject's set of similar problem days, the coping scale that was used most often on those days was located. The average proportion of days that the scale was reported was .70. This indicated that when the same problem is coped with on several occasions, subjects tend to be consistent in their manner of coping with it.

Taken together, the results of this study offered preliminary support for the validity of the DCA. The instrument proved to be well suited for daily use, an important consideration when coping is viewed as a dynamic process that demands detailed assessment. Subjects used the form reasonably; they reported moderate frequencies of each coping category and provided written descriptions of their ways of coping that were appropriate to the categories in which they had been placed. The extent of the agreement found between the written-in content and the checked category provided an important confirmation of content validity. The relationships of coping rates to problem appraisals and the interrelationships among coping strategies provided further support for the use of this instrument. As generally predicted by the transactional model of stress and coping, psychological appraisals of the problem were strongly related to coping rates. The interrelationships among the coping strategies were conceptually reasonable, with direct action being negatively correlated with more emotion-focused strategies and positively related to another mode of action, seeking social support. Finally, we found that, when confronted by similar types of problems, individuals tend to be consistent in their use of coping methods.

SUBSEQUENT RESULTS WITH THE DCA

Several questions concerning coping have been examined using the complete version of the dataset we have described. One report looked at end-of-day positive and negative mood as a measure of coping efficacy (for a summary, see Stone, Neale, & Shiffman, 1993). Same-day mood represents only a narrow view of coping efficacy, as it ignores all but the immediate association between coping and mood as well as functioning in other relevant areas such as health and psychological functioning. However, mood is commonly believed to link perceptions of the environment with psychological and health outcomes; it is conveniently measured on a daily basis; and it may be an indicator for subsequent major health changes. Thus, the observed relationship between coping efforts and same-day mood may provide relevant information on the stress-health link.

One portion of the data collected on a daily basis was a modified Nowlis Mood Adjective Checklist (Nowlis & Green, 1957; Stone, 1981). Community-residing married men completed this mood scale each night over a period of 84 days. Their wives also completed the Nowlis based on their observations of their husbands' moods, thereby increasing the reliability of the mood measure (Stone, 1981). We report only those associations where coping related in the same way to both self- and observer-reported mood. Within-subject analyses, controlling for problem stressfulness (which is itself a strong predictor of mood), yielded significant relationships with the coping methods used to handle the most bothersome problem of the day and same-day positive and negative mood (Stone, Kennedy-Moore, & Neale, 1992). Higher levels of negative mood were associated with the use of catharsis and seeking social support, and the use of acceptance was related to lower levels of negative mood. Higher levels of positive mood were associated with the use of distraction, acceptance, and relaxation. These results support the contention that coping efforts have both beneficial and detrimental effects on mood.

Another report examined the way in which individuals cope with daily work problems (Schwartz & Stone, 1993). Although a substantial amount of research has been conducted on the potential consequence of job stress for job satisfaction and physical and mental health, relatively few studies have specifically examined coping at work. Conceptually, coping could moderate the impact of job stressors, although this was not explicitly examined in this study. Therefore, this study contrasted coping with two frequently reported daily work problems, negative interactions with coworkers and heavy workload, to coping with two frequently reported daily nonwork problems, marital tension and personal illness and injury. Analyses controlling for personal attributes such as age, sex, years of education, and income, the type of problem, and problem appraisals yielded the following results. Heavy workload was associated with more use of relaxation and less distraction than negative interactions with coworkers. Marital tension was associated with more distraction and catharsis and less redefinition, direct action, and seeking social support than negative interactions with coworkers; these differences are particularly interesting because both types of problems are interpersonal in nature. Personal illness and injury were associated with more distraction and relaxation and less redefinition and catharsis than the other problems.

This study also examined between-subject relationships between personal attributes and problem appraisal and coping. Women were found to use more distraction, social support, and relaxation than men. Older subjects used more distraction, direct action, seeking social support, and less religion than their younger counterparts. More education was associated with greater use of distraction, seeking social support, and religion, whereas more income had the opposite effects as well as being negatively related to the use of relaxation.

Stone (1987) looked at the effect of the temporal status of the problem on coping efforts. The transactional model of stress and coping states that past and anticipated problems as well as immediate problems are all relevant to the assessment of coping. However, current state-oriented coping assessments typically focus on current or recent events. Thus, little is known about how people deal with past and anticipated problems. It is important to note that the subjects in this study were instructed to indicate what they were currently doing to handle past or anticipated problems, and not how they imagined they would cope with hypothetical problems or how they remembered coping with past problems at the time they were occurring.

As described earlier, subjects were asked to describe "the most bothersome event or issue of the day" and to indicate whether it was something that happened that day, happened in the past, or was anticipated to happen. Of the 16,264 problems reported by these subjects, 14,264 (90%) were current problems, 629 (4%) were past problems, and 979 (6%) were anticipated problems. An ipsative strategy was employed in which each subject's average on all variables for past, present, and anticipated problems was computed. The ipsatized means for appraisal variables and coping modes were subjected to repeated measures analysis of variance with the temporal status of the problems as a repeated measure factor. Results indicated that temporal status does affect coping. Distraction and religion were each used most often with past problems and least often with current problems. Catharsis was used least with anticipated problems and the same amount with past and current problems. There were trends for the most use of acceptance with current problems and social support with past problems. These relationships remained significant after controlling for problem appraisal.

A final analysis, based on 75 couples who completed at least 4 weeks of report-ing, examined gender differences in the use of the nine coping strategies (Porter & Stone, 1995). After controlling for problem content and appraisal, preliminary re-sults indicated that women used more distraction, social support, relaxation, reli-gion, and other coping strategies than men, and that women used a greater number of coping strategies of all types in dealing with their problems. These results are consistent with others (Billings & Moos, 1981; Carver et al., 1989; Endler & Parker, 1990; Pearlin & Schooler, 1978; Ptacek, Smith, & Zanas, 1992; Vinger-hoets & Van Heck, 1990) showing that women use more emotion-focused coping and are more likely to seek social support than men, but they do not support the contention (e.g., Billings & Moos, 1981; Pearlin & Schooler, 1978; Ptacek et al., 1992; Vingerhoets & Van Heck, 1990) that men use more problem-focused coping than women. In addition, these results indicate that there are gender differences in coping that cannot be attributed to differences in the types of problems experi-enced or problem appraisals. In contrast, the majority of previous studies that examined this possibility (e.g., Billings & Moos, 1981; Folkman & Lazarus, 1980; Hamilton & Fagot, 1988) found that gender differences in coping disappeared once problem content was taken into account.

STRENGTHS AND LIMITATIONS OF
THE DCA APPROACH

The DCA supplements and complements other approaches to assessing coping. The questions previously examined illustrate some of strengths offered by the daily, prospective approach over situation-specific measures used retrospec-tively. First, the daily coping approach, characterized by frequent and repeated assessments of coping, can capture the dynamics proposed by the transactional theory of stress and coping, whereas assessments that condense these fluctua-tions over long time periods cannot. By assessing coping on a daily basis, the pre-ceding reports were able to address questions concerning relationships between coping and same-day mood, problem characteristics, and person characteristics that would have not been feasible if coping efforts had been assessed retrospec-tively or on a single occasion. This is particularly salient in the study examining the association between coping efforts and same-day mood; this data would have been difficult to extract from any but a daily, prospective design.

Another strength of repeated daily measurements of coping is that they permit the analysis of within-person as well as between-person effects. It has been estab-lished that there are large individual differences in the magnitude of the relation-ship between stress and negative mood (DeLongis, Folkman, & Lazarus, 1988; Stone, 1981). Similarly, there are likely to be individual differences in the associ-ation between coping efforts and outcome variables; what works well for one person does not necessarily work well for all. Therefore, questions concerning coping efficacy should ideally be addressed using a within-subject design. For ex-ample, the associations between coping and mood reported by Stone, Kennedy-Moore, Newman, et al. (1992) may well have been masked by between-person effects had they not been removed. This is not to say that the between-subjects effects should be ignored; the strength of this methodology is that the repeated measurements allow for the examination of potential environmental and personality correlates of individual differences in the coping-outcome relationships, while simultaneously providing information on the within-subject relationships.

The repeated measures daily design is also advantageous for examining the association between coping efforts and problem characteristics. Just as with the coping-outcome relationship, there are likely to be large individual differences in the relationship between coping and problem characteristics that will be missed if each subject reports on only one stressful encounter. Interpretations of results that do not include within-subject effects or are based on single time point assessments will be misleading, as the coping-problem associations will confound between- and within-subject effects. Schwartz and Stone (1993) utilized the benefits of the repeated measures design in examining the question of how people cope with stressful work-related events versus nonwork events by running within-subject analyses that controlled for person characteristics and subsequently looking at the relationships between personal attributes and coping.

Another important strength of the daily approach to coping assessment is that reducing the intervals in which subjects are asked to recall their coping efforts reduces the biases and distortions associated with retrospective reporting. Aside from the biases resulting from the normal operation of autobiographical memory, reports of coping efforts tend to become more traitlike as the time interval of assessment increases. It is likely that subjects' reports of their typical coping responses, as assessed by trait-oriented coping measures, do not correspond to what they actually do when faced with a stressful encounter (Lazarus, 1993). With retrospective situation-specific questionnaires, the more time that has elapsed between the events the subjects report on and the time of assessment, the more subjects will tend toward dispositional rather than actual accounts of their behavior (Moore et al., 1979; Peterson, 1980). Therefore, shorter time intervals are desirable in that they both reduce the biases associated with retrospective recall and produce the most valid data concerning situation-specific coping.

The final strength we mention pertains to a specific feature of the DCA as opposed to daily coping assessments in general. The features previously mentioned apply to most methods of assessing coping, including, for instance, daily administration of the WOC. In developing the DCA, we discovered several potential problems with the WOC-like assessments that ultimately results in our using the dichotomous questionnaire approach for the DCA. To our minds, the main strength is that the intention-oriented approach of the DCA—having the subject indicate the intention behind coping thoughts and actions—does not limit our understanding of coping the way WOC-type assessments do. Any thought or action may be assigned to any of the coping categories based on how the subject perceives the action. This is an important conceptual difference between the DCA and other coping assessments.

Despite our enthusiasm for the daily approach to coping assessment, it does have several limitations. First, assessing coping at the end of the day results in a narrow view of the coping process; it fails to capture the way stress is experienced throughout the day (Stone & Shiffman, 1993). Subjects are asked to summarize the day's experience and their coping efforts in the face of inevitable within-day variability, and they are not given any guidelines for doing so. Thus, they must make implicit decisions on how to integrate these variations. They may simply count up the number of coping strategies they used to handle a problem, or the amount of time spent in one strategy, or the amount of effort expended in executing a strategy. These decisions will vary from subject to subject, and this information is not available to the investigators.

A related concern is recall accuracy. Although the shorter recall interval minimizes recall biases and distortions, it does not eliminate them. A shorter recall interval does not guarantee easy accurate recall, and there are still many sources of potential bias. For instance, because assessments take place on a daily basis, we may be asking subjects to recall more minor events, making the recall task equally difficult and bias-prone. Furthermore, end-of-the-day reports may bias recall toward the most recent events, or the most salient events of the day, or subjects may recall coping efforts for resolved but not unresolved problems. This issue is addressed in the discussion of experience sampling methodology in the following section.

Although the problem is not particular to daily approaches to coping, questionnaire approaches—daily or longer retrospective periods—are limited to subjects' awareness of their thoughts and actions. This automatically excludes the measurement of certain types of coping, such as denial, that may be conceptually important. Furthermore, these measures rely on self-report, leading to potential problems of subject biases in both interpretation and response. It is possible that subjects interpret the task or the questionnaire items differently, leading to some of the problems noted earlier, including differences in the way events and coping efforts are recalled and/or summarized. Future studies should compare subject self-reports with other reports, such as the observations of a spouse or a trained observer, or results from experimental studies measuring coping.

FUTURE DIRECTIONS

Many questions remain unanswered concerning the role of coping as a moderator in the stress-health link, and many of these have not been adequately addressed by current assessment techniques. We have two suggestions for future directions in coping assessment that may more fully capture the experience and impact of stress and coping. The first is the modification of existing daily coping assessment measures to examine episodes of stress and coping. The second is to turn to within-day methods that address some of the limitations of daily assessment that we have discussed.

A potentially exciting modification of daily coping assessments involves examining episodes of stress and coping to more fully capture the coping process. Stressors and subsequent coping efforts have natural durations that do not generally correspond to assessment periods. Capturing the natural course of these episodes and describing their topographies with regard to characteristics such as their duration, their intensity, and the degree to which the subject focused on the eliciting event, could lead to insights concerning the psychological experience of the event and the coping efforts used to handle it. The concept of affective episodes has recently received attention (Frijda, Mesquita, Sonnemans, & Van Goozen, 1991), as have episodes of symptoms (Stone, Porter, & Neale, 1993), and this proposal would extend the concept to coping episodes.

One difficulty with this proposal is that episodes of stress and coping are not clearly defined, and there are no explicit rules concerning the criteria that should be used to define them. Investigators will have to make decisions concerning criteria based on the phenomena under study and the hypotheses being tested. A possible method of defining episodes with daily coping assessments would be to track specific problems across days. The investigator could focus on several problems that occurred within one day, assessing their frequency, duration, and appraisal. Daily assessment of each problem would then continue until the subject no longer feels that the problem is significant. Although this could be accomplished with paper-and-pencil questionnaires, telephone interviews may be particularly well suited for this task (Stone, Kessler, & Haythornthwaite, 1991) if they utilized a branching, programlike scheme that would diminish subject burden.

An additional modification of daily coping assessments that we suggest pertains specifically to the DCA, and that is the division of the coping item "Direct Action" into two items. As defined in the DCA, Direct Action consists of both thinking about solutions to the problem and gathering information about it *and* doing something to solve the problem. Ideally, these should be two distinct items, as in the COPE (Carver et al., 1989), which includes the items "Active Coping" (the process of taking active steps to solve the problem) and "Planning" (thinking about how to handle the problem). Both activities are problem focused, but they are conceptually distinct and should be assessed separately.

Another possibility for future directions in coping assessment that addresses some of the limitations of the daily approach is to further intensify the assessment. A highly intensive approach that is gaining prominence is Experience Sampling Method (ESM; see DeVries, 1992). ESM attempts to capture subjects' experiences by randomly sampling their immediate state many times throughout the day. Subjects typically carry beepers or programmable watches that prompt them at random intervals to complete assessments about their current thoughts, feelings, and activities. We have embarked on a study that uses handheld computers to both prompt subjects and store data. Information on coping collected in this way will be used to validate the DCA.

Momentary assessment of coping eliminates virtually all retrospective recall biases as well as the necessity for subjects to summarize the variety of experiences that occur throughout the day. However, the sampling approach means that short-lived stressors occurring between prompts may be missed entirely. The intensiveness of the assessment also makes it intrusive and often reactive; the burden to subjects can lead to noncompliance and attrition, and the length of the observation must be limited. Highly intensive assessment strategies such as ESM are also extremely expensive to implement. When well conducted, however, these studies can provide an incredibly rich database. Although both momentary assessment and the enhancement of daily coping assessments have limitations of their own and need to be more fully explored and developed, these options hold considerable potential for the study of stress and coping.

REFERENCES

Billings, A., & Moos, R. (1981). The role of coping responses and social resources in attenuating the stress of life events. *Journal of Behavioral Medicine, 4,* 139–157.

Bolger, N. (1990). Coping as a personality process: A prospective study. *Journal of Personality and Social Psychology, 59*(3), 525–537.

Bower, G. (1981). Mood and memory. *American Psychologist, 36,* 129–148.

Carver, C. S., Scheier, M. F., & Weintraub, J. K. (1989). Assessing coping strategies: A theoretically based approach. *Journal of Personality and Social Psychology, 56*(2), 267–283.

DeLongis, A., Folkman, S., & Lazarus, R. (1988). The impact of daily stress on health and mood: Psychological and social resources as mediators. *Journal of Personality and Social Psychology, 54,* 486–495.

DeVries, M. (1992). *The experience of psychopathology.* Cambridge, England: Cambridge University Press.

Donner, E., & Young, M. (1991, October). *Mood variability and accuracy of recall for depression.* Paper presented at the annual meeting of the Society for Research in Psychopathology, Cambridge, MA.

Eisenhower, D., Mathiowetz, N., & Morganstein, D. (in press). Recall error: Sources and bias reduction techniques. In P. Beimer, R. Groves, L. M. N. Lyberg, & S. Sudman (Eds.), *Measurement error in surveys.* New York: Wiley.

Endler, N., & Parker, J. (1990). Multidimensional assessment of coping: A critical evaluation. *Journal of Personality and Social Psychology, 58*(5), 844–854.

Felton, B., Revenson, T., & Hinrichsen, G. (1984). Stress and coping in the explanation of psychological adjustment among chronically ill adults. *Social Science and Medicine, 18*(10), 889–898.

Folkman, S. (1984). Personal control and stress and coping processes: A theoretical analysis. *Journal of Personality and Social Psychology, 46*(4), 839–852.

Folkman, S., & Lazarus, R. S. (1980). An analysis of coping in a middle-aged community sample. *Journal of Health and Social Behavior, 21,* 219–239.

Folkman, S., Lazarus, R. S., Dunkel-Schetter, C., DeLongis, A., & Gruen, R. (1986). The dynamics of a stressful encounter: Cognitive appraisal, coping, and encounter outcomes. *Journal of Personality and Social Psychology, 50,* 992–1003.

Frijda, N., Mesquita, B., Sonnemans, J., & Van Goozen, S. (1991). The duration of affective phenomena or emotions, sentiments and passions. In K. Strongman (Ed.), *International review of studies on emotion* (pp. 187–225). New York: Wiley.

Goldstein, M. (1959). The relationship between coping and avoiding behavior and response to fear-arousing propaganda. *Journal of Abnormal and Social Psychology, 58,* 247–252.

Goldstein, M. (1973). Individual differences in response to stress. *American Journal of Community Psychology, 1,* 113–137.

Hamilton, S., & Fagot, B. (1988). Chronic stress and coping styles: A comparison of male and female undergraduates. *Journal of Personality and Social Psychology, 55*(5), 819–823.

Lazarus, R. S. (1984). On the primacy of cognition. *American Psychologist, 59,* 124–129.

Lazarus, R. S. (1993). Coping theory and research: Past, present, and future. *Psychosomatic Medicine, 55,* 234–247.

Lazarus, R. S., & Folkman, S. (1984). *Stress, appraisal and coping.* New York: Springer.

McCrae, R. (1984). Situational determinants of coping responses: Loss, threat, and challenge. *Journal of Personality and Social Psychology, 46,* 919–928.

Miller, S. (1987). Monitoring and blunting: Validation of a questionnaire to assess styles of information seeking under threat. *Journal of Personality and Social Psychology, 52,* 345–353.

Moore, B., Sherrod, D., Liv, T., & Underwood, B. (1979). The dispositional shift in attribution over time. *Journal of Experimental Social Psychology, 15,* 553–569.

Nowlis, V., & Green, R. (1957). *The experimental analysis of mood.* [Tech. Rep., Office of Naval Research: Contract No. Nonr-668(12)]. Washington, DC: Office of Naval Research.

Pearlin, L., & Schooler, C. (1978, March). The structure of coping. *Journal of Health and Social Behavior, 19,* 2–21.

Peterson, C. (1980). Memory and the "dispositional shift." *Social Psychology Quarterly, 43,* 372–380.

Porter, L., & Stone, A. (1995). Are there really gender differences in coping?: A reconstruction of previous data and results from a daily study. *Journal of Social and Clinical Psychology, 14*(2).

Ptacek, J., Smith, R., & Zanas, J. (1992). Gender, appraisal, and coping: A longitudinal analysis. *Journal of Personality, 60*(4), 747–770.

Schwartz, J., & Stone, A. (1993). Coping with daily work problems: Contributions of problem content, appraisal, and person factors. *Work and Stress, 7*(1), 47–62.

Shipley, R. H., Horwitz, B., & Farby, J. E. (1978). Preparation for a stressful medical procedure: Effect of amount of stimulus preexposure and coping style. *Journal of Consulting and Clinical Psychology, 46,* 499–507.

Stone, A. (1981). The association between perception of daily experiences and self- and spouse-related mood. *Journal of Research in Personality, 15,* 510–522.

Stone, A. (1987). *Present, past, and anticipated problems: Appraisals and coping.* Unpublished manuscript.

Stone, A., & Kennedy-Moore, E. (1991). Assessed situational coping: Potential conceptual and methodological issues. H. Friedman (Ed.), *Hostility, coping, and health* (pp. 203–214). Washington, DC: American Psychological Association.

Stone, A., Kennedy-Moore, E., & Neale, J. (1992). *Daily coping efforts predict daily mood.* Unpublished manuscript, State University of New York at Stony Brook.

Stone, A., Kennedy-Moore, E., Newman, M., Greenberg, M., & Neale, J. (1992). Conceptual and methodological issues in current coping assessments. B. Carpenter (Ed.), *Personal coping: Theory, research, and application.* New York: Praeger.

Stone, A., Kessler, R., & Haythornthwaite, J. (1991). Measuring daily events and experiences: Decisions for the researcher. *Journal of Personality, 59*(3), 575–607.

Stone, A., & Neale, J. (1984). New measure of daily coping: Development and preliminary results. *Journal of Personality and Social Psychology, 46*(4), 892–906.

Stone, A., Neale, J., & Shiffman, S. (1993). How mood relates to stress and coping: A daily perspective. *Annals of Behavioral Medicine, 15,* 8–16.

Stone, A., Porter, L., & Neale, J. (1993). Daily events and mood prior to the onset of respiratory illness episodes: A nonreplication of the 3–5 day "desirability dip." *British Journal of Psychology, 66,* 383–393.

Stone, A., Reed, B., & Neale, J. (1987). Changes in daily event frequency precede episodes of physical symptoms. *Journal of Human Stress, 13*(2), 70–74.

Stone, A., & Shiffman, S. (1993). Reflections on the intensive measurement of stress, coping, and mood, with an emphasis on daily measures. *Psychology and Health, 7,* 115–129.

Strongman, K., & Russell, P. (1986). Salience of emotion in recall. *Bulletin of the Psychonomic Society, 24,* 25–27.

Vingerhoets, A., & Flohr, P. (1984). Type A behaviors and self-reports of coping preferences. *British Journal of Medical Psychology, 57,* 15–21.

Vingerhoets, A., & Van Heck, G. (1990). Gender, coping and psychosomatic symptoms. *Psychological Medicine, 20,* 125–135.

CHAPTER 8

Daily Processes in Coping with Chronic Pain: Methods and Analytic Strategies

HOWARD TENNEN and GLENN AFFLECK

Models of stress and coping are being used increasingly to explain individual differences in adaptation to chronic pain (Jensen, Turner, Romano, & Karoly, 1991). Jensen et al. (1991) conclude their comprehensive review of this literature with three concerns and corresponding recommendations. First, they note that although our theoretical models posit causal relations among stress, coping, and adaptation (e.g., Lazarus & Folkman, 1984), the correlational nature of most empirical work in this area has been unsuitable to test causal relations. They call for research designs better suited to address causal processes. Jensen et al. also remind us that whereas theory (e.g., Wills, 1981) elucidates factors that might moderate the pain experience, research has not aggressively pursued tests of moderational models. They urge the field to move in this direction. Finally, Jensen et al. note that single-subject designs are rare, and call for such designs because they are "uniquely suited to understanding an individual's coping process over time" (p. 280). Our goal in this chapter is to describe an approach to the study of stress and coping that addresses each of Jensen et al.'s concerns: It strengthens our causal inferences, evaluates theoretically relevant moderators, and examines individuals over time. It is an *idiographic-nomothetic* method.

The authors are listed in reverse alphabetical order and share equal responsibility for this chapter. The study described in this chapter was funded by National Institute of Arthritis, Musculoskeltal, and Skin Diseases Grant #AR-20621. We wish to express our gratitude to Susan Urrows and Pamela Higgins for their many contributions to this study; to Micha Abeles, Edward Feinglass, Lisa Fitzgerald, Joseph Korn, Ann Parke, Steven Padula, Naomi Rothfield, Ethan Weiner, and Robert Wong for referring their patients; to Arthur Stone for his consultation on the design of the study; to Debra Begin for her preparation of the data for analysis; and to the participants for their extraordinary commitment.

AN IDIOGRAPHIC-NOMOTHETIC METHOD FOR STRESS AND COPING RESEARCH

The dominant tradition in behavioral research is the nomothetic approach. This asks whether there are lawful relations among variables across individuals. The overall success of this approach to psychological inquiry has had an untoward effect: Alternative methods have been eschewed or at least shown benign neglect. One such method, the idiographic approach, is particularly relevant to the mission of this volume. Whereas the nomothetic approach asks whether variables relate *across* individuals, the idiographic approach examines relations among variables *within* an individual. Thus, the individual is the unit of analysis, and the focus is on the relations of variables across situations or over time in that individual's life. The original distinction between nomothetic and idiographic research was made by Gordon Allport (1937) as part of his vision for the science of personality. Allport believed that to best examine how personality expresses itself over time or across situations, individuals need to be studied as separate entities.

The applicability of the idiographic method to current conceptions of coping turns on its potential to examine unfolding processes. Lazarus and Folkman (1984), who offer the most widely accepted definition of coping, describe it as "constantly changing cognitive and behavioral efforts to manage specific external and/or internal demands . . ." (p. 141). Their call for microanalytic, process-oriented research to capture these changing efforts has not been well heeded. As we hope to demonstrate, the idiographic analysis of coping efforts captures the change Lazarus and Folkman describe as well as the traitlike qualities of coping, which they believe have not been well demonstrated.

In this chapter, we argue for the benefits of an approach to the study of coping that combines the strengths of the idiographic and nomothetic traditions. This idiographic-nomothetic approach to coping research requires investigators to ask: *Are there relations among coping-relevant variables within individuals over time that generalize across individuals or that relate to differences between individuals?* Answering this question requires that we first examine relations among variables over time for each individual we study. We must then return to the population level in two ways: by determining if the within-person relations generalize across persons, and by discerning how they relate to differences between individuals. As we will demonstrate, relating within-person associations to between-persons differences yields rich insights into the process of coping with chronic pain. The virtues of the idiographic-nomothetic approach were first advanced by Epstein (1983) and have been applied in Larsen's (e.g., Larsen & Kasimatis, 1991) investigations of daily emotions and physical symptoms.

Unique Advantages of Idiographic Assessment

We believe that the virtues of the idiographic-nomothetic method are unique because the questions one can address cannot be answered nor can the information derived be obtained by more traditional nomothetic designs and measurement strategies. Succinctly stated, a time-intensive idiographic design will allow the investigator to (a) capture proximal stressors and coping efforts closer to their actual occurrence; (b) track change in rapidly fluctuating processes, such as mood and pain, closer to their "real-time" moments of change; and (c) minimize recall error associated with most measurement approaches to stress and coping.

Tracking individuals intensively offers the best chance to study proximal stressors in their own right, as they influence health and well being, and as a consequence of major life events. An alternative to intensive individual tracking is to ask research participants to summarize daily stressful experiences during the prior week or month. The Hassles Scale (Kanner, Coyne, Schaefer, & Lazarus, 1981) was designed to obtain such summaries. Indeed, daily hassles have been linked to emotional distress among individuals with fibromyalgia, a musculoskeletal pain syndrome with no known organic cause (Dailey, Bishop, Russell, & Fletcher, 1990), to the use of less adaptive coping strategies among individuals with rheumatoid arthritis (Beckham, Keefe, Caldwell, & Roodman, 1991), and to greater disease activity among people with severe inflammatory bowel disease (Garrett, Brantley, Jones, & McKnight, 1991; cf. Bradley, Haile, & Jaworski, 1992). But recall is likely to be far from perfect, and cause-effect relations can easily be obscured by summary measures.

Coping efforts are also best measured close to when they occur. In most studies, including our own prior work (Affleck, Tennen, & Rowe, 1991; Stanton, Tennen, Affleck, & Mendola, 1992), research participants complete a retrospective questionnaire summarizing their coping activities. Although widely used measures of coping such as the Ways of Coping scale (Folkman & Lazarus, 1985) and the COPE (Carver, Scheier, & Weintraub, 1989) as well as pain-specific coping inventories such as the Coping Strategies Questionnaire (Rosensteil & Keefe, 1983) and the Vanderbilt Pain Management Inventory (Brown & Nicassio, 1987) differ in their conceptual underpinnings and the aspects of coping they assess (see Schwarzer & Schwarzer, Chapter 6, this volume for a review and critique of some of these measures), each measures coping efforts retrospectively. If coping is truly a process, it needs to be studied as such. Intensive assessment of individuals over time provides the opportunity to examine day-by-day changes in this process.

A second unique advantage of idiographic assessment is that it allows investigators to measure closer to *real time* those outcomes that are closely linked to coping: mood, somatic complaints, and most important to our own work, pain intensity among people with a chronic pain disorder. If we believe that emotional and physical well-being change in response to coping efforts, then both coping and the adaptational outcomes they are thought to influence must be measured near to the time they occur.

A third advantage of idiographic assessment is that it should minimize random and systematic error in recall. A legitimate concern with retrospective appraisals is an individual's ability to accurately recall any aspect of a stressful encounter. Intensive, day-by-day prospective assessment should provide intrinsically superior data to that obtained through recall of the same time period. Although intuitively appealing, this argument needs to be put to empirical test. As an initial test of this prediction, we asked respondents in a daily prospective study of coping with rheumatoid arthritis (RA) pain to provide a 30-day summary of their pain, mood, coping efforts and daily events. We took their daily ratings as a benchmark and then made prospective—retrospective comparisons (Larsen, 1992).

The comparison of retrospective pain recall with average daily pain calculated from participants' prospective reports supported our suspicions. Although pain intensity from ongoing reports correlated highly with pain intensity recalled, participants as a group remembered having significantly more pain than they actually "encoded" day-to-day. This finding, which is consistent with other research on chronic pain recall bias (Erskine, Morley, & Pearce, 1990), supports our argument that retrospective accounts of fluctuating processes are liable to be inaccurate.

We also compared participants' recollection of the number of days they had used each of seven pain coping strategies appearing on a modified version of the Daily Coping Assessment (DCA; see Porter & Stone, Chapter 7, this volume) with the tally of strategies taken from their daily reports over the same period. Again, there were high correlations between the retrospective and prospective versions of each coping variable. The prospective data, however, yielded a significantly richer repertoire of pain coping than the retrospective data made apparent. That is, the average person reported using more *forms* of coping from day to day than he or she recalled having ever used in the past month. Not surprisingly, strategies that someone had used relatively rarely (less than 5 days that month) were most likely to be missed in the coping recollection task.

More important than inaccuracy per se is the *source* of the error. We need to be concerned not only with random error, but especially with *systematic* error in the recall of pain, coping, and events. Individuals who differ on other study variables (or worse, in key ways not measured) may report differentially accurate data or use different cognitive heuristics to assist their recall (Linton, 1991; Neisser, 1991; Affleck, Tennen, Urrows, & Higgins, 1992). In this vein, Larsen (1992) demonstrated that neuroticism predicts not only day-to-day reports of illness symptoms, but also the subsequent accuracy with which these symptoms are later recalled. An idiographic approach, which requires prospective assessment reduces potential recall bias.

AN IDIOGRAPHIC-NOMOTHETIC ANALYSIS OF COPING WITH RHEUMATOID ARTHRITIS PAIN

In the remainder of this chapter, we will demonstrate insights available through idiographic-nomothetic analysis by using as an example a study we have carried out with individuals who have chronic pain from rheumatoid arthritis, a severe and disabling autoimmune disease. Pain from inflamed and eroded joints is the most significant symptom of RA. Individuals with RA call their pain a major stressor in their lives (Affleck, Pfeiffer, Tennen, & Fifield, 1988), which strongly

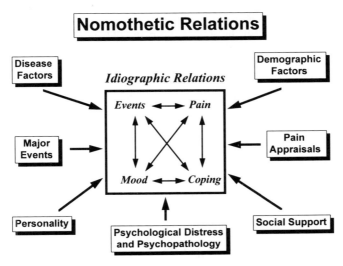

Figure 8.1   A conceptualization of the idiographic-nomothetic approach to coping with rheumatoid arthritis pain.

influences their emotional and physical functioning (Brown, Nicassio, & Wallston, 1989; Peck, Smith, Ward, & Milano, 1989). RA pain appears to be an appropriate context for the study of coping processes.

Figure 8.1 both depicts an idiographic-nomothetic framework that we adopted in our daily study of coping with RA pain and shows our game plan for the remainder of this chapter. At the core of the study are idiographic (within-person) relations among prospectively measured daily events, daily mood, daily pain intensity, and daily ways of coping with pain. After determining whether these within-person relations generalize across persons, we wished to identify those between-persons factors that may explain individual differences in the within-person relations.

Our selection of variables that might moderate within-person relations, like that of more traditional studies of pain coping, was guided by theory to be relevant to the coping process. Nonetheless, it is this aspect of our design and of the idiographic-nomothetic paradigm that remains least satisfying. The problem is in selecting relevant and nonredundant variables (see Katz et al., Chapter 12, this volume). At this point in the coping literature, the selection of between-persons moderators tends to follow the call of Claude Raines in *Casablanca* to "round up the usual suspects." For our study, we selected these "suspects":

- *Demographic Factors* included age, SES, gender, and duration of illness.
- *Disease Activity* was measured approximately every two weeks via a standard clinical examination of joint swelling and erythrocyte sedimentation

rate (ESR), a nonspecific marker of inflammation. Owing to the high autocorrelations of swelling scores and ESRs across exams and the moderate correlation between swelling and ESR, a composite measure of disease activity was computed by summing their standardized scores.

- *Major Life Events* during the 6 months prior to entering the study were assessed with the Life Experiences Survey (LES; Sarason, Johnson, & Siegel, 1978). Forty-five events, excluding "major personal illness or injury" and "change in sleeping patterns" (which may reflect symptom exacerbation) were presented. The negative life change score, which is most likely to relate to health and well-being and which is most relevant to the theme of this volume, was computed.

- *Availability of Social Support* was measured with the Quality of Social Support Scale (QSSS) designed for use by RA patients (Goodenow, Reisine, & Grady, 1990). This scale evaluates perceived availability of support in areas of information, task assistance, opportunity for confiding, physical affection, and personal affirmation.

- *Psychological Distress and Psychopathology* were assessed by the Center for Epidemiological Studies-Depression questionnaire (Radloff, 1977) and by the Diagnostic Interview Schedule (Robins, Helzer, Cottler, & Goldring, 1989), which yielded both current and life-time diagnoses of depression and anxiety disorders.

- Major *personality* variables were neuroticism and optimism. Neuroticism was measured by the *NEO Personality Inventory* (Costa & McCrae, 1985). The facets of neuroticism measured by this scale include dispositional manifestations of depression, anxiety, hostility, self-consciousness, impulsiveness, and vulnerability. Dispositional optimism was measured by the Life Orientation Test (Scheier & Carver, 1985).

- *Pain appraisals* tapping expressions of primary and secondary control, as in perceiving control over pain flares and finding benefits in the chronic pain experience (Rothbaum, Weisz, & Snyder, 1982), were measured by the Inventory of Primary and Secondary Control Beliefs questionnaire (Mendola, 1990; Tennen, Affleck, Urrows, Higgins, & Mendola, 1992).

Several of the selected moderators have been linked in previous research to the magnitude and even the direction of within-person associations between stressful daily events and negative mood (Bolger & Schilling, 1991; Caspi, Bolger, & Eckenrode, 1987; DeLongis, Folkman, & Lazarus, 1988). Although reassuring, the risk associated with rounding up these "usual suspects" is that they may provide only what was already suspected. Fortunately, as we will describe later in this chapter, some of the moderators we selected were uniquely related to the temporal patterning of pain and the sequencing of event-pain relations. But we urge investigators planning idiographic-nomothetic investigations of the coping process to take great care in their selection of moderators of within-person relations.

Description of the Study

Participants in this study were 75 patients diagnosed with classical or definite rheumatoid arthritis. They were recruited from our medical school's faculty practice and from community practices in the same geographic area. As in most studies of RA, participants were mostly white (95%), middle-aged (mean age of 53), middle class, and female (71%). Obtaining representative samples for the study of stress and coping processes has typically not been high on investigators' agendas. This is a problem that needs our full attention.

The study began with the measurement of the between-subject variables we described. Then, for 75 consecutive days, these patients, in waves of eight, completed a structured diary within one hour of bedtime. Completed diaries were returned the next morning through the mail. Although participants were provided a modest financial incentive for timely and complete diaries, we doubt that incentives alone produced the impressive 99.6% compliance rate, with complete data on 5,600 of 5,625 recording days. In fact, we found that many participants had been keeping informal diaries for years in an attempt to understand the waxing and waning of their RA pain.

The main portion of the diary was an assessment of daily events with Stone and Neale's (1982) Daily Life Experience checklist (Stone, Kessler, & Haythornth-waite, 1991; DLE; Stone, Reed, & Neale, 1987). The DLE, designed specifically for use in daily prospective studies, contains 78 items classified under five major activities: *work-related, leisure, activities with family and friends, financial,* and *other activities and happenings.* Each event checked as having occurred was rated for its desirability or undesirability. In addition to the DLE, participants completed the Daily Coping Assessment (see Porter & Stone, Chapter 7, this volume), which was adapted to the pain experience. We selected the DCA rather than existing measures of pain coping such as the Coping Strategies Questionnaire (Rosensteil & Keefe, 1983) because the DCA was designed specifically for daily use. We measured mood each day with an abbreviated version of the Profile of Mood States (POMS-B; Lorr & McNair, 1982). Eighteen adjectives—three each assessing negative mood states of depression, anxiety and hostility and three each assessing the bipolar opposites of elation, calmness, and agreeableness—were used to rate average mood each day, on scales from 0 = "very much unlike this" to 3 = "very much like this." These items were selected because of their high item-total correlations for their respective subscales in a previous study of RA patients (Affleck et al., 1988).

Describing Chronic Pain Processes: Back to Basics

Although the focus of this volume is coping, the study of coping efforts requires an understanding of just what it is that requires coping. Put another way, we seem to know more about coping than we know about the targets of coping. Our own nomothetic studies of coping with threatening medical events mirrors the literature's neglect to coping targets. For example, although we are able to document the coping strategies of women with impaired fertility (Stanton et al., 1992), we know little about what aspects of infertility require coping. Is it the threat of not achieving a cherished goal? The role change that emerges as one's friends become pregnant and have children? Or the intrusive nature of the treatment? Perhaps all these aspects of infertility require coping efforts, with different strategies best applied to each aspect at different times as this threatening encounter unfolds.

A distinct advantage of examining a phenomenon intensively over time is that it allows us to look at individual differences in the *variability* of that which our research participants are coping (in this case pain) as well as how it is patterned over time (its *temporal configuration*). Investigators of stress and coping are used to examining mean differences. But an idiographic analysis of daily events and coping with chronic pain provides the unique opportunity to document individual differences in pain and coping *patterns* at the descriptive level. This descriptive analysis, though not conceptually "sexy," is critical to any adequate definition of a phenomenon including pain and the nature of coping itself. We will describe two important yet overlooked characteristics of pain over time: trending and autocorrelation. We will then describe characteristics of pain coping over 75 days.

Pain Patterns over Time: Trending

Our first step toward this goal was to examine the ebb and flow of daily pain and to document individual differences in the day-to-day experience of chronic pain in RA (Affleck, Tennen, Urrows, & Higgins, 1991). One indicator of daily joint pain intensity was drawn from the Rapid Assessment of Disease Activity in Rheumatology (RADAR; Mason et al., 1992). Participants made separate ratings for each of 20 joints or joint groups (from 0 = no pain or tenderness to 3 = severe pain or tenderness), which were then summed. Pain ratings from the RADAR correlate significantly with physicians' independent assessments of joint pain (Mason & Meenan, 1983).

Figure 8.2 depicts the more common pain series reported over the 75 days of our study. Some of these patterns are not surprising. For example, we see differences in the general level of pain: Some participants reported pain of high intensity with little variability, whereas others reported low intensity pain with little variation. We also found pain series demonstrating variable intensity pain, and others that might best be described as skewed or episodic pain.

We were somewhat surprised, however, by the high frequency of *trending* pain, and we are entertaining two hypotheses about these trends. One is that we have tapped into a far broader secular trend that began before we began our measurements and that may continue long after participation in our study. In other words, we may be capturing a 75-day slice of a broader cycle. In fact, both patients and clinicians describe this disease as having broad cycles of flaring and remitting activity.

Our second hypothesis is that these trends reflect measurement reactivity. This hypothesis is supported by participants' own reflections. After subjects

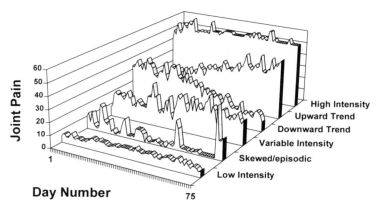

Figure 8.2   Common pain patterns over 75 days.

completed their last diary entry, we conducted a detailed debriefing interview, asking each participant about problems in daily recording and how he or she experienced the entire self-monitoring procedure. We learned that some patients, through the process of keeping track of pain, events, and their coping efforts, were detecting contingencies. These individuals began to assess the efficacy of their coping strategies by recording these strategies at the end of each day. One might reasonably argue that there was some cognitive or behavioral response to the monitoring task that in itself produced a downward trend in pain.

As Figure 8.2 demonstrates, however, there were also those who showed upward trends in pain across the 75 days. Could daily measurement have a pain-reducing effect among some patients yet potentiate pain for others? We believe so. In fact, we suspect that just as downward trends in pain may reflect changed coping strategies in response to daily monitoring, so upward trends may result from an untoward effect of daily monitoring on preferred coping strategies. During debriefing, some patients said that they found monitoring extremely aversive precisely because it forced them to keep track of their pain. These were individuals who had found that their most effective coping strategy was distraction (Endler & Parker, 1990a, 1990b). Dispositionally, they might be what Miller (1987, 1992) calls "blunters" (see Schwarzer & Schwarzer, Chapter 6, this volume). By forcing them to focus on their pain, we may have interfered with a preferred coping strategy, which in turn increased pain over time.

For now, our hypotheses regarding pain trending, coping, and daily monitoring are no more than informed speculation. Yet we hope investigators will follow this speculation to testable predictions. Linear trends in adaptational outcomes have not been discussed in the coping literature. We need to know far more about these trends because we have to take them into account when we examine idiographic connections among daily process variables including daily coping. We will be returning to this issue shortly.

Pain Patterns over Time: Autocorrelation and Cyclycity

In addition to examining trends in our pain series, we investigated autocorrelation within the pain data. Autocorrelation refers to the serial correlation, day to day, of a variable measured repeatedly. Two contrasting series are depicted in Figure 8.3. The shaded series, which is not autocorrelated, is essentially a random pattern of pain over time. Pain ratings on a given day are unrelated to ratings on any other day at a 1-day lag, a 2-day lag, or a 3-day lag. Among time series analysts (e.g., Johnston, 1984), this would be called a "random walk." The unshaded series, on the other hand, represents a highly autocorrelated pain series. Even visual inspection reveals what appear to be day-to-day connections in pain reports. The correlation of pain on day t with pain on day $t + 1$ is .70.

Each of the time series in Figure 8.3 represents a single participant. When we conducted an autocorrelation analysis for each of the patients in our study, we found that the mean autocorrelation (the average day-to-day relation) was .40. Seventy percent of our participants produced a significant successive day correlation. Very few produced a random walk. Fewer still had a more complicated pattern of autocorrelation such that pain on a particular day was correlated not only with pain the next day, but with pain 2, 3, or 4 days later. For most patients, the predictability of pain was from one day to the next day. This phenomenon is called a first-order autoregressive process, which simply means that pain was predictable on consecutive days. Even most of the pain series that were autocorrelated over longer intervals could be explained sufficiently by the correlation of pain on consecutive days.

A complete autocorrelation analysis requires controls for other factors that might contribute to any lagged (from one day to the next) associations. One such factor is day of the week. A first-order autoregressive process could be the result of pain typically being more intense on one day of the week and less intense on the following day. When we controlled for day of the week, including weekdays versus weekends, the first-order process still emerged.

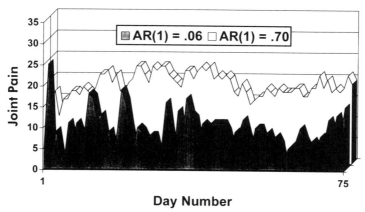

Figure 8.3   Examples of an autocorrelated and uncorrelated daily pain series.

An even more likely candidate for influencing day-to-day pain associations is trending in the series itself. A significant trend can itself produce some degree of autocorrelation: In an upwardly trending series, pain on a given day is likely to be followed by a day with more intense pain, whereas in a downwardly trending series, pain on a given day is likely to be followed by a day with less intense pain. When we "detrended" each pain series (removed its trend component), we continued to observe a sizable autocorrelation pattern.

Another search for regularities in daily pain experience comes from testing models in the frequency domain, known as frequency or spectral analysis (see West & Hepworth, 1991, for applications in daily process data). Modeling a series for its linear trend and autocorrelation components will not necessarily capture cycles of pain experience. A small handful of the daily pain series of our 75 participants still exhibited a significant 7-day cycle even after they had been stripped of serial dependencies due to linear trending and autocorrelation.

What we hope is now clear is that chronic pain is itself a process rather than a static experience. It's a "moving target" that, for many of the RA patients we studied, was predictable only from one day to the next. For some, the pain was relatively invariable. For others, it was episodic. For still others, it was waxing or waning over the 75 days. Moving targets cannot be understood well through snapshots, even two or three snapshots. They require continuous monitoring. And such targets may require coping strategies that change in kind. It is to these coping efforts that we now turn.

Patterns of Daily Pain Coping

We adapted Stone and Neale's (1982; see Porter & Stone, Chapter 7, this volume) Daily Coping Assessment for determining chronic pain coping. Participants were asked to describe what they did or thought to contend with the arthritis pain they experienced that day by checking "yes" or "no" to each of seven coping categories. The seven coping functions and the item presented to depict each were:

1. *Direct Action.* "Did something specific to try to reduce the pain."
2. *Relaxation.* "Did something to help me relax."
3. *Distraction.* "Diverted attention from the pain by thinking about other things or engaging in some activity."
4. *Redefinition.* "Tried to see the pain in a different light that made it more bearable."
5. *Emotional Expression.* "Expressed emotions to reduce my anxiety, frustration or tension about the pain."
6. *Spiritual Comfort.* "Sought spiritual support or comfort concerning my pain."
7. *Emotional Support.* "Sought emotional support from loved ones, friends, or professionals concerning my pain."

The eighth DCA coping strategy, "accepting the problem and that nothing could be done about it," was omitted because pilot testing revealed that respondents had difficulty with its dual meaning. We begin our discussion of coping strategies with a reminder that even without examining day-to-day changes, aggregated daily coping reports provide an unusually reliable indicator of coping. We then present evidence consistent with the concept of coping style as well as situationally determined strategies. Next, we relate coping to pain intensity. Finally, we describe how gender, disability, perceived pain control, and neuroticism are associated with daily coping efforts.

Whether our focus is coping, emotional well-being, daily events, pain, or how these aspects of adaptation relate to one another, it should be apparent that aggregated daily assessments provide an unusually reliable construct indicator. Earlier in this chapter, we demonstrated this in relation to pain. We (Tennen et al., 1992) have applied an aggregation strategy to examine how daily pain moderates the relation between control beliefs and adjustment as well as the relation between benefit appraisals and adjustment. We found that perceived personal control over arthritis pain and the ability to derive benefits from the pain predicted, albeit in different ways, daily well-being. Greater perceived control at the outset was associated with less daily pain over the next 75 days. But among those who experienced more severe pain after believing they could control their pain, greater perceived control was associated with more daily emotional distress (see Jensen & Karoly, 1991). Benefit appraisals did not predict emotional well-being, but did predict the number of days on which pain interfered with daily activities. This relation too was dependent on pain severity. Individuals with more severe pain reported *fewer* days of pain-limited activities when they initially derived more benefits from their illness pain.

Although we believe that the obtained interaction between benefit appraisals and pain severity in forecasting activity limitations is unique in the stress and coping literature, and that this interaction owes much to our daily measurement strategy, it would hardly have been worth the effort if aggregation had been our ultimate goal. Nonetheless, the reliability of aggregated indicators is appealing, and as we soon will demonstrate, aggregated measures of daily pain show significant associations with daily coping efforts.

We begin with a description of the pain-coping efforts employed by these RA patients (see Affleck, Urrows, Tennen, & Higgins, 1991). Figure 8.4 portrays the relative frequency of use for each of the seven DCA coping strategies and the proportion of patients who fell into each category of use. Most of these strategies are fairly skewed in their use, being used rarely. Some strategies, such as *redefining the pain to make it more bearable*, were *never* employed by a substantial number of participants. The distributions of other coping strategies, such as *taking direct action* and *seeking spiritual comfort,* appear bimodal. A large number of patients rarely employed these strategies, but a small number used them on most days. We suspect that these bimodal distributions reflect coping styles or strategies that some people never or rarely use but that others use with great regularity. Use of

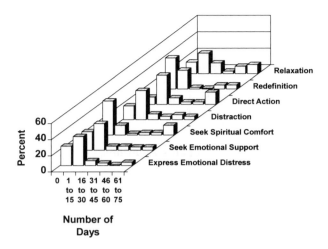

Figure 8.4   The relative frequency of daily pain-coping strategies.

relaxation tactics was the daily strategy most often used on moderate numbers of days, suggesting its status as a situationally driven coping response.

These coping strategies relate to our aggregate measure of pain intensity. As one might expect, people who experience more pain do more overall coping. Controlling for the amount of coping through the transformation of these coping ratings into *relative* scores by including the total number of coping efforts as the denominator (Vitaliano, Maiuro, Russo, & Becker, 1985), we found that patients who expressed emotions more frequently as a coping strategy and those who sought spiritual comfort more frequently also reported more pain. Those who used more relaxation strategies as part of their coping repertoire reported less pain across the reporting period.

Women reported more coping efforts even after controlling for differences in pain. Women were also more likely than men to seek support, which is a common finding in the stress and coping literature (Burda, Vaux, & Schill, 1984). We also found that after controlling for pain intensity, the perception of control over pain was related to a greater use of relaxation strategies and to less use of emotional expression as a coping strategy.

Affleck, Tennen, Urrows, and Higgins (1991) also examined associations of daily pain coping with the extent and direction of *linear* changes in daily pain over the 75-day recording period. Independent of all other factors studied, including the severity of daily pain, patients who reported a higher frequency of coping efforts showed a more pronounced *linear decline* in pain intensity. Thus, despite the possibility that individuals who engaged in more coping may have done so because they were in greater pain, these extensive efforts may have been rewarded by gradual improvement in daily pain, an effect that could only have been observed by assessing pain on a daily basis.

Although these findings are conceptually meaningful and consistent with previous cross-sectional findings, and although they are based on unusually reliable data collected day by day, they remain in the between-persons nomothetic tradition because the data was aggregated over time. We now turn to the unique contribution of idiographic daily monitoring studies—their ability to provide data for within-person analyses, which in turn strengthen the causal inferences permitted by nonexperimental studies of stress and coping.

Within-Person versus Between-Persons Relations: The Difference That Makes a Difference

There are three specific data analytic advantages to the idiographic-nomothetic approach to the study of stress and coping: (a) A within-person design eliminates potential sources of between-persons confounding by stable dispositions or situations; (b) these designs preserve temporal sequences, which in turn (c) strengthens our causal inferences. We will illustrate the first benefit by examining more closely two variables from our study: desirable daily events and undesirable daily events, both derived from the DLE. We wish to show that the findings from a between-persons correlation can depart markedly from those of a within-person correlation, and also show that attempts to answer *intra*individual questions with *inter*individual analytic approaches are likely to miss the mark.

In our cohort of RA patients, the most frequently reported *undesirable* daily events were family duties, illness in a friend or relative, the bothersome routines of daily living, and negative interactions with children and in the workplace. The most prevalent *desirable* events were close interactions and positive interactions, housework, and home maintenance activities. It is noteworthy that household routines were described as desirable events on some days and undesirable events on other days. This should alert us to an important constraint on the use of daily event checklists: They require for each event an appraisal of whether the event was desirable or undesirable.

The between-persons correlation of the aggregate numbers of desirable events with undesirable events was .50: People who reported more desirable events also reported more undesirable events. But as we suspect for many between-persons correlations appearing in the stress and coping literature, this relation was confounded. One might expect that a reporting bias could contribute to the obtained association because some people simply differ in their thresholds for what they call any event, desirable or undesirable. But one need not turn to nuances in response tendencies to explain this finding. Three background factors—gender, work outside the home, and children living at home—account fully for the desirable event-undesirable event correlation. When we controlled for these factors, the correlation approached zero. The moderately positive association apparently reflects that women who work outside the home and have young children experience both more desirable and more undesirable events.

The question addressed by the (confounded) between-persons correlation is whether people who experience more undesirable daily events also experience more desirable daily events. The more interesting question, in our opinion, is "How are desirable and undesirable events patterned in an individual's life?" Is a day with more undesirable events also a day with more desirable events? The between-persons analysis cannot answer this question. It requires calculation of a within-person measure of association. Figure 8.5 depicts the results of our series of within-person analyses. As a moment of self-reflection would suggest, desirable and undesirable events connect within individuals in an *inverse* way. The figure displays the within-person correlation for each of our 75 participants. It illustrates strikingly that not a single participant showed the significant positive association between desirable and undesirable events that was found when the data were analyzed between persons. In fact, the mean within-person correlation was −.25, with a preponderance of significant *negative* correlations. Even many of those who reported a large number of both desirable and undesirable events showed an inverse relation when these events were examined on a within-subject basis.

This comparison of between-persons and within-person correlations is intended to highlight three points: (a) Within-person analysis eliminates potential sources of between-persons confounding; (b) both the magnitude and direction of associations can change when research questions are framed in within-person terms; and (c) although it is common in the coping literature to draw within-person inferences from between-persons associations, they address different questions. Some of the most interesting and clinically relevant questions demand within-person analytic strategies.

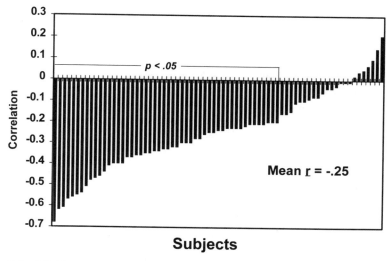

Figure 8.5   Within-person correlations between desirable and undesirable daily events.

Stress-Reactive Chronic Pain: An Idiographic-Nomothetic Conceptualization

Aside from eliminating potential sources of between persons confounding, a within-person design preserves temporal sequences and thus strengthens our causal inferences (West & Hepworth, 1991). We will now demonstrate the power of this approach by turning to the relation between day-to-day undesirable events and changes in pain, which we have addressed in a recent article in greater detail (Affleck, Tennen, Urrows, & Higgins, 1994). Most relevant to the coping process is the possibility of documenting "stress reactivity" and individual differences in its manifestations. We begin with a conceptual rationale for studying stress reactivity. We then describe evolving data analytic strategies and demonstrate the application to our data of a particularly promising strategy.

Several lines of evidence led us to investigate stress-reactive pain. First, previous work (Affleck, Pfeiffer, Tennen, & Fifield, 1987) suggested that from the patient's point of view undesirable events were related to symptom changes. When asked to make causal attributions for such changes, half of our participants noted worsening during stressful episodes. In fact, psychological stress was the single most common attribution for negative symptom changes. Similarly, aside from medication changes, freedom from stress was the most common attribution for symptom improvement. These self-perceptions are consistent with nomothetic research reviewed by Achterberg-Lawlis (1982) and by Anderson, Bradley, Young, McDaniel, and Wise (1985), which provide indirect support for the stress-pain relation. After reviewing this literature, Koehler (1985) hypothesized that stressful incidents might aggravate RA pain by increasing muscle tension around affected joints, by inducing hormonal changes, or by altering the immune system. These intriguing speculations require fully prospective, idiographic studies to document that RA pain is aggravated by exposure to psychological stressors.

In fact, a number of studies have documented "lagged" effects of daily events on episodes of minor illness (DeLongis et al., 1988; Stone et al., 1987), on migraine headaches (Kohler & Haimerl, 1990; Mosely et al., 1991), and on chronic disease symptom fluctuations (King & Wilson, 1991). As we have suggested, these lagged effects strengthen causal inference by establishing temporal precedence.

We also saw in the concept of stress reactivity the opportunity to fully exploit an idiographic-nomothetic analysis. Not every RA patient will report increased pain in response to stressful events. Some may show no change in symptoms and still others may experience *less* pain following a more stressful day. These anticipated individual differences begged the inclusion of several of the person and situation moderators we described earlier: major life events in the 6 months before entering the study, disease activity, neuroticism, and perceived social support. Although we suggested earlier that selecting appropriate moderators was akin to rounding up suspects, the suspects we selected had a documented record in the daily mood literature. For example, the magnitude of within-person associations between stressful daily events and negative mood has been related to neuroticism

(Bolger & Schilling, 1991), recent major life events (Caspi et al., 1987), and social support (Caspi et al., 1987). In fact, Caspi et al. (1987) found that social support influenced not only the magnitude of the stress-mood relation, but its direction. Individuals with relatively modest support showed an increase in negative mood following a more stressful day, whereas those experiencing greater support showed a decrease in negative mood after a more stressful day.

Within-Person Analysis of Prospective Daily Data

New analytic approaches relevant to studies of coping (Benson & Hagtvet, Chapter 5, this volume) and to acute pain episodes (Chapman, Donaldson, & Jacobson, 1992) are beginning to appear in the literature. Strategies for the within-person analysis of prospective daily data are still evolving. We (Affleck et al., 1994) described two broad strategies: a *target-control period* approach (Stone et al., 1987), and what West and Hepworth (1991) call a *concomitant time series* approach. When one is interested in the adaptational effects of unusually stressful days, the target-control period approach is most appropriate. Adaptational outcomes such as well-being or symptoms on atypical days and several subsequent days can be compared with outcomes during periods set off by a low stress control day. Because the designation of high- and low-stress days is necessarily restrictive, subjects may need to be excluded from the final analysis. The concomitant time series approach does not address atypical days. Rather, it allows the investigator to examine how stressors on *each* day are related to adaptational outcomes on that day and subsequent days. Because all subjects are retained, moderators can be more easily incorporated into the analysis.

One approach to concomitant time series analysis is to model within-person associations by pooling data across participants and time points. Cutrona (1986) and Michela (1990) have illustrated how between-person variance can be removed from these associations using subject vector dummy variables, and Jaccard and Wan (1993) have provided a cogent summary of the statistical underpinnings of this strategy. An important limitation of such pooled models is that they obscure almost certain individual differences in the deterministic components of the time series (e.g., their linear trends, cycles, or autocorrelation patterns) (West & Hepworth, 1991). Hierarchical linear modeling of pooled data (Bryk & Raudenbush, 1987) allows for the inclusion of individual differences in slopes and intercepts. Bolger and Schilling (1991) have already produced a creative application of this approach for the analysis of daily stress data.

West and Hepworth (1991) present another approach that preserves individual differences while identifying commonalities. First, idiographic effect sizes are estimated. Because autocorrelation and linear trending can inflate cross-correlations between variables (e.g., between stress and mood), both need to be statistically controlled. The next step involves combining idiographic statistics to determine whether individual within-person associations can be generalized to the cohort. Investigators have taken varied approaches to combining individuals' series. Some have examined whether the number of individuals who exhibit significant associations exceeds that expected by chance (e.g., Halford, Cuddihy, & Mortimer, 1990). Others have calculated the significance of the average within-person correlation (e.g., Emmons, 1991), or have tested the differences of the average correlation from zero (e.g., Affleck, Tennen, Urrows, & Higgins, 1992; Wood, Saltzberg, Neale, Stone, & Rachmiel, 1990).

An intriguing alternative, recommended by West and Hepworth (1991) is to combine within-person findings through meta-analysis, in which each subject's series represents a single subject study and an "independent replication." Following the logic of meta-analysis, the number of "studies" is the number of subjects, and the "sample size" of each study is the number of days in his or her series. Because each subject provides data on the same number of days, the analysis is based on equal sample sizes. Moreover, because all subjects are included in the analysis, problems of publication bias or "file drawer effects" are avoided. And the fact that every study employs the same measures and investigator makes this a particularly appealing application of meta-analytic strategy (Durlak & Lipsey, 1991). Finally, just as meta-analysis can be used to examine differences among studies as sources of variance in obtained relations (Larsen & Sinnett, 1991), it can be used to determine how differences *between* individuals affect the temporal patterning of relations *within* individuals.

Individual Differences in Stress-Reactive Chronic Pain

We followed West and Hepworth's (1991) meta-analytic approach to fully exploit the idiographic-nomothetic nature of the data (see Affleck et al., 1994, for a complete description). The target of the analysis was daily stress reactivity, defined as the unique relation between events and next-day pain. The following regression model for the prediction of pain from the previous day's events are presented to demonstrate the logic of the approach. The regression model for predicting pain from undesirable events occurring on the previous day (events$_{t-1}$), controlling for the autocorrelation (AR) in pain, recording day (to control for linear trend), and day of the week (to control for weekday/weekend cyclicity) took the following form:

$$\text{Pain}_t = \beta(\text{AR}) + \beta(\text{Recording day}) + \beta(\text{Day of week}) + \beta(\text{Mood}_t) + \beta(\text{Events}_t) + \beta(\text{Events}_{t-1}) + e_t + c.$$

The reason for entering same-day mood prior to same-day events is that we wanted to assess the unique relation between undesirable events and pain controlling for possible mood-dependent pain descriptions. The beta for the Events$_{t-1}$ term was conceptualized as the "event reactivity" coefficient.

Following Hunter and Schmidt's (1990) recommendations for conducting the meta-analysis, we considered each subject's series a separate study, taking the event reactivity coefficient coefficient (β_i) as the effect size parameter. Specifically, the observed variance ($s_o{}^2$) across our 75 within-person studies with 75 days of data each equals $\Sigma[75(\beta_i - \bar\beta)^2]/75 \times 75$, and the expected sampling error variance (s_e^2) equals $(1 - \bar{\beta}^2)^2/(75 - 1)$. Thus, the estimated variance of the population regression coefficients (s_p^2) equals $s_o^2 - s_e^2$, and the square root of s_p^2 serves as the standard error in the test that the mean regression coefficient $= 0$ in the population: $z = \bar{\beta}/s_p$. West and Hepworth (1991) provide a full description of the use of this procedure to combine within-person study findings.

The results of this meta-analysis showed no reliable effect size across the 75 participants in predicting next day pain. Although the effect was not reliable for the entire group, we had the opportunity to determine whether the between-persons factors we described earlier predicted individual differences in the regression coefficients. The results were encouraging. Controlling for the distributional characteristics of each subject's daily series, the relation between more undesirable events and greater next-day pain was higher for those who reported more negative life changes at the start of the study and who had more active disease during the study. The effects of these two moderators were additive.

To supplement the analysis for this volume on coping, we also looked at whether each of the aggregate DCA scores (transformed to their relative values) were associated with individual differences in the event-reactive pain coefficients. Interestingly, two of the coping strategies that were associated with more or less daily pain (Affleck, Urrows, Tennen, & Higgins, 1992) also predicted individual differences in stress-reactive pain. Specifically, those who used relaxation coping more prominently were less likely to exhibit increased pain after a day with more undesirable events, but those who used emotional expression as a relatively prominent strategy were more likely to do so. These findings not only speak to the potential of idiographic-nomothetic approaches to stress and coping research; they also remind us that coping is a process that requires a process-oriented research approach.

CHALLENGES OF A DAILY PROCESS APPROACH TO STRESS AND COPING

Three major challenges face investigators interested in pursuing a daily process approach to the study of stress and coping. First, as should be apparent, this line of inquiry places significant burdens on both participants and researchers. For participants, it means a commitment to weeks or months of daily monitoring and daily submission of data. This requires staying power and a willingness to share the details of one's daily life and inner experiences with a stranger. For investigators, it means obsessively monitoring the data collection process and waiting patiently for data that arrives ever so slowly. Because missing data creates problems for time series analysis, and because the quality of the data needs to be monitored throughout the study, we recommend that no more than six to eight subjects participate simultaneously. The researcher, therefore, needs to be willing to collect data for years before submitting a single manuscript for publication.

A second challenge involves managing the data set, keeping together thousands of person-days of data, being able to access data when necessary, and keeping track simultaneously of what amounts to a separate study for each participant. This in itself is a major task requiring the investigator to learn new data management and data analytic approaches.

Finally, there is the potentially serious threat to validity posed by the possible reactive effects of intensive self-monitoring. The most obvious threat, well known to behavior therapists who use it to therapeutic advantage, is that people might alter their behavior as monitoring helps them detect contingencies between events and pain, mood and pain, or coping efforts and pain. As we suggested in our discussion of linear trends, for some individuals, self-monitoring might interfere with distraction as a preferred coping strategy. But perhaps the most insidious threat to validity is that the very task of asking people to become self-focused may create or cement the very linkages we then "discover." An emerging experimental (Croyle & Uretsky, 1987; Salovey & Birnbaum, 1989) and field study (Larsen & Cowan, 1988) literature demonstrates how self-focused attention may create linkages between stress, somatic symptoms, and emotional distress. We believe that the challenges just enumerated are far outweighed by the promise of a daily process methodology.

FUTURE DIRECTIONS IN DAILY PROCESS RESEARCH

We feel secure in predicting that a growing number of stress and coping investigators will be using process-oriented designs to find new answers to old questions or answers to new questions that can be pursued only with this approach (Tennen, Suls, & Affleck, 1991a, 1991b). To bring our chapter to a close, we highlight a daily experience study in progress of individuals with primary fibromyalgia—a syndrome characterized by widespread musculoskeletal pain and low pain thresholds at tender points—that offers new directions and innovations in the time-intensive assessment of chronic pain and other daily experiences.

Most daily stress researchers have ignored the likely prospect that different stressors affect different people in different ways. Some investigators have shown that the most distressing daily stressors occur in the domains of family life and work (Stone et al., 1987), denote interpersonal conflict (Bolger et al., 1989), are "self-produced" (Epstein & Katz, 1992), or are focused on the self (Wood et al., 1990). Studies accounting for individual differences in responses to various types of events have been rare, however. One exception is Emmons's (1991) demonstration that personal strivings determine those daily events that are more or less distressing. Our aim is both to elucidate individual differences in the types of undesirable daily events that affect pain perception or pain-mood linkages and to identify the personal characteristics that potentiate these effects. We are interested principally in the impact of *goal-relevant* events that advance, or interfere with, personal commitments, goals, or strivings (Cantor et al., 1991; Emmons, 1991; Karoly, 1991). Our fibromyalgia subjects are tracking their progress in accomplishing personal goals in the arenas of health and interpersonal relationships to teach us whether goal attainment, alone or in combination with goal-relevant events, is an antecedent or consequence of symptom change. We suspect that relations at the within-person level could well be predicted by between-person differences in the basic personality traits of neuroticism (in the case of health-related goals) or extraversion-introversion (in the case of interpersonal goals).

Most investigators of daily processes have also relied on end-of-the-day reports to summarize a person's symptoms, behaviors, feelings, or thoughts. Virtually without exception, they find the strongest associations are concurrent, or same-day relations. Unfortunately, such same-day associations do not permit the strong inference that is afforded by demonstrating temporal precedence. In preparing for our study of individuals with primary fibromyalgia, we were struck by their descriptions of major shifts in pain intensity and even location throughout the day. By deciding to assess both pain and mood several times each day, we hoped to reduce the error in daily summaries and to isolate sequential processes operating within a day.

Of particular interest, therefore, are innovative techniques for gathering data more than once a day. Until recently, the procedure of choice was to signal subjects in some way, either through electronic pagers (Wong & Csikszentmihalyi, 1991) or watch alarms (Marco & Suls, 1993), that data should be recorded on paper. But without a way to monitor compliance with these requests, the investigator is in the dark about subjects' adherence to the data collection schedule. With the availability of programmable palm-top computers that mediate both the presentation and recording of data and that time-stamp the responses, it is now possible to overcome this constraint on within-day assessment in field studies of stress and coping (see Porter & Stone, Chapter 7, this volume). Several other investigators have demonstrated the feasibility of using such computerized diaries in natural settings (Haythornthwaite, Anderson, & Moore, 1992; Shiffman et al., 1994; Totterdell & Folkard, 1992). They and we have learned that the advantages of this method extend beyond compliance monitoring. As Stone et al. (1991) note, equivalent information can be recorded in less time than with traditional paper-and-pencil questionnaires, and complex "response trees" can be more easily presented. Further, because computerized diaries can be programmed to allow subjects some control over data recording (as in instructing the device to signal again in a few minutes when it would be more convenient to answer questions or to suspend any alarms for the next hour during which responding would be impossible), they may be less likely than other procedures to interfere with daily life. In these ways, computerized diaries can both monitor and improve compliance with demanding daily process studies of stress and coping.

CONCLUSION

We have described an idiographic-nomothetic approach to the study of coping with chronic pain that we believe is ideally suited to test current transactional models of coping and adaptation. By preserving the temporal sequencing of events, coping efforts and adaptational outcomes, this approach strengthens our causal inferences.

Its within-person focus eliminates potential confounding by stable dispositions or situations. We demonstrated how this method incorporates theoretically anticipated moderators, how it captures proximal stressors and coping efforts as they unfold, and how it minimizes recall error. The findings we described linking daily events to next-day pain could not have been derived through traditional nomothetic approaches.

By forcing us to examine trending, autocorrelation, and cyclicity in our data, this approach also compels us to conceptualize stressful events, coping and adaptational outcomes as changing processes rather than static entities. In this way, it begins to close the enormous gap between process-oriented *theories* of coping and the empirical literature meant to evaluate these theories. For all its potential, this approach runs the risk of influencing or interfering with the very appraisals and coping strategies it was designed to measure. A future challenge for investigators will be to capture the temporal processes involved in coping without changing them.

REFERENCES

Achterberg-Lawlis, J. (1982). The psychological dimensions of arthritis. *Journal of Consulting and Clinical Psychology, 50,* 984–992.

Affleck, G., Pfeiffer, C., Tennen, H., & Fifield, J. (1987). Attributional processes in rheumatoid arthritis patients. *Arthritis and Rheumatism, 30,* 927–931.

Affleck, G., Pfeiffer, C., Tennen, H., & Fifield, J. (1988). Social support and psychosocial adjustment to rheumatoid arthritis: Quantitative and qualitative findings. *Arthritis Care and Research, 1,* 71–77.

Affleck, G., Tennen, H., & Rowe, J. (1991). *Infants in crisis: How parents cope with newborn intensive care and its aftermath.* New York: Springer-Verlag.

Affleck, G., Tennen, H., Urrows, S., & Higgins, P. (1991). Individual differences in the day-to-day experience of chronic pain: A prospective daily study of rheumatoid arthritis patients. *Health Psychology, 10,* 419–426.

Affleck, G., Tennen, H., Urrows, S., & Higgins, P. (1992). Neuroticism and the pain-mood relation in rheumatoid arthritis: Insights from a prospective daily study. *Journal of Consulting and Clinical Psychology, 60,* 119–126.

Affleck, G., Tennen, H., Urrows, S., & Higgins, P. (1994). Person and contextual features of stress reactivity: Individual differences in relations of undesirable daily events with negative mood and chronic pain intensity. *Journal of Personality and Social Psychology, 66,* 329–340.

Affleck, G., Urrows, S., Tennen, H., & Higgins, P. (1992). Daily coping with rheumatoid arthritis pain: Patterns and correlates. *Pain, 51,* 221–279.

Allport, G. W. (1937). *Personality: A psychological interpretation.* New York: Holt, Rinehart & Winston.

Anderson, K. O., Bradley, L. A., Young, L. D., McDaniel, L. K., & Wise, C. M. (1985). Rheumatoid arthritis: Review of psychological factors related to etiology, effects, and treatment. *Psychological Bulletin, 98,* 358–387.

Beckham, J. C., Keefe, F. J., Caldwell, D. S., & Roodman, A. A. (1991). Pain coping strategies in rheumatoid arthritis: Relationship to pain, disability, depression, and daily hassles. *Behavior Therapy, 22,* 113–124.

Bolger, N., DeLongis, A., Kessler, R., & Schilling, E. (1989). Effects of daily stress on negative mood. *Journal of Personality and Social Psychology, 57,* 808–818.

Bolger, N., & Schilling, E. A. (1991). Personality and the problems of everyday life: The role of neuroticism in exposure and reactivity to daily stressors. *Journal of Personality, 59,* 335–386.

Bradley, L. A., Haile, J. M., & Jaworski, T. M. (1992). Assessment of psychological status using interviews and self-report instruments. In D. C. Turk & R. Melzack (Eds.), *Handbook of pain assessment* (pp. 193–213). New York: Guilford.

Brown, G., & Nicassio, P. (1987). The development of a questionnaire for the assessment of active and passive coping strategies in chronic pain patients. *Pain, 31,* 53–65.

Brown, G., Nicassio, P., & Wallston, K. (1989). Pain coping strategies and depression in rheumatoid arthritis. *Journal of Consulting and Clinical Psychology, 57,* 652–657.

Bryk, A. S., & Raudenbush, S. W. (1987). Application of hierarchical linear models to assessing change. *Psychological Bulletin, 101,* 147–158.

Burda, P. C., Vaux, A., & Schill, T. (1984). Several support resources: Variations across sex and sex role. *Personality and Social Psychology Bulletin, 10,* 119–126.

Cantor, N., Norem, J., Langston, C., Zirkel, S., Fleeson, W., & Cook-Flannagan, C. (1991). Life tasks and daily life experience. *Journal of Personality, 59,* 425–452.

Carver, C. S., Scheier, M. F., & Weintraub, J. K. (1989). Assessing coping strategies: A theoretically based approach. *Journal of Personality and Social Psychology, 56,* 267–283.

Caspi, A., Bolger, N., & Eckenrode, J. (1987). Linking person and context in the daily stress process. *Journal of Personality and Social Psychology, 52,* 184–195.

Chapman, C. R., Donaldson, G. W., & Jacobson, R. C. (1992). Measurement of acute pain states. In D. C. Turk and R. Melzak (Eds.), *Handbook of pain assessment* (pp. 332–343). New York: Guilford.

Costa, P. T., & McCrae, R. R. (1985). *The NEO Personality Inventory Manual.* Odessa, FL: Psychological Assessment Resources.

Croyle, R. T., & Uretsky, M. B. (1987). Effects of mood on self-appraisal of health status. *Health Psychology, 6,* 239–253.

Cutrona, C. E. (1986). Behavioral manifestations of social support: A microanalytic investigation. *Journal of Personality and Social Psychology, 51,* 201–208.

Dailey, P. A., Bishop, G. D., Russell, I. J., & Fletcher, E. M. (1990). Psychological stress and fibrositis/fibromyalgia syndrome. *Journal of Rheumatology, 17,* 1380–1385.

DeLongis, A., Folkman, S., & Lazarus, R. S. (1988). The impact of daily stress on health and mood: Psychological and social resources as mediators. *Journal of Personality and Social Psychology, 54,* 486–495.

Durlak, J. A., & Lipsey, M. W. (1991). A practitioner's guide to meta-analysis. *American Journal of Community Psychology, 19,* 291–331.

Emmons, R. A. (1991). Personal strivings, daily life events, and psychological and physical well-being. *Journal of Personality, 59,* 453–472.

Endler, N. S., & Parker, J. D. A. (1990a). *CISS: Coping Inventory for Stressful Situations Manual.* Toronto, Canada: Multi-Health Systems.

Endler, N. S., & Parker, J. D. A. (1990b). The multidimensional assessment of coping: A critical evaluation. *Journal of Personality and Social Psychology, 58,* 844–854.

Epstein, S. (1983). A research paradigm for the study of personality and emotions. In M. Page (Ed.), *Personality—Current theory and research: Nebraska Symposium on Motivation* (pp. 91–154). Lincoln: University of Nebraska Press.

Epstein, S., & Katz, L. (1992). Coping ability, stress, productive load, and symptoms. *Journal of Personality and Social Psychology, 62,* 813–825.

Erskine, A., Morley, S., & Pearce, S. (1990). Memory for pain: A review. *Pain, 41,* 255–265.

Folkman, S., & Lazarus, R. S. (1985). If it changes it must be a process: A study of emotion and coping during three stages of a college examination. *Journal of Personality and Social Psychology, 48,* 150–170.

Garrett, V. D., Brantley, P. J., Jones, G. N., & McKnight, G. T. (1991). The relation between daily stress and Crohn's disease. *Journal of Behavioral Medicine, 14,* 87–96.

Goodenow, C., Reisine, S., & Grady, K. E. (1990). Quality of social support and associated social and psychological functioning in women with rheumatoid arthritis. *Health Psychology, 9,* 266–284.

Halford, W. K., Cuddihy, S., & Mortimer, R. H. (1990). Psychological stress and blood glucose regulation in Type I diabetic patients. *Health Psychology, 9,* 516–528.

Haythornthwaite, J., Anderson, D., & Moore, L. (1992). Social and behavioral factors associated with episodes of inhibitory breathing. *Journal of Behavioral Medicine, 15,* 573–588.

Hunter, J. E., & Schmidt, F. L. (1990). *Methods of meta-analysis: Correcting error and bias in research findings.* Newbury Park, CA: Sage.

Jaccard, J., & Wan, C. (1993). Statistical analysis of temporal data with many observations: Issues for behavioral medicine data. *Annals of Behavioral Medicine, 15,* 41–50.

Jensen, M. P., & Karoly, P. (1991). Control beliefs, coping efforts, and adjustment to chronic pain. *Journal of Consulting and Clinical Psychology, 59,* 431–438.

Jensen, M. P., Turner, J. A., Romano, J. M., & Karoly, P. (1991). Coping with chronic pain: A critical review of the literature. *Pain, 47,* 249–283.

Johnston, J. (1984). *Econometric methods.* New York: McGraw-Hill.

Kanner, A. D., Coyne, J. C., Schaefer, C., & Lazarus, R. S. (1981). Comparison of two modes of stress measurement: Daily hassles and uplifts versus major life events. *Journal of Behavioral Medicine, 4,* 1–39.

Karoly, P. (1991). Goal systems and health outcomes across the life span: A proposal. In H. E. Schroeder (Ed.), *New directions in health psychology assessment* (pp. 65–93). New York: Hemisphere.

King, R., & Wilson, G. (1991). Use of a diary technique to investigate psychometric relations in atopic dermatitis. *Journal of Psychosomatic Research, 35,* 697–706.

Koehler, T. (1985). Stress and rheumatoid arthritis: A survey of empirical evidence in human and animal studies. *Journal of Psychosomatic Research, 29,* 655–663.

Kohler, T., & Haimerl, C. (1990). Daily stress as a trigger of migraine attacks: Results of thirteen single subject studies. *Journal of Consulting and Clinical Psychology, 58,* 870–872.

Larsen, R. (1992). Neuroticism and bias in the encoding and recall of physical symptoms: Evidence from a combined prospective–retrospective study. *Journal of Personality and Social Psychology, 62,* 480–488.

Larsen, R. J., & Cowan, G. S. (1988). Internal focus of attention and depression: A study of daily experience. *Motivation and Emotion, 12,* 237–249.

Larsen, R. J., & Kasimatis, M. (1991). Day-to-day physical symptoms: Individual differences in the occurrence, duration, and emotional concomitants of minor daily illnesses. *Journal of Personality, 59,* 387–424.

Larsen, R. J., & Sinnett, L. M. (1991). Meta-analysis of experimental manipulations: Some factors affecting the Velten mood induction procedure. *Personality and Social Psychology Bulletin, 17,* 323–334.

Lazarus, R., & Folkman, S. (1984). *Stress, appraisal and coping.* New York: Springer.

Linton, S. (1991). Memory for chronic pain intensity: Correlates of accuracy. *Perceptual and Motor Skills, 72,* 1091–1095.

Lorr, M., & McNair, D. (1982). *Profile of Mood States—B.* San Diego: Educational and Industrial Testing Service.

Marco, C., & Suls, J. (1993). Daily stress and the trajectory of mood: Spillover, response assimilation, contrast, and chronic negative affectivity. *Journal of Personality and Social Psychology, 64,* 1053–1063.

Mason, J. H., Anderson, J. J., Meenan, R. F., Haralson, K. M., Lewis-Stevens, D., & Kaine, J. L. (1992). The Rapid Assessment of Disease Activity in Rheumatology Questionnaire: Validity and sensitivity to change of a patient self-report of joint count and clinical status. *Arthritis and Rheumatism, 35,* 156–162.

Mason, J., & Meenan, R. (1983). *Rapid assessment of disease activity in rheumatology.* Unpublished manuscript, Boston University School of Medicine, Boston, MA.

Mendola, R. (1990). *Coping with chronic pain: Perceptions of control and dispositional optimism as moderators of psychological distress.* Unpublished doctoral dissertation, University of Connecticut, Storr, CT.

Michela, J. (1990). Within-person correlational design and analysis. In C. Hendrick & M. Clark (Eds.), *Research methods in personality and social psychology* (pp. 279–328). Newbury Park, CA: Sage.

Miller, S. M. (1987). Monitoring and blunting: Validation of a questionnaire to assess styles of information seeking under threat. *Journal of Personality and Social Psychology, 52,* 345–353.

Miller, S. M. (1992). Individual differences in the coping process: What to know and when to know it. In B. N. Carpenter (Ed.), *Personal coping: Theory, research, and application* (pp. 77–91). Westport, CT: Praeger.

Mosely, T., Penzien, D., Johnson, C., Wittrock, D., Brantley, P., Seville, J., & Andrew, M. (1991, March). *Social support as a moderator of the stress-headache relationship.* Paper presented at the annual meeting of the Society of Behavioral Medicine, Washington, DC.

Neisser, U. (1991). A case of misplaced nostalgia. *American Psychologist, 46,* 34–36.

Peck, J., Smith, T., Ward, J., & Milano, R. (1989). Disability and depression in rheumatoid arthritis: A multi-trait, multi-method investigation. *Arthritis and Rheumatism, 32,* 1100–1106.

Radloff, L. (1977). The CES-D scale: A self-report depression scale in the general population. *Applied Psychological Measurement, 1,* 385–401.

Robins, L., Helzer, J., Cottler, L., & Goldring, E. (1989). *NIMH Diagnostic Interview Schedule: Version III Revised.* Unpublished manual, Washington University, St. Louis, MO.

Rosensteil, A. K., & Keefe, F. J. (1983). The use of coping strategies in low-back pain patients. Relationship to patient characteristics and current adjustment. *Pain, 17,* 33–40.

Rothbaum, F., Weisz, J., & Snyder, S. (1982). Changing the world and changing the self: A two process model of perceived control. *Journal of Personality and Social Psychology, 42,* 5–37.

Salovey, P., & Birnbaum, D. (1989). Influence of mood on health-relevant cognitions. *Journal of Personality and Social Psychology, 57,* 539–551.

Sarason, I. G., Johnson, J. H., & Siegel, J. M. (1978). Assessing the impact of life changes: Development of the Life Experiences Survey. *Journal of Consulting and Clinical Psychology, 46,* 932–946.

Scheier, M., & Carver, C. (1985). Optimism, coping, and health: Assessment and implications of generalized outcome expectancies. *Health Psychology, 4,* 219–247.

Shiffman, S., Fischer, L., Paty, J., Gnys, M., Hickcox, M., & Kassel, J. (1994). Drinking and smoking: A field study of their association. *Annals of Behavioral Medicine, 16,* 203–209.

Stanton, A., Tennen, H., Affleck, G., & Mendola, R. (1992). Coping and adjustment to infertility. *Journal of Social and Clinical Psychology, 11,* 1–13.

Stone, A. A., Kessler, R. C., & Haythornthwaite, J. A. (1991). Measuring daily events and experiences: Decisions for the researcher. *Journal of Personality, 59,* 575–608.

Stone, A. A., & Neale, J. M. (1982). Development of a methodology for assessing daily experiences. In A. Baum & J. Singer (Eds.), *Advances in environmental psychology, environment and health* (Vol. 4, pp. 49–83). New York: Erlbaum.

Stone, A. A., Reed, B. R., & Neale, J. M. (1987). Changes in daily event frequency precede episodes of physical symptoms. *Journal of Human Stress, 13,* 70–74.

Tennen, H., Affleck, G., Urrows, S., Higgins, P., & Mendola, R. (1992). Perceiving control, construing benefits, and daily processes in rheumatoid arthritis. *Canadian Journal of Behavioral Science, 24,* 186–203.

Tennen, H., Suls, J., & Affleck, G. (Eds.). (1991a). Personality and daily experience [Special issue]. *Journal of Personality, 59,* 313–662.

Tennen, H., Suls, J., & Affleck, G. (1991b). Personality and daily experience: The promise and the challenge. *Journal of Personality, 59,* 313–338.

Totterdell, P., & Folkard, S. (1992). In situation repeated measures of affect and cognitive performance. *Behavior Research Methods, Instruments, and Computers, 24,* 545–553.

Vitaliano, P., Maiuro, R., Russo, J., & Becker, J. (1985). Raw versus relative scores in the assessment of coping strategies. *Journal of Behavioral Medicine, 10,* 1–18.

West, S. G., & Hepworth, J. T. (1991). Statistical issues in the study of temporal data: Daily experiences. *Journal of Personality, 59,* 609–662.

Wills, T. A. (1981). Downward comparison principles in social psychology. *Psychological Bulletin, 90,* 245–271.

Wong, M., & Csikszentmihalyi, M. (1991). Motivation and academic achievement: The effects of personality traits and the quality of experience. *Journal of Personality, 3,* 537–574.

Wood, J. V., Saltzberg, J. A., Neale, J. M., Stone, A. A., & Rachmiel, T. B. (1990). Self-focused attention, coping responses, and distressed mood in everyday life. *Journal of Personality and Social Psychology, 58,* 1027–1036.

PART THREE

Facets of Coping

CHAPTER 9

On Coping Adaptively with Daily Hassles

PAUL M. KOHN

Hassles are mundane everyday stressors that can range "from minor annoyances to fairly major pressures, problems, and difficulties" (Kanner, Coyne, Schaefer, & Lazarus, 1981, p. 25). Time pressure, disliking work or studies, conflict with a romantic partner, and social mistreatment by acquaintances and friends are general categories of hassles that have emerged in factor analyses of existing hassles measures (Kohn, Lafreneire, & Gurevich, 1990; Kohn & Macdonald, 1992b; Kohn & Milrose, 1993). Cash-flow difficulties, getting a lower work evaluation than expected, and getting cheated in the purchase of goods are specific everyday hassles that are itemized in existing measures (see preceding references).

Typically, research on hassles considers the impact of cumulative exposure to a large variety of hassles over an extended time frame, commonly one month, on well-being, physical (e.g., De Longis, Coyne, Dakof, Folkman, & Lazarus, 1982) or mental (e.g., Kanner et al., 1981). Other research focuses more narrowly on such specific daily hassles as university exams (Abella & Heslin, 1989; Edwards & Trimble, 1992; Folkman & Lazarus, 1985), job and financial problems (Headey & Wearing, 1990), and conflict with friends (Lee, Chan, & Yik, 1992).

It has been claimed that, when encountering daily hassles, the individual engages in "primary appraisal" to determine their personal significance (Folkman, 1984; Folkman & Lazarus, 1980, 1990; Lazarus & Folkman, 1987). The person may variously classify them as threats to future well-being, harms to immediate well-being, or challenges that, if successfully met, will prevent harm or loss, and possibly create some benefit. Theoretically, the person also engages in "secondary appraisal" to determine the adequacy of personal and social resources for dealing with the stressor. The result bears on how serious the threat, harm, or challenge is. These processes have clear emotional implications: Threat, for example, should evoke anxiety; and harm or loss, depression. Challenge could provide an opportunity for emotional uplift and personal growth,

The work reported was facilitated by Grant No. 410-92-1751 from the Social Sciences and Humanities Research Council of Canada. The author gratefully acknowledges the contributions of Brian D. Hay and John J. Legere.

especially if successfully met; however, theoretically, the individual might encounter too many hassles, however categorized, over too long a time, which
would evoke the emotional exhaustion of "burnout" (Bhagat, Allie, & Ford,
1991; Holt, Fine, & Tollefson, 1987; Johnson & Stone, 1986; Leiter, 1990;
Nowack, 1991). Thus, the implications of hassles for subjective distress and
mental health seem clear.

In relation to physical health, researchers have argued that chronic stress impairs immune response (Ballieux & Heijnen, 1989; Jabaaij et al., 1993), especially if accompanied by an avoidant style of coping with threat-relevant
information (Davey, Tallis, & Hodgson, 1993). Furthermore, physiological responses to chronic stress, such as the maintenance of high levels of epinephrine
and norepinephrine, cause wear and tear on organ systems (Baum, Fleming, &
Singer, 1982). Such responses provide a physiological foundation for fight or
flight (Martin & Pihl, 1985), which, although appropriate to many stressful circumstances presumably encountered by our cave-dwelling ancestors, are less
often relevant to most of us now. The practical upshot may be that failure to
"work off" the stress-based arousal exacerbates organic damage. (This is a possible rationale for exercise as a component in programs of stress management.)
Thus, through both wear and tear on organ systems and suppression of immune
response, stress, whether from hassles, major traumas, or negative major life
events, such as job loss, divorce, or bereavement, should increase susceptibility
to various physical ailments.

This chapter considers the possible moderating effects of coping on the adverse impact that hassles have on subjective distress and on physical and mental
health. After reviewing pertinent literature on the measurement and consequences of hassles-based stress and of various modes of coping, this chapter reviews research on the moderating role of coping in relation to the adverse impact
of hassles. Finally, it is suggested that a more fruitful approach to the process of
coping may be in terms of skilled performance rather than either style or response, the currently dominant conceptualizations.

To date, most research on coping approaches it either as a response—an
attempt to adapt to specific stressors; or as a style—a consistent, dispositional
manner of adapting (Cohen, 1987; Dewe, Cox, & Ferguson, 1993; Edwards &
Trimble, 1992). It will be argued that which mode of coping will prove most adaptive (e.g., task-oriented, emotion-oriented, or avoidant) depends on circumstance
(Abella & Heslin, 1989; Bhagat, Allie, & Ford, 1991; Felton & Revenson, 1984;
Folkman & Lazarus, 1980; Forsythe & Compas, 1987; Hobfoll et al., 1991). Thus,
the most important thing about how a person copes with everyday hassles and, indeed, stressors generally is its circumstantial appropriateness, how well it fits the
specific demands of the situation. This depends on a combination of judgmental
astuteness on one hand and determination and self-control on the other. Determination will be needed for situations that require active problem-oriented coping in
the face of inhibiting factors (e.g., fear of hurting a friend's feelings or of confronting a bad-tempered superior at work). Self-control is called for when the situation requires passive coping despite contrary impulses (e.g., keeping one's

temper despite strong and tactically deliberate provocation or standing fast in the face of attempted intimidation).

HASSLES: THEIR ASSESSMENT AND IMPACT

Global Measures of Hassles

Hassles or mundane stressors apparently affect physical and mental health adversely (e.g., De Longis et al., 1982; Flannery, 1986a, 1986b; Johnson & Stone, 1986; Kanner et al., 1981; Lichtenberg, Swensen, & Skehan, 1986; Miller, Wilcox, & Soper, 1985; Nakano, 1988). In fact, their negative impact on well-being apparently far exceeds that of major life events (e.g., Holahan, Holahan, & Belk, 1984; Ivancevich, 1986; Landreville & Vezina, 1992; Monroe, 1983; Weinberger, Hiner, & Tierney, 1987).

Critics have ascribed these findings, at least in part, to hassles measurement that is contaminated in content and format with negative well-being (Burks & Martin, 1983; B. P. Dohrenwend & Shrout, 1985; B. S. Dohrenwend, B. P. Dohrenwend, Dodson, & Shrout, 1984; Ewedmi & Linn, 1987; Green, 1986; Marziali & Pilkonis, 1986; Reich, Parrella, & Filstead, 1988). For example, some items of Kanner et al.'s (1981) Hassles Scale, the first and most commonly used measure of hassles, concern alcohol and drug use, sexual difficulties, physical illness, and personal fears. These could be viewed as symptoms of subjective distress or compromised health, physical or mental, rather than contributing causes.

Also, with the Hassles Scale (Kanner et al., 1981), subjects are instructed to indicate the severity of each hassle experienced in the past month, and hassles are explicitly named and defined. Subjects' responses are made on a scale that runs from "somewhat severe" to "extremely severe," thus excluding the possibility that an itemized event might not be experienced as severe or even negative. Therefore, correlations between the Hassles Scale and measures of negative well-being are ambiguous in their implications: The scale could *reflect* distress rather than predicting it. The desirability of testing the relations between hassles and negative well-being with a *decontaminated* hassles measure, whose format and content do not directly imply negative well-being, thus becomes obvious (Flannery, 1986b, p. 1004).

Decontaminated measures of hassles exposure have been recently developed for college students (Kohn, Lafreniere, & Gurevich, 1990), adults (Kohn & Macdonald, 1992b), and high school students (Kohn & Milrose, 1993). The construction of these scales had the following significant features: (a) elimination of items obviously referring to respondents' subjective distress and physical or mental health; (b) subjects' rating of hassles for degree of exposure only, thus excluding consideration of judged severity, desirability, or adverse impact; and (c) use of innocuous titles (e.g., *Survey of Recent Life Experiences*). To retain the element of subjective appraisal of stressfulness despite eliminating severity ratings, we adopted an "indirect approach" (Kohn & Gurevich, 1993): We selected items from our initial pools based on their correlating positively and significantly with the Perceived Stress Scale (PSS; Cohen, Kamarck, & Mermelstein, 1983), an independent measure of subjectively appraised stress. Our assumption was that people generally perceive many of the same events as stressful (Brown, 1990; Costa & McCrae, 1990; Moos & Swindle, 1990; Repetti, 1987), at least within cultures.

All three scales show good internal consistency and correlate highly with subjectively appraised stress as measured by the PSS (Kohn et al., 1990; Kohn & Macdonald, 1992b; Kohn & Milrose, 1993). As well, the factor-based subscales of each measure intercorrelate much less highly than the corresponding subscales of Kanner et al.'s (1981) Hassles Scale, as reported by B. P. Dohrenwend and Shrout (1985). The latter authors ascribed the startlingly high intercorrelations among factor-based subscales to their common contamination by negative well-being. If one accepts that interpretation, in my view a plausible one, it would follow that the Inventory of College Students' Recent Life Experiences (ICSRLE; Kohn et al., 1990), the Survey of Recent Life Experiences (SRLE; Kohn & Macdonald, 1992b), and the Inventory of High-School Students' Recent Life Experiences (IHSSRLE; Kohn & Milrose, 1993) are less contaminated. Finally and most importantly, recent work with two of these decontaminated measures, the ICSRLE and the SRLE, reinforces earlier observations of strong relations between hassles on one hand and physical and mental health on the other (Kohn & Gurevich, 1993; Kohn, Gurevich, Pickering, & Macdonald, 1994; Kohn, Lafreniere, & Gurevich, 1991; Kohn & Macdonald, 1992a).

In fairness to Lazarus and his associates who developed the Hassles Scale (Kanner et al., 1981), he now maintains that hassles measurement should incorporate not only the content of daily stressful experiences and the subjective intensity of responses to them, but also fluctuations in content and intensity over time (Lazarus, 1990). De Longis, Folkman, and Lazarus (1988) have accordingly developed a new measure, the Hassles and Uplifts Scale, which asks respondents to indicate how much of a hassle (as well as how much of an uplift) each of 53 items was *that day* (e.g., *your spouse, your health,* and *legal matters*). In my view, this new measure is *more* vulnerable than the original Hassles Scale to the criticism of criterion contamination because it asks people to make judgments about areas of their life that are likely to reflect strongly respondents' immediate states of subjective well-being and mental health (Krohne, 1990). Furthermore, despite De Longis et al.'s (1988, p. 488) claim to have "eliminated items and words that suggested psychological and somatic symptoms," suspect items do remain (e.g., *your smoking, your drinking, mood-altering drugs,* and *your health*).

Specific Hassles

Despite the vulnerability of early (and continuing) work to the criticism of criterion contamination, the relationship between hassles exposure and negative well-being still holds up in more recent research with decontaminated hassles measures. Such work emphasizes the adverse impact of cumulative global exposure to hassles of many kinds.

What do we know, though, about the adverse impact of specific classes of hassles, taken singly, such as traffic congestion and family discord? The experience of traffic congestion in commuting or as part of one's work (e.g., as a bus driver) has been found to relate to the following indicators of stress: elevated levels of adrenaline and noradrenaline in urine samples (Evans & Carrere, 1991); work absenteeism because of illness, frequency of colds and flu, negative mood at home, and chest pain (Novaco, Stokols, & Milanesi, 1990); and feelings of tension and nervousness, and elevated systolic blood pressure (Stokols, Novaco, Stokols, & Campbell, 1978).

Marital difficulties apparently contribute to both subjective distress (Felton, Lehmann, Brown, & Liberatos, 1980) and elevated blood pressure (Ewart, Taylor, Kraemer, & Agras, 1991). For subjective distress, a major contributor is discordance between the individuals preferred and actual state of cohabitation versus separation from his or her spouse—cohabiting when the person prefers separation or living separately when he or she desires cohabitation (Felton et al., 1980). Specific contributors to elevated blood pressure during acute disagreements are, in women, hostile outbursts on their part, and, in men, accelerated speech on theirs (Ewart et al., 1991). Unfortunately, suppression of anger by wives, and withdrawal and passivity by husbands augur poorly for marital survival, whatever their contributions might be to cardiovascular health. A possible solution is training in techniques such as anger management, turn taking, role reversal, and fair fighting.

For the children of maritally discordant families, a particular risk is blaming themselves for failing to intervene successfully, on the assumption that they could make a difference (Rossman & Rosenberg, 1992). Typically, children's efforts at intervention are unsuccessful and soon extinguish from the lack of payoff (Luepnitz, 1979). Where violence occurs between the parents, children report a high rate of somatic complaints (Rossman & Rosenberg, 1992).

In summary, intense, prolonged, or repetitive exposure to specific kinds of hassles, such as traffic congestion and marital disagreements, can contribute to subjective distress, elevated blood pressure and catecholamine levels, susceptibility to minor ailments, and absenteeism from work.

MODES OF COPING: THEIR ASSESSMENT AND CONSEQUENCES

Coping may be defined as adapting consciously to stressors (in contrast to "defense," which is unconscious). It can involve either reaction to an immediate stressor (coping response) or a consistent manner of dealing with stressors across time and situations (coping style). The stressors in question include hassles as well as traumas and negative major life events.

Although some experts argue that situational factors are more important than personally consistent styles in determining adaptive response (Cohen, 1987; Compas, Malcarne, & Fondacaro, 1988; Fleishman, 1984; Lazarus & Folkman, 1987), more recent evidence suggests considerable stability in individuals' coping styles over time (Carver, Scheier, & Weintraub, 1989; Endler & Parker, 1990b;

Miller, 1990). Two consistently identified modes of coping have been problem-focused coping, which is directed at remedying a threatening or harmful external situation, and emotion-focused coping, which may be variously directed at ventilating, managing, or palliating an emotional response to such a situation (Carver et al., 1989; Endler & Parker, 1990b; Folkman & Lazarus, 1980). Some experts have identified a third general mode, avoidance-focused coping, which entails the attempt to disengage mentally or even physically from threatening or damaging situations (Amirkhan, 1990; Billings & Moos, 1981; Carver et al., 1989; Cornelius & Caspi, 1987; Endler & Parker, 1990b; Feifel & Strack, 1989; Miller, 1990).

Attempts to measure modes of coping have encountered strong psychometric criticism (e.g., Cohen, 1987; Parker & Endler, 1992; Tennen & Herzberger, 1985). In a critical review of some 14 measures of coping style or coping response, Parker and Endler (1992) pointed to the following flaws as each applying to at least one of the measures reviewed: low reliabilities; no information on factor structure; no data on construct validity; no cross-validation of reported factor structures; difficulty in replicating an initially reported factor structure; inadequate description of procedures and findings in the development of scales; overfactoring through use of the minimum eigenvalue of 1.00 procedure; inadequate sample size for factor analysis, given the number of items; failure to report test-retest reliabilities; and failure formally to substantiate the claim of similar factor structures across samples (e.g., through the use of congruence coefficients).

Endler and Parker's (1990a, 1990b) own measure, the Coping Inventory for Stressful Situations (CISS), was carefully developed to avoid most of these pitfalls in its measurement of task-oriented, emotion-oriented, and avoidance-oriented coping styles. One criticism, however, of the CISS is that its Emotion-Oriented Coping subscale almost entirely concerns emotional ventilation (e.g., *Take it out on other people*) and failure to cope (e.g., *Freeze and don't know what to do*) and hardly touches on emotional self-management or palliation (e.g., *Try to look on the bright side*). (The first two examples come from the CISS's Emotion-Oriented Coping subscale, whereas the third does not.)

The remaining literature review on coping that follows is based in large part on the very measures that have been so heavily criticized. Obviously, this qualifies, if not compromises, its conclusiveness; nonetheless, for the sake of brevity and because, with all its limitations, it reflects the closest approximation we presently have to knowledge in this area, we shall belabor the point no further. *Caveat emptor* henceforth.

Research indicates that problem-focused coping is significantly, if modestly, predictive of positive adaptation (Bhagat, Allie, & Ford, 1991; Billings & Moos, 1981; Compas et al., 1988; Cornelius & Caspi, 1987; Endler & Parker, 1990a, 1990b, 1990c; Headey & Wearing, 1990; Mitchell, Cronkite, & Moos, 1983; Vitaliano, DeWolfe, Maiuro, Russo, & Katon, 1990). Emotion-focused coping, in contrast, has consistently proven to be associated with negative adaptation (Edwards & Trimble, 1992; Endler & Parker, 1990a, 1990b, 1990c; Forsythe & Compas, 1987; Lobel, Gilat, & Endler, 1993; Mitchell et al., 1983; Turner,

King, & Tremblay, 1992). The evidence on avoidance-focused coping is more mixed: Whereas some studies attribute negative adaptive consequences to avoidance-focused coping (Aldwin & Revenson, 1987; Beiler & Terrell, 1990; Billings & Moos, 1981; Davey et al., 1993; Endler & Parker, 1990a; Felton & Revenson, 1984; Headey & Wearing, 1990; Mullins, Olson, Reyes, Bernardy, Huszti, & Volk, 1991), others claim positive adaptive consequences (Miller, 1990; Miller, Brody, & Summerton, 1988), and still others report no significant impact for avoidance-focused coping (Lobel et al., 1993).

CUMULATIVE HASSLES EXPOSURE AND COPING STYLES

An important observation has been that coping and stress-coping interactions explain little additional variance in negative well-being beyond that accounted for by hassles alone (Kohn, Hay, & Legere, 1994; Lu, 1991; Nakano, 1991). For example, Kohn et al. reported two studies, one with university students and one with high school teachers, on the effects of daily hassles and coping styles on physical and mental health and subjective distress. Although the specific findings differed somewhat by population, the major findings were that coping and hassles-coping interactions had little impact beyond hassles alone on mental health and subjective distress, and none on minor physical ailments. Lu (1991) and Nakano (1991), using quite different designs and measures, made similar observations.

A possible explanation for the limited impact of coping styles in themselves and in conjunction with hassles is that *style* is not the most useful way of conceptualizing dispositional coping, because which style is most effective will vary with circumstance. Indeed, the commonness of relevant circumstances may differ across populations in such a way as to alter the relationships between coping styles and negative well-being. This could explain, for example, why avoidance-oriented coping alleviates the perception of stress in high school teachers but not in university students (Kohn et al., 1994). Reinhold Niebuhr (Bartlett, 1968, p. 1024) probably expressed it best in praying for "serenity to accept what cannot be changed, courage to change what should be changed, and wisdom to distinguish the one from the other."

The notion that active coping (problem-focused) and passive coping (emotion-focused and avoidance-focused) are each effective but under different circumstances has representation in psychology as well as religion (e.g., Felton & Revenson, 1984; Folkman & Lazarus, 1980; Forsythe & Compas, 1987; Hobfoll et al., 1991). The evidence suggests that people are more likely to cope actively in subjectively controllable situations that are perceived as subject to constructive change than in uncontrollable ones (Carver et al., 1989; Catanzaro & Greenwood, 1994; Folkman & Lazarus, 1980; Forsythe & Compas, 1987). Some studies further indicate that active coping is more effective in controllable situations (Compas et al., 1988; Knight, 1987, 1990), at least in normal populations but apparently not in psychiatric populations (Vitaliano et al., 1990). Not all studies, however, have found the expected interaction between coping style and controllability (e.g., Felton & Revenson, 1984). Aldwin and Revenson (1987) suggested that the effectiveness of problem-focused coping in reducing stress depends on whether the specific action taken solves the stress-inducing problem. In any event, the upshot appears to be that what modes of coping are likeliest to occur and likeliest to be adaptive depends on circumstance. The following section reviews research on specific hassles such as university examinations, familial discord, noise, and traffic congestion to determine whether the same analysis applies.

COPING WITH INDIVIDUAL HASSLES

University Examinations

Academic examinations are a familiar hassle to college students. Accordingly, how students cope with them has been a subject of some study.

Folkman and Lazarus (1985) demonstrated that the source of stress and manner of coping change from before an exam (Time 1) through the interval between the exam and availability of marks (Time 2) to after the marks are available (Time 3). Students' perceptions of their situation as one of threat or challenge declined from Time 1 and Time 2 to Time 3, whereas perceptions of harm and benefit correspondingly rose. The vast majority of students, over 90% in each case, reported using some coping responses of both problem-focused and emotion-focused kinds at all three time points. Problem-focused coping declined from Time 1 to Time 3, presumably because such action was most practical before the exam (e.g., studying, seeking help in weak areas, consulting old exams). Emotion-focused coping varied inversely with the grade obtained, presumably because poor performance, unlike good performance, would probably evoke emotional palliation or emotional ventilation.

Abella and Heslin (1989) found that the emotional response to problem-focused and avoidance-focused coping depended on students' expectations as to their performance on an exam. Students with favorable expectations reacted positively after highly problem-focused coping but negatively after highly avoidance-focused coping, whereas students with unfavorable expectations showed the opposite pattern.

Edwards and Trimble (1992) examined the impact of both coping style and coping response on exam-related state anxiety, exam grade, and course grade. They found that an emotion-oriented coping response contributed positively to exam-related state anxiety. (Because they used the CISS for coping styles and a modification of it for coping responses, their measure of emotion-focused coping response probably reflects emotional ventilation more than emotional palliation.) Task-focused response predicted exam grade positively, whereas emotion-focused response proved a negative predictor. In terms of course grade, task-focused response contributed positively, whereas avoidant coping style detracted. Thus, academic performance seems to depend on a specific problem-focused investment rather than a problem-focused style. The distinction is meaningful because occasionally individuals with a general problem-oriented coping style will be unable to apply it to the occasion of a specific exam, or for periods of time in a course due to health problems, competing demands, or other preoccupations. In contrast, an avoidance-oriented coping *style* might detract from general academic performance because it is inimical to problem-focused response; for example, it might evoke excessive procrastination.

Cooley and Klinger (1989) showed how students' general attributional styles for success and failure influenced their coping responses for an upcoming test. Those who give external attributions for failure tend not to show much problem-focused coping. In contrast, more avoidant responses positively reflect external attributions for success *and* failure.

Thus, in line with the previously cited literature, it appears that what works best emotionally in an exam situation depends on a variety of circumstances: point in time (e.g., before exam, before grades are available, after grades are available); students' expectation as to performance; and general style of attribution for success and failure. Nonetheless, actual *performance* on exams seems generally to reflect problem-focused action.

Familial Discord

In comparing distressed and nondistressed couples, Sabourin, Laporte, and Wright (1990) found the following characteristics to distinguish distressed couples: avoidance of problem-solving activities; lack of confidence in their problem-solving abilities; and poor strategies of self-control. Distressed couples were less likely to make optimistic comparisons with others, less likely to negotiate, more resigned to their lot, and more emotionally explosive. Optimistic comparison for both genders and problem solving for men were particularly predictive of marital satisfaction. A problem with such cross-sectional associations is that it remains unclear whether the differing coping styles explain distress or its absence, result from distress or its absence, or reflect the operation of such third variables as level of exposure to other stressors (e.g., financial problems, social isolation, or difficult children).

Felton et al. (1980) reported that unwanted separation and unwanted cohabitation increased subjective distress in both genders. The same was true of traditionalistic beliefs concerning the roles of men and women. In women, traditionalism was even more counterproductive when their preferences concerning cohabitation versus separation were met than otherwise. These findings suggest that attempting to force a solution inconsistent with either spouse's preferences (e.g., staying together for the children) is likely to evoke a great deal of unhappiness. It also seems possible that traditional sex-role ideology doesn't particularly help people to meet their own needs or deal effectively with current external realities (e.g., to support a family on the husband's income alone, or to expect as much housework from an externally employed wife as from a full-time housewife).

In a retrospective study of college students whose parents had divorced, Luepnitz (1979) observed a variety of coping responses: somatization which was rare among older children (e.g., vomiting, ulcers, drastic weight change, and hair loss); social withdrawal; fantasy, which was usually temporary and best treated in a laissez-faire manner; attempted intervention in the parents' disagreements, which was generally ineffective and consequently soon extinguished; the cultivation of alternative sources of gratification (e.g., school, sports, and clubs); avoidance of home; social support (e.g., from one parent, a sibling, a best friend, or a teacher); interpretation or cognitive restructuring by the child of his or her circumstances; and help from an external agency (e.g., psychotherapy).

Rossman and Rosenberg (1992) found that the false belief of control over their parents' conflict decreased confidence in their competence by children from discordant homes. Moreover, this effect was more severe, the greater the parental conflict was. Self-calming or emotional palliation, on the other hand, was effective in reducing the total amount of problem behavior reported by the children's mothers.

Grych and Fincham (1993) used analogue experiments with fifth graders to determine the circumstances under which children use various coping strategies. They found that, when the conflict appeared to center on the child, intervention was likely. If the dispute was fairly low key, children indicated an intention to intervene directly (e.g., by siding with one parent); however, if the disagreement was severe, indirect intervention was likelier, such as the child's offering to reform his or her behavior in the area under dispute (e.g., to do school homework right after supper). Finally, when the conflict did not pertain to the child, the expressed likelihood of intervention was low.

In summary, it seems that, for both spouses and children, a problem-oriented approach is likeliest to occur and, for spouses, to succeed when the problem is perceived as soluble (e.g., when both spouses are committed to either maintaining the marriage or dissolving it, or when the child's intervening in the parental dispute is at least topic-relevant). It also seems that misjudged attempts at active intervention can cost dearly, whereas emotional palliation works better when the problem is insoluble (e.g., when circumstances do not permit the person to exercise his or her preference concerning cohabitation versus separation or when the parents' marital issues do not really center on the child).

Noise and Noise-Induced Damage

Noise can be defined as sound that is physiologically arousing and subjectively annoying. Topf (1985) studied how postsurgical patients coped with hospital noise. The main finding was that objective noise level, patient's sensitivity to noise, and noise-induced stress all contributed positively to active coping. This could include using available earplugs or an available transistor radio with earphones, or cognitive-control techniques such as mentally tuning out ambient noise or distracting oneself. Patients most commonly used cognitive-control techniques.

Hallberg, Erlandsson, and Carlsson (1992) examined the coping strategies of male subjects with noise-induced hearing loss, comparing those without tinnitus, with mild tinnitus, and with severe tinnitus. (Tinnitus refers to perception of internal noises, mainly with a perceived origin inside the head, which occur without an external acoustic source.) Three styles of coping were considered: active coping, passive acceptance, and escape coping (e.g., drinking, wishful thinking, and religion). Subjects with severe tinnitus were more likely than those with mild tinnitus or no tinnitus to resort to escape coping.

Thus, in the areas of noise control and coping with noise-induced hearing damage, people seem to cope actively when that strategy is convenient and effective but passively when it is not.

Traffic Congestion

Novaco, Stokols, and Milanesi (1990) found that changing to a job that reduced exposure to traffic-based impedance in commuting to work was an effective means of coping with stress based on such impedance. Correspondingly, they observed that subjective impedance (the person's evaluation of the severity of traffic-based impedance) reflected not only objective impedance, as defined by the distance commuted and the time consumed therein, but also the commuter's perception of choice in the car driven, the route followed, and the location of residence. This highlights that finding a residentially more convenient job is an alternative not open to everybody, especially in economically difficult times.

Evans and Carrere (1991) studied the relations among traffic congestion, perceived control, and psychophysiological stress in urban bus drivers. They found no effects for any of their coping measures, either alone or in interaction with traffic congestion, on their indexes of psychophysiological stress, urinary catecholamines. They did, however, show that perceived control mediated the adverse impact of traffic impedance on stress; specifically, heavy traffic impeded the bus drivers' ability to stay on schedule by adjusting their driving speeds which, in turn, increased stress.

Once more, this time in relation to traffic congestion, it appears that active coping is the method of choice—but only if there is a choice, which often there isn't.

Crowding

Crowding is distinguished from physical density, e.g., persons per acre. Specifically, crowding has been defined as a stressor based on the perceived need for space exceeding the available supply. Why wouldn't crowding then be simply isomorphic with density? The answer is that context can justify high density or increased demand for space under low density. On one hand, people cheerfully accept high density when watching major public athletic events (e.g., during the Olympics); on the other hand, competitors in such athletic events as shot-putting, hammer-throwing, discus, and javelin require what would normally be inordinate space for themselves while competing.

Stokols (1976) suggested in a theoretical paper that crowding entailed several "substressors," each with its own adverse cognitive and emotional consequences and likely adaptational responses. For example, stimulation-overload predisposes confusion and fatigue to which overt or covert withdrawal is a likely adaptational response. (This might include Milgram's, 1970, selective attention to environmental inputs, stringent time-allocation per input, and aloofness to strangers.) Constraint or impedance of an individual's endeavors might be expected to produce reactance (Brehm, 1966) or motivation to counteract perceived infringements of freedom to which he or she could respond by either leaving the situation or negotiating improved coordination with others. Finally, overmanning or scarcity of unique roles should lead to marginalization and concomitant loss of social standing to which the response might be attempted self-aggrandizement and empire building. (The term "overmanning" was coined before the current emphasis on nonsexist terminology.) These theoretical ideas are interesting and again suggest that whether active coping (e.g., negotiating with others, aggrandizing one's own role) or passive coping (e.g., aloofness to strangers) occurs depends very much on the circumstance and the perceived prospect of adaptational success.

An earlier experiment (Stokols, Rall, Pinner, & Schopler, 1973) indicates that humor and laughter are often used as ways of coping with unavoidable crowding during task performance. This could be viewed as emotional palliation in the absence of opportunity to cope actively.

COPING WITH EVERYDAY HASSLES: A PERSPECTIVE AND ITS IMPLICATIONS

Niebuhr's famous prayer for serenity, courage, and wisdom (Bartlett, 1968, p. 1024) deserves consideration as a source of research hypotheses. I would, however, substitute the terms, *self-control, determination,* and *judgment,* respectively, for greater precision. (One must make allowances for homiletic license.) Essentially, a person who encounters a stressful situation in everyday life typically is aware of a variety of alternative responses. Some will be more adaptive than others; commonly, some are quite maladaptive. Adaptive choice requires astute judgment, but, this is not sufficient for adaptive response. On any given occasion, the adaptive choice could either constitute active coping (problem-focused) or passive coping (emotion-focused or avoidance-focused). In the former instance, determination might be required to overcome inhibiting factors (e.g., the prospect of hurting a friend's feelings, being rejected by a romantic partner, or provoking a bad-tempered colleague); in contrast, passive coping may require self-control in the face of contrary impulses (e.g., keeping one's temper in check despite strong and deliberate provocation, or standing fast in the face of serious attempted intimidation).

There are some psychometric implications: Researchers would need to measure the resultant quality, for which *adaptiveness* would seem a good name. An obvious technique would be to use items that confront the subject with a common, everyday stressful situation and several alternative responses—say one each of a problem-focused, emotionally palliative, emotionally ventilative, and avoidance-focused nature. In each case, the subjects' task would be to indicate what they think would be their likeliest response. Scoring would be based on experts' prior rank-ordering of the alternatives for adaptiveness. For approximately half the items, the best response would be active, and, for the rest, it would be passive.

A number of measures have been developed that reflect a similar conceptualization of coping: the Constructive Thinking Inventory (CTI; Epstein & Meier, 1989), the Everyday Problem Solving Inventory (EPSI; Cornelius & Caspi, 1987), the Personal Problem-Solving Inventory (PPSI; Heppner & Peterson, 1982), and the Social Problem Solving Inventory (SPSI; D'Zurilla & Nezu, 1990). Of these, the EPSI comes closest to the format we have suggested, but it has a very laborious scoring method. The PPSI has been shown to account by itself and in interaction with major life events for substantial variability in depression among university students (Nezu, Nezu, Saraydarian, Kalmar, & Ronan, 1986).

At a more advanced stage, separate measures of judgment, determination, and self-control could be developed. The judgment measure could use items resembling those used for adaptiveness, but ask subjects to identify what they consider the "best" response rather than their likeliest response. The determination scale could be based on hypothetical stressful situations where the person's judgment has elected an active response as most adaptive, but where there are strong inhibiting factors. The format would require the subject to indicate his or her subjective probability of actually executing that response. In contrast, the self-control scale could be based on hypothetical stressful situations where the person's judgment has elected a passive response as most adaptive, but where there are strong contrary impulses. Again, the task would be for the subject to indicate his or her probability of actually executing the chosen response. Avoiding serious social-desirability bias might be a problem in developing measures of determination and self-control.

The preceding measures would have utility for both research and application. Researchers could use them to test the hypothesis that, additively and interactively, judgment, determination, and self-control are the major determinants of adaptiveness (in effect, an attempt to establish whether Reinhold Niebuhr prayed for the right stuff). Clinicians could apply them to pinpoint the precise adaptive weaknesses of counseling and therapy clients, thus providing possible remedial objectives.

In fact, the entire scheme has important treatment implications. It suggests separate treatment modules for judgment, determination, and self-control. This makes sense because a client's adaptive problems could involve any subset of these components. For example, one individual could have excellent judgment and self-control, but lack the determination to execute in situations calling for an active coping response. Others could have excellent determination, but lack either judgment or self-control, or both—and so on.

Training in judgment could involve specific tuition and practice in generating alternative responses to real and hypothetical situations, considering the likely consequences of each alternative, if chosen, and assessing those consequences against personal values. The effectiveness of such techniques in therapy and counseling has been recognized for about 40 years (Rotter, 1954). Problems of self-control and determination would lend themselves well to treatment by existing techniques of social-skills training, assertiveness training (for determination), role playing, and role reversal (to illustrate how lack of self-control or determination can make the individual a tempting target for manipulation).

In any event, it seems possible that conceptualizing coping as adaptiveness—an amalgam of judgment, determination, and self-control—holds promise for advancing our knowledge and interventive capabilities in the area of stress beyond what the conceptualization of coping as a style or a response has done to date.

CONCLUSION

This chapter concerned coping adaptively with everyday hassles, which were defined as mundane stressors ranging in seriousness from minor annoyances to fairly major problems (Kanner et al., 1981). Time pressure, alienation from work or studies, and social mistreatment are examples of hassles. Coping was defined as conscious adaptation to stressors, including hassles as well as traumas and major life events. Most research treats coping as either a situational reaction (coping response) or a consistent manner of dealing with stress across time and situations (coping style).

Research was reviewed on the assessment and impact of daily hassles. Early studies demonstrated that hassles had substantial adverse impact on mental and physical health and subjective well-being, in fact, apparently considerably more adverse impact than major life events had. Critics, however, suggested that the apparent effects of hassles were sizably inflated by criterion contamination from the health and distress implications of the Hassles Scale's (Kanner et al., 1981) items and format. Accordingly, the present author and his associates developed "decontaminated" hassles measures for college students (Kohn et al., 1990), high school students (Kohn & Milrose, 1993), and adults (Kohn & Macdonald, 1992b). The decontaminated measures also strongly predicted subjective distress, psychiatric symptomatology, and minor physical ailments (e.g., Kohn et al., 1991; Kohn & Macdonald, 1992a).

Next, research on the assessment of coping and the relations between coping and well-being was reviewed. There are serious psychometric difficulties with most existing measures of coping. Endler and Parker's (1990a, 1990b) Coping Inventory for Stressful Situations (CISS) is one of the better measures in this area, psychometrically speaking. In line with much theorization and research in the area, it distinguishes among task- (or problem-) focused coping, emotion-focused coping, and avoidance-focused coping. Much research suggests that problem-focused coping is significantly, if modestly, predictive of positive adaptation. In contrast, emotion-focused coping appears to be associated with negative adaptation, whereas the findings on avoidance-focused coping are mixed and conflicting.

Studies suggest that the explanatory contributions to negative well-being of coping styles and their interactions with hassles are quite modest compared with those of hassles alone (Kohn, Hay, & Legere, 1994; Lu, 1991; Nakano, 1991). In line with much commentary from others, it seems likely that different modes of coping, (e.g., active vs. passive) are adaptive under different circumstances.

Research studies on coping with such specific hassles as university examinations, family discord, noise, traffic congestion, and crowding were reviewed next, partly to determine whether the preceding analysis, that what works best differs with circumstances, notably that of controllability, held in those areas. In my view, it did.

The concept of adaptiveness—responding appropriately to the demands of stressful situations—may be a suitable alternative conceptualization to coping response and coping style. Adaptiveness was defined in this chapter as an amalgam of judgment, determination, and self-control. A broad method was suggested for the assessment of adaptiveness, and allusions were made to closely related existing measures. Proposals were also offered for the measurement of judgment, determination, and self-control as separate components of adaptiveness. Uses were outlined for the proposed measures in both research and applied work. Finally, possible applications of the present conceptualization were suggested for the treatment of stress-management problems.

REFERENCES

Abella, R., & Heslin, R. (1989). Appraisal processes, coping, and the regulation of stress-related emotions in a college examination. *Basic and Applied Social Psychology, 10,* 311–327.

Aldwin, C. M., & Revenson, T. A. (1987). Does coping help? A reexamination of the relation between coping and mental health. *Journal of Personality and Social Psychology, 53,* 337–348.

Amirkhan, J. H. (1990). A factor analytically derived measure of coping: The Coping Strategy Indicator. *Journal of Personality and Social Psychology, 59,* 1066–1074.

Ballieux, R. E., & Heijnen, C. J. (1989). Stress and the immune response. In H. Weiner, I. Florin, R. Murison, & D. Hellhammer (Eds.), *Frontiers of stress research* (pp. 51–55). Toronto, Canada: Huber.

Bartlett, J. (1968). *Bartlett's familiar quotations* (14th ed.). Boston: Little, Brown.

Baum, A., Fleming, R., & Singer, J. E. (1982). Stress at Three Mile Island: Applying psychological impact analysis. In L. Bickman (Ed.), *Applied social psychology annual* (Vol. 3, pp. 217–248). Beverly Hills, CA: Sage.

Beiler, M. E., & Terrell, F. (1990). Stress, coping style, and problem solving ability among eating-disordered patients. *Journal of Clinical Psychology, 46,* 592–599.

Bhagat, R. S., Allie, S. M., & Ford, D. L., Jr. (1991). Organizational stress, personal life stress and symptoms of life strains: An inquiry into the moderating role of styles of coping. *Journal of Social Behaviour and Personality, 6*(7), 163–184.

Billings, A. G., & Moos, R. H. (1981). The role of coping responses and social resources in attenuating the stress of life events. *Journal of Behavioral Medicine, 4,* 139–157.

Brehm, J. W. (1966). *A theory of psychological reactance.* New York: Academic Press.

Brown, G. W. (1990). What about the real world? Hassles and Richard Lazarus. *Psychological Inquiry, 1,* 19–22.

Burks, N., & Martin, B. (1983). Everyday problems and life-change events: Ongoing versus acute sources of stress. *Journal of Human Stress, 11,* 27–35.

Carver, C. S., Scheier, M. F., & Weintraub, J. K. (1989). Assessing coping strategies: A theoretically based approach. *Journal of Personality and Social Psychology, 56,* 267–283.

Catanzaro, S. J., & Greenwood, G. (1994). Expectancies for negative mood regulation, coping, and dysphoria among college students. *Journal of Counseling Psychology, 41,* 34–44.

Cohen, F. (1987). Measurement of coping. In S. V. Kasl & C. L. Cooper (Eds.), *Stress and health: Issues in research methodology.* New York: Wiley.

Cohen, S., Kamarck, T., & Mermelstein, R. (1983). A global measure of perceived stress. *Journal of Health and Social Behavior, 24,* 385–396.

Compas, B. E., Malcarne, V. L., & Fondacaro, K. M. (1988). Coping with stressful events in older children and young adolescents. *Journal of Consulting and Clinical Psychology, 56,* 405–411.

Cooley, E. J., & Klinger, C. R. (1989). Academic attributions and coping with tests. *Journal of Social and Clinical Psychology, 8,* 359–367.

Cornelius, S. W., & Caspi, A. (1987). Everyday problem solving in adulthood and old age. *Psychology and Aging, 2,* 144–153.

Costa, P. T., Jr., & McCrae, R. R. (1990). Personality: Another "hidden factor" in stress research. *Psychological Inquiry, 1,* 22–24.

Davey, G. C. L., Tallis, F., & Hodgson, S. (1993). The relationship between information-seeking and information-avoiding coping styles and the reporting of psychological and physical symptoms. *Journal of Psychosomatic Research, 37,* 333–344.

De Longis, A., Coyne, J. C., Dakof, G., Folkman, S., & Lazarus, R. S. (1982). Relationships of daily hassles, uplifts and major life events to health status. *Health Psychology, 1,* 119–136.

De Longis, A., Folkman, S., & Lazarus, R. S. (1988). The impact of daily stress on health and mood: Psychological and social resources as mediators. *Journal of Personality and Social Psychology, 54,* 486–495.

Dewe, P., Cox, T., & Ferguson, E. (1993). Individual strategies for coping with stress at work: A review. *Work and Stress, 7,* 5–15.

Dohrenwend, B. P., & Shrout, P. E. (1985). "Hassles" in the conceptualization and measurement of life-stress variables. *American Psychologist, 40,* 780–785.

Dohrenwend, B. S., Dohrenwend, B. P., Dodson, M., & Shrout, P. E. (1984). Symptoms, hassles, social supports and life events: Problem of confounded measures. *Journal of Abnormal Psychology, 93,* 222–230.

D'Zurilla, T. J., & Nezu, A. M. (1990). Development and preliminary evaluation of the Social Problem-Solving Inventory. *Psychological Assessment, 2,* 156–163.

Edwards, J. M., & Trimble, K. (1992). Anxiety, coping, and academic performance. *Anxiety, Stress, and Coping, 5,* 337–350.

Endler, N. S., & Parker, J. D. A. (1990a). *Coping Inventory for Stressful Situations: Manual.* Toronto, Canada: Multi-Health Systems.

Endler, N. S., & Parker, J. D. A. (1990b). Multidimensional assessment of coping: A critical evaluation. *Journal of Personality and Social Psychology, 58,* 844–854.

Endler, N. S., & Parker, J. D. A. (1990c). State and trait anxiety, depression and coping styles. *Australian Journal of Psychology, 42,* 207–220.

Epstein, S., & Meier, P. (1989). Constructive thinking: A broad coping variable with specific components. *Journal of Personality and Social Psychology, 57,* 232–250.

Evans, G. W., & Carrere, S. (1991). Traffic congestion, perceived control, and psychophysiological stress among urban bus drivers. *Journal of Applied Psychology, 76,* 658–663.

Ewart, C. K., Taylor, C. B., Kraemer, H. C., & Agras, W. S. (1991). High blood pressure and marital discord: Not being nasty matters more than being nice. *Health Psychology, 10,* 155–163.

Ewedmi, F., & Linn, M. W. (1987). Health and hassles in older and younger men. *Journal of Clinical Psychology, 43,* 347–353.

Feifel, H., & Strack, S. (1989). Coping with conflict situations: Middle-aged and elderly men. *Psychology and Aging, 4,* 26–33.

Felton, B. J., Lehmann, S., Brown, P., & Liberatos, P. (1980). The coping function of sex-role attitudes during marital disruption. *Journal of Health and Social Behavior, 21,* 240–248.

Felton, B. J., & Revenson, T. A. (1984). Coping with chronic illness: A study of illness controllability and the influence of coping strategies on psychological adjustment. *Journal of Consulting and Clinical Psychology, 52,* 343–353.

Flannery, R. B. (1986a). Major life events and daily hassles in predicting health status: Methodological inquiry. *Journal of Clinical Psychology, 42,* 485–487.

Flannery, R. B. (1986b). Negative affectivity, daily hassles, and somatic illness: Preliminary inquiry concerning hassles measurement. *Educational and Psychological Measurement, 46,* 1001–1004.

Fleishman, J. A. (1984). Personality characteristics and coping patterns. *Journal of Health and Social Behavior, 25,* 229–244.

Folkman, S. (1984). Personal control and stress and coping processes: A theoretical analysis. *Journal of Personality and Social Psychology, 46,* 839–852.

Folkman, S., & Lazarus, R. S. (1980). An analysis of coping in a middle-aged community sample. *Journal of Health and Social Behavior, 21,* 219–239.

Folkman, S., & Lazarus, R. S. (1985). If it changes it must be a process: Study of emotion and coping during three stages of a college examination. *Journal of Personality and Social Psychology, 48,* 150–170.

Folkman, S., & Lazarus, R. S. (1990). Coping and emotion. In N. Stein, B. Leventhal, & T. Trabasso (Eds.), *Psychological and biological approaches to emotion.* San Francisco: Erlbaum.

Forsythe, C. J., & Compas, B. E. (1987). Interaction of cognitive appraisals of stressful events and coping: Testing the goodness of fit hypothesis. *Cognitive Therapy and Research, 11*, 473–485.

Green, B. L. (1986). On the confounding of hassles and stress outcome. *American Psychologist, 41*, 714–715.

Grych, J. H., & Fincham, F. D. (1993). Children's appraisals of marital conflict: Initial investigations of the cognitive–contextual framework. *Child Development, 64*, 215–230.

Hallberg, L. R. -M., Erlandsson, S. I., & Carlsson, S. G. (1992). Coping strategies used by middle-aged males with noise-induced hearing loss with and without tinnitus. *Psychology and Health, 7*, 273–288.

Headey, B. W., & Wearing, A. J. (1990). Subjective well-being and coping with adversity. *Social Indicators Research, 22*, 327–349.

Heppner, P. P., & Peterson, C. H. (1982). The development and implications of a Personal Problem-Solving Inventory. *Journal of Counseling Psychology, 29*, 66–75.

Hobfoll, S. E., Spielberger, C. D., Breznity, S., Figley, S., Folkman, S., Lepper-Green, B., Meichenbaum, D., Milgram, N. A., Sandler, I., Sarason, I., & van der Kolk, B. (1991). War-related stress: Addressing the stress of war and other traumatic events. *American Psychologist, 46*, 848–855.

Holahan, C. K., Holahan, C. J., & Belk, S. S. (1984). Adjustment in aging: The roles of life stress, hassles and self-efficacy. *Health Psychology, 3*, 315–328.

Holt, P., Fine, M. J., & Tollefson, N. (1987). Mediating stress: Survival of the hardy. *Psychology in the Schools, 24*, 51–58.

Ivancevich, J. M. (1986). Life events and hassles as predictors of health symptoms, job performance and absenteeism. *Journal of Occupational Behavior, 7*, 39–51.

Jabaaij, L., Grosheide, P. M., Heijtink, R. A., Duivenvoorden, H. J., Ballieux, R. E., & Vingerhoets, A. J. J. M. (1993). Influence of perceived psychological stress and distress on antibody response to low dose rDNA hepatitis B vaccine. *Journal of Psychosomatic Research, 4*, 361–369.

Johnson, M., & Stone, G. L. (1986). Social workers and burnout: A psychological description. *Journal of Social Service Research, 10*(1), 67–80.

Kanner, A. D., Coyne, J. C., Schaefer, C., & Lazarus, R. S. (1981). Comparison of two modes of stress measurement: Daily hassles and uplifts versus major life events. *Journal of Behavioral Medicine, 4*, 1–39.

Knight, E. A. (1987). Perceived control, coping style, and stress arousal in a job setting. In J. H. Humphrey (Ed.), *Human stress: Current selected research* (Vol. 2, pp. 55–72). New York: AMS Press.

Knight, E. A. (1990). Perceived control and actual outcomes of hassles situations on the job. *Psychological Reports, 67*, 891–898.

Kohn, P. M., & Gurevich, M. (1993). On the adequacy of the indirect method of measuring the primary appraisal of hassles-based stress. *Personality and Individual Differences, 14*, 679–684.

Kohn, P. M., Gurevich, M., Pickering, D. I., & Macdonald, J. E. (1994). Alexithymia, reactivity, and the adverse impact of hassles-based stress. *Personality and Individual Differences, 16*, 805–812.

Kohn, P. M., Hay, B. D., & Legere, J. J. (1994). Hassles, coping style, and negative well-being. *Personality and Individual Differences, 17,* 169–179.

Kohn, P. M., Lafreniere, K., & Gurevich, M. (1990). The Inventory of College Students' Recent Life Experiences: A decontaminated hassles scale for a special population. *Journal of Behavioral Medicine, 13,* 619–630.

Kohn, P. M., Lafreniere, K., & Gurevich, M. (1991). Hassles, health, and personality. *Journal of Personality and Social Psychology, 61,* 478–482.

Kohn, P. M., & Macdonald, J. E. (1992a). Hassles, anxiety, and negative well-being. *Anxiety, Stress, and Coping, 5,* 151–163.

Kohn, P. M., & Macdonald, J. E. (1992b). The Survey of Recent Life Experiences: A decontaminated hassles scale for adults. *Journal of Behavioral Medicine, 15,* 221–236.

Kohn, P. M., & Milrose, J. A. (1993). The Inventory of High-School Students' Recent Life Experiences: A decontaminated measure of adolescents' hassles. *Journal of Youth and Adolescence, 22,* 43–55.

Krohne, H. W. (1990). Personality as a mediator between objective events and their subjective representation. *Psychological Inquiry, 1,* 26–29.

Landreville, P., & Vezina, J. (1992). A comparison of daily hassles and major life events as correlates of well-being in older adults. *Canadian Journal on Aging, 11,* 137–149.

Lazarus, R. S. (1990). Theory-based stress measurement. *Psychological Inquiry, 1,* 3–13.

Lazarus, R. S., & Folkman, S. (1987). Transactional theory and research on emotions and coping. *European Journal of Personality, 1,* 141–169.

Lee, H. B., Chan, D. W., & Yik, M. S. M. (1992). Coping style and psychological distress among Chinese adolescents in Hong Kong. *Journal of Adolescent Research, 7,* 494–506.

Leiter, M. P. (1990). The impact of family resources, control coping, and skill utilization on the development of burnout: A longitudinal study. *Human Relations, 11,* 1067–1083.

Lichtenberg, P. A., Swensen, C. H., & Skehan, M. W. (1986). Further investigation of the role of personality, lifestyle and arthritic severity in predicting pain. *Journal of Psychosomatic Research, 30,* 327–337.

Lobel, T. E., Gilat, I., & Endler, N. S. (1993). The Gulf War: Distressful reactions to SCUD missiles attacks. *Anxiety, Stress, and Coping, 6,* 9–23.

Lu, L. (1991). Daily hassles and mental health: A longitudinal study. *British Journal of Psychology, 82,* 441–447.

Luepnitz, D. (1979). Which aspects of divorce affect children? *Family Coordinator, 28,* 79–85.

Martin, J. B., & Pihl, R. O. (1985). The stress-alexithymia hypothesis: Theoretical and empirical considerations. *Psychotherapy and Psychosomatics, 43,* 169–176.

Marziali, E. A., & Pilkonis, P. A. (1986). The measurement of subjective response to stressful life events. *Journal of Human Stress, 12,* 5–12.

Milgram, S. (1970). The experience of living in cities. *Science, 167,* 1461–1468.

Miller, M. J., Wilcox, C. J., & Soper, B. (1985). Measuring hassles and uplifts among adolescents: A different approach to the study of stress. *School Counsellor, 33,* 107–110.

Miller, S. M. (1990). To see or not to see: Cognitive informational styles in the coping process. In M. Rosenbaum (Ed.), *Learned resourcefulness: On coping skills, self-control, and adaptive behavior* (pp. 95–126). New York: Springer.

Miller, S. M., Brody, D. S., & Summerton, J. (1988). Styles of coping with threat: Implications for health. *Journal of Personality and Social Psychology, 54,* 142–148.

Mitchell, R. E., Cronkite, R. C., & Moos, R. H. (1983). Stress, coping, and depression among married couples. *Journal of Personality and Social Psychology, 92,* 433–448.

Monroe, S. M. (1983). Major and minor life events as predictors of psychological distress: Further issues and findings. *Journal of Behavioral Medicine, 6,* 189–205.

Moos, R. H., & Swindle, R. W., Jr. (1990). Person-environment transactions and the stressor-appraisal-coping process. *Psychological Inquiry, 1,* 30–32.

Mullins, L. L., Olson, R. A., Reyes, S., Bernardy, N., Huszti, H. C., & Volk, R. J. (1991). Risk and resistance factors in the adaptation of mothers of children with cystic fibrosis. *Journal of Pediatric Psychology, 16,* 701–715.

Nakano, K. (1988). Hassles as a measure of stress in a Japanese sample: Preliminary research. *Psychological Reports, 63,* 252–254.

Nakano, K. (1991). The role of coping strategies on psychological and physical well-being. *Japanese Psychological Research, 33,* 160–167.

Nezu, A. M., Nezu, C. M., Saraydarian, L., Kalmar, K., & Ronan, G. F. (1986). Social problem solving as a moderating variable between negative life stress and depressive symptoms. *Cognitive Therapy and Research, 10,* 489–498.

Novaco, R. W., Stokols, D., & Milanesi, L. (1990). Objective and subjective dimensions of travel impedance as determinants of commuting stress. *American Journal of Community Psychology, 18,* 231–257.

Nowack, K. M. (1991). Psychosocial predictors of health status. *Work and Stress, 5,* 117–131.

Parker, J. D. A., & Endler, N. S. (1992). Coping with coping assessment: A critical review. *European Journal of Personality, 6,* 321–344.

Reich, W. P., Parrella, D. P., & Filstead, W. J. (1988). Unconfounding the Hassles Scale: External sources versus internal responses to stress. *Journal of Behavioural Medicine, 11,* 239–249.

Repetti, R. L. (1987). Individual and common components of the social environment at work and psychological well-being. *Journal of Personality and Social Psychology, 52,* 710–720.

Rossman, B. B. R., & Rosenberg, M. S. (1992). Family stress and functioning in children: The moderating effects of children's beliefs about their control over parental conflict. *Journal of Child Psychology and Psychiatry and Allied Disciplines, 33,* 699–715.

Rotter, J. B. (1954). *Social learning and clinical psychology.* Englewood Cliffs, NJ: Prentice-Hall.

Sabourin, S., Laporte, L., & Wright, J. (1990). Problem-solving self-appraisal and coping efforts in distressed and nondistressed couples. *Journal of Marital and Family Therapy, 16,* 89–97.

Stokols, D. (1976). The experience of crowding in primary and secondary environments. *Environment and Behavior, 8,* 49–86.

Stokols, D., Novaco, R. W., Stokols, J., & Campbell, J. (1978). Traffic congestion, Type A behavior, and stress. *Journal of Applied Psychology, 63,* 467–480.

Stokols, D., Rall, M., Pinner, P., & Schopler, J. (1973). Physical, social, and personal determinants of the perception of crowding. *Environment and Behavior, 5,* 87–115.

Tennen, H., & Herzberger, S. (1985). Ways of Coping Scale. In D. J. Keyser & R. C. Sweetland (Eds.), *Test critiques* (Vol. 3, pp. 686–697). Kansas City, MO: Test Corporation of America.

Topf, M. (1985). Noise-induced stress in hospital patients: Coping and nonauditory health outcomes. *Journal of Human Stress, 11,* 125–134.

Turner, R. A., King, P. R., & Tremblay, P. F. (1992). Coping styles and depression among psychiatric outpatients. *Personality and Individual Differences, 13,* 1145–1147.

Vitaliano, P. P., DeWolfe, D. J., Maiuro, R. D., Russo, J., & Katon, W. (1990). Appraised changeability of a stressor as a modifier of the relationship between coping and depression. *Journal of Personality and Social Psychology, 59,* 582–592.

Weinberger, M., Hiner, S. L., & Tierney, W. M. (1987). In support of hassles as a measure of stress in predicting health outcomes. *Journal of Behavioral Medicine, 10,* 19–31.

CHAPTER 10

Coping in Occupational Settings

SUE CARTWRIGHT and CARY L. COOPER

We spend a considerable amount of our lives at work. While work can be challenging and satisfying in fulfilling an individual's needs and providing a sense of purpose (Warr, 1982), it has become increasingly recognized that the workplace can also be stressful. Stressful work contexts have been linked to a wide range of negative outcomes that impair the effective functioning of both employees and their employing organizations.

Research has demonstrated that occupational stress can adversely affect physical and mental health (Cartwright & Cooper, 1993; Cooper, Cooper, & Eaker, 1988), job satisfaction and performance (Cooper & Roden, 1985), and labor turnover (Hendrix, Ovalle, & Troxler, 1985), and also result in increasing incidents of aggressive behaviors, accidents, and theft in the workplace (Chen & Spector, 1992; Sutherland & Cooper, 1990). Against a background of mounting research evidence (Cooper & Payne, 1988), there can be little dispute that work-related stress is responsible for immense humanistic and financial costs. In terms of sickness, absence, and premature death or retirement due to alcoholism, stress costs the economy of the United Kingdom £2 billion per annum (Cartwright & Cooper, 1994). The annual cost of stress-related absence and sickness, reduced productivity, and associated health and compensation costs in the United States is estimated to be more than $150 billion a year (Karasek & Theorell, 1990). Between 60% to 80% of all job accidents are estimated to be stress related. The indirect costs of stress are also reflected in the increasing level of substance abuse, rising divorce rates, and deaths from lung cancer.

Furthermore, occupational stress appears to be a growing problem as many organizations increasingly find themselves functioning in rapidly changing internal and external environments. However, it is not just change and its attendant uncertainty that are the significant precursors of stress in the 1990s. As organizations have become leaner and more aggressively competitive, this has had the effect of increasing individual workloads, as well as fueling endemic fears concerning future job security.

The extent to which organizations and their individual members learn to cope effectively with the stresses and strains of work has important implications for their continued survival and for society generally. In this chapter, we focus on the ways in which the problem of work stress can be addressed at the individual, workgroup, and organizational level. Given the complexity and inherent constraints that limit the range of coping mechanisms available to the individual in an occupational setting, stress reduction can only be effectively achieved if the organization shares the responsibility for coping. In support of this argument, we will discuss the limitations of individual coping and the extent to which organizational initiatives have sought to extend these resources. Current organizational practices in the area of stress management have generally given insufficient attention to modifying or eliminating the *stressors* in the work environment, many of which are not within the direct control of the individual.

STRESS AND COPING

Earlier definitions within the literature conceptualize stress as being an external stimulus, a physiological response, or an environmental condition. Later definitions have emphasized the active role played by the individual in the stress process (Cox, 1978) and have suggested that stress is best understood as resulting from the interaction or some imbalance between the individual and aspects of the environment. Within cybernetic theory (Edwards, 1988), stress is defined as a negative discrepancy between an individual's perceived and desired state, provided that the presence of this discrepancy is considered important by the individual. Consequently, consistent to both definitions, the meaning individuals give to a particular encounter is important in determining whether a situation is experienced as stressful and identified as a threat. Therefore, different individuals are likely to perceive different situations as being stressful, and also deal with those situations in different and various ways.

Within both the transactional and cybernetic framework, there is widespread consensus among researchers that coping is an important moderator in the stress process. Having appraised an event or situation as threatening or stressful, coping refers to any response or effort made by the individual to prevent, avoid, or control emotional distress and/or reduce anxiety (Aldwin & Revenson, 1987). A response that successfully buffers the stress-strain relationship constitutes an effective coping strategy.

Despite the recognized importance of coping, the current literature has been variously described as being diverse (Endler & Parker, 1990), difficult to organize (Edwards, 1988), and laden with problems (Cohen, 1987). There are particular difficulties surrounding the measurement of coping. Dewe, Cox, and Ferguson (1993) suggest the area will remain problematic until there is a clear differentiation between coping *style,* which is a context-free construct, and coping *behavior,* which is context-dependent. Scales also vary considerably in the specificity of the completion instructions given to respondents, making any comparative analysis difficult. Furthermore, despite the growing volume of occupational stress research, relatively few studies have specifically addressed employees' efforts to cope with the stresses and strains of the workplace (Schwartz & Stone, 1993), which may be appraised and coped with differently than general life stress. This issue again raises the question of situational influence. Similarly, stress from daily work-related problems or hassles (e.g., negative interpersonal relationships), may differ from more chronic job-induced stress (e.g., job loss or a corporate takeover).

Sources of Workplace Stress

Whereas stress may have common manifestations and symptomology (e.g., raised blood pressure, irritability, insomnia, depressed mood), the potential sources of workplace stress are many and various, and are not necessarily easy for the individual or the organization to identify, nor to deal with systematically and effectively. According to the model proposed by Cooper and Marshall (1978), the sources of occupational stress can be considered as falling within six broad categories:

1. *Factors Intrinsic to the Job.* These include qualitative and quantitative work overload, poor physical working conditions or badly designed work environments, disruptive work patterns (e.g., shift work), uneven workload demands, long working hours, risk or danger, new technology, and travel.

2. *Role in the Organization.* Three critical factors—role ambiguity, role conflict and the degree of responsibility for others—are identified as major sources of potential stress.

3. *Relationships at Work.* Research has established both a theoretical basis and strong empirical evidence for a causal impact of social relationships on health (Vahtera, 1993). Most studies have concluded that a psychological sense of support and trust in coworkers and colleagues is a powerful determinant of well-being (French & Caplan, 1972). Poor relationships at work (with superiors, colleagues, subordinates, and customers/clients) not only can be primary sources of stress but also adversely affect the development of supportive relationships that act as a stress moderator or buffer. In a recent study of 112 employed subjects, Schwartz and Stone (1993) found that negative interactions or happenings with coworkers, employees, supervisors, and/or clients were the most frequently reported source of work-related problems, followed by heavy workload pressure.

4. *Career Developments.* These factors include problems of over/underpromotion, having reached one's career plateau, early retirement, or an unclear career future. Job insecurity and career development have increasingly become a source of stress during the merger and acquisition boom of the 1980s and seem likely to continue throughout the recessionary 1990s.

5. *Organizational Structure and Climate.* Potential stressors in this category can broadly be described as factors that relate to being in a particular organization and its culture. They include poor communication; incompatible

managerial style; and lack of participation, feedback, and effective consultation.

6. *Home–Work Interface.* Finally, managing the interface between work and home is a potential source of stress, particularly for dual-career couples (Cooper & Lewis, 1993), and those who may be experiencing financial difficulties or life crises. Balancing the often-conflicting demands and responsibilities of home and work life produces especial pressure for individuals in the current economic climate of job uncertainty and increased individual workloads, and may result in a spillover effect.

In their analysis of everyday life problems, Schwartz and Stone (1993), found that 80% of all reported daily problems emanated from the nonwork domain. The two most frequently cited types of problem were marital tension and personal injury or illness. This is consistent with earlier research (Cooper & Sadri, 1991), that analyzed the problems presented to workplace counselors in the U.K. Post Office.

As research studies based on this model (e.g., Cartwright, Cooper, & Barron, in press; Cooper & Bramwell, 1992; Cooper & Roden, 1985; Duffy & McGoldrick, 1990) have demonstrated, the potential sources of stress are likely to vary between occupational groups, between organizations, and even between departmental or workgroups within the same organization. Furthermore, in terms of the main outcome measures incorporated in these studies—job satisfaction and physical and mental health—the stressors predicted these outcomes are often different. For example, money handling and the risk of personal assault were found to be major occupational stressors among bus drivers in the U.K. transport industry (Duffy & McGoldrick, 1990), whereas the major source of stress for U.K. income tax officers was autocratic management style and lack of consultation (Cooper & Roden, 1985). Consequently, the action required by an organization to reduce or eliminate workplace stress will vary according to kinds of stressors operating. In the examples cited, stress reduction might suggest a possible ergonomic solution in the case of bus drivers, but a change in management style in the case of income tax officers.

Individual Moderators in the Stress Process: Coping and Personality

In terms of the transactional model of stress (Lazarus, 1966), individual differences not only influence the perception of stress in the environment and the extent to which its demands exceed or tax the individual's resources (termed the primary appraisal), but also moderate the stress-strain relationship and affect the way in which individuals cope with stress. Personality variables are regarded as internal coping resources (Wylie, 1979) that influence coping strategy. Individuals who exhibit Type A behavior pattern (Friedman & Rosenman, 1989) are considered to be particularly vulnerable to stress because of their heightened perception to environmental stressors, lifestyle, and behaviors, and identified tendency toward maladaptive coping strategies such as smoking (Howard, Rechnitzer, & Cunningham, 1986).

In contrast, personality factors such as "hardiness" (Kobasa, Maddi, & Carrington, 1981) locus of control (Rotter, 1966) self-esteem (Fleishman, 1984), and sense of coherence (Antonovsky, 1979) have all been identified as playing a role in stress resistance. The concept of individual control or mastery, whether it be actual or perceived, is considered to be an important factor in the stress process. Internal locus of control is a central characteristic of both hardiness and a sense of coherence. Because individuals with a high internal locus of control believe that they are able to control the stressors they encounter, their perception of the threat they pose is lessened. Rotter (1975) suggests that generalized control expectancies affect the individual's ability to cope with novel and ambiguous situations. High internals are more likely to appraise such situations as controllable, whereas externals will tend to doubt their self-efficacy to deal with the situation effectively. In terms of coping behavior, it is suggested that compared with externals, internals will display a bias for action and are more likely to adopt active problem-solving behaviors. Anderson (1977), in a study of managerial responses to a flood disaster, found that managers with an internal locus of control displayed more task-oriented ways of dealing with stress compared with more externally oriented managers, who responded with anger, hostility, and greater anxiety—employing more emotion-focused strategies. Similarly, individuals with higher levels of self-esteem have a preference for action (Holahan & Moos, 1987). The moderating relationship between stress and personality in all three stages of the stress process—the primary appraisal (the degree of threat), the secondary appraisal (the "What can I do?"), and the actual coping strategy subsequently adopted—would seem to suggest that certain personalities will consistently be predisposed to adopt more effective coping methods than others.

Despite the theoretical persuasiveness of this proposition, as Edwards (1988) points out, the relationship between personality and coping tends to have been inferred rather than empirically measured, particularly as concerns workplace coping. Although such factors have been presented as being global and stable across time, research studies have produced contradictory evidence to suggest they may actually be situation-specific (Reid, Haas, & Hawkins, 1977). Measures such as Rotters' (1966) Locus of Control scale is a generalized rather than specifically work-related measure. Perceptions of control may be more state- than trait-dependent. Externality may be influenced by certain life events such as unemployment (O'Brien & Kabanoff, 1979) or major organizational change (Callan, 1993; Cartwright & Cooper, 1992), in that such events are experienced as universally stressful and appear to be little moderated by personality characteristics (Ashford, 1988). Because different personality types have been shown to adopt similar coping styles when placed in similar situations (Folkman & Lazarus, 1985), the limited research evidence to date, which has tended to focus on general rather than specifically work-related coping, suggests that situational factors are more influential than personality in determining coping strategies.

Schwartz and Stone (1993) in comparing work and non-work-related problems concluded that coping differences were pronounced among problem types. Although appraisal differences were found to significantly affect coping, they did not play a major role in mediating the effect of problem type on coping. In general terms, work-related problems tended to be addressed with more active problem-focused coping efforts than non-work-related problems. This study examined demographic variables such as age, gender, education and social class, but it did not include personality trait/type measures. Gender and age differences in coping were found. Compared with males, females were more likely to use distraction/diversionary activities, social support, and relaxation. Similarly the use of distraction and social support was more frequent among older subjects. Although personality characteristics may affect appraisal and problem attitude, the interactive relationship between personality and actual coping behavior is complex and as yet not clearly understood. A contingency-based approach to coping, particularly in the workplace, is an area in need of further research.

TYPOLOGIES OF COPING

Coping is generally classified according to (a) the nature and method of coping and (b) the focus or target of coping. According to Billings and Moos (1981), coping methods fall into three categories defined as active-cognitive, active-behavioral, and avoidance. Active-cognitive refers to intrapsychic attempts made by the individual to manage his or her appraisal of the stressful event or situation. Such attempts usually involve some effort at cognitive restructuring through constructive mental dialogue, positive comparisons between present and past predicaments, or analogical problem-solving techniques. Active-behavioral methods refer to overt behavioral attempts made by the individual to deal directly with the stressful event or situation. Finally, the individual may attempt to avoid the problem altogether and adopt avoidance methods of coping.

Schonfeld (1990) suggests that the target or focus of coping can take three possible forms. It can be directed toward (a) modifying the meaning of the stressors, (b) modifying the stressors, and (c) managing distress. Arguably, coping can also take a further form or dimension and be anticipatory (prestressor). A common distinction (Lazarus & Folkman, 1984) is made between problem-focused strategies aimed at directly solving the problem, and emotion-focused strategies aimed at dealing with emotional distress through either controlling emotions or by discharging them.

Although conceptualizing coping in terms of specific methods or foci provides a useful taxonomy for describing coping (Edwards, 1988), operationally it is often difficult to distinguish between methods and foci in that coping efforts may involve a variety of methods and be multifocused. The Ways of Coping Checklist (WCCL; Aldwin, Folkman, Schaefer, Coyne, & Lazarus, 1980) is probably the most commonly used measure of coping; it intended to distinguish between problem- and emotion-focused coping but is composed of items concerned with methods or behaviors rather than foci. Seeking advice or social support, for example, may be classified as both emotion- and problem-focused coping.

Of prime importance are the consequences of coping and their effectiveness in moderating the stress-strain relationship. If the coping response is effective, then the deleterious impacts of stress are reduced and well-being is improved. The distinction is usually drawn between maladaptive and adaptive coping strategies. Maladaptive coping strategies can be defined as actions taken by the individual to temporarily alleviate stress that are usually perceived to be effective in the short term, but that are likely to have a negative impact on health and well-being if continued in the long term. Compensatory or comfort behaviors (e.g., excessive eating, smoking, or drinking) are commonly cited examples of maladaptive coping strategies. In many circumstances, avoidance behavior would fall into the same category. In terms of research evidence relating to coping in an occupational setting, assessment of the range and types of coping employed by individuals has received considerably more attention than any direct empirical measurement of its efficacy in terms of outcome.

According to Janis and Mann (1977), under conditions of threat, the individual first decides whether there are serious risks if no action or the most salient action is taken. Having decided to take action, the individual then considers whether there are alternative courses of action available and sufficient time to search for and deliberate these alternatives. Inherent in such an approach is the notion that the individual can conduct some form of mental calculus to evaluate alternatives systematically and sequentially in terms of appropriateness, effort, and likely outcomes. This view has been challenged by Edwards (1988), who suggests that when under severe and unexpected stress, individuals are only capable of generating a limited number of alternatives. Furthermore, they are likely to evaluate these alternatives in a confused "superficial and erroneous manner" and to accept a solution that they perceive will achieve a minimum rather than an optimal level of well-being.

Theoretical models of coping tend to emphasize the importance of the feedback loop, whereby the individual assesses the success or otherwise of the coping response. The problem with this, however, is that feedback may be delayed, and so an individual may continue inadvertently to cope "badly" with a recurring situation. For example, taking a day off work may seem to be a reasonably satisfactory way of coping to the individual and, in the short term, may not have any adverse repercussions. But if the individual continues to adhere to this method of coping in the longer term, it is likely to have serious and more stressful consequences in leading to disciplinary procedures or dismissal. Indeed, the implementation of a novel coping response, despite its rational or intuitive appeal, may in itself be regarded as stressful, and ultimately may be rejected in favor of the "safer" habitual dominant response.

Schonpflug (1993) has suggested that individuals may even adopt a rational cost-benefit analysis approach to workplace stress, whereby they consider and subsequently accept that the job-derived benefits (e.g., financial rewards, security, status) are greater than the personal costs and risks to their health and well-being. They accept that work has a price in the same way as other human activities such as smoking, drinking, and overeating. These behaviors are recognized to be harmful but nevertheless are continued because the discomfort associated with their discontinuance is considered to outweigh the risks.

INDIVIDUAL RESPONSE TO WORKPLACE STRESS

The literature on coping generally has focused on internal (dispositional) resources for coping with stress and external (environmental) resources, notably social support. Increasingly, the influence of problem type or content, and the distinction between dealing with work and general life stresses, is recognized as playing a major role in determining coping strategies.

As has been discussed, the research evidence to date suggests that work-related problems, or at least routine daily work hassles, elicit more task-oriented than emotion-focused strategies, perhaps because the opportunities to discharge emotions in the workplace are generally restricted. The type of organizational culture operating, the degree of empowerment, and the perceived level of organizational support are therefore external factors, likely to influence employee coping, and are an area for future research.

Problem-focused strategies presuppose an element of individual control. However, workplace stress emanating from environmental stressors over which the individual employee exercises little or no control have become a consistent feature and problem for modern organizations. During the 1980s, widescale uncertainty and concern for job security resulted from major and unexpected organizational changes of a radical rather than incremental nature. Mergers, acquisitions, and corporate restructuring were coupled with massive job losses, particularly in the manufacturing sector. Although, as Callan (1993) suggests, the responsibility for coping with such change often seems to stop with the individual, a small but growing body of research evidence (Ashford, 1988; Cartwright & Cooper, 1992, 1993) indicates that the majority of individuals do not cope well with organizational change and suffer long-term adverse mental health. Compared with routine problems where the individual can apply past experience, such events represent circumstances in which individuals perceive themselves to have no control and no appropriate coping strategy to deal with the stress. In a study of middle managers affected by a merger (Cartwright & Cooper, 1993), the social support of family and friends was the strategy relied on by almost half the sample. Nineteen percent of managers affected reported that they had coped badly with meger stress and had failed to develop any strategy for dealing with the situation. Even though coping with the stress of organizational change would seem to require organizational initiative, studies that have examined the impact of employee involvement in redundancy situations have provided mixed evidence as to its success in employee outcomes (Greenhalgh, 1983; Guest & Peccei, 1992). A study by Schweiger and DeNisi (1991) did find that merger-related communication programs had a positive impact on job satisfaction and employee perceptions of organizational trustworthiness, honesty, and caring.

In occupational settings, coping has to be considered in terms of its functionality and outcomes for both the employee and the employing organization. Methods of coping that the individual may adopt to alleviate stress (e.g., leaving the organization), can have negative organizational outcomes (e.g., the loss of a talented and experienced employee). Research evidence (George, Brief, & Webster, 1991) suggests that overall job satisfaction and specific job stressors are important predictors of the extent to which the individual will seek to adopt a way of coping that is consistent with organizational goals.

ORGANIZATIONAL INITIATIVES TO REDUCE WORKPLACE STRESS

So far, our discussion has focused on individual coping; however, workplace stress is both an individual and organizational problem. Coping, as problem-solving behavior, is the dual responsibility of both the individual and the organization. For the solution to be effective, the methods of coping adopted by the individual and the organization must result in satisfactory and compatible outcomes for both parties.

DeFrank and Cooper (1987) suggest that interventions to reduce workplace stress can focus on the individual, the organization, or the individual/organizational interface. Interventions that focus on the individual include stress education activities, relaxation programs, and employee skill training in areas such as time management and assertion. Organizationally focused interventions seek to reduce stress by changing and improving macrofactors operating within the organization (e.g., restructuring, selection and training policies, organizational development (OD) initiatives). Interventions that focus on the individual-organizational interface are concerned with aspects of the person-environment fit, improving personal relationships, role issues, and so forth. Murphy (1988) also emphasizes three levels of intervention; primary (e.g., stressor reduction), secondary (e.g., stress management) and tertiary (e.g., employee assistance programs). Primary level interventions (stressor reduction) are essentially concerned with modifying environmental stressors by direct action to eliminate or reduce their negative impact on the individual. In contrast, secondary and particularly tertiary level interventions focus on managing distress and dealing with the outcomes or consequences of the stress process. To a lesser extent, they may also help the individual modify the meaning of the stressor(s). Ivancevich and Matteson (1988) pinpoint three possible areas for intervention: (a) reducing the intensity and number of stressors to change the stress potential of a situation, (b) helping individuals to modify their perception or appraisal of a potentially stressful situation, and (c) improving employee coping methods and strategies in terms of range and competence.

Although organizationally focused interventions offer considerable potential for reducing or eliminating the stressors directly responsible for employee ill health, most workplace initiatives have focused on enhancing and extending employees' physical and psychological resources and helping them cope with distress. In the main, this is achieved by improving the adaptability of workers to the existing work environment, by changing their behavior and improving their lifestyle or stress management skills (Cartwright & Cooper, 1993). Newman and Beehr (1979) suggest that individual coping strategies can be divided into four categories:

1. Those aimed at psychological conditions; planning ahead, managing one's life; making realistic self-assessments.
2. Those aimed at physical or physiological conditions such as diet, exercise, and sleep.
3. Those aimed at changing one's behavior; becoming less Type A, relaxing, taking time out, and developing social support networks.
4. Those aimed at changing one's work environment; changing to a less demanding job or organization.

Organizational approaches that focus exclusively on extending and improving individual coping skills are commonly described as the Band-Aid or inoculation treatment. Inherent in this approach is the notion that the organization and its working environment will not change, therefore, the individual must learn ways of coping that help him or her to "fit in" better—or remove him- or herself from the organization.

There has been an enormous growth in the number of organizations providing amenities and/or programs to increase individual stress resilience and promote health and well-being in the workplace. These have taken a variety of forms, including the provision of "on-site" fitness facilities, health screening, dietary control, cardiovascular fitness programs, relaxation classes, stress and health education, or psychological counseling. Often, such programs take a multimodular form. In particular, there has been a pronounced increase in the provision of employee assistance programs (EAPs), which it has been estimated are now established in over 75% of all Fortune 500 companies plus about 12,000 smaller companies (Feldman, 1991). Berridge and Cooper (1993) define an EAP as:

> A programmatic intervention at the workplace, usually at the level of the individual employee, using behavioural science knowledge and methods for the control of certain work related problems (notably alcoholism, drug abuse and mental health) that adversely affect job performance, with the objective of enabling the individual to return to making her or his full contribution and to attaining full functioning in personal life. (p. 89)

Secondary and tertiary level interventions have proved more popular with organizations than primary level interventions for several reasons:

1. The cost-benefit analysis of such programs has produced some impressive results. For example, the New York Telephone Company's "wellness" program

designed to improve cardiovascular fitness saved the organization $2.7 million in absence and treatment costs in one year alone (Cooper, 1985).

2. The professional "interventionists," the counselors, physicians, and clinicians responsible for health care feel more comfortable with changing individuals than changing organizations (Ivancevich, Matteson, Freedman, & Phillips, 1990).

3. It is considered easier and less disruptive to business to change the individual than to embark on any extensive and potentially expensive organizational development program—the outcome of which may be uncertain (Cooper & Cartwright, 1994).

4. They present a high-profile means by which organizations can "be seen to be doing something about stress" and taking reasonable precautions to safeguard employee health. This is likely to be important, not only in terms of the message which it communicates to employees, but also to the external environment. This latter point is particularly important, given the increasing litigation fears that now exist among employers throughout the United States and Europe. It is not difficult to envisage that the existence of an EAP, regardless of whether or not an individual chooses to use it, may become an effective defense against possible legal action.

Overall, evidence as to the success of interventions that focus at the individual level suggests that such interventions can make a difference in temporarily reducing experienced stress (Murphy, 1988). Evidence as to the success of stress management training is generally confusing and imprecise (Elkin & Rosch, 1990), which possibly reflects the idiosyncratic nature of its form and content. Recent studies, which have evaluated the outcomes of stress management training, have found a modest improvement in self-reported symptoms and psychophysiological indexes of strain (Reynolds, Taylor, & Shapiro, 1993); Sallis, Trevorrow, Johnson, Hovell, & Kaplan, 1987), but little or no change in job satisfaction, work stress, or blood pressure. Similarly, studies that have assessed the impact of psychological counseling (Allison, Cooper, & Reynolds, 1989; Cooper & Sadri, 1991) have shown significant improvements in the mental health and absenteeism of counseled employees, but little change in levels of organizational commitment and job satisfaction. Firth-Cozens and Hardy (1992) suggest that when symptom levels drop as a result of clinical treatment for stress, job perceptions are likely to become more positive. However, such changes are likely to be short term if employees return to an unchanged work environment and its indigenous stressors. If, as has been discussed, such initiatives have little impact on improving job satisfaction, then it is more likely that the individual will adopt a way of coping that may have positive individual outcomes, but has negative implications for the organization.

The evidence concerning the impact of health promotion activities has reached similar conclusions. Research findings that have examined the impact of lifestyle and health habits provide further support that any benefits may not necessarily be sustained. Lifestyle and health habits appear to have a strong direct effect on strain outcomes, in reducing anxiety, depression, and psychosomatic distress, but do not necessarily moderate the stressor-strain linkage. Although cardiovascular fitness programs, such as the New York Telephone Company's "wellness" program, may dramatically improve employee health, any benefit may be relatively short term. Some research suggests that 70% of individuals fail to maintain a long-term commitment to exercise habits and are likely to revert to their previous lifestyle after a few years (Ivancevich & Matteson, 1988).

Furthermore, as most stress management programs or lifestyle change initiatives are voluntary, researchers must consider the characteristics and health status of those employees who elect to participate. According to Sutherland and Cooper (1991), participants tend to be the "worried well" rather than the extremely distressed. Consequently, these incentives do not reach the employees who need most help and are coping badly. Also, access to such programs is sometimes restricted to managers and relatively senior personnel within the organization. Because smoking, alcohol abuse, obesity, and coronary heart disease are more prevalent among lower socioeconomic groups, and these workers are likely to occupy positions within the organizational structure that afford them little or no opportunity to change or modify the stressors in their working environment, stress management programs frequently do not address potential health problems or arguably the most at-risk individuals.

Finally, the positive psychological or psychophysiological effects reported by employees who have participated in lifestyle change programs may be more the result of their own expectations than the program content itself, although the outcomes may be falsely attributed to the intervention. Such programs may also enhance employee perceptions of the organization as a caring employer, willing to invest in their health and well-being, and this may create a "feel good" factor. As Ivancevich and Matteson (1988) powerfully argue, the placebo problem in lifestyle change programs and similar initiatives is an area necessitating further research.

Providing access to EAPs, relaxation training, stress management programs, and other means of dampening stress-related symptoms may be ways that organizations can help employees cope with stress. However, organizational initiatives aimed at improving individual coping essentially are concerned with "damage limitation," in addressing the consequences rather than the sources of occupational stress. If, as has been discussed, experienced stress is related to the individual's appraisal of an event or situation, an organization can reduce stress by altering the objective situation, (e.g., by redesigning jobs to better suit the individual's abilities, needs, and preferences). Because perceptions of control also play a significant role in determining both appraisal and subsequent coping behavior, an organization can take a variety of possible actions to increase employee perceptions of control (e.g., by involving employees in setting performance standards and/or modifying unattainable standards).

Elkin and Rosch (1990), summarize a useful range of possible organization-directed strategies to reduce stress:

- Redesign the task.
- Redesign the work environment.
- Establish flexible work schedules.
- Encourage participative management.
- Include the employee in career development.
- Analyze work roles and establish goals.
- Provide social support and feedback.
- Establish fair and family-friendly employment policies.
- Share the rewards.

These parallel an earlier list of strategies suggested by Newman and Beehr (1979) that identifies three possible foci for organizational action:

1. Changing organizational characteristics:
   Alter structure.
   Modify processes (e.g., reward systems; selection, training, and development systems; socialization processes; job transfer and rotation policies; more employee-oriented supervision).
   Develop health services.
2. Changing role characteristics:
   Redefine roles.
   Reduce role overload.
   Reduce role conflict.
   Increase participation in decision making.
3. Change task characteristics:
   Design jobs that match workers' abilities and preferences.
   Use workers' preferences in selection and placement.
   Provide training programs.
   Individualize the treatment of workers.

Again, not a great deal of research evidence has evaluated the impact of such interventions on employee health and well-being. However, in contrast with stress management programs to date, this has been consistently positive. In particular, it has shown the long-term beneficial effects of organizational-level interventions in stress reduction. Quick (1979) examined the stress reduction impact of goal setting in reducing role stress among insurance company personnel over a 14-month period. Measures taken 5 months after training was completed showed a significant decline in role conflict and role ambiguity. Levels of absenteeism also declined, but these did not reach statistical significance. Follow-up measures taken 3 months later, in Month 8, again indicated significant reductions in role conflict and role ambiguity, but no significant differences in absenteeism rates. Similarly, initiatives designed to increase employee participation and consultation (Jackson, 1983) were found to have a significant negative effect on role conflict and ambiguity, and a positive effect on perceived influence among university hospital staff. Evaluations of initiatives to increase job autonomy (Wall & Clegg, 1981) and work schedule autonomy (Pierce & Newstrom, 1983) have also demonstrated benefits in employee emotional health.

STRESS AUDIT AND IDENTIFICATION

In practice, the problem of workplace stress often constitutes an ill-defined problem for both the individual and the organization. Frequently, both the individual and the organization respond to the symptoms and manifestations of stress as the coping target rather than the stressor(s) itself. For the individual, the problem of "being under stress" develops into a generalized cumulative and indifferentiated experience with which he or she must cope. For the organization, the motivation to act tends to arise in response to a problem of escalating sickness and absence. Other less obvious indexes might include high labor turnover rates, high error and accident rates, escalating insurance costs and poor claims ratios, tardiness, low levels of job satisfaction, and falling morale.

To be able to modify or eliminate the stressors operating in the work environment, a diagnosis is critical. At the individual level, stressor identification can be achieved by the maintenance of a stress diary. Over a period of time, by daily recording of the incidents, types of situation, and person(s) that cause distress, it will reveal any significant themes or common stressor patterns and help individuals to identify specific problems or problem areas. It is also likely to be useful for individuals to record how they responded to the situation at the time, whether the strategy was successful in both the short and long term, and how on reflection, they might have handled it better. This information can help workers move toward developing an action plan to eliminate, change, or modify the stressor or explore ways of accepting and dealing with it more effectively, if the stressor cannot be changed. By cataloging current responses and coping methods, and reviewing these with the benefit of retrospection, employees can (a) identify areas where they could improve their coping skills and (b) develop a repertoire of successful contingency-based coping methods to apply in similar future situations. The review process is particularly important, as has been suggested, when individuals are under severe stress. In such circumstances, cognitive processes are frequently impaired to the extent that the possible alternative strategies for coping are unlikely to be fully considered or be poorly evaluated. An awareness of potential stressors can also arguably help the individual develop anticipatory (prestressor) coping strategies.

At the organizational level, regular diagnostic stress audits can be used to assess and monitor employee health and well-being, and to identify the stressors that may be operating throughout the organization or at a departmental or work-group level. It is only at this stage, following stress assessment and problem identification, that interventions can be designed, installed, and evaluated. Instruments such as the Occupational Stress Indicator (OSI) devised by Cooper, Sloan, and Williams (1988) and the Occupational Stress Inventory (Osipaw & Spokane, 1988) have been increasingly used as diagnostic instruments in occupational stress research. Both instruments measure a wide range of job stressors and employee resources for coping with stress, and have established reliability and normative data (Cartwright, Cooper, & Murphy, 1994).

Stress audits can be particularly advantageous in directing organizations to areas where they can engage in anticipatory coping strategies, and so arrest the stress process before its negative impact on employee health manifests itself. This would be true in circumstances where the perceived stress levels among employees are high, but the outcome measures of physical and mental health and job satisfaction are comparable with normative data. At the workgroup level, potential stressors can be identified through less formal means such as regular group review meetings or quality circle initiatives.

CONCLUSION

The relationship between stress and individual coping, particularly in the work context, is an area worthy of further research. As Burke (1993) observes, there is still a large gap between work stress researchers and practitioners, particularly in the area of evaluation of intervention activities.

For the individual, coping with the hassles and stress of work is relatively more complex than dealing with stressful events that occur outside the work domain. This is because of the inherent constraints within the work environment, which restrict the range of acceptable coping responses and behaviors available to the individual and limit the control the individual has to directly modify the stressors. Stress education and stress management training serve a useful function in helping individuals to recognize their own stress symptomology and to overcome much of the negativity and stigma still associated with the stress label. Such initiatives are also useful in extending the individual's skills, resilience, and coping repertoire. However, although individual coping has been shown to be effective in symptom management, activities such as exercise and relaxation techniques have been found to little moderate the stress-strain relationship, particularly in the longer term.

The individual may be able to directly modify or eliminate some workplace stressors, perhaps through personal negotiation (e.g., problems of work overload, role ambiguity) or skill improvement (e.g., exercise of better time management). However, the individual is likely to perceive him- or herself as lacking the resource or potential power to change many potential sources of stress (e.g., the structure, management style, or culture of the organization).

In summary, secondary and tertiary level interventions are likely to be insufficient in maintaining employee health without the complimentary approach of primary/stressor reduction initiatives. Secondary and tertiary level interventions may extend the physical and psychological resources of the individual, particularly in relation to stressors that cannot be changed, but these resources are ultimately finite. Tertiary level interventions, such as counseling services, are likely to be particularly effective in dealing with non-work-related stress. Finally, as has been emphasized in this chapter, workplace stress has adverse implications for both the individual and the organization, and is a joint problem. To achieve an optimal and long-term solution requires recognizing that both parties should also share the responsibility for coping with that problem by combining resources and developing an integrated approach to workplace stress.

REFERENCES

Aldwin, C. M., Folkman, S., Schaefer, C., Coyne, J. C., & Lazarus, R. S. (1980, September) *Ways of coping: A process measure.* Paper presented at the meeting of the American Psychological Association, Montreal, Canada.

Aldwin, C. M., & Revenson, T. A. (1987). Does coping help? A re-examination of the relation between coping and mental health. *Journal of Personality and Social Psychology, 53,* 337–348.

Allison, T., Cooper, C. L., & Reynolds, P. (1989). Stress counseling in the workplace—The Post Office experience. *The Psychologist,* 384–388.

Anderson, C. R. (1977). Locus of control, coping behaviours and performance in a stress setting: A longitudinal study. *Journal of Applied Psychology, 62,* 446–451.

Antonovsky, A. (1979). *Health, stress and coping.* Washington, DC: Jossey-Bass.

Ashford, S. J. (1988). Individual strategies for coping with stress during organizational transitions. *Journal of Applied Psychology, 62,* 446–451.

Berridge, J., & Cooper, C. L. (1993). Stress and coping in US organizations: The role of the Employee Assistance Programme. *Work and Stress, 7*(1), 89–102.

Billings, A. G., & Moos, R. H. (1981). The role of coping responses and social resources in attenuating the stress of life events. *Journal of Behavioral Medicine, 4,* 139–157.

Burke, R. J. (1993). Organizational-level interventions to reduce occupational stress. *Work and Stress, 7*(1), 77–87.

Callan, V. J. (1993). Coping with organizational change. *Work and Stress, 7*(1), 63–75.

Cartwright, S., & Cooper, C. L. (1992). *Mergers and acquisitions: The human factor.* Oxford: Butterworth-Heinemann.

Cartwright, S., & Cooper, C. L. (1993). The psychological impact of merger and acquisition on the individual: A study of building society managers. *Human Relations, 46*(3), 327–347.

Cartwright, S., & Cooper, C. L. (1994). *No hassle: Taking the stress out of workplace situations.* London: Century Business.

Cartwright, S., Cooper, C. L., & Barron, A. (in press). Manager stress and road accidents. *Journal of General Management.*

Cartwright, S., Cooper, C. L., & Murphy, L. (1994). Diagnosing a healthy organization: A proactive approach to stress in the workplace. In G. P. Keita & S. Sauter (Eds.), *Job stress intervention: Current practice & future directions.* Washington, DC: American Psychological Association.

Chen, P. Y., & Spector, P. E. (1992). Relationships of work stressors with aggression, withdrawal, theft and substance use: An exploratory study. *Journal of Occupational and Organizational Psychology, 65,* 177–184.

Cohen, F. (1987). Measurement of coping. In S. V. Kasl & C. L. Cooper (Eds.), *Stress and health: Issues in research methodology.* Chichester: Wiley.

Cooper, C. L. (1985). The road to health in American firms. *New Society, September,* 335–336.

Cooper, C. L., & Branwell, R. (1992). Predictive validity of the strain components of the occupational stress indicator. *Stress Medicine, 8,* 57–60.

Cooper, C. L., & Cartwright, S. (1994). Healthy mind; healthy organization: A proactive approach to stress management. *Human Relations, 47*(4), 455–471.

Cooper, C. L., Cooper, R. D., & Eaker, L. (1988). *Living with stress.* London: Penguin.

Cooper, C. L., & Lewis, S. (1993). *The workplace revolution: Managing today's dual career families.* London: Kogan Page.

Cooper, C. L., & Marshall, J. (1978). *Understanding executive stress.* London: Macmillan.

Cooper, C. L., & Payne, R. (1988). *Causes, coping and consequences of stress at work.* Chichester: Wiley.

Cooper, C. L., & Roden, J. (1985). Mental health and satisfaction amongst tax officers. *Social Science Medicine, 21*(7), 477–451.

Cooper, C. L., & Sadri, G. (1991). The impact of stress counselling at work. *Journal of Social Behaviour and Personality, 6*(7), 411–423.

Cooper, C. L., Sloan, S. J., & Williams, S. (1988). *Occupational stress indicator: Management guide.* Windsor, England: NFER Nelson.

Cox, T. (1978). *Stress.* London: Macmillan.

DeFrank, R. S., & Cooper, C. L. (1987). Worksite stress management interventions: Their effectiveness and conceptualization. *Journal of Managerial Psychology, 2,* 4–10.

Dewe, P., Cox, T., & Ferguson, E. (1993). Individual strategies for coping with stress at work: A review. *Work and Stress, 7*(1), 5–15.

Duffy, C. A., & McGoldrick, A. (1990). Stress and the bus driver in the UK transport industry. *Work and Stress, 4*(1), 17–27.

Edwards, J. R. (1988). The determinants and consequences of coping with stress. In C. L. Cooper & R. Payne (Eds.), *Causes, coping and consequences.* Chichester: Wiley.

Elkin, A. J., & Rosch, P. J. (1990). Promoting mental health at the workplace: The prevention side of stress management. *Occupational Stress: State of the Art Review, 5*(4), 739–754.

Endler, N. S., & Parker, J. D. A. (1990). Multidimensional assessment of coping: A critical evaluation. *Journal of Personality and Social Psychology, 58,* 844–854.

Feldman, S. (1991). Today's EAPs make the grade. *Personnel, 68,* 3–40.

Firth-Cozens, J., & Hardy, C. E. (1992). Occupational stress, clinical treatment, change in job perception. *Journal of Occupational and Organizational Psychology, 65,* 81–88.

Fleishman, J. A. (1984). Personality characteristics and coping patterns. *Journal of Health and Social Behaviour, 25,* 229–244.

Folkman, S., & Lazarus, R. S. (1985). "If it changes it must be a process: A study of emotion and coping during three stages of a college examination. *Journal of Personality and Social Psychology, 48,* 150–170.

French, J. R. P., & Caplan, R. D. (1972). Organizational stress and individual strain. In A. Marlow (Ed.), *The failure of success*. New York: Amacom.

Friedman, M., & Rosenman, R. H. (1989). Association of specific over behaviour pattern with increases in blood cholesterol, blood clotting time, incident of arcus senilis and clinical coronary artery disease. *Journal of the American Medical Association, 169*, 1286–1296.

George, J. M., Brief, A. P., & Webster, J. (1991). Organizationally intended and unintended coping: The case of an incentive compensation plan. *Journal of Occupational Psychology, 64*, 193–205.

Greenhalgh, L. (1983). Managing the job insecurity crisis. *Human Resources Management, 4*, 431–434.

Guest, D., & Peccei, R. (1992). Employment involvement: Redundancy as a critical case. *Human Resource Management Journal, 2,*(3), 34–59.

Hendrix, W. H., Ovalle, N. K., & Troxler, G. (1985). Behavioural and physiological consequences of stress and its antecedent factors. *Journal of Applied Psychology, 70*, 188–201.

Holahan, C. J., & Moos, R. H. (1987). Personal and contextual determinants of coping strategies. *Journal of Personality and Social Psychology, 51*, 389–395.

House, J. S., Umberson, D., & Landis, K. R. (1988). Structures and processes of social support. *Annual Review of Sociology, 14*, 293–318.

Howard, T. H., Rechnitzer, P. A., & Cunningham, D. A. (1986). Role ambiguity Type A behaviour and job satisfaction: Moderating effects on cardiovascular and biochemical responses associated with coronary risk. *Journal of Applied Psychology, 71*, 95–101.

Ivancevich, J. M., & Matteson, M. T. (1988). Promoting the individual's health and well being. In C. L. Cooper & R. Payne (Eds.), *Causes, coping and consequences of stress at work*. Chichester: Wiley.

Ivancevich, J. M., Matteson, M. T., Freedman, S. M., & Phillips, J. S. (1990). Worksite stress management interventions. *American Psychologist, 45*, 252–261.

Jackson, S. E. (1983). Participation in decision making as a strategy for reducing job related strain. *Journal of Applied Psychology, 68*, 3–19.

Janis, I. L., & Mann, L. (1977). *Decisionmaking*. New York: Free Press.

Karasek, R., & Theorell, T. (1990). *Healthy work: Stress productivity and the reconstruction of working life*. New York: Wiley.

Kobasa, C. S., Maddi, S. R., & Carrington, S. (1981). Personality and constitution as mediators in the stress-illness relationship. *Journal of Personality and Social Psychology, 37*, 1–11.

Kuhlman, T. M. (1990). "Coping with occupational stress among urban bus and tram drivers. *Journal of Occupational Psychology, 63*, 89–96.

Lazarus, R. S. (1966). *Psychological stress and the coping process*. New York: McGraw-Hill.

Lazarus, R. S., & Folkman, S. (1984). *Stress, appraisal and coping*. New York: Springer.

Murphy, L. R. (1988). Workplace interventions for stress reduction and prevention. In C. L. Cooper & R. Payne (Eds.), *Causes, coping and consequences of stress at work*. Chichester: Wiley.

Newman, J. D., & Beehr, T. (1979). Personal and organizational strategies for handling job stress: A review of research and opinion. *Personnel Psychology, 32,* 1–43.

O'Brien, Q. E., & Kabanoff, B. (1979). Comparison of unemployed and employed workers on work values, locus of control and health variables. *Australian Psychologist, 14,* 143–154.

Osipaw, S. H., & Spokane, A. R. (1988). *A manual for measures of occupational stress.* New York: Wiley.

Pierce, J. L., & Newstrom, J. W. (1983). The design of flexible work schedules and employee responses: Relationships and processes. *Journal of Occupational Behaviour, 4,* 247–262.

Quick, J. C. (1979). Dyadic goal setting and role stress in field study. *Academy of Management Journal, 22,* 241–252.

Reid, D. W., Haas, G., & Hawkins, D. (1977). Locus of desired control and positive self concept of the elderly. *Journal of Gerontology, 32,* 441–450.

Reynolds, S., Taylor, E., & Shapiro, D. A. (1993). Session impact in stress management training. *Journal of Occupational and Organizational Psychology, 66,* 99–113.

Rotter, J. B. (1966). Generalised expectancies for internal versus external control of reinforcement. *Psychological Monographs, 80,* 1–28.

Rotter, J. B. (1975). Some problems and misconceptions related to the construct of internal versus external control of reinforcement. *Journal of Consulting and Clinical Psychology, 32,* 56–67.

Sallis, J. F., Trevorrow, T. R., Johnson, C. C., Hovell, M. F., & Kaplan, R. M. (1987). Worksite stress management: A comparison of programmes. *Psychology and Health, 1,* 237–255.

Schonfeld, I. S. (1990). Coping with job related stress: The case of teachers. *Journal of Occupational Psychology, 63,* 141–149.

Schonpflug, W. (1993, July). *Coping strategies—Personal and situational determinants.* Paper presented at the III European Congress of Psychology, Tampere, Finland.

Schwartz, J. E., & Stone, A. A. (1993). Coping with daily work problems. Contributions of problem content, appraisals and person factors. *Work and Stress, 7*(1), 47–62.

Schweiger, D. M., & DeNisi, A. A. (1991). Communication with employees following a merger: A longitudinal field experiment. *Academy of Management Journal, 34,* 110–135.

Sutherland, V. J., & Cooper, C. L. (1991). *Understanding stress.* London: Chapman & Hall.

Vahtera, J. (1993, July). *The Raisio study: Job control, social support and health.* Paper presented at the III European Congress of Psychology, Tampere, Finland.

Wall, T. O., & Clegg, C. W. (1981). A longitudinal study of group work redesign. *Journal of Occupational Behaviour, 2,* 31–39.

Warr, P. D. (1982). A national study of non-financial employment commitment. *Journal of Occupational Psychology, 55,* 297–312.

Wylie, R. C. (1979). *The self concept: Theory and research on selected topics.* Lincoln: University of Nebraska Press.

CHAPTER 11

Coping with Chronic Diseases

STAN MAES, HOWARD LEVENTHAL, and DENISE T. D. DE RIDDER

In this chapter, we present and discuss the relevant literature on coping with chronic diseases. We will discuss first why coping with chronic disease is a major problem, after which we will sketch the key requirements for a model of coping with these diseases and then present an overview of Lazarus and Folkman's stress coping model, the most widely used model for the analysis of stress and coping in chronic illness. We then review some of the published studies on stress and coping with chronic illness selecting examples to illustrate some of the conceptual and methodological limitations of the Lazarus-Folkman model. Next, an expanded stress coping model is presented. In the final sections, we emphasize the findings on coping with coronary heart disease, cancer, asthma, diabetes, and rheumatic diseases, before formulating conclusions and indications for future research.

CHRONIC ILLNESS: A PROBLEM FOR CONTEMPORARY WESTERN SOCIETIES

In comparison with the 19th century, during which infectious illnesses in early life were the major causes of mortality, chronic diseases are now responsible for about 80% of the deaths in Western countries (McKinlay & McKinlay, 1977). Improvements in hygiene and diet that greatly reduced infectious illness as causes of death resulted in a vast increase in the life span, a major increase in the number of elderly individuals who must adapt to chronic illness during their later years, and substantial increases in the cost of medical care. For example, van den Berg and van den Bos (1989) calculate that one quarter to one third of the adult population in the Netherlands has a chronic disease (an irreversible illness that one must live with for weeks, months, or years). It is extremely important to recognize that there is no single, universally accepted medical definition of chronic illness because there are vast differences in the causes, course, changeability, and consequences among chronic conditions. The chronic conditions of greatest concern are typically the most prevalent (afflict large numbers of individuals and/or are long-lasting), have a major impact on the health care system (e.g., many days in hospital and high costs of treatment), and have a high rate of mortality. Virtually all the heart and vessel diseases, most of the cancers, asthma and chronic obstructive pulmonary diseases, diabetes mellitus and rheumatic diseases satisfy the criteria of prevalence, longevity, and high cost. Many other chronic diseases (e.g., Parkinson's disease, multiple sclerosis, epilepsy, migraine, muscle diseases, Crohn's disease, colitis ulcerosa, chronic renal insufficiency and psoriasis) also have a substantial impact on quality of life and may be susceptible to psychological intervention, but their lesser prevalence and lesser impact on mortality removes them somewhat from the focus of public attention.

MEDICAL AND PSYCHOLOGICAL VIEWS OF CHRONIC DISEASE

As mentioned earlier, there are vast differences in the causes, course, and final outcome among different chronic conditions. Differences also exist among individuals afflicted with the "same" condition; individual differences in the life span of AIDS patients is a current example that is frequently mentioned in the media. These differences will reflect a host of biomedical factors affecting the virulence of the underlying disease process such as the extent of exposure and the type of underlying disease agent and the vigor of host defenses.

In addition, chronic conditions are unstable; they change over time nearly all having episodes of exacerbation, and many accumulating strength as they progress. Cassileth et al. (1984) and others have found that patients in the initial and end stages of disease report higher levels of stress and lower levels of well-being than comparable healthy subjects. In an attempt to characterize these stages, Morse and Johnson (1991) developed their illness constellation model, which postulates the following four stages in the psychological development of an illness representation:

1. Uncertainty, a stage during which patients attempt to understand the meaning and the severity of the first symptoms.
2. Disruption, when it becomes obvious that the individual is affected by a serious disease (because of the disease state or communication of the diagnosis). During this stage the patient experiences a crisis that is characterized by intense levels of stress and a high degree of dependence on professionals and/or relatives.
3. A striving for recovery of the self, during which patients try to gain control over their illness with the help of their environment by using various forms of coping behavior.
4. Restoration of well-being, which indicates that the patient has attained a new equilibrium within *his or her* environment since *he or she* has now accepted the illness and its consequences.

This model shows that adaptation to chronic disease is largely dependent on the evaluation of the stressor by the individual, the effectiveness of coping behavior, and the social support the patient will receive in attempts to gain control over the stressor. Thus, on biomedical grounds alone (ignoring social and psychological factors), we can expect to observe substantial individual differences in the type and intensity of emotional distress, disruption of daily life and adaptive demands as a consequence of type and duration of condition, and host resistance.

It is essential, however, to separate the "medical" view of a disease from the way it is experienced by the patient, as an individual's perception and/or representation of an illness may have only a modest correlation with its medically defined characteristics. Although a patient's experience of a chronic illness will reflect its biology and developmental history, the degree to which it is a source of psychological stress will also depend on the individual's personal and social resources; these factors will moderate the perceived threat of a disease and facilitate or pose barriers to adaptation. In addition, it is important to recognize that the absence of cures for the vast majority of chronic conditions means that their adaptive demands will extend over a lifetime. Disease duration in conjunction with the resources available to the individual will determine, therefore, whether adaptation can be maintained. What is less clear is whether the individual's social and psychological situation can affect the actual history of the underlying disease process thereby adding to or subtracting from the impact of the disease as a life stressor.

Despite the images of doom and the realities of disability accompanying the most severe chronic conditions, empirical studies show that most patients adapt to chronic disease. Cassileth et al. (1984) and others have also shown that most outpatients with diabetes, cancer, rheumatic diseases, and renal and skin disease do not report higher levels of stress and lower levels of well-being throughout the history of their diseases in comparison with similar healthy subjects, the exceptions being the initial and end stages already mentioned. This emphasizes once again the importance of not relying on simple comparisons between groups of patients and matched controls; adaptation must be examined in relation to the specific time point in the individual's disease history.

Not only do the manifestations of illness differ from one chronic disease to another and from one patient to another, each disease itself represents a complex set of ever-changing stressors. For example, a patient with rheumatoid arthritis can experience a varying set of stressors beginning with the tests and medical communications involved in the detection and diagnosis of the disease, a varying set of somatic sensations including pain that fluctuates in severity, varying disabilities of upper and lower extremities that can interfere with locomotion and management of everyday tasks such as toileting and dressing, and problems with recovery and rehabilitation from surgery. In addition, disease and disability can generate a host of comorbid life stressors ranging from economic (job loss) and social loss (divorce) to the sacrifice of life goals that are critical for self-definition (e.g., giving up a career due to physical disability). These losses in the inter- and intrapersonal domains may appear most often with increased duration of a disease.

What they illustrate most clearly is that the full impact of a chronic condition is not confined to its biological aspect. These added, and perhaps unanticipated, stressors can disrupt whatever equilibrium a patient has achieved with the biological condition. Consequently, although our understanding of stress impact is enhanced by a model that incorporates the distinctive features of a disease and its temporal development, it is impossible to fully appreciate the impact of a chronic disease without considering its interaction with the individual's social environment and life goals.

STRESS COPING MODELS

Individual adaptation processes are described best by means of stress-coping models, of which the Lazarus and Folkman (1984) model is the best known and most widely used. Before describing the model and its application to chronic disease problems, we will list what we believe to be the key factors faced by any individual attempting to adapt to the demands of a life-threatening chronic illness. This will provide a set of five criteria against which to evaluate the stress-coping model.

Our review of the features of the chronic illness domain has of necessity been brief, but it provides a picture of the following key adaptive demands of chronic illness that must be addressed by any stress-coping model:

1. *Representation as a Guide to Problem Solving.* The model must reflect the individual's ongoing efforts at solving the problems he or she will confront with a specific, chronic illness. Thus, the model must be able to represent the features of the illness (the factors that demand problem solving) and must represent both those features that are common to a wide range of chronic illnesses and those that are unique (Leventhal & Nerenz, 1983).

2. *Construction over Time.* The model must be iterative (it must allow for continual updating of the illness representation and procedures for problem solving).

3. *Parallel Processing of Subjective Reality and Emotion.* The model must represent the psychological reality of the disease (its representation), the individual's emotional reactions to the disease, and the interactions among them because the construction of the psychological reality of disease and the emotional reactions to it represent partially independent processes (Leventhal, 1970). A fully developed model will also describe the processing system that generates the psychological reality of the disease and the affective response to it.

4. *Separate Construction of Representation and Response Plans and Performance.* The model must represent the wide range of procedures, both individual and social, for coping with the disease. As a large number of response-specific and personal factors affect the selection of coping responses (e.g., response-specific barriers such as cost and outcome expectations re. cure, personal barriers, and performance expectations), the model must accommodate the reality that a substantial degree

of independence will exist among the factors generating the disease representation from those influencing planning and performance of a specific coping procedure (Leventhal, 1970).

5. *Interaction with Context.* Both the representation of disease threats and the selection and performance of specific procedures for their management are heavily influenced by features of the surrounding context. These moderators of ongoing problem-solving performance include the personal biases of the individual, inputs from the immediate social environment, and information respecting diseases and procedures for problem solution in the cultural context (e.g., media, religious institutions). There is also feedback from the problem-solving space to the context, the experience with specific diseases affecting cultural beliefs and norms and generating societal institutions for disease management. Despite its importance, this last causal pathway will not be discussed further.

The Lazarus and Folkman Stress-Coping Model

The basic assumption of the Lazarus-Folkman model is that people who are confronted with a stressor (in this case, various aspects and consequences of a chronic disease) evaluate this stressor, and that this evaluation determines their emotional or behavioral reactions. Lazarus and Folkman (1984) distinguish two kinds of evaluation or appraisal processes: primary and secondary appraisal. Primary appraisal assesses the personal meaning of an event and indicates whether the event or the stressor has positive, neutral, or negative meaning for the individual. Positive emotions result if the interpretation is positive (e.g., because the stressor is seen as a challenge), negative emotion if the stressor threatens the physical and/or psychological self (which is to be expected in the case of events related to chronic illness). Two classes of negative outcome are distinguished: feelings of anxiety if the stressor is perceived as a threat, and feelings of anger and/or grief if the stressor augurs personal damage or loss. As these negative interpretations and their effects are often most evident during the initial stages of confrontation with the stressor, it is not surprising that studies report strong emotional reactions of anxiety, depression, and anger on confrontation with the initial signs of or with unexpected changes in the features of a chronic illness. For example, patients with myocardial infarction generally suffer from heightened levels of anxiety during the few first days at the coronary care unit and are said to become depressed shortly afterward, but for the majority of patients, these increased levels of distress seem to drop quite rapidly during hospitalization or shortly afterward (Doehrman, 1977; Van Elderen, 1991). Other stressors such as returning to work, sexual intercourse, complications, or coronary bypass surgery may, however, be forthcoming events that can once again cause high levels of anxiety or depression. Comparably, immediate reactions to the discovery of having insulin-dependent diabetes mellitus may encompass grief and mourning and fear of death, which decrease over time, whereas specific stressors such as states of severe hypoglycemia may be regular sources of anxiety and depression (Pennings-Van der Eerden & Visser, 1990). Anxiety and depression, to a lesser extent, are characteristic for asthmatic patients, but after a period of adaptation, anxiety is especially associated with an asthmatic attack (Maes & Schlosser, 1987). Confusion, anxiety, sorrow, and grief are typical reactions to the diagnosis of cancer, which are also subject to change over time (Couzijn, Ros, & Winnubst, 1990).

Affective changes during the course of illness may also result from secondary appraisal, or responses to the question, "What can I do about it?" These processes refer to thoughts through which the person explores his or her capacities to reduce the threat, damage, or loss caused by the event, also called coping capacities. Coping is defined as any effort to manage external or internal demands, which are appraised as negative or challenging. External demands refer to the event itself, internal demands refer to the emotional reactions to the event. This distinction led the authors to differentiate between problem-focused coping (responses directed at the external event) and emotion-focused coping (responses directed at the individual's emotional reactions or internal state). An example of the two different forms of coping can be seen in patients with asthma who engage in problem-focused coping by taking medication to suppress oncoming asthmatic attacks, and emotion-focused coping when they engage in relaxation or avoidant thinking to reduce anxiety. Every example that will come to mind will be consistent with the proposition that coping is a process rather than an event, and the majority, if not all, will also suggest that the intent of the response, rather than the response itself, is the basis of this distinction (e.g., the asthmatic could use relaxation to short-circuit the attack).

During this process, thoughts and actions directed at both the external and internal stressor may coincide or alternate and give rise to emotional and behavioral consequences. In turn, each response can have complex consequences: A response may produce effects that require further coping (e.g., a treatment may have side-effects that require additional treatment) in addition to having an intended effect on the disease and/or the individual's emotions. Additionally, coping behavior may vary greatly over time and from person to person. This explains why there are differences in effectiveness of coping behavior, but also why some patients adapt more quickly and easily to stressors associated with chronic disease, whereas others do not. How people cope with each aspect of a chronic disease will have important psychological, social, and physical consequences.

Limitations of Lazarus and Folkman's Stress-Coping Model

Although our understanding of the factors affecting adaptation to chronic disease has expanded from the empirical studies using the stress-coping model, the studies typically have not led to increased specification of the model's concepts nor have they removed its limitations. First, this model (Lazarus & Folkman, 1984) is more of a frame of reference than a model because it fails to meet our first criterion—it does not incorporate concepts respecting the common and specific features of a chronic illness so as to establish goals and standards for evaluating coping. Thus, although Lazarus and Folkman (1984) state that a stress-coping model must describe person-situation transactions, the situation dimension is poorly represented in this and most other models. Indeed, as Perez and Reicherts (1992) have argued, since Lewin's early attempts, relatively few social-psychological theories have invested effort in describing the psychological situation. Important developments in this direction within personality psychology (Endler & Magnusson, 1976; Pervin & Lewis, 1978) did not lead to application of such theories to applied stress research. As Perrez and Reicherts (1992) state: "Cognitive psychology has—in the tradition of rationalistic philosophy—incorporated the situation dimension in the cognitive dimension. It has done this primarily by granting this dimension significance as the cognitive achievement of situation interpretation" (p. 20). In an attempt to enlarge Lazarus's model from this perspective, Perrez and Reicherts (1992) distinguish the following objective dimensions of situations: (a) valence (or the inherent stressfulness of a situation), (b) controllability (the inherent opportunities for control within a situation), (c) changeability (the probability that the situation will change by itself), (d) ambiguity (the degree to which a situation is inherently lacking in sufficient information, which distorts the meaning of the situation that needs to be ascertained) and (e) recurrence (the inherent likelihood of the stressful situation happening again).

One might question whether Perrez and Reicherts (1992) have removed the deficit they identify, as their "dimensions" appear to be properties of an individual's cognitive system rather than cognitive representations of environmental attributes. Leventhal's commonsense model (Leventhal, 1970; Leventhal & Nerenz, 1983) may be somewhat more successful in this regard as empirical studies from this frame of reference have differentiated five sets of attributes of illness threats that appear to describe an individual's representation of the features of a disease threat. These include the identity or label and disease-specific symptoms of the illness, its time line or duration (acute, cyclic, chronic), its causes (genetic, infection, food poisoning, etc.), consequences (fatal, painful, etc.), and its controllability (susceptible to medical treatment). Although these descriptors overlap in part with those of Perrez and Reicherts (1992), they are more concrete and situationally oriented (e.g., Perrez and Reicherts's factors of ambiguity and valence arise from identity—symptom and label—and consequences).

Chronic disease episodes can be described along these dimensions, and we can hypothesize that confrontation with a chronic disease having a high threat valence (e.g., labeled as cancer with painful symptoms, low controllability via medical interventions, and an unchangeable or chronic time line) will have a powerful impact on the individual and require complex revision of the self and its relation to the social context. Acceptance of the chronicity of the condition is likely to be essential for adaptation. But acceptance of chronicity can be accompanied by a fusion of the entire self with the disease: "I am a cancer," which generates depression and a sense of hopelessness and despair; or the acceptance can involve a compartmentalization of the stressor: "I have a cancer and I adopt the role of a cancer patient at the hospital but I remain myself at home" (Leventhal & Nerenz, 1980). Diseases that are prototypical of such adaptive demands include metastatic breast cancer, lung cancer, and AIDS. In contrast, disease-related stressors with medium valence, high controllability and/or changeability, medium ambiguity, and low likelihood of recurrence will have less impact and leave more room for active problem-oriented forms of coping, as is the case for patients who are confronted with asthma, diabetes, and some forms of epilepsy. Future research should investigate the ability to assess different groups of chronically ill patients and their adjustment on the basis of such a situational analysis.

Because the model has functioned more as a frame of reference than a theory and has failed to deal with the specific features of disease stressors, empirical research has often been highly general in its treatment of coping rather than describing coping with specific diseases at specific points in time. For example, coping with asthma in general is different from coping with a specific attack (Maes & Schlosser, 1987). Coping with arthritis in general is different from coping with a specific pain episode (Zautra & Manne, 1992), and coping with diabetes in daily life varies from coping processes during a state of hypoglycemia (Pennings-van der Eerden & Visser, 1986).

Second, the model has neglected interactions with the context, or influence that other life events may have on the coping process. For example, the psychological focus of the model gave insufficient attention to the importance of social support and other environmental factors on coping and adjustment. The model also ignored the way in which life events extrinsic to the chronic disease may directly impact a chronic condition, by exacerbating its adverse biological effects, in addition to affecting the individual emotionally via the appraisal process. For example, research has found that diabetic patients who have recently experienced stressful life events have more problem with their metabolism (Cox & Gonder-Frederick, 1992).

Finally, by focusing exclusively on the way the stressor shapes coping behavior, this and other models have overlooked the effects of the individual's life goals and social relationships on the meaning or representation of the disease and the selection of coping procedures. For example, a diabetic patient may violate diet regulations because it is more important to him to please his host than to prevent a state of hyperglycemia, or a coronary heart patient who is perfectly able to return to work may stop working because it is more important to him to spend more time with his partner. Lazarus (1991) has recently agreed with this perspective and states:

> Until recently I discussed coping without reference to goal commitment or intentions. . . . However, if one takes seriously that coping is an effort to accomplish something or if one speaks of coping functions, intentions or goals are implied.
> . . . One way to think of the coping process is as a set of lower order goals (or intentions) that serve as methods of achieving higher order goals, as in means-ends relationships. (pp. 830–831)

In summary, the original model neglected that coping may be the consequence not only of situational demands but also of life goals or—in expectancy-value terms—values.

These comments led to an elaboration of the stress-coping model (see Figure 11.1), which is based on Lazarus's (1991) recent insights, but also on the work of others (Hobfoll, 1988, 1989; Moos, 1988; Moos & Schaefer, 1993; Taylor, 1991).

THE STRESS-COPING MODEL AND MEASUREMENT OF COPING WITH CHRONIC DISEASE

Perhaps the most important effect of the Lazarus-Folkman model and similar models on the assessment of coping with chronic illness has been to focus

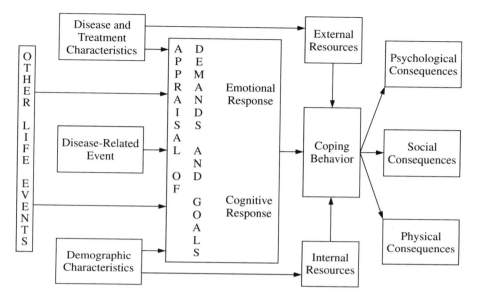

Figure 11.1   Model for coping with chronic disease.

assessment on coping behaviors to the virtual exclusion of assessment of the disease representation and coping outcomes. Thus, there has been a proliferation of coping scales to assess both cognitive and overt actions used to manage the environmental stressors and the emotional responses accompanying exposure to the stressor, that is, the distinction between problem-based and emotion-based coping (see Lazarus & Folkman, 1984; Leventhal, 1970). This narrow focus has sacrificed both the transactional and systems perspective that is the foundation of the stress-coping model.

There are well over 20 coping scales in use that differ in their level of abstraction in describing coping acts and the nature and function of the assessed coping behavior (Aldwin & Revenson, 1987). One group of measures considers coping as a relatively stable personality variable. A good example of this is the Millon Behavioral Health Inventory (Millon, Green, & Meagher, 1982), a self-report questionnaire that measures 8 coping styles: confident, cooperative, forceful, inhibited, introversive, respectful, sensitive, and sociable. The Miller Behavioral Style Scale (Miller, 1987) assesses blunting and monitoring coping preferences on the basis of answers to hypothetical stressors (Miller, 1987). Although this scale has the major advantage that it takes characteristics of the stressor into account, the four hypothetical situations are not disease specific. The frequently used Ways of Coping Inventory (WCI) of Folkman and Lazarus (1988), which consists of the subscales Problem-Focused Coping, Wishful Thinking, Detachment, Seeking Social Support, Focusing on the Positive, Self-Blame, Tension Reduction, and Keeping to Oneself, is based on transactional theory. However, the scale is also not disease specific and postulates that the same coping dimensions will be found at confrontation with different stressors. There are many adaptations of the WCI, resulting in different factor structures and thus measuring coping mechanisms, which are not comparable with the eight original strategies (Felton & Revenson, 1984; Regan, Lorig, & Thoresen, 1988), and even the WCI itself has been used in different ways. Some professionals use this instrument to assess the way people cope overall with a disease such as arthritis (Zautra & Manne, 1992), whereas others use it to assess coping with specific stressors such as osteoarthritis knee pain (Keefe et al., 1989).

Additionally, there are instruments for the general assessment of coping with chronic diseases. Some of these instruments, such as the Medical Coping Modes Questionnaire (Feifel, Strack, & Nagy, 1987a), assess three forms of coping with medical illness: confrontation, avoidance, and acceptance or resignation. Other instruments measure coping with specific problems; for example, the Coping Strategies Questionnaire (Rosentiel & Keefe, 1982) measures coping with low back pain, and the Vanderbilt Pain Management Inventory assesses active and passive forms of coping with pain (Brown & Nicassio, 1987). Furthermore, questionnaires such as the Coping Questionnaire for Heart Patients (Maes & Bruggemans, 1990) or the Coping Questionnaire for Asthmatic Patients (Maes & Schlosser, 1987) are instruments that assess approach and avoidance strategies in problem situations. Items for coronary heart patients include questions such as "When I am experiencing cardiac complaints, I . . ."; "When I'm worrying about my heart disease, I . . ." and "When other people treat me as a patient, I. . . ."

Consequently, general scales tend not to be sensitive enough to evaluate the way people cope with specific disease-related stressors, whereas specific scales (such as pain scales) only inform us about coping with specific problems or symptoms. In addition, specific scales do not differentiate or compare different diseases or disease-related stressors. A combination of both approaches is probably the most advisable, allowing comparisons between different disease-related stressors and adequate assessment of cognitive and behavioral responses to a specific stressor. A similar issue concerns whether coping should be assessed at a general superstrategy level (as, e.g., problem-focused vs. emotion-focused; approach vs. avoidance; active vs. passive coping) or at a situation-specific, observable behavioral level. It is obvious that conceptualizing coping only at a higher-order level cannot provide the entire concept of the coping process. Krohne (1993) suggests a hierarchical distinction between three levels of coping including the generalized coping preferences, coping strategies, and coping acts or responses, future research can determine whether it will be possible to design instruments that will be able to assess these different levels. Another puzzling aspect is that most studies assess coping by means of self-reports; however, not much is known about the relationships between various measures of coping with chronic diseases, including self-report, observer report and physiological measures. Finally, many authors define coping as a process, but do not make use of a longitudinal design, and if they do, it is not always clear whether the coping measures used are sensitive enough to measure changes over time.

AN EXTENDED MODEL FOR COPING WITH CHRONIC DISEASES

On the basis of the preceding comments, we are introducing an extended model for coping with chronic diseases (see Figure 11.1).

According to this model, other important *life events* contribute to the appraisal of disease-related events. Research suggests that life events may, in some cases, be related to disease itself. This was concluded from a study on patients with multiple sclerosis. In this study (Grant, McDonald, Patterson, & Trimble, 1989), it appeared that 62% of the MS patients had experienced an important life event within 6 months before the onset of the disease. This was apparent in only 15% of the controls. There is also some evidence for the impact of life events on the onset of chronic pain and rheumatoid arthritis (Creed, 1993; Martin & Theunissen, 1993). The results of most studies in which an association is sought between severe life events and the onset of chronic organic diseases do not, however, support this hypothesis (Creed, 1993), most likely because such an hypothesis does not match the multicausal nature of these chronic diseases (Maes, Vingerhoets, & Van Heck, 1987). However, severe life events can influence the confrontation with a chronic disease. For example, a patient who is facing the diagnosis of a renal disease will probably evaluate this event in a different way if the diagnosis is made a few weeks after the death of his partner or the loss of his job.

In addition, disease and treatment characteristics can have a major impact on the appraisal of and thus coping with the event. In terms of *disease characteristics,* the previously described criteria of Leventhal and Nerenz (1983) and Perrez and Reicherts (1992) come to mind. Research in this domain points at a positive relationship between valence and avoidant or passive forms of coping (Dunkel-Schetter, Feinstein, Taylor, & Falke, 1992). Other authors showed lack of controllability to be related to more avoidant, emotion-focused coping in rheumatic patients and controllability to active problem-focused coping in patients with diabetes mellitus (Andersson & Ekdahl, 1992). Comparable relationships between controllability and coping have also been observed in other groups of chronic patients (Schüssler, 1992). Other studies show that there is an association between changeability and confrontive, problem-oriented forms of coping in a general patient population (Vitaliano, De Wolfe, Maiaro, Russo, & Katon, 1990) and in patients who have recently been confronted with chronic diseases such as coronary heart disease and cancer (Feifel et al., 1987b). Heim (1988) found that ambiguity was related to passive forms of emotion-focused coping in women with suspicion of breast cancer, and research conducted by Warren, Warren, and Cockerill (1991) showed that there was an association between likelihood of recurrence with avoidance- and emotion-focused forms of coping in multiple sclerosis patients.

Not only characteristics of the disease, but also *treatment characteristics* contribute to the appraisal of the disease-related event. Many studies indicated that hospital admission, medical examinations, surgery, or other forms of treatment such as chemotherapy contribute to changes in the patient's perception and experience of the illness (Johnston, Weinman, & Marteau, 1990; Taylor & Aspinwall, 1993).

It is also known that relatively stable *demographic characteristics* such as age, gender, race, and social class contribute to the interpretation of chronic illness and thus influence coping with chronic disease, although many researchers do not take adequate account of these variables. Limited data support this view; however, research has indicated that females, the lower educated, and especially older chronic patients tend to use more avoidant and/or emotion-focused coping (de Ridder & Schreurs, 1994).

As mentioned earlier, the *appraisal* of the event is not only determined by event characteristics, but also by goals or values, according to the expectancy-value theory. Expectancies can be defined as people's degree of confidence of attaining their goals. As Carver, Scheier, and Pozo (1992) explain, when expectancies are favorable, then people will invest effort to attain their goals. If expectancies are not favorable, then people may cease their effort. Consequently, putting in effort to attain a goal or succumbing are basic, adaptive forms of behavior. Problems arise, however, when a person wants to pursue his goal(s) or to disengage, but cannot because of a situational demand. Confrontation with a serious illness demonstrates this point of view because it may imply that a person cannot continue to pursue his or her current goals in life. Giving up, in this case, is giving up the most important values in life and can further lead to self-destruction. The more goals are threatened by the stressor and the more important these goals are, the more stressful the experience will be. As a result, stress can be defined as the result of a demand/goal appraisal. This is in accordance with recent insights made by Lazarus and Smith (1988) and Smith (1991), who distinguish two components of primary appraisal: motivational relevance, which is an evaluation of the extent to which the problem situation touches on personal goals, and motivational congruence, referring to the extent to which a transaction blocks or facilitates personal goals.

Actual coping behavior not only is the result of demand/goal appraisals but also depends on demand-resources and goal-resources appraisals. According to Hobfoll (1988, p. 54), resources can be defined as "those objects, conditions, personal characteristics, or energies that are valued by the individual or that serve as a means for attainment of valued resources." In our terminology, valued resources are personal goals, and we will refer to resources as internal or external conditions that can be used to cope with demand/goal conflicts. *External resources* consist of money, time, and distance from professional help as well as the social support on which a patient can rely. It is a known that there is a relationship between social support and adaptation to chronic disease and that there is even a relationship between social support and disease progression, although such a relationship seems to be stronger for some chronic diseases than for others (Leppin & Schwarzer, 1988). It is not clear, however, whether this is a buffering effect (influencing appraisals, and thus coping with stressful events) or a main effect (suggesting a beneficial effect of social relationships irrespective of the experience of stress). Social support may determine how a person will cope with the situation. While seeking help can be a coping strategy in itself, lack of social support may also affect the way patients cope with the stresses of illness. Manne and Zautra (1989) found that rheumatoid arthritis (RA) patients with critical, less supportive spouses are more inclined to use maladaptive coping behaviors such as wishful thinking, whereas patients with supportive spouses reported more problem-focused coping. Feifel et al. (1987a) found that men with good social support networks rely more on confrontive coping with medical illness. There is also evidence for the effects of coping on social support; Newman (1990) found that RA patients with the best psychological adjustment were coping in an active and expressive way but did not seek support from others, probably because internal resources were already sufficient to solve the problem.

Internal resources consist of the energy or physical strength a person possesses as well as personality characteristics such as intelligence, trait anxiety, depression, optimism, autonomy, ego-strength, hardiness, locus of control, or self-efficacy. Research has found several personality characteristics to be related to appraisal, coping, and adaptation (Carver, Scheier, & Weintraub, 1989; Moos & Schaefer, 1993). For example, pessimists report higher levels of hostility and depression on the day before coronary artery bypass surgery than optimists and also report less relief and happiness postsurgery than optimists (Carver, Scheier, & Pozo, 1992). Optimistic patients seem to cope in a more active, problem-oriented way, whereas pessimistic patients tend to show more passive or avoidant forms of coping. There is also evidence for a relationship between intelligence and information seeking and between ego strength and more active, adaptive forms of coping in chronic patients (Friedman & Di Matteo, 1984). Research with cancer, chronic pain, and rheumatic patients found a relationship between external locus of control and passive-avoidant coping and also between internal locus of control and active problem- or emotion-focused coping (de Ridder & Schreurs, 1994). It is not clear, however, whether personality factors have a direct effect on coping. Carver et al. (1989) have pointed out that the impact of personality characteristics on coping is modest and that coping preferences exist independent of personality factors. Although coping preferences can also be seen as personality characteristics, they may influence coping indirectly through their impact on appraisal. Most of the research on the relationship between personality characteristics and coping is not longitudinal and it may be argued that this type of research could show stronger relationships.

These many different aspects affect *coping behavior.* As stated earlier, it is important to differentiate between coping actions or actual ways to deal with the problem and coping functions that refer to the goals these actions intend to achieve (Leventhal, Suls, & Leventhal, 1993). Only a hierarchical model of coping, as proposed by Krohne (1993), can adequately deal with these different concepts. At the highest level, individuals would then dispose of generalized coping intentions, preferences, or dispositions (e.g., avoidance of risk, conservation of energy, or vigilance). At the intermediate level, coping strategies occur, and the lowest or behavioral level consists of specific coping acts and responses (Krohne, 1993). Research on coping with chronic diseases has been done on various levels, without being able to distinguish between them, and has caused inconsistent results. At the higher-order level, an important distinction is between problem- and emotion-focused coping. Because actions can be directed either at the problem or toward the person's internal state or emotions, researchers can distinguish between problem-focused and emotion-focused coping (Lazarus & Folkman, 1984) or danger control and fear control (Leventhal, 1970). Other higher-order approaches distinguish between approach and avoidance (Krohne, 1993; Roth & Cohen, 1986; Suls & Fletcher, 1985). These concepts have been used under different labels for more than 30 years to describe coping in different groups of patients. The approach dimension refers to a tendency to approach, focus on or even maximize the significance of the stressful event. The avoidance dimension, on the other hand, refers to a tendency to avoid, ignore, deny, or minimize the significance of the threat.

Although these higher-order approaches may be too general to assess actual disease-specific coping behavior, they facilitate comparison of coping behavior between various disease-related stressors and thus allow general conclusions on coping behavior and coping effectiveness. Coping effectiveness implies a relationship between coping behavior and various outcomes. Cohen and Lazarus (1983) distinguish three kinds of outcomes: psychological, social, and physiological. They state that effectiveness of coping is related to the domain of outcome, the point in time (short or long term) and the context. On the basis of the existing research literature, one could differentiate between effects of passive/avoidant emotion-focused and more active problem-focused coping strategies on psychosocial and physical adjustment, including self-management and compliance. Research conducted at this level has relatively consistent findings: Patients who use avoidant emotion-focused strategies have more difficulty in adjusting to chronic disease than those who use the active problem-focused strategies.

The research literature includes studies of patients with sickle cell disease (Thompson et al., 1992) showing that less use of emotion-focused coping was related to a better psychological functioning, which was measured by the Symptom Checklist (SCL-90). Research with diabetes patients showed a comparable relationship between avoidant emotion-focused coping and poor psychological adjustment (White, Richter, & Fry, 1992) and an association between active problem-focused coping and successful adaptation (Pollock, 1986, 1989). In HIV subjects, the escape/avoidance coping strategy proved to be a strong predictor of both anxiety and depression (Crystal, Bilder, & Sambamoorthi, 1993). Studies conducted on patients with rheumatoid arthritis (Brown, Nicassio, & Wallston, 1989; Jensen, Turner, Romano, & Karoly, 1991; Keefe, Brown, Wallston, & Caldwell, 1989; Newman, 1990; Smith & Wallston, 1992) demonstrated that active problem-focused strategies, including active pain-coping strategies, predict a better adjustment and passive or avoidant emotion-focused strategies a poorer psychological adjustment and physical functioning in terms of depression, well-being, self-esteem, pain and/or functional disability.

Other studies in patients with coronary heart and liver diseases (Kunzendorff, Wilhelm, Scholl, & Scholl, 1991; Muthny, 1992), renal diseases and multiple sclerosis (O'Brien, 1993; Woller et al., 1992) confirm that avoidant emotion-focused strategies are associated with lower quality of life and/or that the use of active problem-focused strategies is related to higher self-esteem, life satisfaction, and/or compliance with medical advice. Studies that compare several subpopulations of patients such as the study by Bombardier, D'Amico, and Jordan (1990) in neurological, chronic pain, cardiovascular, gastroenterological, and oncology patients, and the study by Sherbourne et al. (1992) in patients with hypertension, diabetes, and heart diseases show very few differences in coping behavior between the patient groups confirming a general trend: Avoidant emotion-focused coping strategies are related to poor psychological adjustment and poor adherence to medical advice concerning life style changes, medication, and self-management; whereas active problem-focused forms of coping show a positive relationship with successful psychological and physical adjustment.

Although there is a general trend across these studies, there seem to be less evidence for the effect of active problem-focused strategies. This may be because most studies concentrate on later stages of adaptation, when emotion-focused strategies are more prevalent (Dunkel-Schetter, Feinstein, Taylor, & Falke, 1992), in contrast to the initial stages, which are characterized by active, problem-focused forms of coping (Heim et al., 1987). Second, many studies used Folkman and Lazarus's Ways of Coping Inventory; it assesses six emotion-focused, one mixed, and only one problem-focused strategy, which may lead to an important bias. Also, in the cited studies, avoidant emotion-focused coping especially showed the described negative relationship. Other studies, such as the study by Felton, Revenson, and Hinrichsen (1984) show a positive relationship between other forms of emotion-focused coping, such as cognitive restructuring and adjustment.

COPING WITH SPECIFIC CHRONIC DISEASES

It is beyond the scope of this chapter to make an exhaustive survey of coping with the wide array of specific diseases. For this reason, we include brief comments on current research only for some diseases that have received considerable attention in the literature: asthma, cancer, coronary heart disease, diabetes, and rheumatoid arthritis.

Coping with Asthma

There are only a few studies that investigated the relation between coping and relevant outcome variables in asthmatic patients. Woller et al. (1992) conducted a study on attack-related coping styles in 80 patients with bronchial asthma. They found "minimizing/self-confident" coping to be a predictor for the number of days spent in the hospital, whereas a "diverting" coping strategy predicted poor management of attacks in patients who were using oral corticosteroids. In a study with 379 asthmatic patients, Maes and Schlosser (1987) found that patients who focused on their asthma in daily life were more likely to be hospitalized. Furthermore, patients who maintained a restrictive lifestyle and who reacted emotionally during an attack were more likely to be absent from work because of their asthma. These results indicate that avoidance or losing emotional control in attack situations is as inadequate as concentrating on the illness in daily life when no problems are experienced. These results may show that general conclusions on the effectiveness of coping strategies frequently neglect the nature of the disease process. As a consequence, intervention programs should improve patients' abilities to cope effectively with problems or attacks by increasing their self-management skills and reducing their preoccupation with their illness during attack-free periods.

Promoting an increase in self-management and/or compliance can be seen as supporting an active, problem-focused way of coping. As Bauman (1993) states, asthma self-management programs use numerous approaches. They vary from behavioral skills development to goal setting and from behavioral contracting and self-observation to social learning theory based approaches that focus on increasing the individual's self-efficacy. Self-efficacy can be improved by performing the target behavior, observing role models performing this behavior, receiving encouragement, and learning coping skills to perform the behavior under stressful conditions. Asthma self-management programs focus, for example, on the skills of inhaler use, peak flow monitoring, attack prevention, and early initiation of help-seeking behavior. A meta-analysis, based on data from 24 self-management studies, shows a relatively strong beneficial effect of these programs on measures of self-management, compliance, and psychological measures (Bauman, 1993). Coping was explicitly used as an outcome measure in only two studies. A controlled study by Maes and Schlosser (1987) showed that eight weekly 2-hour group sessions aiming at increasing self-management, produced beneficial effects in terms of a reduction in anxiety, anger, and use of corticosteroids, but these effects were not paralleled by intervention effects on coping with asthma in daily life or coping with asthmatic attacks.

A replication study (Schlösser, 1992) included a larger group of patients ($N = 75$), randomly assigned to an experimental ($N = 38$) and a control condition ($N = 37$). The study found that there were beneficial intervention effects on (a) adherence with medical advice concerning the use of breathing exercises and prescribed medication and (b) perceived restrictions in daily activities and in social life. Of the six coping strategies measured (minimizing the seriousness of the attack, rational action in attack situations, reacting emotionally in attack situations, hiding asthma in daily life, focusing on asthma in daily life, and maintaining a restrictive lifestyle), only rational action in attack situations showed a significant intervention effect, which was due to a decrease in the control group. It should be mentioned, however, that an intervention effect was found on perceived control in favor of the control group. What we can infer from these studies is that positive intervention effects are not necessarily paralleled by changes in coping strategies, which seem hard to obtain and/or to measure.

Coping with Cancer

The literature on coping with cancer covers about 30% of all studies on coping with chronic disease published since 1985 (de Ridder & Schreurs, 1994). Therefore, many remarks made earlier on coping with chronic diseases apply to coping with cancer. Although the first studies on coping with cancer (in the 1950s) emphasized unconscious defenses and maladaptive coping behavior (Meyerowitz, 1983), many coping researchers have adopted the Lazarus and Folkman (1984) model in which coping is studied in an effort to bring about relief or restore emotional equilibrium. Besides the emotion-focused versus problem-focused dimension of coping, an approach-avoidance dimension has also been used to describe coping behavior of cancer patients. Generally, three major strategies can be identified: problem-focused coping, avoidant (or passive) emotion-focused coping and active emotion-focused coping (de Ridder & Schreurs, 1994). A study conducted by Dunkel-Schetter, Feinstein, Taylor, and Falke (1992) showed that cancer patients do not limit themselves to only one or two strategies: 67% of them ($N = 668$) used at least four out of five strategies to adapt to the stressors cancer imposed on them. Nevertheless, cancer patients, like most other patients suffering from chronic conditions, mainly use passive emotion-focused strategies, such as escape-avoidance or wish-fulfilling fantasy (de Ridder & Schreurs, 1994; Dunkel-Schetter et al., 1992; Filipp, Klauer, Freudenberg, & Ferring, 1990). It should be mentioned that this apparent preference might be due to a bias in coping questionnaires. For example, in the Dunkel-Schetter study, only strategies such as distancing and behavioral or cognitive escape-avoidance were assessed. Neither the type of cancer involved, nor its duration seem to affect the preference for emotion-focused coping (Dunkel-Schetter et al., 1992; Felton & Revenson, 1984). Additionally, typical stressors accompanying cancer such as life threat or lack of control also had no effect on the preference for emotion-focused coping. Cancer patients do not differ from patients suffering from rheumatoid arthritis or hypertension, diseases which are characterized by only one of these two stressors (Felton & Revenson, 1984). Furthermore, the issue of disease-specific adaptive tasks and the way they affect coping remains unclear as the Felton and Revenson study was never replicated. There is some evidence that the psychosocial impact of cancer, rather than cancer itself, might affect coping, because fear or uncertainty about the future and limitations in physical ability, which are among the most distressing aspects of cancer, also bring about higher levels of emotion-focused coping (Dunkel-Schetter et al., 1992). Other data suggest that it is not only the amount of threat that affects coping, but also its context. This means that threatening events during the early stage of cancer allow more use of active emotion-focused or problem-focused strategies, including planful problem solving or positive reappraisal (Heim et al., 1987). This may be because diagnosis brings relief and diminishes uncertainty (cf. Andersen, 1992). The issue of adaptive tasks might also be important in interpreting effects of coping on well-being, but it is seldom practiced. However, in contrast with the widespread assumption that only problem-focused coping might reduce levels of anxiety and depression, studies among cancer patients have shown also that active emotion-focused coping strategies, such as positive reappraisal or self-control, can be helpful (Felton et al., 1984; Mishel & Sorenson, 1991; Taylor, Lichtman, & Wood, 1984). Some authors claim that even passive emotion-focused strategies, such as escape-avoidance or self-blaming, can bring about relief or reduce the level of anxiety (Filipp et al., 1990; Steptoe, Sutcliffe, Allen, & Coombes, 1991). It must be noted that research on the effects of coping with cancer is problematic. Effect sizes are weak, and they become even weaker, for example, when controlled for initial level of distress (Ell,

Mantell, Hamovitch, & Nishimoto, 1989) or when the number (instead of type) of strategies is taken into account (Manuel, Roth, Keefe, & Brandley, 1987). Much more research is needed to understand in which way coping might buffer the distressing aspects of cancer on well-being. Promising areas of research concern the development of more proximal outcome measures such as uncertainty or fear (instead of depression or anxiety; Hilton, 1989) and a shift of attention to physical measures like pain or impairment (Lang & Faller, 1992) or even the immunological system (Kiecolt-Glaser & Glaser, 1988). As most of the studies suggest, interventions with cancer patients are aimed at improving their emotional well-being. In reviewing these studies, Andersen (1992) concludes that most interventions are moderately effective, especially when high-risk groups (in the final stage of cancer) are concerned. Nevertheless, much work remains to be done; for example, there are hardly any interventions designed for minorities. Also, it seems to be quite difficult to point out effective components of intervention programs. In the light of the previously mentioned studies, we question whether the focus on enhancing active coping strategies is always helpful. Manuel and coworkers (1987) point out that cancer patients should be allowed to use the strategies they prefer because encouragement to adopt active ways of coping may prevent them from finding their own way in restoring or maintaining emotional equilibrium.

Coping with Coronary Heart Disease (CHD)

Because coping can be broadly defined, including concepts such as denial, there is a long research tradition concerning coping and CHD. Gentry, Foster, and Haney (1972) were among the first to investigate the role of denial as a determinant of anxiety and perceived health status in a coronary care unit. Results indicated that patients with myocardial infarction who deny their illness experience less anxiety than nondenying patients, but have a less realistically perceived health status. Levenson, Kay, Monteferrante, and Herman (1984) found that unstable angina patients in the coronary care unit who were identified as deniers, became medically stabilized twice as quickly as nondeniers. Levine et al. (1987) investigated the relationship between denial and recovery in patients with CHD. They found that strong deniers spent fewer days in the coronary care unit and had fewer signs of cardiac dysfunction during their hospitalization compared with weak deniers. In contrast, during the year following discharge, strong deniers were less compliant with medical recommendations and were rehospitalized more often than nondeniers. To some extent, these studies are similar to the results of the meta-analyses obtained by Mullen and Suls (1982) and Suls and Fletcher (1985), and with the widely accepted clinical opinion that denial can be regarded as an adaptive coping strategy during the first days following acute myocardial infarction. At later stages of the illness, however, it is less adaptive than more active problem-focused coping (Soloff, 1978). In a study conducted by Muthny (1992), active problem-focused coping (including placing trust in doctors, developing compliance-related strategies, having a fighting spirit, and information seeking) proved to be adaptive in a large sample of patients who had experienced a myocardial infarction about a year earlier. Although a general trend emerges from these studies, two points need to be discussed. First, the results may depend largely on the types of outcome behavior studied, as at least one study demonstrates that denial may have beneficial effects on return to work (Stern, Pascale, & Macloone, 1976). Second, other studies by Stern, Pascale, and Ackerman (1977); Dimsdale and Hackett (1982); and Shaw et al. (1985) did not find any significant relationship between denial and medical outcome in coronary patients after hospital discharge. In addition, a more recent study (Maes & Bruggemans, 1990) on 174 CHD patients, at an average of about 5 years after the incident, showed that avoidant coping was negatively associated with anxiety, depression, anger, displeasure, feelings of invalidity, social inhibition, and the use of medical resources, whereas approach strategies were positively associated with these outcome variables. However, approach was measured in this study as focusing on medical, psychological, and social problems rather than on active problem solving and avoidance as distracting from these problems. Despite a general trend suggesting that avoidance may be more beneficial in earlier stages of the disease and active problem-focused coping in later stages, coping effectiveness largely depends on the outcome variable used, and on the way that avoidance or vigilant coping strategies are defined and assessed.

These studies suggest that interventions aiming at increasing active problem-focused coping should not be offered during the first stage of the disease. This may be why many psychosocial interventions in this stage tend to be supportive rather than confrontive. There are over 30 controlled studies of structured psychosocial interventions offered to patients with CHD after dismissal from the coronary care unit. Two types of intervention can be identified. On the one hand, there are stress management interventions that aim at improving quality of life and at affecting morbidity and mortality through psychosocial changes. On the other hand, there are educational interventions that try to affect morbidity and mortality through lifestyle changes and/or compliance with medical advice. Both types of interventions try to stimulate an active, problem-solving way of coping with different consequences of the disease (stress vs. behavior and lifestyle changes). A review of the research literature shows that both types of interventions can have beneficial effects on morbidity and mortality, but that stress management interventions tend to have more favorable effects on emotional distress and quality of life, whereas health education more frequently produces positive effects on health-promotive behavior and risk factors (Van Elderen, 1991). It is evident that a combination of both approaches is expected to result in more general and powerful beneficial effects. Although these conclusions suggest that these effects are most probably paralleled by changes in coping behavior, very few studies have assessed the possible effects on coping. In two comparable studies (Maes, 1987; Van Elderen, 1991), beneficial effects of a psychoeducational group intervention for CHD patients and their partners were found on smoking cessation, healthy eating habits, knowledge related to CHD, and the number of consultations of the family physician. These effects were however not paralleled by changes in coping behavior. In conclusion, changes in coping behavior as a result of intervention are difficult to bring about or to demonstrate.

Coping with Diabetes

Coping with diabetes is different from some of the other chronic diseases because it is one of the rare chronic diseases that allow patients to control their own well-being to a large extent. Recent literature views diabetes as a process of behavioral self-regulation because patients are required to behaviorally regulate metabolic processes that are normally automatically performed (Cox & Gonder-Frederick, 1992). The resultant psychological burden is high because patients consider themselves responsible for their health. Patients must comply to the extremely demanding requirements of their regimen and therefore often fear failure (Wulsin, Jacoson, & Lawrence, 1987). In addition, despite their efforts, they will probably encounter many complications as diabetes progresses (e.g., heart disease, blindness, or amputations). However, many diabetes patients seem to be able to fulfill the demands their disease imposes on them as many succeed in coping in a problem-focused way (Band, 1990; Frenzel, McCaul, Glasgow, & Schafer, 1988; Grey, Cameron, & Thurber, 1991; Lang & Faller, 1992; Spirito et al., 1991). The study conducted by Frenzel et al. (1988) demonstrated that up to 80% of coping efforts used by diabetes patients concerned active (cognitive or behavioral) strategies. Furthermore, diabetes patients also reported higher levels of internal control (Perrin & Shapiro, 1985). These findings suggest that the adaptive tasks of chronic diseases may influence coping because only with diabetes patients is active coping quite dominant (Felton & Revenson, 1984). Many diabetes patients manage rather well; however, some authors claim that this is the result of the use of active problem-focused strategies (Cox & Gonder-Frederick, 1992). Many studies report that it is only through active coping that patients are able to maintain their demanding regimen (Band, 1990; Grey et al., 1991; Spirito et al., 1991). Some authors question the contribution of coping to compliance and suggest that active coping might have a direct effect on glycemic control (Frenzel et al., 1988; Hanson et al., 1989; Lang & Faller, 1992). Other studies note that factors besides active coping may be involved in compliance, such as social support from the patients' families (Glasgow & Toobert, 1988). Studies concerning coping and emotional well-being of diabetes patients are rare, but some of them report interesting findings. Research by Sinzato et al. (1985) demonstrated that diabetes patients who used avoidant or passive coping strategies report lower levels of depression and anxiety. These findings show that avoiding the distress of demanding adaptive tasks can help to maintain emotional equilibrium, but at the cost of future complications (cf. Suls & Fletcher, 1985). Generally, coping with the highly demanding task of compliance, as well as the threat of complications deserves more attention in future research on coping with diabetes (Cox & Gonder-Frederick, 1992). This is also true for intervention. Overall, educational and psychosocial interventions have a moderate but significant effect, especially on physical outcome and knowledge, followed by psychological status and compliance (Padgett, Mumford, Hynes, & Carter, 1988). However, the role of coping in these interventions remains unclear, especially regarding its effects on compliance and glycemic control. Furthermore, an issue that deserves more attention is the identification of patients at high risk for self-care problems; these passive copers face an enhanced risk of complications because of failure to stick to their regimen (Rubin, Peyrot, & Saudek, 1989).

Coping with Rheumatoid Arthritis (RA)

As Zautra and Manne (1992) state in a review of the research literature on coping with RA, basically two different approaches are found in the literature. One approach has taken a general focus based on the model proposed by Lazarus and Folkman, described earlier. The second is based on models for coping with chronic pain.

The first approach examines efforts to cope with arthritis in terms of emotion-focused and problem-focused strategies. In this tradition, Lambert (1985) showed that emotion-focused coping was associated with lower levels of well-being, whereas problem-focused strategies were unrelated to well-being. Felton and Revenson (1984) found that wish-fulfilling fantasy was related to psychological maladjustment in RA patients, whereas information seeking was associated with higher levels of well-being. Parker et al. (1988) found that cognitive restructuring was associated with lower levels of depression and wishful thinking and self-blame with higher levels. In the same tradition, Manne and Zautra (1989) found information seeking and cognitive restructuring in RA patients to be associated with higher levels of well-being and wishful thinking with lower levels. Furthermore, Zautra and Manne (1992) state that these data are the result of cross-sectional studies. Studies using a longitudinal design show less strong associations and suggest that future research should examine coping as a flexible process rather than examining various components of the coping process separately.

Some studies on coping with chronic pain in RA patients concentrate on active and passive coping. Active coping reflects attempts to be able to function, despite pain or because of distraction from pain. Passive coping reflects the tendency to depend on others for pain control, to engage in wishful thinking or to restrict functioning because of pain. A study by Brown and Nicassio (1987), using the Vanderbilt Pain Management Inventory demonstrates that active coping leads to lower levels of depression and higher levels of self-efficacy, and that passive coping predicts higher levels of pain, depression, helplessness, and lower self-efficacy. The most commonly used instrument for assessing coping with pain is the Coping Strategies Questionnaire (CSQ) (Rosentiel & Keefe, 1982). This instrument has frequently been used as a predictor of functional status and depression in RA patients. Park (1994) states that the most striking finding from studies that use the CSQ is not that there are coping strategies related to adequate self-regulation of pain and dysfunction, but rather that some coping strategies appear to be maladaptive. Two factors of the CSQ were identified: the Coping Attempts factor (e.g., praying and hoping, increasing activity, ignoring pain, diverting attention) and the Pain Control and Rational Thinking factor (e.g., items related to helplessness and catastrophizing, and items related to the patient's belief in pain controllability). The second factor proved to be associated with physical and psychological disability in several studies. These findings suggest that it is important to train patients with rheumatoid diseases not to catastrophize and to restructure their beliefs on disease controllability so that they can improve pain control.

There is extensive literature on psychological interventions in patients with rheumatic disorders. Park (1994) states that this literature suggests the need to take illness representations into account. To illustrate this point, Park (1994) describes a study by Parker et al. (1984). In this study, RA patients were offered a 7-hour educational program. Even though patients' knowledge on RA in the intervention group increased, they reported more pain and disability than the patients in the control group. The reason for this is that the intervention probably increased the patients' sense of vulnerability and thus failed to contribute to adequate self-regulation. Other studies that were reviewed by Park (1994) indicate other puzzling conclusions. In a study by Lorig et al. (1989), an arthritis self-management program proved to have beneficial effects on knowledge, pain, and disability, but specific changes in behavior (as, e.g., the increase in exercise) were not related to these changes. In another study by Parker et al. (1988), RA patients were offered cognitive behavior therapy, including patient education and training in various strategies, such as coping, problem solving, distraction, and self-management. The patients in the intervention group reported significantly less catastrophizing and an increased perception of control over pain. These effects did not result in decreases in experienced pain or depression.

Other studies show comparable results, suggesting that effects on pain, disability, and depression are not related to behavioral changes or that changes in coping behavior do not result in changes in health status. Furthermore, a better understanding and measurement of the coping process is probably needed to discover the mechanisms that relate changes in coping patterns to changes in relevant outcome measures.

CONCLUSION: FUTURE RESEARCH DIRECTIONS

Although research on coping with chronic diseases has increased noticeably over the past decade, much of this research seems not to have been guided by an integrated theory or model such as the one introduced in this chapter. Consequently, many questions on determinants of coping remain unanswered. These questions concern how coping behavior is affected by life events; various forms of treatment; demographic characteristics such as age, gender, and social class; external resources including social support; internal resources of personality characteristics; and finally, the appraisal of the disease-related event.

Many researchers even seem to forget that coping is a mediator between a specific disease-related stressor and several outcomes. They study coping independent of an appraisal of the characteristics of the stressor and mostly concentrate on psychological outcomes. We believe only studies that take into account characteristics of the stressor can lead to a full understanding of the coping process and its success. As Zautra and Manne (1992) state, the interactionist approach, for example, suggests that passive coping with chronic illness is adaptive under helpless circumstances but leads to otherwise poor adjustment. If the researcher takes into account that patients may perceive characteristics of the illness as being controllable or changeable, it becomes evident why Mattlin, Wethington, and Kessler (1990) found that passive coping (measured as low frequency of any coping efforts) was positively related to adjustment in a group of patients with chronic illnesses, whereas others found the opposite effect (Brown et al., 1989). Vitaliano et al. (1990) found support for this hypothesis when they discovered that patients showed more problem-focused and less emotion-focused coping, which resulted in lower levels of depression, if they perceived the stressor as changeable, whereas they observed the opposite if they perceived the situation as unchangeable. In conclusion, relating specific types of coping, irrespective of the circumstances to specific types of outcomes, is not in accordance with the transactional coping models.

In general, definitions of adjustment are too simplistic. Most studies operationalize adjustment in terms of psychological outcomes, thus neglecting effects on medical and even more frequently on social outcomes. Studies should include outcome measures related to each of these domains because a positive effect on psychological adjustment is not necessarily parallel to beneficial effects concerning work absenteeism, compliance, or the use of medical resources. More than 10 years ago, Watson and Kendall (1983) suggested that researchers would profit from a consideration of the following measures: patient self-ratings of pain and discomfort; patient self-ratings of mood; physical activity including functional ability measures; assessments of the use of the health-care system; ratings of the vocational rehabilitation; measures of family and social life, including marital satisfaction, family role, sexual functioning, and social activity measures; assessment of medication use; measures of cognitive functioning; cost-effectiveness measures; assessment of coping of the patient's social environment; and specific predictor variables to identify patients who drop out of treatment or those for whom the treatment is more successful. Even though their suggestions are valuable, not many researchers benefited from them. Other critical remarks can be made about the outcome measures used. Anxiety, depression, or well-being are undoubtedly important outcome measures for chronic patients, but assessment of specific everyday life behaviors may be more relevant in terms of practical consequences.

The research literature indicates that avoidant, emotion-focused coping strategies are related to less efficient coping strategies and active, problem-focused coping leads to a better adjustment to chronic illness. However, these conclusions neglect characteristics of the disease-related stressor, the complexity of the coping process, and the variety of possible outcomes. This may be why the relationships with adaptation generally are weak, both for avoidant, emotion-focused and active problem-focused strategies. In addition, the evidence found may even be related only to specific points in time, since the use of a longitudinal research design does not seem to increase the significance of the relationship. For example, cross-sectional studies consistently show that cognitive restructuring is associated with lower levels of depression and wishful thinking with higher levels in patients with rheumatoid arthritis, whereas two studies using a longitudinal design showed very modest to negligible effects of coping on adjustment including depression in RA patients (Zautra & Manne, 1992).

That most research concentrates on higher-order coping strategies at one moment in time implies a certain weakness. What this approach neglects is that coping is a highly dynamic process which attempts to influence a changing stressor, and it would therefore be more advisable to study a variety of specific coping strategies in a longitudinal design to discover which patterns of disease-related coping are related at which stage with relevant outcomes. Some research suggests that this approach may be promising because the type of coping would not be crucial from this point of view, but rather whether patients cope or not, and whether they do so in a flexible, complete way. In a study with diabetic patients, Wikblad and Montin (1992) found that patients who use more complete coping strategies (trying to tackle all possible aspects of the disease) had significantly higher scores on self-esteem. Blalock, McEvoy, DeVellis, Holt, and Hahn (1993) found that rheumatoid arthritis patients who can be characterized as flexible copers (using many different coping strategies for different or the same problems over time) have a better psychological adjustment than inflexible copers. Manuel and colleagues (1987), who categorized patients as "low copers" (low on passive/avoidant and low on active/problem-focused coping), "average copers" (high on one and low on the other dimension) or "high copers" (high on both dimensions), showed that high copers had the best adjustment, suggesting that it is probably more important to do as much as possible than to cope in a specific way. As stated earlier, however, it is apparent also that perceived characteristics of the stressors should be integrated in this approach because the results of the study by Mattlin et al. (1990), which indicated favorable effects of passive coping, would otherwise be inconsistent with this conclusion.

Another argument for more longitudinal research within a real transactional paradigm is that controlled intervention studies with a repeated measures design in patients with chronic diseases showed positive intervention effects on adjustment, whereas these effects were not paralleled by changes in coping strategies (Maes, 1987; Schaffner, 1994; Watson & Kendall, 1983). Although there is some relationship of coping with adjustment, the mechanisms are at least not well understood, possibly because intervention studies concentrate too much on the assessment of basic (and thus more traitlike) modes of coping, and not enough on actual, situation-dependent coping behavior. There is also a tendency in the literature to concentrate only on the patient's coping. Usually, many patients are highly dependent on the way their professional and family environment copes with the illness, and the social environment likewise is affected by the way the patient copes. Consequently, measures that assess coping of partners, parents, or health-care providers should be used more frequently both as determinants of patient's coping and as outcome measures (Coyne & Fiske, 1992; Jacobs, 1992).

This brings us to the issue of assessment of coping with chronic disease. The number of coping instruments increased considerably over the past decade, but there seems to be a lack of disease-specific coping instruments; observational and physiological methods for the validation of self-report measures; instruments that assess coping at various levels, including preferences, strategies, and actual situation-specific coping behavior; and agreement on common measures.

Additionally, many studies have shortcomings in their methodology, such as the use of small samples, heterogeneous samples (e.g., consisting of patients at various stages of the disease), and the lack of longitudinal designs. For these reasons, some authors believe the field is in a mess (de Ridder & Schreurs, 1994). In our opinion, the research on coping with chronic diseases would greatly profit from the establishment of an international task force, which should formulate guidelines for future research and stimulate cooperative research between various groups of researchers. The field does not seem to suffer from a lack of research but rather from a lack of agreement between researchers on a relevant theoretical base and methodological requirements.

REFERENCES

Aldwin, C. M., & Revenson, T. A. (1987). Does coping help? A reexamination of the relation between coping and mental health. *Journal of Personality and Social Psychology, 53,* 337–348.

Andersen, B. L. (1992). Psychological interventions for cancer patients to enhance the quality of life. *Journal of Consulting and Clinical Psychology, 60,* 552–568.

Andersson, S. I., & Ekdahl, C. (1992). Self-appraisal and coping in out-patients with chronic disease. *Scandinavian Journal of Psychology, 33,* 289–300.

Band, E. B. (1990). Children's coping with diabetes: Understanding the role of cognitive development. *Journal of Pediatric Psychology, 15,* 27–41.

Bauman, A. (1993). Effects of asthma patient education upon psychological and behavioural outcomes. In S. Maes, H. Leventhal, & M. Johnston (Eds.), *International Review of Health Psychology* (Vol. 2, pp. 199–212). Chichester: Wiley

Becker, M. H., & Maiman, L. A. (1975). Sociobehavioral determinants compliance with health and medical care recommendations. *Medical Care, 13,* 10–24.

Blalock, S. J., McEvoy DeVellis, B., Holt, K., & Hahn, P. M. (1993). Coping with rheumatoid arthritis: Is one problem the same as another? *Health Education Quarterly, 20*(1), 119–132.

Bombardier, C. H., D'Amico, C., & Jordan, J. S. (1990). The relationship of appraisal and coping to chronic illness adjustment. *Behavioral Research and Therapy, 28*(4), 297–304.

Brown, G. K., & Nicassio, P. M. (1987). Development of a questionnaire for the assessment of active and passive coping strategies in chronic pain patients. *Pain, 31,* 53–64.

Brown, G. K., Nicassio, P. M., & Wallston, K. A. (1989). Pain coping strategies and depression in rheumatoid arthritis. *Journal of Consulting and Clinical Psychology, 57,* 652–657.

Carver, C. S., Scheier, M. F., & Pozo, C. (1992). Conceptualizing the process of coping with health problems. In S. Friedman (Ed.), *Hostility, coping and health* (pp. 167–187). Washington, DC: American Psychological Association.

Carver, C. S., Scheier, M. F., & Weintraub, J. K. (1989). Assessing coping strategies: A theoretically based approach. *Journal of Personality and Social Psychology, 56,* 267–283.

Cassileth, B. R., Lusk, E. J., Strouse, T. B., Miller, D. S., Brown, L. L., Cross, P. A., & Tenaglia, A. N. (1984). Psychosocial status in chronic illness. *The New England Journal of Medicine, 311,* 506–511.

Cohen, F., & Lazarus, R. (1983). Coping and adaptation in health and illness. In D. Mechanic (Ed.), *Handbook of health, illness and social adaptation* (pp. 607–635). New York: Free Press.

Couzijn, A. L., Ros, W. J. G., & Winnubst, J. A. M. (1990). Cancer. In A. A. Kaptein, H. M. van der Ploeg, B. Garssen, & R. Beunderman (Eds.), *Behavioural medicine* (pp. 231–247). New York: Wiley.

Cox, D. J., & Gonder-Frederick, L. (1992). Major developments in behavioral diabetes research. *Journal of Consulting and Clinical Psychology, 60*, 628–683.

Coyne, J. C., & Fiske, V. (1992). Couples coping with chronic and catastrophic illness. In T. J. Akamatsu, M. A. Parris Stephens, S. E. Hobfoll, & J. H. Crowter (Eds.), *Family health psychology* (pp. 129–149). Washington, DC: Hemisphere.

Creed, F. (1993). Stress and psychosomatic disorders. In L. Goldberger & S. Breznitz (Eds.), *Handbook of stress, theoretical and clinical aspects* (pp. 496–510). New York: Free Press.

Crystal, S., Bilder, S., & Sambamoorthi, U. (1993, October 17). *Social support, coping and psychological distress among persons with HIV.* Paper presented at the American Public Health Association, San Francisco, CA.

Dana, R. H. (1984). Assessment for health psychology. *Clinical Psychological Review, 4*, 459–476.

de Ridder, D. T. D., & Schreurs, K. M. G. (1994). *Coping en Sociale Steun van Chronisch Zieken* [Coping and social support in patients with chronic diseases]. Report for the Dutch Commission for Chronic Diseases. Utrecht: Section of Clinical and Health Psychology.

Dimsdale, J. E., & Hackett, T. P. (1982). Effect of denial on cardiac health and psychologial assessment. *American Journal of Psychiatry, 139*, 1477–1480.

Doehrman, S. R. (1977). Psycho-social aspects of recovery from coronary heart disease: A review. *Social Science and Medicine, 11*, 199–218.

Dunkel-Schetter, C., Feinstein, L., Taylor, S. E., & Falke, R. (1992). Patterns of coping with cancer and their correlates. *Health Psychology, 11*, 79–87.

Ell, K. O., Mantell, J. E., Hamovitch, M. B., & Nishimoto, R. H. (1989). Social support, sense of control, and coping among patients with breast, lung or colorectal cancer. *Journal of Psychosocial Oncology, 7*, 63–89.

Endler, N. S., & Magnusson, D. (Eds.). (1976). *Interactional psychology and personality.* Washington, DC: Hemisphere.

Feifel, H., Strack, S., & Nagy, V. T. (1987a). Coping strategies and associated features of medically ill patients. *Psychosomatic Medicine, 49*, 616–625.

Feifel, H., Strack, S., & Nagy, V. T. (1987b). Degree of life threat and differential use of coping modes. *Journal of Psychosomatic Research, 31*, 91–99.

Felton, B. J., & Revenson, T. A. (1984). Coping with chronic illness: A study of illness controllability and the influence of coping strategies on psychological adjustment. *Journal of Consulting and Clinical Psychology, 52*, 343–353.

Felton, B. J., Revenson, T. A., & Hinrichsen, G. A. (1984). Stress and coping in the explanation of psychological adjustment among chronically ill adults. *Social Science & Medicine, 18*, 889–898.

Filipp, S. H., Klauer, T., Freudenberg, E., & Ferring, D. (1990). The regulation of subjective well-being in cancer patients: An analysis of coping effectiveness. *Psychology & Health, 4*, 305–317.

Folkman, S., & Lazarus, R. S. (1988). *Manual for the Ways of Coping Questionnaire.* Palo Alto, CA: Consulting Psychologist Press.

Frenzel, M. P., McCaul, K. D., Glasgow, R. E., & Schafer, L. C. (1988). The relationship of stress and coping to regimen adherence and glycemic control of diabetes. *Journal of Social and Clinical Psychology, 6,* 77–87.

Friedman, H. S., & Di Matteo, M. R. (1984). *Health Psychology.* Englewood Cliffs, NJ: Prentice-Hall.

Gentry, W. D., Foster, S., & Haney, T. (1972). Denial as a determinant of anxiety and perceived health status in the Coronary Care Unit. *Psychosomatic Medicine, 34,* 39–44.

Glasgow, R. E., & Toobert, D. J. (1988). Social environment and regimen adherence among type II diabetic patients. *Diabetes Care, 11,* 377–386.

Grant, I., McDonald, W. L., Patterson, T., & Trimble, M. R. (1989). Multiple sclerosis. In G. W. Brown & T. O. Harris (Eds.), *Life events and illness.* New York: Guilford.

Grey, M., Cameron, M. E., & Thurber, F. W. (1991). Coping and adaptation in children with diabetes. *Nursing Research, 40,* 144–149.

Hanson, C. L., Cigrang, J. A., Harris, M. A., Carle, D. L. (1989). Coping styles in youths with insulin-dependent diabetes mellitus. *Journal of Consulting and Clinical Psychology, 57,* 644–651.

Heim, E. (1988). Coping und Adaptivitat: Gibt es geignetes oder ungeignetes coping? [Coping and adaptation: Is there something as adaptive or maladaptive coping?]. *Psychotherapie, Psychosomatik, Medizinische Psychologie, 38,* 8–18.

Heim, E., Augustiny, K., Blaser, A., Burki, C. (1987). Coping with breast cancer. A longitudinal prospective study. *Psychotherapy and Psychosomatics, 48,* 44–59.

Hilton, B. (1989). The relationship of uncertainty, control, commitment, and threat of recurrence to coping strategies used by women diagnosed with breast cancer. *Journal of Behavioral Medicine, 12,* 39–54.

Hobfoll, S. E. (1988). *The ecology of stress.* New York: Hemisphere.

Hobfoll, S. E. (1989). Conservation of resources: A new attempt at conceptualizing stress. *American Psychologist, 44,* 513–524.

Jacobs, J. (1992). Understanding family factors that shape the impact of chronic illness. In T. J. Akamatsu, M. A. Parris Stephens, S. E. Hobfoll, & J. H. Crowther (Eds.), *Family health psychology* (pp. 111–127). Washington, DC: Hemisphere.

Jensen, M. P., Turner, J. A., Romano, J. M., & Karoly, P. (1991). Coping with chronic pain: A critical review of the literature. *Pain, 47,* 249–283.

Johnston, M., Weinman, J., & Marteau, T. M. (1990). Health psychology in hospital settings. In A. A. Kaptein, H. M. van der Ploeg, B. Garssen, P. J. G. Schreurs, & R. Beunderman (Eds.), *Behavioural medicine* (pp. 13–32). New York: Wiley.

Keefe, F. J., Brown, G. K., Wallston, K. A., & Caldwell, D. S. (1989). Coping with rheumatoid arthritis pain: Catastrophizing as a maladaptive strategy. *Pain, 37,* 51–56.

Kiecolt-Glaser, J. K., & Glaser, R. (1988). Behavioral influences on immune function: Evidence for the interplay between stress and health. In T. Field, P. M. McCabe & N. Schneiderman (Eds.), *Stress and coping across development.* Hillsdale, NJ: Erlbaum.

Krohne, H. W. (1993). Attention and avoidance. Two central strategies in coping with aversiveness. In H. W. Krohne (Ed.), *Attention and avoidance* (pp. 3–15). Seattle, WA: Hogrefe.

Kunzendorff, E., Wilhelm, M., Scholl, U., & Scholl, M. (1991). Coping-Prozesse bei ausgewahlten Gruppen chronisch Kranker [Coping processes in selected groups of chronic patients]. *Zeitschrift fur gesamte Innere Medizin, 46,* 690–696.

Lambert, V. A. (1985). Study of factors associated with psychological well-being in rheumatoid arthritic women. *Journal of Nursing Scholarship, 17*(2), 343–353.

Lang, H., & Faller, H. (1992). Coping and adaptation in pancreatectomized patients. A somatopsychic perspective. *Psychotherapy & Psychosomatics, 57,* 17–28.

Lazarus, R. S. (1991). Progress on a Cognitive-Motivational-Relational Theory of emotion. *American Psychologist, 46*(8), 819–834.

Lazarus, R. S., & Folkman, S. (1984). *Stress, appraisal and coping.* New York: Springer.

Lazarus, R. S., & Smith, C. A. (1988). Knowledge and appraisal in the cognition-emotion relationship. *Cognition and Emotion, 2,* 281–300.

Leppin, A., & Schwarzer, R. (1988). Social support and physical health: An updated meta-analysis. In L. R. Schmidt, P. Schwenkmezger, J. Weinman, & S. Maes (Eds.), *Theoretical and applied aspects of health psychology* (pp. 185–202). Chur, Switzerland: Harwood.

Levenson, J. L., Kay, R., Monteferrante, J., & Herman, M. V. (1984). Denial predicts favorable outcome in unstable angina pectoris. *Psychosomatic Medicine, 46,* 25–32.

Leventhal, E. A., Suls, J., & Leventhal, H. (1993). Hierarchical analysis of coping: Evidence from life-span studies. In H. W. Krohne (Ed.), *Attention and avoidance* (pp. 71–99). Seattle, WA: Hogrefe.

Leventhal, H. (1970). Findings and theory in the study of fear communications. In L. Berkowitz (Ed.), *Advances in experimental social psychology* (pp. 119–186). New York: Academic Press.

Leventhal, H., Meyer, D., & Nerenz, D. (1980). The common sense representation of illness danger. In S. Rachman (Ed.), *Contributions to medical psychology* (Vol. 2, pp. 7–30). New York: Pergamon.

Leventhal, H., & Nerenz, D. R. (1983). A model for stress research with some implications for the control of stress disorders. In D. Meichenbaum & M. Jaremko (Eds.), *Stress reduction and prevention* (pp. 5–38). New York: Plenum.

Levine, J., Warrenburg, S., Kerns, R., Schwartz, G., Delaney, R., Fontana, A., Gradman, A., Smith, S., Allen, S., & Cascione, R. (1987). The role of denial in recovery from coronary heart disease. *Psychosomatic Medicine, 49,* 109–117.

Lorig, K., Seleznick, M., Lubeck, D., Ung, E., Chastain, R. L., & Holman, H. R. (1989). The beneficial outcomes of the arthritis self-management course are not adequately explained by behavior change. *Arthritis and Rheumatism, 32,* 91–95.

Maes, S. (1987). Reducing emotional distress in chronic patients, a cognitive approach. *Communication and Cognition, 20*(2/3), 261–275.

Maes, S., & Bruggemans, E. (1990). Approach-avoidance and illness behaviour in coronary heart patients. In L. R. Schmidt, P. Schwenkmezger, J. Weinman, & S. Maes (Eds.), *Theoretical and applied aspects of health psychology* (pp. 297–308). Chur, Switzerland: Harwood.

Maes, S., & Schlosser, M. (1987). The role of cognition and coping in health behaviour outcomes of asthmatic patients. *Current Psychological Research and Reviews, 6,* 79–90.

Maes, S., Vingerhoets, A., & Van Heck, G. (1987). The study of stress and disease, some developments and requirements. *Social Science and Medicine, 25*(6), 567–578.

Manne, S., & Zautra, A. J. (1989). Spouse criticism and support: Their association with coping and psychological adjustment among women with rheumatoid arthritis. *Journal of Personality and Social Psychology, 56*(4), 608–617.

Manuel, G. M., Roth, S., Keefe, F. J., & Brandley, B. (1987). Coping with cancer. *Journal of Human Stress, 13,* 149–158.

Martin, P. R., & Theunissen, C. (1993). The role of life event stress, coping and social support in chronic headaches. *Headache, 7*, 301–306.

Mattlin, J. A., Wethington, E., & Kessler, R. C. (1990). Situational determinants of coping and coping effectiveness. *Journal of Health and Social Behavior, 31*, 103–122.

McKinlay, J. B., & McKinlay, S. M. (1977). The questionable contribution of medical measures to the decline of mortality in the United States in the twentieth century. *Milbank Memorial Fund Quarterly/Health and Society* (pp. 405–428).

Meyerowitz, B. E. (1983). Postmastectomy coping strategies and quality of life. *Health Psychology, 2*, 117–120.

Miller, S. M. (1987). Monitoring and blunting: Validation of a questionnaire to assess styles of information-sensitivity lection under threat. *Journal of Personality and Social Psychology, 52*, 345–353.

Millon, T., Green, C. J., & Meagher, R. B. (1982). A new psychodiagnostic tool for clients in rehabilitation settings: The MBHI. *Rehabilitation Psychology, 27*, 23–35.

Mishel, M. H., & Sorenson, D. S. (1991). Uncertainty in gynecological cancer. A test for the mediating functions of mastery and coping. *Nursing Research, 40*, 167–171.

Moos, R. H. (1988). Life stressors and coping resource influence health and well-being. *Psychological Assessment, 4*, 133–158.

Moos, R. H., & Schaefer, J. A. (1993). Coping resources and processes: Current concepts and measures. In L. Goldberger & S. Breznitz (Eds.), *Handbook of stress* (pp. 234–257). New York: Free Press.

Morse, J. M., & Johnson, J. L. (1991). Towards a theory of illness: The Illness Constellation Model. In J. M. Morse & J. L. Johnson (Eds.), *The illness experience* (pp. 315–342). London: Sage.

Mullen, B., & Suls, J. (1982). The effectiveness of attention and rejection as coping styles: A meta-analysis of temporal differences. *Journal of Psychosomatic Research, 26*, 43–49.

Muthny, F. A. (1992). Krankheitsverarbeitung im Vergleich von Herzinfarkt-, Dialyse und MS-Patienten. *Zeitschrift fur Klinische Psychologie, 21*(4), 372–391.

Newman, S. (1990). Coping with chronic illness. In P. Bennet, J. Weinman, & P. Spurgeon (Eds.), *Current developments in health psychology* (pp. 159–175). Chur, Switzerland: Harwood.

O'Brien, M. T. (1993). Multiple sclerosis: The relationship among self-esteem, social support, and coping behaviour. *Applied Nursing Research, 6*(2), 54–63.

Padgett, D., Mumford, E., Hynes, M., & Carter, R. (1988). Meta-analysis of the effects of educational and psychosocial interventions on management of diabetes mellitus. *Journal of Clinical Epidemiology, 41*, 1007–1030.

Park, D. C. (1994). Self-regulation and control of rheumatic disorders. In S. Maes, H. Leventhal, & M. Johnston (Eds.), *International Review of Health Psychology* (Vol. 3, pp. 189–217). Chichester: Wiley.

Parker, J. C., Frank, R. G., Beck, N. C., Smarr, K. L., Buescher, K. L., Phillips, L. R., Smith, E. I., Anderson, S. K., & Walker, S. E. (1988). Pain management in rheumatoid arthritis patients: A cognitive-behavioral approach. *Arthritis and Rheumatism, 31*, 593–601.

Parker, J. C., Singsen, B. H., Hewett, J. E., Walker, S. E., Hazelwood, S. E., Hall, P. J., Holsten, D. J., & Rodon, C. M. (1984). Educating patients with rheumatoid arthritis: A prospective analysis. *Archives of Physical Medicine Rehabilitation, 65*, 771–774.

Pennings-Van der Eerden, L., & Visser, A. Ph. (1990). Diabetes mellitus. In A. A. Kaptein, H. M. van der Ploeg, B. Garssen, P. J. G. Schreurs, & R. Beunderman (Eds.), *Behavioural medicine* (pp. 247–265). New York: Wiley.

Perrez, M., & Reicherts, M. (1992). *Stress, coping and health*. Seattle, WA: Hogrefe & Huber.

Perrin, E. C., & Shapiro, E. (1985). Health locus of control beliefs of healthy children, children with chronic physical illness and their mothers. *Journal of Pediatrics, 107,* 627–633.

Pervin, L. A., & Lewis, M. (1978). *Perspectives in interactional psychology*. New York: Plenum.

Pollock, S. E. (1986). Human responses to chronic illness. *Nursing Research, 35,* 90–95.

Pollock, S. E. (1989). Adaptive responses to diabetes mellitus. *Western Journal of Nursing Research, 11,* 265–280.

Regan, C. A., Lorig, K., & Thoresen, C. (1988). Arthritis appraisal and ways of coping, scale development. *Arthritis Care and Research, 3,* 139–150.

Rosentiel, A. K., & Keefe, F. J. (1982). The use of coping strategies in chronic low back pain patients: Relationships to patient characteristics and current adjustment. *Pain, 17,* 33–44.

Roth, S., & Cohen, L. J. (1986). Approach, avoidance and coping with stress. *American Psychologist, 41,* 813–819.

Rubin, R. R., Peyrot, M., & Saudek, C. D. (1989). Effect of diabetes education on self-care, metabolic control, and emotional well-being. *Diabetes Care, 12,* 673–679.

Schaffner, L. (1994). Psychosoziale Interventionen bei Krebspatiënten, Ein Ubersicht [Psychological interventions in cancer patients, a review]. *Jahrbuch der Medizinischen Psychologie, 10,* 170–191.

Schlösser, M. (1992). *Self-management and asthma*. Leiden, The Netherlands: DSWO Press.

Schüssler, G. (1992). Coping strategies and individual meanings of illness. *Social Science and Medicine, 34,* 427–432.

Shaw, R. E., Cohen, F., Doyle, B., & Palesky, J. (1985). The impact of denial and egressive style on information gain and rehabilitation outcomes in myocardial infarction patients. *Psychosomatic Medicine, 47,* 262–273.

Sherbourne, C. D., Hays, R. D., Ordway, L., Di Matteo, M. R., & Kravits, R. L. (1992). Antecedents of adherence to medical recommendations: Results from the medical outcomes study. *Journal of Behavioural Medicine, 15*(5), 447–468.

Sinzato, R., Fukino, O., Tamai, H., Isizu, H., Nakagawa, T., & Ikemi, Y. (1985). Coping behaviors of severe diabetics. *Psychotherapy and Psychosomatics, 43,* 219–226.

Smith, C. A. (1991). The self, appraisal & coping. In C. R. Snyder & D. R. Forsyth (Eds.), *Handbook of social and clinical psychology* (pp. 116–137). New York: Pergamon.

Smith, C. A., & Wallston, K. A. (1992). Adaptation in patients with chronic rheumatoid arthritis: Application of a general model. *Health Psychology, 11*(3), 151–162.

Soloff, P. H. (1978). Denial and rehabilitation of the post-infarction patient. *International Journal of Psychiatry in Medicine, 8,* 125–132.

Spirito, A., Ruggiero, L., Bowen, A., & McGarvey, S. T. (1991). Stress, coping and social support as mediators of the emotional status of women with gestational diabetes. *Psychology & Health, 5,* 111–120.

Steptoe, A., Sutcliffe, I., Allen, B., & Coombes, C. (1991). Satisfaction with communication, medical knowledge, and coping style in patients with metastatic cancer. *Social Science & Medicine, 32,* 627–632.

Stern, M. J., Pascale, L., & Ackerman, A. (1977). Life adjustment post myocardial infarction: Determining predictive variables. *Archives of Internal Medicine, 137,* 1680–1685.

Stern, M. J., Pascale, L., & Macloone, J. B. (1976). Psychosocial adaptation following an acute myocardial infarction. *Journal of Chronic Disease, 29,* 513–526.

Suls, J., & Fletcher, B. (1985). The relative efficacy of avoidant and non-avoidant coping strategies: A meta-analysis. *Health Psychology, 4,* 249–288.

Taylor, S. E. (1991). *Health Psychology.* New York: McGraw-Hill.

Taylor, S. E., & Aspinwall, L. G. (1993). Coping with chronic illness. In L. Goldberger & S. Breznitz (Eds.), *Handbook of stress, theoretical and clinical aspects.* New York: Free Press.

Taylor, S. E., Lichtman, R. R., & Wood, J. V. (1984). Attributions, beliefs about control, and adjustment to breast cancer. *Journal of Personality and Social Psychology, 46,* 489–502.

Thompson, R. J., Gil, K. M., Abrams, M. R., & Philips, G. (1992). Stress, coping and psychological adjustment of adults with sickle cell disease. *Journal of Consulting and Clinical Psychology, 60*(3), 433–440.

van den Berg, J., & van den Bos, G. A. M. (1989). Het (meten van het) voorkomen van chronische aandoeningen 1974–1987. *Maandbericht Gezondheid (CBS), 3,* 4–21.

Van Elderen, T. (1991). *Health education in cardiac rehabilitation.* Leiden, The Netherlands: DSWO Press.

Vitaliano, P. P., De Wolfe, D. J., Maiaro, R. D., Russo, J., & Katon, W. (1990). Appraised changeability of a stressor as a modifier of the relationship between coping and depression: A test of the hypothesis of fit. *Journal of Personality and Social Psychology, 59,* 582–592.

Warren, S., Warren, K., & Cockerill, R. (1991). Emotional stress and coping in multiple sclerosis exacerbations. *Journal of Psychosomatic Research, 35,* 37–47.

Watson, D., & Kendall, P. C. (1983). Methodological issues in research on coping with chronic disease. In T. G. Burish & L. A. Bradley (Eds.), *Coping with chronic disease* (pp. 39–81). New York: Academic Press.

White, N. E., Richter, J. M., & Fry, C. (1992). Coping, social support and adaptation to chronic illness. *Western Journal of Nursing Research, 14*(2), 211–224.

Wikblad, K. F., & Montin, K. R. (1992). Coping with a chronic disease. *The Diabetes Educator, 18*(4), 316–320.

Woller, W., Kruse, J., Alberti, L., Kraut, D., Richter, B., Worth, H., & Tress, W. (1992). Affektiv-kognitive Anfallsverarbeitung und Krankheitsverhalten bei Patienten mit Asthma Bromchiale [Coping with attacks and illness behaviour in patients with bronchial asthma]. *Psychotherapie Psychosomatik und Medizinische Psychologie, 42,* 63–70.

Wulsin, L. R., Jacoson, A. M., & Lawrence, I. R. (1987). Psychosocial aspects of diabetic retinopathy. *Diabetes Care, 10,* 367–373.

Zautra, A. J., & Manne, S. L. (1992). Coping with rheumatoid arthritis: A review of a decade of research. *Annals of Behavioral Medicine, 14*(1), 31–39.

CHAPTER 12

Coping with Chronic Pain

JOEL KATZ, PAUL RITVO, M. JANE IRVINE, and MARLA JACKSON

Pain serves the protective function of informing us of injury or disease and usually remits when healing is complete or the condition is cured. The aversive quality of pain provides the impetus for reflex withdrawal and goal-directed behaviors designed to alleviate pain and promote healing. A sprained ankle reliably elicits pain on weight bearing thus limiting further tissue damage and encouraging recuperation. In contrast, when pain persists and cannot be controlled, it ceases to protect. Chronic, intractable pain interferes with all aspects of living. It demands attention, impairs concentration and drains the individual of energy. The person with chronic pain becomes preoccupied with the meaning of the pain and daily life deteriorates into a single-minded and relentless search for relief.

Despite the intimate experience each of us has with pain, it is surprisingly difficult to define. The International Association for the Study of Pain (IASP) defines pain as "an unpleasant sensory and emotional experience associated with actual or potential tissue damage, or described in terms of such damage" (International Association for the Study of Pain [IASP], 1979, p. 250). We now know that pain is not simply the end-product of a direct pathway that faithfully transmits neural impulses from peripheral nociceptors to a pain center in the brain. The pioneering work of Melzack and Wall (1965) made it clear that the brain exerts a powerful inhibitory influence on selective spinal cord cells thus providing a mechanism by which psychological and emotional processes may modulate the sensory signal. The gate control theory of pain (Melzack & Wall, 1965) paved the way for the widespread acceptance of psychological factors in pain (Melzack & Wall, 1988). It is now well established that pain is a psychological experience. The perception of pain involves sensory-discriminative, motivational-affective, and cognitive-evaluative dimensions and is determined by many factors including cultural influences, the meaning of the situation, past experience, and level of arousal (Melzack & Wall, 1988).

The present chapter deals with coping among persons with chronic nonmalignant pain. This term refers to pain that has persisted for 6 months or longer and is not associated with cancer. Patients with chronic low back pain (CLBP) form the largest subclass of chronic nonmalignant pain conditions, which also include

252

rheumatoid arthritis,[1] osteoarthritis,[2] myofascial pain,[3] and headache. Although there is some evidence that coping efforts and outcomes may be condition specific (Anderson & Rehm, 1984; Keefe et al., 1991; Keefe & Dolan, 1986), it is our belief that there are many more similarities than differences among the various chronic pain conditions that permit general commentary and conclusions.

We begin by presenting a brief overview of the questionnaires that have been used to measure coping followed by a presentation of the classification systems that have arisen in an attempt to categorize the myriad coping strategies people have been reported to use in their daily efforts to cope with chronic pain. We then highlight strategies for coping with pain that consistently have been associated with more or less pain and functional impairment. This is followed by sections on the role of social support in coping with chronic pain and situational aspects of coping among chronic pain patients. The importance of prevention programs and interventions designed to enhance pain coping efforts are covered in a section that deals with primary prevention and early detection, secondary prevention, relapse prevention, and prevention of related difficulties that commonly co-occur with chronic pain. In the final section, we present a risk-adaptation model to guide interventions with patients suffering chronic pain and other distressing conditions. Applying this model involves addressing the risks represented by the pain as well as the inevitable adaptation problems that accompany the experience of chronic pain. Throughout the chapter, we emphasize current conceptual and methodological issues that have led to important advances in our understanding of how people cope with chronic pain as well as those that we believe have hampered progress in the field. We conclude with a critical review of research directions that have limited utility and comment on some of the complexities of coping with chronic pain that need to be addressed.

COPING AND PAIN

Coping with chronic pain may be defined as the thoughts and actions people engage in in their efforts to manage pain on a daily basis. These diverse efforts include interventions as global as cognitive-behavior therapy and other self-management programs developed to help patients cope with a multitude of problems associated with pain to specific strategies designed to manage the sensory intensity of a discrete episode of pain. This diversity highlights the

---

[1] Rheumatoid arthritis is associated with intermittent aching and/or burning joint pain due to systemic inflammatory disease. It is characterized by flare-ups and remissions and affects about 1% of the population (Task Force on Taxonomy, 1994).

[2] Osteoarthritis is a degenerative disease process that most commonly affects the cartilage in the joints of the hands, knees, hips, and spine. The pain is usually described as a deep aching in the joints and surrounding muscle (Task Force on Taxonomy, 1994).

[3] Myofascial pain syndromes are associated with diffuse, aching musculoskeletal pain and tenderness. Specific myofascial pain syndromes include fibrositis, myalgia, muscular rheumatism, and nonarticular rheumatism (Task Force on Taxonomy, 1994).

importance of specifying exactly what is meant by coping with chronic pain (Keefe, Salley, & Lefebvre, 1992). In addition to the burden of pain, patients must contend with many secondary lifestyle changes that inevitably arise when pain becomes chronic. Among the downstream effects of chronic pain are loss of employment and income, mood disturbances such as depression and anxiety, changes in the marital relationship and family dynamics, and a reduction in social and leisure activities (Hitchcock, Ferrell, & McCaffery, 1994).

Although chronic pain has much in common with other life stressors, it has aspects that make the task of coping with pain especially difficult and unique. For one, the familiarity we all have with pain is deceptive. Because of its inherently subjective nature, we can never really know what another person is experiencing when he or she complains of pain. The subjective nature of pain makes the experience a lonely one. In addition, the relationship between physical activity and subsequent pain is variable and often is not immediate. For example, pain resulting from an especially strenuous effort may not be apparent for a day or more. The variable temporal link between specific behaviors and pain makes it very difficult for patients to determine whether or not a contingency exists between their actions and the pain. This sets the stage for the development of superstitious beliefs and behaviors, widespread avoidance, and a pervasive sense of helplessness and hopelessness.

Diagnostic uncertainty is commonplace in the field of chronic pain. Many pains persist in the absence of peripheral pathology. For others, the pathology is poorly related to the degree of pain (Wall, 1994). Outdated but persisting dualistic notions imply that pain in the absence of physical findings or pain that does not conform to the observed pathophysiology is evidence of psychopathology, malingering or secondary gain (Gamsa, 1994). Thus not only must patients cope with pain and its sequelae as previously outlined, but also with the uncertainty of diagnosis and the nagging doubts about the authenticity of the pain occasionally displayed by concerned family, friends, and helping professionals.

PAIN-COPING QUESTIONNAIRES

The empirical literature on coping with pain has developed through two quite different approaches to the assessment of coping strategies among chronic pain patients (Keefe et al., 1992). The more traditional approach has been to assess coping using questionnaires that request patients to specify and respond to the primary stressor in their life—whether or not it is pain (Folkman & Lazarus, 1980; Lazarus & Folkman, 1984). Another approach has been to develop stressor-specific coping questionnaires that request patients to report the manner in which they cope with chronic pain (Rosenstiel & Keefe, 1983). These two approaches may yield very similar results for chronic pain patients who consider the pain to be the primary stressor in their lives. However, chronic pain patients who do not rate pain as the primary stressor may differ in important ways from pain patients who rate another stressor as primary (Turner, Clancy, & Vitaliano,

1987). The choice of which approach to use obviously depends on the purpose of the assessment. Use of pain-specific coping questionnaires has the advantage of reducing response variability and generally is to be preferred when selecting cognitive or behavioral targets for chronic pain management. Use of a general coping questionnaire provides the potential to elucidate whether pain patients engage in context-dependent coping efforts. We now present a brief description of the main questionnaires currently used to assess coping among chronic pain patients, both to introduce readers to these instruments and to provide a context for subsequent reference.

The Ways of Coping Checklist (WCC)

The WCC (Folkman & Lazarus, 1980) and revised Ways of Coping Checklist (WCC-R) (Lazarus & Folkman, 1984) provide general measures of coping for which the respondent is instructed to indicate the thoughts, feelings, and actions engaged in when coping with the various demands of a respondent-specified stressor. The WCC has undergone further revision by Vitaliano, Russo, Carr, Maiuro, and Becker (1985) to consist of 42 items that measure the frequency with which respondents use each of the following coping strategies: Problem-Focused (e.g., concentrated on something good that could come out of the whole thing), Social Support Seeking (e.g., accepted sympathy and understanding from someone), Avoidance (e.g., went on as if nothing had happened), Self-Blame and Wishful Thinking (e.g., hoped a miracle would happen). Respondents are asked to read a number of coping strategies and indicate, using a 4-point scale (0 = not used, 3 = used a great deal), to what extent they used each in a particular instance that required them to cope with pain or other related stressors.

Vanderbilt Pain Management Inventory (VPMI)

The VPMI (Brown & Nicassio, 1987) is a 27-item, self-report questionnaire that requests respondents to indicate, on a 5-point rating scale, the frequency with which they engage a variety of cognitive and behavioral coping strategies when attempting to manage pain of at least moderate intensity. Items include statements such as "restricting social activities," "praying for relief," and "depending on others for help with daily tasks." Two internally reliable scales, Active Coping and Passive Coping were derived using factor analytic techniques. Active coping techniques were found to be associated with reports of lower pain scores, less depression, less functional impairment, and higher self-efficacy than passive coping strategies.

The Coping Strategies Questionnaire (CSQ)

The CSQ (Rosenstiel & Keefe, 1983) is a 44-item questionnaire assessing the extent to which respondents report engaging in six different cognitive coping strategies and two behavioral coping strategies when they experience pain. The six cognitive strategies include diverting attention (e.g., I count numbers in my head or run a song through my mind), reinterpreting pain sensations (e.g., I just think of it as some other sensation, such as numbness), coping self-statements (e.g., I tell myself to be brave and carry on despite the pain), ignoring pain sensations (e.g., I tell myself it doesn't hurt), praying or hoping (e.g., I pray to God it won't last long), and catastrophizing (e.g., I worry all the time about whether it will end). The two behavioral strategies include increasing activity level (e.g., I do something active, like household chores or projects) and increasing pain behavior (e.g., I take my medication). Using a 7-point rating scale for each item, respondents indicate how often they use each strategy from "never" to "always." Respondents also rate their overall effectiveness in coping with pain. These ratings assess how much control respondents believe they have over pain and how much they are able to decrease the pain.

The Pain-Related Self-Statements Scale (PRSS)

The PRSS (Flor, Behle, & Birbaumer, 1993) consists of 35 pain-related cognitions typically engaged in by chronic pain patients when they experience severe pain. The respondents are asked to rate, on a 6-point scale, the frequency with which they engage in each item from "almost never" to "almost always." The scale focuses on pain-related cognitions that occur throughout a situation-specific pain experience. Factor analysis of the PRSS reveals that it consists of two 9-item subscales labeled catastrophizing and coping. Examples of items indicative of catastrophizing include "cannot stand pain," "cannot change pain," "will never stop," and "cannot go on." In contrast, items that reflect coping efforts include "better when I relax," "can do something," and "can help myself."

STRATEGIES PEOPLE USE IN COPING WITH PAIN

The literature contains a bewildering array of coping strategies people use in their attempts to cope with chronic pain (Table 12.1). Many of these strategies are poorly defined. Some researchers have used different names to refer to what appears to be the same strategy whereas others have used the same name to refer to two seemingly different strategies. Several systems of classifying these strategies have naturally developed both in response to the increasing number of coping strategies identified and in an attempt to develop coherent models specified by a relevant few dimensions that capture the essence of the process of coping with chronic pain.

One common method of classification distinguishes between problem-focused and emotion-focused coping (Lazarus & Folkman, 1984). With respect to chronic pain, individuals who use problem-focused coping strategies might direct their energies at reducing or eliminating the pain per se. In contrast, individuals who rely on emotion-focused coping would attempt to manage the stress and negative emotions that co-occur with chronic pain. The distinction between problem-focused

TABLE 12.1   Pain-Coping Strategies Classified According to Two Frequently Used Dimensions

	Cognitive	Behavioral
Attentional	Catastrophizing	Hypnosis
	Praying/hoping	Operant conditioning
	Imagery	Modeling
	Stress inoculation	Exercise
	Self-statements	Attention seeking
	Reappraisal	Emotional expression
	Self-blame	Information seeking
	Focus on pain	Social support seeking
	Rationalization	Increased pain behavior
Avoidant	Diverting attention	Resting/relaxation
	Ignoring pain sensations	Taking medication
	Distancing	Reading/watching television
	Denial	Leisure activities
	Wishful thinking	Restricting activities
	Threat minimization	Increasing activities
	Dissociation	Keeping busy
	Suppression	Isolation

and emotion-focused coping is by no means clear-cut because successful resolution using a problem-focused strategy usually also reduces associated emotional distress. Furthermore, when coping with a stressor such as pain, the distinction between problem-focused and emotion-focused coping is even less clear given the IASP (1979) definition of pain as an unpleasant sensory and emotional experience.

Another system of classification is to categorize coping strategies as cognitive or behavioral (Fernandez, 1986). Cognitive strategies include attempts to manage pain through techniques such as counting, distraction, and imagery. Behavioral strategies refer to actions carried out in an attempt to manage pain (e.g., taking pain medication, seeking social support, resting in bed). There is a controversy over whether pain-coping strategies are best defined as cognitive processes or behaviors. Whereas some call for a greater research focus on behavioral strategies for coping with pain (Jensen, Turner, Romano, & Karoly, 1991), others (Keefe et al., 1992) argue for a strictly cognitive definition, questioning the usefulness of defining coping strategies in behavioral terms, which, in their view blurs the distinction between a coping strategy and its outcome. For example, what one investigator considers a behavioral coping strategy (e.g., taking medication), another researcher may view as simply an outcome of the attempt to cope with the pain (Keefe et al., 1992).

Within these broad classification systems, coping strategies can be further classified to reflect a passive or active style. Active coping strategies would require a person suffering in pain to intentionally initiate some activity in an attempt to relieve the pain. Passive coping strategies generally involve withdrawal or giving up and relinquishing control to something or someone else. Brown and Nicassio (1987) consider active coping to involve efforts to deal with the pain and to carry on in spite of it (e.g., deliberate distraction, engaging in leisure or physical activities) whereas passive coping strategies involve an avoidance of the pain or a reliance on outside sources to help manage the pain (e.g., wishful thinking and praying, restricting activities, taking medication).

Finally, some researchers further classify coping strategies according to whether they are attentional or avoidant (e.g., Suls & Fletcher, 1985). An individual in pain who focuses attention directly on the source of the pain in an attempt to manage it would be using attentional techniques (e.g., stretching or exercising the area of pain). In contrast, a person who avoids thinking about or acting on the source of the pain would be using avoidant strategies to cope (e.g., denying pain sensations, distraction, attention-diversion).

ADAPTIVE AND MALADAPTIVE STRATEGIES FOR COPING WITH PAIN

The definition of a coping strategy as maladaptive or adaptive depends on the individual patient, the nature and chronicity of the pain problem, the specific situation, the anticipated degree of pain relief, and many other factors (Turner, 1991). What is effective in reducing pain for one person at a particular time may be ineffective at another time or for another person. It is also true, however, that the coping literature has demonstrated certain coping strategies or classes of strategies are consistently associated with increased pain, functional disability, and poorer psychosocial adaptation, whereas others are associated with less severe pain, improved functional ability, and better psychosocial adjustment. As noted later in this chapter, the correlational nature of these studies does not permit conclusions about the direction of causality between coping variables and measures of pain and psychosocial impairment. In addition, a review of the empirical literature indicates that it is not always possible to identify single strategies as adaptive or maladaptive because studies often use factor analytic techniques to facilitate interpretation by combining multiple coping strategies into a limited number of composite measures. In this section, we review the most consistent findings in the pain-coping literature showing that certain coping strategies or classes of strategies are associated with variable degrees of pain, physical disability, and psychosocial adjustment. Readers are referred to the review by Jensen et al. (1991) for a detailed examination of studies that have examined the relationship between use of specific coping strategies and adjustment to chronic pain.

Active Versus Passive Coping

Factor analytic studies of the CSQ, VPMI, and WCC frequently yield factors that are identified as passive and active coping. In addition, there is considerable evidence that the use of passive coping strategies (e.g., praying, hoping, wishful thinking) is associated with increased pain (Brown, Nicassio, & Wallston, 1989), depression (Brown et al., 1989; Parker et al., 1989), disability (Parker et al., 1989), and poorer psychological adjustment (Brown et al., 1989; Manne & Zautra, 1990; Parker et al., 1989). By contrast, active coping (e.g., problem solving, information seeking) has been found to be negatively correlated with depression (Brown & Nicassio, 1987; Spinhoven, Ter Kuile, Linssen, & Gazendam, 1989) and physical disability (Brown & Nicassio, 1987). The majority of studies are correlational, leaving open the question of the direction (if any) of causality: We do not know whether disability and pain lead to passive coping efforts or use of these strategies leads to pain and disability. Moreover, it has been suggested that passive coping is actually a feature of depressive cognition implying that the findings among chronic pain patients previously reviewed reflect the confounding effects of concurrent depression (Weickgenant et al., 1993). Further research is required to elucidate the relationships among chronic pain, depression, and active and passive coping.

Although it is tempting to operationally define active coping as adaptive and passive coping as maladaptive (Brown & Nicassio, 1987), there is sufficient disagreement about what constitutes passive and active coping that such definitions may prove simplistic and premature. The distinction between active and passive coping has recently been criticized on conceptual grounds (Keefe et al., 1992). For example, specific items (e.g., taking pain medication and calling a doctor or nurse) loading highly on what was identified as the "passive coping" factor of the VPMI (Brown & Nicassio, 1987) may actually involve active, goal-directed behaviors expressly carried out in an attempt to manage pain. Unless the intention or cognition that precedes a coping effort is assessed, it may be impossible to determine to what extent any behavior truly reflects active versus passive coping. These considerations suggest caution in interpreting the chronic pain literature on active and passive coping; these terms have been defined differently depending on the specific questionnaire used and whether that particular questionnaire includes cognitions and/or behaviors as coping strategies.

Maladaptive Strategies

Catastrophizing

There is considerable inconsistency in the literature about the status of catastrophizing as a pain-coping strategy. Much effort has been directed at understanding the relationship between chronic pain and catastrophizing, a cognitive process defined by negative self-statements and excessively negative beliefs about the future. It is characterized by the patient's unrealistic belief that the current situation will lead to the worst possible outcome (Keefe, Brown, Wallston, & Caldwell, 1989; Rosenstiel & Keefe, 1983).

Although some researches consider catastrophizing a strategy for coping with pain (Keefe et al., 1989), the worrisome cognitions, overconcern, and negative expectancies are not congruent with the definition of coping as an intentional effort to manage stress (Turner, 1991). Catastrophizing cognitions and emotions may be more reflective of patients' appraisals of their ability to cope than their attempts to cope (Jensen et al., 1991; Turner, 1991). Despite the inconsistent use of the term, catastrophizing deserves further study as it appears to be a ubiquitous and clinically relevant correlate of inadequate coping (Lawson, Reesor, Keefe, & Turner, 1990).

Perhaps the most commonly used instrument to assess catastrophizing among pain patients is the Catastrophizing subscale of the Coping Strategies Questionnaire (CSQ) (Rosenstiel & Keefe, 1983). This subscale includes the following 6 items that patients endorse on a 6-point rating scale from "never do when in pain" to "very frequently do when in pain":

1. It is terrible and I feel it is never going to get any better.
2. It is awful and I feel it overwhelms me.
3. I feel my life isn't worth living.
4. I worry all the time about whether it will end.
5. I feel I can't stand it anymore.
6. I feel like I can't go on.

More recently, Flor et al. (1993) described the use and validation of the Pain-Related Self-Statements Scale (PRSS), which contains a 9-item catastrophizing subscale.

The tendency to catastrophize has been associated with poorer outcomes including the presence of medically incongruent chronic back pain (Reesor & Craig, 1988), depression (Sullivan & D'Eon, 1990), psychosocial dysfunction (Jensen, Turner, & Romano, 1992), and pain intensity (Flor & Turk, 1988; Keefe et al., 1989). In addition, when factor analytic or principal component techniques are used to identify the factor structure of the CSQ relative to specific samples of chronic pain patients, studies often identify a factor that includes the negative thinking characteristic of catastrophizing (e.g., helplessness, pain control and rational thinking, self-control and rational thinking). In general, these factors tend to be strongly correlated with depression, measures of physical impairment, and poor psychosocial adjustment. Clearly, patients who catastrophize tend to be worse off than those who do not.

Keefe et al. (1989) used a longitudinal design to assess the predictive validity of catastrophizing (as measured by the CSQ) among a group of 223 patients with rheumatoid arthritis. Patients were assessed on two occasions separated by 6 months. The results of the baseline assessment showed that catastrophizing scores were significantly correlated with baseline assessments of pain intensity, physical disability, and depression. More importantly, catastrophizing scores at the first assessment predicted depression 6 months later after controlling for initial levels of depression, pain, and disability. These results suggest that a cognitive behavioral approach designed to reduce catastrophizing among patients with persistent pain due to rheumatoid arthritis might prove beneficial in reducing pain and depressive symptoms. Turner and Clancy (1986) demonstrated a reduction in the extent of "helplessness" (a factor loading highly on the catastrophizing subscale of the CSQ) among chronic low back pain patients who received eight weekly sessions of group cognitive behavioral or group behavioral therapy.

Jensen et al. (1991) conclude that one of the few consistent findings in the pain-coping literature is that patients who avoid catastrophizing about their predicament seem to fare better than patients who catastrophize. This conclusion is consistent with results from Turner and Clancy (Turner & Clancy, 1986), who found that following either cognitive-behavioral or operant behavioral therapy, a reduction in catastrophizing was associated with lower pain and improved psychosocial functioning. Furthermore, Flor et al. (1993) found that degree of catastrophizing was reduced significantly from pre- to posttreatment among patients who improved but not among patients who did not. In contrast, improvement was not accompanied by a strengthening of adaptive self-statements and beliefs. The association between lower pain and a reduction in the use of catastrophizing but not a strengthening of adaptive self-statements and beliefs suggests that maladaptive cognitions may have a stronger influence on negative outcomes than the utilization of adaptive coping strategies. In other words, it may be more important not to catastrophize than to engage in positive self-statements.

Catastrophizing is obviously not unique to chronic pain patients. It is a hallmark feature of depressive cognition (Beck, Rush, Shaw, & Emery, 1979). Accordingly, it has been suggested that catastrophizing (at least as measured by the CSQ) may be more related to vulnerability to depression or current depression than to pain severity (Sullivan & D'Eon, 1990). This issue, however, is far from resolved. For example, in the study by Keefe et al. (1989), even though depression and catastrophizing were significantly correlated, catastrophizing and not depression, was found to account for a significant proportion of the variance in pain severity. This suggests that depression does not mediate the relationship between pain and catastrophizing. A study that examines coping and catastrophizing in (a) depressed, CLBP patients, (b) depressed, pain-free patients, (c) nondepressed, CLBP patients, and (d) healthy controls would help to elucidate this issue.

Avoidance Behaviors and Fear-Avoidance Beliefs

The general class of coping strategies collectively referred to as avoidant includes both active and passive cognitive processes as well as behaviors designed to reduce ongoing pain and anticipated increases in pain. Avoidance behaviors include a reduction in the frequency of physical activities and exercise that might be generally expected to increase pain, but most importantly, extend to behaviors that do not necessarily predict or cause pain. Recent work shows that avoidance exhibited by chronic pain patients mostly involves a withdrawal from social activities

(Philips, 1987a; Philips & Jahanshahi, 1986). Although avoidance by withdrawal and inactivity (escape) may reduce ongoing pain, particularly in the early recovery phase, a long-term effect of these behaviors is reinforcement of the belief that avoidance prevents further pain. Such fear-avoidance beliefs are specific expectations about the consequences of certain actions (e.g., physical activity, work) on pain (Waddell, Newton, Henderson, Somerville, & Main, 1993).

Specific avoidance behaviors (e.g., guarding, limping, social withdrawal) are part of coping with ongoing pain or anticipated increases in pain. Some of these behaviors, however, also serve as maladaptive coping responses to concurrent life difficulties. Unpleasant work obligations, aversive household chores, marital strife, and interpersonal difficulties may thus be avoided by the person in pain. Those pain behaviors that serve the dual purpose of avoiding expected flare-ups in pain as well as other unpleasant life events are at high risk of becoming entrenched due to the multiple sources of negative reinforcement (Fordyce, 1989).

There is a paradoxical element to coping with pain through avoidance. Patients' fear-avoidance beliefs and expectancies about the consequences of their actions lead to extensive avoidance designed to reduce anticipated increases in pain. Nonetheless, although withdrawal from activity negatively reinforces the belief that increases in pain have been prevented, pain severity usually remains stable (Philips, 1987a). Avoidance confirms the belief that further pain has been prevented, but it does not reduce pain severity. Avoidance behaviors tend to increase in frequency as a function of pain duration (chronicity) so that pain behaviors and pain intensity become increasingly decoupled (Philips, 1987a). This desynchrony sets the stage for reduced self-efficacy beliefs and further avoidance (Philips, 1987b). Thus, in attempts to gain control over the pain through avoidant coping, patients actually report an increasing loss of control over the pain. Self-management programs focused on behavioral exposure and nonavoidance lead to improved self-efficacy and a reduction in preoccupation with pain because patients acquire increasingly realistic appraisals of the relationship between pain and behavior (Philips, 1987b).

Although use of avoidant cognitive coping strategies for pain may be beneficial under certain circumstances, such as when pain is acute (Holmes & Stevenson, 1990), long-term use of such strategies among chronic pain patients is associated with impaired psychosocial functioning, intense pain, increased disability, and loss of employment (Holmes & Stevenson, 1990; Philips, 1987a; Philips & Jahanshahi, 1986; Waddell et al., 1993). Chronic pain patients who employ attentional coping strategies are more socially active, less depressed, and less anxious than those who cope through avoidance (Holmes & Stevenson, 1990). In contrast, among patients with pain of recent onset, psychological and behavioral measures of adjustment are higher for those engaged in avoidant coping versus attentional coping (Holmes & Stevenson, 1990). Although studies such as these do not permit conclusions about the role of avoidance in determining psychosocial adjustment to pain, they are consistent with the hypothesis that avoidant coping strategies are adaptive in the early period following an injury because they minimize ongoing pain, reduce the risk of exacerbation through further injury, and thus promote healing. Once healing has occurred, however, these strategies become maladaptive because they promote continued isolation, inactivity, and faulty reality testing. Implications for preventing a maladaptive transition from acute pain to chronic pain are discussed in the section on preventive programs.

Adaptive Strategies

Distraction/Attention-Diversion

Perhaps the simplest and most effective method of coping with chronic pain is by means of cognitive and/or behavioral strategies that divert the patient's attention away from pain to some other activity, object, or event. The scope of distracting and attention-diverting strategies is extensive, covering direct intentional efforts to reduce pain awareness through techniques such as relaxation, transformational imagery (Hanson & Gerber, 1990), and control of appraisal processes (Turk, Meichenbaum, & Genest, 1983) as well as indirect approaches that accomplish similar goals without distraction or diversion of attention as a primary objective (e.g., reading, painting, socializing). Although direct and indirect approaches appear equally effective in reducing awareness of pain, they may result in important differences in patients' awareness of the reduction in pain and in patients' attributions and self-efficacy beliefs regarding pain control. The effectiveness of distraction also appears to approach a limit as pain intensity increases (McCaul & Malott, 1984).

Distraction and attention-diverting strategies are effective for many reasons (McCaul & Malott, 1984), and it appears that multiple mechanisms are involved. For example, relaxation and related activities that require sustained, focused attention may actually reduce pain intensity, as well as pain awareness, by decreasing sympathetic nervous system activity (Katz, 1993). Engaging in distracting, social interactions with others may alter the frequency and use of maladaptive strategies such as catastrophizing and avoidance, in part because of response-incompatibility and in part due to improved mood. At the same time, socializing may also lead to a reduced emphasis on the importance of pain. The vast array of cognitive and behavioral activities that fall within the class of distracting and attention-diverting coping strategies, and the diverse mechanisms of action, raise the issue of whether this classification is truly useful. The problem seems linked in part to the paradox inherent in the definition of distraction as a process of not attending to pain.

SOCIAL SUPPORT, COPING, AND PAIN

A growing body of literature documents the importance of social support in mediating the relationship between life stress and health outcomes. The beneficial effects of social relationships have been proposed to act as a buffer, and more directly, as a main effect against life stress and chronic illness (Sarason, Sarason, & Pierce, 1990). The evaluation of potentially advantageous and detrimental effects of social relationships in the lives of chronic pain patients is in its infancy. Only recently have researchers begun to widen their field of inquiry from the individual in pain to the chronic pain patient and his or her immediate social environment.

A major impetus for investigating the social context affecting the chronic pain patient comes from evidence that chronic pain behaviors may in part be maintained by an operant conditioning model (Fordyce, 1976). From this perspective, specific pain behaviors (sighing, grimacing, groaning, limping, taking pain medication) may be positively reinforced (e.g., by attending to the patient) or negatively reinforced (e.g., patient avoids or escapes unpleasant duties) by the spouse and/or other family members leading to an increase in the frequency of occurrence of pain behaviors. Recent studies have shown that spouses of chronic pain patients may become discriminative cues not only for their partner's pain behaviors (Flor, Kerns, & Turk, 1987; Lousberg, Schmidt, & Groenman, 1992; Romano et al., 1992), but also for ratings of pain severity (Block, Kremer, & Gaylor, 1980; Flor, Kerns, & Turk, 1987; Lousberg et al., 1992).

These results have potentially important implications when considered in conjunction with studies showing a positive relationship between satisfaction with social support and increased pain behaviors. For example, patients who score relatively high on self-report measures of satisfaction with social support tend to exhibit more pain behaviors (e.g., guarding and rubbing) than patients who report less satisfaction (Gil, Keefe, Crisson, & Van Dalfsen, 1987). However, the complex interactions that occur between patients and solicitous-supportive spouses need to be studied in more detail to better understand the positive outcomes that are also associated with the support of chronic pain patients. Solicitous spouses of chronic pain patients report higher levels of marital satisfaction (Flor, Kerns, & Turk, 1987). Furthermore, levels of solicitousness appear to interact with pain severity and marital satisfaction: pain is equally low among high and low maritally satisfied patients who view their spouses as low in solicitousness but is high among relatively highly maritally satisfied patients when perceived solicitousness is high (Kerns, Haythornthwaite, Southwick, & Giller, 1990).

Other findings that underscore the complexity of the interactions among social support, satisfaction, and pain indicate that more solicitous spouses report better mood and a greater sense of control despite the significant interference their partner's pain has on their life (Flor, Kerns, & Turk, 1987). Notwithstanding these data, it appears that living with a person in chronic pain takes a toll on spouse and children (Turk, Flor, & Rudy, 1987). Eighty-three percent of spouses reported emotional, physical, and social health disturbances that they attributed to their partner's pain. These included heightened nervousness, irritability, sleep and appetite disturbances, headaches, gastrointestinal distress, and being housebound (Rowat & Knafl, 1985). The prevailing emotional response was often a sense of helplessness at effecting any change in their partner's pain. Coping strategies proven useful in overcoming other life crises were not helpful in dealing with their partner's pain. A major source of the spouse's distress stemmed from global uncertainty: family life became ill-defined and indeterminate, the nature of the chronic pain itself was seen as questionable and a sense of impotence was commonly experienced by spouses. Significant disturbances in family functioning have also been reported in families where one parent suffers with chronic pain when compared with no-illness control families. For example, families in which the mother has a chronic pain problem show more relationship dysfunction including reduced cohesion and more conflict. Generally, mothers, fathers, and children were significantly more depressed in chronic pain families than in no-illness families (Dura & Beck, 1988).

In widening the perspective to include reciprocal interactions between the patient and his or her immediate social support system, we confront an increasing complexity in the issues associated with chronic pain. The importance of identifying and addressing the multiple factors that influence the chronic pain patient's ability to cope cannot be overemphasized (Kerns & Jacob, 1992). Despite the obvious need for more study in these areas, little empirical work has evaluated the relationship between chronic pain and family functioning in terms of how coping efforts on behalf of the chronic pain sufferer are facilitated or hindered by the family system and how the family as a unit copes when one member of the parental dyad is afflicted with pain. Since overall adaptation is influenced by multiple, interdependent factors, the patient's success in coping must be assessed using multifactorial methods that evaluate the pattern of coping across variables. Unless such a multivariable approach is adopted, results may be misleading. For example, the growing body of research on the effects of spouse solicitousness has generally been interpreted as support for the operant model of pain. The findings that pain patients whose spouses are solicitous (e.g., provide sympathy and attention to pain behaviors and complaints) exhibit more pain behaviors and increased pain intensity have been taken to indicate that solicitous behaviors are, for the most part, detrimental to the patient. However, if the evaluation is extended to additional factors, a discontinuity between pain behaviors and overall psychological status may be uncovered, such that at least some patients may evidence both more pain behavior and better overall status, with the spouse faring globally better as well. Moreover, spouse solicitousness and familial social support requires thorough study both from functional and motivational perspectives (see, e.g., the work of Coyne, Ellard, & Smith, 1990; Coyne, Wortman, & Lehman, 1988) to assess whether differences in modes of support predict coping outcomes.

These available data and related issues have important implications for the development of effective chronic pain management programs, specifically in terms of how the family can be positively mobilized in support of effective patient coping (Flor, Turk, & Rudy, 1987). Incorporating the spouse and other solicitous family members into the treatment regimen may prove helpful in reducing the frequency of pain behaviors and increasing adaptive coping responses, particularly if family members are taught to provide selectively contingent support (Radojevic, Nicassio, & Weisman, 1992) (e.g., reinforcing behaviors incompatible with the expression of pain and withholding reinforcement for pain behaviors). Although we do not know the direction of causality between variables in studies dealing with support and spouse solicitousness, we need to be aware that modifying pain behaviors by altering reinforcement contingencies within the couple or family may have untoward repercussions on marital and family satisfaction. The advantages and disadvantages of such interventions must be considered and either integrated into approaches that combine contingency management and the enhancement of supportive environments or integrated into a "best trade-off" of advantages and disadvantages. Including family members in treatment may also increase the likelihood that positive treatment effects are maintained and generalized outside and beyond the treatment context (but see Radojevic et al., 1992). However, few studies have assessed the effectiveness of spousal and/or family involvement in the treatment of chronic pain (Bradley et al., 1987; Moore & Chaney, 1985; Radojevic et al., 1992). Studies of patients with rheumatoid arthritis (Bradley et al., 1987; Radojevic et al., 1992) have thus far shown little additional benefit of including the spouse or other family members over standard group treatment. The absence of positive findings in this patient group may be related to the negative association between pain intensity ratings and levels of solicitous responding from family members (Anderson & Rehm, 1984). This could mean that patients with rheumatoid arthritis do not readily communicate about the intensity of their pain, are more independent than other patients with chronic pain, and consequently are less likely to display helpless behaviors typically reinforced by a caring spouse. Further studies of the role of family support in the lives of patients with chronic pain will further define the multidimensional nature of what it means to cope with a chronic pain condition.

SITUATIONAL ASPECTS OF COPING AMONG CHRONIC PAIN PATIENTS

Lazarus and Folkman (1984) define coping as a dynamic process that varies, in part, as function of the nature of the stressful situation. According to their definition, chronic pain patients should engage in context-dependent coping efforts. A better understanding of the context-dependent nature of coping among chronic pain patients is important because treatment implications differ for patients who, for example, fail to engage in adaptive coping efforts regardless of the situation and those who fail to use adaptive coping strategies in response to pain, but do so when coping with other stressful life events.

Weickgenant et al. (1993) evaluated the relationship between pain, coping, depressed mood and type of stressor in depressed, chronic low back pain (CLBP) patients, nondepressed CLBP patients and healthy control subjects who were neither depressed nor in pain. Subjects completed the revised WCC (Vitaliano et al., 1985) in relation to the foremost stressor currently in their lives, and again in reaction to a standardized scenario involving an episode of low back pain. The results showed that whereas both the control subjects and the nondepressed CLBP patients responded to the standardized pain scenario with more evidence of avoidant and wishful thinking than they did to their current primary life stressor, the depressed CLBP patients employed avoidant and wishful thinking with equal frequency across stressors. The similarity in response patterns between the two nondepressed groups leads to the speculation that emotional distress in the form of depression, rather than the presence of chronic pain, determines the pervasive use of passive-avoidant coping.

The study of Weickgenant et al. (1993) also found that the three groups differed in social-support-seeking activities with regard to the two stressors. Nondepressed CLBP patients showed no difference in the frequency of their social-support-seeking behavior in response to the two stressors. However, healthy controls and depressed CLBP patients showed the opposite pattern: controls endorsed support seeking more frequently for the standardized pain scenario and less frequently for the primary stressor, whereas the depressed CLBP patients endorsed support seeking less frequently for the standardized pain scenario and more frequently for the primary stressor. These results are consistent with Lazarus and Folkman's (Lazarus & Folkman, 1984) view that coping efforts are stressor-specific and context-dependent.

PREVENTIVE PROGRAMS AND INTERVENTIONS TO ENHANCE COPING WITH PAIN

Primary Prevention

Until recently, the issues of primary prevention and early detection of individuals at risk for developing chronic pain have not received the attention they deserve. Keefe et al. (1992) advocated use of longitudinal designs in which subjects are identified and assessed in terms of coping strategies prior to the development of chronic pain. Following these individuals over time would clarify the relationship between pain-coping strategies and the development of persistent pain. This task might be accomplished best by targeting patient populations at relatively high risk for developing long-term pain problems. For example, it has been estimated that 80% of amputees continue to report phantom limb pain up to 7 years after amputation (Sherman & Arena, 1992). Lateral thoracotomy incision for chest surgery is associated with persistent chest wall pain in 60% of patients 2 years after surgery (Katz, Jackson, Kavanagh, & Sandler, 1994). These long-term pain problems are iatrogenic (i.e., treatment-induced); although they are triggered by surgery, we know little about the maintaining factors and the role of coping efforts in their development.

Secondary Prevention

As noted earlier, patients with pain of recent onset (<4 weeks) and those with chronic pain (>6 months) can be differentiated on the basis of the relative frequency with which they engage in attentional versus avoidant coping strategies (Holmes & Stevenson, 1990). Within the group of chronic pain patients, anxiety and depression scores were significantly higher and levels of social activity were lower for avoidant versus attentional copers. This pattern of results was reversed for patients with pain of recent onset. Avoidant copers showed better psychosocial adjustment than attentional copers. This time-strategy interaction may be one important factor that influences the transition from acute to chronic pain and determines the extent to which adaptation is successful. What works in the short term may not be best for long-term adaptation and functioning. Prevention efforts directed at altering coping strategies from avoidant to attentional as time in pain lengthens may help to divert some patients away from developing the lifestyle of a chronic pain patient. Early intervention to prevent chronicity has been recommended on the basis of the strong relationship between fear-avoidance beliefs and disability on the one hand and the absence of a relationship between these beliefs and biomedical characteristics of the pain, including its severity (Waddell et al., 1993). The importance of implementing these preventive measures is underscored by the finding that fear-avoidance beliefs are fostered by diagnostic uncertainty, a quality that characterizes many patients with chronic pain.

Relapse Prevention

Recent efforts have been directed at developing programs and interventions designed to prevent relapse after treatment and to prevent escalation of pain during flare-ups or particularly intense episodes. The cognitive behavioral approach to pain management is designed to help patients learn to cope with much more than simply the pain problem. In fact, it is not uncommon for some patients to reach the end of treatment with pain intensity levels not much lower than at the start of the program yet to report improvements in mood and in personal, social, and family functioning. Outcomes such as these highlight the multidetermined nature of chronic pain problems. One of the challenges facing patients and helpers is to develop means of preventing relapses in pain from acquiring the deteriorating qualities and course that characterized the pain prior to treatment. In general, self-management programs operating from a cognitive behavioral perspective address the problem of relapse prevention from the start of treatment through regular homework assignments and by incorporating family members into the treatment program whenever possible. These interventions are designed to increase the likelihood of generalization when the treatment is completed.

A common theme stressed throughout many self-management programs for chronic pain patients is the nonlinearity inherent in recovery and rehabilitation. As part of the process of reconceptualizing the pain problem, patients are encouraged to continually assess their progress in learning new ways to cope. By building into the treatment program, specific strategies designed to deal with the very high likelihood of relapse and flare-ups, it is possible to teach patients to prevent or attenuate the recurrence of their earlier reactions to inevitable flare-ups in pain. Getting patients to view their recovery from a stages-of-change perspective, in which they view recovery as a process involving a spiral model of change (Prochaska, DiClemente, & Norcross, 1992), may help them to alter their view of the problem and to cope better with the possibility of relapse. Patients may be reminded of previous episodes in which they successfully managed episodes of intense pain and stress. Equally important are those times when they may not have been successful. By discussing the very real possibility of relapse and stressing the nonlinear course of recovery, patients are less likely to catastrophize when and if flare-ups in pain occur, and they may draw on their past experiences within and without treatment to remind them of similar episodes. Patients are encouraged to anticipate flare-ups and to develop a personal plan for coping including coping self-statements, coping activities, reactivating stress management skills and engaging in relaxation exercises (Turner & Romano, 1989).

Pain problems of a chronic but periodic nature with a clear onset and offset (e.g., migraine headaches, dysmennohrea, bouts of phantom limb pain with obvious triggers) are particularly amenable to preventive measures. Through a self-management approach (e.g., Hanson & Gerber, 1990), patients with classic migraine headaches, for example, are taught to become attuned to the sensory cues (e.g., visual disturbance or aura) that precede the onset of pain and to intervene on their own by engaging in active coping efforts such as relaxation, deep breathing, physical exercise, identifying and altering pain modifiers, and removing themselves whenever possible from the source of stress.

Primary Prevention of Adjustment Disorders among Children Whose Parents Have Chronic Pain

It is becoming increasingly clear that families, spouses, and children of chronic pain patients are at risk for developing a variety of stress-related disorders and behavior problems. The reduced quality of life that comes to define the lives of many chronic pain patients clearly has an impact on the patient's spouse and other close relatives as well. However, only recently have researchers begun to document the nature of the problems among children of chronic pain patients. The results of these studies suggest that offspring from families in which one parent suffers from chronic pain may be at greater risk for developing childhood adjustment disorders than children from healthy families or families in which one parent has a chronic disease. For example, children from families in which the father had CLBP were found to have significantly more behavior problems at school, to have missed more days of school, and to have visited the school nurse significantly more often than either control children or children whose parent was diabetic (Rickard, 1988). In addition, they had a significantly higher frequency of complaints, including crying and whining, and avoidance and dependency behaviors and they scored significantly higher on the external subscale of the Child Health Locus of Control questionnaire suggesting that they felt less in control of their environment.

Other studies have shown that children of mothers with chronic low back or neck pain reported increased levels of depressive symptomology (Dura & Beck, 1988) and offspring of mothers with temporomandibular pain and dysfunction syndrome[4] were reported (by their mothers) to have excessive illness rates relative

---

[4] This pain syndrome involves the musculoskeletal system of the jaw and is usually described by an aching in the muscles involved in chewing (Task Force on Taxonomy, 1994).

to controls (Raphael, Dohrenwend, & Marbach, 1990). Other negative effects observed among children of chronic pain patients include a greater frequency of behavior problems and lower levels of social competence (Chun, Turner, & Romano, 1993).

At the present time, the etiology and developmental course of these adjustment problems are unknown. It is unclear the extent to which the behavior problems observed among offspring of chronic pain patients stem from parental modeling, socialization, reinforcement contingencies, global family stress (Rickard, 1988), or genetic influences and whether they represent precursors of a chronic pain disorder. Nevertheless, these findings indicate that children of chronic pain patients are at risk for developing adjustment problems. Early detection of children who are at risk and early implementation of interventions that teach children how to cope with the inevitable disruptions in family functioning that arise over the course of a parent's chronic pain problem may attenuate or prevent the development of childhood adjustment disorders when one parent suffers from chronic pain.

A RISK-ADAPTATION MODEL FOR COPING WITH CHRONIC PAIN

From the preceding discussion, it is obvious that a variety of therapeutic approaches exist for enhancing pain-coping processes, each implicitly guided by assumptions about coping and the nature of pain reactivity. We have been investigating whether communicating guiding assumptions about coping and pain reactivity helps our patients derive clearer perspectives about autonomous change processes. This has resulted in a risk-adaptation model (RAM) that elucidates pain-coping processes (Ritvo, 1994). According to the RAM (Figure 12.1), patients face issues of both risk and adaptation when coping with pain. These issues involve reciprocally relevant efforts to reduce risk (which requires adaptation) and to adapt (which requires risk confrontation). In developing the RAM, we distilled four essential factors from past theoretical frameworks (Janz & Becker, 1984; Maddux & Rogers, 1983; Prentice-Dunn & Rogers, 1986; Self & Rogers, 1990; Weinstein, 1988). Modifiability is the perceived likelihood that an action will reduce risk and improve adaptation significantly. Individuals act on options offering the greatest likelihood of positively modifying risk-adaptation status by the greatest degree. Consequentiality consists of the perceived likelihood of positive (and negative) consequences occurring if a risk is (not) reduced and adaptation is (not) improved, the likely severity of such consequences as well as the negative and positive consequences associated with making modification attempts. Attention regulation refers to the degree to which people focus attention functionally while engaged in decision making about risk-adaptation problems. This factor reflects our belief that people must focus sufficient attention on relevant factors (those affecting modifiability and consequentiality) to make rational choices likely to optimize outcomes. Evidence for the effect of optimism and pessimism on health behaviors and outcomes prompted us to include

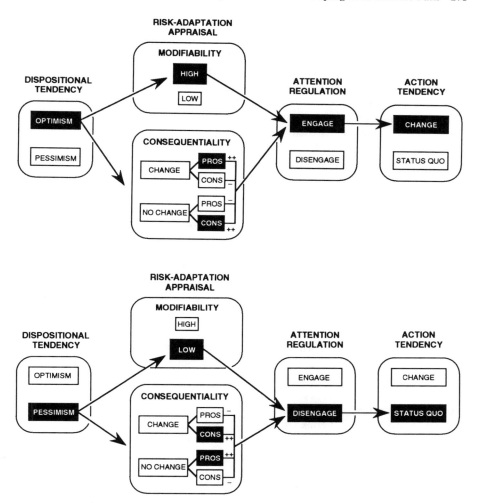

Figure 12.1   Schematic diagram of the risk-adaptation model (RAM). The top figure shows a prototypical constellation of factors depicting an optimistic individual with risk-adaptation appraisal processes conducive to positive change. These include a high degree of perceived modifiability, a positive expectancy of favorable outcomes associated with the anticipated consequences of change (consequentiality), and functional attention regulation processes engaged in decision making about the current risk-adaptation problem. The bottom figure shows a prototypical constellation of factors depicting a pessimistic individual with risk-adaptation appraisal processes conducive to maintaining the status quo (e.g., low perceived modifiability, negative perceived consequences of change, positive perceived consequences associated with current level of adaptation, and dysfunctional attention regulation processes).

optimistic-pessimistic expectancies as a crucial factor. Optimism predisposes people to develop positive expectancies about the modifiability of risk-adaptation status, thereby increasing motivation and decreasing avoidance of helpful health information (including psychological interventions). Optimism concerning (favorable) outcome also reinforces efforts to adhere to a given behavior change because the consequences of such change are more likely perceived as positive.

In assessing and treating people with chronic pain, we have found it helpful to have them clarify their own decisional processes through application of the RAM. For example, consider an individual who has sustained a work injury resulting in lower back pain. The medical diagnosis is ambiguous, offering no definitive information. Some of the key questions in need of clarification are whether and when to return to work, whether returning to work will aggravate the pain, what further professional health services may ameliorate the condition or provide more information about the source of the pain. Returning to work without additional assessment or intervention means confronting the risk of further injury and pain, whereas terminating employment involves a decrease in adaptation (reduced family income, increased stress). Judgments of modifiability, (e.g., beliefs that continuing to work may or may not reduce pain; further treatment may or may not help) are thus balanced with judgments of consequentiality (e.g., beliefs that continuing to work may or may not cause more injury and disabling pain; further treatment may or may not waste time and resources). These judgments are, in turn, influenced by how optimistic or pessimistic the individual is generally, and specifically with regard to overcoming the injury and/or finding another form of employment. The judgments, themselves, are likely to be accurate or inaccurate, helpful or unhelpful, in accord with the individual's attention-regulation processes. If he or she devotes little functional attention to modifiability-consequentiality issues, the judgments are more likely inaccurate and unhelpful. An individual may devote considerable nonfunctional attention (e.g., worrying, fretting, catastrophizing) and minimal amounts of functional attention (e.g., consulting physicians, working with a physiotherapist, systematically varying work regimens and observing the effects). The optimal pathway for intervention and/or autonomous change involves redirection or support of the individual in engaging in functional attention-regulation, clarification and rational consideration of modifiability-consequentiality issues, and realistic optimism regarding outcome (based on confidence in the plans derived for investigation and action). Intrinsic to the RAM is its applicability to therapeutic intervention, autonomous change processes, social support, and their combination.

CONCLUSION

Research progresses according to the inspirations of investigators and the availability of research funding. It is unrealistic to expect an even development of the various areas of research relevant to coping with chronic pain. In some areas, investigation has been intense; in others there is great need for further study. In this chapter, we have provided a critique of areas of research that have led to important advances in our understanding of how people cope with chronic pain. In this concluding section, we present a critical overview and offer a perspective on coping that we have found helpful with our patients.

As pointed out earlier, the precise classification of a coping strategy as adaptive or maladaptive depends on the context in which the coping process takes place. The contexts of coping previously deemed helpful in classifying strategies relate to the individual characteristics of the patient, the nature and chronicity of the pain problem, the specific situation in which coping occurs, and the anticipated degree of pain relief (Turner, 1991). We maintain that a precise classification of coping strategies can only occur within specified contexts in relation to two primary goals that motivate most pain coping efforts: (a) pain prevention and reduction and (b) maximization of lifestyle and quality of life despite pain. Using this aggregation helps to clarify that the most adaptive strategies are those that enable patients to progress toward both goals, whereas the most maladaptive strategies are those that impede progress toward both goals. This approach further illuminates the complex trade-offs involved in the employment of strategies adaptive for one goal but maladaptive for the other. Research in chronic pain has, for the most part, avoided the complexity of such trade-offs, although clinicians are well aware of their pragmatic significance. Researchers have attempted instead to define specific coping strategies (active/passive, problem-focused/emotion-focused, cognitive/behavioral, and avoidant/attentional) as adaptive or maladaptive across contexts. Such anticontextual definitions are of limited utility. Employing the two primary goals to aggregate contexts represents a progressive step toward a context-dependent definition of coping with chronic pain.

The shortcoming of assessing strategies out of context extends to classifying specific interaction patterns between patient and family. Although it is understandable that researchers would gravitate to the simplicity and apparent success of the operant conditioning model in pain management, its emphasis on training family members to supply contingent support denies the wider context of family functioning. Current social support theory acknowledges the importance of defining the context of any support attempt to assess its effectiveness. It also acknowledges the interdependent nature of support interactions such that any interaction can be positively supportive for both participants, undermining for both, or supportive for one and undermining for the other (Coyne et al., 1988; Coyne et al., 1990). It is obvious that a precise assessment of support interactions in chronic pain must include an evaluation of specific trade-offs frequently implicit in one form of support versus another for each participant. An interesting example can be found in the study by Flor, Kerns, and Turk (1987) in which the solicitous spouses of chronic pain patients reported higher levels of marital satisfaction, better mood, and more control of their lives (all positive features of solicitousness) while also registering more interference of the patient's pain in their lives.

The goal is to formulate trade-offs such as these so that they can be better understood within the clinical context and by patients themselves. Recently, we have employed a risk-adaptation model to guide interventions with patients suffering chronic pain and other distressing conditions (Ritvo, 1994). Applying this model involves addressing the risks represented by the pain as well as the inevitable adaptation problems that accompany chronic pain. Specifically, pain experience is viewed as a risk signal (e.g., that the pain may worsen if action is not taken or if an undetected disease process is not treated). Pain is also viewed as an adaptation problem concerned with reducing pain and maximizing lifestyle despite pain. Any specific encounter with pain thus involves judgments regarding which dimension (risk or adaptation) is most salient, how modifiable each dimension is perceived to be and the perceived consequences of attempting or not attempting modification.

Models such as this one require a more complex investigative perspective on coping than views that currently dominate the field. It is our belief that progress depends on addressing the multiple contexts relevant to pain coping and the balance between the risk of further pain and the adaptation problems people encounter in their attempts to deal with pain.

REFERENCES

Anderson, L. P., & Rehm, L. P. (1984). The relationship between strategies of coping and perception of pain in three chronic pain groups. *Journal of Clinical Psychology, 40,* 1170–1177.

Beck, A. T., Rush, A. J., Shaw, B. F., & Emery, G. (1979). *Cognitive therapy of depression.* New York: Guilford.

Block, A. R., Kremer, E. F., & Gaylor, M. (1980). Behavioral treatment of chronic pain: The spouse as a discriminative cue for pain behavior. *Pain, 9,* 243–252.

Bradley, L. A., Young, L. D., Anderson, K. O., Turner, A. R., Agudelo, C. A., McDaniel, L. K., Pisko, E. J., Semble, E. L., & Morgan, T. M. (1987). Effects of psychological therapy on pain behavior of rheumatoid arthritis patients. Treatment outcome and six-month follow-up. *Arthritis and Rheumatism, 30,* 1105–1114.

Brown, G. K., & Nicassio, P. M. (1987). Development of a questionnaire for the assessment of active and passive coping strategies in chronic pain patients. *Pain, 31,* 53–64.

Brown, G. K., Nicassio, P. M., & Wallston, K. A. (1989). Pain-coping strategies and depression in rheumatoid arthritis. *Journal of Consulting and Clinical Psychology, 57,* 652–657.

Chun, D. Y., Turner, J. A., & Romano, J. M. (1993). Children of chronic pain patients: Risk factors for maladjustment. *Pain, 52,* 311–317.

Coyne, J. C., Ellard, J. H., & Smith, D. A. F. (1990). Social support, interdependence, and the dilemmas of helping. In B. R. Sarason, I. G. Sarason, & G. R. Pierce (Eds.), *Social support: An interactional view* (pp. 129–150). New York: Wiley.

Coyne, J. C., Wortman, C. B., & Lehman, D. R. (1988). The other side of support. Emotional overinvolvement and miscarried helping. In B. H. Gottlieb (Eds). *Marshaling social support* (pp. 305–330). Beverly Hills, CA: Sage.

Dura, J. R., & Beck, S. J. (1988). A comparison of family functioning when mothers have chronic pain. *Pain, 35,* 79–89.

Fernandez, E. (1986). A classification system of cognitive coping strategies for pain. *Pain, 26,* 141–151.

Flor, H., Behle, D. J., & Birbaumer, N. (1993). Assessment of pain-related cognitions in chronic pain patients. *Behaviour Research and Therapy, 31,* 63–73.

Flor, H., Kerns, R. D., & Turk, D. C. (1987). The role of spouse reinforcement, perceived pain, and activity levels of chronic pain patients. *Journal of Psychosomatic Research, 31,* 251–259.

Flor, H., & Turk, D. C. (1988). Chronic back pain and rheumatoid arthritis: Predicting pain and disability from cognitive variables. *Journal of Behavioral Medicine, 11,* 251–265.

Flor, H., Turk, D. C., & Rudy, T. E. (1987). Pain and families: II. Assessment and treatment. *Pain, 30,* 29–45.

Folkman, S., & Lazarus, R. S. (1980). An analysis of coping in a middle-aged community sample. *Journal of Health and Social Behavior, 21,* 219–239.

Fordyce, W. E. (1976). *Behavioral methods for chronic pain.* St. Louis, MO: Mosby.

Fordyce, W. E. (1989). The cognitive/behavioral perspective on clinical pain. In J. D. Loeser & K. J. Egan (Eds.), *Managing the chronic pain patient* (pp. 51–64). New York: Raven Press.

Gamsa, A. (1994). The role of psychological factors in pain: II. A critical appraisal. *Pain, 57,* 17–29.

Gil, K. M., Keefe, F. J., Crisson, J. E., & Van Dalfsen, P. J. (1987). Social support and pain behavior. *Pain, 29,* 209–217.

Hanson, R. W., & Gerber, K. E. (1990). *Coping with chronic pain. A guide to patient self-management.* New York: Guilford.

Hitchcock, L. S., Ferrell, B. R., & McCaffery, M. (1994). The experience of chronic nonmalignant pain. *Journal of Pain and Symptom Management, 9,* 312–318.

Holmes, J. A., & Stevenson, C. A. Z. (1990). Differential effects of avoident and attentional coping strategies on adaptation to chronic and recent-onset pain. *Health Psychology, 9,* 577–584.

International Association for the Study of Pain. (1979). The need of a taxonomy. *Pain, 6,* 247–252.

Janz, N. K., & Becker, M. H. (1984). The Health Belief Model: A decade later. *Health Education Quarterly, 11,* 1–47.

Jensen, M. P., Turner, J. A., & Romano, J. M. (1992). Chronic pain coping measures: Individual vs. composite scores. *Pain, 51,* 273–280.

Jensen, M. P., Turner, J. A., Romano, J. M., & Karoly, P. (1991). Coping with chronic pain: A critical review of the literature. *Pain, 47,* 249–283.

Katz, J. (1993). The reality of phantom limbs. *Motivation and Emotion, 17,* 147–179.

Katz, J., Jackson, M., Kavanagh, B. P., & Sandler, A. N. (1994). *Pre-emptive analgesia: Two-years after thoracic surgery.* Unpublished manuscript.

Keefe, F. J., Brown, G. K., Wallston, K. A., & Caldwell, D. S. (1989). Coping with rheumatoid arthritis pain: Catastrophizing as a maladaptive strategy. *Pain, 37,* 51–56.

Keefe, F. J., Caldwell, D. S., Martinez, J., Nunley, J., Beckham, J., & Williams, D. A. (1991). Analyzing pain in rheumatoid arthritis patients. Pain coping strategies in patients who have had knee replacement surgery. *Pain, 46,* 153–160.

Keefe, F. J., & Dolan, E. (1986). Pain behavior and coping strategies in low back pain and myofascial pain dysfunction syndrome patients. *Pain, 24,* 49–56.

Keefe, F. J., Salley, A. N. J., & Lefebvre, J. C. (1992). Coping with pain: Conceptual concerns and future directions. *Pain, 51,* 131–134.

Kerns, R. D., Haythornthwaite, J., Southwick, S., & Giller, E. L., Jr. (1990). The role of marital interaction in chronic pain and depressive symptom severity. *Journal of Psychosomatic Research, 34,* 401–408.

Kerns, R. D., & Jacob, M. C., (1992). Assessment of the psychosocial context of the experience of chronic pain. In D. C. Turk & R. Melzack (Eds.), *Handbook of Pain Assessment* (pp. 235–253). New York: Guilford.

Lawson, K., Reesor, K. A., Keefe, F. J., & Turner, J. A. (1990). Dimensions of pain-related cognitive coping: Cross validation of the factor structure of the Coping Strategy Questionnaire. *Pain, 43,* 195–204.

Lazarus, R. S., & Folkman, S. (1984). *Stress, appraisal, and coping.* New York: Springer.

Lousberg, R., Schmidt, A. J. M., & Groenman, N. H. (1992). The relationship between spouse solicitness and pain behavior: Searching for more experimental evidence. *Pain, 51,* 75–79.

Maddux, J. E., & Rogers, R. W. (1983). Protection motivation and self-efficacy: A revised theory of fear appeals and attitude change. *Journal of Experimental Social Psychology, 19,* 469–479.

Manne, S. L., & Zautra, A. J. (1990). Couples coping with chronic illness: Women with rheumatoid arthritis and their healthy husbands. *Journal of Behavioral Medicine, 13,* 327–342.

McCaul, K. D., & Malott, J. M. (1984). Distraction and coping with pain. *Psychological Bulletin, 95,* 516–533.

Melzack, R., & Wall, P. D. (1965). Pain mechanisms: A new theory. *Science, 150,* 971–979.

Melzack, R., & Wall, P. D. (1988). *The challenge of pain* (2nd ed.). New York: Basic Books.

Moore, J. E., & Chaney, E. F. (1985). Outpatient group treatment of chronic pain: Effects of spousal involvement. *Journal of Consulting and Clinical Psychology, 53,* 326–334.

Parker, J., Smarr, K., Buescher, K., Phillips, L., Frank, R., Beck, N., Anderson, S., & Walker, S. (1989). Pain control and rational thinking: Implications for rheumatoid arthritis. *Arthritis Rheum, 32,* 984–990.

Philips, C., & Jahanshahi, M. (1986). The components of pain behaviour report. *Behaviour Research and Therapy, 24,* 117–125.

Philips, H. C. (1987a). Avoidance behaviour and its role in sustaining chronic pain. *Behaviour Research and Therapy, 25,* 273–279.

Philips, H. C. (1987b). The effects of behavioral treatment for chronic pain. *Behaviour Research and Therapy, 25,* 365–377.

Prentice-Dunn, S., & Rogers, R. W. (1986). Protection Motivation Theory and preventive health: Beyond the Health Belief Model. *Health Education Research, 1,* 153–161.

Prochaska, J. O., DiClemente, C. C., & Norcross, J. C. (1992). In search of how people change: Applications to addictive behaviors. *American Psychologist, 47,* 1102–1114.

Radojevic, V., Nicassio, P. M., & Weisman, M. H. (1992). Behavioral intervention with and without family support for rheumatoid arthritis. *Behavior Therapy, 23,* 13–30.

Raphael, K. G., Dohrenwend, B. P., & Marbach, J. J. (1990). Illness and injury among children of temporomandibular pain and dysfunction syndrome (TMPDS) patients. *Pain, 40,* 61–64.

Reesor, K., & Craig, K. D. (1988). Medically incongruent chronic back pain: Physical limitations, suffering, and ineffective coping. *Pain, 32,* 35–45.

Rickard, K. (1988). The occurrence of maladaptive health-related behaviors and teacher-rated conduct problems in children of chronic low back pain patients. *Journal of Behavioral Medicine, 11,* 107–116.

Ritvo, P. G. (1994). Quality of life and prostate cancer treatment: Decision-making and rehabilitative support. *Canadian Journal of Oncology, 4*(Suppl. 1), 43–45.

Romano, J. M., Turner, J. A., Friedman, L. S., Bulcroft, R. A., Jensen, M. P., Hops, H., & Wright, S. F. (1992). Sequential analysis of chronic pain behaviors and spouses responses. *Journal of Consulting and Clinical Psychology, 60,* 777–782.

Rosenstiel, A. K., & Keefe, F. J. (1983). The use of coping strategies in low-back pain patients: Relationship to patient characteristics and current adjustment. *Pain, 17,* 33–40.

Rowat, K. M., & Knafl, K. A. (1985). Living with chronic pain: The spouse's perspective. *Pain, 23,* 259–271.

Sarason, B. R., Sarason, I. G., & Pierce, G. R. (Eds.). (1990). *Social support: An interactional view.* New York: Wiley.

Self, C. A., & Rogers, R. W. (1990). Coping with threats to health: Effects of persuasive appeals on depressed, normal, and antisocial personalities. *Journal of Behavioral Medicine, 13,* 343–357.

Sherman, R. A., & Arena, J. G. (1992). Phantom limb pain: Mechanisms, incidence, and treatment. *Clinical Reviews in Physical and Rehabilitation Medicine, 4,* 1–26.

Spinhoven, P., Ter Kuile, M. M., Linssen, A. G. C., & Gazendam, B. (1989). Pain coping strategies in a Dutch population of chronic low back pain patients. *Pain, 37,* 77–83.

Sullivan, M. J. L., & D'Eon, J. L. (1990). Relation between catastrophizing and depression in chronic pain patients. *Journal of Abnormal Psychology, 99,* 260–263.

Suls, J., & Fletcher, E. (1985). The relative efficacy of avoidant and non-avoidant coping strategies: A meta analysis. *Health Psychology, 4,* 249–288.

Task Force on Taxonomy. (1994). *Classification of chronic pain. Descriptions of chronic pain syndromes and definitions of pain terms.* (H. Merskey & N. Bogduk Eds., 2nd ed.). Seattle, WA: IASP Press.

Turk, D. C., Flor, H., & Rudy, T. E. (1987). Pain and families: I. Etiology, maintenance, and psychosocial impact. *Pain, 30,* 3–27.

Turk, D. C., Meichenbaum, D., & Genest, M. (1983). *Pain and behavioral medicine. A cognitive-behavioral perspective.* New York: Guilford.

Turner, J. A. (1991). Coping and chronic pain. In M. R. Bond, J. E. Charlton, & C. J. Woolf (Eds.), *Proceedings of the VIth World Congress on Pain* (pp. 219–227). Amsterdam: Elsevier Science Publishers BV.

Turner, J. A., & Clancy, S. (1986). Strategies for coping with chronic low back pain: Relationship to pain and disability. *Pain, 24,* 355–364.

Turner, J. A., Clancy, S., & Vitaliano, P. P. (1987). Relationship of stress, appraisal and coping, to chronic low-back pain. *Behavior Research and Therapy, 25,* 281–288.

Turner, J. A., & Romano, J. M. (1989). Cognitive-behavioral therapy for chronic pain patients. In J. D. Loeser & K. J. Egan (Eds.), *Managing the chronic pain patient* (pp. 95–104). New York: Raven Press.

Vitaliano, P. P., Russo, J., Carr, J. E., Maiuro, R. D., & Becker, J. (1985). The Ways of Coping Checklist: Revision and psychometric properties. *Multivariate Behavior Research, 20,* 3–26.

Waddell, G., Newton, M., Henderson, I., Somerville, D., & Main, C. J. (1993). A Fear-Avoidance Beliefs Questionnaire (FABQ) and the role of fear-avoidance beliefs in chronic low back pain and disability. *Pain, 52,* 157–168.

Wall, P. D. (1994). Introduction to the edition after this one. In P. D. Wall & R. Melzack (Eds.), *The textbook of pain* (pp. 1–7). Edinburgh: Churchill Livingstone.

Weickgenant, A. L., Slater, M. A., Patterson, T. J., Atkinson, J. H., Grant, I., & Garfin, S. R. (1993). Coping activities in chronic low back pain: Relationship with depression. *Pain, 53,* 95–103.

Weinstein, N. D. (1988). The precaution adoption process. *Health Psychology, 7,* 355–386.

CHAPTER 13

Coping and Substance Abuse: A Theoretical Model and Review of the Evidence

THOMAS ASHBY WILLS and A. ELIZABETH HIRKY

This chapter considers theory and research on the relation of coping processes to risk for substance abuse, an outcome variable with both societal and theoretical implications. From the societal standpoint, smoking- and alcohol-related problems are a significant part of the disease burden in the U.S. population (Helzer, 1987; U.S. Department of Health and Human Services [USDHHS], 1988). From a theoretical standpoint, coping may be involved in individual-difference effects. For example, having an alcoholic parent increases risk for alcohol problems among offspring, but that only a minority of children of alcoholics (about 25% in most surveys) develop alcoholism as adults (Russell, 1990). The interplay of biological, environmental, and personal factors during childhood and adolescence may influence whether individuals at risk become involved in early substance use and whether they develop problems with substance abuse and related issues such as HIV-risk behaviors (Leigh & Stall, 1993; Tarter, Moss, & Vanyukov, 1995; Zucker, 1993).

In this chapter, we consider theoretical models of coping and substance use and discuss research conducted with adolescents and adults. The scope of the chapter includes research on *initiation* of substance use, *ongoing* substance use, and *cessation* of substance use, because findings on coping-outcome relationships are strikingly consistent across these phases of substance use. We note that research in this area has explicitly tried to identify adaptive versus nonadaptive types of coping, because the dependent variables (e.g., cessation vs. relapse) lend themselves to this task. In these paradigms, when appropriate designs are employed, the research has the potential to indicate which types of coping are adaptive and which are non-adaptive.

Research on coping and substance use has distinguished between *occasional use* and *high-intensity use*. Occasional use is temporally infrequent, presents no health problems for the user, and would be regarded as normal from a societal

---

Preparation of this chapter was supported in part by Grant #R01-DA-05950 and #R01-DA-08880 from the National Institute on Drug Abuse.

standpoint (e.g., having one or two drinks at a party). High-intensity use involves more frequent use and larger amounts of consumption (e.g., getting drunk at a party), may cause immediate or delayed problems for the user, and may involve drugs or behaviors that would be regarded as deviant in terms of general social norms. This type of use occurs with a 6-month prevalence of 5% to 10% in community samples (Helzer, 1987; Regier et al., 1990). Coping research typically focuses on predicting high-intensity use, because it is likely to be motivated by personal distress and more likely to have negative implications for the adjustment of the individual. Studies of quitting fall under this rubric because substance use is acknowledged as maladjustive with respect to the individual's own goals.

In the following sections, we first present a theoretical model of the relation between coping and substance abuse. Then we use this theoretical perspective to discuss recent research on initiation, ongoing substance abuse, and relapse. Finally, we discuss recent work on coping-skills approaches to prevention of substance abuse.

THEORETICAL APPROACHES

Theoretical models of the relation between coping and substance use differ from strict behavioral models, which construe substance use as a learned behavior acquired and maintained in response to social cues and social pressure (Biglan & Lichtenstein, 1984), or deviancy models, which construe substance use as a form of deviant behavior motivated by rejection of conventional societal values and adoption of a deviant life style (Jessor & Jessor, 1977). Although coping models do not reject evidence from these alternative models (e.g., substance users tend to have deviant attitudes and friends who use substances), they provide postulates about other factors that are predicted to place a person at increased risk.

Coping Functions of Substance Use

Coping models all depend on some construal of the coping functions of substance use; if substance use itself produced no effects on subjective well-being, there would be nothing to explain. There are three basic positions about coping functions of substance use, derived from known or speculated physiological effects of substances (e.g., Gilbert, 1979; Hull & Bond, 1986), and studies of perceived motives for use of tobacco and alcohol (Pandina, Johnson, & Labouvie, 1992; Wills & Cleary, 1995).

There are three basic models of coping functions. A model of *direct affect regulation* posits that substances produce change in affective states. For example, the tension-reduction model of alcohol use posits that alcohol reduces anxiety (e.g., Cappell & Greeley, 1987). Other versions posit that substance use has functions for (a) reducing negative affect and (b) increasing positive affect. These functions may be dose-dependent, and they may all be utilized on different occasions by the same user (Labouvie, 1986; Wills & Shiffman, 1985). An alternate view is that substance use assists coping by providing *distraction from problems,* through a physiological process that operates to divert attention temporarily from unpleasant self-awareness (Alexander & Hadaway, 1982; Hull & Bond, 1986; Steele & Josephs, 1990). A third suggestion is that substance use may provide *performance enhancement* through physiological effects on arousal or other mechanisms. For example, tobacco use in some situations may result in performance improvement because of attentional focusing and arousal-based enhancement of well-learned responses (Grobe, Perkins, Breus, & Fonte, 1991; Revell, Warburton, & Wesnes, 1985). Literature on expectancy models, specifically derived for alcohol use, represents some combination of these coping functions (e.g., Brown, Goldman, & Christiansen, 1985; Christiansen, Smith, Roehling, & Goldman, 1989; Marlatt, 1987). It is assumed that coping functions are learned through initial exposure to a substance and subsequent use in different situations, hence the salience of particular functions should show considerable variation across individuals.

Coping Processes: Transactional Model

Because substance use produces effects on subjective well-being, a theoretical question is the interplay between substance use and other types of coping, considering how the level of other coping processes makes substance use more or less likely. Theory on the relationship of coping to outcomes has generally proceeded from the transactional model of Lazarus and Folkman (1984). This theory implicitly assumes that individuals have expectations about the probable effectiveness of the coping responses in their current repertoire. The transactional theory recognizes conditions where people would not invest effort in adaptive coping, for example, when the problem was appraised as severe and expectancies about effectiveness of coping (other than substance use) were unfavorable. The original transactional model proposed the distinction between problem-focused coping and emotion-focused coping (see Parker & Endler, Chapter 1, this volume). The Lazarus and Folkman model predicts that both types of coping are protective with respect to substance use, problem-focused coping because it reduces the level of problems that could create stress, and emotion-focused coping because it reduces the level of internal emotional distress.

Coping Processes: Approach-Avoidance Models

Some concerns about the transactional model were addressed in alternative models of coping, based on theory and observation, which are discussed under the general label of *active coping versus avoidant coping* (e.g., Moos & Schaefer, 1993; Roth & Cohen, 1986). In these models, the primary distinction is between responses that involve investment of effort in dealing with the problem versus responses in which a person disengages from investing effort in trying to cope (Carver, Scheier, & Weintraub, 1989; Endler & Parker, 1990). Responses such as problem-focused coping (also termed behavioral or direct action), cognitive coping (also termed appraisal), and social coping (seeking social support) are all grouped under the rubric of *approach coping* because they involve active investment of effort in the coping process. In contrast, a separate domain of *avoidant coping* includes responses such as distraction, withdrawal, wishful thinking, or daydreaming, plus a category termed "emotional discharge" that involves venting of negative emotions on other people. In some studies, use of drugs and medications is explicitly included in the category of avoidant coping because it clusters empirically with other avoidant mechanisms (e.g., Rohde, Lewinsohn, Tilson, & Seeley, 1990).

The general prediction in these models has been that approach coping will lead to better outcomes, whereas avoidant coping will lead to worse outcomes (Blechman & Wills, 1992; Stone, Kennedy-Moore, Newman, Greenberg, & Neale, 1992). As discussed subsequently, there is considerable evidence for this proposition.[1] The implicit assumption in these models is that the more effort invested in coping, the more likely a favorable outcome. However, there is little direct evidence for this central assumption of the theory. Available evidence comes from a study of self-change by Perri (1985), which showed that for several problems (e.g., weight loss), the more different productive coping strategies that were applied over the course of the change effort, the better the outcome. Other examples are discussed subsequently.

Coping Processes: Stage Models

Another model of coping derives from studies of relapse, focusing on situations in which a person must use coping processes to remain abstinent in the face of temptation to use the substance (e.g., going to a party and feeling the urge to smoke). Shiffman (1985) has termed this "temptation coping" because it involves dealing with a specific temptation, in contrast to dealing with general life stressors. In this area, researchers have tended to develop scales specific to coping with relapse temptations, often through eliciting statements from subjects about how they coped with relapse crises and then using these as a basis for further research (e.g., Shiffman, 1982).

Stages of Change

The stages-of-change model (Prochaska, DiClemente, & Norcross, 1992) is a general model applicable to cessation situations. This model postulates that readiness for change can be classified on a 5-step scale ranging from Precontemplation (not currently ready for change) through Contemplation, Preparation, Action, and Maintenance of Change. Studies of smoking and alcohol cessation show it is typical for a person to go through a cycle of cessation and relapse several times before achieving permanent abstinence. Thus Prochaska et al. (1992) illustrate change as a spiral model in which the person goes through cessation and relapse, back to contemplation or preparation, but always with a more favorable starting point than in the previous cycle.

---

[1] Coping through mechanisms such as avoidance or distraction may be in some situations, for example, in coping with physical pain (e.g., Suls & Fletcher, 1985). Our discussion is not meant to suggest that any given type of coping is universally effective or ineffective. Consideration should always be given to the specific context of coping.

Processes of Change

The stage model postulates that use of particular coping mechanisms is what moves persons from one stage to another. The coping mechanisms studied in this model were originally derived from studies of self-change of psychological distress and were subsequently used with smoking cessation (DiClemente & Prochaska, 1985). The stage model predicts, for example, that moving from precontemplation to preparation involves behavioral coping mechanisms such as information seeking (termed "consciousness raising" by Prochaska et al., 1992) and considering different alternatives ("environmental reevaluation"). Moving from preparation to action involves making a decision and implementing the plan of action ("self-liberation"), and moving from action to maintenance involves use of social support from significant others ("helping relationships"). Evidence for the application of coping strategies at particular stages of change is discussed by Prochaska et al. (1992).

Vulnerability to Substance Abuse

A final issue for the coping model is consideration of why some individuals are more vulnerable to substance abuse in the first place. This is a complex topic involving variables at several levels (e.g., Galizio & Maisto, 1985; Newcomb, Maddahian, & Bentler, 1986; Tarter, 1988). Here we briefly note three domains of variables and discuss how they are relevant to the coping model. *Biological factors* are relevant. With regard to gender, for instance, alcohol abuse shows a male differential (Helzer, 1987), whereas use of tranquilizers shows a female differential (e.g., Cafferata, Kasper, & Bernstein, 1983). It is believed that these effects are at least partly related to differences in affect states and drug effects between men and women. Also, there is evidence for a genetic component in alcoholism, as children with an alcoholic parent are at increased risk for alcoholic abuse, (Tarter, 1988), and children of alcoholics show a greater stress-dampening effect from alcohol consumption (Levenson, Oyama, & Meek, 1987). Temperamental characteristics such as activity level are also related to risk for substance abuse (Tarter, 1988). The *social/cultural environment* conveys particular norms about substance use and may involve embedded strains that have effects on both children and parents (Pearlin, 1993; Wills, McNamara, & Vaccaro, 1995). Finally, *life stress* itself is a risk factor for substance initiation, abuse, or relapse (e.g., Chaney & Roszell, 1985; Cohen & Williamson, 1988; Wills, 1990). This suggests that the tendency for substance abuse will be increased when individuals have a great many demands to face and lack sufficient coping resources for dealing with them.

Theoretical Model

The coping model of substance abuse integrates the concepts previously discussed. It is assumed that a person may be at increased risk for substance use because of temperamental factors (e.g., high activity level), social factors (e.g., an environment with few models of adaptive coping skills), or stress factors (e.g., many negative life events). These background factors increase vulnerability because they elevate subjective distress, reduce reinforcement from the social environment, and make the perceived coping functions of substance use more attractive. These coping functions include regulation of affective states, distraction from unpleasant self-awareness, or "magical enhancement" of situations. To the extent that an individual had several background risk factors, had prior experience with substances, and perceived many coping-related functions from substance use, then he or she would be predicted to be vulnerable to high-intensity substance use (Wills & Cleary, 1995).

The coping model posits that particular types of coping may decrease or increase risk for substance abuse when vulnerability factors are present. Avoidant types of coping are predicted to increase risk because the individual is not disposed to deal with problematic situations but rather to seek the path of least resistance toward restoring affective balance. To the extent that a person tends to cope by denying the existence of problems, seeking distraction from unpleasant self-awareness, and withdrawing from engagement with normative (but more effortful) sources of reinforcement, then the path to substance use as a coping mechanism would be more likely. In contrast, active types of coping are predicted to decrease risk. A problem-solving approach is more likely to resolve problematic situations, increase feelings of self-efficacy and self-esteem, and attract others to assist in the problem-solving process. This is likely to produce a "positive cycle," in which initial efforts at problem solving produce some beneficial effects on problem situations and attract supporters, so that further active coping is encouraged. Avoidant coping is likely to produce a "vicious cycle," in which withdrawal from coping effort only leaves problem situations worse than they started, and venting of anger on others only serves to drive away supporters and decrease the amount of social support available for further problem solution (Wills, McNamara, Vaccaro, & Hirky, 1995). For cessation as well, the belief that one can cope is likely to influence whether a person actually does something to resist temptation (vs. not coping at all) when a temptation arises (Shiffman, 1985).

There is a theoretical paradox in this formulation. Substance use may itself be construed as a coping mechanism, but it also may be a product of deficits in other coping mechanisms. To the extent that alternative modes of coping are well developed, the perceived coping function(s) of substance use can be diminished. To the extent that normative modes of coping and social reinforcement are unavailable, then substance use may appear as a more attractive mode of coping, and the tendency to use it would be increased. Ultimately, this question may have to be approached as a dynamic system like Boyle's law.[2] If active modes of coping are decreased, then the perceived coping function of substance use may be enhanced, with further consequences for use of active coping. If avoidant modes of coping are increased, then the tendency to gravitate toward substance use would

---

[2] Boyle's law describes the relationship among temperature, pressure, and volume of a gas. The general form of the law is $pv = kt$ where p = pressure, v = volume, t = temperature, and k = a gas constant.

be enhanced and the perceived coping function of substance use would be affected (Wills, in press).

In the sections that follow, we present and discuss evidence on coping and substance use with respect to the coping-theoretical model. The presentation is not encyclopedic, but rather aims to discuss recent research that is particularly relevant to the coping model. Previous works have considered earlier research on various aspects of this topic (see, e.g., Chaney & Roszell, 1985; Khantzian, 1990; Moos, Finney, & Cronkite, 1990; Shiffman et al., 1986; Wills & Shiffman, 1985).

COPING AND SUBSTANCE USE INITIATION

Research on initiation of substance use is typically conducted with subjects in the age range of 12 to 14 years and focuses on studying onset of tobacco and alcohol use (see Christie et al., 1988; Robins & Przybeck, 1985). Coping is sometimes measured with self-report inventories indexing how subjects cope with general adolescent life stressors (e.g., Wills, 1986), sometimes with observational procedures that assess coping responses in specific situations (e.g., Pentz, 1985). A relationship between life stress and substance use has been demonstrated in a number of studies with adolescent samples (e.g., Wills, Vaccaro, & McNamara, 1992), so it is known that high stress is a vulnerability factor.

Behavioral coping is consistently indicated as a protective factor in this research. For example, Wills (1986) used two different self-report measures to assess coping with generic life stressors ("problems at school or home") with mid-size sample of younger adolescents. A measure of behavioral coping, which includes information seeking, decision making, and direct action, is consistently related to lower levels of tobacco and alcohol use (Wills, 1986; Wills, McNamara, Vaccaro, & Hirky, 1995). Typical effect sizes are standardized regression coefficients of .15 to .20. Similar results have been found among adolescents (Glyshaw, Cohen, & Towbes, 1989) and adults (Nezu & Ronan, 1985), with psychological symptoms as the outcome.

Buffering effects for behavioral coping have been suggested in several studies. For example, Dubow and Tisak (1989) studied a sample of 361 third- to fifth-grade students, using a vignette measure that assessed how subjects coped with situations involving conflict with parents or peers; parents independently completed a measure of recent life stress. Coding of responses indicated the predominant categories were problem solving (assertiveness or direct action) versus aggressive responding. Results showed a Stress × Coping interaction for problem solving, consistent in form with stress-buffering; that is, the relationship between life stress and maladjustment was reduced among students who scored high on problem solving. Analogous results were found by Wills, McNamara, Vaccaro, and Hirky (1995) using composite indexes for adaptive coping (behavioral + cognitive + exercise) and maladaptive coping (avoidance + helplessness + anger), with substance use as the outcome. Results showed interactions of Adaptive

× Maladaptive Coping: The level of adaptive coping reduced the impact of maladaptive coping on substance use.

Several types of evidence on avoidant coping are available. Kaplan, Martin, Johnson, and Robbins (1986) examined high-intensity marijuana use in a sample of 2,158 adolescents, first surveyed in seventh grade and followed up in young adulthood. A coping measure termed Avoidance, based on items about daydreaming, spending much time by oneself, and avoiding competition, was related to escalated marijuana use. Hirschman, Leventhal, and Glynn (1984) studied initial smoking episodes in a sample of 386 students in Grades 2–10. A measure of Helplessness, indexing the approach of not trying to cope with problems, was related to rapid progression to subsequent smoking after initial trial.

Our research with adolescents has distinguished among various aspects of avoidant coping. Using both factorial measures and intention-based measures, we obtain separate measures for the construct of avoidant coping as measured by others (general avoidant action, distraction, and withdrawal) as well as separate measures for helplessness and for anger. Results from multivariate analyses show that avoidant coping is nonsignificant, whereas helplessness and anger coping have significant unique effects, both related to greater substance use. This does not mean that avoidance has no relationship with substance use; the zero-order correlation of avoidant coping with substance use always is significant, but avoidance has no unique effect in the multivariate models because of its correlation with helplessness and anger. This is interpretable as suggesting that a tendency for avoidant coping leads to higher levels of helplessness and anger, and the latter variables are more proximal factors for substance use (Wills, Vaccaro, McNamara, & DuHamel, 1992).

Two variant forms of avoidant coping have been indicated as increasing risk for substance use. For example, Labouvie, Pandina, White, and Johnson (1990) studied a sample of 874 older adolescents with a coping measure that assessed whether the subject engaged in emotional outbursts (getting angry, screaming and yelling at others, blaming or criticizing others) when he/she was bothered by a problem. This measure of coping through anger was related to high-intensity substance use. This is consistent with other findings from adolescent samples, which show anger coping related to higher levels of substance use (Swaim, Oetting, Edwards, & Beauvais, 1989; Wills, McNamara, Vaccaro, & Hirky, 1995). Comparable results were found in another study (Farrell, Danish, & Howard, 1992; Farrell & Danish, 1993) for the Ventilating Feelings scale from McCubbin and Thompson's (1987) inventory, which may assess the same construct. Prospective analyses (Wills, McNamara, Vaccaro, & Hirky, 1995) indicate coping through anger is related to increased substance use over time (controlling for levels of other types of coping), so angry emotion is not simply a reaction to unsuccessful coping.

There has been relatively little research on perceived coping functions of substance use among adolescents. Newcomb and colleagues (Newcomb, Chou, Bentler, & Huba, 1988; Stacy, Newcomb, & Bentler, 1991) studied an adolescent sample and administered an inventory assessing perceived functions of alcohol and marijuana use for negative affect reduction, positive affect enhancement, social cohesion, and addiction. The functional dimensions were analyzed as a single latent construct reflecting perceived functions of substance use. Longitudinal analyses showed the perceived-functions score predicted increase in frequency and quantity of substance use. In a recent study with 10th-grade students, an index of coping functions of tobacco and alcohol use (for anxiety reduction, mood regulation, and relaxation) was uncorrelated with either curiosity or social motives (social pressure and perceived consensus for use) and only moderately correlated with motives for dealing with boredom and increasing self-confidence (Wills & Cleary, 1995). A multiple-regression analysis showed coping motives were strongly related to level of use (betas of .45 to .55), and only boredom motives showed an independent effect (beats of .08 to .12). Thus a comparative test shows that perceived coping functions are an important predictor of high-intensity use in adolescence.

The only investigators so far to study coping effort are Sussman, Brannon, Dent, Hansen, Johnson, and Flay (1993). They conducted a study with a sample of 125 seventh-grade students, administering a number of coping strategy scales and separate measures of the extent to which subjects felt they put effort into not smoking cigarettes. Main-effect analyses showed that a coping measure termed Getting Revenge (anger coping) and a measure termed Partying both were positively related to substance use. The latter measure (which included hanging out with other kids and going to parties) was associated with a higher level of stress and seemed to reflect a tendency to deal with problems through distraction or diversion derived from entertainment activities. Coping effort was found to interact with current stress level: The relationship between stress and smoking was reduced among those subjects who indicated they put more effort into coping with temptation.

COPING AND ONGOING SUBSTANCE ABUSE

In this section, we consider research on how coping mechanisms are related to level of ongoing substance abuse and related problems in adult samples. This research is conducted with sizable samples of adults and uses as criterion variable an index of high-intensity substance use, such as a quantity-frequency index that combines the frequency of alcohol consumption and the typical amount consumed per occasion, or a DSM-III diagnosis of substance abuse. Some recent studies have also used indexes of HIV-risk behavior.

Life stress is consistently related to substance use in adult samples. This has been found for cigarette smoking, heavy drinking, psychotropic drug use, and illicit drug use (e.g., Cafferata et al., 1983; Caplan et al., 1984; Cohen & Williamson, 1988; McKirnan & Peterson, 1988), with effect sizes comparable to Pearson correlations in the range of .20 to .30. Experimental studies have shown effects of stress on smoking (USDHHS, 1988) and alcohol use (Hull & Bond, 1986), supporting the conclusion of a causal relationship. Gender differences are more prominent in this literature, with alcoholism and antisocial diagnoses more prevalent among men, whereas tranquilizer use and anxiety diagnoses are more prevalent among women (Cafferata et al., 1983; Helzer, 1987; Parker, Parker, Harford, & Farmer, 1987).

Avoidant coping has been linked to substance abuse in several community studies. For example, Cronkite and Moos (1984) studied a representative sample of 242 respondents using a measure of avoidant coping (from Moos's original inventory) that included items on selective ignoring, withdrawal, and emotional discharge (e.g., "Took it out on others"). Concurrent analyses indicated the measure of avoidant coping was related to more alcohol use. Interaction analyses indicated this effect was stronger when the spouse was high on depressive or physical symptoms and hence, by implication, was less available as a source of social support. Similar effects for a revised inventory of approach and avoidance coping were found by Moos, Brennan, Fondacaro, and Moos (1990) for distinguishing problem drinkers from nonproblem drinkers in a sample of adults aged 55 to 65. Problem drinkers were more likely to use coping strategies classified as avoidant (particularly emotional discharge and cognitive avoidance) and less likely to use approach mechanisms such as positive reappraisal and seeking social support.

Rohde et al. (1990) conducted a 1-year longitudinal study with a sample of 742 older adults using a 65-item coping inventory (from Parker, Brown, & Blignault, 1986) that included items on behavioral coping and self-control, various avoidant types of coping, and helplessness. Factor analysis indicated three factors. The Active Coping factor combined items on behavioral coping (e.g., "Approach the solution in a systematic way") and cognitive coping ("Tell myself the problem is not so catastrophic"), hence reflecting a general dimension of approach coping. The second factor was loaded by a variety of avoidant coping mechanisms including general avoidance ("Postpone making a decision"; "Stay in bed"), withdrawal ("Keep away from people"), helplessness ("Do nothing in particular"), daydreaming ("Daydream about a better time or place"), and substance use ("Take tablets or medicine," "Take a tranquilizer whenever I feel tense or nervous"). The third factor reflected social support seeking ("Spend time with a relative or close friend"). Results showed avoidant coping was related to increased risk for depression, and interaction analyses showed avoidance coping increased the impact of current life stress. In contrast, social support coping acted as a stress buffer: A higher level of support coping reduced the impact of negative life events on depression.

Research on perceived coping functions of substance use also shows relationships to high-intensity use. For example, Cooper, Russell, and George (1988) conducted a household interview study with a representative community sample of 1,067 adults, of whom 11% met DSM-III criteria for current alcohol abuse or dependence. Measures were obtained for general avoidant coping (from Moos's inventory), alcohol expectancies, alcohol use to cope, and overall alcohol consumption (quantity-frequency index). A path analysis indicated avoidant coping was significantly related to (a) drinking to cope and (b) overall alcohol consumption, each of which had an independent relationship to alcohol abuse. Relationships of avoidant coping to other variables were particularly strong among persons who had positive expectancies about coping functions of alcohol for tension reduction and mood enhancement.

Other studies have found an interaction of life stress, expectancies, and avoidant coping in prediction of substance abuse. Timmer, Veroff, and Colten (1985) studied alcohol and psychotropic drug use as coping mechanisms in a representative national sample. They found coping through alcohol and drug use was related to low social support and high life stress, and was moderated by perceived control. McKirnan and Peterson (1988) studied an urban homosexual sample, obtaining measures of heavy drinking and illicit drug use (mostly marijuana). Stress was indexed by measures of subjective distress and by a scale of negative events linked to discrimination. Results showed coping expectancies (e.g., tension reduction or mood enhancement) were related to both indexes of substance abuse. There was a particularly strong relationship between stress and substance abuse among persons scoring high on coping expectancies (cf. Cooper, Russell, Skinner, Frone, & Mudar, 1992, with a community sample).

An area of recent interest is how coping is related to HIV-risk behavior, which includes unprotected sex and multiple partners. McKirnan and Peterson (1989) investigated this question with data from their metropolitan sample. Results showed tension-reduction expectancies, stress-related substance use, and low perceived control were related to indexes of sexual risk behavior. This general relationship between substance abuse and risky behavior has also been found in other samples (see Leigh & Stall, 1993).

Folkman, Chesney, Pollack, and Philips (1992) studied coping in a sample drawn from an AIDS-risk cohort study with an all-male homosexual sample. The study was based on 366 respondents who were nonmonogamous and not diagnosed with AIDS; the coping measure was a 19-item version of the Ways of Coping Scale (Lazarus & Folkman, 1984); and the definition of risk behavior was unprotected anal intercourse in the previous month. An item was also included to index the extent to which the respondent used sex as a way of coping with stress. Results indicated the perceived coping function of sex was a significant predictor of risk behavior. Two coping mechanisms, seeking social support and religious coping, were related to lower levels of risky behavior (cf. Rohde et al., 1990; Timmer et al., 1985). One avoidant coping mechanism, based on items about social withdrawal and keeping feelings to oneself, was related to higher levels of risky behavior. This study suggests that the function of sexual behavior as a means of coping with life stress is an important factor for predicting high-risk outcomes.

Gender differences are a third area of current interest. For example, Cooper et al. (1992) examined gender differences in alcohol abuse in a community sample. Interaction tests suggested the effect of life stress on drinking problems, and the relationship between avoidant coping and drinking problems, occurred primarily among males. Wilsnack, Klassen, Schur, and Wilsnack (1991) conducted a five-year longitudinal study with a national probability sample of 1,313 respondents that was stratified to include a sizable proportion (40%) of female heavy drinkers. Prospective analyses showed that variables predicting onset of drinking problems (among women who drank initially but were without problems) were previous use of other drugs in addition to alcohol, cohabiting versus being married, low self-esteem at baseline, and depressive episodes during the follow-up interval. For predicting chronicity of drinking problems, the most important variables were sexual dysfunction at baseline, depression at baseline, and depressive episodes over the follow-up interval. Unemployment and partner's drinking status were also significant predictors of chronicity. These data are consistent with findings from a community sample of employed adults (Parker et al., 1987), which found depression correlated with alcohol abuse among both males and females.

These investigators summarized their results by suggesting that role deprivation increases the risk of alcohol abuse by reducing feelings of self-esteem and availability of social support. They also suggested chronicity of drinking was related to "a tendency of problem-drinking women to self-medicate sexual difficulties with alcohol" (Wilsnack et al., 1991, p. 315), and that "onset of problem drinking may be facilitated by a woman's long-term tendency to use various psychoactive drugs to feel better, to have a good time, or to cope with problems" (p. 316). Thus these findings are consistent in interpretation with a coping model of substance abuse.

COPING AND RELAPSE

Research on the relation between coping and likelihood of relapse is typically conducted with samples of long-term users who are trying to quit. This research studies situations in which the subject was tempted to lapse from a period of cessation, and indexes coping mechanisms used in response to a specific temptation. The evidence is mostly from field studies but includes some research using laboratory paradigms (Abrams et al., 1987; Perkins & Grobe, 1992).

Research on relapse has consistently shown stress as a precipitating factor, with observed commonality for tobacco, alcohol, opiate, and cocaine relapse (Chaney & Roszell, 1985; Shiffman, 1985; McMahon & Kouzekanani, 1991; Wills, 1990): Persons are much more likely to relapse when they are under stress. This research has included measures of perceived stress, negative life events, and negative affect states such as anger, anxiety, or depression (Carey, Kalra, Carey, Halperin, & Richards, 1993; Cohen & Lichtenstein, 1990; Hall, Munoz, Reus, & Sees, 1993). Some evidence for gender differences has been noted; for example, Swan et al. (1988) found daily hassles were related to relapse among men, whereas work strain was the only unique stress predictor for women. Situational cues, such as seeing other persons smoking, are also an important situational predictor of relapse (Bliss, Garvey, Heinold, & Hitchcock, 1989; Shiffman, 1985). The coping model posits that stress situations activate cues associated with coping functions of substance use (e.g., anxiety reduction); that this evokes craving for the substance; and that this temptation may lead to relapse if not effectively counteracted through appropriate coping (see, e.g., Shadel & Mermelstein, 1993).

The measures of temptation-coping strategies define behavioral coping as actions such as employing planning to avoid substance use stimuli (e.g., throwing all cigarettes out of the house), using physical activity (e.g., exercising) to deal with temptation, using relaxation to reduce stress, enlisting social support from family or friends, or actively leaving a tempting situation. Cognitive coping involves strategies such as thinking about health benefits of abstinence, thinking about social consequences (e.g., "Spouse and kids will be pleased"), using distraction strategies that involve thinking about alternative pleasant activities, or simple delay ("I'll just wait this out"). Nonadaptive strategies are defined as using "willpower" (coded only when a cognitive strategy did not involve other activity), wishful thinking, helplessness, or self-punitive strategies (e.g., "I can't do this," "I'm a weakling").

Research has indicated that any productive attempt to cope with a relapse crisis is effective, compared with no attempt to cope (see Curry & Marlatt, 1985; Shiffman, 1985). A combination of behavioral and cognitive coping is usually more effective than either used alone. For example, Bliss et al. (1989) found, in a sample of 232 self-initiated quitters, that subjects who combined cognitive and behavioral temptation-coping strategies were significantly more likely to abstain than subjects who used any one strategy during a relapse crisis. Among subjects who used no coping, almost all (95/96) relapsed. Similar results were found by Carey et al. (1993) with a generalized stress-coping measure.

The relation of coping effort to initial lapses and subsequent outcomes was studied by Baer, Kamarck, Lichtenstein, and Ransom (1989) in a sample of 102 heavy smokers in a formal treatment program. Lapse was defined as any smoking followed by at least a week of abstinence; relapse was defined as return to regular smoking. Results showed that use of either cognitive or behavioral coping differentiated subjects who were tempted (but remained abstinent) from those who lapsed. Longitudinal analyses showed that initial lapse was a powerful predictor of subsequent relapse. Thus the implied mechanism is that coping effort is effective primarily for averting small, initial lapses, the occurrence of which would increase the risk of subsequent relapse.

Some research has considered general affect-regulation strategies in addition to specific mechanisms used for coping with relapse temptations. For example, Kamarck and Lichtenstein (1988) used a 32-item inventory of mood-regulation techniques such as relaxation, humor, and talking to others about feelings, which was administered at the end of a formal cessation program. The mood-regulation measure was related to lower probability of relapse at 1 and 2 months after treatment. The treatment program included training in self-monitoring and self-control for dealing with relapse crises, and measures of these dimensions were found to be independent predictors of (less) relapse from 2 months through 1 year posttreatment. The suggestion is that mood-related coping is most relevant during the first few weeks after cessation, when subjective distress from withdrawal symptoms and loss of coping functions of smoking is elevated, whereas long-term maintenance is more dependent on the ability to cope with situations where smoking cues may be present. Similarly, Hall et al. (1993) found that depressed smokers assigned to a condition that involved training in strategies for mood management showed lower rates of relapse.

Some null results have been noted in the relapse area. In a prospective study of 104 cocaine treatment patients, Hall, Havassy, and Wasserman (1991) found effects for a temptation coping inventory in relation to relapse to cocaine use among Caucasians, but not among African Americans. Though the coping inventory used in this study was different from measures used in other research, the findings are consistent with results from Chaney and Roszell (1985), who found that a characteristic of intravenous drug users was a very low level of any kind of coping. Brandon, Tiffany, Obremski, and Baker (1990) followed a sample of 147 persons who completed a smoking cessation program and obtained retrospective measures of what had transpired in lapse episodes. These investigators found that a temptation-coping measure did not predict latency from lapse to relapse. However, they did not study whether coping was related to initial lapse, as was done by Baer et al. (1989). In this study, only 29% of subjects used any coping response after the lapse episode, so the results suggest a generally low level of coping in this sample.

Recent research has examined extensions of concepts from smoking research to other types of relapse. For example, among a group of 57 obese individuals with Type II diabetes, cognitive and behavioral coping responses to relapse crises were found to be equally related to maintaining a dietary regimen (Grilo, Shiffman, & Wing, 1989). It was noted that 37% of the relapse crises produced no coping execution and each of these episodes resulted in a lapse (an overeating incident).

We also note similarities to research on relapse to HIV-risk behaviors, for example, reverting to unprotected sex among persons who have previously adopted safer sex practices. Relapse to risky behavior has been related to life stress and negative affect, particularly among persons without regular partners (Stall, Ekstrand, Pollack, McKusick, & Coates, 1990), and to the perceived reinforcement value of the behavior (Kelly, Kalichman, et al., 1991), as well as other predictors (e.g., romantic feelings, belief that condoms reduce pleasure). Kelly, St. Lawrence, and Brasfield (1991) found several coping strategies were prevalent among persons who successfully resisted temptations to engage in unsafe sex. These included cognitive strategies involving health consequences ("Thought how important it is to be in good health") and self-reinforcement ("Knew how good I'd feel about myself if I stayed safe"), planning and direct action ("Decided ahead of time what I would do," "Actively guided our actions to stay safe"), and eschewal of drug use ("Didn't drink or use drugs before sex so I could be clearheaded"). Thus coping theory may have significant applications for further research on relapse in the area of HIV-risk behavior.

PRIMARY AND SECONDARY PREVENTION

Here we consider research focused on coping skills training as a preventive strategy, either among persons who have not initiated any substance use (primary prevention) or among persons with problematic substance use (secondary prevention). Detailed discussion of methods for coping skills training are presented in several sources (see Foreman, 1993 for primary prevention; Hester & Miller, 1989 for treatment).

With adolescents, several projects have used training in coping skills as an approach to deterring initiation of cigarette or alcohol use. Pentz (1985) focused on social coping skills, conducting an 8-session school-based program in which sequenced modeling and feedback were used to teach skills for social problem-solving in a variety of everyday situations involving teachers, peers, parents, and other adults. This study used an observational method for assessing social coping: Subjects' responses to standardized situations were recorded and subsequently coded for coping skill by independent raters. Process data showed increases in socially competent responding and evaluation data showed the program reduced alcohol use in the training group (relative to controls), particularly for students who were more aggressive at baseline. Other effective multimodal programs have combined social competence training with instruction in general stress-coping skills such as relaxation or cognitive coping (e.g., Botvin & Wills, 1985). Multimodal approaches have also been included in community-based prevention programs (MacKinnon et al., 1991; Pentz et al., 1989). Outcome results have shown preventive effects for tobacco, alcohol, and marijuana; a process analysis suggested these effects occurred in part through altering the perceived social environment for substance use (MacKinnon et al., 1991).

Some innovative recent studies have been designed for populations with high levels of risk: students in special high schools (Sussman et al., 1993) and teenagers in high-crime urban areas (Pentz, Gong, & Pentz, 1993). These projects have used a new combination of methods to deal with the needs of these populations, because of recent evidence that the refusal-skill approach to prevention does not work as well in these populations (Sussman et al., 1993). The program by Pentz et al. (1993) was conducted in ethnically diverse urban areas with high levels of gang activity. Participants were randomly assigned to a personal coping program, a social influences program, or a control condition. In the personal coping program, peer modeling was used to teach decision making, cognitive coping strategies, relaxation, social support seeking, appropriate assertiveness skills, dealing with gangs, and coping with anger. Outcome data showed the program reduced cigarette and marijuana use, compared with either the social influence curriculum or the control condition. The authors suggested that in high-stress environments, interventions aimed at teaching adolescents to cope with stress may have more beneficial effects than other approaches.

The application of coping theory to treatment and relapse prevention has been explored for smoking (Stevens & Hollis, 1989), alcohol abuse (Hester & Miller, 1989), and opiate or cocaine addiction (Chaney & Roszell, 1985; McMahon, Kouzekanani, & Kelley, 1993). In the alcohol area, the approach of behavioral self-control training has been extensively evaluated. This treatment approach involves training in self-monitoring of drinking behavior, assertiveness in refusing drinks, learning alternative coping skills other than drinking, and self-reinforcement for achieving goals. Alternative coping mechanisms may involve cognitive mood management skills and relaxation, communication and compromise skills for marital stressors, and assertion skills for low-power situations, such as job stressors. This approach has been shown effective in randomized trials (e.g., Miller & Joyce, 1979; Sanchez-Craig, Annis, Bornet, & MacDonald, 1984). The self-control approach is indicated as more effective for persons beginning to show high-intensity drinking, but less effective for chronic alcoholics with severe dependence and biomedical deterioration (Cooney, Kadden, Litt, & Getter, 1991; Miller & Hester, 1986). Several guides to coping skills training are available for treatment of alcohol problems (see Hester & Miller, 1989; Monti, Abrams, Kadden, & Cooney, 1989; Moos, Finney, & Cronkite, 1990).

CONCLUSION

In this chapter, we have developed a theoretical model of the relationship between coping and substance use and have discussed research on substance use with respect to this model. We note several conclusions. First, coping is related to substance use. Second, the relation of coping mechanisms to substance use is strikingly consistent across the three phases of use (initiation, maintenance, and relapse). Thus there is a considerable amount of evidence showing that coping processes are related to a significant external criterion, substance use. Results are consistent with theory, and the consistency of findings across phases of substance use with what would seem to be very different demands (e.g., initiation at 12 years of age vs. relapse at 52 years of age) lends support to the view that coping processes have meaningful effects across different parts of the life span. The clinical significance of coping processes is most clearly evident for relapse, where evidence shows that persons who try to cope are relatively protected, whereas among persons who do not cope, almost all relapse immediately. We also noted that life stress is a risk factor across the different phases, with a high level of life stress representing a risk factor for initiation of use, for higher levels of ongoing substance use, and for relapse. Thus the evidence shows that stress constructs are an integral part of a stress-coping theory of substance use (Wills & Cleary, 1995; Wills & Filer, in press).

Our theoretical model makes the distinction between active coping and avoidant coping. The evidence we have discussed is consistent in showing avoidant coping to be maladaptive, being related to higher likelihood of initiation, higher levels of ongoing substance abuse, and greater probability of relapse (cf. Zeidner & Saklofske, Chapter 22, this volume). Evidence on active (behavioral and cognitive) coping as a protective factor is more consistent for initiation and relapse, less consistent for ongoing substance abuse in adult samples. It may be that effects of active coping are most important at transition points, or more relevant for reducing the impact of maladaptive coping (Wills, McNamara, Vaccaro, & Hirky, 1995).

We see many directions for further research on coping and substance use. At the psychometric level, there is a need for further studies of the dimensionality of coping, with an eye toward understanding, respectively, the intercorrelation between measures of problem solving and cognitive strategies for dealing with internal emotional distress (here classified as active coping), and the corresponding intercorrelation among measures of anger, helplessness, and wishful thinking (here classified as avoidant coping). At the pharmacological level, there is a need for research on how the physiological effects of tobacco, alcohol, or other substances are related to perceived coping functions, so this is an area where interdisciplinary efforts are necessary. Coping should also be investigated in high-risk samples (cf. Seracini, Siegel, Wills, Nunes, & Goldstein, 1995). Predictions can be tested about the dynamic relationship among active coping, avoidant coping, and the perceived coping function of substance use. This type of investigation may provide a new perspective on the relation of coping to the observed comorbidity of substance use and mental disorder (Helzer & Przybeck, 1988; Regier et al., 1990). Longitudinal research is still greatly needed to clarify the temporal relationships among problem solving, social support coping, and various types of outcomes, as well as the relationships over time of different aspects of avoidant coping (e.g., helplessness, anger). There is potential for studying how previous research on coping and relapse can be used to design cessation treatments that are tailored to individual motives and situations. Finally, new research is needed to explore the potential of coping processes to predict high-risk behavior such as may place persons at risk for HIV infection.

REFERENCES

Abrams, D. B., Monti, P. M., Pinto, R. P., Elder, J. P., Brown, R. A., & Jacobus, S. I. (1987). Psychosocial stress and coping in smokers who relapse or quit. *Health Psychology, 6,* 289–303.

Alexander, B. K., & Hadaway, P. F. (1982). Opiate addiction: The case for an adaptive orientation. *Psychological Bulletin, 92,* 367–381.

Baer, J. S., Kamarck, T., Lichtenstein, E., & Ransom, C. C., Jr. (1989). Prediction of smoking relapse: Analyses of temptations and transgressions after initial cessation. *Journal of Consulting and Clinical Psychology, 57,* 623–627.

Biglan, A., & Lichtenstein, E. (1984). A behavior-analytic approach to smoking acquisition. *Journal of Applied Social Psychology, 14,* 207–223.

Blechman, E. A., & Wills, T. A. (1992). Process measures in interventions for drug-abusing women: From coping to competence. In M. M. Kilbey & K. Asghar (Eds.), *Methodological issues in epidemiological, prevention, and treatment research on drug-exposed women and their children* (pp. 314–343). Rockville, MD: National Institute on Drug Abuse.

Bliss, R. E., Garvey, A. J., Heinold, J. W., & Hitchcock, J. L. (1989). The influence of situation and coping on relapse crisis outcomes after smoking cessation. *Journal of Consulting and Clinical Psychology, 57,* 443–449.

Botvin, G., & Wills, T. A. (1985). Personal skills training: Cognitive behavioral approaches to substance abuse prevention. In C. S. Bell & R. Battjes (Eds.), *Deterring drug abuse among children and adolescents* (pp. 8–49). Rockville, MD: National Institute on Drug Abuse.

Brandon, T. H., Tiffany, S. T., Obremski, K. M., & Baker, T. B. (1990). Postcessation cigarette use: The process of relapse. *Addictive Behaviors, 15,* 105–114.

Brown, S. A., Goldman, M. S., & Christiansen, B. A. (1985). Do alcohol expectancies mediate drinking patterns of adults? *Journal of Consulting and Clinical Psychology, 53,* 512–519.

Cafferata, G. L., Kasper, J., & Bernstein, A. (1983). Family roles, structure, and stressors in relation to sex differences in obtaining psychotropic drugs. *Journal of Health and Social Behavior, 24,* 132–143.

Caplan, R. D., Abbey, A., Abramis, D. J., Andrews, F. M., Conway, T. L., & French, J. R. P., Jr. (1984). *Tranquilizer use and well-being: A longitudinal study of social and psychological effects.* Ann Arbor: Institute for Social Research.

Cappell, H., & Greeley, J. (1987). Alcohol and tension reduction. In H. T. Blane & K. E. Leonard (Eds.), *Psychological theories of drinking and alcoholism* (pp. 15–54). New York: Guilford.

Carey, M. P., Kalra, D. L., Carey, K. B., Halperin, S., & Richards, C. S. (1993). Stress and unaided smoking cessation: A prospective investigation. *Journal of Consulting and Clinical Psychology, 61,* 831–838.

Carver, C. S., Scheier, M. F., & Weintraub, J. K. (1989). Assessing coping strategies. *Journal of Personality and Social Psychology, 56,* 267–283.

Chaney, E. F., & Roszell, D. K. (1985). Coping in opiate addicts maintained on methadone. In S. Shiffman & T. A. Wills (Eds.), *Coping and substance use* (pp. 267–293). Orlando, FL: Academic Press.

Christiansen, B. A., Smith, G. T., Roehling, P. V., & Goldman, M. S. (1989). Using alcohol expectancies to predict adolescent drinking behavior after one year. *Journal of Consulting and Clinical Psychology, 57,* 93–99.

Christie, K. A., Burke, J. D., Regier, D. A., Rae, D. S., Boyd, J. H., & Locke, B. Z. (1988). Epidemiologic evidence for early onset of mental disorders and higher risk of drug abuse in young adults. *American Journal of Psychiatry, 145,* 971–975.

Cohen, S., & Lichtenstein, E. (1990). Perceived stress, quitting smoking, and smoking relapse. *Health Psychology, 9,* 466–478.

Cohen, S., & Williamson, G. M. (1988). Perceived stress in a probability sample of the United States. In S. Spacapan & S. Oskamp (Eds.), *The social psychology of health* (pp. 31–67). Newbury Park, CA: Sage.

Cooney, N. L., Kadden, R. M., Litt, M. D., & Getter, H. (1991). Matching alcoholics to coping skills or interactional therapies: Two year follow-up results. *Journal of Consulting and Clinical Psychology, 59,* 598–601.

Cooper, M. L., Russell, M., & George, W. H. (1988). Coping, expectancies, and alcohol abuse. *Journal of Abnormal Psychology, 97,* 218–230.

Cooper, M. L., Russell, M., Skinner, J. B., Frone, M. R., & Mudar, P. (1992). Stress and alcohol use: Moderating effects of gender, coping, and alcohol expectancies. *Journal of Abnormal Psychology, 101,* 139–152.

Cronkite, R. C., & Moos, R. H. (1984). The role of predisposing and moderating factors in the stress-illness relationship. *Journal of Health and Social Behavior, 25,* 372–393.

Curry, S. G., & Marlatt, G. A. (1985). Unaided quitters' strategies for coping with temptations to smoke. In S. Shiffman & T. A. Wills (Eds.), *Coping and substance use* (pp. 243–265). Orlando, FL: Academic Press.

DiClemente, C. C., & Prochaska, J. O. (1985). Processes and stages of change: Coping and competence in smoking behavior change. In S. Shiffman & T. A. Wills (Eds.), *Coping and substance use* (pp. 319–343). Orlando, FL: Academic Press.

Dubow, E. F., & Tisak, J. (1989). The relation between stressful life events and adjustment in elementary school children: The role of social support and problem-solving skills. *Child Development, 60,* 1412–1423.

Endler, N. S., & Parker, J. D. A. (1990). Multidimensional assessment of coping: A critical evaluation. *Journal of Personality and Social Psychology, 58,* 844–854.

Farrell, A. D., & Danish, S. J. (1993). Peer drug associations and emotional restraint: Causes or consequences of adolescent's drug use. *Journal of Consulting and Clinical Psychology, 61,* 327–334.

Farrell, A. D., Danish, S. J., & Howard, C. W. (1992). Risk factors for drug use in urban adolescents: Identification and cross-validation. *American Journal of Community Psychology, 20,* 263–286.

Folkman, S., Chesney, M. A., Pollack, L., & Philips, C. (1992). Stress, coping and high-risk sexual behavior. *Health Psychology, 11,* 218–222.

Foreman, S. G. (1993). *Coping skills interventions for children and adolescents.* San Francisco: Jossey-Bass.

Galizio, M., & Maisto, S. A. (Eds.). (1985). *Determinants of substance abuse.* New York: Plenum.

Gilbert, D. G. (1979). Paradoxical tranquilizing and emotion-reducing effects of nicotine. *Psychological Bulletin, 86,* 643–661.

Glyshaw, K., Cohen, L. H., & Towbes, L. C. (1989). Coping strategies and psychological distress: Prospective analyses of early and middle adolescents. *American Journal of Community Psychology, 17,* 607–623.

Grilo, C. M., Shiffman, S., & Wing, R. R. (1989). Relapse crises and coping among dieters. *Journal of Consulting and Clinical Psychology, 57,* 488–495.

Grobe, J. E., Perkins, K. A., Breus, M., & Fonte, C. (1991, March). *Paradoxical effects of smoking on subjective stress vs. cardiovascular arousal.* Paper presented at the Society of Behavioral Medicine, Washington, DC.

Hall, S. M., Havassy, B. E., & Wasserman, D. A. (1991). Effects of commitment to abstinence, moods, stress, and coping on relapse to cocaine use. *Journal of Consulting and Clinical Psychology, 59,* 526–532.

Hall, S. M., Munoz, R. F., Reus, V. I., & Sees, K. L. (1993). Nicotine, negative affect, and depression. *Journal of Consulting and Clinical Psychology, 61,* 761–767.

Helzer, J. E. (1987). Epidemiology of alcoholism. *Journal of Consulting and Clinical Psychology, 55,* 284–292.

Helzer, J. E., & Pryzbeck, T. R. (1988). The co-occurrence of alcoholism with other psychiatric disorders in the general population and its impact on treatment. *Journal of Studies on Alcohol, 49,* 219–224.

Hester, R. K., & Miller, W. R. (1989). Self-control training. In R. K. Hester & W. R. Miller (Eds.), *Handbook of alcoholism treatment approaches* (pp. 141–149). Elmsford, NY: Pergamon.

Hirschman, R. S., Leventhal, H., & Glynn, K. (1984). The development of smoking behavior: Cross-sectional survey data. *Journal of Applied Social Psychology, 14,* 184–206.

Hull, J. G., & Bond, C. F., Jr. (1986). Social and behavioral consequences of alcohol consumption and expectancy. *Psychological Bulletin, 99,* 347–360.

Jessor, R., & Jessor, S. L. (1977). *Problem behavior and psychosocial development.* New York: Academic Press.

Kamarck, T. W., & Lichtenstein, E. (1988). Program adherence and coping strategies as predictors of success in a smoking treatment program. *Health Psychology, 7,* 557–574.

Kaplan, H. B., Martin, S. S., Johnson, R. J., & Robbins, C. A. (1986). Escalation of marijuana use. *Journal of Health and Social Behavior, 27,* 44–61.

Khantzian, E. J. (1990). Self-regulation and self-medication factors in alcoholism and the addictions: Similarities and differences. In M. Galanter (Ed.), *Recent developments in alcoholism* (Vol. 8, pp. 255–271). New York: Plenum.

Kelly, J., Kalichman, S., Kauth, M., Kilgore, H., Hood, H., Campos, P., Rao, S., Brasfield, T., & St. Lawrence, J. (1991). Situational factors associated with AIDS risk behavior lapses and coping strategies used by gay men who successfully avoid lapses. *American Journal of Public Health, 81,* 1335–1338.

Kelly, J., St. Lawrence, J., & Brasfield, T. (1991). Predictors of vulnerability to AIDS risk behavior relapse. *Journal of Consulting and Clinical Psychology, 59,* 163–166.

Labouvie, E. W. (1986). The coping function of adolescent alcohol and drug use. In R. K. Silbereisen, K. Eyferth, & G. Rudinger (Eds.), *Development as action in context* (pp. 229–240). New York: Springer.

Labouvie, E. W., Pandina, R. J., White, H. R., & Johnson, V. (1990). Risk factors of adolescent drug use: An affect-based interpretation. *Journal of Substance Abuse, 2,* 265–285.

Lazarus, R. S., & Folkman, S. (1984). *Stress, appraisal, and coping.* New York: Springer.

Leigh, B. C., & Stall, R. (1993). Substance use and risky sexual behavior for exposure to HIV. *American Psychologist, 48,* 1035–1045.

Levenson, R. W., Oyama, O. N., & Meek, P. S. (1987). Greater reinforcement from alcohol for those at parental and personality risk. *Journal of Abnormal Psychology, 96,* 242–253.

MacKinnon, D. P., Johnson, C. A., Pentz, M. A., Dwyer, J. H., Hansen, W. B., Flay, B. R., & Wang, E. Y. -I. (1991). Mediating mechanisms in a school-based drug prevention program. *Health Psychology, 10,* 164–172.

Marlatt, G. A. (1987). Alcohol, the magic elixir: Stress, expectancy, and the transformation of emotional states. In E. Gottheil, K. A. Druley, S. Pashdo, & S. P. Weinstein (Eds.), *Stress and addiction* (pp. 302–322). New York: Brunner/Mazel.

McCubbin, H. I., & Thompson, A. I. (1987). *Family assessment inventories for research and practice.* Madison: University of Wisconsin Press.

McKirnan, D. J., & Peterson, P. L. (1988). Stress, expectancies, and vulnerability to substance abuse. *Journal of Abnormal Psychology, 97,* 461–466.

McKirnan, D. J., & Peterson, P. L. (1989). AIDS-risk behavior among homosexual males: The role of attitudes and substance abuse. *Psychology and Health, 3,* 161–171.

McMahon, R. C., & Kouzekanani, K. (1991, August). *Stress, social support, and the buffering hypothesis in the prediction of cocaine abuse relapse.* Paper presented at the meeting of the American Psychological Association, San Francisco.

McMahon, R. C., Kouzekanani, K., & Kelley, A. (1993, August). *Personality and coping in the prediction of cocaine treatment dropout.* Paper presented at the meeting of the American Psychological Association, Toronto, Canada.

Miller, W. R., & Hester, R. K. (1986). The effectiveness of alcoholism treatment: What research reveals. In W. R. Miller & N. Heather (Eds.), *Treating addictive behaviors: Processes of change* (pp. 121–174). New York: Plenum.

Miller, W. R., & Joyce, M. A. (1979). Prediction of abstinence, controlled drinking, and heavy drinking outcomes following behavioral self-control training. *Journal of Consulting and Clinical Psychology, 47,* 773–775.

Monti, P. M., Abrams, D. B., Kadden, R. M., & Cooney, N. L. (1989). *Treating alcohol dependence: A coping skills training guide.* New York: Guilford.

Moos, R. H., Brennan, P. L., Fondacaro, M. R., & Moos, B. S. (1990). Approach and avoidance coping responses among older problem and nonproblem drinkers. *Psychology and Aging, 5,* 31–40.

Moos, R. H., Finney, J. W., & Cronkite, R. C. (1990). *Alcoholism treatment: Context, process, and outcome.* New York: Oxford University Press.

Moos, R. H., & Schaefer, J. A. (1993). Coping resources and processes: Current concepts and measures. In L. Goldberger & S. Bresnitz (Eds.), *Handbook of stress* (2nd ed., pp. 234–257). New York: Free Press.

Newcomb, M. D., Chou, C. -P., Bentler, P. M., & Huba, G. J. (1988). Cognitive motivations for drug use among adolescents as predictors of changes in drug use. *Journal of Counseling Psychology, 35,* 426–438.

Newcomb, M. D., Maddahian, E., & Bentler, P. M. (1986). Risk factors for drug use among adolescents: Concurrent and longitudinal analyses. *American Journal of Public Health, 76,* 525–531.

Nezu, A. M., & Ronan, G. F. (1985). Life stress, current problems, problem solving, and depressive symptoms: An integrative model. *Journal of Consulting and Clinical Psychology, 53,* 693–697.

Pandina, R. J., Johnson, V., & Labouvie, E. W. (1992). Affectivity: A central mechanism in the development of drug dependence. In M. D. Glantz & R. W. Pickens (Eds.), *Vulnerability to drug abuse* (pp. 179–209). Washington, DC: American Psychological Association.

Parker, D. A., Parker, E. S., Harford, T. C., & Farmer, G. C. (1987). Alcohol use and depression symptoms among employed men and women. *American Journal of Public Health, 77,* 704–707.

Parker, G. B., Brown, L. B., & Blignault, I. (1986). Coping behaviors as predictors of the course of clinical depression. *Archives of General Psychiatry, 43,* 561–565.

Pearlin, L. I. (1993). The social contexts of stress. In L. Goldberger & S. Bresnitz (Eds.), *Handbook of stress* (2nd ed., pp. 303–315). New York: Free Press.

Pentz, M. A. (1985). Social competence and self-efficacy as determinants of substance use in adolescence. In S. Shiffman & T. A. Wills (Eds.), *Coping and substance use* (pp. 117–142). Orlando, FL: Academic Press.

Pentz, M. A., Dwyer, J. H., MacKinnon, D. P., Flay, B. R., Hansen, W. B., Wang, E. Y. I., & Johnson, C. A. (1989). A multicommunity trial for primary prevention of adolescent drug abuse: Effects on drug use prevalence. *Journal of the American Medical Association, 261,* 3259–3266.

Pentz, M. A., Gong, A., & Pentz, C. A. (1993, August). *Relative effectiveness of social influence and stress coping programs for adolescent drug prevention.* Paper presented at the meeting of the American Psychological Association, Toronto, Canada.

Perkins, K. A., & Grobe, J. E. (1992). Increased desire to smoke during acute stress. *British Journal of Addiction, 87,* 231–234.

Perri, M. G. (1985). Self-change strategies for the control of smoking, obesity, and problem drinking. In S. Shiffman & T. A. Wills (Eds.), *Coping and substance use* (pp. 295–317). Orlando, FL: Academic Press.

Prochaska, J. O., DiClemente, C. C., & Norcross, J. C. (1992). In search of how people change: Applications to addictive behaviors. *American Psychologist, 47,* 1102–1114.

Regier, D. A., Farmer, M. E., Rae, D. S., Locke, B. Z., Keith, S. J., Judd, L. L., & Goodwin, F. K. (1990). Comorbidity of mental disorders with alcohol and other drug abuse: Results from the Epidemiologic Catchment Area (ECA) Study. *Journal of the American Medical Association, 264,* 2511–2518.

Revell, A. D., Warburton, D. M., & Wesnes, K. (1985). Smoking as a coping strategy. *Addictive Behaviors, 10,* 209–224.

Robins, L. N., & Przybeck, T. R. (1985). Age of onset of drug use as a factor in drug and other disorders. In C. L. Jones & R. J. Battjes (Eds.), *Etiology of drug abuse* (DHHS Publication No. ADM 87–1335, pp. 178–192). Rockville, MD: National Institute on Drug Abuse.

Rohde, P., Lewinsohn, P. M., Tilson, M., & Seeley, J. R. (1990). Dimensionality of coping and its relation to depression. *Journal of Personality and Social Psychology, 58,* 499–511.

Roth, S., & Cohen, L. J. (1986). Approach, avoidance, and coping with stress. *American Psychologist, 41,* 813–819.

Russell, M. (1990). Prevalence of alcoholism among children of alcoholics. In M. Windle & J. S. Searles (Eds.), *Children of alcoholics: Critical perspectives* (pp. 9–38). New York: Guilford.

Sanchez-Craig, M., Annis, H. M., Bornet, A. R., & MacDonald, K. R. (1984). Evaluation of a cognitive-behavioral program for problem drinkers. *Journal of Consulting and Clinical Psychology, 52,* 390–403.

Seracini, A. M., Siegel, L. J., Wills, T. A., Nunes, E. V., & Goldstein, R. B. (1995, August). *Coping, social support, and adjustment in children of heroin addicts.* Paper presented at the meeting of the American Psychological Association, New York, NY.

Shadel, W. G., & Mermelstein, R. J. (1993). Cigarette smoking under stress: The role of coping expectancies among smokers in a clinic-based smoking cessation program. *Health Psychology, 12,* 443–450.

Shiffman, S. (1982). Relapse following smoking cessation: A situational analysis. *Journal of Consulting and Clinical Psychology, 50,* 71–86.

Shiffman, S. (1985). Coping with temptations to smoke. In S. Shiffman & T. A. Wills (Eds.), *Coping and substance use* (pp. 223–242). Orlando, FL: Academic Press.

Shiffman, S., Abrams, D. B., Cohen, S., Garvey, A., Grunberg, N. E., & Swan, G. E. (1986). Models of smoking relapse. *Health Psychology, 5*(Suppl. 1), 13–27.

Stacy, A. W., Newcomb, M. D., & Bentler, P. M. (1991). Cognitive motivation and drug use: A 9-year longitudinal study. *Journal of Abnormal Psychology, 100,* 502–515.

Stall, R., Ekstrand, M., Pollack, L., McKusick, L., & Coates, T. J. (1990). Relapse from safer sex: The next challenge for AIDS prevention efforts. *Journal of AIDS, 3,* 1181–1187.

Steele, C. M., & Josephs, R. A. (1990). Alcohol myopia: Its prized and dangerous effects. *American Psychologist, 45,* 921–933.

Stevens, V. J., & Hollis, J. F. (1989). Preventing smoking relapse using an individually tailored skills-training technique. *Journal of Consulting and Clinical Psychology, 57,* 420–424.

Stone, A. A., Kennedy-Moore, E., Newman, M. G., Greenberg, M., & Neale, J. M. (1992). Conceptual and methodological issues in current coping assessments (pp. 15–29). In B. N. Carpenter (Ed.), *Personal coping: Theory, research and application.* Westport, CT: Praeger.

Suls, J., & Fletcher, B. (1985). The relative efficacy of avoidant and non-avoidant coping strategies. *Health Psychology, 4,* 249–288.

Sussman, S., Brannon, B. R., Dent, C. W., Hansen, W. B., Johnson, C. A., & Flay, B. R. (1993). Relations of coping effort, perceived stress, and cigarette smoking among adolescents. *International Journal of the Addictions, 28,* 599–612.

Sussman, S., Dent, C. W., Stacy, A. W., Sun, P., Craig, S., Simon, T. R., Burton, D., & Flay, B. R. (1993). Project Towards No Tobacco Use: One-year behavior outcomes. *American Journal of Public Health, 83,* 1245–1250.

Swaim, R. C., Oetting, E. R., Edwards, R. W., & Beauvais, F. (1989). Links from emotional distress to adolescent drug use: A path model. *Journal of Consulting and Clinical Psychology, 57,* 227–231.

Swan, G. E., Denk, C. E., Parker, S. D., Carmelli, D., Furze, C. T., & Rosenman, R. H. (1988). Risk factors for late relapse in male and female ex-smokers. *Addictive Behaviors, 13,* 253–266.

Tarter, R. E. (1988). Are there inherited behavioral traits that predispose to substance abuse? *Journal of Consulting and Clinical Psychology, 56,* 189–196.

Tarter, R. E., Moss, H. B., & Vanyukov, M. M. (1995). Behavior genetic perspective of alcoholism etiology. In H. Begleiter & B. Kissin (Eds.), *Alcohol and alcoholism* (Vol. 1, pp. 294–326). New York: Oxford University Press.

Timmer, S. G., Veroff, J., & Colten, M. E. (1985). Life stress, helplessness, and use of alcohol and drugs to cope. In S. Shiffman & T. A. Wills (Eds.), *Coping and substance use* (pp. 171–198). Orlando, FL: Academic Press.

U.S. Department of Health and Human Services. (1988). *Surgeon General's report on health consequences of smoking: Nicotine addiction* (DHHS Publication No. CDC 88–8406, pp. 394–413). Washington, DC: U.S. Government Printing Office.

Wills, T. A. (1986). Stress and coping in early adolescence: Relationships to substance use in urban school samples. *Health Psychology, 5,* 503–529.

Wills, T. A. (1990). Stress and coping factors in the epidemiology of substance use. In L. T. Kozlowski, H. M. Annis, H. D. Cappell, F. B. Glaser, M. S. Goodstadt, Y. Israel, H. Kalant, E. M. Sellers, & E. R. Vingillis (Eds.), *Research advances in alcohol and drug problems* (Vol. 10, pp. 215–250). New York: Plenum.

Wills, T. A. (in press). Coping relates to important external criteria. In T. Pickering (Ed.), *Concepts and controversies in behavior medicine.* Hillsdale, NJ: Erlbaum.

Wills, T. A., & Cleary, S. D. (1995). Stress-coping model for alcohol/tobacco interactions in adolescence. In J. Fertig & J. Allen (Eds.), *Alcohol and tobacco: From basic science to policy.* Rockville, MD: National Institute on Alcohol Abuse and Alcoholism.

Wills, T. A., & Filer, M. (in press). Stress-coping model of adolescent behavior problems. In T. H. Ollendick & R. J. Prinz (Eds.), *Advances in clinical child psychology* (Vol. 18). New York: Plenum.

Wills, T. A., McNamara, G., & Vaccaro, D. (1995). *Parental education related to adolescent stress-coping and substance use. Health Psychology, 14,* 464–478.

Wills, T. A., McNamara, G., Vaccaro, D., & Hirky, A. E. (1995). *Coping and substance use: Relationships over time in a community sample of adolescents.* Manuscript submitted for publication.

Wills, T. A., & Shiffman, S. (1985). Coping and substance use: A conceptual framework. In S. Shiffman & T. A. Wills (Eds.), *Coping and substance use* (pp. 3–24). Orlando, FL: Academic Press.

Wills, T. A., Vaccaro, D., & McNamara, G. (1992). The role of life events, family support, and competence in adolescent substance use: A test of vulnerability and protective factors. *American Journal of Community Psychology, 20,* 349–374.

Wills, T. A., Vaccaro, D., McNamara, G., & DuHamel, D. (1992, August). *Coping and substance use among urban adolescents.* Paper presented at the meeting of the American Psychological Association, Washington, DC.

Wilsnack, S. C., Klassen, A. D., Schur, B. E., & Wilsnack, R. W. (1991). Predicting onset and chronicity of women's problem drinking: Five-year longitudinal analysis. *American Journal of Public Health, 81,* 305–318.

Zucker, R. A. (1993). Pathways to alcohol problems and alcoholism: A developmental account of the evidence for multiple alcoholisms and contextual contributions to risk. In R. A. Zucker, J. Howard, & G. M. Boyd (Eds.), *The development of alcohol problems* (pp. 255–289). Rockville, MD: National Institute on Alcohol Abuse and Alcoholism.

CHAPTER 14

Coping with Unusual Stressors: Criminal Victimization

IRENE HANSON FRIEZE and JAMILA BOOKWALA

No matter how well a person copes with the everyday events in life, he or she may be confronted with an unusual or traumatic stressor. It could be a criminal act committed against the person, a serious accident, or a natural disaster. Such events are unexpected and stressful. Typically, they are one-time events occurring within a limited time period although those who suffer from violence from another family member may experience repeated victimization over many years. In this chapter, we focus on those unexpected traumatic events. Other chapters address problems associated with community disasters and other shared traumatic events, so these are not discussed in detail in this chapter. Our particular concern is the reactions of those who are suddenly victimized by the negative and intentional acts of another person or group of people. We examine the psychological reactions to such victimization and the types of coping mechanisms typically employed by these victims. We also briefly examine therapeutic implications of the issues discussed in the chapter. In addressing such questions, we center our attention on the criminal victim.

REACTIONS TO TRAUMATIC VICTIMIZATION

Researchers have studied the reactions of victims of rape, burglary, domestic violence, and robbery, as well as those of victims of other traumatic events, and have found surprising commonality in their reactions (Figley, 1985; Frieze, Hymer, & Greenberg, 1987). First, there is an immediate emotional reaction that may take the form of denial, disbelief, numbness, or disorientation (Maguire, 1980; Symonds, 1976; Veronen, Kilpatrick, & Resick, 1979). After the initial shock, victims might experience any of a variety of emotions including anxiety, helplessness, and psychosomatic symptoms (Krupnik, 1980). These are typically labeled as short-term reactions.

After this initial reaction ends, other reactions appear and change over time. In many cases, symptoms disappear quickly. Leymann (1985) found that for a large sample of bank clerks involved in a bank robbery, all symptoms had disappeared in the large majority within 3 weeks. For many types of traumatic victimization, reactions diminish gradually within 6 months; but for others, they may persist for years or even a lifetime.

Evidence for quite long-term effects is seen in a variety of studies (e.g., Sales, Baum, & Shore, 1984). In a study of psychiatric patients, Carmen, Rieker, and Mills (1984) found that half of them had histories of physical or sexual abuse, most often from family members. Thus, Carmen et al. argue that the effects of family violence can cause lifetime disruption in the victims. Other types of victimization can also have severe consequences, as demonstrated by Kilpatrick et al. (1985). In a random telephone survey of over 2,000 women, Kilpatrick and his colleagues found that overall, victims of rape, sexual molestation, robbery, or aggravated assault were more likely to have had a nervous breakdown and to have attempted suicide than those who had never been victimized by these criminal acts. About half of the sample reported being a crime victim at least once. Rape experiences were the most traumatic of the crimes studied in this research.

Many researchers have argued for a stage model of reactions (e.g., Bard & Sangrey, 1986; Burgess & Holmstrom, 1979), but empirical evidence for clearly defined stages is difficult to find (Silver & Wortman, 1980). It appears that there are wide individual differences in the specific symptoms and the order in which they are experienced by victims of trauma. There are some commonalities, however, no matter what the source of the traumatic stress. Psychiatrists have labeled such reactions as posttraumatic stress disorder (PTSD), which is a formal diagnostic category in the DSM-III (American Psychiatric Association [APA], 1994). The criteria include:

1. Existence of an external stressor that would evoke anxiety symptoms in everyone.

2. Reexperiencing of the trauma via memories or dreams.

3. Numbing of responsiveness demonstrable by feelings of detachment from others, constricted affect, or diminished interest in significant activities.

4. At least two of the following symptoms absent before the trauma: (a) exaggerated startle response; (b) sleep disturbance; (c) guilt; (d) memory impairment or trouble concentrating; (e) phobias about activities triggering recollection of the event; (f) intensification of symptoms via exposure to events associated symbolically or in actuality with the traumatic event.

EXPLAINING THE REACTIONS OF TRAUMA VICTIMS

Any of the traumatic events being discussed here involve some type of physical loss (of property) or injury, or both. Rapes, for example, are often associated with varying degrees of injury for the victim (Burt & Katz, 1985). Property loss is central to many crimes as well. But, in many cases, the reactions of the victims of such events appear to be much more severe than one might expect based on what was lost or the level of physical injury. The psychological injury appears to be as important, if not more important, than the physical injury.

In general, people perceive themselves as indestructible and invulnerable to victimization (Janoff-Bulman, 1992; Perloff, 1983). Perloff described this perception as a person's belief in his or her own "unique invulnerability" (p. 42). We do not expect to be in accidents or to have our homes robbed or to be the victims of drive-by shootings. According to Janoff-Bulman (1992), our feelings of invulnerability stem from our "fundamental assumptions." These are internal representations that form the core of our conceptual system and reflect and guide our interactions in the world. There are three fundamental assumptions:

1. The world is a benevolent place (there is a preponderance of positive outcomes over negative ones).
2. The world is meaningful (we directly control what happens to us through our own actions, a belief stemming from a perception of self-outcome contingency).
3. The self is worthy.

These assumptions are partly illusory, and as such, they operate on an illusion of invulnerability or unrealistic optimism (Taylor, 1989).

In some ways, such illusions are especially surprising in the realm of crime because we are so often confronted with images of crime victims in the media. Heath (1984) found that newspaper reports of crime were especially likely to raise fears about being a crime victim if the crimes occurred locally and appeared to be random. Hearing about friends and neighbors who have been robbed or had other crime experiences is also likely to raise one's own fear of crime (Tyler, 1984).

Because most of us are exposed to evidence that we may not be safe and invulnerable and that we too could become crime victims, how do we maintain beliefs in our own invulnerability? Janoff-Bulman (1992) argues that a basic tendency to maintain our beliefs against conflicting information is one explanation. Another explanation is that we arrange our lives in ways that keep us out of danger. Even in situations of potential danger, many people have developed rules for use in their daily lives that they feel will keep them safe. Scheppele and Bart (1983) describe such rules used by women to avoid being raped. Other rules used by men and women may include avoiding areas they feel are dangerous. Perhaps because of this, individual levels of fear of crime are unrelated to the general crime rate (Tyler, 1984).

The general tendency to feel safe and invulnerable does not apply to everyone, though. Several groups of people, often those with the fewest resources and the least ability to control their lives, feel vulnerable to crime. These include the elderly, ethnic minorities, and women (Normoyle & Lavrakas, 1984; Riger & Gordon, 1981). In response to such fears, women may not go out alone or after dark, and may become isolated in their homes (Riger & Gordon, 1981). In such cases, personal safety rules may become maladaptive.

Given the widespread beliefs in our invulnerability, when people do become victims, they must cope not only with the direct consequences of whatever has happened, but also with threats to the loss of their belief in invulnerability. Thus, crime victims "feel humiliated, depressed, angry and vengeful in response to what [has] happened to them . . . and fearful and anxious about what [might] happen to them in the future" (Greenberg, Ruback, & Westcott, 1983, p. 86). Those who have become victims fear that it could happen again (Friedman, Bischoff, Davis, & Person, 1982; Stinchcombe et al., 1980). For example, Stinchcombe et al. (1980) noted that people who have been previously robbed are more likely to report being afraid of crime than are their neighbors. Interviews with victims of crime in New York City revealed that 48% were fearful of future victimization (Friedman, Bischoff, Davis, & Person, 1982). This may be a result of the experience of victimization being more "available" (Vitelli & Endler, 1993). If one is able to easily visualize being a victim because of personal experience or exposure to media images of victims, the idea of victimization is said to be more cognitively available or readily called to mind. Fears about the future can also result from the knowledge that personal safety rules have failed (Scheppele & Bart, 1983). Victims may now see themselves as living in a less safe world, and, more important, become painfully aware of their own mortality. Victims of crime and other negative events can no longer assume that they have control over negative outcomes or that they will reap benefits because they are "good" individuals. Janoff-Bulman (1992) expounds that victims must deal with a double dose of anxiety associated, first, with the realization that their survival is no longer secure and, second, with the survival of their disintegrated conceptual system resulting from shattered fundamental assumptions.

Research has indicated that victimization does not always lead to shattered assumptions. At least for certain types of traumatic events, people may be able to protect against such destruction by seeing their potential vulnerability as more limited. In one demonstration of this, university students who experienced the 1989 California earthquake showed no loss of feelings of invulnerability to a heart attack, divorce, mugging, or a nervous breakdown 3 days after the earthquake. However, they saw themselves as vulnerable to being seriously hurt in a natural disaster such as an earthquake 3 days and 3 months after their personal experience with this event (Burger & Palmer, 1992). Such ability to compartmentalize fears may also be related to a more general pattern of separating feelings of control into various components. Bryant (1989) factor analyzed ratings of control, finding four distinct aspects—the ability to avoid negative outcomes; cope with negative outcomes; obtain positive outcomes; and savor positive outcomes. Feelings of vulnerability (and low self-esteem) were found to be especially related to the person's perceptions of being able to avoid bad things and secondarily to the sense of being able to cope with bad things. Perceived control over positive events was not related to vulnerability.

COPING WITH TRAUMATIC VICTIMIZATION

Even though most survivors, regardless of type of victimization, feel more vulnerable, the effects of lack of control or feelings of helplessness following a traumatic event present only one side of the picture (Kleber & Brom, 1992). Victims often actively attempt to regain control over the situation to battle the feelings of helplessness. Such control may be cognitive or behavioral. Regaining a sense of control is essential to mental health (Thompson & Spacapan, 1991).

Cognitive Coping Strategies

Denial of the Traumatic Event

As already discussed, people tend to have ideas about the world and the events in their lives that are relatively stable and resistant to change (Janoff-Bulman, 1992). As new information is made available, it tends to be assimilated into these existing belief systems. However, events that are too inconsistent to be incorporated into one's knowledge structures may be dealt with in some other way. One mechanism commonly used to cope with highly discrepant information is denial or developing an alternative interpretation of the negative event (Janoff-Bulman & Timko, 1987). Even though traditionally, denial has been viewed as a maladaptive coping strategy because it interferes with the accurate interpretation of reality, some researchers propose that denial can be adaptive in protecting the victim from being too overwhelmed by the event (Horowitz, 1983; Janoff-Bulman & Timko, 1987). Positive aspects of denial are most likely when it occurs immediately following the traumatic event and is short-lived. For example, for victims of crime, denial has been found to be an essential part of the healing process soon after the victimization (Bard & Sangrey, 1986).

For the victim of a traumatic event, outright denial may be very difficult. But there is evidence that a person can minimize what happened by denying its true nature. Bard and Sangrey (1986) report that, in such circumstances, denial can take a hyperactive form (e.g., throwing oneself into an activity unrelated to the crime and thus, appearing constantly busy) or emotional detachment and apathy. Still other victims may cognitively deny the severity of the crime. For example, Scheppele and Bart (1983) report that some of the women, according to legal definitions, who had been raped, perceived themselves as having escaped rape because they had been penetrated anally or with an object. Similarly, far more battered women are willing to describe themselves as being "forced to have sex" than as being "raped" by their husbands (Frieze, 1983).

Other research with college students shows a similar trend to deny one's status as a victim. After reporting that they had experienced at least one of the events typically studied by victimization researchers, the students were asked if they considered themselves "a victim." Many said "no," citing explanations such as "I didn't consider it a very severe thing" or "Because I felt partly responsible" or

"I just had my purse stolen. It could happen to anyone and besides in a way it was my fault for being so careless" (Frieze, 1985).

Redefinitions of the Event

Lazarus and Folkman (1984) have emphasized the fundamental importance of people's appraisal of an event in determining their stress reactions. Whether an individual perceives himself or herself as a victim depends on the cognitive appraisal of the event, which in turn serves to minimize, maximize, or nullify the situation as an instance of victimization. Lazarus and Folkman (1984) distinguish between two types of appraisal, one involving evaluations about whether the person is being threatened (primary appraisal), the other involving judgments about the alternatives and resources the person has access to in managing the potential harm (secondary appraisal). According to this cognitive-affective approach, whether the person is a victim depends largely on whether he or she cognitively evaluates the situation as a harmful stressor. Thus, although one individual who is raped might experience posttraumatic symptoms, another might perceive herself as fortunate to have escaped further harm or death (e.g., Scheppele & Bart, 1983).

According to Janoff-Bulman (1992), a third type of appraisal process becomes evident in the case of traumatic events. This process becomes apparent not during the initial confrontation with the negative event (as do primary and secondary appraisal), but instead represents the reinterpretation and redefinition of the event over the course of coping and adjustment. These cognitive strategies contribute to the difficult process of rebuilding the victim's shattered inner world by maximizing the possibility of perceiving, once again, benevolence in the world, meaningfulness, and self-worth. Such strategies include comparing oneself with others (either real or imagined, especially victims), interpreting one's own role in the victimization, and reinterpreting the negative event in terms of benefits and purpose.

Victims' cognitive reinterpretation can take the form of reinterpreting the negative event itself, their own coping capacities, or the negative emotions arising from the trauma (Houston, 1987). For example, victims of sexual assault may cope with the trauma by perceiving the assault to be less severe than it actually was or by overassessing their capacity to cope with the assault. Indeed, the latter may facilitate positive reinterpretation of attack as well as lessen their conception of personal responsibility for the assault. Factors that can facilitate such reinterpretation include seeking the company of others who think similarly about the event, convincing others of the reinterpretation, gathering evidence to support the reinterpretation, or the less useful behavioral mechanisms of alcohol and drug abuse (Houston, 1987).

Taylor (1989) also asserts that victims of negative events such as life-threatening attacks, illness, and natural disasters engage in systematic and selective perceptions and evaluations that help them to control their view of themselves as victims. This may be done by comparing their trauma and its effects to what could have been ("it could always be worse") or engaging in downward social comparisons, especially comparisons with less fortunate others. Downward social comparisons have a self-enhancing quality and are conducive to subjective well-being. For example, Burgess and Holmstrom (1979) found that rape victims often make downward comparisons. Comparing herself to another victim who suffered even more than she did enables the victim to rebuild her self-esteem. And self-esteem has been found to be critical in the process of coping with rape because higher levels of self-esteem are related to a shorter time to recovery. Alternatively, rape victims have been found to note that they could have been killed or subjected to even more humiliating circumstances than did occur (Burgess & Holmstrom, 1979).

Other mechanisms of coping through downward social comparisons include selective abstraction of positive attributes (e.g., a victim of rape may overrecall her positive attributes and underrecall her negative ones), selective focus or target choice (e.g., a victim of a mugging incident may compare himself or herself to a target of a brutal mugging so as to provide a favorable self-comparison), or derogation of others (Wills, 1987a). Thus, strategically constructed social comparisons are useful coping mechanisms because they enable the victim to perceive the self as strong and capable enough to deal with an extreme situation and to redefine the situation as less tragic (Janoff-Bulman, 1992). However, Greenberg, Ruback, and Westcott (1982) warn that such downward comparisons can be maladaptive when the victim's stress derives from feelings of being vulnerable to future victimization.

People can also minimize victimization by engaging in a "search for meaning" that involves, reconstructing the event as one resulting in personal growth or some other benefit (Taylor, 1989). For example, Taylor cited a woman who had been severely beaten, shot in the head, and left to die, but who survived and was able to describe in a newspaper interview how the assault had led to a "joyful reconciliation with her mother" (p. 32). Such searches for meaning often evolve around religious themes. Others feel that their experiences have made them stronger people. Many victims are unable to find such meaning and experience recurrent thoughts about "Why me?" throughout their lives.

Self-Blame

When people are victimized, they begin to ask, either during the crime or shortly thereafter, "Why me?" or "What did I do to provoke this attack?" (Bard & Sangrey, 1986; Katz & Burt, 1988). Self-blaming and further attribution of the victimization to enduring and pervasive factors within the self is likely to result in hopelessness about the future. Nevertheless, many victims tend to blame themselves for their victimization (Janoff-Bulman & Lang-Gunn, 1988; Katz & Burt, 1988; Wortman, 1976). For example, victims of unprovoked sexual assaults or of battering have been found to take personal responsibility for the crime (Frieze, 1979; Janoff-Bulman, 1979; Wyatt, Notgrass, & Newcomb, 1990). However, these feelings of personal responsibility tend to diminish over time (Katz & Burt, 1988).

Attribution theory would suggest that self-blame would be maladaptive for the victim's recovery. In general, taking responsibility for negative events is associated with more negative affect (Weiner, 1979). Consistent with what the theory would predict, research has demonstrated that self-blame is associated with post-rape depression and rape victims' negative initial and lasting attitudes toward sex and intimacy (Wyatt et al., 1990). Negative effects were also obtained by Katz and Burt (1988), who found self-blame immediately following rape to be associated with higher levels of psychological distress and lower levels of self-esteem. In addition, self-blaming rape victims reported spending more hours of counseling after the rape and felt it took longer for them to "recover" from the trauma.

In contrast, Janoff-Bulman (1979, 1992) proposes that self-blame can be quite functional. She distinguishes between characterological self-blame (esteem-related and focused on the person's character or enduring qualities) and behavioral self-blame (control-related and focused on one's own behavior—acts or omissions one believes causally contributed to the outcome). According to Janoff-Bulman, behavioral self-blame, especially in the absence of characterological self-blame, may be adaptive for the victim's coping and recovery.

Janoff-Bulman (1979) found that rape victims who made characterological attributions saw their victimization as more deserved, whereas rape victims who attributed their rapes to behavioral factors were more confident about avoiding future rapes. In addition, behavioral self-blame has been found to be associated with high self-esteem and the perception of the avoidability of subsequent victimization (Janoff-Bulman, 1992).

More recent research, however, has failed to replicate the association between behavioral self-blame by victims and adaptive outcomes. In one study, both behavioral and characterological self blame were associated with more depression after victimization (Frazier, 1990). A similar failure to demonstrate positive effects of self blame was found for rape victims, where it was found that all forms of self blame were associated with poorer postrape adjustment (Meyer & Taylor, 1986). Abbey (1987) argues that those victims who feel responsible for rapes may dwell on the circumstances of the rape and what they might have done differently. By focusing on these issues, it may be difficult for victims to resolve their feelings about what happened and move on to other concerns. It may also be true that those victims who are most depressed would be more likely to blame themselves. Thus, the causal direction of these relationships is not entirely clear.

The effects of self-blame may also depend on the victims' personalities and their resources or abilities to change the circumstances of their lives. McCann and Pearlman (1990) suggest that self-blame may be functional for individuals with strong resources and capacities, who have high needs for independence. Conversely, self-blaming attributions are likely to be destructive for persons with impaired capacities for affect regulation and low self-concept.

There may also be a distinction between the answer to the question, "Why me?" and self-blame (Abbey, 1987). In a qualitative study of rape victims, Abbey found that nearly all could explain why they had been raped (typically interpreted as "self-blame"). Answers cited being in the wrong place, not having an alarm system, or being a different type of person. Such answers, because they refer to aspects of the victim that may have contributed to the crime, are normally classified as self-blame (Frieze, 1979). But, when asked in the research reported by

Abbey if they were responsible or their assailant was, the modal response was that the assailant was [totally] responsible. Thus, these victims may not have been thinking of their responses as indicative of self-blame, even though they were classified in that way.

Behavioral Coping Strategies

Most people take some action after being victimized. They may seek to change their behavior on their own, or they may seek out other people to help them. This section discusses some of these strategies.

Informal Sources of Assistance: Self-Help

Janoff-Bulman (1992) suggests that victims may respond to the challenge of regaining control by immersing themselves vigorously into life's activities. For example, a victim may deliberately implement changes in his or her life (e.g., relocation to new place, a change of career, a new home security system). Such actions may convey to victims quite concretely that once again they have control over the activities and events in their lives. Indeed, one study reports that the use of locks by adults who had recently experienced a crime buffered the effects of fear of crime on generalized distress (Norris & Kaniasty, 1992). A common strategy for first-time victims of a crime is to do things that will increase their personal safety and rebuild a sense of invulnerability (Kidder & Cohn, 1979; Lavrakas, 1981). For example, rape victims reported becoming more vigilant in scanning their environment and generally becoming more cautious (Scheppele & Bart, 1983). Those whose homes have been robbed may install burglar alarm systems, extra locks, window bars, outdoor lighting, or purchase a dog (Conklin, 1975).

Other strategies may be more extreme. Moving to a new residence or changing telephone numbers are common reactions of rape victims (Burgess & Holmstrom, 1979). Avoidance of social contact and staying home rather than going out whenever possible have also been reported strategies used by rape victims (Scheppele & Bart, 1983) and by elderly crime victims (Friedman et al., 1982). Although apparently intended as safety measures, such responses may not reduce feelings of vulnerability or fears of future victimization (Kidder & Cohn, 1979). As noted earlier, fear of crime can cause people to behave in such ways even before ever being personally victimized. Such behavior in response to fear is associated with feelings of vulnerability and continuing fear (Burt & Katz, 1985).

Other strategies appear to be directed at anger rather than fear reactions in victims. It is not uncommon for a victim to retaliate against an assailant at a later time (Frieze & Browne, 1989). There is also evidence that youthful victims of property crimes who don't know their victimizer may react by stealing from others (Van Dijk & Steinmetz, 1979). Such responses to frustration have been labeled as "reactance" and appear to be an alternative to feelings of helplessness (Wortman, 1976).

Finally, although there is little, if any, research on this, people may try to resolve their feelings by reading one of the many self-help books available. Bard and Sangrey's (1986), *The Crime Victim's Book* is an example of such a book. Advice may also be sought on a face-to-face basis, the topic of the next section.

Informal Sources of Assistance Family and Friends

Positive social support after victimization is very important to the traumatized victim (Cobb, 1976; Silver & Wortman, 1980). Family members and friends appear to help victims in several ways (Frieze et al., 1987). First, by being available to talk with the person after the event, they allow the victim to express emotions. Having companions and being able to disclose one's feelings about the event have been found to be highly important for successful coping (Greenberg & Stone, 1992; Pennebaker & Beall, 1986). Family and friends can also provide affirmation of self-worth. The need for this type of outlet for emotions may continue for months or even years. A second form of support is to assist the victim in thinking through what should be done (Hirsch, 1980). Tangible help is also provided by others.

As necessary and important as support can be for the victim, it is not always readily available. In general, people who are more comfortable receiving help, higher in self-esteem, and more religious are more likely to receive help from others in dealing with any type of stress (Dunkel-Schetter, Folkman, & Lazarus, 1987). But, social support for victims of trauma presents special problems. Others may avoid interacting with victims because they don't want to deal with their depression or upset. Another difficulty in receiving needed social support is the negative stigma that is so often attached to the crime victim or the victim of some other traumatic event. People in general have the same initial assumptions about the world that were described earlier for the victim him- or herself. They believe that bad things happen to bad people and that people should be able to control their lives so that they are safe. Hence, others may blame the victims for their fate or see them as somehow responsible (e.g., Lerner, 1980; Ryan, 1971). Or, if they do come into contact with a recent victim, they may express these negative beliefs, causing further trauma for the victim. Symonds (1980) has labeled this all-too-often occurrence as the "second injury"—this harm can be caused by friends and family, as well as by institutional helpgivers.

Female victims of male aggression may have particular difficulties in receiving social support because of the high degree of societal blame attributed to these women (Frieze, 1987; Frieze & Browne, 1989). And, male rape victims may be even more stigmatized because the rape victim is so often assumed to be female. Even for victims of disasters, those who blame themselves are less likely to seek help from others (Solomon, Regier, & Burke, 1989).

Formal Helpgivers

In addition to informal sources of help, crime victims can obtain aid from formal helpers who provide psychotherapy and the criminal justice system. Many crimes are reported to the police. In general, the more serious the crime, the more likely it is to be reported (Bureau of Justice Statistics, 1985).

Notification of the police can serve the victim in several ways (Greenberg, Ruback, & Westcott, 1983). If the offender is caught and punished for the crime, this can reduce the victim's sense of injustice and can reestablish the victim's sense of control and feelings of safety. But, many crime victims do not report the crimes to the police. Two frequently cited reasons for not doing so are the belief that "nothing can be done" or that "the police would not want to be bothered" (Bureau of Justice Statistics, 1985). As a general rule, people prefer informal sources of help when dealing with any traumatic event (Wills, 1987b).

Victims may also resist calling the police if they do not want to become involved with the criminal justice system. Being forced to undergo long interviews about the circumstances of the crime can be stressful. And, if the offender is caught and brought to trial, the victim must relive the experience while testifying at the trial. Such legal processes can lead to a number of negative symptoms, long after achievement of the initial recovery (Sales et al., 1984).

Comparing Different Traumatic Events

Although we have been combining all types of trauma victims in this discussion, not all reactions are the same. One of the important determinants of the level of psychological trauma appears to be the level of threat to one's life (Sales et al., 1984; Wilson, Smith, & Johnson, 1985). A related finding was that the level of violence determined the level of stress in a sample of battered women (Mitchell & Hodson, 1983). Green (1990) mentions threats to one's life and also lists severe physical harm or injury and the receipt of intentional harm or injury from another person as key criteria for something to be labeled as "traumatic." All of these are often associated with criminal victimization. Green also describes other definitions of "trauma" that would apply to events described in other chapters of this book: exposure to others who are dead, injured, or mutilated; the sudden loss of a loved one; witnessing or learning about violence done to a loved one; exposure to environmental threats; and causing death or severe harm to someone else.

Another consideration in classifying different types of traumatic events and the reactions to these events is whether the trauma is repeated. For some types of trauma, such as environmental disasters, having previous experience can be predictive of less severe reactions, but this does not appear to apply to victims of crimes (Norris, 1990). Frazier and Borgida (1988) found that having been raped before was one of the strongest predictors of poor outcome among recent rape victims. This is consistent with data reported by Leymann (1985) in a longitudinal study of bank clerks victimized by bank robbers. Repeated involvement in a series of bank robberies resulted in more stress reactions, perhaps because of feelings on the part of these clerks that their lives lacked safety and that nothing would prevent yet another victimization.

Special problems exist for the battered wife or abused child because the victimization is often repeated and the victim is intimately involved with the victimizer

(Miller & Porter, 1983; Silver et al., 1983). In many ways, the reaction of this type of victim is similar to that of the hostage, with feelings of helplessness and fears for the future, and life-threatening injuries (Dutton, 1988). For these victims, basic assumptions are even more fundamentally shaken. A trust in the benevolence of people is especially difficult if the victim's assailant is a loved family member.

Defining Successful Coping

Coping is defined as including responses whose purpose it is to reduce or avoid psychological stress and accompanying negative emotions (Houston, 1987). Such responses may or may not be successful in actually reducing the stress, or they may be successful in the short run but less successful in the long run (or vice versa). Yet, an important issue in the study of coping with negative events is the adaptive value or "success" of various coping processes—are some coping processes more or less effective than others? It is difficult to answer this question conclusively because, in lay terminology, individuals are said to have coped with being raped or assaulted if they have overcome the demands of the situation successfully; to say one did not cope implies ineffectiveness and inadequacy (Lazarus & Folkman, 1991).

Traditionally, direct coping efforts (e.g., seeking information, obtaining support from friends and family) have been viewed as more effective than palliative thoughts or actions whose goal is to relieve the emotional impact of stress (e.g., denial) (Monat & Lazarus, 1991; Lazarus & Folkman, 1991). However, there is growing conviction today that all coping processes, including those traditionally considered inadequate (e.g., denial), have both positive and negative consequences. Monat and Lazarus suggest that the adaptiveness of coping efforts be evaluated after taking into account the diverse levels of analysis (physiological, psychological, and sociological) for which a particular strategy may have implications, the short-term versus long-term consequences of using that strategy, and the specific situation in question. For example, a rape victim's use of denial immediately following the trauma may have adaptive value. Moreover, behavioral withdrawal from the negative situation (relocation following rape) may have psychological gains that are offset by psychosocial losses in the form of lost social support. And, downward social comparisons following a burglary may be less beneficial than those following a rape in alleviating stress. Hence, there is no one "successful" coping process—instead, such judgments must necessarily take the entire context into account. According to Houston (1987), the adaptiveness or maladaptiveness of coping behavior depends on several criteria including how realistic the coping behavior is, how acceptable it is to others, and the short-term and long-term consequences of the effort for other areas of functioning.

These concerns make it especially difficult to know what specific recommendations can be made for assessing successful coping in the trauma victim. Although many would argue that the trauma victim should ideally have a realistic view of the event and should not blame him- or herself for what happened, theory and research does not always support this view (Frieze et al., 1987; Silver & Wortman, 1980). For example, a realistic assessment of the criminal act done to oneself may not be adaptive (Scheppele & Bart, 1983). And, illusions may be quite functional (Taylor, 1989). In cases involving physical injury, however, distorting reality by denying the seriousness of the physical problems may lead to inadequate care and to later complications of the initial injuries (Silver & Wortman, 1980).

THERAPEUTIC IMPLICATIONS

As this chapter has outlined, the victim of crime or other trauma typically experiences both short- and long-term stress reactions. These may disappear quickly, within a matter of hours or days, or they may persist for a lifetime, depending on the level of trauma. In many ways, the traumatic events described in this chapter are no different from other types of stressors (Kasl, 1990). In fact, researchers have recently begun to question the psychiatric posttraumatic stress disorder (PTSD) diagnosis as unnecessary because the reactions to trauma are so similar to those of other stressors (e.g., Breslau, 1990).

Looking at the research on various forms of victimization shows there is much validity in the argument that criminal victimization is no different from other forms of trauma. Studies done of accident and disaster victims show exactly the same types of reactions as discussed in this chapter. But, there are unique aspects to criminal victimization. That the event is intentionally caused by another person gives the criminal victim unique concerns about whether or not other people can be trusted. This would necessarily lead to more fundamental threats to basic assumptions about the world, what Janoff-Bulman labels as the "shattering" of basic beliefs.

The first form of treatment for crime victims is often medical. The physician must look for signs of physical injury and for signs of sexually transmitted disease or pregnancy in cases involving sexual assault. Once these medical needs are taken care of, if symptoms persist and the person's own coping mechanisms are not effective, the victim may then seek psychological counseling. In many cases, this occurs weeks, months, or even years after the victimizing event (Koss & Harvey, 1987). Counseling programs have been most developed for victims of rape (Allison & Wrightsman, 1993). The counseling provided may be one-to-one therapy for these victims, but more often, it is done in self-help groups. Rape crisis centers provide such services in many parts of the United States.

The theoretical and empirical research reviewed in this chapter would suggest that a major goal of counseling would be helping the victim to regain a sense of control and to restore a belief in a safe and benevolent world. A variety of specific techniques could be used to do this. For example, Ledray (1988) evaluated the relative efficacy of two techniques of treatment for rape victims—supportive crisis counseling and goals-oriented counseling. The supportive crisis counseling is widely used. It stresses early intervention and assumes that the individual in crisis is a normal person dealing with an overwhelming crisis. No assumption of underlying psychopathology is made. The counseling goals are oriented toward helping the victim regain control in his or her life. Ledray found that both treatments were effective in reducing symptomatology in rape victims with guidance to goals being somewhat more effective than supportive crisis counseling.

Other therapeutic techniques also work to rebuild assumptions through a variety of supportive activities that resemble the needs sometimes met through informal sources of social support. As Kleber and Brom (1992) argue, not every victim needs specialized therapy, but most would benefit from some form of support and advice. Even though victims of violence may not immediately seek counseling, it can be helpful if they do. For Kleber and Brom, early preventive intervention is the major goal. Helping individuals in an early stage can prevent serious disorders in a later period. Psychological interventions can be provided in different ways at different times in the recovery process. They identified three separate goals of assistance after serious life events: stimulating a healthy process of coping, early recognition of disorders, and providing group or individual assistance. As this chapter has discussed, the victim of violence often has immediate, highly distressed emotional reactions to the event. It may be difficult for the person to return to normal functioning. The first goal of intervention is to return the individual to a stable level of functioning. This can be achieved by providing practical and helpful information (e.g., referrals to specialized institutions, answers to medical questions, information about the process of coping, and the kind of help that can be expected). Another early intervention is to provide support after the serious event to create a safe and quiet environment that enables the victim to realize the trauma is really over. This will provide opportunities for reality testing and permit the coping process to begin. A second goal is to determine if the victim will have special needs. Finally, the counselor can provide more direct therapeutic assistance either in individual or in group counseling.

In looking at interventions for victims, many researchers and therapists or counselors who work with these victims argue that the real need is for prevention rather than for treatment. Within the literature on rape, in particular, there is much concern about stopping rapes from happening in the first place. A number of programs have been designed for this purpose (Koss & Harvey, 1987). Another approach is to teach self-defense to the potential victim so that he or she can fight back and prevent the crime from being carried out. Such programs would combat the sometimes debilitating fears of crime discussed earlier. Rozee, Bateman, and Gilmore (1991) suggested a three-tiered, community-based preventive educational program to increase societal responsibility for rape, and to build individual awareness and self-protection. They argue that rape awareness programs on college campuses are needed, along with interventions aimed specifically at behavior change. They also recommend that women examine their "safety rules" in terms of how realistic they are and weigh the safety gained from these rules against quality of life.

FUTURE RESEARCH ON THE PSYCHOLOGY OF VICTIMIZATION

As this review has suggested, there are many things we do not know about victims. Although researchers have identified a number of common reactions to a victimizing event, it is still not clear which of these are more and less functional in terms of recovery from the initial trauma. An important goal of future research would be to develop criteria for determining what an effective coping response would be and then to determine which of the reactions are most and least likely to lead to effective coping.

A second issue concerns the similarities and differences among the various victims of violence and other crimes. In the very early research on crime victims, different types of victims were assessed in separate studies. Once a body of such studies was available, researchers were able to draw similarities across different types of crime victims (e.g., Frieze et al., 1987). This led to some very important theoretical developments. But, perhaps we now need to go back to studies of different types of victims, using the insights gained from the theories developed to explain the reactions of all types of victims. What are the important differences between victims? Are the differences primarily a function of the type of crime? Or, are other variables more important?

REFERENCES

Abbey, A. (1987). Perceptions of personal avoidability versus responsibility: How do they differ? *Basic and Applied Social Psychology, 8,* 3–19.

Allison, J. A., & Wrightsman, L. S. (1993). *Rape: The misunderstood crime.* Newbury Park, CA: Sage.

American Psychiatric Association. (1994). *Diagnostic and statistical manual of mental disorders* (4th ed.). Washington, DC: Author.

Bard, M., & Sangrey, D. (1986). *The crime victim's book* (2nd ed.). New York: Brunner/Mazel.

Bureau of Justice Statistics. (1985). *Reporting crimes to the police.* Washington, DC: U.S. Department of Justice.

Burger, J. M., & Palmer, M. L. (1992). Changes in and generalizations of unrealistic optimism following experiences with stressful events: Reactions to the 1989 California earthquake. *Personality and Social Psychology Bulletin, 18,* 39–43.

Burgess, A. W., & Holmstrom, L. L. (1979). Adaptive strategies and recovery from rape. *American Journal of Psychiatry, 136,* 1278–1282.

Burt, M. R., & Katz, B. L. (1985). Rape, robbery, and burglary: Responses of actual and feared criminal victimization, with special focus on women and the elderly. *Victimology: An International Journal, 10,* 325–358.

Breslau, N. (1990). Stressors: Continuous and discontinuous. *Journal of Applied Social Psychology, 20,* 1666–1673.

Bryant, F. B. (1989). A four-factor model of perceived control: Avoiding, coping, obtaining, and savoring. *Journal of Personality, 57,* 773–797.

Carmen, E. (Hilberman), Rieker, P. P., & Mills, T. (1984). Victims of violence and psychiatric illness. *American Journal of Psychiatry, 141,* 378–383.

Cobb, S. (1976). Social support as a moderator of life stress. *Psychosomatic Medicine, 38,* 300–314.

Conklin, J. E. (1975). *The impact of crime.* New York: Macmillan.

Dunkel-Schetter, C., Folkman, S., & Lazarus, R. S. (1987). Correlates of social support receipt. *Journal of Personality and Social Psychology, 53,* 71–80.

Dutton, D. G. (1988). *The domestic assault of women: Psychological and criminal justice perspectives.* Boston: Allyn and Bacon.

Figley, C. R. (1985). *Trauma and its wake: The study and treatment of post-traumatic stress disorder.* New York: Brunner/Mazel.

Frazier, P. A. (1990). Victim attributions and post-rape trauma. *Journal of Personality and Social Psychology, 59*(2), 298–304.

Frazier, P. A., & Borgida, E. (1988, August). *Multiple victimization experiences in rape victims.* Paper presented at the American Psychological Association Convention, Atlanta, GA.

Friedman, K., Bischoff, H., Davis, R., & Person, A. (1982). *Victims and helpers: Reactions to crime.* New York: Victim Services Agency.

Frieze, I. H. (1979). Perceptions of battered wives. In I. H. Frieze, D. Bar-Tal, & J. S. Carroll (Eds.), *New approaches to social problems: Applications of attribution theory.* San Francisco: Jossey-Bass.

Frieze, I. H. (1983). Investigating the causes and consequences of marital rape. *Signs: Journal of Women in Culture and Society, 8,* 532–553.

Frieze, I. H. (1985, March). *Female and male reactions to potentially victimizing events.* Invited address for the Tenth National Conference of the Association for Women in Psychology, New York.

Frieze, I. H. (1987). The female victim: Rape, wife beating and incest. In G. R. VandenBos & B. K. Bryant (Eds.), *Cataclysms, crises, and catastrophies: Psychology in action* (pp. 109–146). Washington, DC: American Psychological Association.

Frieze, I. H., & Browne, A. (1989). Violence in marriage. In L. Ohlin & M. Tonry (Eds.), *Family violence* (pp. 163–218). Chicago: University of Chicago Press.

Frieze, I. H., Hymer, S., & Greenberg, M. S. (1987). Describing the crime victim: Psychological reactions to victimization. *Professional Psychology: Research and Practice, 18*(4), 299–315.

Green, B. L. (1990). Defining trauma: Terminology and generic stressor dimensions. *Journal of Applied Social Psychology, 20,* 1632–1642.

Greenberg, M. A., & Stone, A. A. (1992). Emotional disclosure about traumas and its relation to health: Effects of previous disclosure and trauma severity. *Journal of Personality and Social Psychology, 63,* 75–84.

Greenberg, M. S., Ruback, R. B., & Westcott, D. R. (1982). Decision-making by crime victims: A multimethod approach. *Law & Society Review, 17,* 47–84.

Greenberg, M. S., Ruback, R. B., & Westcott, D. R. (1983). Seeking help from the police: The victim's perspective. In A. Nadler, J. D. Fisher, & B. DePaulo (Eds.),

Applied perspectives on help-seeking and receiving (pp. 71–103). New York: Academic Press.

Heath, L. (1984). Impact of newspaper crime reports on fear of crime: Multimethodological investigation. *Journal of Personality and Social Psychology, 47,* 263–276.

Hirsch, B. J. (1980). Natural support systems and coping with major life changes. *American Journal of Community Psychology, 8,* 159–172.

Horowitz, M. J. (1983). Psychological response to serious life events. In S. Bresnitz (Ed.), *The denial of stress.* New York: International Universities Press.

Houston, B. K. (1987). Stress and coping. In C. R. Snyder & C. E. Ford (Eds.), *Coping with negative life events* (pp. 373–399). New York: Plenum.

Janoff-Bulman, R. (1979). Characterological versus behavioral self-blame: Inquiries into depression and rape. *Journal of Personality and Social Psychology, 37,* 1798–1809.

Janoff-Bulman, R. (1992). *Shattered assumptions.* New York: Free Press.

Janoff-Bulman, R., & Lang-Gunn, L. (1988). Coping with disease, crime, and accidents: The role of self-blame attributions. In L. Y. Abramson (Ed.), *Social cognition and clinical psychology: A synthesis* (pp. 116–147). New York: Guilford.

Janoff-Bulman, R., & Timko, C. (1987). Coping with traumatic life events: The role of denial in light of people's assumptive worlds. In C. R. Snyder & C. E. Ford (Eds.), *Coping with negative life events* (pp. 135–159). New York: Plenum.

Kasl, S. V. (1990). Some considerations in the study of traumatic stress. *Journal of Applied Social Psychology, 20,* 1655–1665.

Katz, B., & Burt, M. (1988). Self-blame: Help or hindrance in recovery from rape? In A. Burgess (Ed.), *Rape and sexual assault II* (pp. 151–168). New York: Garland.

Kidder, L. H., & Cohn, E. S. (1979). Public views of crime and crime prevention. In I. H. Frieze, D. Bar-Tal, & J. S. Carroll (Eds.), *New approaches to social problems: Applications of attribution theory* (pp. 237–264). San Francisco: Jossey-Bass.

Kilpatrick, D. G., Best, C. L., Veronen, L. J., Maick, A. E., Villeponteaux, L. A., & Ruff, G. A. (1985). Mental health correlates of criminal victimization: A random community survey. *Journal of Consulting and Clinical Psychology, 53,* 866–873.

Kleber, R. J., & Brom, D. (1992). *Coping with trauma: Theory, prevention, and treatment.* Amsterdam: Stwets & Zeitlinger.

Koss, M., & Harvey, M. (1987). *The rape victim: Clinical and community treatment approaches to treatment.* Lexington, MA: Stephen Green Press.

Krupnick, J. (1980). Brief psychotherapy with victims of violent crime. *Victimology: An International Journal, 10,* 376–396.

Lavrakas, P. J. (1981). On households. In D. A. Lewis (Ed.), *Reactions to crime* (pp. 67–85). Beverly Hills, CA: Sage.

Lazarus, R. S., & Folkman, S. (1984). *Stress, appraisal, and coping.* New York: Springer.

Lazarus, R. S., & Folkman, S. (1991). The concept of coping. In A. Monat & R. S. Lazarus (Eds.), *Stress and coping: An anthology* (3rd ed., pp. 189–206). New York: Columbia University Press.

Ledray, L. E. (1988). Responding to the needs of rape victims: Research findings. In A. W. Burgess (Ed.), *Rape and sexual assault II* (pp. 187–190). New York: Garland.

Lerner, M. J. (1980). *The belief in a just world: A fundamental delusion.* New York: Plenum.

Leymann, H. (1985). Somatic and psychological symptoms after the experience of life threatening events: A profile analysis. *Victimology: An International Journal, 10,* 512–538.

Maguire, M. (1980). Impact of burglary upon victims. *British Journal of Criminology, 20,* 261–275.

McCann, I. L., & Pearlman, L. A. (1990). *Psychological trauma and the adult survivor.* New York: Brunner/Mazel.

Miller, D. T., & Porter, C. A. (1983). Self-blame in victims of violence. *Journal of Social Issues, 39*(2), 139–152.

Meyer, C., & Taylor, S. (1986). Adjustment to rape. *Journal of Social and Personality Psychology, 50,* 1226–1234.

Mitchell, R. E., & Hodson, C. A. (1983). Coping with domestic violence: Social support and psychological health among battered women. *American Journal of Community Psychology, 11,* 629–654.

Monat, A., & Lazarus, R. S. (1991). Introduction to stress and coping—Some current issues and controversies. In A. Monat & R. S. Lazarus (Eds.), *Stress and coping: An anthology* (pp. 1–15). New York: Columbia University Press.

Normoyle, J., & Lavrakas, P. J. (1984). Fear of crime in elderly women: Perceptions of control, predictability, and territoriality. *Personality and Social Psychology Bulletin, 10,* 191–202.

Norris, F. H. (1990). Screening for traumatic stress: A scale for use in the general population. Traumatic stress: New perspectives in theory, management, and research [Special issue]. *Journal of Applied Social Psychology, 20*(2), 1704–1718.

Norris, F. H., & Kaniasty, K. (1992). A longitudinal study of the effects of various crime prevention strategies on criminal victimization, fear of crime, and psychological distress. *American Journal of Community Psychology, 20*(5), 625–648.

Pennebaker, J. W., & Beall, S. (1986). Confronting a traumatic event: Toward an understanding of inhibition and disease. *Journal of Abnormal Psychology, 95,* 274–281.

Perloff, L. S. (1983). Perceptions of vulnerability to victimization. *Journal of Social Issues, 39*(2), 41–62.

Riger, S., & Gordon, M. T. (1981). The fear of rape: A study in social control. *Journal of Social Issues, 37*(4), 71–92.

Rozee, P. D., Bateman, P., & Gilmore, T. (1991). The personal perspective of acquaintance rape prevention: A three-tier approach. In A. Parrot & L. Bechhofer (Eds.), *Acquaintance rape: The hidden crime* (pp. 337–354). New York: Wiley.

Ryan, W. (1971). *Blaming the victim.* New York: Vintage Books.

Sales, E., Baum, M., & Shore, B. (1984). Victim readjustment following assault. *Journal of Social Issues, 40*(1), 117–136.

Scheppele, K. L., & Bart, P. B. (1983). Through women's eyes: Defining danger in the wake of sexual assault. *Journal of Social Issues, 40*(1), 27–38.

Silver, R. L., Boon, C., & Stones, M. H. (1983). Searching for meaning in misfortune: Making sense of incest. *Journal of Social Issues, 39*(2), 81–102.

Silver, R. L., & Wortman, C. B. (1980). Coping with undesirable life events. In J. Barber & M. E. P. Seligman (Eds.), *Human helplessness* (pp. 279–375). New York: Academic Press.

Solomon, S. D., Regier, D. A., & Burke, J. D. (1989). Role of perceived control in coping with disaster. *Journal of Social and Clinical Psychology, 8,* 376–392.

Stinchcombe, A. L., Adams, R., Heimer, C. A., Scheppele, K. L., Smith, T. W., & Taylor, D. G. (1980). *Crime and punishment: Changing attitudes in America.* San Francisco: Jossey-Bass.

Symonds, M. (1976). The rape victim: Psychological patterns of response. *American Journal of Psychoanalysis, 35,* 27–34.

Symonds, M. (1980). The "second injury" to victims. *Evaluation and Change,* 36–38.

Taylor, S. E. (1989). *Positive illusions.* New York: Basic Books.

Thompson, S. C., & Spacapan, S. (1991). Perceptions of control in vulnerable populations. *Journal of Social Issues, 47*(4), 1–21.

Tyler, T. R. (1984). Assessing the risk of crime victimization: The integration of personal victimization experience and socially transmitted information. *Journal of Social Issues, 40*(1), 27–38.

Van Dijk, J. J. M., & Steinmetz, C. H. D. (1979). *The RDC Victim Surveys 1974–1979.* The Hague, The Netherlands: Research and Documentation Centre, Ministry of Justice.

Veronen, L. G., Kilpatrick, D. G., & Resick, P. A. (1979). Treating fear and anxiety in rape victims: Implications for the criminal justice system. In W. H. Parsonage (Ed.), *Perspectives on victimology* (Sage Research Progress Series in Criminology, Vol. 11, pp. 148–159). Beverly Hills: Sage.

Vitelli, R., & Endler, N. S. (1993). Psychological determinants of fear of crime: A comparison of general and situational prediction models. *Personality and individual differences, 14,* 77–85.

Weiner, B. (1979). A theory of motivation for some classroom experiences. *Journal of Educational Psychology, 71,* 3–23.

Wills, T. A. (1987a). Downward comparison as a coping mechanism. In C. R. Snyder & C. E. Ford (Eds.), *Coping with negative life events* (pp. 243–368). New York: Plenum.

Wills, T. A. (1987b). Help-seeking as a coping mechanism. In C. R. Snyder & C. E. Ford (Eds.), *Coping with negative life events: Clinical and social psychological perspectives* (pp. 19–50). New York: Plenum.

Wilson, J. P., Smith, W. K., & Johnson, S. K. (1985). A comparative analysis of PTSD among various survivor groups. In C. R. Figley (Ed.), *Trauma and its wake: The study and treatment of post-traumatic stress disorder.* New York: Brunner/Mazel.

Wortman, C. B. (1976). Causal attributions and personal control. In J. H. Harvey, W. J. Ickes, & R. F. Kidd (Eds.), *New directions in attributions research* (Vol. 1, pp. 23–52). Hillsdale, NJ: Erlbaum.

Wyatt, G. E., Notgrass, C. M., & Newcomb, M. (1990). Internal and external mediators of women's rape experiences. *Psychology of Women Quarterly, 14*(2), 153–176.

CHAPTER 15

Coping in Reaction to Extreme Stress: The Roles of Resource Loss and Resource Availability

STEVAN E. HOBFOLL, JOHN R. FREEDY, BONNIE L. GREEN, and
SUSAN D. SOLOMON

Extreme stressors, such as disasters and war, are unlikely to occur to any given individual in any week, month, or year. During the course of people's lives, however, it is inevitable that they will encounter extreme stressors. When extreme
stressors occur, individuals', families', and communities' coping ability will be
severely challenged. This chapter will examine how the resources that underlie
coping are both influenced by extreme stress and how resources set the course for
people's reactions to extreme stress. Research on extreme stressors has tended to
look at the resources that underlie coping behaviors, rather than examining coping
per se. This approach may stem from extreme stress challenging a more basic
level of functioning than coping behavior, or from a flattening effect of extreme
stress, such that differences in ways of coping become less influential and the person's basic ability to survive takes precedence.

Since the 1970s, nearly 200 or more English language articles concerning the
psychological impact of natural and technological disasters have been published
(Blake, Albano, & Keane, 1992) along with a great increase in interest in war-
related trauma (Hobfoll, Lomranz, Eyal, Bridges, & Tzemach, 1989; Milgram,
1986). Despite this level of attention, much remains to be learned concerning the
linkage between extreme stress and psychological adjustment. A major problem
within this body of literature concerns the rarity of theoretical models. Although
conceptual models have been suggested (see Baum, 1987; Freedy, Kilpatrick, &
Resnick, 1993a; Freedy, Resnick, & Kilpatrick, 1992; Solomon, 1989), research
studies seldom test proposed models. Consequently, there are limits to available
knowledge concerning the relationship between extreme stress and subsequent
psychosocial functioning. Moreover, this literature has tended not to focus on
coping behaviors per se, but has tended to address the psychosocial resources
people employ to adapt successfully.

It is widely recognized that extreme stressors may create both acute (e.g., Freedy, Kilpatrick, & Resnick, 1993b) and prolonged psychological distress (e.g., see Green, Lindy, et al., 1990). However, ambiguity exists regarding the elements of disaster exposure responsible for adjustment difficulties. Most conceptual definitions emphasize acute factors such as injury or extreme threat, whereas other definitions emphasize ongoing factors including a range of adversities within the postdisaster environment (e.g., residential displacement, job disruption) (Freedy, Resnick, & Kilpatrick, 1992).

We will frame our thesis within the context of Conservation of Resources (COR) theory (Hobfoll, 1988, 1989, 1991; Hobfoll & Lilly, 1993). COR theory is a general stress framework that applies to the process of stress within the psychosocial context. We will specifically apply COR theory to the process of coping with extreme stress and rely on this general explanatory framework for helping to understand and predict when extreme stressors will take their worst toll and how and when people will best withstand the deleterious effects of extreme stressors. In this regard, people's reactions to extreme stress, although certainly negative, range in severity and longevity from moderate and short term to very severe and long term. Likewise, some communities are paralyzed by the occurrence of a disaster or war, whereas others manage to effectively mobilize in the face of extreme stressors. A theory that would help us organize and predict these differences would be helpful indeed.

First, we will present the basic parameters of COR theory. Then we will examine how COR theory can be applied to short-term responding to extreme stress. Next, we will explore the implications of a resource perspective on long-term responding to extreme stress. Finally, we will look at personal, social, and community resources that are particularly important in the face of such circumstances as disasters and war. We will concentrate on community stress events that influence a large segment of a community or an entire community and on how such events influence resources. We will not address extreme stressors that occur on an individual level, such as rape and violent assault. By focusing on the community context, we hope to uncover principles that apply to the individual, group, and organizational levels.

CONSERVATION OF RESOURCES THEORY

COR theory is based on an underlying motivational tenet: *Individuals strive to obtain, retain, and protect that which they value.* These valuables as well as the means of obtaining or protecting them are termed resources. From this tenet, it follows that psychological stress will occur in any of three contexts:

1. Stress will occur when people's resources are threatened.
2. Stress will occur when people experience loss of resources.
3. Stress will occur when people invest their resources and fail to achieve subsequent, adequate gain of resources following their investment.

Hobfoll (1988, 1989) has suggested our general categories of resources. These are (a) object resources, (b) condition resources, (c) personal resources, and (d) energy resources. Extreme stressors are likely to threaten, cause the loss thereof, or result in failure to gain resources in each of these categories, as we will illustrate in this chapter. Each of these resource categories aid coping efforts.

Object resources include physical objects such as home, car, jewels, and clothing. They provide a safe "base of operations" for coping and often are necessary to act in a problem-solving manner. For example, transportation can be a key to evacuation prior to a disaster and to house repairs or getting to treatment following a disaster or tragedy.

Condition resources are the conditions that themselves are valued by people or that facilitate acquisition or protection of valued resources. These include seniority at work, stable employment, a good marriage, and being a member of a family. The disaster response, and therefore people's abilities to act in a problem-focused mode, is tied to conditions of employment and social status. This includes formal processes, such as medical insurance, and informal process, such as having contacts who can provide the resources necessary for coping.

Personal resources are characteristics or skills that individuals possess. Key personal resources include job skills, social prowess, and sense of personal efficacy. Carver, Scheier, and Weintraub's (1989) and Endler and Parker's (1990) work on active coping suggest that those who have greater self-esteem and personal sense of mastery, will be more likely to use these more problem-focused efforts.

Energy resources facilitate other resource attainment; they are only valued to the extent they allow access to other resources. Energy resources include money, credit, owed favors, and knowledge. Again, coping demands have energy resources, and when individuals' and communities' energy resources are depleted, they will tend to use less active coping and the use of more passive or emotion focused coping efforts is likely to increase.

Yates, Axsom, Bickman, and Howe (1989) further suggest that individuals need to be aware of their resources to enable problem-focused coping efforts. Extreme stress may cause people to question their resources or become disoriented, and service providers may enhance coping efforts by helping people identify the resources they possess that may aid coping or by actively filling in for absentee resources (Myers, 1989).

Hobfoll (1988, 1989) has outlined a number of principles that follow from COR theory. These principles will be presented next.

Principle 1. Loss Is the Primary Axis of Stress

It follows from COR theory that loss is the primary operating mechanism driving stress reactions. This is a departure from most stress theories, which depict loss as one of many situations that may create stress. We can briefly argue why loss is so central to stress.

First, it has long been held that the most severe events are clearly loss events: the loss of loved ones, loss of health, loss of freedom (imprisonment), and loss of income or employment. Some researchers have taken the position that stress occurs whenever the individual perceives an event as stressful (Lazarus, 1990), but we would argue along with others that this merely confounds stress reactions with neurotic processes. If a wholly positive event, say, is viewed as stressful, this would suggest that the perception was embodied in the individual's neurosis, not in the stressful nature of the event (see also Dohrenwend, Dohrenwend, Dodson, & Shrout, 1984).

Part of the confusion on the issue of what aspect of the event is stressful emerged from the earliest work by Holmes and Rahe (1967). By using vaguely worded items such as "Change in health status," or "Change in financial status," they illustrated correlations between change and negative stress outcomes. However, reanalysis of such data that separated positive change from negative change indicated that only negative change resulted in psychological distress or negative health outcomes (Thoits, 1983). Negative change means loss, such as when respondents report poorer health, loss of income, reduced health status, or loss of loved ones. In fact, gain events have been found to be related to lower distress and act as a buffer, limiting the negative influence of other loss events (Cohen & Hoberman, 1983). For example, not only is an increase in income or improvement in health not stressful, it also buffers the negative influence of other losses, such as a setback at work.

Research on life transitions has also contributed to some confusion about the nature of stressful events. If transitions are stressful, then positive transitions should also produce negative stress reactions. Kessler, Turner, and House (1989) find, however, that positive job transitions fully reverse the negative influence of loss transitions. Specifically, the regaining of employment virtually reverses the untoward effect of a job layoff. Moving to a new location has also been taken as evidence that transitions are stressful. However, when the losses and gains involved in a move are considered, then it can be seen that only when losses outweigh gains are the effects of moves negative (Brett, 1982; Munton, 1990). Life is one transition after another, and if positive transitions had a negative impact, then it could be argued that there would be little motivation but to guard the status quo. This does not seem to be the case.

Hobfoll and Lilly (1993) examined how loss and gain of resources influenced people in a direct test of our thesis. They found that only losses were related to greater psychological distress. In fact, resource gains were related to lower psychological distress, particularly following other losses. In other words, resource gain was generally not related to psychological distress, but did have a positive effect when individuals were faced with other losses. We will see this process emerge in research on extreme stress in instances where even small initial gains people make following disaster result in their more successful long-term coping.

Implied in this first principle is the notion that loss is much more negative in impact than gain is positive in impact. This is an important point in understanding extreme stress because not only are losses likely to occur, but the promise of future gain does not compensate for loss once having occurred. This bias in favor of overweighting loss's impact may possibly stem from evolutionary pressures, such that resource loss may translate to failure to survive, whereas resource gain means little in terms of improved survival. In fact, the importance of resource gain to survival is to prevent devastating effects of future resource loss that may occur, such as the case where lack of earlier gains makes food or shelter unavailable for winter's onslaught. Although evolutionary arguments are speculative, it is clear that this bias in favor of loss is a general cognitive attribute of people (Tversky & Kahneman, 1981).

Principle 2. Resources Act to Preserve and Protect Other Resources

The second principle of COR theory helps explain people's reactions to extreme stressors: Resources are what people use to preserve, protect, and build other resources. Sometimes people use the same resource to build that resource further. For example, self-esteem may be employed to face the serious challenge of extreme stress and not back down, resulting in further increase in self-esteem. Often, one resource or a group of resources is used to gain other resources. Money and time may be invested to rebuild one's home following a tornado. Mastery and social support may be employed to prevent loss of self-esteem in reaction to job loss when a disaster destroys a community's employment base.

Hobfoll and Leiberman (1987) found, for example, that women who were high in self-esteem made good use of social support. However, those who lacked self-esteem misused social support. The resource of self-esteem was interpreted as providing a framework for being able to positively translate the messages communicated in social support. Those low in self-esteem, in contrast, may have misunderstood the social support to mean that they were personally inadequate. Similarly, Hobfoll and Lerman (1989) found that having strong personal resources led to greater intimacy. Those who lacked personal resources, in comparison, experienced further reductions in social resources as the stress process unfolded. In a study of Israeli combatants, it was similarly found that men whose units provided strong support were more likely to retain a feeling of attachment to their units. Those who lost this sense of attachment were at greater risk of experiencing breakdown in combat (Solomon, Mikulincer, & Hobfoll, 1987).

Principles 3 and 4: Loss and Gain Spirals

By combining the first two COR principles, a third principle emerges. Since, stress results from the loss or threat of loss of resources, and since people use resources to offset loss, *Principle 3 suggests that following stressful circumstances people tend to have an increasingly depleted resource pool to combat future stressful circumstances.* As more stressors are confronted, the individual or group is decreasingly capable of meeting stress challenges, resulting in loss spirals. Gain spirals (Principle 4) can also occur, as one gain makes for a more robust organism or group that, in turn, is more capable of achieving further gains. However, because loss is more highly weighted than gains, loss spirals occur with greater intensity and velocity than gain spirals. By velocity, we mean the speed at which losses occur in reaction to stressful conditions.

If, as we have suggested, resources underlie the ability to successfully employ coping efforts, then individuals will be increasingly less able to assert themselves in an active coping posture. This may mean that they cope actively, but ineffectively, or it may mean that they must rely on more emotional and internal resources.

The influence and course of loss and gain spirals is a critical concept for appreciating the impact of extreme stressors. Rather than seeing such stressors as single events, they should be conceptualized as chains of events that contain multiple losses and threats to loss, and even appreciable opportunity for gains. Reconceptualizing the general "event" into its components can be termed "unpacking" the event. The initial disaster, even in the case of a defined event such as a single-shock earthquake that comes without warning, produces a wake of following events. Loss of life may translate to loss of income, tension may create marital conflict, community support and contact may dissolve, reappear, and dissolve again. Some individuals may have to leave their homes, whereas others may find their homes intact, but their place of employment destroyed. Some of these homes may be rebuilt, others may be declared unsafe at any time. Some businesses may reopen, others may decide to leave the area or go bankrupt. These chains of events will interact with the personal, familial, and community chains of losses and gains that follow the initial impact.

This picture of loss spirals becomes even more complicated when we realize that the initial stressor event is seldom well defined. Many extreme events follow a prolonged period of preparation and warning, whereas others begin with no forewarning. Still other extreme events, such as the "silent disasters" that we will discuss later in this chapter, may have a vague beginning and course. Some extreme stressors come in multiple shock waves, and these may follow at unpredictable lengths of time. When we unpack extreme stressors into their component events, we can better appreciate that extreme stressors are actually a film of interrelated events that reverberate between the individual, family, and community level, rather than a snapshot of a single event. This highlights the importance of depicting loss and gain spirals on the individual, group, and community level.

Unpacking extreme stressors leads to adoption of a developmental perspective (Freedy, Kilpatrick, & Resnick, 1993a; Freedy, Resnick, & Kilpatrick, 1992). According to this view, individual and environmental factors existing before, during, and following the focal event may have either a positive or a negative impact on individual psychological adjustment. Salient *predisaster, within-disaster,* and *postdisaster* factors all influence the loss and gain cycles accompanying extreme stress.

Hobfoll, London, and Orr (1988) noted how loss and gain cycles might operate in a study of soldiers who experienced varying levels of exposure to war-related stressors such as being in combat, having contact with dead or wounded, and themselves being wounded during the past year. They noted that those exposed to such circumstances, who also lacked social resources (developmentally available to them from before the war), were likely to both experience psychological distress and to have problems at work and in their social lives. This, in turn, would be likely to lead to compounding of the original stressors as they experienced relationship discord and possible negative repercussions at work.

Studying patients' responses to loss related to severe physical disease, Lane and Hobfoll (1992) also noted that disease-related resource loss resulted in increased anger. Anger, in turn, cycled to alienate potential supporters. Thus, the patients were not only losing their developmentally available resources due to their disease, but losing social resources as a consequence of their response to the disease. A similar process has been noted by Kaniasty and Norris (1993) in response to losses associated with a major flood. Original resource loss made victims more vulnerable to loss when secondary stressors occurred.

COR and Extreme Stress

There are also a number of special properties of extreme stress that separate it from more garden variety stressors and even what have been called major stress events, such as job loss, loss of income, and threat to personal health. The rapidity and degree of devastation that accompanies extreme stress may be related to five aspects of extreme stress (Hobfoll, 1991):

1. They attack people's most basic values (e.g., life, shelter).
2. They make excessive demands.
3. They often come without warning.
4. They are outside the realm for which resource utilization strategies have been practiced and developed.
5. They leave a powerful mental image that is evoked by cues associated with the event.

First, extreme stress often results in rapid loss of resources. Earthquakes, floods, and war can destroy people's homes, lives, places of work, and community infrastructure in a blink of the eye. This is not always the case, and some disasters, such as toxic exposure, are more insidious and slow in their effects. However, most extreme stressors have a more rapid influence on resource loss than are generally associated with other kinds of stress events.

A second aspect of how extreme stressors affect resources is in the breadth of devastation. Extreme stressors tend to influence a broad band of resources at the same time. Floods affect people's homes, communities, livelihood, social contacts, and health. Not only is the individual affected, but he or she also finds that the widespread loss impacts family, friends, colleagues, and other community members. Because of this broad sweep of loss, potential resources are lost on all these levels, thus impeding the process of recovery. In this regard, most research on coping behaviors have addressed the individual level. This may assume that external resources that the person calls on in active or problem-focused coping are available to respond. In the case of disasters, these calls for aid and response may be left unanswered.

Disasters may or may not occur with prior warning. In cases where there is not adequate warning, individuals and communities will be unable to organize their coping resources in a preventive manner. Such preparation must occur on the object, conditions, personal characteristics, and energy resource levels. Many other kinds of stressful life events can also come without warning, however, preparation for extreme stressors differs also because of the lack of an established repertoire or plan for combating the kinds of threats and losses that might occur. Likewise, this repertoire or plan may be available in the community or among family for other stressors (e.g., how to cope with death of a loved one), but such knowledge and experience may be lacking for extreme stressors.

This highlights the importance of warning time, because with warning a theoretical plan, at least, can be put into place. Also, forewarning allows for mental preparation and anticipatory coping. Yates et al. (1989) suggest that coping efforts will be aided by either prior experience with a similar situation or the ability to formalize a coping plan. This is especially important for disaster response teams, who know that they will be encountering extreme stress and can rehearse their coping response.

The issue of leaving an etched mental image that evokes negative emotions associated with the original event is only known to occur for extreme stressors and deserves some special mention (Horowitz, Wilner, & Alvarez, 1979). It acts as a special challenge to emotion-focused coping (Lazarus & Folkman, 1984), because the emotions that need to be addressed will keep resurfacing over many years. When alcohol and drugs are used as means of emotion focused coping, this could be particularly devastating, as there may be a life long need to attempt to overcome these distressing emotions.

Hobfoll (1991) has speculated that the images of the stressor and the accompanying emotions are related to survival because they alert the victim to the possible threat of a repetition of the original event. They serve as a critical mechanism for the ongoing conservation of the most critical resource—survival of the self. For example, a soldier who lives through an ambush in which he witnesses the gruesome death of comrades, will be more likely to respond to the cues that foretell the possible onset of another similar episode. He will be highly sensitized to the sights, sounds, and smells that are associated with the event. And so it went with saber-tooth tigers. The problem is that this survival mechanism is typically of less use in modern society, where repetitions of a disaster are either unlikely or where technological warning systems have replaced human-sensory warning systems. As such, victims are left with an indelible image that interferes with their functioning and causes ongoing emotional pain (van der Kolk, 1987).

Before exploring the short- and long-term consequences of extreme stress exposure, we wish to emphasize that we are discussing the events on a community level. This means that not all those individuals in the community have the same stress exposure. Some individuals experience threat to their lives, loss of loved ones, and destruction of their property. Others experience only the threat of such loss and emerge relatively unscathed from the event. War and disaster carry great potential threat, but the experience of those involved is highly varied. When we consider events on a community level, we do not necessarily know what occurred to any given individual. This differs from the study and understanding of the experience of individual victims of extreme stressors, such as rape or violence, or even from the study of individual victims who are identified as known to have directly experienced a travesty due to war or disaster. These are closely related questions, but the differences are often marked and should be underscored.

IMMEDIATE RESPONDING TO CRISES AND DISASTER

The Nature of Responses to Resource Loss

Having identified that the availability and the maintenance of resources are crucial to adaptation following disasters and other extreme stressors, we will now look at how engendered resource loss relates to immediate functioning. We will first identify the time framework for the psychological reactions to be discussed. Immediate psychological adjustment will be defined as including experiences occurring during the focal stress event and during the hours, days, and weeks following. We will define immediate psychological reactions as those extending up to approximately 6 months following the onset of the event.

Research has seldom focused on immediate psychosocial reactions to disaster. This situation is related to the logistical difficulties inherent in studying natural and technical disasters; such environments are chaotic and research participation is not a high priority for impacted persons (Baum, Solomon, & Ursano, 1987; Raphael, Lundin, & Weisaeth, 1989). Nevertheless, some creative research efforts have succeeded in collecting valuable information. These studies provide insight into the nature of immediate postdisaster psychological reactions.

With regard to psychological states existing during and in the hours immediately following extreme stress, it is typical for victims to experience a range of intense psychological reactions: surprise, sadness, feelings of helplessness, fear, emotional numbness or shock, anger, and disorientation or confusion (Freedy, Resnick, Kilpatrick, & Saunders, 1993; Freedy, Kilpatrick, & Resnick, 1993b; Milgram, 1986). Most often, initially intense psychological reactions resolve in the weeks and months following the onset of the event (Cook & Bickman, 1990; Freedy, Kilpatrick, & Resnick, 1993a, 1993b; Rubonis & Bickman, 1991).

COR stress theory may be used to suggest a process underlying postdisaster recovery. In particular, it appears that the vast majority of individuals escape prolonged adjustment difficulties due to natural or technical disasters or war (Milgram, 1986; Summers & Cowan, 1991). From the perspective of COR theory, this may be because the majority of disaster victims, soldiers, or civilians in a war area do not experience irreversible resource loss (e.g., death of a family member, disabling injury, irreversible financial ruin) (Freedy, Shaw, Jarrell, &

Masters, 1992). However, experiences associated with extreme resource loss (e.g., deaths, extreme property loss, destruction of entire communities) can produce severe initial and prolonged periods of demand and misery for some individuals (Green, Lindy, et al., 1990; Rubonis & Bickman, 1991; Solomon, Noy, & Bar-On, 1986). In essence, broad or extreme resource loss may threaten the physical, psychological, or social survival. The breadth and intensity of resource loss should correspond to the intensity and duration of psychosocial complaints.

It is also critical to address severe initial reactions at the time of crisis because initial loss of functioning can usually be restored with immediate professional attention. Experience with severe reactions among combatants suggests that replenishing their liquids and nutrients, providing shelter for peaceful sleep, and offering positive expectations and a psychological sense of community are important intervention ingredients (Solomon & Benbenishty, 1986). These resources help restore a sense of control, optimism, and normalcy to the victim.

However, if initial loss in functioning is treated in a traditional psychiatric manner, relying on hospitalization and treatment that places the victim on hold for even a few days before treatment with the expectation for long-term dysfunction, then the initial loss of functioning is often exacerbated and made more permanent. One interpretation of this finding is that traditional psychiatric treatment encourages emotion-focused coping and insight coping; whereas crisis intervention encourages a combination of active coping and emotion-focused coping. It would appear that the latter combination is more effective.

Research Examples from Disasters and War

Two research studies have specifically applied COR stress theory in an effort to predict immediate psychological functioning following a disaster. The first study concerned Hurricane Hugo, which devastated the South Carolina coast on September 22, 1989. At that point in time, Hugo was the costliest natural disaster in U.S. history with 7.5 billion dollars in mainland damage (B. Case, National Hurricane Center, personal communication, January 1990). In addition, Hurricane Hugo had the following characteristics: sustained winds of 138 miles per hour, a storm surge of 10.4 feet, 7 inches of local rain, and 13 deaths in South Carolina (Lawrence, 1989).

Freedy, Shaw, Jarrell, and Masters (1992) conducted a study of acute psychological reactions to Hurricane Hugo. In particular, 490 faculty and professional staff from the Medical University of South Carolina at Charleston completed a set of questionnaires approximately 3 months following the hurricane. Standardized measures of demographic characteristics, resource loss, coping behavior, and psychological distress were included. Three major findings were supported. First, resource loss (e.g., loss of the following: a daily routine, time, a sense of control, possessions, social involvement or companionship) was associated with increased levels of psychological distress. Second, among all predictors of psychological distress (resource loss, demographic factors, and coping), resource loss was the most powerful predictor accounting for 34.1% of psychological distress variance. Third, elevated levels of resource loss were associated with clinically significant elevations in the level of psychological distress reported.

A second research study applied COR theory in an attempt to predict acute psychological distress following the Sierra Madre earthquake (Freedy, Saladin, Kilpatrick, Resnick, & Saunders, 1994). This earthquake struck residents of the San Gabriel valley in California on June 28, 1991. The Sierra Madre earthquake was moderate in size, as indicated by the following characteristics: 5.8 on the Richter scale, 33.5 million dollars in damages, two deaths, and approximately 100 injuries (J. D. Goltz, Southern California Earthquake Preparedness Project, personal communication, August 1991).

Researchers interviewed a community sample of 229 adults by telephone between 4 and 7 months following the Sierra Madre earthquake. Standardized questions assessed the following characteristics: demographic characteristics, history of previous traumatic events (e.g., another natural disaster, sexual assault), history of low magnitude stressors in the past 12 months (e.g., divorce, death of a close family member, serious illness/injury), earthquake-related threat to life, resource loss (e.g., a sense of control, a daily routine, time with loved ones, companionships), and current psychological distress. The 75% participation rate strengthens confidence in the findings (Freedy et al., 1994).

Three basic findings emerged regarding resource loss and acute psychological adjustment following the Sierra Madre earthquake. These findings are consistent with findings from the Hurricane Hugo study (Freedy et al., 1992). First, resource loss was positively associated with psychological distress. Second, resource loss remained an important predictor of psychological distress (accounting for 11.2% of psychological distress variance) even when other potential predictors were controlled (demographics, traumatic event history, low magnitude events in the past 12 months, and earthquake-related life threat). Third, resource loss was associated with elevations of psychological distress that may be considered clinically meaningful (Freedy et al., 1994).

Work by McFarlane illustrates that prognosis for individuals in an affected community is generally favorable, as long as the extent of devastation to the community's resources does not pass a certain threshold at which the resources available for recovery are damaged or lost along with the resources held by individuals (McFarlane, 1992). Community resources constitute a backup for individual and family resources and can be metered out to support members of a community. When community resources are overcome, however, this safety net is unavailable. For example, if community disaster organizations such as fire and rescue are destroyed, or crisis psychological help cannot be offered due to the inability to gain access to victims, then assistance to families and businesses may have to wait until the avenues for community response are rebuilt.

Research on combatants suggests that resource loss and availability are also critical in this domain. Soldiers who possess support from officers and comrades are less likely to experience dysfunctional reactions than those who lack these social resources (Solomon, Mikulincer, & Hobfoll, 1987). Personal sense of self-efficacy also acts to limit negative psychological reactions to the realities of combat (Solomon & Mikulincer, 1990). This line of research also suggests that positive coping can be trained, because troops with low psychiatric breakdown rates are "overtrained" in their coping responses to difficult situations. Further, they are taught to continue to behave as a team under pressing circumstances and to offer mutual support.

Despite the positive contribution of coping resources, the degree of direct loss experienced by the soldier is a risk factor for negative psychological reactions and debilitation of functioning (Hobfoll, London, & Orr, 1988). Indeed, if exposure continues over long periods of time, even well-trained, resourceful soldiers are likely to experience psychiatric breakdown (Marlowe, 1979). This phenomenon is noted both at the high-stress time of invasion and at around Day 25 following prolonged combat exposure (Marlowe, 1979).

Resource availability and maintenance before, during, and after both disaster and war appear to be crucial in determining the intensity and duration of short- to mid-term psychological reactions. Intense, broad, or nonreversible forms of resource loss (e.g., death, disabling injury, financial ruin) in particular are likely to produce intense or persistent distress. Psychosocial resources may counteract these deleterious effects, but prolonged extreme exposure may cause deterioration of individuals, groups, or communities well endowed with resources.

LONG-TERM REACTIONS TO DISASTER

As previously noted, it is difficult to do research on the very early effects of disaster. Therefore, we have considerably more information about the longer term responses to these events. This information generally supports the assertion that (a) loss associated with both natural and human-caused disasters and war may result in negative mental health impacts, (b) that personal, social, and community resources may reduce these negative sequelae in extent and duration, and (c) that resource loss cycles may take a continued toll on survivors. This section of the chapter will briefly summarize research on the long-term effects of extreme stress, what is known about the types of reactions to disaster and war, and the longevity of responses. Several studies will be used to indicate how different factors interact to predict long-term responses, and how the nature of the response may vary by the type of event.

A number of studies have assessed the overall impact of disaster events when survivors are compared with individuals not exposed to such events (Green & Solomon, in press). A few will be mentioned here as examples, but the trends evidenced in these studies have been shown in other events as well. Several studies looked at the mental health effects of the Mt. St. Helen's volcanic eruption and showed higher levels of post-traumatic stress disorder, anxiety, depression, and somatic symptoms in survivors than in unexposed controls within a 2-year period following the event (Murphy, 1984; Shore, Tatum, & Vollmer, 1986). Adams and Adams (1984) also used archival records to examine community effects of this event 7 months following the initial event. Accompanying these changes, disaster-related increases in mental health visits, substance abuse visits, medical visits, court cases and domestic violence reports, have also been noted at first, but tend to decline markedly after the first year. Phifer and Norris (1989a, 1989b) showed increased anxiety and depression symptoms at 3 to 6 months in a prospective study controlling for predisaster symptoms levels. Canino and colleagues (Canino, Bravo, Rubio-Stipec, & Woodbury, 1990), in a prospective study of mudslides and floods in Puerto Rico, found significantly increased symptoms of depression, generalized anxiety, and PTSD, from pre- to postdisaster.

Similar effects, but perhaps more long term, have been found for "human-caused" or "technological" events. For example, Holen (1991) studied survivors of an oil rig collapse in the North Sea where many coworkers were killed, and found, at 5 years, higher current levels of intrusion and avoidance symptoms, as well as general distress symptoms, in this group than in workers on a rig that did not collapse. Sick leave was also used more by the exposed group, and psychiatric diagnoses were higher. Baum, Schaeffer, Lake, Fleming, and Collins (1986) studied individuals around the Three Mile Island plant about 1½ years after the nuclear leak there. Exposed individuals were higher on overall distress, as well as somatic, anxiety, and alienation symptoms. They also showed lower performance on a proofreading task and higher levels of epinephrin, norepinephrine, and urinary cortisol than controls. Blood pressures were elevated, and physicians rated more problems in these individuals, indicating effects across a range of potential reactions.

Robins et al. (1986) and Smith, Robins, Pryzbeck, Goldring, and Solomon (1986) found significantly increased PTSD and depression symptoms in individuals exposed to floods, tornadoes, radioactivity, and dioxin in a prospective study where initial levels could be taken into account. The most common new (since disaster) symptoms in the residents were somatization and depression. Green, Grace, et al. (1990) showed higher levels of depression, anxiety, and lifetime PTSD in survivors of a dam collapse disaster 14 years after the disaster than in an unexposed comparison group. Taken together, these studies indicate clear-cut effects of disasters regardless of the type of event, and even when predisaster levels were taken into account. Consistent effects were demonstrated in the areas of PTSD symptoms, depression, and anxiety. Measurable physiological symptoms have been documented to be associated with these events, as well as health visits of all sorts, indicating that the effects can be pervasive. Subjects most at risk will be described later in the chapter.

The preceding studies indicate that disaster events may cause prolonged impacts as well as short-term effects. Furthermore, the research to date is quite supportive of the generalization that human-caused events may have more lasting impacts than natural disasters. Longitudinal studies of natural disasters have usually shown declines in symptoms over time, with functioning often returning to normal community levels 7 months following the initial event (e.g., Adams & Adams, 1984; Cook & Bickman, 1990; Phifer & Norris, 1989b; Shore et al.,

1986). Technological disasters show effects lasting years after these events (e.g., Davidson, Fleming, & Baum, 1986; Green, Grace, et al., 1990; Holen, 1991). The longest follow-up, by Green et al., showed effects into the second decade.

Long-term consequences of war-related stress show a similar trend. Survivors of the Dutch underground who fought the German army during World War II have been found to have increased risk for PTSD more than 40 years after the war's conclusion (Aarts, 1992). Long-term risk is highest for those who have had severe initial reactions. Soldiers who broke down in combat, for example, have high rates of impairment for many years following their traumatic combat experience (Milgram, 1986).

Models Predicting Long-Term Outcome

Numerous studies have investigated factors that contribute to long-term outcomes following disaster and war. Because mediators of extreme stress response are discussed in detail later in the chapter, this section will highlight several studies that have focused on resource loss and its role in long-term outcomes. Traumatic stress is a special case of resource loss (Hobfoll, 1991). Disasters have the potential to cause loss of life, and thus of friends and loved ones. Being exposed to a life-threatening situation may result in the loss of one's sense of safety or invulnerability, as would observing the results of destruction of life and property. Such losses may occur rapidly and overtax usual resources to an extreme degree (Hobfoll, 1991). Such stress might be expected to produce negative outcomes, particularly in people who suffered more extreme losses, and who might be vulnerable for other reasons.

A study of the effects of a supper club fire in northern Kentucky in 1977 examined several different aspects of loss associated with exposure to this human-caused event in which 165 were killed (Green, Grace, & Gleser, 1985). Researchers evaluated 117 survivors at 1 year postdisaster, and 67 of those at 2 years. Objective resource loss included extent of loss (bereavement) (closeness of relationship to lost person), life threat (warning, exposure to the smoke and fumes, etc.), injury, and prolonged waiting to learn the fate of a loved one, in addition to exposure to dead bodies. Victims' subjective stress was also assessed. Age, education, intervening life events, social supports, and coping were all assessed and tested in a regression model, which predicted interviewer-rated affective distress (anxiety, depression, somatic concerns, social isolation, suicidal thoughts, etc.) and total score on the Symptom Checklist (SCL-90). Resource loss, operationalized as the preceding stressors, accounted for the most variance in outcome (45% of affective distress, and 30% of SCL-90 total), with 60% and 57% of the total variance accounted for, respectively. Subjective stress and demographic factors predicted additional significant variance in the SCL measure. Measures of hostility, belligerence, and substance abuse were predicted at much lower levels. At 2 years, the objective stress continued to significantly predict rated affective distress, but at this point also predicted substance abuse. The experience of exposure to grotesque death was particularly important in that relationship. This study indicated an important role for resource loss in long-term functioning.

Another study that used such a model and focused on resource loss was a study of a dam collapse in West Virginia in 1972 (Gleser, Green, & Winget, 1981). Survivors were originally studied in the context of a lawsuit against the coal company that built the defective dam, but were later followed up with a sample of nonplaintiffs. The disaster devastated the small Appalachian community and caused 125 deaths. In addition to resource loss, demographic factors and postdisaster events were assessed. The losses and threats of loss included life threat, bereavement, subsequent hardships, displacement from original geographic location, and identification of bodies. At 2 years postdisaster, these losses accounted for 20% of the variance in rated overall impairment for both men and women, out of a total variance of 40% for men and 32% for women. Prediction was somewhat less for self-reported symptoms.

Researchers followed up a subsample of the flood victims at 14 years postevent, long after the lawsuit had been settled. At this point, 28% of those originally assessed still had PTSD (Green, Lindy, et al., 1990). In the follow-up, additional variables were assessed, including predisaster diagnoses. At this later point, the disaster losses no longer significantly predicted the global impairment rating, which was more dependent on prior diagnosis, education, and social support available, with resource gain in the form of social support producing a more positive outcome. On the other hand, the PTSD diagnosis was still predictable from aspects of the disaster experience, specifically prolonged exposure to the elements in the several days following the disaster, when water and electricity were not available and survivors were still being rescued. Lower education and existence of prior (to the disaster) psychiatric diagnoses also predicted PTSD (Green, 1992).

Other studies of the long-term effects of disaster, including those of natural disasters, also support the critical role of immediate resource loss in the unfolding of disaster-related problems over time. For example, Phifer and Norris (1989b) and Norris, Phifer, and Kaniasty (in press) demonstrated that the extent of personal (property) loss was associated with negative affect (anxiety, sadness) among older adults up to 18 months after a series of floods struck their Kentucky community. Extent of community destruction, on the other hand, was associated with a decline in positive affect. Persons with both types of losses were doing the worst. Studies by Bravo, Rubio-Stipec, Canino, Woodbury, and Ribera (1990) and by McFarlane (1987) also show the long-term impact of these experiences, with significant outcome predictions from 8 months to 2 years postdisaster.

Ayalon and Soskis (1986) qualitatively studied long-term reactions of victims of terrorism. They found that those who experienced greatest resource loss were likely to have prolonged psychological problems. In addition to noting the helpfulness of crisis intervention, they also noted that survivors who received ongoing supportive intervention benefited further. Such intervention included availability of psychological services, rehabilitation, and family intervention. Survivors who lacked family support or whose families blamed them in some way for having been exposed to terrorism or for their behavior while a hostage also had more negative reactions. It may be noted here that for good adjustment not only would individuals have had to cope by seeking support, but support had to be available in response to their efforts.

Jaffe and Rosenfeld (1982) found that war-related neuroses (this study was conducted prior to use of PTSD diagnosis) were evidenced 3 years following the 1973 Israel Yom Kippur War. Such reactions were most common in veterans who displayed field dependence, inward-directed hostility, and inadequate sexual identification. They argued that these personality characteristics were most likely to have been evidenced prior to veterans' war experience. Because these traits were measured following the war, their argument is open to dispute. Solomon, Noy, and Bar-On (1986) found that recurrence of combat-related trauma response was no more likely in those who had previously experienced breakdown than in combatants who had never experienced breakdown. They concluded from this finding that premorbid conditions are unlikely to affect long-term psychological responding as much as environmental factors related to the degree of trauma exposure.

Combatants who use more emotion-focused coping and less problem-focused coping may also have poorer recovery and greater risk for PTSD (Mikulincer & Solomon, 1989). When soldiers related their problems to stable and uncontrollable causes, they tended to use more emotion-focused coping responses. This, in turn, increased their likelihood for PTSD 2 and 3 years following the war-related trauma. However, the authors noted that a likely causal route for these effects may be circular, as suggested by Lazarus, DeLongis, Folkman, and Gruen (1985). As such, people's threat appraisal may influence their inner state, which, in turn, influences their coping response, followed by further reappraisal and a continuation of the cycle.

Outcomes Associated with Different Types of Losses

The studies just mentioned imply that not all types of loss are equivalent. The Norris studies suggested that personal loss, compared with community destruction, had somewhat different impacts on long-term outcome. The longitudinal studies suggested that technological, human-caused events may have more persistent impact. A specific case of technological disaster might provide some further information about how characteristics of events may influence the long-term outcome. This is the "silent" disaster (e.g., the radioactivity leak, the toxic exposure) that does not cause any visible damage.

A few studies of silent disasters have been mentioned but should be highlighted because the resource losses associated with them are vaguer than is the case for acute or visible events. The features associated with this type of event have been described by Green, Lindy, and Grace (in press) and include lack of warning or indication that the hazard has occurred until it is underway or over, the stigma associated with exposure and contamination and the chronicity of the threat. Baum, Fleming, and Davidson (1983) have referred to this latter characteristic as the absence of a "low point" where the disaster is clearly over and no threat of loss remains. Rather, exposure to radioactivity increases the likelihood of the development, many years later, of a variety of illnesses including leukemia and other forms of cancer, decreased effectiveness of the immune system, and genetic anomalies. This type of loss is different from that associated with a visible destruction of property or loss of loved ones, and it might be expected to have a somewhat different effect. It is not clear at this point the extent to which symptom outcomes associated with silent disasters are different from those associated with other human-caused events. However, some interesting findings from two such events suggest that in addition to the more common symptoms of anxiety, depression, and PTSD, these events may leave lingering effects related to mistrust and alienation.

Davidson et al. (1986), in their 5-year follow-up of residents exposed to the Three Mile Island leak, found that many symptoms had actually increased over the course of time, but hostility and suspiciousness showed particularly dramatic increases to become among the highest scores. Green, Lindy, and Grace (in press) studied individuals exposed to radioactive contamination from a nuclear weapons plant, about which authorities had given out misleading or incorrect information for years. Subjects were rated for earlier (worst period) and present distress and impairment. The findings indicated that decreases occurred over time for anxiety, depression, daily routine impairment, belligerence, and agitation. However, elevations remained for somatic concerns, social isolation, and suspiciousness. Self-reported symptoms (SCL-90) were relatively high (compared with norms) on somatization, obsessive-compulsive symptoms, hostility, paranoid thinking and interpersonal sensitivity (e.g., feeling that others cannot be trusted). Victims reported avoidance symptoms that were higher than intrusion symptoms; they coped by using "problem avoidance," with levels of "wishful thinking" and "social withdrawal" similar to patients who had just been told they had cancer (Green, Lindy, & Grace, in press). Although subjects for this study were involved in a lawsuit, and were likely more distressed than their uninvolved neighbors, the pattern of symptoms fits those found by Baum and colleagues (SCL profiles were quite similar in both elevation and pattern). The common symptoms of somatization found by Smith et al. after dioxin and radioactivity are also consistent with this picture.

Taken together, these studies suggest the hypothesis that although diffuse, human-caused disasters may produce symptoms common to other events (e.g., anxiety and depression), they may also produce somatic reactions, suspicion, and mistrust, along with avoidance of dealing directly with the reality of the event. These findings have potential implications for how such information is given to the public in the first place, as well as for ongoing educational and policy efforts (Wandersman & Hallman, 1993) and mental health prevention after the fact.

MEDIATORS OF EXTREME STRESS RESPONSES

We have made the case that severity of exposure to extreme stress is of primary importance, but many community, social, and individual resources can affect psychological outcomes as well. Resources and conditions that facilitate or impede the employment of resources play a central role in determining how victims react to extreme stressors, and what physical and mental health consequences these reactions produce. Studies of the effects of resources and resource-facilitating circumstance help identify those victims likely to develop prolonged effects.

Community Resources

The community context is an important class of disaster resources. Community circumstances that can affect psychological response include the extent of community disruption, the centrality (e.g., an airplane crash involving a group of strangers would be peripheral rather than central; see Green, 1982), the setting of the community (e.g., rural vs. urban), and the nature of the community's official disaster response (e.g., adequate vs. ineffective).

Community-level factors may be more important than the event itself in predicting individual outcomes. Golec (1983) found that an unusually positive community response to the 1976 Teton Dam collapse resulted in remarkably rapid recovery. Despite considerable property loss and disruption (70% of the homes in the county were severely damaged or totally destroyed), recovery was optimized by several community characteristics: adequate warning (resulting in a low death/injury rate), a homogeneous (Mormon) population, maintenance of social networks, adequate financial compensation, a surplus of resources for immediate needs, and an effective local disaster response.

A study by Steinglass and Gerrity (1990) suggests that the natural social network in particular may be critical in determining long-term recovery. Their study compared two communities hit by natural disaster: one by tornado, the other by flood. Of particular interest is that although the tornado-hit community was the *more* effective community in the delivery of disaster relief services, its residents experienced higher long-term levels of posttraumatic stress disorder PTSD than did those in the flooded community. This happened, even though the recovery process had been substantially completed by the time of 16-month data collection in the tornado-stricken community, whereas in the flooded community recovery was only partial, with many families (mostly uninsured) still living in temporary housing. Yet, the absence of an effective disaster response in the flooded community did not appear to prolong the psychiatric symptomatology of its residents.

Steinglass and Gerrity (1990) speculated that the key factor was the nature of the relationship established between affected families and the larger community. The tornado community characterized its extremely effective recovery efforts as directed at assisting the "victims," and may have thereby inadvertently contributed to the alienation of disaster-impacted families from the rest of the community. Victims are not encouraged to be empowered and to cope by actively doing something. In contrast, the flood was from the first conceptualized as a community-level disaster. Even though recovery was agonizingly slow, relocated families may have been less likely to feel estranged from the community as a whole, since everyone felt victimized by the flood. This may have encouraged a community-problem solving focus and facilitated appropriate and mutual support-seeking coping. Such an interpretation is consistent with the increasing recognition in coping research that support seeking is a critical aspect of people's coping response (Endler & Parker, 1990).

Phifer and Norris's (1989a, 1989b) analysis of the psychological responses of flood victims in several Kentucky communities provides further illumination of the preceding findings. These investigators found that while personal losses were more closely associated with persistent (2 year postdisaster) increases in negative affect (e.g., sadness, anxiety, discouragement, worry, and agitation), extent of community destruction was more closely associated with declines in positive affect (e.g., feeling less enthusiasm, less energy, and less enjoyment of life). Thus whereas being singled out for disaster losses may serve to increase psychiatric symptomatology, widespread community destruction may rob even those without personal losses of the qualities that make living in their community a worthwhile experience.

Social Resources

Victims' social networks include family, friends, neighbors, and community gatekeepers. Like community response, the immediate social environment can be an important mediator of individuals' outcomes following exposure to extreme stress.

Children may be particularly vulnerable to social mediators. For example, a study by McFarlane, Policansky, and Irwin (1987) indicated that the mother's response to Australian bushfires was a better predictor of the child's response than was the extent of the child's exposure to the disaster. This relationship was particularly affected by the extent of intrusive symptoms experienced by the mother, and by her changed pattern of parenting (overprotection). A study of the Three Mile Island (TMI) nuclear disaster by Bromet, Hough, and Connell (1984) found that there was no relationship between adverse TMI experiences and the child's outcome (social competence, self-esteem, behavioral problems) in families with a good milieu, but more adverse experiences *did* predict outcome in families with a poor milieu. These findings suggest that parents who can themselves model successful coping behavior and can continue to cope successfully in their parental role may sustain a more protective environment for their children.

As the preceding findings suggest, social involvement has the potential to cause both positive and negative effects following disaster (see Solomon, 1986, for a review). Although providing support under normal conditions may benefit the provider as well as the recipient, Shumaker and Brownell (1984) point out that large-scale emergencies force providers to give support at a time when they too need it, thereby making the supportive role in itself a source of stress.

Along these lines, a study of St. Louis victims of floods and dioxin found that for women, mid-range levels of support availability were associated with the most favorable outcomes, whereas women victims with high-support availability did more poorly (Solomon, Smith, Robins, & Fischbach, 1987; see also Z. Solomon's, 1985, study of TMI-exposed mothers of preschool children).

Because women are more often called on to provide emotional support than are men (Fischer, 1982; Gove & Hughes, 1984), household exposure to disaster may serve to overload the capacity of women to provide the nurturance asked of them. Along these lines, Gleser et al. (1981) found that married women who were victims of the Buffalo Creek disaster showed higher psychopathology than did women who lived alone; further, a spouse's anxiety or depression more seriously distressed women than men. Gleser et al.'s findings suggest that women may be responding more to their husband's mental health problems than to the disaster that precipitates them. These results suggest the possibility that, for women in particular, strong family ties may be more burdensome than supportive in times of extreme stress (see Solomon, Smith, Robins, & Fischbach, 1987). Hobfoll and London (1986) noted a similar pattern among Israeli women whose loved ones were called into service during the 1982 Israel-Lebanon War. The more support these women received, the greater was their psychological distress. They termed this phenomenon the "pressure cooker" effect because researchers noted that women's negative reactions to support may have been due to the fact that social interactions concentrated on talking about worries and all the potential negative consequences of the war. Those who received more support were thus also receiving ongoing reminders of the risk to their loved ones.

A recent study by Kaniasty and Norris (1993) showed that although support from both kin and nonkin members of the social network declined following Kentucky floods, it was only the loss of nonkin support that led to increased levels of depression. And even those who suffered no personal loss were more likely to be depressed 2 years postdisaster, if their community experienced widespread destruction and weak social ties were disrupted. The investigators noted that relatives typically provide instrumental (material) support, but people generally turn to friends, neighbors, and co-workers for companionship and emotional support (Rook, 1985, 1990). These findings suggest that support-seeking coping may need to be better differentiated than it is in available measures of coping. Kaniasty and Norris's (1993) findings indicate that long-term depression may relate more to declines in emotional support and social participation than to the loss of instrumental support. Other research suggests that single parents appear to be at particularly high risk for losing access to emotional support following a disaster, and may therefore be a particularly high-risk group for psychological problems in a disaster's wake (Solomon, Bravo, Rubio-Stipec, & Canino, 1993).

Individual Resources

Other moderators of disaster response relate to personal resources of the victims. Individual characteristics most frequently studied in disasters tend to be demographic variables, such as gender and age. Some studies suggest that women may be at greater risk than men for PTSD and other mental health problems following exposure to disaster (e.g., Bromet, Parkinson, Schulberg, Dunn, & Gondek, 1982; Gleser et al., 1981; Green et al., 1991; Steinglass & Gerrity, 1990). Although these and other studies suggest that women are more vulnerable, it may actually depend on the circumstances (see preceding discussion) as well as which particular outcome is measured. For example, women victims tend to have higher rates of anxiety and depression, while male victims may be more likely to abuse alcohol (e.g., Solomon, Smith, Robins, & Fischbach, 1987). With respect to age, studies suggest that elderly victims are *less* vulnerable to psychological problems than are younger victims; further, middle-aged subjects are at most risk for these problems, perhaps because this group tends to be responsible for both children and for parents in the event of a crisis (Green, Gleser, Lindy, Grace, & Leonard, in press; Lomranz, Hobfoll, Johnson, Eyal, & Tzemach, in press).

Other individual personal characteristics that can modify disaster effects include cognitive and emotional factors such as prior psychiatric history, the specific coping response, perceived control, and attributions of blame for the event. People who are vulnerable to psychopathy are at particular risk. For example, Smith et al. (1986) found that disasters appeared to exacerbate preexisting depressions rather than to initiate symptoms of the disorder in those previously symptom free.

According to Taylor (1983), an important aspect of successful adjustment to trauma is gaining a sense of control over the emergency event, so as to either manage its effects or prevent its recurrence. It is possible that individuals suffering the most psychological disturbance in the wake of disaster are those whose sense of mastery over their lives has been most undermined. Sustaining a positive sense of mastery allows individuals to remain in a problem-directed coping mode, rather than in typically less successful forms of coping, such as avoidance and drinking.

Along these lines, results of a study by Solomon, Regier, and Burke (1989) indicate that the degree of distress varies according to both type of disaster exposure and victims' explanations for their misfortune. These investigators found that assigning blame (particularly to the self) impeded both help seeking and psychological recovery following a flood; however, assigning blame (to others) enhanced psychological recovery following exposure to dioxin. Natural disasters may better lend themselves to active, problem-focused responses, such as seeking agency assistance for flood relief. However, in more ambiguous disaster situations, such as exposure to dioxin or other technological hazards, the external environment is less amenable to individual control (see Baum, Fleming, & Singer, 1983).

In situations where direct control over consequences is not possible, Taylor (1983) suggests that successful adjustment will require the ability to summon cognitions that impart the *illusion* of control. In the Solomon et al. (1989) study, blaming other human agents for the dioxin damage may have provided such an illusion of control, by fostering the belief that the identified guilty party would be forced to assume the responsibility for finding solutions to dioxin-related problems. Similarly, after the actual stressor has departed and initially high levels of support have dissipated, people may not have a clear target for problem-directed coping efforts. Yet, sustaining a problem focus is important, once again illustrating that people might do better to create targets for their control. This may also help explain why intact communities do better following a disaster, because individuals can continue their problem-focused efforts with others in survivor groups, memorial programs, and projects to rebuild the community.

CONCLUSION

We have presented the basic framework of COR theory and offered it as a possible explanatory model for the study of coping with extreme stressors. We have illustrated the support for the basic tenets and principles of the theory and outlined how it might be applied to the study of extreme stressors. We used the theory as a heuristic for examining short- and long-term reactions to extreme stressors and for pointing toward particularly critical resources in the process of extreme stress.

COR theory may be particularly applicable to extreme stress owing to the extent to which resources are lost and challenged in such circumstances. Extreme stress often produces a rapid and widespread devastation to resources and the consequences of such circumstances are often long term as well, lasting many years. Focusing on resources also helps us appreciate that extreme stress affects people, groups, and communities on the level of personal and social resources, the conditions that create and foster resources, and the community attributes that sustain resources. It also highlights that these different resource levels are interrelated and produce a web of interactions that must be understood if we are to explain people's extreme stress reactions.

Extreme stressors set a ball into motion that threatens and challenges resources and can result in the loss of the most precious of resources. How well individuals respond depends, in part, on the degree of resources that are lost and the extent to which they can preserve resources for a coping process that includes the management of recovery, rehabilitation, and rebuilding. When resources are available, victims seem to be more capable of entering a survivor role that allows them to cope using both problem-directed and emotion-directed coping. When personal and community resources are lacking, coping tends to take the form of emotion- and cognition-directed behaviors and the emotion-focused attempts tend to be more self-defeating; consequently, those affected have difficulty emerging from a victim into the survivor role. The interaction between resources, coping behavior, and outcomes is complex, and COR theory is an explanatory mechanism for untangling this web, making predictions, and intervening to offset the extent of loss and resultant dysfunction and distress.

Future research might attempt to further investigate how coping behavior and resources interact. We suggest two specific avenues of investigation. First, it is essential to examine how coping behavior affects people in the presence or absence of critical resources. Does a problem-oriented focus aid adjustment for those low in self-esteem, social support, or those lacking employment opportunities in their locale? Because extreme stressors often decimate resources, this question takes on even greater meaning in extreme stress situations. Second, we encourage investigation of the social aspects of coping. This means not just the seeking of social support, but also coalition building, social joining, and social protection (acting to protect others) (Hobfoll, Dunahoo, Ben-Porath, & Monnier, 1994). In this way, coping research must merge its control-mastery orientation with a social communal orientation (Riger, 1993) if it hopes to unravel the intricacies of how people cope in a social world. Such efforts will bring coping research in confrontation with more ecologically valid questions. These questions will also be more complex, but the basis from individualistic research is solid enough to tackle such new challenges.

REFERENCES

Aarts, P. (1992, June). Late onset symptomatology in elderly Dutch resistance veterans. *Abstract of the World Conference of the International Society for Traumatic Stress Studies* (p. 58). Amsterdam, The Netherlands.

Adams, P., & Adams, G. (1984). Mount Saint Helen's ashfall. *American Psychologist, 39,* 252–260.

Ayalon, O., & Soskis, D. (1986). Survivors of terrorist victimization: A follow-up study. In N. A. Milgram (Ed.), *Stress and coping in time of war: Generalizations from the Israeli experience.* New York: Brunner/Mazel.

Baum, A. (1987). *Toxins, technology, and natural disasters.* In G. R. VandenBos & B. K. Bryant (pp. 9–53). Washington, DC: American Psychological Association.

Baum, A., Fleming, R., & Davidson, L. (1983). Natural disaster and technological catastrophe. *Environment and Behavior, 15,* 333–354.

Baum, A., Fleming, R., & Singer, J. E. (1983). Coping with victimization by technological disaster. *Journal of Social Issues, 39*(2), 117–138.

Baum, A., Schaeffer, M., Lake, R., Fleming, R., & Collins, D. (1986). Psychological and endocrinological correlates of chronic stress at Three Mile Island. *Perspectives on Behavioral Medicine, 2,* 201–217.

Baum, A., Solomon, S., & Ursano, R. (1987). Emergency/disaster research issues: A guide to the preparation and evaluation of grant applications dealing with traumatic stress. *Proceedings of the Workshop on Research Issues: Emergency, Disaster, and Post-Traumatic Stress.* Bethesda, MD: Uniformed Services University of the Health Sciences.

Blake, D. D., Albano, A. M., & Keane, T. M. (1992). Twenty years of trauma: Psychological Abstracts 1970 through 1989. *Journal of Traumatic Stress, 5,* 1–8.

Bravo, M., Rubio-Stipec, M., Canino, G., Woodbury, M., & Ribera, J. (1990). The psychological sequelae of disaster stress prospectively and retrospectively evaluated. *American Journal of Community Psychology, 18,* 661–680.

Brett, J. M. (1982). Job transfer and well-being. *Journal of Applied Psychology, 67,* 450–463.

Bromet, E., Hough, L., & Connell, M. (1984). Mental health of children near the Three Mile Island reactor. *Journal of Preventive Psychiatry, 2,* 275–301.

Bromet, E. J., Parkinson, D. K., Schulberg, H. C., Dunn, L. O., & Gondek, P. C. (1982). Mental health of residents near the Three Mile Island reactor: A comparative study of selected groups. *Journal of Preventive Psychiatry, 1*(3), 225–274.

Canino, G., Bravo, M., Rubio-Stipec, M., & Woodbury, M. (1990). The impact of disaster on mental health: Prospective and retrospective analyses. *International Journal of Mental Health, 19,* 51–69.

Carver, C. S., Scheier, M. F., & Weintraub, J. K. (1989). Assessing coping strategies: A theoretically based approach. *Journal of Personality and Social Psychology, 56,* 267–283.

Cohen, S., & Hoberman, H. M. (1983). Positive events and social supports as buffers of life change stress. *Journal of Applied Social Psychology, 13*(2), 99–125.

Cook, J., & Bickman, L. (1990). Social support and psychological symptomatology following a natural disaster. *Journal of Traumatic Stress, 3*(4), 541–556.

Davidson, L., Fleming, I., & Baum, A. (1986). Post-traumatic stress as a function of chronic stress and toxic exposure. In C. Figley (Ed.), *Trauma and it's wake* (Vol. 2). New York: Brunner/Mazel.

Dohrenwend, B. S., Dohrenwend, B. P., Dodson, M., & Shrout, P. E. (1984). Symptoms, hassles, social support, and life events: Problem of confounded measures. *Journal of Abnormal Psychology, 93,* 222–230.

Endler, N. S., & Parker, J. D. A. (1990). Multidimensional assessment of coping: A critical evaluation. *Journal of Personality and Social Psychology, 58,* 844–854.

Fischer, C. S. (1982). *To dwell among friends: Personal networks in town and city.* Chicago: University of Chicago Press.

Freedy, J. R., Kilpatrick, D. G., & Resnick, H. S. (1993a). Natural disasters and mental health: Theory, assessment, and intervention. *Journal of Social Behavior and Personality, 8*(5), 49–103.

Freedy, J. R., Kilpatrick, D. G., & Resnick, H. S. (1993b). *The psychological impact of the Oakland Hills fire.* Final report for supplement to National Institute of Mental Health (NIMH) grant no. 1R01 MH 47508-01A1. Submitted to NIMH Violence and Traumatic Stress Research Branch, Washington, DC.

Freedy, J. R., Resnick, H. S., & Kilpatrick, D. G. (1992). A conceptual framework for evaluating disaster impact: Implications for clinical intervention. In L. S. Austin (Ed.), *Responding to disaster: A guide for mental health professionals.* Washington, DC: American Psychiatric Press.

Freedy, J. R., Resnick, H. S., Kilpatrick, D. G., & Saunders, B. E. (1993). *Adult psychological functioning after earthquakes.* Final report for National Institute of Mental Health (NIMH) grant no. R03 MH 49485. Submitted to NIMH Violence and Traumatic Stress Research Branch, Washington, DC.

Freedy, J. R., Saladin, M. E., Kilpatrick, D. G., Resnick, H. S., & Saunders, B. E. (1994). Understanding acute psychological distress following natural disaster. *Journal of Traumatic Stress, 7,* 257–273.

Freedy, J. R., Shaw, D., Jarrell, M. P., & Masters, C. (1992). Towards an understanding of the psychological impact of natural disaster: An application of the conservation resources stress model. *Journal of Traumatic Stress, 5*(3), 1992.

Gleser, G. C., Green, B. L., & Winget, C. N. (1981). *Prolonged psychosocial effects of disaster: A study of Buffalo Creek.* New York: Academic Press.

Golec, J. A. (1983). A contextual approach to the social psychological study of disaster recovery. *International Journal of Mass Emergencies and Disasters, 1*(2), 255–276.

Gove, W. R., & Hughes, M. (1984). *Overcrowding in the household.* New York: Academic Press.

Green, B. L. (1982). Assessing levels of psychosocial impairment following disaster: Consideration of actual and methodological dimensions. *The Journal of Nervous and Mental Disease, 17*(9), 544–552.

Green, B. L. (1992, August). *PTSD following a disaster: Comparison of first and second decade predictors.* Paper presented at the annual meeting of the American Psychological Association as a part of symposium entitled "Traumatic Stress: Theory to Practice." Washington, DC.

Green, B. L., Gleser, G. C., Lindy, J. D., Grace, M. C., & Leonard, A. (in press). Age related reactions to the Buffalo Creek dam collapse: Second decade effects. In P. E. Ruskin & J. A. Talbott (Eds.), *Aging and posttraumatic stress disorder.* Washington, DC: American Psychiatric Press.

Green, B., Grace, M., & Gleser, G. (1985). Identifying survivors at risk: Long-term impairment following the Beverly Hills Supper Club fire. *Journal of Consulting and Clinical Psychology, 53,* 672–678.

Green, B., Grace, M., Lindy, J., Gleser, G., Leonard, A., & Kramer, T. (1990). Buffalo Creek survivors in the second decade: Comparison with unexposed and nonlitigant groups. *Journal of Applied Social Psychology, 20,* 1033–1050.

Green, B. L., Korol, M., Grace, M. C., Vary, M. G., Leonard, A. C., Gleser, G. C., & Smitson-Cohen, S. (1991). Children and disaster: Age, gender, and parental effects on PTSD symptoms. *Journal of the American Academy of Child and Adolescent Psychiatry, 30*(6), 945–951.

Green, B. L., Lindy, J. D., & Grace, M. C. (in press). Psychological effects of toxic contamination. In R. Ursano, B. McCaughey, & C. Fullerton (Eds.), *Individual and community responses to trauma and disaster.* Cambridge, UK: Cambridge University Press.

Green, B., Lindy, J., Grace, M., Gleser, G., Leonard, A., Korol, M., & Winget, C. (1990). Buffalo Creek survivors in the second decade: Stability of stress symptoms. *American Journal of Orthopsychiatry, 60*(1), 43–54.

Green, B. L., & Solomon, S. D. (in press). The mental health impact of natural and technological disasters. In J. R. Freedy & S. E. Hobfoll (Eds.), *Traumatic stress: From theory to practice.* New York: Plenum.

Hobfoll, S. E. (1988). *The ecology of stress.* Washington, DC: Hemisphere.

Hobfoll, S. E. (1989). Conservation of resources: A new attempt at conceptualizing stress. *The American Psychologist, 44,* 513–524.

Hobfoll, S. E. (1991). Traumatic stress: A theory based on rapid loss of resources. *Anxiety Research, 4,* 187–197.

Hobfoll, S. E., Dunahoo, C. L., Ben-Porath, Y., & Monnier, J. (1994). Gender and coping: The dual-axis model of coping. *American Journal of Community Psychology, 22,* 49–82.

Hobfoll, S. E., & Leiberman, J. (1987). Personality and social resources in immediate and continued stress-resistance among women. *Journal of Personality and Social Psychology, 52,* 18–26.

Hobfoll, S. E., & Lerman, M. (1989). Predicting receipt of social support: A longitudinal study of parents' reactions to their child's illness. *Health Psychology, 8,* 61–77.

Hobfoll, S. E., & Lilly, R. S. (1993). Resource conservation as a strategy for community psychology. *Journal of Community Psychology, 21,* 128–148.

Hobfoll, S. E., Lomranz, J., Eyal, N., Bridges, A., & Tzemach, M. (1989). Pulse of a nation: Depressive mood reactions of Israelis to the Israel-Lebanon war. *Journal of Personality and Social Psychology, 56*(6), 1002–1012.

Hobfoll, S. E., & London, P. (1986). The relationship of self-concept and social support to emotional distress among women during war. *Journal of Social and Clinical Psychology, 4*(2), 189–203.

Hobfoll, S. E., London, P., & Orr, E. (1988). Mastery, intimacy, and stress-resistance during war. *Journal of Community Psychology, 16,* 317–331.

Holen, A. (1991). A longitudinal study of the occurrence and persistence of post-traumatic health problems in disaster survivors. *Stress medicine, 7,* 11–17.

Holmes, T. H., & Rahe, R. H. (1967). The social readjustment rating scale. *Journal of Psychosomatic Research, 11*(2), 213–218.

Horowitz, M., Wilner, N., & Alvarez, W. (1979). Impact of event scale: A measure of subjective stress. *Psychological Medicine, 41,* 209–218.

Jaffe, Y., & Rosenfeld, H. (1982). Field dependence, handling of hostility, and sexual identification of posttraumatic Yom Kippur War veterans: Three years after the war. In C. D. Spielberger & I. G. Sarason (Eds.), *Stress and anxiety* (Vol. 8). Washington, DC: Hemisphere.

Kaniasty, F., & Norris, F. H. (1993). A test of the social support deterioration model in the context of natural disaster. *Journal of Personality and Social Psychology, 64*(3), 395–408.

Kessler, R. C., Turner, J. B., & House, J. S. (1989). Unemployment, reemployment, and emotional functioning in a community sample. *American Sociological Review, 54,* 648–657.

Lane, C., & Hobfoll, S. E. (1992). How loss affects anger and alienates potential supporters. *Journal of Consulting and Clinical Psychology, 60,* 935–942.

Lawrence, M. (1989). *Preliminary report: Hurricane Hugo.* Unpublished manuscript, National Hurricane Center, Miami, Florida.

Lazarus, R. S. (1990). Theory-based stress measurement. *Psychological Inquiry, 1,* 3–13.

Lazarus, R. S., DeLongis, A., Folkman, S., & Gruen, R. (1985). Stress and adaptational outcome: The problem of confounded measures. *American Psychologist, 40,* 770–779.

Lazarus, R. S., & Folkman, S. (1984). *Stress, appraisal, and coping.* New York: Springer.

Lomranz, J., Hobfoll, S. E., Johnson, R., Eyal, N., & Tzemach, M. (in press). *A nation's response to attack: Stressful events do result in depressive mood.*

Marlowe, D. H. (1979). *Cohesion, anticipated breakdown, and endurance in battle: Considerations for severe- and high-intensity combat.* Unpublished manuscript, Division of Neuropsychiatry, Walter Reed Army Institute of Research, Washington, DC.

McFarlane, A. H. (1987). Family functioning and overprotection following a natural disaster: The longitudinal effects of post-traumatic morbidity. *Australian and New Zealand Journal of Psychiatry, 21,* 210–218.

McFarlane, A. H. (1992). Avoidance and intrusion in posttraumatic stress disorder. *Journal of Nervous and Mental Disease, 180*(7), 439–445.

McFarlane, A. H., Policansky, S., & Irwin, C. (1987). A longitudinal study of the psychological morbidity in children due to a natural disaster. *Psychological Medicine, 17*, 727–738.

Mikulincer, M., & Solomon, Z. (1989). Causal attribution, coping strategies, and combat-related post-traumatic stress disorder. *European Journal of Personality, 3*, 269–284.

Milgram, N. A. (1986). *Stress and coping in time of war: Generalizations from the Israeli experience*. New York: Brunner/Mazel.

Munton, A. G. (1990). Job relocation stress and the family. *Journal of Organizational Behavior, 11*, 401–406.

Murphy, S. (1984). Stress levels and health status of victims of a natural disaster. *Research in nursing and health, 7*, 205–215.

Myers, D. G. (1989). Mental health and disaster: Preventive approaches to intervention. In R. Gist & B. Lubin (Eds.), *Psychosocial aspects of disaster* (pp. 190–228). New York: Wiley.

Norris, F., Phifer, J., & Kaniasty, K. (in press). Individual and community reactions to the Kentucky floods: Findings from a longitudinal study of older adults. In R. Ursano, B. McCaughey, & C. Fullerton (Eds.), *Individual and community responses to trauma and disaster*. Cambridge, UK: Cambridge.

Phifer, J. F., & Norris, F. H. (1989a). Psychological and physical sequelae of natural disaster: Differential vulnerability among older adults. *Psychology and Aging, 5*, 412–420.

Phifer, J. F., & Norris, F. H. (1989b). Psychological symptoms in older adults following natural disaster: Nature, timing, duration, and course. *Journal of Gerontology: Social Sciences, 44*, 207–217.

Raphael, B., Lundin, T., & Weisaeth, L. (1989). A research method for the study of psychological and psychiatric aspects of disaster. *Acta Psychiatrica Scandinavia, 80*(353), 1–75.

Riger, S. (1993). What's wrong with empowerment. *American Journal of Community Psychology, 21*, 279–292.

Robins, L. N., Fischbach, R. L., Smith, E. M., Cottler, L. B., Solomon, S. D., & Goldring, E. (1986). Impact of disaster on previously assessed mental health. In J. Shore (Ed.), *Disaster stress studies: New methods and findings*. Washington, DC: American Psychiatric Press.

Rook, K. S. (1985). Functions of social bonds: Perspectives from research on social support, loneliness and social isolation. In I. G. Sarason & B. R. Sarason (Eds.), *Social support: Theory, research and application*. Dordrecht, The Netherlands: Martinus Nijhoff.

Rook, K. S. (1990). Social relationships as a source of companionship: Implications for older adults' psychological well-being. In B. R. Sarason, I. G. Sarason, & G. R. Pierce (Eds.), *Social support: An interactional view* (pp. 219–250). New York: Wiley.

Rubonis, A. V., & Bickman, L. (1991). Psychological impairment in the wake of disaster: The disaster-psychopathology relationship. *Psychological Bulletin, 109*(3), 384–399.

Shore, J., Tatum, E., & Vollmer, W. (1986). Psychiatric reactions to disaster: The Mount St. Helens experience. *American Journal of Psychiatry, 143*, 590–595.

Shumaker, S. A., & Brownell, A. (1984). Toward a theory of social support: Closing conceptual gaps. *Journal of Social Issues, 40*(4), 11–36.

Smith, E. M., Robins, L. N., Pryzbeck, T. R., Goldring, E., & Solomon, S. D. (1986). Psychosocial consequences of a disaster. In J. H. Shore (Ed.), *Disaster stress studies: New methods and findings.* Washington, DC: American Psychiatric Press.

Solomon, S. D. (1986). Mobilizing social support networks in times of disaster. In C. Figley (Ed.), *Trauma and its wake* (Vol. 2). New York: Brunner/Mazel.

Solomon, S. D. (1989). Research issues in assessing disaster's effects. In R. Gist & Lubin (Eds.), *Psychosocial aspects of disaster* (pp. 308–340). New York: Wiley.

Solomon, S. D., Bravo, M., Rubio-Stipec, M., & Canino, G. (1993). Effect of family role on response to disaster. *Journal of Traumatic Stress, 6*(2), 255–269.

Solomon, S. D., Regier, D. A., & Burke, J. D. (1989). Role of perceived control in coping with natural and technological disaster. *Journal of Clinical and Social Psychology, 8*(4), 376–392.

Solomon, S. D., Smith, E. M., Robins, L. N., & Fischbach, R. L. (1987). Social involvement as a mediator of disaster-induced stress. *Journal of Applied Social Psychology, 17*(12), 1092–1112.

Solomon, Z., & Benbenishty, R. (1986). The role of proximity, immediacy, and expectancy in frontline treatment of combat stress reaction among Israelis in the Lebanon War. *American Journal of Psychiatry, 143*(5), 613–617.

Solomon, Z., & Mikulincer, M. (1990). Life events and combat-related posttraumatic stress disorder: The intervening role of locus of control and social support. *Military Psychology, 2,* 241–256.

Solomon, Z., Mikulincer, M., & Hobfoll, S. E. (1987). The effects of social support and battle intensity on loneliness and breakdown during combat. *Journal of Personality and Social Psychology, 51,* 1269–1276.

Solomon, Z., Noy, S., & Bar-On, R. (1986). Who is at high risk for a combat stress reaction syndrome? In N. A. Milgram (Ed.), *Stress and coping in time of war: Generalizations from the Israeli experience.* New York: Brunner/Mazel.

Steinglass, P., & Gerrity, E. (1990). Natural disasters and post-traumatic stress disorder: Short-term versus long-term recovery in two disaster-affected communities. *Journal of Applied Social Psychology, 20,* 1746–1765.

Summers, G. M., & Cowan, M. L. (1991). Mental health issues related to the development of a national disaster response system. *Military Medicine, 156*(1), 30–32.

Taylor, S. E. (1983). Adjustment to threatening events: A theory of cognitive adaption. *American Psychologist, 38*(11), 1161–1173.

Thoits, P. A. (1983). Multiple identities and psychological well-being: A reformulation and test of the social interaction hypothesis. *American Sociological Review, 48,* 174–187.

Tversky, A., & Kahneman, D. (1981). The framing decisions and the psychology of choice. *Science, 24,* 453–458.

van der Kolk, B. A. (1987). *Psychological trauma.* Washington, DC: American Psychiatric Press.

Wandersman, A. H., & Hallman, W. K. (1993). Are people acting irrationally?: Understanding public concerns about environmental threats. *American Psychologist, 48,* 681–686.

Yates, S., Axsom, D., Bickman, L., & Howe, G. (1989). Factors influencing help seeking for mental health problems after disasters. In R. Gist & B. Lubin (Eds.), *Psychosocial aspects of disaster* (pp. 163–189). New York: Wiley.

CHAPTER 16

Coping with Multiple Stressors in the Environment

STEPHEN J. LEPORE and GARY W. EVANS

It is not uncommon for people to cope with diverse stressors in their day-to-day life. People living in urban environments may be taxed by intense and competing demands on their sensory systems from a multitude of environmental stimuli including noise, crowding, and pollution. Poor people must cope with unsafe and substandard housing, face relentless financial pressure, and are frequently victims of crime. Parents of a disabled child cope with multiple stressors related to caregiving, ongoing financial difficulties, and anxiety about their child's health. It is also easy to imagine multiple stressors arising from demands in the different social roles we occupy, such as parent, spouse, and employee.

Although stressors commonly occur in multiples, we know little about the adaptive consequences of coping with multiple stressors. Moreover, we know very little about how coping with one stressor affects people's ability to cope with another stressor. The capacity to cope with a stressor, as well as the effectiveness of coping efforts, presumably depends on the availability of coping resources (e.g., social support) and the particular coping response (e.g., avoidance) the person makes. Does the expenditure of coping resources on one stressor make us less adept at coping with another stressor, or somehow constrain our coping options? Are there instances in which coping with one stressor somehow enhances our ability to cope with another stressor?

INTRODUCTION TO TERMS

The term *stressors* will be used to refer to physical and social environmental conditions that the average person would perceive as actually or potentially

We are very grateful to Sheldon Cohen, Martin Greenberg, Krys Kaniasty, and Ron Kessler for their comments on an earlier version of this chapter. Preparation of this chapter was partially supported by the National Heart Lung and Blood Institute, R01 HL47325-01A1, the American Cancer Society, IRG-58-33, and the National Institutes of Mental Health R03 MH54455-01.

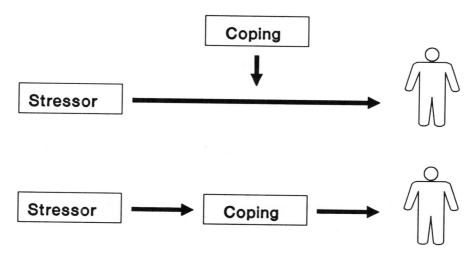

Figure 16.1 Schematic diagram of moderating (top) and mediating (bottom) role of coping in the link between stressors and health outcomes.

threatening, damaging, harmful, or depriving. Individuals' evaluations of stressors are *stress appraisals* (Lazarus & Folkman, 1984). Biological responses to stressors are physiological *stress reactions.*

We also distinguish between coping resources and coping responses. *Coping responses* are behaviors and cognitions that a person uses to adjust to a stressor. Coping responses may be aimed at managing and resolving a stressor or at ameliorating its negative emotional or bodily effects. *Coping resources* are properties of individuals (e.g., self-efficacy), their social environment (e.g., social support), and physical environmental resources (e.g., privacy) that enable them to respond to stressors.

Coping responses and resources are intended to protect people from the negative effects of stressors on psychological and physical health. When the effects of a stressor are conditioned by a person's coping responses or resources, coping acts as a moderator (see Figure 16.1, top). The relationship between a stressor and some outcome may either be increased or decreased by the presence of a particular coping response or resource. Coping responses and resources might also mediate the effects of stressors (see Figure 16.1, bottom). That is, a stressor might influence a person's coping responses or resources, which, in turn, may influence some outcome (for discussion on the mediator-moderator distinction in relation to coping, see Evans & Lepore, in press).

MULTIPLE EXPOSURES TO ENVIRONMENTAL STRESSORS

As indicated in Figure 16.2, a person might be exposed to multiple stressors because one stressor causes additional, secondary stressors to occur (top, middle)

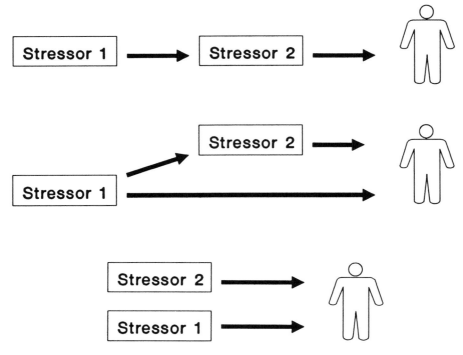

Figure 16.2   Schematic diagram of different types of exposures to multiple stressors using a two-stressor example. In the top diagram, Stressor 1 influences a person's adjustment indirectly by increasing exposure to Stressor 2. In the middle diagram, Stressor 1 has direct and indirect effects on a person's adjustment. In the bottom diagram, Stressor 1 and Stressor 2 have independent, direct effects on a person's adjustment.

or because two or more unrelated stressors from independent, or discrete origins, co-occur (bottom). In addition, a person could be exposed to different combinations of related and unrelated stressors with discrete or common causes. Multiple stressors also may be perceived as causally related or stemming from a common underlying cause even though they are objectively independent from one another in the external environment. There have been relatively few analyses of how different environmental stressors are related, partly because of assumptions many investigators have adopted from the stressful life events tradition of research that conceptualizes stressors as discrete, perhaps even random, occurrences with additive effects.

As shown in Table 16.1, environmental stressors can be sorted into five general categories: cataclysmic events, major life events, daily stressors, ambient stressors, and role stressors. Much empirical stress research focuses on how people cope with one of these general categories of stressors. However, a close inspection of the characteristics of these stressors reveals that each of them represents not a

TABLE 16.1 Five General Categories of Stressors and Their Characteristics

Category	Typical Characteristics	Examples
Cataclysms	Sudden, tumultuous, irrevocable events that impose great adaptive demands on many people. Cataclysms tend to be severe stressors to the average person.	Natural disasters, such as floods, hurricanes, and earth-quakes; technological or human-made catastrophes, such as nuclear accidents, war, plane wrecks, collapsing bridges or buildings.
Major life events	Episodic and often irrevocable events that tend to impose great adaptive demands on one or few individuals. Major life events tend to be severe stressors to the average person.	Social losses through divorce, death, relocation, or other life transitions; job loss; criminal victimization; serious illness or disability.
Daily stressors	Constellations of related and ongoing stressors experienced in day-to-day life. Daily stressors can range from being relatively minor to severe to the average person.	Financial problems, such as inability to buy basic necessities; bureaucratic inefficiencies; trouble getting work done because of interruptions.
Ambient stressors	Often intractable environmental conditions that impose ongoing demands on people. Ambient stressors can range from relatively minor and unnoticed to severe to the average person.	Noise, crowding, pollution, traffic congestion, extreme temperatures.
Role stressors	Ongoing difficulties related to fulfilling role obligations; problematic social relations encountered while perform-ing role-related obligations. Role stressors are typically severe to the average person, especially when they occur in personally important roles (e.g., marital or work roles).	Competing role expectations and demands, excessive workload, role ambiguity, too many responsibilities for people or objects, lack of social support or cohesion, lack of control or appropriate decision latitude.

singular, or unique source of threat, damage, harm, or loss to an individual, but instead comprises a wide range of unique combinations of interrelated stressors of varying magnitudes and durations.

For example, cataclysmic events obviously can exert direct negative effects on people, such as permanent physical injury, but they also can generate secondary stressors that are detrimental to individuals' well-being. Norris and Uhl (1993) found that people who sustained hurricane-related injuries and losses were likely to experience increases in chronic daily stressors (e.g., marital, parental, and financial stressors) that, in turn, were correlated with elevated psychological distress symptoms 1 year after the hurricane. The secondary stressors associated with the cataclysmic event seem to have been responsible for the negative effects of the cataclysm on psychological well-being exhibited in some victims long after the cataclysm ended.

Major life events also can generate secondary stressors that might contribute to physical and psychological health problems. Major life events seem to increase the frequency of daily stressors, such as interruptions, having to wait, or misplacing things (Kanner, Coyne, Schaefer, & Lazarus, 1981). Daily stressors associated with major life events seem to have a mediating role in the link between major life events and psychosomatic complaints and psychological distress symptoms (DeLongis, Coyne, Dakof, Folkman, & Lazarus, 1982; Kanner et al., 1981). Life events also can generate role-related stressors, such as work and family stressors, that might be detrimental to well-being. For example, people who experience job disruptions may have increased financial stressors and associated increases in depressive symptoms relative to people who have not experienced job disruption (Pearlin, Lieberman, Menaghan, & Mullan, 1981). Role stressors also can spill over from one role domain to another (Eckenrode & Gore, 1990). For example, individuals who take a cut in pay might experience increased stressors at home if they cannot contribute enough to the family economy.

The preceding examples show how people come to be exposed to multiple stressors through the cascade effect of one stressor leading to another. Individuals also might be exposed to multiple stressors from other underlying causes, such as economic (e.g., poverty) and social (e.g., crime) conditions. Some individuals are at higher risk than others for exposure to multiple stressors because of their social status or social roles. For example, multiple ambient stressors such as noise and vibration or crowding and heat are quite common in blue-collar work settings as a result of industrial processes (Poulton, 1978). Among the urban poor, residences are often overcrowded and noisy, as are the neighborhoods in which they are located (Lepore, 1994).

In summary, when people cope with a focal stressor, such as a cataclysm or major life event, they often are coping with the focal stressor and a cascade of other stressors triggered by the focal stressor. In addition, some people are more prone to be exposed to multiple stressors because of their personal characteristics or social roles. Finally, some stressors, such as ambient stressors (e.g., noise and crowding) have a tendency to covary.

EFFECTS OF MULTIPLE STRESSORS ON ADJUSTMENT

Social, psychological, and biological effects of coping with one stressor may influence a person's ability to cope with concurrent or subsequent stressors. Some theorists argue that there are benefits of coping with multiple stressors. Exposure to some stressors might inoculate people or help them to develop coping resources and strategies so that they are less harmed by subsequent stressors. Presumably, the more past experience individuals have in coping with stressors, the better equipped they will be at coping with subsequent stressors. In contrast, other theorists argue that there are direct and indirect costs of coping with a stressor. Coping with one stressor might deplete a person's resources or otherwise attenuate his or her ability to cope with subsequent stressors. Although coping is not the only factor that influences adjustment to multiple stressors, we believe it is central to understanding whether multiple stressors will have an additive or multiplicative effect on adjustment. Before elaborating on the specific ways that coping might influence adjustment to multiple stressors, we will define and illustrate what we mean by additive versus multiplicative effects of multiple stressors on adjustment.

Figure 16.3 illustrates the distinct ways that multiple stressors might influence outcomes using a two-stressor (A and B) example. Higher scores represent more adjustment problems, or stronger stress reactions. The first two bars show

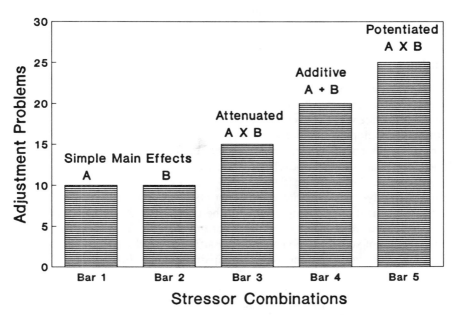

Figure 16.3   Illustration of main effects (bars 1 and 2), additive effects (bar 4), and multiplicative effects (bars 3 and 5) of stressors using a two-stressor, A and B, example.

the independent or simple main effects of exposure to either A or B. On average, a person who experiences either stressor A or stressor B can be expected to score 10 points on our adjustment problem scale. According to an additive model, the joint effects of stressors A and B on adjustment problems should be equivalent to the sum of the independent effects of A and B (10 + 10 = 20), as shown in the fourth bar in Figure 16.3. In statistical terms, the additive model indicates that there are no unique effects of being exposed to both stressor A and B above and beyond their combined independent effects.

The third and fifth bars in Figure 16.3 show two different multiplicative effects of combining stressors A and B. Here the combined effect of stressors A and B is not equal to the sum of the independent effects. The attenuation model (third bar) indicates that the joint effect of stressors A and B is less than would be expected from the additive model. The potentiation model (fifth bar) indicates that the joint effect of stressors A and B is greater than would be expected from the additive model.

In the following sections, we will briefly review some of the empirical findings related to additive and multiplicative (attenuation or potentiation) effects of multiple stressors. This review is illustrative rather than comprehensive. Many life events studies that we reviewed are not included because we could not determine the effects of the multiple stressors. Some researchers aggregated multiple stressors into a single stressor score. Other investigators who have analyzed the unique and interactive effects of diverse multiple stressors did not include plots of the interactions or tables of the means, which made it difficult to accurately interpret the interactive effect.

Additivity

The assumption that multiple stressors have additive effects on adjustment is implicit in most studies in which investigators create aggregate stress scores. This practice is prevalent in life events studies that follow the Holmes and Rahe (1967) tradition of developing cumulative stress scores by summing the number of major life events a person has experienced, or summing the magnitude of change scores of the life events. A number of scholars have challenged the additivity assumption (e.g., Brown & Harris, 1978; Thoits, 1983). For example, in her review of data published by Myers, Lindenthal, and Pepper (1971), Thoits (1983) noted that the events-impairment relationship seemed to be curvilinear. As the number of life events increased from one or more to two or more, there was a large decrease in the proportion of subjects who could be classified as psychiatrically unimpaired; however, the change in proportion of unimpaired people dropped off rapidly at higher levels of exposure to life events. Thoits did not test the additive or interactive effects of various combinations of stressors.

An alternative to the life events approach is to expose people to multiple stressors in a laboratory. Myrtek and Spital (1986) examined responses on cardiovascular and psychological tension measures after subjects were exposed to single, double, or triple stressors (mental arithmetic, cold pressor, physical exercise).

Most of the physiological outcomes indicated additive effects of the multiple stressors. There was no evidence of potentiation of physiological responses when multiple acute stressors were present. Psychological and somatic tension scores did not exceed the level they achieved following the most potent single stressor. Thus, a ceiling, or attenuation, effect was apparent.

In summary, very few investigators studying stressful life events have directly tested the additivity assumption. Instead, they have tended to examine associations between cumulative measures of presumably discrete, independent stressors and outcomes. Therefore, we have little information about when, if ever, multiple life event stressors produce an additive effect on psychological outcomes. When multiple life stressors are aggregated, it is difficult to detect underlying interactions, or the attenuating and potentiating effects that different stressors can exert on one another. There is emerging experimental data suggesting that multiple acute stressors may have additive effects on short-term physiological arousal but not on psychological outcomes.

Potentiation

Psychological Distress and Negative Mood

Lepore, Evans, and Palsane (1991) found an interactive effect of household crowding (person per room) and daily stressors from housemates on psychological distress symptoms. Social stressors were positively associated with psychological distress symptoms among people living in crowded households, but were unrelated to distress in people living in relatively uncrowded households. In another study, an interaction was obtained between air pollution and major life events: There was a positive association between air pollution and psychological distress in people who had experienced 1 or more stressful life events in the prior 3 months, but no relation between pollution and distress among people who had not experienced any recent stressful events (Evans, Jacobs, Dooley, & Catalano, 1987).

Caspi, Bolger, and Eckenrode (1987) found a significant interactive effect of poor neighborhood quality and daily social stressors on women's mood. A higher level of daily social stressors was more strongly associated with poorer mood in women who believed their neighborhood was unsafe than in women who believed their neighborhood was relatively safe. In another study of mood, Ruback and Pandy (1992) found that high temperatures and crowding combined interactively to reduce positive mood. Increasing the number of people in a taxi dampened riders' positive mood much more in hot months than in relatively cool months.

Physiological Outcomes

Schaubroeck and Ganster (1993) found that workers in chronically demanding occupations tended to have higher resting levels of diastolic blood pressure and to exhibit lower heart rate, blood pressure, and skin temperature responses during exposure to acute laboratory challenges than workers in less demanding occupations. In addition, after cessation of the acute laboratory stressor, individuals in more demanding occupations took longer to recover to resting physiological levels than their counterparts in less demanding occupations. Siegrist and Klein (1990) found a similar pattern of psychophysiological reactions to acute stressors among blue-collar workers facing different levels of job-related chronic stressors.

The general pattern of reduced responsivity to an acute stressor, delayed recovery to basal levels, and higher resting diastolic blood pressure in chronically stressed workers suggests that chronic stressors alter workers' initial physiological state and reduce their ability to respond to acute stressors. Perhaps chronic stress degenerates the peripheral sympathetic nervous system, thereby reducing adaptive arousal during acute challenge and interfering with recovery after challenge. Diminished physiological capacity for responding to challenge may reflect conditioned tendencies to avoid active coping responses, or an inability to marshal coping energies. Therefore, diminished physiological responses to an acute stressor may be interpreted as a maladaptive response (Dienstbier, 1989). In addition, sustained elevations in blood pressure might put people at risk for cardiovascular diseases; therefore, failure to return to baseline quickly after the removal of a stressor may be maladaptive.

Fleming, Baum, Davidson, Rectanus, and McArdle (1987) found that residents of crowded neighborhoods had higher chronic psychological distress symptoms and higher chronic urinary catecholamines than did uncrowded residents. During an acute laboratory stressor, crowded residents had higher blood pressure reactivity than did uncrowded residents. In addition, it took crowded residents longer than uncrowded residents to habituate to the acute stressor, as indicated by a measure of their half-recovery. The slower cardiovascular habituation of crowded versus uncrowded residents in response to acute challenge is consistent with the findings from Schaubroeck and Ganster (1993) and Siegrist and Klein (1990), who found that chronically stressed workers took longer to reach their baseline level of cardiovascular functioning after exposure to an acute stressor relative to workers not facing chronic stressors. The slower habituation reported by Fleming and colleagues also is consistent with the notion that chronic stressors can potentiate, or increase, the negative physiological effects of acute stressors. However, the finding that crowded subjects had higher cardiovascular reactivity to the acute stressor seems to be inconsistent with the findings from Schaubroeck and Ganster (1993) and Siegrist and Klein (1990). One possible reason that the latter researchers obtained different responsivity results than Fleming et al. is that they used a different type of responsivity index.[1]

In summary, chronic ambient stressors, such as crowding, pollution, and poor neighborhood quality, when combined with major life events or daily stressors,

---

[1] In the Fleming et al. study, responsivity was measured by subtracting the baseline cardiovascular measures from the average of 8 cardiovascular measurements taken during the acute stressor. In contrast, the studies by Schaubroeck and Ganster and by Siegrist and Klein used maximal, or peak, increases over resting blood pressures and heart rate to assess cardiovascular responsiveness. It is possible that crowded individuals in the Fleming et al. study could have had lower peak cardiovascular responses (e.g., peak increase in blood pressure as a percentage of baseline) and higher average responses during the acute stressor in comparison with their uncrowded counterparts.

seem to potentiate psychological distress and negative mood states. In addition, individuals experiencing chronic role stressors and major life events tend to be less able to marshal physiological resources for responding to acute stressor challenge and take longer to return to their basal levels of arousal on cessation of acute stressors than individuals not exposed to other stressors. Exposure to one stressor, particularly a chronic stressor, can reduce an individual's ability to adapt to another stressor and even increase vulnerability to subsequent stressors.

Attenuation

Psychological Distress and Negative Mood

McGonagle and Kessler (1990) found some indications that depression created by acute life stressors is less pronounced among women who have preexisting chronic difficulties than among those without such difficulties. In their study, all events people had experienced less than 12 months prior to the study were classified as acute, including point-in-time events such as death of a loved one; more enduring events were classified as chronic. The authors examined over 40 different Chronic Stressor × Acute Stressor interactions, using the total aggregated chronic and acute stressor scores, as well as chronic and acute stressors disaggregated by life domains (e.g., finance, marriage, health). The aggregated interaction analyses (total Chronic Stressor score × total Acute Stressor score) indicated a negative interaction on depressive symptoms in women. To identify the locus of this effect, the authors conducted additional analyses of the interactions between chronic and acute stressors disaggregated by domain. They found one significant negative interaction between chronic and acute interpersonal conflicts in women. No other negative or positive interactions were statistically significant after controlling for simultaneous significance.

In some circumstances, major life transitions may not be experienced as stressful and could even relieve a person from an ongoing stressor (Wheaton, 1990). For example, divorce following a bad marriage might be less distressing than if it followed a relatively good marriage. Wheaton (1990) identified people experiencing different transition events (e.g., job loss, divorce) and measured their role problems prior to the transition. He concluded from his findings that having prior role stress reduced the negative impact of life events on mental health for people experiencing many of the transition events. For example, he found that increases in baseline-adjusted distress symptoms were smaller in young, unmarried men who had lost a relatively high-stress job than in their counterparts who had lost a relatively low-stress job. Furthermore, 6 out of 10 such attenuation interaction effects in different age and sex groups were statistically significant. Two potentiation interaction effects were nonsignificant.

There are some problems in interpreting Wheaton's results as evidence of stress relief or attenuation effects of multiple stressors. For instance, whether or not workers had relatively stressful or stress-free jobs to begin with, they tended to experience increases in distress symptoms following loss of job. No group experienced a decline in symptoms, or relief, following job loss. In addition, the distress measure was a residualized variable (symptoms in 1981 controlling for symptoms in 1977). The absolute value of distress before and after job loss for people in stressful versus unstressful jobs was not shown in Wheaton's paper. It is possible that individuals in the less favorable job conditions were near the ceiling on the distress symptoms measure before becoming unemployed. If this were so, following the loss of their job, workers from high-stress jobs could not exhibit large increases in symptoms.

Caspi and colleagues (1987) examined the interactive effect of major life events and neighborhood quality on women's mood. They found a weaker relation between exposure to ambient stressors and negative mood among women who had experienced negative life events than among women who had not. Caspi and colleagues argued that following a major life stressor a person's threshold for detecting acute stressors is higher than it would be in the absence of the major life stressor, therefore reducing the psychological impact of acute stressors.

In another study on mood, the negative effects of multiple arguments (e.g., argument with spouse and child on same day) seemed to be smaller than the combined effects of multiple arguments when they occurred on separate days (Bolger, DeLongis, Kessler, & Schilling, 1989). However, this effect was only statistically significant among women. Other combinations of multiple minor stressors occurring on the same day also had negative coefficients, suggesting a reduction in negative mood when multiple stressors occurred on a single day rather than on separate days. However, these latter effects were not statistically significant. There were no instances in which a positive effect (potentiation) of multiple minor stressors on the same day reached statistical significance.

In summary, several studies find mixed evidence of attenuation effects between multiple stressors on psychological symptomatology and mood. The studies reviewed in this section also provided very little evidence of potentiation effects. Indeed, the studies by Wheaton (1990) and McGonagle and Kessler (1990) provided many opportunities to find potentiation effects if they existed, but they failed to do so. Thus, although the evidence for attenuation effects following exposure to multiple stressors is not very strong in these studies, neither is the alternative type of multiplicative effect, stress potentiation.

Physiological Outcomes

Dienstbier (1989) has argued that some forms of intermittent stressor exposure can result in physiological "toughening." A toughened organism is one that becomes conditioned to stressors, as indicated by "resistance to central catecholamine depletion, increased peripheral catecholamine availability, increased beta-receptor sensitivity, and suppression of cortisol responses" (p. 95). A toughened organism demonstrates a low level of basal arousal, a strong sympathetic-adrenal-medullary (SAM) response in the presence of a stressor (strong arousal during stressor), and a quick decline to baseline levels of arousal after the removal of the stressor. In contrast, the untoughened organism, may exhibit elevated basal arousal, weak SAM response, and slow return to baseline arousal after removal of the stressor.

The mechanisms that lead to conditioned toughening or untoughening in humans are not well established. Most of the experimental evidence on this effect is from animal studies (see Dienstbier, 1989), but some human studies show effects consistent with toughening. Ursin (1978) found that among Norwegian paratrooper trainees there was a dramatic reduction in physiological reactivity as their training progressed. During the first parachute practice jump, there was a great increase in arousal—as indicated by a number of physiological parameters (e.g., cortisol, testosterone, catecholamines). On subsequent jumps, however, there was reduced reactivity or no reactivity at all relative to baseline measures. An exception to this general decreased reactivity was the pattern of heart rate and epinephrine: Heart rate showed a pronounced increase at every jump and epinephrine increased at every jump but to a smaller degree after multiple jumps. The persistent increased heart rate prior to every jump, a suppression of cortisol, and availability of systemic epinephrine after multiple exposures is consistent with toughening.

The empirical findings related to toughening reveal little about the effects of multiple concurrent stressors, or the effects of exposure to an acute stressor in the context of an ongoing stressor. It would be interesting to learn whether toughening can occur under continuous stressor exposures, or whether it is important to have recovery periods between exposures. In the Norwegian paratrooper studies, the jumps were separated by several or more days. Another important question is whether toughening will condition a person to highly specific stressors or toughen a person to diverse stressors. For instance, would paratroopers toughened to jump stressors be toughened to other stressors, such as military combat?

COPING WITH MULTIPLE STRESSOR EFFECTS

There are diverse psychological and biological responses to different patterns of multiple stressors. The severity and duration of the stressor, the timing of multiple exposures, measurement artifacts (e.g., ceiling effects), and the outcome all seem to contribute to the results of the various studies previously described. However, coping processes also may play an important role in people's reactions to multiple stressors. In this section, we develop a framework for considering the role of coping in explaining individuals' reactions to multiple stressors.

There are instances in which coping with one stressor has no implication for a person's ability or willingness to cope with another stressor. All other things being equal, we would predict that the effects of two stressors in this situation would be additive. This could explain the additive effects of exposure to multiple acute stressors on cardiovascular reactivity obtained by Myrtek and Spital (1986). The coping demands associated with mental arithmetic might be independent of those associated with submerging one's hand in ice water, therefore the combined effects of these two tasks on cardiovascular arousal should be equal to their independent effects. This makes sense considering that the mental arithmetic task requires active coping (mental problem solving), whereas the cold pressor task requires passive acceptance. These two stressors also might be tapping a more general resource, such as stamina, which could get depleted under particularly prolonged exposures, creating a multiplicative effect. Nevertheless, we would expect the combined effects of two stressors to be additive when one stressor does not deplete one's coping resources, taps a different reservoir of resources than that tapped by another stressor, or when the coping response to one stressor is independent of, or does not compete with, the coping response to another stressor. With so few tests of the additivity assumption in the literature, it is difficult to evaluate these speculations.

There are other instances in which coping with one stressor does have implications for coping with another stressor. Coping with one stressor might increase or decrease the person's ability or willingness to cope with another stressor. In these situations, we would expect a multiplicative effect of the combined stressors. When coping with one stressor has negative implications for coping with another stressor, we refer to it as a cost of coping, or a stress potentiation model. When coping with one stressor has positive implications for coping with another stressor, we refer to it as a benefit of coping, or a stress attenuation model.

Costs of Coping

The notion that behavioral and psychological coping responses can have negative consequences has been discussed previously (Cohen, 1980; Cohen, Evans, Stokols, & Krantz, 1986; Dubos, 1965; Glass & Singer, 1972). These theorists propose that adaptive costs are associated with coping processes used to remove stressors or to ameliorate their negative biological, emotional, and psychological effects. Adaptive cost theories have direct implications for coping with multiple stressors. Specifically, coping with a stressor can have negative adaptive consequences by interfering with a person's capacity (resources, ability) or motivation (incentive) to cope with subsequent stressors. These are important considerations in most stress studies because, as noted earlier, stressors often occur in multiples. Our expanded cost of coping model goes beyond examining the direct negative implications of coping processes by highlighting the ways that coping with one stressor can increase individuals' vulnerability to other stressors. Table 16.2 summarizes the various costs of coping to be discussed in this section.

Stereotypic Coping

When people maintain a coping behavior in the absence of the triggering stressor, they are exhibiting overgeneralization of that coping behavior. To envision this problem, imagine a fish that bites a baited hook but escapes following a vicious struggle. If the fish learns from its brush with death to avoid eating delectable looking worms and other such creatures, it might soon perish from starvation. Overgeneralization of a coping behavior may be a result of overlearning a coping response (Cohen et al., 1986). Thus, we might expect overgeneralization to be most common following chronic or repeated stressors. We use the term stereotypic coping to refer to the tendency of people to use a persistent coping strategy indiscriminately in the face of diverse stressors. This is slightly different from a

TABLE 16.2 Costs of Coping

Mechanism	Description	Implication
Stereotypic coping	Indiscriminate application of a coping response or resource to diverse stressors.	Mismatch between demands of stressors and coping response may amplify the negative effects of stressors.
Behavioral constraints	Coping response to one stressor is incompatible with coping response to another stressor.	Inability to cope with competing demands because of coping response incompatibilities may lead to frustration and helplessness and amplify the negative effects of stressors.
Residual arousal & fatigue	Coping with one stressor alters a person's physiological and psychological state by increasing arousal or fatigue before the onset of another stressor.	Residual arousal or fatigue resulting from coping with one stressor can reduce capacity to respond to other stressors, thereby increasing the negative effects of other stressors.
Resource depletion	Loss of social, material, and psychological coping resources as a result of coping with a stressor.	Depletion of resource during coping with one stressor could increase the negative effects of another stressor that could have been alleviated by the depleted resource.
Helplessness	Coping with a stressor can lead individuals to have generalized expectancies of a lack control over environmental demands.	Helplessness resulting from coping with one stressor can lead to passive and emotion-focused coping with stressors that are resolved best by using active or instrumental coping responses. Failure to cope with controllable stressors because of helplessness should increase the negative effects of those stressors.
Reappraisals	Perceived threat of a stressor is increased or perceived coping capacity is decreased when the stressor co-occurs with another stressor.	Exaggerated appraisals of threat and underestimates of coping capacity could diminish incentive to cope and exacerbate the negative effects of stressors.

simple overgeneralization of a coping response. Overgeneralized coping occurs when a coping behavior is maintained after a stressor has terminated (in the absence of a stressor), whereas stereotypic coping occurs when a coping behavior is routinely used in response to diverse stressors.

There currently seems to be no coping strategy or resource that is helpful in all stressful situations (Cohen & Edwards, 1988). Even having or seeking control in a stressful situation, which is generally thought to be positive, can have negative effects on adjustment (Evans, Shapiro, & Lewis, 1993). Thus, stereotypic coping can have negative consequences for people contending with multiple stressors. The greatest problems are likely to occur when there is a mismatch between the stereotypic coping style and the demands of the diverse stressors. For instance, if a person adopts a general coping style of avoiding or denying anxiety-arousing stimuli, this strategy will sometimes be helpful but other times be unhelpful and potentially dangerous. When a stressful event is uncontrollable and intractable, such as paralysis or death of a loved one, it might be best to avoid efforts to alter the event or ruminate about it. However, if avoidance becomes generalized to a potentially controllable situation, a person might miss an opportunity to resolve or prevent a major problem. For example, avoiders who delay seeking medical assistance when they are experiencing illness symptoms (e.g., lump in breast, chest pain) might diminish their chances for effective interventions.

An example of a coping strategy that has been overgeneralized to other stressors is social withdrawal, or social disengagement. Several investigators have observed overgeneralized patterns of withdrawal in people living in chronically crowded housing (see Baum & Paulus, 1987; Evans & Lepore, 1992). A negative implication of this behavior is that crowded individuals might be less able to obtain social support to help them cope with stressors other than crowding. In a recent study, Evans and Lepore (1993) found that people who had been chronically exposed to crowded living conditions exhibited elevated levels of social withdrawal (e.g., reading magazines, not looking at confederate) in a laboratory setting relative to their uncrowded counterparts. More importantly, they found that after the experimenter gave the subjects negative feedback about their performance on a writing task, subjects from crowded residences were less likely to attend to and respond to supportive comments made to them by a confederate than were subjects from uncrowded residences. Repetti (1992) has reported that social withdrawal is sometimes adopted by people employed in stressful occupations (e.g., air traffic controllers) as a method of unwinding at the end of the day. Problems could emerge if this behavior is used to avoid dealing with other stressors, such as marital or family demands, which might require open communication to reach resolution.

Behavioral Constraints

Coping can be constrained in the face of multiple stressor because of response competitions. For example, a person cannot be in two places at once, so demands that require a person to be in two separate locations (e.g., work and home demands) could create a unique tension that exceeds the tension that would be created by the independent demands had they occurred serially rather than in parallel. A parent who is interrupted during an important conference at work and told to retrieve his or her sick child from school might experience such tension.

In some stressful situations, the stressor itself can interfere with a person's ability to cope with another stressor by constraining behavioral options or limiting behavioral control. In such instances, options for coping with a second stressor might be constrained. There is some evidence that constraints on coping options might exacerbate the stress associated with multiple stressors. For example, Lepore, Evans, and Schneider (1992) found that there was a stronger inverse association between daily social stressors and perceived environmental control among crowded residents than among uncrowded residents. In addition, lower perceived control was associated with higher psychological distress symptoms. The authors argued that social stressors are more likely to reduce perceived control over the environment and increase psychological distress symptoms for crowded residents because they are less able to escape or avoid the social stressors than residents from uncrowded homes.

Residual Arousal and Fatigue

The physiological and psychological changes caused by one stressor might reduce a person's capacity to respond to another stressor. That is, the initial physiological and psychological state of the organism at the onset of a second stressor may be altered by exposure to another stressor, potentially compromising a person's behavioral control over the second stressor.

Stress-reactivity studies have provided mixed evidence regarding the costs of residual arousal. For example, Kallus (1987) found that subjects who were prestressed by electrical stimulation, and hence aroused, had lower finger temperature response during a subsequent speech stressor task. However, contrary to his prediction, skin conductance and anger levels were enhanced during the speech in subjects who were prestressed. Evidence from other studies suggests that independent of baseline arousal a person's initial state can have a negative effect on his or her capacity to actively respond to a stressor. Siegrist and Klein (1990) found that workers with high levels of chronic occupational stress responded to an acute laboratory stressor (Stroop) with lower peak cardiovascular reactivity than did workers with lower occupational stress. However, workers' baseline levels of blood pressure were not associated with their blood pressure reactivity. Moreover, the poorer cardiovascular responses to challenge exhibited by the chronically stressed workers did not disappear after statistically adjusting for hypertensive status, smoking, or age—again indicating that residual arousal levels probably do not explain the lower responsivity.

It is possible that people can suffer from residual physical and cognitive fatigue as a result of effort expended in coping with a stressor. The fatigue associated with coping with one stressor can degrade a person's ability to respond to the physical (e.g., stamina, strength) or cognitive (e.g., memory, perception, attention) demands required for actively coping with stressors. Cognitive fatigue produces a number of deficits in behavioral control, which might stem from problems in sustaining attention or concentrating on tasks (Cohen, 1980). During physical fatigue, the body's regulatory system is compromised. For example, the endocrine organs and reflexive innervation processes cannot respond fully more than once (Ursin, 1978). Thus, fatigued persons might have lowered availability of catecholamines, dampened adrenomedullary arousal, and poor recovery to baseline arousal levels when stressors are terminated (Schaubroeck & Ganster, 1993). Physiological and cognitive fatigue have obvious implications for a person's ability to cope with multiple stressors. Empirical evidence to date suggests that residual fatigue is most likely to occur following chronic stressors and has the potential to interfere with a person's ability to actively cope with subsequent acute stressors in a laboratory.

Resource Depletion

Residual fatigue can be conceived as a particular form of a more general cost of coping known as resource depletion. For example, the availability of catecholamines is an important resource for actively responding to a challenge. If a stressor diminishes the availability of catecholamines, then it can be said to have depleted that resource. Coping resources, however, do not just include biological resources; they include environmental and social resources (e.g., supportive social ties), material resources (e.g., money), and individual, or dispositional resources (e.g., self-esteem). If an individual depletes resources in coping with one stressor, he or she might be less resilient to subsequent stressors than if the antecedent stressor had not occurred.

There are many ways that a stressor might diminish social coping resources (see Lepore, in press). If people rely too heavily on their social network for support, they might wear out the network members. People who are in need of support can elicit feelings of vulnerability, resentment, and distress in potential support providers, leading the providers to avoid the support seeker or withdraw support (cf. Coates, Wortman, & Abbey, 1979). Some stressors, such as major floods (Kaniasty & Norris, 1993), can diminish opportunities for supportive exchanges by destroying communal gathering places and disrupting daily social routines. Other stressors might erode social support because they cause friction between support providers and seekers. For example, homeless families that double-up with friends often end up in shelters because of the tensions created by crowding (cf. Weitzman, Knickman, & Shinn, 1990). In several studies, we have found that over time social relationships become increasingly strained in crowded households: people become less willing to discuss their problems with one another and levels of perceived social support among housemates diminish (Lepore, Evans, & Schneider, 1991; Lepore, Palsane, & Evans 1991). Other chronic stressors, such as ongoing parenting difficulties (Quittner, Glueckauf, & Jackson, 1990) also seem to diminish social support. Strained or unsupportive social relationships may be a direct source of stress and psychological distress (Lepore, 1992) or may cause people to have heightened vulnerability to other stressors (Lepore, Silver, Wortman, & Wayment, in press).

There are also ways in which a stressor might alter a person's dispositional qualities that are usually viewed as positive attributes for coping with stressors. If a stressful experience were to diminish a person's self-concept or feelings of personal control and self-efficacy, then that person might be more vulnerable to subsequent stressors (Cohen & Edwards, 1988). People's beliefs that they are invulnerable, that the world is just (bad things do not happen to good people), and that they can somehow control their own destiny, are challenged and sometimes destroyed in the face of major life stressors or chronic, intractable situations (Evans et al., 1993). Beliefs that once sustained people in the face of challenges may fall away after some major stressors and be replaced by feelings of insecurity, uncertainty, and self-doubt—that could undermine a person's coping efforts in the face of subsequent stressors.

Finally, there are instances in which material resources might be depleted in coping with a stressor, thereby leaving a person unable to apply the same types of resources to other stressors. Many major life stressors, such as long-term hospitalization, divorce, or loss of a spouse, drain financial assets. If a person allocated substantial assets to deal with one stressor, such as hospitalization, then he or she would be in a major predicament if another stressor arose, such as job loss, that also required financial resources. We expect that the joint effect of two stressors that both rely on a limited resource, such as money, should be greater than the discrete, additive effect of those stressors.

Helplessness

In animal research, it has been observed that pretreatment with an inescapable shock seems to inhibit responses to future escapable shock (e.g., Seligman & Groves, 1970). Presumably, animals learn in the pretreatment phase that shock termination is not contingent on their own behavior. This learning interferes with subsequent formation of an association between behavior and shock termination in escapable shock situations, and diminishes the animal's incentive to attempt to escape. This effect has been observed in humans as well. Performance deficits occur on tasks identical to the pretreatment task as well as on novel tasks (e.g., Hiroto & Seligman, 1975), suggesting that interference with learning and motivation might be a general effect following exposure to uncontrollable stressors. Other work suggests that the generalizability of helplessness in humans is a function of the attributions people make about their failures (Abramson, Seligman, & Teasdale, 1978).

A number of investigators have examined the links between exposure to chronic stressors and motivational processes related to helplessness. Social learning research suggests that people exposed to prolonged, uncontrollable events such military conscription (McArthur, 1970) and disasters (Edelstein, 1988) acquire an external locus of control. Chronic exposure to uncontrollable ambient stressors, such as crowding and noise, seems to increase susceptibility to helplessness, perhaps by decreasing expectancies for control. It is easier to induce helplessness in adolescents from crowded households than in their peers from uncrowded households (Rodin, 1976). High-density housing also seems to be associated with increased helplessness in college students (Baum & Paulus, 1987). People residing near airports report high levels of annoyance, but they tend not to complain to officials or take other actions to reduce noise levels (Jue, Shumaker, & Evans, 1984). The effects of noise on helplessness are also apparent in children (Evans & Lepore, 1993).

Another way to consider helplessness as a cost of coping with stressors is to examine the influence of stressor exposure on individuals' coping strategies. Evans, Jacobs, and Frager (1982) found that migrants to a city with high levels of air pollution tended to use palliative, emotion-focused coping strategies if they had previous exposure to high levels of air pollution. In contrast, migrants to a high-pollution city with no previous exposure to high levels of air pollution tended to use instrumental coping strategies. Those without prior exposure to pollutants were more likely to notice perceptual cues of pollution in their new community and to follow pollution health advisories to reduce potential health risks. Palliative coping strategies used by migrants with prior exposure to pollutants included denying that their new community had pollution problems, underestimating the potential health threats from pollution, and ignoring health advisories during pollution alerts.

Thus, chronic exposure to uncontrollable ambient stressors seems to increase motivational deficiencies, external locus of control, beliefs associated with helpless behaviors, and palliative rather than instrumental coping strategies. These findings suggest that people who become helpless after exposure to one stressor might not respond actively to remove or avoid subsequent stressors that are potentially controllable. Thus, people who are helpless might be exposed to stressors needlessly or for extended durations because they do not take actions to reduce exposure.

Reappraisals

Exposure to multiple stressors could alter the way people appraise the threat value of stressors or the adequacy of their coping resources. Multiple stressors can affect both primary appraisals and secondary appraisals (Lazarus & Folkman, 1984). According to some theorists, stress responses increase as perceived threat of a stressor increases and perceived adequacy of coping resources decreases. Individuals experiencing a stressor might perceive it to be more threatening or their coping resources to be less adequate when that stressor co-occurs with another stressor than when it occurs by itself. Brown and Harris (1978) contend that major life events can trigger clinical depression in women experiencing ongoing stressors; presumably because major life events can heighten the unfavorable implications of women's ongoing life stressors. For example, a woman who has an unwanted pregnancy at a period when she also has been having ongoing difficulties with the father might be more distressed by the pregnancy than a women having an unwanted pregnancy in the course of a good relationship with the father because of the different implications the pregnancy has in these respective situations.

In addition to altering threat appraisals, cumulative stressors might alter individuals' appraisals of their coping abilities. A person's actual and perceived capacity to cope with a current stressor can be diminished by demands from previous or ongoing stressors (Schonpflug, 1986). To the extent that coping resources are perceived to be insufficient, subjective stress should be elevated and motivation to actively respond to a stressor could be diminished, perhaps leading to helpless behaviors. It is important to distinguish this phenomenological model from the behavioral constraint and resource depletion models described previously. The emphasis of the constraint and depletion models is on changes in actual coping resources, options, and strategies that result from coping with multiple stressors. A web of multiple stressors might reduce the individual's resources and options for dealing with any particular stressor in that web. The reappraisal model maintains that constraints on coping options and resources are to some extent self-imposed because of individuals' construal of their situation. Whether or not a tangible constraint exists does not matter if an individual perceives that it is present and behaves accordingly.

Benefits of Coping

Some stressor combinations produce detrimental effects with regard to some outcomes, but beneficial effects with regard to other outcomes. For example, the combination of sleep deprivation and chronic exposure to loud noise at work might increase a person's levels of psychological anxiety and depression. However, noise on the job might counter the negative effects of sleep deprivation on a worker's concentration by increasing arousal. Thus, whereas psychological distress might be exacerbated by the combined effects of noise and sleep deprivation, attention and job performance might be enhanced by this combination of stressors (Poulton, 1978). In this section, we consider several ways in which coping with one stressor might enhance or facilitate coping with another stressor.

As indicated earlier, there are strands of evidence that multiple stressors can have negative multiplicative effects on psychological outcomes (e.g., mood, depressive symptoms). That is, the combined effects of exposure to two or more stressors may be less than we would expect based on the independent effects of each stressor (see attenuation effect in Figure 16.3). We believe that although an attenuation effect is plausible, it is likely to be rare; the current empirical evidence of attenuation effects is not very strong, especially when physiological stress reactions are investigated. Nevertheless, it is intriguing to consider the conditions under which coping with multiple stressors might have some beneficial effects. Table 16.3 presents a summary of the benefits of coping to be discussed in this section.

Resiliency

Resiliency is the tendency of some people to thrive despite experiencing personal atrocities and being exposed to extremely stressful physical and social environments. Research on resiliency attempts to identify personal, environmental, and social resources that help people flourish when they are by most objective indicators at risk for developing various pathologies. The concept of inoculation often is applied to explain such resiliency. Children who develop into healthy, high-functioning, and well-adjusted adults despite their exposure to multiple risk factors (e.g., poverty, divorce, racial discrimination) often share the characteristic of having successfully negotiated aversive environmental stimuli early in life (Garmezy, 1983). Early exposure to and mastery over stressors thus seems to

TABLE 16.3   Benefits of Coping

Mechanism	Description	Implication
Resiliency	Mastery experiences with a stressor teaches a person how to respond effectively to environmental challenges, or toughens an individual.	Individuals may transfer successful coping responses from one stressor to another, thereby reducing the impact of stressors.
Resource mobilization	Coping with a stressor mobilizes social support networks or enhances self-concept.	Support networks that are on alert, or mobilized, might intervene more quickly and effectively to minimize the impact of diverse and multiple stressors. Enhanced self-concept following successful coping with one stressor can promote adaptive appraisals during subsequent stressors, thereby reducing their impact.
Reappraisal	Perceived threat of a stressor is decreased or perceived coping capacity is increased when the stressor co-occurs with another stressor.	Diminished appraisals of threat and exaggerated perceptions of coping capacity could enhance incentive to cope and decrease the negative effects of stressors.

inoculate people from subsequent stressors and to play a key role in success later in life. Elder (1974) has noted that many children who survived the U.S. economic depression of the 1930s became imbued with a sense of mastery. He also suggested that the feeling of having made it through tough times enhanced the subsequent coping abilities of depression-era survivors. Unfortunately, the data related to resiliency and inoculation effects are primarily retrospective and self-report based, thus raising questions about the validity of this model.

The notion that mastery over stressors contributes to resiliency seems to be consistent with some of the details of Dienstbier's (1989) toughening hypothesis. Organisms that have early, repeated exposure to stressors seem to become physiologically toughened or inoculated by the experience. A close reading of Dienstbier's review suggests that intermittent rather than continuous stressor exposure is associated with toughening. The data also seem to suggest that sufficient time for recovery during interstressor intervals is necessary for toughening to occur. Dienstbier has suggested that there are psychological correlates of toughening as well. He has argued that because the toughened organism is responsive rather than helpless in the face of stressors, its appraisals of coping abilities are positive (e.g., confidence), it may view demands as challenges rather than threats, and it will have a more positive mood. In contrast, the untoughened organism will be helpless in the face of stressors, see demands as threats, and have a negative mood.

From the available evidence, we speculate that experiences of mastery over stressors may provide some inoculative effect that makes people more resilient in the face of subsequent stressors. We predict that this is most likely to happen when the stressor exposures are intermittent rather than continuous; when there is an opportunity to apply coping strategies or resources that are effective in reducing the impact of the stressors; and when the experience of coping with the stressors leaves the person with a generalized sense of control or self-efficacy. The extent to which a new stressor is seen as novel or distinct from previously mastered stressors might be a salient factor in influencing whether coping with multiple stressors can have salutary effects.

We would also predict that concurrent rather than sequential stressor exposures are less likely to foster opportunities for successful coping and the development of resiliency. Another interesting issue to consider is the generalizability of the development of competency, or a sense of mastery, in response to diverse stressors. If a person has an early experience of successful mastery over the stress and challenges of being crowded or of having no privacy at home, does this inoculate that person from other sources of unwanted social interactions or generalize to various social and nonsocial stressors?

Resource Mobilization

A sense of personal competence growing out of experiences of successfully coping with a stressor may engender greater self-confidence and lower perceived threat in the face of subsequent environmental demands. This could happen because of a heightened sense of control—or the feeling that no problem is too tough to tackle. There is an abundant literature on the benefits of perceived control in coping with stressors (Evans et al., 1993). There is some evidence that a heightened sense of perceived control in the face of stressor might increase a person's coping flexibility. Recall, for example, Evans et al.'s (1982) finding that people who moved to a polluted environment from another polluted environment were less likely to respond appropriately to pollution emergencies than were people who had migrated from a relatively unpolluted environment to a polluted one. People without prior exposure to air pollution had a more flexible coping repertoire: they considered multiple responses to a pollution emergency, including restricting their outdoor activity and denying or intellectualizing the possible harmful effects of pollution on health. However, what if the group with a history of pollution exposure had learned some effective ways to cope with the pollution in their previous community? Under such circumstances, we would expect them to cope at least as well if not better than those people who had no prior experience with pollution. In short, if prior experience has provided people with an opportunity to apply a successful coping response, mobilization of an effective coping response should be enhanced during subsequent exposures.

There are several other ways that coping with one stressor might increase psychological and social resources for coping with another stressor. One potential mechanism is improved self-concept that might accompany successful adaptation to or eradication of a stressor. Individuals who experience a sense of mastery or increased self-esteem as a result of effectively coping with a stressor might be more confident and less threatened by another stressor as a result of improvements in their self-concept. High self-esteem should reduce vulnerability to a stressor because people who possess it tend not to internalize stressful events, or blame themselves for negative outcomes (cf. Cronkite & Moos, 1984).

Resources also might be enhanced for individuals coping with multiple stressors through social support mobilization. Support mobilization refers to those situations in which support providers supply the help that a person needs. Support providers might recognize needs for support in a person who has just confronted a major stressor, who has solicited help, or who appears distressed (Eckenrode & Wethington, 1990). For example, friends of a young mother who has suddenly lost her husband in an automobile accident might take turns providing emotional comfort to the mother and assisting with housekeeping and child care. The friends also might increase their contact with the mother and with one another to help her through her crisis. During this period in which the network is mobilized to help the mother, she might receive support for a wide range of life stressors and demands that she might not have received had her network not been on alert. In addition, there may be burdens that a support provider would only take on for a person who is facing a major life stressor. Thus, following some stressors, people might experience an increase in social coping resources that could be helpful to them if they are confronted by subsequent stressors.

Reappraisal

The appraisal of a stressor plays a central role in its consequences (Lazarus & Folkman, 1984). Experience with prior stressors can influence the appraisal process in ways that might lead to nonadditive, negative interactions between multiple stressors. As noted previously, some stressful events can potentially reduce or eliminate more severe environmental demands (Wheaton, 1990). For example, death of a chronically ill and suffering patient might bring relief to family caregivers, divorce can terminate chronic marital difficulties, and job loss can remove a person from work-related stressors. In each of these situations, the stressful event—death, divorce, job loss—is not necessarily pleasant, but relative to the situations that these events are capping off, the net effect could be less perceived stress.

There is another way in which reappraisal can function to attenuate the effects of multiple stressors. Caspi et al. (1987) have argued that the perceived threat or magnitude of one stressor can pale by comparison to a more serious or major stressor. Similarly, Helson (1964) has argued that a person's criterion for judging a phenomenon (e.g., magnitude estimation) is a negative function of prior experiences with that phenomenon. Thus, a person carrying a heavy object prior to judging the weight of a lighter object would tend to underestimate the weight of the lighter object. However, if the initially held object was very light relative to the judged object, a person would tend to overestimate the weight of the judged object. This effect has been shown in studies of people judging ambient stressors. For example, people from large cities who move to medium-size cities judge them to be less crowded, polluted, noisy, and congested than people who move to them from smaller towns (Wohlwill & Kohn, 1973).

SUMMARY AND FUTURE RESEARCH ISSUES

Although people often cope with multiple environmental demands, much of the research on coping has focused on single stressor-coping transactions or on the role of coping with aggregated, cumulative stressors. Examination of stress and coping processes in isolation from the ecological context in which they typically occur may distort estimates of the effects of stress and coping processes on human adjustment. In addition, summary stressor scores that ignore potential interactive effects of diverse stressors also could lead to biased estimates of stressor effects and of the coping demands of multiple stressors. In this chapter, we have reviewed much empirical evidence that multiple stressors often do not have a simple additive effect on people's physical or psychological functioning. We also have shown that many of the potentially adverse effects of multiple stressors on human beings are potentially a function of the coping processes invoked to deal with multiple stressors.

The effects of multiple stressors can be moderated by coping processes. Alternatively, coping processes can act as underlying, mediating mechanisms that both directly and indirectly affect individuals' stress reactions. Furthermore, stressors can occur independently of one another but frequently are, in fact, interdependent. As an illustration, major life events may be have long-term negative effects on people because of the series of negative, daily stressors they can create. The negative outcomes associated with a major life event may be best understood by examining the disruptions and enduring challenges that it brings about in people's day-to-day lives. Efforts to cope with the ongoing and persistent daily stressors created by a major life event may also contribute to stress reactions.

Coping processes may explain the complex array of multiple stressor effects observed in humans. Under some circumstances, multiple stressors seem to cause greater adversity than would be predicted based on summing the unique effects of each stressor in the multiple stressor constellation. Exposure to multiple stressors might potentiate negative stress reactions if people engage in stereotypic coping, face behavioral restraints, engage in negative reappraisal processes, or experience residual arousal and fatigue, resource depletion, and helplessness. However, under some circumstances coping with multiple stressors may attenuate stress reactions. We suspect that stressor attenuation can result from resiliency developed during the course of coping, resource mobilization, or positive stressor reappraisals. We also expect multiple stressor effects to be attenuated in circumstances where there is a large interval between exposures or a person has recovered from one stressor before being exposed to another one.

Two central challenges remain for researchers interested in the consequences of coping with multiple stressors in the environment. First, there is scant data on basic parameters of multiple stressors and coping transactions. Little is known, for example, about the psychological or physiological consequences of multiple exposures to different types of stressors or stressors of different durations. We also do not have adequate conceptualizations of the demands posed by various stressors to examine the importance of matching individuals' coping resources and response capacities to particular patterns of stressors. Nor do we have enough data to determine if patterns of potentiation, attenuation, and additivity occur across diverse outcomes or tend to be limited to particular types of measures (e.g., self-reports of distress vs. psychophysiological parameters). Second, and more challenging, is the problem of specifying a theoretical model that can explain the diverse effects of multiple stressors on human adaptation, which seem to include additive, potentiation (cost of coping with more than one stressor), and attenuation (benefit of coping with more than one stressor) effects. This chapter provides a starting point for considering both of these challenges.

REFERENCES

Abramson, L., Seligman, M. E. P., & Teasdale, J. (1978). Learned helplessness in humans: Critique and reformulation. *Journal of Abnormal Psychology, 87,* 49–74.

Baum, A., & Paulus, P. B. (1987). Crowding. In D. Stokols & I. Altman (Eds.), *Handbook of environmental psychology* (Vol. 1, pp. 533–570). New York: Wiley.

Bolger, N., DeLongis, A., Kessler, R. C., & Schilling, E. A. (1989). Effects of daily stress on negative mood. *Journal of Personality and Social Psychology, 57,* 808–818.

Brown, G. W., & Harris, T. W. (1978). *The social origins of depression: A study of psychiatric disorders in women.* New York: Free Press.

Caspi, A., Bolger, N., & Eckenrode, J. (1987). Linking person and context in the daily stress process. *Journal of Personality and Social Psychology, 52,* 184–195.

Coates, D., Wortman, C. B., & Abbey, A. (1979). Reactions to victims. In I. H. Frieze, D. Bar-Tal, & J. S. Carroll (Eds.), *New approaches to social problems* (pp. 21–52). San Francisco: Jossey-Bass.

Cohen, S. (1980). After effects of stress on human performance and social behavior: A review of research and theory. *Psychological Bulletin, 88,* 82–108.

Cohen, S., & Edwards, J. R. (1988). Personality characteristics as moderators of the relationship between stress and disorder. In R. W. J. Neufeld (Ed.), *Advances in the investigation of psychological stress* (pp. 235–283). New York: Wiley.

Cohen, S., Evans, G. W., Stokols, D., & Krantz, D. S. (1986). *Behavior, health, and environmental stress.* New York: Plenum.

Cronkite, R. C., & Moos, R. H. (1984). The role of predisposing and moderating factors in the stress-illness relationship. *Journal of Health and Social Behavior, 25,* 372–393.

DeLongis, A., Coyne, J. C., Dakof, G., Folkman, S., & Lazarus, R. S. (1982). Relationships of daily hassles, uplifts, and major life events to health status. *Health Psychology, 1982,* 1, 119–136.

Dienstbier, R. A. (1989). Arousal and physiological toughness: Implications for mental and physical health. *Psychological Review, 96,* 84–100.

Dubos, R. (1965). *Man adapting.* New Haven, CT: Yale University Press.

Eckenrode, J., & Gore, S. (Eds.). (1990). *Stress between work and family.* New York: Plenum.

Eckenrode, J., & Wethington, E. (1990). The process and outcome of mobilizing social support. In S. Duck & R. C. Silver (Eds.), *Personal relationships and social support* (pp. 83–103). London: Sage.

Edelstein, M. R. (1988). *Contaminated communities: The social and psychological impacts of residential toxic exposure.* Boulder, CO: Westfield.

Elder, G. H., Jr. (1974). *Children of the Great Depression.* Chicago: University of Chicago Press.

Evans, G. W., Jacobs, S. V., Dooley, D., & Catalano, R. (1987). The interaction of stressful life events and chronic strains on community mental health. *American Journal of Community Psychology, 15,* 23–34.

Evans, G. W., Jacobs, S. V., & Frager, N. B. (1982). Behavioral responses to air pollution. In A. Baum & J. Singer (Eds.), *Advances in environmental psychology* (Vol. 4, pp. 99–121). Hillsdale, NJ: Erlbaum.

Evans, G. W., & Lepore, S. J. (1992). Conceptual and analytic issues in crowding research. *Journal of Environmental Psychology, 12,* 163–173.

Evans, G. W., & Lepore, S. J. (1993). Household crowding and social support: Aquasiexperimental analysis. *Journal of Personality and Social Psychology, 65,* 308–316.

Evans, G. W., & Lepore, S. J. (in press). Moderating and mediating processes in environment-behavior research. In G. T. Moore & R. W. Marans (Eds.), *Advances in environment, behavior, and design* (Vol. 4). New York: Plenum.

Evans, G. W., Shapiro, D. H., & Lewis, M. A. (1993). Specifying dysfunctional mismatches between different control dimensions. *British Journal of Psychology, 84,* 255–273.

Fleming, I., Baum, A., Davidson, L. M., Rectanus, E., & McArdle, S. (1987). Chronic stress as a factor in physiologic reactivity to challenge. *Health Psychology, 6,* 221–237.

Garmezy, N. (1983). Stressors of childhood. In N. Garmezy & N. Rutter (Eds.), *Stress, coping, and development in children* (pp. 43–84). New York: McGraw-Hill.

Glass, D., & Singer, J. E. (1972). *Urban stress.* New York: Academic Press.

Helson, H. (1964). *Adaptation-level theory: An experimental and systematic approach to behavior.* New York: Harper.

Hiroto, D. S., & Seligman, M. E. P. (1975). Generality of learned helplessness in humans. *Journal of Personality and Social Psychology, 31,* 311–327.

Holmes, T., & Rahe, R. (1967). The social readjustment rating scale. *Journal of Psychosomatic Research, 11,* 213–218.

Jue, G., Shumaker, S. A., & Evans, G. W. (1984). Community opinion toward airport noise abatement alternatives. *Journal of Environmental Psychology, 4,* 337–345.

Kallus, K. W. (1987). Effects of initial state on psychophysiological stress reactions: Experimental evidence. In H. Weiner, I. Florin, R. Murison, & D. Hellhammer (Eds.), *Frontiers of stress research* (pp. 379–382). Toronto, Canada: Huber.

Kaniasty, K., & Norris, F. (1993). A test of the social support deterioration model in the context of natural disaster. *Journal of Personality and Social Psychology, 64,* 395–408.

Kanner, A. D., Coyne, J. C., Schaefer, C., & Lazarus, R. S. (1981). Comparison of two modes of stress measurement: Daily hassles and uplifts versus major life events. *Journal of Behavioral Medicine, 4,* 1–39.

Lazarus, R. S., & Folkman, S. (1984). *Stress, appraisal, and coping.* New York: Springer.

Lepore, S. J. (1992). Social conflict, social support, and psychological distress: Evidence of cross-domain buffering effects. *Journal of Personality and Social Psychology, 63,* 857–867.

Lepore, S. J. (1994). Crowding: Effects on health and behavior. In V. S. Ramachandran (Ed.), *Encyclopedia of human behavior* (Vol. 2, pp. 43–51). San Diego: Academic Press.

Lepore, S. J. (in press). Social-environmental influences on the chronic stress process. In B. H. Gottlieb (Ed.), *Coping with chronic stress.* New York: Plenum.

Lepore, S. J., Evans, G. W., & Palsane, M. N. (1991). Social hassles and psychological health in the context of chronic crowding. *Journal of Health and Social Behavior, 32,* 357–367.

Lepore, S. J., Evans, G. W., & Schneider, M. (1991). Dynamic role of social support in the link between chronic stress and psychological distress. *Journal of Personality and Social Psychology, 61,* 899–909.

Lepore, S. J., Evans, G. W., & Schneider, M. (1992). Role of control and social support in explaining the stress of hassles and crowding. *Environment and Behavior, 24,* 795–811.

Lepore, S. J., Palsane, M. N., & Evans, G. W. (1991). Daily hassles and chronic strains: A hierarchy of stressors? *Social Science and Medicine, 33,* 1029–1036.

Lepore, S. J., Silver, R. C., Wortman, C. B., & Wayment, H. (in press). Social constraints, intrusive thoughts, and depressive symptoms among bereaved mothers. *Journal of Personality and Social Psychology.*

McArthur, L. (1970). Luck is alive and well in New Haven. *Journal of Personality and Social Psychology, 16,* 316–318.

McGonagle, K. A., & Kessler, R. C. (1990). Chronic stress, acute stress, and depressive symptoms. *American Journal of Community Psychology, 18,* 681–706.

Myers, J., Lindenthal, J. J., & Pepper, M. P. (1971). Life events and psychiatric impairment. *Journal of Nervous and Mental Disease, 152,* 149–157.

Myrtek, M., & Spital, S. (1986). Psychophysiological response patterns to single, double, and triple stressors. *Psychophysiology, 23,* 663–671.

Norris, F. H., & Uhl, G. A. (1993). Chronic stress as a mediator of acute stress: The case of hurricane Hugo. *Journal of Applied Social Psychology, 23,* 1263–1284.

Pearlin, L. I., Lieberman, M. A., Meneghan, E. G., & Mullan, J. T. (1981). The stress process. *Journal of Health and Social Behavior, 22,* 337–356.

Poulton, E. C. (1978). Blue collar stressors. In C. L. Cooper & R. Payne (Eds.), *Stress at work* (pp. 51–79). New York: Wiley.

Quittner, A. L., Glueckauf, R. L., & Jackson, D. N. (1990). Chronic parenting stress: Moderating versus mediating effects of social support. *Journal of Personality and Social Psychology, 59,* 1266–1278.

Repetti, R. L. (1992). Social withdrawal as a short-term coping response to daily stressors. In H. S. Friedman (Ed.), *Hostility, coping, and health* (pp. 151–165). Washington, DC: American Psychological Association.

Rodin, J. (1976). Crowding, perceived choice, and response to controllable and uncontrollable outcomes. *Journal of Experimental Social Psychology, 12,* 564–578.

Ruback, R. B., & Pandy, J. (1992). Very hot and really crowded: Quasi-experimental investigations of Indian "tempos." *Environment and Behavior, 4,* 527–554.

Schaubroeck, J., & Ganster, D. C. (1993). Chronic demands and responsivity to challenge. *Journal of Applied Psychology, 78,* 73–85.

Schonpflug, W. (1986). Behavior economics as an approach to stress theory. In M. Appley & R. Trumbull (Eds.), *Dynamics of stress: Physiological, psychological, and social perspectives* (pp. 81–98). New York: Plenum.

Seligman, M. E. P., & Groves, D. P. (1970). Nontransient learned helplessness. *Psychonomic Science, 19,* 191–192.

Siegrist, J., & Klein, D. (1990). Occupational stress and cardiovascular reactivity in blue-collar workers. *Work & Stress, 4,* 295–304.

Thoits, P. A. (1983). Dimensions of life events that influence psychological distress: An evaluation and synthesis of the literature. In H. B. Kaplan (Ed.), *Psychosocial stress: Trends in theory and research* (pp. 33–103). New York: Academic Press.

Ursin, H. (1978). Activation, coping, and psychosomatics. In H. Ursin, E. Baade, & S. Levine (Eds.), *Psychobiology of stress: A study of coping in men* (pp. 201–228). New York: Academic Press.

Weitzman, B. C., Knickman, J. R., & Shinn, M. (1990). Pathways to homelessness among New York City families. *Journal of Social Issues, 46*(4), 125–140.

Wheaton, B. (1990). Life transitions, role histories, and mental health. *American Sociological Review, 55,* 209–223.

Wohlwill, J. F., & Kohn, I. (1973). Dimensionalizing the environmental manifold. In S. Wapner, S. Cohen, & B. Kaplan (Eds.), *Experiencing the environment* (pp. 19–54). New York: Plenum.

PART FOUR

Individual Differences

CHAPTER 17

Individual Differences in Coping

HEINZ WALTER KROHNE

Theoreticians and researchers in the stress domain have long been preoccupied with individual differences in coping with stress (cf. Lazarus, 1966). In recent years, however, approaches that focus on personality dispositions (traits) for predicting an individual's behavior in stress situations have become subject to criticism. Critics call to abandon trait constructs and, instead, to adopt concepts like coping process or coping strategy to describe and predict stress-related behavior and behavior outcomes (see, e.g., Folkman & Lazarus, 1985).

The present chapter includes an analysis of this controversy and is organized as follows:

- Objections against a personality-centered approach are critically examined.
- A system for classifying different theoretical and empirical approaches is presented.
- One group of these approaches, the microanalytic conceptions of coping, is discussed in more detail.
- The next section is a presentation of macroanalytic coping conceptions. First, the traditional repression-sensitization construct and its major shortcomings are discussed. Some authors have tried to overcome the flaws of the repression-sensitization concept by proposing a multivariable assessment of coping dispositions. A presentation of these approaches concludes this section.
- Finally, two macroanalytic approaches are discussed in detail: the "monitoring-blunting" hypothesis proposed by Miller (1987) and the two-dimensional "model of coping modes" elaborated in our research group (cf. Krohne, 1989).

COPING RESEARCH AND THE CONCEPT OF TRAITS

A controversy has evolved concerning the usefulness of the trait concept for predicting a person's actual coping behavior and its consequences. The main objection against a trait- or personality-centered approach, which has been put forward in particular by Lazarus and colleagues (cf. Folkman & Lazarus, 1985; Lazarus, 1990a, 1990b; Lazarus & Folkman, 1984, 1987), points to the variability in behavior observed for the majority of individuals in stressful situations. Lazarus characterizes this intraindividual variability in coping behavior as a process. He contrasts this process with structure, which refers to stable factors such as personality traits. Because these traits are assumed to be intraindividually invariable, or static, it is argued that "structural approaches cannot reveal changes in stress-related phenomena" (Folkman & Lazarus, 1985, p. 151). Consequently, the empirical indicators of traits (e.g., personality scales) are considered to be unsuitable for adequately explaining or predicting the variability in coping behavior. "The assessment of coping traits actually has had very modest predictive value with respect to coping processes" (Lazarus & Folkman, 1984, p. 288). Lazarus has therefore called for a shift away from trait concepts as the focal point in the analysis of stress and coping. Instead, the emphasis should be placed on the contingencies of situational demands and specific patterns of coping behavior (cf. Folkman, Lazarus, Dunkel-Schetter, DeLongis, & Gruen, 1986; Lazarus, 1990a, 1990b; Lazarus & Folkman, 1987).

Several authors have argued against this view and suggested to reconsider the potential of trait concepts (and trait measurement) to clarify phenomena of coping (cf. Ben-Porath & Tellegen, 1990; Costa & McCrae, 1990; Krohne, 1986, 1990, 1993b; Watson, 1990). Ben-Porath and Tellegen (1990), for example, call to discard the "strawman view of traits as transituational 'situation blind' action tendencies" (p. 15), which they think Lazarus and colleagues have in mind. My opinion is that this view of traits originated from a confusion of "stable" with "static," as put forward by the Lazarus group (cf. Folkman & Lazarus, 1985; Lazarus, 1990b). In a commentary to a target article by Lazarus (1990b), I argued that an antagonism between personality trait (or structure) and process (changes in coping behavior during a stressful encounter) does not exist as described by Lazarus and colleagues (Krohne, 1990). The central points can be summarized as follows (cf. Krohne, 1993b, p. 20):

1. The terms *process* and *structure* represent different conceptual levels. Although process refers to a stream of *observed* events, the term structure implies the regularity that one might recognize in such a process and the constellation of *inferred* mechanisms that affect this process. A prerequisite of structure and regularity is the concept of "system."

2. Change and stability do not exclude each other because *stable* is not the same as *static*. Static, in fact, means "no change." Changes, however, can be stable or unstable. Instability refers to the inability to put a boundary on a system's states along the time course of some encounter. Unstable changes generally indicate the breakdown of a system (Ashby, 1956). Stability of change, on the other hand, implies that a process is *replicable*. This is only possible when the crucial effect mechanisms that this process is based on have been previously identified (cf. Herrmann, 1973). Of

course, the replicability of a process is restricted by the fact that nobody can be confronted with exactly the same situation more than once.

3. Crucial effect mechanisms are identified by using both methods of induction and deduction. First, a fine-grained analysis of a stream of events is applied, thus obtaining initial evidence for a cross-temporal or cross-situational consistency in this process (Laux & Weber, 1987). In this way, ideas about effect mechanisms can be developed inductively. Regularity or stability in this stream of behavior, however, can only be detected by deduction (by applying specific theoretical concepts to the behavioral analysis). What appears to be irregular from a certain point of view can be described as an ordered or *stable sequence of events* when a different theoretical construct is applied.

4. To modify an inadequately operating system (e.g., a person with malfunctioning coping strategies), a mere description of actual coping behavior with its antecedents and consequences is not satisfactory. Instead, it is crucial to identify the rules that the system follows in regulating itself. This is precisely the point where structure and process meet—where personality-oriented coping research begins to focus on process.

A later section of this chapter will present personality models based on a more process-oriented view of coping. Next, however, I will discuss a system for classifying different approaches in coping research. This system may be helpful in evaluating the status of a coping model in terms of trait- or state-orientation.

CLASSIFICATION OF COPING MODELS

Approaches to describe and measure different forms of coping may be classified according to two independent aspects: (a) trait-oriented versus state-oriented and (b) microanalytic versus macroanalytic research strategies. Trait-oriented (or dispositional) and state-oriented (or actual) research strategies have different objectives: The *dispositional* strategy primarily aims at an early identification of those individuals whose coping resources and tendencies are inadequate for the demands of a specific stress situation. Stressful encounters investigated in this respect are, for example, surgery (cf. Johnston, 1988; Krohne, 1992; Krohne, Slangen, & Kleemann, in press; Ludwick-Rosenthal & Neufeld, 1988; Miller, 1980; Slangen, Kleemann, & Krohne, 1993) or critical situations during an athletic competition (Hackfort & Spielberger, 1989; Krohne & Hindel, 1988). An early identification of persons with inadequate coping resources will offer the opportunity for establishing a selection procedure or a successful primary prevention program.

Research approaches that center around *actual coping* reactions have a more general objective. They analyze the relationships between coping strategies applied by a person and self-reported or objectively registered coping efficiency, emotional reactions accompanying and following certain coping efforts, and variables of adaptational outcome such as health status or performance measures (Becker, 1985; Folkman & Lazarus, 1985; Folkman, Lazarus, Gruen, & DeLongis, 1986; McCrae & Costa, 1986; Stone & Neale, 1984). Thereby, this research strategy intends to lay the foundation for a general (modification) program to improve personal coping competency.

Microanalytic approaches study a large number of specific coping strategies, whereas *macroanalytic* analysis operates at a higher level of aggregation, or abstraction, thus concentrating on more fundamental constructs in coping research (cf. Laux & Weber, 1990; Lazarus & Folkman, 1987). This distinction is important for the assignment of single coping acts to specific coping categories as well as for the problem of transituational consistency or variability of certain coping strategies applied by an individual (cf. Stone & Neale, 1982). The more microanalytic the distinction among coping strategies, the more likely it is to observe transsituational variability among these strategies (and the lower the retest correlations between measures of these strategies, cf. Folkman & Lazarus, 1980).

The remainder of this chapter concentrates on dispositional (or trait-oriented) conceptions, beginning discussion with microanalytic and then concluding with macroanalytic conceptions. When considering the discussion of structure versus process approaches in coping research, readers should keep in mind, however, that several models (e.g., Lazarus & Folkman, 1987; Billings & Moos, 1984; McCrae, 1984; cf. McCrae & Costa, 1986) that apparently deal with actual coping can also be regarded as describing coping dispositions.

MICROANALYTIC TRAIT-CONCEPTIONS OF COPING

Considering the preceding arguments, it is not surprising that most microanalytic coping conceptions are more state- than trait-oriented. Typical examples are the approaches presented by Lazarus and coworkers in their "Ways of Coping Checklist/Questionnaire" (Folkman & Lazarus, 1980, 1985, 1988), by McCrae (1984; McCrae & Costa, 1986), by Carver and colleagues (COPE: Carver, Scheier, & Weintraub, 1989; see also Carver & Scheier, 1993), or by Stone and Neale (1984). Compared with the other conceptions, the Stone and Neale approach is insofar particular as it is the only one that takes into account the personal *coping intentions* underlying coping acts (for a detailed description of measurement instruments originating from these conceptions see Schwarzer & Schwarzer, Chapter 6, this volume).

A clear exception is the model and the instruments elaborated by Janke and colleagues (Janke, Erdmann, & Kallus, 1985). The authors postulate that coping strategies applied by an individual are *temporally constant,* independent of the specific type of stressor encountered (*situationally constant*), and *independent* of the type of stress reaction. The latter postulate implies that coping strategies are global with respect to the reduction or control of specific stress reactions, such as an increase in heart rate.

The authors specify a multitude of coping strategies that they consider to be independent of each other. This should imply the possibility of describing individuals by their profile of actually applied coping strategies rather than by their standing on one or two central dimensions of coping, (e.g., repression-sensitization; Byrne, 1961). Finally, these coping dimensions are considered to be independent of other personality variables (cf. Janke et al., 1985, p. 8ff). The authors point out that all the postulated independencies are only "relative," which makes the testing of this model an uncertain enterprise.

To measure individual coping tendencies, Janke and coworkers constructed a coping questionnaire, the "Streβverarbeitungsfragebogen" (SVF). In its most recent version (Janke et al., 1985), an individual's standing on 19 habitual coping strategies (such as minimization, attention deployment, positive self-instruction, avoidance tendencies, resignation, aggression, or taking drugs) can be assessed separately. It is not quite evident how Janke theoretically derived his 19 coping strategies. The fact that the number of categories specified fluctuated between 16 and 24 in the course of test construction (cf. Janke et al., 1985), makes it likely that test and model developed from a sort of dialogue between an a priori classification and subsequent test-statistical analyses. Principal component analyses of the SVF yielded three well-defined factors, while three additional factors referred to less circumscribed areas. The three main factors could be interpreted as "emotional distress and resignation," "active control attempts," and "cognitively avoidant reappraisal," thus manifesting a strong correspondence with the dimensions of some macroanalytically oriented measurement approaches in this area (e.g., Endler & Parker, 1990).

The central problem of microanalytic coping conceptions is their lack of theoretical foundation. This becomes obvious in the Janke model, but is also evident in the more state-oriented approaches mentioned earlier (Carver et al., 1989; Folkman & Lazarus, 1985; McCrae & Costa, 1986; Stone & Neale, 1984). In general, no theoretically intelligible deduction of coping strategies is presented. Instead, the number and definition of these strategies seems to be arbitrary. When mathematical analyses of the respective coping instruments are applied (e.g., principal component analysis), solutions are generally instable, changing with subject sample and situational context. In addition, interrelationships between these coping strategies often remain unclear. Are these strategies independent of each other and located at the same conceptual level, as the application of factor analysis seems to indicate? This is highly unlikely because some strategies have a similar meaning (e.g., Janke's strategies "self-pity" and "self-accusation"), whereas others obviously exclude each other (e.g., "minimization" and "aggressive confrontation"). Furthermore, some strategies are preferably applied at distinct time points during a stressful encounter and may therefore form a chain of dependencies. For example, planning how to cope with a problem ("situation control") is a strategy applied early during an episode, whereas resignation is very likely a late response to an uncontrollable stressor. Finally, not all coping dimensions are located at the same conceptual level. Attention diversion, for example, is a broad category, almost identical with the fundamental concept of cognitive avoidance. Such a strategy would rank high in a hierarchy of coping concepts (cf. Krohne, 1993b). On the other hand, a strategy like taking drugs is specific, thus ranking lower in such a hierarchy.

Even if an elaborated coping theory is presented (e.g., Lazarus's theory; cf. Lazarus & Launier, 1978), a considerable theoretical distance between the model and its empirical realization can be observed. Lazarus, for example, defines stress and coping as a transactional process, a relationship "constantly changing as a result of the continual interplay between the person and the environment" (Lazarus, 1990b, p. 4). However, the assessment of coping, which is of central significance for empirically testing the model, is based on an instrument that largely lacks theoretical basis. This instrument (the "Ways of Coping Check-list") yields a structure that resulted from factor-analytic methods, that is, from a linear-additive model for explaining the variance of observed coping behavior. This structure-based measurement model is completely inappropriate with respect to the transactional, process-oriented theory.

MACROANALYTIC CONCEPTIONS: REPRESSION-SENSITIZATION AND MULTIVARIABLE APPROACHES

The Repression-Sensitization Construct

The repression-sensitization concept (Byrne, 1961, 1964; Eriksen, 1952) is a traditional example of a macroanalytic approach. Different forms of dispositional coping are related to a unidimensional bipolar construct. When confronted with an aversive situation, persons located at one pole of this dimension ("repression") tend to deny or to minimize its existence, fail to verbalize feelings of anxiety, and avoid thinking about the consequence of this encounter. Persons at the opposite pole ("sensitization") react to threat cues by way of enhanced information search and obsessive and ruminative worrying. The concept is theoretically founded in research on perceptual defense (Bruner & Postman, 1947; Eriksen, 1952), an approach that incorporated psychodynamic ideas as well as the functionalistic behavior analysis of Brunswik (1947).

The development of a reliable, easily administered, and objectively scored instrument to measure this personality characteristic, the Repression-Sensitization (R-S) Scale (Byrne, 1961; Byrne, Barry, & Nelson, 1963), instigated a rapidly growing body of research in this area (for reviews, see Bell & Byrne, 1978; Byrne, 1964; Krohne, 1975, 1995). Although numerous studies yielded results consistent with expectations derived from the construct, a number of investigations failed to support these hypotheses. As these inconsistent results accumulated, it became inevitable that certain critical issues arose eventually leading to the decline of this research area. However, some of these objections stimulated a fruitful reconceptualization of the construct, which will therefore be presented briefly here.

Although theory predicts a curvilinear relationship between repression-sensitization and emotional adjustment, with highest adjustment scores for subjects in the middle area of the data distribution (so-called "neutrals"), empirical results show, in fact, a highly linear association between repression-sensitization and different measures of adjustment, especially tests of trait anxiety and defensiveness. This lack of discriminant validity between the R-S Scale and measures of anxiety and defensiveness has led to the question "what does the R-S Scale measure"? Several authors claim that repression-sensitization is simply a component of a second-order factor that might be called "emotionality" or, in the terms of Watson and Clark (1984), "negative affectivity." However, this definition does not take into account that the repression-sensitization construct, as compared with other constructs in this field (e.g., anxiety, emotional lability-stability, defensiveness) has generated *independent theoretical expectations.* To name but a few: Repressers are supposed to show greater physiological reactivity to threat than do sensitizers; in incidental learning situations repressers should have greater difficulty in recalling threatening material than do sensitizers; and finally, when confronted with ambiguous stimuli containing threat cues (e.g., double entendre words), sensitizers should be more likely to perceive the threatening and repressers the neutral meaning (for an overview, see Bell & Byrne, 1978; Eriksen, 1966; Krohne, 1978, 1995).

Multivariable Conceptions of Coping

The major problem of the repression-sensitization construct is its unidimensional conception (a) making a distinction between repressers and truly low-anxious individuals as well as sensitizers and highly anxious individuals impossible and (2) giving intermediate subjects an unclear status.

Some authors have tried to overcome this problem by proposing a *multivariable* assessment of coping dispositions (Boor & Schill, 1967; Hill, 1971; Hill & Sarason, 1966; Holroyd, 1972; Kogan & Wallach, 1964; Krohne & Rogner, 1985; Lefcourt, 1969; Ruebush, Byrum, & Farnham, 1963; Weinberger, Schwartz, & Davidson, 1979). The simplest approach of this kind would be the simultaneous application of an anxiety scale (for example, the Manifest Anxiety Scale MAS; Taylor, 1953) and a test of the social desirability tendency (Crowne & Marlowe, 1960; Edwards, 1957). Whereas the meaning of anxiety scales is unequivocal (anxiety scales are supposed to measure the interindividually varying tendency to appraise situations as threatening), the definition of social desirability scales is somewhat controversial. For some authors (e.g., Crandall, 1966; Hill, 1971; Krohne & Rogner, 1985; Millham & Jacobson, 1978), scales of social desirability measure *defensiveness* (the tendency to avoid or deny threat, especially in evaluative situations, as well as corresponding negative affects like anxiety). On the other hand, Weinberger et al. (1979) think of social desirability scales as measures of a person's *search for social approval.* Because tests of anxiety and social desirability are in general only modestly correlated, four approximately equal groups of subjects with different patterns of anxiety and social desirability emerge when a median split of the respective data distribution is applied. These clusters can be defined in terms of specific coping tendencies (cf. Figure 17.1).

Persons scoring low on both variables can be defined as "nondefensive" (Krohne & Rogner, 1985) or "truly low-anxious" subjects (Asendorpf & Scherer, 1983; Weinberger et al., 1979). Individuals who are high in social desirability and low in anxiety should be repressers in the sense of Byrne's conceptualization. The definition of the two remaining clusters is controversial, depending on the interpretation of the social desirability tendency. Krohne and Rogner (1985) have defined the configuration of high self-reported anxiety and low social desirability (defensiveness) as "sensitization," and persons who score high both on tests of anxiety and social desirability as "unsuccessful defenders" or "truly high-anxious" persons. On the other hand, Weinberger et al. (1979) define the cluster high anxiety and low social desirability (search for social approval) as "high anxiety," while subjects with high scores on both variables are designated "defensively high-anxious" (cf. Asendorpf & Scherer, 1983). In many studies, however, the latter group is excluded from further data analysis (cf. Newton & Contrada, 1992; Weinberger et al., 1979).

In a more recent approach, Weinberger and Schwartz (1990) have replaced the anxiety and social desirability variables with the global dimensions of "distress" (being very similar to negative affectivity) and "self-restraint" (e.g., affect inhibition). By distinguishing two distress (low vs. high) and three (low, moderate, high)

| | Social Desirability | |
	Low	High
Low Trait-Anxiety	Nondefensive (Truly Low-anxious)	Repressive
High Trait-Anxiety	Sensitive (High-anxious)	Unsuccessfully Defensive/ Truly High-anxious (Defensively High-anxious)

Figure 17.1   A two-dimensional classification of dispositional coping modes. Definitions proposed by Krohne and Rogner (1985) and (in parentheses) Weinberger et al. (1979).

self-restraint groups, the authors present a typology that closely corresponds to the one proposed by Krohne and Rogner, if those subjects low in self-restraint are excluded: Individuals scoring high in subjective distress and moderate in self-restraint are called "sensitized," whereas the "low distress/high restraint" configuration is named "repressive." Persons being moderate in self-restraint and low in distress are termed "self-assured," and subjects scoring high on both dimensions are considered to be "oversocialized." Persons of the latter pattern are defined as being low in self-expression and self-concept, manifesting high neurotic symptoms, proneness to personality disorders of the type avoidant and dependent, physical illness, and low impulse gratification. This designation is very similar to Krohne and Rogner's "unsuccessful defender" or "truly high-anxious" person, and the description of self-assured individuals (e.g., persons low in neurotic symptoms) is very close to the concept of nondefensiveness.

The joint use of two dimensions of emotional adjustment (anxiety or distress and social desirability/defensiveness or self-restraint) to define dispositional coping styles has stimulated a considerable amount of research (for overviews, see Asendorpf & Wallbott, 1985; Kohlmann, 1990, 1993a; Krohne, 1995; Krohne & Rogner, 1985). Especially the *repressive coping style* has attracted much interest with respect to health-related variables (cf. the monograph by Singer, 1990). One of the theoretically most important predictions derived from the two-dimensional conception of coping dispositions is the *"discrepancy hypothesis."* This hypothesis is based on formulations of the Lazarus group (Lazarus, 1966; Weinstein, Averill, Opton, & Lazarus, 1968). It states that repressers and sensitizers differ in subjective and objective (physiological or behavioral-expressive) stress reactions: Repressers exhibit a lowered level in the subjective and an elevation (and/or longer duration) in the objectively measured response system, whereas sensitizers show the opposite response configuration. In contrast, individuals of the coping modes low anxiety, or nondefensiveness (low social desirability and low anxiety scores) and high anxiety (high social desirability and high anxiety scores) should manifest consistently low (nondefensiveness) or high profiles across subjective and objective (physiological-behavioral-expressive) response modalities (cf. Figure 17.2).

Results are inconsistent with respect to confirming this hypothesis. Although some studies observed the expected response dissociation only for repressers (e.g., Asendorpf & Scherer, 1983; King, Taylor, Albright, & Haskell, 1990; Newton & Contrada, 1992; Weinberger et al., 1979), others found that only subjects with the pattern "anxiety high/social desirability low" (sensitizers) exhibited a discrepancy between self-reported and physiological data (cf. Kohlmann, Singer, & Krohne, 1989). In a more recent study, Wallbott and Scherer (1991) observed complex interactive effects of type and degree of stress, coping mode (as assessed by the method of Weinberger et al., 1979), and gender on vocal parameters of stress. Obviously, the subject's evaluation of the stress situation is jointly influenced by gender and coping disposition, thus resulting in differential reaction patterns.

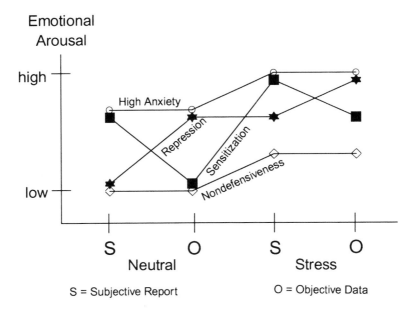

Figure 17.2   Hypothetical profiles of the four coping modes for two data sources (subjective, objective) across two situations (neutral, stress). Adapted from "Coping with Stress: Dispositions, Strategies, and the Problem of Measurement" by H. W. Krohne. In *Dynamics of Stress: Physiological, Psychological, and Social Perspectives* edited by M. H. Appley and R. Trumbull, 1986, New York: Plenum Press. Copyright 1986 by Plenum Press.

This section closes by presenting two studies that either employ an alternative two-dimensional conception of coping or report interesting findings for the often neglected group of high-anxious persons (high trait-anxiety and high social desirability). Miller (1993) replaced the trait-anxiety dimension by measures of *anger expression* (Spielberger, Jacobs, Russel, & Crane, 1983). The author found that persons high in defensiveness (social desirability) and low in expression of anger exhibited elevated heart rate and systolic blood pressure compared with other subjects only in a task where avoidance of the possibility of electric shock was made contingent on video game performance. He interprets this finding as a response of anger-defensive individuals in situations involving evaluative threat. However, in my opinion, these individuals were more likely affected by the anticipation of emotional arousal associated with the electric shock, leading to intensified task involvement and, as a consequence, to increased physiological arousal. The interpretation of repressive coping behavior as being stimulated by the anticipation of emotional arousal will be outlined in more detail in the next section of this chapter.

Esterling, Antoni, Kumar, and Schneiderman (1993) investigated the relationship between coping modes (as operationalized by the approach of Weinberger and coworkers) and differences in antibody titer to Epstein-Barr viral capsid antigen (EBV-VCA) in a normal, healthy college population previously exposed to EBV, a latent, ubiquitous herpes virus. High levels of antibody of EBV-VCA indicate a lowered cellular immune competence, (a state in which there is an infection or reactivation of latent virus). The authors found that *high-anxious students* (high anxiety/high defensiveness) had significantly higher antibody titers to EBV-VCA than low-anxious students (individuals low in anxiety and defensiveness). Titers for the two other coping groups lay between these modes. The literature on personality and immune functioning has as yet only related *individual differences in repressive coping* (especially emotional repression) to indexes of immunity (cf. Jamner, Schwartz, & Leigh, 1988; Pennebaker, Kiecolt-Glaser, & Glaser, 1988; Temoshok, 1987). The finding of Esterling et al., however, indicates that a combination of emotional repression and high vulnerability to stress may be critical in predicting immune competence.

Many approaches that employ multivariable assessment in determining coping dispositions are deficient insofar as they do not analyze main and interaction effects of the two classification variables (trait-anxiety and social desirability). Instead, coping groups are defined by a cross-classification of the two (median-split) variables and subsequently compared by one-way analysis of variance. In a careful analysis, Kohlmann (1993a) demonstrated that most differences between coping groups could be explained by two main effects: (a) High trait-anxiety is associated with the reporting of high subjective distress, and (b) high social desirability leads to intense task involvement, which is accompanied by increased physiological arousal. Both results are expected and almost trivial if one considers the established validity of trait-anxiety and social desirability scales.

Approaches using traditional trait scales to assess different coping modes have a number of deficits. With such instruments, reactions to stressors can be assessed only indirectly and on a global level. The items on such scales refer neither to concrete anxiety-arousing situations nor do they require subjects to describe specific coping behaviors. Instead, subjects are only instructed to comment on certain distressing circumstances and highly generalized response tendencies. Consequently, the researcher learns very little about the strategies preferred by a person in a given situation. The theoretical distance between such inventories and the definition of certain coping modes seems to be too far apart to allow for satisfactory prediction of concrete behaviors based on these instruments. In the following section, concepts and assessment procedures will be presented that are more closely related to the idea of dispositional coping modes.

TWO-DIMENSIONAL COPING THEORIES

Vigilance and Avoidance: Two Central Coping Strategies

Current studies on coping have established two constructs central to an understanding of the cognitive response to stress: (a) *vigilance* (or *sensitization*), the orientation toward the threat-related aspects of an aversive situation, and

(b) *cognitive avoidance,* that is averting attention from threatening cues (cf. Janis, 1983; Krohne, 1978; Krohne & Rogner, 1982; Roth & Cohen, 1986; Singer, 1990; Suls & Fletcher, 1985). Approaches corresponding to these conceptions are, among others, "Sensitization/Repression" (Byrne, 1964), "Monitoring/Blunting" (Miller, 1980, 1987), "Attention/Rejection" (Mullen & Suls, 1982), and "Vigilance/Cognitive Avoidance" (Krohne, 1986, 1989, 1993a, 1993b).

With regard to the dimensionality of these two constructs, Byrne explicitly specifies a unidimensional, bipolar structure, whereas the approaches of Miller as well as Mullen and Suls leave this question open. Krohne (1986), on the other hand, postulates an independent functioning of these dimensions. The advantage of this two-dimensional conceptualization is that one can distinguish between those people who employ an increased amount of both vigilance *and* cognitive avoidance in stressful situations and those who do not tend toward either form of coping. Most models are conceptualized as *partial-area* theories: Unlike approaches with a mere descriptive orientation (e.g., Billings & Moos, 1981, 1984; Janke et al., 1985; Stone & Neale, 1984) these models do not claim to cover the full range of possible coping strategies. Instead, in concentrating on two specific, albeit fundamental, dimensions of coping, these theories attempt to describe and *explain* individual differences in behavioral regulation under stressful conditions.

Monitoring and Blunting

The monitoring-blunting hypothesis (Miller, 1980, 1987, 1989; Miller, Combs, & Kruus, 1993) originated from the same basic assumptions formulated earlier by Eriksen (1966) for the repression-sensitization construct. Miller's hypothesis states that individuals who encounter an aversive situation (e.g., surgery) react with anxiety or, more generally, arousal according to the amount of attention they direct to this stressor. Conversely, the arousal level can be lowered, if an individual succeeds in reducing the impact of threat cues by employing intrapsychic strategies such as distraction, denial, or reinterpretation. However, these strategies, called "blunting," should only be adaptive if the aversive event is *uncontrollable.* If control is available, strategies called "monitoring" (seeking information about the stressor, monitoring the source of stress) are the more adaptive and, hence, preferred forms of coping. Although initially these strategies are associated with increased arousal, they enable the individual to gain control over the stressor in the long run, thus reducing the impact of threat.

This general relationship can be moderated by situative and personal influences. First, threat-related cues may be so intense that blunting strategies (e.g., attentional diversion) are ineffective with respect to reducing arousal. Second, as described in the approaches presented earlier in this chapter, there are relatively stable individual differences in the inclination, or ability, to employ blunting or monitoring techniques when encountering a stressor. As Miller is primarily interested in interindividual differences in the processing of *information* in threatening situations, monitoring and blunting are also called "cognitive informational styles" (Miller, 1989).

To assess individual differences in the inclination to seek out or to cognitively avoid and transform threat-related information, Miller and coworkers (Miller, 1987, Miller & Mangan, 1983) devised a new self-report instrument according to the idea of stimulus-response inventories in anxiety assessment (cf. Endler, Hunt, & Rosenstein, 1962). This "Miller Behavioral Style Scale" (MBSS) consists of four hypothetical stress-evoking scenes of an uncontrollable nature. Each scene is followed by eight statements that represent monitoring or blunting ways of coping with the situation. Subjects mark all the statements following each scene that might apply to them. Three measures are derived from the scale. The monitoring score is the sum of all the items endorsed on the respective subscale. Subjects scoring above the median are high monitors, those scoring below are low monitors. A blunting measure is the sum of all the items endorsed on the blunting subscale, again identifying high and low blunters based on median-split. Finally, a monitoring-blunting measure is obtained by subtracting the total number of items endorsed on the blunting subscale from the total number of endorsed monitoring items. Subjects scoring above the median of this data distribution are monitors, and those scoring below are blunters.

This scale has been validated in laboratory studies and in those relying on real-life stressors. Laboratory experiments showed that high monitors (or low blunters, respectively) typically seek out information relevant to physical and psychological threats. In contrast, low monitors (or high blunters) prefer to avoid threat-relevant information, for example by applying distraction (cf. Efran, Chorney, Ascher, & Lukens, 1989; Miller, 1987). Findings with real-life (especially medical) stressors are consistent with these results. Miller and Mangan (1983) studied gynecological patients at risk for cervical cancer who were about to undergo colposcopy, an aversive diagnostic procedure. They found that monitors generally desired more sensory and procedural information than they had received and were more interested in obtaining information relevant to aversive medical procedures than were blunters. After receiving such information, they felt less anxious (for similar findings, see Miller, Brody, & Summerton, 1988; Phipps & Zinn, 1986; Steptoe & O'Sullivan, 1986; Watkins, Weaver, & Odegaard, 1986; for an overview, cf. Miller et al., 1993).

A major problem with the Miller approach is the relatively arbitrary selection of the described scores as a predictor of outcome variables. In one study, differences in a dependent variable (e.g., employment of a certain coping strategy) are predicted from the monitoring subscale, the next time from the blunting subscale and, again, in another investigation from the difference score. Because both scales are negatively correlated (Miller, 1987), application of the difference score would be most advisable. However, this procedure would again lead to a unidimensional conception of coping tendencies, similar to Byrne's approach and, hence, be subject to the same criticism.

A further problem arises because the MBSS only contains fictitious *un*controllable situations. Within such a design, the manifestation of monitoring behavior, which is more likely unadaptive in those situations, can indeed be related to habitual tendencies ("traits"). For blunting, however, which is in general an adaptive form of coping in uncontrollable situations (cf. Krohne, 1986), it remains open whether it is determined by situative or by habitual factors.

The Model of Coping Modes

The personality model of coping modes (Krohne, 1986, 1989, 1993b) attempts to describe and explain individual differences in behavioral regulation under stressful conditions. The model concentrates on those processes of *attention orientation* that can be observed when an individual is confronted with threat cues. Two fundamental concepts have been introduced to describe these processes: vigilance (the intensified intake and processing of threatening information) and cognitive avoidance (the turning away from threat-related cues). Subsequent to developments in research on perceptual defense (cf. Erdelyi, 1974; Krohne, 1978), the allocation of attention in threatening situations is defined as a two-phase process; after a (perhaps only rudimentary) identification of threat-related cues, attention is turned toward or away from such stimuli.

It is assumed that individuals can be differentiated according to the way they dispositionally react in threatening situations. They can react with either vigilant or cognitive avoidant strategies. Vigilance and cognitive avoidance are conceived conceptually and operationally as *separate personality dimensions.* The specific configuration of a person's standing on both personality dimensions (e.g., high vigilance and low cognitive avoidance) is called *coping mode.*

The model extends beyond other similar approaches in coping research (e.g., repression/sensitization or monitoring/blunting) in that it relates the descriptive constructs vigilance and cognitive avoidance to an explicative basis. According to a number of theoretical approaches and empirical studies (summarized in Epstein, 1972), most situations that evoke anxiety can be characterized by two general aspects: *the presence of aversive stimuli* (Epstein: "primary overstimulation") and a *high degree of ambiguity* ("cognitive incongruity"). Ambiguity in aversive situations is an important factor in triggering anxiety, because it counteracts the immediate employment of open reactions aimed at removing danger. Corresponding to these general aspects, it is postulated that two reactions will be triggered in persons confronted with an aversive situation: the *experience of uncertainty* (as related to ambiguity) and the *perception of somatic arousal* (caused by the presence of aversive stimuli). For the present, these two reactions are viewed as *elementary feeling states* that could lead to more complex anxiety reactions. Thus, "elementary" uncertainty, which manifests itself in questions such as "what does that mean?" can lead to a more complex cognitive anxiety reaction as a result of appraising the relevant situational aspects, especially the imminence of danger and the degree of predictability and controllability of the situation. This reaction can be described as apprehension toward being surprised by negative developments in the situation (Krohne, 1989). On the other hand, the perception of somatic arousal, when confronted with aversive stimuli, could lead to the expectation of a further increase in emotionality that might not be controllable as it arises. It is additionally postulated that the intensified experience of uncertainty should release behavioral impulses characteristic of vigilance. In contrast, the perception or anticipation of intense somatic arousal should initiate the tendency to avoid threat-related cues.

At this point, vigilance can be more precisely defined as a class of coping strategies employed to reduce uncertainty or to prevent a further increase in the same (*uncertainty-motivated* behavior, cf. Krohne, 1993b). Thus, individuals strive to construct a schema of the aversive situation and its eventual course to prevent the possibility of being negatively surprised. Cognitive avoidance, in contrast, designates a class of coping strategies aimed at shielding the organism from stimuli that induce arousal (*arousal-motivated* behavior). An existing emotional state experienced as too intensive would thereby be reduced, or an impending strong and possibly uncontrollable increase in arousal would be prevented.

Dispositional preferences for vigilance and cognitive avoidance are explained by the constructs *intolerance of uncertainy* and *intolerance of emotional arousal* (cf. Figure 17.3). Individuals are assumed to habitually vary in the extent to which they can tolerate uncertainty or emotional arousal. Individuals high in intolerance of uncertainty should tend to employ vigilant coping. On the other hand, intolerance of emotional arousal should be associated with cognitive avoidant strategies.

Individuals with the configuration "high intolerance of uncertainty, low intolerance of arousal" are especially affected by the ambiguity inherent in threatening situations. Their prime concern is to construct a cognitive schema of the

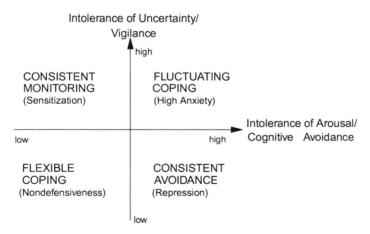

Figure 17.3   The two-dimensional model of dispositional coping modes. Adapted from "Coping Variables as Predictors of Perioperative Emotional States and Adjustment" by H. W. Krohne, K. Slangen, and P. P. Kleemann, in press, *Psychology and Health,* Montreux, Switzerland: Harwood Academic Publishers. Copyright Harwood Academic Publishers.

impending danger and, hence, to avoid a "negative surprise." Correspondingly, they manifest a comparatively consistent vigilant behavior and direct their attention continuously to threat-relevant information *(consistent monitoring)*. Although emotional arousal is thereby unintentionally intensified, vigilant behavior can still stabilize because persons of this mode are comparatively insensitive to such stress. According to the traditional terminology in coping research, individuals with this configuration are called "sensitizers" (Krohne, 1986, 1989). The emotional (somatic) arousal produced by the perception of threat-related cues is the central problem for individuals with the configuration "high intolerance of arousal, low intolerance of uncertainty." They encounter this state by ignoring such cues *(consistent avoidance)* and endure the subsequent increase of uncertainty, because it is not particularly stressful for them. These individuals are called "repressers."

Those individuals who are highly intolerant of both arousal and uncertainty are able to withstand neither the uncertainty nor the emotional arousal induced by cues in aversive situations. When they attempt to reduce the uncertainty that they experience as stressful by increased preoccupation with the stressor, they simultaneously heighten their emotional arousal to a level exceeding their level of tolerance. If they turn away from the stressor to reduce this unbearable state of arousal, then their uncertainty will increase together with the stress resulting from it. Because the employment of vigilant as well as cognitive avoidant behavior results in intolerable unintended consequences for individuals of this mode, they are faced with a conflict that should lead to coping actions of only short duration and, consequently, a *fluctuating* coping behavior. As these individuals are preoccupied with both threats, being negatively surprised as well as being overwhelmed by strong emotions, they should be unable to wait and see if a strategy has been effective. This should then hinder the employment of situation-related, particularly instrumental, coping behavior. This is assumed to be manifested in an intensified tendency to employ intrapsychic (vigilant *and* avoidant) coping. Such a fluctuating and therefore less efficient behavior could be designated as "high-anxious or unsuccessful coping."

Individuals, who are characterized by a low intolerance of both factors can withstand both uncertainty and arousal relatively well in aversive situations. Because of their higher tolerance for uncertainty and arousal, they can pursue a certain strategy long enough to determine if it is effective or not. Their orientation is not necessarily directed toward an analysis of all threat-relevant aspects of the situation or toward evasion of cues that induce arousal. Therefore, they are able to *flexibly* adapt their behavior to the important demands of each situation; for example, they intensify their search for information when this enables them to improve their control over the situation, act instrumentally when this is the best way to bring about a desired effect, or neglect threat-related stimuli in an aversive situation whose eventual course is beyond their control. Such individuals are called "nondefensives." Regarding the relationship of this pattern to vigilance and cognitive avoidance, one restriction has to be emphasized: Nondefensives tend toward a comparatively low employment of intrapsychic (vigilant or avoidant) coping strategies, but not all individuals with this coping pattern can be designated as 'nondefensives." Extreme tolerance and thereby a low tendency to employ vigilant or avoidant coping behavior could also indicate a lack of sensitivity to uncertainty and emotional arousal and perhaps a general deficit in coping resources.

Taking the lead from stimulus-response inventories in anxiety research (cf. Endler et al., 1962), the Mainz Coping Inventory (MCI) was constructed for the separate measurement of the dimensions "vigilance" and "cognitive avoidance" (Krohne, 1989; Krohne, Rösch, & Kürsten, 1989; Krohne, Schumacher, & Egloff, 1992; Schumacher, Krohne, & Kohlmann, 1989). As a first step, descriptions of various situations potentially capable of eliciting anxiety were developed. On the one hand, these situations were supposed to represent the two large groups of threat described in the literature—*ego-threat* and *physical threat*. On the other hand, these situations had to contain varying degrees of controllability and predictability. In this manner, eight situations were constructed, four of which represented ego-threat and four others physical threat (for more details, see Krohne, 1989). Second, equally large repertoires of vigilant and cognitive avoidant coping strategies were assigned to every situational description. Examples of vigilant coping strategies are "anticipation of negative events," "information search," or "recalling negative events," whereas avoidant coping includes strategies such as "attentional diversion," "self-enhancement," or "denial." Depending on the purpose of a study, only the parts "physical threat" or "ego-threat" are used. The answers that are summed separately with regard to vigilance and cognitive avoidance items across the four situations of one part serve as scores of dispositional coping. Empirical investigations with this instrument, described in more detail elsewhere (Krohne, 1989; Krohne & Kürsten, 1989; Krohne et al., 1989; Krohne, Schumacher, & Egloff, 1992; Schumacher et al., 1989), yield the following results:

1. The four fictitious situations of each part met the criteria for variable predictability and controllability. That is, the instrument contains situations that are described as being both relatively predictable and controllable as well as situations lacking predictability and controllability. Other configurations (e.g., high predictability and low controllability) are also included in the instrument.

2. With coefficients around .85, internal consistency (Cronbach's Alpha) proved to be satisfactory.

3. The results of principal component analyses yielded a two-factor structure (cf. Krohne, 1989). Based on this solution, a clear separation between vigilant and cognitive avoidant coping strategies could be achieved. These results support the assumption underlying the model of coping modes, which postulates an independent functioning of the dispositional preferences for vigilant and avoidant coping.

To test assumptions derived from the model, laboratory studies as well as field research have been conducted. Limited space does not permit a more detailed presentation of these investigations and their findings. Instead, Table 17.1 gives an overview of the issues that were analyzed.

TABLE 17.1   Empirical Investigations of the Model of Coping Modes

Authors	Results
Krohne & Hindel (1988)	Successful top athletes (table-tennis players) were characterized by few interfering worry cognitions, little vigilant coping, and an extended use of cognitively avoidant self-regulatory techniques.
Krohne (1993b)	Sensitizers, compared with repressers, appraised an exam as being more difficult and important and manifested a lower self-efficacy concerning expected performance. Although both groups performed equally well when preparation for the exam was structured, sensitizers decreased and repressers increased in their performance in a condition of unstructured preparation.
Hock (1993)	Taken as an indicator of attention orientation in socially threatening situations, looking behavior has a twofold function: it is an integral part of a person's warning system, and an important arousal regulation device. Dispositional determinants of looking at or away from a source of threat were analyzed. Furthermore, sequential relationships between looking behavior (as an indicator of attention) and bodily arousal (as an indicator of emotion) during the anticipation of a potentially aversive event were investigated.
Hock & Krohne (1992)	In a moderately stress-inducing laboratory setting, sensitizer children (14 years) showed a close visual orientation toward their mother. Although repressers exhibited a heightened frequency of gazes at their mothers, their total looking time was comparatively short. In high-anxious children, frequency of gazes as well as total looking time were low.
Krohne & Fuchs (1991)	When anticipating an aversive stimulus, sensitizers exhibited the highest degree of instrumental (information search) as well as cognitive (self-reported attention deployment) orientation toward this event, whereas repressers cognitively, but not instrumentally, avoided stress-related information.
Krohne & Hock (1993)	Repressers solved more anagrams than high-anxious subjects. For persons high in cognitive avoidance, state-anxiety was positively correlated with the later recognition of success items (solved anagrams), whereas for individuals low in avoidance, anxiety was negatively associated with the recognition of unsolved anagrams.
Hock, Krohne, & Kaiser (1995)	Vigilant, compared with nonvigilant, individuals appraised ambiguous (potentially threatening) descriptions as being more aversive. They were also better able to later recognize the disambiguated threatening versions of these items, while their recognition performance was inferior with nonthreatening versions.

TABLE 17.1   *(Continued)*

Authors	Results
Krohne, Hock, & Kohlmann (1992)	Two experiments aimed at analyzing information processing characteristics associated with dispositional vigilance and avoidance. The first study investigated the relationships between these coping dimensions and the intake and retention of threat-related information; the second study dealt with the influence of vigilance and cognitive avoidance on the degree to which autonomous arousal as well as situational cues are taken into account when experiencing anxiety.
Kohlmann & Krohne (1991)	Sensitizers exhibited the highest scores on a symptom-emotion checklist to be completed 5 times per day on 7 consecutive days.
Krohne & Kohlmann (1991)	Although male sensitizers reported an about equal amount of positive and negative affects, the remaining three (male) coping modes scored significantly higher for positive than for negative affects. Nondefensives were especially low in negative affect. Differences between males high and low in vigilance increased (with vigilant Ss reporting more intense affects) as the time frame for reporting affects (past days, weeks, year) lengthened. Female avoiders reported a lower intensity of negative affects than nonavoiders, however only for longer time frames.
Kohlmann, Weidner, & Messina (in press)	Avoidant, compared with nonavoidant, Ss showed verbal autonomic response dissociation across experimental trials (speech preparation and delivery): Their systolic blood pressure increases were stronger in relation to their increases in self-reported anxiety.
Kohlmann (1993b)	The study tested the influence of personality variables (vigilance, cognitive avoidance) and gender on the self-estimation of physiological activity (blood pressure). While coping dispositions were unrelated to the accuracy of self-perception, cognitive avoidance was related to the reliance on internal or external cues in estimating this activity. For Ss high in avoidance, the percentage of variance in estimated blood pressure accounted for by external situational cues was comparatively high.
Hodapp & Knoll (1993)	Good heartbeat perception ability is associated with lower emotionality (affect intensity and anxiety), lower dispositional vigilance, and high scores in cognitive avoidance.
Krohne, Kleemann, Hardt, & Theisen (1990)	Sensitizers manifested more state-anxiety than the other coping modes when anticipating surgery. After admittance to hospital, high avoiders showed stronger physiological stress reactions (free fatty acids) than low avoiders; and immediately before surgery, low avoiders manifested a stronger increase in physiological stress reactions than high avoiders.

(Continued)

TABLE 17.1   *(Continued)*

Authors	Results
Slangen, Kleemann, & Krohne (1993)	Patients who expressed their preoperative anxiety more freely showed a lower level of stress reactions immediately before surgery (as measured by doses of the narcotic agent at anesthesia induction). Furthermore, the maladaptive effects of vigilant coping reported in the literature could be confirmed. However, patients, who primarily employed avoidance prior to surgery also received higher doses of narcotic agents.
Krohne, Slangen, & Kleemann (in press)	The study analyzed the influence of coping dispositions (vigilance, cognitive avoidance) and gender on intra- and postoperative adaptation in surgical patients. Dispositionally vigilant female patients received higher doses of thiopentone (the narcotic agent for anesthesia induction) than low vigilant patients. No such differences were found in male patients. However, low vigilant male patients differed from their female counterparts in that they received significantly higher thiopentone doses. Patients high in avoidance had a higher risk for an unstable hemodynamic course during surgery than patients low in avoidance. High-anxious and nondefensive patients had a much lower chance of taking analgesics postoperatively than either repressers or sensitizers, with sensitizers having by far the greatest probability of taking analgesics.

CONCLUSION

Without doubt, personality dispositions play an important role in predicting and explaining variance in coping behavior and its consequences (e.g., performance level, health status). To accomplish this, however, it is necessary that personality concepts themselves have an explicative basis. The mere elaboration of "descriptive" constructs, mostly originating in the observed variation in some measure of (generally self-reported) coping behavior, is insufficient. In this way, only "empirical" (more or less theory-free) validations of predictors of coping behavior can be achieved. What is needed, however, is the elaboration of "explicative" constructs, whose indicators can be validated along the lines of a "nomological network" (Feigl, 1958) as outlined in the approach of construct validation (Cronbach & Meehl, 1955).

Vigilance and cognitive avoidance are relevant personality dimensions for describing the intake of aversive information as well as processes that determine the short-term and long-term effects of this information. This is true for both the processing of *external* threat-related cues and for experiencing *symptoms* and *emotions*. The constructs *intolerance of uncertainty* and *intolerance of emotional arousal* appear to be relevant for explaining disposition-related differences within these areas.

So far, not much attention has been paid to gender differences in coping (cf. Miller & Kirsch, 1987). Two types of differences have to be distinguished. First, differences between men and women in the employment of certain coping strategies in specific situations. In general, men manifest more avoidant and women more vigilant coping (Krohne, Schumacher, & Egloff, 1992; Miller & Kirsch, 1987; Weidner & Collins, 1993). Although the greater use of avoidant strategies appears to be more adaptive when handling everyday short-term stressors, vigilance (paying attention to warning signals) may be more appropriate in severe stress situations of longer duration (see Weidner & Collins, 1993). This might explain why men, compared with women, are better protected from emotional distress and display overall lower rates of depression (cf. Nolen-Hoeksema, 1987). On the other hand, women are better adapted to long-term stressors (e.g., stressful life changes such as loss of a spouse; cf. Stroebe & Stroebe, 1983). In addition, women pay more attention to their physical well-being, thus increasing the likelihood of seeking medical care early and preventing serious illness.

The second type of difference is related to gender as a moderator between coping variables and outcome. The same coping strategy can lead to different results in men and women. For example, Slangen, Krohne, Stellrecht, and Kleemann (1993) observed that men who exhibited a high rate of somatic anxiety symptoms when anticipating surgery and who employed "positive restructuring" as a coping strategy showed the highest risk for an unstable hemodynamic state during surgery. On the other hand, women with the same pattern (high somatic anxiety, high positive restructuring) showed the lowest risk for an unstable state during surgery. Obviously, positive restructuring has a different significance for male and female patients. Men may use positive restructuring to repress or deny the threatening aspects of the situation. By not paying attention to situational cues, they may feel overwhelmed when the confrontation is imminent. This could result in an increased arousal immediately prior to surgery. In contrast, women who exhibit an elevated state of anxiety may employ positive restructuring as a means of developing cognitive skills required for successful coping with the severe stressor (for further results, see Krohne et al., in press).

In general, the relationships among gender, coping, and outcome variables (such as health status) are very complex (for an overview, see Miller & Kirsch, 1987; Weidner & Collins, 1993). This fact calls for the inclusion of men and women in studies of coping so that all data can be analyzed for gender differences. Furthermore, it also seems necessary to register the *intentions* underlying the employment of certain coping strategies. The same coping strategy (e.g., positive restructuring) can yield different relationships with outcome variables, depending on the intention behind it. Applied to gender differences, this idea calls for adoption of a broader conceptualization of gender that includes socially determined aspects such as life- and gender-roles (cf. Weidner & Collins, 1993).

REFERENCES

Asendorpf, J. B., & Scherer, K. R. (1983). The discrepant repressor: Differentiation between low anxiety, high anxiety, and repression of anxiety by autonomic-facial-verbal patterns of behavior. *Journal of Personality and Social Psychology, 45,* 1334–1346.

Asendorpf, J. B., & Wallbott, H. G. (1985). Formen der angstabwehr: Zweidimensionale Operationalisierung eines Bewältigungsstils [Modes of coping: A two-dimensional operationalization of a coping style]. In K. R. Scherer, H. G. Wallbott, F. J. Tolkmitt, & G. Bergmann (Eds.), *Die streßreaktion: Physiologie und Verhalten* (pp. 39–49). Göttingen, Germany: Hogrefe.

Ashby, W. R. (1956). *An introduction to cybernetics.* London: Chapman & Hall.

Becker, P. (1985). Bewältigungsverhalten und seelische Gesundheit [Coping behavior and mental health]. *Zeitschrift für Klinische Psychologie, 14,* 169–184.

Bell, P. A., & Byrne, D. (1978). Repression-sensitization. In H. London & J. E. Exner (Eds.), *Dimensions of personality* (pp. 449–485). New York: Wiley.

Ben-Porath, Y. S., & Tellegen, A. (1990). A place for traits in stress research. *Psychological Inquiry, 1,* 14–17.

Billings, A. G., & Moos, R. H. (1981). Social support functioning among community and clinical groups: A panel model. *Journal of Behavioral Medicine, 3,* 295–311.

Billings, A. G., & Moos, R. H. (1984). Coping, stress, and social resources among adults with unipolar depression. *Journal of Personality and Social Psychology, 46,* 877–891.

Boor, M., & Schill, T. (1967). Digit symbol performance of subjects varying in anxiety and defensiveness. *Journal of Consulting Psychology, 31,* 600–603.

Bruner, J. S., & Postman, L. (1947). Emotional selectivity in perception and reaction. *Journal of Personality, 16,* 69–77.

Brunswik, E. (1947). *Systematic and representative design of psychological experiments: With results in physical and social perception.* Berkeley: University of California Press.

Byrne, D. (1961). The Repression–Sensitization Scale: Rationale, reliability, and validity. *Journal of Personality, 29,* 334–349.

Byrne, D. (1964). Repression–sensitization as a dimension of personality. In B. A. Maher (Ed.), *Progress in experimental personality research* (Vol. 1, pp. 169–220). New York: Academic Press.

Byrne, D., Barry, J., & Nelson, D. (1963). Relation of the revised Repression–Sensitization Scale to measures of self-description. *Psychological Reports, 13,* 323–334.

Carver, C. S., & Scheier, M. F. (1993). Vigilant and avoidant coping in two patient samples. In H. W. Krohne (Ed.), *Attention and avoidance. Strategies in coping with aversiveness* (pp. 295–320). Seattle: Hogrefe & Huber.

Carver, C. S., Scheier, M. F., & Weintraub, J. G. (1989). Assessing coping strategies: A theoretically based approach. *Journal of Personality and Social Psychology, 56,* 267–283.

Costa, P. T., & McCrae, R. R. (1990). Personality: Another "hidden factor" in stress research. *Psychological Inquiry, 1,* 22–24.

Crandall, V. J. (1966). Personality characteristics and social and achievement behaviors associated with children's social desirability response tendencies. *Journal of Personality and Social Psychology, 4,* 477–486.

Cronbach, L. J., & Meehl, P. E. (1955). Construct validity in psychological tests. *Psychological Bulletin, 52,* 281–302.

Crowne, D. P., & Marlowe, D. (1960). A new scale of social desirability independent of psychopathology. *Journal of Consulting Psychology, 24,* 349–354.

Edwards, A. L. (1957). *The social desirability variable in personality assessment and research.* New York: Dryden.

Efran, J. S., Chorney, R. L., Ascher, L. M., & Lukens, M. D. (1989). Coping style, paradox, and the cold pressor task. *Journal of Behavioral Medicine, 12,* 91–103.

Endler, N. S., Hunt, J. M., & Rosenstein, A. J. (1962). An S–R inventory of anxiousness. *Psychological Monographs, 76*(17, Whole No. 536).

Endler, N. S., & Parker, J. D. (1990). Multidimensional assessment of coping: A critical evaluation. *Journal of Personality and Social Psychology, 58,* 844–854.

Epstein, S. (1972). The nature of anxiety with emphasis upon its relationship to expectancy. In C. D. Spielberger (Ed.), *Anxiety: Current trends in theory and research* (Vol. 2, pp. 291–337). New York: Academic Press.

Erdelyi, M. H. (1974). A new look at the New Look: Perceptual defense and vigilance. *Psychological Review, 81,* 1–25.

Eriksen, C. W. (1952). Defense against ego-threat in memory and perception. *Journal of Abnormal and Social Psychology, 47,* 230–235.

Eriksen, C. W. (1966). Cognitive responses to internally cued anxiety. In C. D. Spielberger (Ed.), *Anxiety and behavior* (pp. 327–360). New York: Academic Press.

Esterling, B. A., Antoni, M. H., Kumar, M., & Schneiderman, N. (1993). Defensiveness, trait anxiety, and Epstein-Barr viral capsid antigen antibody titers in healthy college students. *Health Psychology, 12,* 132–139.

Feigl, H. (1958). The "mental" and the "physical." In H. Feigl, M. Scriven, & G. Maxwell (Eds.), *Minnesota studies in the philosophy of science* (Vol. 2, pp. 370–497). Minneapolis: University of Minnesota Press.

Folkman, S., & Lazarus, R. S. (1980). An analysis of coping in a middle-aged community sample. *Journal of Health and Social Behavior, 21,* 219–239.

Folkman, S., & Lazarus, R. S. (1985). If it changes it must be a process: Study of emotion and coping during three stages of a college examination. *Journal of Personality and Social Psychology, 48,* 150–170.

Folkman, S., & Lazarus, R. S. (1988). *Manual for the Ways of Coping Questionnaire.* Palo Alto, CA: Consulting Psychologist Press.

Folkman, S., Lazarus, R. S., Dunkel-Schetter, C., DeLongis, A., & Gruen, R. J. (1986). The dynamics of a stressful encounter: Cognitive appraisal, coping, and encounter outcomes. *Journal of Personality and Social Psychology, 50,* 992–1003.

Folkman, S., Lazarus, R. S., Gruen, R. J., & DeLongis, A. (1986). Appraisal, coping, health status, and psychological symptoms. *Journal of Personality and Social Psychology, 50,* 571–579.

Hackfort, D., & Spielberger, C. D. (Eds.). (1989). *Anxiety in sports: An international perspective.* Washington, DC: Hemisphere.

Herrmann, T. (1973). *Persönlichkeitsmerkmale: Bestimmung und verwendung in der psychologischen Wissenschaft* [Personality concepts: Definition and use in psychology]. Stuttgart, Germany: Kohlhammer.

Hill, K. T. (1971). Anxiety in the evaluative context. *Young Children, 27,* 97–118.

Hill, K. T., & Sarason, S. B. (1966). The relation of test anxiety and defensiveness to test and school performance over the elementary school years: A further longitudinal study. *Monographs of the Society for Research in Child Development, 31*(2, Serial No. 104).

Hock, M. (1993). Coping dispositions, attentional direction, and anxiety states. In H. W. Krohne (Ed.), *Attention and avoidance. Strategies in coping with aversiveness* (pp. 139–169). Seattle: Hogrefe & Huber.

Hock, M., & Krohne, H. W. (1992). Anxiety and coping dispositions as predictors of the visual interaction between mother and child. *Anxiety Research, 4,* 275–286.

Hock, M., Krohne, H. W., & Kaiser, J. (1995). *Coping dispositions and the interpretation of ambiguous stimuli.* Manuscript in preparation.

Hodapp, V., & Knoll, J. F. (1993). Heartbeat perception, coping, and emotion. In H. W. Krohne (Ed.), *Attention and avoidance. Strategies in coping with aversiveness* (pp. 191–211). Seattle: Hogrefe & Huber.

Holroyd, K. (1972). Repression–sensitization, Marlowe–Crowne defensiveness, and perceptual defense. *Proceedings of the 80th Annual Convention of the American Psychological Association* (Vol. 7, pp. 401–402). Washington, DC: American Psychological Association.

Jamner, L. D., Schwartz, G. E., & Leigh, H. (1988). The relationship between repressive and defensive coping styles and monocyte, eosinophile, and serum glucose levels: Support for the opiod peptide hypothesis of repression. *Psychosomatic Medicine, 50,* 567–575.

Janis, I. L. (1983). Stress inoculation in health care: Theory and research. In D. Meichenbaum & M. Jaremko (Eds.), *Stress reduction and prevention* (pp. 67–99). New York: Plenum.

Janke, W., Erdmann, G., & Kallus, W. (1985). *Streßverarbeitungsfragebogen (SVF), Handanweisung* [Coping Inventory (SVF), Manual]. Göttingen, Germany: Hogrefe.

Johnston, M. (1988). Impending surgery. In S. Fisher & J. Reason (Eds.), *Handbook of life stress, cognition and health* (pp. 79–100). Chichester, UK: Wiley.

King, A. C., Taylor, C. B., Albright, C. A., & Haskell, W. L. (1990). The relationship between repressive and defensive coping styles and blood pressure responses in healthy, middle-aged men and women. *Journal of Psychosomatic Research, 34,* 461–471.

Kogan, N., & Wallach, M. A. (1964). *Risk taking: A study in cognition and personality.* New York: Holt.

Kohlmann, C. -W. (1990). *Streßbewältigung und Persönlichkeit. Flexibles versus rigides Copingverhalten und seine Auswirkungen auf Angsterleben und physiologische Belastungsreaktionen* [Coping and personality. Flexible versus rigid coping behavior and its effects on anxiety and physiological stress reactions]. Bern, Switzerland: Huber.

Kohlmann, C. -W. (1993a). Development of the repression–sensitization construct: With special reference to the discrepancy between subjective and physiological stress reactions. In U. Hentschel, G. Smith, W. Ehlers, & J. G. Draguns (Eds.), *The concept of defense mechanisms in contemporary psychology: Theoretical, research, and clinical perspectives* (pp. 184–204). New York: Springer-Verlag.

Kohlmann, C. -W. (1993b). Strategies in blood pressure estimation: The role of vigilance, cognitive avoidance, and gender. In H. W. Krohne (Ed.), *Attention and avoidance. Strategies in coping with aversiveness* (pp. 213–238). Seattle: Hogrefe & Huber.

Kohlmann, C. -W., & Krohne, H. W. (1991, July). *The coping dispositions vigilance and cognitive avoidance: Associations with symptom reporting.* Paper presented at the 6th annual meeting of the International Society for Research on Emotions, Saarbrücken, Germany.

Kohlmann, C. -W., Singer, P., & Krohne, H. W. (1989). Coping disposition, actual coping, and the discrepancy between subjective and physiological stress reactions. In P. F. Lovibond & P. Wilson (Eds.), *Proceedings of the XXIV International Congress of Psychology* (Vol. 9, pp. 67–78). Amsterdam, The Netherlands: Elsevier.

Kohlmann, C. -W., Weidner, G., & Messina, C. (in press). *Avoidant coping style and verbal-cardiovascular response dissociation. Psychology and Health.*

Krohne, H. W. (1975). *Angst und Angstverarbeitung* [Anxiety and coping]. Stuttgart, Germany: Kohlhammer.

Krohne, H. W. (1978). Individual differences in coping with stress and anxiety. In C. D. Spielberger & I. G. Sarason (Eds.), *Stress and anxiety* (Vol. 5, pp. 233–260). Washington, DC: Hemisphere.

Krohne, H. W. (1986). Coping with stress: Dispositions, strategies, and the problem of measurement. In M. H. Appley & R. Trumbull (Eds.), *Dynamics of stress. Physiological, psychological, and social perspectives* (pp. 207–232). New York: Plenum.

Krohne, H. W. (1989). The concept of coping modes: Relating cognitive person variables to actual coping behavior. *Advances in Behaviour Research and Therapy, 11,* 235–248.

Krohne, H. W. (1990). Personality as a mediator between objective events and their subjective representation. *Psychological Inquiry, 1,* 26–29.

Krohne, H. W. (1992). Streßbewältigung bei Operationen [Coping with surgery]. In L. R. Schmidt (Ed.), *Jahrbuch der Medizinischen Psychologie* (Vol. 7, pp. 55–73). Heidelberg: Springer-Verlag.

Krohne, H. W. (Ed.). (1993a). *Attention and avoidance. Strategies in coping with aversiveness.* Seattle: Hogrefe & Huber.

Krohne, H. W. (1993b). Vigilance and cognitive avoidance as concepts in coping research. In H. W. Krohne (Ed.), *Attention and avoidance. Strategies in coping with aversiveness* (pp. 19–50). Seattle: Hogrefe & Huber.

Krohne, H. W. (1995). Repression–sensitization. In M. Amelang (Ed.), *Enzyklopädie der Psychologie: Differentielle Psychologie und Persönlichkeits-forschung: Vol. 3. Individuelle Unterschiede: Temperament und Persönlichkeit.* Göttingen, Germany: Hogrefe.

Krohne, H. W., & Fuchs, J. (1991). Influence of coping dispositions and danger-related information on emotional and coping reactions of individuals anticipating an aversive event. In C. D. Spielberger, I. G. Sarason, J. M. T. Strelau, & J. Brebner (Eds.), *Stress and anxiety* (Vol. 13, pp. 131–155). Washington, DC: Hemisphere.

Krohne, H. W., & Hindel, C. (1988). Trait anxiety, state anxiety, and coping behavior as predictors of athletic performance. *Anxiety Research, 1,* 225–234.

Krohne, H. W., & Hock, M. (1993). Coping dispositions, actual anxiety and the incidental learning of success- and failure-related stimuli. *Personality and Individual Difference, 15,* 33–41.

Krohne, H. W., Hock, M., & Kohlmann, C. -W. (1992). Coping dispositions, uncertainty, and emotional arousal. In K. T. Strongman (Ed.), *International review of studies on emotion* (Vol. 2, pp. 73–95). Chichester, UK: Wiley.

Krohne, H. W., Kleemann, P. P., Hardt, J., & Theisen, A. (1990). Relations between coping strategies and presurgical stress reactions. In L. R. Schmidt, P. Schwenkmezger, J. Weinman, & S. Maes (Eds.), *Theoretical and applied aspects of health psychology* (pp. 423–429). London: Harwood.

Krohne, H. W., & Kohlmann, C. -W. (1991, July). *Vigilance, cognitive avoidance, and the reporting of positive and negative affects.* Paper presented at the 6th annual meeting of the International Society for Research on Emotions, Saarbrücken, Germany.

Krohne, H. W., & Kürsten, F. (1989). *Die Messung von Angstbewältigungsdispositionen: III. Die Erfassung erlebter Kontrollierbarkeit und Vorhersagbarkeit von Belastungssituationen* [The assessment of coping dispositions: III. Measurement of perceived controllability and predictability of stress situations]. Mainz, Germany: Johannes Gutenberg-Universität, Psychologisches Institut.

Krohne, H. W., & Rogner, J. (1982). Repression-sensitization as a central construct in coping research. In H. W. Krohne & L. Laux (Eds.), *Achievement, stress and anxiety* (pp. 167–193). New York: McGraw-Hill.

Krohne, H. W., & Rogner, J. (1985). Mehrvariablen-Diagnostik in der Bewältigungsforschung [Multivariate assessment in coping research]. In H. W. Krohne (Ed.), *Angstbewältigung in Leistungssituationen* (pp. 45–62). Weinheim, Germany: Edition Psychologie.

Krohne, H. W., Rösch, W., & Kürsten, F. (1989). Die Erfassung von Angstbewältigung in physisch bedrohlichen Situationen [The assessment of coping in physical-threat situations]. *Zeitschrift für Klinische Psychologie, 18,* 230–242.

Krohne, H. W., Schumacher, A., & Egloff, B. (1992). *Das Angstbewältigungs-Inventar (ABI)* [The Mainz Coping Inventory (MCI)]. (Mainzer Berichte zur Persönlichkeitsforschung No. 41). Mainz, Germany: Johannes Gutenberg-Universität, Psychologisches Institut.

Krohne, H. W., Slangen, K., & Kleemann, P. P. (in press). Coping variables as predictors of perioperative emotional states and adjustment. *Psychology and Health.*

Laux, L., & Weber, H. (1987). Person-centered coping research. *European Journal of Personality, 1,* 193–214.

Laux, L., & Weber, H. (1990). Bewältigung von Emotionen [Coping with emotions]. In K. R. Scherer (Ed.), *Enzyklopädie der Psychologie: Motivation und Emotion: Vol. 3. Psychologie der Emotion* (pp. 560–629). Göttingen, Germany: Hogrefe.

Lazarus, R. S. (1966). *Psychological stress and the coping process.* New York: McGraw-Hill.

Lazarus, R. S. (1990a). Author's response. *Psychological Inquiry, 1,* 41–51.

Lazarus, R. S. (1990b). Theory-based stress measurement. *Psychological Inquiry, 1,* 3–13.

Lazarus, R. S., & Folkman, S. (1984). Coping and adaptation. In W. D. Gentry (Ed.), *The handbook of behavior medicine* (pp. 282–325). New York: Guilford.

Lazarus, R. S., & Folkman, S. (1987). Transactional theory and research on emotions and coping. *European Journal of Personality, 1,* 141–169.

Lazarus, R. S., & Launier, R. (1978). Stress-related transactions between person and environment. In L. A. Pervin & M. Lewis (Eds.), *Perspectives in interactional psychology* (pp. 287–327). New York: Plenum.

Lefcourt, H. M. (1969). Need for approval and threatened negative evaluation as determinants of expressiveness in a projective test. *Journal of Consulting and Clinical Psychology, 33,* 96–102.

Ludwick-Rosenthal, R., & Neufeld, R. W. J. (1988). Stress management during noxious medical procedures: An evaluative review of outcome studies. *Psychological Bulletin, 104,* 326–342.

McCrae, R. R. (1984). Situational determinants of coping responses: Loss, threat, and challenge. *Journal of Personality and Social Psychology, 46,* 919–928.

McCrae, R. R., & Costa, P. T. (1986). Personality, coping, and coping effectiveness in an adult sample. *Journal of Personality, 54,* 385–405.

Miller, S. B. (1993). Cardiovascular reactivity in anger-defensive individuals: The influence of task demands. *Psychosomatic Medicine, 55,* 78–85.

Miller, S. M. (1980). When is a little information a dangerous thing? Coping with stressful life events by monitoring versus blunting. In S. Levine & H. Ursin (Eds.), *Health and coping* (pp. 145–169). New York: Plenum.

Miller, S. M. (1987). Monitoring and blunting: Validation of a questionnaire to assess styles of information seeking under threat. *Journal of Personality and Social Psychology, 52,* 345–353.

Miller, S. M. (1989). Cognitive informational styles in the process of coping with threat and frustration. *Advances in Behaviour Research and Therapy, 11,* 223–234.

Miller, S. M., Brody, D. S., & Summerton, J. (1988). Styles of coping with threat: Implications for health. *Journal of Personality and Social Psychology, 54,* 142–148.

Miller, S. M., Combs, C., & Kruus, L. (1993). Tuning in and tuning out: Confronting the effects of confrontation. In H. W. Krohne (Ed.), *Attention and avoidance. Strategies in coping with aversiveness* (pp. 51–69). Seattle: Hogrefe & Huber.

Miller, S. M., & Kirsch, N. (1987). Sex differences in cognitive coping with stress. In R. C. Barnett, L. Biener, & G. K. Baruch (Eds.), *Gender and stress* (pp. 278–307). New York: Free Press.

Miller, S. M., & Mangan, C. E. (1983). Interacting effects of information and coping style in adapting to gynecologic stress: Should the doctor tell all? *Journal of Personality and Social Psychology, 45,* 223–236.

Millham, J., & Jacobson, L. (1978). The need for approval. In H. London & J. E. Exner (Eds.), *Dimensions of personality* (pp. 365–390). New York: Wiley.

Mullen, B., & Suls, J. (1982). The effectiveness of attention and rejection as coping styles: A meta-analysis of temporal differences. *Journal of Psychosomatic Research, 26,* 43–49.

Newton, T. L., & Contrada, R. J. (1992). Repressive coping and verbal-autonomic response dissociation: The influence of social context. *Journal of Personality and Social Psychology, 62,* 159–167.

Nolen-Hoeksema, S. (1987). Sex differences in unipolar depression: Evidence and theory. *Psychological Bulletin, 101,* 259–282.

Pennebaker, J. W., Kiecolt-Glaser, J. K., & Glaser, R. (1988). Disclosure of traumas and immune function: Health implications for psychotherapy. *Journal of Consulting and Clinical Psychology, 56,* 239–245.

Phipps, S., & Zinn, A. B. (1986). Psychological response to amniocentesis: II. Effects of coping style. *American Journal of Medical Genetics, 25,* 143–148.

Roth, S., & Cohen, L. J. (1986). Approach, avoidance, and coping with stress. *American Psychologist, 41,* 813–819.

Ruebush, B. K., Byrum, M., & Farnham, L. J. (1963). Problem solving as a function of children's defensiveness and parental behavior. *Journal of Abnormal and Social Psychology, 67,* 355–362.

Schumacher, A., Krohne, H. W., & Kohlmann, C. -W. (1989). *Die Messung von Angstbewältigungsdispositionen: IV. Angstbewältigung in selbstwertbedrohlichen Situationen* [The assessment of coping dispositions: IV. Coping in ego-threat situations]. Mainz, Germany: Johannes Gutenberg-Universität, Psychologisches Institut.

Singer, J. L. (Ed.). (1990). *Repression and dissociation. Implications for personality theory, psychopathology, and health.* Chicago: University of Chicago Press.

Slangen, K., Kleemann, P. P., & Krohne, H. W. (1993). Coping with surgical stress. In H. W. Krohne (Ed.), *Attention and avoidance. Strategies in coping with aversiveness* (pp. 321–348). Seattle: Hogrefe & Huber.

Slangen, K., Krohne, H. W., Stellrecht, S., & Kleemann, P. P. (1993). Dimensionen perioperativer Belastung und ihre Auswirkungen auf intra- und postoperative Anpassung von Chirurgiepatienten [Dimensions of perioperative stress and their effects on intra- and postoperative adjustment of surgical patients]. *Zeitschrift für Gesundheitspsychologie, 1,* 123–142.

Spielberger, C. D., Jacobs, G., Russel, S., & Crane, R. J. (1983). Assessment of anger: The State-Trait-Anger-Scale. In J. N. Butcher & C. D. Spielberger (Eds.), *Advances in personality assessment* (Vol. 2, pp. 161–189). Hillsdale, NJ: Erlbaum.

Steptoe, A., & O'Sullivan, J. (1986). Monitoring and blunting coping styles in women prior to surgery. *British Journal of Clinical Psychology, 25,* 143–144.

Stone, A. A., & Neale, J. M. (1982). Development of a methodology for assessing daily experiences. In A. Baum & J. Singer (Eds.), *Advances in environmental psychology: Environment and health* (Vol. 4, pp. 49–83). New York: Erlbaum.

Stone, A. A., & Neale, J. M. (1984). New measure of daily coping: Development and preliminary results. *Journal of Personality and Social Psychology, 46,* 892–906.

Stroebe, M. S., & Stroebe, W. (1983). Who suffers more? Sex differences in health risks of the widowed. *Psychological Bulletin, 93,* 279–301.

Suls, J., & Fletcher, B. (1985). The relative efficacy of avoidant and non-avoidant coping strategies: A meta-analysis. *Health Psychology, 4,* 249–288.

Taylor, J. A. (1953). A personality scale of manifest anxiety. *Journal of Abnormal and Social Psychology, 48,* 285–290.

Temoshok, L. (1987). Personality, coping style, emotion and cancer: Towards an integrative model. *Cancer Surveys, 6,* 545–567.

Wallbott, H. G., & Scherer, K. R. (1991). Stress specificities: Differential effects of coping style, gender, and type of stressor on autonomic arousal, facial expression, and subjective feeling. *Journal of Personality and Social Psychology, 61,* 147–156.

Watkins, L. O., Weaver, L., & Odegaard, V. (1986). Preparation for cardiac catheterization: Tailoring the content of instruction to coping style. *Heart & Lung, 15,* 382–389.

Watson, D. (1990). On the dispositional nature of stress measures: Stable and nonspecific influences in self-reported hassles. *Psychological Inquiry, 1,* 34–37.

Watson, D., & Clark, L. A. (1984). Negative affectivity: The disposition to experience aversive emotional states. *Psychological Bulletin, 96,* 465–490.

Weidner, G., & Collins, R. L. (1993). Gender, coping, and health. In H. W. Krohne (Ed.), *Attention and avoidance. Strategies in coping with aversiveness* (pp. 241–265). Seattle: Hogrefe & Huber.

Weinberger, D. A., & Schwartz, G. E. (1990). Distress and restraint as superordinate dimensions of self-reported adjustment: A typological perspective. *Journal of Personality, 58,* 381–417.

Weinberger, D. A., Schwartz, G. E., & Davidson, R. J. (1979). Low-anxious, high-anxious, and repressive coping-styles: Psychometric patterns and behavioral and physiological responses to stress. *Journal of Abnormal Psychology, 88,* 369–380.

Weinstein, J., Averill, J. R., Opton, E. M., & Lazarus, R. S. (1968). Defensive style and discrepancy between self-report and physiological indexes of stress. *Journal of Personality and Social Psychology, 10,* 406–413.

CHAPTER 18

Personality Traits and the Coping Process

PAUL L. HEWITT and GORDON L. FLETT

Different people cope with stressors in different ways and with varying results. This is a reasonably well-accepted maxim and an extension of this maxim is also well-accepted—that personality factors are linked closely with coping processes (Ben-Porath & Tellegen, 1990; Lazarus & Folkman, 1984; Moos & Schaeffer, 1993). It has been proposed extensively that both personality and coping are involved directly or indirectly in the production and maintenance of various kinds of maladjustment (see Snyder & Ford, 1987). This chapter presents an overview of the literature on personality and coping. We describe current research on coping and selected personality traits including the traits represented by the five-factor model; locus of control; optimism; and traits that reflect achievement-related tendencies, notably, Type A behavior and perfectionism. In addition to describing research on the extent to which these personality traits are related to coping dimensions, we examine some key issues in the personality and coping literature, including the central question of whether coping styles represent personality traits. Finally, we highlight some important directions for future research.

MODELS OF PERSONALITY, COPING, AND STRESS

It has long been held that assessing the links between coping and particular personality variables may help to explain why certain personality factors are related to maladjustment or negative outcomes. Within extant research on personality and coping, at least three models appear to pertain to the relationship between the variables. The first model, Figure 18.1, top, assumes that personality determines the particular coping strategy or style that is used during stressful times. Studies that test this model assess the association between levels of particular dispositional variables that have been proposed as pathogenic (e.g., neuroticism) and particular coping strategies or styles (e.g., avoidance; Endler & Parker, 1990; McCrae & Costa, 1986), or assess coping and maladjustment in samples of individuals who are high or low on some pathogenic personality trait (Pittner, Houston, &

410

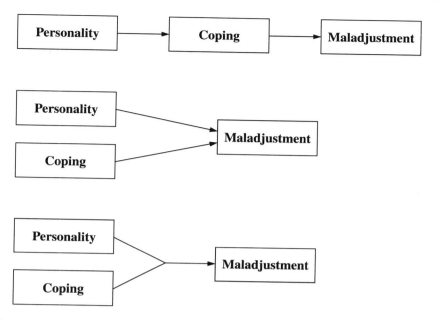

Figure 18.1   Three models of personality, coping, and maladjustment: A mediational model (top), an additive model (middle), and an interactive model (bottom).

Spiridigliozzi, 1983). These studies try to determine whether certain personality variables or types produce coping styles that may result in pathology.

The second model, Figure 18.1, middle, is an additive model wherein both personality and coping are hypothesized to make independent contributions to maladjustment. The model assumes that certain personality variables and coping strategies are related uniquely to maladjustment and each is relevant in the prediction of symptoms (e.g., Parkes, 1986). Finally, the third model, Figure 18.1, bottom, is an interactive model whereby certain personality variables interact with coping variables to produce or maintain maladjustment (e.g., Wheaton, 1983). Many of these formulations are diathesis-stress models (Taylor, 1990) that are evaluated by testing the interaction effects of personality and coping in predicting maladjustment. Numerous personality variables have been examined within the context of one or more of these models, with the majority of the research examining the mediational approach rather than the additive or interactional models. In the sections that follow, we present a brief overview of some of this research on personality and coping.

COPING, NEUROTICISM, AND THE FIVE-FACTOR MODEL

Historically, there has been much interest in reducing the myriad personality constructs into a smaller number of superordinate traits (Cattell, 1950; Fiske, 1949).

Although researchers have found varying numbers of traits that explain personality (e.g., Cattell, Eber, & Tatsuoka, 1970; Eysenck & Eysenck, 1985), one of the more recently revived attempts involves the five-factor model as originally espoused by Tupes and Christal (1961) and more recently elaborated by several researchers (for a review, see John, 1990). Costa and McCrae (1985) suggested that the five traits of neuroticism, extraversion, openness, agreeableness, and conscientiousness represent the core components of personality. The majority of work on coping and these traits has focused on neuroticism, probably because neuroticism involves instability and coping efforts directed at emotionality.

Most research has found that neuroticism is linked with maladaptive coping. For example, Endler and Parker (1990) found that neuroticism was correlated with increased emotion-focused coping in both men and women and with lower task-focused coping in women (also see Endler, 1993). Likewise, Epstein and Meier (1989) showed that neuroticism is associated negatively with a broad coping variable labeled constructive thinking that involves thinking constructively versus destructively regarding potentially stressful events. Costa and McCrae (1990) described a retrospective study of coping with the accident at Three Mile Island to clarify the role of neuroticism in coping. They found that neuroticism was related to increased neurotic coping and decreased mature coping, suggesting that neuroticism may not only enhance poor or maladaptive coping strategies but also promote fewer adaptive strategies. They also raised the important issue that maladaptive components of coping (e.g., self-blame, hostile reactions) may simply be components of neuroticism and not coping strategies in and of themselves.

Other research indicates that the link between neuroticism and coping is complex and depends, in part, on contextual factors. Parkes (1986) tested both additive and interactive models of personality and coping in a study of neuroticism, extraversion, environmental factors, and coping. Consistent with other research, Parkes found that neuroticism was related to less direct or problem-centered coping, whereas extraversion was related to more direct forms of coping. Moreover, she demonstrated that intraindividual, environmental, and situational factors were all important in predicting coping responses. An interactional model was shown to be more appropriate than additive models in this work. For instance, the interaction of neuroticism, work demand, and importance of stressor predicted suppression (ignore situation and not act impulsively). Furthermore, Parkes also showed that neuroticism and extraversion interacted to predict levels of suppression, supporting the usefulness of looking at the interaction of personality variables in coping. Along a similar vein, Bolger (1990) assessed whether coping strategies would mediate the relation between neuroticism and maladjustment. He found that neuroticism led to ineffective coping and subsequent increases in distress and that neuroticism also interacted with coping to predict distress.

McCrae and Costa (1986) also provided evidence for a link between neuroticism and emotion-oriented coping, but they included measures of extraversion and openness. It was found that neuroticism was related to a variety of specific emotion-focused strategies and to an overall factor called neurotic coping. Extraversion was associated with adaptive strategies such as increased rational thinking, substitution, and restraint, as well as an overall factor called mature coping. This is consistent with others' findings (e.g., Rim, 1986) as well as with reports that extraversion may contribute to positive emotionality (Watson & Clark, in press). Finally, openness was associated with increased use of humor and decreased use of faith, although the relations between openness and the broader factors of neurotic and mature coping were not reported. McCrae and Costa concluded that the ". . . most pervasive and replicable factors in coping are closely related to the major personality dimensions of neuroticism and extraversion" (p. 394). Moreover, in light of the finding that some associations between coping and outcome were attenuated when personality variables were partialed, they suggested further that personality variables such as extraversion may be important in coping and adjustment for not only reducing distress, but also in maintaining good spirits during stressful times.

The research to date has provided some information as to the role of neuroticism in coping and, to a lesser extent, the nature of the relationship between extraversion and coping. There has been little coping research done using the other three components of the five-factor model—openness, conscientiousness, and agreeableness. McCrae (1991) suggested that these three factors may be important especially in accessing coping resources such as therapists or social support more generally, although no work has addressed this issue. One reason for the lack of research on other components of the five-factor model may be the hesitance of clinical researchers to use this model, which is described as comprising the traits of normal personality (Ben-Porath & Waller, 1992). More work is certainly needed in these areas to clarify the relation between dimensions of personality and coping strategies. Likewise, there are other major facets of personality, such as psychoticism (Eysenck & Eysenck, 1985) that have received little attention with respect to coping, despite some indications of their relevance to emotion-focused coping (e.g., Endler & Parker, 1990; Rim, 1986). Moreover, assessment of concurrent and specific stressors and premorbid levels of personality is needed to elucidate the relations between such traits and coping (for a discussion, see Bolger, 1990). Finally, tests of the mediation and interaction models are promising in terms of understanding how neuroticism and extraversion predispose individuals to the adverse consequences of stress.

COPING STYLES IN OPTIMISM-PESSIMISM AND LOCUS OF CONTROL

Research on locus of control and coping has been predominant throughout the past two decades, reflecting the more general impact of the locus of control construct (Lefcourt, 1992). Locus of control involves individual differences in beliefs about control over reinforcement. Individuals with an internal locus of control perceive personal mastery over outcomes, whereas individuals with an external locus of control perceive that reinforcements are due to external factors. An extensive literature indicates that individuals with an external locus of control exhibit a wide range of maladaptive coping responses when confronted with stressors (see Folkman, 1984). This locus of control is related to primary appraisals of threats and challenges, as well as subsequent coping efforts (Folkman, 1984). For example, Parkes (1986) examined locus of control, appraisal, and coping in a sample of nurses. The overall pattern of results indicated that an internal locus of control was associated with more adaptive coping responses. Amirkhan (1990) examined how the three subscales of his Coping Strategy Indicator (problem solving, avoidance, and seeking support) related to personality measures of locus of control, repression-sensitization, and social support. An external locus of control was associated with less problem-solving coping, whereas repression was associated with less problem-solving coping and less support seeking. Related research has found that personality dispositions that may contribute to an internal locus of control (hardiness, personal mastery, and feelings of self-efficacy and personal confidence) are correlated with more adaptive coping responses (see Holahan & Moos, 1987; Litt, 1988). In summarizing the existing literature, Compas, Banez, Malcarne, and Worsham (1991) concluded that a consistent finding is that an internal locus of control is associated with problem-focused coping but that locus of control and emotion-focused coping tend to be unrelated.

There are two important qualifications to the general finding that an external locus of control is associated with more maladaptive coping responses or with fewer adaptive responses. First, the coping associated with an external locus of control may be adaptive under certain circumstances. Following observations by Folkman (1984), Forsythe and Compas (1987) reported evidence indicating that problem-focused coping is adaptive when a stressor is seen as controllable, but emotion-focused coping is adaptive when a stressor is seen as uncontrollable. Other research indicates that avoidance may be adaptive in a problem situation that fosters unfavorable expectancies (Abella & Heslin, 1989). Thus, the association among locus of control, coping, and adjustment is rather complex and may vary as a function of the qualitative nature of the stressor and extant situational factors.

Second, statements about locus of control and coping should be qualified by the fact that the locus of control construct is multidimensional (Lefcourt, 1991). That is, individuals may be differentiated in terms of their locus of control beliefs for achievement, interpersonal, and health outcomes. Research that focuses on a specific control domain and coping responses when confronted with a matching problem, such as health locus of control and coping with a health problem (e.g., Crisson & Keefe, 1988) should yield more robust associations between personality and coping.

The literature on coping and locus of control has been supplemented by a wealth of research on coping and dispositional levels of optimism-pessimism. Rather than examining expectancies about control over reinforcement, research on optimism-pessimism focuses more generally on the valence of expected outcomes, irrespective of the source of reinforcement. Research by Scheier and Carver (e.g., Scheier & Carver, 1985, 1987, 1992) and associates has been influential in establishing the link between dispositional optimism and a variety of health-related outcomes. This research has shown consistently that their general measure of optimism, the Life Orientation Test (LOT), is associated with adaptive coping responses to physical challenges (Scheier, Weintraub, & Carver, 1986) and completion of alcoholism recovery programs (Strack, Carver, & Blaney, 1987). Moreover, other work by Fontaine and Manstead (1993) shows significant associations between optimism and active coping and negative associations between optimism and venting emotions.

A study by Carver et al. (1993) is particularly helpful in clarifying the associations among optimism, coping, and distress. Their study was a longitudinal investigation of 59 breast cancer patients. Subjects provided reports of levels of optimism, coping, and distress at various time points (e.g., time of diagnosis, 1 day presurgery, and 10 days, 3 months, 6 months, and 12 months postsurgery). It was found that optimism was related negatively to distress at each time point, even after controlling for initial distress level. In terms of the link between optimism and coping tendencies, optimists tended to express more frequent use of positive coping responses (positive reframing and acceptance) and less frequent use of negative coping responses (denial and disengagement). Finally, a series of path analyses underscored the complex association among optimism, coping, and distress by indicating that certain coping styles (e.g., disengagement) mediated the association between optimism and distress. It was found, for instance, that optimists were less likely to disengage from the problem and this, in turn, resulted in lower levels of distress.

In addition to the work by Scheier and Carver, other researchers have confirmed the associations among pessimism, coping, and maladjustment (Zeidner & Ben-Zur, 1993). Zeidner and Hammer (1992), in a longitudinal study of 261 adults during the Persian Gulf War, found that higher levels of pessimism were correlated with higher levels of anxiety, depression, and physical symptoms. However, pessimism was not directly related to any of the adjustment outcome variables once other predictor variables had been taken into account. Small but significant correlations were also obtained between the pessimism measure and indexes of emotion-focused and palliative coping and it was shown that pessimism was linked with palliative coping that, in turn, predicted levels of health symptoms, anxiety, and cognitive functioning. The link between pessimism and maladaptive coping is consistent with observations that pessimism drains available coping resources (e.g., Wong, 1993).

Although Scheier and Carver (1992) have argued effectively for the need to focus on generalized outcome expectancies rather than domain-specific outcomes in coping and health, focusing on domain-specific outcome expectancy beliefs for related problems may be fruitful. Initial evidence supporting this observation has been provided by Taylor et al. (1992). These researchers investigated optimism, coping, psychological adjustment, and risk-taking behavior in a sample of homosexual men. The measures in this study included a general measure of optimism (the LOT) as well as event-specific measures, including indexes of AIDS-specific optimism (a belief in invulnerability to AIDS) and fatalistic vulnerability (pessimism regarding the belief in the inevitability of contracting AIDS). The need to examine general and specific outcome expectancies was underscored by the weak, positive association obtained between scores on the LOT and the measure of AIDS-specific optimism ($r = .18$, $p < .05$). Additional analyses indicated that the pattern of findings varied as a function of the outcome expectancy measure used. The general measure of optimism did not predict risk-related sexual behavior, but it was associated with more positive psychological adjustment. The authors concluded that optimism may be adaptive without necessarily jeopardizing the individual's health status. In contrast, the domain-specific measure was less strongly correlated with psychological adjustment ($r = -.12$, $p < .01$), but this domain-specific measure predicted coping avoidance of AIDS. Moreover, HIV-seropositive men differed from HIV-seronegative men in AIDS-specific optimism but not in generalized optimism.

There are other indications that different results emerge with general versus domain-specific outcome expectancy measures. We have assessed the predictive usefulness of a new measure of social pessimism versus more global measures of pessimism (see Flett, Hewitt, & Gayle, 1993). Our results consistently indicate that individual differences in negative social expectancies account for substantial degrees of unique variance in adjustment outcomes after removing variance associated with more general measures of outcome expectancy, such as the Hope Scale (Snyder et al., 1991) and the Hopelessness Scale (Beck, Weissman, Lester, & Trexler, 1974). The relevance of a domain-specific approach to the coping process was illustrated in a recently completed study (Flett, Hewitt, & Belanger, 1993a). We administered our new measure of social pessimism, along with the Hope Scale and the Hopelessness Scale to a sample of 119 high school students. These adolescents also completed measures of depression, social anxiety, and the Causey and Dubow (1992) coping measure with respect to a psychosocial stressor (a quarrel with a peer). Our results showed that a dispositional tendency to have negative social expectancies was associated strongly with depression, social anxiety, and maladaptive coping responses involving avoidance, distancing, and emotion-oriented responses reflecting internalizing and externalizing tendencies. Importantly, even though our new measure was substantially correlated with more general measures of hope and hopelessness, the correlations with depression, social anxiety, and maladaptive coping responses remained significant after removing variance associated with hope and hopelessness. These data are consistent with other indications that pessimism for interpersonal events is a strong predictor of distress in a variety of populations, and they attest further to the usefulness of examining general and specific optimism-pessimism in life domains.

COPING STYLES AND ACHIEVEMENT-ORIENTED TRAITS

Type A Behavior Pattern

There is a recent interest and a growing literature on coping and achievement-related variables that involve planfulness, goal striving, and purposive actions. The Type A behavior pattern (TABP) is a well-known personality construct that is clearly linked to coping processes and health outcomes. This construct was defined originally as an action-emotion complex that involves specific behavioral dispositions, specific behaviors, and emotional responses. It is characterized by competitive achievement strivings, hostility, impatience, and accelerated pace of activities (Friedman & Rosenman, 1959). Interest in the construct began when it was shown that TABP was linked with coronary heart disease (Friedman & Rosenman, 1959), primarily due to an hostility component of TABP (Contrada, Leventhal, & O'Leary, 1990). Furthermore, recent work has established that the TABP is also associated with psychological symptoms (Suls & Wan, 1989) indicating that it is associated widely with maladjustment.

It has been suggested that TABP is either associated with maladaptive coping or is a coping strategy in and of itself. For example, Glass (1977) indicated that TABP is a style of dealing with the environment and Type A individuals utilize rigid and maladaptive behavior when confronted with stressors that signify a lack of personal control. Others have suggested that the TABP produces coping styles that compromise the individual's efforts to deal with environmental exigencies (Defares, 1982; Vingerhoets & Flohr, 1984).

The empirical evidence has confirmed as association between the TABP and maladaptive coping. Pittner et al. (1983) demonstrated that Type A persons, as assessed by the Activity subscale of the Thurstone Temperament Schedule, tended to use cognitive or defensive strategies encompassing denial and projection, but not rationalization or intellectualization. Similarly, a factor analysis by Endler, Parker, and Butcher (1993) yielded a factor composed jointly of emotion-oriented coping and the Type A measure from the MMPI-2 further supporting a link. In related research, Endler and Parker (1990) showed that increased Type A behavior, as measured by the Survey of Work Styles (Jackson & Gray, 1989) was associated with emotion-focused coping (also see Greenglass, 1988) and that Type A males reported a tendency to engage in avoidant-oriented coping in the form of distraction. Other work has also demonstrated that TABP tends to be related to avoidance-withdrawal forms of coping (see Carver, Coleman, & Glass, 1976; Helman, 1987).

In contrast, other research indicates that the TABP may be associated positively with more adaptive and active forms of problem-focused coping. For example, Vingerhoets and Flohr (1984) had 300 male subjects complete the Jenkins Activity Survey (JAS; Chesney, Black, Chadwick, & Rosenman, 1981) and the Ways of Coping Checklist (Folkman & Lazarus, 1988). They found that Type A people tended to be lower on acceptance but significantly higher on problem-focused coping. These findings are similar to other findings showing that problem-focused coping characterizes Type A individuals (Evans & Fearn, 1985; Hart, 1988; Smith & Brehm, 1981). Finally, some researchers have reported no association between TABP and coping strategies (see Burke, 1982; Kliewer, 1991) indicating the lack of consistency across studies.

Several factors may account, in part, for the lack of consistent findings. First, methodological issues such as the manner in which TABP has been assessed may be particularly important. Vickers, Hervig, Rahe, and Rosenman (1981) assessed coping styles (conscious and flexible dealings with stressors) and defensive processes (unconscious and inflexible dealings with stressors) and Type A behavior, using both the JAS and the Structured Interview (SI; Rosenman, 1978). Whereas the SI was not at all related to coping or defenses, the JAS subscale of Job Involvement was related to better coping skills, Speed and Impatience was related to high defensiveness, and Hard Driving was related to poorer coping skills. A second issue is the Type A component that is being assessed. In a study of 364 healthy young men, Keltikangas-Jarvinen and Raikkonen (1993) found that whereas a global index of TABP was not useful in characterizing coping strategies, two components of TABP were relevant. Engagement-Involvement was related to problem-focused coping, whereas the Hard Driving factor was related to a passive style of withdrawal. Finally a third method issue involves gender differences. Keltikangas-Jarvinen and Jokinen (1989) found that whereas TABP in girls was related to aggressive coping, TABP in boys was related negatively to aggression and positively with constructive coping. The authors suggest that studies assessing subcomponents and gender differences might shed light on the controversy over TABP and active versus passive coping (also see Endler & Parker, 1990).

Another factor that may account for the discrepant findings can be found in the process models of coping (Lazarus & Folkman, 1984). Defares (1982) suggested that on initial confrontation with a stressor, Type A's use active, problem-focused strategies to deal with the event. After repeated failures to cope, the Type A person move into a passive helpless phase characterized by withdrawal and avoidance. Thus, depending on where in the coping process measures are administered, TABP may be associated with seemingly opposite coping styles.

A final possibility is that there are subtypes of Type A individuals who are particularly prone to disorders, and these subtypes are differentiated by their coping strategies. Keltikangas-Jarvinen and Raikkonen (1993) postulated a subtype of "at-risk" Type A individuals who rely on passive withdrawal forms of coping. According to this formulation, a pattern of engagement-involvement may be a protective factor, whereas a hard-driving style or avoidance may be pathogenic. Indirect evidence for the subtype notion has been provided by Denollet and De Potter (1992). These investigators attempted to delineate coping subtypes of individuals with heart disease on the basis of their scores on three superordinate trait measures of negative affectivity, positive affectivity, and self-deception. Cluster analysis was used to differentiate various subtypes, including a group of high negative affect individuals who were characterized jointly by high negative affectivity, high social inhibition, and low levels of self-deception. These individuals had the highest levels of Type A and distress, and appeared to have the greatest risk.

In general, there are few definitive conclusions regarding coping and TABP. Although work has been directed at trying to establish consistent relations, the findings tend to be equivocal. The literature on Type A personality and coping is instructive in that it highlights the general need for meta-analytic investigations that could empirically examine this association from a broad perspective. A meta-analysis could control for sources of variance that influence the findings in this area, such as coping and TABP measures used (Booth-Kewley & Friedman, 1987), the specific subcomponents of TABP assessed (Vickers et al., 1981), and even the cultural background of subjects used in the studies (see Helman, 1987).

Perfectionism

Perfectionism is another personality construct that involves a high level of achievement motivation as well as a focus on the attainment of goals in a nonimpulsive manner (Hewitt & Flett, 1993). There are many reasons why perfectionism would be seen as a relevant variable in coping processes. Perhaps what is most important is that perfectionists experience a great deal of stress. Hewitt and Flett (1993) theorized that excessive levels of perfectionism influence the generation or instigation of stress. That is, perfectionistic behavior increases both the frequency of stressful events or failures and the negative psychological impact of stressful events. Perfectionists have been described as having stringent criteria for success, to the extent that even minor shortfalls are experienced as major failures (see Hewitt & Flett, 1993). Also, because perfectionists tend to equate self-worth and performance, any interruptions in meeting standards may be interpreted as failures with implications for the self-concept (Hewitt, Flett, Turnbull-Donovan, & Mikail, 1991; Hewitt & Genest, 1990; Hewitt, Mittelstaedt, & Wollert, 1989).

Given that perfectionists should experience stress consistently, a key question is how they respond to stressors and failures. Past accounts suggest that perfectionists cope with stress in self-defeating ways such as perseverative maintenance of unrealistic standards, ruminative thought, self-blame, overgeneralization of failure, and the tendency to experience negative emotions (see Flett, Hewitt, Blankstein, & Koledin, 1991; Hewitt et al., 1991).

We have confirmed an empirical link between perfectionism and coping, but the results vary depending on the perfectionism dimension in question. Whereas past research on perfectionism has adopted a unidimensional view that focused on the attainment of self-standards, recent conceptualizations have treated perfectionism as a multidimensional construct that involves personal and social components (Frost, Marten, Lahart, & Rosenblate, 1990; Hewitt & Flett, 1990, 1991a). For instance, the Multidimensional Perfectionism Scale (MPS; Hewitt & Flett, 1991b) assesses self-oriented, other-oriented, and socially prescribed perfectionism with three distinct subscales. Whereas self-oriented perfectionism involves unrealistic self-standards and motivation for oneself to be perfect, other-oriented perfectionism involves unrealistically high expectations for others. Finally, socially prescribed perfectionism involves the belief that others expect perfection.

The available evidence suggests that the perfectionism dimensions may be distinguished in terms of their link with measures of problem-solving confidence as well as the actual strategy used to cope with difficulties. Flett, Hewitt, Blankstein, Solnik, and Van Brunschot (1993) administered the MPS, the Social Problem-Solving Inventory (SPSI; D'Zurilla & Nezu, 1990), and a measure of depression to college students. The SPSI assesses self-reports of problem-solving orientation (high or low confidence) and problem-solving skills. It was found that individuals with high levels of socially prescribed perfectionism had a negative problem-solving orientation, even after removing variance due to depression. It was concluded that the link between socially prescribed perfectionism and a negative problem-solving orientation was due, in part, to the feelings of noncontingency and learned helplessness that accompany the belief that others are imposing impossibly high expectations on the self. A more direct investigation of dimensions of perfectionism and coping responses was conducted by Hewitt, Flett, and Endler (1995). A sample of 121 psychiatric patients completed the MPS (Hewitt & Flett, 1991b) and the Coping Inventory for Stressful Situations (CISS; Endler & Parker, 1990). The CISS provides measures of task-oriented coping, emotion-oriented coping, and two avoidance-oriented coping subscales (Distraction and Social Diversion). Our results showed that both self-oriented and socially prescribed perfectionism were associated with maladaptive coping tendencies, but the results varied by gender. Emotion-oriented coping was correlated with self-oriented perfectionism for women, whereas emotion-oriented coping was correlated with socially prescribed perfectionism for men. The data imply that men may respond or cope less adaptively to perfectionistic social expectations, whereas women may respond or cope less adaptively to perfectionistic self-related expectations. Finally, Flett, Russo, and Hewitt (1993) examined the link between the MPS and the coping variable of constructive thinking, as assessed by the Constructive Thinking Inventory (see Epstein, 1992; Epstein & Meier, 1989). This coping measure assesses tendencies to engage in constructive versus destructive thinking and provides an assessment of thoughts involving emotional coping and behavioral coping as well as superstitious, esoteric, and categorical thinking. Analyses revealed a pervasive link between socially prescribed perfectionism and an absence of constructive thinking across most of the CTI subscales. Other-oriented perfectionism was unrelated to the CTI; however, self-oriented perfectionism was linked with positive aspects of constructive thinking (greater behavioral coping) as well as elements of destructive thinking indicating a lack of self-acceptance in stressful situations.

In addition to examining zero-order correlations between perfectionism and coping, we have also tested predictions derived from self-regulation models of standards and adjustment (e.g., Kanfer & Hagerman, 1981). These models posit an interactive relationship such that individuals with perfectionistic standards will be especially prone to maladjustment if they are characterized jointly by perfectionism and maladaptive coping responses, typically in the form of self-blame. In the Hewitt et al. (1995) study, some support for these models was obtained in that hierarchical regression analyses found that the interaction of self-oriented perfectionism and emotion-oriented coping predicted unique variance in depression. In an earlier study with college students, researchers found that socially prescribed perfectionism was associated with low learned resourcefulness and individuals characterized jointly by the perceived presence of unrealistic social expectations and low learned resourcefulness were especially prone to depressive symptoms (see Flett, Hewitt, Blankstein, & O'Brien, 1991). These results combine to suggest the associated coping style is a factor that makes perfectionists vulnerable to psychological distress.

In contrast to the voluminous literature on Type A behavior, research on perfectionism and coping is just beginning, and several significant issues remain to be investigated. A particularly important issue is how perfectionism and coping are associated in interpersonal situations with significant others. Coyne and Smith (1991) observed that existing approaches to the study of coping are highly individualistic and ignore important factors such as environmental and life circumstances. In one of our studies, we examined the relations among the interpersonal dimensions of perfectionism and coping tendencies of couples (Hewitt, Flett, & Mikail, 1993). A sample of 82 couples completed the MPS and the Marital Coping Inventory as part of a larger assessment battery. The coping measure assesses forms of coping (e.g., positive approach coping) and maladaptive forms of coping (e.g., conflict coping and avoidance coping). Analyses that focused on the individual respondent found that self-oriented perfectionism was related to the person's own increased conflict coping (criticism, sarcasm, and revenge) and decreased positive approach coping (gestures of affection and fun). Socially prescribed perfectionism was related widely to negative coping strategies reflecting increased conflict, self-blame, self-interest (e.g., increased activity outside the home), and avoidance. Socially prescribed perfectionists also reported less approach coping. Other-oriented perfectionism was not related to the individual's own coping efforts. The results were similar for both partners in the marriage, suggesting some consistency in the relation between perfectionism and coping in marriage.

A more complex pattern emerged when we assessed perfectionism in one partner and coping strategies in the other partner. Analyses for the dyad indicated that wives were especially likely to rely on avoidance coping if their husbands were high on other-oriented perfectionism. Wives were also likely to rely on conflict coping if their husbands were high on socially prescribed perfectionism. As for the men, husbands used greater avoidance coping and decreased approach coping if their wives had high levels of socially prescribed perfectionism. The results of this study suggest that assessing personality and coping variables with respect to specific kinds of stressful experiences can enhance our understanding of the interplay of personality, coping, and stress. In this case, both the intrapersonal and interpersonal aspects of perfectionism may differentially influence coping strategies. The results illustrate that multifaceted assessments of personality and coping in certain stressful situations with significant others can clarify and extend our knowledge of personality and coping.

CONTROVERSIAL ISSUES AND DIRECTIONS FOR FUTURE RESEARCH

The general research area of personality, stress, and coping has not been without controversy. There are those who suggest that models of stress, coping, and adjustment must take personal factors into account (Costa & McCrae, 1990; Moos & Schaefer, 1993), whereas others suggest that personality variables are artifacts or nuisance factors (Brown & Harris, 1978). Perhaps the most critical question in the area is the extent to which coping responses can be regarded as personality traits. In response to observations raised by Endler and Parker (1990), Lazarus (1993) noted that there is a distinction between a trait approach and a process approach to coping measurement, and many coping measures are process measures that do not represent personality variables. This observation raises the question of whether coping measures are tapping a personality construct. Studies assessing temporal stability and cross-situational consistency would initially address this question.

The initial work on coping was based on the notion that coping is a stable trait, and this view has been subsumed by a process-oriented approach to coping (for a review, see Stone, Greenberg, Kennedy-Moore, & Newman, 1991). Overall, few studies have directly examined the "coping as personality trait" issue, but test-retest studies of coping measures tend to indicate that they have temporal stability. For instance, Billingsley, Waehler, and Hardin (1993) administered the COPE Scale (Carver, Scheier, & Weintraub, 1989) on two occasions to a sample of 82 students. The one month test-retest correlations for each COPE subscale were significant, with correlations ranging from .47 to .87. Similarly, a longitudinal study, over 7 years, of elderly individuals yielded moderate correlations in the degree to which particular coping mechanisms were used over time (McCrae, 1989). Amirkhan (1990) investigated the reliability coefficients of his coping measure in samples of university students and community residents. The test-retest interval ranged from 4 to 8 weeks and the average test-retest values were .81 and .82 across the three subscales of Problem Solving, Avoidance, and Seeking Support. Holahan and Moos (1987) examined coping in a community sample and a patient sample over a 1-year period. The respective stability coefficients for the community and patient samples were .38 and .46 for active-cognitive coping, .46 and .44 for active-behavioral coping, and .54 and .53 for avoidance coping. Similar results were reported in a 3-year longitudinal study by Swindle, Cronkite, and Moos (1989). Rohde, Lewinsohn, Tilson, and Seeley (1990) reported test-retest correlations of .53 or greater with a 2-year interval between coping assessments. Finally, a prospective study of coping in Israeli soldiers yielded high stability coefficients (Solomon, Mikulincer, & Avitzur, 1988), as did a study of individuals with chronic illnesses (Felton & Revenson, 1984).

Another way to examine the "coping as personality trait" issue is to examine the cross-situational stability issue. Rather than examine responses in different situations, coping researchers often compare coping responses to two or more distinct stressors. Existing evidence indicates that scores on particular coping dimensions are correlated significantly across problem types. For example, Causey and Dubow (1992) compared the coping responses of children to a hypothetical achievement problem versus a hypothetical social problem. Comparison of problem types showed consistency in the use of particular coping strategies. For instance, they reported a significant correlation of .56 between level of problem-solving coping if one is coping with a poor grade versus coping with a peer argument.

Another test of this issue is to examine the use of coping dimensions across actual life problems rather than hypothetical events. Once again, data indicate a fair amount of consistency. Stone and Neale (1984) had 120 married people complete a measure of daily coping with actual life problems for 21 consecutive days. They found that similar types of problems experienced by an individual result in the stable use of coping mechanisms. People with recurring problems tended to rely on the same coping mechanism when the problem recurred. Compas, Forsythe, and Wagner (1988) had a sample of college students complete the same coping measure used by Stone and Neale (1984) so as to rate their coping responses to an achievement stressor and an interpersonal stressor. Weekly ratings for each stressor were obtained over a 4-week period. Compas et al. (1988) reported that there was a tendency for subjects to use a consistent coping pattern when rating the same problem on different occasions. However, they also noted that consistency was lower when ratings across the two different problem types were compared. Compas et al. (1988) concluded by noting that it is commonly found that temporal consistency is greater than cross-situational consistency.

This evidence of consistency notwithstanding, a growing number of studies have indicated the extent to which situational factors influence the link between coping and adjustment (e.g., Bolger, 1990; McCrae, 1984; Parkes, 1986). Bolger's (1990) prospective study of neuroticism, coping, and anxiety in students taking a medical school entrance examination found that the situational factor (time of measurement) accounted for more variance than did neuroticism or the Neuroticism × Situation interaction. These data underscore that the seemingly opposing concepts of coping as trait versus coping as a dynamic process are not necessarily mutually exclusive. Responses will depend on the personality traits of the individual, the coping period being assessed, and the type of problem confronting the individual. Because various coping strategies will be utilized and abandoned depending on where in the process of coping the researcher measures the variables of interest (see Defares, 1982; Krohne, 1986), we might speak of a coping repertoire that encompasses several dispositional coping styles or traits that become salient at certain points during the coping process. This would be consistent with work promoting the importance of Person × Situation interactions in predicting behavior (Endler & Magnusson, 1976).

PERSONALITY AND THE COPING PROCESS FROM A BROADER PERSPECTIVE

Although there is a vast literature on personality and coping, the research is limited by the adoption of a narrow view of personality, and by few attempts to investigate the relevance of personality to the entire coping process. First, there is a decided imbalance to the field in that some personality variables (neuroticism, optimism, locus of control) have received extensive empirical attention, whereas others have received surprisingly little attention. Also, although many studies use a diathesis-stress model to explain personality factors and stress in various types of maladjustment, these studies seldom assess coping. For example, despite indications that emotion-focused coping and a depressive attributional style are closely linked (Bruder-Mattson & Hovanitz, 1990), few of the studies in the voluminous literature on attributional style, life stress, and depression have examined the role of individual differences in coping. Moreover, a variable representing coping style is not incorporated in existing attribution models. Another prime example of the lack of a focus on coping resources is in recent work dealing with personality and depression that derives from Beck's (1983) observations. Beck proposed two personality variables that predispose individuals to experience significant depression. The two variables are sociotropy (dependency) and autonomy, and the two variables are assumed to make one vulnerable to depression because self-esteem becomes based on specific goals or activities. Whereas the sociotropic person derives self-esteem from maintenance of dependent relationships, the autonomous person derives self-esteem from attaining lofty achievement goals. Depression ensues during times when congruent ego-involving stressors are present (see Hewitt & Flett, 1993, for a related discussion). Although there is some support for this specific vulnerability model (Hammen, Ellicott, & Gitlin, 1989; Segal, Shaw, & Vella, 1989; Zuroff & Mongrain, 1987), the results are equivocal (Hammen, Ellicott, Gitlin, & Jamison, 1989; Robins & Block, 1988). One reason for the lack of consistent findings in this work is an implicit assumption that the specific environmental stress experienced by the vulnerable individual is assumed to exert its full distressing properties of the individual. Only a few authors (e.g., Bolger, 1990; Reynolds & Gilbert, 1991) have considered the possibility that the stressor may be coped with and the negative impact of the stressor reduced differentially as a function of the personality variable in question.

Second, despite some noteworthy exceptions (e.g., Aspinwall & Taylor, 1992; Contrada, 1989), there is still an overall shortage of research that examines multiple traits within the same investigation. Ideally, researchers should include numerous personality measures, including measures reflecting broader conceptual schemes, to assess the relative ability of personality traits to predict coping tendencies. An excellent example of the usefulness of this approach was provided by Aspinwall and Taylor (1992) who reported the results of a longitudinal study of 672 college students. Subjects completed a wide range of variables at various time points, including measures of optimism, locus of control, desire for control, self-esteem, coping, social support, and measures of health symptoms and psychological adjustment to college. It was shown that optimism could be distinguished from the other personality traits by its direct link with psychological adjustment. In contrast, the link between most of the other personality measures and psychological adjustment was more indirect and mediated by coping styles. Future research that adopts a similar approach examining overall personality structure will clarify the relative roles of personality factors in coping and the adjustment process. The need to study the structure of personality is stated by Lazarus (1993), who observed the following:

> Although coping approaches are better able to encompass specific coping thoughts and actions in diverse stressful contexts that call for coping, they have their own limitations. The most important one is that the measures are not usually formulated

to link up with the whole person, who has a particular goal hierarchy and situational intentions, belief systems, and a life pattern of plans and social connections. Coping process measures would be far more meaningful and useful if we knew more about the persons whose coping thoughts and actions in specific contexts are being studied. Now they tend to be disembodied, as it were, from that person. (Lazarus, 1993, p. 242)

Third, the field needs to be expanded considerably by investigating personality and coping from a broader perspective that acknowledges not only the nature of the coping effort itself, but also the antecedents and consequences of coping. Most research on personality and coping adopts a focus on perceptions of threat (primary appraisal), perceptions of available coping resources (secondary appraisal), and the actual coping effort without considering the possibility that personality is also involved in the initial creation or recognition of the stressful event, and subsequent reactions to coping outcomes. People differ markedly in stress susceptibility. Personality factors should vary substantially in terms of the frequency and types of life problems with which they are associated; certain personality factors such as neuroticism and perfectionism may be more relevant to the coping process simply because these variables are more closely linked with subjective stress reactions (see Cohen & Edwards, 1988) and the generation of stress (Hewitt & Flett, 1993).

In addition to being associated with the stress levels as well as coping appraisals and coping strategies, certain traits may also be linked with coping outcomes and reactions to coping outcomes. Aldwin and Revenson (1987) drew attention to the need to examine both coping effectiveness (how well the coping efforts reduced distress) and coping efficacy (the perception that coping efforts were successful in achieving coping goals). Similarly, Zautra and Wrabetz (1991) made the important point that a great deal of research has examined coping in terms of perceptions of the stressor and attempts to cope with the stressor, but there are very few studies on the outcome of the coping process and related reactions. Specifically, they highlighted the lack of research on perceptions of coping success or failure and the ongoing consequences of perceived success or failure. Many findings emerged from their study, including some data suggesting that internal locus of control is associated with perceived coping success. Dissatisfaction with the coping effort and responses to this dissatisfaction are critical aspects of the coping process, but these aspects have gone untapped by personality researchers.

The relevance of perceived coping success is illustrated by a consideration of perfectionism. Because perfectionists are troubled greatly by failure, perceptions of coping failure should represent a substantial source of distress. Once it is acknowledged that coping efforts are not succeeding, then some adjustments in coping strategies need to be made, but these adjustments may prove to be quite difficult for perfectionists. Brandtstadter and Renner (1990, 1992) have provided a framework for examining this issue with a model of coping and adjustment that centers on how individuals react to the discrepancy between aspirations and achievement. Their research has revealed that flexible goal adjustment is an important component of the coping process. Personality traits may be associated differentially with the flexibility of goal adjustment. Our own research with a sample of elderly people (e.g., Flett, Hewitt, & Belanger, 1993b) has established that perfectionism is distinguished from other personality traits by its robust negative association with flexible goal adjustment. An inability or unwillingness to modify goals is a factor that should influence not only the response to life problems, but also the likelihood of experiencing certain problems. These observations combine to suggest that personality may influence not only the presence or absence or degree of a particular coping style, but also general coping ability, flexibility of coping styles, breadth of coping repertoire, choice of particular coping strategy, access to coping resources, the number of stressors that must be coped with, and, as we showed earlier, coping strategies of others.

The preceding discussion makes evident that a great deal of work has been done on personality and coping, but much work remains to be done, especially concerning the mechanisms involved in personality and coping. We began with the observation that the link between personality and coping is generally accepted by most researchers. Ironically, the relevance of personality traits to the coping process is probably understated because of the gaps that currently exist in the research literature. A broader focus that incorporates more personality traits and all aspects of the coping process should further elucidate the role of personality traits in coping and the nature of coping itself.

REFERENCES

Abella, R., & Heslin, R. (1989). Appraisal processes, coping, and the regulation of stress-related emotions in a college examination. *Basic and Applied Social Psychology, 10,* 311–327.

Aldwin, C. M., & Revenson, T. A. (1987). Does coping help? A reexamination of the relation between coping and mental health. *Journal of Personality and Social Psychology, 53,* 337–348.

Amirkhan, J. H. (1990). A factor analytically derived measure of coping: The Coping Strategy Indicator. *Journal of Personality and Social Psychology, 59,* 1066–1074.

Aspinwall, L. G., & Taylor, S. E. (1992). Modeling cognitive adaptation: A longitudinal investigation of the impact of individual differences and coping on college adjustment and performance. *Journal of Personality and Social Psychology, 63,* 989–1003.

Beck, A. T. (1983). Cognitive therapy of depression: New perspectives. In P. J. Clayton & J. E. Barrett (Eds.), *Treatment of depression: Old controversies and new approaches* (pp. 265–290). New York: Raven Press.

Beck, A. T., Weissman, A., Lester, D., & Trexler, L. (1974). The measurement of pessimism: The Hopelessness Scale. *Journal of Consulting and Clinical Psychology, 42,* 861–865.

Ben-Porath, Y., & Tellegen, A. (1990). A place for traits in stress research. *Psychological Inquiry, 1,* 14–16.

Ben-Porath, Y., & Waller, N. G. (1992). "Normal" personality inventories in clinical assessment: General requirements and the potential for using the NEO Personality Inventory. *Psychological Assessment, 4,* 14–19.

Billingsley, K. D., Waehler, C. A., & Hardin, S. I. (1993). Stability of optimism and choice of coping strategy. *Perceptual and Motor Skills, 76,* 91–97.

Bolger, N. (1990). Coping as a personality process: A prospective study. *Journal of Personality and Social Psychology, 59,* 525–537.

Booth-Kewley, S., & Friedman, H. S. (1987). Psychological predictors of heart disease: A quantitative review. *Psychological Bulletin, 101,* 343–362.

Brandtstadter, J., & Renner, G. (1990). Tenacious goal pursuit and flexible goal adjustment: Explication and age-related analysis of assimilative and accommodative strategies of coping. *Psychology and Aging, 5,* 58–67.

Brandtstadter, J., & Renner, G. (1992). Coping with discrepancies between aspirations and achievements in adult development: A dual-process model. In L. Montada, S. -H. Filipp, & M. J. Lerner (Eds.), *Life crises and experiences of loss in adulthood* (pp. 301–319). Hillsdale, NJ: Erlbaum.

Brown, G. W., & Harris, T. O. (1978). *Social origins of depression: A study of psychiatric disorder in women.* London: Tavistock Publications.

Bruder-Mattson, S. F., & Hovanitz, C. A. (1990). Coping and attributional styles as predictors of depression. *Journal of Clinical Psychology, 46,* 557–565.

Burke, R. J. (1982). Interpersonal behavior and coping styles of Type A individuals. *Psychological Reports, 51,* 971–977.

Carver, C. S., Coleman, E. A., & Glass, D. C. (1976). The coronary-prone behavior pattern and the suppression of fatigue on a treadmill test. *Psychosomatic Medicine, 33,* 460–466.

Carver, C. S., Pozo, C., Harris, S. D., Noriega, V., Scheier, M. F., Robinson, D. S., Ketcham, A. S., Moffat, F. L., Jr., & Clark, K. C. (1993). How coping mediates the effect of optimism on distress: A study of women with early stage breast cancer. *Journal of Personality and Social Psychology, 65,* 375–390.

Carver, C. S., Scheier, M. F., & Weintraub, J. K. (1989). Assessing coping strategies: A theoretically-based approach. *Journal of Personality and Social Psychology, 56,* 267–283.

Cattell, R. B. (1950). *Personality: A systematic, theoretical, and factual study.* New York: McGraw-Hill.

Cattell, R. B., Eber, H. W., & Tatsuoka, M. M. (1970). *Handbook for the Sixteen Personality Factor Questionnaire.* Champaign, IL: Institute for Personality and Ability Testing.

Causey, D. L., & Dubow, E. F. (1992). Development of a self-report coping measure for elementary school children. *Journal of Clinical Child Psychology, 21,* 47–59.

Chesney, M. A., Black, G. W., Chadwick, J. H., & Rosenman, R. H. (1981). Psychological correlates of the coronary-prone behavior pattern. *Journal of Behavioral Medicine, 4,* 217–229.

Compas, B. E., Banez, G. A., Malcarne, V., & Worsham, N. (1991). Perceived control and coping with stress: A developmental perspective. *Journal of Social Issues, 47,* 23–34.

Compas, B. E., Forsythe, C. J., & Wagner, B. M. (1988). Consistency and variability in causal attributions and coping with stress. *Cognitive Therapy and Research, 12,* 305–320.

Contrada, R. J. (1989). Type A behavior, personality hardiness, and cardiovascular responses to stress. *Journal of Personality and Social Psychology, 57,* 895–903.

Contrada, R. J., Leventhal, H., & O'Leary, A. (1990). Personality and health. In L. A. Pervin (Ed.), *Handbook of personality: Theory and research* (pp. 638–669). New York: Guilford.

Costa, P. T., Jr., & McCrae, R. R. (1985). *The NEO Personality Inventory manual.* Odessa, FL: Psychological Assessment Resources.

Costa, P. T., Jr., & McCrae, R. R. (1989). Personality, stress, and coping: Some lessons from a decade of research. In K. S. Markides and C. L. Cooper (Eds.), *Aging, stress, and health.* Chichester: Wiley.

Costa, P. T., Jr., & McCrae, R. R. (1990). Personality: Another "hidden factor" in stress research. *Psychological Inquiry, 1,* 22–24.

Coyne, J. C., & Smith, D. A. F. (1991). Couples coping with a myocardial infarction: A contextual perspective on wife's distress. *Journal of Personality and Social Psychology, 61,* 404–412.

Crisson, J. E., & Keefe, F. J. (1988). The relationship of locus of control to pain coping strategies and psychological distress in chronic pain patients. *Pain, 35,* 147–154.

Defares, B. P. (1982, March). *Coping with stress.* Paper presented at the Workshop on Heart and Stress, Bilthoven, The Netherlands.

Denollet, J., & De Potter, B. (1992). Coping subtypes for men with coronary heart disease: Relationship to well-being, stress, and Type A behaviour. *Psychological Medicine, 22,* 667–684.

D'Zurilla, T. J., & Nezu, A. M. (1990). Development and preliminary evaluation of the Social Problem-Solving Inventory (SPSI). *Psychological Assessment, 2,* 156–163.

Endler, N. S. (1993, July). *Neuroticism: Its utility as a multidimensional construct.* Paper presented at the sixth meeting of the International Society for the Study of Individual Differences, Baltimore, Maryland.

Endler, N. S., & Magnusson, D. (1976). Toward an interactional psychology of personality. *Psychological Bulletin, 83,* 956–974.

Endler, N. S., & Parker, J. D. A. (1990). Multidimensional assessment of coping: A critical evaluation. *Journal of Personality and Social Psychology, 58,* 844–854.

Endler, N. S., Parker, J. D. A., & Butcher, J. N. (1993). A factor analytic study of coping styles and the MMPI-2 content scales. *Journal of Clinical Psychology, 49,* 523–527.

Epstein, S. (1992). Constructive thinking and mental and physical well-being. In L. Montada, S. -H. Filipp, & M. J. Lerner (Eds.), *Life crises and experiences of loss in adulthood* (pp. 385–409). Hillsdale, NJ: Erlbaum.

Epstein, S., & Meier, P. (1989). Constructive thinking: A broad coping variable with specific components. *Journal of Personality and Social Psychology, 57,* 332–350.

Evans, P. D., & Fearn, J. M. (1985). Type A behavior pattern, choice of active coping strategy and cardiovascular activity in relation to threat of shock. *British Journal of Medical Psychology, 58,* 95–99.

Eysenck, H. J., & Eysenck, M. W. (1985). *Personality and Individual Differences.* New York: Plenum.

Felton, B. J., & Revenson, T. A. (1984). Coping with chronic illness: A study of illness controllability and the influence of coping strategies on psychological assessment. *Journal of Consulting and Clinical Psychology, 52,* 343–352.

Fiske, D. W. (1949). Consistency of the factorial structures of personality ratings from different sources. *Journal of Abnormal and Social Psychology, 44,* 329–344.

Flett, G. L., Hewitt, P. L., & Belanger, S. (1993a). *The assessment of pessimistic social expectations in adolescents: Psychometric qualities and correlates of the Social Hopelessness Questionnaire.* Manuscript in preparation.

Flett, G. L., Hewitt, P. L., & Belanger, S. (1993b, November). *Personality correlates of depression and life satisfaction in the elderly.* Paper presented in the 27th annual meeting of the Association for the Advancement of Behavior Therapy, Atlanta, Georgia.

Flett, G. L., Hewitt, P. L., Blankstein, K. R., & Koledin, S. (1991). Dimensions of perfectionism and irrational thinking. *Journal of Rational-Emotive and Cognitive-Behavior Therapy, 9,* 185–201.

Flett, G. L., Hewitt, P. L., Blankstein, K. R., & O'Brien, S. (1991). Perfectionism and learned resourcefulness in depression and self-esteem. *Personality and Individual Differences, 12,* 61–68.

Flett, G. L., Hewitt, P. L., Blankstein, K. R., Solnik, M., & Van Brunschot, M. (1993). *Dimensions of perfectionism and social problem-solving ability.* Manuscript submitted for publication.

Flett, G. L., Hewitt, P. L., & Gayle, B. (1993, August). *The Social Hopelessness Questionnaire: Development, validation, and association with adjustment.* Paper presented at the 101st annual conference of the American Psychological Association, Toronto, Ontario.

Flett, G. L., Russo, F., & Hewitt, P. L. (1993). *Dimensions of perfectionism and constructive thinking as a coping strategy.* Manuscript in preparation.

Folkman, S. (1984). Personal control and stress and coping processes: A theoretical analysis. *Journal of Personality and Social Psychology, 46,* 839–852.

Folkman, S., & Lazarus, R. S. (1988). *Manual for the Ways of Coping Questionnaire.* Palo Alto, CA: Consulting Psychologist Press.

Fontaine, K. R., & Manstead, A. S. (1993). Optimism, perceived control over stress, and coping. *European Journal of Personality, 7,* 267–281.

Forsythe, C. J., & Compas, B. B. (1987). Interaction of cognitive appraisals of stressful events and coping: Testing the goodness of fit hypothesis. *Cognitive Therapy and Research, 11,* 473–485.

Friedman, M., & Rosenman, R. H. (1959). Association of specific overt behavior pattern with blood and cardiovascular findings. *Journal of the American Medical Association, 169,* 1286–1296.

Frost, R., Marten, P., Lahart, C., & Rosenblate, R. (1990). The dimensions of perfectionism. *Cognitive Therapy and Research, 14,* 449–468.

Glass, D. C. (1977). *Behavior patterns, stress, and coronary disease.* Hillsdale, NJ: Erlbaum.

Greenglass, E. R. (1988). Type A behavior and coping strategies. *Applied Psychology: An International Review, 37,* 271–288.

Hammen, C., Ellicott, A., & Gitlin, M. (1989). Vulnerability to specific life events and prediction of course of disorder in unipolar depression. *Canadian Journal of Behavioural Science, 21,* 377–388.

Hammen, C., Ellicott, A., Gitlin, M., & Jamison, K. R. (1989). Sociotropy/autonomy and vulnerability to specific life events in unipolar and bipolar patients. *Journal of Abnormal Psychology, 98,* 154–160.

Hart, K. E. (1988). Association of Type A behavior and its components to ways of coping with stress. *Journal of Psychosomatic Research, 32,* 213–219.

Helman, C. C. (1987). Heart disease and the cultural construction of time: The Type A Behavior Pattern as a western culture-bound syndrome. *Social Science and Medicine, 25,* 969–979.

Hewitt, P. L., & Flett, G. L. (1990). Perfectionism and depression: A multidimensional analysis. *Journal of Social Behavior and Personality, 5,* 423–438.

Hewitt, P. L., & Flett, G. L. (1991a). Dimensions of perfectionism in unipolar depression. *Journal of Abnormal Psychology, 100,* 98–101.

Hewitt, P. L., & Flett, G. L. (1991b). Perfectionism in the self and social contexts: Conceptualization, assessment, and association with psychopathology. *Journal of Personality and Social Psychology, 60,* 456–470.

Hewitt, P. L., & Flett, G. L. (1993). Dimensions of perfectionism, daily stress, and depression: A test of the specific vulnerability hypothesis. *Journal of Abnormal Psychology, 102,* 58–65.

Hewitt, P. L., & Flett, G. L. (1993). Perfectionism and goal orientation in impulsive and suicidal behavior. In W. McCown, M. Shure, & J. Johnson (Eds.), *The impulsive client: Theory, research, and treatment* (pp. 247–264). Washington, DC: American Psychological Association.

Hewitt, P. L., Flett, G. L., & Endler, N. S. (1995). Perfectionism, coping, and depression symptomatology in a clinical sample. *Clinical Psychology and Psychotherapy, 2,* 47–58.

Hewitt, P. L., Flett, G. L., & Mikail, S. F. (1993). *Perfectionism in the marital context.* Manuscript in preparation.

Hewitt, P. L., Flett, G. L., Turnbull-Donovan, W., & Mikail, S. F. (1991). The Multidimensional Perfectionism Scale: Reliability, validity, and psychometric properties in psychiatric samples. *Psychological Assessment: A Journal of Consulting and Clinical Psychology, 3,* 464–468.

Hewitt, P. L., & Genest, M. (1990). Ideal-self: Schematic processing of perfectionistic content in dysphoric university students. *Journal of Personality and Social Psychology, 59,* 802–808.

Hewitt, P. L., Mittelstaedt, W., & Wollert, R. (1989). Validation of a measure of perfectionism. *Journal of Personality Assessment, 53,* 133–144.

Holahan, C. J., & Moos, R. H. (1987). Personal and contextual determinants of coping strategies. *Journal of Personality and Social Psychology, 52,* 946–955.

Jackson, D. N., & Gray, A. (1989). *Survey of Work Styles manual: Research edition.* Port Huron, MI: Research Psychologists Press.

John, O. P. (1990). The "big five" factor taxonomy: Dimensions of personality in the natural language and in questionnaires. In L. A. Pervin (Ed.), *Handbook of personality: Theory and research* (pp. 21–65). New York: Guilford.

Kanfer, F. H., & Hagerman, S. (1981). The role of self-regulation. In L. Rehm (Ed.), *Behavior therapy for depression: Present status and future directions* (pp. 143–179). New York: Academic Press.

Keltikangas-Jarvinen, L., & Jokinen, J. (1989). Type A behavior, coping mechanisms and emotions related to somatic risk factors of coronary heart disease in adolescents. *Journal of Psychosomatic Research, 33,* 17–27.

Keltikangas-Jarvinen, L., & Raikkonen, K. (1993). Emotional styles and coping strategies characterizing the risk and non-risk dimensions of Type A behavior in young men. *Personality and Individual Differences, 14,* 667–677.

Kliewer, W. (1991). Coping in middle childhood: Relations to competence, Type A behavior, monitoring, blunting, and locus of control. *Developmental Psychology, 27,* 689–697.

Krohne, H. W. (1986). Coping with stress: Dispositions, strategies, and the problem of measurement. In M. H. Appley & R. Trumbull (Eds.), *Dynamics of stress: Physiological, psychological, and social perspectives.* New York: Plenum.

Lazarus, R. S. (1993). Coping theory and research: Past, present, and future. *Psychosomatic Medicine, 55,* 234–247.

Lazarus, R. S., & Folkman, S. (1984). *Stress, appraisal, and coping.* New York: Springer.

Lefcourt, H. M. (1991). Evaluating the growth of helplessness literature. *Psychological Inquiry, 2,* 33–35.

Lefcourt, H. M. (1992). Durability and impact of the locus of control construct. *Psychological Bulletin, 112,* 411–414.

Litt, M. D. (1988). Cognitive mediators of stressful experiences: Self-efficacy and perceived control. *Cognitive Therapy and Research, 12,* 241–260.

McCrae, R. R. (1984). Situational determinants of coping responses: Loss, threat, and challenge. *Journal of Personality and Social Psychology, 46,* 919–928.

McCrae, R. R. (1989). Age differences and changes in the use of coping mechanisms. *Journal of Gerontology: Psychological Sciences, 44,* 161–169.

McCrae, R. R. (1991). The five-factor model and its assessment in clinical settings. *Journal of Personality Assessment, 57,* 399–414.

McCrae, R. R., & Costa, P. T., Jr. (1986). Personality, coping, and coping effectiveness in an adult sample. *Journal of Personality, 54,* 385–405.

Moos, R. H., Schaeffer, J. A. (1993). Coping resources and processes: Current concepts and measures. In L. Goldberger & S. Breznitz (Eds.), *Handbook of stress: Theoretical and clinical aspects* (pp. 234–257). New York: Free Press.

Parkes, K. R. (1986). Coping in stressful episodes: The role of individual differences, environmental factors, and situational characteristics. *Journal of Personality and Social Psychology, 51,* 1277–1292.

Pittner, M. S., Houston, B. K., & Spiridigliozzi, G. (1983). Control over stress, Type A Behavior Pattern, and response to stress. *Journal of Personality and Social Psychology, 44,* 627–637.

Reynolds, S., & Gilbert, P. (1991). Psychological impact of unemployment: Interactive effects of vulnerability and protective factors on depression. *Journal of Counseling Psychology, 38,* 76–84.

Rim, Y. (1986). Ways of coping, personality, age, sex, and family structural variables. *Personality and Individual Differences, 7,* 133–116.

Robins, C. J., & Block, P. (1988). Personal vulnerability, life events, and depressive symptoms: A test of a specific interactional model. *Journal of Personality and Social Psychology, 54,* 847–852.

Rohde, P., Lewinsohn, P. M., Tilson, M., & Seeley, J. R. (1990). Dimensionality of coping and its relation to depression. *Journal of Personality and Social Psychology, 58,* 499–511.

Rosenman, R. H. (1978). The interview method of assessment of the coronary-prone behavior pattern. In T. Dembroski, S. Weiss, J. Shields, S. Haynes, & M. Feinleib (Eds.), *Coronary-prone behavior.* New York: Springer.

Scheier, M. F., & Carver, C. S. (1985). Optimism, coping, and health: Assessment and implications of generalized outcome expectancies. *Health Psychology, 4,* 219–247.

Scheier, M. F., & Carver, C. S. (1987). Dispositional optimism and physical well-being: The influence of generalized outcome expectancies on health. *Journal of Personality, 55,* 169–210.

Scheier, M. F., & Carver, C. S. (1992). Effects of optimism on psychological and physical well-being: Theoretical overview and empirical update. *Cognitive Therapy and Research, 16,* 201–228.

Scheier, M. F., Weintraub, J. K., & Carver, C. S. (1986). Coping with stress: Divergent strategies of optimists and pessimists. *Journal of Personality and Social Psychology, 51,* 1257–1264.

Segal, Z. V., Shaw, B. F., & Vella, D. D. (1989). Life stress and depression: A test of the congruency hypothesis for life event content and depressive subtype. *Canadian Journal of Behavioural Science, 21,* 389–400.

Smith, T. W., & Brehm, S. S. (1981). Cognitive correlates of the Type A coronary-prone behavior pattern. *Motivation and Emotion, 3,* 215–223.

Snyder, C. R., & Ford, C. E. (1987). *Coping with negative life events.* New York: Plenum.

Snyder, C. R., Harris, C., Anderson, J. R., Holleran, S., Irving, L., Sigmon, S., Yoshinobu, L., Gibb, J., Langelle, C., & Harney, P. (1991). The will and the ways: Development and validation of an individual difference measure of hope. *Journal of Personality and Social Psychology, 60,* 570–585.

Solomon, Z., Mikulincer, M., & Avitzur, E. (1988). Coping, locus of control, social support, and combat-related posttraumatic stress disorder: A prospective study. *Journal of Personality and Social Psychology, 55,* 279–285.

Stone, A. A., Greenberg, M. A., Kennedy-Moore, E., & Newman, M. G. (1991). Self-report situation-specific coping questionnaires: What are they measuring? *Journal of Personality and Social Psychology, 61,* 648–658.

Stone, A. A., & Neale, J. M. (1984). New measure of daily coping: Development and preliminary results. *Journal of Personality and Social Psychology, 46,* 892–906.

Strack, S., Carver, C. S., & Blaney, P. H. (1987). Predicting successful completion of an aftercare program following treatment for alcoholism: The role of dispositional optimism. *Journal of Personality and Social Psychology, 53,* 579–584.

Suls, J., & Wan, C. K. (1989). The relation between Type A behavior and chronic emotional distress: A meta-analysis. *Journal of Personality and Social Psychology, 57,* 503–512.

Swindle, R., Cronkite, R., & Moos, R. (1989). Life stressors, social resources, coping, and the 4-year course of unipolar depression. *Journal of Abnormal Psychology, 98,* 468–477.

Taylor, S. E. (1990). Health psychology. *American Psychologist, 45,* 40–50.

Taylor, S. E., Kemeny, M. E., Aspinwall, L. G., Schneider, S. G., Rodriguez, R., & Herbert, M. (1992). Optimism, coping, psychological distress, and high-risk sexual behavior among men at risk for Acquired Immunodeficiency Syndrome (AIDS). *Journal of Personality and Social Psychology, 63,* 460–473.

Tupes, E. C., & Christal, R. C. (1961). *Recurrent personality factors based on trait ratings.* (Technical Rep. No. ASDTR–61–97). Lackland Air Force Base, TX: U.S. Air Force.

Vickers, R. R., Hervig, L. K., Rahe, R. H., & Rosenman, R. H. (1981). Type A Behavior Pattern and coping and defense. *Psychosomatic Medicine, 43,* 381–396.

Vingerhoets, A. J. J. M., & Flohr, P. J. M. (1984). Type A behaviour and self-reports of coping preferences. *British Journal of Medical Psychology, 57,* 15–21.

Watson, D., & Clark, L. A. (in press). Extraversion and its positive emotional core. In R. Hogan, J. A. Johnson, & S. R. Briggs (Eds.), *Handbook of personality psychology.* San Diego, CA: Academic Press.

Wheaton, B. (1983). Stress, personal coping resources, and psychiatric symptoms: An investigation of interactive models. *Journal of Health and Social Behavior, 24,* 208–229.

Wong, P. T. P. (1993). Effective management of life stress: The resource-congruence model. *Stress Medicine, 9,* 51–60.

Zautra, A. J., & Wrabetz, A. B. (1991). Coping success and its relationship to psychological distress for older adults. *Journal of Personality and Social Psychology, 61,* 801–810.

Zeidner, M., & Ben-Zur, H. (1993). Coping with a national crisis: The Israeli experience with the threat of missile attacks. *Personality and Individual Differences, 14,* 209–224.

Zeidner, M., & Hammer, A. L. (1992). Coping with missile attack: Resources, strategies, and outcomes. *Journal of Personality, 60,* 709–746.

Zuroff, D. C., & Mongrain, M. (1987). Dependency and self-criticism: Vulnerability factors for depressive affective states. *Journal of Abnormal Psychology, 96,* 14–22.

CHAPTER 19

Coping and Social Support

GREGORY R. PIERCE, IRWIN G. SARASON, and BARBARA R. SARASON

Coping refers to a complex process that involves personality characteristics, personal relationships, and situational parameters. Discussions of coping often take as their starting point the time at which a specified event occurs. Lazarus's model of coping, with its emphasis on primary and secondary appraisals, falls into this category (Lazarus & Folkman, 1984). Temporality also plays a role in the buffering hypothesis in the social support literature because social support is presumed to be beneficial only when individuals are coping with stressful events. Social support is hypothesized to have no positive effect during periods when life events are not being confronted (Cohen & Wills, 1985). However, this focus on events once they have happened ignores the role that various factors may play in whether such life events actually occur. In this chapter, we discuss the roles of personality, relationships, and situational context in coping and in stress prevention; these factors not only can affect coping responses toward events that have occurred but also can influence whether the individual can completely avoid certain types of stressful events.

It is puzzling that researchers have devoted so little attention to determining why some individuals experience certain types of difficulties, whereas others do not (see Bandura, 1986, for an exception). It appears likely that certain personality characteristics play a role in the way individuals construct their environments. For example, one person—fearing the possibility of another Great Depression—may save considerable sums of money to deal with this eventuality. Another person, less concerned about an economic slump, may spend money freely, without thinking about the future. If the economy were to turn downward, the implications of this situation—in terms of the life events each would face—would be quite different for these two individuals. Coping researchers investigating only those persons who have faced or are facing a major economic hardship would identify only the latter person, thus overlooking that the former person avoided the problem by "coping" with the event *prior* to its occurrence.

This example illustrates one way in which personal behavior may influence whether stressful life events occur at all. Social relationships may play a similar role. Consider two people who are looking for a job. The friends and relatives of one person may be on the lookout for jobs, alerting the person to promising opportunities. Members of the other person's network may not assist the individual, or may be ineffective. Thus, one person may experience long-term unemployment, whereas the other person may quickly find a job. Our point here is that life events are not randomly assigned to individuals. Instead, people—and their social networks—play important roles in whether they experience, and how they respond to, stressful life events.

This chapter focuses on how social support influences coping with stressful life events and their prevention. In doing so, we will also discuss the issues of the conceptualization and assessment of the social support construct. Specifically, we will describe three conceptualizations of social support: (a) perceived social support, (b) supportive relationships, and (c) supportive networks. Perceived social support has been defined as the general perception that others are available and desire to provide assistance should the individual need it (Pierce, B. R. Sarason, & I. G. Sarason, 1990). Supportive relationships are those dyadic social bonds from which individuals are able to derive resources that may aid in coping. An individual's supportive relationships, in combination, make up her or his supportive network.

Each of these ways of defining social support has grown out of, rather than led to, particular assessment procedures. For this reason, we will briefly describe some available instruments that have been used to assess each of these features of social support. We will then discuss some of the implications of our observations regarding the conceptualization and measurement of social support for research and theory development on social support and coping (I. G. Sarason & B. R. Sarason, 1986).

THREE CONCEPTUALIZATIONS OF SOCIAL SUPPORT

Before discussing each of the three conceptualizations of social support mentioned earlier, we need to deal with two important issues. First, these conceptualizations are not mutually exclusive; instead, they are interconnected. Our aim is not to argue that one conceptualization of social support is more accurate than another, nor is it to claim that one conceptualization is more appropriate or sufficient in a particular context. A comprehensive understanding of the role of social support processes in coping requires attention to each—and all—of these conceptualizations. In fact, a major point to be made in this chapter is that *none* of the conceptualizations of social support in isolation is sufficient to lead to an adequate understanding of its role in coping and well-being. However, for ease of presentation, we will discuss each of these views of social support separately, and then link them together at the end of the chapter.

Second, we wish to distinguish between social support viewed as a personal resource or a coping response. When conceptualized as a personal resource, social support encompasses the supportive provisions potentially available from specific relationship partners within the individual's social network; these resources may include the availability of tangible assistance (e.g., money), cognitive guidance (e.g., advice, information), and emotional support (e.g., someone to listen to one's problems). When defined in terms of a coping response, social support refers to the receipt of supportive behaviors from others in an individual's social network. This assistance may be neither solicited nor desired by the person receiving the aid. Evidence suggests that the availability of social support, as well as its receipt, may influence the manner in which an individual copes with a situation as well as the outcome of these coping efforts.

Perceived Social Support

Most measures of social support probably assess, in one way or another, perceptions of social support. This statement in part results from the observation that the majority of instruments are self-report questionnaires that ask the respondent to describe one or more facets of her or his relationships with others. However, the term perceived social support has been used to refer to the extent to which an individual believes others value, care for, and desire to aid her or him (B. R. Sarason, Shearin, Pierce, & I. G. Sarason, 1987). Perceived social support therefore reflects a belief about the nature of social relationships, and in this sense might be seen as an attitude, with the object of this attitude being others in the person's social network. Specifically excluded from this definition has been reference to the particular types of assistance that these relationships might offer (e.g., advice, physical affection, or tangible aid).

Assessing Perceived Social Support

The Social Support Questionnaire (SSQ) illustrates measures of perceived social support (I. G. Sarason, Levine, Basham, & B. R. Sarason, 1983). The SSQ yields two scores. The Number or Availability score (SSQN) represents the average number of persons perceived to be available as potential supporters across 27 situations. Sample items include, "Whom can you really count on to be dependable when you need help?" and "Whom can you count on to console you when you are very upset?" Subjects respond to each item by listing the initials of up to nine individuals to whom they believe they could turn in that particular situation. The Satisfaction score (SSQS), which reflects how satisfied the respondent reports being with the perceived available support, is the average satisfaction rating obtained on a 6-point scale (1 = very dissatisfied, 6 = very satisfied) for each of the 27 situations. A 6-item short form of the SSQ also yields availability and satisfaction scores (I. G. Sarason, B. R. Sarason, Shearin, & Pierce, 1987). The SSQ was developed on the assumption that, as a person aggregates his or her perceptions of support across many interactions, a general sense of support develops that reflects expectations of how forthcoming the social environment is likely to be. A person high in perceived social support seems to be something of a social optimist, believing that the social environment can generally be counted on to provide help and support when needed.

This feature of social support appears to be stable over periods of up to 3 years, even during transitional events that lead to major changes in network composition (I. G. Sarason, B. R. Sarason, & Shearin, 1986). Perceived social support indexes have also been shown to correlate negatively with measures of neuroticism and trait-anxiety, and to correlate positively with measures of extraversion (B. R. Sarason et al., 1987; I. G. Sarason et al., 1983). In addition, instruments assessing perceived support predict social behavior occurring between family members and peers (Heller & Lakey, 1985; Procidano & Heller, 1983; B. R. Sarason, Pierce, & I. G. Sarason, 1992). For these reasons, several researchers have hypothesized that perceived social support may itself be a personality characteristic (Heller & Swindle, 1983; I. G. Sarason et al., 1986).

Perceived Social Support and Coping

Perceived social support may influence coping through the appraisal of personal characteristics. B. R. Sarason et al. (1991) found that individuals high in perceived social support were more accurate in estimating the personal characteristics of their peers than were others. They also found high perceived support subjects to ascribe to themselves more positive and less negative attributes than did other subjects, and that these ratings were positively related to their parents' and peers' perceptions of them. In combination, these findings suggest that perceived social support may foster more accurate and more positive appraisals of self and others. In turn, this may enable individuals to develop more effective and realistic coping strategies for dealing with particular situations.

Besides promoting more accurate appraisals of personal resources, perceived social support may also enable individuals to confront challenges more effectively because they believe others will help them if the challenge exceeds their personal resources. For example, subjects high in perceived social support experience fewer distracting cognitions while completing intellective tasks, and correctly solve more problems, than do other subjects (I. G. Sarason & B. R. Sarason, 1986). Research also suggests that high perceived support individuals are more interpersonally effective than others (e.g., are better able to assume a leadership role and are more considerate in their interactions with others) (I. G. Sarason et al., 1986). Thus, perceived social support may serve to promote personal effectiveness that enhances the individual's coping repertoire.

Interactions with others are based in part on expectations about how those others will respond. Whereas high perceived support individuals approach others for support based on their expectation that others are likely to provide help, those low in perceived social support may avoid asking others for assistance because they fear aid will not be forthcoming. One reason for this difference may be that high perceived support individuals feel loved and valued by others, and may therefore be less concerned about how others might perceive them should they need to request assistance. Other evidence supporting this hypothesis comes from an experimental study of social support in which subjects interacted with a confederate trained to provide one of two types of social support to subjects who were preparing to give a speech (Pierce & Contey, 1992). Despite the extensive training given to confederates (who were blind to subjects' level of perceived social support), when randomly assigned to subjects low in perceived social support, confederates provided fewer acts of emotional (positive feedback) or instrumental (advice) support than they did to subjects high in perceived social support. These results indicate that those high in perceived social support may provide potential support providers with more opportunities to administer support.

These observations suggest that perceived social support, acting as a personality characteristic, may influence coping in three distinct ways. It might lead individuals to (a) structure situations so that stressful life events are relatively unlikely to occur, (b) develop effective personal coping skills, and (c) seek and obtain assistance when it is needed. Bowlby's theory of attachment (1988) and related research suggest that the social environment, even early in life, contributes to the development and quality of adult relationships. This may happen because attachment experiences in infancy and subsequent interpersonal relationships are sources of cognitive structures or working models related to the self and relationship partners. A secure attachment enhances exploratory behavior from which coping skills develop. In turn, these coping skills enhance feelings of personal effectiveness or self-efficacy. This view of perceived social support meshes with and is reinforced by the current emphasis in psychology on cognitive appraisals and the influence over behavior of cognitive schemata. It also fits well with the early conceptualizations of social support offered by Cassel (1976) and Cobb (1976). Thus, one of the ironies of perceived social support may be that, by promoting effective personal coping, it reduces an individual's need to seek help when confronting challenging situations.

Supportive Relationships

Although people have relatively well-formed perceptions, expectations, and attributions about available support in general, they also have specific expectations about the availability of support from significant people in their lives. Pierce et al. (1990) and I. G. Sarason, Pierce, and B. R. Sarason (1990) have argued that relationship-specific expectations are not simply the building blocks for general perceptions of available support. They have contended that, although people's general and relationship-specific expectations for social support may be related, they reflect different aspects of perceived social support and each may play an important and unique role in coping and well-being.

Assessing Supportive Relationships

The Quality of Relationships Inventory (QRI) was constructed to measure relationship-specific support (Pierce, I. G. Sarason, & B. R. Sarason, 1991). This 25-item measure assesses both relationship-specific perceptions of available support and perceptions of interpersonal conflict and depth for specific relationships. It can be used to assess any significant relationship in a person's life (e.g., mother, father, spouse, friend). Respondents to the QRI answer such questions as, "To what extent can you turn to this person for advice about problems?" "How significant is this relationship in your life?" and "How often does this person make you feel angry?" Factor analyses have shown that the QRI is composed of three dimensions: support, depth, and conflict. Items that load on the *support* dimension measure the extent to which the individual can rely on the other person (e.g., mother, father) for assistance in a variety of situations. Items that load strongly on the *depth* dimension assess the extent to which the individual is committed to the relationship and positively values it. Items that load on the *conflict* dimension reflect the extent to which the individual experiences angry, ambivalent feelings regarding the other person.

Pierce et al. (1991) used both the SSQ and QRI to study the associations of global and relationship-specific support perceptions with loneliness. Their results suggest that previous studies establishing an association between perceived social support and personal adjustment have given insufficient attention to the contribution of relationship-specific support. They found that (a) perceptions of available support from specific relationships are distinct from global perceptions of available support and (b) these two aspects of support have separate and distinct impacts on personal adjustment. For example, the QRI support scores for specific relationships were found to be only moderately correlated with perceived social support (as measured by the SSQ). Thus, the SSQ and the QRI seemed to be tapping related but not identical constructs. Furthermore, the SSQ and QRI each made a significant and unique contribution to the prediction of loneliness. The fact that the QRI scales predicted loneliness after removing variance associated with perceived social support demonstrates the existence of an independent link between relationship-specific perceptions of support and loneliness. This suggests that perceived social support and supportive relationships are not competing features of the social support construct, but rather are both important facets of the construct and play important roles in personal outcomes.

Other aspects of specific relationships assessed, particularly interpersonal conflict, also made unique contributions to predicting loneliness. This finding reinforces our observation that the conceptualization and assessment of social support requires attention to each of the several facets of the construct, rather than a focus on only a single feature. Furthermore, interpersonal conflict, as well as social support, predicted loneliness suggesting that there may be negative features associated with social support processes. Grissett and Norvell's (1992) investigation of the quality of relationships among bulimic and non-eating-disordered women also underscores the role of conflict in supportive relationships. Individuals may feel guilty or indebted as a result of receiving support, or they may feel resentful and angry because support is withheld. Research suggests that supportive and conflictual features of relationships are nearly orthogonal (Hirsch, 1979; Pierce et al., 1991). Thus, individuals who have high levels of support available to them may experience either high or low levels of ambivalence regarding the support they receive from family members and friends; conversely, individuals who experience low levels of social support may not necessarily have highly conflictual relationships within their network. Thus, social support may have both costs and benefits, and the relative weighting of these two aspects of supportive interactions may be different for each individual. These findings suggest the need to adopt a multidimensional view to supportive relationships that considers the positive and negative features of interpersonal ties.

Supportive Relationships and Coping

Although perceived social support has often been a useful predictor of clinical outcomes, the clinical literature also provides evidence of the importance of relationship-specific support in predicting outcomes and adjustment. Dakof and Taylor (1990) found that support from a spouse is particularly critical in enhancing well-being and encouraging adaptive behaviors in cancer patients. Coyne and DeLongis (1986) reported that inappropriate, poorly timed, or oversolicitous support from a spouse could be quite stressful for chronically ill patients. Kulik and Mahler (1993) inquired into the relationship of support from a wife to the preoperative anxiety and postoperative recovery of coronary-bypass patients. Support, defined in this study as how often the wife visited the husband in the hospital, was positively related to clinical outcome measures. For example, husbands who were highly supported by their wives were released 1.26 days sooner on the average than their less-supported counterparts.

The ability of a significant other to provide support to a patient may be linked to identifiable aspects of her or his own life. Revenson and Majerovitz (1990) studied supportive interactions between rheumatoid arthritis patients and their spouses and found that although spouses were important sources of support for their patients, the amount and quality of extrafamilial support available to the spouses influenced how supportive they were able to be toward the patients. Thus, in clinical and nonclinical settings, both specific relational support and perceived social support seem to play a role (I. G. Sarason et al., 1990).

Even though research has demonstrated that relationship-specific support and general perceived social support are distinct, these two features of social support are clearly related. For example, evidence suggests that perceived social support grows out of a history of supportive experiences, especially with family members (e.g., parents). The general expectations an individual has about the forthcomingness of others, in turn, influence whether and how that person will approach others to form new potentially supportive relationships. Perceived social support, as a working model of relationships, may be especially influential in the formative stages of a relationship before individuals have developed clear expectations about how their relationship partner, as opposed to others in general, will respond in particular situations. As the relationship progresses and relationship-specific expectations develop, each person's general expectations may become less influential, or may influence relationship processes through their impact on developing expectations for the partner's behavior.

It is also possible for expectations that develop within a specific relationship to influence general perceptions of social support. For example, one of the goals of psychotherapy is to provide the client with an interpersonal context in which to revise general working models regarding personal relationships. By developing a therapeutic alliance, the client and therapist can interact in ways that help the client create healthier, more positive views of relationships. This work is often made possible by interpretation of the transference relationship, in which the client responds to the therapist based on previously established working models of early relationships (which we might suppose reflect, in part, the client's general perceptions of social support).

Our discussion of relationship-specific support has focused primarily on its role in coping with events once they have occurred. However, relationships may also enable individuals to prevent stressful events. For example, advice about establishing a realistic sum for a house payment may help keep a person from overextending his or her finances. In this sense, we may talk about *preventive* coping as being actions that minimize or avert potential unwanted events. Divorce provides another instance in which the development of supportive relationships may render a person less likely to encounter a specific stressful situation. Personal characteristics of spouses, and the quality of the relationship they establish with each other, play important roles in marital outcomes (Buehlman, Gottman, & Katz, 1992). Thus, some individuals are at greater risk to divorce as evidenced by the higher rate of divorce among those who have already divorced once, as opposed to those who have never been divorced (Cherlin, 1981). This observation does not imply that individuals who become divorced are incapable of developing a supportive spousal relationship, or that their spouses were never a source of support for them, or might not be a source of support at some point in the future. But it does seem likely that the quality of relationship spouses establish and maintain over time will be an important determinant for whether or not they will divorce.

An additional issue concerns whether a specific life event occurs primarily to one or both individuals within a dyadic relationship. Some events challenge an individual. A student taking an examination is one example of this type of event. However, other events may challenge both members of a dyad. As we mentioned, divorce is one example. When a spouse loses a job, each family member must cope with the financial implications of the event. Similarly, the birth of a child is not typically a situation that confronts only one person; instead, both parents (and siblings) must adjust to the new family member. This point is illustrated by Coyne and his colleagues' work on spouses who experience a myocardial infarction (Coyne, Ellard, & Smith, 1990). They found that the wives of men who had experienced a myocardial infarction had, themselves, to cope with events that stemmed from this situation. The wives had to face the possibility of losing their husband, to assist in the husband's recovery, and to adjust significant elements of their former lifestyle. This study showed that stressful life events are not specific to a particular individual, but instead may occur to dyads, or even to larger social units.

These observations suggest that supportive relationships may influence coping by (a) rendering an individual less vulnerable to experiencing a specific life event or (b) providing assistance in coping with a stressful event once it has occurred. In addition, we wish to emphasize that the development, maintenance, and dissolution of supportive relationships are influenced by participants' working models of perceived social support. In turn, supportive relationships may contribute to significant revisions in these working models.

Supportive Networks

So far, we have discussed supportive relationships in dyadic terms. But this view neglects that all dyadic relationships are themselves a part of larger social structures that impact—and are influenced by—these dyadic relationships. Research on the family underscores this point. Many studies have documented the impact that parents' marital relationship may have on their ability to parent effectively (Emery, 1982). Events occurring between parents and their children may become a source of conflict in the parents' marital relationship. In other words, these relationships mutually influence one another and do not operate in isolation. In addition, these family relationships may be influenced by events occurring with members of the extended family or with friends.

Assessing Supportive Networks

Network measures deal with individuals and those people with whom they have direct personal links or those people who through significant or important ties provide the individual with support. Some measures concentrate on particular populations, for example, the elderly; others can be applied to a general population. The measures also differ in whether or not they limit the number of network members whom the respondents are asked to identify. Some ask for a particular number of supporters; others specify the relationships with supporters, for example, by limiting the inquiry to a list of those judged most significant in the respondent's life. Research suggests that it may not be necessary to move beyond a person's closest relationships. House and Kahn (1985) note that gathering data on more than 5 to 10 individuals in the subject's network yields rapidly diminishing returns.

Network instruments also identify different network components. Some of them look at the network's structure and measure its relationships, size, and density. Others ask about the qualities of each relationship in terms of its durability, frequency of contact, and intensity. Still others explore the functions of each of the network members, such as the type of help he or she provides.

Supportive Networks and Coping

Although most network measures focus primarily on relatively small social spheres, research suggests that larger, community-based networks may influence the clinical outcomes of specific members (Henderson, 1992). For example, there are wide regional and cultural differences in a large country like the United States. According to a survey done some years ago, the town of Roseto, Pennsylvania, had a remarkably low death rate, especially from heart attacks. The coronary death rate for men was 100 per 100,000 and the rate for women was almost half that figure (Wolf, 1969). Moreover, residents of Roseto had low rates of several other stress-related disorders, such as stomach ulcers. These low rates seemed surprising because both the men and women of Roseto tended to be overweight and their diets, smoking, and exercise patterns were similar to those in other communities. Apparently, what contributed most to the relatively low death rate was the way people lived. Almost all Roseto's residents were of Italian descent, and the town's neighborhoods were very cohesive. Family relationships were extremely close, supportive, and traditional. Men were likely to be the uncontested heads of their families, and personal and family problems tended to be worked out with the help of relatives, friends, and the local priest.

Although Roseto had these stable features, like all American communities, it had begun undergoing change. Young men and women were marrying non-Italians from other towns, the birth rate was declining, church attendance was down, and the people were moving outside the old areas into more distant suburban neighborhoods. By the mid-1970s, after many of these changes had occurred, a striking increase in the rate of heart attacks and sudden death was noticed, particularly among men under 55 (Greenberg, 1978). It appeared that this social change was weakening Roseto's sources of social and emotional security, with important consequences for the health and longevity of its inhabitants. Obviously, many factors contributed to change in Roseto over the years, but the change in social networks appeared to be a salient feature.

An important point illustrated by the research on the inhabitants of Roseto and others is the impact that community-level relationships can have on whether or not individuals experience particular types of life events. Prior to the 1970s, Roseto residents were relatively unlikely to face events such as heart attacks and other coronary heart diseases. Thus, social support at the community level may prevent the occurrence of, as well as facilitate coping with, particular types of life events.

The role of social losses and social isolation (the lack of a social network) in recovery from heart attacks has also been explored in a number of studies. In one investigation, 2,320 male survivors of myocardial infarctions were assessed to identify factors predictive of how long they would live after having had a heart attack (Ruberman, Weinblatt, Goldberg, & Chaudhary, 1984). One important factor was education, with the better educated subjects living longer. Life stress and social isolation, both alone and in combination, also emerged as significant predictors of mortality. Life stress was defined by subjects' reports concerning such problems as job difficulties, divorces and separations, accidents, and criminal victimization. Social isolation was defined in terms of contacts with friends and relatives and membership in social, church, and fraternal organizations. When the effects of life stress and social isolation were evaluated simultaneously, each of these factors was significantly associated with increased probability of mortality.

A major finding of this study was that the risk of death for men who were high in life stress was double the risk for men who were low in life stress. A similar relationship was found when comparing men who were high and low in social isolation. For men who were high in both life stress and social isolation, the risk of dying was four times greater than for men who were low in both life stress and social isolation. These findings suggest that the effects of personal cataclysms interact with less intense but persistent aspects of a person's lifestyle such as interactions with other people and general levels of social support.

These two studies are especially suggestive in light of the wide variety of studies that have identified relationships among social support, coping, and health status (Wallston, Alagna, DeVellis, & DeVellis, 1983). Family, friends, and other social contacts ease the emotional stress resulting from injuries incurred in automobile accidents (Porrit, 1979). Burn victims experience higher self-esteem and general life satisfaction if they have support from friends and family (Davidson, Bowden, & Tholen, 1979). Patients with kidney disease who have support from spouses and cohesive families have higher morale and show fewer changes in social functioning during hemodialysis than do those with less support (Dimond, 1979). Research on psychosocial processes in immune function also provides some promising leads. Kennedy, Kiecolt-Glaser, and Glaser (1990) have reported evidence suggesting that social support may be related to immune system functioning.

The three conceptualizations of social support we have focused on in this chapter are not exhaustive. One of the difficult—and stimulating—features of social support research has been the range of ways in which researchers have approached the construct. One conceptualization of social support that we have not described has been labeled "received support." This term refers to the aid an individual receives from others when faced with a challenging situation. This facet of the construct plays an important role in each of the other ways of thinking about social support. For example, evidence suggests that perceived social support grows out of a history of supportive experiences; that is, it stems from experiences with received support (I. G. Sarason et al., 1986). We chose not to focus on this aspect of the social support construct because it emphasizes the role of social support in coping after a stressful event has occurred and ignores the potential role of social support in preventing the occurrence of challenging situations. In addition, research focusing on received support without considering other facets of the construct has not yielded impressive findings (Coyne & DeLongis, 1986).

IMPLICATIONS FOR THEORY AND RESEARCH ON SOCIAL SUPPORT AND COPING

An exciting, as well as complicating, feature of research on social support and coping is that the processes involved are complex and interactive. Social support affects how individuals cope with stressful events; and how individuals cope, particularly in terms of the outcome of their coping efforts, may influence their use of social support in the future. This view of social support and coping has several implications for further research in this area.

We agree with Newcomb's (1990) call for the abandonment of the conception of social support as simply a provision of resources from the external social environment to the individual. Social support theories need to incorporate the complexity of those situational, interpersonal, and intrapersonal processes that shape individuals' perceptions of their social interactions with the significant people in their lives. The study of social support requires a focus, not only on general perceptions of social support, but also on the diversity of cognitions, emotions, and behaviors associated with specific personal relationships that shape behavior and well-being under diverse circumstances.

A theoretical perspective that encompasses situational, interpersonal, and intrapersonal processes has implications for the research agenda of the future. What are the cognitive models that lead people to relate to others as they do? Can these models and the behavior that flows from them be influenced, for example, by particular interventions? How do relationships between people and the personal meanings attached to them change over time? The realization that neither social support nor personal relationships are invariant or guaranteed for life has implications for a systems view of the individual. Although the individual is, at any point in time, part of a system that includes situational, interpersonal, and intrapersonal vectors, this multidimensional system undergoes changes over time. We need to improve our ability to describe these processes and their outcomes.

Conceptualizing and Assessing Social Support

Conceptualizing social support as, in part, a personality characteristic requires that measurement strategies be developed to assess this facet of the construct. Several self-report measures, such as the SSQ, appear to tap this feature of social support. Although these perceptions pertain to the social environment, however, they are not specific to a particular relationship. Instead, perceived social support reflects the belief that others, in general, are willing and able to provide assistance if needed. Further research is warranted to establish other methods of assessing the underlying cognitive models relating to perceived social support. One promising avenue is social-cognitive approaches employing computer-assisted presentation of stimuli to which subjects respond. For example, Yee, Pierce, Paul, and Rosenbaum (1993) have used computers to collect subjects' responses to measures of social support. They have obtained support for their hypothesis that subjects for whom social support is schema-consistent (they believe others are available to aid them should they need it) respond more quickly to items asking about this aspect of their lives than do other subjects.

Perceived social support is probably associated with personality characteristics related to the ability to enter into intimate relationships with other people (Brown & Harris, 1978; Hobfoll, Nadler, & Lieberman, 1986). In fact, Reis (1984) suggested that social support is linked more strongly with the capacity for intimacy than with any other aspect of social interaction. Thus, personality characteristics, including perceived social support, may play an important role in the development of supportive relationships. Advances in assessment methods will facilitate our understanding of the mechanisms by which personality characteristics influence interpersonal outcomes. For example, we need to know more about the processes that shape perceptions of specific relationships, the developmental antecedents of these perceptions, and the pathways that lead from social support—either perceived social support or relationship-specific—to personal adjustment, well-being, and health.

Although research on supportive relationships is beginning to flourish, we still know relatively little about whether and to what degree relationship phenomena occurring in one category of relationship (e.g., family) correspond to processes occurring in other relationship categories (e.g., friends). In this regard, Rook's (1990) work has been particularly helpful in delineating differences between the supportive activities that take place and are valued within the context of family versus peer relationships among the elderly. Her work suggests that a developmental perspective may be helpful in examining the manner in which supportive relationships change over time, as well as the ways in which individuals make use of them.

A variety of paper-and-pencil measures are available to assess various features of social networks. Because conceptual developments have lagged behind assessment efforts, we still need to identify the most salient factors of the social environment and to understand their role in coping efforts. To what extent and in which circumstances is the size of one's network pertinent? While measures of such features as density and interconnectedness are available, how can we quantify interactions occurring among network members? And how are we to measure the nature and impact of particular relationships on others in the network? How can we account for the separate, additive, and interactive impact of multiple relationships? Some researchers have noted that evidence for network measures' usefulness in studying the relations between health and social support has not been impressive compared with the more economically administered measures of social support that simply ask for the number of relationships in the network (House & Kahn, 1985). However, our own view is that an adequate understanding of social support processes probably should take into account the interconnectedness of a person's supportive relationships; the network approach offers a promising avenue by which to pursue an understanding of these phenomena.

Investigating Social Support

Although new assessment techniques are needed, so too are research designs that permit evaluation of specific mechanisms by which the various facets of social support exert their impact on coping. One paradigm that has not been employed systematically or frequently involves the experimental manipulation of pertinent features of stressors and support that is available to the individual. Evidence from available studies, however, suggests that this approach may yield valuable information about social support processes. For example, I. G. Sarason and B. R. Sarason (1986) successfully manipulated social support so that it positively influenced subjects' performance on an evaluative task. In their study, social support was manipulated by having an experimenter tell students, "I'll be next door while you work on the anagrams. If you need me for any reason or if you have any questions, don't hesitate to come in. I appreciate your being in this experiment, and I'd like to be helpful if you should need any help." The results of this study are particularly intriguing because none of the subjects ever came to ask the experimenter for assistance. Instead, the positive impact of this manipulation on subjects' performance appears to have been a function of subjects' belief that the other person was available and desired to provide aid, rather than specific assistance rendered by the experimenter. Heller and his coworkers (Heller & Swindle, 1983; Procidano &

Heller, 1983), on the other hand, investigated the effects of the presence of others, intimates or strangers, on performance in stressful laboratory situations in which overall support was analyzed as an individual difference variable.

Experimental studies are also needed that investigate social support processes within the context of established relationships. This is particularly important if research is to examine the unique impact that working models of perceived social support, as well as relationship-specific expectations of support (e.g., mother, father), have on coping and well-being. For example, Pierce, B. R. Sarason, and I. G. Sarason (1992) demonstrated that the QRI predicted participants' perceptions of specific social behaviors. In that study, 54 undergraduates and their mothers participated in a series of social interactions. In one of the interactions, the mother was taken to another room while the student was asked to prepare and give a speech (which would be videotaped). The mother was then asked to copy in her own handwriting two standardized notes that were provided to her. At two different times while completing the speech task, the student received one of the two notes and rated his or her perceptions of the supportiveness of the mother's message. Using a series of multiple regression analyses, the students' QRI ratings of their relationship with their mother, but not with either their father or a same-sex best friend, were found to predict the students' perceptions of their mother's notes.

Because life events, stress coping efforts, and supportive relationships, may have an impact on health and well-being over time, longitudinal designs are needed to permit evaluation of specific mechanisms. In particular, studies are needed that follow individuals who have not experienced a particular life stressor to identify the mechanisms by which some individuals are rendered less likely to experience the event in the first place. Attention needs to be given both to the active efforts individuals and their networks engage in to avoid problems (such as saving money to deal with future expenses) as well as indirect mechanisms (e.g., investment in work that fosters self-esteem and self-efficacy).

Much of the interest in social support has stemmed from the hope that research on this topic may yield information to aid in the development of interventions that enhance coping. As Gottlieb (1992) has noted, it is important to analyze the experience or situation concerning which an individual needs support. For example, Jacobson (1990) analyzed stress and support in stepfamily formation and found that a central task in the process is family members' review and reorganization of their assumptions concerning family interactions and responsibilities and the structure of meaning they entail. The process of remarriage calls for revision and disassembly of the microculture of the first marriage and the creation of a new social system. From this perspective, support includes information that enables individuals to undertake a process of cognitive restructuring. Such support offers feedback that alters the way in which a person views and experiences the world and the self or environment. Self-help groups provide contexts in which individuals can reflect on the ideas that shape their behavior and then begin developing alternative perspectives from which to evaluate and establish the meaning of circumstances in which they find themselves. Such research may require that investigators familiarize themselves with the issues confronting particular groups of individuals by gathering information informally from group members. Coyne's work, described earlier, on spouses coping with a partner who has suffered a myocardial infarction, provides an excellent illustration of this approach. The study had two phases. In the pilot phase, postmyocardial infarction couples (who were similar to those who were to take part in the survey phase), helped to design the study. The investigators participated in group focus sessions in which key issues confronting these couples were identified, and the couples then reviewed the proposed research to provide feedback about its relevance for the phenomena under investigation. Although time consuming, this strategy permitted the researchers to tailor a study to the specific needs of the group being investigated.

It is becoming increasingly clear that social support functions as a buffer against stress—it helps individuals to cope with life's challenges. Yet social support also serves as a coping facilitator by encouraging exploration of the environment. What kinds of social support function as a coping facilitator? What does the facilitating? Is it one's perception of the general forthcomingness of the social environment? Is it social support from specific relationships? What additional features of supportive relationships (e.g., low levels of conflict, high levels of intimacy) make them particularly likely to be facilitators that lead individuals to acquire personal coping skills? Answers to these questions are important if we are to develop a comprehensive theoretical framework to understand the role of social support in coping.

The development of supportive interventions will also require careful study of supportive interactions between different groups of individuals. For example, what features of parent-child interactions make them facilitative, not for coping with particular challenges, but also for developing effective personal coping skills? And are these features of parent-child interactions the same as those occurring in student-teacher relationships? We suspect that intervention efforts that do not pay careful attention to the intrapersonal, interpersonal, and situational features of a person's life are likely to meet with little success.

CONCLUSION

The concept of social support is multifaceted, encompassing features of personality, personal relationships, and larger social structures. Questions focusing on which facet of social support has the greatest impact on coping are likely to be counterproductive. Instead, we need to develop theories of social support and coping that focus on how these three features of social support influence, and are influenced by, an individual's efforts to cope with specific life events. In addition, their role in reducing the likelihood of particular types of events from occurring needs to be examined.

Research and theory on how individuals confront, respond to, and resolve life events has documented the important role played by characteristics of the individual and the social environment. Recognition that these characteristics influence health as well as psychological outcomes has provided increased impetus to discover the mechanisms by which they exert their influence. If the enormous strides made in the past several decades can be used as a predictor of continued progress, the future does indeed look promising.

REFERENCES

Bandura, A. (1986). *Social foundations of thought and action: A social cognitive theory.* Englewood Cliffs, NJ: Prentice-Hall.

Bowlby, J. (1988). Developmental psychiatry comes of age. *American Journal of Psychiatry, 145,* 1–10.

Brown, G. W., & Harris, T. (1978). *Social origins of depression.* New York: Free Press.

Buehlman, K. T., Gottman, J. M., & Katz, L. F. (1992). How a couple views their past predicts their future. *Journal of Family Psychology, 5,* 295–318.

Cassel, J. (1976). The contribution of the social environment to host resistance. *American Journal of Epidemiology, 104,* 107–123.

Cherlin, A. (1981). *Marriage, divorce, remarriage.* Cambridge, MA: Harvard University Press.

Cobb, S. (1976). Social support as a moderator of life stress. *Psychosomatic Medicine, 38,* 300–314.

Cohen, S., & Wills, T. A. (1985). Stress, social support, and the buffering hypothesis. *Psychological Bulletin, 98,* 310–357.

Coyne, J. C., & DeLongis, A. (1986). Going beyond social support: The role of social relationships in adaption. *Journal of Consulting and Clinical Psychology, 54,* 454–460.

Coyne, J. C., Ellard, J. H., & Smith, D. A. F. (1990). Social support, interdependence, and the dilemmas of helping. In B. R. Sarason, I. G. Sarason, & G. R. Pierce (Eds.), *Social support: An interactional view* (pp. 129–149). New York: Wiley.

Dakof, G. A., & Taylor, S. E. (1990). Victims' perspective of social support: What is helpful to whom? *Journal of Personality and Social Psychology, 58,* 80–89.

Davidson, T. N., Bowden, L., & Tholen, D. (1979). Social support as a moderator of burn rehabilitation. *Archives of Physical Medicine and Rehabilitation, 60,* 55–60.

Dimond, M. (1979). Social support and adaptation to chronic illness: The case of maintenance hemodialysis. *Research in Nursing and Health, 2,* 101–108.

Emery, R. E. (1982). Interparental conflict and the children of discord and divorce. *Psychological Bulletin, 92,* 310–330.

Gottlieb, B. H. (1992). Quandaries in translating support concepts to intervention. In H. O. F. Veiel & U. Baumann (Eds.), *The meaning and measurement of social support* (pp. 293–309). New York: Hemisphere.

Greenberg, J. (1978). The Americanization of Roseto. *Science News, 113,* 378–382.

Grissett, N. I., & Norvell, N. K. (1992). Perceived social support, social skills, and quality of relationships in bulimic women. *Journal of Consulting and Clinical Psychology, 60,* 293–299.

Heller, K., & Lakey, B. (1985). Perceived support and social interaction among friends and confidants. In I. G. Sarason & B. R. Sarason (Eds.), *Social support: Theory, research, and applications* (pp. 287–300). The Hague, The Netherlands: Martinus Nijhoff Publishers.

Heller, K., & Swindle, R. W. (1983). Social networks, perceived social support, and coping with stress. In R. D. Felner, L. A. Jason, J. M. Moritsugu, & S. S. Farber (Eds.), *Preventive psychology: Theory, research and practice* (pp. 87–103). Elmsford, NY: Pergamon.

Henderson, A. S. (1992). Social support and depression. In H. O. F. Veiel & U. Baumann (Eds.), *The meaning and measurement of social support* (pp. 85–92). New York: Hemisphere.

Hirsch, B. (1979). Psychological dimensions of social networks: A multimethod analysis. *American Journal of Community Psychology, 7,* 263–277.

Hobfoll, S. E., Nadler, A., & Lieberman, J. (1986). Satisfaction with social support during crisis: Intimacy and self-esteem as critical determinants. *Journal of Personality and Social Psychology, 51,* 296–304.

House, J. S., & Kahn, R. L. (1985). Measures and concepts of social support. In S. Cohen & S. L. Syme (Eds.), *Social support and health* (pp. 83–108). Orlando, FL: Academic Press.

Jacobson, D. (1990). Stress and support in stepfamily formation: The cultural context of social support. In B. R. Sarason, I. G. Sarason, & G. R. Pierce (Eds.), *Social support: An interactional view* (pp. 199–218). New York: Wiley.

Kennedy, S., Kiecolt-Glaser, J. K., & Glaser, R. (1990). Social support, stress, and the immune system. In B. R. Sarason, I. G. Sarason, & G. R. Pierce (Eds.), *Social support: An interactional view* (pp. 253–266). New York: Wiley.

Kulik, J. A., & Mahler, H. I. M. (1993). Emotional support as a moderator of adjustment and compliance after coronary bypass surgery: A longitudinal study. *Journal of Behavioral Medicine, 16,* 45–63.

Lazarus, R. S., & Folkman, S. (1984). *Stress, appraisal, and coping.* New York: Springer.

Newcomb, M. D. (1990). What structural equation modeling can tell us about social support. In B. R. Sarason, I. G. Sarason, & G. R. Pierce (Eds.), *Social support: An interactional view* (pp. 26–63). New York: Wiley.

Pierce, G. R., & Contey, C. (1992). *An experimental study of stress, social support, and coping.* Unpublished manuscript.

Pierce, G. R., Sarason, B. R., & Sarason, I. G. (1990). Integrating social support perspectives: Working models, personal relationships, and situational factors. In S. Duck with R. C. Silver, (Eds.), *Personal relationships and social support* (pp. 173–189). London: Sage.

Pierce, G. R., Sarason, B. R., & Sarason, I. G. (1992). General and specific support expectations and stress as predictors of perceived supportiveness: An experimental study. *Journal of Personality and Social Psychology, 63,* 297–307.

Pierce, G. R., Sarason, I. G., & Sarason, B. R. (1991). General and relationship-based perceptions of social support: Are two constructs better than one? *Journal of Personality and Social Psychology, 61,* 1028–1039.

Porrit, D. (1979). Social support in crisis: Quantity or quality? *Social Science and Medicine, 124,* 715–721.

Procidano, M. E., & Heller, K. (1983). Measures of perceived social support from family and friends: Three validation studies. *American Journal of Community Psychology, 11,* 1–24.

Reis, H. T. (1984). Social interaction and well-being. In S. Duck (Ed.), *Personal relationships: Vol. 5. Repairing personal relationships.* London: Academic Press.

Revenson, T. A., & Majerovitz, D. (1990). Spouses' support provision to chronically ill patients. *Journal of Social and Personal Relationships, 7,* 575–586.

Rook, K. S. (1990). Social relationships as a source of companionship: Implications for older adults' psychological well-being. In B. R. Sarason, I. G. Sarason, & G. R. Pierce (Eds.), *Social support: An interactional view* (pp. 219–250). New York: Wiley.

Ruberman, J. W., Weinblatt, E., Goldberg, J. D., & Chaudhary, B. S. (1984). Psychological influences on mortality after myocardial infarction. *New England Journal of Medicine, 311,* 552–559.

Sarason, B. R., Pierce, G. R., & Sarason, I. G. (1992). *Personality, relationship, and task-related factors in parent–child interactions: Two observational studies.* Unpublished manuscript.

Sarason, B. R., Pierce, G. R., Shearin, E. N., Sarason, I. G., Waltz, J. A., & Poppe, L. (1991). Perceived social support and working models of self and actual others. *Journal of Personality and Social Psychology, 60,* 273–287.

Sarason, B. R., Shearin, E. N., Pierce, G. R., & Sarason, I. G. (1987). Interrelationships of social support measures: Theoretical and practical implications. *Journal of Personality and Social Psychology, 52,* 813–832.

Sarason, I. G., Levine, H. M., Basham, R. B., & Sarason, B. R. (1983). Assessing social support: The Social Support Questionnaire. *Journal of Personality and Social Psychology, 44,* 127–139.

Sarason, I. G., Pierce, G. R., & Sarason, B. R. (1990). Social support and interactional processes: A triadic hypothesis. *Journal of Social and Personal Relationships, 7,* 495–506.

Sarason, I. G., & Sarason, B. R. (1986). Experimentally provided social support. *Journal of Personality and Social Psychology, 50,* 1222–1225.

Sarason, I. G., Sarason, B. R., & Shearin, E. N. (1986). Social support as an individual difference variable: Its stability, origins, and relational aspects. *Journal of Personality and Social Psychology, 50,* 845–855.

Sarason, I. G., Sarason, B. R., Shearin, E. N., & Pierce, G. R. (1987). A brief measure of social support: Practical and theoretical implications. *Journal of Social and Personal Relationships, 4,* 497–510.

Wallston, B. S., Alagna, S. W., DeVellis, B. M., & DeVellis, R. F. (1983). Social support and physical illness. *Health Psychology, 2,* 367–391.

Wolf, S. (1969). Psychosocial factors in myocardial infarction and sudden death. *Circulation, 39,* 74–83.

Yee, P. L., Pierce, G. R., Paul, J., & Rosenbaum, L. B. (1993). *Social-cognitive approaches to social support.* Unpublished manuscript.

CHAPTER 20

Coping with Stress in Childhood and Adolescence

MONIQUE BOEKAERTS

This chapter has the following objectives: (a) Briefly review major ways of measuring coping in childhood and adolescence and discuss the outcomes; (b) provide an overview of inter- and intraindividual differences in coping with stress, highlighting adaptive and maladaptive coping strategies; (c) review intervention studies and delineate needed areas of research with respect to coping in childhood and adolescence.

In this chapter, coping is understood as the individual's efforts to deal with taxing situations. These efforts may be thoughts or acts that the individual uses to manage the external or internal demands of a particular person-environment transaction previously appraised as stressful. I will focus only on adaptational responses involving effort, thus excluding instinctive mechanisms that are beyond the youngster's introspection and control. However, coping is not limited to successful efforts. It includes all deliberate attempts, even those that have become automatic after being used several times as well as those deemed maladaptive. Folkman and Lazarus (1988) explained that any stressful event has more than one implication for well-being and several options for coping. This implies that the same stressor may elicit multiple and often conflicting emotions in different individuals and even in the same individual (e.g., being happy to demonstrate competence in front of the class and at the same time feeling scared that something may go wrong). To understand these emotions and the range of cognitive and behavioral strategies that individuals use to maintain or restore their well-being and to change the situation for the better, it is important to take account of a person's appraisals, coping intentions, and coping strategies.

TWO MAJOR COPING FUNCTIONS

Two major functions of coping have been recognized by researchers working within the transactional framework. The first function deals with the problem itself (problem-focused coping) and the second function concerns regulating emotions (emotion-focused coping). Problem-focused coping involves attempts to alter the stressor, as in confrontive coping or planful problem solving. Emotion-focused coping refers to attempts to regulate negative emotional reactions to the stressor, for example, through distancing or self-control. By using a slightly different framework, Suls and Fletcher (1986) made a distinction between approach and avoidance as qualities of coping. Approach is defined as an individual's cognitive, emotional and behavioral efforts directed toward the stressor (e.g., monitoring, aggression, seeking information), whereas avoidant coping strategies entail cognitive, emotional and behavioral efforts that are directed away from the stressor in an attempt to avoid it (e.g., blunting, distancing, ignoring). Still another research group (Rothbaum, Weisz, & Snijder, 1982) has differentiated between primary and secondary control. Primary control is aimed at influencing objective conditions or events (e.g., modifying aspects of the situation in such a way that symptoms are relieved). Secondary control allows a person to come to terms with unalterable circumstances. It may provide some degree of control when certain aspects of stress are not modifiable, as in the case of a chronic disease.

These different conceptualizations of dichotomized coping functions refer to similar, though not identical, underlying concepts of coping. They can be viewed as coping styles. These styles should not be regarded as personality traits. Rather, a coping style characterizes a person's tendency to respond in a habitual or preferred way across a range of stressful situations that share the same distinctive features. On the basis of the adult literature, it is hypothesized that when youngsters believe that something can be done to affect the stressor directly, their coping will be characterized predominantly by problem-focused strategies, approach, or primary control. By contrast, when youngsters perceive that the stressor must be endured for the time being, indirect strategies (emotion-focused coping, avoidance, secondary control) will predominate.

STRESSORS: LIFE EVENTS AND DAILY HASSLES

Children and adolescents display specific coping strategies in relation to different classes of stressors because they have developed and internalized distinct personal reasons to cope with a domain of stressors in a particular way. In his review of the literature on stress in childhood and adolescence, Compas (1987) made an attempt to classify various types of stressors. He distinguished between acute and chronic stimuli that exert a demand on the child or adolescent and require an adaptational response. Acute demands consist of specific events, such as life transitions (e.g., first date, first menstruation) and atypical events (e.g., outbreak of war). Furthermore, acute demands may also derive from more cumulative experiences, including major life events (e.g., sickness or loss of a loved one) and everyday difficulties (e.g., getting into trouble at school). These acute demands should be distinguished from chronic demands, which refer first to recurring life events (e.g., maternal depression), second to personal conditions that create a handicap or liability (e.g., a chronic disease such as asthma), and third to environmental conditions of deprivation and disadvantage (e.g., financial family stressors).

Although it is possible to use this classification to organize the literature on coping with stress, it is, in my opinion, not fruitful to do so. In the first place, the most important reason for my reluctance to use Compas's categorization is that I learned from my interviews with children and adolescents that their conceptualizations of stressful events do not fit the orderly categories proposed by Compas. In the second place, a categorization formulated at the molar level introduces ambiguity because it characterizes stressful events, such as sudden outbreak of war, death or illness of a loved one, as acute demands. Granted, these demands disrupt existing conditions and involve deprivation and disadvantage for a short while, thus creating an environment in which the youngster must meet a sudden stream of threats and challenges. A serious pitfall of such a characterization, however, is that it ignores the fact that an acute stressor may turn into a chronic stressor and that it is not clear at what point in time the label must be changed (after a few weeks or months, when the event has recurred several times, or when chronic psychosocial adversity is apparent). A similar remark could be made concerning stressful events traditionally classified as chronic events. For example, separation from a loved one could, on the macro level, be conceptualized as a chronic life event. But, this stressful event could also be viewed as a sequence of several acute episodes. Furthermore, daily hassles (e.g., being bullied at school) could trigger off the next microepisode. For this reason it is not fruitful to draw a sharp line between acute and chronic life events on the one hand and life events and daily hassles on the other.

Following Lazarus et al.'s proposal for research on the effects of coping with daily hassles on adjustment, several researchers have turned their attention to the study of irritating, frustrating, and anxiety-provoking situations that occur in everyday life. In the adult literature, the relation between daily hassles and a wide range of physiological, psychological, and social symptoms have been well documented, and the overall conclusion is that the impact of daily burdens on maladjustment may well exceed that of life events (for a review, see Kohn, Chapter 9, this volume). Developmental psychologists have argued that children and adolescents are in a period of cognitive, physical, and psychosocial development, and that the stressful episodes they view as uncontrollable and/or unchangeable at a specific moment in time may turn into controllable and changeable events some months later when their coping strategies have become increasingly diverse and sophisticated. Evidence is slowly building up that the strategies youngsters develop for coping with everyday burdens are highly predictive of their coping response to life stressors when the latter arise. For example, Wagner, Compas, and Howell (1988) found that in late adolescence life events were not linked directly to symptomatology, but that the effect was mediated by daily hassles.

COPING RESPONSES, COPING STRATEGIES, AND INTENTIONS

If we want to shed some light on children's and adolescents' coping efforts, a distinction should be made between various components of the coping process. In Figure 20.1, a model of coping is presented that distinguishes between various components. Component 1 represents the youngster's perception of the stressful situation. Component 2 refers to an individual's coping repertoire in which specific coping responses are located, such as looking at the ceiling during a painful medical treatment, or hitting a younger child when feeling frustrated. Learned sequences for controlling specific problems and regulating specific emotions may also be stored in the coping repertoire (e.g., first try to manage by oneself by putting in more effort; then look for social support; if that is not available, give up). It is assumed that through experience with stressors and modelling, the individual's coping repertoire widens, but that only some of the available coping responses will become part of the coping preferences linked to the coping goals. Component 3 consists of an individual's generalized coping goals and his or her conceptions and misconceptions about how to restore well-being and deal with various stressors. Coping goals are a subset of general goals. They are linked to self-schemata, the belief system (including beliefs about personal and social resources), personality traits (intelligence, self-esteem, optimism, neuroticism, etc.) and coping preferences.

The model posits that individuals actively construct and regulate their environment. Each stressful situation triggers a network of highly specific connotations because it impinges on a person's personal strivings and vulnerabilities. The uniqueness of the meta-representation of a stressor is represented in the model by linking a dynamic working memory (WM), in which the contents of the three components are constantly fed, to the appraisals (component 4). It is further theorized that individuals represent the stressor on the basis of a number of dimension-wise judgments of the stressful situation. These appraisals and their concomitant emotions are shaping and reshaping the meta-representation of the stressor and at the same time are acting as a steering mechanism for taking decisions to act or not to act, and in what way (coping intention symbolized in component 5). As such, appraisals and emotions steer the selection of coping strategies (component 6) from the coping repertoire via coping intention(s). Coping intentions and coping strategies are linked to the coping repertoire and to the coping goals so that flexible selection and combination of coping responses is possible. The model also describes a double feedback system. One feedback loop (7) links the outcomes of the coping efforts to the coping goals and preferences. It symbolizes the continuous assessment that takes place as the stressful encounter unfolds, which then leads to a reevaluation of alternative coping strategies or to a change of the coping goal. The other feedback loop (8) extends or modifies the repertoire of coping responses and strategies.

Perrez and Reicherts (1992) proposed six dimension-wise judgments to represent stressors (see Table 20.1). Understanding how youngsters of both sexes, of

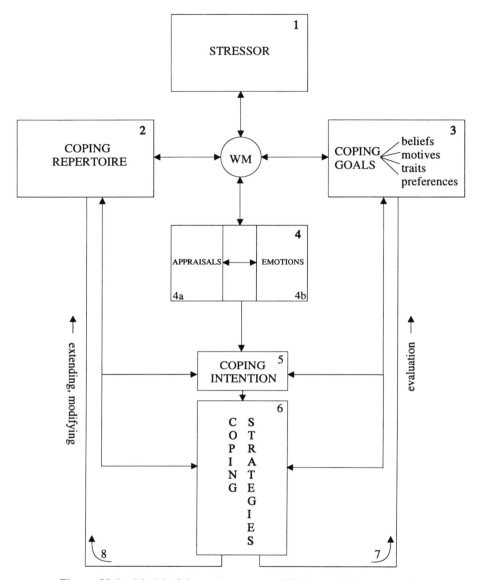

Figure 20.1   Model of the coping process (WM = working memory).

different age groups and of different cultures classify and represent stressors in terms of these six dimension-wise judgments will shed some light on their situation-specific coping intentions, on the unique ways in which coping intentions are linked to coping goals and preferences, and to the selection of specific coping strategies. Reference shall be made to these dimensions when reporting on the salience of the coping strategies found in past research on coping in youngsters.

TABLE 20.1   Subjective Dimensions of Stressful Situations

Valence	The subjective meaning of a situation in terms of its relevance and severity of negative quality
Controllability	The subjective appraisal of personal ability to control the stressful situation
Changeability	The subjective appraisal that the situation will change by itself
Ambiguity	The subjective appraisal of the uncertainty created by the situation
Recurrence	The subjective appraisal that the situation will strike again
Familiarity	The extent of personal experience with that type of situation

Note: Adapted from *Stress, Coping, and Health* by M. Perrez and M. Reicherts, 1992, p. 26. Copyright 1992 by Hogrefe & Huber Publishers. Adapted by permission.

WAYS OF MEASURING COPING IN YOUNGSTERS

Researchers have used various techniques (checklists, interviews, self-reports, group discussions, card-sorting tasks, and observations) to achieve a better understanding of children's appraisals of stressful events and of their coping strategies. The first attempts to study stress in youngsters focused on the occurrence of negative life events and the psychological symptoms these events caused, without taking into account the youngsters' coping efforts. There is a vast body of research documenting that in children and adolescents, as in adults, negative life events are related to immediate and long-term physiological, psychological, and social effects. The correlations vary between .10 and .68, with the majority falling between .20 and .30. More specifically, major life events have been associated with a wide range of psychological symptoms such as increased trait-anxiety, depression, and anger. Negative life events have also been implicated in long-term physiological, psychological, and social dysfunctioning, including childhood depression, suicide attempts, deviant behavior, health complaints, increased school absences and lower grades (for review, see Compas, 1987; Johnson, 1986). Rarely more than 15% of the variance in symptomatology is accounted for by major life events (e.g., illness of a friend or family member). A problem with most of these studies is that they do not address the causality issue. Typically, a broad range of childhood variables is sampled in the hope of detecting early signs (predictors) of later disorders. In some studies, all the data were collected at a single point in time, and respondents were asked to describe stress and symptoms retrospectively. Such a design does not provide a basis for establishing causal links between stressors and symptomatology. Data from prospective studies show that in 10- to 15-year-olds only 2% of the variance in subsequent adjustment could be explained by the occurrence of stressful events measured at an earlier point in time (Compas, Wagner, Slavin, & Vannatta, 1986) and that after controlling for seventh and eighth graders' adjustment at an initial measurement point, controllable life events, but not uncontrollable events, significantly predicted adjustment measured several months later

(Cohen, Burt, & Bjorck, 1987). These results raise questions concerning the link that has been described between stressful life events and subsequent adjustment, and they draw our attention to the coping process. Indeed, research based on the transactional stress model has demonstrated that not all youngsters become distressed or perform poorly under stress. The literature offers much evidence of considerable individual differences in the degree to which adverse symptoms are associated with various life stressors. Findings suggest that whether youngsters become distressed or remain resilient during negative life events has to do with the quality of their *coping strategies* and with *personality characteristics.*

There is little agreement in the literature concerning the conceptualization and measurement of coping strategies in children and adolescents. Nevertheless, there has been an explosion of instruments for the measurement of coping responses to general and specific stressors. Most research groups started from scratch and constructed their own instruments to assess children's and adolescents' efforts to deal with various types of stressors, without taking into account the instruments that already existed. Most of the research to date has focused on the identification of frequently used coping strategies. These studies will be reviewed next. Technically speaking, coping instruments can be grouped into three broad categories: (a) observation and case studies, (b) life event studies, (c) coping with unspecified stressors and with specific daily stressors.

Observation and Case Studies

Although Compas (1987) made an attempt to integrate the literature on attachment with the field of stress, it is not clear whether this is a productive approach. Traditionally, attachment researchers (see Karraker & Lake, 1991) classify infants into three basic categories: (a) securely attached infants, (b) ambivalent or resistant infants, and (c) avoidant infants. This classification system is based on observations of the infants' coping behavior in separation and reunion situations. But, as La Greca (1990) explained, it is more the researcher's interpretation of observed behavior or the caretaker's view assessed via structured interviews or checklists, than the child's appraisal that is taken into account in research with very young children. Nonetheless, it must be assumed that differences in young children's coping responses are due to differences in their primary and secondary appraisals. Because of the complications in the collection of accurate, reliable and valid information about the appraisals made by the very young children, this age group will be excluded from the present review. In a similar vein, the evidence from several case studies set up from a psychoanalytic perspective should be excluded. For example, Caty, Ellerton, and Ritchie (1984) reexamined the findings from 39 published nursing case studies of hospitalized children from a transactional perspective. They noted that coping efforts entailing cognitive strategies were totally absent from the database. To date, most of the research is set up from the transactional perspective and the range of valid and reliable instruments for assessing children's interpersonal, behavioral and affective functioning is currently expanding. Several authors have argued that from the age of 7 years onward children can provide accurate and reliable reports of episodes they have experienced, provided that (a) questions are phrased in a grammar the child can understand, (b) demands for verbalizations are minimized, and (c) the instrument is sensitive to the child's capacities (see, La Greca, 1990).

Coping with Life Events

Dise-Lewis (1988) developed the Life Events and Coping Inventory (LECI) for 12- to 14-year-olds. This inventory consists of 125 life events such as "Your mom or dad moved out of the house," "Your family had financial problems," "You got suspended from school," "You got caught stealing." The life events rating scale requires children to evaluate each item on the basis of how stressful it would be for them if the event occurred. Attached to these stressors are 42 coping response items, and the children are asked to assess whether they would use these coping responses in the respective situations. Five factors were empirically extracted: aggression (e.g., throw things or break things), stress-recognition (e.g., cry, scream, write or talk to somebody), distraction (e.g., do something you enjoy), self-destruction (e.g., take drugs, do something dangerous), and endurance (e.g., clench your teeth, go away to be alone). Distraction was the coping strategy most frequently reported (61%), followed by stress-recognition (56%). Self-destruction had the lowest frequency (16%). Girls displayed higher average stress ratings and scored significantly higher on stress-recognition than boys. It is important to note, however, that the life events scale used by Dise-Lewis is a mixture of nonnormative and normative life events, which means that about half of the items are completed in a hypothetical mode.

Groër, Thomas, and Shoffner (1992) developed the Adolescent Life Change Event Scale (ALCES). Coping with 38 life events is measured in a longitudinal panel study with an open-ended questionnaire (see Table 20.2). Life events include nonnormative events, such as "death of a loved one," "losing a favorite pet," "flunking a grade," "parents divorced or separated," "arrested by the police," "wrecking a car" as well as normative events, such as "hassling with parents," and "making new friends." Coding of the students' coping responses was done according to the coping categories identified by Dise-Lewis. Respondents (13–15 and 16–18 years of age) reported using a lot of active distraction (e.g., walking, exercise) followed by passive distraction (e.g., reading, music, sleep). Endurance, stress-recognition, aggression, and self-destruction were not used often. Use of these coping strategies was quite stable across time.

Coping with Daily Hassles

Some authors introduced inventive techniques for interacting with the younger age groups to learn about the typical way they cope with daily hassles. For example, Jenkins, Smith, and Graham (1989) read children stories about parental quarrels and asked them to predict what the child in the story would do, as well as what they themselves would do in the depicted situation. They found that most

TABLE 20.2   Categories of Coping Strategies Identified in Children and Adolescents

Groër et al. (1992) $N = 467$ (ages 13–18)	Seiffge-Krenke (1993) $N = 2,000$ (ages 15–19)	Ryan (1989) $N = 103$ (ages 8–12)
—Coping with 38 normative and nonnormative life events —longitudinal study with open-ended coping questions	—Coping with 8 normative problem-domains —Questionnaire	—Coping with self-defined stressor in recent past —Group discussion questionnaire

Salience of Higher Order Coping Strategies			

	Age 13–15 16–18		(%)		(%)
		German Sample			
1. Active distraction	72.9% 58.4%	1. Active coping	52–55	1. Social support	17.6
2. Passive distraction	15.7 22.0	2. Internal coping	22	2. Avoidant activity	15.6
3. Endurance	3.1 2.5	3. Withdrawal	21	3. Emotional behavior	12.2
4. Aggression	1.2 3.6			4. Behavior distraction	9.5
5. Self-destruction	1.2 5.4	Israeli Sample		5. Cognitive activity	9.1
6. Stress-recognition	2.8 5.5			6. Behavior aggression	6.9
7. Other	3.1 4.0	1. Active coping	33–36	7. Physical exercise	6.6
		2. Internal coping	44	8. Isolating action	6.2
		3. Withdrawal	16	9. Verbal aggression	4.3
				10. Relaxation	3.5
				11. Ticks	2.5
				12. Spiritual action	6.8
				13. Other behavior	5.6

Note: IP = Interpersonal stressor; AC = Academic stressor. % means different things in different studies. In the studies by Groër et al., Seiffge-Krenke, and Ryan % = percentage distribution of X coping strategies computed on the basis of Y coping responses used by (different groups of)

children suggested approach strategies, such as directly intervening or comforting parents after the quarrel, but attempts to appraise the episode positively were also frequent. Altshuler and Ruble (1989) also used stories successfully to interact with children ranging from 5 to 12 years. Other techniques that were used to gain information about children's coping responses to daily stressors include structured or unstructured interviews (e.g., Brotman Band, 1990; Compas, Malcarne, & Fondacaro, 1988; Wertlieb, Weigel, & Feldstein, 1987), checklists (e.g., Spirito, Stark, Grace, & Stamoulis, 1991; Stark, Spirito, Williams, & Guevremont, 1989), and straightforward questions, such as "What do you do when you experience difficulties or trouble?" (Rauste-von Wright, 1987).

The literature on daily hassles could roughly be divided into (a) studies that explore coping with unspecified stressors, and (b) studies investigating how children and adolescents cope with specific minor stressors. An example of the former type of study is Ryan's. She (Ryan, 1989) described 518 different coping responses that children, aged between 8 and 12, reported spontaneously using in response to recently experienced, *undefined stressors* (e.g., ride my bike, hit my brother, lock

Boekaerts et al. (1993) N = 500 (ages 10–12)		Rost and Schermer (1987) several studies (ages 14–20)		
—Coping with 4 academic and 4 interpersonal stressors —Questionnaire with 10 coping responses per situation		—Coping in response to anxiety-provoking school situations —Questionnaire with 51 coping responses		

		Salience of Higher Order Coping Strategies		
	IP (%)	AC (%)		
Problem-Focused Coping				
1. Confrontive approach	47	46	1. Danger control	$x = 42.0$ $SD = 10.4$
2. Social support	15	56	2. Anxiety control	$x = 24.8$ $SD = 7.6$
3. Aggressive behavior	72	—	3. Anxiety repression	$x = 41.6$ $SD = 10.8$
4. Problem solving	—	97	4. Situation control	$x = 31.1$ $SD = 9.8$
Emotion-Focused Coping				
5. Avoidant activity	82	67		
6. Behavior distraction	82	47		
7. Cognitive distraction	71	39		

respondents. In the study by Boekaerts, % refers to the prevalence of each coping strategy, independent of the other coping strategies.

myself into the closet, take a deep breath, cuddle a stuffed animal). She grouped these coping responses into 12 meaningful coping categories (see Table 20.2); 65% of all reported coping responses fell into the five first coping categories—social support, avoidant activities, emotional behavior, behavioral distraction, and cognitive activities. The children perceived social support and cognitive activities as most helpful, whereas emotional behavior and verbal aggression were viewed as least helpful. Ryan also reported age differences: The 8-year-olds named social support more frequently than older children. Nine-year-olds relied more than the other age groups on verbal aggression and avoidant activities, 11-year-olds displayed most physical activities, and 12-year-olds used more relaxation, cognitive activities, and distraction than the younger children (for a review of the literature, see also Ryan-Wenger, 1992).

Frydenberg and Lewis (1991) constructed the adolescent coping scale (ACS) to measure how adolescents cope with *general concerns*. This is an 80-item checklist. Students are asked to indicate on 5-point scales whether the coping activity described is used a great deal, often, sometimes, very little, or not at all. Eighteen different coping strategies commonly used by adolescents were identified: seek social support (e.g., talk to people to help me sort it out), social action (e.g., join with people who have the same concern), seek professional help (e.g., discuss the problem with teacher or counselor), seek to belong (e.g., improve my relationship with others), invest in close friends (e.g., spend more time with boy/girl friend), wishful thinking (e.g., hope for the best), worry, work hard and achieve, focus on solving the problem, seek relaxing diversions, physical recreation, focus on the positive, not coping (e.g., I have no way of dealing with the situation), ignore the problem, tension reduction (e.g., make myself feel better by taking cigarettes, alcohol, drugs), self-blame, keep to self, seek spiritual support. Frydenberg (in press) described seven studies spanning a 5-year period in which the ACS was used to study Australian adolescents' coping behavior. She reported that adolescents (12–16 years of age) generally nominate no more than three responses when asked to describe the ways in which they cope. Findings revealed that in middle adolescence, youngsters attempt to deal directly with the causes of their concerns. The most frequently used coping strategies were work hard, focus on solving the problem, invest in close friends, wishful thinking, seek to belong, worry, seek social support. The strategies that were least frequently used were seek spiritual support, social action, and seek professional help. The oldest students in the sample (15–16) reported less "work hard" strategies and more self-blame and tension reduction strategies than did the youngest students in the sample (11–13). Even though a specific form of the ACS allows for measurement of responses to self-nominated concerns, Ryan as well as Frydenberg and Lewis measure coping independent of the characteristics of the stressor.

Seiffge-Krenke (1990, 1993) investigated in a large sample of German adolescents (ages 15–19) how they cope with critical, normative developmental stress related to eight problem domains, viz.: parents, peers, opposite sex, self, future, leisure time, studies, and teachers. The stressor related to a problem domain was specified (e.g., I had an argument with my parents) and youngsters were asked to indicate how they would react to the stressor (anticipatory coping), choosing as many of the 20 coping responses as they thought appropriate (e.g., I try to let steam off with loud music, wild dancing, sports). Three higher-order coping strategies were extracted: (a) internal coping, (b) active coping, and (c) withdrawal. The first two labels refer to the problem-focused coping mode, whereby the term "internal coping" is reserved for techniques that are characterized by internal reflection on possible solutions (e.g., I analyze the problem and think of various possible solutions), whereas the term "active coping" is used for responses that reflect active and constructive attempts to solve the problem by gathering information about it or by eliciting social support (e.g., I discuss the problem with my friends). Finally, withdrawal (e.g., I retreat because I am unable to change the situation) includes defensive responses that inhibit actions that might produce more stress, lead to embarrassment, or get him or her into trouble. Seiffge-Krenke reported that 52% to 55% of the coping responses in relation to the domains "teachers," "parents," "future," and "opposite sex" could be classified as active coping. In the domains of "study" and "peers," active coping was also the most frequently used coping strategy (40%). Only about 15% to 20% of all reactions could be classified as withdrawal. This coping category was most salient (30%) in relation to the domains "leisure time" and "self." Closer analysis of the coping responses that students used vis-à-vis the different types of stressors revealed that the responses used within one domain were highly consistent, but that adolescents relied on different coping responses for different domains (e.g., family vs. studies). The use of the three coping strategies was relatively stable over time (she tested three times over 18 months), but girls made more use of active coping and withdrawal than did boys. There was a modest correlation between internal and active coping, whereas both were independent from withdrawal.

Seiffge-Krenke described 10% to 20% of the original sample of 2,000 adolescents as a "clinical group" in the sense that they were drug abusers, had interpersonal problems, or reported depression. Among this group, withdrawal was a prominent coping strategy that was applied fairly indiscriminantly across different life problems, but active coping and internal coping did not differ significantly from that of the "normal" group. It seems that these youngsters do not take account of situational demands, but repeatedly use the same coping strategy regardless of the type of stressor. It is interesting though that being in treatment reduced the withdrawal score to a level comparable to that of the nonclinical group. Seiffge-Krenke further reported that situational invariant withdrawal is strongly influenced by family climate. Cross-sectional research with German, Scandinavian, and Israeli adolescents displayed that those who came from families characterized by poor cohesion, minimal expression of feelings, interpersonal conflict and high control over their children, had the highest withdrawal scores.

The Stress and Coping Inventory (SCI) that Boekaerts, Hendriksen, and Maes (1987) constructed measures coping in response to *specific stressors*. The SCI was constructed for 10- to 12-year-olds and later extended and adapted for older age groups (12–15). Youngsters are presented with situations depicting different academic and interpersonal hassles. They are asked how frequently they encounter each stressor and to give an indication of the amount of stress each stressor elicits. An example of an academic stressor is "The teacher wants you to copy from the blackboard and he or she is going fast." An example of an interpersonal stressor is "You are being bullied at school." The inventory lists 10 different coping responses per stressor and respondents are asked to indicate the frequency with which they use each coping response. The data were aggregated for interpersonal stressors and academic stressors respectively and two higher order categories were inducted: emotion-focused coping and problem-focused coping. Emotion-focused coping was the dominant response pattern for interpersonal stressors. Avoidant activities (e.g., Pretend that I don't hear anything) and behavioral distraction (e.g., Go and do something else) were most frequently used in relation to this type of stressor, followed by cognitive distraction (e.g., Think about something else) and aggressive behavior (e.g., Get angry with that student). In relation to academic stressors, planful problem solving showed the highest frequency (e.g., try harder), but avoidant activities were also frequently used (e.g., I don't care about it). Confrontive coping (e.g., I tell them to stop doing that) and seeking social support had the lowest frequency. Boekaerts (1994) found that, on average, 5 coping responses (out of 10) were reported in relation to the respective stressors. The data do not allow further suggestions about the selection of various coping responses and about the temporal order in which they were used. Because there is no correlation between emotion-focused and problem-focused coping in relation to interpersonal stressors, however, children may combine approach and avoidant coping responses in attempting to cope with this type of stressor. The modest negative correlation between the two coping modes in relation to academic stressors signals, on the other hand, suggests that children may prefer using either one of these modes when coping with stressful academic situations.

The last instrument that will be discussed is Rost and Schermer's (1987, 1992) inventory to assess adolescents' coping with anxiety-provoking situations. They presented students with the general statement: "To cope with my test-anxiety, . . ." followed by 51 coping responses such as, ". . . , I try to control my breathing". Four coping strategies that adolescents use to reduce, accept, or come to terms with threatening academic situations were identified: (a) danger control, (b) anxiety control, (c) anxiety repression, and (d) situation control. Danger control and anxiety control are regarded as preventive ways of coping with anxiety. The former type of coping strategy refers to active attempts to control the perceived danger. For example, an increase in study behavior makes good grades more probable. Anxiety control represents coping strategies that attempt to reduce psychic and somatic anxiety symptoms (e.g., controlling one's breathing). Anxiety repression and situation control refer to avoidant strategies. Both of these techniques may lead to effective relief of anxiety, but neither of them modifies the underlying causes: Anxiety repression may temporarily calm down the student (e.g., by thinking, I have survived in the past, I will survive this time), whereas situation control may help the student to evade the taxing demands in the confrontation phase (e.g., by cheating, or reporting sick). The authors reported that the use of the four coping strategies was stable over time (they tested twice in 6 weeks). Danger control and anxiety repression were the most salient coping strategies used by German adolescents (between 14 and 20), and anxiety control was the least salient coping strategy. No age differences were reported. Girls scored higher on danger control and anxiety repression than boys. There is a moderate correlation between danger control and anxiety control, and between anxiety repression and the three other forms of control.

Conclusions

In the previous pages, various ways of measuring coping in youngsters were described. In an attempt to reduce the rich variety of coping responses that respondents used into a manageable set of categories, most authors have developed their own category system, either a priori or post hoc. This situation makes it complicated to compare and contrast the results from the different studies and limits general conclusions. However, the reported findings allow for the following inferences:

1. Children and adolescents use a wide range of coping responses.
2. They use different coping responses for different domains.
3. Coping responses can be reliably grouped into higher-order coping strategies that prove to be relatively stable over time.
4. The most salient coping strategies are various forms of active coping, such as danger control and seeking social support; various forms of internal coping, such as planful problem solving, active and passive distraction.
5. The least salient coping strategies are self-destruction, aggression, confrontive coping, withdrawal, relaxation, ticks, and anxiety control.

A better understanding of coping in children and adolescents would be achieved if the constructs that each coping instrument attempts to measure were classified in a standard way across studies. Furthermore, coping instruments should reflect rather than simplify reality. These instruments should be based on an integrated theory or model such as the one introduced in this chapter. Many questions on the determinants of coping in children and adolescents remain unanswered. These questions relate to inter- and intraindividual differences in coping with stress and to the effects of interventions on dealing with adversity. In the next section, an attempt will be made to enlarge the systematic knowledge base regarding the psychological and functional correlates of the different coping strategies that children and adolescents use. In the last section, the results of interventions will be reported.

INTER- AND INTRAINDIVIDUAL DIFFERENCES IN COPING WITH STRESS

Age Differences in Perception of Stressors

The types of event that may produce stress drastically change with development. Compas, Phares, and Ledoux (1989) provided some evidence to this effect. In children and young adolescents (through the age of 14) *family stressors* were found to be most predictive of psychological symptoms. In middle adolescence (ages 15 to 17), only *peer stressors* were predictive of psychological symptoms, and among 18- to 20-year-olds, *academic stressors* were the best predictors. This suggests that some stressors are closely tied to a specific period during development. It does not imply that youngsters who have already passed through a particular period are no longer vulnerable to the stressors associated with that period. As Caspi, Bolger, and Eckenrode (1987) explained, exposure to a stressful event is unlikely to be static. Youngsters may be more vulnerable to the effects of a stressor when they are first confronted with it, because at that point they may have access neither to a fully mature social support system nor to adequate self-regulating skills (e.g., skills to make an adequate meta-representation of the stressor or to elicit social support). In terms of the coping model depicted in Figure 20.1 this implies that as children get older and become more familiar with different types of situations, their skill at appraising the situation in terms of the six dimension-wise judgments summarized in Table 20.1 develops. Spivack and Shure (1982) attempted to explain these and related issues. They identified six component skills that are essential to the process of solving interpersonal problems. These cognitive skills include sensitivity to social problems, role taking, anticipating the consequences of personal and social acts, generation of alternative solutions, development of means-end thinking, and social-causal reasoning. Their research demonstrated that some of these skills emerge early in life. For example, the ability to generate alternative solutions emerges around the age of 4 or 5, whereas other skills, such as means-end thinking, emerge in children at 8 to 10 years of age. In a comparison of youngsters with emotional and behavioral problems with well-adjusted peers, these authors found a strong association between interpersonal problem-solving skills and level of adjustment.

Developmental changes such as the ones reported by Spivack and Shure may explain Rutter's (1983) results concerning hospital admission. This experience produces most stress in children between 6 months and 4 years of age. Below the age of 6 months, infants have not developed selective attachments and hence experience less separation anxiety. Children older than 4 years may be less vulnerable because they can generate alternative solutions to a problem situation and hold these alternatives in memory simultaneously. In other words, they have the necessary cognitive skills to appraise the stressor because they understand that separation does not lead to abandonment. In terms of the six dimension-wise judgments depicted in Table 20.1, children older than 4 may perceive this type of loss situation as changeable, whereas younger children may not. In a similar vein, Macobby (1983) reported that older children understand the finality of death, which makes the loss of a loved one more acute. She also refers to a vast body of research documenting that younger children have a smaller repertoire of coping strategies tailored to specific threats. Their all-purpose prepared response to danger is "Run to the attachment figure(s)." Little attention has been given to the forms and functions of attachment to significant others (e.g., parents, members of the extended family, teachers) in the middle childhood years and adolescence. However, it is generally accepted that the obedient stance toward adult authority taken by most preadolescents constitutes a buffer against stress. Macobby explained that when instructions given by a trustworthy adult proved to have negative consequences, children were partly protected from anxiety and a sense of failure and guilt.

An interesting question is whether older and younger children differ in the way they perceive situational constraints and incorporate them into their meta-representation of a stressor. More specifically, is there evidence of age differences in the perception of controllability and changeability, and if so, are these differences reflected in the coping strategies selected from the coping repertoire?

Age Differences in Coping with Uncontrollable Stressors

There is some evidence that older children and adolescents tend to use cognitive coping strategies in response to uncontrollable stressors. These forms of inner reflection enable the individual to turn away from a salient unpleasant stimulus and focus on other events, which in turn, helps the individual to reduce negative emotions and learn to come to terms with existing conditions. Ignoring salient cues may, however, be beyond the capacities of children below the age of 7 (see Brotman Band & Weisz, 1988; Mischel, 1974). Brotman Band and Weisz (1988) provided evidence that children between 6 and 12 years of age take account of situational constraints when selecting a strategy for coping with stressors in three domains (school failure, separation, and medical stress). With increasing age, primary control (trying to modify aspects of the situation in a way that relieves symptoms) declined and secondary control (trying to come to terms with unalterable circumstances) increased, especially in relation to medical stress. In an effort to study how youngsters deal with their emotions during uncontrollable situations, several authors have investigated how they cope with chronic illness and invasive medical procedures. For example, Brotman Band (1990) showed developmental trends in the way youngsters cope with diabetes. Most children (mean age 8.8 years) directed their coping at concrete, modifiable aspects of diabetes (getting an injection and other direct self-care activities that changed the symptoms). Although all respondents tended to emphasize primary over secondary control, the older group (mean age 14.6 years) reported significantly more secondary control (e.g., come to terms with low sugar intake by changing cognitions about sugar) than the younger group. Blount, Landolf-Fritsche, Powers, and Sturges (1991) reviewed the literature and reported that older children were more aware than younger children that when escape/avoidance is not possible, partial avoidance can be achieved. Older children and those who had more experience with the medical procedures tended to use a greater number of coping strategies than younger children and those with less experience.

Altshuler and Ruble (1989) suggest that with increasing age children have more access to their own thoughts and strategies, which may help them to expand their repertoire of situationally relevant coping techniques. They drew a distinction between cognitive and behavioral distraction and asked children in three age groups (ranging from 5 to 12 years) how the child in various stories might reduce his or her excitement or fear. Cognitive distraction was less available to the younger than to the older children, but behavioral distraction (e.g., looking at the ceiling) was the avoidant strategy most frequently selected by children in all three age groups. These authors explained that children must understand that "unobservable" methods (such as inner reflection or cognitive distraction) constitute a viable way of reducing stress and pain if they are to begin using these subtle means on their own initiative. Nevertheless, some forms of secondary control require complex thinking that may well be beyond the capacities of children below the age of 11 (e.g., lowering one's expectations to minimize future disappointment).

Differences in the Perception of Situational Dimensions

In an achievement context, teachers and educators tend to think of most learning situations as high in valence, low in ambiguity, low in changeability, but high in controllability. It has been argued elsewhere (Boekaerts, 1993, 1994) that most learners may not perceive learning opportunities as low in ambiguity and high in controllability. Elias (1989) also maintained that in an educational system that is too heavily oriented around a narrow notion of academic success, many students may become caught in cycles of perceived failure and self-blame. He reported that perception of excessive academic demands and stressors related to low decision latitude were associated with various maladaptive coping strategies, (e.g., self-reported substance abuse in middle school). In my own research (see Boekaerts, 1993), it was predicted that students would react differently to uncontrollable and controllable failure in achievement situations. It was found that children aged 10 to 12 who reported frequent confrontation with unavoidable failure (e.g., they have not prepared well for an exam that is about to start) preferred avoidance as a coping mode. However, students who reported state anxiety in these situations favored approach (e.g., cramming in the time left before the exam starts). Apparently, students low on state anxiety perceived the situation depicted in the questionnaire as low on controllability and opted for a form of secondary control (e.g., coming to terms with the negative consequences). The students who expressed anxiety may have represented the stressor as valuable, unchangeable, but controllable, thus contemplating that approach could still keep them out of danger (cf. Rost & Schermer, 1987). Alternatively, approach could also signal primary control through an attempt to alleviate or attenuate unpleasant bodily symptoms elicited in response to an uncontrollable stressor (having a plan of action may temporarily alleviate symptoms and thus restore well-being). Schönpflug and Battman (1988) reported that with increasing discrepancy between task difficulty and intellectual capacity, individuals first react with increased effort, but switch to a form of avoidance when the stressful experience unfolds. They noted that in everyday activities, disengagement, conceptualized as giving up, is a common response to experienced or anticipated loss of personal resources. They argued that giving up should be viewed as an adaptive coping strategy if the stressor is uncontrollable or if the task taxes a person's resources too heavily. In such a context, approach should be seen as a costly coping strategy.

In another study, Boekaerts (1994) compared the coping data from primary school students (ages 10–12 years) with those of adolescents (14–15). This study concerned *controllable* academic stressors (e.g., You are in class and the teacher wants you to take notes, but he or she is going fast) and interpersonal stressors (e.g., You are being bullied at school). All students used more problem-focused coping in response to academic stressors than interpersonal stressors. The correlations between problem-focused coping in relation to the two types of stressors was modest to moderate, whereas there was no correlation between emotion-focused coping. Further, primary school students did not differ from secondary school students in their use of problem-focused coping in relation to controllable academic stressors. They made, however, less use of emotion-focused coping than the older students in relation to this type of stressor. The difference was most marked between the older and the younger girls. Also, younger students used significantly more problem-focused coping in response to interpersonal stressors than did older students. Girls displayed dual-focused coping when dealing with social conflict; they reported using both more problem-focused and more emotion-focused strategies than did boys.

Several authors have substantiated the view that the frequency with which emotion-focused coping and problem-focused coping is used and the rated efficacy of these coping strategies differ with age and gender. Ryan (1989) found that younger children (8–12) view emotional behavior and verbal aggression as least helpful and social support and cognitive activities as must helpful in reducing their stress. Frydenberg (in press) stated that the youngest students in her sample (12-year-olds) reported using more "hard work" and less "tension reduction" than did older students (13–16), whereas the oldest students in the sample (16-year-olds) reported using the least "hard work" and the most "tension reduction" and "self-blame" of all students. Referring to an ongoing longitudinal study, Seiffge-Krenke (1993) informed that most age-related changes occurred in the internal coping scale. As they grow older, adolescents rely more on internal forms of coping and make less use of specific forms of active coping, such as discussions with parents. Social support from peers, on the other hand increases continuously between 12 and 19.

Gender and Culture Differences

The consistent pattern of gender differences in the literature may reflect differential understanding and representation of stressful situations. Seiffge-Krenke (1990) found that male and female adolescents differ in their appraisal of the same normative demands: Girls assess the same events, such as getting bad marks at school and conflict with family members, as being four times more threatening than do boys of the same age. Girls evaluate the same problem as more complex, more internally caused, and when a stressful event is over, they continue to go on thinking about it. They are also significantly more affected by observing stress experienced by others in their social network. Groër et al. (1992) demonstrated that adolescent girls are more stressed than boys about interpersonal relationships. These gender differences in appraisals may explain coping preferences and differences in adjustment. For example, Frydenberg (in press) reported that adolescent girls generally use more seeking social support, wishful thinking and tension reduction strategies than did boys, whereas boys rely more on physical recreation than do girls. Seiffge-Krenke also documented striking gender differences in the use of coping strategies. Regardless of the type of problem, girls address problems immediately, talk about them frequently with significant others and usually try to solve the conflict with the person concerned. Boys, on the other hand, seem to tackle problems when these are imminently present, but do not put themselves under as much pressure as females do. They attempt to manage by themselves rather than look for social support and may more easily try to forget and adopt a wait-and-see policy. At 13, the difference between the sexes in seeking social support is marginal, but as they grow older, girls seek advice, help, comfort, or sympathy from others more often than boys do, independent of the type of stressor.

Rauste-von Wright (1987) reported on the basis of a longitudinal study with Scandinavian adolescents that gender differences in coping with stress decreased with age. She asked respondents what they did when they experienced difficulties or trouble at age 13, and again at ages 15 and 18. The coping strategies reported by the adolescents could be grouped into four categories: talking with someone, attempting to manage by oneself, escape-avoidance, and emotional reactions. Escape-avoidance was most salient at age 15, but the type of coping response reported by individual students at the various measurement points remained rather stable. This was especially the case for the strategy of attempting to manage by oneself. Students who reported using escape-avoidance strategies at age 18 had also largely done so at ages 13 and 15. Consonant with the findings reported by Seiffge-Krenke, girls more often sought social support, whereas boys tried to manage by themselves. However, in contrast to the findings reported by Seiffge-Krenke, this difference was most pronounced at age 13 and decreased as the students grew older. This discrepancy could be due to the different ways of measuring social support, but it could also be attributed to cross-cultural differences in self-concept and coping preferences.

Although many developmental tasks are universal, cultures differ in their child-rearing techniques. This may imply that children and adolescents are provided with different models for coping with stressors and are allowed and even stimulated to use different coping strategies. Some studies have been set up to explore these cross-cultural differences. For example, Diaz-Guerrero (1973) supervised a study carried out in eight different countries, among others, Mexico, the United States, Great Britain, and Italy. Findings show that in agricultural societies such as Mexico, adolescents use more passive modes of coping than in industrialized countries, where active modes are more salient. Seiffge-Krenke (1990) reported the results of a cross-cultural study featuring the self-concept and coping behavior of German and Israeli adolescents. She reported that self-related cognitions are comparable with respect to their dimensional structure and to gender differences, but that for coping behavior, cultural differences were more marked. Although active coping and internal coping exceeded withdrawal in both samples, the German sample scored twice as high as the Israeli sample on withdrawal in response to problems in the domains "leisure time" and "self." In stressful situations involving parents and teachers, both samples had about the same withdrawal rate, but Israeli adolescents used significantly more forms of internal coping, whereas German adolescents used more active coping. The same conclusion holds for the domains "opposite sex" and "future." Across all the stressors, the Israeli emphasis on internal forms of coping was twice as high as that in the German sample (44% vs. 22%). In both samples, similar results were noted regarding gender differences: Seeking social support and asking for advice were used significantly more by female adolescents (see also Frydenberg, in press).

A possible explanation for these gender and culture differences may lie in different child-rearing patterns (for a discussion, see Bush & Simmons, 1987). For example, social support may be more readily provided to girls and the reinforcement patterns for soliciting social support from parents may be at variance for boys and girls, and for children in different cultures. Several studies have demonstrated that parents and other members of a youngster's social network are catalysts of coping behavior. For example, a study by Blount et al. (1991) has shown that all children who were undergoing painful medical treatment wanted their parents to be present, but that children who were separated from their parents during the painful procedure displayed less distress than those who underwent the procedure with their parents present. Interestingly, parents of children who coped well with their distress engaged in more behaviors that promoted their child's coping (e.g., distracting conversation, coaching the child in deep breathing) than did the parents of children who had difficulty coping with the stressful situation. Adult behaviors that were associated with increases in child distress were reassurance, agitation or criticism, empathy, and giving control to the child.

It stands to reason that the way in which parents console their children when they are confronted with adversity provides a powerful mechanism for shaping their coping strategies. When attachment figures are always there to take over the regulation of stress, children will not learn to appraise various stressors in terms of their unique dimensions (Table 20.1) and neither will they learn to act on the basis of this information (form context-specific coping intentions and select coping strategies in accordance with these intentions). Further, when parents model or reinforce an urgent, direct-action approach to ongoing stress, the child's behavior will be governed by the determination to reduce stress symptoms as fast as possible (tension reduction). To gain quick control over stressful situations, these children will prefer to use direct actions and thus may get into the habit of alleviating symptoms (primary control) rather than learning to adapt to stressors. By contrast, when children learn to adapt flexibly to upcoming and ongoing daily burdens, a nonurgent approach to stressors will develop. Not only will these children learn to adapt to stressors in a context-sensitive way (e.g., trying to manage by themselves, distracting themselves, or finding relaxation in creative activities and sports), the occurrence of a stressor may not automatically impair their performance by mood disturbance and a decrease in confidence rating (cf. Boekaerts, 1994).

Adaptive and Maladaptive Coping Strategies

A question that has appealed to educators and developmental psychologists is whether youngsters become more effective in dealing with stressful situations as they get older and/or more experienced. This question is difficult to answer because it is nearly impossible to determine unequivocally when a coping strategy is effective or adaptive and when it is not. Successful adaptation to minor and major stressors requires that youngsters achieve a fit between themselves (their internal environment, including perception of personal and social resources, values, motives, and beliefs) and different physical and social environments. The individual's ability to achieve a good fit is based on his or her capacity (a) to represent the stressor adequately (components 1, 2, 3, 4 in Figure 20.1) and (b) to select from the coping repertoire those coping responses that best fit the situational demands (components 5 and 6 in combination with 2 and 3). There are no universally adaptive responses that are suitable for all individuals in all situations all the time. A coping strategy may be adaptive for some youngsters and not for others; it may be effective in a particular context and not in another. The question is always: Does the coping response take account of the demands and constraints of the concrete situation?

On the basis of a meta-analysis of studies on adults' coping with stressful life events, Suls and Fletcher (1986) suggest that avoidance is the superior response to short-term threats, whereas approach is the more effective response when the threat persists over time, mainly because it enables the individual to make cognitive and behavioral efforts to deal with long-term adverse effects. A meta-analysis of studies on coping in youngsters has not yet been carried out. Nevertheless, there is growing evidence that both problem-focused coping and emotion-focused coping are important in successful adaptation to stress. Most researchers studying coping in children and adolescents seem to forget that coping is a mediator between a specific stressor and adjustment variables. They study coping independent of the youngster's representation of the stressor and his or her coping goals and intentions. As mentioned earlier, only studies that take account of the individual's perception of the characteristics of the stressor, can shed some light on the coping process and its success.

A study by Compas et al. (1988) illuminated the effect of the perception of controllability on coping. They reported that older children and young adolescents appraised academic stressors as more controllable than interpersonal stressors. A modest-to-moderate consistency in their use of coping strategies across the two types of stressors was noted, but problem-focused strategies were more frequently used for coping with academic stressors. An increase in the use of emotion-focused coping strategies was noted between 12 and 14 years of age, and girls used more emotion-focused coping in response to academic stressors. Close inspection of the coping strategies revealed that when there was a match between the student's perception of control in a situation and the selected coping mode (e.g., low perceived control and emotion-focused coping, or high perceived control and problem-focused coping) the intensity of reported stress was low, whereas the reverse was true when there was a mismatch. Furthermore, the number of problem-focused coping strategies reported in relation to interpersonal stressors was negatively related to self-reports and maternal reports of emotional and behavioral problems. By contrast, a positive link was noted between the use of emotion-focused strategies and emotional and behavioral problems (cf. Spivack & Shure, 1982).

Following the line of argument put forward by Perrez and Reicherts (1992), judgment about the effectiveness and appropriateness of concrete coping efforts presupposes knowledge about the way in which a person construes the stressor and its consequences, about the knowledge he or she has of coping-relevant features of the stressful event, and about his or her coping intentions. These authors assume that the appropriateness of coping efforts can be judged in terms of a double correspondence, mainly between objective features of the situation and the individuals' subjective representation thereof and between these appraisals and the selected coping strategies. In this framework, maladaptive coping can be caused by perceptual and representational deficits and/or by the nonavailability of coping competencies in spite of appropriate perception and representation. Perrez and Reicherts proposed the following six behavioral rules that link the appraisal and representation of a stressor to the selection stage of coping strategies:

1. If the valence is perceived as high, the changeability as low, but the controllability as high active coping is predicted.
2. If the changeability is perceived as higher than or similar to the controllability, passivity is a likely reaction.
3. If the valence is perceived as high, but both changeability and controllability are perceived as low, escape or avoidance is probable.
4. If the ambiguity of the stressor is perceived as high, active search for information becomes more probable, more so the higher the perceived controllability.
5. If the ambiguity of the stressor is perceived as low but the controllability is also perceived as low, suppression of information becomes more likely.
6. If the controllability of short-term stressors is perceived as low and the valence is perceived as low, a reevaluation of the situation is likely.

To illustrate Rules 1, 2, and 3, an example will be given that is situated at the interface of three domains—"school," "peers," and "teacher":

> Imagine that the math teacher tells Howard that he can get a better grade in math if he is willing to do extra assignments supervised by an assistant teacher. Howard highly values a good grade for math. He also knows that extracurricular work is not endorsed by his friends and against the current school culture. *Rule 1* predicts that Howard will opt for active coping when he believes that he will not get a good enough grade without the extra assignments (low changeability), but that expending effort will guarantee him a better grade (high controllability). Active coping could take on many forms, such as trying to convince one's friends that a good grade in math is absolutely essential to get into a highly valued course. *Rule 2* predicts that Howard will decide to wait and see (lose time in indecision) when he believes that there is a chance that he will get a good enough grade without extra assignments. Finally, *Rule 3* predicts that if Howard believes that extra work is essential (low changeability) but not sufficient (low controllability) to guarantee him a better grade, he may decide that it is not worth a try and give up on ever getting a good grade for math.

Rules 4, 5, and 6 will be exemplified with a vignette from the domains "peers," "leisure time," and "parents":

Imagine that Howard's friends try to persuade him to go on holiday with them to the south of France. Howard would love to go with them, but he knows that there was a lot of trouble last year. Apparently, they met with their French friends who use hard drugs. There are some stories around that they have been picked up by the police for dangerous driving and stealing. But he is not sure what happened exactly. Although Howard highly values a good social support network and does not want to risk losing his buddies, he also does not want to get into trouble with his parents. He finds the situation highly stressful and has postponed the decision for weeks. *Rule 4* predicts that Howard will search for more information when he believes that he can stay out of trouble while being in the south of France (high controllability). *Rule 5* predicts that Howard will suppress information when he doubts whether he will be able to stand his ground. Finally, *Rule 6* predicts that if Howard has doubts about his strengths and weaknesses (low controllability) and can convince himself that he does not really want to go to the south of France (low valence), a reevaluation of the stressful situation will follow.

Most of these rules seem to be in line with the empirical findings presented earlier. For example, Rules 1, 2, and 3 seem to hold true especially for academic stressors. Together, these rules specify that when youngsters are convinced that they can and must do something because the situation will not change for the better, the dominant coping mode will be active coping. On the contrary, when they believe that the situation is uncontrollable, they will opt for a form of avoidance. The findings reported by Compas, Malcarne, and Fondacaro (1988), and by Boekaerts (1993) provide evidence for this prediction. Academic stressors were perceived by older children and young adolescents as more controllable than interpersonal stressors, and more problem-focused coping was reported in response to the former type of stressor. No age or gender differences were apparent. The modest negative correlation between emotion-focused coping and problem-focused coping suggests that students may give preference to either coping mode. Adolescents relied more on emotion-focused coping than did children in response to academic stressors. This finding could be interpreted as indirect evidence that older students differ from younger students in the way they make sense of academic situations (degree of perceived controllability and changeability). Rost and Schermer reported that danger control (a form of problem-focused coping) and anxiety repression (a form of emotion-focused coping) were both dominant coping strategies in older adolescents. This and similar findings suggest that as they grow older, adolescents may display more dual-focused coping, but research needs to further examine how different coping responses are selected from the coping repertoire and combined into a coping strategy as the stressful experience unfolds.

On the basis of the cross-sectional data reported in this chapter, it could be speculated that the younger age groups use less emotion-focused coping than the older groups in relation to academic stressors because they realize that emotion-focused coping is considered by their parents and teachers to be a maladaptive response to controllable stressors. As Macobby remarked, the obedient stance toward adult authority taken by most preadolescents may be a powerful mechanism that protects them from stress. Peers take up a more prominent position in the social support network of older adolescents, and unlike parents and teachers, they may consider emotion-focused coping adaptive when the stressor is over-taxing personal resources. This shared knowledge may explain the increase in emotion-focused coping in response to academic stressors when children are be-tween 12 and 14 years of age.

Rule 3 can also be applied to the studies on uncontrollable medical stressors, where the effectiveness of distraction and reframing (emotion-focused coping) has been well established. In relation to this domain of stressors, older children tended to use a greater number of coping strategies, and more secondary control, than did younger and less experienced children. Rules 5 and 6 can be utilized in relation to interpersonal stressors (cf. example of Howard). It remains a chal-lenge for future research to test these and other related hypotheses in a more sys-tematic way.

Coping responses, however, are not merely triggered by situation characteris-tics. The way youngsters cope with various stressors is also influenced by per-sonality variables that relate to their goals, motives, commitments, and values. For example, a student who perceives a math exam as stressful because he or she appraises the situation as unchangeable and uncontrollable may normally expend little effort to prepare for the exam (in line with Rule 3). Knowing that a partic-ular student wants to please his grandfather with a passing grade helps one un-derstand that the situation has high valence for the student and will prompt him to react with approach instead of with avoidance. In a different situation, a stu-dent who appraises an upcoming exam as important, ambiguous, but controllable, would be expected to approach rather than avoid (Rule 4). When this student fails the exam because she did not prepare well, Rule 4 seems to be violated. Informa-tion about personal goals and motives may provide the missing link to explain her behavior. For example, the student's boyfriend broke up their relationship, and she thought it more important to make it up with her boyfriend than to prevent negative study outcomes.

Personality Characteristic and Coping

Individual differences in personal variables help explain why the same situation may be appraised as a threat by one person and as a challenge by another. Re-searchers in search of factors that condition the effects of stress have identified a number of variables that interact with stress in producing outcome variables. In the discussion of moderator variables, a distinction can be made between variables that are believed to be ameliorative (protective factors) and those that increase vulnerability (risk factors). Although there is an extensive literature on vulnerability and resilience in youngsters (for a review, see Luthar & Zigler, 1991), it is not always clear whether a particular variable should be viewed as a risk factor, as a protective factor, or merely as a variable related to adjustment. From a clinical perspective, one would hope to identify moderator variables that would reduce the impact of stress on adjustment. Studies of "invulnerables" have enabled us to think about capacities and conditions that allow youngsters to handle (multiple) stressors. This type of research (see, e.g., Werner & Smith, 1982) has described several factors that contribute to stress resistance, such as the child's temperament, optimism, perceived personal control, familial factors (family cohesion and shared values, or a loving, patient relationship with at least one parental figure), and the availability of social support.

Several variables have been cataloged as risk factors, including prenatal and birth complications, low intelligence, low self-esteem, being poorly accepted by one's peers, anxiety and neuroticism, and low socioeconomic status. There is ample evidence that youngsters who score high on neuroticism or trait-anxiety experience more negative emotions and cognitions that distract them from the task at hand. Yet, such intrusive feelings and thoughts do not seem to debilitate performance directly but elicit a "costly coping style" (cf. Schönpflug & Battman, 1988). Rauste-von Wright (1987) reported associations between adolescents' preferred coping strategies and their self-rated anxiety and self-esteem. At 13 years of age, those who tried to avoid or escape problems tended to be more anxious than those who tried to manage by themselves. At age 15, youngsters who managed by themselves were less anxious than those who used other coping strategies. At age 18, adolescents who tried to manage by themselves had on average higher self-esteem than those who reacted emotionally or tried to escape or avoid difficulties.

The ways in which various moderators interact with stress in predicting coping and adjustment are still poorly understood. Some investigators have demonstrated the protective effect of specific moderators, whereas other studies have failed to find such effects. A better theoretical framework and more theory-guided research is necessary to understand how person and situation variables are linked to stress, coping with it, and adjustment or maladjustment.

INTERVENTIONS AND DIRECTIONS FOR FUTURE RESEARCH

In the final section of this chapter, some attention will be given to intervention programs. It has been argued so far that successful adaptation to minor and major stressors requires that youngsters achieve a balance between themselves and different physical and social environments, and that the youngster's ability to achieve a good balance is based on his or her capacity (a) to represent the stressor adequately, and (b) to select from the coping repertoire those coping responses that best fit the situational demands. Research has shown that there are wide divergences between the knowledge, spontaneous verbalizations, and preferences voiced by youngsters in various age groups in relation to different coping strategies. In addition, it has become clear that understanding a stressful event and having knowledge about the effectiveness of the coping strategies available in one's coping repertoire do not guarantee that less stress will be experienced or that these coping strategies will be used effectively or flexibly. Hence, intervention programs that are primarily providing youngsters with normative information or with information about the hazards associated with maladaptive coping strategies and the benefits of adaptive strategies are most likely going to fail. Leventhal and Cameron (1994) refer to empirical findings documenting that the behavioral effects of threatening messages are enhanced when they are combined with practicing action information. They urged program constructors to encourage participants to review their own routines in relation to a stressor and identify concrete situations in which new action plans could be inserted. To make sure that these new action plans become part and parcel of their coping repertoire (cf. component 2 of Figure 20.1) and coping preferences (component 3), participants should be given ample opportunity to mentally rehearse or role-play the action in a number of suitable situations.

Most current intervention programs combine the informational approach with techniques that originated in social learning theory and behavior therapy. They can be subdivided into programs tailored to coping with a specific stressor or to the acquisition of specific skills, on the one hand, and multifarious intervention programs on the other. Examples of the former type of intervention programs are the Children of Divorce Intervention Program; Herzfeld and Powell's "Coping for Kids" program; Lord's "Death at School" program; relaxation training; the treatment of school refusal; and Spivack and Shure's Interpersonal cognitive problem-solving skills. Multifarious intervention programs differ from these programs in that they concentrate on the acquisition of several types of skills, including skills to enhance the self-concept; skills to regulate stress, social behavior and motivation; and decision-making skills. Training modules may consist of audiovisual-presented information, modeling exercises, sharing threatening episodes, group discussions, role-play, cooperative learning, posters, making catchy slogans. Most of these programs are school-based, targeted to a specific age group and to the conditions of the participating schools. An example of a multifarious program is Elias's Social Decision Making and Life Skills Development Program. This widely applied program was originally designed to assist children in coping with the transition to middle school by building the necessary skills for both social and academic learning. The present program concentrates on eight primary skill areas: notice feelings in oneself and others; identify issues or problems; determine and select goals; generate alternative solutions; envision possible consequences; select your best solution; plan your actions and make a final check for obstacles; notice what happened and use the information for future decision making and problem solving. For more information on these and other intervention programs and for further references, the reader is referred to Cohen and Fish's (1993) *Handbook of School-Based Interventions*.

Currently, a wide variety of well-validated, interrelated, curriculum-based programs exist for helping teaching staff and parents promote effective coping in youngsters. These programs have been shown to have beneficial effects on several outcome variables, including increases in self-esteem, academic performance, ability to handle academic stress, and ability to deal with social conflict, and decreases in absenteeism and emotional and behavioral problems. Unfortunately, the difference between treatment groups and control groups tends to shrink or disappear in follow-up studies that are conducted some years later.

This is why most program constructors recommend annual booster sessions. There is no clear evidence favoring any particular type of training program over another in specific developmental stages. In the absence of such evidence, I would recommend two basic ways to help children and adolescents to enhance their coping skills and alleviate stress: (a) Make concentrated efforts at the brink of major transition periods; and (b) make self-regulation skills explicit educational targets.

The former type of training could make youngsters more resistent to transition stress. I would like to see major transition periods—physical changes; beginning to go to school, to middle school, or college; first dating; first menstruating; first dealing with disease or handicap; first admission to a hospital—studied as periods of growth in coping skills. In such periods, youngsters are confronted with new challenges, in relation to which their existing adaptive potential may prove to be inadequate or unacceptable. The reason for this is that youngsters may (a) not be able to represent the new stressful episode adequately due to lack of expertise, (b) have low self-efficacy to cope with these new stressors, and (c) lack knowledge of and practice with adequate coping responses. A wealth of data documents the disturbance caused at the beginning of middle school (cf. Elias, 1989; Simmons, Carlton-Ford, & Blyth, 1987). We found (Boekaerts, Seegers, & Van den Goor, 1993) that students who reported stress symptoms in the first few weeks following the transition from elementary school to secondary school highlighted that they felt uncertain and unhappy due to a multitude of stressors, including complex timetables, long hours, complex grading system, quantity of homework, many school subjects each with their own teachers using different methods, evaluation procedures, and management styles. Seven percent of the students did not report stressful episodes. These students emphasized that they were already familiar with the new situation (e.g., because they had an older brother or sister) and that they had a good network of friends in the new school. In a similar vein, Compas et al. (1986) found that 64% of the variance in psychological symptoms at the time of entrance to college could be accounted for by measures administered 3 months earlier: prior symptoms, satisfaction with social support, and life events. Once students were past this transition period (3 months after entering college), neither life events nor social support were predictive of developing symptoms. Compas et al. suggest that leaving home to go to college involves separation from family and friends as well as adjustment to a new environment, including the building up of favorable selves and a new social support system. On the basis of the model of coping presented in Figure 20.1, intervention programs focusing on transition stress should give participants a preview of what to expect and demonstrations of how others have successfully navigated the same transition (modeling). This will allow them to adequately represent the new stressor(s) in terms of the six dimension-wise judgments and identify action plans that they could insert into their own coping repertoire. In addition, they should be given plenty of opportunities to rehearse these action plans either mentally or in a role-play situation, so that they become part of their coping preferences. Youngsters should also be given ample opportunities to build up or extend their social network and experience self-confidence in using that network (e.g., through physical or creative recreation).

The second type of intervention should be carried out in actual classrooms by the regular teachers. I have explained elsewhere (Boekaerts, 1992, 1995) that specific properties of the education system may cause ill-being in students, for example, an emphasis on obligatory commitments rather than on self-related commitments, a focus on norms and set standards rather than on self-assessment, allotting time for teacher-imposed activities and course requirements rather than for student-initiated activities. Such a teacher-dominant school culture may instill in students a sense of low autonomy and low decision latitude. When youngsters experience low task autonomy in class, and low decision authority at home, they may not learn to behave according to self-related commitments. In other words, functional deficits in self-regulation, including coping with stress, may be seen as properties of the educational system (see also Elias, 1989). Nevertheless, there are plenty of opportunities both in the home and at school to provide students with scaffolding for and feedback on context-sensitive ways of dealing with personal strivings and vulnerabilities. In this respect, it is important that educators realize that any spontaneous or systematic learning opportunity finds the learner at a certain level of skill development and at a certain level of confidence in relation to the required skill. As they acquire new knowledge and skills, youngsters should therefore be assisted in developing confidence and in making use of their coping repertoire in a context-sensitive way. On the basis of the model of coping presented in Figure 20.1 students should develop an understanding of different stressful academic and interpersonal stressors and learn to cope with them in a context-sensitive way. The following objectives should be explicitly targeted:

1. To find a way to reduce negative emotions when stress is encountered so that rational thinking becomes possible.
2. To develop the skill to classify and represent various stressors on the basis of the six dimension-wise judgments.
3. To consider alternative actions for different stressors and evaluate the short-term and long-term consequences of these actions.
4. To clarify and reflect on one's coping goals and intentions.
5. To plan and reflect on selected courses of action, and to initiate, monitor, terminate, and evaluate them.

Such a systematic approach to the development and extension of a youngster's coping repertoire may help the child to explore different coping responses and their effect in relation to the new learning skill and its context. Coping strategies that prove to be effective in that context and do not violate personal values may swiftly be incorporated into the individual's coping repertoire, whereas strategies that are deemed effective by the child's parents, teachers, or peers, yet prove to be cumbersome, embarrassing, or unacceptable, may be forgone.

Needed Areas of Research

On the basis of a review of the literature, it became clear that most studies on coping with stress in children and adolescents are cross-sectional in nature. Hence, no causal links can be inferred. Numerous coping scales and checklists have been constructed without a strong theoretical basis. Some of these checklists provide youngsters with specific stressors and measure stressor-specific coping. Others measure coping in response to undefined general concerns, problems, or difficulties without much attention to the characteristics of the stressor. The latter studies cannot provide insight into the complexity of the coping process. Current research on coping in childhood and adolescence suggests first, that emotion-focused coping, internal coping, and secondary control increase with age. Second, there are no consistent developmental changes in problem-focused coping (some studies report no changes in relation to academic stressors; others found that problem-focused coping decreased with age in relation to interpersonal stressors). Third, strategies that reflect an ambivalent reaction pattern (coping attempts that are characterized by both emotion-focused and problem-focused coping) increase with age and are most evident in females and in clinical samples. These findings, which are largely based on cross-sectional research, suggest that during childhood youngsters acquire a direct, urgent form of coping through observational learning. Less observable and more complex forms of coping may be acquired in adolescence when meta-cognitive skills become part and parcel of the self-regulatory system (cf. Boekaerts, 1995).

Efforts should be directed at creating a more comprehensive theoretical model of coping with stress in childhood and adolescence in which the components and the relations between the components depicted in Figure 20.1 are incorporated. Future research on coping with stress in childhood and adolescence must differ from past research in its approach to data collection and analysis. An attempt should be made to construct instruments that can measure coping at various levels, including coping goals, preferences, and intentions as well as the actual selection and timing of coping responses. Greater clarity is needed with regard to the processes through which boys and girls achieve successful coping in various domains at different ages. Only theory-driven research programs can shed light on continuity and discontinuity of (a) the various procedures youngsters use in constructing their stress representations; (b) coping goals, intentions, and preferences within and between stress domains; and (c) the causal role of personality and environmental variables on various aspects of resilience and vulnerability to stress. Other issues that warrant further investigation are the relation between coping with daily hassles and with life events, and the mediating role of coping between domain-specific stressors and adjustment. Intervention studies have provided evidence that coping strategies can be changed and that such training has a positive effect on various indexes of adjustment. What is needed urgently are comprehensive research programs in which longitudinal designs are used to follow youngsters through major transition periods. The aim of this research should be to describe stressor-specific patterns of coping and how they are linked to various outcome variables as the stressful episodes unfold. In addition, it should be researched whether intervening in developmental trajectories yields unequivocal positive results for boys and girls; for gifted and nongifted students, and for youngsters from different ethnic groups. Such an ambitious and challenging task can only be successfully realized through a productive interplay between theory construction and empirical data, including data from intervention studies. I hope that the data reviewed in this chapter will provide a foundation for meeting this challenge.

REFERENCES

Altshuler, J. L., & Ruble, D. N. (1989). Developmental changes in children's awareness of strategies for coping with uncontrollable stress. *Child Development, 60,* 1337–1349.

Blount, R. L., Landolf-Fritsche, B., Powers, S. W., & Sturges, J. W. (1991). Differences between high and low coping children and between parent and staff behaviours during painful medical procedures. *Journal of Pediatric Psychology, 16,* 795–809.

Boekaerts, M. (1992). The adaptable learning process: Initiating and maintaining behavioural change. *Applied Psychology: An International Review, 41*(4), 377–397.

Boekaerts, M. (1993). Being concerned with well-being and with learning. *Educational Psychologist, 28*(2), 149–167.

Boekaerts, M. (1994, April). *The other side of learning: Allocating resources to restore well-being* (ERIC Document No. ED 378 668). Paper presented at the annual conference of the American Educational Research Association, New Orleans, LA.

Boekaerts, M. (1995). The interface between intelligence and personality as determinants of classroom learning. In D. H. Saklofske & M. Zeidner (Eds.), *Handbook of personality and intelligence.* New York: Plenum.

Boekaerts, M., Hendriksen, J., & Maes, S. (1987). *The Stress and Coping Inventory:* Leiden, The Netherlands: Leiden University, Centre for the Study of Education and Instruction.

Boekaerts, M., Seegers, G., & Van den Goor, J. (1993). *Stress bij leerlingen van 12 tot 16 jaar* [Stress in adolescents from 12 to 16 year of age]. Leiden, The Netherlands: Leiden University, Centre for the Study of Education and Instruction.

Brotman Band, E. (1990). Children's coping with diabetes: Understanding the role of cognitive development. *Journal of Pediatric Psychology, 15,* 27–41.

Brotman Band, E., & Weisz, J. R. (1988). How to feel better when it feels bad: Children's perspectives on coping with everyday stress. *Developmental Psychology, 24,* 247–253.

Bush, D. M., & Simmons, R. (1987). Gender and coping with the entry into early adolescence. In R. C. Barnett, L. Biener, & B. K. Baruch (Eds.), *Gender and stress* (pp. 185–218). New York: Free Press.

Caspi, A., Bolger, N., & Eckenrode, J. (1987). Linking person and context in the daily stress process. *Journal of Personality and Social Psychology, 52,* 184–195.

Caty, S., Ellerton, M. L., & Ritchie, J. A. (1984). Coping in hospitalized children: An analysis of published case studies. *Nursing Research, 33,* 277–282.

Cohen, J. J., & Fish, M. C. (1993). *Handbook of school-based interventions.* San Francisco: Jossey-Bass.

Cohen, L. H., Burt, C. E., & Bjorck, J. P. (1987). Life stress and adjustment: Effects of life events experienced by young adolescents and their parents. *Developmental Psychology, 23,* 583–592.

Compas, B. E. (1987). Stress and life events during childhood and adolescence. *Clinical Psychology Review, 7,* 275–302.

Compas, B. E., Malcarne, V. L., & Fondacaro, K. (1988). Coping with stressful events in older children and young adolescents. *Journal of Consulting and Clinical Psychology, 56,* 405–411.

Compas, B. E., Phares, V., & Ledoux, N. (1989). Stress and coping preventive interventions for children and adolescents. In L. A. Bond & B. E. Compas (Eds.), *Primary prevention and promotion in the schools* (pp. 319–340). Newbury Park: Sage.

Compas, B. E., Wagner, B. M., Slavin, L. A., & Vannatta, K. (1986). A prospective study of life events, social support, and psychological symptomatology during the transition from high school to college. *American Journal of Community Psychology, 14,* 241–257.

Diaz-Guerrero, R. (1973). Interpreting coping styles across nations from sex and social class differences. *International Journal of Psychology, 8,* 193–203.

Dise-Lewis, J. E. (1988). The Life Events and Coping Inventory: An assessment of stress in children. *Psychosomatic Medicine, 50,* 484–499.

Elias, M. J. (1989). School as a source of stress to children: An analysis of causal and ameliorative influences. *Journal of School Psychology, 27*(4), 393–407.

Folkman, S., & Lazarus, R. S. (1988). The relationship between coping and emotion: Implications for theory and research. *Social Science & Medicine, 26,* 309–317.

Frydenberg, E. (in press). Coping and its correlates. What the Adolescent Coping Scale tells us. *Australian Educational and Developmental Psychologist.*

Frydenberg, E., & Lewis, R. (1991). Adolescent coping styles and strategies. Is there functional and dysfunctional coping? *Australian Journal of Guidance and Concelling, 1,* 35–43.

Groër, M. W., Thomas, S. P., & Shoffner, D. (1992). Adolescent stress and coping: A longitudinal study. *Research in Nursing & Health, 15,* 209–217.

Jenkins, J. M., Smith, M. A., & Graham, P. J. (1989). Coping with parental quarrels. *Journal of the American Academy of Child and Adolescent Psychiatry, 28,* 182–189.

Johnson, J. H. (1986). *Life events as stressors in childhood and adolescence.* Beverly Hills, CA: Sage.

Karraker, K. H., & Lake, M. (1991). Normative stress and coping processes in infancy. In E. M. Cummings, A. L. Greene, & K. H. Karraker (Eds.), *Life-span developmental psychology. Perspectives on stress and coping* (pp. 85–109). Hillsdale, NJ: Erlbaum.

La Greca, A. M. (1990). Issues and perspectives on the child assessment process. In A. M. La Greca (Ed.), *Through the eyes of the child: Obtaining self-report from children and adolescents* (pp. 3–17). Boston: Allyn and Bacon.

Leventhal, H., & Cameron, L. (1994). Persuasion and health attitudes. In S. Shavitt & T. C. Brock (Eds.), *Persuasion: Psychological insights and perspectives* (pp. 219–249). Boston: Allyn and Bacon.

Luthar, S. S., & Zigler, E. (1991). Vulnerability and competence: A review of research on resilience in childhood. *American Journal of Orthopsychiatry, 61*(1), 6–22.

Macobby, E. E. (1983). Social-emotional development and response to stressors. In N. Garmezy & M. Rutter (Eds.), *Stress, coping and development in children* (pp. 217–234). New York: McGraw-Hill.

Mischel, W. (1974). Processes in delay of gratification. In L. Berkowitz (Ed.), *Advances in experimental social psychology* (Vol. 7, pp. 249–292). New York: Academic Press.

Perrez, M., & Reicherts, M. (1992). *Stress, coping, and health*. Seattle, WA: Hogrefe & Huber.

Rauste-von Wright, M. (1987). *On the life process among Finnish adolescents: Summary report of a longitudinal study*. Helsinki, Finland: Societas Scientiorun Fennica.

Rost, D. H., & Schermer, F. J. (1987). The assessment of coping with test anxiety. In R. Schwarzer, H. M. van der Ploeg, & C. B. Spielberger (Eds.), *Advances in test anxiety research* (Vol. 6, pp. 179–191). Amsterdam: Stwets & Zeitlinger.

Rost, D. H., & Schermer, F. J. (1992). "Reactions to tests" (RTT) and "manifestations of test-anxiety" (DAI-MAN): Same or different concepts. In K. A. Hagtvet & T. Backer Johnsen (Eds.), *Advances in test anxiety research* (Vol. 7, pp. 114–129). Amsterdam: Stwets & Zeitlinger.

Rothbaum, F., Weisz, J. R., & Snijder, S. S. (1982). Changing the world and changing the self: A two-process model of perceived control. *Journal of Personality and Social Psychology, 42*, 5–37.

Rutter, M. (1983). Stress, coping, and development: Some issues and some questions. In N. Garmezy & M. Rutter (Eds.), *Stress coping and development in children* (pp. 1–41). New York: McGraw-Hill.

Ryan, N. M. (1989). Stress-coping strategies identified from school age children's perspective. *Research in Nursing & Health, 12*, 111–122.

Ryan-Wenger, N. M. (1992). A taxonomy of children's coping strategies: A step toward theory development. *American Journal of Orthopsychiatry, 62*(2), 256–263.

Schönpflug, W., & Battman, W. (1988). The costs and benefits of coping. In S. Fisher & J. Reason (Eds.), *Handbook of life stress, cognition and health* (pp. 699–713). New York: Wiley.

Seiffge-Krenke, I. (1990). Developmental processes in self-concept and coping behaviour. In H. Bosma & S. Jackson (Eds.), *Coping and self-concept in adolescence* (pp. 51–68). Berlin, Germany: Springer.

Seiffge-Krenke, I. (1993). Coping behavior in normal and clinical samples: More similarities than differences? *Journal of Adolescence, 16*, 285–303.

Simmons, R. G., Carlton-Ford, S. L., & Blyth, D. A. (1987). Predicting how a child will cope with the transition to junior high school. In R. M. Lerner & T. T. Foch (Eds.), *Biological-psychological interactions in early adolescence: A life-span perspective* (pp. 1–6). Hillsdale, NJ: Erlbaum.

Spirito, A., Stark, L. J., Grace, N., & Stamoulis, D. (1991). Common problems and coping strategies reported in childhood and early adolescence. *Journal of Youth and Adolescence, 20*, 531–544.

Spivack, G., & Shure, M. B. (1982). The cognition of social adjustment: Interpersonal cognitive problem solving thinking. In B. B. Lahey & A. E. Kazdin (Eds.), *Advances in clinical child psychology* (Vol. 5, pp. 323–372). New York: Plenum.

Stark, L. J., Spirito, A., Williams, C., & Guevremont, D. (1989). Common problems and coping strategies. *Journal of Abnormal Child Psychology, 17,* 203–212.

Suls, J., & Fletcher, B. (1986). The relative efficacy of avoidant and nonavoidant coping strategies: A meta-analysis. *Health Psychology, 4,* 249–288.

Wagner, B. M., Compas, B. E., & Howell, D. C. (1988). Daily and major life events: A test of an integrative model of psychosocial stress. *American Journal of Community Psychology, 16,* 189–205.

Werner, E. E., & Smith, R. S. (1982). *Vulnerable but invincible: A study of resilient children.* New York: McGraw-Hill.

Wertlieb, D., Weigel, C., & Feldstein, M. (1987). Stress, social support, and behavior symptoms in middle childhood. *Journal of Clinical Child Psychology, 16*(3), 204–211.

CHAPTER 21

Age Differences, Coping, and the Adult Life Span

STEPHEN STRACK and HERMAN FEIFEL

Our aim in this chapter is to look at the broad horizon of the adult life span to find clues to the role that age plays in the process of adaptation. To gaze steadily and well across such an expanse requires distance. From the point of view of writing a succinct chapter, this means that we shall cover a lot of territory in a brief space and must distill many elements. Wherever meaningful, we shall direct readers to sources that provide greater depth of coverage. The chapter is divided into four sections. The first covers theories, models, and hunches provided by a number of influential thinkers concerning age-related processes in coping. The second addresses methodological issues in studying interactions between coping and age. The third presents current research findings, and the fourth offers a summary and suggestions for future research.

CHANGES IN COPING ASSOCIATED WITH AGE: DEVELOPMENTAL AND SITUATIONALIST PERSPECTIVES

Researchers and clinicians in the area of aging and coping are guided by a variety of theories, models, and hunches offered by a number of theorists and empiricists over the past 50 years. Most of these provide *developmental* perspectives, that is, ways of viewing adaptation within the context of individual growth over the life span. Essentially, these ideas have been offered by ego analysts who posited a relationship between chronological or physical age, intrapsychic functioning, and coping behavior. In the past 30 years, a second group of investigators have emerged with views of aging and coping that focus on individual responses to specific stress encounters. These *situationalist* conceptions downplay intrapsychic processes and typically do not specify age-related changes in adaptation. Rather, they focus on the phenomenological and socioenvironmental context of the stress-coping process, in particular, the role of stress appraisal in the activation of coping behavior.

Contemporary developmental models of aging and coping are reflected in the work of Carl Jung (e.g., 1933, 1959). Informed by empirical study, self-analysis, and clinical observation, he viewed human beings as innately driven toward fulfillment of endowed potentials. From birth to death, we are engaged in a maturational process that he termed *individuation.* Akin to ripening, aging was viewed as a dynamic process by which we achieve greater differentiation and integration of selfhood. Conceived in terms of steps or stages, Jung saw adult development as a dialectical process. Advancing age brings new tasks to be mastered. By grappling with these tasks, we further our ability to cope and increase our comprehension of the meaning of life. Old age is a time of fulfillment when—at least psychologically and spiritually—we are at the apex of our existence.

Erik Erikson (1963) also viewed aging and coping in terms of life-span development. He envisioned eight stages that bring critical tasks to be mastered. As we mature biologically, our coping abilities are challenged in new ways. Although Jung saw the development process as being primarily motivated from within the individual, Erikson perceived external reality as equally motivational. Ready or not, we must acquire a sense of individual identity in adolescence and a sense of meaning and purpose in adulthood. According to Erikson, if we successfully grapple with life challenges as they are presented, we further develop and strengthen our coping abilities so we are better able to contend with succeeding challenges. For example, development of a secure identity provides us with critical skills that are required to integrate intimate relationships as adults. Similar to Jung, Erikson viewed the ultimate outcome of this process as one of fulfillment and harmony in later years. Unlike Jung, however, Erikson emphasized that individual differences in endowed abilities, along with social circumstances, profoundly affect life outcomes. Thus, although Erikson conceptualized aging in terms of enhancement of coping skills, for him aging, in itself, did not automatically result in positive growth.

On the basis of a number of cross-cultural investigations, David Guttman (1964, 1974, 1987) noted that individuals are inclined to move from active coping in early adulthood to passive coping and a form of "magical mastery" beginning at age 50. He surmised that these changes reflect internal psychodynamic processes as well as physical aging processes. Accompanying physical deterioration that usually begins in middle age, there is a spreading psychic regression and disengagement from the outside world. This results in what Guttman called a "country of old men," namely, a group of persons who are relatively withdrawn, focused inward, and settled in "a dominion that they do not share even with their own sons" (1974, p. 118). This does not mean that old persons are bereft of good coping skills; in fact, passive coping and magical mastery may well be suited to the types of circumstances that many old people face, for example, physical limitations, shrinking social resources, and chronic illness.

Clinical attention, and study of both healthy and ill elderly persons, led Eric Pfeiffer (1977) to assert that aging brings along with it increased use of regressed and primitive coping mechanisms. Throughout childhood and into young adulthood people typically develop an increasingly involved set of coping mechanisms. Healthy young adults may be considered at the height of their coping power, at once possessing physical and mental strength and the inclination to use a full repertoire of mature, high-level coping skills such as active mastery. Although some persons continue to use a wide range of adaptive coping mechanisms through middle age and into old age, "most return to the use of more primitive . . . types of defense mechanisms . . . [such as] depression-withdrawal, projection, somatization, and denial. . . ." (p. 651). Characteristically rigid and inflexible, many older persons are susceptible to psychopathology and need assistance from younger family members or professionals.

George Vaillant's (1976, 1977; G. L. Vaillant, Bond, & C. D. Vaillant, 1986) longitudinal studies have led him to conclude that use of healthy, mature coping strategies increases markedly from age 20 through middle adulthood. Vaillant believes that coping resources evolve primarily during childhood and adolescence in tandem with other physical and cognitive maturational processes. However, rather than stagnate and decline during adulthood as some physical attributes do, coping resources continue to mature slowly through the elderly years. As with Erikson (1963), Vaillant views life demands as having potentially salutary effects on coping, with successful coping further enhancing the utility of existing resources. At least among fairly healthy persons, aging is associated with greater use of such coping mechanisms as suppression, sublimation, altruism, anticipation, and humor, and decreased use of such presumed immature mechanisms as projection, denial, and repression.

In contrast with ego-analytic interpretations of coping, Richard Lazarus and his associates (Folkman, 1991; Lazarus, 1966; Lazarus & Folkman, 1984) developed a phenomenological-situationalist view of adapting to stress. In their model, coping is defined as what the person thinks and does to manage the demands of a particular encounter—no attempt is made to infer unconscious dynamics. Coping is perceived as a changing process that is not necessarily related to personality traits or ingrained dispositions. Furthermore, effectiveness and maturity of coping efforts are evaluated in the context of the situation in which the stress arises. Thus, no coping strategy is judged to be "good" or "mature" in and of itself; the overall value of an individual's coping efforts must be examined in reference to the demands, constraints, and resources of the particular context. In this model, age may affect stress appraisal and thus choice of coping strategies, but aging is not considered a major determinant of adaptation behavior or coping effectiveness. Across the life span, people are expected to use a wide variety of potent problem-focused and emotion-focused coping strategies to adapt to shifting stressors.

Another situationalist view of adaptation was offered by Robert McCrae and Paul Costa (Costa & McCrae, 1993; Costa, Zonderman, & McCrae, 1991; McCrae, 1989; McCrae & Costa, 1990). Their empirical work suggested that coping, like personality, changes little during adulthood. Individuals who are competent in managing everyday life events by age 30 are very likely to remain competent in accommodating to fluctuating vicissitudes through old age.

Conversely, those who exhibit coping deficiencies in early adulthood are likely to remain inadequate throughout their lives unless interventions are made. These researchers interpret the adaptation process similarly to Lazarus but believe that personality can strongly effect both appraisal of stress and choice of coping strategies. For example, individuals high on traits of neuroticism may succumb more readily to pressure than other people because of their emotional sensitivity and low threshold for negative affect.

There are also a number of additional theorists and researchers whose work impacts our current conceptions of coping across the adult life span. Space limitations prevent us from covering them adequately here, but the interested reader will do well to seek out P. B. Baltes and M. M. Baltes (1990), Block (1971), Haan (1977), Havighurst (1972), Loevinger (1976), Millon (1969, 1981, 1990), Moos (1986; Moos & Schaefer, 1993), B. L. Neugarten (1972, 1977; B. L. Neugarten & D. A. Neugarten, 1986), Shanan (1990), and Thomae (1987; Rudinger & Thomae, 1990).

METHODOLOGICAL ISSUES

In spite of the differing viewpoints delineated in the preceding section, most investigators in the field agree that coping and age are intertwined (e.g., Feifel & Strack, 1989; Lazarus & Folkman, 1984; Moos & Schaefer, 1993; Thomae, 1987). It is generally agreed that human beings develop and change physically and psychologically throughout adulthood and, at the same time, life brings new demands to be mastered. There is awareness that individuals vary greatly in how they grapple with stress and trauma at different time points, and that intraindividual differences in coping should be given scrutiny as well as differences between individuals and among age groups. Furthermore, the age-coping association must be considered within a larger context of society, culture, and physical environment.

Experimental, Nonexperimental, Cross-Sectional, and Longitudinal Designs

Age and coping are linked with many sorts of variables, and it is doubtful that any single methodology can capture all the contributory elements involved. Nevertheless, well-designed experimental studies can yield relatively unambiguous findings and intimate causative relationships between variables. They are typically limited, however, to narrowly defined problems that are amenable to investigation in restricted settings such as the laboratory. Also, experimental results are often difficult to generalize to real-life circumstances. Nonexperimental studies, on their part, do not require random sampling and there is usually little manipulation of study variables. As a result, findings are often unclear, and causation cannot be directly inferred. On the plus side, nonexperimental studies permit investigation of a wider range of problems (for a discussion of the strengths and limitations of various research designs, see Kazdin, 1992).

Experimental and nonexperimental studies can be either cross-sectional or longitudinal in nature. Cross-sectional studies normally use two or more groups of subjects that are similar on all variables except those under inspection. In the age-coping area, groups usually differ in age but are matched on other important demographic variables such as gender and socioeconomic status. By comparing the behavior and self-reported tendencies of people in the groups, investigators can ferret out relevant differences and similarities based on the grouping variable(s). However, even when cross-sectional age groups are thoroughly matched, significant differences found between them may still be accounted for by cohort effects. Cohort effects refer to differences between generations of people. Individuals in the same age group (cohorts) are considered to have a number of things in common because of their shared sociocultural-environmental upbringing. Individuals of different generations may exhibit significant divergences in type and level of education received and in varying attitudes. Physical and emotional disparities may also be apparent across generations because of particular hardships that are unique to certain age groups, such as an economic depression and war. Because generations may be dissimilar with respect to physical and emotional resources, as well as in the kinds of stress encountered, coping behavior may well differ across age groups.

Longitudinal studies, in which one or more groups of people are followed over extended periods of time, bypass cohort effects. Measures are taken at various time intervals and results are examined in terms of age changes within individuals (or within cohorts). Longitudinal investigations can address theoretical formulations that posit changes over significant periods of time, for example, those of Jung, Erikson, Pfeiffer, and Vaillant. Because of unpredictable events that can impact both subjects and investigators in longitudinal studies, it can be quite difficult to prove that age per se was a substantial cause of observed changes (Tomlinson-Keasey, 1993).

Measurement

Just as there is no consensus concerning the best way to conceptualize coping, there is no accepted taxonomy of coping responses. Coping measures currently available to researchers and clinicians vary greatly in their derivation, application, and the number and types of coping responses assessed (for recent reviews, see Haan, 1993; Moos & Schaefer, 1993; Parker & Endler, 1992). For example, although most instruments were developed specifically to measure coping responses, many were created for broader purposes, such as evaluating personality, ego resources, and defense mechanisms. In addition, a number of instruments have scales with the same or similar names even though item content may be quite dissimilar across measures.

The kind of assessment device the researcher chooses will be determined largely by his or her concepts about the nature of coping and the types of stress situations to be examined. Psychoanalytic conceptualizations usually focus on intrapsychic adaptation processes. In addition to the *Thematic Apperception Test,*

Rorschach, and sentence completion measures, psychodynamic researchers have frequently used the *Defense Style Questionnaire* (DSQ) (Bond, Gardner, Christian, & Sigel, 1983; Bond et al., 1989) and *Defense Mechanisms Inventory* (DMI) (Cramer, 1988; Ihilevich & Gleser, 1986), to assess generalized coping styles conceived in terms of ego defenses. The DSQ measures maladaptive, image-distorting, self-sacrificing, and mature response styles. The DMI assesses projection, intellectualization, reversal, turning against object, and turning against self.

Carver, Scheier, and Weintraub (1989) recently developed a theory-based, multidimensional inventory called COPE to measure dispositional forms of coping. Subjects are asked to respond to 60 statements on 4-point Likert scales in terms of what they "generally do and feel" when experiencing stressful encounters. The inventory contains 15 four-item scales that appraise problem-focused and emotion-focused coping, venting of emotions, behavioral disengagement, and mental disengagement. Although COPE has been used most frequently to measure generalized coping styles, instructions can be altered to assess responses to single stress encounters.

A number of promising measures have recently been developed to gauge situation-specific coping. General situations can be examined with the *Coping Inventory for Stressful Situations* (Endler & Parker, 1990, 1991), which assesses task-oriented, emotion-oriented, and avoidance-oriented coping; the *Coping Responses Inventory* (Moos, 1992), which measures logical analysis, guidance and support seeking, cognitive avoidance, and seeking alternative rewards; and the *Ways of Coping Questionnaire* (Folkman & Lazarus, 1988), which taps confrontation, distancing, self-control, social support seeking, acceptance of responsibility, escape-avoidance, planful problem-solving, and positive reappraisal. Each of these instruments asks subjects to respond vis-à-vis a single, self-selected stressful event that occurred in the recent past. Responses to multiple stressors can be obtained by having subjects complete the inventory for a number of different encounters. The *Life Situations Inventory* (Feifel & Strack, 1989) provides coping measures of problem solving, avoidance, and resignation. It is somewhat different from other instruments in that subjects are asked to record their coping responses to stressful events that occurred in five well-defined conflict areas: decision making, defeat in competition, general frustration, dealing with authority figures, and peer disagreement. Responses to the five specific conflicts can be compared with one another, or they can be summed to provide measures of generalized coping.

Instruments developed specifically for studying adaptation to illness include the *Medical Coping Modes Questionnaire* (Feifel, Strack, & Nagy, 1987a, 1987b), which has scales to assess confrontation, avoidance, and acceptance-resignation, and the *Coping with Health, Injuries, and Problems Scale* (Endler, Parker, & Summerfeldt, 1992), which evaluates distraction, palliative coping, instrumental coping, and negative emotion. Both of these instruments ask subjects to respond in reference to a current problem.

RECENT RESEARCH FINDINGS

Cross-Sectional Studies

One of the first modern cross-sectional studies to examine coping and aging was conducted by Pearlin and Schooler (1978) with a sample of 2,300 men and women between the ages of 18 and 65 who were representative of residents in the Chicago area. Subjects were asked to report typical stressors and to indicate their use of 17 coping responses. Several age differences were noted. For example, in coping with marital problems, older people were less likely to seek advice from others and more likely to engage in controlled reflection than were young adults. Effective coping was noted in most subjects, and neither the young nor old appeared to have an advantage in this regard.

Billings and Moos (1981) found no reliable association between aging and coping in their sample of fairly healthy San Francisco Bay Area residents. They studied the responses of 338 primarily young and middle-aged men and women (mean age 43–45 years) who were asked to recall stressful events that occurred in the recent past. Subjects of all ages used a variety of coping methods (active-cognitive, active-behavioral, and avoidance) that were both problem focused and emotion focused.

Quayhagen and Quayhagen (1982) measured the interpersonal coping strategies of healthy, middle-class men ($n = 77$) and women ($n = 141$) ranging in age from 40 to 70 years. Grouping subjects by decades, they found that 60- to 70-year-olds used more affective coping and less problem-solving coping than 40- to 50-year-olds and 50- to 60-year-olds. The three age groups were found to differ with respect to help-seeking, with the youngest group reporting more help-seeking than the middle group, and the oldest group reporting less help-seeking than the youngest and middle groups. A significant gender difference was also noted, with women using more help-seeking than men across all age groups. Comparing relative use of coping strategies, Quayhagen and Quayhagen reported that problem solving was the most frequently used method for handling interpersonal stress among all subjects.

Bäckman and Molander (e.g., 1986a, 1986b, 1991) conducted a series of experimental studies that focused on age differences in performance and physiological arousal among young, middle-aged, and elderly miniature golf players. Under competitive conditions they consistently found that middle-aged and elderly persons coped less well than did younger persons. Older players exhibited a decline in performance skills, greater physiological arousal (e.g., increased heart rate), and more self-reported anxiety than younger players. They attributed the poorer coping skills of the middle-aged and elderly subjects to age-related declines in task-relevant cognitive abilities such as concentration and memory.

Everyday problem-solving skills were examined by Cornelius and Caspi (1987) in a well-educated, central New York community sample of 126 men and women, ages 20 to 78. They had subjects record their responses to a number of hypothetical problem situations, for example, dealing with a landlord about repairs and being passed over for a job promotion. Coping responses were categorized in terms of problem-focused action, cognitive problem analysis, passive-dependent behavior, avoidant thinking, and denial. In addition, trained judges rated the effectiveness of coping responses to each situation. Results showed that use of effective problem-solving skills increased steadily with age. Young adults (20–34) were significantly less effective than the older adults (55–78), whereas middle-aged subjects (35–54) placed between the young and old.

In the realm of medical illness, Felton and Revenson (1987) studied coping in 151 men and women, ages 41 to 89, who suffered from chronic hypertension, rheumatoid arthritis, diabetes, and cancer. Using the original version of the *Ways of Coping Questionnaire,* they found minor but significant age differences in the use of information seeking, emotional expression, and self-blame, but not in cognitive restructuring, wish-fulfilling fantasy, or threat minimization. Contrasted with middle-aged subjects, the elderly used information seeking, emotional expression, and self-blame less often in managing their illnesses.

Feifel, Strack, and Nagy (1987a) used the *Medical Coping Modes Questionnaire* to measure use of confrontation, avoidance, and acceptance-resignation coping in a sample of 223 middle-aged men, ages 40 to 64, suffering from a variety of chronic and life-threatening illnesses. They found no relationship between age and frequency of use of coping modes. Patients of all ages favored use of confrontation over avoidance and acceptance-resignation.

Coping responses, ego development, and defense mechanisms were studied by Labouvie-Vief, Hakim-Larson, and Hobart (1987) in 100 upper-middle-class male and female subjects ranging in age from 10 to 77. Using a composite score based on coping response and defense maturity, they found age-related improvements in coping-defending during childhood and young adulthood but not during the adult years. However, when the variables of ego level and source of stress were used as predictors of developmental change in coping-defending, they indicated that developmentally mature adults used less escape-avoidance and distancing coping as they grew older (into the elderly years).

Folkman and colleagues (Folkman, Lazarus, Pimley, & Novacek, 1987) compared the everyday coping responses of 75 married couples, ages 35 to 44, with those of 141 men and women ranging in age from 65 to 74. Eight types of coping responses were scored based on a revised *Ways of Coping Questionnaire.* Individual differences in response rates were controlled by statistical analyses. They found that younger adults used proportionately more confrontation, social support seeking, and planful problem solving than did the older adults. On their side, older subjects used more distancing, acceptance of responsibility, and positive reappraisal than did the younger subjects. In an earlier study, Folkman and Lazarus (1980) discovered no relationship between age and coping in a sample of 100 fairly healthy, primarily white, middle-aged (45–64) men and women. This research differed from their later work in that here they measured only two forms of coping (problem-focused and emotion-focused), and used raw scores rather than proportions, which may have masked potential age differences.

Irion and Blanchard-Fields (1987; see also Blanchard-Fields & Irion, 1988) examined the relationship between age, coping, and perceived control in a healthy community sample of 60 males and females ranging in age from 14 to 46. They found that younger subjects endorsed more emotion-focused strategies than older subjects, irrespective of whether the stressor was appraised as controllable. Older participants employed problem-focused coping more frequently than emotion-focused coping in stressful situations perceived as controllable, and emotion-focused coping more frequently than problem-focused coping in situations perceived as uncontrollable.

The coping responses of community dwelling middle-aged (40–64 years, $n = 76$) and elderly (65–92 years, $n = 106$) men to five well-defined, everyday conflict situations were investigated by Feifel and Strack (1989). Findings showed a significant interaction between age, coping, and type of stressful situation. Elderly persons used avoidance coping significantly less often than did middle-aged persons in handling decision making and authority-conflict situations, but not when managing defeat in competition, general frustration, and peer disagreement. No differences were noted between the age groups in use of problem solving or resignation. Both middle-aged and elderly subjects favored use of problem solving in managing all types of conflict.

A multivariate analysis that included age, coping responses, and coping efficacy was conducted by Aldwin (1991). Findings were based on the questionnaire responses of 228 community-dwelling men and women, 18 to 78 years of age, who were essentially college-educated whites. She reported that older persons used escapist coping techniques less frequently than did younger adults. Older persons were also found to be just as effective in managing conflict situations as were their younger counterparts.

Costa, Zonderman, and McCrae (1991) reported correlations between age and self-reported use of a number of defense mechanisms in men and women volunteers between the ages of 20 to 92 (n ranged from 182 to 477). Age was positively associated with use of principalization, reversal, repression, denial, intellectualization, and self-sacrifice, and negatively associated with turning against object, projection, and maladaptive action. There was no relationship between age and use of turning against self, regression, displacement, projection, doubt, image distortion, and adaptive responding. Generally, older people appeared to be less prone to frustration and more willing to meet adversity cheerfully than did younger persons.

Findings from these cross-sectional studies suggest that more often than not, age differences in coping exist among young, middle-aged, and elderly persons when dealing with everyday life situations and medical illnesses. The strength and direction of the age-coping association is not entirely clear because of differing samples, measures, and the stress situations involved. For example, increased use of problem solving was sometimes found to be positively correlated with age (Cornelius & Caspi, 1987; Irion & Blanchard-Fields, 1987) and sometimes not (Feifel & Strack, 1989; Folkman et al., 1987). Nevertheless, people of all ages appear to use a variety of coping strategies in managing stress, and many favor a problem-solving approach over other coping tactics.

Longitudinal Studies

As noted previously, because generations differ in such areas as education and exposure to stress, there is reason to believe that cohort effects may confound the results of numerous cross-sectional studies. The only investigations that can truly bypass cohort effects are longitudinal. Few longitudinal studies have focused on adaptation, and most of these were not designed to assess coping responses directly. For example, the classic investigations of Helson (Helson, 1967; Helson & Wink, 1992), Terman (e.g., Terman & Oden, 1959), Thomae (1987; Rudlinger & Thomae, 1990), and Shanan (1990) were set up primarily to study adult development and personality. Although data from these studies can be obliquely coupled with mainstream coping literature, findings are frequently vague and difficult to interpret in a coping context.

G. L. Vaillant's (1976, 1977; G. L. Vaillant et al., 1986) model of coping and aging (presented earlier) was based on a 40-year prospective study of the ego defenses and psychological health of 95 well-functioning men. Vaillant categorized subjects' coping responses to a variety of situations in terms of 18 ego defenses. The defenses were arranged in a hierarchy from least adaptive to most adaptive, and further categorized as psychotic (e.g., denial of external reality, distortion), immature (e.g., projection, unrealistic fantasy), neurotic (e.g., repression, reaction formation), and mature (e.g., sublimation, suppression). Examined from the point of view of three age categories: adolescence (less than 20 years), young adulthood (20–35 years), and middle adulthood (over 35 years), Vaillant described a clear increase in the use of mature coping mechanisms, and a corresponding decrease in the use of immature mechanisms, from adolescence to middle adulthood. Consistent with his view that maturational processes stabilize during adulthood, the change in coping behavior from adolescence to young adulthood was more striking than that from young adulthood to middle adulthood.

McCrae (1989) reported on a 7-year follow-up of two cross-sectional studies that he conducted in 1980 (McCrae, 1982). He gave a 118-item coping questionnaire based on the original *Ways of Coping Questionnaire* to 398 fairly healthy men and women ranging in age from 20 to 93. Approximately half of the sample had completed the questionnaire 7 years earlier. Responses were scored for 28 specific coping mechanisms and two broad factors of neurotic and mature coping. To rule out as many potential confounds as possible, cross-sequential and time-sequential investigations were conducted in addition to longitudinal analyses. Cross-sequential analyses compare groups of people born at the same time but tested at different times. Because of this, cohort and practice effects can be ruled out. Time-sequential analyses compare individuals tested at the same ages but at different times, and allow for an estimation of time-of-measurement effects. Cross-sectional results evidenced modest age and cohort differences in the use of several coping mechanisms. For example, older persons were less likely to use expression of feelings, escapist fantasy, positive thinking, and hostile reaction than younger persons. However, longitudinal and cross-sequential results revealed no consistent age-related differences in the use of coping mechanisms. Seven-year test-retest coefficients showed a surprising degree of stability for some of the strategies (e.g., neurotic coping $r = .51–.55$; withdrawal $r = .33–.55$; expression of feeling $r = .39–.43$). McCrae concluded that aging had little overall effect on his subjects' use of coping modes.

Vaillant's and McCrae's studies are rather different, so direct comparison between them is perplexing. Nevertheless, their findings point to some measure of stability in the use of major coping mechanisms, and that developmental changes in adaptive behavior may continue as we age, albeit more gradually. One should recall that McCrae's work covered a relatively narrow 7-year period, and Vaillant's conclusions were based on subjects who had not yet attained elderly status.

SUMMARY AND FUTURE DIRECTIONS

The relationship between aging and coping is manifestly complex so that it will be some time before we can put all the puzzle pieces together. Certainly, it is premature to make summary judgments about the role that aging may play in adaptation (cf. Costa & McCrae, 1993). This overview of coping and aging suggests that the field awaits the emergence of a paradigm that can offer a competent explanation for adaptive behavior within a biopsychosocial context, and a satisfactory taxonomy of coping responses. At this point, we have a variety of models, theories, glimmers, and measurement devices that conceptualize and assess the age-coping relation quite differently. Most of the models and methods appear equally viable at this stage because no resolving research is available, and because of the difficulty in meaningfully combining empirical evidence across studies. Current findings do not clearly support either an age-graded developmentalist or situationalist interpretation of coping. Both of these viewpoints appear to underline valuable aspects of the equation, but the essence of their explanatory power appears maximized in an *interactionist* perspective of their individual contributions (cf. Feifel & Strack, 1989). Further, there is no robust answer as to whether people cope better or worse as they age. However, it appears that those who cope well tend to employ a wide range of strategies (cf. Weisman, 1984). Future research would also benefit from a focus on age changes within groups of people as well as on changing intraindividual constellations over the adult life span.

What momentum there is in the field has been shaped primarily by the work of Lazarus and his colleagues, most notably in the area of measurement (Folkman

& Lazarus, 1988; Lazarus & Folkman, 1984). Lazarus's situationalist approach posits that the way we appraise stress determines how we respond to it, but it is somewhat atheoretical with respect to the types and kinds of coping behavior that people use. Because of this, he cast his nets widely in conceptualizing and measuring adaptation responses. The *Ways of Coping Questionnaire* was initially developed to measure as many kinds of coping responses as he and his colleagues thought were empirically viable. Although the inventory itself has been criticized on a number of fronts, many others have followed this broad-based approach with good results (e.g., Endler & Parker, 1991; McCrae, 1982, 1989).

Before we begin narrowing our sights on a single group of parsimoniously defined strategies we need to be certain that we are capturing the entire range of variability in adaptation. We expect that continued endeavors to develop measures of coping that are not bound by strict theories will be helpful in moving us toward the goal of creating a satisfactory taxonomy of adaptation responses. Such an approach is responsible for substantial gains made in developing a taxonomy of normal personality traits (John, 1990). This is not to gainsay the importance of continuing efforts to link methodology to a theory-based milieu.

It is also important to develop better standards for age classifications across the life span. In this regard, we can no longer afford to categorize elderly persons into one "65 years-of-age and older" unit. Neugarten (1977) and others have suggested that we distinguish the *young–old* (65–74 years) from the *old–old* (75 + years). Although this dichotomy may prove to be overly simplistic, it can serve to sensitize us in differentiating this heterogeneous group of persons (cf. Feifel & Strack, 1987).

Much of the coping literature is based on subjects' retrospective reports of their responses to single stress events. As we are now aware, people of different ages cope the same in some situations and differently in others. Future studies must focus on accommodation to multiple stressor from a variety of domains (e.g., work, family, peer relationships). In addition, we must study coping *in medias res,* that is, while subjects are in the throes of contending with their stressful situations (cf. Feifel, 1990).

Just as we must be more sensitive to age groupings and the type of stress encounters measured, research efforts must become more seasoned in assessing multiple determinants of coping behavior. Although it is widely recognized that dispositional factors such as personality, and demographic, physical, social, and environmental variables contribute to adaptation behavior, only a few studies have attempted to examine the interaction of these variables. More investigations of this type are required before we can fully comprehend the forces that shape adaptation responses, and the role of coping behavior within the larger context of human functioning.

Most people cope fairly successfully with the vicissitudes of life. Some, however, find that their skills are not adequate for managing particular life crises, such as a divorce or retirement, or that their coping resources have been attenuated due to accident, illness, financial difficulties, and the like. Developing coping interventions that address age-related changes is an important goal for researchers and clinicians. In this respect, empirical findings have demonstrated a number of physical changes that occur during adulthood and old age that may impact considerably on coping efforts. As people age, some cannot necessarily perform physically and mentally as well as they did when they were younger. Rehabilitation programs must consider that older persons cannot bring into play certain coping responses, and that the ability of a number of people to learn new responses will be affected by memory impairments and higher cortical deficits (Hartke, 1991; Shanan, 1990).

In addition to the physical aging process, coping interventions must consider the role of personality, environment, and culture (e.g., Jackson, Antonucci, & Gibson, 1991; Lawton, 1977). Behavioral dispositions and temperaments can strongly determine how people perceive themselves and consequently react to stress effectively. For example, certain introverted persons are solitary in nature, interpersonally passive, and lacking in both social interests and social skills (Millon, 1981, 1990). The coping repertoire of these persons does not ordinarily include socially directed responses, and these persons are unlikely to find social coping modes to be of much value (for additional perspectives on personality and coping, see Costa & McCrae, 1993; Scheier, Weintraub, & Carver, 1986). Intervention programs should also be cognizant of the individual's living circumstances and the personal availability of social supports. Furthermore, cultural and spiritual beliefs can frequently shape the meaning of various stressors as well as choice of coping responses. In some cultures, confrontive coping strategies are frowned on, whereas in others they are encouraged (Mead, 1935).

All things considered, it appears that innovative hypothesizing, use of multidimensional measures of coping, and appreciation of disparities in the kinds of events and situations experienced by persons along the life-span continuum will advance and enhance our understanding of developments in coping that occur with age. Seldom simple and straightforward, coping is an individual and complex process at all age ranges, with hints that not even presumably stable or enduring coping preferences are constant in the same individual contending with differing stress and conflict situations. In sum, the field in its present state mandates us to amplify our own creative coping responses.

REFERENCES

Aldwin, C. M. (1991). Does age affect the stress and coping process? Implications of age differences in perceived control. *Journal of Gerontology, 46,* 174–180.

Bäckman, L., & Molander, B. (1986a). Adult age differences in the ability to cope with situations of high arousal in a precision sport. *Psychology and Aging, 1,* 133–139.

Bäckman, L., & Molander, B. (1986b). Effects of adult age and level of skill on the ability to cope with high-stress conditions in a precision sport. *Psychology and Aging, 1,* 334–336.

Bäckman, L., & Molander, B. (1991). On the generalizability of the age-related decline in coping with high-arousal conditions in a precision sport: Replication and extension. *Journal of Gerontology, 46,* 79–81.

Baltes, P. B., & Baltes, M. M. (Eds.). (1990). *Successful aging: Perspectives from the behavioral sciences.* New York: Cambridge University Press.

Billings, A. G., & Moos, R. H. (1981). The role of coping responses and social resources in attenuating the impact of stressful life events. *Journal of Behavioral Medicine, 4,* 139–157.

Blanchard-Fields, F., & Irion, J. C. (1988). Coping strategies from the perspective of two developmental markers: Age and social reasoning. *Journal of Genetic Psychology, 149,* 141–151.

Block, J. (1971). *Lives through time.* Berkeley, CA: Bancroft Books.

Bond, M., Gardner, S. T., Christian, J., & Sigel, J. (1983). Empirical study of self-rated defense styles. *Archives of General Psychiatry, 40,* 333–338.

Bond, M., Perry, C., Gautier, M., Goldenberg, M., Oppenheimer, J., & Simand, J. (1989). Validating the self-report of defense styles. *Journal of Personality Disorders, 3,* 101–112.

Carver, C. S., Scheier, M. F., & Weintraub, J. K. (1989). Assessing coping strategies: A theoretically-based approach. *Journal of Personality and Social Psychology, 56,* 267–283.

Cornelius, S. W., & Caspi, A. (1987). Everyday problem solving in adulthood and old age. *Psychology and Aging, 2,* 144–153.

Costa, P. T., Jr., & McCrae, R. R. (1993). Psychological stress and coping in old age. In L. Goldberger & S. Breznitz (Eds.), *Handbook of stress: Theoretical and clinical aspects* (pp. 403–412). New York: Free Press.

Costa, P. T., Jr., Zonderman, A. B., & McCrae, R. R. (1991). Personality, defense, coping, and adaptation in older adulthood. In E. M. Cummings, A. L. Greene, & K. H. Karraker (Eds.), *Life-span developmental psychology: Perspectives on stress and coping* (pp. 277–293). Hillsdale, NJ: Erlbaum.

Cramer, P. (1988). The Defense Mechanisms Inventory: A review of research and discussion of the scales. *Journal of Personality Assessment, 52,* 142–164.

Endler, N. S., & Parker, J. D. A. (1990). Multidimensional assessment of coping: A critical evaluation. *Journal of Personality and Social Psychology, 58,* 844–854.

Endler, N. S., & Parker, J. D. A. (1991). *Coping Inventory for Stressful Situations: Manual.* Toronto, Canada: Multi-Health Systems.

Endler, N. S., Parker, J. D. A., & Summerfeldt, L. J. (1992). *Coping with health problems: Developing a reliable and valid multidimensional measure* (Department of Psychology Rep. No. 204). Toronto, Canada: York University.

Erikson, E. (1963). *Childhood and society* (2nd ed.). New York: Norton.

Feifel, H. (1990). Psychology and death: Meaningful rediscovery. *American Psychologist, 45,* 537–543.

Feifel, H., & Strack, S. (1987). Old is old is old? *Psychology and Aging, 2,* 409–412.

Feifel, H., & Strack, S. (1989). Coping with conflict situations: Middle-aged and elderly men. *Psychology and Aging, 4,* 26–33.

Feifel, H., Strack, S., & Nagy, V. T. (1987a). Coping strategies and associated features of medically ill patients. *Psychosomatic Medicine, 49,* 616–625.

Feifel, H., Strack, S., & Nagy, V. T. (1987b). Degree of life-threat and differential use of coping modes. *Journal of Psychosomatic Research, 31,* 91–99.

Felton, B. J., & Revenson, T. A. (1987). Age differences in coping with chronic illness. *Psychology and Aging, 2,* 164–170.

Folkman, S. (1991). Coping across the life span: Theoretical issues. In E. M. Cummings, A. L. Greene, & K. H. Karraker (Eds.), *Life-span developmental psychology: Perspectives on stress and coping* (pp. 3–19). Hillsdale, NJ: Erlbaum.

Folkman, S., & Lazarus, R. S. (1980). An analysis of coping in a middle-aged community sample. *Journal of Health and Social Behavior, 21,* 219–239.

Folkman, S., & Lazarus, R. S. (1988). *Manual for the Ways of Coping Questionnaire.* Palo Alto, CA: Consulting Psychologist Press.

Folkman, S., Lazarus, R. S., Pimley, S., & Novacek, J. (1987). Age differences in stress and coping processes. *Psychology and Aging, 2,* 171–184.

Guttman, D. L. (1964). An exploration of ego configurations in middle and later life. In B. L. Neugarten (Eds.), *Personality in middle and later life* (pp. 114–148). New York: Atherton.

Guttman, D. L. (1974). The country of old men: Cross-cultural studies in the psychology of later life. In R. L. LeVine (Ed.), *Culture and personality: Contemporary readings* (pp. 95–122). Chicago: Aldine.

Guttman, D. L. (1987). *Reclaimed powers: Toward a psychology of men and women in later life.* New York: Basic Books.

Haan, N. (1993). The assessment of coping, defense, and stress. In L. Goldberger & S. Breznitz (Eds.), *Handbook of stress: Theoretical and clinical aspects* (pp. 258–273). New York: Free Press.

Hartke, R. J. (1991). The aging process: Cognition, personality, and coping. In E. M. Cummings, A. L. Greene, & K. H. Karraker (Eds.), *Life-span developmental psychology: Perspectives on stress and coping* (pp. 45–71). Hillsdale, NJ: Erlbaum.

Havighurst, R. J. (1972). *Developmental tasks and education* (3rd ed.). New York: David McKay Company.

Helson, R. (1967). Personality characteristics and developmental history of creative college women. *Genetic Psychology Monographs, 76,* 205–256.

Helson, R., & Wink, P. (1992). Personality change in women from the early 40s to the early 50s. *Psychology and Aging, 7,* 46–55.

Ihilevich, D., & Gleser, G. (1986). *Defense mechanisms: Their classification, correlates, and measurement with the Defense Mechanisms Inventory.* Owosso, MI: DMI Associates.

Irion, J. C., & Blanchard-Fields, F. (1987). A cross-sectional comparison of adaptive coping in adulthood. *Journal of Gerontology, 42,* 502–504.

Jackson, J. S., Antonucci, T. C., & Gibson, R. C. (1991). Social relations, productive activities, and coping with stress in late life. In M. A. P. Stephens, J. J. Crowther, S. E. Hobfoll, & D. L. Tennenbaum (Eds.), *Stress and coping in later-life families* (pp. 193–212). New York: Hemisphere.

John, O. P. (1990). The "Big Five" factor taxonomy: Dimensions of personality in the natural language and in questionnaires. In L. Pervin (Ed.), *Handbook of personality theory and research* (pp. 66–100). New York: Guilford.

Jung, C. G. (1933). *Modern man in search of a soul.* New York: Harcourt, Brace & World.

Jung, C. G. (1959). The soul and death. In H. Feifel (Ed.), *The meaning of death* (pp. 3–15). New York: McGraw-Hill.

Kazdin, A. (1992). *Research design in clinical psychology* (2nd ed.). Boston: Allyn and Bacon.

Labouvie-Vief, G., Hakim-Larson, J., & Hobart, C. J. (1987). Age, ego level, and the life-span development of coping and defense processes. *Psychology and Aging, 2,* 286–293.

Lawton, M. P. (1977). The impact of the environment on aging and behavior. In J. E. Birren & K. W. Schaie (Eds.), *Handbook of the psychology of aging* (pp. 276–301). New York: Van Nostrand-Reinhold.

Lazarus, R. L. (1966). *Psychological stress and the coping process.* New York: McGraw-Hill.

Lazarus, R. S., & Folkman, S. (1984). *Stress, appraisal, and coping.* New York: Springer.

Loevinger, J. (1976). *Ego development: Conceptions and theories.* San Francisco: Jossey-Bass.

McCrae, R. R. (1982). Age differences in the use of coping mechanisms. *Journal of Gerontology, 37,* 454–460.

McCrae, R. R. (1989). Age differences and changes in the use of coping mechanisms. *Journal of Gerontology, 44,* 161–169.

McCrae, R. R., & Costa, P. T., Jr. (1990). *Personality in adulthood.* New York: Guilford.

Mead, M. (1935). *Sex and temperament in three primitive societies.* New York: William Morrow.

Millon, T. (1969). *Modern psychopathology.* Philadelphia: Saunders.

Millon, T. (1981). *Disorders of personality.* New York: Wiley.

Millon, T. (1990). *Toward a new personology.* New York: Wiley.

Moos, R. H. (Ed.). (1986). *Coping with life crises: An integrated approach.* New York: Plenum.

Moos, R. H. (1992). *Coping Responses Inventory manual.* Palo Alto, CA: Center for Health Care Evaluation, U.S. Department of Veterans Affairs and Stanford University Medical Centers.

Moos, R. H., & Schaefer, J. A. (1993). Coping resources and processes: Current concepts and measures. In L. Goldberger & S. Breznitz (Eds.), *Handbook of stress: Theoretical and clinical aspects* (pp. 234–257). New York: Free Press.

Neugarten, B. L. (Ed.). (1972). *Middle age and aging.* Chicago: University of Chicago Press.

Neugarten, B. L. (1977). Personality and aging. In J. E. Birren & K. W. Schaie (Eds.), *Handbook of the psychology of aging* (pp. 626–649). New York: Van Nostrand-Reinhold.

Neugarten, B. L., & Neugarten, D. A. (1986). Age in the aging society. *Daedelus, 115,* 31–49.

Parker, J. D. A., & Endler, N. S. (1992). Coping with coping assessment: A Critical review. *European Journal of Personality, 6,* 321–344.

Pearlin, L. I., & Schooler, C. (1978). The structure of coping. *Journal of Health and Social Behavior, 19,* 2–21.

Pfeiffer, E. (1977). Psychopathology and social pathology. In J. E. Birren & K. W. Schaie (Eds.), *Handbook of the psychology of aging* (pp. 650–671). New York: Van Nostrand-Reinhold.

Quayhagen, M. P., & Quayhagen, M. (1982). Coping with conflict. *Research on Aging, 4,* 364–377.

Rudinger, G., & Thomae, H. (1990). The Bonn longitudinal study of aging: Coping, life adjustment, and life satisfaction. In P. B. Baltes & M. M. Baltes (Eds.), *Successful aging: Perspectives from the behavioral sciences* (pp. 265–295). New York: Cambridge University Press.

Scheier, M. F., Weintraub, J. K., & Carver, C. S. (1986). Coping with stress: Divergent strategies of optimists and pessimists. *Journal of Personality and Social Psychology, 51,* 1257–1264.

Shanan, J. (1990). Coping styles and coping strategies in later life. In M. Bergener & S. I. Finkel (Eds.), *Clinical and scientific psychogeriatrics: Vol. 1. The holistic approaches* (pp. 76–111). New York: Springer.

Terman, L. M., & Oden, M. H. (1959). *Genetic studies of genius: Vol. 5. The gifted group at midlife.* Stanford, CA: Stanford University Press.

Thomae, H. (Ed.). (1987). *Patterns of aging: Findings from the Bonn longitudinal study on aging.* Basel, Switzerland: Karger.

Tomlinson-Keasey, C. (1993). Opportunities and challenges posed by archival data sets. In D. C. Funder, R. D. Parke, C. Tomlinson-Keasey, & K. Widaman (Eds.), *Studying lives through time: Personality and development* (pp. 65–92). Washington, DC: American Psychological Association Press.

Vaillant, G. L. (1976). Natural history of male psychological health: 5. The relation of choice of ego mechanisms of defense to adult adjustment. *Archives of General Psychiatry, 33,* 535–545.

Vaillant, G. L. (1977). *Adaptation to life.* Boston: Little, Brown.

Vaillant, G. L., Bond, M., & Vaillant, C. O. (1986). An empirically validated hierarchy of defense mechanisms. *Archives of General Psychiatry, 42,* 597–601.

Weisman, A. D. (1984). *Coping capacity: On the extent of being mortal.* New York: Human Sciences Press.

PART FIVE

Clinical Parameters: Adaptive Coping and Interventions

CHAPTER 22

Adaptive and Maladaptive Coping

MOSHE ZEIDNER and DONALD SAKLOFSKE

> It is not stress that kills us. It is the effective adaptation to stress that permits us to live.
>
> *Vaillant, 1977, p. 374*

An understanding of the relationship between coping processes and adaptational outcomes has become a major concern among stress researchers (Lazarus, 1993). Current transactional stress models (e.g., Lazarus & Folkman, 1984b) view stress as a multivariate process involving inputs (person and environmental variables), outputs (immediate and long-term effects), and the mediating activities of appraisal and coping. Implicit in descriptions of coping is the notion of effectiveness: The prime importance of appraisal and coping processes is that they affect adaptational outcomes (Lazarus & Folkman, 1984b). Coping is hypothesized to explain outcome variability, even when the stressors are essentially identical. Thus, additional outcome variance, beyond personality and situational factors, should be predicted from the inclusion of coping data.

Initial research demonstrated only a small association between life event stress and outcome measures, suggesting that coping may be a critical moderating factor or even a more important determinant of outcome than the frequency and severity of the stressor (Zeidner & Hammer, 1990). Furthermore, the shift in perspective from an emphasis on pathology to a concern with stress resistance and adaptive processes has led research to focus on the adaptive value of effective coping strategies (Holahan et al., Chapter 2, this volume). This recent focus on the adaptive value of effective coping may help to address several outstanding questions. An understanding of adaptive coping strategies should assist in predicting outcomes to both normative and nonnormative events. We may then be better able to diagnose maladaptive coping and prescribe more effective coping techniques. This is especially important because some responses to stress may alleviate the problem or reduce the resulting distress, others may actually exacerbate the problem or become problems or interfere with outcomes (Carver et al., 1993), and other coping strategies may not result in any benefit (Aldwin & Revenson, 1987).

This chapter examines current thinking and research related to adaptive coping. The outstanding question is whether variations in coping strategies are associated with variations in outcomes such as emotional adjustment and physical health. We shall consider both conceptual and methodological complexities in describing adaptive coping, summarize some research literature on coping in various criterion groups, and finally present some preliminary conclusions and generalizations about adaptive coping and ways of training coping skills.

CONCEPTUAL ISSUES

Adaptive Coping

The concepts of adaptation and adjustment are central to studying coping effectiveness. Adaptation in the psychological sense refers to processes employed to manage environmental demands (Lazarus & Folkman, 1984a). Adjustment is an achievement, accomplished well or badly, or a process whereby people adjust under different circumstances. Earlier, Freud (1933) identified various defense mechanisms such as displacement, sublimation, projection, reaction formation, regression, rationalization, repression, and suppression that were unconsciously activated to discharge the stress resulting from id-superego conflicts. The a priori classification of behavior as adaptive or maladaptive has led Haan (1977) and Vaillant (1977) to differentiate between lower-level defensive behaviors (rigid, unconscious, automatized, pushed from the past, distorting, process-based, permits impulse gratification through subterfuge coping) and higher-level coping behaviors (flexible, conscious, purposive, future-oriented, reality-focused, and permits ordered and open impulse gratification).

Current psychological writings view coping as an active and conscious process, interacting with other factors such as personality and stress management experience. Coping is more than simple adjustment; it is the pursuit of human growth, mastery, and differentiation allowing us to evolve in an ever-changing world. Functional coping behavior both buffers the immediate impact of stress and ensures a sense of self-worth and wholeness with one's past and anticipated future. Within the context of coping research, "adaptive" refers to "the effectiveness of coping in improving the adaptational outcome" (Lazarus, 1993, p. 237). Deciding whether particular coping strategies are adaptive or not requires an examination of situational factors (e.g., nature of the stressor, degree and chronicity) and personal factors (e.g., personality, beliefs about coping resources and their effectiveness). Further, the selection and efficacy of coping strategies must be viewed in relation to interactions between the person and the situation; a change in any element may affect the process and product.

Basic Working Assumptions

The transactional model (Lazarus, 1993; Lazarus & Folkman, 1984a) offers several basic working assumptions that impact current conceptualizations about coping. Coping strategies should not be prejudged as adaptive or maladaptive. Rather, the concern must be for whom and under what circumstances a particular coping mode has adaptive consequences rather than the wholesale categorization of coping as adaptive versus maladaptive. Because coping is a process embedded in context, coping responses may vary across contexts and change over time in response to life conditions, and as a function of the skill with which the coping is applied. Another assumption is that coping effectiveness must be empirically demonstrated. Finally, coping efforts should not be confounded with outcomes (Lennon, Dohrenwend, Zautra, & Marbach, 1990).

Mechanisms Underlying Coping-Outcome Relationships

Coping may protect us by eliminating or modifying the conditions that produce stress or by keeping the emotional consequences within manageable bounds (Zeidner & Hammer, 1990). Coping may affect outcomes through its impact on the frequency, intensity, duration and patterning of physiological stress reactions and the resultant affective and somatic outcomes. The impact on emotional distress may be related to both controllable and uncontrollable stressful encounters. Health may be negatively affected when coping involves risk taking (high speed car racing) or substance abuse (alcohol).

Further, coping strategies may impede rather than promote health-related behaviors. Although denial and wishful thinking may delay seeking life-saving medical attention for chest pains, so might the overuse of information-seeking strategies. Coping and health have been linked in two recent models (Aldwin & Revenson, 1987). The main or additive effects model suggests that coping has similar effects on well-being regardless of the kind or amount of stress. The interactive model suggests that coping moderates the impact of stressful episodes to varying degrees, depending on the type or severity of stress. The stress-coping interaction has also led to the view that coping provides a buffer effect (Wills, 1986). Thus, if a coping strategy has a buffering effect it will be of significant value under moderate to high stress conditions but of much less value under low stress conditions or vice versa. Research results provide mixed support for both models (Felton & Revenson, 1984) although interactive effects may be more prevalent for problem-focused coping and main effects for emotion-focused coping (Aldwin & Revenson, 1987).

Major Considerations in Assessing Coping Effectiveness

The Theoretical Model

Defining effective coping is mainly determined by the theoretical model or paradigm guiding research (Folkman, Chesney, McKussick, Ironson, Johnson, & Coastes, 1991). Psychodynamic models generally assume a hierarchy of coping and defense in which some processes are seen as superior to others. Haan (1977) categorizes ego processes as adaptive or maladaptive depending on their relative freedom from reality distortion, future orientation, allowance for impulse gratification, and expression of affect. In contrast, the transactional stress model focuses on the changing cognitive and behavioral efforts required to manage specific demands appraised as taxing or exceeding the person's resources (Folkman et al., 1991). A contextual definition of coping effectiveness (what is said, thought, or done in a specific situation) is demanded by interactional models. Thus, coping efficacy is determined by its effects and outcomes within a particular situation.

Criteria for Assessing Coping Outcomes

Appropriate and valid criteria of good or poor adjustment are necessary to evaluate coping effectiveness (Lazarus, 1969). Ideally, adaptive coping should lead to a permanent problem resolution with no additional conflict or residual outcomes while maintaining a positive emotional state (Pearlin & Schooler, 1978). The following are the most salient and prevalent criteria for judging coping effectiveness (Meneghan, 1982; Pearlin & Schooler, 1978; Taylor, 1986):

1. *Resolution of the Conflict or Stressful Situation.* Coping with a problem should be instrumental in alleviating or removing the stressful situation, where possible.

2. *Reduction of Physiological and Biochemical Reactions.* Coping efforts are judged to be successful if they reduce arousal and its indicators (e.g., heart rate, blood pressure, respiration, skin conductivity).

3. *Reduction of Psychological Distress.* Adaptive coping usually involves success in controlling emotional distress and keeping anxiety within manageable limits.

4. *Normative Social Functioning.* Adaptive coping involves normative patterns of social functioning that reflect realistic appraisal of events. Deviation of behavior from socially acceptable norms is taken to be a sign of maladaptive coping.

5. *Return to Prestress Activities.* To the extent that people's coping efforts enable them to resume their routine activities, coping may be judged to be effective. (Note that substantial life change following a stressful encounter may be a sign of successful rather than unsuccessful coping, particularly if the person's prior living situation was not in some sense ideal.)

6. *Well-Being of Self and Others Affected by the Situation.* This criterion includes spouses, children, parents, coworkers, friends, neighbors.

7. *Maintaining Positive Self-Esteem.* Negative self-esteem is commonly viewed as indicative of poor adjustment.

8. *Perceived Effectiveness.* This involves the respondents' claims that a particular strategy or approach was helpful to them in some way. Such testimonials, however, may have an uncertain relation to observed effects.

Coping effectiveness, however, is both context-specific and related to the specific encounter. Relevant outcome measures of hospital patients undergoing first-time coronary bypass surgery might include length of stay in hospital, progress toward walking and pace of recovery (Carver, Scheier, & Pozo, 1992). Studying the effects of technological disaster may include symptom checklists, cognitive and behavioral performances, and biochemical assessments (Baum, Fleming, & Singer, 1983).

There are no universal criteria for assessing coping effectiveness that may further vary across research paradigms, context, and even sociocultural settings; a coping response might be judged successful relative to one outcome criteria but not another. Indeed, the resolution of one coping task might even come at the expense of another (e.g., working long hours for both financial and professional gain but contributing to marriage breakdown). Coping is a complex process that must be viewed as a multivariate construct and judged according to a number of criteria.

Context of Coping: Cultural and Social Factors

Coping effectiveness must be examined in the context in which problems occur: "Without information about the social context we would have half the story" (Lazarus & Folkman, 1984a, p. 299). Also, evaluations of coping effectiveness must be sensitive to broader social (Weidner & Collins, 1992) and cultural factors (Marsella, DeVos, & Hsu, 1985) including social values (Lazarus & Launier, 1978). Preferred coping methods and perceived effectiveness must be appraised relative to a social or cultural group, values, norms, world view, symbols, and orientation. For example, in the case of a mother who devotes herself to her ill parents at the expense of her newborn baby, the evaluation of this coping approach is not merely a scientific but a moral matter and may differ in traditional versus modern child-centered societies. Evaluating coping effectiveness must be further addressed relative to people's normative response to a stressor. Virtually all bereaved persons manifest distress, with depression being a common feature, so that freedom from distress may not signal good coping skills. However, normative standards must be used cautiously when judging coping efficacy, especially under extremely adverse conditions.

Adaptational Tasks

Coping efforts are centered and structured around certain goals, issues, and patterns of challenges referred to as coping tasks (Cohen & Lazarus, 1979). Successful coping depends on the successful resolution of coping tasks. For example, the tasks of children of divorced parents range from acknowledging the marriage breakup, disengagement from parental conflict, coming to terms with multiple losses associated with divorce, and resolving feelings of self-blame and anger (Wallerstein, 1983). Coping generally centers on five main tasks (Cohen & Lazarus, 1979): (a) to reduce harmful environmental conditions and enhance prospects of recovery; (b) to tolerate or adjust to negative events or realities; (c) to maintain a positive self image; (d) to maintain emotional equilibrium and decrease emotional stress; and (e) to maintain a satisfying relationship with the environment.

Personal Agendas and Coping Styles

The individual's aspirations and goals are critical in evaluating coping outcomes. Also, a good match between actual coping and preferred coping style, as well as between coping strategies and personal values, is important in ensuring positive outcomes. When the amount of received information "fits" the individual's personal coping style (e.g., "monitors" receiving high information), there is less indication of affective and physiological distress (Miller & Mangan, 1983). Person variables also determine how we interpret and manage stress and judge coping effectiveness. For example, persons with high personal and social resources rely more on active coping and less on avoidance, thus impacting their coping effectiveness (Holahan & Moos, 1987; also see Costa et al., Chapter 3, this volume; and Hewitt & Flett, Chapter 18, this volume).

ASSESSING COPING EFFECTIVENESS

Various methodological problems plague research on coping effectiveness thereby limiting the validity of the generalizations about coping-outcome relations. The following discussion looks at the more important methodological problems (see also Beehr & McGrath, Chapter 4, this volume).

Methodological Issues

Correlational Research Designs

Most coping effectiveness research has been cross-sectional rather than longitudinal in design. This provides weak evidence of causality because coping and outcome variables are correlated at any given time (Stone, Helder, & Schneider, 1988), hampering the pinpointing of direction in the coping-adjustment relationship. Thus, the question remains: Does the association of a particular strategy with fewer symptoms or lower distress mean that coping reduces distress (coping → distress) or that people with fewer problems or in better mental health tend to employ a particular strategy (distress → coping)? Further, coping efforts and outcomes should not be confounded in assessing their relative contribution to adjustment, a problem of cross-sectional research (Cohen, 1987; Lennon, Dohrenwend, Zautra, & Marbach, 1990).

Variations in Outcome May Arise from Some Third, Unmeasured, Preexisting Factor such as Personality

The relationship between coping and outcomes may reflect an underlying disposition (e.g., neuroticism) so the association between coping and distress could be explained by the individual's disposition toward distress (McCrae & Costa, 1986). Coping efforts may provide the causal mechanism linking personality and well-being but they may also be an epiphenomenon, with no real impact on stress and life adaptation.

Level of Analysis

The tendency in coping research is to aggregate and combine a number of coping behaviors into one category. Global categories (e.g., problem-focused coping) prevent the more refined and differentiated analysis that might come from examining tactics such as humor, confrontation, and information seeking (cf. Carver, Scheier, & Weintraub, 1989; Schwarzer & Schwarzer, Chapter 6, this volume). Different coping tactics within a general category may have different implications for a person's coping success. A particular coping strategy (say emotion-focused coping) is quite a broad category, including several subclasses; adaptive coping may be positively associated with one subclass (e.g., positive reinterpretation, or emphasizing the positive side of a situation) and inversely related with others (e.g., denial, wishful thinking). It is a gross oversimplification to treat different strategies as one group, and we need to clarify the meaning and function of a particular response at a level that permits meaningful generalizations about coping-outcome relations.

Missing Information about the Parameters of Additional Stressors

McCrae and Costa (1986) state that coping-outcome relationships are meaningful if the stressful event under consideration represents a significant portion of the designated time period, and similar coping methods are employed with other stressors during that time. Thus, if we are comparing people who are not only simultaneously using different coping responses but also grappling with different stressors and coping with them differently, we really don't know exactly which factor contributes to outcome variability. A complete coping-outcome model must include all stressful events and coping strategies occurring at a particular time.

Multiple Meanings and Functions of Coping Behaviors

Each coping act may have more than one function, depending on the psychological context in which it occurs. Problem-focused coping, for example, may also regulate emotion as in public speaking training that also decreases stage fright. Thus, the function of a coping strategy may not be fully inferred from the act. Similarly, emotion-focused strategies (e.g., humor, relaxation exercises, tranquilizers) can have problem-focused functions if they are effective in decreasing anxiety or other aversive emotions that impede functioning. One really needs to know what the specific function of the coping behavior is rather than the act itself to assess the effectiveness of a particular strategy. The missing information would certainly limit the internal validity and generalizability of coping-outcome relationships.

Reliance on Self-Report in the Assessment of Coping

There is heavy reliance on self-report measures (e.g., questionnaires, checklists) to determine both coping behaviors and outcomes. This raises the issue of common method variance that may yield inflated correlations between self-reported coping and outcome responses. Retrospective self-reports may also suffer from memory distortions. Further, outcome may bias retrospective reports of the perceived adaptiveness of the coping behaviors. Multimethod and multisource data would reduce the method variance problem and effects due to memory and attitudes.

Anchoring of Coping Scales

Most coping questionnaires ask about coping behaviors and frequency of usage. Accordingly, respondents are typically presented with an inventory of coping items (e.g., "I tackle the problem step by step," "I pray," "I consume alcohol") and are asked to indicate how frequently they use each tactic in coping with a particular situation (e.g., "almost all the time" to "not at all"). However, this does not provide information about the coping strategy-situation fit, personality of the coper, success in carrying out the coping efforts, outcome, and the like. Thus, we may be erroneously assuming that correlating the frequency of use of some strategy with outcome measures will have uniform effects regardless of the qualitative aspects of the person, situation, and execution of the strategy.

Multiple Criteria for Assessing Coping Outcomes

Conclusions about coping effectiveness vary depending on the choice of outcome criteria (Meneghan, 1982). A coping strategy may have differential affects on different criterion measures. Moreover, the various indexes of effective coping may causally influence one another. For example, a person who employs avoidance-type behaviors to deal with occupational stressors might be judged to cope effectively based on self-report measures of symptom-reduction but judged to cope maladaptively based on the supervisor's assessment of functioning on the work site. Moreover, the various indexes of effective coping may causally influence one another. For example, the amount of time spent in studying for an upcoming exam may also impact the subject's state of subjective well-being by reducing anxiety and enhancing self-esteem.

Reciprocal Determinism in Coping-Outcome Relationships

Causal relationships among coping strategies and outcome indexes are likely to be multidirectional rather than linear (Carver & Scheier, in press; Lazarus & Folkman, 1984a). Furthermore, there may be a mutually reinforcing causal cycle between severe stressors, poor outcomes, and maladaptive coping strategies. Coping indexes, often seen as dependent variables, might also serve as independent variables in a complex process of reciprocal and unfolding transactions over time. In fact, it might not make sense to conceptualize indexes of effective coping as dependent variables, since they in turn serve as independent variables in a complex process of reciprocal and unfolding transactions over time.

Interactions between Coping and Other Factors

Coping invariably interacts with situational parameters in impacting both adaptive and maladaptive outcomes. For example, avoidance behaviors (e.g., wishful thinking, distancing, procrastination) would be nonefficacious when used by college students who are on probation—when they should instead be attending to their study problems. On the other hand, distancing might be an adaptive response for these same individuals when confronted with a negative and unalterable situation, such as a serious illness in the family. As a stressful episode evolves and develops over time, there is a continuous interplay between appraisal, coping, and emotional and somatic responses, each fluctuating as the transaction unfolds (Lazarus & Folkman, 1984a). Thus, a particular coping strategy may be more effective at one stage of a stressful encounter or in one time period than another (Auerbach, 1989). For example, whereas emotion-focused coping might be more adaptive following an exam, active-oriented coping would probably be more adaptive prior to the exam, when something could be done to change the outcome (cf. Folkman & Lazarus, 1985). Also, coping strategies found useful in one time period may not be useful in a different period. For example, resigning from a tenured research position in academia on account of conflictual encounters with the dean might be a more adaptive coping strategy in time of high institutional demand for academics than in time of high unemployment, when academic positions are scarce.

Ipsative or Normative Comparisons

Most coping outcome studies use normative or interindividual comparisons (see Porter & Stone, Chapter 7, this volume; Tennen & Affleck, Chapter 8, this volume). In fact, the apparent relations between appraisal and coping processes may differ depending on whether one studies coping responses within persons (ipsative) or across (normative) persons. Furthermore, what may matter is not an individual's overall level of coping compared with other individuals but whether the individual shows more or less coping relative to previous baseline coping. Thus, it is important to know of how a shift away from the person's typical style of appraisal or baseline coping affects outcomes.

Inconsistent Results

The methodological variance in subject samples, coping and outcome measures may well account for some inconsistencies in studies of the influence of coping strategies on adjustment (Aldwin & Revenson, 1987). Aggregation of results in meta-analytic studies should be done cautiously.

Future Research

The preceding analysis would suggest that future research on coping effectiveness should include more precise theoretical statements, continuous and longitudinal data collection, and situational and personal variables, including secondary stressors. Employing multiple assessment points, repeated measures of coping efforts, and various indexes of outcomes at regular intervals over meaningful time spans would enhance the exploration of the complex pathways of effects. Coping effectiveness could be better understood through both normative and ipsative comparisons. By examining how people cope with different problems, we may then clarify whether shifting strategies based on the situation requirements results in more effective coping than relying on particular strategies across problem areas (Kessler, Price, & Wortman, 1985).

EMPIRICAL RESEARCH ON COPING EFFECTIVENESS

In spite of recent advances in theory, research, and assessment, the issue of coping effectiveness is still open to debate. Which coping behaviors are most effective in the short and long term, in which contexts, and for whom—these questions pose a conceptual and empirical puzzle (Carver & Scheier, in press). We will provide a brief description of the research on the effectiveness of three basic coping categories (problem-focused, emotion-focused coping, avoidance) and an examination of the coping patterns observed in various criterion groups.

Problem-Focused, Emotion-Focused, and Avoidance Coping

Theorists have frequently emphasized the positive effects of problem-focused coping and negative effects of emotion-focused coping on psychological outcomes, especially when the threatening situation can be ameliorated by the subject's responses (Lazarus & Folkman, 1984a). Although emotion-focused coping or avoidance may help in maintaining emotional balance, an adaptive response to remediable situations still requires problem-solving activities to manage the threat. Active coping is preferred by most persons and is highly effective in stress reduction (Gal & Lazarus, 1975). Active coping provides a sense of mastery over the stressor, diverts the person's attention from the problem, when engaged in task-oriented behavior and discharges energy following exposure to threat. Non-problem-solving strategies are increasingly used when the source of stress is unclear, when there is a lack of knowledge about stress modification, or when the person can do little to eliminate stress (Pearlin & Schooler, 1978).

The research evidence on the adaptiveness of avoidance coping is mixed. On one hand, a wealth of data indicates that avoidance coping in general is positively tied to concurrent distress and may have negative consequences (Aldwin & Revenson, 1987; Billings & Moos, 1981; Mullins et al., 1991). A review of the literature by Carver & Scheier (in press) suggests that "avoidance" coping (e.g., wishful thinking, escapism, overt effort to deny, and self-distraction and mental disengagement) typically works against people rather than to their advantage. On the other hand, some research evidence shows that cognitive avoidance may be an effective way to cope with short-term stressors (e.g., noise, pain, and uncomfortable medical procedures; Suls & Fletcher, 1985). Avoidance coping may be useful at times because it gives the person a psychological breather and an opportunity to escape from the constant pressures of the stressful situation (Carver et al., 1992).

Some coping strategies appear to be inherently maladaptive in managing stress. Alcohol and drugs may provide brief relief, but ultimately the person is worse off. Factor analytic studies have suggested a cluster of theoretically adaptive strategies: active coping, planning, suppression of competing activities, restraint coping, positive reinforcement, seeking social support, and positive reappraisal. The second cluster included denial, behavioral disengagement, focus on emotions, and alcoholism (Carver et al., 1989). However, whereas some research supports the relationship between active coping and well-being (Aldwin & Revenson, 1987; Aspinwall & Taylor, 1992), the opposite effect has been reported with a focal stressor (Bolger, 1990; Mattlin, Wethington, & Kessler, 1990). Similarly, some research suggests that emotion-focused coping is maladaptive and increases stress (Lazarus & Folkman, 1984a, 1984b), but the opposite pattern is also reported (Baum et al., 1983).

As discussed earlier and throughout this book, some overall conclusions may be drawn about the relative efficacy of coping processes. However, the outcome of specific strategies depends on personal and contextual factors, reliance on other coping responses, and the match between stressor characteristics, appraisal, and coping.

Coping in Various Criterion Groups

The coping strategies employed in four different but salient human conditions in modern society are now described: (a) depression—a prevalent mental disorder; (b) loneliness—a major social problem; (c) health—the range of acute and chronic, and minor and major somatic conditions; (d) posttraumatic stress—the sequelae of an earlier stressor. These should serve as useful illustrations of adaptive versus maladaptive coping. However, such data must be interpreted cautiously so as to not infer that a particular coping method is always effective or ineffective or is critical and causal to the condition.

Depression

In the mental health field, depression is one of the most researched and written about problems. Coping is regarded as an important variable in descriptions of depression. Depressed persons are more likely to employ emotional and avoidance coping responses in contrast to task-coping and problem-solving strategies. Zeidner (1994) and Saklofske (1993) reported that university students scoring high on the Beck Depression Inventory preferred an emotion-focused coping style in contrast to students reporting no depression. Other studies support the relationship between increased reliance on emotion-focused and avoidance coping and decrease in problem-focused coping in depressed persons. Some features of depression affect the selection of coping strategies and their actual and perceived effectiveness. These include the mood and self preoccupation of depressed subjects (Endler & Parker, 1990b), their difficulty in decision making (Coyne, Aldwin, & Lazarus, 1981), less well-developed social problem-solving skills (Nezu, 1986), more negative views of themselves as problem solvers (Mayo & Tanaka-Matsumi, 1993), higher self-oriented and socially prescribed perfectionism (Hewitt & Flett, 1991), greater tendency to not feel in control of either good or bad outcomes (Mirowsky & Ross, 1990), and greater experience of stressful life events (Billings, Cronkite, & Moos, 1983). Employing problem-focused coping requires more of an external focus, skill in defining problems, and access to a menu of appropriate coping strategies for managing both stressors and emotional reactions.

The links between coping and depression are neither simple nor necessarily direct. Negative events and ongoing strains can influence the choice of coping strategies in depressed and nondepressed persons (Fondacaro & Moos, 1989). Depressed mood is negatively related to problem-focused coping and positively to emotion-focused coping when the stressor is appraised as changeable (Vitaliano, DeWolfe, Maiuro, Russo, & Katon, 1990). Moos and colleagues demonstrated that coping, social resources, and stress are "additively predictive" of depressed patients' functioning (Billings & Moos, 1984). Avoidant coping strategies, lower family support, and personality characteristics such as low self-esteem are predictive of depression (Holahan & Moos, 1987). More effective coping strategies are employed by depressed persons who have strong family and work resources (Fondacaro & Moos, 1987). Holahan and Moos (1990, 1991) reported that changes in depressive symptoms over one year are best predicted by initial resources (family support, easygoingness, self confidence) under low stress but indirectly through approach coping strategies under high stress. They concluded, "Under high stressors, adaptive personality characteristics and family support function prospectively as coping resources; coping, in turn, mediates between initial resources and later health status" (p. 36).

Coping assumes an important role in the treatment of mood disorders. Burns and Nolen-Hoeksema (1991) showed that patients employing active strategies for coping with negative moods manifested less depression at intake and after 12 weeks of treatment than those scoring lower on this factor. Although the frequency of active coping and belief in its helpfulness before starting cognitive behavioral therapy were not related to complying with self-help homework or with recovery, patients who were more willing to learn positive coping strategies showed greater recovery. These studies suggest that depressed individuals tend to frequently employ maladaptive coping strategies but that coping must be further viewed in the context of other critical person and situation variables.

Loneliness

From the viewpoint of social psychology, loneliness is a relational deficit reflecting social and interpersonal relationships that the individual defines as deficient in meeting his or her needs. As such, loneliness may result from evaluations that one's person-network is qualitatively inadequate or quantitatively too small. Loneliness may be specific to deficits in romantic, friendship, family, and social/community relationships. Of concern is that loneliness has been associated with physical and mental health problems ranging from substance abuse to depression and suicide. The coping strategies that are employed to deal with loneliness must be considered critical in determining the eventual physical and psychological well-being of the person.

Saklofske and Yackulic (1989) reported that general loneliness was negatively associated with problem-focused coping and positively correlated with wishful thinking for both male and female university students. Problem-focused coping was also negatively correlated with specific kinds of loneliness (romantic, family, social) for males but only social loneliness for females. Wishful thinking was positively related to the three kinds of loneliness for females; denial was not correlated with general or specific loneliness.

It is interesting to speculate on the outcomes of various strategies for coping with loneliness. Problem solving has the potential for finding solutions to perceived loneliness (e.g., call an acquaintance, join a club, visit a family member). Wishful thinking may serve a role if the process then leads to some action; however, wishing in itself may only compound the realization that one is lonely and the situation is not improving. A rich fantasy life is useful as an escape or diversion from everyday problems, or for buying time to recover from stress, and may even serve a role in creativity. It would, however, appear maladaptive if it becomes the exclusive coping style and in turn, becomes the person's reality (akin to living vicariously through TV soap operas).

Other research on loneliness extends these findings to suggest that lonely individuals may employ a mixture of coping strategies. Rubenstein and Shaver (1980) reported that lonely adults employed such coping strategies as "active solitude" (a creative use of time spent alone), "spending money" (a distracting response), "social contact" (an attempt to deal directly with the problem of isolation and the need for interpersonal relationships), and "sad passivity" (a maladaptive response reflecting "lethargic self-pity"). Van Buskirk and Duke (1991) noted that both lonely and nonlonely adolescents may employ sad passivity but the latter group used this only as a temporary coping strategy and in preparation for initiating more active coping methods. Thus such passivity may be adaptive (e.g., sit and think, do nothing, watch TV) in the short term by giving individuals some quiet time to regroup or even stabilize themselves before following through with active coping strategies such as visiting a friend or inviting some guests for a party. It is when this coping style becomes both chronic and the dominant style for managing loneliness that it becomes maladaptive.

Finally, social support can be a major factor in influencing reactions to stress. The importance of friends and family in providing social and emotional support and buffering us against stress has been extensively described in the research literature (Heller, Swindler, & Dusenbury, 1986) and further examined in the context of loneliness. Although social support networks are important in buffering the effects of stress, including social and emotional loneliness, lonely individuals may also behave and think in ways that undermine the supportive role that might come from social relationships.

Physical Health Problems

Coping is an important variable in health psychology research. Special series of major journals have been devoted to topics such as "Coping with Medical Illness and Medical Procedures" (Peterson, 1989). Methodological concerns are apparent (Endler, Parker, & Summerfeldt, 1993), but research evidence suggests that adjustment to and recovery from health problems are related to coping. However, it is apparent that "coping is inherently a dynamic, sequential process; and that emotion- and problem-focused coping modes may thus sometimes overlap and become indistinguishable as people deal with complex situations" (Auerbach, 1989, p. 393).

There is evidence for and against the adaptiveness of particular coping strategies in health-related areas, as in the example of cardiac and hypertensive patients. Whereas distraction may interfere with the recognition and response to novel symptoms of cardiovascular dysfunction (Nolan & Wielgosz, 1991), active coping (monitoring and scanning for threat-relevant information) may also be "a contributing factor in either onset or exacerbation" of hypertension (Miller, Leinbach, & Brody, 1989). Whether or not high monitoring is of short- or long-term benefit in the treatment of and recovery from hypertension is still unclear.

Studies of cancer patients suggest that multiple coping strategies are required to effectively manage the many stressors associated with this disease. Prostate cancer patients undergoing radiation therapy showed reduced disruption in their daily lives when they received information that increased their understanding of their experiences and reduced inconsistencies between expectations and actual experiences (Johnson, Lauver, & Nail, 1989). The negative effects of avoidant coping strategies contrast with the reduced distress shown when acceptance, humor, and positive reframing were employed by breast cancer patients (Carver et al., 1993). A 12-year follow-up of children previously diagnosed with acute lymphoblastic leukemia showed that coping and adjustment were correlated with age, mother's coping, positive reappraisal, seeking social support, and low use of escape and avoidance strategies. Good psychological adjustment was linked with higher efficacy expectation, family functioning, and less use of palliative coping and negative thinking in adults with sickle cell disease (Thompson, Gil, Abrams, & Philips, 1992).

Collins et al. (1990) observed that a number of different coping efforts were associated with positive changes following cancer:

> Because victimizing events produce many problems and disruptions, different aspects of the event are likely to be amenable to different strategies of coping. For example, physical limitations are particularly amenable to active problem solving . . . in contrast the regulation of emotions may depend on methods of cognitive restructuring. A repertoire of responses may allow individuals to take maximum advantage of each situation to facilitate positive perceptions and experience. (p. 280)

Bulimia and other eating disorders such as anorexia nervosa have received extensive attention over the past decade. Recent attention has been directed to the role played by both early life stressors (Lacey, Coker, & Birtchnell, 1986) and contemporary stressors (Cattanach, Malley, & Rodin, 1988). Lacey et al. (1986) suggests that bulimic women may be less effective in coping with stress. Avoidance and emotion-focused coping have been associated with bulimia in contrast to less use of cognitive and behavioral strategies (Mayhew & Edelman, 1989; Shatford & Evans, 1986). Janzen, Kelly, and Saklofske (1992) have reported that bulimic symptomatology was negatively correlated with task-oriented scores of the Coping Inventory for Stressful Situations (CISS; Endler & Parker, 1990a) but positively related to emotion-focused scores; the relationship with avoidance was not significant. Also of interest was the finding of a significant correlation with Neuroticism (N). These studies would indicate that women who manifest bulimia or bulimic symptoms are more likely to manage stress with emotional coping, involving self-deprecation, guilt, anger, anxiety and worry.

Further research on coping and health problems suggest that a wide array of key variables influence the choice of adaptive or maladaptive coping behaviors and outcomes. These range from hardiness (Williams, Wiebe, & Smith, 1992), psychiatric factors (Vitaliano, Katon, Maiuro, & Russo, 1989), to appraisal of the illness as changeable (Dorland & Hattie, 1992) or acceptance of the illness (Revenson & Felton, 1989). Many health studies point to the positive effects of information-seeking (Peterson, 1989) and problem-focused coping (Vitaliano et al., 1989) in contrast to emotion-focused and avoidance coping. However, Auerbach (1989) concludes that the challenge remains to differentiate among the various coping techniques that may be successfully employed to manage stressors at particular times and then to teach patients how and when to use them.

Posttraumatic Stress Disorder

Coping responses are reported to be meaningful predictors of postdisaster stress. Studies of U.S. (Nezu & Carnavale, 1987) and Israeli combat veterans (Solomon, Avitzur, & Mikulincer, 1989; Solomon, Mikulincer, & Avitzur, 1988) found that the severity of posttraumatic stress disorder (PTSD) was positively related to emotion-focused coping and negatively associated with problem-focused coping. PTSD in combat-stressed soldiers has been meaningfully predicted by greater appraisal of threat during the war, more negative emotions following stress reactions, and use of emotion-focused strategies for coping with combat stress (Solomon, Mikulincer, & Benbenishty, 1989). Vietnam combat veterans with PTSD and adjustment disorders reported less effective coping reactions and poorer problem solving than well-adjusted veterans.

Zeidner and Ben-Zur (1994) examined the posttraumatic reactions of Israelis exposed to missile attacks during the Persian Gulf War. Emotion-focused coping was related to high levels of posttraumatic stress, anxiety, and bodily symptoms following the war. Emotion-focused coping and trait anxiety were the most salient predictors of stress-related outcomes. Active coping strategies were not meaningful predictors of outcome variables, except for postcrisis attitude changes (Joseph, Cairns, & McCollam, 1993). Alternatively, Northern Irish children living in areas of high versus low political violence showed no difference in depression scores. Denial and depression were not related although an indirect measure of social support was associated with lower depression scores.

Research also suggests that emotion-focused coping may be an effective strategy in moderating emotional arousal and enhancing adaptation in situations where people have no objective control, such as during combat or disaster situations (Baum et al., 1983). By contrast, postdisaster situations require mobilization of adaptive resources (e.g., problem-focused responses); also there is more control over events and problems. Thus, emotion-focused coping may be less adaptive in postdisaster situations.

SOME TENTATIVE GENERALIZATIONS ABOUT ADAPTIVE COPING

Research findings on coping effectiveness must be considered as tentative at present. The same coping techniques may contribute to different outcomes and not all coping strategies are equally effective in managing stress. Stress is best managed when effective methods are used for removing the stressor or its cause and coping with reactions and emotions. Stress reduction behaviors associated with a difficult university course might include increased study time, peer assistance, or dropping the course until a later time. In the process, effective strategies for addressing the concurrent anxiety, worry, and depressed mood must be implemented. In instances where the stressor cannot be changed (e.g., loss of a loved one, war, diagnosis of terminal cancer), personal management is critical in determining short- and long-term psychological adjustment to such stress.

Although few unequivocal principles have been uncovered in three decades of coping research, we now put forward some generalizations about adaptive coping (see also Lazarus's review on coping research, 1993). We will not discuss in any detail the role of specific coping tactics in adjustment, as these will be handled in the various domain-specific chapters of this Handbook.

Coping Strategies Work with Modest Effects, Sometimes, with Some People

Some kinds of coping responses to some kinds of situations and exigencies do make a difference. However, the magnitude of such differences is frequently disappointing (Pearlin, 1991) offering little justification for the power of coping in the stress outcome process. Methodological difficulties and weaknesses may account for some of these less than robust findings. The hypothesis that coping is a significant moderator of stress-outcome relations remains to be demonstrated.

Coping Responses Are Not Uniformly Adaptive

The results of a given coping style are determined by the interaction of personal needs and preferences and the constraints of the current situation. Thus, applying the same coping strategies across all situations is not likely to be adaptive (Collins et al., 1990). Specific coping strategies are more or less effective depending on the type of stress encountered (Pearlin & Schooler, 1978). For example, role-related distress (interpersonal relationship problems) was more responsive to coping efforts than occupational and economic distress, where the individual has little direct control.

Strategies often viewed as maladaptive (e.g., avoidance, distancing) may be adaptive under some circumstances and vice versa. Though many advocate that keeping emotional distress within manageable bounds reflects good adjustment, research shows that some people (e.g., cancer patients, spinal cord injuries) may be better off in the long run if they initially express their emotions rather than behaving in a restrained manner (Wortman, 1983). Furthermore, Pearlin and Schooler (1978) found that distancing strategies were most successful for coping with stressful impersonal situations. Conversely, strategies by which individuals remained committed and engaged with relevant others were most successful in reducing emotional distress in more personal situations. M. J. Miller (1989) described how illusions may be used as effective mechanisms in coping with painful experiences. Also, the initial expression of emotion may be more facilitative in managing emotional distress than acting with restraint (Wortman, 1983). Finally, qualitative differences between stressors are relevant to an examination of coping effectiveness. Important parameters of stressful events include "entrance"-"exit," acute-chronic, expected-unexpected, positive-negative, and "off-time"-"on-time."

Coping Patterns Should Fit the Context and the Individual

Coping effectiveness is related to its appropriateness to the internal/external demands of the situation. This "matching" hypothesis suggests that adaptive coping requires a good fit between the person-environment transaction, the person's appraisal of the transaction, and the consequent coping behavior (Lazarus, 1993; Lazarus & Folkman, 1984a). Inappropriate appraisal of a situation may result in unnecessary coping or conversely, a lack of necessary anticipatory coping.

A good fit between the realities of the situation and coping methods is important. Problem-focused coping is more adaptive in situations viewed as changeable whereas emotion-focused is best used in unalterable situations (Lazarus & Folkman, 1984a). Controllability also determines or moderates the effectiveness of strategies that directly address the problem or those that aim at alleviating the emotional distress caused by the problem (Felton & Revenson, 1984). Baum et al. (1983) reported that emotion-focused coping was adaptive in dealing with technological disaster because it increased the sense of perceived control. Coping must also be matched to appraisals of control and personal factors (e.g., values, goals, beliefs). Optimal functioning requires that the individual stay with or abandon goals depending on circumstances.

Coping Strategies Vary between and within Individuals

Task-focused efforts (e.g., studying) may be activated by certain individuals on announcement of an exam. Others procrastinate or complain about the course or instructor, yet they may use adaptive coping methods to manage other stressors. Person-situation interactions also occur; for example, one student uses problem-focused coping with little skill and is less successful than another who uses emotion-focused coping to alleviate anxiety. Coping strategies may change over time to manage both short- and long-term effects of a stressful event, such as the loss of a family member. However, continued life stressors may result in the use of less effective strategies (Fondacaro & Moos, 1989).

Furthermore, coping with a particular stressor (e.g., death of a family member) may change over time so that the person eventually is able to deal with the event and continue on. Yet it is also recognized that the life stressors themselves may wear down the individual and lead to the use of less effective coping strategies under continued stress (Aldwin & Revenson, 1987; Fondacaro & Moos, 1989).

Adaptive Coping Involves a Flexible Repertoire and Combined Use of Coping Strategies

People tend to employ both emotion- and problem-focused coping in managing most stressful events. This would appear to be functional for it allows for both the regulation of emotion and management of the stressor (Lazarus & Folkman, 1984a). For example, a theft of a personal possession may certainly cause some anger and the victim may ventilate this in conversation with friends while hoping for the "worst" to befall the culprit; but at the same time, the person will report the theft to police, call the insurance company for compensation, and increase security (such as installing a better door).

A large repertoire of coping resources, and flexibility and creativity in their use may increase coping adaptiveness. Both emotion- and problem-focused coping are commonly viewed as functional for regulating emotion and managing the actual stressor. Thus, trying different strategies in different combinations may be a better way to manage stress rather than responding reflexively with the same limited response to varying stressors. To ensure personal coping efficacy, it is necessary to incorporate relevant problem-solving skills (e.g., social skills, decision-making) and/or emotion-focused skills (e.g., relaxation). Although greater flexibility may relate to better emotional adjustment (Mattlin et al., 1990), multiple coping reactions within a given period may reflect ineffective coping (Carver et al., 1993).

A number of studies (cf. Mattlin et al., 1990; Pearlin & Schooler, 1978) suggest that having a versatile coping profile is associated with good adjustment, though the effects are rather modest. This does not hold true across the board; for example, in occupational stress being able to call on more mechanisms does not minimize the chances that role strains will result in emotional stress (Pearlin & Schooler, 1978).

Coping Responses May Influence Some but Not Other Outcomes

A particular coping behavior may differentially influence various outcomes (Silver & Wortman, 1980). Various coping indexes are not highly correlated. Further, each coping strategy has both its benefits and costs. For example, denying the seriousness of a partner's illness may reduce emotional distress but also negatively affect the care given to the spouse. Each coping strategy has its benefits as well as costs.

Adaptive Coping May Differ for Chronic versus Acute Stressors

There is some evidence that engaging in coping may be less effective among people exposed to a chronic difficulty than to acute stressors (cf. Wethington & Kessler, 1991). Thus, the power of coping strategies to promote adjustment may become weaker as stress continues. Furthermore, some situations may be so intractable that endurance is more efficacious than action.

Coping Adaptiveness May Vary across Phases of a Stressful Encounter

Coping is a process; it is a transaction between a person and event that plays across time and changing circumstances. The relevance and effectiveness of a coping reaction varies with the phase of the transaction. For example, denial may interfere with the early detection and treatment of breast cancer. By contrast, following diagnosis, denial of one's emotional reaction or the life-threatening implications of the disease may have very different effects (Carver et al., 1993). Timing is also an important aspect of adaptive coping. Avoidance strategies may be effective for short-term stressors, but nonavoidant strategies are effective for long-term stressors (Suls & Fletcher, 1985). A response positively associated with short-term well-being (e.g., maintaining hope that a husband missing in action will be found) may be negatively associated with well-being if it persists for a number of years.

TRAINING ADAPTIVE COPING BEHAVIORS

A critical question that arises for both researchers and practitioners is whether coping skills can be effectively taught and implemented within stress management and various other therapeutic programs. If, as suggested in the literature, maladaptive coping behaviors may be implicated in causing, maintaining, and even exacerbating mental and physical ill health, then it might follow that teaching more adaptive coping strategies would be an effective intervention and prevention strategy. A number of studies have examined the effects and effectiveness of developing and modifying existing coping behaviors.

The kind and extent of coping efforts that are activated and implemented by an individual are the result of both primary and secondary appraisals (Folkman & Lazarus, 1985). Cognitive-behavioral methods such as cognitive restructuring (Ellis, 1977) may have considerable effectiveness for altering faulty and dysfunctional perceptions and beliefs that, in turn, determine human behaviors including coping. Thus, modifying the stress appraisal process may be a critical step in determining ensuing coping strategies. Of further relevance is the recognition of a reciprocal relationship between the outcome effectiveness of the enacted coping strategies and the appraisal of future stressful events.

Secondary appraisal includes the learners' evaluations of their coping resources as more or less effective in managing perceived stress. MacNair and Elliott (1992) state that as persons' perceptions of their coping effectiveness increase, they are more likely to employ problem-focused coping. Further, problem-focused coping is more likely to be used in situations viewed as changeable in contrast to unchangeable ones (Folkman et al., 1986). These findings suggest that modifying the appraisal of both the stressor and one's coping effectiveness may be a critical factor in the effective management of stress (cf. Folkman et al., 1991).

Because secondary appraisal is more directly related to the topic of coping, the following comments will focus mainly on attempts to create, modify, and select coping strategies. One example of training more effective coping behaviors is problem solving (D'Zurilla & Goldfried, 1971; Janis & Mann, 1977). Problem-solving strategies have been incorporated into various cognitive-behavioral therapies and are defined as efforts to identify or create effective and adaptive coping behaviors (D'Zurilla & Goldfried, 1971). In relation to depression (discussed earlier), deficient and ineffective problem solving has been implicated in this major mental health disorder (Dobson & Dobson, 1981). Nezu (1986) has also reported that depressed patients benefit from social problem-solving therapy. Training in problem-solving skills has been incorporated into programs for the prevention of health-care problems (e.g., diet, tobacco use) among Native American youth (Schinke & Singer, 1994).

Teaching coping skills is part of various cognitive-behavioral programs ranging from specific techniques such as self-instruction training (Meichenbaum, 1977) to comprehensive health-care programs (Schinke & Singer, 1994). For example, Meichenbaum's (1977) stress inoculation training program is intended to teach more effective coping skills in the management of stress. During the skills acquisition and rehearsal phase, participants are trained in both instrumental and palliative coping skills as required. The self-instruction component further includes the generation of self-statements designed to cope effectively with feelings of being overwhelmed.

Another example of coping skills training is found in programs designed to prevent relapse following the termination of treatment (Granvold & Wodarski, 1994). Training effective coping skills is important in successfully managing both old and new stressors that may cause a relapse of such behaviors as smoking (Baer, Kamarck, Lichtenstein, & Ransom, 1989). Further, the use of multiple coping behaviors in smoking cessation programs appears to increase the effectiveness of the treatment thereby reducing the likelihood of relapse (Bliss, Garvey, Heinold, & Hitchcock, 1989). A recent study of unaided smoking cessation suggested that quitters more often than nonquitters, used problem-solving coping strategies and cognitive restructuring in contrast to wishful thinking, self-criticism, and social withdrawal (Carey, Kalra, Carey, Halperin, & Richards, 1993). These studies provide important insights into the role of coping and the need to train more effective coping behaviors to ensure greater treatment success and relapse prevention.

Lastly, the research literature has provided some important data on the use of coping versus mastery models in coping skills training programs. During the acquisition and rehearsal of new coping strategies, it appears that coping models who make mistakes in the process of finally reaching an appropriate solution are more effective than mastery models (models who correctly select and enact the correct coping behavior each and every time). Coping models are found in various programs for teaching social skills (Kendall & Braswell, 1986), for instructing parents (Cunningham, 1990) and residential staff (Cunningham, Davis, Bremner, Dunn, & Rzasa, 1993), and for treating anxiety (Sarason, 1975).

An examination of various criterion groups, both clinical and normal, offers considerable insight into defining adaptive and maladaptive coping behaviors and describing effective coping. Studies of procedures that teach more effective coping skills provide even further opportunity to examine the short- and long-term effectiveness of such training. Preliminary evidence offers some support for the need to change both primary and secondary appraisals in efforts to promote enhanced well-being.

CONCLUSION

In spite of research that indicates there are particular coping behaviors in certain criterion groups, and further that coping training may be an effective component in cognitive and behavioral therapies, the process and causal directions in the stress-coping-outcome literature do not permit bold and conclusive statements. At present, there is no consensus about which coping strategies are most effective and adaptive in promoting positive outcomes. Further research is needed to clarify how a coping strategy resolves problems, relieves emotional distress, and prevents future difficulties (Aldwin & Revenson, 1987). Associations between stress and outcome are mainly concurrent; it is not clear whether coping influences adjustment, whether coping tactics covary with adjustment, or whether coping and distress are mutually intertwined reflections of yet some other human condition or characteristic. Future research should help clarify the kind and extent of the effect that coping behavior has on well-being.

REFERENCES

Aldwin, C. M., & Revenson, T. T. (1987). Does coping help? A reexamination of the relation between coping and mental health. *Journal of Personality and Social Psychology, 53,* 337–348.

Aspinwall, L. G., & Taylor, S. E. (1992). Modelling cognitive adaptation: A longitudinal investigation of the impact of individual differences and coping on college adjustment and performance. *Journal of Personality and Social Psychology, 63,* 989–1003.

Auerbach, S. M. (1989). Stress management and coping research in the health care setting: An overview and methodological commentary. *Journal of Consulting and Clinical Psychology, 57,* 388–395.

Baer, J. S., Kamararck, T., Lichtenstein, E., & Ransom, C. C., Jr. (1989). Prediction of smoking relapse: Analyses of temptations and transgressions after initial cessation. *Journal of Consulting and Clinical Psychology, 57,* 623–627.

Baum, A., Fleming, R. E., & Singer, J. E. (1983). Coping with technological disaster. *Journal of Social Issues, 39,* 117–138.

Billings, A. G., Cronkite, R. C., & Moos, R. H. (1983). Social-environmental factors in unipolar depression: Comparison of depressed patients and nondepressed controls. *Journal of Abnormal Psychology, 92,* 119–133.

Billings, A. G., & Moos, R. H. (1981). The role of coping responses and social resources in attenuating the impact of stressful life events. *Journal of Behavioural Medicine, 4,* 139–157.

Billings, A. G., & Moos, R. H. (1984). Coping, stress, and social resources among adults with unipolar depression. *Journal of Personality and Social Psychology, 46,* 877–891.

Bliss, R. E., Garvey, A. J., Heinhold, J. W., & Hitchcock, J. L. (1989). The influence of situation and coping on relapse crisis outcomes after smoking cessation. *Journal of Consulting and Clinical Psychology, 57,* 443–449.

Bolger, N. (1990). Coping as a personality process: A prospective study. *Journal of Personality and Social Psychology, 59,* 525–537.

Burns, D. D., & Nolen-Hoeksema, S. (1991). Coping styles, homework compliance, and the effectiveness of cognitive-behavioral therapy. *Journal of Consulting and Clinical Psychology, 59,* 305–311.

Carey, M. P., Kalra, D. L., Carey, K. B., Halperin, S., & Richards, C. S. (1993). Stress and unaided smoking cessation: A prospective investigation. *Journal of Consulting and Clinical Psychology, 61,* 831–838.

Carver, C. S., Pozo, C., Harris, S. D., Noriega, V., Scheier, M. F., Robinson, D. S., Ketchan, A. S., Moffat, F. L., Jr., & Clark, K. C. (1993). How coping mediates the effect of optimism on distress: A study of women with early stage breast cancer. *Journal of Personality and Social Psychology, 65,* 375–390.

Carver, C. S., & Scheier, M. F. (in press). Situational coping and coping dispositions in a stressful transaction. *Journal of Personality and Social Psychology.*

Carver, C. S., Scheier, M. F., & Pozo, C. (1992). Conceptualizing the process of coping with health problems. In H. S. Friedman (Ed.), *Hostility, coping, and health* (pp. 167–199). Washington, DC: American Psychological Association.

Carver, C. S., Scheier, M. F., & Weintraub, J. K. (1989). Assessing coping strategies: A theoretically based approach. *Journal of Personality and Social Psychology, 56,* 267–283.

Cattanach, L., Malley, R., & Rodin, J. (1988). Psychologic and physiologic reactivity to stressors in eating disorder individuals. *Psychosomatic Medicine, 50,* 591–599.

Cohen, F. (1987). Measurement of coping. In S. V. Kasl & C. L. Cooper (Eds.), *Stress and health: Issues in research methodology* (pp. 283–305). New York: Wiley.

Cohen, F., & Lazarus, R. (1979). Coping with the stresses of illness. In G. C. Stone, F. Cohen, & N. E. Adler (Eds.), *Health psychology: A handbook.* San Francisco: Jossey-Bass.

Collins, R. L., Taylor, S. E., & Skokan, L. A. (1990). A better world or a shattered vision? Changes in life perspectives following victimization. *Social Cognition, 8,* 263–285.

Coyne, J. C., Aldwin, C., & Lazarus, R. S. (1981). Depression and coping in stressful episodes. *Journal of Abnormal Psychology, 90,* 439–447.

Cunningham, C. E. (1990). A family systems oriented parent training program. In R. A. Barkley (Ed.), *Attention deficit hyperactivity: A handbook for diagnosis and treatment* (pp. 432–461). New York: Guilford.

Cunningham, C. E., Davis, J. R., Bremner, R., Dunn, K. W., & Rzasa, T. (1993). Coping modeling problem solving versus mastery modeling: Effects on adherence, in-session process, and skill acquisition in a residential parent-training program. *Journal of Consulting and Clinical Psychology, 61,* 871–877.

Dobson, D. J., & Dobson, K. S. (1981). Problem-solving strategies in depressed and nondepressed college students. *Cognitive Therapy and Research, 5,* 237–249.

Dorland, S., & Hattie, J. (1992). Coping and repetitive strain injury. *Australian Journal of Psychology, 44,* 45–49.

D'Zurilla, T. J., & Goldfried, M. R. (1971). Problem solving and behavior modification. *Journal of Abnormal Psychology, 78,* 107–126.

Ellis, A. (1977). Rational-emotive therapy: Research data that supports the clinical and personality hypotheses of RET and other modes of cognitive-behavior therapy. *The Counseling Psychologist, 7,* 2–42.

Endler, N. S., & Parker, J. D. (1990a). *Coping Inventory for Stressful Situations (CISS): Manual.* Toronto, Canada: Multi-Health Systems.

Endler, N. S., & Parker, J. D. (1990b). State and trait anxiety, depression, and coping styles. *Australian Journal of Psychology, 42,* 207–220.

Endler, N. S., Parker, J. D., & Summerfeldt, L. J. (1993). Coping with health problems: Conceptual and methodological issues. *Canadian Journal of Behavioural Science, 25,* 384–399.

Felton, B. J., & Revenson, T. A. (1984). Coping with chronic illness: A study of illness controllability and the influence of coping strategies on psychological adjustment. *Journal of Consulting and Clinical Psychology, 52,* 343–353.

Folkman, S., Chesney, M., McKussick, L., Ironson, G., Johnson, D. S., & Coastes, T. J. (1991). Translating coping theory into an intervention. In J. Eckenrode (Ed.), *The Social Context of Coping* (pp. 239–260). New York: Plenum.

Folkman, S., & Lazarus, R. S. (1985). If it changes it must be a process: Study of emotion and coping during three stages of a college examination. *Journal of Personality and Social Psychology, 48,* 150–170.

Folkman, S., Lazarus, R. S., Gruen, R. J., & DeLongis, A. (1986). Appraisal, coping, health status, and psychological symptoms. *Journal of Personality and Social Psychology, 50,* 571–579.

Fondacaro, M. R., & Moos, R. H. (1987). Social support and coping: A longitudinal analysis. *American Journal of Community Psychology, 15,* 653–673.

Fondacaro, M. R., & Moos, R. H. (1989). Life stressors and coping: A longitudinal analysis among depressed and nondepressed adults. *Journal of Community Psychology, 17,* 330–340.

Freud, S. (1933). *New introductory lectures on psychoanalysis.* New York: Norton.

Gal, R., & Lazarus, R. (1975). The role of activity in anticipation and confronting stressful situations. *Journal of Human Stress, 1,* 4–20.

Granvold, D. K., & Wodarski, J. S. (1994). Cognitive and behavioral treatment: Clinical issues, transfer of training, and relapse prevention. In D. K. Granvold (Ed.), *Cognitive and behavioral treatment: Method and applications* (pp. 353–375). Pacific Grove: Brooks/Cole.

Haan, N. (1977). *Coping and defending: Processes of self-environmental organization.* New York: Academic Press.

Heller, K., Swindle, R. W., & Dusenbury, L. (1986). Component social support processes. *Journal of Consulting and Clinical Psychology, 54,* 466–470.

Hewitt, P. L., & Flett, C. L. (1991). Perfectionism in the self and social contexts: Conceptualization, assessment, and association with psychopathology. *Journal of Personality and Social Psychology, 60,* 456–470.

Holahan, C. J., & Moos, R. H. (1987). Personal and contextual determinants of coping strategies. *Journal of Personality and Social Psychology, 52,* 946–955.

Holahan, C. J., & Moos, R. H. (1990). Life stressors, resistance factors and psychological health: An extension of the stress-resistance paradigm. *Journal of Personality and Social Psychology, 58,* 909–917.

Holahan, C. J., & Moos, R. H. (1991). Life stressors, personal and social resources, and depression: A 4-year structural model. *Journal of Abnormal Psychology, 100,* 31–38.

Janis, I., & Mann, L. (1977). *Decision making.* New York: Free Press.

Janzen, B. L., Kelly, I. W., & Saklofske, D. H. (1992). Bulimic symptomatology and coping in a nonclinical sample. *Perceptual and Motor Skills, 75,* 395–399.

Johnson, J. E., Lauver, D. R., & Nail, L. M. (1989). Process of coping with radiation therapy. *Journal of Consulting and Clinical Psychology, 57,* 358–364.

Joseph, S., Cairns, E., & McCollam, P. (1993). Political violence, coping, and depressive symptomatology in Northern Irish Children. *Personality and Individual Differences, 15,* 471–474.

Kendall, P. C., & Braswell, L. (1986). The medical applications of cognitive-behavioral interventions with children. *Journal of Developmental and Behavioral Pediatrics, 7,* 257–264.

Kessler, R. C., Price, R. H., & Wortman, C. B. (1985). Social factors in psychopathology: Stress, social support, and coping processes. *Annual Review of Psychology, 36,* 531–572.

Lacey, J. H., Coker, S., & Birtchnell, S. A. (1986). Bulimia: Factors associated with its etiology and maintenance. *International Journal of Eating Disorders, 5,* 475–487.

Lazarus, R. S. (1969). *Patterns of adjustment and human effectiveness.* New York: McGraw-Hill.

Lazarus, R. S. (1993). Coping theory and research: Past, present and future. *Psychosomatic Medicine, 55,* 237–247.

Lazarus, R. S., DeLongis, A., Folkman, S., & Gruen, R. (1985). Stress and adaptational outcomes: The problem of confounded measures. *American Psychologist, 40,* 770–779.

Lazarus, R. S., & Folkman, S. (1984a). Coping and adaptation. In W. D. Gentry (Ed.), *The handbook of behavioral medicine* (pp. 282–325). New York: Guilford.

Lazarus, R. S., & Folkman, S. (1984b). *Stress, appraisal, and coping.* New York: Springer.

Lazarus, R. S., & Launier, R. (1978). Stress-related transactions between person and environment. In L. Pervin & M. Lewis (Eds.), *Perspectives in international psychology* (pp. 287–327). New York: Plenum.

Lennon, M. C., Dohrenwend, B. P., Zautra, A. J., & Marbach, J. J. (1990). Coping and adaptation to facial pain in contrast to other stressful life events. *Journal of Personality and Social Psychology, 59,* 1040–1050.

MacNair, R. R., & Elliott, T. R. (1992). Self-perceived problem solving ability, stress appraisal, and coping over time. *Journal of Research in Personality, 26,* 150–164.

Marsella, A. J., DeVos, G., & Hsu, F. (Eds.). (1985). *Culture and self: Asian and Western perspectives.* London: Tavistock.

Mattlin, J. A., Wethington, E., & Kessler, C. (1990). Situational determinants of coping and coping effectiveness. *Journal of Health and Social Behavior, 31,* 103–122.

Mayhew, R., & Edelman, R. J. (1989). Self esteem, irrational beliefs, and coping strategies in relation to eating problems in a non-clinical population. *Personality and Individual Differences, 10,* 581–584.

Mayo, V. D., & Tanaka-Matsumi, J. (1993, August). *Emotion versus problem-focused approaches to an interpersonal problem by depressives.* Paper presented at 101st annual Convention of the American Psychological Association, Toronto, Canada.

McCrae, R. R., & Costa, P. T. (1986). Personality, coping, and coping effectiveness in an adult sample. *Journal of Personality, 54,* 383–405.

Meichenbaum, D. (1977). *Cognitive-behavior modification: An integrative approach.* New York: Plenum.

Meneghan, E. (1982). Measuring coping effectiveness: A panel analysis of marital problems and coping efforts. *Journal of Health and Social Behavior, 23,* 220–234.

Miller, M. J. (1989). The importance of holding on to illusions. *Counseling and Values, 33,* 146–151.

Miller, S. M., Leinbach, A., & Brody, D. S. (1989). Coping style in hypertensive patients: Nature and consequences. *Journal of Consulting and Clinical Psychology, 57,* 333–337.

Miller, S. M., & Mangan, C. E. (1983). Interacting effects of information and coping style in adapting to gynecologic stress: Should the doctor tell all? *Journal of Personality and Social Psychology, 45,* 223–236.

Mirowsky, J., & Ross, C. (1990). Control or defense? Depression and the sense of control: Good and bad outcomes. *Journal of Health and Social Behavior, 31,* 71–86.

Mullins, L. L., Olson, R. A., Reyes, S., Bernardy, N., Huszti, H. C., & Volk, R. J. (1991). Risk and resistance factors in the adaptation of mothers of children with cystic fibrosis. *Journal of Pediatric Psychology, 16,* 701–715.

Nezu, A. M. (1986). Efficacy of a social problem solving therapy approach for unipolar depression. *Journal of Consulting and Clinical Psychology, 54,* 196–202.

Nezu, A. M., & Carnevale, G. J. (1987). Interpersonal problem solving and coping reactions of Vietnam Veterans with post-traumatic stress disorder. *Journal of Applied Psychology, 96,* 155–157.

Nolan, R., & Wielgosz, A. T. (1991). Assessing adaptive and maladaptive coping in the early phase of acute myocardial infarction. *Journal of Behavioral Medicine, 14,* 111–124.

Pearlin, L. I. (1991). The study of coping: An overview of problems and directions. In J. Eckenrode (Ed.), *The Social Context of Coping* (pp. 261–276). New York: Plenum.

Pearlin, L. I., & Schooler, C. (1978). The structure of coping. *Journal of Health and Social Behavior, 19*, 2–21.

Peterson, L. (1989). Coping by children undergoing stressful medical procedures: Some conceptual, methodological, and therapeutic issues. *Journal of Consulting and Clinical Psychology, 57*, 380–387.

Revenson, T. A., & Felton, B. J. (1989). Disability and coping as predictors of psychological adjustment to rheumatoid arthritis. *Journal of Consulting and Clinical Psychology, 57*, 344–348.

Rubenstein, C., & Shaver, P. (1980). Loneliness in two north eastern cities. In J. Hartog, J. R. Audy, & Y. A. Cohen (Eds.), *Anatomy of loneliness* (pp. 319–337). New York: International Universities Press.

Saklofske, D. H. (1993, July). The position of N with non-clinical groups. *Proceedings of the 6th meeting of the International Society for the Study of Individual Differences* (p. 32). Baltimore: International Society for the Study of Individual Differences.

Saklofske, D. H., & Yackulic, R. A. (1989). Personality predictors of loneliness. *Personality and Individual Differences, 10*, 467–472.

Sarason, I. G. (1975). Test anxiety and the self-disclosing model. *Journal of Consulting and Clinical Psychology, 43*, 148–153.

Schinke, S. P., & Singer, B. R. (1994). Prevention of health-care problems. In D. K. Granvold (Ed.), *Cognitive and behavioral treatment: Method and applications* (pp. 285–298). Pacific Grove, CA: Brooks/Cole.

Shatford, L. A., & Evans, D. R. (1986). Bulimia as a manifestation of the stress process: A LISREL causal modeling analysis. *International Journal of Eating Disorders, 5*, 451–473.

Silver, R. L., & Wortman, C. (1980). Coping with undesirable life events. In J. Garber & M. E. P. Seligman (Eds.), *Human helplessness* (pp. 279–340). New York: Academic Press.

Solomon, Z., Avitzur, M., & Mikulincer, M. (1989). Coping resources and social functioning following combat stress reactions: A longitudinal study. *Journal of Social and Clinical Psychology, 8*, 87–96.

Solomon, Z., Mikulincer, M., & Avitzur, E. (1988). Coping, locus of control, social support, and combat-related post-traumatic stress disorder. *Journal of Personality and Social Psychology, 55*, 279–285.

Solomon, Z., Mikulincer, M., & Benbenishty, R. (1989). Locus of control and combat related post-traumatic stress disorder: The intervening role of battle intensity threat appraisal and coping. *British Journal of Clinical Psychology, 28*, 131–144.

Stone, A. A., Helder, L., & Schneider, M. M. (1988). Coping with stressful events: Coping dimensions and issues. In L. H. Cohen (Ed.), *Life events and psychological functioning: Theoretical and methodological issues* (pp. 182–210). Newbury Park, CA: Sage.

Suls, J., & Fletcher, B. (1985). The relative efficacy of avoidant and nonavoidant coping strategies: A meta-analysis. *Health Psychology, 4*, 249–288.

Taylor, S. E. (1986). *Health psychology*. New York: Random House.

Thompson, R. J., Gil, K. M., Abrams, M. R., & Philips, G. (1992). Stress, coping, and psychological adjustment of adults with sickle cell disease. *Journal of Consulting and Clinical Psychology, 60*, 433–440.

Vaillant, G. E. (1977). *Adaptation to life.* Boston: Little, Brown.

Van Buskirk, A. M., & Duke, M. P. (1991). The relationship between coping style and loneliness in adolescents: Can "sad-passivity" be adaptive? *Journal of Genetic Psychology, 152,* 145–157.

Vitaliano, P. P., DeWolfe, D. J., Maiuro, R. D., Russo, J., & Katon, W. (1990). Appraised changeability of a stressor as a modifier of the relationship between coping and depression: A test of the hypothesis of fit. *Journal of Personality and Social Psychology, 59,* 582–592.

Vitaliano, P. P., Katon, W., Maiuro, R. D., & Russo, J. (1989). Coping in chest pain patients with and without psychiatric disorders. *Journal of Consulting and Clinical Psychology, 57,* 338–343.

Wallerstein, J. S. (1983). Children of divorce: The psychological tasks of the child. *American Journal of Orthopsychiatry, 53,* 230–243.

Weidner, G., & Collins, R. L. (1992). Gender, coping, and health. In H. W. Krohne (Ed.), *Attention and avoidance: Strategies in coping with aversiveness* (pp. 241–265). Gottingen: Hogrefe & Huber.

Williams, P. G., Wiebe, D. J., & Smith, T. W. (1992). Coping processes as mediators of the relationship between hardiness and health. *Journal of Behavioral Medicine, 15,* 237–255.

Wills, T. A. (1986). Stress and coping in early adolescence: Relationships to substance use in urban high schools. *Health Psychology, 5,* 503–529.

Wortman, C. (1983). Coping with victimization: Conclusions and implications for future research. *Journal of Social Issues, 39,* 195–221.

Zeidner, M. (1994). Personal and contextual determinants of coping and anxiety in an evaluative situation: A prospective study. *Personality and Individual Differences, 16,* 899–918.

Zeidner, M., & Ben-Zur, H. (1994). Individual differences in anxiety, coping, and posttraumatic stress in the aftermath of the Persian Gulf War. *Personality and Individual Differences, 16,* 459–476.

Zeidner, M., & Hammer, A. L. (1990). Life events and coping resources as predictors of stress symptoms in adolescents. *Personality and Individual Differences, 11,* 693–703.

CHAPTER 23

Defensive Control Processes: Use of Theory in Research, Formulation, and Therapy of Stress Response Syndromes

MARDI J. HOROWITZ, HANS J. ZNOJ, and CHARLES H. STINSON

This chapter will focus on the cognitive processes by which individuals accomplish coping and defense. This focus is important in planning interventions for reducing maladaptive responses to stressor life events. The control process categories to be considered are those that influence conscious thought and interpersonal communication of ideas and feelings. Knowledge gained about these areas of preconscious information processing can lead to formulations of how to intervene in psychotherapy and prevention.

BASIC CONCEPTS AND BACKGROUND

Coping strategies have been related both to formation of psychopathology in stress-response syndromes and to recovery from stressor events in terms of normal resilience and adaptive functioning (Perrez & Reicherts, 1992). Some coping strategies seem to be more possible with less severe stressor events and harder to use for more traumatic events. As the magnitude of the stress increases, people may turn from use of internal information-processing capacities to use of external agents such as drugs, group rituals (Park & Cohen, 1993; Portes et al., 1992; Roper, Rachman, & Hodgson, 1973; Salzman, 1979), or therapy.

We focus on *defensive control processes* following what Lazarus referred to as emotional coping through cognitive processes (Folkman & Lazarus, 1988; Folkman, Lazarus, Dunkel-Schetter, DeLongis, & Gruen, 1986; Lazarus, 1993). We add an integrated cognitive-psychodynamic perspective (Horowitz, 1988a, 1988b) that draws from defense mechanisms theory, stemming from Freud

This chapter is based on research supported by the Program on Conscious and Unconscious Mental Processes of the John D. and Catherine T. MacArthur Foundation. The second author is supported by the Swiss National Foundation (SNF 8210-037067). Andreas Maercker, Francisco Gonzalez, and Raphael Gray made important contributions in judging videotape on these constructs.

(1900/1958) and reaching to Vaillant (1992). But, we do not retain the classical psychoanalytic definitions of defense; a newer approach seemed necessary (Horowitz, 1988a; Horowitz, Markman, Stinson, Fridhandler, & Ghannan, 1990; Horowitz & Stinson, 1995).

This new approach evolved over many years of study of stress response syndromes, during which defensiveness was clearly apparent and empirically validated. For example, evidence for periods of denial/avoidance as well as other aspects of phases in prototypical stress response syndromes, as shown in Figure 23.1, have been demonstrated (Horowitz, 1992). Confronting defensiveness, making information processing safe, and aiding reschematization of beliefs to accord to new realities are all parts of a brief and effective approach to phase-oriented treatment of such stress disorders as posttraumatic stress disorder and pathological grief reaction. Important therapist activities include interpretation of defenses and warded-off contents, as well as dysfunctional beliefs, as illustrated in the summary of a sample therapy in Table 23.1. Careful qualitative and quantitative studies of what happens in video records of such treatments led to our modification of existing psychoanalytic theory and a cognitive-dynamic integration.

On repeated reviews of video-recorded treatment sessions and over the course of therapy, we observed that operational definitions of repression, dissociation, undoing, reaction formation, and similar ego defense mechanisms could not easily be applied to the immediacy of expression of conflictual topics and complex medleys of expressed and stifled emotions. Debates developed between observers because the operational definitions contained blends of content and form that were often confusing. Moreover, we noted that even habitual styles of regulating emotional expression in a single subject varied from state to state of that subject. Because of differences in use of even habitual defensive control processes, a memory of a traumatic event might seem real in one state, unreal in another state, forgotten in a third state, and experienced in a depersonalized way in yet another kind of state.

A task force of scientists examined the same recorded case material to contrast and compare methods of classification of regulatory behaviors based on control process theory with those of classical defense mechanisms theory. The results have been published and indicate the fine-grained nature of the defensive control process theory we have been developing: It specifies in more detail and with more precise temporal localization what cognitive operations are being used to modulate conscious thought and interpersonal communication. Defense mechanisms theory, in contrast, is more useful in examining lifelong stories of how an individual adapts from year to year (Horowitz et al., 1992).

There are two main issues in the psychotherapy of persons who have a stress-response syndrome such as PTSD or pathological grief after a major terror, injury, or loss. One is *shock mastery*—the integration into a belief structure the meaning of terrible perceptions and intense frights. Sequelae to traumas include unbidden images, fears of repetition, and general alarm reactions (physiological and hormonal as well as brain-based) to unthreatening stimuli. These signs and symptoms occur until shock mastery is accomplished. The second main issue in

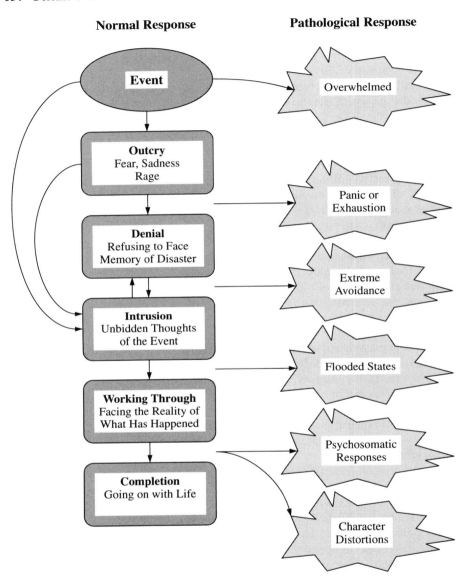

Figure 23.1   Normal and pathological phases of poststress response.

TABLE 23.1   Treatment for Stress Disorders: A Sample 12-Session Cognitive-Dynamic Approach

Session	Relationship Issues	Patient Activity	Therapist Acitvity
1	Initial positive feeling for helper.	Patient tells story of event.	Preliminary focus is discussed.
2	Lull as sense of pressure is reduced.	Event is related to previous life.	Takes psychiatric history. Gives patient realistic appraisal of syndrome.
3	Patient testing therapist for various relationship possibilities.	Patient adds associ- ations to indicate ex- panded meaning of event.	Formulation leads to focus. Resistances are interpreted.
4	Therapeutic alliance deepened.	Implications of event in the present are contemplated.	Defenses and warded-off contents are interpreted.
5	Obstacles to frank communication may block sharing.	Themes that have been avoided are worked on.	Active confrontation of contradictions on feared topics. Reengagement in adaptive activities is en- couraged. Unrealistic transferences are interpreted.
6	The treatment relation- ship is transient.	The future is contemplated.	Time and manner of termination is discussed.
7–11	Transference reactions interpreted and linked to other configurations. Acknowledgment of pending separation repeated.	Central conflicts are worked through.	Central conflicts are identified and adaptive integrations or choices are proposed as possibilities.
12	Saying good-bye.	Work that is to be continued on own and plans for the future are discussed.	Real gains and summary of future work for patient to do on own are clarified.

Note: Modified from Horowitz, 1992.

psychotherapy is the *reschematization of personal beliefs* to accord with new real- ities, exemplified by a mourning process. Signs of maladaptive behavior may per- sist until such reschematization is accomplished (Horowitz, 1986, 1991). Both mastery of shocks and reschematization are forms of information processing.

Mastery of Shocks

A supportive relationship often facilitates mastery of shock-related ideas and feelings and biological alarm reactions. Within a therapeutic alliance, a therapist can use treatment techniques that help a person move from failing levels of self-regulatory capacity toward more adaptive levels of control of emotion. The person is helped to progress from dysregulation in phases of intrusion to working states in which problem-filled ideas and feelings are contemplated without a sense of chaos.

Mastery of shock-related topics is aided by a dose-by-dose approach to tumultuous themes. There is no expectation of completing the train of thought about a stressful topic in one sitting. Rather, there is an expectation that there will be repeated and intermittent efforts to explore aspects of the topic within safe limits of toleration for unpleasant emotions. Usually, it is best to focus first on the most intrusive topics including topics that subsequently became intrusive often being warded off during a phase of relative denial. A dose-by-dose approach means *both* facilitating a focus of attention on the topic *and* learning deliberate deflection of attention away from the topic when there is a threat of excessive flooding with emotion. With practice, the person learns that they can control both remembering and a shift of attention away from an emotionally distressing topic.

The purpose of the set of techniques for pulling attention toward and away from shocking topics is to advance an associate examination of a topic to a point of relative completion of appraisal and to learn to associate the topic with increasing levels of self-control and a sense of mastery. Earlier theories about catharsis as emptying the mind of excessive stimulation have been replaced by this emphasis on learning to integrate news of shocking perceptions into a sense of the overall continuity and self-coherence.

Memory is not a camera. Recollection of trauma produces composites of information derived from perceptions of the event and preexisting meaning structures, including both realistic and fantastic associations to the meanings of the event. At first, shocking events may be recalled as if they were unreal, then there may be a period in which unbidden images feel like accurate flashbacks of real events. Only over time is there a growing sense of what was real and what was fantasy. Differentiating reality and fantasy is an important aspect of personal event processing and social communication.

Adaptive Reschematization

In addition to mastery of shocks, stressor event processing is often followed by adaptive reschematization of personal beliefs and structures of identity and affiliation meanings. Reschematization, as in processes of mourning of forced development of new self-concepts, may be facilitated by expressive treatment techniques, behavioral rehearsals, and supportive approaches. The person is helped to recognize focal discrepancies and contradictions between beliefs, and between beliefs and social or worldly actualities. New belief structures and integrations are encouraged. New behavioral practices, based on adaptive beliefs, are supported until the person rehearses and repeats them enough to acquire appropriate habit patterns. Behavioral repetitions etch in the new, adaptive schematizations and scenarios of how to best articulate self to the surrounding world.

Obstacles to Mastery and Reschematization

Mastery of shocks and adaptive reschematizations improve a person's coping capacity. The main obstacles to mastery of shocks and changing beliefs are states of dysregulation (the person is flooded by alarm reactions) or excessive regulation (information processing is blocked to avoid excessive emotional arousal). The person does not adequately contemplate new action plans and outmoded beliefs.

Other obstacles include activation of latent irrational ideas as ways of explaining the occurrence of a stressor life event. Social support that might otherwise be helpful is shunted aside. Different persons who have experienced the same type of shocking stressor event may nonetheless manifest different types of defensive control processes and irrational beliefs. The classification theory of types of control processes we present can lead to more detailed plans for how to intervene to counter excessive defensiveness and to address irrational beliefs.

Defensiveness

For many years, we used defense mechanism theory from psychoanalysis. But as we attempted empirical studies and modern case formulations, we found it difficult to apply to videotapes of psychotherapy. We gradually developed a fine-grained defensive control process theory that incorporated object relations and self-psychological perspectives with more classical ego psychological perspectives. Defensive distortions in self-concept and views of roles of relationship with others were important components in this integrative effort (Horowitz, 1988a, 1988b).

States and Person Schemas Theory

Person schemas theory assumes that each person has a repertoire of multiple self-concepts as possible organizers of states. Each self-concept might be contained and stabilized in enduring role relationship models (Horowitz, 1989, 1991). These self and other schemas would lead to different organizations of memory and emotion in different states (Eells, Horowitz, Stinson, & Fridhandler, 1993; Horowitz, Fridhandler, & Stinson, 1991). Control processes would affect which topics were a focus of attention and which person schemas organized views of that topic.

The arduous and important work by Haan (1977, 1993) preceeded our attempt. We have kept her basic approach as a format, but believe she erred in keeping too close to classical psychoanalytic ego defense mechanisms. We believed that to converge with cognitive science, we needed to redefine what we mean by "mechanisms" (Erdelyi, 1984; Miller, Galanter, & Pribram, 1960; Singer, 1990; Wegner & Pennebaker, 1992). The classical set of defenses is more a set of outcomes of processes than the processes themselves. Haan's idea, following Kroeber (1963), was to define basic processes and then to consider variants that led to adaptive outcomes, maladaptive ones, or to failures in regulation. We retain that approach, but redefine processes.

DEFINITIONS USED IN DEFENSIVE CONTROL
PROCESSES THEORY

We use the term "control" to imply various ways in which incipient topics, schemas, and modes of representing thoughts and feelings might be inhibited or facilitated. In the Tables 23.2–23.4, we organize the classification according to *regulation of content, form, and person schemas.* We relate these sets of processes to outcome categories.

To categorize outcome, we have to consider the goals of using control. *Purposes* of control can be judged in a clinical context. In the denial phase that might follow reaction to a serious life event, one purpose might be to maintain emotional intensity within tolerable limits, to avoid an out-of-control state. Inhibition of topics might be adaptive if judged in relation to this purpose.

At the same time, another purpose might be to arrive at a decision about the meaning of the life event to the self and what to do about it. Warding off the topic might be maladaptive to this purpose (see also Wegner, Schneider, Carter, & White, 1987). That is why outcome categories have fuzzy, approximate boundaries. The usual inferred purpose of controls, for these outcome categories, is to avoid entry into states that are flooded with emotions, states in which the person is cognitively disrupted, or states in which the person might express feelings or ideas in ways that may incur social disapproval.

Following these assumptions, we define *defensive control processes* as mental activities that can change a state of mind by shifting a setting for how information is selected, formed, and organized. *Control* refers to processes of shifting mental activities; the state of regulation or modulation describes the outcome effects of controls. An *outcome state* may feel or appear to be well modulated, or under- or overmodulated; shimmering states indicate oscillating controls. Emotional regulation can be judged in terms of outcome to be *adaptive* or *maladaptive,* and an outcome of relative lack of regulation to be *dysregulation.* These outcomes are judged in relation to any specified standard of what states are desirable or useful to the individual in his or her social biological context.

Control *processes* change set points that influence the transition from preconscious processing to conscious representation or from conscious representation to social representation. Set points can be seen as limited numbers of possible settings for any kind of feedback regulations, as in a thermostat. In the following classification scheme, we differentiate between (a) processes that control what *contents* will become conscious, (b) processes that control the *form* of the conscious representation, and (c) processes that control *person schemas* as organizers of consciousness. We view these organizers as existing within learned repertoires of schemas.

The classification scheme consists of the types of set points of each of the three main categories (control of content, form, and person schemas) and of three different types of outcome regulation (adaptive, maladaptive, and dysregulation) specific to the type of setpoint. We aim at empirical evidence and so must define outcomes in terms of what could be recorded. Interpersonal communication can be

TABLE 23.2 Control of Contents: Interpersonal Outcome

	Outcome of Regulation		
Types of Set Points	Adaptive	Maladaptive	Outcome of Dysregulation
1. Altering the focus of attention.	Expresses a potentially stressful topic to another person to a degree that both can tolerate the emotion or conflict evoked with a balanced focus on feelings of self and reactions of other.	Unbalanced focus so that disruptively attentive only to self or too attuned to other to be sufficiently attentive to topics of importance to self; does not present stressful topic; selects obscuring or misleading alternative topic(s).	Sudden shifts into emotionally overwhelming topics.
2. Altering concepts and frame of attention.	Communicates key facts, emotions, and significance to self; contemplation of implications and possible solutions to problem; alert to cues of others.	Communicative reluctance; misleading others who are potentially helpful; giving misinformation; generalizing when specifying is indicated; avoidance of expressing a concept that might prove useful in solving problems; switching back and forth regarding the facts; interruption or overriding of other to prevent clarification or useful give and take; refusal to follow useful cues or leads provided by others.	Fragmented and hard-to-follow communication.
3. Altering the importance to self of a chain of concepts.	Careful appraisal of alternatives; maintenance of and/or clear changes in values, commitments, and shared meanings.	Vacillation when taking a stance is essential; facile face-saving at the expense of reasonable shared estimates of the truth; rationalizing the irrational.	Disruptive or chaotic shifts in values and appraisals.
4. Altering threshold for decision on a focus or frame of attention.	Shares the decision-making process; makes decisions when in the best position to do so; selects the best topics and shows links between topics; accepts lead from others where that is best.	Avoids desirable actions to prevent inner tensions; acts in impairing manner so to get a tense situation over prematurely.	Uncontrolled instinctive or reflexive action.

539

TABLE 23.3 Control of Form: Interpersonal Outcome

Types of Set Points	Outcome of Regulation		
	Adaptive	Maladaptive	Outcome of Dysregulation
1. Altering modes of representation.	Coherent mixes of verbalization, facial signals, imagery metaphors, and bodily gestural movements.	Disruptive image metaphors; flat verbiage; discordant prosodics across words, voice, face, and body leading to distortion, confusion, or a sense that something is warded off or being concealed.	Jumbles of signals in different expressive media; raw enaction of emotions.
2. Altering time span.	Coherent framing of time being discussed as to past, present, future, or imagery perspectives.	Disruptive or confusing shifts in temporal perspective.	Chaotic time sense.
3. Altering logic level.	Balance between rational planning (reflexive analyses) and restorative or creative fantasy (brainstorming); restorative humor or banter.	Disruptive or confusing shifts between analytic reasoning and fantasy; avoidant humor, joking, or banter.	Inability to follow a thread of intended meaning.
4. Altering level of action.	Appropriate and shared choices of when to talk and when to act; taking turns in a dialogue.	Avoidant disruption of turn-taking in a dialogue; acting out without recognition or sharing intentions in a dialogue; avoidant dialogue when acting is indicated; restless jittering to avoid thinking and feeling.	Impulsive actions; paralysis of action.
5. Altering vigilance.	Appropriate lulls, silences, excitements, and turn-takings; useful cycles of activity and inactivity in complementary actions.	Excessive speed or slowing of dialogue or shared actions to avoid ideational or emotional implication.	Unavailable to shared communication because of excessive speed, impulsivity, or slowing down.

TABLE 23.4 Control of Person Schemas and Role Relationship Models: Interpersonal Outcome

	Outcome of Regulation		
Types of Set Points	Adaptive	Maladaptive	Outcome of Dysregulation
1. Altering self schema.	Increases in competence and resilience within a situation; improved fit of behavior to the situation.	Jarring shift in "personality"; acting in a too-superior or too-inferior way; using others as if they were part of or extension of the self.	Inability to use relationships with others to stabilize a sense of identity.
2. Altering schema of other person.	Increases in understanding the intentions, motives, and predictable patterns of other (empathy); "reading" of another during an interaction.	Reacting by an internal misperception of the other; provoking the other to conform to an internal misperception (projective identification); short circuiting to an inappropriate all-good or all-bad view of other; changing the object of a feeling, wish, source of threat from the most pertinent one to a less pertinent one (displacement).	Chaotic views about another in a situation.
3. Altering role relationship models.	Useful trials of a new pattern for a situation.	Disguising or undoing an intended script sequence by running an alternative, compromise, or opposite one (undoing, passive-aggression); shimmering alternations of contradictory patterns; pretense of roles that are not felt authentically; acting out an "obligatory script" rather than acting flexibly as situation unfolds; switching working models into all-good or all-bad views of the relationship; changing the agent or source of an activity, wish, or feeling from self to other or other to self.	Inflexible preservation of an inappropriate interaction pattern.

(Continued)

541

TABLE 23.4 *(Continued)*

Types of Set Points	Outcome of Regulation		Outcome of Dysregulation
	Adaptive	Maladaptive	
4. Altering value schemas (critic roles).	Pointing out following of or deflections from values, rules, commitments in self and others in a useful way to give rewards, pride, or to improve situation in future.	Irrational assumptions of other's values to avoid a social tension; inhibition of spontaneity by excessive monitoring; attributing blame outward irrationally to protect self-esteem.	Impulsive, punitive, or revenge behaviors against self or others.
5. Altering executive-agency schemas.	Acting responsible to care for others and to care for self as situations demand.	Unrealistic abnegation of self; suddenly selfish or autistic acts that disrupt relationships.	Inability to take care of others.

recorded and scientifically reviewed. That is why we define *outcomes in terms of interpersonal and communicative patterns and types of relationship transactions.* These outcomes have the advantage of enabling operational definitions that can lead to reliable measure and to quantitative studies. We have, however, reported outcome definitions in terms of the more conventional psychoanalytic language of conscious and unconscious intrapsychic processes, which may be of interest to some readers (Horowitz & Stinson, 1995).

CONTROL OF CONTENT: DEFINITIONS

Control of contents contains four levels that can shift (a) the focus of attention, (b) the sequencing of concepts within that focus, (c) the weighting of relative importance of chains of concepts or elements within the chains, and (d) the threshold for deciding to interrupt or close a topic:

1. *Focus of Attention.* The setpoint for attentional focus determines in part the probabilities for the next topics for conscious representation. The assumption is that topics of importance are related to intentions and that they may be selectively inhibited or facilitated relative to one another. Changing these setpoints may lead to a shift in attention from one topic to another.

2. *Concepts.* Concepts are elements of meaning within an overall topic. These elements may be derived from external perception, internal sensation, and stored internal knowledge. Shifts in settings at this level may facilitate or inhibit different types of concepts relative to one another. The settings will affect how a chain of concepts on the topic of attention is formed and represented. The frame of attention may range from wide to narrow in terms of amplifying or diminishing (even to the point of excluding) concepts associated with a topic. This can affect how one topic is linked to or segregated from another topic.

3. *Appraisal of Importance of a Chain of Concepts.* Chains of concepts are weighted according to their relative importance in terms of their implications for the motives or intentions of self and others. By shifting the appraisal and valuation of a chain of concepts, a person can alter the emotional consequences of ideas, memories, fantasies, or plans that are involved. The significance to the self and others of a given chain of concepts can be exaggerated or minimized relative to alternative chains of weighting and will determine, in part, the course of conscious contemplation.

4. *Threshold for Decision or Interruption.* One may change the threshold for shifting attention to a new topic, allowing a point of decision or interruption. Such shifts may occur on completion of processing a topic, or may serve to avoid emotional tension when a topic is conflictual.

The interpersonal behavioral outcomes of these control processes that affect ideational/emotional contents are found in Table 23.2.

CONTROL OF FORM: DEFINITIONS

Processes that control the form of conscious representation can shift (a) the modes of representation, (b) orientations to time span, (c) the quality and rule sets for logical or nonlogical contemplation, (d) level of threshold for action planning, and (e) levels of general arousal:

1. *Modes of Representation.* The setting of modes of representation determines the predominance of words, images, or enactions in the sphere of conscious representation. Controls may emphasize semantic or nonsemantic modes as well as the degree of translation among modes.

2. *Time Span.* The setting of time span establishes a focus of considering a topic in terms of past, present, or future as well as a temporal range from very short to very long periods. A short span primes for the here-and-now; a long time span primes for reconstructing past memories and reconsidering future implications.

3. *Quality of Logic.* The setting for type of logic and organization determines in part the forms that will be used for the simultaneous and sequential organization of concepts. The forms used may vary from the logic of rational problem solving to use of reverielike fantasy (including more primary or secondary process, realistic or magical thinking, socially valued or autistic behavior).

4. *Level of Action.* Settings for level of action planning may vary from using thought as nonaction, to thought as trial action, to rehearsal of action, to direct or reflexive actions.

5. *Arousal Levels.* The setting of arousal level involves thresholds for excitation or dampening of various systems of mental activity in terms of reacting to input from other systems.

The communicative contextual—the interpersonal behavioral—outcomes of control processes that affect the form of organizing and associating meanings are found in Table 23.3.

CONTROL OF PERSON AND VALUE SCHEMAS: DEFINITIONS

Processes that control within repertoires of person schemas can be divided into (a) schemas of self, (b) schemas of other persons, (c) role relationship models, (d) value schemas (critic roles), and (e) executive-agency schemas:

1. *Self Schemas.* We assume each individual has a repertoire of multiple schematizations of self. In any state of mind, one of several potential self-schemas tends to be dominant. Shifting which schema is primed may change which state of mind is present, how topics are thought about, and how actions are planned and carried out.

2. *Other Person Schemas.* We assume that each person can view another person as characterized by a variety of roles, characteristics, and attributes. Shifting which schema is primed from this repertoire will affect how the behaviors, intentions, and motives of the other person are interpreted. By shifting the schemas selected for interpreting the other person, a subject may alter current emotional responses to an interpersonal situation.

3. *Role Relationship Models.* Schemas of self and other scripts for expected interactions may be combined into a type of interpersonal schematization called role relationship models. These include expected sequences of action and reaction (e.g., "If I am trusting, the other person will exploit me"). By shifting which role relationship model is used for interpreting an interpersonal situation, a person may change mood, states, plans, and actions, and may alter how a topic is contemplated.

4. *Value Schemas (Critic Roles).* The appraisal of a topic, chain of concepts, or remembered action sequence includes judgments in relation to sets of values. This critical appraisal can lead to pride or shame, esteem or guilt. The judgments can range from harsh to accepting views. Judgments can be experienced in thought as if they were made by critics, including self and others. A person may have as schematic structures introjects of people, spirits, or ideological groups. By shifting which schemas and which sets of values are currently amplified a person may vary the degree of praise and blame.

5. *Executive-Agency Schemas.* A person may view the body and mind as that of an individual (I, me) or as that belonging to another person or larger group (we, us). For example, a person may prime as his or her current agency an "I" or a "we" (marital unit, family, group, ideology, tribe, nation) that transcends the framework of his or her individuality. Shifts in emotionality and how topics are viewed may occur with changes in which executive schemas are currently primed.

Definitions of the behavioral outcomes of control processes that affect person and value schemas are found in Table 23.4.

EMPIRICAL STUDY OF DEFENSIVE CONTROL PROCESSES IN STRESSOR CONTEXTS

The advantage of specifying signs of defensive control processes in terms of interpersonal actions is that they are behaviors that can be observed and recorded for scientific scrutiny. In the following sections, we will discuss empirical findings related to control processes as they emerged from ongoing studies of reactions to loss events requiring shock mastery and adaptive reschematization for recovery.

Two instruments have been developed recently for a self-report and observer report based on the classification system in Tables 23.2–23.4. The observer-based method applies a Q-sort technique to recorded discourse from therapy or evaluation interviews. It includes very short scales of control processes. Forced Q-sort methodology has both advantages and disadvantages. For an ipsative (see Lazarus, 1991) strategy, however, the advantages are the relatively high reliabilities that come automatically with this procedure (Block, 1961; Neff & Cohen, 1967) and the power to focus attention repeatedly on key definitions (Stephenson, 1979). We have achieved relatively high reliabilities between raters, as illustrated by the following case example.

CASE EXAMPLE

The patient is a woman who suddenly lost her husband in an unusually violent incident. The traumatic death happened more than one year earlier. She had some treatment that helped with shock mastery, but she had not reschematized her identity and relationship patterns. At this time, over a year after the loss, she met diagnostic criteria for both posttraumatic stress disorder and major depressive disorder. Brief dynamic-cognitive psychotherapy consisted of 28 sessions (case reported in Horowitz, Stinson, Fridhandler, et al., 1993). To demonstrate the application of control process rating procedures, we excerpted a 5-minute segment (minutes 37.00′–41.00′) from the 4th hour, focusing specifically on observable signs of control in a 30-second block (40.30′–41.00′).

The patient begins the 5 minutes saying that her dead husband and daughter were really close and that he put the child to bed more often than she did. She concluded that her daughter had good reason to be extremely hurt losing him. Then she said that any man trying to come into her daughter's life has "tough shoes to fill" because he was such a good father. In the prior discourse, the patient had been elaborating on her daughter's reaction to the impact of the patient's new relationship to another man, an important and conflictual topic. The therapist uttered some supporting "mhms," which led the patient to go further, saying that her daughter was not ready to be open to someone new and—after a pause—that most of her week consisted of difficulties in dealing with her. She was then silent and the therapist asked what she was thinking about. The patient, hesitantly, says that she was thinking about her daughter missing her father and that she was "not ready to give her another one." Then she said, "This is going to be a battle." The therapist said: "It is not so simple to give her another one either, it isn't just the matter of plugging in a new replacement." Here the 30-second frame starts:

PATIENT: (Sighing.) It's all complicated.

THERAPIST: Yeah.

PATIENT: And I have not been able to sit down and do any of the paperwork I need to do, you know, just to keep my life in order. God, it's just this mountain, keeps growing.

THERAPIST: Hm.

PATIENT: God, I should (end of the 30 seconds) probably just hire a secretary.

Here, looking for control processes related to ideational/emotional content, we have a clear change of the current relevant topic (conflict over her new intimate relationship and how it affects her daughter and her) to a more peripheral one. Her pitch of voice is changing, indicating relief. She also lifts her eyebrows, gives a shy smile, and looks more relaxed on shifting the topic; as if asking if this shift, to a less conflictual topic of work pressures, is all right with the therapist.

On a Q-sort, judges of this 30-second block within this five minute context rated the following control processes as predominant: abruptly terminating contemplation of a major topic; blocking of potentially painful memories; avoiding emotional arousals; and moving from the emotional heart of a topic to its periphery.

On the same segment, using the Q-sort, raters also assigned control processes affecting the form of ideational/emotional communication. Those were excessive speeding of dialogue; focusing on small, relatively unimportant logical steps; expressing herself with discordant prosodics and meanings across verbalization, facial action, and bodily gesture; making confusing shifts in temporal perspective; and shifting from an internal to an external locus of attention.

For control processes affecting person schemas, raters saw a shift of the wish, threat, or feeling from an important to a less important object.

These ratings involved six raters watching the 5-minute segment twice before rating the 30-second segment as a focus of evidence. This segment was then rated by six raters in three groups of two each. Each group independently ordered the Q-sort cards in this distribution: 2, 4, 8, 20, 8, 4, 2 reaching from very characteristic to very uncharacteristic. The averaged interrater correlation for the three teams was satisfactory (Pearson $r = .6$).

STUDIES ON DEFENSIVE CONTROL PROCESS THEORY: OTHER PRELIMINARY EMPIRICAL RESULTS

Defensive Control Process Theory (DCPT) led us to develop instruments that could be applied to a whole therapy. Frequent signs of control, such as those that affect verbal communication of ideas and those that affect nonverbal communication or stifling of emotion, were operationally defined. This led to new and reliable measures of dyselaboration (verbal warding off; Horowitz, Milbrath, Reidbord, & Stinson, 1993) and states of expressing or stifling affect (Horowitz, Milbrath, Ewert, & Sonneborn, 1994).

Horowitz, Stinson, Curtis, et al. (1993) then investigated how these measures related to disclosure of important topics in psychotherapy to resolve a stress response syndrome. The transcripts of an early, a middle, and a late therapy hour were sampled from a brief psychotherapy, transcribed in a standardized manner, and then segmented according to topic. The records were independently scored on expressive and control process variables. Three topics—relationship with the deceased, current intimacy, and work—were used to segment the discourse records. Nontopic variables were contrasted. The results support the hypothesis that, during discourse on the most emotionally distressing topics (relationship with a deceased brother), there were more signs of defensive control.

Another single case study (Horowitz, Milbrath, Jordan, et al., 1994), using the paradigm of defensive control process theory, replicated and extended these findings. Using cluster and factor analysis, the researchers examined specific topics based on the measures related to control—nonverbal warding off, states of mind, dyselaboration and elaboration of verbal behavior, and structural analysis of social behavior (SASB; Benjamin, 1974)—combined with interpersonal behavior and physiological measures of autonomic activity. Signs of defensive control processes varied systematically with topic.

These empirical studies validate the construct of signs of outcome of processes of defensive control process. The results also show a consistent pattern of control mechanisms: Emotionally loaded topics are highly correlated with *both* patterns of avoidance and of recurrence of these topics. This concords with studies showing correlations of intrusions and avoidance experiences using the Impact of Events Scale (Horowitz, Wilner, & Alvarez, 1979). We interpret this as a kind of approach and avoidance conflict that is part of a dose-by-dose working-through process to change beliefs and modify underlying problematic schemas.

Signs of defensive control processes may be useful as a way to detect which topics may be unresolved and problematic for individuals. This leads to formulations and plans for treatment that reduce excessive controls and enable shock mastery and reschematization.

FORMULATION AND TREATMENT PLANNING

States, person schemas, and defensive control process theories can help therapists to treat people with prolonged maladaptive responses to stressor life events, including posttraumatic stress disorders, dissociations, adjustment reactions, brief reactive psychoses, reactive depressions, and pathological grief; these formulations may also be useful with poststressor event character distortions. The person may be helped to associate the bad news of stressor events to an inner repertoire of enduring beliefs and schemas, leading to recognition of areas of necessary identity change and changes from an accustomed lifestyle, and to reality testing of irrational beliefs that may be used to explain the event.

After the therapist has arrived at a diagnosis, the formulation links the salient signs, symptoms, and problems of living to reasons for their formation. The salient phenomena depicted in Figure 23.1 are related to unintegrated, unresolved topics activated by the stressor event. The therapist can develop a formulation and treatment strategy by attending to these four questions:

1. What are states in which these salient phenomena are or are not experienced?
2. What are the defensive control processes that keep the person from reaching an integration of the unresolved topics raised by the stressor life event and its sequelae?

3. How might the patient be helped to recover from dysregulation by treatments that teach adaptive control processes, reduce unnecessary levels of defensive control processes, and modify dysfunctional beliefs?

4. What are the enduring beliefs and schemas of self and other that are now dysfunctional and/or in discord or contradictory to the present and the realistic possible future? How may adaptive schemas be learned and repeated?

In complex cases, in which the stressor event is confounded by personality-based issues, the therapist will find it hard to arrive at answers to questions 3 and 4. The reason is that the dysfunctional beliefs and schemas may be obscured by the action of regulatory efforts that prevent emotional flooding when traumatic memories and discordant schemas are thought about consciously or discussed with others. That is why the therapist creates a safe situation, fosters a therapeutic alliance, and then affects attention deployment to usually warded-off topics. With time and patience, answers to questions 3 and 4 will emerge.

The therapist usually affects attention deployment by shifting the set point of the kinds of control processes presented in Tables 23.2–23.4. Once conflicts, discrepancies, discords, dilemmas, and contradictions in belief are identified, the therapist can help the patient shift from dysfunctional beliefs and develop adaptive ones. Specific examples of how to do this in persons who use histronic, narcissistic, compulsive, and other styles of habitual defensive control processes are presented elsewhere (Horowitz, 1992; Horowitz et al., 1984).

The general form of such integrations was shown in Table 23.1. Now, issues of defensive control process modification as a treatment technique can be considered briefly in relation to the prototypical phases of a stress response as shown in Figure 23.1.

In the *outcry phase,* social support may supply time and activity structure that serves as a control enhancer. In treatment contexts, the therapist may focus attention to the availability of such social support and modify obstacles to use it. The patient is helped to shift time frame set points to consider the here-and-now, not issues of the past ("Why me?") or the future ("How will I be happy again?"). Issues that do not require immediate decisions can be postponed. Forms for rational thinking in words and step-by-step plan framing can be emphasized. This will reduce the emotional flooding for image-based thinking and the feeling of hopelessness engendered by considering long-range implications. Activities that give a sense of being in control, even as to whether a bed light is on or off, help in and of themselves.

In the *denial phase,* attention may be focused on topics that have been postponed during the outcry phase, after a period of restoration of equilibrium. A supportive interpersonal relationship can be established. It is sometimes necessary directly to confront inhibitions when a denial phase has been maladaptively prolonged. Topic selection, moving to the emotional heart of a topic, and attention to sensory image memory may then be important. Also, attention may be drawn to warded-off views of self and others, and to value schemas that are being walled away. Attention focuses on the implications of the traumatic event in terms of self-organization, goals, and beliefs.

A therapeutic alliance helps consciously counteract excessive preconscious inhibitory controls. The therapist may model a dose-by-dose approach to emotionally difficult topics in this effort at teaching conscious control maneuvers.

In the *intrusive phase,* the gradual telling and restructuring of the disastrous events helps subjects to differentiate reality from fantasy. Magical thinking about wishes or activities that might have caused the catastrophic event can be counteracted by rational interpretation. The therapist may bolster realistic attributes of the patient that indicate competence and worth. It is important to supply a structure for scattered fragments of ideas and emotions during the intrusive phase. By placing each concept into a time frame and sequence, the therapist helps the person gain a sense of reality and integration about what happened.

Often, memories of disastrous events at first feel unreal and the person may feel depersonalized. During an intrusive phase, it is important to reduce external demands to focus on the heart of the reaction to help integrate the reality of events and to restore a sense of competent identity. The most important conflicted self-schemas should be addressed by interpretations that help integrate contradictions in belief and help modify irrational conceptualizations. At the same time, the therapist should provide models for how to be more self-efficacious (Bandura, 1977) and how to engage—if necessary—in effective remorse activities rather than guilty self-loathing.

Alarm reactions that occur because new realities do not accord with expectations based on prior schemas should be clarified. If the person understands intrusive experiences, this will reduce the anxiety of going out of control, losing a sense of reality, or "going crazy." Fear of repetition is also a universal topic. It is the worry that, in the future, either oneself or a loved one will suffer the same fate as the victim. This may also be mixed with survivor guilt and self-blame.

Each topic should be addressed in a manner that chains concepts, realistically appraises the result of the chain, and leads to a schema of how the topic is closed so that the mind can open to a new topic.

In the *working-through phase,* the therapeutic task for attention deployment of patient and clinician is often toward schemas and dilemmas that need modification. These issues are often related to preevent personality attributes. Previous conflicts—neurotic complexes—may be activated by the stressor life event and/or by the work of reacting to the stressor event. The topics may include activated memories and fantasies of earlier traumas. Working through can be aided if the therapist juxtaposes dysfunctional and functional beliefs to emphasize attention to differences. New meanings will be formed; facilitating their repetition will foster adaptive reschematization.

For example, in mourning the loss of a loved one, the issue is not only what was lost but who the self becomes in current reality without the deceased. Concepts of self as worthless, incompetent, bad, shamed, guilty, or weak without the deceased may be clarified and challenged. To do so, the therapist may seek to help the patient consciously modify the set points for role relationship models, value schemas, and executive-agency schemas. Maladaptive outcomes will give way to adaptive outcomes allowing the patient to move to the final phase shown at the end of Figure 23.1: *going on with life.*

CONCLUSION

The phases of stress-response syndromes include periods of high and low signs of defensive control processes, as in extreme experiences of intrusion and denial. Classical psychoanalytic theory of defense mechanisms and lists of coping processes do not get down to the details of how individuals regulate ideas and emotions to produce these experiences. For that reason, we have developed a theory of defensive control processes, operationally defined interpersonal outcomes, and empirically tested some derivatives of this theory. The results indicate how to formulate individual cases and consider treatment options.

REFERENCES

Bandura, A. (1977). Self-efficacy: Toward a unifying theory of behavior change. *Psychological Review, 84*, 191–215.

Benjamin, L. S. (1974). Structural analysis of social behavior. *Psychological Review, 81*, 392–425.

Block, J. (1961). *The Q-sort method in personality assessment and psychiatric research.* Springfield, IL: Thomas.

Eells, T. B., Horowitz, M. J., Stinson, C. H., & Fridhandler, B. (1993). Self-representation in anxious states of mind: A comparison of psychodynamic models. In Z. V. Segal & S. J. Blatt (Eds.), *The self in emotional distress: Cognitive and psychodynamic perspectives* (pp. 100–128). New York: Guilford.

Erdelyi, M. H. (1984). The recovery of unconscious (inaccessible) memories: Laboratory studies of hypermnesia. In G. Bower (Ed.), *The psychology of learning and motivation: Advances in research and theory.* New York: Academic Press.

Folkman, S., & Lazarus, R. S. (1988). The relationship between coping and emotion: Implications for theory and research. *Society of Scientific Medicine, 26*(3), 309–317.

Folkman, S., Lazarus, R. S., Dunkel-Schetter, C., DeLongis, A., & Gruen, R. (1986). Dynamics of a stressful encounter: Cognitive appraisal, coping, and encounter outcomes. *Journal of Personal and Social Psychology, 50*(5), 992–1003.

Freud, S. (1958). *The interpretation of dreams.* London: Hogarth Press. (Original work published 1900)

Haan, N. (1977). *Coping and defending.* New York: Academic Press.

Haan, N. (1993). The assessment of coping, defense, and stress. In L. Goldberger & S. Breznitz (Eds.), *Handbook of stress: Theoretical and clinical aspects* (pp. 258–273). New York: Free Press.

Horowitz, M. J. (1986). *Stress response syndromes.* Northvale, NJ: Jason Aronson.

Horowitz, M. J. (1988a). *Introduction to psychodynamics. A new synthesis.* New York: Basic Books.

Horowitz, M. J. (Ed.). (1988b). *Psychodynamics and cognition.* Chicago: University of Chicago Press.

Horowitz, M. J. (1989). Relationship schema formulation: Role relationship models and intrapsychic conflict. *Psychiatry, 52*, 260–274.

Horowitz, M. J. (Ed.). (1991). *Person schemas and maladaptive interpersonal patterns.* Chicago: University of Chicago Press.

Horowitz, M. J. (1992). Stress response syndromes: A review of post traumatic and adjustment disorders. In J. Wilson & B. Raphael (Eds.), *International handbook of traumatic stress syndromes*. New York: Plenum Press.

Horowitz, M., Cooper, S., Fridhandler, B., Perry, C. J., Bond, M., & Vaillant, G. (1992). Control processes and defense mechanisms. *Journal of Psychotherapy Practice and Research, 1*(4), 324–336.

Horowitz, M. J., Fridhandler, B., & Stinson, C. (1991). Person schemas and emotion. *Journal of the American Psychoanalytic Association, 39,* 173–208.

Horowitz, M. J., Markman, H. C., Stinson, C. H., Fridhandler, B., & Ghannam, J. H. (1990). A classification theory of defense. In J. L. Singer (Ed.), *Repression and dissociation. Implication for personality theory, psychopathology, and health* (pp. 61–84). Chicago: The University of Chicago Press.

Horowitz, M. J., Marmar, C., Krupnick, J., Wilner, N., Kaltreider, N., & Wallerstein, R. (1984). *Personality stiles and brief psychotherapy*. New York: Basic Books.

Horowitz, M. J., Milbrath, C., Ewert, M., & Sonneborn, D. (1994). Cyclical patterns of states of mind in psychotherapy. *American Journal of Psychiatry, 151*(12), 1767–1770.

Horowitz, M. J., Milbrath, C., Jordan, D. S., Stinson, C. H., Mary, E., Redington, D. J., Fridhandler, B., Reidbord, S. P., & Hartley, D. (1994). Expressive and defensive behavior during discourse on conflicted topics: A single case study. *Journal of Personality, 62*(4), 527–563.

Horowitz, M., Milbrath, C., Reidbord, S., & Stinson, C. (1993). Elaboration and dyselaboration: Measures of expression and defense in discourse. *Psychotherapy Research, 3*(4), 278–293.

Horowitz, M. J., & Stinson, C. (1995). Consciousness and processes of control. *Psychotherapy: Research & Practice, 4,* 123–139.

Horowitz, M. J., Stinson, C., Curtis, D., Ewert, M., Redington, D., Singer, J., Bucci, W., Mergenthaler, E., Milbrath, C., & Hartley, D. (1993). Topics and signs: Defensive control of emotional expression. *Journal of Consulting and Clinical Psychology, 61*(3), 421–430.

Horowitz, M. J., Stinson, C., & Field, N. (1991). Natural disasters and stress response syndromes. *Psychiatric Annals, 21*(9), 556–562.

Horowitz, M. J., Stinson, C., Fridhandler, B., Milbrath, C., Redington, D., & Ewert, M. (1993). Vivid representation of psychotherapeutic processes. Pathological grief: An intensive cases study. *Psychiatry, 56*(11), 356–374.

Horowitz, M. J., Wilner, N., & Alvarez, W. (1979). Impact of Events Scale: A measure of subjective stress. *Psychosomatic Medicine, 41*(3), 209–218.

Kroeber, T. C. (1963). The coping functions of the ego mechanisms. In R. White (Ed.), *The study of lives*. New York: Atherton.

Lazarus, R. S. (1991). *Emotion and adaption*. New York: Oxford University Press.

Lazarus, R. S. (1993). Coping theory and research: Past, present, and future. *Psychosomatic Medicine, 55,* 234–247.

Miller, G. A., Galanter, E., & Pribram, K. H. (1960). *Plans and the structure of behavior*. New York: Holt, Rinehart & Winston.

Neff, W. S., & Cohen, J. (1967). A method for the analysis of the structure and internal consistency of Q-sort arrays. *Psychological Bulletin, 68*(5), 361–368.

Park, C. L., & Cohen, L. H. (1993). Religious and nonreligious coping with the death of a friend. *Cognitive Therapy and Research, 17*(6), 561–577.

Perrez, M., & Reicherts, M. (1992). *Stress, coping, and health.* Seattle, WA: Hogrefe & Huber.

Portes, P. R., Howell, S. C., Brown, J. H., & Eichenberger, S., et al. (1992). Family functions and children's postdivorce adjustment. *American Journal of Orthopsychiatry, 62*(4), 613–617.

Roper, G., Rachman, S., & Hodgson, R. (1973). An experiment on obsessional checking. *Behaviour Research & Therapy, 11*(3), 271–277.

Salzman, L. (1979). Psychotherapy of the obsessional. *American Journal of Psychotherapy, 33*(1), 32–40.

Singer, J. L. (Ed.). (1990). *Repression and dissociation: Implications for personality theory, psychopathology, and health.* Chicago: University of Chicago Press.

Stephenson, W. (1979). Q methodology and Newton's fifth rule. *American Psychologist, 34*(4), 354–357.

Vaillant, G. E. (Ed.). (1992). *Ego mechanisms of defense: A guide for clinicians and researchers.* Washington, DC: American Psychiatric Press.

Wegner, D., & Pennebaker, J. (Ed.). (1992). *Handbook of mental control.* New York: Prentice-Hall.

Wegner, D. M., Schneider, D. J., Carter, S. R., III, & White, T. L. (1987). Paradoxical effects of thought suppression. *Journal of Personality and Social Psychology, 53*(1), 5–13.

CHAPTER 24

Coping and Adaptation to Trauma and Loss

MARIO MIKULINCER and VICTOR FLORIAN

In the modern world, individuals have to deal with many types of misfortune: natural and human-made disasters, the loss of a loved one, the diagnosis of chronic illnesses with their consequent physical disabilities, and so on. These situations seem particularly important for psychological study because they have the power to transform individual and family lives, almost always drain personal resources, and have potential impact on well-being and adjustment. Moreover, the knowledge gained from these studies may provide theoretical and applied insight into the processes involved in successful and unsuccessful coping. In fact, coping is a multifaceted process. Coping strategies that provide benefits in one situation may prove ineffective in another. Even within the same situation, contextual, interpersonal, and intrapsychic factors may alter the adequacy of attempts to cope with stressful events. On this basis, a basic task of theory and research is to examine which coping strategies may be beneficial in specific situations.

In our opinion, the best way to approach this task is to compare the effectiveness of coping strategies in regard to the unique human experiences of trauma and losses. Like other traumatic events, the experience of loss demands from the individual a major investment of coping efforts to reach a new and proper level of adaptation (Kleber, Brom, & DeFares, 1992). Loss, however, differs from other traumas in a number of ways. First, loss is a specific event that has occurred, which has an element of immediacy. Second, loss involves an objective referent, the disappearance of a significant object or person. Third, the adaptation to loss is a long-lasting process that may have consequences for the entire life span. The main objective of the present chapter is to analyze the existing relevant literature on the adaptational effects of coping strategies in dealing with a widely researched traumatic event—war experience—and two well-recognized losses—death of a loved one and physical disability.

A CLASSIFICATION OF COPING RESPONSES

The complex pattern of relationships among stress, coping, and mental health has intrigued both researchers and theorists for the past three decades. In reviewing the various chapters of this volume, readers may easily observe the wide variety of coping strategies that people report using in diverse stressful situations as well as the theoretical attempts to categorize these strategies. These attempts seem to reflect a transition from Lazarus and Folkman's (1984) classic bipartite classification (problem-focused vs. emotion-focused) to more complex categorizations. For example, Scheier, Weintraub, and Carver (1986) and Endler and Parker (1990) proposed a tripartite categorization, in which emotion-focused coping strategies are divided into those that reflect a cognitive and affective "stay" in the stressful situation (emotion-focused/approach) and those that avoid facing the stress (emotion-focused/avoidance).

We believe that the preceding tripartite categorization is still insufficient to explain the encounter with stressful events and, particularly, the process of coping with irreversible personal losses. A further division of the emotion-focused/approach category is still required. Although all the strategies in this category aim at intrapsychic changes, they are not homogeneous in the purpose and product of these changes. We propose to differentiate between reorganization and reappraisal strategies. "Reorganization" strategies entail the accommodation of existing cognitive-motivational structures to reality constraints. "Reappraisal" strategies entail the positive reinterpretation of external events so that inner structures remain basically intact. Moreover, whereas "reorganization" results in the acceptance of the new reality, like the loss, and its incorporation into mental structures, "reappraisal" results in a partial denial of the threat (Lazarus, 1983) and its disassociation from inner structures. Finally, "reorganization" can lead to real adjustment by stabilizing the situation and sometimes finding substitute goals, whereas "reappraisal" can provide only an "illusory," temporary relief, and, in fact, may delay a real solution of the problem until possible changes occur in the environment or the person.

On this basis, we propose four higher-order categories of coping: (a) problem-focused strategies, (b) reappraisal, (c) reorganization, and (d) avoidance strategies. Problem-focused coping consists of a vast array of cognitive and behavioral maneuvers that attempt to make changes in the environment that will eliminate the external sources of stress. Although several studies indicate that problem-focused coping has beneficial adaptational outcomes (e.g., Epstein & Meier, 1989; McCrae & Costa, 1986), other research has pointed out the possible limitations of this type of coping particularly in uncontrollable situations (e.g., Forsythe & Compas, 1987).

Reappraisal involves the use of selective attention on positive information, the creation of positive illusions, and the partial denial of negative aspects of reality (Lazarus & Folkman, 1984; Taylor & Brown, 1988). The effectiveness of discovering something positive in stressful events has been documented in several investigations (for reviews, see Taylor & Brown, 1988; Snyder & Higgins, 1988).

Reorganization coping implies a series of intrapsychic steps (acceptance, working through the experience, and restructuring of inner structures) that entail better accommodation to reality. It involves the pursuit of more realistic goals and the adoption of a more appropriate view of oneself. It may also result in a more flexible and rich self-system, as people become aware of their strengths and weaknesses and renew their sense of self-worth. Reorganization coping has been implied in Lindemann's (1944) concept of "grief work" and Janis's (1958) concept of the "work of worrying," and it has been empirically validated in factor analytic studies of coping strategies (Carver, Scheier, & Weintraub, 1989; McCrae, 1984).

Avoidance coping seems to encompass two large groups of strategies. The first consists of cognitive maneuvers, which attempt to prevent the intrusion of threat-related thoughts into consciousness (e.g., Carver et al., 1989; Folkman & Lazarus, 1980). The second group of strategies reflects an attempt to behaviorally disengage from the stressful situation either by actively withdrawing problem-focused efforts or by consuming and abusing substances like drugs and alcohol (e.g., Carver et al., 1989; Stone & Neale, 1984). Although avoidance coping may initially have a beneficial effect by reducing distress, in the long run it has a detrimental effect on the person's adaptational efforts (Lazarus, 1983; Roth & Cohen, 1986). The literature consistently validates the negative impact of avoidance coping, though Collins, Baum, and Singer (1983) found that avoidance may sometimes facilitate psychological adjustment when employed in uncontrollable situations such as the Three Mile Island nuclear incident.

At this point, a lot of caution is required because we acknowledge that additional coping strategies may exist. However, our assumption is that a careful analysis of these strategies would allow their incorporation within one or more of the preceding four higher-order categories. For example, seeking support may be related to problem-focused coping (e.g., information seeking), reappraisal (e.g., making social comparisons with other people), and even avoidance (e.g., talking about distracting subjects with others). Similarly, blaming others may be a particular case of reappraisal, whereas blaming oneself may be viewed as an initial step in the reorganization process.

In the following sections, we review relevant literature on the relationships between the preceding four higher-order coping categories and adaptation to particular trauma and loss situations, specifically, war trauma, the death of a loved one, and physical disability.

COPING STRATEGIES AND THE PSYCHOLOGICAL CONSEQUENCES OF WAR TRAUMA

Since ancient times, combat and related war experiences have been recognized as being severely traumatic for human beings. War exposes both military personnel and civilians to many real stressors, such as the danger of death and injury to self and friends, lack of food, drink, shelter, and rest (Stauffer, 1949; Titchener &

Ross, 1974). Although literature and art had long documented the psychological damage suffered by people during and after war-related exposures, only after World War II did social scientists begin empirical examinations of these consequences of war trauma. Their studies indicate that participation in war may challenge the coping resources of most individuals and in some cases may produce an array of psychological difficulties in the battlefield (Grinker & Spiegel, 1945; Titchener & Ross, 1974). The most common diagnosable problem is labeled "combat stress reaction" (CSR), which is marked by labile polymorphic manifestations, such as overwhelming anxiety or total withdrawal (Kardiner, 1947). The common element in all these reactions is that people cease to function efficiently and may endanger themselves and their comrades.

Research has also demonstrated that war trauma may have potential long-lasting effects. In some cases, emotional equilibrium may be restored and combat stress reactions may evaporate with the end of the war. In other cases, however, these reactions may be consolidated into more chronic psychological problems that leave individuals emotionally vulnerable (Solomon, Weisenberg, & Schwarzwald, 1985). The most common psychological disorder observed among those returning from war is posttraumatic stress disorder (PTSD), which is characterized by reexperiencing the traumatic event, numbing of responsiveness to or reduced involvement with the world, and a variety of dysphoric and cognitive symptoms (American Psychiatric Association [APA], 1987). It may be accompanied by functioning and somatic problems (Solomon & Mikulincer, 1992).

Most of the research effort has been devoted to delineating the nature, manifestations, correlates, and course of both combat stress reactions and PTSD (e.g., Solomon et al., 1985). Although only few studies have examined the etiology of CSR, many investigations have examined situational and personality factors that can explain the development of PTSD after the war (e.g., Solomon et al., 1985; Solomon & Mikulincer, 1992). A number of investigators have particularly focused on the contribution of coping strategies to postwar adaptation.

In a retrospective study, Fairbank, Hansen, and Fitterling (1991) examined the association between coping strategies and PTSD four decades after World War II (WWII). Three groups of WWII male veterans (prisoners of war with current diagnosis of PTSD, prisoners of war without PTSD, and veterans who were not prisoners of war) were asked to complete the Ways of Coping Checklist with regard to WWII memories and recent stressors. Results indicate that PTSD was associated with more frequent use of wishful thinking, self-blame, and self-isolation in coping with both war memories and recent stressors. In addition, it was found that among prisoners of war without PTSD the most frequently reported coping strategy was emphasizing the positive. The authors suggest that reappraisal coping may serve as an emotional buffer against the development of war-related PTSD.

Several studies on Vietnam War veterans have examined the relationship between coping strategies and the diagnosis of PTSD a decade after the war. Green, Lindly, and Grace (1988) assessed how Vietnam veterans with and without current PTSD coped with their war memories. Using Horowitz and Wilner's (1980) inventory, they found that four emotion-focused coping responses—event processing, time out for reflection, religion, and denial—were more frequently reported by PTSD than by non-PTSD veterans. In another study, Nezu and Carnevale (1987) found that Vietnam veterans with PTSD reported less use of problem-focused responses and more use of distancing strategies in dealing with current interpersonal problems (as measured by Moos & Billings, 1982) when compared with non-PTSD veterans. In a different study carried out on female nurses who served in the army during the Vietnam War, Leon, Ben-Porath, and Hjemboe (1990) examined how retrospective accounts of coping strategies used during the war contribute to current psychological functioning. Finding meaning in the traumatic events (caring for the wounded and dying) was related to good psychological functioning, whereas self-blame and withdrawal were associated with poor current adjustment. The authors interpret their finding in line with Taylor's (1983) ideas on the positive effects of searching for meaning. It is possible that those nurses who were able to find meaning in their war experiences emerged from them with a newfound appreciation of life, transforming the negative experience into a positive one.

The 1982 Lebanon War provided an opportunity for the systematic study of the impact of soldiers' coping strategies on the long-term effects of psychological breakdown during battle. In a series of carefully designed studies, the Israel Defence Forces' Mental Health Department documented the psychological and psychiatric outcomes of war trauma among a large group of Israeli soldiers who participated in the Lebanon War and suffered from CSR. Solomon, Mikulincer, and Benbenishty (1989) found that retrospective accounts of the coping responses employed during battle, as recorded from structured interviews, predicted the intensity of PTSD a year later: The more the soldiers reported having used wishful thinking and denial, the more intense the PTSD symptomatology. Follow-up studies carried out in the same population 2 and 3 years after the war employed the Ways of Coping Checklist for assessing the coping strategies veterans used to deal with current stressors. These studies revealed that problem-focused coping was inversely related to PTSD intensity (Solomon, Mikulincer, & Avitzur, 1988), difficulties in social functioning (Solomon, Avitzur, & Mikulincer, 1989), psychiatric symptomatology (Solomon, Avitzur, & Mikulincer, 1990), and somatic complaints (Solomon, Mikulincer, & Habershaim, 1990). In contrast, wishful thinking and distancing coping were found to correlate positively with those outcome measures. Additional findings indicate that although problem-focused coping diminished the effects of stressful events and maladaptive causal attribution on the intensity of PTSD, avoidance coping exacerbates these detrimental effects (Mikulincer & Solomon, 1989; Solomon, Mikulincer, & Flum, 1988).

Whereas all the preceding studies have focused on the psychological reactions of military personnel to war trauma, the unique situation created by the Scud missile attacks to Israeli cities during the Gulf War (1991) allowed the examination of war trauma among civilian population. Several studies have assessed the impact of coping with the trauma of missile attacks on emotional and psychiatric reactions during and after the war. Based on data gathered during the Gulf War from structured interviews with Israeli adolescents and adults, Zeidner (1993), Zeidner and Hammer (1992), and Zeidner and Ben-Zur (1993) found that active coping (seeking of information, planning, taking action) did not significantly predict anxiety and physical symptoms during the crisis, whereas palliative coping (a wide variety of emotion-focused strategies, like reappraisal, denial, ventilation) were positively related to these negative stress reactions. In a study conducted 2 weeks after the war, Mikulincer, Florian, and Weller (1993) assessed retrospective accounts of coping strategies during the war, as measured by the Ways of Coping Checklist, among a sample of undergraduate students. Results indicated that problem-focused coping was negatively related to depression, anxiety, hostility, somatization, and PTSD-related responses, whereas wishful thinking and distancing were positively related to these psychological reactions. Interestingly, in a study of schoolchildren, Weisenberg, Schwarzwald, Waysman, Solomon, and Klingman (1993) found that more frequent use of problem solving and less frequent use of avoidance response in a sealed room, wherein children cannot do anything to escape the threat, were associated with more postwar stress reactions.

Following the Gulf War, a task force of American and Israeli mental health professionals compiled guidelines for coping with war trauma (Hobfoll et al., 1991). The task force recommends that the most effective coping strategy involves two main ways of problem-focused coping. One implies ". . . breaking down major problems into more manageable subcomponents" (p. 850). The second includes "to become part of the solution of others' problems" (p. 851). The authors also identified coping strategies that may have detrimental effects on the individual's mental health after war: excessive self-blame, prolonged avoidance of problems, substance abuse, cynicism, and prolonged social withdrawal.

Based on our theoretical framework, it seems that the empirical findings regarding coping with war trauma revealed that problem-focused coping and reappraisal have beneficial effects on mental health. With respect to adults' coping in controllable situations, avoidance strategies usually seem to have a detrimental effect. At this point, however, there is no empirical information about the effectiveness of reorganization coping in dealing with war trauma. It seems to us that this pattern of findings may reflect the nature of the adaptational task that veterans and civilians should accomplish after their encounter with war trauma: the reintegration to family and work activities and the return to daily routines. Although the war trauma may be initially uncontrollable, these postwar activities are potentially controllable and may therefore demand the use of active problem-focused coping. In this case, any avoidance strategy, which may counteract problem solving, may impede successful adaptation and exacerbate the negative impact of war trauma on the individual's mental health.

COPING STRATEGIES AND ADJUSTMENT TO LOSS

The concept of loss and the behavioral reactions that follow on loss have been used to help us understand the stressful nature of a number of human situations

(Alexi, 1980; Ben-Sira, 1983; Marris, 1974; Parkes, 1972). The most common type of loss is related to death, the loss of a significant other—interpersonal loss. The other major category of loss is related to the loss of a limb or a physical function—personal loss. In their comprehensive model of reactions to loss, Katz and Florian (1986) analyzed the common psychological reactions to these types of loss and pointed out the process of adaptation to these conditions. In this section, we will examine the psychological effects of using different kinds of coping strategies in dealing with the consequences of each of the two types of losses.

Coping with Interpersonal Loss

An extensive review of the literature dealing with grief and bereavement reveals that most of the studies have not adopted the classical stress-coping theoretical framework. In fact, only few studies have examined the process of adjustment to loss in terms of the preceding framework. Littlewood, Cramer, Hoekstra, and Humphrey (1991) assessed how mothers and fathers cope with the death of their child and found that during the 18 months after the loss these bereaved parents used less problem-focused strategies than a normative sample. Similarly, Schwab (1990) found that bereaved persons did not mention the use of problem-focused strategies in coping with their loss. Instead, different categories of emotion-focused coping were usually employed such as seeking release of tension, avoiding painful thoughts and feelings, ruminating about the deceased, using a cognitive framework to understand the loss, seeking emotional support, and relying on religious beliefs. Only one study conducted on a sample of widows and widowers found that the use of problem-focused coping strategies had some beneficial effects on psychosocial health status (Gass & Chang, 1989).

Usually, the bereavement literature focuses on the assumption that adaptation to loss should involve the working through of the death of the loved one and that avoidance of the new reality is basically maladaptive. This assumption is based on the approaches of Freud (1918), Lindemann (1944), Bowlby (1981), and Marris (1974) emphasizing the need for "grief work" involving the process of confronting the death of the loved one, going over the events before and after the loss, focusing on feelings and memories related to the deceased, and restructuring the thoughts about the loss experience and the new reality (Stroebe, 1993). Moreover, this assumption implies that the failure to work through the grief and the suppression of loss-related feelings and thoughts could have a long-lasting detrimental effect. Practitioners in the area of bereavement (e.g., Worden, 1982) recommend against the use of distraction and sedative drugs in the early stages of mourning because they may interfere with the grief work and could lead to subsequent abnormal reactions. Moreover, Rando (1984) stated that "for the griever who has not attended to his grief, the pain is as acute and fresh 10 years later as it was the day after" (p. 114).

Even though the grief work assumption has not directly emerged from a stress-coping framework, it seems to us that the psychological mechanisms involved in grief work may reflect the action of intrapsychic coping. According to our analysis, grief work may be a particular case of reorganization coping. In both cases, people deal with a stressful experience by confronting their own negative feelings, recollecting thoughts about, and analyzing the causes, meaning, and consequences of this experience, and reframing their schemas about their selves and the changed reality within which they must now live. In addition, both grief work and reorganization coping are activated when the stressful events (loss) cannot be changed by the individual's own instrumental efforts and demand an inner change in schemas, values, and goals to reach a better adaptation to reality. In light of this theoretical analysis, empirical studies dealing with grief work may be interpreted without our theoretical formulation of reorganization coping.

Although some empirical efforts have been invested in examining the validity of the grief work hypothesis, the results are still inconclusive. In a study of reactions to widowhood, Pennebaker and O'Heeron (1984) found that one aspect of the grief work—recollecting thoughts about the loss and speaking about it with others—was negatively correlated with physical health problems. However, another aspect of this work, involving rumination about the spouse's death, was positively correlated with illness rates. Similar findings have been also reported by Remondet, Hansson, Rule, and Winfrey (1987). In our terms, this last finding should not be viewed necessarily as contradicting the grief work hypothesis. Although we conceptualize reorganization coping as implying the ability to reflect on the loss experience without being overwhelmed by it, Pennebaker and O'Heeron's rumination construct involves the automatic, overwhelming stream of loss-related thoughts that may even interfere with more controllable reframing activities. Indeed, these authors reported an inverse correlation between the "confiding in others" aspect of the grief work and rumination.

In two studies with pathologically bereaved individuals, Mawson, Marks, Ramm, and Stern (1981) and Sireling, Cohen, and Marks (1988) found that encouraging the grief work (to face cues concerning the loss experience) improved mental health many weeks after the therapy ended (10 to 20 weeks). In addition, Martinson and Campos (1991) found that avoiding confrontation with the death of a sibling leads to negative health outcomes among adolescents. However, Stroebe and Stroebe (1991) reported that grief work immediately after the loss of a spouse had beneficial effects on mental health and adjustment 2 years later among widowers but not among widows. It was also found that widowers who employed avoidance strategies (distraction, suppressing feelings) showed more maladjustment than widowers who did not use these strategies.

Data from two longitudinal studies on the bereavement process do not provide empirical support for the grief work hypothesis. Parkes and Weiss (1983) found that bereaved persons who face the loss in the initial stages of mourning (e.g., yearning and pining for the deceased) showed poorer mental and physical health 1, 2, and 4 years later than those who avoid the grief work. In a study of parents whose child had died from the sudden infant death syndrome, Wortman and Silver (1987) found that grief work 3 weeks after the loss, operationalized as searching for the causes of the child's death, thinking about how the death could have been avoided, and preoccupation with thoughts about the loss, was positively correlated with distress 18 months later. However, these findings are criticized by Stroebe (1993), since they cannot be taken as serious indicators of grief work. Yearning seems to be a symptom of depression rather than an aspect of grief work. Accordingly, Wortman and Silver's operationalization seems to be more related to useless rumination rather than to constructive reframing of the loss. In Stroebe's own words, "Wortman and Silver's results can be interpreted as showing that the more depressed parents are simply more disturbed and preoccupied with loss initially . . ." (p. 24).

McIntosh, Silver, and Wortman (1993) reformulated the operationalization of the reorganization task by assessment of responses indicating "that individuals are engaged in integrating the new data of the traumatic event to their old schemata" (p. 815) and found a beneficial long-term effect of the grief work. Parents who initially engaged in the cognitive processing of the sudden death of their child were found to show more well-being and less distress 18 months later than those who did not engage in grief work. Interestingly, this cognitive integrative effort was found to have less positive effects when well-being and distress were measured only 3 weeks after the loss. This finding further emphasizes the differential contribution of reorganization coping in short- versus long-term assessments.

An overall view of data related to the coping with interpersonal loss indicates that, in terms of our coping classification, problem-solving strategies seem not to be so relevant in the adjustment process. In contrast, reorganization coping appears to provide a better solution in dealing with this type of loss. However, the data also show the complexity of the reorganization task. First, reorganization may involve the arousal of loss-related painful feelings (e.g., yearning) that, when acting alone, may appear as immediate emotional problems. Second, reorganization may also demand rumination over the causes and meaning of the loss, which, in turn, may be an additional source of distress. Third, reorganization coping may be a long-lasting process, and, in some cases, even a never-ending task. Therefore, its adaptational outcomes should be examined over much longer periods of time than those assessed in previous studies. In our terms, even if reorganization coping may lead to short-term distress, it still may have a long-term alleviating effect whenever it is used for reframing the loss experience.

Coping with Personal Loss

Coping with personal loss refers to the ways individuals deal with the permanent loss of bodily function, the loss of particular body parts, and the disability resulting from chronic physical illness (Katz & Florian, 1986). In her classic theoretical formulation, Wright (1983) proposed to differentiate between two major ways of dealing with disability: coping versus succumbing. Coping is related to strategies that lead to adjustment, such as emphasizing positive strivings and possibilities, efficient body care procedures, and reduced negative expectancies. Coping involves mourning the loss of ability or function, relinquishing the idolization of normal standards, recognizing still existing life triumphs and satisfactions, and viewing oneself as a person with a physical disability rather than a disabled person. In the acceptance of disability, value changes occur that subordinate the importance of the physical and enhance the mental and personality spheres of the person. The orientation of coping is toward seeking solutions and discovering new satisfactions in living. Succumbing, on the other hand, refers to all those strategies that lead to maladjustment—wishful thinking; cognitive and behavioral disengagement; and increased negative views of body care requirements, the self, and the world. Succumbing concentrates on difficulties not on challenges, and on what the person cannot do; disability is central and the person as an individual is lost.

In terms of our theoretical framework, Wright's coping construct seems to involve a configuration of problem solving, reappraisal, and reorganization strategies. Investing efforts in efficient body care procedures can be viewed as an example of problem-solving strategies; maintaining positive expectancies is an example of reappraisal strategies; and accepting the disability and searching for new satisfactions are examples of reorganization coping. On the other hand, Wright's succumbing construct seems to reflect the action of avoidance strategies, which may lead to poor adjustment.

An extensive review of literature reveals that the preceding theoretical ideas receive empirical support in studies carried out in different relevant populations using different methodologies and instruments. Using a case study approach, Adams and Lindemann (1975) examined the adaptation to spinal cord injury of two late adolescent boys. In one case, the individual denied the permanent nature of disability and remained depressed, uncooperative with helpers, and complaining of pain. In the other case, the individual shifted from the unrealistic initial hope to walk again to the acceptance of disability and reframed his loss experience, which, in turn, was reflected in good adjustment and functioning. In a more controlled and extensive study, Bulman and Wortman (1977) found that individuals with spinal cord injuries showed poor adjustment during the first year after the injury when they denied personal responsibility for their physical condition by blaming others. Accordingly, Buckelew, Baumstark, Frank, and Hewett (1990) found that wishful thinking was a predictor of high distress among a group of persons with spinal cord injuries over and above age, time since injury, or level of injury.

A group of more carefully conducted studies assessed the direct association between coping and adjustment among patients with different chronic illnesses. In a germinal study, Felton and Revenson (1984) examined the coping strategies (Ways of Coping Checklist) of four groups of patients with chronic illness: arthritis, diabetes, cancer, and hypertension. Regardless of the type of the illness, they found that wishful thinking, a cognitive avoidance strategy, was a predictor of poor adjustment and negative feelings, whereas information seeking, a problem-solving strategy, had beneficial effects on the individual's positive feelings.

Several studies focusing on rheumatoid arthritis patients revealed that problem-focused coping has been associated with less depression (Brown & Nicassio, 1987) and less distress (Manne & Zautra, 1989; Newman, Fitzpatrick, Lamb, & Shipley, 1984). In addition, reappraisal strategies, such as downward comparisons, have been found to be related to good adjustment (Affleck, Tennen, Pfeiffer, &

Fifield, 1988; Affleck, Tennen, Pfeiffer, Fifield, & Rowe, 1987) and reorganization to less distress (Manne & Zautra, 1989). Finally, cognitive and behavioral avoidance strategies have been found to be positively associated with depression and distress (Manne & Zautra, 1989; Parker, Singsin, Hewett, & Davis, 1984; Parker, Smarr, Buescher, & Hewett, 1989; Smith & Wallston, 1992). Zautra and Manne (1992), in their extensive review, concluded that individuals with arthritis who adopt avoidance coping show poor adaptation, whereas those who adopt reappraisal and reorganization strategies show positive outcomes.

Less consistent findings have been found about the effectiveness of coping strategies among patients with diabetes. Kovacs and colleagues have identified several strategies that individuals adopt to cope with juvenile diabetes (e.g., enrollment in self-help diabetes groups, seeking information about diabetes, minimization of the seriousness of the illness), but they failed to find significant associations between these strategies and psychological functioning (Kovacs, Brent, Steinberg, Paulauskas, & Reid, 1986; Kovacs et al., 1985). Similarly, Frenzel, McCaul, Glasgow, and Schafer (1988) found that coping strategies were not associated with adherence to treatment. However, Delamater, Kurtz, Bubb, White, and Santiago (1987) found that youths who used avoidance strategies in coping with insulin-dependent diabetes mellitus showed poorer metabolic control and lower adherence to treatment than those who did not use avoidance coping.

In the process of adjustment to cancer, several investigators pointed out the positive effects of reorganization and reappraisal strategies and the detrimental effects of avoidance coping. On the one hand, acceptance of the illness, a basic step in the reorganization process, was found to be the most common coping response among breast cancer patients during the first year after surgical intervention (Carver et al., 1993), and it was associated with low levels of negative affect (Carver et al., 1993) and good adjustment (Klein, 1971; Weisman & Worden, 1976). Similarly, focusing on the positive, the most common reappraisal strategy, was found to contribute to better mental health (Dunkel-Schetter, Feinstein, Taylor, & Falke, 1992; Felton, Revenson, & Hinrichsen, 1984).

On the other hand, Weisman (1979), Felton et al. (1984), Friedman, Nelson, Baer, Lane, and Smith (1990) and Bloom (1982) found that several aspects of avoidance coping were positively related to distress in cancer patients. Moreover, Stanton and Snider (1993) revealed that the use of avoidance coping before a biopsy for breast cancer predicted higher levels of distress after the surgery. In a study of a large number of cancer patients, Dunkel-Schetter et al. (1992) found that the use of cognitive and behavioral escape-avoidance strategies was related to emotional distress. Carver et al. (1993) also reported that the use of avoidance 3 months after surgery predicted distress 3 months later among breast cancer patients.

The adaptation to personal loss not only is an individual task, but also may involve the intervention of significant others, particularly in the case of children with physical disability. The demands required from the parents of such children expose them to many kinds of stressors, with which they should cope on a daily basis during the life span (Anstey & Spence, 1986; Singer & Irvin, 1989).

Numerous case studies examining coping strategies in families of disabled children are available (e.g., Houser & Seligman, 1991; Stevens, 1988); however, large-sample correlational studies using comparison groups are less common. For example, Frey, Greenberg, and Fewell (1989) and Miller, Gordon, Daniele, and Diller (1992) found that avoidance strategies (as measured by the Ways of Coping Checklist) were related to higher distress, whereas problem-focused coping was related to lower levels of psychological distress in mothers of physically disabled children. Similar findings concerning the negative effects of avoidance strategies were found among both parents of children with severe motor disability (Sloper & Turner, 1993) and among mothers of children with cancer (Rosko, Youll, Huszti, Nitschke, & Mullins, 1990). In a large study with families who have a medically fragile child, Patterson and Leonard (in press) found that parents change their worldview regarding the meaning of their life so that it fits the new reality of their child and contributes to adjustment.

In general, the reviewed studies provide support to Wright's conceptualization of the process of adaptation to physical disability. The configuration of problem solving, reappraisal, and reorganization—Wright's coping construct—seems to facilitate adaptation; whereas avoidance coping—Wright's succumbing construct—seems to lead to maladaptation. Moreover, this pattern seems to be generalizable across different chronic illnesses and disability conditions.

CONCLUSION

An overview of the empirical findings reviewed in this chapter revealed some basic similarities and certain differences in the psychological outcomes of coping with the three traumatic conditions that we examined. A comparative analysis indicates that avoidance strategies usually have no beneficial effects in dealing with the consequences of war trauma, bereavement, and chronic physical illnesses. In contrast, problem solving, reappraisal, and reorganization strategies seem to be more effective in coping with such conditions. However, the three beneficial strategies appear to differ in their relative effectiveness in each of the assessed traumatic conditions. In the case of war trauma, problem solving has been found to be the most efficient strategy in reducing posttraumatic symptomatology and improving psychological and social functioning. After the death of a loved one, the irreversible nature of the loss makes problem-focused strategies irrelevant and exposes the individual to long-term emotional turmoil. In such situations, reorganization coping, as involved in the grief work, has some potential beneficial effects in ameliorating distress and improving adjustment to the new reality. In the process of coping with chronic illness and disability, our analysis indicates that individuals can use a configuration of problem solving, reappraisal, and reorganization, which prove to be efficient ways for the adaptation to the challenges of the changed life.

In clinical terms, our review endorses the approach of several authors who develop special training programs for enhancing coping skills (e.g., Folkman et al.,

1991; Hobfoll et al., 1991). Our review also points to the possible differences between people who have to cope with various traumas and losses and to the importance of finding the proper fit between coping training and the particular type of stressor. In dealing with war trauma, interventions should focus mainly on enhancing problem-solving strategies. For example, the Israel Defence Forces have developed a comprehensive intervention program that should be carried out near as possible to the battlefield, immediately after the combat breakdown. It focuses on the enhancement of problem-solving skills and the reestablishment of adequate functioning (Solomon et al., 1985).

In cases of grief and bereavement, coping training should encourage people to work through the loss, reorganize their schemas and values, and attempt to find new meanings in life. Although many therapeutic techniques are available in dealing with bereavement, some of them, as reviewed by Raphael, Middleton, Martinek, and Misso (1993), seem to be more relevant to the above intervention aims. For example, "guided mourning" therapy involves intense reliving of painful memories and affects associated with the bereavement; "regrief work" therapy emphasizes the reliving, revisiting, and reviewing the relationships with the deceased person until the loss is resolved; and the "therapeutic rituals" technique encourages verbalization of feelings and recollection of the deceased, helping the mourner to identify and work through the loss.

In dealing with physical disability, our conclusions point to the importance of enriching the individual's repertoire of coping strategies so that the person can flexibly select the most adequate strategy for his or her unique condition. Moreover, intervention programs should include the enhancement of self-esteem and mastery, the teaching of social skills, the review of values and priorities, and the acceptance of the new reality to reestablish adequate social function and achieve proper rehabilitation goals (Wright, 1983). These suggestions should be viewed with caution because the process of coping with loss is a long-term venture and adjustment should not be taken for granted.

Based on our review, future studies should explore the validity of the proposed taxonomy of coping strategies in regard to particular trauma and losses. These studies should also inquire into the effectiveness of the various coping strategies in dealing with the specific demands posed by the new realities in the different stages of the adaptation process. Important research questions should address the individual, familial, and cultural contexts in which the coping and adaptation processes take place. Finally, investigations should focus on the efficacy of intervention programs to change inadequate coping strategies and to teach more appropriate ways of coping.

REFERENCES

Adams, J. E., & Lindemann, E. (1975). Coping with long-term disability. In J. V. Coelho, D. A. Hamburg, & J. E. Adams (Eds.), *Coping and adaptation.* New York: Basic Books.

Affleck, G., Tennen, H., Pfeiffer, C., & Fifield, J. (1988). Social comparisons in rheumatoid arthritis: Accuracy and adaptational significance. *Journal of Social and Clinical Psychology, 6,* 219–234.

Affleck, G., Tennen, H., Pfeiffer, C., Fifield, J., & Rowe, J. M. (1987). Downward comparison and coping with serious medical problems. *American Journal of Orthopsychiatry, 57,* 125–141.

Alexi, W. D. (1980). Coping with loss: The principal theme postulate. *Rehabilitation Literature, 41,* 66–71.

American Psychiatric Association. (1987). *Diagnostic and statistical manual of mental disorders* (3rd ed. rev.). Washington, DC: Author.

Anstey, T. J., & Spence, N. (1986). Factors associated with stress in mothers of intellectually disabled children. *Australia and New Zealand Journal of Developmental Disabilities, 12,* 249–255.

Ben-Sira, Z. (1983). Loss stress and readjustment: The structure of coping with bereavement and disability. *Social Science and Medicine, 17,* 1619–1632.

Bloom, J. R. (1982). Social support, accommodation to stress, and adjustment to breast cancer. *Social Science and Medicine, 16,* 1329–1338.

Bowlby, J. (1981). *Attachment and loss: Vol. 3. Loss, sadness, and depression.* Harmondsworth, England: Penguin Books.

Brown, G. K., & Nicassio, P. M. (1987). Development of a questionnaire for the assessment of active and passive coping strategies in chronic pain patients. *Pain, 31,* 53–64.

Buckelew, S. P., Baumstark, K. E., Frank, R. G., & Hewett, J. E. (1990). Adjustment following spinal cord injury. *Rehabilitation Psychology, 35,* 101–109.

Bulman, R., & Wortman, C. B. (1977). Attributions of blame and coping in the "real world": Severe accident victims react to their lot. *Journal of Personality and Social Psychology, 35,* 351–363.

Carver, C. S., Pozo, C., Harris, S. D., Noriega, V., Scheier, M. F., Robinson, D. S., Ketchman, A. S., Moffat, F. L., & Clark, K. C. (1993). How coping mediates the effect of optimism on distress: A study of women with early stage breast cancer. *Journal of Personality and Social Psychology, 65,* 375–390.

Carver, C. S., Scheier, M. F., & Weintraub, J. K. (1989). Assessing coping strategies: A theoretically based approach. *Journal of Personality and Social Psychology, 56,* 267–283.

Collins, D. L., Baum, A., & Singer, J. E. (1983). Coping with chronic stress at Three Mile Island: Psychological and biochemical evidence. *Health Psychology, 2,* 149–166.

Delamater, A. M., Kurtz, S. M., Bubb, J., White, N. H., & Santiago, J. V. (1987). Stress and coping in relation to metabolic control of adolescents with Type 1 diabetes. *Developmental and Behavioral Pediatrics, 8,* 136–140.

Dunkel-Schetter, C., Feinstein, L. G., Taylor, S. E., & Falke, R. L. (1992). Patterns of coping with cancer. *Health Psychology, 11,* 79–87.

Endler, N. S., & Parker, J. D. (1990). Multidimensional assessment of coping: A critical evaluation. *Journal of Personality and Social Psychology, 58,* 844–854.

Epstein, S., & Meier, P. (1989). Constructive thinking: A broad coping variable with specific components. *Journal of Personality and Social Psychology, 57,* 332–350.

Fairbank, J. A., Hansen, D. J., & Fitterling, J. M. (1991). Patterns of appraisal and coping across different stressor conditions among former prisoners of war with and without posttraumatic stress disorder. *Journal of Consulting and Clinical Psychology, 59,* 274–281.

Felton, B. J., & Revenson, T. A. (1984). Coping with chronic illness: A study of illness controllability and the influence of coping strategies on psychological adjustment. *Journal of Consulting and Clinical Psychology, 52,* 343–353.

Felton, B. J., Revenson, T. A., & Hinrichsen, G. A. (1984). Stress and coping in the explanation of psychological adjustment among chronically ill adults. *Social Science and Medicine, 18,* 889–898.

Folkman, S., Chesney, M., McCusick, L., Ironson, G., Johnson, D. S., & Coates, T. J. (1991). Translating coping theory into an intervention. In J. Eckenrode (Ed.), *The social context of coping.* New York: Plenum.

Folkman, S., & Lazarus, R. S. (1980). An analysis of coping in a middle-aged community sample. *Journal of Health and Social Behavior, 21,* 219–239.

Forsythe, C. J., & Compas, B. E. (1987). Interaction of cognitive appraisals of stressful events and coping: Testing the goodness of fit hypothesis. *Cognitive Therapy and Research, 11,* 473–485.

Frenzel, M. P., McCaul, K. D., Glasgow, R. E., & Schafer, L. C. (1988). The relationship of stress and coping to regimen adherence and glycemic control of diabetes. *Journal of Social and Clinical Psychology, 6,* 77–87.

Freud, S. (1918). *Mourning and melancholy.* London: Hogarth Press.

Frey, K. S., Greenberg, M. T., & Fewell, R. R. (1989). Stress and coping among parents of handicapped children: A multidimensional approach. *American Journal of Mental Retardation, 94,* 240–249.

Friedman, L. C., Nelson, D. V., Baer, P. E., Lane, M., & Smith, F. E. (1990). Adjustment to breast cancer: A replication. *Journal of Psychosocial Oncology, 8,* 27–40.

Gass, K. A., & Chang, A. S. (1989). Appraisals of bereavement, coping, resources, and psychosocial health dysfunction in widows and widowers. *Nursing Research, 38,* 31–36.

Green, B. L., Lindly, J. D., & Grace, M. C. (1988). Long-term coping with combat stress. *Journal of Traumatic Stress, 1,* 399–412.

Grinker, R. R., & Spiegel, J. P. (1945). *Men under stress.* Philadelphia: Blakistan.

Hobfoll, S. E., Spielberger, C. D., Breznitz, S., Figley, C., Folkman, S., Leeper-Green, B., Meichenbaum, D., Milgram, N. A., Sandler, I., Sarason, I., & Van der Kolk, B. (1991). War-related stress: Addressing the stress of war and other traumatic events. *American Psychologist,* 848–855.

Horowitz, M. J., & Wilner, N. (1980). Life events, stress, and coping. In L. Poon (Ed.), *Aging in the 1980's.* Washington, DC: American Psychiatric Association.

Houser, R., & Seligman, M. (1991). Differences in coping strategies used by fathers of adolescents with disabilities and fathers of adolescents without disabilities. *Journal of Applied Rehabilitation Counseling, 22,* 7–10.

Janis, I. L. (1958). *Psychological stress.* New York: Wiley.

Kardiner, A. (1947). *War stress and neurotic illness.* New York: Holber.

Katz, S., & Florian, V. (1986). A comprehensive theoretical model of psychological reaction to loss. *International Journal of Psychiatry in Medicine, 16,* 325–345.

Kleber, R. J., Brom, D., & DeFares, P. B. (1992). *Coping with trauma: Theory, prevention, and treatment.* Alphen a/d Rijn, The Netherlands: Stwets & Zeitlinger.

Klein, R. A. (1971). A crisis to grow. *Cancer, 28,* 1660–1665.

Kovacs, M., Brent, D., Steinberg, T. F., Paulaskas, S., & Reid, J. (1986). Children's self-report of psychological adjustment and coping strategies during first year of insulin-dependent diabetes mellitus. *Diabetes Care, 9,* 472–479.

Kovacs, M., Feinberg, T. L., Paulaskas, S., Finkelstein, R., Pollock, M., & Crouse-Novak, M. (1985). Initial coping responses and psychosocial characteristics of children with insulin-dependent diabetes mellitus. *Journal of Pediatrics, 106,* 827–834.

Lazarus, R. S. (1983). The costs and benefits of denial. In S. Breznitz (Ed.), *The denial of stress* (pp. 1–30). New York: International Universities Press.

Lazarus, R. S., & Folkman, S. (1984). *Stress, appraisal, and coping.* New York: Springer.

Leon, G. R., Ben-Porath, Y. S., & Hjemboe, S. (1990). Coping patterns and current functioning in a group of Vietnam and Vietnam-era nurses. *Journal of Social and Clinical Psychology, 9,* 334–353.

Lindemann, E. (1944). Symptomatology and management of acute grief. *American Journal of Psychiatry, 101,* 15–27.

Littlewood, J. L., Cramer, D., Hoekstra, J., & Humphrey, G. B. (1991). Gender differences in parental coping following their child's death. *British Journal of Guidance and Counseling, 19,* 139–148.

Manne, S., & Zautra, A. J. (1989). Spouse criticism and support: Their association with coping and psychological adjustment among women with rheumatoid arthritis. *Journal of Personality and Social Psychology, 56,* 608–617.

Marris, P. (1974). *Loss and change.* New York: Pantheon.

Martinson, I. M., & Campos, R. G. (1991). Adolescent bereavement: Long-term responses to a sibling's death from cancer. *Journal of Adolescent Research, 6,* 54–69.

Mawson, D., Marks, I. M., Ramm, L., & Stern, R. S. (1981). Guided mourning for morbid grief: A controlled study. *British Journal of Psychiatry, 138,* 185–193.

McCrae, R. R. (1984). Situational determinants of coping responses: Loss, threat, and challenge. *Journal of Personality and Social Psychology, 46,* 918–928.

McCrae, R. R., & Costa, R. T. (1986). Personality, coping, and coping effectiveness in an adult sample. *Journal of Personality, 54,* 385–405.

McIntosh, D. N., Silver, R. C., & Wortman, C. B. (1993). Religion's role in adjustment to a negative life event: Coping with the loss of a child. *Journal of Personality and Social Psychology, 65,* 812–821.

Mikulincer, M., Florian, V., & Weller, A. (1993). Attachment styles, coping strategies, and post-traumatic psychological distress: The impact of the Gulf War in Israel. *Journal of Personality and Social Psychology, 64,* 817–826.

Mikulincer, M., & Solomon, Z. (1989). Causal attribution, coping strategies, and combat-related post-traumatic stress disorder. *European Journal of Personality, 3,* 269–284.

Miller, A. C., Gordon, R. M., Daniele, R. J., & Diller, L. (1992). Stress, appraisal, and coping in mothers of disabled and nondisabled children. *Journal of Pediatric Psychology, 17,* 587–605.

Moos, R. H., & Billings, A. (1982). Conceptualizing coping resources and processes. In L. Goldberger & S. Breznitz (Eds.), *Handbook of stress: Theoretical and clinical aspects.* New York: Macmillan.

Newman, S., Fitzpatrick, R., Lamb, R., & Shipley, M. (1984). Patterns of coping in rheumatoid arthritis. *Psychology and Health, 95,* 516–533.

Nezu, A. M., & Carnevale, G. J. (1987). Interpersonal problem solving and coping reactions of Vietnam veterans with posttraumatic stress disorder. *Journal of Abnormal Psychology, 96,* 358–367.

Parker, J., Singsin, B., Hewett, J., & Davis, M. (1984). Educating patients with rheumatoid arthritis: A prospective analysis. *Archives of Physical Medicine and Rehabilitation, 65,* 771–774.

Parker, J., Smarr, K., Buescher, K. L., & Hewett, J. (1989). Pain control and rational thinking. *Arthritis and Rheumatism, 32,* 984–990.

Parkes, C. M. (1972). *Studies of grief in adult life.* London: Penguin.

Parkes, C. M., & Weiss, R. (1983). *Recovery from bereavement.* New York: Basic Books.

Patterson, J. M., & Leonard, B. J. (in press). Caregiving and children. In E. Kahana, D. E. Biegel, & M. Wykle (Eds.), *Family caregiving across the lifespan.* Newbury Park, CA: Sage.

Pennebaker, J., & O'Heeron, R. C. (1984). Confiding in others and illness rate among spouses of suicide and accident death victims. *Journal of Abnormal Psychology, 93,* 473–476.

Rando, T. A. (1984). *Grief, dying, and death: Clinical interventions for caregivers.* Champaign, IL: Research Press.

Raphael, B., Middleton, W., Martinek, N., & Misso, V. (1993). Counseling and therapy of the bereaved. In M. S. Stroebe, W. Stroebe, & R. O. Hansson (Eds.), *Handbook of bereavement: Theory, research, and intervention.* New York: Cambridge University Press.

Remondet, I., Hansson, R. O., Rule, B., & Winfrey, G. (1987). Rehearsal for widowhood. *Journal of Social and Clinical Psychology, 5,* 285–297.

Rosko, C. K., Youll, L., Huszti, H. C., Nitschke, R., & Mullins, L. L. (1990). *Factors associated with maternal adaptation to pediatric cancer.* Unpublished manuscript, University of Oklahoma.

Roth, S., & Cohen, L. J. (1986). Approach, avoidance, and coping with stress. *American Psychologist, 41,* 813–819.

Scheier, M. F., Weintraub, J. K., & Carver, C. S. (1986). Coping with stress: Divergent strategies of optimists and pessimists. *Journal of Personality and Social Psychology, 51,* 1257–1264.

Schwab, R. (1990). Paternal and maternal coping with the death of a child. *Death Studies, 14,* 407–422.

Singer, G., & Irvin, L. (Eds.). (1989). *Support for caregiving families: Enabling positive adaptation to disability.* Baltimore: Brookes.

Sireling, L., Cohen, D., & Marks, I. (1988). Guided mourning for morbid grief: A controlled replication. *Behavior Therapy, 19,* 121–132.

Sloper, P., & Turner, S. (1993). Risk and resistance factors in the adaptation of parents of children with severe physical disability. *Journal of Child Psychiatry, 34,* 167–188.

Smith, C. A., & Wallston, K. A. (1992). Adaptation in patients with chronic rheumatoid arthritis: Application of a general model. *Health Psychology, 11,* 151–162.

Snyder, C. R., & Higgins, R. L. (1988). Excuses: Their effective role in the negotiation of reality. *Psychological Bulletin, 104,* 24–35.

Solomon, Z., Avitzur, E., & Mikulincer, M. (1989). Coping resources and social functioning following combat stress reaction: A longitudinal study. *Journal of Social and Clinical Psychology, 8,* 87–96.

Solomon, Z., Avitzur, E., & Mikulincer, M. (1990). Coping styles and post-war psychopathology among Israeli soldiers. *Personality and Individual Differences, 11,* 451–456.

Solomon, Z., & Mikulincer, M. (1992). Aftermaths of combat stress reactions: A three-year study. *British Journal of Clinical Psychology, 31,* 21–32.

Solomon, Z., Mikulincer, M., & Avitzur, E. (1988). Coping, locus of control, social support, and combat-related posttraumatic stress disorder: A prospective study. *Journal of Personality and Social Psychology, 55,* 279–285.

Solomon, Z., Mikulincer, M., & Benbenishty, R. (1989). Locus of control and combat-related post traumatic stress disorder: The intervening role of battle intensity, threat appraisal, and coping. *British Journal of Clinical Psychology, 28,* 131–144.

Solomon, Z., Mikulincer, M., & Flum, H. (1988). Negative life events, coping responses, and combat-related psychopathology: A prospective study. *Journal of Abnormal Psychology, 97,* 302–307.

Solomon, Z., Mikulincer, M., & Habershaim, N. (1990). Life events, coping strategies, social resources, and somatic complaints among combat stress reaction casualties. *British Journal of Medical Psychology, 63,* 137–148.

Solomon, Z., Weisenberg, M., & Schwarzwald, J. (1985). *Psychological adjustment of soldiers experiencing combat stress disorder during Operation Peace for Galilea* (Scientific Rep.). IDF Medical Corps, Department of Mental Health.

Stanton, A. L., & Snider, P. R. (1993). Coping with a breast cancer diagnosis: A prospective study. *Health Psychology, 12,* 16–23.

Stauffer, S. A. (1949). *The American soldier: Combat and its aftermath.* Princeton, NJ: Princeton University Press.

Stevens, M. S. (1988). Application of a stress and coping framework to one adolescent's experience of hospitalization. *Maternal-Child Nursing Journal, 17,* 51–61.

Stone, A. A., & Neale, J. M. (1984). New measure of daily coping: Development and preliminary results. *Journal of Personality and Social Psychology, 46,* 892–906.

Stroebe, M. (1993). Coping with bereavement: A review of the grief work hypothesis. *Omega, 26,* 19–42.

Stroebe, M., & Stroebe, W. (1991). Does "grief work" work? *Journal of Consulting and Clinical Psychology, 59,* 479–482.

Taylor, S. E. (1983). Adjustment to threatening events: A theory of cognitive adaptation. *American Psychologist, 38,* 1161–1173.

Taylor, S. E., & Brown, J. D. (1988). Illusion and well-being: A social psychological perspective on mental health. *Psychological Bulletin, 103,* 193–210.

Titchener, J. L., & Ross, W. O. (1974). Acute or chronic stress as determinants of behavior, character and neuroses. In S. Arieti & F. B. Brody (Eds.), *Adult Clinical Psychiatry: American Handbook of Psychiatry.* New York: Basic Books.

Weisenberg, M., Schwarzwald, J., Waysman, M., Solomon, Z., & Klingman, A. (1993). Coping of school-age children in the sealed room during scud missile bombardment and postwar stress reactions. *Journal of Consulting and Clinical Psychology, 61,* 462–467.

Weisman, A. D. (1979). *Coping with cancer.* New York: McGraw-Hill.

Weisman, A. D., & Worden, J. W. (1976). The existential plight in cancer: Significance of the first 100 days. *International Journal of Psychiatry in Medicine, 7,* 1–15.

Worden, J. W. (1982). *Grief counseling and grief therapy: A handbook for the mental health practicioner.* New York: Springer.

Wortman, C., & Silver, R. (1987). Coping with irrevocable loss. In G. R. VandenBos & B. K. Bryant (Eds.), *Cataclysms, crises, and catastrophes: Psychology in action.* Washington, DC: American Psychological Association.

Wright, B. A. (1983). *Physical disability—A psychosocial approach.* New York: Harper & Row.

Zautra, A. J., & Manne, S. L. (1992). Coping with rheumatoid arthritis: A review of a decade of research. *Annals of Behavioral Medicine, 14,* 31–39.

Zeidner, M. (1993). Coping with disaster: The case of Israeli adolescents under threat of missile attack. *Journal of Youth and Adolescence, 22,* 89–108.

Zeidner, M., & Ben-Zur, H. (1993). Coping with a national crisis: The Israeli experience with the threat of missile attacks. *Personality and Individual Differences, 14,* 209–224.

Zeidner, M., & Hammer, A. L. (1992). Coping with missile attack: Resources, strategies, and outcomes. *Journal of Personality, 60,* 709–746.

CHAPTER 25

Attentional Processes, Dysfunctional Coping, and Clinical Intervention

GERALD MATTHEWS and ADRIAN WELLS

THEORETICAL BASES FOR INTERRELATING ATTENTION AND COPING

In this chapter, we examine the influence of attentional processes on choice of coping strategy, and the clinical implications of dysfunctional attention. The research reviewed is based on three types of psychological theory: the transactional theory of stress (Lazarus & Folkman, 1984), the cognitive psychology of attention, and Beck's (e.g., 1967) schema theory of clinical depression and anxiety. Some of the defining characteristics of the three types of theoretical framework are summarized in Table 25.1. The concept of coping originates from transactional theory. It is claimed that stress symptoms are generated by the person's appraisal of the personal significance of potentially threatening or harmful events, and the success of subsequent attempts to cope with perceived demands of the encounter. Stress may be expressed through various symptom measures; in this chapter, we are concerned primarily with emotional distress as a stress outcome measure.

Transactional Theory of Stress

The transactional approach has been particularly useful in providing a taxonomy of the types of processing contributing to stress reactions. In particular, Endler and Parker (1990) have proposed a three-dimensional structural model of broad dimensions of coping. *Task-focused coping* (also termed problem-focused coping) refers to active efforts to change the external situation (e.g., by formulating and implementing a plan of action). *Emotion-focused coping* comprises attempts to alter one's cognitive and emotional reactions, without directly influencing external reality (e.g., by accepting blame or trying to learn something from the encounter). *Avoidance* is the ostrichlike strategy of trying not to think about the event, often through self-distraction. Clinical patients suffering from affective disorders such as depression and various anxiety conditions tend to show a

TABLE 25.1   Three Theoretical Frameworks for Investigating Coping

Theoretical Framework	Main Source of Data	Antecedents of Coping	Consequences of Coping	Associated Therapies
Transactional theory of stress (Lazarus & Folkman, 1984)	Self-reports of reactions to specific stressful encounters	Appraisal of the personal meanings of encounters, and of coping capabilities	Stress outcomes: emotion, psycosocial functioning and health	Stress management techniques
Cognitive psychology of attention	Experimental studies of selective, focused, and divided attention	Voluntary selection of plans and strategies, using capacity-limited processing	Changes in efficiency of performance, and in focus of attention	
Schema theory of emotional disorders (Beck, 1967)	Case studies and clinical trials	Self-knowledge, as represented by the self-schema, including dysfunctional beliefs and attitudes	Confirmation or modification of dysfunctional self-knowledge	Cognitive therapy

distinct pattern of coping. The broad trend is for both depression (e.g., Holahan & Moos, 1987) and anxiety (e.g., Dusenberg & Albee, 1988) to relate to increased emotion-focus and avoidance, and reduced task-focus. In normal individuals, neurotic personality is associated with a similar pattern of coping (Endler & Parker, 1990).

Attention: Resources and Selection

The shortcoming of transactional theory is its vagueness about the specific information processing that supports appraisal and coping. Experimental research on attention suggests two features of processing are of special importance. First, the efficiency of certain kinds of processing is limited by availability of attentional capacity or resources. Although there are various technical difficulties with the resource concept (e.g., Navon, 1984), it is probable that people's ability to cope is constrained by capacity limitations. Second, coping is likely to be influenced by selectivity of attention. Selection of information for action or further processing is, in part, guided by top-down strategies (Neisser, 1976), which in turn requires access of knowledge from long-term memory (LTM), in procedural or declarative form (see Anderson, 1982). Hence, selection of a coping strategy depends on processes controlling interrogation or search of LTM for knowledge relevant to the encoding of the event. The coping strategy chosen is itself likely to guide subsequent selection, such that coping and selective attention are dynamically and reciprocally related.

Schema Theory of Affective Disorder

The third type of theory with which we are concerned, schema theory (Beck, 1967), articulates the nature of the knowledge base in clinical patients in more detail. A schema is an organized representation of generic knowledge of a common concept, event, or activity that may influence selective attention, memory and reasoning. According to Beck (1967), affective disorder patients are characterized by a schema for the self composed of dysfunctional negative beliefs (e.g., that one is a worthless person). These beliefs have consequences for coping. For example, a belief that one is powerless to influence events is likely to discourage task-focused coping, whereas a belief that one is to blame for a mishap is likely to encourage self-criticism, an emotion-focused strategy. The outcomes of using coping strategies such as self-criticism may tend to confirm and strengthen negative self-beliefs. Different types of dysfunctional schema generate different types of affective disorder (e.g., Beck, Emery, & Greenberg, 1985), though in this chapter we are more concerned with elements common to the various affective disorders than with the differences between them. Mild dysfunction may give rise to neurotic personality rather than clinical pathology (Martin, 1985; Matthews, Pitcaithly, & Mann, 1995). Various criticisms of schema theory have been made (e.g., Segal, 1988), but it is convenient to use "schema" as a shorthand for the generic knowledge that contributes to the individual's choice of coping strategy in any given situation.

COPING AND ATTENTIONAL PROCESSES

Attentional Impairment in Stress States and Affective Disorder

It is widely accepted that states of stress and negative emotion reduce the quantity of attentional resources available for processing information. Several distinct dimensions of subjective experience have been implicated in such effects, including anxiety (Sarason, 1978), worry (Morris, Davis, & Hutchings, 1981), depression (Hartlage, Alloy, Vazquez, & Dykman, 1993), and fatigue (Matthews, Davies, & Lees, 1990). Matthews et al. (1990) and Hartlage et al. (1993) make the essential point that strategic or "controlled" processing is more sensitive to shortfalls in resources and stress-related impairment than is involuntary or "automatic" processing. Hence, stress states will tend to impair efforts at coping to the extent that such efforts require strategic rather than involuntary processing.

The transactional model of stress emphasizes that choice of coping strategy is often highly variable across occasions (e.g., Folkman, Lazarus, Gruen, & DeLongis, 1986). Although there are clear individual differences in coping style (e.g., Endler & Parker, 1990), people appear to show considerable flexibility in adapting coping to the needs imposed by specific situations. So, choice and implementation of coping strategies are not usually stereotypical, and are unlikely to be automatized. Hence, in this chapter we conceptualize coping as primarily strategic in nature, requiring volitional choice and the allocation of attentional resources, although two provisos should be made. First, some specific components of coping responses may become automatized through practice, reducing, but not eliminating, capacity demands. Second, choice of coping strategy may be biased, though not fully determined, by unconscious processing of situational cues (cf. Higgins, 1987).

Two factors complicate the prediction of coping in states of stress and negative affect. First, coping strategies differ in their resource requirements. Wells and Matthews (1994b) argue that task-focused strategies, which require the most engagement with external stimuli, are likely to be the most resource-demanding, and avoidance strategies, which require little active processing, the least resource-demanding. Resource requirements will also vary with the specific strategy adopted; for example, a task-focused strategy that is easy to implement will require few resources, and so is likely to be insensitive to stress. Second, it is important to distinguish the person's choice of strategy from its effectiveness. We expect that people's selection of cognitive strategies will tend to be constrained by their perceptions of current mental efficiency, so that individuals reporting frequent attentional failures are more likely to adopt avoidance strategies (Matthews, Coyle, & Craig, 1990). Hence, there is likely to be a general bias against choosing complex, resource-demanding strategies in stress states. However, particularly if the content of schematic knowledge introduces strong bias into the strategy choice process, stressed individuals may sometimes choose strategies they cannot implement effectively. Stress effects on strategy choice are moderated by characteristics of the person's repertoire of available strategies such as their complexity and strength.

The most direct evidence for ineffective coping in stress states is provided by performance studies. It is widely accepted that the worry associated with anxiety is primarily responsible for its detrimental effects on performance (Morris et al., 1981). Worry during performance is associated with negative self-preoccupation and with evaluation of negative aspects of the self (Sarason, Sarason, & Pierce, 1990). Worry may be conceptualized as an outcome of forms of emotion-focused coping associated with self-regulation (see Wells, 1994, for a more detailed account of the functional significance of worry). Performance studies also demonstrate stress-related impairment of task-focused coping, evidenced by decreased motivation and effort. For example, the aftereffects of loud, uncontrollable noise on performance are characterized by reduced performance and persistence (Cohen, 1980). Depression is associated with reduced processing effort on memory tasks (Johnson & Magaro, 1987), and with reluctance to change strategy in response to task stimuli (Griffin, Dember, & Warm, 1986). Test-anxious individuals characteristically wish to avoid the situation (Geen, 1987). However, the case of anxiety may be more complex, in that anxious subjects may sometimes increase effort (increased task-focus) to compensate for the detrimental effects of worry (Eysenck, 1992; Matthews & Westerman, 1994). In general, though, distressed individuals are prone to cope with performance of demanding tasks by an increased reliance on negative emotion-focused coping strategies, and decreased task-focus.

Attentional Bias in Anxiety and Depression

Negative affect influences not just the efficiency of attentional processing, but also the direction of selective attention. There is now extensive evidence that most or all affective disorders, including anxiety, depression, panic, and posttraumatic stress disorder, are associated with a bias toward selection of stimuli associated with the disorder (A. Wells & Matthews, 1994a). Such effects are most clearly demonstrated on the emotional Stroop test, on which subjects are required to name the ink colors of words that include emotional terms. Patients tend to respond more slowly to words related to their pathology and personal concerns. For example, spider phobics color-name words such as "WEB" more slowly, implying that their attention has been diverted toward the semantic content of the word (Watts, McKenna, Sharrock, & Tresize, 1986). Various other attentional tasks have also been used to demonstrate bias (see MacLeod & Mathews, 1991).

Williams, Watts, MacLeod, and Mathews (1988) have suggested that anxiety-related biases of this kind are preattentive and are driven by an involuntary mechanism for attention allocation. If this hypothesis is correct, then these clinically significant biases may lie outside the field of coping; the patient is simply a passive victim of unconscious biases in the information-processing machinery. A contrary view has been advanced by A. Wells and Matthews (1994a). Several features of the experimental evidence suggest that bias is introduced after initial attentional selection, as a result of expectancy-based or strategic processing. For example, attentional bias associated with both anxiety (Richards & French, 1992) and depression (Segal & Vella, 1990) is sensitive to semantic priming effects operating at time intervals of >300 ms, which are believed to be expectancy-based rather than dependent on automatic activation (Neely, 1991). These results imply that attentional bias may be a consequence of strategies for coping with threat stimuli, rather than the result of early, involuntary processing operating prior to strategy selection, as suggested by Williams et al. (1988).

A. Wells and Matthews (1994a) suggest that affective disorder patients tend to adopt a specific task-focused strategy of maintaining the focus of attention on stimuli, to monitor potentially threatening or important stimuli. Eysenck (1992) makes a somewhat similar point in suggesting that anxious individuals are hypervigilant for danger. Hence, although depressed patients in particular often appear to be deficient in task-focused coping, it is simplistic to posit a generalized impairment in affective disorder patients. When task stimuli are congruent with personal concerns, affective disorder patients show a distinct style of task-focused coping associated with bias in selective attention. Although we cannot exclude the possibility that preattentive processing makes some contribution to attentional bias, it appears that control of attentional focus is closely linked to choice of coping strategy.

Maladaptive Coping: A Cause or a Symptom of Attentional Dysfunction?

The styles of coping typical of affective disorder patients are maladaptive in two respects. First, performance studies suggest that the quality of attentionally demanding performance is commonly impaired. These impairments may result from a tendency to engage in emotion- rather than task-focused coping. Everyday efforts at problem-solving and direct action may be similarly impaired (Nezu & D'Zurilla, 1989). Second, habitually focusing attention on negative stimuli may be adaptive in some contexts (Matthews & Dorn, 1995). However, the benefits of heightened threat sensitivity are likely to be outweighed by the costs of failure to attend to signals of possible personal gain or reward, and of adopting a generally pessimistic worldview. For example, bias in selective attention may contribute to the negative biases in evaluation and judgment shown by anxious and depressed individuals (see Forgas & Bower, 1987).

The nature of the causal links between maladaptive coping, attentional bias and affective disorder is somewhat uncertain. It has been suggested (MacLeod & Rutherford, 1992) that attentional bias is itself a cause of pathological anxiety. However, this hypothesis is challenged by evidence that, typically, recovered clinical patients (who remain vulnerable to future pathology) do not reliably show attentional bias (see Eysenck, 1992). Similarly, it is difficult to see coping style as the primary causal agent because, as Zeidner and Saklofske (Chapter 22, this volume) point out, coping styles are typically adaptive in some situations, and maladaptive in others. It is possible that inflexible use of emotion-focused coping, even when the situation requires task-focus coping (as in a performance study), predisposes to pathology. Existing cognitive theories of depression (e.g., Beck, 1967) would tend to suggest that the primary causal agent is the maladaptive self-schema that generates both maladaptive coping and attentional bias as symptoms. However, schema theory neglects the possibility that dysfunctional coping style and attentional bias feedback into changes in self-knowledge, a possibility that we will return to subsequently.

SELF-FOCUSED ATTENTION AND COPING

Experimental Studies in Normal and Clinical Groups

Thus far, we have reviewed relationships between coping and attention in a variety of contexts related to affective distress. Next, we turn to a more specific issue: the relationship between self-focus of attention and coping. "Self-focus," or self-consciousness, refers to the extent to which attention is predominantly directed toward the self, as opposed to external events or internal thoughts unrelated to the self. It may be conceptualized as either a stable personality trait (Fenigstein, Scheier, & Buss, 1975), or as a temporary state of mind. Fenigstein et al. (1975) distinguish private self-consciousness, referring to self-scrutiny and reflection from public self-consciousness, which is awareness of aspects of the self available to the scrutiny of others. In this chapter, we are primarily concerned with private self-consciousness, although both dispositional factors may contribute to states of self-consciousness. Heightened self-focus is a feature of a variety of affective disorders and may play a part in the etiology and/or maintenance of pathology (Ingram, 1990). Experimental studies suggest that self-focus is reciprocally related to negative mood. Inducing a sad mood heightens self-focus (Wood, Saltzberg, & Goldsamt, 1990), but increased self-focus intensifies emotional experience (Scheier & Carver, 1977), so that self-focus resulting from depression is likely to amplify the negative mood experienced. Self-focus is of special interest in the present context as a concept linking style of selective attention to emotional distress and disorder.

Theories of self-focus predict that it should affect selection of coping strategy. Carver and Scheier (1981) propose that self-focus contributes to self-regulation by comparison of current behavioral status with a standard. Action is then directed toward reducing any discrepancy between current state and the ideal standard, with negative affect resulting when the probability of discrepancy reduction is appraised as low. Hence, self-focus should exaggerate task-focused efforts when success is expected. Low expectancy of discrepancy reduction results in behavioral withdrawal or mental disengagement (Carver & Scheier, 1988)—in other words, increased avoidance coping and decreased task-focused coping. The role of self-focus in increasing attention to internal states is also suggestive of increased emotion-focused coping. Hence self-regulation theory predicts that self-focus will interact with perceptions of success likelihood, or confidence, in its influence on coping. The combination of high self-focus and low confidence should generate a pattern of coping similar to that seen in depression (e.g., Holahan & Moos, 1987): substitution of avoidance and emotion-focus for task-focus, even in situations affording opportunities for external action.

Experimental evidence for this prediction is broadly supportive, particularly in the case of increased avoidance. Self-focused individuals are more likely to withdraw from threats such as approaching a feared object or submission to strong electric shock (Carver & Blaney, 1977; Scheier, Carver, & Gibbons, 1981). Support has also been obtained for Carver and Scheier's (1981) prediction that effects of self-focus on task-directed effort depend on "confidence" and related variables. Carver, Peterson, Follansbee, and Scheier (1983) showed that self-focus enhanced anagram solution performance in low test-anxious individuals, but impaired performance in high test-anxious individuals. The latter group reported a shift in attention from the concrete elements of the task to task-irrelevant thoughts, implying a shift to emotion-focused coping. In a second study, Carver et al. (1983) showed that self-focused test-anxious subjects showed less persistence on an impossible anagram, suggesting that avoidance was substituted for task-focused coping. (Note that giving up on an impossible problem is an adaptive response!) Rich and Woolever (1988) have reported similar findings to those of Carver et al. (1983), but a further study (Strack, Blaney, Ganellen, & Coyne, 1985) failed to show that attentional focus and expectancy of success consistently interacted in a sample of depressives. In one of their studies, a task-focusing manipulation enhanced performance irrespective of whether or not a positive expectancy was induced.

Questionnaire Studies of Self-Focus and Coping

If a person has to deal with an encounter whose outcome is likely to be negative, the Carver and Scheier (1981) model predicts that self-focus should enhance avoidance and emotion-focused coping, and reduce task-focused coping. Wood, Saltzberg, Neale, Stone, and Rachmiel (1990), on the basis of a daily diary study, showed increased passive and ruminative coping in self-focused men, consistent with the prediction. Private self-focus, rumination, and reduced direct action were all associated with global negative mood in this study. A. Wells and Matthews (1994b) asked a sample of 139 nurses to complete questionnaires on their reactions to a recent, severely stressful situation. The prediction of reduced task-focused coping in self-focused individuals was confirmed. However, self-focus effects on other dimensions of coping were moderated by appraisal of the controllability of the situation. Self-focus was negatively related to emotion-focus and to suppression (avoidance) when controllability was appraised as mixed or ambiguous, but was not related to these forms of coping when controllability was unequivocally low or high. These negative associations between self-focus and emotion-focus and avoidance appear to be inconsistent with the Carver and Scheier (1981) hypothesis, and with other findings, such as those of Wood et al. (1990). A. Wells and Matthews (1994b) suggest that the demand for attentional resources imposed by ambiguous situations, in which it is difficult to decide what form of coping is most suitable, is sufficient to impair all forms of coping in self-focused individuals. In other words, self-focus effects are moderated not only by expectancies of success, but also by the attentional demands of coping. Predictions from the Carver and Scheier (1981) model are more likely to be confirmed when attentional demands are low or moderate.

A further study (Matthews, Mohamed, & Lochrie, in press; see also A. Wells & Matthews, 1994a, pp. 174–177) investigated styles of coping with less severe everyday stressors. A group of 141 postgraduate student respondents rated their appraisal and coping for nine scenarios previously shown to be common sources of stress for this group. No linear associations between dispositional private self-focus and coping were found; instead, self-focus effects were moderated by the perceived changeability of the situation. The general trend for the sample was for problem-focused coping to increase with appraised changeability, as might be expected. However, the relationship between changeability and problem-focused coping was particularly strong in low self-focus subjects, whereas in high self-focus subjects changeability and problem-focused coping were largely independent. In other words, self-focused individuals fail to show the normal tendency toward increased use of problem- or task-focus when the situation is open to change, and task-focus is relatively likely to be adaptive. High self-focused subjects also tended to use more reappraisal (an emotion-focused strategy) when the situation was appraised as changeable, relative to low self-focused subjects, and to appraise the situation as more threatening. Thus, the expected shift from task- to emotion-focus in self-conscious individuals was found only when the person appraised the situation as changeable. The indecisiveness of high self-focus subjects under these circumstances suggests that they are poorly adapted to a category of encounters that would normally be relatively easy to cope with.

In conclusion, the relationship between private self-consciousness and coping in everyday life appears to be somewhat complex. Even in dealing with severe events, self-focused individuals do not necessarily show the maladaptive pattern of coping associated with affective disorder patients, as predicted by the Carver and Scheier (1981) model. Self-focus effects are moderated by attentional demands and situational appraisals, such that self-focus is maladaptive only in certain conditions. First, when attentional resources are overloaded, there may be a general *impairment* of all types of coping in the self-focused person. Second, when the situation appears to afford potential for change, the self-focused person is most likely to show maladaptive *patterning* of coping: decreased task-focus and increased emotion-focus and avoidance.

Attentional Basis for Self-Focus Effects on Coping

The data reviewed in the previous section suggest two distinct mechanisms for self-focus effects on coping: overload of resources and bias in retrieval of strategies from long-term memory, perhaps associated with processing of discrepancies between actual and ideal state (cf. Carver & Scheier, 1981). Experimental studies of self-focus and attention have shown both overload and biasing effects. The clearest demonstration of overload has been provided by Kanfer and Stevenson (1985), in a study using a continuous learning task. After each trial block, self-regulating subjects were required to self-monitor and evaluate their performance. Learning performance in these subjects was impaired, relative to subjects in a control condition. Self-regulating subjects also showed reduced persistence in voluntarily completing extra trial blocks after the "end" of the experiment, indicating reduced task-directed effort. It appears that the predominantly emotion-focused coping required by the self-regulation instructions impaired subsequent task-oriented coping. Self-focus also influences appraisal of attentional efficiency, in that self-focused individuals report a greater incidence of cognitive failures in everyday life (Matthews & Wells, 1988).

Biasing effects of self-focus have also been demonstrated experimentally. Geller and Shaver (1976) ran a version of the Stroop test requiring subjects to name the colors of self-referent words. Interference was greater when self-focus was increased by having the subject perform the task in front of a camera and a mirror. Generally comparable findings were obtained by Segal and Vella (1990), who showed that Stroop responses of self-focused normal subjects were similar to those of clinical depressives. Self-focus may also influence memory bias, inasmuch as personal involvement in the task seems to enhance mood-congruence in memory (Ucros, 1989).

Clinical Implications

Self-focus amplifies negative moods, increases loss of functional resources, increases attentional bias to negative self-referent stimuli, and increases bias toward retrieval of negative information. Hence, the heightened self-focus associated with affective disorder (Ingram, 1990) probably contributes to the development and maintenance of individual, acute episodes of negative affect and cognitive dysfunction. The relationship between self-focus and acute distress is likely to be reciprocal, in that heightened negative emotion and awareness of personal shortcoming is itself likely to raise self-focus. In a panic attack, for example, the panicker's initial self-consciousness may contribute to perceptions of minor somatic sensations such as cardiac acceleration as indicating an imminent catastrophe, such as cardiac arrest (see Clark, 1988). The immediate consequences of this appraisal are diversion of attention to cardiac symptoms, worry and loss of functional resources, retrieval of knowledge about heart attacks and how to cope with them, and emotional anxiety. The negative emotion is itself likely to raise self-focus. Additionally, coping by worrying about personal consequences of the heart attack is itself likely to have a similar effect. Given the reciprocal relationship, we can see how a vicious circle may develop, such that in a severe panic attack the person's attention is wholly occupied by negative, self-referent thoughts. The diversion of attentional resources to processing such thoughts may preclude any effective coping at all. A less dramatic vicious circle is that associated with extended rumination on personal faults and inadequacies, in which continued accessing of negative self-beliefs is likely to maintain self-focus and negative emotion, which in turn prolong rumination (A. Wells & Matthews, 1994a).

Hence, self-focus may contribute to affective disorder symptoms by interfering with effective coping. We have argued that in normal individuals self-focus is not necessarily detrimental in coping with everyday stressors. However, in affective disorder patients, factors moderating self-focus effects, such as attentional demands and situational appraisals, are likely to work to exacerbate detrimental effects of self-focus. First, patients will be more vulnerable than normal individuals to resource overload resulting from self-focus because of their proneness to worry. Second, cognitive therapies for affective disorder normally require some commitment to changing behavior on the basis of restructured beliefs. As we have seen in both experimental studies (Carver & Scheier, 1981) and questionnaire studies (Matthews et al., 1994), entering a situation where direct action is required may be particularly threatening for the self-focused individual. Self-focus may especially interfere with the patient's capacity to change undesirable behaviors. Third, rumination may, paradoxically, block access to dysfunctional knowledge so it cannot be modified (A. Wells, 1994). Morgan, Matthews, and Winton (in press) found that dispositional self-focus was associated with anxiety in individuals subjected to a traumatic experience, loss of possessions in a flood. Self-focused individuals showed a pattern of posttraumatic stress symptoms associated with heightened numbing but reduced arousal, suggesting that they were detached from their normal life goals and activities because of lack of access to self-knowledge. Self-conscious individuals also reported more use of worry-related coping strategies.

In the next section, we describe a theoretical model of the interrelationships between self-focus of attention, attentional information processing, coping strategy, and emotional distress and pathology. The model is based on Anderson's (1982) theory of skill and knowledge, not discussed in this chapter (a full account of the model is provided by Wells & Matthews, 1994a). We then consider current therapies directed toward enhancing effective coping in the light of the model and suggest some theory-driven alternative techniques.

A THEORETICAL MODEL OF STRESS PROCESSES, ATTENTION, AND COPING

The A. Wells and Matthews (1994a) model proposes that emotional distress is intimately linked to a cognitive-attentional syndrome described as self-referent executive function (SREF), characterized by self-focus of attention, on-line strategic processing of negative self-beliefs and retrieval of generic, schemalike negative self-knowledge. SREF processing is goal directed; it is driven by control loops that aim to reduce discrepancies between actual and ideal state. The SREF syndrome may be initiated by both externally and internally generated signals. Initiating cues from the external environment are those that tend to signal personal inadequacy, such as failure feedback and criticism by other people, and cues that increase state self-consciousness such as being the center of attention in a social group. SREF activity may also be initiated by intruding negative thoughts generated by unconscious automatic processing, or through internal retrieval from long-term memory (LTM) of information about discrepancies between actual and ideal state. Hence, a tendency to adopt a ruminative, self-directed emotion-focused coping style is one of several factors predisposing the syndrome. However, the predisposing factors described do not necessarily activate the SREF; other factors such as positive self-beliefs and positive emotion will tend to reduce the likelihood of SREF initiation.

The direct effect of SREF initiation is to bias retrieval from LTM of the high-level plans that control thought and action, toward those that aim to reduce discrepancies in self-knowledge. It is supposed, as in Higgins' (1987) theory of self-knowledge, that LTM contains representations of (a) the person's beliefs about their actual state of being, and (b) beliefs about ideal states held by themselves and by significant others. Broadly, discrepancies arise when actual state falls short of personal ideals, or fails to match the standards of others (see Higgins, 1987, for a full account of self-discrepancy). Frequently, plans linked to self-discrepancy specify coping options in the form of procedural knowledge that specifies action in generic terms. Further central processing is necessary to develop a plan that may be applied to the current situation. Often, multiple generic plans will be activated, requiring additional processing to select and integrate plans. For example, a panicker experiencing chest pain may retrieve plans that specify resting and seeking medical help. The person must still process environmental cues, using resource-demanding controlled processing, to decide how to implement these general strategies. The indirect effect of SREF operation is to allocate attentional resources to internal processing, which may interfere with task-directed processing. Resource demands of plan formulation will vary with factors such as the familiarity and complexity of the strategy, and the compatibility of concurrently activated multiple plans.

Implications of the Model for Coping

Selection of coping strategies is a key component of SREF function, and many of the observed consequences of emotional distress, such as attentional bias, may result from biasing of retrieval of generic coping strategies. As with processing generally, SREF activation has direct and indirect effects on coping. The direct effect is the accessing from LTM of strategies linked to the salient problem or discrepancy. These strategies may be highly person- and/or situation-specific, and may specify task-focus, emotion-focus, or avoidance. Thus, in accord with the empirical evidence, the model does not assume any rigid association between self-focus and a specific pattern of coping.

However, the prevalence of worry in emotionally distressed individuals suggests that emotion-focused plans that generate active worry and rumination are commonly retrieved by the SREF. Worry in part results from *metacognitive* beliefs about the functioning of the person's internal cognitions. For example, worry may result from a belief that rumination is helpful for dealing with life difficulties (A. Wells, 1994). Similarly, patients may believe that it is important to punish themselves by self-criticism for actions appraised as mistakes, or that it is beneficial to monitor one's thoughts for negative content (see A. Wells & Hackmann, 1993). Alternatively, the act of worrying may itself by appraised negatively on the basis of metacognitive self-knowledge. In such cases, the individual may divert SREF processing effort to attempts at suppressing or controlling worry, which in turn may exacerbate the problem (Wegner, Schneider, Carter, & White, 1987; Wells, 1994). Another plan that appears to be common in affective disorder is task- rather than emotion-focused: monitoring for threats by maintaining focused attention on sources of negative stimuli. Operation of this plan accounts for biasing effects of emotional distress on selective attention, as in Stroop test studies.

Indirect effects of SREF activity on coping derive from the loss of processing resources resulting from active worry and rumination. The person must time-share plans for worry with plans for other coping activities, with consequent risk of resource overload. Because overload is more likely with task-focused coping, the model predicts the general trend toward a negative association between self-focus and task-focused coping evident in the research literature (e.g., A. Wells & Matthews, 1994b). Conversely, the attractiveness of avoidant strategies such as behavioral withdrawal and disengagement (Carver & Scheier, 1981) may be increased by their low resource demands. However, these trends may be overridden by plans strongly activated within a given individual and situation. The individual may sometimes choose a complex, resource-demanding task-focused strategy, even though loss of functional resources may make it difficult to implement effectively. Application of the SREF model to coping is shown in Figure 25.1: Coping outcomes of SREF activity listed are typical rather than obligatory. Feedback loops from outcomes to the executive system have also been omitted. In fact, appraisal of outcomes will influence appraisal of coping options, choice of strategy and modification of self-beliefs dynamically.

Implications for Clinical Theory and Practice

Like Beck's (1967) schema theory, the SREF model emphasizes the importance of negative self-knowledge in generating pathology, but it extends and modifies Beck's theory in several respects. First, much of the relevant self-knowledge is stored in procedural rather than declarative form. That is, self-knowledge is represented as a set of "programs" for processing self-relevant information, which are activated by specific cues and goals, rather than as explicit propositions that can be stated verbally (see Anderson, 1982). In the case of coping, plans

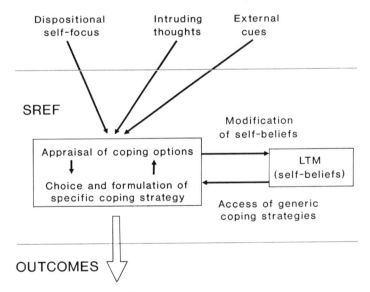

Figure 25.1 Factors predisposing initiation of self-referent executive function (SREF) model of attention, coping, and emotional distress, with feedback loops omitted (see Wells & Matthews, 1994a).

are activated by contextual cues, such that the person is aware (at least partially) of how he or she is coping, but is unaware of the derivation of the coping strategy implemented from generic knowledge. Hence, seeking to modify self-beliefs directly may be ineffective; the proper target for therapy is the unconscious procedural knowledge that gives rise to conscious, verbalizable beliefs. Second, the emphasis on procedural knowledge highlights the person's scope for action, functional or dysfunctional, in response to situational cues, including social cues. Therapy must be directed not to abstracted self-knowledge, but to the cognitive bases for action in specific, problematic situations. Coping strategies are an important category of actions, and understanding pathology requires understanding why, in patients, situations evoke strategies that are unlikely to deal successfully with a particular problem.

Third, the model emphasizes the role of dynamic factors in generating and maintaining both acute emotional distress, and chronic pathology. The mutual facilitation of self-focus, negative emotion, and negative self-beliefs in acute distress has already been discussed. Chronic pathology may derive from the changes in self-knowledge resulting from such episodes. Generally, the knowledge base is modified by the outcomes of running procedures such as coping strategies, and strategy change resulting from a distress episode may influence the probability and circumstances of future episodes. Consider the panic patient described previously. If the consequence of the panic attack is that the panicker strengthens generic strategies for monitoring cardiac perceptions, and for evaluating them as symptoms of disease, the chance of future panic attacks is likely to be enhanced. Conversely, if the panicker strengthens strategies for dismissing the perceptions as unimportant (adaptive avoidance), or for implementing relaxation procedures, the probability of future attacks may be lessened. It may be the effects on self-knowledge in LTM that distinguish episodes of everyday, nonpathological unhappiness from clinical disorder.

Finally, the model posits the co-occurrence of direct and indirect effects of SREF activity on coping and behavior. The person's scope for action is constrained by loss of available resources, so that he or she is cognitively ill equipped to deal with the dysfunction, and has difficulty restructuring cognitions and modifying the knowledge base. Hence, the importance of relaxation techniques in therapy may derive not so much from the relaxation itself, but in freeing attentional resources from self-referent processing so that the person can cope effectively and modify dysfunctional self-knowledge.

IMPLICATIONS FOR THERAPY: I. TRAINING OF SPECIFIC COPING SKILLS

In the remainder of this chapter, we review the role of coping and attention in common techniques used in the treatment of stress-related problems and affective disorders, such as various forms of self-control training and cognitive therapy. We present a brief overview of some of the main psychological treatments for emotional problems, and their limitations. Most techniques influence either task- or emotion-focused coping, or both. Therapists generally see avoidance as undesirable, although we shall discuss some evidence for beneficial effects of distraction. We also derive some new implications for treatment based on the A. Wells and Matthews (1994a) cognitive-attentional model of emotional distress. Biological as well as cognitive factors may contribute to affective disorders, but biologically based treatments for anxiety and depression are beyond the scope of this chapter.

Training of Specific Behaviors and Task-Focused Coping

Traditional behavioral approaches are based on the learning theories of Skinner (1953), Pavlov (1927), and Bandura (1977). These approaches share the assumption that emotional responses, particularly fears, are learned by the individual and can therefore be unlearned by modifying the behavioral and affective contingencies that maintain the problem. The behavior therapies most commonly applied to affective disorders, such as systematic desensitization, discussed in the next section, are directed toward the conditioning of emotional responses. However, if the problem is seen as one of more overt behaviors, then training a behavior that affords more positive reinforcement is a suitable therapy. The behaviorist, of course, rejects the cognitive theory of coping. However, the aim of behavioral training is similar to that of task-focused coping; to change the efficacy with which the person acts on the external, objective environment. Hence, from the cognitive standpoint, such efforts are, in effect, training the person in a specific, task-focused coping strategy.

A good example of behavioral training is social skills training; social phobia and depression have both been linked to skills deficits. Therapy is directed toward identifying and rectifying specific instances of skill deficiency (e.g., Trower, Bryant, & Argyle, 1978). Training may include skills in conversation, in observing and listening to another speaker, and in nonverbal communication. Means of instruction include direct reinforcement, modeling and role-play. Several studies, reviewed by Edelmann (1992), show improvements in social anxiety following social skills training. However, Edelmann (1992) cautions that there is little evidence for its efficacy for extreme social anxiety, and that not all socially anxious patients have inadequate skills. There is also little evidence that behavioral deficits in socially anxious individuals are due to lack of social skills, rather than failure to implement skills effectively due to competing worries and cognitive interference. Other behaviors that may be directly trained include assertiveness (e.g., McFall & Twentyman, 1973) and handling difficult people (Bramson, 1981).

A more general application of behavior training as a treatment for depression is achieved through activity scheduling (Lewinsohn, 1976), which has three phases: assessment, baseline, and treatment. In the assessment phase, the therapist attempts to determine activities that may be intrinsically rewarding to the patient, and draws up a list of activities likely to be mood enhancing. In the baseline phase, the patient completes a daily diary concerning mood and participation in the activities listed. Correlations between activities and mood may then be established. In the treatment phase, the patient is encouraged to participate in those activities most strongly associated with positive mood. One of the difficulties encountered may be that the patient finds it difficult to engage in the activity successfully. In this case, a *graded task assignment* may be adopted, such that the therapist initially sets easy tasks for the patient to accomplish and progressively increases difficulty (Williams, 1992).

Nezu, Nezu, and Perri (1989) have developed problem-solving therapy (PST) for depression to counteract depressives' observed lack of success in social problem solving. Treatment is based on an analysis of the problem-solving process (Nezu & D'Zurilla, 1989), which discriminates five interacting components:

1. *Problem Orientation.* Adopting a cognitive set that encourages problem solving efforts.
2. *Problem Definition and Formulation.* Clarifying the specific nature of the problem.
3. *Generation of Alternatives.* Maximizing the likelihood of a successful solution.
4. *Decision Making.* Choosing the alternative best suited to the problem at hand.
5. *Solution Implementation and Verification.* The final stage of the process.

Patients are explicitly trained in all five components of social problem solving. Nezu and D'Zurilla (1989) review studies suggesting that such training is more effective in reducing depression than general discussion of current problems, with improvements maintained at 6-month follow-up. The problem-orientation component, whose inclusion increases clinical effectiveness, indicates that it is important to train beliefs that task-focus is likely to be successful, as well as specific problem-solving skills.

Teaching problem-solving skills may also benefit some anxiety patients. For example, Kleiner, Marshall, and Spevack (1987) instructed agoraphobics in recognizing and dealing with interpersonal problems. Patients also participated in an (emotion-focused) coping skills training program, in which they learned techniques for relaxation and modification of negative thoughts. Patients treated with problem-solving and coping packages showed more improvement at 6-month follow-up than patients treated with the coping package alone.

Training Relaxation Skills and Emotion-Focused Coping

It is often difficult to identify specific problem behaviors, so that techniques which directly address the person's emotional state are preferred. A behavioral treatment used extensively in the treatment of anxiety and phobic states is systematic desensitization. This procedure, developed by Wolpe (e.g., 1958), is based on the concept of counterconditioning in which a learned response, such as a fear of crowds, can be blocked by substituting an activity antagonistic to it, most often relaxation. Counterconditioning is achieved by exposing the individual to the feared situation or approximations of the situation in gradual steps while the individual reduces anxiety through relaxation. To achieve desensitization, treatment is presented in a number of stages. The first stage consists of training in relaxation such as progressive relaxation (Jacobsen, 1938) or autogenics (Schultz & Luthe, 1969). Once relaxation has been mastered, the person practices relaxation while visualizing being in a feared situation. The degree of threat is progressively increased, until the patient can reliably imagine highly frightening scenes without anxiety. Systematic desensitization is typically practiced in conjunction with real-life exposure to feared situations. As in the case of specific behavioral training, the therapy makes no reference to cognitive processes. However, it would appear that progressive desensitization improves the person's control over emotional state, and so facilitates effective emotion-focused coping.

An alternative approach to alleviating anxiety is *applied relaxation training* (Öst, 1988), in which the patient learns to relax in response to internal cues that anxiety or panic is developing. Training progresses through stages in which the length of time required to achieve relaxation is progressively shortened. Homework practice is an important part of the treatment. At the outset, patients are presented with a rationale emphasizing that relaxation is a skill that can be learned and applied to breaking the vicious circle of anxiety and panic. Initially, individuals keep a diary of the earliest signs of stress and anxiety; these become the cues for practicing relaxation during the later stages of treatment. Stage 1 is *progressive relaxation,* which involves systematic tensing and releasing of specified muscle groups. Stage 2 is *release-only relaxation,* which is aimed at reducing the time needed to relax, and uses only the release phase learned previously. In Stage 3, *cue controlled relaxation* is taught. This shortens the time taken for relaxation to 2 to 3 minutes and focuses on slow breathing and the forming of an association between the self-suggestion "relax" and feelings of relaxation. Stage 4 of the procedure involves *differential relaxation,* which consists of practicing cue-controlled relaxation during body movements and then full activities such as walking. Stage 5, *rapid relaxation,* aims to reduce the time needed to relax to 20 to 30 seconds. It requires the practice of cue-controlled relaxation many times a day in response to seeing a particular cue, such as red dots that are placed at varying locations in the person's work and social settings. Stage 6, the final stage of applied relaxation, is *application training* in which individuals are instructed to practice relaxation in anxiety-provoking situations. This stage is most often combined with exposure exercises in which individuals enter feared situations while controlling anxiety. Öst (1988) showed that applied relaxation training was more effective in treating panic than the purely physiological procedure of progressive muscle relaxation.

Training Hybrid Coping Skills

The treatments so far reviewed can be readily categorized as oriented toward either behavior in the external world, or internal emotional states. Other skill-training approaches aim to teach a package of coping skills, including both task- and emotion-focused coping. *Anxiety management training* (AMT: Suinn, 1976,

1984) teaches the control of anxiety primarily through the use of relaxation skills that can be applied to a range of problematic situations. It combines relaxation training, cognitive procedures, exposure to anxiety-inducing situations and skills training, in the form of treatment packages aimed at teaching individuals to cope with anxiety more effectively. AMT is effective in reducing anxiety in nonclinical samples (Edelmann, 1992) and (in modified form) in generalized anxiety disorder patients (Butler, Cullingham, Hibbert, Klimes, & Gelder, 1987).

Another hybrid treatment is *stress inoculation training* (Meichenbaum & Cameron, 1983), which aims to teach coping skills during exposure to a manageable degree of stress. The person learns to recognize dysfunctional cognitions, and to apply coping strategies across a variety of stressful situations. For example, Novaco (1975, 1979) has developed an inoculation procedure for anger control, which has been applied to the stresses of police work. The person learns (a) general information about anger, (b) how to discriminate anger-evoking situations, (c) how to identify maladaptive aspects of anger, and (d) how to use anger and confrontation management techniques. Such techniques include both emotion-focused techniques intended to reduce emotional response to provocation, and problem-focused techniques for resolving conflict without resorting to aggressive behavior. Similarly, J. K. Wells, Howard, Nowlin, and Vargas (1986) showed that use of a three-phase inoculation procedure was effective in reducing anxiety and speeding recovery in elective surgery patients. Phases of information provision and training in a variety of coping skills are practiced and rehearsed in the final phase.

Limitations of the Skills Approach

Skill-based therapies are limited both in their efficacy and in the coherence of the psychological rationales from which they are derived. Some specific problems are described in the following subsections.

Superficiality of Therapy

A familiar criticism of behavior therapy is that it addresses symptoms rather than underlying causes. Lazarus and Folkman (1984) make a related criticism of skills training, that it downplays or even denigrates the subjective distress of the patient. Skills training may also be unsuccessful in dealing with emotional distress because it fails to address the dysfunctional cognitive biases that obstruct the learning of social and cognitive skills.

Prevention of Disconfirmation of Dysfunctional Beliefs

Teaching control of anxiety responses may prevent disconfirmation of fears that individuals have concerning the experience of anxiety. For example, persons who believe that anxiety will lead to total mental breakdown would be unable to discover the erroneous nature of this belief if they controlled their anxiety. The nonoccurrence of the catastrophe could be attributed to their control behavior (e.g., Salkovskis, 1991; A. Wells, Clark, Salkovskis, Ludgate, Hackmann, & Gelder, in press). In this way, they would maintain vulnerability to misinterpreting arousal in a catastrophic way. In other words, some forms of training may provide short-term relief at the expense of undermining the ability to confront dysfunctional beliefs.

Loss of Functional Capacity

The practice of control strategies that are cognitively demanding may reduce capacity for effective task-focused performance and for problem solving. Emotion-focused strategies are likely to increase self-focus of attention, which, as previously described, may impair efforts at active coping (see Kanfer & Stevenson, 1985). Hence, anxiety control strategies, as a type of emotion-focus, may require attentional capacity that is diverted from other activities, such as the processing required for direct, task-focused action.

Priming of Negative Beliefs

Certain control strategies may be counterproductive because they prime low-level processing units for detection of threats and for threat responses to generate intruding thoughts. For example, the literature on thought suppression demonstrates that attempting not to think particular thoughts can have a counterproductive effect of increasing the frequency of the unintended thought (Wegner et al., 1987). Morgan et al. (in press) found that use of thought suppression was associated with more severe PTSD symptoms and emotional distress.

Rationales for Training Effects

Even with effective training programs, it may not actually be modification of specific behaviors that is responsible for observed improvements. In the case of social skills training, it may be exposure to social situations that reduces social phobia through desensitization (Stravynski & Greenberg, 1989). Alternatively, cognitive restructuring that results from successful performance in the therapeutic environment may be responsible for benefits, rather than increased skill per se (Edelmann, 1992). In the case of composite and somewhat eclectic training packages, such as AMT or stress inoculation, a further difficulty is that it is unclear which components of the package are responsible for changes in symptoms. The underlying theoretical model for such packages is frequently obscure. Such treatment approaches may fail to optimize cognitive change because they are prescriptive and technique driven rather than theory driven in nature.

IMPLICATIONS FOR THERAPY: II. MODIFYING THE ANTECEDENTS OF MALADAPTIVE COPING

Cognitive Therapy and Coping

Cognitive behavior therapy approaches assume that the proximal determinant of stress reactions is the individual's appraisal of events or beliefs about events (Beck, 1976; Meichenbaum, 1977). For example, Ellis's (1962) Rational Emotive

Therapy seeks to train patients to recognize and restructure harmful irrational beliefs. According to Beck's (1967) schema theory, the dysfunctional negative appraisals associated with depression derive from the self-schema, so that the patient's style of appraisal is traced back to the person's store of self-knowledge in long-term memory. Biased appraisals and certain behaviors maintain emotional dysfunction by interfering with disconfirmation of the individual's negative beliefs and appraisals. For example, a depressed individual may appraise his current situation as hopeless and so will retire from coping attempts. This behavior will block opportunities for mastery of problems and for pleasure, thus restricting opportunities for disconfirmation of belief and contributing to feelings of hopelessness. In another example, a health-anxious individual who believes that she has a life-threatening illness may become hypervigilant for bodily sensations, may discount personal medical information that contradicts her health fears, and may avoid certain behaviors that are believed to be risky, such as vigorous exercise. These cognitive and behavioral factors prevent disconfirmation of belief in the spurious appraisal of serious physical illness, thereby contributing to a maintenance of health anxiety.

Beck's cognitive therapy (e.g., Beck et al., 1985; Beck, Rush, Shaw, & Emery, 1979) is based on an idiosyncratic formulation of the cognitive and behavioral factors that serve to maintain emotional problems. Therapy proceeds by the collaborative modification of belief at the level of situational appraisals and of more stable knowledge. This is accomplished by behavioral and verbal procedures intended to optimize belief change. Thus, exposure to real-life stressors is presented as a behavioral experiment in which the patient is encouraged to test out the likelihood that his or her feared catastrophes will occur. For example, the misinterpretations of bodily sensations as a sign of mental or physical calamity, which are considered to result in panic attacks (Clark, 1988), can be challenged by engaging in behaviors that are likely to make the catastrophe happen. The nonoccurrence of the catastrophe then facilitates disconfirmatory learning. Although this requires a high level of therapist skill, feared catastrophes are seldom realistic and safeguards are built into therapy to minimize the risk of confirmatory experiences. Verbal reattribution techniques in cognitive therapy are also important in modifying belief in situational appraisals and in more stable self-knowledge. These strategies involve identifying and questioning negative appraisals and generating more realistic responses. In Beck's cognitive therapy, realistic responses are derived from collaborative experimental and verbal analysis of the validity of thoughts.

Hence, cognitive therapy focuses on modifying the knowledge base from which coping derives, but deemphasizes specific training of emotion- and problem-focused coping skills. Cognitive therapy has a stronger rationale than the somewhat ad hoc stress management techniques previously described. However, although the therapy is often efficacious (Williams, 1992), the assumptions of schema theory have attracted considerable criticism (e.g., Segal, 1988). It has also been argued that cognitive therapy does not fundamentally change the patient's self-knowledge; instead, the patient learns compensatory meta-cognitive, problem-solving, and planning strategies to cope with his or her problems (Barber & DeRubeis, 1989). Meta-cognitive strategies are those directed toward the processing of internal thoughts, such as questioning negative self-beliefs. In general, the theory does not distinguish between automatic and strategic processes, and it does not specify the role of the attentional processes discussed in the first part of this chapter. In the next section, we consider the contribution of the SREF model to improving the rationale for therapy and its outcome.

Treatment Implications of the SREF Model

The various treatments that we have described often do not take account of the range of processing characteristics that serve to maintain the individual's dysfunction. The model of stress vulnerability advanced by A. Wells and Matthews (1994a) assumes that treatments are effective when they modify the dysfunctional self-knowledge responsible for perseverative negative self-relevant processing. The model clarifies the processes of knowledge modification in several respects, described in the following subsections.

The Role of Attentional Bias

Bias of selective attention toward negative or threatening stimuli tends to confirm existing negative beliefs, and to maintain access to plans for dysfunctional coping strategies that contribute to overestimation of threat, styles of thinking characterized by worry, and frequent maladaptive emotion-focused coping attempts. The more emotion-focused aspects of cognitive therapy, such as the identification and questioning of negative appraisals, may facilitate control over selective attentional bias. The SREF model suggests that plans may be modified by pursuing questions that focus on the patient's dynamic processing strategies, such as: "How did I form this judgement?" "How do I know my thoughts are realistic?" and "What do I pay attention to in a given situation?" In contrast, questions in standard cognitive therapy are directed more toward specific items of self-knowledge (see Beck et al., 1985, pp. 201–209).

The Role of Attentional Overload

The loss of functional resources typically resulting from SREF activation leads to general cognitive impairment, including reduced ability to challenge and modify dysfunctional beliefs. Hence, capacity-demanding perseverative processing such as worry or overanalytic thinking should be reduced early in treatment so that SREF capacity is freed for disconfirmatory processing. To achieve this, the individual maintains personal detachment during observation of negative appraisal processes; this prevents activation of full-blown SREF perseveration. Relaxation therapies may be a useful adjunct to cognitive therapy to the extent that they reduce active worry.

The Role of Meta-Cognitive Processing

Meta-cognitive beliefs about the nature and significance of internal thoughts play an important part in choice of dysfunctional coping strategies such as perseverative worry. Some individuals may actually be motivated to choose worry as a coping strategy, because they believe it aids problem solving or averts dangers associated with optimism (e.g., A. Wells, 1994; A. Wells & Hackmann, 1993). Treatment based on the SREF model should focus on identifying and modifying meta-cognitive knowledge by challenging declarative beliefs about cognition, and by the practice of replacement processing strategies under stressful conditions.

The Role of Dispositional Variables

High dispositional self-focus is a marker for the likelihood of activation of the SREF, and is indicative of a tendency to cope through ruminative self-focused processing. Hence, the self-focused individual is at particular risk that the SREF will become starved of resources for disconfirmatory processing. Worry then leads to an "incubation" of intrusive stress-related thoughts as a symptom of failed emotional processing (cf. Borkovec & Hu, 1990; Rachman, 1980). Neuroticism may be a marker for the presence of a negative self-schema or other representations of negative self-beliefs (Matthews et al., in press). Hence, therapy may benefit from personality assessment to indicate which causes of chronic SREF activation are most salient for the individual.

Attentional Therapies

The SREF model implies that direct manipulation of attentional focus may sometimes improve therapeutic outcome. Distraction is quite well established as a potentially beneficial intervention. For example, reading a story reduces anxious behavior in children undergoing dental treatment (Stark et al., 1989), and directing attention to slides of outdoor scenes alleviates depression in some patient groups (Fennell, Teasdale, Jones, & Damle, 1987). Diversion of attention from depressive thinking may explain the paradoxical improvements in depressives' performance sometimes found when task demands are increased (e.g., Krames & MacDonald, 1985). However, as A. Wells and Matthews (1994a) point out, distraction is not always effective, and the rationales for distraction-based therapies are often obscure. For example, Shapiro's (1989) eye-movement desensitization (EMD) treatment for anxiety requires the patient to follow rapid movements of the therapist's finger with the eyes, while simultaneously maintaining images and thoughts concerning the source of anxiety. It appears that the division of attention between external and internal stimuli is beneficial, but the mechanism is unclear.

A. Wells (1990) has developed a theory-based attentional training procedure for treatment of panic in which the patient is instructed in selective attention, attentional switching, and divided attention. Initial results (see A. Wells & Matthews, 1994a, pp. 240–241) suggest that the technique is effective in producing decrements in anxiety that are stable over time. It is hypothesized that the reduction in self-focus reduces attention to negative thoughts in emotional states, and frees up attentional resources for processing belief-incongruent information. In other words, contrary to much cognitive theory, modifying attentional focus without directly attacking negative thoughts may be beneficial. Attentional training is not a replacement for conventional cognitive therapy, but a technique that may facilitate the work of the cognitive therapist in modifying dysfunctional knowledge structures.

TABLE 25.2   Therapies That Influence Coping

Approach to Therapy	Examples of Therapy	Application
Skill-Based Approaches		
Training task-focused coping	Social skills training (Trower et al., 1978)	Social phobia, depression
	Activity scheduling and task assignment (Lewinsohn, 1976)	Depression, anxiety
	Problem-solving therapy (Nezu et al., 1989)	Depression
	Interpersonal problem solving (Kleiner et al., 1987)	Agoraphobia
Training emotion-focused coping	Systematic densitization (Wolpe, 1958)	Anxiety, phobias
	Progressive relaxation (Jacobsen, 1938)	Anxiety, stress symptoms
	Applied relaxation training (Öst, 1988)	Anxiety, stress symptoms
Training hybrid coping skills	Anxiety management training (Suinn, 1976)	Anxiety, stress symptoms
	Stress inoculation training (Meichenbaum & Cameron, 1983)	Stress symptoms
Approaches Modifying the Antecedents of Coping		
Cognitive therapies	Rational emotive therapy (Ellis, 1962)	Various affective disorders
	Beck's (1967) cognitive therapy— various specific techniques, including detecting negative automatic thoughts, reality testing, and changing dysfunctional assumptions	Various affective disorders
Attentional therapies	Eye-movement desensitization (Shapiro, 1989)	Anxiety
	Attentional training (A. Wells, 1990)	Panic disorder

CONCLUSION

In the first part of this chapter, we saw that states of emotional distress may impair coping in two respects: a general impairment of coping associated with worry and loss of resources, and a bias toward selection of maladaptive coping strategies such as rumination. Such impairments may be related to a cognitive-attentional syndrome characterized by heightened self-focus of attention. This distress syndrome may be modeled as a dynamic interaction between retrieval of generic plans for action from LTM and on-line formulation of coping strategies and other responses. Some coping strategies may contribute to maintaining or enhancing representations of negative self-beliefs in LTM, putting the person at risk of clinical affective disorder. These dysfunctional strategies are of several types, including perseverative worry (emotion-focused), monitoring for external threat (task-focused), and thought suppression (avoidance).

Table 25.2 summarizes the therapies described in this chapter. Although training of specific coping strategies and skills has had some therapeutic success, intervention is likely to be most successful when based on a theoretical model of dysfunctional self-knowledge, and systematic analysis of the individual's styles of attention and coping. The key to therapeutic success is the modification of dysfunctional self-knowledge. Existing cognitive therapies may be enhanced by discriminating the roles of selective bias, overload of attention, meta-cognitive belief, and dispositional vulnerability factors, and by attentional training that reduces excessive self-focus of attention.

REFERENCES

Anderson, J. R. (1982). Acquisition of cognitive skill. *Psychological Review, 89,* 369–406.

Bandura, A. (1977). Self-efficacy: Toward a unifying theory of behavioural change. *Psychological Review, 84,* 191–215.

Barber, J. P., & DeRubeis, R. J. (1989). On second thoughts: Where the action is in cognitive therapy for depression. *Cognitive Therapy and Research, 13,* 441–457.

Beck, A. T. (1967). *Depression: Causes and treatment.* Philadelphia: University of Pennsylvania Press.

Beck, A. T. (1976). *Cognitive therapy and the emotional disorders.* New York: International Universities Press.

Beck, A. T., Emery, G., & Greenberg, R. L. (1985). *Anxiety disorders and phobias: A cognitive perspective.* New York: Basic Books.

Beck, A. T., Rush, A. J., Shaw, B. F., & Emery, G. (1979). *Cognitive therapy of depression.* New York: Guilford.

Borkovec, T. D., & Hu, S. (1990). The effect of worry on cardiovascular response to phobic imagery. *Behaviour Research and Therapy, 28,* 69–73.

Bramson, R. M. (1981). *Coping with difficult people.* New York: Doubleday.

Butler, G., Cullingham, A., Hibbert, G., Klimes, I., & Gelder, M. (1987). Anxiety management for persistent generalized anxiety. *British Journal of Psychiatry, 151,* 535–542.

Carver, C. S., & Blaney, P. M. (1977). Perceived arousal, focus of attention and avoidance behaviour. *Journal of Abnormal Psychology, 86,* 154–162.

Carver, C. S., Peterson, L. M., Follansbee, D. J., & Scheier, M. F. (1983). Effects of self-directed attention and resistance among persons high and low in test-anxiety. *Cognitive Therapy and Research, 7,* 333–354.

Carver, C. S., & Scheier, M. F. (1981). *Attention and self-regulation: A control-therapy approach to human behavior.* Berlin, Germany: Springer-Verlag.

Carver, C. S., & Scheier, M. F. (1988). A control-process perspective on anxiety. *Anxiety Research, 1,* 17–22.

Clark, D. M. (1988). A cognitive model of panic attacks. In S. Rachman & J. D. Maser (Eds.), *Panic: Psychological perspectives* (pp. 71–89). Hillsdale, NJ: Erlbaum.

Cohen, S. (1980). After effects of stress on human performance and social behavior: A review of research and theory. *Psychological Bulletin, 88,* 82–108.

Dusenberg, L., & Albee, G. W. (1988). Primary prevention of anxiety disorders. In C. G. Last & M. Hersen (Eds.), *Handbook of anxiety disorders* (pp. 571–583). New York: Pergamon.

Edelmann, R. J. (1992). *Anxiety: Theory, research and intervention in clinical and health psychology.* Chichester, UK: Wiley.

Ellis, A. (1962). *Reason and emotion in psychotherapy.* New York: Lyle Stuart.

Endler, N. S., & Parker, J. (1990). Multi dimensional assessment of coping: A critical review. *Journal of Personality and Social Psychology, 58,* 844–854.

Eysenck, M. W. (1992). *Anxiety: The cognitive perspective.* Hillsdale, NJ: Erlbaum.

Fenigstein, A., Scheier, M. F., & Buss, A. H. (1975). Public and private self-consciousness: Assessment and theory. *Journal of Consulting and Clinical Psychology, 43,* 522–527.

Fennell, M. J. V., Teasdale, J. D., Jones, S., & Damle, A. (1987). Distraction in neurotic and endogenous depression: An investigation of negative thinking in major depressive disorder. *Psychological Medicine, 17,* 441–452.

Folkman, S., Lazarus, R. S., Gruen, R. J., & DeLongis, A. (1986). Appraisal, coping, health status, and psychological symptoms. *Journal of Personality and Social Psychology, 50,* 571–579.

Forgas, J. P., & Bower, G. H. (1987). Affect in social and personal judgements. In K. Fiedler & J. Forgas (Eds.), *Affect, cognition and social behavior: New evidence and integrative attempts* (pp. 183–208). Lewiston, NY: Hogrefe.

Geen, R. G. (1987). Test anxiety and behavioral avoidance. *Journal of Research in Personality, 21,* 481–488.

Geller, V., & Shaver, P. (1976). Cognitive consequences of self-awareness. *Journal of Personality and Social Psychology, 12,* 99–108.

Griffin, J. A., Dember, W. N., & Warm, J. S. (1986). Effects of depression on expectancy in sustained attention. *Motivation and Emotion, 10,* 195–205.

Hartlage, S., Alloy, L. B., Vazquez, C., & Dykman, B. (1993). Automatic and effortful processing in depression. *Psychological Bulletin, 113,* 247–278.

Higgins, E. T. (1987). Self-discrepancy: A theory relating self and affect. *Psychological Review, 94,* 319–340.

Holahan, C. J., & Moos, R. H. (1987). Personal and contextual determinants of coping strategies. *Journal of Personality and Social Psychology, 58,* 909–917.

Ingram, R. E. (1990). Self-focused attention in clinical disorders: Review and a conceptual model. *Psychological Bulletin, 107,* 156–176.

Jacobson, E. (1938). *Progressive relaxation.* Chicago: University of Chicago Press.

Johnson, M. H., & Magaro, P. A. (1987). Effects of mood and severity on memory processes in depression and mania. *Psychological Bulletin, 101,* 28–40.

Kanfer, F. H., & Stevenson, M. K. (1985). The effects of self-regulation on concurrent cognitive processing. *Cognitive Therapy and Research, 9,* 667–684.

Kleiner, L., Marshall, W. L., & Spevack, M. (1987). Training in problem-solving and exposure treatment for agoraphobics with panic attacks. *Journal of Anxiety Disorders, 1,* 219–238.

Krames, L., & MacDonald, M. R. (1985). Distraction and depressive cognitions. *Cognitive Therapy and Research, 9,* 561–573.

Lazarus, R. S., & Folkman, S. (1984). *Stress, appraisal and coping.* New York: Springer.

Lewinsohn, P. M. (1976). Activity schedules in the treatment of depression. In J. D. Krumbolz & C. E. Thoresen (Eds.), *Counselling methods.* New York: Holt, Rinehart & Winston.

MacLeod, C., & Mathews, A. (1991). Cognitive-experimental approaches to the emotional disorders. In P. R. Martin (Ed.), *Handbook of behaviour therapy and psychological science: An integrative approach* (pp. 116–149). Oxford: Pergamon.

MacLeod, C., & Rutherford, E. M. (1992). Anxiety and the selective processing of emotional information: Mediating roles of awareness, trait and state variables, and personal relevance of stimulus materials. *Behaviour Research and Therapy, 30,* 479–491.

Martin, M. (1985). Neuroticism as predisposition towards depression: A cognitive mechanism. *Personality and Individual Differences, 6,* 353–365.

Matthews, G., Coyle, K., & Craig, A. (1990). Multiple factors of cognitive failure, and their relationships with stress vulnerability. *Journal of Psychopathology and Behavioral Assessment, 12,* 49–65.

Matthews, G., Davies, D. R., & Lees, J. L. (1990). Arousal, extraversion, and individual differences in resource availability. *Journal of Personality and Social Psychology, 59,* 150–168.

Matthews, G., & Dorn, L. (1995). Personality and intelligence: Cognitive and attentional processes. In D. Saklofske & M. Zeidner (Eds.), *International handbook of personality and intelligence* (pp. 367–396). New York: Plenum.

Matthews, G., Mohamed, A., & Lochrie, B. (in press). Dispositional self-focus of attention and individual differences in appraisal and coping. In J. Bermudez, A. M. Perez, A. Sanchez-Elvira, & G. L. van Heck (Eds.), *Personality psychology in Europe* (Vol. 6). Tilburg, Netherlands: Tilburg University Press.

Matthews, G., Pitcaithly, D., & Mann, R. E. (1995). Mood, neuroticism, and the encoding of affective words. *Cognitive Therapy and Research, 19,* 565–589.

Matthews, G., & Wells, A. (1988). Relationships between anxiety and self-consciousness, and cognitive failure. *Cognition and Emotion, 2,* 123–132.

Matthews, G., & Westerman, S. J. (1994). Energy and tension as predictors of controlled visual and memory search. *Personality and Individual Differences, 17,* 617–626.

McFall, R. M., & Twentyman, C. T. (1973). Four experiments on the relative contribution of rehearsal, modeling and coaching to assertion training. *Journal of Abnormal Psychology, 81,* 199–218.

Meichenbaum, D. (1977). *Cognitive-behavior modification: An integrative approach.* New York: Plenum.

Meichenbaum, D., & Cameron, R. (1983). Stress inoculation training: Toward a general paradigm for training coping skills. In D. Meichenbaum & M. E. Jeremko (Eds.), *Stress reduction and prevention.* New York: Plenum.

Morgan, I. A., Matthews, G., & Winton, M. (in press). Coping and personality as predictors of post-traumatic intrusions, numbing, avoidance and general distress: A study of the victims of the Perth flood. *Behavioral and Cognitive Psychotherapy.*

Morris, L. W., Davis, M. A., & Hutchings, C. H. (1981). Cognitive and emotional components of anxiety: Literature review and a revised worry-emotionality scale. *Journal of Educational Psychology, 73,* 541–555.

Navon, D. (1984). Resources—A theoretical soup stone? *Psychological Review, 91,* 216–234.

Neely, J. H. (1991). Semantic priming effects in visual word recognition: A selective review of current findings and theories. In D. E. Besner & G. Humphreys (Eds.), *Basic processes in reading* (pp. 264–337). Hillsdale, NJ: Erlbaum.

Neisser, U. (1976). *Cognition and reality.* San Francisco: Freeman.

Nezu, A. M., & D'Zurilla, T. J. (1989). Social problem solving and negative affective conditions. In P. C. Kendall & D. Watson (Eds.), *Anxiety and depression: Distinctions and overlapping features* (pp. 285–315). New York: Academic Press.

Nezu, A. M., Nezu, C. M., & Perri, M. G. (1989). *Problem-solving therapy for depression: Theory, research and clinical guidelines.* New York: Wiley.

Novaco, R. W. (1975). *Anger control: The development and evaluation of an experimental treatment.* Lexington, MA: Heath.

Novaco, R. W. (1979). The cognitive regulation of anger and stress. In P. C. Kendall & S. D. Hollon (Eds.), *Cognitive-behavioral interventions: Theory, research, and procedures.* New York: Academic.

Öst, L. -G. (1988). Applied relaxation vs progressive relaxation in the treatment of panic disorder. *Behaviour Research and Therapy, 26,* 13–22.

Pavlov, I. P. (1927). *Conditioned reflexes.* London: Oxford University Press.

Rachman, S. (1980). Emotional processing. *Behaviour Research and Therapy, 18,* 51–60.

Rich, A. R., & Woolever, D. K. (1988). Expectancy and self-focused attention: Experimental support for the self-regulation model of test anxiety. *Journal of Social and Clinical Psychology, 7,* 246–259.

Richards, A., & French, C. C. (1992). An anxiety-related bias in semantic activation when processing threat/neutral homographs. *Quarterly Journal of Experimental Psychology, 45A,* 503–525.

Salkovskis, P. M. (1991). The importance of behaviour in the maintenance of anxiety and panic: A cognitive account. *Behavioural Psychotherapy, 19,* 6–19.

Sarason, I. G. (1978). The Test Anxiety Scale: Concepts and research. In C. D. Spielberger & I. G. Sarason (Eds.), *Stress and anxiety* (Vol. 5, pp. 193–215). Washington, DC: Hemisphere.

Sarason, I. G., Sarason, B. R., & Pierce, G. R. (1990). Anxiety, cognitive interference, and performance. *Journal of Social Behavior and Personality, 5,* 1–18.

Scheier, M. F., & Carver, C. S. (1977). Self-focused attention and the experience of emotion: Attraction, repulsion, elation, and depression. *Journal of Personality and Social Psychology, 35,* 625–636.

Scheier, M. F., Carver, C. S., & Gibbons, F. X. (1981). Self-focused attention and reactions to fear. *Journal of Research in Personality, 15,* 1–15.

Schultz, J. H., & Luthe, W. (1969). *Autogenic therapy: Vol. 1. Autogenic methods.* New York: Grune and Stratton.

Segal, Z. V. (1988). Appraisal of the self-schema construct in cognitive models of depression. *Psychological Bulletin, 103,* 147–162.

Segal, Z. V., & Vella, D. D. (1990). Self-schema in major depression: Replication and extension of a priming methodology. *Cognitive Therapy and Research, 14,* 161–176.

Shapiro, F. (1989). Eye movement desensitization: A new treatment for post-traumatic stress disorder. *Journal of Behaviour Therapy and Experimental Psychiatry, 20,* 211–217.

Skinner, B. F. (1953). *Science and human behaviour.* New York: Macmillan.

Stark, L. J., Allen, K. D., Hust, M., Nash, D. A., Rigney, B., & Stokes, T. F. (1989). Distraction: Its utilization and efficacy with children undergoing dental treatment. *Journal of Applied Behavioral Analysis, 22,* 297–307.

Strack, S., Blaney, P. H., Ganellen, R. J., & Coyne, J. C. (1985). Pessimistic self-preoccupation, performance deficits and depression. *Journal of Personality and Social Psychology, 49,* 1076–1085.

Stravynski, A., & Greenberg, D. (1989). Behavioural psychotherapy for social phobia and dysfunction. *International Review of Psychiatry, 1,* 207–218.

Suinn, R. (1976). Anxiety management training to control general anxiety. In J. Krumboltz & C. Thoresen (Eds.), *Counseling methods.* New York: Holt, Rinehart & Winston.

Suinn, R. (1984). Generalized anxiety disorder. In S. Turner (Ed.), *Behavioral theories and treatment of anxiety.* New York: Plenum.

Trower, P., Bryant, B., & Argyle, M. (1978). *Social skills and mental health.* London: Methuen.

Ucros, C. G. (1989). Mood state-dependent memory: A meta-analysis. *Cognition and Emotion, 3,* 139–167.

Watts, F. N., McKenna, F. P., Sharrock, R., & Tresize, L. (1986). Processing of phobic stimuli. *British Journal of Clinical Psychology, 25,* 253–261.

Wegner, D. M., Schneider, D. J., Carter, S. R., III, & White, T. L. (1987). Paradoxical effects of thought suppression. *Journal of Personality and Social Psychology, 53,* 5–13.

Wells, A. (1990). Panic disorder in association with relaxation-induced anxiety: An attentional training approach to treatment. *Behavior Therapy, 21,* 273–280.

Wells, A. (1994). Attention and the control of worry. In G. L. C. Davey & F. Tallis (Eds.), *Worrying: Perspectives on theory, assessment and treatment* (pp. 91–114). Chichester, UK: Wiley.

Wells, A., Clark, D. M., Salkovskis, P. M., Ludgate, J., Hackmann, A., & Gelder, D. M. (in press). Social phobia: The role of in-situation safety behaviors in maintaining anxiety and negative beliefs. *Behavior Therapy.*

Wells, A., & Hackmann, A. (1993). Imagery and core beliefs in health anxiety: Content and origins. *Behavioural and Cognitive Psychotherapy, 21,* 265–273.

Wells, A., & Matthews, G. (1994a). *Attention and emotion: A clinical perspective.* Hove, England: Erlbaum.

Wells, A., & Matthews, G. (1994b). Self-consciousness and cognitive failures as predictors of coping in stressful episodes. *Cognition and Emotion, 8,* 279–295.

Wells, J. K., Howard, G. S., Nowlin, W. F., & Vargas, M. J. (1986). Presurgical anxiety and postsurgical pain and adjustment: Effects of a stress inoculation procedure. *Journal of Consulting and Clinical Psychology, 54,* 831–835.

Williams, J. M. G. (1992). *The psychological treatment of depression* (2nd ed.). London: Routledge.

Williams, J. M. G., Watts, F. N., MacLeod, C., & Mathews, A. (1988). *Cognitive psychology and emotional disorders.* Chichester, UK: Wiley.

Wolpe, J. (1958). *Psychotherapy by reciprocal inhibition.* Stanford, CA: Stanford University Press.

Wood, J. V., Saltzberg, J. A., & Goldsamt, L. A. (1990). Does affect induce self-focused attention? *Journal of Personality and Social Psychology, 58,* 899–908.

Wood, J. V., Saltzberg, J. A., Neale, J. M., Stone, A. A., & Rachmiel, T. B. (1990). Self-focused attention, coping responses, and distressed mood in everyday life. *Journal of Personality and Social Psychology, 58,* 1027–1036.

CHAPTER 26

Coping with Emotion and Psychopathology

LAURA J. SUMMERFELDT and NORMAN S. ENDLER

The coping literature has traditionally identified as one of its chief concerns the relationship between efforts to manage stress and the experience of psychological distress. This is mirrored, in both clinical research and practice, by an interest in the role of an individual's adaptational resources in the genesis and maintenance of psychopathology. Despite this clear commonality, the bodies of research and theory on coping and psychopathology have evolved in relative isolation from one another, with surprisingly little mutual influence. This may arise, in part, from the former field's rather insular and well-delineated approach to what constitutes coping itself—a definition that can be distinguished from those offered in the clinical realm by its almost exclusively empirical roots (see Folkman, 1992). These circumstances may have impeded the development of a clinically relevant body of coping research. A number of rich literatures, however, may serve to conceptually bridge these two areas. By providing a conceptual integration of a number of current clinical and empirical formulations with the issues most commonly addressed within the field of coping, this chapter seeks to explore this possibility.

This is a timely effort. In recent years, a small body of psychodynamically-oriented clinicians have published several arguments regarding the utility of considering defensive functioning as a diagnostic category (e.g., Skodol & Perry, 1993). This proposal was considered by the authors of the most recent edition of the *Diagnostic and Statistical Manual of Mental Disorders* (DSM-IV; American Psychiatric Association [APA], 1994) to require further study, and was appended thereto in order to facilitate this. Nonetheless, the terminology adopted in this proposal is worthy of note, for the terms *defense mechanism* and *coping style* have been used synonymously. Furthermore, its definition of defense provides little information to those seeking to conceptually distinguish it from the coping construct: "defense mechanisms mediate the individual's reaction to emotional conflicts and to internal and external stressors" (APA, 1994, p. 751). Clearly,

The authors would like to acknowledge the general support provided during the writing of this chapter by the Social Sciences and Humanities Research Council of Canada (SSHRC), both in the form of a Doctoral Fellowship to the first author and a Research Grant (#410-94-1473) to the second author.

there is growing clinical interest in concepts similar to those that have long been addressed by coping research.

Two functional relationships are often specified in the coping literature: Coping may serve to mediate between stress and such outcomes as psychopathology, or, alternatively, coping may take place in response to psychological distress. Our primary emphasis, as indicated in the title, will be on the latter. However, the two are not easily disentangled; in the words of Leventhal, Suls, and Leventhal (1993): "Coping procedures have dual objectives, as they have functions in the problem space and in the information processing system, the latter set being broader but including the regulation of emotional states" (p. 87). Relevantly, our review of conceptual bridges relies heavily on an interpretation of much coping in terms of emotional regulation. The use of the term "regulation" in this context is consistent with such recent general conceptualizations as that of Karoly (1993): "It implies modulation of thought, affect, behaviour, or attention via deliberate or automated use of specific mechanisms or supportive metaskills" (p. 25). Three diagnostic categories will be discussed: personality disorders, anxiety, and depression. Others, for which neurological conceptualizations are useful, such as schizophrenia, or where situational determinants seem primary, such as adjustment disorders, will not be addressed.

As is made unmistakable elsewhere in this volume, the question of the stability of coping responses has remained controversial and is one of the long-standing disciplinary disputes that defines the field of research on coping. However, any treatment of coping as it pertains to those issues addressed by the field of clinical psychology must acknowledge the conceptual overlap, within that field, of the broad topic of personality and the pattern of efforts to respond to demands from both the internal and external environment that is called "coping." The difficulties inherent in extricating coping efforts from the person's more general pattern of adaptation were made apparent over 50 years ago, by Gordon Allport (1937): "Personality is the dynamic organization within the individual of those psychophysical systems that determine his unique adjustments to his environment" (p. 48). Inherent in this conceptualization are the ideas of personal adaptive endeavours (Staub, 1980), and an ongoing pattern of regulatory efforts that is unique for each individual. The important feature of this classic definition, though, is its insistence on some pattern that *can* be organized.

One cannot dispute the role of situational determinants in an individual's coping responses, but there is increasing recognition of the contribution made by the person to the very circumstances to which he or she may have to adjust. Situational appraisal has long been thought to be among the mechanisms by which this takes place (Lazarus & Folkman, 1984; Terry, 1991). The constructive nature of the individual's engagement with the world is a central focus of many seeking to understand the role of personality variables in adjustment (Magnusson & Torestad, 1993). The pertinence of this to the understanding of coping has been made explicit by Lazarus (1993), who, seeking to clarify the nature and source of emotional experience, has written: "Coping theory must become more concerned than formerly with the motivational implications of person-environment relationships, which underlie the different emotions" (p. 16). In this view, appraisals (and hence the goal of an individual's coping efforts) are the crucial intersection between environmental contingencies and the motives and beliefs of the individual. Dispositional contributions are also found in the self-generation of stressors associated with some forms of psychopathology. What has been considered a methodological nuisance is now being acknowledged as a valuable link in reciprocal models of stress and psychological disorder (e.g., Lakey, Baltman, & Bentley, 1993; Watson, Clarke, & Harkness, 1994). Stable individual differences in the capacity to identify, discriminate among, and articulate emotional states (see Salovey & Mayer, 1990; Taylor, 1984) are also clinical variables of clear relevance to coping models.

In short, although contextual determinants of coping responses must be acknowledged, all dimensions of coping—initial appraisal of environmental events; emotional responses, and the ability to monitor, identify and regulate them; and the occurrence and experience of contextual stressors—are influenced by the personal characteristics brought to the situation. This may explain why, in the words of a recent researcher: "The evidence suggests that how people cope in response to a new event appears to be, in part, a function of how they coped in the past" (Terry, 1994, p. 907). Pearlin (1991) has noted that unlike problem-focused strategies, emotionally regulatory coping responses seem less influenced by situational contingencies than by stable predispositions. By acknowledging these factors, we wish to emphasize the inextricable web of interrelationship among coping, personality, and the general maladjustment found in all forms of psychopathology. Semantic and conceptual clarity and consensus are indisputable components of any discipline. Nonetheless, we would join Nolen-Hoeksema, Parker, and Larson (1994) in suggesting that by restricting their considerations to the empirically driven roots of their field, coping researchers may have failed to benefit from a much more diffuse literature. A broader approach may have considerable potential for elucidating the interplay among the individual's efforts at regulating both internal and external environment and the experience, etiology, and maintenance of psychopathology.

COPING AND PERSONALITY DISORDER

Our brief discussion of the conceptual (rather than empirical) difficulties inherent in any effort to disentangle personality functioning from coping is perhaps nowhere more evident than in the case of personality disorders. The adoption of a multiaxial format in the third edition of the DSM (APA, 1980) marked a significant turning point in approaches to clinical diagnosis. The inclusion of disorders of personality in the separate but important Axis II represented an acknowledgment that a diagnosis based on manifest symptoms is often incomplete without consideration of the context provided by more enduring dispositional resources (Millon, 1990a). Such an orientation, integral to diathesis-stress approaches to psychopathology (see Watson et al., 1994) places implicit emphasis on deficits in the availability, breadth, type, and application of coping strategies. This is made explicit by Millon (1981): "[It is] the patient's personality pattern—that is, coping skills and adaptive flexibilities—that will determine whether or not the person will master or succumb to his/her psychosocial environment" (p. 6). Different orientations have forged similar sentiments. Vaillant (1992, 1994) has written of the importance of patient's defensive style or consistent emotional regulation strategies: "It is often not life stress but the patient's idiosyncratic response to it that leads to psychopathology" (Vaillant, 1994, p. 49).

Conventional clinical approaches to this form of psychopathology, guided as they are by diagnostic frameworks, have not been hampered by ongoing debates in the field of personality about the best definition of its subject matter, a debate echoed in the empirical coping literature since its inception (Folkman, 1992). Axis II, by definition, represents an acknowledgment of patterns of cognitive and behavioral consistency. According to the DSM-IV (APA, 1994), it is only when the associated characteristics, or traits, are inflexible and maladaptive, and cause either substantial impairment or subjective distress, that they may be considered personality disorders. The point on the continuum at which a coordinated constellation of traits constitutes a disturbance is far from clear. Millon (1969, 1990a), a recognized authority, has proposed three chief differentiating features, all of which are crucial to an appreciation of the interplay between personality pathology and various components of the coping process.

The first, *functional inflexibility,* describes the rigid imposition of characteristic modes of relating, thinking, and perceiving on even those situations not amenable to such an approach. It represents a basic inability to adjust one's strategies to contextual demands. The genesis and maintenance of *vicious circles* is the second distinguishing feature. Habitual modes of framing demands and coping therewith may restrict experience in such a way that one's problems are continually reinforced: "Personality disorders are themselves pathogenic . . . (they) set into motion self-defeating sequences that cause their already established difficulties not only to persist, but to be further activated" (Millon, 1990a, p. 342). Finally, Millon has proposed *structural instability,* or these patterns' lack of integrity under conditions of stress, to be a feature distinguishing normal functioning from pathology.

Such conceptual and clinical guidelines make apparent the connections that exist among coping efforts, adjustment, and personality pathology, as do theoretical and clinical accounts (e.g., Kantor, 1992; Millon, 1981; Vaillant, 1994). Although these authors differ in theoretical orientation and approach to etiology, they share an emphasis on the restricted range of responses available to those with Axis II disorders when faced with demands requiring adjustment. This is made clear in Millon's (1981) description of the effects of experience: "(the) initial range of behaviours gradually becomes narrowed, selective, and, finally, crystallized into preferred ways of relating to others and coping with this world" (p. 4). The rigidity, restricted range, and overapplication of these strategies is recognized in diagnostic criteria and clinical definitions (APA, 1987).

Inflexibility of Coping Styles

General rigidity in response strategies has been the focus of increasing attention within the coping literature. Terry (1994), discussing the context-specific differential adaptiveness of emotion-focused versus problem-focused coping (e.g., Conway & Terry, 1992; Vitaliano, DeWolfe, Maiuro, & Russo, 1990) has suggested that flexibility, or the ability to adjust strategies in accordance with demands, may be the key factor whereby personality traits act on general adjustment. Similar conceptualizations have been expressed in the literature on defense, a construct which those writing about personality disorders often do not distinguish from coping (e.g., Morey, 1993), or differentiate in terms of adaptiveness or association with psychopathology, rather than function, structure, or psychological dissimilarities (see Haan, 1993). Most importantly, clinically the two terms are often used in a complementary way. Contemporary conceptualizations of defenses, which emphasize efforts to regulate both one's internal (emotional) and external (interpersonal) environment, and on the employment of cognitive distortion to this end (see Vaillant, 1993, 1994) are almost indistinguishable from current approaches to what is commonly termed "emotion-oriented coping." Lazarus (1993) has suggested that "emotion-focused coping change(s) the way we attend to or interpret what is happening" (p. 8). In such cases, the distinction between coping and defense is a fragile one. Reference to the nonvoluntary aspect of defense is similarly unproductive. Although individuals may be aware of the behavioral indexes of their coping efforts, underlying motivations and patterns of consistency may entail minimal insight.

In view of this, it is worth noting that Cramer (1991) has catalogued three characteristics of pathological defenses: rigidity, extensiveness, and overgeneralization (or their use in connection with an inappropriately wide range of people or situations). Such observations have been recently echoed in the empirical coping literature. Amirkhan (1994) has suggested that much of the lack of consensus in the person/situation debate in the coping field has resulted from researchers' failure to recognize consistency itself as a behavioral dimension along which people vary. According to this view, one must recognize individual differences in two aspects of consistency (Cohen, 1987): that exhibited within a situation, often displayed as a refusal or inability to abandon an unsuccessful strategy, and that displayed, cross-situationally, seen in a propensity to repeatedly apply a similar coping approach and often referred to as "coping style." Thus, while some consistency may represent an adaptive effort to benefit from previous coping experiences, a rigid inability to adjust coping to fit the objective demands of the situation typifies the maladaptive end of the continuum (see Kohlmann, 1993, for a pertinent demonstration using a laboratory manipulation).

Thus we see the importance placed on flexibility, both in the coping literature and in that on personality pathology. Although manifested in different ways, each of the Axis II disorders displays its own unique pattern of inflexibility in response to environmental demands. A good illustration is provided by obsessive-compulsive personality disorder. An all-encompassing striving for control and completion, manifested in a pervasive pattern of perfectionism and rigidity, characterizes individuals with this disorder (APA, 1994). Although their meticulousness and attention to detail often results in others' perception of obsessionals as conscientious and well-adjusted (Reed, 1985), it is in fact a manifestation of a highly limited coping style. As described by Millon (1990a): "[He/she] constructs the world in terms of rules, regulations, time schedules, and social hierarchies" (p. 366). This leaves these individuals ill-prepared to cope with less well-structured life demands, particularly interpersonal and emotional ones. The consequent avoidance of such situations results, as Freeman, Pretzer, Fleming, and Simon (1990) have noted, in deficits both in the ability to evoke and benefit from social support, and in adaptive emotional regulation—subjects of key import to coping researchers. To employ the language of coping researchers: Although the behavior of the obsessional may appear "problem-focused," it is not so, phenomenologically. The rigid application of rules of conduct and procedure, rather than a systematic analysis of situational demands, underlie these behaviors (Beck & Freeman, 1990; Kantor, 1992). In a laboratory investigation of the response of individuals high in obsessional traits to potentially threatening situations, Summerfeldt (1991) found that an objectively benign control condition was most evocative of anxiety and perceived threat. In fact, this context was the least suited to obsessionals' habitual coping techniques, as it involved a lack of direction, reflection on one's internal state rather than an external problem, and few clear-cut expectations. The heightened discomfort reported by obsessionals in this condition may be seen as compelling evidence for the limited range of their coping style. It leaves the individual unprepared to deal with experiences not amenable to clearly defined choices. It is because a great many of life's tasks take this form that this personality disorder may be associated with the onset of more severe forms of psychopathology (Millon, 1981).

Self-Generation of Stressors

The coping styles associated with personality disorders may themselves evoke additional stress, thereby initiating a self-perpetuating cycle. Accordingly, the stress-coping relationship may not be a unidirectional one (Leventhal et al., 1993). A number of mechanisms may be identified in this process. A valuable explanatory construct is that of *cognitive style,* a term referring to self-consistent modes of perceiving and organizing information and thought, considered by Millon (1990b) to be "among the most useful indices to the clinician of the patient's distinctive way of function" (p. 146). The selective modes of processing information exhibited by those with personality disorders may be the primary determinants of what the coping task in any one situation is thought to be. Relevantly, Lazarus (1991, 1993), making implicit reference to the related *schema* construct, has hypothesized the presence of "cognitive-motivational configurations" that operate idiosyncratically to shape appraisals of situations which may generate emotional responses not entirely congruent with their objective qualities. Such responses, having interpersonal consequences, in turn contribute to the coping task.

Thus, cognitive distortions and appraisals may be one mechanism involved in the self-perpetuation of personality disorders and stress. Behavioral manifestation of coping styles is another. This is well illustrated in the case of paranoid personality disorder, which has long been considered among the more serious of these disorders "due to the inelasticity and constriction of their coping skills" (Millon, 1981, p. 372). Patients with this disorder show an enduring tendency to interpret a wide variety of occurrences, particularly in interpersonal contexts, as having negative and threatening intent. Clinicians and theorists of diverse orientations emphasize the role played in the generation of paranoid features by efforts to cope with anxiety regarding one's own general inadequacy. These authors differ in their formulations of the source of these anxieties, but they all interpret resulting responses as misguided efforts at self-regulation: "The paranoid cognitive style is . . . motivated and perpetuated by its distress-reducing effects" (Freeman et al., 1990).

Also commonly recognized is the self-fulfilling nature of the hypervigilant, confrontational interpersonal coping style. As these individuals will habitually act on the expectation that others are hostile and deceptive, they frequently evoke in others responses congruent with their own belief systems (Kantor, 1992). This stance, which Freeman et al. (1990) have termed the "expectation of malevolence-defensiveness-hostility of others cycle," is one reason these authors have targeted the paranoid coping style, rather than its unknown psychodynamic underpinnings, for therapeutic intervention (see also Beck & Freeman, 1990). As in the case of other Axis II disorders, the coping style itself becomes a generator of the specific sorts of stress that may reinforce it. Researchers interested in the misguided attempts at adjustment integral to this form of psychopathology should pay special attention to such reciprocal relationships.

Integrity under Stress

The third defining characteristic of personality disorders, structural instability, is highly pertinent to our conceptualization of them as coordinated yet maladaptive constellations of coping strategies. The ultimate insufficiency of these patterns of adjustment is acknowledged in the DSM-IV, which makes reference to their frequent association with more personally distressing symptom syndromes, or Axis I disorders. In the words of Kantor (1992): "there is an almost organic affinity between each personality disorder and at least one . . . neurosis or psychosis for which the personality disorder provides the premorbid or residual state" (p. 12). Such characterological vulnerabilities may also contribute to the recently noted chronicity of a wide range of symptom disorders (Watson et al., 1994). This tenuous stability, indicative of a lack of resilience under conditions of subjective stress, is closely tied to the inflexibility already discussed. When one's coping repertoire is restricted, multiple demands or even single ones not amenable to that adaptational strategy may result in decompensation, or a marked deterioration in psychological functioning. Perry (1988), for example, has reported that the best predictor of psychotic symptoms and depression in a group of subjects diagnosed

with borderline personality disorder was the predominant use of distorting defenses (e.g., acting out and splitting) in coping with the year's life events. Life
events alone were not predictive of such deterioration. Millon (1981) has provided
a fitting analysis: "symptom syndromes are viewed as a reaction to a situation for
which the individual's personality is notably vulnerable" (p. 10).

The diathesis-stress emphasis of this conceptualization is echoed in the mainstream empirical literature on coping, with reference to coping predispositions
more circumscribed than the coordinated patterns evident in Axis II disorders.
Such approaches are commonly subsumed under the umbrella provided by "goodness-of-fit" models (see Folkman, 1992). In the case of personality disorders, exposure to situations not suited to their adjustive efforts may result not only in
distress but in disruption of the pattern of coping strategies itself. Illustratively,
the avoidant personality pattern involves a pervasive and enduring pattern of sensitivity to the disapproval of others, and overestimation of the probability of failure and rejection. As the appellation suggests, such individuals also tend to avoid
situations where their fears might be realized (APA, 1994). This active withdrawal
represents deficits in three widely recognized coping domains: intentional efforts
to approach and resolve interpersonally stressful situations (problem-focused),
drawing on the resources of others through affiliation (support seeking), and regulating one's emotional state, perhaps by desensitizing oneself to anxiety (emotion-
oriented). It also represents a heightened vigilance for, and vulnerability to,
potential confirmation of one's beliefs regarding personality inefficacy (see Beck
& Freeman, 1990). Given the coping pattern's minimal adaptiveness, such experiences are almost inevitable. Accordingly, a considerable literature has arisen addressing this pattern's utility in the understanding of agoraphobia and forms of
phobic disorder (e.g., Hoffart & Martinsen, 1992; Starcevic, 1992). Characteristic
modes of appraising and responding to experiences, involving considerable distortions of reality (Vaillant, 1994), are associated in this case with the development
of debilitating patterns of behavior.

In summary, the descriptive criteria offered by Millon as a framework for
understanding personality disorders may also serve to illustrate the utility
of characterizing them in terms of broad coping styles. Their inflexibility,
self-perpetuating nature, and tenuous stability under stress may be potentially
fruitful areas of study for those wishing to bridge the existing gap between
mainstream coping research and the rich clinical literature on personality and
psychopathology. Our discussion has also revealed patterns congruent with the
conceptual frameworks adopted by coping researchers. Authors seeking to delineate clearly established dimensions of coping have commonly identified three
classes: (a) emotional regulation, involving the modulation of internal states
through such strategies as self-focusing, emotional expression, attentional deployment, and cognitive distortion, (b) task-oriented attempts to modify the environmental source of stress, and (c) the seeking out and utilization of social
support. Behavioral avoidance, as a coping factor, appears to be functionally related both to emotional regulation, and to the ability to draw on social resources
(see Endler & Parker, 1990a). The foci of the first two dimensions have their

personological equivalents in the DSM-IV's definition of personality traits as "enduring patterns perceiving, relating to, and thinking about the environment and one's self" (APA, 1994, p. 630). Its diagnostic emphasis on impairment in social and interpersonal functioning applies clearly to the remaining coping class. This, and emotional regulation, as they are inextricably related, will be discussed.

Emotional Regulation and Social Support

Deficits in emotional regulation, both in oneself and others, are a central feature of the Axis II disorders. The emotional intelligence construct is a useful one in the clarification of this feature. It is thought to involve "the ability to monitor one's own and others' feelings and emotions, to discriminate among them, and to use this information to guide one's thinking and actions" (Salovey & Mayer, 1990, p. 189). Emotional regulation constitutes a major component of this general competence; it entails the ability to modify negative emotions through both strategic and automatic cognitions and behaviors, in ways that facilitate adaptive functioning. Although mainstream coping researchers have commonly neglected the framework provided by models of self-regulation, the strategy labeled with variants of the term "emotion-oriented" (e.g., Carver, Scheier, & Weintraub, 1989; Endler & Parker, 1990a; Lazarus & Folkman, 1984) would seem to access regulatory functions. Theoretical and empirical analysis of the affect regulation construct is to be found almost solely in the psychological defense literature (e.g., Costa, Zonderman, & McCrae, 1991; Ilhilevich & Gleser, 1993). Similarly, measures of defense mechanisms are considered appropriate operationalizations of regulatory operations (e.g., Aronoff, Stollack, & Woike, 1994). Personality disorders have all, to varying degrees, been associated with the use of under-developed and minimally adaptive defenses (Vaillant, 1994). In the words of Vaillant (1993): "Immature defenses are the building blocks of personality disorder" (p. 266).

Clinicians working with personality-disordered individuals have long been familiar with manifestations of affect dysregulation and associated deficits in the ability to identify, discriminate among, and express emotional states (see Taylor, 1984, for a highly pertinent discussion of the alexithymia construct). One sees examples in the histrionic patient's indiscriminant ventilation of fleeting affect and accompanying lack of insight, and in the emotional constriction of the obsessional. In their proposed therapeutic foci for such individuals, writers from diverse theoretical orientations have emphasized the need for acquisition of skills for the regulation of emotion (e.g., Freeman et al., 1990; Kantor, 1992; Meissner, 1985).

Seeking social support, another coping dimension, deserves some mention due to its relation to the previous topic and to the centrality of interpersonal factors in clinical accounts. There have even been suggestions that diagnostic schemas should be revised to incorporate an interpersonal taxonomy (see Morey, 1993). In a classic treatise, Schneider (1923, 1950) described disordered personalities as those who "either suffer personally because of their abnormality or make a community suffer because of it" (p. 3). Individuals with Axis II disorders rarely enter therapy due to perceived problems with the self, but rather seek help with perceived difficulties in interpersonal adjustment (Freeman et al., 1990). The ability to cultivate, maintain, and benefit from supportive and stable relationships is a particular area of impairment. It is worth noting that emotional intelligence is often seen as a subset of "social" or "interpersonal" intelligence (Salovey & Mayer, 1990; Walters & Gardner, 1986). This entails the individual's understanding of the needs, moods, intentions, and motives of others, or knowledge about the social environment that is acquired through implicit cues (Sternberg & Frensch, 1990). Deficits in these competencies are evident in the often-observed trail of failed relationships that marks the passage of the individual with personality disorder (Millon, 1990a). As interpersonal coping styles, the ambivalent resistance of the passive-aggressive personality, the demanding self-aggrandizement of the narcissistic pattern, and the manipulative dependence of the histrionic pattern commonly serve ultimately to sabotage available social support networks.

Deficits in emotional regulation and relational skills are inextricably linked. Insight regarding one's own internal environment has been hypothesized to be highly related to insight regarding the emotional cues provided by others (see Gardner, 1983). This issue has generally been neglected in the coping literature, where social support is conventionally viewed as an environmental supplement to personal resources rather than a partial function of them (see Carpenter, 1992; Thoits, 1986). However, a growing trend in the recent literature on defense and affect regulation has been to emphasize their role in the individual's social environment (Greenspan, 1989). A recent investigation of the role of regulatory operations in the capacity to evince behaviors reflecting interpersonal engagement, such as facial displays of emotion, found less mature defenses to be associated with a more restricted range of emotion and fewer indexes of engagement (Aronoff et al., 1994). The authors interpreted this as evidence for the interpersonal adaptiveness of the ability to identify in one's self, express, and encourage in others a wide range of emotions. This study underscores the need for researchers interested in coping and personality pathology to simultaneously consider capacities for emotional regulation and relational experience.

There is considerable overlay in the emphases of both those interested in the clinical diagnosis and conceptual clarification of disorders of personality, and those seeking to understand the role of coping in the emotional and interpersonal adjustment of the individual. Despite this, personality disorders have been notably absent from the mainstream empirical coping literature. Individuals likely develop an idiosyncratic pattern of adaptive efforts; the flexibility, range, and appropriateness of this constellation of coping strategies may distinguish ultimate adjustment from psychopathology. Relatively stable patterns of appraising and responding to demands for adjustment are an integral part of this form of psychopathology. The embeddedness of these acquired patterns in the larger network of beliefs and self-definitions comprising one's personality contributes to their resistance to change.

COPING AND DEPRESSION

Depressive psychopathology, subsumed under the category of mood disorders in the DSM-IV, includes major depression and dysthymia, and the more temporally limited category of major depressive episode. These share a common feature of depressed affect, characterized by feelings of sadness, disappointment, and despair. Co-occurring features include reduced interest, feelings of guilt and worthlessness, and impairment in concentration. Dysthymia is a form of minor depression evidenced in habitual gloominess and preoccupation with personal inadequacy (see Akiskal, 1983). This category may be likened to the "depressive personality" which, although familiar to clinicians, does not have formal classificatory status (see Phillips, Hirschfeld, Shea, & Gunderson, 1993).

The relationship between coping efforts and depression has received considerable attention in the mainstream empirical literature, with some degree of agreement regarding the implicit nature and direction of the relationship. Coping is commonly thought to mediate between stressful events and such psychological outcomes as depression (Endler & Parker, 1990c). An examination of literatures that are external, but highly pertinent to, this body of work reveals a comparable emphasis on the interacting effects of exogenous factors, such as environmental demands, and endogenous vulnerabilities. Such models are generally subsumed under the term "diathesis-stress." Even a superficial review is beyond the scope of the present chapter. Nor, however, do we wish to restrict our review to those findings commonly considered the exclusive domain of coping researchers. In the following section we will discuss three disparate areas of study that, despite their pertinence to the present topic, have been neglected by coping investigators. Their consideration derives from a view of emotion-oriented coping as affect regulation, and from our belief that, as in the case of personality disorders, misguided coping efforts may themselves contribute to perceived stressors.

Emotional Dysregulation and Ruminative Coping

One of the few observations in the empirical coping literature about which there is considerable consensus is the association of emotion-oriented coping with psychological distress, primarily depression (Stanton, Danoff-Burg, Cameron, & Ellis, 1994). Supportive findings are reported with both clinical and nonclinical samples. Moeller, Richards, Hooker, and Ursino (1992), for example, in a longitudinal study with college students, identified emotion-focused coping as a foremost predictor of chronic mild depressed mood, or dysphoria, over a period of several weeks. Inpatients hospitalized with major depression have reported higher use of emotion-focused coping than controls (McNaughton, Patterson, Irwin, & Grant, 1992). The association in clinical subjects of depressed mood with emotion-oriented strategies even beyond acute episodes has been demonstrated by Turner, King, and Tremblay (1992).

A plethora of similar findings has contributed to disciplinary consensus regarding the relationship between emotion-oriented strategies and depression (for contradictory findings see Coyne & Downey, 1991; Holohan & Moos, 1991). Nonetheless, the clinical value of such findings is quite limited. As Nolen-Hoeksema et al. (1994) and Stanton et al. (1994) have observed, the "emotion-focused" label has been applied to a disparate group of coping responses—including ventilation, suppression or denial, and preoccupation with one's internal state—that exhibit marked conceptual and functional differences (see Carver et al., 1989). The precise nature and direction of the relationship is also unclear. Stanton et al. (1994) have observed that what many coping researchers and test developers have labeled as indexes of emotion coping are in fact symptoms of distress and this confound has led to spurious and ininterpretable empirical relationships between the two variables.

Popular measures have often neglected subscales that tap emotional expressiveness and understanding, potentially "positive" aspects of emotion coping (see Stanton et al., 1994). This may reflect the coping field's insularity; a considerable literature exists in the area of emotional inhibition and health on the adaptiveness of emotional reflection and disclosure (see Pennebaker, 1993). Despite this, criticisms such as that of Stanton et al. (1994) may be somewhat misguided, as the implicit message is that objectively maladaptive responses (e.g., "focus on my general inadequacies"; Endler & Parker, 1990a) should not be considered examples of coping. Lazarus and Folkman (1984) made an important distinction between coping efforts and adaptational outcomes. As paraphrased by Stanton et al. (1994), "Coping strategies in and of themselves are neither adaptive nor maladaptive" (p. 350). Although this should serve as a cautionary suggestion to scale developers regarding conceptual clarity, it may also be taken as an argument for the inclusion in scales of items potentially indicative of affect *dysregulation*. This line of thought is supported by the research program of Susan Nolen-Hoeksema and her colleagues on ruminative response styles and depression. As this literature, despite its potential clinical utility, has been somewhat neglected by coping researchers, it is worthy of some attention.

Clinicians frequently note individual differences in the duration of depressive episodes. Nolen-Hoeksema (1987, 1991) has suggested that such discrepancies are determined, to a large part, by some individuals' proclivity to engage in passive ruminative responses to their depressed mood. This general response style is thought to involve "behaviours and thoughts that focus one's attention on one's depressive symptoms and on the implications of these symptoms" (Nolen-Hoeksema, 1991, p. 569). These may be contrasted with distraction as a response style, which involves active deployment of attention toward unrelated events (see Krohne, 1993b). Important to the present discussion is the conceptualization of such ruminative responses as a misguided form of coping through affect regulation, or a critical component of emotion-focused coping (Nolen-Hoeksema et al., 1994). Such activities and cognitions as isolating oneself, focusing on symptoms, and passively worrying about their outcome are regarded in this way; the ruminative passive *style* of such activities, rather than their content, is of foremost interest. It is noteworthy that elaboration of the "monitoring" construct by coping researchers (Ahles, Blanchard, & Leventhal, 1983) has established that while heightened attendance to information regarding the source of stress may well be highly adaptive, reducing distress, similar monitoring of emotional reactions in fact amplifies it: "Indeed, painful or catastrophic interpretations and monitoring emotion seem ideal conditions for sensitization or the intensification and prolongation of emotional reactions" (Leventhal et al., 1993, p. 90). Clinical accounts of the phenomenon of double depression, often described as "depression about depression" would seem to support this (see Barlow, 1991).

A programmatic series of studies has shed considerable light on the nature of the relationship between ruminative coping and depression, although the predominant use of nonclinical subjects continues to be a recognized limitation (see Burns & Nolen-Hoeksema, 1991, for an exception). In studies in which subjects were encouraged to engage in experimental analogues of "response styles," it has been found that the least remediation of induced depressive affect results from engagement in passive-ruminative responses (e.g., silently reading emotion-focusing sentences; Morrow & Nolen-Hoeksema, 1990). These findings have been replicated (e.g., Lyubomirsky & Nolen-Hoeksema, 1993), in some cases with naturally occurring depressed mood (Nolen-Hoeksema & Morrow, 1993). These studies, though suggestive, prompted subjects' response styles and were therefore not able to address individual differences in the spontaneous expression of ruminative response styles. In a longitudinal study designed to remedy this, Nolen-Hoeksema, Morrow, and Fredrickson (1993) found that 83% of their nonclinical subjects showed consistency in their use of either ruminative or distracting strategies. Furthermore, a significant relationship was found between ruminative responses and duration of depressed mood, even when mood severity was controlled for (see also Nolen-Hoeksema et al., 1994; Wood, Saltzberg, Neale, Stone, & Rachmiel, 1990). Thus, relatively enduring tendencies to engage in ruminative coping would appear to be a dispositional vulnerability for prolonged or recurrent episodes of depressed mood. This interpretation is lent further credence by the finding that in a sample of individuals at risk for depression due to the terminal illness of a loved one, people with a predominantly ruminative coping style were significantly more likely to have a history of clinical depression (Nolen-Hoeksema et al., 1994).

A number of mechanisms have been proposed to account for the ruminative response style's perpetuation of depression (detailed discussions are found in Mussen & Alloy, 1988; Nolen-Hoeksema, 1991; Nolen-Hoeksema et al., 1994). A chief feature is their interference with more instrumental externally oriented behaviors that would otherwise engender feelings of personal control and agency. Lyubomirsky and Nolen-Hoeksema (1993) found that highly ruminative individuals, although able to articulate the pleasantness of distracting activities, reported less willingness to participate in them than did control subjects. This was thought to be indicative of the inhibitory influence of ruminations on appraisals of self-efficacy and on the initiation of instrumental activities. Interestingly, this finding parallels the frequent observation of clinically depressed persons' limited employment of task-oriented coping strategies (e.g., Billings & Moos, 1984, 1985). An additional mechanism may be the influence of rumination on information processing. Cognitive biases and depression will be discussed elsewhere. However, preoccupation with one's affective state (ruminative coping), rather than the depressed affect per se, may be most predictive of the disproportionate availability, to depressives, of negatively valenced memories and self-evaluations. A vicious cycle may be thus maintained, with information that confirms and reinforces the person's depressed state dominating cognitive processes. A number of studies provide evidence of the self-perpetuating reciprocal influence of depressed mood and negatively toned thought (e.g., Abramson, Metalsky, & Alloy, 1989; Haaga, Dyck, & Ernst, 1991).

In short, there appears to be some utility in elaborating on the "emotion-focused coping" construct, the breadth of which may lend it little clinical utility. When one emphasizes the regulatory nature of such coping efforts, then potential dysregulation becomes a possible avenue of research. The misguided adjustive efforts represented by these strategies were clearly evident in the study reported by Lyubormirsky and Nolen-Hoeksema (1993). It was here found that dysphoric individuals who were forced to ruminate reported an enhanced perception of insightfulness into themselves. The authors have suggested that self-focused rumination may be reinforced by the person's belief that it affords greater insight into feelings and symptoms, and may thus facilitate adjustment. As they have indicated, however, it also paradoxically leads to perpetuation of the negative mood, and the frustration of more active efforts to overcome it. Accordingly, rumination may be most usefully conceptualized as a misguided attempt at coping through affect regulation.

Emotional Dysregulation and Cognitive Biases

A mechanism proposed by Nolen-Hoeksema and her colleagues to account for the perpetuation of depressed mood by ruminative coping is its effect on information processing. This alludes to a vast literature on depressive cognition that has, with few exceptions, been neglected by mainstream coping researchers. This is somewhat surprising, given the increasing importance that such literature places on attentional deployment and biased cognitive appraisal as aspects of coping (see Krohne, 1993a; Lazarus, 1993). Illustratively, Miller (1992) has described the focus of her research program on dispositional cognitive coping as "individual differences in the ability and/or inclination to seek out or to cognitively avoid and transform threat-relevant information" (p. 79). Because of such concerns, coping researchers might do well to familiarize themselves with the example of affect dysregulation evident in research on selective information processing and emotional disorders (Dagleish & Watts, 1990; for reviews, see Mathews & MacLeod, 1994).

In light of clinical observations of depressives' construal of their present state as the result of an unbroken chain of personal inadequacies, much empirical attention has been given to the association of depression with memory biases for emotionally congruent material. Studies on naturally occurring mood in clinically depressed subjects, this mood in nonclinical samples, and the consequences of mood induction have fairly consistently demonstrated the clear association of depression with superior recall for emotionally negative material in a number of forms (cf. MacLeod, 1990). These range from life experiences (Pyszczynski, Hamilton, Herring, & Greenberg, 1989; Williams & Scott, 1988) to such manipulated stimuli as emotionally valenced words (Bellew & Hill, 1991; Caballero & Moreno, 1993) and emotional phrases (Forgas & Bower, 1987). Much recent work has focused on the mediating influence of such stimuli's personal relevance, finding that self-referent negative semantic material is particularly vulnerable to recall bias (e.g., Edwards, Pearce, Collett, & Pugh, 1992).

It would seem that depressed individuals may be unable to extricate themselves from a web of cognitions which serve to affirm and perpetuate their own feelings of worthlessness, despair, and preoccupations with negative depressive experiences. The cognitive biases underlying such a failure in affect regulation may also manifest themselves in the individual's characteristic way of approaching a variety of life experiences, including person-perception (Bradley & Mathews, 1988) and interpersonal relationships (Forgas & Bower, 1987). It may reflect the impact not only of elevated state depression, but of relatively enduring cognitive tendencies, suggesting a general vulnerability to experience recurrent depressive episodes. Evidence for this is found in studies reporting processing biases in recovered depressives (e.g., Bradley & Mathews, 1988; Bellew & Hill, 1991). As Mathews and MacLeod (1994) have suggested: "A persisting tendency to selectively process emotionally threatening material represents the cognitive mechanism underlying vulnerability to emotional disorder" (p. 41). Clarifying this, they have also proposed that the interaction of this stable trait factor with stressful events may result in a positive feedback loop between biased processing and mood state, ultimately culminating in clinical disorder. This dispositional vulnerability may account, in part, for the underappreciated chronicity of depressive disorder remarked on in recent works (e.g., Watson et al., 1994). In short, the affect dysregulation manifested in information-processing biases may, in interaction with specific types of stressors (see Teasdale, 1988; Barnard & Teasdale, 1991) result in the self-maintaining downward spiral characteristic of this disorder.

Social Support and the Self-Generation of Stressors

Our discussion has made explicit the role of emotion-focused coping efforts (defined in an idiosyncratic but conceptually useful way) in an individual's vulnerability to severe and persistent depression. Both areas of research discussed have made explicit the interactive role of environmental stressors in the genesis and maintenance of depressive symptomatology (see also DeVellis & Blalock, 1992). Nolen-Hoeksema et al. have maintained that, in contrast to self-regulatory self-focus models (e.g., Pyszczynski & Greenberg, 1987; Pyszczynski, Greenberg, Hamilton, & Nix, 1991) their conceptualization of the self-perpetuating properties of depressive rumination does not rely on the presence of negative life events (Nolen-Hoeksema, 1991; Nolen-Hoeksema et al., 1994). Nonetheless, the role played by environmental demands in conventional models of the stress-coping process (see Folkman, 1992; Gruen, 1993), justifies a brief discussion of the self-generation of stressors in depression.

As Monroe and Simmons (1991) have noted (see also Coyne, Burchill, & Stiles, 1990), there is increasing acknowledgment among depression researchers of the possibility that individuals with this disorder may act in ways that create particular types of environments. In the most widely recognized program of research, Constance Hammen and her colleagues (e.g., Hammen, 1992; Hammen, Davila, Brown, Ellicott, & Gitlin, 1992) have suggested that the stress-depression relationship is not unidirectional: "Depressed persons shape their environments . . . and the consequences of their depression and behaviours may serve to generate stressful conditions and events, which in turn cause additional symptomatology" (Hammen, 1991, p. 555). This is thought to operate primarily in the interpersonal domain. In one illustrative longitudinal study, Hammen (1991) has found that women with unipolar depression experienced significantly more stressful interpersonal events *to which they had contributed* than demographically matched subjects with no disorder, or with other psychiatric or medical conditions. In short, mechanisms of affect regulation, such as the biased cognitive processing already discussed (see Hammen, 1992), or maladroit efforts to elicit the support of important others, may paradoxically create added stressors, thus further taxing already burdened coping resources. It would seem that depressive coping styles may undermine the availability of much-needed social support (see Pennebaker, 1993). Paradoxically, Hirschfeld (1994) has concluded that interpersonal dependency is the trait most associated with clinical depression. Greater familiarity with such findings might prove informative for coping researchers seeking to answer clinically relevant questions. Despite frequent endorsement in the coping field of interactional, process-oriented models (see Folkman & Lazarus, 1985; Folkman, 1992), empirical investigations have conventionally adopted quite mechanistic and linear methods. These may be of limited value to those seeking to understand why the best consistent predictor of future depression is past depression (cf. Lewinsohn, Zeiss, & Duncun, 1989; Watson et al., 1994).

In summary, our discussion has expanded on the frequently cited association of depression and emotion-focused coping—a relationship of such breadth that it has questionable explanatory value. We have identified three areas of study which we feel are relatively disregarded by coping researchers, whose discipline has been driven, for the most part, by empirical rather than conceptual considerations. When one acknowledges the self-regulatory aspect of the emotion-coping construct, a number of possible foci of investigation of clear clinical import become evident. Among them is affect dysregulation, approached here from the perspective of discrete literatures on ruminative response styles and selective recall biases. Stress-generative depressive responses, the final topic, represents another important contribution to the process of adjustment. Perhaps because of the ease with which analogue depression or dysphoria can be identified, induced, and measured in nonclinical populations, undergraduate populations have been the mainstay of research on coping and what is euphemistically termed "psychological distress" (see also Vredenburg, Flett, & Krames, 1993). The value of such an approach for a true understanding of the depressed person in context, with specific reference to experienced stressors, has been questioned by Hammen (1992). The topic of anxiety has been treated similarly; clinical anxiety disorders have not received much attention in the coping literature. As in the case of depression, however, a number of lines of work of potential interest to coping researchers and theorists may be identified.

COPING AND ANXIETY

Unlike depression, the adaptive qualities of anxiety are clearly apparent, and in many ways serve to identify the point in the continuum where a "normal" anxiety response may be considered a clinical disorder. The differences are not solely quantitative; anxiety disorders cannot be merely regarded as an excess of anxiety (Andrews, 1991; Edelmann, 1992). Clinically significant anxiety, and the behavioural and cognitive responses associated therewith, appear to be as self-perpetuating as the depressive disorders. This feature contrasts dramatically with the transitory quality of normal anxiety responses. Anxiety, then, is a feature both of adaptive functioning and a number of forms of psychopathology. Despite its prominence in the psychological literature, the lack of a satisfactory definition and its confusion with the "stress" construct are frequently noted (e.g., Edelmann, 1992; Endler, 1988). Barlow (1991) has concluded that anxiety might be best conceptualized as "a loose cognitive-affective structure which is composed primarily of high negative affect, a sense of uncontrollability, and a shift in attention to a primary self-focus or a state of self-preoccupation" (p. 60). It is generally defined in terms of its cognitive and emotional features, including elevated arousal and pronounced apprehensiveness regarding the possibility of threat or danger (cf. Barlow, 1991; Ingram & Kendall, 1987). Avoidance is considered a chief behavioral component.

Although the experience of anxiety is invariably aversive (Lilienfeld, Turner, & Jacob, 1993), it is accompanied by enhanced arousal and vigilance; as such, it may have a highly adaptive function, enabling a state of psychological and physiological readiness to meet challenges and avoid harm (Beck & Emery, 1985). As Barlow (1991) has indicated: "[It] is a future-oriented mood state where one is ready or prepared to cope with upcoming negative events" (p. 235). Despite this, anxiety often occurs with such severity or frequency, and may be associated with such aversive symptoms, that it significantly interferes with one's ability to function; it may then be considered a clinically significant form of psychopathology. Anxiety disorders, the corresponding DSM-IV classification, include panic disorder with or without agoraphobia, agoraphobia, social and simple phobias, obsessive-compulsive disorder, and generalized anxiety disorder.

Although there is some consensus regarding general features of anxiety, there have been a number of refinements in its conceptualization. One is the primary distinction between state- and trait-anxiety (Endler, 1980, 1983; Spielberger, 1972). The latter represents a relatively enduring predisposition to respond anxiously to stressors. This construct's distinctiveness from several broader umbrella traits, such as neuroticism and negative emotionality, has been a topic of considerable debate (e.g., Watson & Clark, 1992a, 1992b). Clarifying its unique features, Endler, Edwards, and Vitelli (1991) have proposed four distinct facets of trait-anxiety: social evaluation, physical danger, ambiguous, and daily routines, reflecting the type of perceived situational context in which the individual is predisposed to experience anxiety. State-anxiety is the transient arousal most commonly referred to as anxiety. Its features have been summarized by Andrews (1991): "the arousal is experienced as symptoms consistent with those of the fight-or-flight response" (p. 294). Inherent in Andrew's depiction is a recognition of the potential adaptiveness of transient anxious arousal, or its function as a preparatory set or signal mobilizing coping responses to deal with external threat. In the case of anxiety disorders, however, anxiety and its associated symptoms themselves become the focus of coping efforts. In this way, the debilitating effects of clinical anxiety are not limited by reality-based resolution of environmental demands; efforts to regulate one's emotional state predominate.

Symptoms as Coping Efforts

The defining features of a number of anxiety disorders have themselves been long regarded as misguided efforts to alleviate anxious arousal, or, in the spirit of the present discussion, emotionally regulatory coping efforts. Often this is accomplished through behavioral avoidance, a fact evident in diagnostic considerations (e.g., APA, 1994). This is true even in the case of obsessive-compulsive disorder, whose unusual qualities have prompted suggestions that it be differentiated from other anxiety disorders. The much-cited distinction made by Rachman and Hodgson (1980) between *passive avoidance,* or distancing oneself from a threatening stimulus, and *active avoidance,* represented by preventive rituals and compulsions, is noteworthy. Both categories have been regarded by the authors as learned, and ultimately maladaptive strategies for coping with anxiety. Evidently, there may be considerable clinical utility in viewing many symptoms as acquired coping strategies.

It has been suggested that it is advantageous to consider coping efforts as responses to stress that have outcome expectancies attached (Carpenter, 1992). Applying this to the symptoms of anxiety disorders, one might conclude that the outcome expected is that of alleviation of anxiety rather than resolution of environmental stressors (problem-focused coping). Relevantly, coping researchers have identified behavioral avoidance as a key factorial dimension (e.g., Endler & Parker, 1990a). However, as most clinicians familiar with the delivery of behavioral therapy to such individuals recognize, the "quick fix" of anxious arousal provided by avoidance or rituals is both short-lived and self-perpetuating (cf. Freeman et al., 1990). In fact, it serves to amplify the aversive qualities of both the feared stimulus and the anxious apprehension associated with it, while impeding the acquisition of more constructive responses. In this way, misguided emotionally regulatory coping responses serve to maintain the disorder. The demonstrated efficacy of therapies combining exposure with response prevention (e.g., Cox, Endler, Lee, & Swinson, 1992) attests to the utility of interrupting this self-perpetuating cycle.

Emotional Dysregulation and Anxiety Sensitivity

Anxiety is an emotion suggestive of engagement and activation (Barlow, 1991). Some individuals, however, seem to be predisposed to be unable to benefit from its adaptive qualities, and may experience their anxiety as more disturbing and less evocative of rational, reality-based coping responses than do others. This phenomenon is prevalent in the anxiety disorders, where it appears illustrative of the inability to successful self-regulate emotional experience. A number of factors, many of them individual differences variables, have been proposed to explain this basic difference. Negative affectivity and neuroticism (see Watson et al., 1994) are constructs that share a common feature: a temperamental sensitivity to negative stimuli leading to a greater likelihood of experiencing negative mood states (see Tellegen, 1985). Such personality characteristics, like trait-anxiety, have been used to account for vulnerabilities to the genesis and maintenance of anxiety disorders. Although there is some consensus on the role of personality predispositions in the development of these clinical disorders, many have questioned the explanatory value of such broad constructs as trait anxiety. Their tautological quality has also been challenged: "The trait anxiety explanation for panic appears circular. That is, it 'explains' the tendency for people to experience anxiety attacks by invoking the tendency to experience anxiety in general" (Donnell & McNally, 1990, p. 84). This criticism is empirically supported: High levels of trait-anxiety in nonclinical samples are not predictive of such symptoms as panic attacks (e.g., Cox, Endler, Norton, & Swinson, 1991).

An important conceptual distinction appears necessary. Whereas trait-anxiety is regarded as a proclivity to experience state-anxiety in response to environmental contingencies, clinical accounts frequently emphasize patients' inability to tolerate, regulate, or derive benefit from their own anxiety-related sensations. Many individuals with anxiety disorder diagnoses appear unable to cope with the specific experience of anxiety itself. This clinical observation is not easily accounted for by the linear progression of stressor, coping strategy, then symptom traditionally investigated by coping researchers. It has, however, prompted interest in two related explanatory constructs: *fear of fear* (Goldstein & Chambless, 1978) and *anxiety sensitivity* (Reiss & McNally, 1985). The latter and more contemporary of the two is a stylistic variable, distinct from trait-anxiety (e.g., McNally, 1989; Taylor, Koch, & Crockett, 1991) and defined by a tendency to hold generalized beliefs about the aversive consequences of the experience of anxiety, and to interpret bodily arousal as threatening. This construct, frequently cited in the anxiety disorders literature, has been particularly useful in explaining why certain individuals engage in the dramatic misinterpretations of bodily sensations thought to underlie panic attacks.

The anxiety sensitivity construct occupies a similar conceptual position relative to anxiety disorder as does the ruminative response style, previously discussed, to depression. The reader will recall that Nolen-Hoeksema (1991) has proposed that individuals' habitual responses to depressed moods influence the duration and ease of alleviation of these moods. The conceptual similarity with anxiety sensitivity is made evident by Wardle, Ahmad, and Hayward (1990): "[Higher levels] will increase alertness about the possibility of becoming anxious and increase worry about becoming anxious" (p. 326). In this way, habitual responses to anxiety in fact serve to amplify its effects. This is most conspicuous in the dramatic manifestations of anxiety found in panic attacks.

A vast research literature has arisen surrounding the role played by anxiety sensitivity in the etiology and maintenance of panic (see Lilienfeld et al., 1993, for a review). Considerable empirical evidence has emerged of its particular salience, but not specificity to, panic disorder. Taylor, Koch, and McNally (1992) have reported that in a subject sample in which each of the DSM-III-R anxiety disorder categories were represented, for all but one clinical group anxiety sensitivity levels were more elevated than those of normal controls. This stylistic variable was, however, most strongly associated with panic disorder (see also Zeitlin & McNally, 1993). A number of causal mechanisms have been hypothesized to underlay this precursor of affect dysregulation. It may reflect interoceptive classical conditioning of such physical sensations as accelerated heartbeat, which in turn become the conditioned stimuli for an acquired anxiety response and panic attacks (e.g., Goldstein & Chambless, 1978). However, more cognitive explanations predominate. One of these, the expectancy model of anxiety (see Reiss, 1991) contrasts with others in its tenet that anxiety sensitivity is a cause rather than a consequence of panic. Those in the area have argued that individual differences in this predisposition may arise from such sources as social learning and physiological overreactivity (e.g., Reiss, Peterson, Gursky, & McNally, 1986).

A cognitive model offered by Barlow (1991) contends that certain anxiety disorders, such as panic, are a consequence of spontaneous "misfirings" of transient arousal, interacting with a stable psychological vulnerability to experience such inappropriate expressions of emotion as threatening. Disorder develops when anxious apprehension arises regarding the possibility of subsequent spontaneous attacks. The associated acute sensitivity to interoceptive cues is hypothesized to function as a self-fulfilling prophecy, although empirical support is mixed (e.g., Asmundson, Sandler, Wilson, & Norton, 1993). An important feature is thought to be previous exposure to events where one's active coping efforts were unsuccessful: "Early experiences with lack of control provide a psychological vulnerability for anxiety" (Barlow, 1991, p. 65). Relevantly, Andrews (1991) has also cited perceived controllability, or beliefs regarding the ability to effect changes in one's environment, as a foremost determinant of a person's preparedness to cope. Telch, Brouilard, Telch, Agras, and Taylor (1989) have similarly highlighted the importance of self-appraisal in their model of panic-related avoidance; a central role is assigned to beliefs in one's ability to execute effective coping strategies. Escalation of anxiety and self-perpetuating avoidance may follow from perceived self-inefficacy. Reports of decreased frequency and reported fear of panic following courses of treatment that incorporate cognitive coping and skills training techniques support this (e.g., Adler, Craske, Kirshenbaum, & Barlow, 1989). An interesting variation has been reported by Catanzaro (1993). In an investigation of the role played by expectancies regarding the outcomes of mood regulation attempts in emotional distress, it was found that in a nonclinical sample those with low self-perceptions of ability to regulate negative moods, and high anxiety sensitivity, reported the highest levels of distress.

It would appear that the coping construct, conceptualized both in terms of affect regulation tendencies and efforts to resolve environmental threat, appears to have a potentially valuable place in models of panic and anxiety disorders. Despite this, anxiety disorders have received little attention in the mainstream coping literature. This may partly reflect the difficulty of identifying such symptoms in frequently utilized undergraduate populations; the qualitative differences between clinical and nonclinical panic attacks, for example, are often remarked on (e.g., Stewart, Knize, & Pihl, 1992). Such individuals more readily dismiss attacks, attribute them to fleeting situational events, and report little apprehension over the potential of future recurrence (Barlow, 1991). It is also likely that the psychometrically derived coping dimensions and linear models investigated by mainstream coping researchers may be particularly ill suited for such clinical disorders, where symptoms themselves may represent adjustive efforts in response to threat, and where the person's perceptions of and reactions to emotional responses may themselves exacerbate the problem. Coping frameworks capable of incorporating variables such as anxiety sensitivity, indicative of individual differences in the ability to regulate the experience of anxiety, would be of value to both clinical research and practice.

Emotional Dysregulation and Cognitive Biases

The discussion thus far has addressed examples of faulty affect regulation that amplify the experience of anxiety; as Andrews (1991) has noted: "When anxiety is too severe it robs capacity, and reduces the individual's ability to perceive, reason, and act appropriately" (p. 295). A large body of research has arisen around this important clinical feature. Anxiety, in accordance with its adaptive role in our evolutionary history, is associated with enhanced vigilance for cues or stimuli associated with sources of apprehension. In some cases, however, this hypervigilance may lead to such a dramatic narrowing of attentional focus that distortions in information processing become likely due to the selective exclusion of neutral nonconfirmatory information. The clinical consequences of such biased processing are acknowledged by researchers in this area: "The more that nervous individuals attend to threatening cues in their environment, the more they will encode information about potential hazards, again allowing a circular relationship between selective processing and anxious mood" (Mathews & MacLeod,

1994, p. 27). Hypervigilant scanning, then, as a strategy for managing feelings of apprehension, instead serves to intensify them.

A growing number of studies indicate the primary role played in the etiology and maintenance of anxiety disorders by biases in information processing at the level of attention. MacLeod (1990) and Mathews and MacLeod (1994) have offered comprehensive summaries of this vast literature. It is also addressed elsewhere in this volume. It is worth noting, however, that this body of knowledge has not generally been acknowledged by coping researchers (see Krohne, 1993b, for an exception). This is quite surprising, given its clear relevance to increasingly cited models of coping that emphasize the role played by attentional deployment (distraction) in the management and successful regulation of negative emotions (see Krohne, 1993a; Miller, 1990, 1992). Representing as they do clear illustrations of failed regulatory mechanisms, information-processing biases in anxiety merit some discussion in the present chapter.

Attentional Biases

Coping researchers and theorists interested in cognitive responses to aversive demands have identified two key dimensions: attention, or one's orientation toward the threat-relevant features of a situation, and *cognitive avoidance,* or the diversion of attention away from such features (e.g., Krohne, 1993b). A number of constructs, among them "sensitization/repression" (Byrne, 1964), "monitoring and blunting" (Miller, 1980, 1987), and "vigilance/cognitive avoidance" (Krohne, 1986, 1989) reflect this basic distinction. Recent reviews of this body of work (e.g., Krohne, 1993a) have acknowledged that several factors, including the nature of the stressor, the stage of engagement with the stressor, and flexibility of strategy, determine the adaptiveness of either of these cognitive strategies. Most authors emphasize that while vigilance aims at reducing uncertainty, the primary goal of cognitive avoidance is to regulate emotional arousal. Even when operationalized simply as looking behavior directed away from or toward a source of threatening information (see Hock, 1993), it would appear that directed attention functions both as a warning signal and, when diverted, as an arousal regulation mechanism. Cognitive rehearsal of threat cues, combined with heightened awareness of one's emotional state and associated vigilance for threat may result in the perpetuation of emotional arousal. Furthermore, as Miller, Combs, and Kruus (1993) have postulated, avoidance attempts may be activated by enhanced vigilance, thereby thwarting full emotional processing of a stressor.

Recent years have witnessed a surge of empirical interest within the field of experimental cognitive psychology in the role of information-processing biases in psychopathology. This is particularly true of the topic of attentional biases, or facilitated processing of affect-congruent information, in anxiety (see Mathews & MacLeod, 1994). This body of research has, in general, found a consistent relationship between anxiety and the disproportionate allocation of attentional resources to threatening stimuli (Mineka & Sutton, 1992). Several studies have used Stroop-type methodologies, which seek to assess the degree of cognitive interference evoked by emotionally valenced words by measuring latencies in the naming of the ink colors in which words are printed. Clinically anxious subjects have been shown to take longer to name groups of threat-relevant words than nonthreatening ones, a trend not exhibited by matched controls (e.g., Mathews & MacLeod, 1985; Mogg, Mathews, & Weinman, 1989). Furthermore, there is some evidence for the specificity of biases to personally relevant fears (e.g., somatic symptoms for panic disorder patients; Zinbarg, Barlow, Brown, & Hertz, 1992). Alternate methodologies for presenting semantic material, such as dichotic listening tasks (e.g., Mathews & MacLeod, 1986) have provided comparable results.

Such findings may reflect active rather than passive cognitive mechanisms. Methodological refinements in the form of visual probe paradigms, adopted to address the possible confound of a bias in response rather than in selective attention, have demonstrated that anxious subjects selectively allocate attentional resources *toward* the location on a screen where a threatening stimulus word occurs (MacLeod, Mathews, & Tata, 1986). Interestingly, this contrasts with nonanxious control subjects' propensity to shift attentional resources away from threat (see also Broadbent & Broadbent, 1988). Hock's (1993) conceptualization of diversion of visual attention as an emotionally regulatory coping strategy seems highly relevant. Writers interested in the clinical consequences of such tendencies (e.g., Beck & Emery, 1985) have noted that facilitated processing of affect-congruent information restricts feedback available to only that material most reinforcing of an anxious state. A cognitive feedback loop results in continued preoccupation with potential threat, unrealistically enhanced vigilance, and anxious arousal. In the anxiety disorders, vigilance and worry, as coping efforts, are actually self-perpetuating (Freeman et al., 1990).

The high correlation found in clinical samples between state- and trait-anxiety makes it somewhat difficult to partial out their unique contributions (see MacLeod, 1990). Reductions in manifest anxiety have been found to be predictive of decreases in some processing biases (e.g., Eysenck, Mogg, May, Richards, & Mathews, 1991). Nonetheless, with respect to attentional biases, there seems to be growing consensus regarding the role of more enduring predispositions. Recovered patients, presumably high in trait-anxiety but not currently anxious, have been shown to exhibit attentional impairment when threat-related disruptions were used (Mathews, May, Mogg, & Eysenck, 1990). In the authors' words: "A bias favouring threat cues during perceptual search is an enduring feature of individuals vulnerable to anxiety, rather than a transient consequence of current mood state" (p. 166). Studies with nonclinical subjects high in trait-anxiety support this observation (e.g., Fox, 1993; MacLeod & Mathews, 1988).

In short, it would seem that processing biases are mediated by the interacting influence of both trait- and state-anxiety (see Mogg, Mathews, Bird, & MacGregor-Morris, 1990, for elaboration). The general vulnerability represented by the former has been discussed by MacLeod (1991), who has suggested that the predisposition alone may reflect a tendency to selectively attend to, or encode, threatening information in the environment. Thus, anxiety proneness may be associated in a causal and reciprocal way, with enduring processing styles. This is congruent with clinical observation of persistent cognitive distortions in anxiety disorders and their influence on situation perception (Freeman et al., 1990). It may also be a key to why the clinical literature and the mainstream body of coping research have had few intersections. A highly influential group of coping researchers has repeatedly deemphasized dispositional facets of coping (Folkman, 1992).

Recent empirical work has provided additional insight into attentional biases. First, it would appear that mood-congruent processing biases in anxiety may be evident only when there is competition for cognitive resources, or when decisions must be made regarding selective allocation of processing resources to tasks (MacLeod & Mathews, 1991). Furthermore, the differences between anxious and nonanxious subjects are most robust on those cognitive tasks requiring active attentional shifts or search strategies when faced with competing stimuli. Importantly, such tasks have been found to be associated with an attentional shift *toward* such material on the part of anxious subjects (Mogg, Mathews, Eysenck, & May, 1991). Nonanxious subjects in these studies, however, commonly show an automatic tendency to divert attention *away* from potentially anxiety-evoking stimuli—a practice evocative of the term "perceptual defense" (Bruner & Postman, 1947). There is some agreement in the cognitive coping literature that vigilance and cognitive avoidance are associated with, respectively, reduction of uncertainty and reduction of emotional arousal (Krohne, 1993a). It would appear that whereas those prone to anxiety disorders may successfully enhance their ability to detect potential danger signals and minimize ambiguity, they fail to benefit from relatively automatic cognitive mechanisms involved in successful emotional regulation.

An additional feature of this bias relevant to the current chapter's emphasis (see Mathews, 1993, for elaboration) is that whereas anxious individuals may be predisposed to engage in enhanced processing at an initial stage (attention), they do not pursue further elaboration of obtained information. Illustratively, anxious subjects, unexpectedly, have been found to show disproportionately poorer memory for threat-related negative information (e.g., Mogg, Gardiner, Stavrou, & Golumbek, 1992). It appears that a bias favoring threat stimuli may not operate at later stages of information processing. Anxiety may preclude the subsequent elaborated processing of stimuli, a phenomenon termed "cognitive avoidance" by Foa and Kozak (1986). Anxious individuals may make an active cognitive effort to minimize extensive processing of relevant information to maintain their selective attentional focus (Harvey, 1984). This tendency has potential clinical consequences. Primarily, it may account for the inability of those with anxiety disorders to retain an image of anxiety-inducing stimuli that is congruent with objective assessments, as reflected in such clinical terms as "catastrophizing" and "magnification" (Freeman et al., 1990). In this way, the individual may be unable to extricate him- or herself from the feedback loop existing between arousal and hypervigilance for danger cues.

Interpretive Biases

The primary role played in coping by appraisal, both of the situation and of its pertinence to one's personal needs and well-being, has long been acknowledged. Current approaches to appraisal, or interpretation, emphasize its often nonvolitional qualities: "Appraisal is not coextensive with consciousness, deliberateness, and rationality" (Lazarus, 1991, p. 361). Biases of interpretation in anxiety, although not as evident as those of attention, have been empirically demonstrated. It would appear that individuals vulnerable to anxious states may habitually impose threat-relevant meanings on ambiguous stimuli.

In one study investigating the role of anxiety in the interpretation of homophones having both neutral and threatening meanings, Eysenck, MacLeod, and Mathews (1987) reported suggestive results. Ambiguous words were embedded in a list of unambiguous buffer items; subjects were directed to listen to a tape of these recorded words and record them as a form of "spelling list." The frequency with which subjects reported the threat-relevant spelling of these words, such as "pain" versus "pane," and "die" rather than "dye," was highly correlated with their scores on a self-report trait-anxiety measure. Studies comparing current and recovered anxious patients and controls have had similar results (e.g., Mathews, Mogg, May, & Eysenck, 1989). In a recent study designed to control for the confounding effects of response selection bias and perceived experimenter expectations, MacLeod and Cohen (1993) have reported consistent findings with a sensitive experimental technique. In accordance with predictions of anxiety-linked interpretive biases, high trait-anxious nonclinical subjects displayed a tendency to appraise ambiguous sentences in a threatening manner.

It would appear, then, that some individuals may be less influenced by objective situational cues signaling the absence of threat than others. If, as Andrews (1991) has suggested, "Reality-based coping means accurate and considered appraisal of the problem" (p. 295), coping researchers might do well to incorporate into their investigative frameworks findings regarding relatively stable individual differences in the tendency to favor threatening interpretations. The value of such an approach has recently been alluded to by Lazarus (1993), who has suggested that a much richer perspective in the study of coping would be afforded by the inclusion of a "relational-motivational" model of emotions. The overlap between this view and the models and empirical findings of the field of experimental cognitive psychopathology is evident:

> We must consider individualized cognitive-motivational-relational configurations that operate idiosyncratically as hidden, irrational, or distorted meanings shaping our appraisals of interpersonal and intrapersonal relationships and, therefore, generating emotions that seem not to fit the consensual premises of observers about what is taking place. (Lazarus, 1991, p. 362)

In summary, for the anxiety disorders we have identified three clinically useful bodies of work exhibiting considerable conceptual overlap with issues germane to the field of coping. The topics discussed—(a) symptoms as misguided acquired coping strategies, and affect dysregulation evidenced in both; (b) anxiety sensitivity; and (c) cognitive biases—all merit attention by coping researchers and theorists. These features are explicitly targeted in cognitive-behavioral therapies for anxiety disorders, whose primary goal is to "eliminate disproportionate fears and any maladaptive patterns of avoiding or preventing anxiety that the individual may have developed" (Freeman et al., 1990, p. 137). Their consideration might foster a body of coping research of clear clinical and theoretical value.

CLINICAL INTERVENTION

Virtually all psychotherapies aim to modify current patterns of adjustment to one's environment in a way more conducive to long-term well-being. Despite this, "coping" as an explicit goal for intervention is articulated most explicitly in cognitive and cognitive-behavioral approaches (e.g., Wollersheim, 1984; see also Folkman et al., 1991). Comprehensive reviews maintain that underlying this form of clinical intervention is the belief that contents and processes of thought play a causal role in many clinical disorders (e.g., Beck & Emery, 1985; Beck & Freeman, 1990; Bergin & Garfield, 1994; Freeman et al., 1990; Warren & Zgourides, 1991). Cognitive therapies seek to produce changes in cognition, thereby influencing affect and behavior. This emphasis is shared by the two most influential models of intervention: Beck's cognitive therapy (BCT; Beck, 1976) and the rational-emotive therapy of Ellis (RET; 1962). Although entailing different techniques (the former emphasizes empirical testing of pathogenic cognitions, the latter their modification through therapeutic debate), these are often used in concert with behavioral procedures to supplant highly limited and self-perpetuating coping responses with more adaptive strategies (Freeman et al., 1990). The mechanism underlying therapeutic change is thought to be cognitive reeducation, accomplished through the modification of existing maladaptive beliefs and behavioral strategies and the acquisition of needed skills. In our discussion of the personality disorders, depression, and anxiety, we have identified several topics of relevance to the field of coping. These include inflexibility of strategy, pathological adjustive efforts in the form of symptoms, emotional dysregulation reflecting the inability to manage, benefit from, and assimilate emotional experience, and the related role of distorted information processing. These features are all specifically targeted by cognitive-behavioral interventions. Although often tailored for specific disorders (see Freeman et al., 1990), a number of common techniques may be identified that have as their goal the very issues discussed throughout this chapter.

Emotional experience is thought to be accompanied by negative thoughts and cognitive distortions in all the disorders discussed; affect dysregulation can be addressed by psychoeducational methods. Cognitive therapists with both BCT (e.g., Clark & Salkovskis, 1991) and RET (Warren & Zgourides, 1991) orientations have emphasized the role of faulty logic in both the misinterpretation of bodily sensations and aversion to anxious arousal (evidenced in anxiety sensitivity) so frequently associated with anxiety disorders. "Catastrophizing," as one of these distortions, can be addressed by challenges and questioning by the therapist, and controlled imagery on the part of the client. The ability to be appropriately attuned to somatic cues in order to abort either panic or anxiety is also valuable: "Coping procedures are skills that may be applied to prevent an attack from developing" (Jacobs, Nadel, & Hayden, 1992). The goal of becoming more "positively emotional," rather than unemotional, is made explicit in RET (Warren & Zgourides, 1991).

Exposure techniques, combined with response (rituals, avoidance) prevention are an essential part of these therapies. Although verbal interventions may help to challenge cognitions and offer alternatives, they often have a limited impact on significant autonomic arousal. The clinical superiority of combining exposure techniques, such as systematic desensitization, with cognitive therapy is attested to by a growing empirical literature (e.g., Chambless & Gillis, 1993; Cox et al., 1992; Durham & Allan, 1993). In the case of personality disorders, an interesting variation on this method encourages both familiarization with one's sensations of emotions and acquisition of a sense of control by combining exposure with imagery in a "scheduled" emotional outburst. This is quite useful with histrionic and narcissistic clients, as is its equivalent, "scheduled worries," for depressive rumination. The feeling of mastery associated with this artificial arrangement may supplant the perception of being victimized by sudden onsets of emotional trauma, and generalize to enhanced regulatory skills. Although traditionally thought by behaviorists to primarily entail deconditioning of a fear response, recent approaches to exposure techniques have deemphasized the cognitive versus noncognitive distinction (see Rapee, 1991; Zinbarg, 1990). A crucial component of these techniques is to experience enhanced self-efficacy and perceived control following successful use of nonsymptomatic coping strategies.

Self-perpetuating patterns of biased information processing are also a target for change. "Cognitive restructuring" directly focuses on such processing tendencies as biases favoring recall of depressogenic material and hypervigilant scanning for threat-congruent information (see Zinbarg et al., 1992). For anxiety disorders, Freeman et al. (1990) have advocated the introduction of "outward focus" coping techniques. Here, attention is strategically diverted from anxiety-inducing foci, such as one's internal state, to more benign environmental stimuli. This tactic, unlike cognitive avoidance, is thought to be an appropriate strategy that disrupts a self-perpetuating cycle.

A chief therapeutic goal, particularly with personality disorders, is to cultivate an increased sense of self-efficacy in problem situations, thereby addressing the tenuous stability of pathological coping patterns under stress. This may be accomplished by challenging clients' overestimation of negative outcomes and underestimation of personal coping skills, in cases where appropriate, or by helping clients recognize their specific insufficiencies and bolstering needed coping skills. In the BCT tradition, behavioral experiments ("homework assignments") provide a practice venue; nonconfirmation of implicit hypotheses can then be discussed. Such opportunities also target patients' exclusive reliance on a narrow repertoire of coping responses.

Although initially developed for the treatment of depression, the efficacy of cognitive-based interventions in a wide variety of disorders is being increasingly recognized (for a review of clinical trials, see Hollon & Beck, 1994). Its long-term effectiveness has been particularly noted; unlike pharmacotherapy it serves to bolster the patients' armamentarium of coping skills against future demands. It has also been lauded for its conscious transformation of coping strategies, a goal somewhat neglected by psychodynamic interventions (e.g., Weston, 1991).

CONCLUSION

We have attempted to review constructs, issues, and empirical findings representing conceptual intersections among several discrete literatures. These all have as a goal the elucidation of the role played by an individual's adaptational resources in the genesis and maintenance of psychopathology. Our discussion has implicated the inadequacy of mainstream coping models and empirical findings for a true understanding of psychopathological mechanisms involved in the management of both external (environmental) and internal (emotional) demands. Despite this, it has also identified several underexploited areas of overlap, whose integration may facilitate the development of a clinically relevant body of knowledge about coping. We have reviewed several issues in our discussion of three diagnostic categories; foremost among these was affect dysregulation, as evidenced in rumination about, and sensitivity to, emotional experience, biased information processing, and cognitive distortions. Self-generation of stressors and symptomatic coping strategies were also addressed. An enhanced appreciation of the integrative potential of these topics may be of some benefit, both to those in the coping field, and to those more specifically interested in the mechanisms involved in psychopathology.

REFERENCES

Abramson, L. Y., Metalsky, G. I., & Alloy, L. B. (1989). Hopelessness depression: A theory-based subtype of depression. *Psychological Review, 96,* 358–372.

Adler, C. M., Craske, M. G., Kirshenbaum, S., & Barlow, D. H. (1989). "Fear of panic": An investigation of its role in panic occurrence, phobic avoidance, and treatment outcome. *Behaviour Research and Therapy, 27,* 391–396.

Ahles, T. A., Blanchard, E. B., & Leventhal, H. (1983). Cognitive control of pain: Attention to the sensory aspects of the cold pressor stimulus. *Cognitive Therapy and Research, 7,* 159–177.

Akiskal, H. S. (1983). Dysthymic disorder: Psychopathology of proposed depressive subtypes. *American Journal of Psychiatry, 26,* 315–317.

Allport, G. M. (1937). *Pattern and growth in personality.* Toronto, Canada: Holt, Rinehart & Winston.

American Psychiatric Association. (1980). *Diagnostic and statistical manual of mental disorders* (3rd ed.). Washington, DC: Author.

American Psychiatric Association. (1994). *Diagnostic and statistical manual of mental disorders.* (4th ed). Washington, DC: Author.

Amirkhan, J. H. (1994). Seeking person-related predictors of coping: Exploratory analyses. *European Journal of Personality, 8,* 13–30.

Andrews, G. (1991). Anxiety, personality, and the anxiety disorders. *International Review of Psychiatry, 3,* 293–302.

Aronoff, J., Stollak, G. E., & Woike, B. A. (1994). Affect regulation and the breadth of interpersonal engagement. *Journal of Personality and Social Psychology, 67,* 105–114.

Asmundson, G. J., Sandler, L. S., Wilson, K. G., & Norton, G. R. (1993). Panic attacks and interoceptive acuity for cardiac sensations. *Behaviour Research and Therapy, 31,* 193–197.

Barlow, D. H. (1991). Disorders of emotion. *Psychological Inquiry, 2,* 58–71.

Barnard, P. J., & Teasdale, J. D. (1991). Interacting cognitive subsystems: A systemic approach to cognitive-affective interaction and change. *Cognition and Emotion, 5,* 1–39.

Beck, A. T. (1976). *Cognitive therapy and the emotional disorders.* New York: International University Press.

Beck, A. T., & Emery, G. (1985). *Anxiety disorders and phobias: A cognitive perspective.* New York: Basic Books.

Beck, A. T., & Freeman, A. (1990). *Cognitive therapy of personality disorders.* New York: Guilford.

Bellew, M., & Hill, A. B. (1991). Schematic processing and the prediction of depression following childbirth. *Personality and Individual Differences, 12,* 943–949.

Bergin, A. E., & Garfield, S. L. (Eds.). (1994). *Handbook of psychotherapy and behavior change* (4th ed.). Toronto, Canada: Wiley.

Billings, A. G., & Moos, R. H. (1984). Coping, stress, and social resources among adults with unipolar depression. *Journal of Personality and Social Psychology, 46,* 877–891.

Billings, A. G., & Moos, R. H. (1985). Psychosocial processes of remission in unipolar depression: Comparing depressed patients with match community controls. *Journal of Consulting and Clinical Psychology, 53,* 314–325.

Bradley, B., & Mathews, A. (1988). Memory bias in recovered clinical depressives. *Cognition and Emotion, 2,* 235–246.

Broadbent, D., & Broadbent, M. (1988). Anxiety and attentional bias: State and trait. *Cognition and Emotion, 2,* 165–183.

Bruner, J. S., & Postman, L. (1947). Emotional selectivity in perception and reaction. *Journal of Personality, 15,* 300–308.

Burns, D., & Nolen-Hoeksema, S. K. (1991). Coping styles, homework assignments, and the effectiveness of cognitive-behavioral therapy. *Journal of Consulting and Clinical Psychology, 59,* 305–311.

Byrne, D. (1964). Repression-sensitization as a dimension of personality. In B. A. Maher (Ed.), *Progress in experimental personality research* (Vol. 1, pp. 169–220). New York: Academic Press.

Caballero, J. A. R., & Moreno, J. B. (1993). Depressed mood, mood-simulation and congruent recall. *Personality and Individual Differences, 14,* 365–368.

Carpenter, B. N. (1992). Issues and advances in coping research. In B. N. Carpenter (Ed.), *Personal coping: Theory, research, and application* (pp. 1–14). London: Praeger.

Carver, C. S., Scheier, M. F., & Weintraub, J. K. (1989). Assessing coping strategies: A theoretically based approach. *Journal of Personality and Social Psychology, 56,* 267–283.

Catanzaro, S. J. (1993). Mood regulation expectancies, anxiety sensitivity, and emotional distress. *Journal of Abnormal Psychology, 102,* 327–330.

Chambless, D. L., & Gillis, M. M. (1993). Cognitive therapy of anxiety disorders. *Journal of Consulting and Clinical Psychology, 61,* 248–260.

Clark, D. M., & Salkovskis, P. M. (1991). *Cognitive therapy with panic and hypochondriasis.* New York: Pergamon.

Cohen, F. (1987). Measurement of coping. In S. V. Kasl & C. L. Cooper (Eds.), *Stress and health: Issues in research methodology* (pp. 283–305). New York: Wiley.

Conway, V. J., & Terry, D. J. (1992). Appraised controllability as a moderator of the effectiveness of different coping strategies. *Australian Journal of Psychopathology, 44,* 1–7.

Costa, P. T., Zonderman, A. B., & McCrae, R. R. (1991). Personality, defense, coping, and adaptation in older adulthood. In E. M. Cummings, A. L. Greene, & K. H. Karraker (Eds.), *Life-span developmental psychology: Perspectives on stress and coping* (pp. 277–293). Hillsdale, NJ: Erlbaum.

Cox, B. J., Endler, N. S., Lee, P. S., & Swinson, R. P. (1992). A meta-analysis of treatments for panic disorder with agoraphobia: Imipramine, alprazolam, and in vivo exposure. *Journal of Behavior Therapy and Experimental Psychiatry, 23,* 175–182.

Cox, B. J., Endler, N. S., Norton, G. R., & Swinson, R. P. (1991). Anxiety sensitivity and nonclinical panic attacks. *Behavior Research and Therapy, 29,* 367–369.

Coyne, J. C., Burchill, S. A., & Stiles, W. B. (1990). An interactional perspective on depression. In C. R. Snyder & D. O. Forsyth (Eds.), *Handbook of social and clinical psychology: The health perspective.* New York: Pergamon.

Coyne, J. C., & Downey, G. (1991). Social factors and psychopathology: Stress, social support, and coping processes. *Annual Review of Psychology, 42,* 401–425.

Cramer, P. (1991). *The development of defense mechanisms: Theory, research, and assessment.* New York: Springer-Verlag.

Dagleish, T., & Watts, F. N. (1990). Biases of attention and memory in disorders of anxiety and depression. *Clinical Psychology Review, 10,* 589–604.

Donnell, C. D., & McNally, R. J. (1990). Anxiety sensitivity and panic attacks in a nonclinical population. *Behavior Research and Therapy, 28,* 83–85.

Durham, R. C., & Allan, T. (1993). Psychological treatment of generalised anxiety disorder: A review of the clinical significance of results in outcome studies since 1980. *British Journal of Psychiatry, 163,* 19–26.

Edelmann, R. J. (1992). *Anxiety: Theory Research and intervention in clinical and health psychology.* Toronto, Canada: Wiley.

Edwards, L., Pearce, S., Collett, B. J., & Pugh, R. (1992). Selective memory for sensory and affective information in chronic pain and depression. *British Journal of Clinical Psychology, 31,* 239–248.

Ellis, A. (1962). *Reason and emotion in psychotherapy.* New York: Lyle Stuart.

Endler, N. S. (1980). Person–situation interaction and anxiety. In I. L. Kutash & L. B. Schlesinger (Eds.), *Handbook on stress and anxiety: Contemporary knowledge, theory and treatment* (pp. 241–266). San Francisco: Jossey-Bass.

Endler, N. S. (1983). Interactionism: A personality model, but not yet a theory. In M. M. Page (Ed.), *Nebraska symposium on motivation 1982: Personality—Current theory and research* (pp. 155–200). Lincoln: University of Nebraska Press.

Endler, N. S. (1988). Hassles, health and happiness. In M. P. Janisse (Ed.), *Individual differences, stress and health psychology* (pp. 24–56). New York: Springer-Verlag.

Endler, N. S., Edwards, J. M., & Vitelli, R. (1991). *Endler Multidimensional Anxiety Scales: Manual.* Los Angeles: Western Psychological Services.

Endler, N. S., & Parker, J. D. A. (1990a). *Coping Inventory for Stressful Situations (CISS): Manual.* Toronto, Canada: Multi-Health Systems.

Endler, N. S., & Parker, J. D. A. (1990b). The multidimensional assessment of coping: A critical evaluation. *Journal of Personality and Social Psychology, 58,* 844–854.

Endler, N. S., & Parker, J. D. A. (1990c). State and trait anxiety, depression, and coping styles. *Australian Journal of Psychology, 42,* 207–220.

Eysenck, M. W., MacLeod, C., & Mathews, A. (1987). Cognitive functioning in anxiety. *Psychological Research, 49,* 189–195.

Eysenck, M. W., Mogg, K., May, J., Richards, A., & Mathews, A. (1991). Bias in interpretation of ambiguous sentences related to threat in anxiety. *Journal of Abnormal Psychology, 100,* 144–150.

Foa, E. B., & Kozak, M. J. (1986). Emotional processing of fear: Exposure to corrective information. *Psychological Bulletin, 99,* 20–35.

Folkman, S. (1992). Making the case for coping. In B. N. Carpenter (Ed.), *Personal coping: Theory, research, and application* (pp. 31–46). London: Praeger.

Folkman, S., Chesney, M., McKusick, L., Ironson, G., Johnson, D. S., & Coates, T. J. (1991). Translating coping theory into an intervention. In J. Eckenrode (Ed.), *The social context of coping* (pp. 239–260). New York: Plenum.

Folkman, S., & Lazarus, R. S. (1985). If it changes it must be a process: A study of emotion and coping during three stages of a college examination. *Journal of Personality and Social Psychology, 48,* 150–170.

Folkman, S., & Lazarus, R. S. (1988). *Manual for the Ways of Coping Questionnaire.* Palo Alto, CA: Consulting Psychologist Press.

Forgas, J. P., & Bower, G. H. (1987). Mood effects in person perception. *Journal of Personality and Social Psychology, 53,* 53–60.

Fox, E. (1993). Allocation of visual attention and anxiety. *Cognition and Emotion, 7,* 207–215.

Freeman, A., Pretzer, J., Fleming, B., & Simon, K. M. (1990). *Clinical applications of cognitive therapy.* New York: Plenum.

Gardner, R. W. (1983). *Frames of mind: The theory of multiple intelligences.* New York: Basic Books.

Goldstein, A. J., & Chambless, D. L. (1978). A reanalysis of agoraphobia. *Behavior Therapy, 3,* 45–53.

Greenspan, S. I. (1989). *The development of the ego.* Madison, CT: International Universities Press.

Gruen, R. J. (1993). Stress and depression: Toward the development of integrative models. In L. Goldberger & S. Breznitz (Eds.), *Handbook of stress: Theoretical and clinical aspects* (pp. 550–569). Toronto, Canada: Free Press.

Haaga, D. A. F., Dyck, M. J., & Ernst, D. (1991). Empirical status of cognitive theory of depression. *Psychological Bulletin, 110,* 215–236.

Haan, N. (1993). The assessment of coping, defense, and stress. In L. Goldberger & S. Breznitz (Eds.), *Handbook of stress: Theoretical and clinical aspects* (pp. 258–273). Toronto, Canada: Free Press.

Hammen, C. (1991). Generation of stress in the course of unipolar depression. *Journal of Abnormal Psychology, 100,* 555–561.

Hammen, C. (1992). Cognitive, life stress, and interpersonal approaches to a developmental psychopathology model of depression. *Development and Psychopathology, 4,* 189–206.

Hammen, C., Davila, J., Brown, G., Ellicott, A., & Gitlin, B. (1992). Psychiatric history and stress: Predictors of severity of unipolar depression. *Journal of Abnormal Psychology, 101,* 45–52.

Harvey, N. (1984). The Stroop effect: Failure to focus attention or failure to maintain focusing? *Quarterly Journal of Experimental Psychology: Human Experimental Psychology, 36,* 89–115.

Hirschfeld, R. M. A. (1994). Major depression, dysthymia, and depressive personality disorder. *British Journal of Psychiatry, 165,* 23–30.

Hock, M. (1993). Coping dispositions, attentional direction, and anxiety states. In H. W. Krohne (Ed.), *Attention and avoidance: Strategies in coping with aversiveness* (pp. 139–169). Toronto, Canada: Hogrefe & Huber.

Hoffart, A., & Martinsen, E. W. (1992). Personality disorders in panic with agoraphobia and major depression. *British Journal of Clinical Psychology, 31,* 213–214.

Hollon, S. D., & Beck, A. T. (1994). Cognitive and cognitive-behavioral therapies. In A. E. Bergin & S. L. Garfield (Eds.), *Handbook of psychotherapy and behavior change* (4th ed., pp. 428–466). Toronto, Canada: Wiley.

Holohan, C. J., & Moos, R. H. (1991). Life stressors, personal and social resources, and depression: A 4-year structural model. *Journal of Abnormal Psychology, 100,* 31–38.

Ilhilevich, D., & Gleser, G. C. (1993). Defense mechanisms. Odessa, FL: Psychological Assessment Resources.

Ingram, R. E., & Kendall, P. C. (1987). The cognitive side of anxiety. *Cognitive Therapy and Research, 11,* 523–536.

Jacobs, W. J., Nadel, L., & Hayden, V. C. (1992). Anxiety disorders. In D. J. Stein & J. E. Young (Eds.), *Cognitive science and clinical disorders* (pp. 211–234). Toronto, Canada: Academic Press.

Kantor, M. (1992). *Diagnosis and treatment of the personality disorders.* St. Louis, MO: Ishiyaku EuroAmerica.

Karoly, P. (1993). Mechanisms of self-regulation: A systems view. *Annual Review of Psychology, 44,* 23–52.

Kohlmann, C. W. (1993). Rigid and flexible modes of coping: Related to coping style? *Anxiety, Stress, and Coping: An International Journal, 6,* 107–123.

Krohne, H. W. (1986). Coping with stress: Dispositions, strategies, and the problem of measurement. In M. H. Appley & R. Trumbull (Eds.), *Dynamics of stress, physiological, psychological, and social perspectives* (pp. 209–234). New York: Plenum.

Krohne, H. W. (1989). The concept of coping modes: Relating cognitive person variables to actual coping behavior. *Advances in Behaviour Research and Therapy, 11,* 235–248.

Krohne, H. W. (Ed.). (1993a). *Attention and avoidance: Strategies in coping with aversiveness.* Toronto, Canada: Hogrefe & Huber.

Krohne, H. W. (1993b). Attention and avoidance: Two central strategies in coping with aversiveness. In H. W. Krohne (Ed.), *Attention and avoidance: Strategies in coping with aversiveness* (pp. 3–15). Toronto, Canada: Hogrefe & Huber.

Lakey, B., Baltman, S., & Bentley, K. (1993). Dysphoria and vulnerability to subsequent life events. *Journal of Research in Personality, 27,* 138–153.

Lazarus, R. S. (1991). Progress on a cognitive-motivational-relational theory of emotion. *American Psychologist, 46,* 819–834.

Lazarus, R. S. (1993). From psychological stress to the emotions: A history of changing outlooks. *Annual Review of Psychology, 44,* 1–21.

Lazarus, R. S., & Folkman, S. (1984). *Stress, appraisal, and coping.* New York: Springer.

Leventhal, E. A., Suls, J., & Leventhal, H. (1993). Hierarchical analysis of coping: Evidence from life-span studies. In H. W. Krohne (Ed.), *Attention and avoidance: Strategies in coping with aversiveness* (pp. 71–99). Toronto, Canada: Hogrefe & Huber.

Lewinsohn, P. M., Zeiss, A. M., Duncun, E. M. (1989). Probability of relapse after recovery from an episode of depression. *Journal of Abnormal Psychology, 97,* 251–264.

Lilienfeld, S. O., Turner, S. M., & Jacob, R. G. (1993). Anxiety sensitivity: An examination of theoretical and methodological issues. *Advances in Behaviour Research and Therapy, 15,* 147–183.

Lyubomirsky, S., & Nolen-Hoeksema, S. (1993). Self-perpetuating properties of dysphoric rumination. *Journal of Personality and Social Psychology, 65,* 339–349.

MacLeod, C. (1990). Mood disorders and cognition. In M. W. Eysenck (Ed.), *Cognitive psychology: An international review* (pp. 9–56). Toronto, Canada: Wiley.

MacLeod, C. (1991). Clinical anxiety and the selective encoding of threatening information. *International Review of Psychiatry, 3,* 279–292.

MacLeod, C., & Cohen, L. (1993). Anxiety and the interpretation of ambiguity: A text comprehension study. *Journal of Abnormal Psychology, 102,* 238–247.

MacLeod, C., & Mathews, A. (1988). Anxiety and the allocation of attention to threat. *Quarterly Journal of Experimental Psychology: Human Experimental Psychology, 38,* 659–670.

MacLeod, C., & Mathews, A. (1991). Biased cognitive operations in anxiety: Accessibility of information or assignment of processing priorities. *Behaviour Research and Therapy, 29,* 599–610.

MacLeod, C., Mathews, A., & Tata, P. (1986). Attentional bias in emotional disorders. *Journal of Abnormal Psychology, 95,* 15–20.

Magnusson, D., & Torestad, B. (1993). A holistic view of personality: A model revisited. *Annual Review of Psychology, 44,* 427–452.

Mathews, A. (1993). Attention and memory for threat in anxiety. In H. W. Krohne (Ed.), *Attention and avoidance: Strategies in coping with aversiveness* (pp. 119–135). Toronto, Canada: Hogrefe & Huber.

Mathews, A., & MacLeod, C. (1985). Selective processing of threat cues in anxiety states. *Behaviour Research and Therapy, 23,* 563–569.

Mathews, A., & MacLeod, C. (1986). Discrimination of threat cues without awareness in anxiety states. *Journal of Abnormal Psychology, 95,* 131–138.

Mathews, A., & MacLeod, C. (1994). Cognitive approaches to emotion and emotional disorders. *Annual Review of Psychology, 45,* 25–50.

Mathews, A., May, J., Mogg, K., & Eysenck, M. (1990). Attentional bias in anxiety: Selective search or defective filtering? *Journal of Abnormal Psychology, 99,* 166–173.

Mathews, A., Mogg, K., May, J., & Eysenck, M. (1989). Implicit and explicit memory bias in anxiety. *Journal of Abnormal Psychology, 98,* 236–240.

McNally, R. J. (1989). Is anxiety sensitivity distinguishable from trait anxiety? Reply to Lilienfeld, Jacob, and Turner (1989). *Journal of Abnormal Psychology, 98,* 193–194.

McNaughton, M. E., Patterson, T. L., Irwin, M. R., & Grant, I. (1992). The relationship of life adversity, social support, and coping to hospitalization with major depression. *Journal of Nervous and Mental Disease, 180,* 491–497.

Meissner, W. W. (1985). A case of phallic-narcissistic personality. *Journal of the American Psychoanalytic Association, 33,* 437–469.

Miller, S. M. (1980). When is a little information a dangerous thing? Coping with stressful events by monitoring vs. blunting. In S. Levine & H. Ursin (Eds.), *Coping and health* (pp. 145–170). New York: Plenum.

Miller, S. M. (1987). Monitoring and blunting: Validation of a questionnaire to assess styles of information seeking under threat. *Journal of Personality and Social Psychology, 52,* 345–353.

Miller, S. M. (1990). To see or not to see: Cognitive informational styles in the coping process. In M. Rosenbaum (Ed.), *Learned resourcefulness: On coping skills, self-regulation, and adaptive behavior.* New York: Springer.

Miller, S. M. (1992). Individual differences in the coping process: What to know and when to know it. In B. N. Carpenter (Ed.), *Personal coping: Theory, research, and application* (pp. 77–92). London: Praeger.

Miller, S. M., Combs, C., & Kruus, L. (1993). Tuning in and tuning out: Confronting the effects of confrontation. In H. W. Krohne (Ed.), *Attention and avoidance: Strategies in coping with aversiveness* (pp. 51–69). Toronto, Canada: Hogrefe & Huber.

Millon, T. (1969). *Modern psychopathology.* Philadelphia: Saunders.

Millon, T. (1981). *Disorders of personality: DSM-III, Axis II.* New York: Wiley.

Millon, T. (1990a). The disorders of personality. In L. A. Pervin (Ed.), *Handbook of personality* (pp. 339–369). New York: Guilford.

Millon, T. (1990b). *Toward a new personology: An evolutionary model.* Toronto, Canada: Wiley.

Mineka, S., & Sutton, S. K. (1992). Cognitive biases and the emotional disorders. *Psychological Science, 3,* 65–69.

Moeller, D. M., Richards, C. S., Hooker, K. A., & Ursino, A. A. (1992). Gender differences in the effectiveness of coping with dysphoria: A longitudinal study. *Counselling Psychology Quarterly, 5,* 349–357.

Mogg, K., Gardiner, J. M., Stavrou, A., & Golumbek, S. (1992). Recollective experience and recognition memory for threat in clinical anxiety states. *Bulletin of the Psychonomic Society, 30,* 109–112.

Mogg, K., Mathews, A., Bird, C., & MacGregor-Morris, R. (1990). Effects of stress and anxiety on the processing of threat stimuli. *Journal of Personality and Social Psychology, 59,* 1230–1237.

Mogg, K., Mathews, A., Eysenck, M., & May, J. (1991). Biased cognitive operations in anxiety: Artefact, processing priorities, or attentional search? *Behaviour Research and Therapy, 29,* 459–467.

Mogg, K., Mathews, A., & Weinman, J. (1989). Selective processing of threat cues in anxiety states: A replication. *Behaviour Research and Therapy, 27,* 317–323.

Monroe, S. M., & Simmons, A. D. (1991). Diathesis-stress theories in the context of life stress research: Implications for the depressive disorders. *Psychological Bulletin, 110,* 406–425.

Morey, L. C. (1993). Psychological correlates of personality disorder. *Journal of Personality Disorders, 7*(Suppl.), 149–166.

Morrow, J., & Nolen-Hoeksema, S. (1990). Effects of responses to depression on the remediation of depressive affect. *Journal of Personality and Social Psychology, 58,* 519–527.

Mussen, R. F., & Alloy, L. B. (1988). Depression and self-directed attention. In L. B. Alloy (Ed.), *Cognitive processes in depression* (pp. 193–220). New York: Guilford.

Nolen-Hoeksema, S. (1987). Sex differences in unipolar depression: Evidence and theory. *Psychological Bulletin, 101,* 259–282.

Nolen-Hoeksema, S. (1991). Responses to depression and their effects on the duration of depressive episodes. *Journal of Abnormal Psychology, 100,* 569–582.

Nolen-Hoeksema, S., & Morrow, J. (1993). The effects of rumination and distraction on naturally-occurring depressed moods. *Cognition and Emotion, 7,* 561–570.

Nolen-Hoeksema, S., Morrow, J., & Fredrickson, B. L. (1993). Response styles and the duration of episodes of depressed mood. *Journal of Abnormal Psychology, 102,* 20–28.

Nolen-Hoeksema, S., Parker, L. E., & Larson, J. (1994). Ruminative coping with depressed mood following loss. *Journal of Personality and Social Psychology, 67,* 92–104.

Pearlin, L. I. (1991). The study of coping: An overview of problems and directions. In J. Eckenrode (Ed.), *The social context of coping* (pp. 261–276). New York: Plenum.

Pennebaker, J. W. (1993). Overcoming inhibition: Rethinking the roles of personality, cognition, and social behaviors. In H. C. Traue & J. W. Pennebaker (Eds.), *Emotion, inhibition and health* (pp. 100–115). Toronto, Canada: Hogrefe & Huber.

Perry, J. C. (1988). A prospective study of life stress, defenses, psychotic symptoms, and depression in borderline and antisocial personality disorders and bipolar type II affective disorder. *Journal of Personality Disorders, 2,* 49–59.

Phillips, K. A., Hirschfeld, R. M. A., Shea, M. T., & Gunderson, J. G. (1993). Depressive personality disorders: Perspectives for DSM-IV. *Journal of Personality Disorders, 7,* 30–42.

Pyszczynski, T., & Greenberg, J. (1987). Depression, self-focused attention, and self-regulatory perseveration. In C. R. Snyder & C. E. Ford (Eds.), *Coping with negative life events: Clinical and social psychological perspectives* (pp. 105–129). New York: Plenum.

Pyszczynski, T., Greenberg, J., Hamilton, J., & Nix, G. (1991). On the relationship between self-focused attention and psychological disorder: A critical reappraisal. *Psychological Bulletin, 110,* 538–543.

Pyszczynski, T., Hamilton, J. C., Herring, F. H., & Greenberg, J. (1989). Depression, self-focused attention, and the negative memory bias. *Journal of Personality and Social Psychology, 57,* 351–357.

Rachman, S. J., & Hodgson, R. J. (1980). *Obsessions and compulsions.* Englewood Cliffs, NJ: Prentice-Hall.

Rapee, R. M. (1991). The conceptual overlap between cognition and conditioning in clinical psychology. *Clinical Psychology Review, 11,* 193–203.

Reed, G. F. (1985). *Obsessional experience and compulsive behaviour: A cognitive-structural approach.* Toronto, Canada: Academic Press.

Reiss, S. (1991). Expectancy model of fear, anxiety, and panic. *Clinical Psychology Review, 11,* 141–153.

Reiss, S., & McNally, R. J. (1985). Expectancy model of fear. In S. Reiss & R. R. Bootzin (Eds.), *Theoretical issues in behavior therapy* (pp. 107–121). New York: Academic Press.

Reiss, S., Peterson, R. A., Gursky, D. M., & McNally, R. J. (1986). Anxiety sensitivity, anxiety frequency, and the prediction of fearfulness. *Behaviour Research and Therapy, 24,* 1–8.

Salovey, P., & Mayer, J. D. (1990). Emotional intelligence. *Imagination, Cognition and Personality, 9,* 185–211.

Schneider, K. (1950). *Psychopathic personalities* (9th ed., English translation). London: Cassell. (Original work published 1923)

Skodol, A. E., & Perry, J. C. (1993). Should an axis for the defense mechanisms be included in the DSM-IV? *Comprehensive Psychiatry, 34,* 108–119.

Spielberger, C. D. (1972). Anxiety as an emotional state. In C. D. Spielberger (Ed.), *Anxiety: Current trends in theory and research* (Vol. 1). New York: Academic Press.

Stanton, A. L., Danoff-Burg, S., Cameron, C. L., & Ellis, A. P. (1994). Coping through emotional approach: Problems of conceptualization and confounding. *Journal of Personality and Social Psychology, 66,* 350–362.

Starcevic, V. (1992). Comorbidity models of panic disorder/agoraphobia and personality disturbance. *Journal of Personality Disorders, 6,* 213–225.

Staub, E. (1980). Social and prosocial behavior: Personal and situation influences and their interactions. In E. Staub (Ed.), *Personality: Basic aspects and current research.* Englewood Cliffs, NJ: Prentice-Hall.

Sternberg, R. J., & Frensch, P. A. (1990). Intelligence and cognition. In M. W. Eysenck (Ed.), *Cognitive psychology: An international review* (pp. 57–103). Toronto, Canada: Wiley.

Stewart, S. H., Knize, K., & Pihl, R. O. (1992). Anxiety sensitivity and dependency in clinical and nonclinical panickers and controls. *Journal of Anxiety Disorders, 6,* 119–131.

Summerfeldt, L. J. (1991). Obsessive-compulsive personality and anxiety: An application of the multidimensional interaction model. Unpublished master's thesis. Toronto, Canada: Psychology Department, York University.

Taylor, G. (1984). Alexithymia: Concept, measurement and implications for treatment. *American Journal of Psychiatry, 141,* 725–732.

Taylor, S., Koch, W. J., & Crockett, D. J. (1991). Anxiety sensitivity, trait anxiety, and the anxiety disorders. *Journal of Anxiety Disorders, 5,* 293–311.

Taylor, S., Koch, W. J., & McNally, R. J. (1992). How does anxiety sensitivity vary across the anxiety disorders? *Journal of Anxiety Disorders, 6,* 249–259.

Teasdale, J. D. (1988). Cognitive vulnerability to persistent depression. *Cognition and Emotion, 2,* 247–274.

Telch, M. J., Brouillard, M., Telch, C. F., Agras, W. S., & Taylor, A. B. (1989). Role of cognitive appraisal in panic-related avoidance. *Behaviour Research and Therapy, 27,* 373–383.

Tellegen, A. (1985). Structures of mood and personality and their relevance to assessing anxiety, with an emphasis on self-report. In A. H. Tuma & J. D. Maser (Eds.), *Anxiety and the anxiety disorders* (pp. 681–706). Hillsdale, NJ: Erlbaum.

Terry, D. J. (1991). Coping resources and situational appraisals as predictors of coping behavior. *Personality and Individual Differences, 12,* 1031–1047.

Terry, D. J. (1994). Determinants of coping: The role of stable and situational factors. *Journal of Personality and Social Psychology, 66,* 895–910.

Thoits, P. (1986). Social support as coping assistance. *Journal of Consulting and Clinical Psychology, 54,* 416–423.

Turner, R. A., King, P. R., & Tremblay, P. F. (1992). Coping styles and depression among psychiatric outpatients. *Personality and Individual Differences, 13,* 1145–1147.

Vaillant, G. E. (1987). A developmental view of old and new perspectives of personality disorders. *Journal of Personality Disorders, 1,* 146–156.

Vaillant, G. E. (1992). The historical origins and future potential of Sigmund Freud's concept of the mechanisms of defence. *International Review of Psycho-Analysis, 19,* 35–50.

Vaillant, G. E. (1993). *The wisdom of the ego.* Cambridge, MA: Harvard University Press.

Vaillant, G. E. (1994). Ego mechanisms of defense and personality psychopathology. *Journal of Abnormal Psychology, 103,* 44–50.

Vitaliano, P. P., DeWolfe, D. J., Maiuro, R. D., & Russo, J. (1990). Appraised changeability of a stressor as a modifier of the relationship between coping and depression: A test of the hypothesis of fit. *Journal of Personality and Social Psychology, 59,* 582–592.

Vredenberg, K., Flett, G. L., & Krames, L. (1993). Analogue versus clinical depression: A critical reappraisal. *Psychological Bulletin, 113,* 327–344.

Walters, J., & Gardner, H. (1986). The crystallizing experience: Discovering an intellectual gift. In R. J. Sternberg & J. E. Davidson (Eds.), *Conceptions of giftedness* (pp. 306–331). New York: Cambridge University Press.

Wardle, J., Ahmad, T., & Hayward, P. (1990). Anxiety sensitivity in agoraphobia. *Journal of Anxiety Disorders, 4,* 325–333.

Warren, R., & Zgourides, G. D. (1991). *Anxiety disorders: A rational-emotive perspective.* Toronto, Canada: Pergamon.

Watson, D., & Clark, L. A. (1992a). Affects separable and inseparable: On the hierarchical arrangement of the negative affects. *Journal of Personality and Social Psychology, 62,* 489–505.

Watson, D., & Clark, L. A. (1992b). On traits and temperament: General and specific factors of emotional experience and their relation to the five-factor model. *Journal of Personality, 60,* 441–476.

Watson, D., Clark, L. A., & Harkness, A. R. (1994). Structures of personality and their relevance to psychopathology. *Journal of Abnormal Psychology, 103,* 18–31.

Weston, D. (1991). Cognitive-behavioral interventions in the psychoanalytic psychotherapy of borderline personality disorders. *Clinical Psychology Review, 11,* 211–230.

Williams, J. M. G., & Scott, J. (1988). Autobiographical memory in depression. *Psychological Medicine, 18,* 689–695.

Wollersheim, J. P. (1984). *Coping therapy: Treatment manual.* Unpublished manuscript, University of Montana at Missoula.

Wood, J. V., Saltzberg, J. A., Neale, J. M., Stone, A. A., & Rachmiel, T. B. (1990). Self-focused attention, coping responses, and distressed mood in everyday life. *Journal of Personality and Social Psychology, 58,* 1027–1036.

Zeitlin, S. B., & McNally, R. J. (1993). Alexithymia and anxiety sensitivity in panic disorder and obsessive-compulsive disorder. *American Journal of Psychiatry, 150,* 658–660.

Zinbarg, R. E. (1990). Animal research and behavior therapy: Part I. Behavior therapy is not what you think it is. *Behavior Therapy, 13,* 171–175.

Zinbarg, R. E., Barlow, D. H., Brown, T. A., & Hertz, R. M. (1992). Cognitive-behavioral approaches to the nature and treatment of anxiety disorders. *Annual Review of Psychology, 43,* 235–236.

CHAPTER 27

Facilitating Coping with Chronic Physical Illness

GERALD M. DEVINS and YITZCHAK M. BINIK

Chronic conditions introduce significant psychosocial challenges and adaptive demands. These can include diagnostic uncertainties. Physical and cognitive disabilities, dependencies on professional expertise and biomedical technology, negative social biases and stigma, and illness intrusiveness (lifestyle disruptions) associated with chronic disease.

DIAGNOSTIC UNCERTAINTIES

The situation presented by chronic illness is often characterized by uncertainties that elicit significant anxiety and emotional distress. Many conditions remain difficult to diagnose until well after the onset of significant symptomatology. Diagnostic uncertainties threaten the sense of security and future predictability (Mushlin, Mooney, Grow, & Phelps, 1994). Such ambiguities may be especially stressful when effective treatments do not yet exist for the condition under investigation, as in Huntington's disease (Wiggins et al., 1992) or HIV/AIDS (Jacobsen, Perry, & Hirsch, 1990). Even in cases where effective treatment is available, aversive side effects or other consequences (e.g., pain, nausea, disfiguration) can introduce significant strains, as in cancer (Devins, Stam, & Koopmans, 1994). In many instances, individuals affected by chronic illness are forced to contend with the threat of death, despite available treatments that offer a good prognosis, as in end-stage renal disease (Devins, Mann, et al., 1990). Unpredictable variability in the course of illness introduces further uncertainties. A number of chronic illnesses follow a progressive course that gradually intensifies and extends across basic functions (e.g., memory, abstract reasoning, balance, fine motor control), although this may be punctuated by unpredictable episodes

Writing of this chapter was supported in part by a National Health Research Scholar Award from Health Canada to Gerald M. Devins. Thanks to Andy Gotowiec for valuable comments and suggestions.

of exacerbation and remission (e.g., multiple sclerosis, rheumatoid arthritis, systemic lupus erythematosus). Still other conditions may be characterized by variability in symptom expression (e.g., epilepsy), contributing to a sense of helplessness (DeVellis, Wallston, & Wallston, 1980).

DISABILITY

Disability is a second common feature of chronic illness (Thompson-Hoffman & Storck, 1991). Disability can involve limitations of mechanical function (e.g., physically disabling conditions may compromise functional capacity or abilities), cognitive control (e.g., neurological conditions often produce impairments of memory, abstract reasoning, and other deficits), or energy (e.g., cardiopulmonary conditions often impair physical strength and stamina) (Badley, Lee, & Wood, 1987). Pain (Binik et al., 1982; Devins, Armstrong, et al., 1990) is also common in chronic illness. In addition to their direct effects of human suffering, disability and pain limit one's ability to maintain involvements in valued activities and interests—contributing to *illness intrusiveness* and further compromising quality of life (Devins, 1994).

DEPENDENCY

Dependency on professional expertise and biomedical technology represents a third common stressful feature. Although all health care consumers can be considered dependent on service providers, the ongoing nature of chronic disease amplifies this aspect of the relationship. End-stage renal disease and its treatment by renal replacement therapy provide a good example. Once an individual has reached the end stage of irreversible kidney failure, ongoing renal replacement therapy by maintenance dialysis or kidney transplantation is required for survival. In the case of hemodialysis, the most widely used mode of dialytic therapy, sessions are typically scheduled three times weekly for an average of 4 to 6 hours per session and are usually delivered in a hospital or satellite center. Patients are immobilized during treatment as their blood is circulated extracorporeally through an artificial kidney to remove toxic metabolic waste products and excess fluid (water). In addition to monitoring interdialytic weight gains (an index of adherence to the relatively strict fluid-intake restrictions that accompany treatment), service providers routinely monitor blood pressure and serum electrolytes to evaluate the patient's adherence to dietary limitations and the complex pharmacological regimen. Individuals who fail to comply adequately are identified and counseled by various members of the treatment team (e.g., nephrologist, dialysis nurse, nutritionist, social worker). Because of comparatively stringent restrictions and the complex regimen associated with treatment, nonadherence is widespread and is considered a serious violation of the dialysis patient's role and responsibilities (Kirschenbaum, 1991). Not surprisingly, adherence to the therapeutic regimen frequently serves as the battleground on which a variety of struggles are played out between dialysis patients and their health care providers (Mars, 1991), resulting in significant interpersonal strain (Devins, Anthony, Mandin, & Taylor, 1983) and stress-related adjustment problems both for patients (Abram, Moore, & Westervelt, 1971; Goldstein, 1980; Somer & Tucker, 1992) and for staff (Devins, Anthony, et al., 1983; De-Nour, 1983).

BIASES AND STIGMA

Individuals with chronic conditions are also often the objects of negative biases (Wright, 1988) and stigma (Susman, 1994). Negative social stereotypes can lead the physically healthy to avoid interaction with the disabled and the chronically ill (Fichten, 1988). Stereotypes have been identified as significant barriers to employment opportunities and to vocational rehabilitation (King, 1994). Negative attitudes may also lead affected individuals to avoid social interaction with their healthier counterparts, further limiting the availability of satisfying and productive interpersonal exchange (Devins et al., 1994). Recent evidence indicates that such effects are insidious and can exert a deleterious impact in subtle and indirect ways. Health service providers who interact frequently with chronically ill individuals, for example, often maintain negative stereotypes that portray affected individuals as helpless and depressed, contributing unwittingly to the development of increased dependency and disillusionment (Devins, 1989). Even media campaigns intended to raise funds in support of efforts to conquer disabling and/or life-threatening conditions can undermine the image of the chronically ill as capable and independent (Adler, Wright, & Ulicny, 1991). In addition to compromising opportunities for productive social exchange and for maintaining involvements in valued activities and interests, social stereotypes and stigma may thus compromise feelings of independence and self-esteem (Crocker, Voelkl, Testa, & Major, 1991).

ILLNESS INTRUSIVENESS

Illness intrusiveness (illness-induced disruptions to valued activities and interests) represents a further adaptive challenge faced by people with chronic conditions (Devins, Binik, et al., 1983). As indicated, interference with lifestyles occurs commonly in chronic disease due to the operation of a variety of illness- and treatment-related factors. Pain, fatigue, disability, and severity of illness all have been identified as significant contributors to increased illness intrusiveness (Devins, Armstrong, et al., 1990; Devins, Edworthy, Guthrie, & Martin, 1992; Devins, Mandin, et al., 1990; Devins, Seland, Klein, Edworthy, & Saary, 1993). Moreover, treatment-related factors, such as differences in therapeutic modalities and the amount of time required for treatment have also been found to influence the extent to which an illness and/or its treatment intrude on important life domains (Binik, Chowanec, & Devins, 1990; Devins, 1989; Devins, Mandin, et al., 1990). Illness intrusiveness has been hypothesized to influence psychosocial well-being and quality of life in chronic illness through two complementary pathways (Devins, 1994; Devins, Edworthy, Guthrie, & Martin, 1992; Devins, Seland, et al., 1993). One involves the direct reduction of positively reinforcing experiences as a result of decreased involvement in valued activities and interests (including social exchange). The second mechanism involves reduced perceptions of personal control that, in turn, further limit the individual's ability to obtain positively valued outcomes and/or avoid negative ones (Devins et al., 1982).

Maintenance of hope, self-esteem, feelings of predictability and control, and a regular schedule of productive and satisfying involvements thus represents a significant challenge to individuals affected by chronic disease. In this chapter, we will review some of the most widely used methods to facilitate coping with chronic physical illness. Although we have organized interventions according to traditional labels (e.g., psychotherapy, cognitive-behavior therapy), we recognize that these categories overlap at times and are not mutually exclusive. Nonetheless, this strategy is heuristically useful since many of the studies predate the recent movement to identify common underlying components that form the basis for different interventions. Given the significance of the problem, this is a voluminous literature that spans several decades and mental health disciplines. In presenting this material, therefore, our coverage will be limited to a representative but not exhaustive review of relevant procedures. It will also be limited to work in which the focus of investigation has been on facilitating coping to achieve psychosocial well-being or to minimize emotional distress. We have not included literature that focuses on more specific problems, such as the management of chronic pain or delivery of diagnostic information, although these are certainly related to the broader issue of coping with chronic illness. Finally, our presentation has been limited largely to controlled experimental research in which the efficacy of therapeutic interventions has been evaluated against a comparison condition (e.g., no-treatment or attention-placebo control groups). We have, however, included uncontrolled investigations in a few special circumstances where they provide a particularly illuminating finding or consideration. Interested readers may wish to consult earlier reviews for additional coverage of these and related issues (e.g., Andersen, 1992; Devins & Hunsley, 1988; Holroyd & Creer, 1986; Massie & Straker, 1989; Mermelstein & Lesko, 1992; Spira & Spiegel, 1993).

PSYCHOTHERAPY

Psychotherapy has been employed to facilitate coping with a broad range of chronic diseases. A number of therapeutic elements have typically been incorporated within this approach. Treatment can be delivered individually or in a group format, time-limited or on an ongoing ("open-ended") basis. Psychotherapeutic efforts to facilitate coping with chronic illness have been guided by a variety of theoretical orientations, including psychoanalytic theory (Nezu, Nezu, & Perri, 1989), crisis intervention (Capone, Good, Westie, & Jacobson, 1980), humanistic psychology (Phillips & Osborne, 1989), and less widely known approaches (e.g., "confrontation problem-solving;" Godbole & Verinis, 1974). In many cases, therapeutic emphasis is placed on the identification and "working through" of intrapsychic conflicts that are believed to underlie difficulties in adapting effectively to the situation of chronic disease. Other psychotherapeutic work appears to be eclectic in orientation and is frequently described as "supportive" without specifying a particular theoretical or conceptual foundation. As a result, "psychotherapy" does not entail a uniquely defined intervention.

Regardless of the conceptual model that informs it, psychotherapy directed at coping with chronic illness typically emphasizes a number of common elements, including (a) interpersonal support; (b) validation of feelings; (c) exploration of issues (e.g., threats imposed by the condition; clarification of the problems with which the individual must contend); (d) corrective or interpretive feedback; and (e) encouragement to maintain hope. Verbal exchange provides the principal medium through which therapy is provided. Each of these components is believed to assist affected individuals in coping effectively with the threats imposed by chronic illness although the specific mechanisms through which these salubrious effects are believed to occur remain to be established. Unlike other verbal therapies (e.g., behavioral self-management, cognitive-behavior therapy), however, psychotherapeutic interventions do not focus on the acquisition of specific skills. Nor does traditional psychotherapy engage in directive challenges to erroneous or irrational assumptions and beliefs.

Group psychotherapy differs from individual approaches by including a number of affected individuals collectively in the therapeutic process. Especially when group composition is limited to individuals who share a common diagnosis, the collective exploration of issues is believed to provide the opportunity for group members to model diverse coping responses to a variety of challenges and issues that are likely to affect each participant at some point in his or her own illness (Mermelstein & Lesko, 1992). Such experiences also offer vicarious opportunities to observe and evaluate the outcomes produced by alternative coping responses, assisting participants in preparing for the time when they, too, will be required to deal with these issues. Group psychotherapy focused on coping with life-threatening conditions often relaxes the usual prohibition against personal contact among group members outside the therapeutic setting. In so doing, it is hoped that participants will experience an enhanced bonding with others in the group and the heightened sense of social support that this can be expected to produce (Spira & Spiegel, 1993). As cautioned by Spira and Spiegel (1993), however, methods that are capable of assisting individuals to cope more effectively can also produce harmful effects. Unstructured groups that lack clear and consistent therapist leadership may contribute to the escalation of anxieties to the detriment of participants. Forceful confrontation of avoidant coping styles (e.g., denial or repression), for example, may be especially destructive if the therapist fails to provide an effective alternative method to manage psychosocial threats and patient anxieties. Skillful direction by a leader can assist group members in confronting difficult issues constructively and effectively.

Table 27.1 summarizes representative studies that have investigated the efficacy of traditional individual and group psychotherapy to facilitate coping with chronic illness. As is evident in this table, investigators have examined a broad range of interventions and an even broader range of therapeutic outcomes. Several studies indicate that group and individual psychotherapeutic interventions can, and in many cases do, assist individuals in coping more effectively with chronic disease. Among the outcomes observed are reductions in both depressive symptoms and emotional distress, improved self-concepts and self-esteem, improved stress management and other coping skills, as well as reduced duration of hospitalization, decreased physical symptomatology, and even improved survival.

Also evident in Table 27.1, however, is that experimental results have been inconsistent. A number of studies have reported no reliable benefit from psychotherapy beyond that produced by no-treatment or usual-care control conditions. The final column in this table lists some of the major methodological strengths and weaknesses of the studies reviewed. Although a number of studies included randomized and controlled experimental designs, several did not. Many studies included standardized instrumentation and repeated assessments (including follow-up well beyond the conclusion of therapeutic involvement). Few studies included effective controls, however, for demand characteristics (Adair & Spinner, 1979) or experimenter-bias effects (Rosenthal & Rubin, 1978). Heterogeneity across participants (e.g., diagnoses, prognoses, severity of illness, stage in the treatment process) further threatens the internal validity of experimental results (Binik, Devins, & Orme, 1989). Few studies clearly described or defined the component interventions that composed the psychotherapy delivered to participants. Such omission of basic procedural details limits the potential for independent replication and inhibits incorporation of experimentally validated techniques into routine clinical practice. Although this literature has succeeded in substantiating the assertion that psychotherapeutic efforts are able to facilitate coping with chronic illness, research has not yet articulated and tested specific hypotheses that identify the mechanism or "active ingredient(s)" responsible for these effects. This gap in our knowledge represents an important challenge for future research.

COGNITIVE-BEHAVIOR THERAPY

As a more recent alternative to psychotherapy to facilitate coping with chronic illness, efforts based on cognitive-behavior therapy (e.g., Kirschenbaum, 1991) overcome many of the foregoing limitations. Two of the working hypotheses underlying the cognitive-behavioral model are similar to those underlying other psychotherapeutic efforts. First, it is the *interpretation* of illness-imposed stressors and constraints that produces psychosocial threats and adaptive demands. Second, it is the individual's *response* to this appraisal that determines whether

TABLE 27.1 Psychotherapy to Facilitate Coping with Illness

Study	Condition	Participants	Component Interventions	Results	Comments
Capone et al. (1980)	Gynecological cancer	97 patients	Individual psychological counseling (crisis intervention), emphasizing behavioral change, throughout hospitalization period.	Significantly reduced emotional distress and improved self-concept. Experimental group demonstrated superior improvements in self-concept, vocational rehabilitation, and sexual functioning compared with control group.	Nonrandomized control group design; repeated assessments at 3, 6, and 12 months posttreatment; standardized instrumentation; no control for demand characteristics
Compton & Purviance (1992)	Various chronic illnesses (including cardiovascular, neurological, rheumatological, and pulmonary)	14 outpatients referred for psychiatric treatment	Time-limited supportive group psychotherapy; twelve 90-minute sessions, emphasizing validation of feelings, interpersonal understanding, and problem solving.	Majority of participants rated treatment as highly helpful. No significant improvements as evidenced by standardized instrumentation. Statistically significant reduction in outpatient clinic visits and health service use.	Uncontrolled pre-post single group design; some standardized instrumentation; no follow-up assessment; small sample; demand characteristics not controlled; referral bias not controlled.
Ferlic et al. (1979)	Advanced cancer	60 recently diagnosed ($M = 7$ months) patients	Six 90-minute supportive psychoeducational group sessions grounded in crisis theory. Meetings occurred three times per week and were co-led by a social worker and a "content expert" (one of physician, nurse, occupational therapist, dietician, chaplain, depending on focus for the session). Sessions incorporated an educational emphasis and covered nursing perspectives, medical aspects, psychological aspects, religion, sexuality, nutrition, and exercise.	Experimental group demonstrated significant improvements in "group aptitude," hospital adjustment, relationship strength, cancer information, death perceptions, and self-concept relative to control group. Six-month follow-up indicated that differences between experimental counseling and control groups persisted after conclusion of intervention.	Controlled trial (not clear whether randomized); some standardized instrumentation (self-concept); 6 month follow-up; small sample; no control for nonspecific effects of experimental intervention (e.g., increased concern and attention); referral bias not controlled.

Ford et al. (1990)	Cancer	39 distressed outpatients	Time-limited group therapy (six 90-min. sessions), emphasizing interpersonal support, not designed to provide treatment information or cognitive-behavioral techniques.	No significant improvement in anxiety or depression resulted from therapy.	Uncontrolled pre-post design; repeated measurement 3 months after completion of therapy; standardized instrumentation; majority of eligible participants (108 of 120, 80%) refused or were unable to participate in therapy; demand characteristics not controlled.
Forester et al. (1985)	Cancer (various sites)	100 outpatients receiving radiotherapy at a tertiary care hospital	10 weekly unstructured 30-minute sessions of "supportive" psychotherapy where patient determined the focus. Treatment was initiated prior to commencement of radiotherapy and continued for 4 weeks following its completion.	All participants demonstrated significant reductions in "emotional distress" (composite of anxiety, depression, pessimism, asymptomatic preoccupation, worry, social isolation, and withdrawal) following conclusion of radiotherapy. Psychotherapy group demonstrated significantly greater reductions compared with the control group. This advantage was maintained 4 weeks following the conclusion of radiotherapy.	Randomized controlled trial; standardized instrumentation (Schedule of Affective Disorders and Schizophrenia); 4-week follow-up; large sample size; heterogeneous subject group; intervention described in global terms.

(Continued)

TABLE 27.1 *(Continued)*

Study	Condition	Participants	Component Interventions	Results	Comments
Godbole & Verinis (1974)	Geriatric patients with various conditions	61 rehabilitation hospital inpatients	Brief "confrontation problem-solving" (individual) psychotherapy (10–15 min. sessions) provided thrice weekly during hospitalization (6–12 sessions).	Both treatment groups demonstrated significantly lower depression and improved self-concept compared with no treatment control group.	Randomized controlled trial: brief psychotherapy with confrontation vs. brief supportive psychotherapy vs. no treatment control; standardized measures of depression and self-concept, staff ratings, discharge plans; no control for demand characteristics; heterogenous diagnostic mix may obscure important effects.
Gruen (1975)	Myocardial infarction	75 patients, aged 40–69	Individual psychotherapy incorporating 10 therapeutic components, emphasizing support, exploration, feedback, and encouragement.	Psychotherapy recipients showed significant benefits: (a) decreased incidence of congestive heart failure; (b) fewer days in hospital, in intensive care, and on monitor; (c) decreased anxiety, depression, and increased surgency.	Randomized controlled trial; multimethod measurement; standardized instrumentation; results were stronger when comparisons excluded "well-adjusted patients."
Harris et al. (1985)	Head and neck cancer	142 patients (males) and 33 family members	Weekly 50-min. support group sessions, primarily intended to provide support and understanding through sharing of feelings and discussion of problems. Also provided opportunities to practice artificial speech and communication.	Impressionistic findings indicated that therapists and other staff believed the group to have been helpful. Group cohesiveness appeared to increase. Tabulation of most common group themes included (in descending order of frequency): anticipation of or reaction to treatment, adaptation following treatment, interaction with family, losses due to cancer, peer support, smoking, and eating difficulties.	Uncontrolled pre-post single group design; unstandardized instrumentation; no follow-up.

Study	Condition	Sample	Intervention	Results	Methodological notes
Ibrahim et al. (1974)	Myocardial infarction	118 postdischarge inpatients who initially required intensive care	50 weekly 90-min. supportive group therapy sessions, emphasizing self-disclosure and shared problems and feelings. Although therapists encouraged self-exploration, groups preferred to limit focus to more practical "here-and-now" concerns (practical realities of everyday living, such as constructive use of leisure time).	No significant benefits observed among therapy group compared with (no treatment) control group. Among individuals with more severe heart disease at intake into the experiment, survival was significantly higher among therapy recipients compared with control group participants.	Randomized controlled trial; primarily standardized instrumentation; large sample.
Linn et al. (1982)	Cancer	120 men with end-stage (IV) cancer	Frequent supportive (individual) counseling according to Kubler-Ross principles, including trusting relationship, reduction of denial and maintenance hope, life review; involvement in meaningful activities.	Significantly greater improvements in depression, life satisfaction, and self-esteem among therapy recipients than controls. No changes or group differences in alienation, locus of control, functional abilities, or survival. Effects of counseling were most pronounced at 3-month follow-up and attenuated by 12-month follow-up.	Randomized controlled trial; repeated measurements at 3, 6, 9, and 12 months post-counseling; standardized instruments; large sample; demand characteristics not controlled; mortality attrition bias not controlled.
Poulsen (1991)	Rheumatoid arthritis or Sjörgren's syndrome	46 women	Time-limited psychodynamic group psychotherapy; twelve 90-minute sessions, biweekly meetings.	Alexithymia and self-reported "well-being" improved in psychotherapy but not control group. No improvements for either group on other standardized instruments.	Randomized controlled trial; standardized instrumentation; referred by attending physicians (referral bias); demand characteristics not controlled; differences not tested statistically.

(Continued)

TABLE 27.1 *(Continued)*

Study	Condition	Participants	Component Interventions	Results	Comments
Spiegel et al. (1981)	Metastatic breast cancer	58 women	Weekly 90-min. supportive group therapy sessions which continued to meet throughout the study period (12 months or longer). Primarily supportive focus, including high cohesion and limited confrontation, self-disclosure, and sharing of mutual concerns; discussions of death and dying; related family problems; difficulties in medical treatment; communication with physicians, and "living as richly as possible in the face of a terminal illness" (p. 529).	Treatment group demonstrated significant reductions in mood disturbance over 12 months of study compared with (no-treatment) control group. Treatment group used fewer "maladaptive" methods of managing stress compared with control group.	Randomized controlled trial; repeated measurements at 4, 8, and 12 months; standardized instrumentation; directly measured coping behavior; demand characteristics not controlled; suggested several theoretical mechanisms to account for results.
Spiegel & Bloom (1983)	Metastatic breast cancer	54 women	Identical to group intervention described for Spiegel et al. (Spiegel, Bloom, & Yalom, 1981) study with one exception: One group was randomly assigned to conclude with a self-hypnosis exercise that was designed to alter the experience of pain. Self-hypnosis instruction was to "filter the hurt out of the pain" by imagining competing sensations.	Self-hypnosis group demonstrated significant reductions in pain compared with control group that received supportive group therapy without hypnosis. Reduced pain correlated significantly with reduced mood disturbance.	Randomized controlled trial; repeated measurements at 4, 8, and 12 months following randomization; standardized instrumentation; directly measured pain; demand characteristics not controlled; suggested a theoretical mechanism to account for results.

the psychosocial consequences of coping efforts will be positive or negative. Whereas traditional psychotherapy has tended to focus on unresolved intrapsychic conflicts and/or to provide nonspecific support, cognitive-behavioral therapies focus specifically on the problematic appraisals (e.g., irrational beliefs, cognitive errors) and coping skill deficits (e.g., stress management) that are hypothesized to account for difficulties in adapting to life with a chronic condition. From this perspective, therefore, assisting affected individuals to acquire or enhance such skills can contribute importantly by bolstering their abilities to cope effectively.

A number of cognitive-behavioral skills can be employed to enhance coping effectiveness (Meichenbaum, 1977). These include stress-management skills, such as progressive relaxation, meditation, breathing control; cognitive restructuring techniques, such as challenging irrational beliefs or cognitive reframing (e.g., reconstruing a potentially threatening situation as a challenge that creates opportunities and motivates one to respond adaptively); and stress inoculation training in which individuals are taught to integrate these skills into their everyday experience to minimize the potentially deleterious effects of repeated daily hassles and other stressful encounters (Meichenbaum, 1985). A number of programs have incorporated problem-solving training (D'Zurilla, 1986) into cognitive-behavioral interventions. Based on the premise that effective problem-solving is fundamental to competent coping, training assists individuals in acquiring skills in several domains, including problem definition and formulation, generation of alternative solutions, decision making, and solution implementation and verification (see also Nezu, Nezu, & Perri, 1989). In some cases (e.g., Edgar, Rosberger, & Nowlis, 1992), problem-solving in the context of coping with chronic disease has been extended to include appropriate methods for accessing health care and related services.

Cognitive-behavioral interventions have been enhanced by the pioneering efforts of Beck and his associates (e.g., Beck, Rush, Shaw, & Emery, 1979) in dealing with depression, a frequent concomitant of chronic disease (Rodin, Craven, & Littlefield, 1991). Although biological (and biochemical) factors are germane to the etiology and treatment of depression and other disorders, a discussion of these factors is beyond the scope of this chapter. Techniques for identifying and challenging cognitive errors and distortions have been adapted and integrated into intervention efforts with some success (Evans, Smith, Werkhoven, Fox, & Pritzl, 1986; Larcombe & Wilson, 1984). Other behavioral techniques that have proven effective in ameliorating depression in clinically depressed but physically healthy populations have also been adapted effectively to facilitate coping with chronic disease. Lewinsohn's (Lewinsohn, Sullivan, & Grosscup, 1982) pleasant event scheduling, for example, as well as training in assertion and social skills have proven effective when incorporated into cognitive-behavioral efforts to facilitate adaptation among the chronically ill (Basler & Rehfisch, 1991; Fiegenbaum, 1981; Telch & Telch, 1986).

Table 27.2 summarizes representative studies of cognitive-behavioral interventions to facilitate coping with a wide variety of chronic diseases. As is evident in

TABLE 27.2   Cognitive-Behavior Therapy to Facilitate Coping with Chronic Illness

Study	Condition	Participants	Component Interventions	Results	Comments
Basler & Rehfisch (1991)	Ankylosing spondylitis	39 self-help group members	12 weekly 90-min. group cognitive-behavior therapy sessions, including training in progressive muscle relaxation, cognitive restructuring, attention-related techniques, and pleasant activity scheduling. Emphasis on increased behavioral self-control.	Significant improvements in depression, anxiety, daily mood, pain, and sleep in therapy (experimental) but not control group at posttreatment; gains maintained at 6-month follow-up. Clearest benefits involved improved psychosocial well-being; least change noted in pain and pain management skills.	Randomized controlled trial; repeated measurements, including pre- & posttreatment, 6-month follow-up; some standardized instrumentation; volunteer selection bias threatens external validity.
DeVellis et al. (1988)	Rheumatoid arthritis	101 outpatients registered with a university-affiliated clinic	All patients participated in a preliminary psychosocial interview that assessed lifestyle arthritis-imposed problems and identified the potential resources that might be mobilized to cope with them. Experimental intervention consisted of an additional 1-hour one-on-one problem-solving intervention composed of six components: problem identification and confirmation; identification of alternative strategies to deal with problem; identification of potential inhibitors; selection of "best" potential solution; development of plan for action; subsequent (2 weeks) follow-up to evaluate need for further intervention.	Intervention group solved significantly more problems in domains of "lifestyle" and adherence to exercise regimen compared with control group. All participants (both experimental and control) reported significant reductions in arthritis symptom severity (e.g., fatigue, stiffness, swelling, pain), impairment with physical activities, and depressive symptoms posttreatment. Intervention and control groups did not differ significantly, however, for these or any of the other outcomes examined (e.g., anxiety, helplessness, self-esteem, internality, dexterity, mobility, physical activities, household activities, activities of daily living, or social activities).	Randomized controlled trial; standardized instrumentation; pretest sensitization due to preliminary psychosocial assessment may account for lack of difference between groups; longer follow-up interval may have helped to detect differences.

| Edgar et al. (1992) | Cancer (predominantly breast cancer but numerous other diagnoses included) | 205 male and female out-patients | Five 1-hour sessions, addressing problem solving, goal setting, cognitive reappraisal, relaxation training, and effective use of health care resources. | Significant improvements in depression, anxiety, intrusive thoughts, and personal control for both immediate and delayed treatment groups. Delayed treatment group demonstrated superior improvements relative to immediate treatment at 8-month follow-up. Group differences did not persist at 12-month follow-up. | Randomized controlled trial, comparing cognitive-behavioral intervention delivered immediately ($M = 10.8$ weeks after diagnosis) vs. following a 4-month delay ($M = 28.2$ weeks after diagnosis); standardized instrumentation; repeated assessments: baseline, 4, 8, and 12 months posttherapy; no controls for "attention" or other nonspecific influences. |
| Evans et al. (1986) | Physical disability | 50 outpatients, discharged from a rehabilitation medicine service within preceding 30 months | Weekly 1-hour group therapy sessions, focussing on problem solving, correcting cognitive distortions and errors, and goal attainment. | 16 of 21 treatment group participants reported achievement of their goals (number of control group members who achieved their goals not reported). Treatment group demonstrated significant reductions in loneliness compared with control group (improvement maintained at 3-month follow-up). No significant changes noted in depression or life satisfaction. | Randomized controlled trial; 3-month follow-up assessed maintenance of therapeutic gains; standardized instrumentation; sample size may not have afforded adequate statistical power; intervention inadequately described; numerous procedural details unreported. |

(Continued)

TABLE 27.2 (*Continued*)

Study	Condition	Participants	Component Interventions	Results	Comments
Fiegenbaum (1981)	Survivors of disfiguring surgery (head/neck cancer)	17 visibly disfigured postsurgical otolaryngology patients	10 weekly 2-hour group social skills training sessions, focusing on social skills: establishing contact; expressing wishes and stating demands; expression of rejection; and tolerance of criticism from others. Behavioral objectives and suggested performance guidelines specified for each of 36 training situations, followed by role-play and behavioral rehearsal. Introductory session presented didactic coverage of reinforcement and self-regulation in social interaction.	Experimental—but not control—group improved significantly in feelings of general insecurity, (social) contact anxiety, ability to express rejection, and anxiety in social situations. Neither group changed in ability to tolerate criticism, to express demands, or feelings of "self-discontent." Posttreatment results remained unchanged at 2-year folow-up.	Matched control group design (not random assignment); long-term follow-up evaluated durability of benefits; focused intervention relevant to problems faced by participants; European (German) questionnaires unfamiliar to many readers; no control for demand characteristics; no direct measure of coping (e.g., social skill).
Foley et al. (1987)	Multiple sclerosis	40 outpatients	Six stress inoculation training sessions, including cognitive-behavior therapy, progressive muscle relaxation training (adapted for MS), self-monitoring of daily stressors, self-statement responses to stressors, role-play and rehearsal of adaptive responses to distressing situations.	Significant improvement in depression, state anxiety, coping with daily stressors, and problem-focused coping in therapy recipients compared with controls. No changes in trait anxiety or locus of control.	Randomized controlled trial, control group received routine treatment that included psychosocial support; standardized instrumentation; multivariate repeated measures statistical analyses; no controls for "attention" or other nonspecific effects.

| Greene & Blanchard (1994) | Irritable bowel syndrome | 20 outpatients (15 female, 5 male) | Ten 1-hour cognitive therapy sessions, emphasizing cognitive determinants of symptomatology, identification and self-monitoring of threatening appraisals and automatic thoughts. Therapy also included elements challenging irrational beliefs, "decentering" (acknowledging idiosyncratic nature of automatic thoughts), and "experiential disconfirmation" via planned behavioral enactments. | Gastrointestinal symptoms decreased more in experimental group than in symptom-monitoring control group. Significant improvements in depression, automatic thoughts, and dysfunctional attitudes among experimental but not control group. Clinically significant improvements persisted for 77% of experimental but less than 50% of control group members at 3-month follow-up. | Randomized controlled trial (control group monitored symptoms while experimental group received therapy); standardized instrumentation; repeated measurements pre- and posttreatment and at 3-month follow-up; component interventions clearly described; measured process variables (automatic thoughts, dysfunctional attitudes) directly; clinical significance of results communicated quantitatively; small sample size; no control for "attention" or other non-specific effects. |
| Greer et al. (1991) | Cancer (various diagnoses) | 44 consecutive outpatients | Six individual "adjuvant psychological therapy" sessions, incorporating identification and challenging of negative automatic thoughts, anticipation and rehearsal of adaptive responses to impending stressful events, relaxation training, cultivation of "fighting spirit" through behavioral homework emphasizing mastery and positive self-image. When operative, denial not challenged directly. | Significant pre- to posttreatment reductions in anxiety, depression, helplessness, anxious preoccupation, and fatalism; significant increase in fighting spirit. No negative effects of therapy. | Uncontrolled pre-post design; standardized instrumentation; no follow-up to assess durability of benefits. |

(Continued)

TABLE 27.2 (*Continued*)

Study	Condition	Participants	Component Interventions	Results	Comments
Greer et al. (1992)	Cancer (all diagnoses except cerebral tumors and nonmelanoma skin cancers)	174 consecutive patients 4–12 weeks after diagnosis or first recurrence who disclosed clinically elevated distress as indicated by psychological tests (e.g., Hospital Anxiety and Depression Scale)	"Adjuvant psychological therapy" comprises six individual 1-hour sessions (conjoint with spouse if patient desired). Therapy focuses on "personal meaning" of cancer and responses to this. Component interventions include identifying personal strengths, overcoming helplessness and fostering a fighting spirit, identification and challenging of negative automatic thoughts, role-play and rehearsal in imagination, pleasant events scheduling, communication between patient and spouse, and progressive relaxation.	Experimental therapy group demonstrated significant benefits at 8 weeks relative to control group for most psychosocial outcomes, including fighting spirit, helplessness, anxious preoccupation, fatalism, anxiety, depression, "psychological symptoms," and positive health care orientation. Benefits persisted at 4-month follow-up with continued improvement differential in favor of experimental group on symptoms of depression and anxiety. Clinical significance of improvements was indicated by proportions of groups whose scores on standardized tests remained in clinically significant range.	Randomized controlled trial; standardized instrumentation; component interventions described clearly; repeated assessments at pre- and posttreatment, 8-weeks, and 4-months follow-up; no controls for "attention" or other nonspecific effects; diagnostically heterogeneous sample.
Kemp et al. (1992)	Various disabling conditions, including rheumatoid arthritis, stroke, osteoporosis, heart disease, and pulmonary disease	41 aged ($M = 74$ yr) individuals meeting DSM-III/RDC criteria for major depression, 18 with a chronic illness and 23 with no physical illness	12 weekly group cognitive-behavior therapy sessions focused on role of cognition and behavior in depression. Therapy also emphasized increased activity level. Groups led by 2 licensed clinical psychologists.	Depressive symptoms improved significantly from pre- to posttherapy for both groups; no change over follow-up period. Rate of improvement did not differ across groups.	Nonequivalent comparison group design; repeated measurements at 6 and 12 weeks, 6 and 12 months posttherapy; standardized instrumentation; nonspecific factors not controlled.

| Larcombe & Wilson (1984) | Multiple sclerosis | 20 depressed outpatients | Six weekly 90-min. group cognitive-behavior therapy sessions adhering to Beck's model, including behavioral activation, self-monitoring and behavioral contracting to increase pleasant activities; monitoring of positive and negative thoughts and moods; identification and challenging of depressogenic thoughts, irrational beliefs, and cognitive distortions. | Significant improvement in depression and mood (both self-report and collateral ratings) in cognitive-behavior therapy group; no change in wait-list control group. No treatment effects on two of six criterion variables (best or average daily mood). Posttreatment improvements maintained at follow-up. | Randomized controlled trial; repeated measurements at pre- & post-treatment, 4-week follow-up; clinically significant reduction in depression among therapy recipients; small sample size; short follow-up interval. |
| Moorey et al. (1994) | Cancer (all diagnoses except cerebral tumors and nonmelanoma skin cancers) | 134 of the participants in the Greer et al. (1992) study who completed 12-month follow-up assessments | Adjuvant psychological therapy (described above for Greer et al.) | Experimental therapy group continued to demonstrate significant improvement, relative to control group, from 4 to 12 months for three outcomes: anxiety, "psychological symptoms," and psychological distress; nonsignificant "deterioration" for other psychosocial measures among experimental group participants. Control group scores remained unchanged from 4-month measurements. | Same methodological strengths as noted for Greer et al.; 12-month follow-up: no attrition since 4-month follow-up; analyses did not control for pretreatment group differences. |

(Continued)

TABLE 27.2 (*Continued*)

Study	Condition	Participants	Component Interventions	Results	Comments
Telch & Telch (1986)	Cancer (heterogeneous with regard to site, stage, duration, and treatment)	41 outpatients experiencing "psychosocial distress"	Six weekly 90-minute group sessions, emphasizing acquisition and rehearsal of cognitive, behavioral, and affective coping strategies via homework assignments, goal setting, self-monitoring, behavioral rehearsal and role-playing, feedback coaching. Separate coping skills modules focused on relaxation and stress management; communication and assertion; problem solving and constructive thinking; feelings management; and pleasant activity planning. Control group participants received either supportive group therapy aimed at emotional catharsis or no psychological intervention.	Significant reductions in mood disturbance in experimental coping skills training group, whereas no-treatment control group demonstrated significant deterioration; outcome measures did not change in supportive control group. Identical pattern of results for perceived self-efficacy in relation to coping with cancer and its treatment. Experimental group also reported significantly fewer cancer-related problems at posttest compared with the two control groups. Results based on self-report inventories were corroborated by standardized interviews.	Randomized controlled trial; standardized instrumentation; posttest data collected 6 weeks following the conclusion of group skills training; coping behavior measured directly; control groups control for attention-placebo and nonspecific effects; therapeutic intervention well specified and clearly described; small sample size.

the table, the consistent approach has been to provide affected individuals with focused training in specific coping skills rather than to address unresolved intrapsychic conflicts. In many cases, the components of cognitive-behavioral interventions have been described in detail. Such description can be especially useful when it facilitates replication efforts and assists readers in incorporating validated intervention components into clinical practice.

The research evidence cited in Table 27.2 indicates clearly that cognitive-behavioral interventions have been effective in producing clinically significant benefits in terms of several psychosocial outcomes. Benefits have included reduced emotional distress (e.g., anxiety, depression, loneliness, worry, and intrusive thoughts) and, in a number of cases, improved psychosocial well-being (e.g., improved mood, happiness, life satisfaction, and self-esteem). Many of these studies have also demonstrated that cognitive-behavioral interventions have succeeded in assisting individuals to acquire useful new coping skills (e.g., increased problem-focused coping, social skills, problem solving) as well as assisting them in reducing dysfunctional attitudes and irrational beliefs. A number of randomized controlled trials have been conducted, generating encouraging support for the clinical efficacy of such efforts. The adoption of widely used psychometrically sound measures also adds to the usefulness of these studies.

Although much of this research has been of a high caliber, important issues remain to be addressed. Foremost, perhaps, is whether the benefits demonstrated in this literature can be attributed specifically to the cognitive-behavioral skills acquired in therapy. Few studies have included attention-placebo conditions or attempted otherwise to control for the therapeutic effects of increased professional interest, social support, or other nonspecific effects implicit in any therapeutic relationship. Such factors can exert powerful influences and may be attributable more to generic features of the helping relationship than to any specific interventions or skills (Frank, 1974; Roberts, Kewman, Mercier, & Hovell, 1993). A second important issue involves the durability of therapeutic benefits. Although the few studies that examined this issue produced encouraging results, most have not yet addressed the long-term maintenance of therapeutic gains. It is not clear that the skills acquired in therapy continue to be used effectively once formal meetings have ended.

SOCIAL SUPPORT INTERVENTIONS

Social exchange and support can facilitate coping with chronic disease. The supportive potential of social contact has long been recognized (Lynch, 1977) and has stimulated the burgeoning of mutual aid and patient self-help groups (Cella, Sarafian, Snider, Yellen, & Winicour, 1993). Typically, the emphasis in such programs is on interpersonal exchange and information sharing in the context of an understanding group that endeavors to provide members with encouragement and mutual support in contending with illness-induced difficulties. Accounts of self-help group experiences testify both to the positive and negative effects that can occur. In addition to enhanced self-esteem and perceived social support, self-help group participants have noted that other members can be especially helpful by modeling effective coping strategies and solutions in response to illness-related problems. Negative effects can accrue, however, when ineffective or inappropriate health behavior is demonstrated. Involvement in self-help groups may also be distressing when other members experience exacerbations or relapses to which participants themselves may be susceptible (such negative effects are not limited to mutual aid groups and can occur in any group comprising chronically ill people). Because of their generally low cost and flexibility to deal with a wide range of problems, self-help groups are frequently cited as a promising alternative to professional treatment. It is somewhat surprising, therefore, that a comparatively small proportion of individuals with chronic conditions actually subscribe to mutual aid groups. As noted by Taylor and Aspinwall (Taylor & Aspinwall, 1990), self-help groups appeal disproportionately to well-educated, middle-class white females, a population already well served by professionally delivered programs. Indeed, many of the same individuals who participate in mutual aid groups regularly access a number of other supportive and professional services (Taylor, Falke, Shoptaw, & Lichtman, 1986).

Formal efforts to design patient support programs and to evaluate their effectiveness are more recent developments. Stimulated, in part, by striking evidence that continued social contact can produce a significant survival advantage among individuals affected by such diverse conditions as breast cancer (Spiegel, Bloom, Kraemer, & Gottheil, 1989), myocardial infarction (Frasure-Smith & Prince, 1985, 1989), and end-stage renal disease (Friend, Singletary, Mendell, & Nurse, 1986), research has begun to document the beneficial effects that can accrue from ongoing supportive contact. Findings that supportive social contact may profoundly impact fundamental health outcomes such as survival or the course of illness are both impressive and surprising, challenging the limits of established knowledge and theory (Ader, 1981; Engel, 1977).

While considering the value of supportive social contact in facilitating coping with chronic illness, however, it is important to recognize that physical disease and ill health often occur in individuals who are comparatively well adjusted psychologically, notwithstanding that a number of chronic conditions may be attributable, at least in part, to maladaptive health behavior (e.g., lifestyle factors, such as smoking, obesity, or alcohol and other substance use) and/or behavioral styles (e.g., type A behavior pattern). The vast majority of affected individuals may thus derive substantial benefit simply from the support provided by regular social contact and exchange. Research in social support has indicated, for example, that ongoing social contact can provide a variety of significant benefits in addition to emotional support and maintenance of self-esteem, including the provision of informational, financial, and instrumental assistance (Ader, 1981; Engel, 1977).

The onset of chronic illness can be highly disorganizing, necessitating a readjustment of lifestyles, activities, and interests (Devins, 1994). Such effects are especially challenging in those cases where the affected individual is also characterized by specific coping deficits. Under such circumstances, more than social support alone may be needed to facilitate effective adaptation. Evidence consistent with this reasoning may be taken from contradictory research findings concerning the benefits of socially supportive interventions. As indicated in Table 27.3, evidence substantiates the claim that socially supportive interventions are associated with psychosocial well-being in chronic illness groups; some results have failed, however, to support this hypothesis. Given the continuing operation of illness-imposed stressors and constraints, additional attention to particular appraisals, coping strategies, and skills is likely necessary to facilitate effective and durable coping even when one has access to a richly supportive social sphere (Devins, 1989, 1991; Lepore, Evans, & Schneider, 1991).

Inconsistent findings may also be attributable, in part, to the failure to address coping appraisals and/or behavior directly in experimental investigations. Indeed, most studies to date have not tested any particular mechanism(s) by which socially supportive interventions may facilitate coping with chronic illness. Many of the positive findings in this literature have actually been serendipitous; experiments were not designed to test specific hypotheses that could account for the unexpected benefits of enhanced social support. Especially troubling are those few instances where initial serendipitous findings have been followed up with more rigorous large-scale investigations that have failed to replicate the psychosocial benefits observed in the initial experiment even though results indicate that the intervention did enhance feelings of social support (e.g., Weinberger, Tierney, Booher, & Katz, 1991).

Although socially supportive relationships may indeed facilitate coping with chronic illness, it is not yet clear how this is achieved. Future research can contribute usefully by specifying testable hypotheses that map out the mechanisms by which socially supportive interventions facilitate effective coping. It may be especially promising to begin focusing on specific methods that can be employed by affected individuals to identify potential sources of social support and to elicit this where available.

PATIENT EDUCATION

One of the earliest and most common strategies to facilitate adaptation to chronic disease has been to provide affected individuals with information about their illness and its treatment with the expectation that they can then employ this knowledge in responding to the constraints introduced by their condition. Emphasis is on predictability and informational control (Averill, 1973) and on providing patients with sufficient information to respond effectively to illness-imposed challenges and demands as they arise. Patient education efforts have been directed at a wide range of chronic conditions (interested readers are referred to earlier reviews, e.g., by Bartlett, 1985; Daltroy & Liang, 1993; Ley, 1989; Lorig, Konkol, & Gonzalez, 1987; Mazzuca, 1982). Traditional patient education efforts have focused almost exclusively on providing information about

TABLE 27.3 Social Support Interventions to Facilitate Coping with Illness

Study	Condition	Participants	Component Interventions	Results	Comments
Evans & Jaureguy (1982)	Visual impairment	84 aged VA outpatients	Eight weekly 1-hour telephone conference calls involving a counselor and three patients. Therapeutic foci included expression of social problem areas, provision of information about resources, problem-solving, development of camaraderie, and building confidence.	Intervention recipients demonstrated significant improvement, relative to controls, in three domains: reduced loneliness, increased outside social activities, and increased performance of household chores. No significant improvements were noted for interpersonal involvement, depression, agitation, substance use, memory, self-care abilities, or motor skills.	Randomized controlled trial; no follow-up to assess maintenance of therapeutic gains; adequate sample size; hypothesized mediator variables measured directly; standardized instrumentation; no controls for "attention" or other nonspecific effects; overlaps between "supportive telephone contact" and group psychotherapy.
Frasure-Smith & Prince (1985)	Myocardial infarction	769 male survivors of recent myocardial infarction	Life stress monitored monthly by questionnaire for 12 months. Individuals whose scores exceeded a threshold value received a telephone call from a nurse who responded to the patient's needs as indicated. Although options included a wide range of referral services, project nurses indicated that "teaching and providing reassurance by supplying information constituted a major portion of their role."	Significantly higher survival rate observed for the experimental life stress monitoring group. This group also demonstrated significantly lower levels of distress compared with the control group that did not receive life stress monitoring.	Randomized controlled trial; standardized instrumentation; large representative sample; 12-month follow-up; no control for pretest sensitization effects.

Study	Illness	Sample	Intervention	Results	Comments
Mermelstein & Holland (1991)	Cancer; ovarian, lymphoma	2 illustrative case studies	Frequent (1–2 times weekly) brief (15–30 minute) telephone contacts. Patients had moved out of city in which they had been hospitalized for cancer treatment. Telephone contact was employed to continue psychotherapeutic support.	Patients reported increased social and emotional support. Continued telephone contact with therapist helped to keep emotional distress within tolerable limits.	Uncontrolled case studies; no standardized instrumentation; no follow-up assessments; overlaps with psycho-therapy; suggests utility of continued contact through telephone.
Taylor et al. (1986)	Cancer	667 southern California residents who either had (n = 400) or had not (n = 267) participated in a support group at some time	Individuals had attended one of a variety of groups, including "Make Today Count," "We Can Do," "I Can Cope," American Cancer Society support group, "Mastectomy Recovery Plus," "Wellness Community," among others.	Support group attenders relied significantly more on others (family, friends, mental health professionals) for social support than did nonattenders. Attenders reported significantly more negative experiences in cancer treatment than did nonattenders. Attenders more frequently described health care providers as "cold" and insensitive than did nonattenders. The groups did not differ, however, in satisfaction with health care. Attenders were slightly less depressed than nonattenders; no other significant differences in mood disturbance.	Nonequivalent comparison group design; large sample but not randomly selected; benefits or effects of participation in support groups were not measured directly; no controls for "Attention" or other nonspecific factors; majority of data obtained via unstandardized questionnaire.

(Continued)

TABLE 27.3 *(Continued)*

Study	Condition	Participants	Component Interventions	Results	Comments
Weinberger et al. (1986)	Osteoarthritis of the knee	193 outpatients attending a municipal hospital general medical clinic	12 biweekly telephone interviews to inquire about daily hassles (minor stressors) and to obtain a self-assessment of health status.	Statistically significant increases in perceived social support (emotional, tangible, and "overall" support) following intervention. Pain and physical disability improved significantly following the intervention. Psychological distress improved marginally (p<.09).	Uncontrolled pre-post single group design; no follow-up assessment; large sample; hypothesized mediator variable (social support) measured directly; standardized instrumentation; no controls for "attention" or other nonspecific factors; intervention resembles continued medical follow-up more than enhancement of social support.
Weinberger et al. (1991)	Osteoarthritis	439 outpatients attending a municipal hospital general medical clinic	12 monthly interviews by trained nonmedical personnel who reviewed the following with the patient: medications (e.g., regimen, side effects, compliance); joint pain; gastrointestinal complaints; early warning signs of common comorbid conditions (e.g., hypertension, diabetes, heart or pulmonary disease); scheduled outpatient visits; mechanism to contact physicians after hours; barriers to keeping appointments; and encouragement to ask questions of service providers.	No statistically significant effects of the intervention on any of the variables, including perceived social support, satisfaction with care, morale, psychological distress).	Randomized controlled trial (no treatment control vs. telephone contact vs. clinic contact vs. telephone-plus-clinic contact); no follow-up assessment; large sample; hypothesized mediator variable (social support) measured directly; standardized instrumentation; intervention resembles continued medical follow-up more than enhancement of social support.

(a) the causes, course, and progression of a condition; (b) nutrition, medications, and treatments, including an outline of intended (therapeutic) and common side effects; and (c) the treatment setting, health care personnel, financial issues, and available social services. Educational media may take the form of short courses, lectures, discussion groups, films, video- or audiotapes, written materials (e.g., booklets, newsletters, or pamphlets), and, more recently, computer programs.

A growing body of evidence supports the value of patient education to facilitate adaptation to chronic disease. Although the majority of studies have failed to evaluate the effectiveness of educational interventions directly (Binik et al., 1993), several studies have demonstrated that such efforts are capable of enhancing illness-related knowledge (e.g., Bill-Harvey et al., 1989; Devins, Binik, et al., 1990; Jacobs, Ross, Walker, & Stockdale, 1983). Experiments have also begun to test the assertion that the provision of illness- and coping-related information can result in improved psychosocial outcomes. Simple minimal contact interventions, such as an introductory letter to new clinic attenders, have been demonstrated in randomized trials to enhance recipients' appraisals of their potential to influence the recovery process (Johnston, Gilbert, Partridge, & Collins, 1992). The subsequent effectiveness of such communications in mobilizing rehabilitation or coping efforts has not yet been examined. More extensive educational interventions have also been investigated. Results have been inconsistent, however, with some studies demonstrating significant improvements in terms of expectations for a positive prognosis, enhanced internal locus of control, and reduced illness intrusiveness; whereas others have failed to replicate these benefits.

An intriguing new approach has capitalized on the potential of computer technology to provide detailed and personalized instruction, contingent on the particular knowledge strengths and weaknesses of individual learners. Wetstone et al., for example, have developed extensive computer-assisted lessons for two common disabling conditions, systemic lupus erythematosus (Wetstone, Pfeiffer, & Rippey, 1988) and rheumatoid arthritis (Wetstone, Sheehan, Votaw, Peterson, & Rothfield, 1993), in which a number of central topics are presented together with detailed multiple-choice questions designed to assess specific knowledge gaps and individual learning needs to direct the user to those topics in need of increased coverage. Randomized controlled trials have produced encouraging initial results supporting the efficacy of these pedagogically and technologically sophisticated new programs. Results in both illness groups have indicated that health care consumers are willing and able to engage in computer-assisted patient education and that significant improvements in illness-related knowledge follow exposure to the program. Expectations for a good prognosis and optimism about the potential for a good life despite chronic disabling illness have also been enhanced significantly. Less clear, at present, are the more distal effects of the program on psychosocial adaptation and quality of life. Future research, involving larger numbers of participants and longer follow-up intervals may be required to enhance statistical power sufficiently to demonstrate such effects.

Representative studies evaluating patient education to facilitate coping with chronic illness are summarized in Table 27.4. A review of these studies indicates

TABLE 27.4 Patient Education to Facilitate Coping with Illness

Study	Condition	Participants	Component Interventions	Results	Comments
Bill-Harvey et al. (1989)	Osteoarthritis	76 aged low-literacy outpatients	Six weekly group classes developed specifically for low-SES, low-literacy urban residents. Topics included exercise, self-help aids and joint protection, medicine, pain-depression spiral and role of relaxation, and unorthodox treatments. Course delivered by health care team consisting of health educator, nurse practitioner, physical therapist, sociologist, rheumatologist, and community helpers.	Significant improvements in illness-related knowledge in experimental group compared with control group. Both groups demonstrated significant improvements in exercise behavior, function, and in use of adaptive equipment. No significant changes in moods.	Separate-sample pretest/posttest quasi-experimental design; no randomization; instrumentation not standardized; no controls for demand characteristics.

| Jacobs et al. (1983) | Hodgkin's disease | 381 chemotherapy patients | One of two interventions. In Study 1, experimental educational group members received an information booklet about their disease, its diagnosis, treatment, treatment problems, and prognosis plus newsletters with updates on recent advances in treatment of Hodgkin's disease. In Study 2, experimental peer support group members participated in 8 weekly 90-minute non-directive sessions, led by a health professional. | In Study 1, the education group demonstrated significant improvements in cancer-related knowledge, anxiety, and reduced treatment problems; "marginally significant" ($p<.10$) improvements were also observed for depression and life disruption, compared with control group members. No significant improvements were observed for interpersonal problems, personal habits, activity, life satisfaction, or self-competency. The education group demonstrated significant *reduction* in social competency relative to the control group.

In Study 2, both the experimental peer support and control groups demonstrated significant improvements in depression, interpersonal problems, anxiety, personal habits, and treatment problems. No significant changes were noted in life satisfaction, self-competency, social competency, or activity. | Randomized controlled trials of two common interventions; unstandardized instrumentation; minimal therapist contact; direct measures of knowledge and social support. |

(Continued)

TABLE 27.4 (*Continued*)

Study	Condition	Participants	Component Interventions	Results	Comments
Johnston et al. (1992)	Physiotherapy patients with a variety of diagnoses	71 outpatients	Routine appointment letter was modified for patients in experimental group to enhance perceived control over recovery. Control group received standard appointment letter. Letters mailed to patients before first appointment.	Relative to controls, experimental group reported significantly more internal locus of control in relation to rehabilitation and greater satisfaction with information received prior to treatment. No differences in accuracy of pretreatment expectations of physiotherapy.	Randomized controlled trial; posttest only design; no check to determine whether participants read or retained content of experimental letter; did not investigate impact of increased perceived control on coping or psychosocial outcomes.
Pruitt et al. (1993)	Recently diagnosed (within 6 weeks) cancer at various sites	31 radiotherapy outpatients at risk for psychological distress	Three individual psychoeducational sessions, delivered by a chaplain (Session 1), nurse (Session 2), and social worker (Session 3). Content included factual information about cancer and radiotherapy, common concerns and coping strategies, and communication with the health care team.	Experimental group demonstrated a significant reduction in depression relative to control group; no other psychosocial differences. Neither group demonstrated changes in illness-related knowledge, and knowledge did not correlate with improved psychosocial outcomes.	Randomized controlled trial; however, groups differed significantly in relevant clinical (e.g., cancer site) and sociodemographic characteristics (e.g., age, gender, marital status) despite randomization, a problem that may have obscured meaningful therapeutic benefits; standardized instrumentation; demand characteristics not controlled.

that there is some support for the effectiveness of educational interventions to enhance patients' knowledge of their illness, its treatment, and the tactics that can be undertaken in responding to the challenges. Inconsistent findings have been reported concerning the effectiveness of educational interventions to influence psychosocial outcomes more directly, however. The impact of education on the implementation of effective coping efforts, for example, is unclear. Patient education studies suffer from many of the same conceptual and methodological limitations identified previously in relation to the literatures concerning psychotherapy, cognitive-behavior therapy, and social support interventions. Methodologically, the majority of studies have failed to employ psychometrically sound measures of illness-related knowledge or expectations about treatment or prognosis. Experimental designs have not controlled for demand characteristics, "Hawthorne effects," or other nonspecific influences. Theoretically, the fundamental hypothesis that increased information will facilitate effective coping has not been specified in sufficient detail to enable investigators to derive testable statements of the mechanisms that may be involved. Moreover, in response to the inconsistency of experimental results, researchers have begun to question the validity of the proposition implicit in the health education approach, that the psychosocial distress accompanying chronic illness is largely attributable to a lack of relevant knowledge. A growing number are beginning to suggest that the acquisition of illness-related information—although quite likely necessary—is not sufficient to enable effective coping (Lorig & Laurin, 1985; Lorig, Lubeck, Kraines, Seleznick, & Holman, 1985). As a result, composite therapeutic approaches have begun to emerge in which patient education entails one of several component interventions required to assist individuals in coping more effectively.

COMPOSITE INTERVENTIONS

A variety of innovative clinical investigators have attempted in recent years to incorporate effective components of psychotherapy, cognitive-behavior therapy, social support enhancement, and patient education into a composite treatment package. Some investigators have developed comparatively simple combinations; for example, antidepressant-supported psychotherapy (Schiffer & Wineman, 1990) or patient education supplemented by supportive counseling plus "environmental manipulation" (providing informational and other supports to health service providers who may not be especially familiar with a particular condition (Gordon et al., 1980). Recent efforts have integrated a more diverse series of components.

A particularly impressive effort has been described by Fawzy et al. (Fawzy, Cousins, et al., 1990; Fawzy et al., 1993; Fawzy, Kemeny, et al., 1990) who combined components of patient education, problem-solving training, relaxation-based stress management, and social support from treatment personnel in developing a brief program of group therapy for cancer patients with melanoma.

Evaluated by a randomized controlled trial, results indicated that therapy participants experienced significantly more vigor at the conclusion of the 6-week
program. Follow-up data collected 6 months later indicated that the benefits produced by the experimental intervention had intensified so that therapy participants were now significantly less depressed, fatigued, or confused than their
"usual care" control group counterparts. Recognizing the importance of measuring coping behavior directly, the investigators also assessed cognitive and behavioral responses employed in coping with disease. Results at the conclusion of
therapy indicated that therapy participants used active-behavioral coping methods significantly more frequently than did the control group. Moreover, the intervention group continued to use significantly more active-behavioral coping as
well as more active-cognitive coping techniques than the control group when
assessed at the 6-month follow-up.

Correlational analyses were undertaken in an attempt to determine whether
coping behavior related systematically to emotional distress (Fawzy, Cousins,
et al., 1990). Analyses were limited to simultaneous bivariate correlations, however, and do not address the crucial issue of whether *changes* in coping styles (occurring as a result of participation in the experimental group therapy) were
responsible for changes in emotional distress. More sophisticated latent variable
or survival analysis techniques are required to examine such complex research
questions (Collins & Horn, 1991). Survival techniques were, in fact, applied in a
subsequent 6-year follow-up (Fawzy et al., 1993) and some evidence emerged to
support the hypothesis that changes in coping can contribute to improved morbidity (e.g., decreased recurrence of disease) and reduced mortality. Therapy-
induced increases in active-behavioral coping significantly predicted increased
6-year survival in a multivariate (Cox's proportional hazards) model that controlled for standard medical prognostic indicators (e.g., tumor depth). A limited
number of patients participated in this experiment, and it is plausible that a
clearer pattern of statistically significant results might have been observed if a
larger sample size had been available to the investigators.

Another especially promising approach has focused on *behavioral self-
management* of chronic disease. Adapting cognitive-behavioral and behavior
modification techniques for the situation of chronic illness, self-management approaches have also borrowed heavily from other disciplines, including health education, nursing, physio- and occupational therapy. Much of this work is grounded
in Bandura's (1986) social cognitive theory, the underlying premise being that individuals affected by chronic conditions can be enlisted to collaborate actively
with health service providers in minimizing—if not outright controlling—disabling symptoms and treatment side effects through the mindful application of
cognitive and behavioral self-management skills. Although self-management programs have been developed for a variety of chronic conditions, including asthma,
diabetes mellitus, hypertension, chronic pain, neurological and neuromuscular
disorders, and gastrointestinal conditions, among others (see Holroyd & Creer's,
1986, excellent review), the approach is perhaps most highly developed in relation

to arthritis, principally osteo- and rheumatoid arthritis (Lorig & Fries, 1986, 1988).

The Stanford Arthritis Self-Management Program (ASMP; Lorig & Fries, 1986) is a structured group program that exemplifies the self-management approach. Developed specifically for people with osteo- and rheumatoid arthritis, the program combines a heterogeneous series of component interventions with the objective of training affected individuals to manage symptoms, collaborate with the health care team in controlling the disease, and thereby minimize its disruptive impact on lifestyles, activities, and interests. The program consists of six weekly 2-hour group sessions (12–20 participants mixed with regard to arthritic diagnoses), led by a lay leader (often an individual who has arthritis him- or herself and who has learned to master arthritis self-management skills). Program components include information sharing (education) about various forms of arthritis (including features of the disease, prognosis, and treatment), myth dispelling, orientation to the self-management philosophy, exercise training (introducing several mobility- and strength-enhancing techniques and establishment of a regular exercise routine), pain management, problem solving, joint protection (e.g., load distribution, body leverage, efficiency principles), energy conservation, sleep hygiene, pleasant event scheduling, mood management, diet and nutrition, medications, and communicating and collaborating with physicians and allied health professionals. Contingency contracting and social support ("buddy system") components are also employed to enhance adherence and to provide encouragement in continuing to follow the program. As noted in Table 27.5, promising initial results have suggested that the Stanford ASMP is effective in teaching participants effective self-management skills. Experimental results have indicated that participants experience significant improvements in a variety of clinical outcomes, including enhanced self-efficacy and psychosocial well-being, and that these persist for as long as 4 years after completion of the program. Given the diverse and complex elements that make up the ASMP, it seems ripe for component analysis research. A reasonable question, for example, is whether participants, especially naive arthritis patients who may not have extensive previous experience with behavioral or other psychological interventions, are capable of absorbing the full range of component interventions presented in the 6-week program. Consistent with the notion that it may not be necessary to master the entire set of self-management skills in the ASMP, Lorig has recently asserted that the individual's enhanced confidence in his or her ability to perform self-management behavior skillfully (self-efficacy) is the single most important factor responsible for improvement (Lenker, Lorig, & Gallagher, 1984; Lorig, Chastain, Ung, Shoor, & Hollman, 1989). This is an intriguing hypothesis that fits well with research in clinical and health psychology more generally (O'Leary, 1985) and merits increased research attention.

Clinical investigators concerned with heart health have been active in developing behavioral interventions that may also facilitate coping with cardiac disease (Razin, 1982). *Cardiac rehabilitation* programs focus principally on maximizing

TABLE 27.5 Composite Interventions to Facilitate Coping with Chronic Illness

Study	Condition	Participants	Component Interventions	Results	Comments
Burgess et al. (1987)	Acute myocardial infarction	180 inpatients (male and female) transferring from CCU to intermediate care; all were employed at least 20 hr/wk prior to MI	Cardiac rehabilitation: challenging maladaptive appraisals and attributions, reframing of perceived threats, relaxation training, assertion training. Effort was made to intervene at the levels of individual patients, family members, and at the workplace. On average, participants received 6.3 contacts.	At 3-month follow-up, experimental group demonstrated significant reductions in "distress" (although not anxiety or depression, measured separately) and significant reductions in family strain relative to "usual care" control group. No other group differences (e.g., occupational rehabilitation). No differences between the groups at 13-month follow-up.	Randomized controlled trial; large sample size; 3- and 13-month follow-up; standardized instrumentation.

| Cain et al. (1986) | Gynecological cancer | 80 consecutive women within 1 month of diagnosis | Eight group sessions combining education and counseling. Sessions provided information about cancer, diet, and communication with family, friends, and health care professionals. Supportive sharing of feelings about impact of illness and treatment on body image, sexuality, and guilt reactions. Behavioral component interventions included progressive relaxation training and encouragement to develop short- and long-term goals. | Individual and group counseling group recipients demonstrated increased illness-related knowledge and more positive attitudes toward treatment staff compared with control group members. Significant posttreatment reductions in anxiety and health concerns in all groups; individual counseling participants demonstrated significantly lower levels than group or standard counseling groups. Both individual and group counseling recipients continued to demonstrate significant reductions in distress at 6-month follow-up compared with standard counseling control group. Moreover, benefits observed in both experimental counseling groups at follow-up extended into several new domains, including functioning at work, at home with domestic chores, in sexual relationships, and in leisure activities. | Randomized controlled trial (individual vs. group vs. standard counseling); repeated measurements at posttreatment and 6 months after conclusion of therapy; standardized instrumentation; controlled for demand characteristics. |

(Continued)

TABLE 27.5 (*Continued*)

Study	Condition	Participants	Component Interventions	Results	Comments
Fawzy, Cousins, et al. (1990a)	Cancer (melanoma)	66 consecutive patients with good prognosis (operationally defined)	Six weekly 90-minute group therapy sessions included health education, enhancement of illness-related problem-solving skills, stress management (relaxation) training, and psychological support.	Treatment group demonstrated significantly greater vigor (positive mood) than control group but no other psychosocial benefit immediately following treatment. Follow-up measures showed greater differentiation of groups: Treatment group reported significantly higher vigor and lower depression, fatigue, confusion, and mood disturbance. Treatment group demonstrated significantly more active coping methods both at completion of treatment and at follow-up.	Randomized controlled trial; repeated measurements posttreatment and at 6-month follow-up; standardized instrumentation; measured coping behavior directly; no-treatment control group does not control for attention-placebo explanation for treatment group effects; therapeutic intervention well specified and clearly described.

| Gordon et al. (1980) | Cancer (breast, lung, or melanoma) | 197 hospital inpatients | Three components, including patient education, counseling, and environmental manipulation. The educational component provided information about cancer, its treatment, the medical system, and how to live with cancer. Counseling focused on personal reactions to and feelings about the disease. Individuals were encouraged to ventilate, interpret thoughts, feelings, and behavior, and to respond more effectively. "Environmental manipulation" involved referrals to appropriate ancillary service providers (e.g., social work, psychology, psychiatry); an "oncology counselor" provided supportive consultation to these professionals to enhance awareness of cancer-specific issues. | Number of psychosocial problems reported by patients declined significantly from hospitalization to postdischarge period for all participants. No significant difference between experimental and control groups. Slightly greater improvement in emotional distress (anxiety) and activities of daily living among experimental compared with control group, especially among lung cancer patients. Experimental group demonstrated significant increase in activities outside the home postdischarge, whereas control group increased participation in solitary activities at home. No significant differences across groups or over time in "psychiatric impairment" or health locus of control. Involvement in paid employment declined significantly for both groups. | Nonequivalent control group design; standardized interview and instrumentation; repeated assessment at hospital admission, hospital discharge, 3 months postdischarge, and 6 months postdischarge; dependent variables assessed by an independent assessor who was blind to experimental vs. control group membership; historical threats to validity controlled by obtaining comparison group data both before and after period when experimental intervention was provided. |

(Continued)

TABLE 27.5 *(Continued)*

Study	Condition	Participants	Component Interventions	Results	Comments
Lorig et al. (1985)	Osteo- and rheumatoid arthritis	190 community volunteers	Stanford Arthritis Self-Management Program (ASMP; Lorig & Fries, 1988): six sessions over 4 months, delivered in a community setting by lay leaders, covering a broad range of self-management strategies and tactics (see text for details). Emphasis on group discussion, knowledge acquisition, behavioral rehearsal, behavioral contracts and diaries to enhance adherence, and weekly feedback. Participants paid a nominal fee ($15–20) to cover expenses.	Significantly greater increases in arthritis knowledge and in frequency of arthritis and relaxation exercises at 4-month assessment in experimental compared with control group. Experimental group also demonstrated significant improvements in pain at 4 months compared with controls. No group differences in disability or number of arthritis-related doctor visits. Data at 8- and 20-month follow-ups indicated that initial gains were generally maintained.	Solomon 4-group quasi-experimental design (controls for pretest sensitization); repeated assessment at pretreatment, 4-, 8-, and 20-month follow-ups; standardized instrumentation; large sample size; substantial durability of therapeutic effects; initial differences in criterion variables between groups; statistical analyses based on difference scores (posttest minus pretest) are unreliable.
Lorig et al. (1993)	Osteo- and rheumatoid arthritis	224 community volunteers, including those in the Lorig et al. (1985) study	Stanford ASMP (as described for Lorig et al., 1985).	Four-year follow-up of Stanford ASMP participants. ASMP participants demonstrated significant reduction in numbers of arthritis-related doctor visits and self-efficacy to cope with the consequence of arthritis despite worsening of disability. Improvement in depression observed at 4-month posttest was not sustained at 4-year follow-up.	Substantial follow-up interval (4 years); large sample size; randomization achieved at 4-month occasion lost because all subjects eventually received ASMP; impressive maintenance of most therapeutic gains long after completion of training.

| Oldridge et al. (1991) | Acute myocardial infarction | 201 "low-risk" (nondistressed) patients identified within 6 weeks of heart attack | Cardiac rehabilitation: Eight 90-minute group sessions focusing on identification and evaluation of thoughts, feelings, and personal reactions to the physical changes, treatment regimens, and behavioral changes associated with recovery; progressive relaxation training; communication training between patients and their spouses. Augmented by sixteen 50-minute exercise sessions. Spouses invited to attend all sessions with patients. Exercise conditioning conducted under supervision of cardiologist. | Significant improvement over the 12 months for both groups, with biggest improvement occurring between baseline and 8 weeks. Small but consistent differences in favor of experimental over control group in terms of emotional well-being, quality of life, and time trade-off measure. No significant group differences in changes in exercise tolerance, anxiety, or depression. | Randomized controlled trial; repeated assessments at pre- and post-treatment, 4-, 8-, and 12-month follow-ups; multifaceted outcome assessment (exercise tolerance, quality of life, time trade-off); feelings of mastery, control, and confidence were hypothesized to mediate therapeutic efficacy of experimental treatment but these were not measured directly; results suggest that early recovery is enhanced by cardiac rehabilitation but that later adaptation may not benefit to the same extent. |

(Continued)

TABLE 27.5 *(Continued)*

Study	Condition	Participants	Component Interventions	Results	Comments
O'Leary et al. (1988)	Rheumatoid arthritis	30 women	Stanford ASMP. Five 2-hour weekly group sessions included educational coverage of the biopsychosocial model of pain, cognitive-behavioral pain management skills (including relaxation, guided imagery, attention-focusing, vivid imagery, dissociation, relabeling, and self-encouragement), goal-setting with self-reward for increased activity, pleasant activity scheduling, and social support through the development of a "buddy" system. Course content was summarized in a treatment manual that was provided to each participant in the experimental and no-treatment control groups.	Therapy group improved significantly in depression, perceived stress, loneliness, and sleep (quantity and quality), whereas control group did not. Therapy group also demonstrated significant improvements in "coping" (to construe arthritis-imposed difficulties as a "challenge" rather than being overwhelmed by them), self-efficacy for arthritis self-management, and significantly reduced pain relative to control group. Groups did not differ, however, in disease activity at conclusion of treatment.	Controlled trial (not stated whether participants were randomly assigned to groups, however); standardized instrumentation; multidimensional assessment incorporated measures of pain and psychosocial outcomes, as well as measures of hypothesized coping mechanism and disease activity; small sample; multiple t-tests inflate experimentwise type I error rate.

Study	Condition	Sample	Intervention	Results	Design Comments
Schiffer & Wineman (1990)	Multiple sclerosis	28 depressed MS patients, meeting RDC criteria for major depression	Antidepressant medication (desipramine, 25 mg) plus structured supportive psychotherapy vs. placebo plus psychotherapy. Psychotherapy sessions met weekly. Trial duration was 30 days.	Blind clinical judgments indicated that significantly higher number of patients in active medication group improved in depression compared with controls although both groups demonstrated significant improvements in depression. At conclusion of trial, 11 (of 13) medication patients and 6 (of 14) placebo patients showed clinically significant improvement. Group differences were not corroborated by standardized test scores (Beck Depression Inventory).	Double-blind randomized controlled trial; blind clinical evaluation plus standardized instrumentation; small sample size; placebo condition controls for nonspecific effects; statistical tests did not control for initial values of depressive symptoms (e.g., analysis of covariance).
Wetstone et al. (1988)	Systemic lupus erythematosus	53 outpatients attending a rheumatology clinic	Computer-based educational lesson covering 19 major topic areas and over 200 multiple choice questions and branch points allowing participants to direct the focus of instruction. After a brief orientation, participants were encouraged to use the lesson as much or as little as they liked.	Experimental group used computer-based lesson for 2 hours and 48 minutes, on average, typically over two sessions. On average, 13.5 out of 19 sections were completed. Experimental group demonstrated significant improvement in illness-related knowledge and significantly increased hope of a good prognosis compared with control group. Groups did not differ in moods or health locus of control.	Randomized controlled trial; standardized instrumentation; powerful intervention delivered in a novel way; demand characteristics not controlled.

(Continued)

TABLE 27.5 *(Continued)*

Study	Condition	Participants	Component Interventions	Results	Comments
Wetstone et al. (1993)	Rheumatoid arthritis	67 rheumatology clinic outpatients	Computer-based educational lesson covering 10 major topic areas, incorporating diverse instructional techniques (e.g., factual information, problem-solving, case study illustrations, practice of new skills, and specific advice). Multiple choice questions at branch points allowed participants to direct the focus of instruction. After a brief orientation, participants were encouraged to use the lesson as much or as little as they liked.	Experimental group used computer-based lesson for 1 hour and 47 minutes, on average, over one to four sessions. Experimental group demonstrated significant improvement in illness-related knowledge relative to controls. Experimental group reported significant improvements in outlook on life, hopefulness for a good prognosis, joint protection, and amount of time resting compared with control group. However, these differences were not corroborated by standardized instruments.	Randomized controlled trial; standardized instrumentation; powerful intervention delivered in a novel way; demand characteristics not controlled.
Worden & Weisman (1984)	Cancer, widely varying sites	117 newly diagnosed cancer patients at "high risk" for psychological distress as indicated by screening instrument	Four sessions in which psychotherapeutic, educational, problem-solving, and progressive relaxation component interventions were delivered.	Significantly lower emotional distress and lower denial in therapy group compared with no-treatment group. Both groups reported similar types and numbers of problems introduced by cancer but therapy group achieved more effective resolutions to cancer-induced problems. No differences between groups in time perspective or in feelings of hopelessness. Psychosocial benefits of therapy persisted throughout the 18 weeks of follow-up.	Nonrandomized comparison group design; standardized instrumentation; individuals most likely to benefit targeted for treatment; no controls for "attention" or other nonspecific effects.

physical and functional recovery following myocardial infarction. Toward this end, such programs emphasize on establishing and maintaining a regular schedule of exercise training. The primary goal is to increase the efficiency of oxygen extraction and metabolism in skeletal muscle, thereby reducing cardiac work and improving coronary artery collateral blood flow (O'Connor et al., 1989). Experimental evaluations of cardiac rehabilitation efforts to reduce mortality and reinfarction have not, however, been especially encouraging. Results have tended to be inconsistent and, even when statistically significant, the magnitude of effects has tended to be small. Recognizing that small effect sizes can obscure the detection of valid therapeutic benefits, two separate meta-analyses have been published, independently concluding that cardiac rehabilitation produces a small but statistically significant and clinically meaningful advantage by reducing rates of reinfarction and mortality (O'Connor et al., 1989; Oldridge, Guyatt, Fischer, & Rimm, 1988).

A second component often included in cardiac rehabilitation programs involves modification of lifestyle and behavioral risk factors (e.g., smoking, obesity, type A behavior) and return to work. These interventions are intended to augment an hypothesized secondary benefit of regular exercise training: reinforcement of appraisals fundamental to effective coping, most notably self-efficacy and self-control. Recent efforts have added cognitive-behavioral components, such as progressive relaxation training and communication between marital partners, with encouraging results (Blumenthal & Emery, 1988; Oldridge et al., 1991; Taylor & Aspinwall, 1990). Oldridge et al. (1991) have added a component focused on spouses that includes management of their own anxiety in relation to their partner's heart attack and how best to provide support for the patient. Communication patterns are reviewed to enhance social support and to reduce hostility, criticism, and overprotective behavior. As indicated, a recent randomized controlled trial demonstrated significant psychosocial and quality-of-life benefits attributable to this innovative addition to the cardiac rehabilitation program. The experiment, however, simply compared the entire composite intervention against usual community care. Moreover, the mediator variables hypothesized to account for therapeutic benefits were not measured or compared directly. It is not possible, therefore, to attribute the observed benefits to any particular therapeutic intervention(s). Future research might profitably begin to dismantle the components that comprise cardiac rehabilitation and to examine more directly the underlying therapeutic factors that are believed to account for improved patient outcomes.

FUTURE DIRECTIONS

The preceding review justifies considerable optimism about the future of psychological efforts to facilitate coping with chronic disease. Research and practice have produced a number of promising strategies and techniques with demonstrated clinical efficacy. Although one might reasonably question the wisdom of psychological prognostication (cf. Boneau, 1992), current developments support at least some speculation.

Matching Interventions to Information-Processing Styles

Given its established efficacy in facilitating coping with chronic disease, patient education is likely to continue as a cornerstone for a wide range of interventions. Increased availability of illness- and treatment-related information may only be helpful, however, to the extent that the patient is willing and/or able to attend to and make use of it. Recent research concerning individual differences in dispositional information-seeking styles may be especially informative in this regard. Miller and her associates (Miller, 1980; Miller, Brody, & Summerton, 1988; Miller & O'Leary, 1992), for example, have hypothesized that under conditions of threat, such as those characterizing the context of life with a chronic life-threatening condition, information-processing behavior can vary along two main dimensions. One involves the extent to which individuals will seek out and *monitor* for information about the threat. The second dimension involves the extent to which they can cognitively distract themselves from and psychologically *blunt* threat-relevant information. To the extent that one's dispositional information-seeking style involves monitoring for threat-relevant cues, the monitoring-blunting hypothesis maintains that the individual will actively seek out such information in a self-regulatory effort to minimize anxiety (e.g., through increased predictability). Individuals characterized primarily by a blunting coping style, on the other hand, are hypothesized to avoid threat-relevant information. Thus, the effectiveness of therapeutic efforts that emphasize illness- and treatment-related information may be compromised to the extent that these fundamental individual differences are ignored (Miller, 1992a).

A sizable body of evidence has accumulated in support of the monitoring-blunting hypothesis (see Miller, 1980, 1989, 1990, 1992b; Miller et al., 1988; Miller & O'Leary, 1992). Much of this work has supported the hypothesis in the health care context. Evidence that informational interventions are more effective when matched to the recipient's monitoring-blunting style have been reported, for example, among women undergoing amniocentesis (Phipps & Zinn, 1986), colposcopy (Miller & Mangan, 1983), and various gynecological procedures (Steptoe & O'Sullivan, 1986), as well as in men and women undergoing cardiac catheterization (Watkins, Weaver, & Odegaard, 1986). Supportive evidence is also available from laboratory cold pressor situations (Efran, Chorney, Ascher, & Lukens, 1989). Studies involving individuals with acute conditions have indicated that compared with individuals characterized primarily by a blunting style, monitors are more highly concerned about the nature of their relationships with health service providers (Miller et al., 1988). Miller (1992a) has speculated that monitors may respond best to health care interactions that enable them freely to ask questions and to discuss their experiences; blunters, on the other hand, may respond best to exchanges that minimize threatening interpretations while leaving open opportunities to obtain instrumental (e.g., procedural) information.

These findings lead to the speculation that alternative interventions to facilitate coping with chronic illness might be selected, in part, on the basis of an individual's monitoring or blunting information-seeking styles. In the context of Lazarus and Folkman's distinction between problem- and emotion-focused coping

(Lazarus & Folkman, 1984), interventions that focus primarily on enhancing problem-focused coping (e.g., patient education, behavioral self-management)— treatment modalities that require the acquisition and manipulation of illness-related information—might be especially well suited for individuals whose primary mode of information seeking is characterized by a monitoring style. Emotion-focused coping interventions (e.g., stress management, social support), on the other hand, do not invoke potentially threatening illness-related information directly and thus might be indicated for individuals characterized predominantly by a blunting style.

Integrating Computer Technology

There is now a significant body of research suggesting that computers may be useful in delivering psychological assessment and therapy (e.g., Binik, Servan-Schreiber, Freiwald, & Hall, 1988; Bloom, 1992; Butcher, 1985; Lawrence, 1986; Selmi, Klein, Greist, Sorrell, & Erdman, 1990; Servan-Schreiber, 1986). In some situations, patients may even prefer interacting with a computer over a human health professional (e.g., Binik, Servan-Schreiber, & Westbury, 1989; Erdman et al., 1992; Ochs, Meana, Pare, Mah, & Binik, 1994). The potential for intelligent programs ("expert systems") to gather relevant data, integrate it into a meaningful assessment, and respond in a contextually sensitive and appropriate manner creates exciting new possibilities for facilitating coping with chronic disease. Moreover, the potential to integrate automated data collection and database features introduces unprecedented opportunities for research and clinical practice. As indicated, early patient education efforts have already produced promising results (Wetstone et al., 1988, 1993). Computer-assisted interventions can transcend the limits of didactic presentation, however, and can actually simulate human therapeutic exchange. Binik et al. (1988) reviewed the literature concerning intelligent computer-based assessment and psychotherapy and outlined considerations relevant to the design of expert systems for these purposes. They conclude with a description of *Sexpert,* an intelligent expert system developed to provide computer-assisted assessment and therapy for sexual dysfunctions.

Evidence in support of the therapeutic efficacy of expert computer systems has been reported by Selmi et al. (1990) who developed a six-session computer-administered cognitive-behavioral treatment for depression and found it to be equally effective when compared with therapist-delivered treatment in a randomized wait-list controlled trial. Results, immediately following the conclusion of treatment and at a 2-month follow-up, indicated that both computer-assisted and human-delivered therapy groups demonstrated significant improvements in depressive symptoms as indicated by a number of standardized self-report and interviewer-based instruments. Improvement was statistically significant despite covariance controls for pretreatment scores and was equivalent across the two therapy groups.

Collectively, the potential to translate effective interventions into intelligent computer programs and the observation that with exposure patients come to view such expert systems as highly credible (Binik et al., 1989) suggest that much can be gained. The challenge will be to develop similar systems to facilitate coping with chronic disease. Inasmuch as the dissemination of such programs can be achieved at a very low cost once initial software development has been completed, and given the high degree of standardization possible with automated procedures, the incorporation of new computer technology will surely continue to contribute importantly by augmenting and simulating the delivery of valuable therapeutic interventions.

Models of Care for a Multicultural Society

The experience of illness and its psychosocial impact are profoundly shaped by culturally based practices, attitudes, and beliefs. Yet, research to date, has ignored these issues in interventions to facilitate coping with chronic disease. Increasing international migration and resettlement are, however, rapidly transforming the globe into a strikingly pluralistic community, resulting in an ever more pressing need for culturally sensitive and appropriate health care, including psychological interventions in support of coping.

Developments in Canada mirror more global trends and provide a representative example. Recent Canadian census data indicate that one in six people living in Canada was born outside the country; in our larger centers, this proportion is as high as one in three. In metropolitan Toronto, recognized by the United Nations as the most ethnically diverse city in the world, residents originate from more than 110 different countries and speak more than 90 different languages. As might be expected, many of these new Canadians speak neither of the two official languages (English and French). The pattern of immigration is also changing significantly. Although most immigrants to Canada migrated from European countries prior to 1980, almost half have immigrated from Asia in more recent years (Canadian Task Force on Mental Health Issues Affecting Immigrants and Refugees, 1988). Given the resulting diversity of ethnocultural backgrounds, it seems reasonable to question the validity and appropriateness of current therapeutic practices insofar as these have been developed, tested, and refined largely within the Euro-American cultural context. Such concerns are not limited to the domain of psychotherapeutic intervention. Many countries in which cultural diversity has continued to increase in recent years—including the United States, England, and Australia, among others—have introduced new initiatives to inform, evaluate, and reform health delivery systems to ensure the availability of ethnoculturally sensitive and appropriate services across the entire spectrum of medical and health care (Masi, 1993). Increasing the availability of services in a variety of languages is an important first step toward this goal. It will be necessary, however, for ethnocultural adaptation to proceed well beyond translation (Devins & Beiser, 1994).

Research in medical anthropology has identified *explanatory models* (Kleinman, 1980), the conceptual frameworks within which the experience of illness is perceived and defined, as powerful influences that can dramatically shape appraisals of the illness experience. Explanatory models "contain explanations for any or all of five issues: etiology; onset of symptoms; pathophysiology; course of sickness (severity and type of sick role); and treatment" (Kleinman, 1978, pp. 87–88). Cross-cultural differences in explanatory models can lead to different interpretations of objectively similar constellations of signs and symptoms, producing marked discrepancies in perceived causes of illness, patterns of distress, anticipated course of illness, and help-seeking behavior (Weiss, 1988; Weiss et al., 1988).

A growing body of ethnographic evidence documents the validity and clinical utility of this perspective. Investigations have begun to link explanatory models to patients' perceived causes of a variety of chronic conditions such as temperomandibular joint pain (Garro, 1994), diabetes mellitus (Hagey, 1984), and leprosy (Weiss et al., 1992). Evidence has begun to emerge that variation in explanatory models can help to account for fascinating cross-cultural differences in medical help-seeking behavior (e.g., Snyder, 1983; Weiss et al., 1992). In an investigation of nonprescribed treatment usage in end-stage renal disease, for example, Snyder (1983) interviewed 122 Hawaiian dialysis patients about the types of interventions they independently sought out for help with problems in a number of domains, including physical well-being, sexual functioning, emotional well-being, relations with others, kidney function, and (increasing) energy. Several ethnic identities were represented among participants, including Caucasian, Chinese, Filipino, Hawaiian, and Japanese, and self-directed help-seeking behavior differed significantly across the groups. Prayer, religious healing, exercise, massage, herbal remedies, and dietary changes were among the most commonly identified alternative treatments. Preferences for one or another of these were influenced significantly by ethnic and gender differences across participants. When respondents were asked specifically about the types of assistance they had sought for help with emotional well-being and with interpersonal relationships, self-selected alternatives differed significantly across ethnic groups. This suggests that the influence of explanatory models may also extend to the domain of coping with chronic disease.

More pedestrian evidence that nonmedically based explanatory models exert an important influence on help-seeking in North America can be gleaned from the recent report (Eisenberg et al., 1993) that as many as one in three American health care consumers are likely to seek out one or more unconventional medical treatments in a given year, at an estimated annual cost of $13.87 billion. These findings also highlight the extent to which the current system is unable to address illness from the patient's perspective. The vast majority (83%) of the 1,539 adults surveyed by telephone had sought treatment for the same condition from both a medical doctor and an alternative practitioner. A substantial proportion of these people (72%), however, had not informed their physician of the unconventional treatment.

Psychosocial stressors and adaptive challenges introduced by chronic illness are contingent on the individual's appraisal of this eventful stressor. Culturally shaped explanatory models exert a powerful influence on such appraisals. The argument to adapt existing interventions in support of effective coping so that they will be appropriate for a wider range of ethnocultural populations is thus all the more timely and compelling.

CONCLUSION

People affected by chronic physical illness must contend with what can often be an overwhelming burden of uncertainty, dependency, disability, pain, fatigue, illness intrusiveness, and the stigma and negative stereotypes imposed by others. Each of these domains introduces significant adaptive challenges and coping demands. The fact that the majority of chronically ill people have been able to achieve a comparatively positive level of psychosocial adjustment bears impressive testimony to the strength and resilience of the human spirit. The likelihood that the vast majority have also benefited from some form of support at some point in their chronic disease is also extremely high. As indicated in this chapter, a number of promising interventions have been developed to facilitate coping with chronic illness. Evidence in support of their efficacy to date is encouraging, but there is much room for improvement. The increasing emphasis on both quality and quantity of life that characterizes current health care philosophy provides much reason for optimism. Continued efforts to enhance the efficacy of our techniques must be informed by sophisticated scientific research directed at increasing our understanding of their mechanisms of action and at adapting effective approaches and procedures for diverse ethnocultural populations. A research focus that combines the investigation of theoretically important issues in relevant clinical populations and settings will likely contribute most profitably toward these ends.

REFERENCES

Abram, H. S., Moore, G. L., & Westervelt, F. B. (1971). Suicidal behavior in chronic dialysis patients. *American Journal of Psychiatry, 127,* 1199–1204.

Adair, J. G., & Spinner, B. (1979). Subjects' access to cognitive processes: Demand characteristics and verbal report. *Journal of Theory and Social Behaviour, 11,* 31–52.

Ader, R. (1981). *Psychoneuroimmunology.* New York: Academic Press.

Adler, A. B., Wright, B. A., & Ulicny, G. R. (1991). Donations and attitudes. *Rehabilitation Psychology, 36,* 231–240.

Andersen, B. L. (1992). Psychological interventions for cancer patients to enhance quality of life. *Journal of Consulting and Clinical Psychology, 60,* 552–568.

Averill, J. R. (1973). Personal control over aversive stimuli and its relationship to stress. *Psychological Bulletin, 80,* 286–303.

Badley, E. M., Lee, J., & Wood, P. H. N. (1987). Impairment, disability, and the ICIDH Model II: The nature of the underlying condition and patterns of impairment. *International Rehabilitation and Medicine, 8,* 118–124.

Bandura, A. (1986). *Social foundations of thought and action: A social cognitive theory.* Englewood Cliffs, NJ: Prentice-Hall.

Bartlett, E. E. (Ed.). (1985). Forum: Patient education. *Preventive Medicine, 14,* 667–818.

Basler, H. E., & Rehfisch, H. P. (1991). Cognitive-behavioral therapy in patients with ankylosing spondylitis in a German self-help organization. *Journal of Psychosomatic Research, 35,* 345–354.

Beck, A. T., Rush, A. J., Shaw, B. F., & Emery, G. (1979). *Cognitive therapy of depression.* New York: Guilford.

Bill-Harvey, D., Rippey, R., Abeles, M., Donald, M. J., Downing, D., Ingenito, F., & Pfeiffer, C. A. (1989). Outcome of an osteoarthritis education program for low-literacy patients taught by indigenous instructors. *Patient Education and Counselling, 13,* 133–142.

Binik, Y. M., Baker, A. G., Kalogeropoulos, D., Devins, G. M., Guttmann, R. D., Hollomby, D. J., Barre, P. E., Hutchinson, T. A., Prud'homme, M., & McMullen, L. (1982). Pain, control over treatment, and compliance in dialysis and transplant patients. *Kidney International, 21,* 840–848.

Binik, Y. M., Chowanec, G. D., & Devins, G. M. (1990). Marital role strain, illness intrusiveness, and their impact on marital and individual adjustment in end-stage renal disease. *Psychology and Health, 4,* 245–257.

Binik, Y. M., Devins, G. M., Barre, P. E., Guttmann, R. D., Mandin, H., Paul, L. C., Hons, R. B., & Burgess, E. D. (1993). Live and learn: Patient education delays the need to initiate renal replacement therapy in end-stage renal disease. *Journal of Nervous and Mental Disease, 181,* 371–376.

Binik, Y. M., Devins, G. M., & Orme, C. M. (1989). Psychological stress and coping in end-stage renal disease. In R. W. J. Neufeld (Ed.), *Advances in the investigation of psychological stress* (pp. 305–342). New York: Wiley.

Binik, Y. M., Servan-Schreiber, D., Freiwald, S., & Hall, K. S. K. (1988). Intelligent computer-based assessment and psychotherapy: An expert system for sexual dysfunction. *Journal of Nervous and Mental Disease, 176,* 387–400.

Binik, Y. M., Servan-Schreiber, D., & Westbury, C. F. (1989). Interaction with a "sex-expert" system enhances attitudes toward computerized sex therapy. *Behaviour Research and Therapy, 27,* 303–306.

Bloom, B. L. (1992). Computer-assisted psychological intervention: A review and commentary. *Clinical Psychology Review, 12,* 169–197.

Blumenthal, J. A., & Emery, C. F. (1988). Rehabilitation of patients following myocardial infarction. *Journal of Consulting and Clinical Psychology, 56,* 374–381.

Boneau, C. A. (1992). Observations on psychology's past and future. *American Psychologist, 47,* 1586–1596.

Burgess, A. W., Lerner, D. J., D'Agostino, R. B., Vokonas, P. S., Hartman, C. R., & Gaccione, P. (1987). A randomized control trial of cardiac rehabilitation. *Social Science and Medicine, 24,* 359–370.

Butcher, J. N. (Ed.). (1985). Perspectives on computerized psychological assessment. *Journal of Consulting and Clinical Psychology, 53,* 429–451.

Cain, E. N., Kohorn, E. I., Quinlan, D. M., Latimer, K., & Schwartz, P. E. (1986). Psychosocial benefits of a cancer support group. *Cancer, 57,* 183–189.

Canadian Task Force on Mental Health Issues Affecting Immigrants and Refugees. (1988). *After the door has been opened: Mental health issues affecting immigrants and refugees in Canada.* Ottawa: Government of Canada.

Capone, M. A., Good, R. S., Westie, K. S., & Jacobson, A. F. (1980). Psychosocial rehabilitation of gynecologic oncology patients. *Archives of Physical Medicine and Rehabilitation, 61,* 128–132.

Cella, D. F., Sarafian, B., Snider, P. R., Yellen, S. B., & Winicour, P. (1993). Evaluation of a community-based cancer support group. *Psycho-Oncology, 2,* 123–132.

Collins, L. M., & Horn, J. L. (1991). *Best methods for the analysis of change: Recent advances, unanswered questions, future directions.* Washington, DC: American Psychological Association.

Compton, A. B., & Purviance, M. (1992). Emotional distress in chronic medical illness: Treatment with time-limited group psychotherapy. *Military Medicine, 157,* 533–535.

Crocker, J., Voelkl, K., Testa, M., & Major, B. (1991). Social stigma: The affective consequences of attributional ambiguity. *Journal of Personality and Social Psychology, 60,* 218–228.

Daltroy, L. H., & Liang, M. H. (1993). Arthritis education: Opportunities and state of the art. *Health Education Quarterly, 20,* 3–16.

De-Nour, A. K. (1983). Staff–patient interaction. In N. B. Levy (Ed.), *Psychonephrology 2: Psychological problems in kidney failure and their treatment* (pp. 31–41). New York: Plenum.

DeVellis, B. M., Blalock, S. J., Hahn, P. M., DeVellis, R. F., & Hochbaum, G. M. (1988). Evaluation of a problem-solving intervention for patients with arthritis. *Patient Education and Counselling, 11,* 29–42.

DeVellis, R. F., Wallston, B. S., & Wallston, K. A. (1980). Epilepsy and learned helplessness. *Basic and Applied Social Psychology, 1,* 241–253.

Devins, G. M. (1989). Enhancing personal control and minimizing illness intrusiveness. In N. G. Kutner, D. D. Cardenas, & J. D. Bower (Eds.), *Maximizing rehabilitation in chronic renal disease* (pp. 109–136). New York: PMA.

Devins, G. M. (1991). Illness intrusiveness and the psychosocial impact of end-stage renal disease. In M. A. Hardy, J. Kiernan, A. H. Kutscher, L. Cahill, & A. I. Bevenitsky (Eds.), *Psychosocial aspects of end-stage renal disease: Issues of our times* (pp. 83–102). New York: Haworth.

Devins, G. M. (1994). Illness intrusiveness and the psychosocial impact of lifestyle disruptions in chronic life-threatening illness. *Advances in Renal Replacement Therapy, 1,* 251–263.

Devins, G. M., Anthony, M. O., Mandin, H., & Taylor, J. L. (1983). The impact of suffering on the dialysis nurse. *Dialysis and Transplantation, 12,* 719–724.

Devins, G. M., Armstrong, S. J., Mandin, H., Paul, L. C., Hons, R. B., Burgess, E. D., Taub, K., Schorr, S., Letourneau, P. K., & Buckle, S. (1990). Recurrent pain, illness intrusiveness, and quality of life in end-stage renal disease. *Pain, 42,* 279–285.

Devins, G. M., & Beiser, M. (1994). *Principles of psychological measurement for multicultural health care research.* Manuscript submitted for publication.

Devins, G. M., Binik, Y. M., Gorman, P., Dattel, M., McCloskey, B., Oscar, G., & Briggs, J. (1982). Perceived self-efficacy, outcome expectancies, and negative mood states in end-stage renal disease. *Journal of Abnormal Psychology, 91,* 241–244.

Devins, G. M., Binik, Y. M., Hutchinson, T. A., Hollomby, D. J., Barre, P. E., & Guttmann, R. D. (1983). The emotional impact of end-stage renal disease: Importance of patients' perceptions of intrusiveness and control. *International Journal of Psychiatry in Medicine, 13,* 327–343.

Devins, G. M., Binik, Y. M., Mandin, H., Letourneau, P. K., Hollomby, D. J., & Prichard, S. (1990). The Kidney Disease Questionnaire: A test for measuring patient knowledge about end-stage renal disease. *Journal of Clinical Epidemiology, 43,* 297–307.

Devins, G. M., Edworthy, S. M., Guthrie, N. G., & Martin, L. (1992). Illness intrusiveness in rheumatoid arthritis: Differential impact on depressive symptoms over the adult lifespan. *Journal of Rheumatology, 19,* 709–715.

Devins, G. M., Edworthy, S. M., Paul, L. C., Mandin, H., Seland, T. P., Klein, G. M., & Shapiro, C. M. (1993). Restless sleep, illness intrusiveness, and depressive symptoms in three chronic illness conditions: Rheumatoid arthritis, end-stage renal disease, and multiple sclerosis. *Journal of Psychosomatic Research, 37,* 163–170.

Devins, G. M., & Hunsley, J. D. (1988). *Psychosocial aspects of diagnostic testing with relevance to human immunodeficiency virus (HIV) antibody testing and the control of the HIV epidemic: An annotated bibliography.* Ottawa: Health and Welfare Canada.

Devins, G. M., Mandin, H., Hons, R. B., Burgess, E. D., Klassen, J., Taub, K., Schorr, S., Letourneau, P. K., & Buckle, S. (1990). Illness intrusiveness and quality of life in end-stage renal disease: Comparison and stability across treatment modalities. *Health Psychology, 9,* 117–142.

Devins, G. M., Mann, J., Mandin, H., Paul, L. C., Hons, R. B., Burgess, E. D., Taub, K., Schorr, S., Letourneau, P. K., & Buckle, S. (1990). Psychosocial predictors of survival in end-stage renal disease. *Journal of Nervous and Mental Disease, 178,* 127–133.

Devins, G. M., Seland, T. P., Klein, G. M., Edworthy, S. M., & Saary, M. J. (1993). Stability and determinants of psychosocial well-being in multiple sclerosis. *Rehabilitation Psychology, 38,* 11–26.

Devins, G. M., Stam, H. J., & Koopmans, J. P. (1994). Psychosocial impact of laryngectomy mediated by perceived stigma and illness intrusiveness. *Canadian Journal of Psychiatry, 39,* 608–616.

D'Zurilla, T. (1986). *Problem-solving therapy: A social competence approach to clinical interventions.* New York: Springer.

Edgar, L., Rosberger, Z., & Nowlis, D. (1992). Coping with cancer during the first year after diagnosis. *Cancer, 69,* 817–828.

Efran, J. S., Chorney, R. L., Ascher, L. M., & Lukens, M. D. (1989). Coping styles, paradox, and the cold pressor task. *Journal of Behavioral Medicine, 12,* 91–103.

Eisenberg, D. M., Kessler, R. C., Foster, C., Norlock, F. E., Calkins, D. R., & Deleanco, T. L. (1993). Unconventional medicine in the United States. *New England Journal of Medicine, 328,* 246–252.

Engel, G. L. (1977). The need for a new medical model: A challenge for biomedicine. *Science, 196,* 129–136.

Erdman, H. P., Klein, M. H., Greist, J. H., Skare, S. S., Husted, J., Robins, L. N., Helzer, J. E., Goldring, E., Hamburger, M., & Miller, J. P. (1992). A comparison of two computer-administered versions of the NIMH diagnostic interview schedule. *Journal of Psychiatric Research, 26,* 85–95.

Evans, R. L., & Jaureguy, B. M. (1982). Phone therapy outreach for blind elderly. *The Gerontologist, 22,* 32–35.

Evans, R. L., Smith, K. M., Werkhoven, W. S., Fox, H. R., & Pritzl, D. O. (1986). Cognitive telephone group therapy with physically disabled elderly persons. *The Gerontologist, 26,* 8–11.

Fawzy, F. I., Cousins, N., Fawzy, N. W., Kemeny, M. E., Elashoff, R., & Morton, D. (1990). A structured psychiatric intervention for cancer patients: 1. Changes over time in methods of coping and affective disturbance. *Archives of General Psychiatry, 47,* 720–725.

Fawzy, F. I., Fawzy, N. W., Hyun, C. S., Elashoff, R., Guthrie, D., Fahey, J. L., & Morton, D. L. (1993). Malignant melanoma: Effects of an early structured psychiatric intervention, coping, and affective state on recurrence and survival 6 years later. *Archives of General Psychiatry, 50,* 681–689.

Fawzy, F. I., Kemeny, M. E., Fawzy, N. W., Elashoff, R., Morton, D., Cousins, N., & Fahey, J. L. (1990). A structured psychiatric intervention for cancer patients: 2. Changes over time in immunological measures. *Archives of General Psychiatry, 47,* 729–735.

Ferlic, M., Goldman, A., & Kennedy, B. J. (1979). Group counseling in adult patients with advanced cancer. *Cancer, 43,* 760–766.

Fichten, C. S. (1988). Students with physical disabilities in higher education: Attitudes and beliefs that affect integration. In H. E. Yuker (Ed.), *Attitudes towards persons with disabilities* (pp. 171–186). New York: Springer.

Fiegenbaum, W. (1981). A social training program for clients with facial disfigurations: A contribution to the rehabilitation of cancer patients. *International Journal of Rehabilitation Research, 4,* 501–509.

Foley, F. W., Bedell, J. R., Larocca, N. G., Scheinberg, L. C., & Reznikoff, M. (1987). Efficacy of stress-inoculation training in coping with multiple sclerosis. *Journal of Consulting and Clinical Psychology, 55,* 919–922.

Ford, M. F., Jones, M., Scannell, T., Powell, A., Coombes, R. C., & Evans, C. (1990). Is group psychotherapy feasible for oncology outpatients attenders selected on the basis of psychological morbidity. *British Journal of Cancer, 62,* 624–626.

Forester, B., Kornfeld, D. S., & Fleiss, J. L. (1985). Psychotherapy during radiotherapy: Effects on emotional and physical distress. *American Journal of Psychiatry, 142,* 22–27.

Frank, J. D. (1974). *Persuasion and healing: A comparative study of psychotherapy* (Rev. ed.). New York: Schocken.

Frasure-Smith, N., & Prince, R. (1985). The ischemic heart disease life stress monitoring program: Impact on mortality. *Psychosomatic Medicine, 47,* 431–445.

Frasure-Smith, N., & Prince, R. (1989). Long-term follow-up of the ischemic heart disease life stress monitoring program. *Psychosomatic Medicine, 51,* 485–513.

Friend, R., Singletary, Y., Mendell, N. R., & Nurse, H. (1986). Group participation and survival among patients with end-stage renal disease. *American Journal of Public Health, 76,* 670–672.

Garro, L. C. (1994). Narrative representations of chronic illness experience: Cultural models of illness, mind and body in stories concerning the temporomandibular joint (TMJ). *Social Science and Medicine, 38,* 775–788.

Godbole, A., & Verinis, J. S. (1974). Brief psychotherapy in the treatment of emotional disorders in physically ill geriatric patients. *The Gerontologist,* 143–148.

Goldstein, A. M. (1980). The "uncooperative" patient: Self-destructive behavior in hemodialysis patients. In N. L. Farberow (Ed.), *The many faces of suicide: Indirect self-destructive behavior* (pp. 89–98). New York: McGraw-Hill.

Gordon, W. A., Freidenbergs, I., Diller, L., Hibbard, M., Wolf, C., Levine, L., Lipkins, R., Ezrachi, O., & Lucido, D. (1980). Efficacy of psychosocial intervention with cancer patients. *Journal of Consulting and Clinical Psychology, 48,* 743–759.

Greene, B., & Blanchard, E. B. (1994). Cognitive therapy for irritable bowel syndrome. *Journal of Consulting and Clinical Psychology, 62,* 576–582.

Greer, S., Moorey, S., & Baruch, J. D. R. (1991). Evaluation of adjuvan psychological therapy for clinically referred cancer patients. *British Journal of Cancer, 63,* 257–260.

Greer, S., Moorey, S., Baruch, J. D. R., Watson, M., Robertson, B., Mason, A., Rowden, L., Law, M. G., & Bliss, J. M. (1992). Adjuvant psychological therapy for patients with cancer: A prospective randomised trial. *British Medical Journal, 304,* 675–680.

Gruen, W. (1975). Effects of brief psychotherapy during the hospitalization period on the recovery process in heart attacks. *Journal of Consulting and Clinical Psychology, 43,* 223–232.

Hagey, R. (1984). The phenomenon, the explanations and the responses: Metaphors surrounding diabetes in Urban Canadian Indians. *Social Science and Medicine, 18,* 265–272.

Harris, L. L., Vogtsberger, K. N., & Mattox, D. E. (1985). Group psychotherapy for head and neck cancer patients. *Laryngoscope, 95,* 585–587.

Holroyd, K. A., & Creer, T. L. (1986). *Self-management of chronic disease: Handbook of clinical interventions and research.* Orlando, FL: Academic Press.

Ibrahim, M. A., Feldman, J. G., Sultz, H. A., Staiman, M. G., Young, L. J., & Dean, D. (1974). Management after myocardial infarction: A controlled trial of the effect of group psychotherapy. *International Journal of Psychiatry in Medicine, 5,* 253–268.

Jacobs, C., Ross, R. D., Walker, I. M., & Stockdale, F. E. (1983). Behavior of cancer patients: A randomized study of the effects of education and peer support. *American Journal of Clinical Oncology, 6,* 347–350.

Jacobsen, P. B., Perry, S. W., & Hirsch, D. A. (1990). Behavioral and psychological responses to HIV antibody testing. *Journal of Consulting and Clinical Psychology, 58,* 31–37.

Johnston, M., Gilbert, P., Partridge, C., & Collins, J. (1992). Changing perceived control in patients with physical disabilities: An intervention study with patients receiving rehabilitation. *British Journal of Clinical Psychology, 31,* 89–94.

Kemp, B. J., Corgiat, M., & Gill, C. (1992). Effects of brief cognitive-behavioral group psychotherapy on older persons with and without disabling illness. *Behavior, Health, and Aging, 2,* 21–28.

King, K. (1994). The issue of vocational rehabilitation in maintenance dialysis patients. *Advances in Renal Replacement Therapy, 1,* 228–239.

Kirschenbaum, D. S. (1991). Integration of clinical psychology into hemodialysis programs. In J. J. Sweet, R. H. Rozensky, & S. M. Tovian (Eds.), *Handbook of clinical psychology in medical settings* (pp. 567–586). New York: Plenum.

Kleinman, A. (1978). Concepts and a model for the comparison of medical systems as cultural systems. *Social Science and Medicine, 12,* 85–93.

Kleinman, A. (1980). *Patients and healers in the context of culture.* Berkeley: University of California Press.

Larcombe, N. A., & Wilson, P. H. (1984). An evaluation of cognitive-behaviour therapy for depression in patients with multiple sclerosis. *British Journal of Psychiatry, 145,* 366–371.

Lawrence, G. H. (1986). Using computers for the treatment of psychological problems. *Computers and Human Behavior, 2,* 43–62.

Lazarus, R. S., & Folkman, S. (1984). *Stress, appraisal, and coping.* New York: Springer.

Lenker, S. L., Lorig, K., & Gallagher, D. (1984). Reasons for the lack of association between changes in health behavior and improved health status: An exploratory study. *Patient Education and Counselling, 6*(2), 69–72.

Lepore, S. J., Evans, G. W., & Schneider, M. L. (1991). Dynamic role of social support in the link between chronic stress and psychological distress. *Journal of Personality and Social Psychology, 61,* 899–909.

Lewinsohn, P. M., Sullivan, J. M., & Grosscup, S. J. (1982). Behavioral therapy: Clinical applications. In A. J. Rush (Ed.), *Short-term psychotherapies for depression* (pp. 50–87). New York: Guilford.

Ley, P. (1989). *Communicating with patients: Improving communication, satisfaction, and compliance.* London: Croom Helm.

Linn, M. W., Linn, B. S., & Harris, R. (1982). Effects of counselling for late stage cancer patients. *Cancer, 49,* 1048–1055.

Lorig, K., Chastain, R. L., Ung, E., Shoor, S., & Hollman, H. (1989). Development and evaluation of a scale to measure perceived self-efficacy in people with arthritis. *Arthritis and Rheumatism, 32,* 37–43.

Lorig, K., & Fries, J. F. (1986). *The arthritis helpbook: A tested self-management program for coping with your arthritis* (Rev. ed.). Reading, MA: Addison-Wesley.

Lorig, K., & Fries, J. F. (1990). *The arthritis helpbook: A tested self-management program for coping with your arthritis* (3rd ed.). Reading, MA: Addison-Wesley.

Lorig, K., Konkol, L., & Gonzalez, V. (1987). Arthritis patient education: A review of the literature. *Patient Education and Counselling, 10,* 207–252.

Lorig, K., & Laurin, J. (1985). Some notions about assumptions underlying health education. *Health Education Quarterly, 12,* 231–243.

Lorig, K., Lubeck, D., Kraines, R. G., Seleznick, M., & Holman, H. R. (1985). Outcomes of self-help education for patients with arthritis. *Arthritis and Rheumatism, 28,* 680–685.

Lorig, K. R., Mazonson, P. D., & Holman, H. R. (1993). Evidence suggesting that health education for self-management in patients with chronic arthritis has sustained health benefits while reducing health care costs. *Arthritis and Rheumatism, 4,* 439–446.

Lynch, J. J. (1977). *The broken heart: The medical consequences of loneliness.* New York: Basic Books.

Mars, D. (1991). Nurses' attitudes, nurse–patient interactions and adherence to treatment by hemodialysis patients. *Psychological Reports, 68,* 733–734.

Masi, R. (1993). Multicultural health: Principles and policies. In R. Masi, L. Mensah, & K. A. McLeod (Eds.), *Health and cultures: Exploring the relationships: Vol. 1. Policies, professional practice and education* (pp. 12–31). Oakville, Ontario: Mosaic Press.

Massie, M. J., & Straker, N. (1989). Psychotherapeutic interventions. In J. C. Holland & J. H. Rowland (Eds.), *Handbook of psychooncology: Psychological care of the patient with cancer* (pp. 455–469). New York: Oxford University Press.

Mazzuca, S. A. (1982). Does patient education in chronic disease have therapeutic value? *Journal of Chronic Diseases, 35,* 521–529.

Meichenbaum, D. (1977). *Cognitive-behavior modification: An integrative approach.* New York: Plenum.

Meichenbaum, D. (1985). *Stress inoculation training.* New York: Pergamon.

Mermelstein, H. T., & Holland, J. C. (1991). Psychotherapy by telephone: A therapeutic tool for cancer patients. *Psychosomatics, 32,* 407–412.

Mermelstein, H. T., & Lesko, L. (1992). Depression in patients with cancer. *Psycho-Oncology, 1,* 199–215.

Miller, S. M. (1980). When is a little information a dangerous thing? Coping with stressful events by monitoring versus blunting. In S. Levine & H. Ursin (Eds.), *Coping and Health* (pp. 145–169). New York: Plenum.

Miller, S. M. (1989). Cognitive informational styles in the process of coping with threat and frustration. *Advances in Behaviour Research and Therapy, 11,* 223–234.

Miller, S. M. (1990). To see or not to see: Cognitive informational styles in the coping process. In M. Rosenbaum (Ed.), *Learned resourcefulness: On coping skills, self-control, and adaptive behavior* (pp. 95–126). New York: Springer.

Miller, S. M. (1992a). Individual differences in the coping process: What to know and when to know it. In B. N. Carpenter (Ed.), *Personal coping: Theory, research, and application* (pp. 77–91). New York: Praeger.

Miller, S. M. (1992b). Monitoring and blunting in the face of threat: Implications for adaptation and health. In L. Montada, S. -H. Filipp, & M. J. Lerner (Eds.), *Life crises and experiences of loss in adulthood* (pp. 255–273). Hillsdale, NJ: Erlbaum.

Miller, S. M., Brody, D. S., & Summerton, J. (1988). Styles of coping with threat: Implications for health. *Journal of Personality and Social Psychology, 54,* 142–148.

Miller, S. M., & Mangan, C. E. (1983). Interacting effects of information and coping style in adapting to gynecologic stress: Should the doctor tell all? *Journal of Personality and Social Psychology, 45,* 223–236.

Miller, S. M., & O'Leary, A. (1992). Cognition, stress and health. In K. Dobson & P. C. Kendall (Eds.), *Cognition and psychopathology.* New York: Academic Press.

Moorey, S., Greer, S., Watson, M., Baruch, J. D. R., Robertson, B. M., Mason, A., Rowden, L., Tunmore, R., Law, M., & Bliss, J. M. (1994). Adjuvant psychological therapy for patients with cancer: Outcome at one year. *Psycho-Oncology, 3,* 39–46.

Mushlin, A. I., Mooney, C., Grow, V., & Phelps, C. E. (1994). The value of diagnostic information to patients with suspected multiple sclerosis. *Archives of Neurology, 51,* 67–72.

Nezu, A. M., Nezu, C. M., & Perri, M. G. (1989). *Problem-solving therapy for depression: Theory, research, and clinical guidelines.* New York: Wiley.

O'Connor, G. T., Buring, J. E., Yusuf, S., Goldhaber, S. Z., Olmstead, E. M., Paffen-barger, R. S., & Hennekens, C. H. (1989). An overview of randomized trials of reha-bilitation with exercise after myocardial infarction. *Circulation, 80,* 234–244.

Ochs, E. P., Meana, M., Pare, L., Mah, K., & Binik, Y. M. (1994). Learning about sex outside the gutter: Attitudes toward a computer sex-expert system. *Journal of Sex and Marital Therapy, 20,* 86–102.

Oldridge, N. B., Guyatt, G. H., Fischer, M. E., & Rimm, A. A. (1988). Cardiac rehabili-tation after myocardial infarction. *Journal of the American Medical Association, 260,* 945–950.

Oldridge, N., Guyatt, G., Jones, N., Crowe, J., Singer, J., Feeny, D., McKelvie, R., Runions, J., Streiner, D., & Torrance, G. (1991). Effects on quality of life with comprehensive rehabilitation after acute myocardial infarction. *American Journal of Cardiology, 67,* 1084–1089.

O'Leary, A. (1985). Self-efficacy and health. *Behaviour Research and Therapy, 27,* 437–451.

O'Leary, A., Shoor, S., Lorig, K., & Holman, H. R. (1988). A cognitive-behavioral treat-ment of rheumatoid arthritis. *Health Psychology, 7,* 527–544.

Phillips, L. J., & Osborne, J. W. (1989). Cancer patients' experiences of forgiveness therapy. *Canadian Journal of Counselling, 23,* 236–251.

Phipps, S., & Zinn, A. B. (1986). Psychological response to amniocentesis: 2. Effects of coping style. *American Journal of Medical Genetics, 25,* 143–148.

Poulsen, A. (1991). Psychodynamic, time-limited group therapy in rheumatic disease: A controlled study with special reference to alexithymia. *Psychotherapy and Psychoso-matics, 56,* 12–23.

Pruitt, B. T., Waligora-Serafin, B., McMahon, T., Byrd, G., Besselman, L., Kelly, D. M., Drake, D. A., & Cuellar, D. (1993). An educational intervention for newly-diagnosed cancer patients undergoing radiotherapy. *Psycho-Oncology, 2,* 55–62.

Razin, A. M. (1982). Psychosocial intervention in coronary artery disease: A review. *Psychosomatic Medicine, 44,* 363–387.

Roberts, A. H., Kewman, D. G., Mercier, L., & Hovell, M. (1993). The power of nonspe-cific effects in healing: Implications for psychosocial and biological treatments. *Clinical Psychology Review, 13,* 375–392.

Rodin, G., Craven, J., & Littlefield, C. (1991). *Depression in the medically ill: An inte-grated approach.* New York: Brunner/Mazel.

Rosenthal, R., & Rubin, D. B. (1978). Interpersonal expectancy effects: The first 345 studies. *Behavioral and Brain Sciences, 3,* 377–415.

Schiffer, R. B., & Wineman, N. M. (1990). Antidepressant pharmacotherapy of depression associated with multiple sclerosis. *American Journal of Psychiatry, 147,* 1493–1497.

Selmi, P. M., Klein, M. H., Greist, J. H., Sorrell, S. P., & Erdman, H. P. (1990). Computer-administered cognitive-behavioral therapy for depression. *American Jour-nal of Psychiatry, 147,* 51–56.

Servan-Schreiber, D. (1986). Artificial intelligence and psychiatry. *Journal of Nervous and Mental Disease, 174,* 191–202.

Snyder, P. (1983). The use of nonprescribed treatments by hemodialysis patients. *Culture, Medicine and Psychiatry, 7,* 57–76.

Somer, E., & Tucker, C. M. (1992). Spouse marital adjustment and patient dietary adherence in chronic hemodialysis: A comparison of afro-americans and caucasians. *Psychology and Health, 6,* 69–76.

Spiegel, D., & Bloom, J. R. (1983). Group therapy and hypnosis reduce metastatic breast carcinoma pain. *Psychosomatic Medicine, 45,* 333–339.

Spiegel, D., Bloom, J. R., Kraemer, H. C., & Gottheil, E. (1989). Effect of psychosocial treatment on survival of patients with metastatic breast cancer. *Lancet, 2,* 888–891.

Spiegel, D., Bloom, J. R., & Yalom, I. (1981). Group support for patients with metastatic cancer. *Archives of General Psychiatry, 38,* 527–533.

Spira, J. L., & Spiegel, D. (1993). Group psychotherapy of the medically ill. In A. Stoudemire & B. S. Fogel (Eds.), *Psychiatric care of the medical patient* (pp. 31–50). New York: Oxford University Press.

Steptoe, A., & O'Sullivan, J. (1986). Monitoring and blunting coping styles in women prior to surgery. *British Journal of Clinical Psychology, 25,* 143–144.

Susman, J. (1994). Disability, stigma and deviance. *Social Science and Medicine, 38,* 15–22.

Taylor, S. E., & Aspinwall, L. G. (1990). Psychosocial aspects of chronic illness. In P. T. Costa & G. R. VandenBos (Eds.), *Psychological aspects of serious illness: Chronic conditions, fatal diseases, and clinical care* (pp. 7–60). Washington, DC: American Psychological Association.

Taylor, S. E., Falke, R. L., Shoptaw, S. J., & Lichtman, R. R. (1986). Social support, support groups, and the cancer patient. *Journal of Consulting and Clinical Psychology, 54,* 608–615.

Telch, C. F., & Telch, M. J. (1986). Group coping skills instruction and supportive group therapy for cancer patients: A comparison of strategies. *Journal of Consulting and Clinical Psychology, 54,* 802–808.

Thompson-Hoffman, S., & Storck, I. F. (1991). *Disability in the United States: A portrait from national data.* New York: Springer.

Watkins, L. O., Weaver, L., & Odegaard, V. (1986). Preparation for cardiac catheterization: Tailoring the content of instruction to coping style. *Heart & Lung, 15,* 382–389.

Weinberger, M., Hiner, S. L., & Tierney, W. M. (1986). Improving functional status in arthritis: The effect of social support. *Social Science and Medicine, 23,* 899–904.

Weinberger, M., Tierney, W. M., Booher, P., & Katz, B. P. (1991). The impact of increased contact on psychosocial outcomes in patients with osteoarthritis: A randomized, controlled trail. *Journal of Rheumatology, 18,* 849–854.

Weiss, M. G. (1988). Cultural models of diarrheal illness: Conceptual framework and review. *Social Science and Medicine, 27,* 5–16.

Weiss, M. G., Desai, A., Jadhav, S., Gupta, L., Channabasavanna, S. M., Doongaji, D. R., & Behere, P. B. (1988). Humoral concepts of mental illness in India. *Social Science and Medicine, 27,* 471–477.

Weiss, M. G., Doongaji, S., Wypij, S. D., Pathare, S., Bhatawdekar, M., Bhave, A., Sheth, A., & Fernandes, R. (1992). The Explanatory Model Interview Catalogue (EMIC): Contribution to cross-cultural research methods from a study of leprosy and mental health. *British Journal of Psychiatry, 160,* 819–830.

Wetstone, S. L., Pfeiffer, C. A., & Rippey, R. M. (1988). Evaluation of a computer-based education lesson for patients with systematic lupus erythematosus. *Arthritis Care and Research, 1,* 5–11.

Wetstone, S. L., Sheehan, T. J., Votaw, R. G., Peterson, M. G., & Rothfield, N. (1993). Evaluation of a computer based education lesson for patients with rheumatoid arthritis. *Journal of Rheumatology, 12,* 907–912.

Wiggins, S., Whyte, P., Huggins, M., Adam, S., Theilmann, J., Bloch, M., Sheps, S. B., Schechter, M. T., & Hayden, M. R. (1992). The psychological consequences of predictive testing for Huntington's disease. *New England Journal of Medicine, 327,* 1401–1405.

Worden, J. W., & Weisman, A. D. (1984). Preventive psychosocial intervention with newly diagnosed cancer patients. *General Hospital Psychiatry, 6,* 243–249.

Wright, B. A. (1988). Attitudes and the fundamental negative bias: Conditions and corrections. In H. E. Yuker (Ed.), *Attitudes toward persons with disabilities* (pp. 3–21). New York: Springer.

Author Index

Subject Index